Wash
Oregon & the Pacific Northwest

Sandra Bao

Brendan Sainsbury, Becky Ohlsen, John Lee

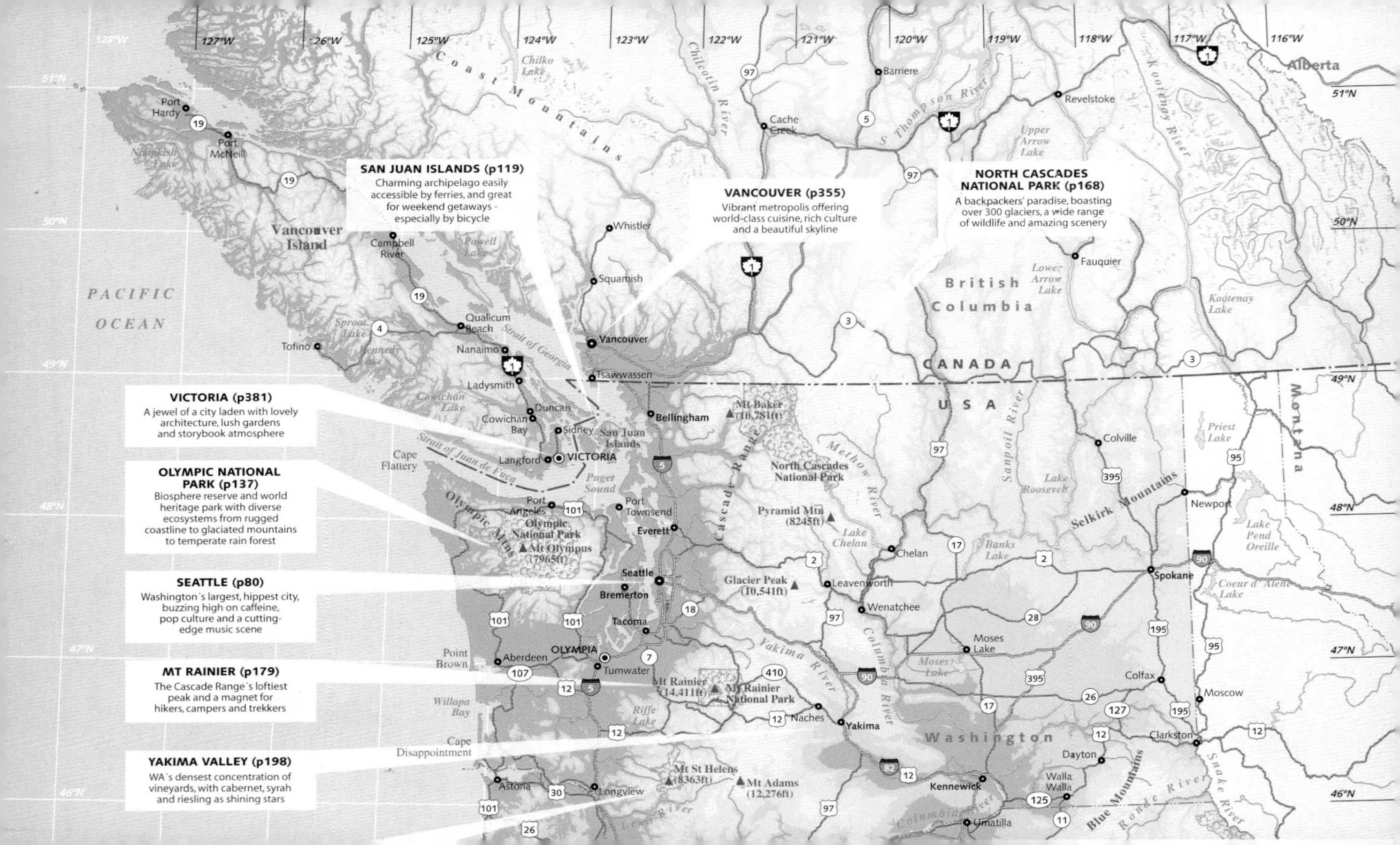
SAN JUAN ISLANDS (p119)
Charming archipelago easily accessible by ferries, and great for weekend getaways - especially by bicycle
VANCOUVER (p355)
Vibrant metropolis offering world-class cuisine, rich culture and a beautiful skyline
NORTH CASCADES NATIONAL PARK (p168)
A backpackers' paradise, boasting over 300 glaciers, a wide range of wildlife and amazing scenery
VICTORIA (p381)
A jewel of a city laden with lovely architecture, lush gardens and storybook atmosphere
OLYMPIC NATIONAL PARK (p137)
Biosphere reserve and world heritage park with diverse ecosystems from rugged coastline to glaciated mountains to temperate rain forest
SEATTLE (p80)
Washington´s largest, hippest city, buzzing high on caffeine, pop culture and a cutting-edge music scene
MT RAINIER (p179)
The Cascade Range´s loftiest peak and a magnet for hikers, campers and trekkers
YAKIMA VALLEY (p198)
WA´s densest concentration of vineyards, with cabernet, syrah and riesling as shining stars
PACIFIC OCEAN
British Columbia
CANADA
USA
Washington
Montana
Alberta
Coast Mountains
Cascade Range
Selkirk Mountains
Blue Mountains
Olympic Mtns
Vancouver Island
Port Hardy
Port McNeill
Campbell River
Qualicum Beach
Nanaimo
Ladysmith
Duncan
Cowichan Bay
Sidney
Langford
VICTORIA
Tofino
Whistler
Squamish
Vancouver
Tsawwassen
Bellingham
San Juan Islands
Port Angeles
Port Townsend
Everett
Seattle
Bremerton
Tacoma
OLYMPIA
Tumwater
Aberdeen
Astoria
Longview
Cache Creek
Barriere
Revelstoke
Fauquier
Colville
Newport
Spokane
Chelan
Leavenworth
Wenatchee
Moses Lake
Yakima
Naches
Kennewick
Umatilla
Walla Walla
Dayton
Colfax
Moscow
Clarkston
Mt Baker (10,781ft)
Pyramid Mtn (8245ft)
Glacier Peak (10,541ft)
Mt Olympus (7965ft)
Mt Rainier (14,411ft)
Mt St Helens (8363ft)
Mt Adams (12,276ft)
North Cascades National Park
Olympic National Park
Mt Rainier National Park
Cape Flattery
Point Brown
Cape Disappointment
Willapa Bay
Puget Sound
Strait of Georgia
Strait of Juan de Fuca
Chilcotin River
S Thompson River
Kootenay River
Methow River
Sanpoil River
Columbia River
Yakima River
Snake River
Lewis River
Chilko Lake
Powell Lake
Sproat Lake
Kennedy Lake
Cowichan Lake
Nimpkish Lake
Upper Arrow Lake
Lower Arrow Lake
Kootenay Lake
Priest Lake
Lake Pend Oreille
Coeur d' Alene Lake
Lake Roosevelt
Banks Lake
Lake Chelan
Moses Lake
Riffe Lake
128°W
127°W
126°W
125°W
124°W
123°W
122°W
121°W
120°W
119°W
118°W
117°W
116°W
51°N
50°N
49°N
48°N
47°N
46°N

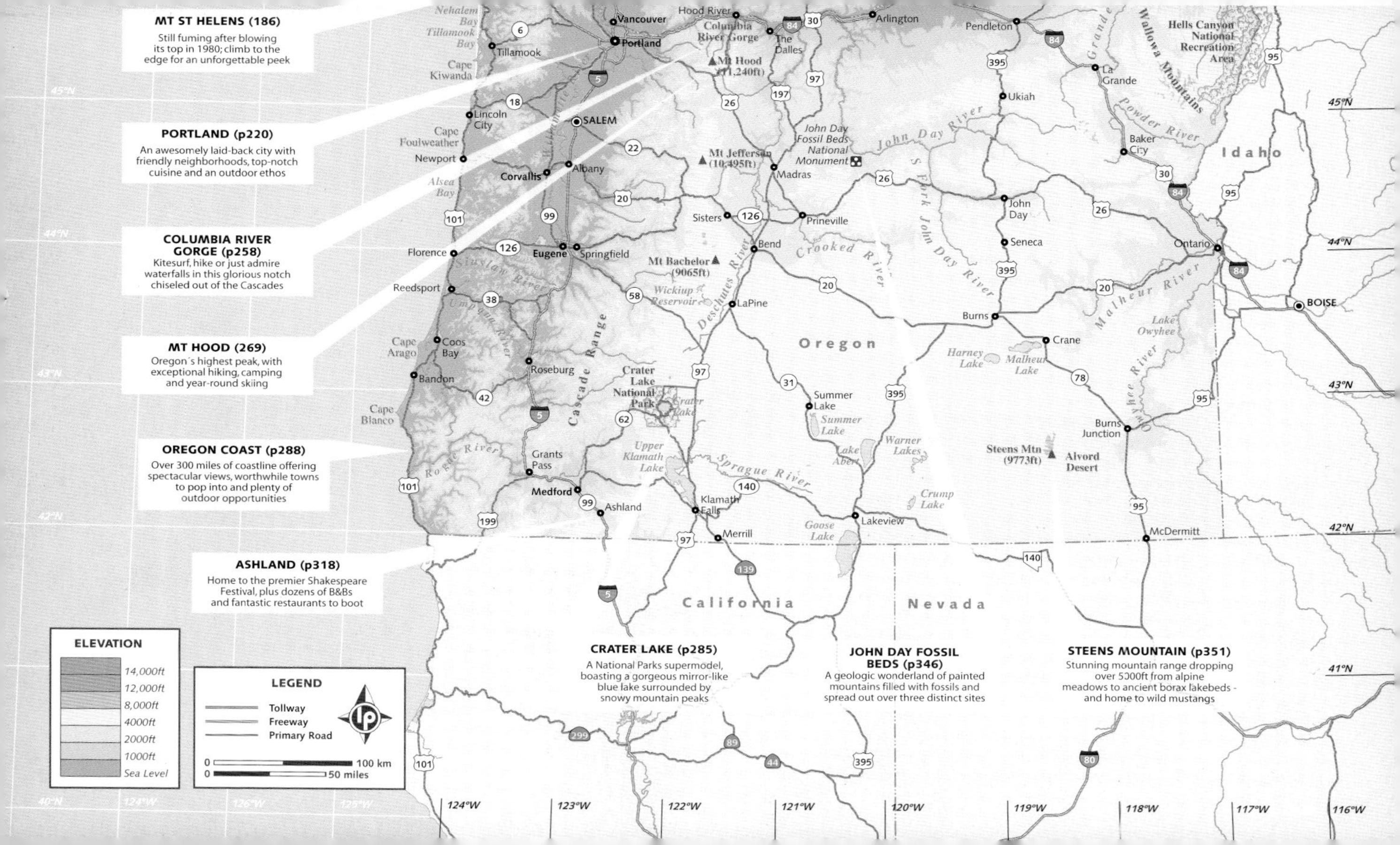
MT ST HELENS (186)
Still fuming after blowing its top in 1980; climb to the edge for an unforgettable peek
PORTLAND (p220)
An awesomely laid-back city with friendly neighborhoods, top-notch cuisine and an outdoor ethos
COLUMBIA RIVER GORGE (p258)
Kitesurf, hike or just admire waterfalls in this glorious notch chiseled out of the Cascades
MT HOOD (269)
Oregon´s highest peak, with exceptional hiking, camping and year-round skiing
OREGON COAST (p288)
Over 300 miles of coastline offering spectacular views, worthwhile towns to pop into and plenty of outdoor opportunities
ASHLAND (p318)
Home to the premier Shakespeare Festival, plus dozens of B&Bs and fantastic restaurants to boot
CRATER LAKE (p285)
A National Parks supermodel, boasting a gorgeous mirror-like blue lake surrounded by snowy mountain peaks
JOHN DAY FOSSIL BEDS (p346)
A geologic wonderland of painted mountains filled with fossils and spread out over three distinct sites
STEENS MOUNTAIN (p351)
Stunning mountain range dropping over 5000ft from alpine meadows to ancient borax lakebeds - and home to wild mustangs
ELEVATION
14,000ft
12,000ft
8,000ft
4000ft
2000ft
1000ft
Sea Level
LEGEND
Tollway
Freeway
Primary Road
0 100 km
0 50 miles
Oregon
Idaho
California
Nevada
Portland
Vancouver
SALEM
Eugene
Springfield
Corvallis
Albany
Medford
Ashland
Grants Pass
Roseburg
Bend
Sisters
Prineville
Madras
LaPine
Klamath Falls
Merrill
Lakeview
Summer Lake
Burns
Crane
Burns Junction
McDermitt
John Day
Seneca
Ukiah
Pendleton
La Grande
Baker City
Ontario
BOISE
Hood River
The Dalles
Arlington
Tillamook
Lincoln City
Newport
Florence
Reedsport
Coos Bay
Bandon
Mt Hood (11,240ft)
Mt Jefferson (10,495ft)
Mt Bachelor (9065ft)
Steens Mtn (9773ft)
Alvord Desert
Crater Lake National Park
Cascade Range
Wallowa Mountains
Hells Canyon National Recreation Area
John Day Fossil Beds National Monument
Cape Kiwanda
Cape Foulweather
Cape Arago
Cape Blanco
45°N
44°N
43°N
42°N
41°N
124°W
123°W
122°W
121°W
120°W
119°W
118°W
117°W
116°W

On the Road

SANDRA BAO Coordinating Author Smith Rock is one of my favorite places in Oregon. Its glorious 400ft formations make for some spectacular scenery and amazing rock climbing. I was here on my 40th birthday, leading my first outdoor 5.10b-ranked climb – very scary but also fun. My friends and I walked along the sinewy Crooked River, scrambling up rock faces and bouldering here and there. It's a magical spot, offering a piece of heaven for picnickers, day hikers and climbers. This time I came to research, and didn't have the time even to scamper down to the riverside. I had only enough of a break for this photo, a few memories and a promise to return in the future.

JOHN LEE It's early evening at Grouse Mountain and I'm combining a snowshoe trek with a feast-like dinner. After a 1½-hour uphill push through the crunchy snow, occasional bursts of pace flicking ice crumbs over my head like confetti, I reach the tree-lined summit overlooking the crags of Vancouver Island shimmering in the moonlight. Barreling back down the slope, I head inside the lodge for some fondue, tucking into pyramids of salmon, scallops, chicken and vegetables.

BECKY OHLSEN The Pacific Northwest coastline is almost never sunny, but when it is, you're morally obligated to stop and enjoy it. This shot was taken by my dad one afternoon at the coast, during a family visit graced by uncannily beautiful weather. No wonder the folks back home never believe me about how much it rains up here.

BRENDAN SAINSBURY Standing on Washington's Ruby Beach, I was caught in one of the region's innumerable spring downpours. In the background, sea stacks do battle with formidable Pacific breakers. The logs scattered all around are evidence of a recent West Coast storm. My son, Kieran, is keeping an eye out for swooping eagles and foraging raccoons. As an expat Brit, I love the 'evergreen' state for its expansive forests, pristine wilderness areas and miles of remote and untamed Pacific coastline.

See full author bios page 429

Pacific Northwest Highlights

Where else but the Pacific Northwest can you wallow in natural hot springs in the morning, take photos of mountains at lunch time, roll up in one of the world's coolest cities by mid-afternoon, sample a mind-boggling assortment of locally brewed beers by evening and rock out until dawn? The Pacific Northwest is a charmer and its offbeat character and quirky sense of humor make it fun to be around and hard to say goodbye to. But these are just some of the reasons why we love the Pacific Northwest: why not let the experts speak for themselves? We asked our own readers, writers and staff what they liked best about the region. Here is what they had to say:

JAY SCHLEGAL/GETTY IMAGES

1 SAN JUAN ISLANDS

For breathtaking scenery, visit the San Juan Islands (p119) in northwestern Washington state. Stop and take the time to watch for orcas, try sea kayaking or simply watch the sun set over the water.

Sarah Eileen, Bluelist contributor

BRENT WINEBRENNE

2 MT RAINIER

I listen to the crunch of snow under my crampons and the rasping of the cold, thin air in my throat as the sun rises on the way to Mt Rainier's (p179) summit. The sun hits the mountain-tops before it hits the rest of the world and I remember seeing a line of orange-pink peaks – Mt St Helens, Mt Adams, Mt Hood – leading south over a dark land all the way into Oregon.

Piers Pickard, Lonely Planet, Melbourne

RICHARD CUMMIN

3 SEATTLE

From Gas Works Park (p91), get an awesome view of the Seattle skyline, fly a kite and picnic beside the picturesquely rusted-out skeletons of industry. And Pike Place Market (p87): sure it's obvious, but it's still great, especially early in the morning, when real Seattleites do their shopping at the labyrinthine old market's fish and produce stands.

Becky Ohlsen, Lonely Planet author, Oregon

VANCOUVER

Standing on the beach at Kits (p364) is the best way to figure out Vancouver at a glance. English Bay in the foreground, filled with sailors and swimmers, while downtown bustles just across the water. Looming over it all in the background is Grouse Mountain (p365), just a short drive from town for the outdoors-focused Vancouverites who love their skiing as much as their Ultimate (Frisbee, that is).

Holly Alexander, Lonely Planet, Melbourne

GLENN VAN DER KNIJFF

VICTORIA

These days, Victoria (p381) is not the clichéd incarnation of olde-worlde England that it used to be. Yes, there are still copious tearooms and great fish 'n chips, but there are also swanky boutique hotels, surprisingly innovative restaurants and a hipster shopping scene on Lower Johnson that rivals much bigger and supposedly cooler cities. So if you've come here with your monocle and pith helmet, wear them ironically and you'll fit right in.

John Lee, Lonely Planet author

5

JOHN ELK III

RICHARD CUMMINS

6

PORTLAND

Portland (p220) is a dream city for urbanites and nature lovers alike. It's vibrant yet relaxed, small in size yet huge in personality, fabulously hip yet not chi-chi, with exquisite restaurants and welcoming residents. The infamous winter rains nurture unparalleled spring blossoms, when the city's streets and gardens come alive with rhododendrons of every color imaginable.

Emily K Wolman, Lonely Planet, Oakland

WASHINGTON CASCADES

We hiked for six days through the lush alpine forests of Washington's Cascade Mountains (p162), refilling our water bottles from glaciers and grabbing handfuls of fresh blueberries along the way. We only laid eyes on a few other people and happily wondered how these mountains had remained such a well-kept secret.

Chris Howard, traveler

7

JOHN ELK I

CRATER LAKE

The water is sapphire blue, the air crisp and the lodge cozy. For the non-adventurous, Crater Lake (p285) offers fantastic views from the many drivable turn-outs. Hike down to the rocky shore, where you'll almost forget about hiking back up.

fongemy, Bluelist contributor

8

ROBERTO GEROMETTA

RYAN F

9

CYCLING

Not to make the people in Ohio feel bad, but the Pacific Northwest is a place where you can cycle from the summit of a mountain to the ocean in a day, where you can tour old highways, historic tunnels, and covered bridges. It's the Halls of Shangri-La for a cyclist and Portland is the New York City of the bike world.

Joe Kurmaskie, author of the Metal Cowboy website

HOT SPRINGS

We found these hot springs (p329), in natural balconies, high above the banks of the Umpqua River in Oregon. After clambering up the slippery mineral rock face we soaked for a while with bikini-clad toe-dippers and fully-submerged naked folk, who had phases of the moon tattooed on their foreheads.

Heather & Chris, travelers

11

FOTOSEARCH

10

ALICE GRULICH-JONES

NATIVE AMERICAN CULTURE

Nearly every site in the Pacific Northwest was visited, touched and honored by its rich native cultures. Countless stories were told of Coyote shaping and naming the land, giving life to the creatures and peoples. These names and stories are still alive and celebrated in ways that might surprise you.

David Lukas, Lonely Planet author

ANN CECIL

OREGON COAST

When I visit family in Portland, we always head west to the Oregon coast for the kitschy vibe at Seaside (p292), rocky tide pools at Cannon Beach (p293), deep-fried Twinkies (seriously) at the Astoria Sunday Market (p290) and miles of secluded beaches where our dogs and kids can run for hours.

Suki Gear, Lonely Planet, Oakland

MT ST HELENS

I remember the incredible drama of living in Portland when Mt St Helens (p186) blew. Clouds of ash towering tens of thousands of feet into the sky threatened to turn night into day, and our beautiful mountain was gone! Today it's possible to drive right up to the crater and relive this amazing event.

David Lukas, Lonely Planet author

13

JIM WARK

JOHN ELK III

14

WALLA WALLA

Walla Walla (p213): so good they named it twice, or so the enamored locals have been heard to quip. It's difficult to disagree. What was once a bucolic Washington backwater is now one of the trendiest, yet most unpretentious, wine-tasting destinations outside California. Get there quick before the cab sav connoisseurs descend en masse.

Brendan Sainsbury, Lonely Planet author

SEAN MCMENAMIN

15

MICROBREWERIES & BEER

It's one thing that the Pacific Northwest is really good looking but quite another that it likes to drink and has a sense of humor. With 28 microbreweries in the Portland area alone and a local chain of fun McMenamins pubs and hotels dotted all over the region, you'll be sampling brews for a long while.

Heather Dickson, Lonely Planet, Oakland

OLYMPIC NATIONAL PARK

You never forget your first bear, especially a cub. But there it was, happily munching berries on the trail amid the massive, moss-covered old-growth conifers. 'Sweet!' we said. 'But where's mom?' We retreated before finding out, back to soak in the hot springs by our camp, deep in Olympic National Park (p137).

Jay Cooke, Lonely Planet, Oakland

16

AARON MCCOY

MT HOOD

Waterfalls, glaciers, the historic Timberline Lodge (p273). Where else can you go summer snowboarding on a potentially active volcano? Just an hour's gorgeous drive through the Gorge from Portland, Mt Hood (p269) *will* surprise you.

Erin Corrigan, traveler

17

JOHN ELK III

STEPHANIE YAO/GETTY IMAGES

18

JOHN DAY FOSSIL BEDS

Visiting the John Day Fossil Beds (p346) is like exploring the surface of another world. Most striking is the barren, dune-like hills with bands of red, orange, green and black that reveal ancient soils and river deposits from Oregon's tropical past. Gape at the monolithic pillars of ancient lava flows that once blanketed the Pacific Northwest. If you're lucky, you may spot a bald eagle overhead or even find a 40-million-year-old fossil!

Kevin O'Dea, traveler

FUNGUS FORAYS

Mushroom-foraging in the dank, lush forests of the Pacific Northwest is the most fun I've had with a butter knife and a canvas bag. After a long afternoon of hiking amidst the pine trees, we returned home to let our mushrooms and our feet dry out by the fire, then cooked up a fungal feast fit for a king.

Jennye Garibaldi, Lonely Planet, Oakland

19

NATIONAL GEOGRAPHIC/GETTY IMAGES

JOHN ELK III

20

HOH RAIN FOREST

I once spent a summer studying spotted owls in the Hoh Rain Forest (p142) and quickly discovered why it's called a rain forest – it rained for weeks on end. I've never been so wet in my life.

David Lukas, Lonely Planet author

JOHN ELK III

21

COLUMBIA RIVER GORGE

Let the sweet juice from the best peaches around dribble down your chin while the satisfying burn in your legs from mountain biking subsides. The Columbia River Gorge (p258) is the ultimate active vacation destination. You can ski in the morning on Mt Hood and then windsurf in the afternoon. Plus the fresh air and fresh fruit here will rejuvenate anybody.

trvlgrl, Bluelist contributor

YAKIMA VALLEY

With old-growth vines and new-school wines, Yakima Valley (p198) is at the heart of Washington's wine country. Fall is the best time to hit the wineries strung out along I-82. Catch the Crush in September or the region-wide tasting over Thanksgiving weekend for a peek at wineries that are usually closed to the public.

Erin Corrigan, traveler

COURTESY OF YAKIMA VALLEY VISITORS & CONVENTION BUREAU

22

WATERFALLS & SPRING-FED RIVERS

As if 300 fire hydrants had been turned on, the Metolius River (p275) explodes from underneath Black Butte in an amazing spectacle of nature's power. See crystal-blue water (so damn cold!) and salmon making their way upriver.

nickwusz, Bluelist contributor

23

D.C LOWE/SUPER STOCK

ED DARACK

24

ELK & OTHER CRITTERS

One of my favorite things is waking up to shuffling noises, looking outside to see a massive bull elk standing next to my tent in the beautiful morning light. Sitting half in, half out of my tent, just watching.

nicb, Bluelist contributor

KAYAKING

Sea-kayaking, amongst the islands near Tofino, feeling life itself beneath me as the water embraces my boat and we move as one along caressing currents and playful waves while sensing the company of others below the ocean's surface.

soultraveller, Bluelist contributor

25

GREG GAWLOWSKI

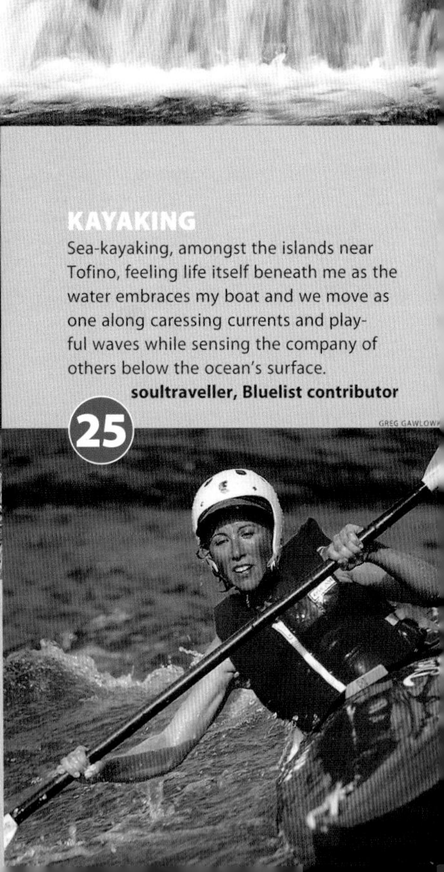

COFFEE

Coffee in the Pacific Northwest is the best coffee there is. It's an entire culture in itself. The coffee-houses are inviting sanctuaries, full of wonderful smells, beautiful people, delicious treats, and wonderful art.

erbsnspices, Bluelist contributor

27

LAWRENCE WORCHESTER

LAWRENCE WORCHESTER

26

MUSICAL ROOTS

First it was Hendrix, then Nirvana and Pearl Jam, who put Seattle on the musical map. You can pay tribute to Jimi at his grave and visit the Frank Gehry–designed Experience Music Project (p88). The city is one of the top 10 for music in the US.

thejourneyer, Bluelist contributor

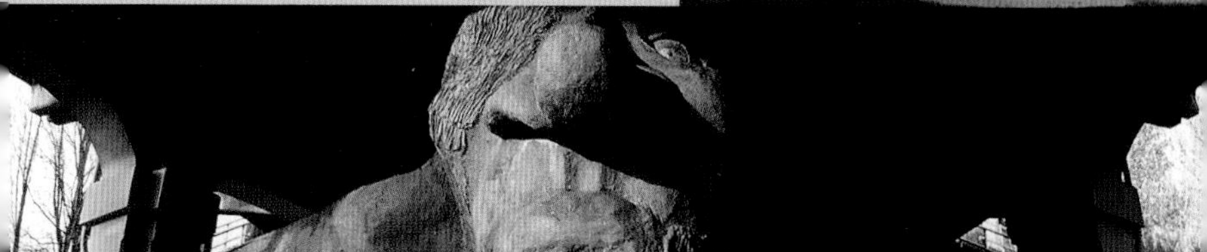

LAWRENCE WORCHESTER

28

WEIRD ART

Located in Seattle's hip and radical Fremont neighborhood is a 7-ton Slovakian bronze statue of Lenin. You can't miss it; it's just down the street from the giant troll under the bridge (p90).

huk, Bluelist contributor

T CHARLES ERICKS

29 OREGON SHAKESPEARE FESTIVAL

We started our drive from San Francisco to Ashland on a Saturday morning and by the evening we were watching *The Two Gentlemen of Verona* in a replica Shakespearian theater (p319). The crowd was enthralled with the show but I couldn't help noticing the sky turn bright orange above the roofless setting.

Heather Dickson, Lonely Planet, Oakland

Contents

Regional Map Contents

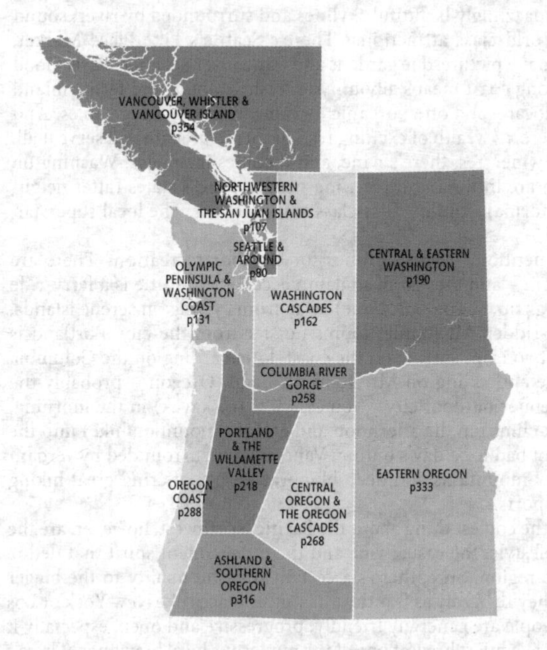

Destination Pacific Northwest

You hold in your hands a guide to one of the most glorious regions in the US. From the early European settlers who first began to trickle into the West 200 years ago to today's flow of modern-day explorers seeking that has-it-all haven, the Pacific Northwest has always exerted a strong pull on the adventurous of spirit. Mention the Northwest to folks outside this area and you'll start a conversation on the region's lush forests, snow-dusted volcanic mountains and amazing waterways and coastlines. Then you might gab about the vibrant economy, up-and-down unemployment rates and computer industry (that's the 'Silicon Forest' to the uninitiated). And certainly you'll discuss the rain (though it doesn't rain here as much as in Florida or Louisiana, believe it or not!). Locals don't mind, though, since it keeps everyone else from moving in, buying up cheap real estate and plopping down in their backyard. (Actually it might already a bit late for that.)

FAST FACTS

Pacific Northwest population: 14.5 million

Regional unemployment rate: 4.8%

Height of Mt Rainier, the highest peak in the Cascades: 14410ft (4392m)

Number of extinct volcanoes within city limits: two (in Bend, OR, and Portland, OR)

Approximate number of breweries in the Pacific Northwest: 220

But grey skies, green forests, high-tech industries and cheap housing aside, there's so much more on offer in the Pacific Northwest. For metro lovers, there are the sophisticated cities of Seattle, Portland and Vancouver. We're talking top-notch museums, refined culture and upscale cuisine, all wrapped in dazzlingly beautiful skylines and surrounded by river, sound or strait. World-class attractions? There's Seattle's Pike Place Market, Portland's many picturesque gardens and Vancouver's Stanley Park. Good food? The long coast means a bounty of fresh seafood, and fertile inland soils mean local – and often organic – grains, meats and vegetables. And of course there's a wealth of exciting restaurants to prepare and serve it all. How about wine? Yes, there's wine, and it comes in spades. Washington and Oregon are in the top three wine-producing US states (after neighboring California). And it's first-class stuff, too – try the local superstar, pinot noir.

Did we mention the possibilities for outdoor recreation? There are *heaps* of them – and they're all so damn accessible! Seattle is a ferry-ride (or kayaking trip, of you fancy one) away from cycling on serene islands, and glacier-ridden Mt Rainier looms not far from the city. Portland is an hour or two from surfing on the coast, kiteboarding on the Columbia River Gorge and skiing on Mt Hood. In Bend, Oregon – probably the region's premier outdoor city – you can hike (or kayak) in the morning, ski (or rock climb) in the afternoon and golf (or mountain bike) into the evening. Not bad for a day's outing. Vancouver is surrounded by verdant forests, lofty mountains and deep-blue waterways, offering great hiking and water sports.

Perhaps the coolest thing about the Pacific Northwest, however, are the laid-back lifestyle, the casual vibe and the independent spirit that define this unique region. Sure, there's a certain stressful quality to the bigger cities, but they're hardly as frantic or taxing as places like New York or Los Angeles. People are generally friendly, progressive and open, especially if you buy them a microbrew at one of the numerous local brewpubs. There's not much of a dress code; with the weather and outdoors so 'in your face,' you can wear Gore-Tex to a fancy restaurant or jeans to the opera and fit right in. Grungy hipsters, nerdy tech-heads, responsible dog-owners and organic gardeners all abound. Hanging out at a coffee shop for hours, drinking the Northwest's premium java and accessing wi-fi on a laptop is so common that you'll wonder if anyone around here has a *real* job. For most who settle in this region, quality of life matters more than a full bank account or a glamorous facelift.

But a laid-back outlook doesn't mean Northwesterners don't care what's going on around them. Quite the opposite: they're highly attuned to the economy and the political bubble of the region, and whatever is going on outside of it. People in the region's major cities tend to lean towards the political left, boasting progressive views and perhaps being part of an activist group, while smaller towns are much more conservative (but still friendly). Almost everyone is quick to voice their own opinion, whether it's the spotted owls versus 'forest management' controversy or personal rights – like Oregon's famous 'death with dignity' act – versus conservative ethics. People are deeply concerned about their environment and what's happening to affect their valued and independent lifestyle here in the Northwest.

This region is also vibrant place in terms of ethnicity. Seattle has attracted a large variety of peoples, and claims a varied palate that includes African American, Hispanic and folk from various Asian cultures. In Portland, while many locals lament the city's white-bread status – at least compared to its sister cities in the Northwest – the city does actually have a fair share of the rainbow, with over 20% of the population possessing non-European blood. British Columbia is Canada's quintessential melting pot of cultures, creeds and ethnicities, making the province as varied in terms of culture as it is in terms of ecology. Minorities here include a large percentage of Chinese and those from the subcontinent.

Dandy as things are in the Pacific Northwest, not everything is perfect. Urban sprawl is a major issue around Seattle, Portland and Vancouver, which have attracted so many transplants from other states (especially California) that they've grown like weeds in the past decade or two. Illegal drug problems do exist, especially methamphetamine abuse. Plenty of people smoke marijuana. And recent drought years, climate change–related or not, have affected the ski industry, broken record temperatures, intensified wildfires, affected coastal whale habitats and killed salmon in too-warm rivers. These are problems that affect many high-density areas, and unfortunately the Northwest hasn't been able to escape all these metropolitan plagues.

Yet the Pacific Northwest's highly livable reputation remains solid (and well deserved), and while the cost of living might be slowly increasing over time, what residents get in return is undeniably worth the trouble. On a clear day, the inspiring spectacle of the outdoors – such as that inspirational volcanic peak – is visible even from the biggest cities. That nature-loving, independent spirit is all around in this often quirky region that tends to shy from the traditional mainstream. Perhaps it's a flashback to those resilient pioneers, fueled by the determination to push ever further into the unknown. Though today's Northwest populations tend to be driven by espresso rather than the desire to chart new territory, there remains a culture founded on restless idealism and the sense that there's still more prospecting to do. Indeed, you're expected to delve into the outdoors and scout on your own, so remember to pack some hiking boots and an adventurous attitude. And remember that no matter how long you're here and how much you end up doing, there will always be something left to explore the next time around – handy, since there's no doubt you'll soon want to come back to the Pacific Northwest.

Getting Started

The Pacific Northwest is an easy, fun and scenic place to travel. Pick a theme if you want – camping, regional festivals, a microbrewery tour, waterfall hikes, crossing all the US–Canadian borders – or combine several. Having your own car makes life much, much easier, especially when exploring those off the beaten paths, of which there are many. Just keep in mind that summertime requires some planning ahead for long ferry lines, full hotels and busy destinations – everyone else wants in on the fun too.

WHEN TO GO

What you want to do should determine when to visit the Pacific Northwest. Summer (generally Memorial Day to Labor Day) is high season, when masses of tourists descend on the beaches, mountains and waterways to camp, hike, swim and generally be outdoors wearing skimpy clothing. Accommodation prices tends to head north at this time as well, but you can't beat the clear skies and warm temperatures. There's a plethora of outdoor festivals, everything is lush and folks are happy to see the sun for long periods.

See Climate Charts (p410) for more information.

Spring and fall can be the best times for some places – the crowds disperse (especially after school starts), prices go down, there's less competition for campsites and hotels, and fall colors emerge or springtime wildflowers bloom. Some services (say, raft rentals or ferry schedules) might be more limited, but still available. Spring weather can be undependable, but Indian summer tends to last through October.

Winter tends to mean overcast days, cool temperatures and plenty of rain. It's a great time for indoor cultural activities in cities, such as music, theater and dance. Outdoors, ice-skating and fishing are possible, but the big draw is downhill skiing – there are some awesome slopes in the region, like Whistler in British Columbia, Crystal Mountain in Washington and Mt Bachelor in Oregon. And winter action doesn't get any bigger than Vancouver's 2010 Winter Olympics.

COSTS & MONEY

Traveling costs in the Pacific Northwest depend on you, of course. Accommodations are the biggest cost, ranging from $10 to $18 for a comfortable campsite to $60 for a cheap motel room, and $120 or more for a nice hotel or B&B room. Avoid public holidays and summertime for the lowest rates (though some snow destinations may cost just as much in winter). Fix your own food (many hotel rooms have kitchenettes) to save on restaurant meals – a good choice for families. Many markets have cheap takeout also.

HOW MUCH?

Cup of coffee $1.50

Midrange motel room $80

Dinner for two at a nice restaurant $60

Movie ticket $10

DON'T LEAVE HOME WITHOUT

- Ear plugs – useful in any hotel anywhere.
- Wet-weather gear – rain jackets, gum boots and umbrellas.
- Mosquito repellent – essential for summer camping.
- Swimsuit – hot springs, pools, beaches, rivers and lakes.
- Binoculars – spotted owls, humpback whales, the Seattle Mariners…
- Bottle openers – to get all those microbrews and wine bottles open.

Car rental rates start from about $150 to $175 per week, depending on the location, dates and vehicle. The best bus route choices are between bigger cities. Car ferries in Washington and British Columbia can be pricey, so check ahead of time if you plan on much island-hopping. See the Transportation chapter (p416) for more information. Parking can be costly in downtown areas, and parking at some hiking trailheads requires a day-use permit of about $5.

Some museums have admission-free or donation days once a week or month, so check their websites or with local visitors centers.

TRAVELING RESPONSIBLY

If anywhere in the USA can be called 'green' it's the Pacific Northwest. Recycling is big, composting is hot and cycling to work is cool. There are hybrid cars on practically every corner, solar-powered parking meters in Portland and biodiesel whale-watching tours in the San Juan Islands. As a visitor to the area, you can also make a difference.

While in Portland, don't miss the world's largest independent bookstore: Powell's Books (www.powells.com).

Getting to the Pacific Northwest

Airplanes are a major polluter. To avoid flying into the area, consider taking the train or bus. Seattle, Portland and Vancouver all have good networks; for details, check out www.greyhoundbuses.com (www.greyhound.ca in Canada) and www.amtrak.com. International flights are pretty much unavoidable, so consider contributing to a carbon offset organization like www.carbonfund.org, www.terrapass.com, www.nativeenergy.com and www.driveneutral.org, who transform your money into support for sustainable practices.

Local travel

Long-distance buses and trains are the best sustainable choice. In big cities, local bus networks are good and biking is a great option (rentals abound). And if you do need a car, think about patronizing www.flexcar.com, a car-sharing program available in Portland and Seattle; try www.zipcar.com for Vancouver. Some car-rental agencies offer hybrid vehicles, so ask.

If you can handle sharing a ride with strangers, check www.craigslist.com, a popular international online bulletin board offering regional rideshares (look under 'community'). Folks here are looking for people to carpool and share the cost of gas.

Go to www.dailycandy.com/seattle/for a dose of everything Seattle has to offer in the worlds of fashion, lifestyle, art and beyond.

Accommodations

Camping is both 'sustainable' and the quintessential summer experience. Yurts are awesome, and many Pacific Northwest campgrounds and resorts have rentals (see p298). Hostels are another green option since their high-density dormitories use less space and energy.

But staying at hotels often can't be helped, of course, but you still have options. Try asking for your linens and towels not be changed for a few days. Utilize only one trash bin in your room to reduce the amount of bin liners wasted. Turn off lights, TV and air con when you leave. Ask the managers if the hotel recycles and composts. Do they use compact fluorescent light bulbs? Less toxic cleaning products? Are they signed up for wind power? And consider not using those inefficient travel-sized sundries.

Portland boasts a couple of hotels with excellent sustainable practices:

Ace Hotel (Portland, OR; p232) Remodeled with eco-friendly materials like US Army jacket fabric couches and reclaimed timber furniture.

Hawthorne Hostel (Portland, OR; p233) Eco-roof, recycling program, bike rentals, use of eco-products use and 100% renewable energy power. Discounts to those traveling by bicycle.

FESTIVAL & EVENTS CALENDAR

January–February

Chinese New Year (Vancouver, BC) Vancouver's large Chinese population has their say with parades, activities, prizes, dragon dances, traditional art and, of course, plenty of great Chinese food.

Oregon Shakespeare Festival (Ashland, OR; p319) Tens of thousands of theater fans party with the Bard at this nine-month-long festival (that's right), highlighted by world-class plays and Elizabethan drama.

March–April

Hood River Valley Blossom Festival (Hood River, OR; p262) Celebrating the fertile Hood River Valley's amazing fruit bounty with food, wine, crafts and a 47-mile festival tour route also known as the Fruit Loop.

Spring Whale-Watching Week (Oregon coast, OR) Spot the gray whale spring migration anywhere along the Pacific Coast, but around Depoe Bay it's semi-organized with docents and special viewpoints.

May

Northwest Folklife Festival (Seattle, WA; p93) This festival is rejoiced with hundreds of musicians, artists and performers from all over the world.

Victoria Day (Victoria, BC; p385) Originally in honor of Queen Victoria's birthday, this Canadian holiday now celebrates the current sovereign's birthday (and unofficial start of the summer season) with parades and fireworks.

June

Portland Rose Festival (Portland, OR; p232) Music concerts, floral parades, children's events, carnival rides, tall sailing ships, dragon-boat races, the naval fleet, fireworks and a half-million spectators.

Britt Festival (Jacksonville, OR; p323) Outdoor summer music celebration featuring world-class jazz, folk, country, and classical music artists, including some mighty big names.

July–August

Oregon Brewers Festival (Portland, OR; p232) Enjoy Portland's prime summer weather at this fun beer festival, where over 50,000 microbrew lovers eat, drink and generally whoop it up.

Seafair (Seattle, WA; p93) Three-week party that includes the arrival of the naval fleet, hydroplane races, a torchlight parade and plenty of music.

September

Pendleton Round-Up (Pendleton, OR; p334) Country music, dances, art shows, a Native American powwow, bronco-breaking and western pageantry preside here, one of the country's most famous rodeos.

Bumbershoot (Seattle, WA; p93) Seattle's biggest arts and cultural event boasts two dozen stages and hundreds of musicians, artists, theater troupes and writers.

October

Oktoberfest (Leavenworth, WA) Oktoberfest in Leavenworth, where men in boyish shorts and vests eat, drink and dance.

Vancouver International Film Festival (Vancouver, BC; p367) Highly regarded film festival screening some 300 international films and documentaries from over 50 countries.

November–December

Victorian Christmas (Jacksonville, OR) A Christmas past; witness a community tree lighting, Victorian ball, Father Christmas parade, carollers and town criers.

New Year's Eve (Seattle, WA) Washington's ground zero for the new year is the Space Needle, where revelers dress up, countdown and drink champagne as fireworks go off.

Restaurants

Plenty of restaurants in the Pacific Northwest use local, organic and seasonal produce, along with 'natural' meats. For a general guide, check www.eatwellguide.org. All three major cities in the region have at least a few eco-minded eateries:

Tilth (Seattle, WA; p100)
Laughing Planet (Portland, OR; p234)
Raincity Grill (Vancouver, BC; p370)

Responsible Travel Links

There are various organizations that identify tourist facilities such as hotels, restaurants and tour operators by a series of sustainable-travel criteria – check www.sustainabletravel.com. And finally, if you're looking to volunteer at an organic farm, see www.organicvolunteers.com and www.wwoofusa.org.

TRAVEL LITERATURE

Rained out for a few days? Read an adventure before the sun comes out again.

Jack Kerouac's *Desolation Angels* was written during a two-month spell as a fire lookout on Desolation Peak in the North Cascade Mountains. An autobiographical novel dealing with psychological struggles and disenchantments with Buddhism.

Echoes of Fury: The Eruption of Mount St Helens and the Lives it Changed Forever by Frank Parchman is a captivating tale that follows the lives of eight people whose lives were changed by the eruption on May 18, 1980. Suspenseful, thrilling and heart breaking.

Check out www.portlandpicks.com for Portland-centric life and style articles.

The Forest Lover by Susan Vreeland tells of ground-breaking Canadian painter Emily Carr's early 1900s travels through the Native American lands, seeking to paint indigenous art and traditions before they died out.

The Good Rain: Across Time and Terrain in the Pacific Northwest, by *New York Times* correspondent and Pulitzer Prize winner Timothy Egan, gives a fantastic insight into the Northwest and its people.

INTERNET RESOURCES

Lonely Planet (www.lonelyplanet.com) The nexus of the world between planning and travel.

Oregon.gov (www.oregon.gov) Oregon's official site, complete with welcome by the esteemed governor.

Oregon Tourism Commission (www.traveloregon.com) Dizzying number of suggestions about what to do in Oregon – this pretty much covers it all.

Seattle Tourism (www.seattle.gov) The emerald city's official site, in 26 different languages! Click on the 'Visiting' tab.

Tourism British Columbia (www.hellobc.com) Official tourism site of British Columbia, with its own little blog section.

United States Forest Service (www.fs.fed.us/r6) Recreational possibilities, campsite descriptions, weather links, permit information, maps, volunteering…

Washington State Tourism (www.experiencewa.com) Look up information on any significant town or city in Washington.

Itineraries

CLASSIC ROUTES

HIGHWAY 101 – LAND'S EDGE TOUR **Two Weeks**

In British Columbia, a stretch of Hwy 101 forms the **Sunshine Coast** (p379), a getaway accessible only by ferry. Skip way south to **Olympia** (p132), where 101 circles the Olympic Peninsula before heading south.

Port Townsend (p145) makes a fun stop before reaching **Lake Crescent** (p140) and its great vistas. Nearby are the mineral waters of **Sol Duc Hot Springs** (p141). Just south (but a long drive around) is the **Hoh Rain Forest** (p142), with its short but magical Hall of Moss Trail. Back on 101, enjoy the wild ocean scenery before reaching **Kalaloch Lodge** (p145); stay here for an exceptional dining and overnight experience. Further south, beautiful **Lake Quinault** (p142) is a scenic glacial lake with more resorts.

Once you cross into Oregon, **Astoria** (p290) features historical attractions. Enjoy the awesome scenery of **Three Capes Drive** (p296), then take a whale-watching excursion at **Depoe Bay** (p299). Newport's first-rate **Oregon Coast Aquarium** (p299) is fantastic, and the **Oregon Dunes** (p305) are unique. **Cape Blanco** (p311) juts way westward and offers exhilarating views. **Gold Beach** (p312) is renowned for its Rogue River fishing, while south of here is Oregon's most magnificent coastal scenery.

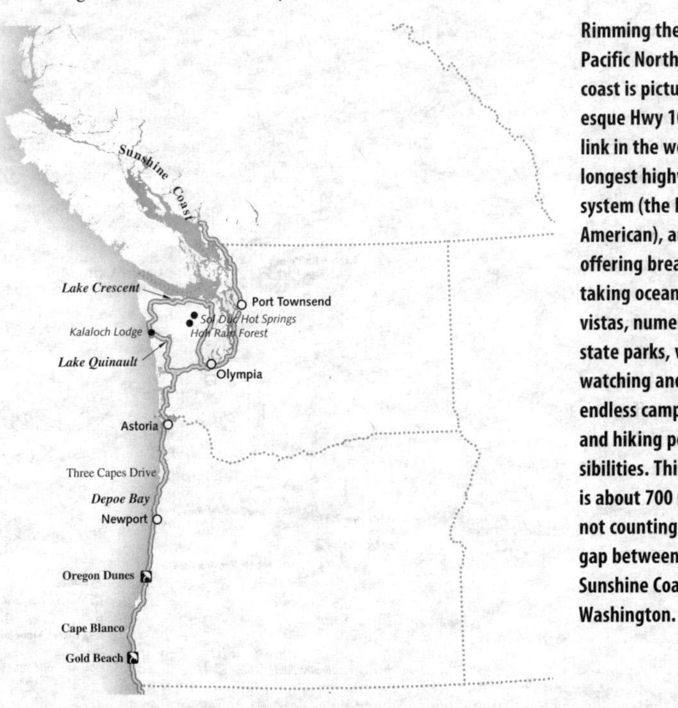

Rimming the Pacific Northwest coast is picturesque Hwy 101, a link in the world's longest highway system (the Pan-American), and offering breathtaking ocean vistas, numerous state parks, whale-watching and endless camping and hiking possibilities. This trip is about 700 miles, not counting the gap between the Sunshine Coast and Washington.

SUMMER WILDLIFE SAFARI – PNW STYLE

Two Weeks

Start by scanning for orcas and minke whales from **Lime Kiln Point State Park** (p123), on San Juan Island in Washington. If you're lucky, you might also spot them while on ferry rides around Puget Sound. A bit east, the **Upper Skagit River Valley** (p167) is the nesting site of up to 20 bald eagles – but you'll see many more in winter. Southwards is **Mt Rainier** (p179), home to endearing marmots and pikas, who like the high altitudes of the Cascade Range (as do black bears).

On the Oregon Coast, **Yaquina Head Outstanding Natural Area** (p300) has some of the region's best viewpoints for shorebirds and various pinnipeds, along with some prime tide pools. Grey whales migrate between Alaska and Mexico from December to June, though you can spot resident pods all year round in **Depoe Bay** (p299). For guaranteed sea lion sightings, stop at touristy **Sea Lion Caves** (p302). Roosevelt elk hang out a bit further south at **Dean Creek Elk Viewing Area** (p307).

Inland and to the east, bird-watchers shouldn't miss the **Klamath Basin National Wildlife Refuges** (p332), which support up to two million waterfowl during peak spring and fall migrations. Hundreds of bald eagles come here from November to February, but you might spot a few outside winter too.

For pronghorn antelope, your best bet is near the southeastern corner of Oregon, at **Hart Mountain National Antelope Refuge** (p352) – if you look hard enough, you might spot some bighorn sheep as well. Wild mustangs have inhabited the nearby **Steens Mountain** (p3510) area for hundreds of years. Finally, just a bit north is **Malheur National Wildlife Refuge** (p350), with more top-notch bird-watching; in spring, Sandhill cranes are a highlight.

Animal lovers have plenty to see in the Pacific Northwest, whose thick forests, alpine mountains and long shoreline offer sanctuary to countless birds, large mammals and marine life. Here's just a taste of what the region has to offer; this general itinerary covers about 1100 miles.

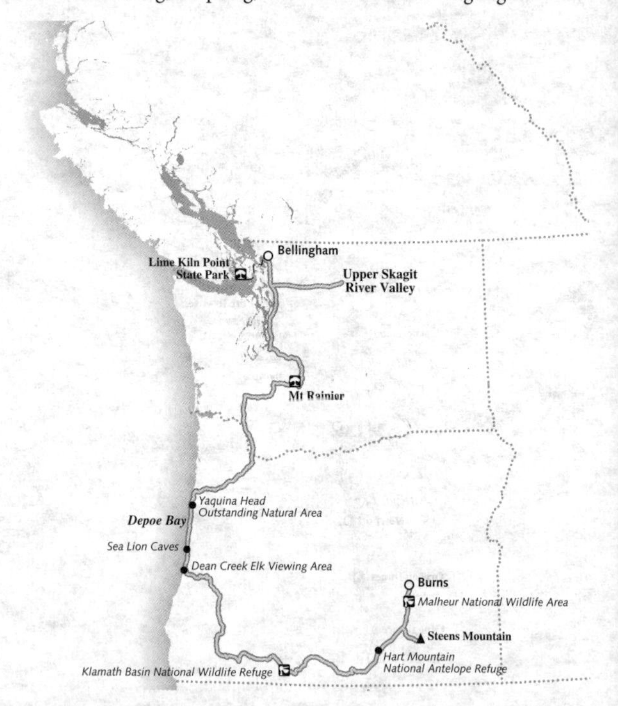

PACIFIC NORTHWEST GRAND TOUR **Six Weeks**

Just want to hit the highlights? Then here's where you should go. **Vancouver's** (p355) ethnic attractions and parks are a must, as are the **Southern Gulf Islands** (p404). For European charm there's no beating **Victoria** (p381). On Vancouver Island, **Tofino** (p399) has great surfing, and for rustic beaches there's **Cape Scott Provincial Park** (p403). Ski-hounds should head to **Whistler** (p376), while the **Sunshine Coast** (p379) makes a great getaway.

In Washington, you can't miss scenic and top-notch **Seattle** (p80). In the San Juans there's beautiful **Orcas Island** (p125), but for the definitive wilderness experience head to **North Cascades National Park** (p168). On the Olympic Peninsula the **Hoh Rain Forest** (p142) boasts a unique ecosystem. **Olympia** (p132) might possibly be the coolest town in Washington, with stunningly gorgeous **Mt Rainier National Park** (p179) not far away. For a vaguely surreal Bavarian experience be sure to hit **Leavenworth** (p191), and for an attractive, laid-back town with awesome wineries head way east to **Walla Walla** (p213).

There's no escaping the attractions in **Portland** (p220) – and you won't want to. Just east are the grand vistas of the **Columbia River Gorge** (p258), while nearby **Mt Hood** (p269) is a must for hiking and the historic Timberline Lodge. To the south, expanding **Bend** (p278) is the ultimate sports town, with nearly limitless outdoor recreational activities. For supreme scenery and geologic wonders there's **Crater Lake National Park** (p285). Shakespeare aficionados beeline to Ashland's famous **Oregon Shakespeare Festival** (p319). Nearby **Jacksonville** (p323) is quaintly historic and worth a visit. Dazzling mountain scenery is on tap at **Steens Mountain** (p351), while just east the **Alvord Desert** (p351) has an equally stunning landscape. Finally there's the grandeur (and seafood cuisine) of the **Oregon Coast** (p288).

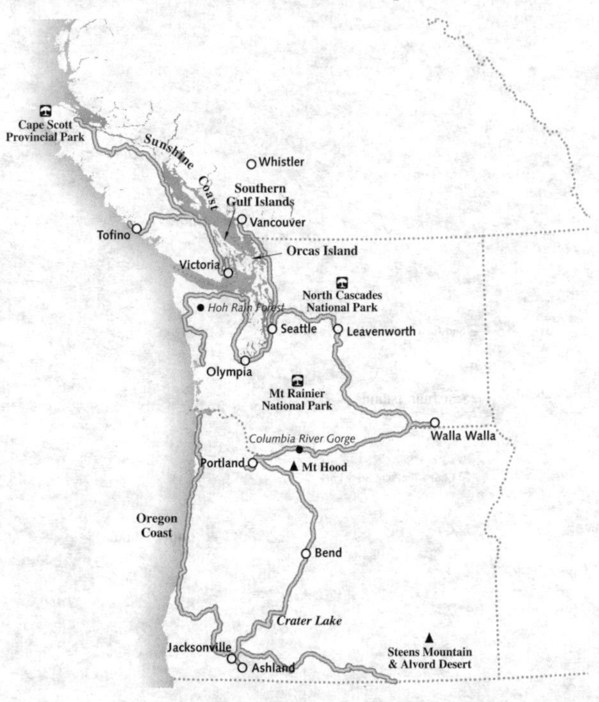

The best of the Pacific Northwest means sophisticated cities nestled on pretty waterways, a spectacular volcanic mountain chain, fantastic hiking opportunities and grand scenery all around. From lush islands to eccentric small towns to stunning desert formations, this tour takes it all in – but doing everything might require driving some 2000 miles, so pick and choose.

ISLAND HOPPING

MERRY GO AROUND THE SAN JUANS **One Week**

Washington's San Juans are an archipelago of hundreds of islands covering some 750 sq miles. Only about 40 are inhabited, and just four are accessible by public ferry. Three of these islands bring thousands of vacationers every year, but all have managed to keep a serene atmosphere and distinct character.

San Juan Island (p122) has the best tourist facilities of the islands, along with the archipelago's only sizeable town, Friday Harbor. **Lime Kiln Point State Park** (p123) has prime whale-watching shores; in June, keep a look out for killer or minke whales feasting on salmon runs. To the north is the English Camp of the **San Juan Island National Historical Park** (p123), with old British military facilities and earthwork fortifications and, on clear days, great mountain views.

The largest of the islands, **Orcas Island** (p125) is probably the most beautiful – and also the poshest. It's laced with fancy homes and resort communities, and the lack of a central town gives it an exclusive neighborhood feel. Stay, or just grab a mud bath, at the swanky **Rosario Resort & Spa** (p126). For less money, check out **Moran State Park** (p126), which offers camping, fishing, hiking and mountain biking. **Mt Constitution** (p126), the highest point in the archipelago, is also here, and features some of the finest views in Washington.

Lopez Island (p129) is the most peaceful island, with friendly locals and pastoral charm. Don't expect too many tourist services – agriculture and farming are the main focus here. The mostly flat island is made for cycling, and there's little vehicular traffic; bike rentals (or kayaks) are available at the marina.

Tropical they're not, but you can still have a blast on the San Juan Islands. Hiking, biking and whale-watching are a few possibilities, as is simply taking in some relaxed island rhythms. Expect to cover around 120 miles on this hop, including a loop around Lopez Island.

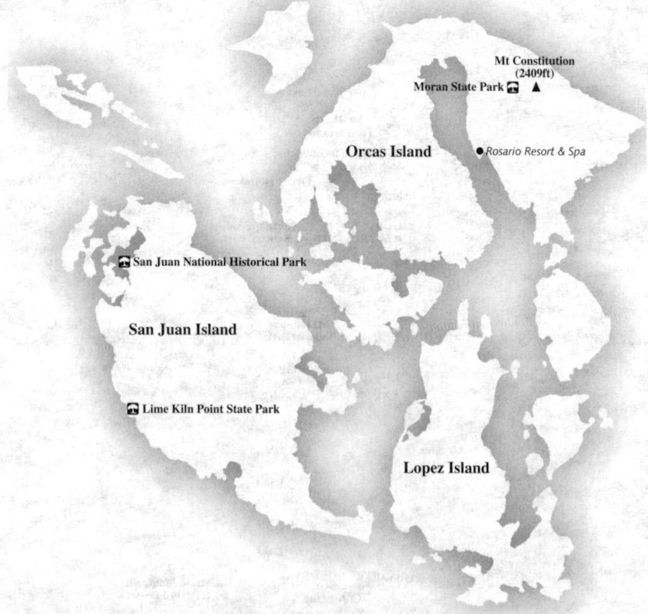

Mt Constitution (2409ft)
Moran State Park
Orcas Island
Rosario Resort & Spa
San Juan National Historical Park
San Juan Island
Lime Kiln Point State Park
Lopez Island

VANCOUVER ISLAND ADVENTURE

10 Days

Start your adventure in lovely **Victoria** (p381), a cosmopolitan city with a variety of ethnic cultures – yet maintaining a touch of old Britain. You can wander through old-world streets and stroll through worthwhile museums, all the while enjoying the city's nicely restored 19th-century architecture. Can't-miss attractions include the world-famous **Butchart Gardens** (p392), a few miles north of town, and high tea at the grand **Empress Hotel** (p388).

Just south of Victoria is the little hamlet of **Sooke** (p393), at the western tip of Vancouver Island. All around are recreational highlights like beachcombing, swimming and hiking. Directly north about 50 miles is **Chemainus** (p394), a town boasting dozens of artsy outdoor murals painted on city buildings – a big tourist draw. Heading west you'll eventually reach the spectacularly located town of **Tofino** (p399), where you can go kayaking, explore gorgeous islands and spot marine life like gray whales. Nearby is **Pacific Rim National Park Reserve** (p397), home to rain forests, crashing coastal surf, adventurous islands and amazing hiking opportunities.

At the heart of the island lies **Strathcona Provincial Park** (p402), Vancouver's largest park and BC's oldest protected area. It's a paradise for fishing, hiking and camping fans, and boasts Canada's highest waterfall. There's more whale-watching toward the northern end of Victoria Island, at **Telegraph Cove** (p402), a village mostly built over the water on wooden pilings; spotting orcas is a highlight here. Finally, head to land's end at **Cape Scott Provincial Park** (p403) and the surrounding area to explore the island's most remote and pristine beaches. Self-sufficient outdoor lovers have miles of challenging trails and backcountry camping opportunities at this isolated park – and the chance to get away from it all.

Explore BC's premiere island, boasting such gems as lovely Victoria, rich with history, architecture and gardens. Outdoor enthusiasts will love the exceptional hiking and wildlife-viewing opportunities, while natural beauty abounds around every corner. You'll cover over 700 miles on this adventure, including some backtracking.

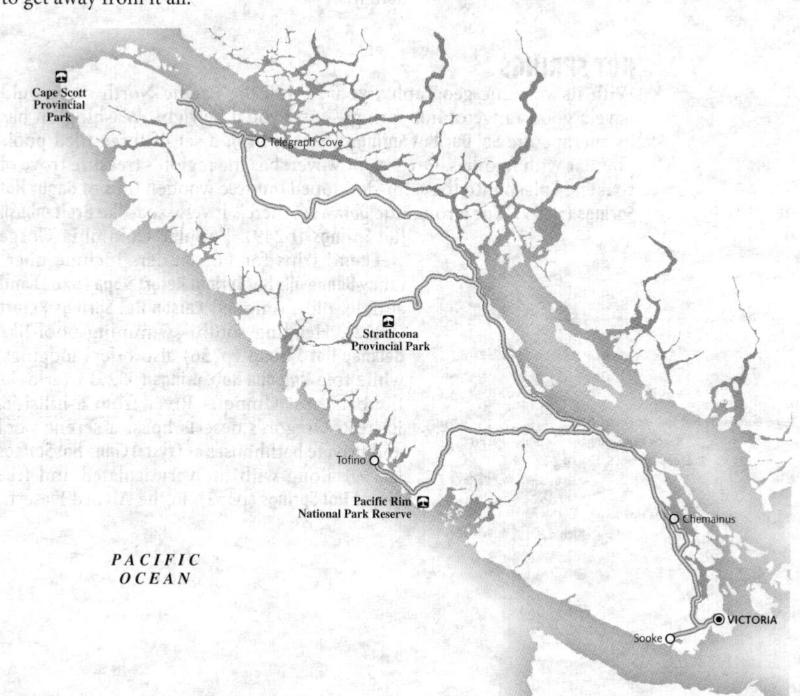

TAILORED TRIPS

MICROBREWERIES

Beer-lovers have hit the jackpot in the Pacific Northwest, which boasts one of the world's highest density of microbreweries. Start quaffing in Vancouver at **Granville Island Brewing** (p364), Canada's first microbrewery – opened in 1984. Now head south to Seattle for a pint at **Hale's Ales Brewery, Pike Pub & Brewery** and **Elysian Brewing Co** (p101) – all with very tasty options. Outside the emerald city, try award-winning **Boundary Bay Brewery** (p112) in Bellingham, McMenamins **Olympic Club Hotel** (p156) in Centralia, small **Fishbowl BrewPub** (p134) in Olympia and worthwhile **Mill Creek Brewpub** (p216) in Walla Walla.

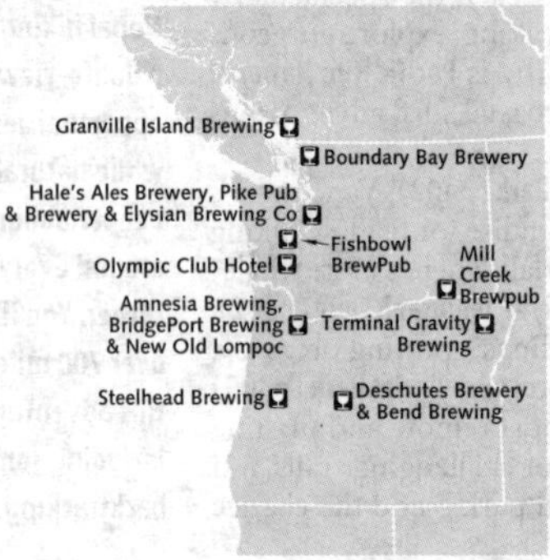

Portland has around 30 microbreweries, the most of any city in the world. Tried and true ones here include **Amnesia Brewing** (p237), **BridgePort Brewpub** (p237) and **New Old Lompoc** (p237) – all have good attached restaurants and outdoor patios. Eugene boasts several of its own, including first-rate **Steelhead Brewing** (p255); in Bend, **Deschutes Brewery** and **Bend Brewing** (p282) are worth a pint or three. And if you find yourself in Enterprise, don't miss **Terminal Gravity Brewing** (p339) – one of Eastern Oregon's finest yeasty delights.

HOT SPRINGS

With its volcanic geography, you'd think the Pacific Northwest would have a good range of hot springs – and you'd be right. Washington has its therapeutic **Sol Duc Hot Springs Resort** (p141), a set of three-tiled pools popular with families. Oregon, however, has the region's treasure trove of soakers. Splash into the semi-developed but free wooden tubs of **Bagby Hot Springs** (p249). For a romantic getaway, there's lovely, spa-like **Breitenbush Hot Springs** (p249). Popular Columbia Gorge weekend trips for Portlanders include uber-fancy **Bonneville Hot Springs Resort & Spa** (p262) and simple, old-fashioned **Carson Hot Springs Resort** (p262). Heading south, swimming-pool-like **Belknap Hot Springs** (p256) also offers lodgings, while free **Umpqua Hot Springs** (p329) overlooks the beautiful Umpqua River from a hillside. Eastern Oregon's deserts boast a serene pool and private bathhouses at **Crystal Crane Hot Springs** (p350) along with the very isolated and free **Alvord Hot Springs** (p352), in the Alvord Desert.

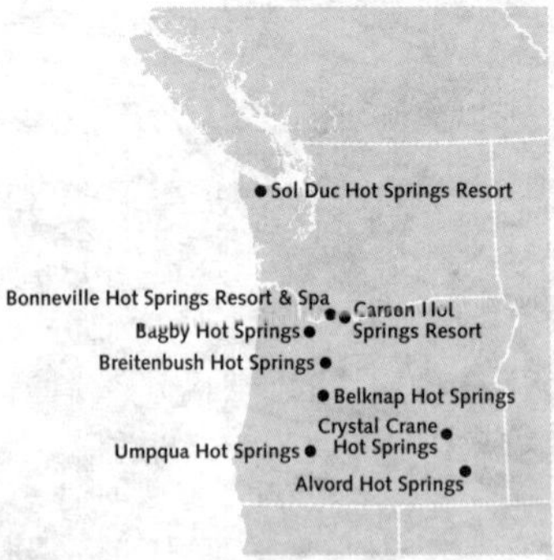

TRAVEL WITH KIDS

Home to millipedes and tarantulas, what could be better than BC's **Victoria Bug Zoo** (p384)? In Vancouver, **Science World** (p363) and the **Vancouver Aquarium** (p362) are fun highlights.

Seattle has a plethora of offerings, from interactive museums to waterfront distractions; see p92. Tacoma's **Point Defiance Zoo & Aquarium** (p106) is a wonderland boasting sharks *and* elephants. In Bellingham, the **Whatcom Children's Museum** (p110) offers imaginative activities and workshops. For warm weather fun, head to **Slidewaters** (p177), a water park at Lake Chelan. Meanwhile, Olympia's **Hands On Children's Museum** (p133) stimulates little brains.

Portland has several cool things for children, from frolicking fountains to a world-class zoo; see p231. Salem has interactive exhibits at the **AC Gilbert's Discovery Village** (p247), though the little squirts might prefer the nearby theme park **Enchanted Forest** (p248). Eugene's **Science Factory** (p251) has hands-on learning displays, while south in Winston there's a real **Wildlife Safari** (p328). Bend's excellent **High Desert Museum** (p278) boasts a sea otter exhibit, and Ashland's **Science Works** (p318) makes the kids think hard. Head to the coast for Newport's world-class **Oregon Coast Aquarium** (p299) and Port Orford's dinosaur-filled **Prehistoric Gardens** (p311).

NATURAL WONDERS

Nature lovers rejoice; the Pacific Northwest holds gorgeous landscapes that will rejuvenate your spirit and stretch your hiker's legs. Here are the region's best places to commune with the outside world.

On the west coast of Vancouver Island in BC is the magnificent **Pacific Rim National Park Reserve** (p397), encompassing three geographically distinct regions. Not far away are the **Southern Gulf Islands** (p404), which have attracted artists with their mild climate and natural beauty.

Nearby, but in Washington, are the **San Juan Islands** (p119), a popular yet tranquil archipelago. To the east, the dramatic peaks of **North Cascades National Park** (p168) feature top-notch panoramas, while glorious **Olympic National Park** (p137) has a wide variety of ecosystems. Inland, **Mt Rainier National Park** (p179) boasts Washington's tallest mountain.

Oregon's **Columbia River Gorge** (p258) is strewn with waterfalls, awesome hikes and spectacular scenery. Way to the east, **Hells Canyon** (p342) is North America's deepest gorge. **Crater Lake** (p285), the state's only national park, offers exquisite scenery. Finally, way to the southeast is **Steens Mountain** (p351) and the **Alvord Desert** (p351) – both boasting unforgettable beauty and isolation.

WINERIES

The Pacific Northwest is a top wine-growing region, with Washington and Oregon ranking second and third (after neighbor California) for state wine grape production. Washington's Columbia Valley and Oregon's Willamette Valley claim the lion's share of the region's wineries.

In Spokane, Washington, gurgle the cabernet at **Caterina Winery** or the Riesling at **Latah Creek Wine Cellars** (p206). For good chardonnay, head to **Woodward Canyon Winery** or **Waterbrook Winery** (p214), both in Walla Walla. In Yakima Valley you can enjoy merlot with a view at **Sagelands Vineyard** (p203).

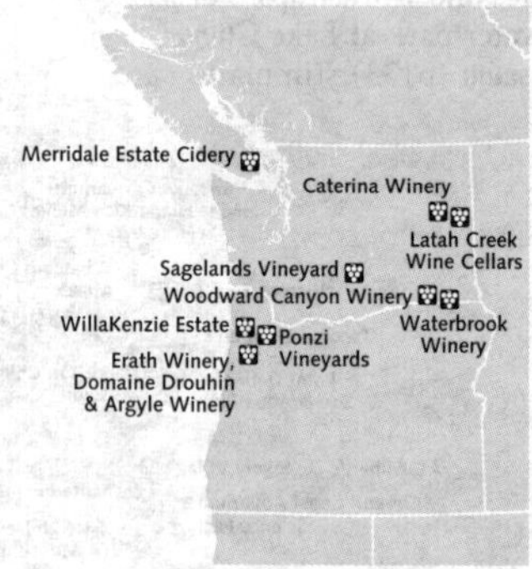

Oregon's Willamette Valley produces some of the world's best pinot noirs. Try a few sips at **Domaine Drouhin** (p244), a luxurious European-style spot with great views. **WillaKenzie Estate** (p244) is also impressive and slightly off the beaten path. **Erath** (p244) and **Ponzi Vineyards** (p244) are two of the oldest wineries in this region and helped pioneer wine-making in Oregon, while **Argyle Winery** (p244) is famous for sparkling wines.

For BC wineries you'll have to head east to the Okanagan Valley, covered in Lonely Planet's *British Columbia* guidebook.

BEST HIKES

If there's one thing the Pacific Northwest has in spades, it's a bounty of great hiking. After all, the area is full of mountains, forests, rivers, coastline and deserts. Listed here are a few favorites – and it's just the very tip of the iceberg!

Vancouver Island has the highly challenging **West Coast Trail** (p398) in the Pacific Rim National Park Reserve; it features rock-face ladders, stream crossings and other adversities.

Washington offers the unforgettable **Wonderland Trail** (p183) – a classic 93-mile circumnavigation of Mt Rainier. Trudge up 6.8 miles to **Desolation Peak** (p171), where novelist Jack Kerouac spent a summer. To witness amazing glaciers, head up to the supremely scenic 3.5-mile **Cascade Pass** (p170). Finally, for a good leg-stretch there's the **Pacific Coastal hike** (p144), stretching 20 miles between Ozette and Rialto Beach.

Oregon's coast has the strenuous 4-mile hike up **Neahkahnie Mountain** (p295), with spectacular views. In the Columbia River Gorge, the 13-mile-long **Eagle Creek Trail** (p261) is a classic, boasting stunning waterfalls and sheer canyons. To the south, the **Timberline Trail** (p271) is a 40-mile loop around lovely Mt Hood. Meanwhile, the **McKenzie River National Recreation Trail** (p256) follows the wild and scenic McKenzie for 26.5 miles through lush forests.

History

FROM ASIA THEY CAME

About 25,000 years ago, humans first stepped into North America via a convenient land bridge from Siberia to Alaska. This area, now underwater, is currently known as the Bering Strait. These early hunter-gatherers became the ancestors of Native Americans, and over millennia spread themselves down through the Americas. A multitude of tribes, each with its own culture and language, existed around the Pacific Northwest.

Coastal inhabitants – who tromped up and down the Pacific Coast, around Puget Sound and along river valleys – went out to sea in pursuit of whales or sea lions, or depended on catching salmon and cod, and collecting shellfish. On land they hunted deer and elk while gathering berries and roots. Life was good during these early days, especially in the Pacific Northwest's glorious warmer months. Plenty of food could be stored for the long winters, when free time could be spent on artistic, religious and cultural pursuits like putting on potlatches (ceremonial feasts), taking part in 'vision quests' (spiritual trances) or carving dancing masks and totem poles. The construction of ornately carved cedar canoes led to extensive trading networks among the permanent settlements that stretched along the coast.

www.oregonpioneers.com/ortrail.htm is specially good for its information on Native Americans. Also has good trivia, such as provisions that pioneers needed for the Oregon Trail.

Inland, on the arid plateaus between the Cascades and the Rocky Mountains, a regional culture based on seasonal migration between rivers and temperate uplands developed. Tribes like the Nez Perce, Cayuse, Spokane, Yakama and Kootenai displayed cultural features of both the coastal Native Americans and the plains Native Americans east of the Rockies. During salmon runs, the tribes gathered at rapids and waterfalls to net or harpoon fish, which they then dried or smoked. Most transportation was overland, with large dogs serving as pack animals until horses arrived in the 18th century.

In the harsh landscapes of Oregon's southern desert, another culture evolved. Tribes such as the Shoshone, Paiute and Bannock were nomadic peoples who hunted and scavenged in the northern reaches of the Great Basin desert. Berries, roots and small game such as gophers and rabbits constituted their meager diet. Clusters of easily transported, woven-reed shelters made up migratory villages. Religious and cultural life focused on shamans, who could tap into the spirit world to heal sickness or bring success in hunting.

Possibly the world's oldest shoes – a pair of sagebrush sandals – were discovered in Oregon and are now displayed in Eugene's University of Oregon Museum of Natural History (p251).

EUROPEANS MAKE A SPLASH

Native peoples were doing fine by themselves until the 16th century, when the white man finally came knocking. The Pacific Northwest was one of the last areas up for grabs for European colonialism and economic exploitation –

TIMELINE

c 13000 BC

Epic glacial floods carve out 4000ft cliffs along an 80-mile section of the Columbia River Gorge. Eventually the river will stretch to 1243 miles long.

c 5600 BC

Mt Mazama erupts in an explosion estimated to be over 40 times more powerful than Mt St Helen's in 1980. Its elevation is reduced by a half-mile, but the subsequent collapsed caldera creates what is now the gorgeous Crater Lake.

AD 1543

Spanish Captain Bartolomé Ferrelo is one of the first Europeans to sight the Pacific Northwest coast, heading as far north as Oregon's Cape Blanco in search of the fabled Northwest Passage.

CHIEF SEALTH

'How can you buy or sell the sky, the warmth of the land?' Chief Sealth (Seattle) of the Duwamish tribe stated in his famous speech. 'If we do not own the freshness of the air and the sparkle of the water, how can you buy them? Every shining pine needle, every sandy shore, every mist in the dark woods, every clearing and humming insect is holy in the memory and experience of my people...'

The Seattle area was originally the homeland of the peaceful Duwamish tribe, who initially welcomed members of the Denny party when they arrived in 1851. Chief Sealth (1786–1866) had urged peaceful coexistence between his tribe and the whites. Relations with other tribes in Puget Sound were not as good however – in 1855, warfare erupted between the natives and European settlers, and in the end the settlers prevailed.

The Duwamish were moved to the port Madison Reservation in 1856 despite their peaceable history. In part to recognize Chief Sealth's aid and pacifist efforts, the settlers renamed their town in the chief's honor. Apparently the honor did not exactly please Chief Sealth: according to Duwamish beliefs, if someone utters a dead person's name, the soul of the deceased is denied everlasting peace.

exactly 300 years passed between Columbus's discovery of America and the discovery of the Columbia River, one of the continent's largest water systems. The reason why is the region's faraway location and its wacky weather, which even today keeps the softies away. The rocky and storm-wracked coasts of the Pacific Northwest didn't make landings easy.

The first Europeans to clap eyes on the area were the crew of Portuguese explorer Juan Rodríguez Cabrillo (sailing for the Spanish). In 1542, his ship took off from Mexico and reached the mouth of the Rogue River in 1543, but the coast was too stormy to attempt a landing (Cabrillo wasn't there – he had unfortunately died along the way). English explorer Sir Frances Drake checked out the region in 1579, but headed back home soon after, also likely discouraged by storms. By the 18th century, the Spanish had colonized the southern parts of California and had begun to explore the northern Pacific Coast in earnest. They were looking for the Northwest Passage, a fabled direct water route from the Pacific Ocean to the Atlantic Ocean. The Spanish were also keen on investigating the land that lay between them and their potential new neighbor to the north, Russia. (The Russians had begun to make claims along the Pacific Coast in the late 18th century, after Peter the Great sent Danish explorer and navigator Vitus Bering on an expedition of the area.) By 1774, Spanish frigates reached as far north as the Queen Charlotte Islands, claiming the Northwest coast for the Spanish crown.

Stan Rogers, a popular Canadian folk singer, wrote the song 'Northwest Passage' in 1981 to mark history's attempts to establish this almost-fabled route.

The British, not to be outdone, were also looking for the Northwest Passage. In 1778, Captain James Cook explored the coast of present-day Oregon, Washington and British Columbia, landing at Nootka Sound on Vancouver Island. With him was George Vancouver, who in 1792 became

1792

American Robert Gray finds the elusive mouth of the Columbia River and sails upstream, becoming the first non–Native American to do so. He names the river after his ship, the *Columbia Rediviva*.

1805

Lewis and Clark finally reach the Pacific Ocean, a year and six months after leaving St Louis, Missouri. They lay important groundwork that immensely aids in future US expansion towards the West.

1811

Pacific Fur Company mogul John Jacob Astor establishes Fort Astoria, the first permanent US settlement on the Pacific Coast, at the mouth of the Columbia River. He later becomes the country's first millionaire.

the first European explorer to sail and chart the waters of Puget Sound. The Spanish attempted to build colonies along the Northwest coast – first in 1790 at Neah Bay, on the Olympic Peninsula, and then at Nootka Sound. However, European politics forced Spain to give up its Northwest claim to Britain in 1792.

The Americans also entered the scene in 1792, when Captain Robert Gray spotted the mouth of the Columbia River past obscuring sandbars and hazardous currents. He sailed up the great waterway, traded with the Native Americans and named his discovery the Columbia, in honor of his ship. The true importance of his discovery would be realized later, when it supported US territorial claims to the area.

In 1793 Scottish fur-trader Alexander Mackenzie became the first European to reach the Pacific Ocean via an overland route. He followed Native American trails across the Canadian Rockies to arrive at present-day Bella Coola, on the British Columbian coast, blazing a path for the fur trade. Mackenzie wrote a book about his adventures, which President Thomas Jefferson read with interest. Thus, an American journey was born.

LEWIS & CLARK

In 1801 Jefferson enlisted his personal secretary, Meriwether Lewis, to lead an expedition to chart North America's western regions. The goal was to find a waterway to the Pacific while exploring the newly acquired Louisiana Purchase and establishing foothold for American interests. Lewis, then 27, had no training in this sort of thing, but couldn't resist this grand opportunity. He managed to get his good friend, 33-year-old William Clark, an experienced frontiersman and army veteran, to tag along. In 1804, the party left St Louis, Missouri, heading west with an entourage of 40 adventurers.

The daily logs of Lewis and Clark, as presented in Bernard DeVoto's carefully edited *Journals of Lewis and Clark*, are full of wild adventures, misspellings and wonderful candor.

The Corps of Discovery – the expedition's official name – fared relatively well, in part because of the presence of Sacagawea. This young Shoshone woman had been sold to and became the wife of Toussaint Charbonneau, a French-Canadian trapper who was part of the entourage. Sacagawea proved invaluable as a guide, translator and ambassador to the area's Native Americans. York, Clark's African American servant, also softened tensions between the group and the Native Americans – his dark skin and stature were both fascinating and intimidating.

The party traveled some 8000 miles (12,900km) in about two years, documenting everything they came across in their journals with such bad spelling that it must have taken historians a few extra years just to sort out what they wrote. Meticulous notes were taken on 122 animals and 178 plants, with some new discoveries being made along the way. In 1805 the party finally reached the mouth of the Columbia River and the Pacific Ocean at Cape Disappointment (p159). The party bedded down for the winter nearby, establishing Fort Clatsop to rest before heading back home.

Undaunted Courage, by Stephen Ambrose, is a compelling account of the Lewis and Clark expedition; it follows the footsteps of their extraordinary journey to the Pacific and back again.

1846

The Oregon Treaty brings an end to Oregon land disputes between the US and the UK. Both countries had jointly occupied the region since the Treaty of 1818.

1851

The first significant gold deposits are discovered near Jacksonville, starting a gold rush in Oregon. Thousands of fortune seekers pour into the state, creating new settlements and small towns.

1858

Cascade Railroad Company becomes the region's first railroad and begins operations in the Columbia River Gorge. It will take 25 years for transcontinental rail lines to finally reach the Pacific Northwest.

Lewis and Clark returned to a hero's welcome in St Louis in 1806. Lewis was later appointed governor of the Louisiana Territory but died a year later, of either murder or more likely suicide. Clark dealt with his fame a bit better and was appointed governor of the Missouri Territory, living to be 68.

OTTERS & BEAVERS LOSE OUT

Although no settlement or permanent trading post resulted from Lewis and Clark's pioneering explorations, the British and Americans were discovering the Northwest's bounty of fur-bearing wildlife. While in the Northwest in 1778, Captain Cook's crew traded with the Native Americans for animal pelts, of which sea otter and beaver were the most valuable. This fur trade would dominate British and US economic interests in the northern Pacific for the next 30 years, until the War of 1812 stuck a thorn in the side of relations between the USA and Britain.

The oldest commercial corporation in North America is Hudson's Bay Company, which once controlled the Pacific Northwest fur trade, conducted early exploration of the region and even functioned as de facto government before the US took over.

Trappers from two competing British fur-trading companies – the Hudson's Bay Company (HBC) and the North West Company – began to expand from their bases around Hudson's Bay and the Great Lakes, edging over the Rocky Mountains to establish fur-trading forts. These trading posts were quite successful, even though each was linked to eastern markets by an 1800-mile (2900km) overland trail. Each fort was given goods to trade with local Native Americans for beaver, otter, fox, wolf or whatever other unfortunate fur-bearing animal had yet to be wiped out. Forts edged closer to the Pacific, and in 1811 the American fur magnate, John Jacob Astor, established a post in Astoria (p290), at the mouth of the Columbia River. During the War of 1812, however, it was sold to North West Company, which merged with the HBC in 1821. With the Americans out of the way, the HBC created a network of relationships with Native American tribes throughout this region, establishing headquarters at Fort Vancouver (p160), which straddled the Willamette and Columbia Rivers.

By 1827 the Northwest's borders were becoming more defined. Spain had withdrawn its claim, establishing the northern border of New Spain at the 47th parallel (the current Oregon–California border). Russian ambitions were limited to the land north of the 54°40' parallel, at the start of the Alaska panhandle, near Prince Rupert, BC. The USA, through the Louisiana Purchase, owned all land south of the 49th parallel and east of the Rocky Mountains, while Britain controlled the territory north of this line. This left a vast territory of present-day British Columbia – the states of Oregon, Washington and Idaho and parts of western Montana and Wyoming – open to claims by both Britain and the USA.

In Chinese markets, an exceptional sea otter pelt could fetch the equivalent of a year's pay for a fur company laborer.

The Treaty of Ghent, which ended the War of 1812, included an amendment that declared a joint custody (of sorts) of the Pacific Northwest: Britain and the USA could continue economic development in the area, but neither could establish an official government.

1859

On February 14th Oregon is admitted into the union and becomes the USA's 33rd state, about nine months after Minnesota achieves its own statehood.

1871

British Columbia, Canada's third largest province in area and population, becomes the country's sixth province to join into Confederation.

1889

On November 11th President Benjamin Harrison signs a bill making Washington the USA's 42nd state.

THE AMERICANS SETTLE IN

Unlike most other early trading posts, which were basically repositories for goods, Fort Vancouver became a thriving, nearly self-sufficient agricultural community complete with mills, a dairy, gardens and fields.

Canadian-born Dr John McLoughlin, often called the 'father of Oregon,' was the capable steward of this post. He encouraged settlement beyond the precincts of the fort, and allowed retired HBC trappers to settle along the Willamette River in an area still called French Prairie. By 1828 these French Canadians, with their Native American wives, began to clear the land and build cabins, becoming the first true settlers in the Northwest. McLoughlin established a mill and incorporated the first town in the Northwest in 1829, at Oregon City. He later built a house there, which today is a museum (see p241).

The decline of the fur trade, along with an influx of American farmers, traders and settlers from the east, all helped loosen the weakening British Empire's grip on the Pacific Northwest. But it was the missionaries who probably played the biggest role. In 1834 New England Methodists Daniel and Jason Lee came to the area and founded a mission just north of present-day Salem. Although the local Native Americans weren't keen on Christianity, the two succeeded in founding the first schools in Oregon. Other missionaries, like Protestants Marcus and Narcissa Whitman, and Henry and Eliza Spalding, arrived in 1836 (Narcissa and Eliza were the first women to cross what would later become the Oregon Trail), establishing missions near today's Walla Walla in Washington, and Lewiston in Idaho.

Losing ground despite the Treaty of Ghent, the HBC hedged its bets and established another center of operations further north at Fort Victoria, on Vancouver Island. After all, this was an era when belief in Manifest Destiny – the idea that it was the USA's natural right to expand its territory to the Pacific Coast – ran mighty strong. However, the federal government did not offer military intervention to rid the area of British stragglers. If the settlers wanted an independent civil authority, they would have to do the dirty work themselves.

In 1850 Congress passed the Donation Land Act, which granted every European settler and 'American half-breed Indian' 320 acres. Married couples could claim 640 acres.

ROUNDING THE TURN AT CHAMPOEG

By the early 1840s the Willamette Valley had become home to a rag-tag mix of 700 French-Canadian farmers, retired trappers, Protestant missionaries and general adventurers. Eager to establish some order to the region, the settlers held a series of meetings and created the framework for a budding government. These meetings led to an 1843 vote at Champoeg, along the Willamette River about 30 miles (48km) south of Portland (now Champoeg State Heritage Area p241). By a razor-thin 52-to-50 margin, a measure was passed to organize a provisional government independent of the HBC. The land north of the Columbia, however, would remain in control of the British – at least for a bit longer.

1899

Mt Rainier National Park is established on March 2, becoming the USA's fifth national park. It contains the highest point in the Cascade Range (over 14,000ft) and encompasses 368 sq miles.

1912

Aided by teacher, journalist and women's rights activist Abigail Scott Duniway, women win the right to vote in Oregon. She becomes the first woman registered to vote in Multnomah County, the state's most populous county.

1916

In Seattle, William Edward Boeing – who made his wealth in the timber industry – incorporates his airplane manufacturing business as Pacific Aero Products, changing the name to Boeing Airplane Company a year later.

Meanwhile, the USA–Canada boundary dispute became a hotbed of contention. There was a fervent settler movement to occupy the Northwest – all the way up to present-day Alaska. The 1844 presidential campaign slogan became '54/40 or fight' (referring to the geographical parallel). The bickering finally ended in 1846 when the British and Americans negotiated the Treaty of Oregon, and agreed to today's present USA–Canada border, which runs along the 49th parallel.

Accepting its inevitable fate, the HBC gave up its headquarters at Fort Vancouver and high-tailed it north to Fort Victoria on Vancouver Island (many British citizens followed, and Vancouver Island was designated a crown colony in 1849). In 1848 Oregon officially became a US territory.

FOLLOW THE OREGON TRAIL

The party was now just getting started. In the Willamette Valley, nearly 900 new settlers arrived in one go, more than doubling the area's population. They were a trickle in what became a flood of migrants following the 2170-mile-long (3500km) Oregon Trail, which edged south around the footsteps of the explorers before them – first Lewis and Clark, then adventurous fur trappers and intrepid missionaries. Between 1843 and 1860, over 50,000 fresh faces arrived to a brand new future in the gorgeous Pacific Northwest.

Learn more about the Oregon Trail at the End of the Oregon Trail interpretive Center in Oregon City (p241) and the National Historic Oregon Trail Interpretive Center in Baker City (p344).

Spanning six states, the long Oregon Trail sorely tested the families who embarked on this perilous trip. Their belongings were squirreled away under canvas-topped wagons, which often trailed livestock. The journey could take up to eight months, and by the time the exhausted settlers reached eastern Oregon their food supplies were running on fumes. And there was one last challenge; when the weary parties arrived at the Columbia River in The Dalles, they had to choose between rafting themselves and all their belongings through the rapids in the Columbia River Gorge or struggling up the flanks of Mt Hood and descending via the precipitous Barlow Trail.

The journey ended at Oregon City, in the Willamette Valley. Here, settlers established farms, businesses and towns. Portland, near the Willamette's confluence with the Columbia River, took on an early importance as a trade center. Oregon City, at the falls of the Willamette River, was the early seat of government, while above the falls, in the river's broad agricultural basin, small farming communities sprang up.

After Fort Vancouver fell to the Americans in 1846, explorers began to mosey up the Cowlitz River into the Puget Sound area, initially planting roots at Tumwater near Olympia. By 1851 a group of Oregon Trail pioneers – led by brothers Arthur and David Denny – set sights on Elliott Bay and founded the port city of Seattle.

In 1846, seeking a route around the daunting Columbia River Gorge, a party of pioneers began to blaze a southern route into the Willamette Valley. This new Applegate Trail cut through the deserts of Nevada and California before turning north through the valleys of southern Oregon. Immigrants

1937

After three years of construction and $80 million, Bonneville Dam is completed on Oregon's Columbia River. The construction provided 4000 crucial jobs during the Great Depression.

1941

The US enters WWII, transforming the population and the economy of the Pacific Northwest and establishing the region as an important financial powerhouse for the country.

1962

Seattle hosts the second major World's Fair since WWII, names it 'Century 21' and gives 10 million people a glimpse of what the future might hold. The Space Needle opens on the first day of the fair, April 21st.

NORTHERN GOLD

Nothing draws fortune-seekers more than the lure of riches. In 1851, gold was discovered in southern Oregon near the Rogue River valley. Prospectors and scoundrels flooded in, boomtowns popped up overnight and native populations were brushed aside. A year later gold was discovered near Scottsburg along the Umpqua River, while along the coast miners washed gold dust out of sands near Coos Bay.

In 1861 the Blue Mountains of eastern Oregon became the next target, but violent clashes again ensued between Native Americans and the newcomers. The result for most Native Americans was forced relocation to reservations, some as far away as Oklahoma. Meanwhile the rush kept moving north into British Columbia's Fraser River and, over the next few decades, beyond into the Yukon Territory.

along this route were the first to settle the upper Willamette Valley and established towns such as Eugene, and scouted the land in the Rogue, Umpqua and Klamath River valleys.

By the late 1850s settlers had staked claim to the best land in the western valleys. Some folks began setting their sights east of the Cascades, particularly the Grande Ronde River valley of present-day Oregon and Walla Walla River valley of what would be Washington. Eastern Oregon didn't become a hot spot until the discovery of gold there in the 1860s (see above).

DECIMATION OF THE NATION OF NATIVE AMERICANS

By 1860 the Pacific Northwest's coast was strung with white settlements, and most major cities had been founded. Unfortunately the area's wildlife, especially the beaver and otter populations, had been nearly extinguished. Even more deplorable, however, was the effect the settlers had on the region's original inhabitants: European diseases devastated whole Native American communities, who had no natural immunity, while alcoholism took its own insidious toll on their culture.

The incidents leading up to, during and after the tragic Whitman Massacre, which had wide-ranging repercussions in Oregon's history are detailed at www.oregonpioneers.com/whitman.htm.

But it was the missionaries who eventually delivered the final blow. In 1847, near Walla Walla, the Whitman mission's attempts to bring Christianity to eastern Washington tribes ended in tragedy. The Cayuse Native Americans slew over a dozen missionaries in revenge for a measles epidemic. Conveniently enough, American settlers now felt justified in removing the Native Americans from their land and incarcerating them on reservations.

Coastal Native Americans were marched or shipped to reservations in 1855 and 1856, where increased illness, starvation and dislocation led to the complete extinction of many tribal groups. Even on Vancouver Island, where British policies were generally more enlightened regarding Native American culture, most of the arable land was given over to European settlers. Christian missionaries worked to make illegal the traditional potlatches that formed the nucleus of coastal Native American religion and social life.

1980

Mt St Helens blows her top, killing 57 people and destroying 250 homes. Her elevation is cut from 9677ft to 8365ft, and where a peak once stood, a mile-wide crater is born.

1988

Nirvana records 10 demos in just six hours, leading to the band being signed to the Sub Pop label. Later in the year they play their first Seattle show, blowing everyone's minds and expectations.

1994

The Vancouver Canucks reach the Stanley Cup finals (hockey's holy grail), only to lose to the New York Rangers in game seven. Night-long riots ensue in downtown Vancouver.

East of the Cascades, Native Americans were more resistant to the US military and settlers. A series of fierce battles were fought between the US Army and various Native American tribes from 1855 to 1877. Especially bloody were the Rogue River and the Modoc Wars, in southern Oregon, and the Cayuse War, near Walla Walla. However, in the end, these Native American groups also ended up on reservations, utterly dependent upon the federal government for subsistence.

The Pacific Northwest and its rich resources were now in control of new tenants, and the region quickly grew into an economic force both on the national and international stage.

Native People of the Northwest: A Travelers Guide to Land, Art and Culture, by Jan Halliday and Gail Chehak, is a hands-on guide to Native American hot spots like galleries, museums and historical sites.

MORE RECENT TIMES

By the 1880s the Northwest's port cities boomed with the region's rich agricultural, fishing and logging resources. The Northern Pacific Railroad linked the Northwest to the eastern USA, making national markets more accessible and bringing in more settlers. Seattle became the area's most important seaport in 1897 when gold was discovered in the Canadian Klondike and prospectors poured into the city.

The World Wars brought further economic fortune to the Pacific Northwest, when the area became the nation's largest lumber producer and both Oregon and Washington's naval yards bustled (along with William Boeing's airplane factory). The region continued to prosper through the second half of the 20th century, attracting new migrations of educated, progressively minded settlers from the nation's east and south. In the 1980s and '90s the economy shifted to the high-tech industry, embodied by Microsoft in Seattle and Intel in Portland.

However, all this growing success has not come without cost. The production of cheap hydroelectricity and the massive irrigation projects along the Columbia have led to the near-irreversible destruction of the river's ecosystem. Dams have all but eliminated most runs of native salmon and have further disrupted the lives of remaining Native Americans who depend on the river. Logging of old-growth forests has left ugly scars, while the 'Silicon Forest' had its own economic collapse at the turn of the century. And while Washington's Puget Sound groans under the weight of its own rapidly growing centers, Oregon's population has created heated political rifts between its liberal and conservative factions.

Still, the Pacific Northwest's inhabitants generally manage to find a reasonable balance between their natural resources and continued popularity. The region continues to be one of the United States' most beautiful and attractive places to visit…and settle down.

In 1990 the Northern Spotted Owl was declared a threatened species, barring timber industries from clear-cutting certain old-growth forests. The controversy sparked debate all across the Pacific Northwest, pitting loggers against environmentalists.

1994

The Death with Dignity Act is established, making Oregon the first and (so far) only US state to give certain terminally ill patients the right to assisted suicide. Attempts at overturning the act prove unsuccessful.

1995

Amazon, one of the first major companies to sell products online, is launched in Seattle. Originally started as a bookseller, it will not become annually profitable until 2003.

2010

Vancouver hosts the Olympic winter games after beating out Pyeongchang, South Korea, and Salzburg, Austria, for the golden prize. It is Canada's third time hosting, and Vancouver's first.

The Culture

REGIONAL IDENTITY

A Texan, a Californian and an Oregonian were sitting around a campfire drinking. The Texan took a swig of whiskey, threw the bottle in the air and shot it with his pistol while yelling 'We have lots more whiskey where I come from!' The Californian sipped his zinfandel, grabbed the Texan's pistol, threw the wine bottle in the air, and shot it while yelling 'We have lots more wine where I come from!' The Oregonian guzzled his microbrew, grabbed the Texan's pistol, threw the empty in the air but caught the bottle and shot the Californian. He said 'We have lots of Californians where I come from, but I need to recycle this beer bottle.'

While not everyone in the Pacific Northwest is a tree-hugging hipster with activist tendencies and a penchant for latte, many locals are proud of their independent spirit, profess a love for nature and yes, will separate their plastics when it's time to recycle. They're a friendly, laid-back lot and, despite the common tendency to denigrate Californians, most are transplants themselves. Why did they come here? Among other things, for the lush scenery, the good quality of life and the lack of hoity-toity-ness that often afflicts bigger, more popular places. Primping up and putting on airs is not a part of Northwestern everyday life, and wearing casual clothing to restaurants, concerts or social functions will rarely raise an eyebrow. A healthy glow is in, while the cosmetic look belongs somewhere else.

Oregon is the only US state to legalize the 'right to die,' with the Death with Dignity Act, by which terminally ill patients are allowed to voluntarily end their lives.

In a broad sense the Northwest shares the general cultures of the US and Canada, but adds its own personal twist. In rural parts of eastern Oregon and Washington, the personality of the Old West is still very much alive. Fishing towns along the coast and islands have a distinctive and often gritty sensibility that comes from making a living on the stormy Pacific Ocean. Urban centers have a reputation for progressive, somewhat maverick politics (it's a long way to the East Coast's political centers, and people tend to look closer to home for leadership). There's a do-it-yourself, no-pain-no-gain, pull-yourself-up-by-the-breeches ethic that streaks through the spirit of your typical Northwesterner. And if you accept who you are, respect the great outdoors and keep the frills to a minimum, you're likely to fit right in.

Some folk do put emphasis on 'old family' legitimacy and connections, however, boasting of ancestors who came across the Oregon Trail or who were early Brits in Victoria. And while most urban Americans and Canadians are tolerant of individual eccentricities, rural Northwesterners in particular may be skeptical of strangers and may resent what they perceive as interference in local matters. Outside the big cities, try not to broadcast your animal-rights convictions in a bar full of hunters or denounce clear-cutting in a mill town – the Pacific Northwest does have a somewhat hidden conservative side (one part of its multifaceted personality). But if you're friendly to locals, whether they're city slickers or country bumpkins, they often can't help but be friendly right back.

Hwy 99 in British Columbia and I-5 through Washington and Oregon creates the Vancouver–Seattle–Portland corridor, passing through the region's three most populated cities.

LIFESTYLE

The region's gorgeous waters, forests and mountains certainly help define the lifestyle of Northwesterners. Here, people can be close to nature without sacrificing the comforts of a sophisticated metropolis. During the week they'll work in city centers, dine at world-class restaurants and take in fine theatrical productions or cutting-edge live music. Then on weekends they'll head to the beach or ski slopes, or hike on the nearest mountaintop (everything is close by – just an hour or so away from the big lights). And while they love their outdoors, Northwesterners can be just as happy inside their warm homes – especially when snow, drizzly rain and gray skies take over in winter. Reading, watching movies and drinking (both microbrew and coffee) are a few popular indoor pastimes, and the area is known for its bookstores, funky cinemas, breweries and cafés.

Seattle and Portland have both been listed as two of the top three most sustainable US cities; see www.sustainlane.com/us-city-rankings.

The Pacific Northwest lifestyle is generally relaxed and notably open, and all sorts of quirky people are tolerated. In fact, a certain degree of eccentricity is expected – that shabbily dressed, green-haired woman next to you at the coffee shop might actually be a software developer at Microsoft. Portland's unofficial motto is 'Keep Portland Weird,' while Seattle's popular Fremont neighborhood proclaims the 'freedom to be peculiar.' And let's not forget gays and lesbians, who are widely accepted and especially attracted to the Northwest's liberal cities. Girls, forget San Francisco – lesbians *love* Portland.

But not everything is perfect in paradise. Urban sprawl is a big headache: Seattle, Portland and Vancouver have all grown past their breeches in one way or another. Rising real-estate markets mean that people are forced to buy houses far from their jobs, which are often in city centers. And more commuting means that freeways are jammed during rush hours, which are becoming longer each year; this is an especially serious issue in the Seattle area. Unemployment has also been a problem in the past (the tech-bubble collapse and lay-offs at Boeing didn't help), though things have been improving in recent years.

Northwesterners are an adaptable lot, however. Like their ancestors, who came over the Oregon Trail (or California, or the East Coast or Hong Kong), they've learned to change with the times. Even if they like to complain the whole way.

ECONOMY

Once covered in lush forests, it's no surprise that the Northwest, with its rich natural resources, invited colonization. Today Oregon and Washington continue to lead the USA in lumber production, while British Columbia (BC) contains nearly 40% of the marketable timber in Canada. However, US federal restrictions now protect much of local forests (many of which have been overharvested for many years), creating a chasm between rural folks, who relied on logging for work, and their city cousins, who tend toward the environmentalist side. BC's timber industry is closely tied to Asia and the US.

Oregon is the home to Nike, Adidas and Columbia Sportswear headquarters, while Washington boasts Starbucks, Nordstrom and REI. Vancouver doesn't care – it scored the 2010 Winter Olympics .

The area's fish populations have also been exploited to the edge of sustainability. The Columbia and other Northwest rivers were once teeming with salmon, but overfishing, dam building and deforestation (which creates runoff that clogs rivers with silt) have nearly wiped out the species. Though much diminished, commercial fishing still plays an important role in the regional economy, and sportfishing remains a viable industry in many small coastal towns.

High Technology

As timber and fishing have receded, the high-tech industry has redefined the region's personality by creating jobs, attracting faraway talent and enriching support industries – though economic cycles do boom and bust on a regular basis, affecting communities and population migrations. Seattle's Puget Sound area is headquarters for many computer-software and telecommunications firms like Microsoft, Nintendo and AT&T Wireless, while star internet companies include Real Networks, Amazon.com and Expedia.com. The area is also home to various biotechnology companies.

Oregon's 'Silicon Forest' is supported by the semiconductor giant Intel, which maintains several campuses and construction plants in Hillsboro (a large suburb west of Portland). Neighbors include branches of Tektronix, Genentech, Sun Microsystems, Epson, Fujitsu and Yahoo! Other high-tech firms with campuses or offices in Oregon are Hewlett-Packard (Corvallis), Symantec (Eugene) and Google (The Dalles).

BC has its own high-tech niches, but Vancouver's vibrant film industry tends to steal the economic spotlight.

Boeing, the world's number-one aircraft manufacturer, moved its corporate offices to Chicago in 2001, but despite layoffs remains responsible for 68,570 Seattle-area jobs. In 2006 it created a partnership with Lockheed Martin and will provide a butt-load of rocket launchers for the US government.

International Trade & Agriculture

The ports of Seattle, Tacoma, Portland and Vancouver are among the largest on the West Coast. Practically all of Canada's trade with Pacific Rim countries passes through Vancouver, the second-busiest port on the North American continent. Electronic gadgets from all over Asia pour through Seattle's docks. Portland, meanwhile, exports more wheat than any other port in the country.

Rainforest: Ancient Realm of the Pacific Northwest by Graham Osboe and Wade Davis is the book to read for stunning photographs and eloquent text on the rain forests of the Pacific Northwest.

The Pacific Northwest is a paradise for agriculture. This essential industry flourishes along the moist valleys of the Rogue, Umpqua, Skagit and Fraser Rivers, as well as in the sprawling temperate grasslands east of the Cascades. Cattle and sheep graze the eastern uplands, and golden wheat fields stretch across volcanic plateaus. The rain-swept valleys along the Pacific Coast are famous for their thriving dairy farms, especially around Tillamook, the Rogue River and Vancouver Island. Along the Columbia and Okanogan Rivers, vast orchards of apples, cherries, peaches and pears are harvested for the international market. Flower bulbs are grown extensively along the Skagit River, in northern Washington.

Oregon's fertile Willamette Valley yields hops, wheat, hazelnuts, berries and, of course, wine grapes. The irrigated vineyards of Washington's Columbia, Walla Walla and Yakima Valleys have come into their own, producing world-class chardonnays and merlots and making the state the second-largest wine producer in the USA after California.

OFFBEAT BELIEFS

Only a quarter of Pacific Northwesterners have a religious affiliation, and a good chunk of those bow to Christianity, Judaism and the Mormon Church. However, strange and exotic religions have claimed footholds in the Northwest – perhaps due to the Celtic gloom that presides here much of the year.

Ramtha's School of Enlightenment, known for channeling and out-of-body experiences, is headquartered in Yelm, Washington (the movie *What the Bleep Do We Know* was filmed in Portland's Bagdad Theatre, and its three directors are devotees). The Living Enrichment Center was a large 'New Thought' church located in Wilsonville, Oregon; it closed in 2004 because of a financial scandal. Bhagwan Shree Rajneesh – an Indian spiritual leader who started the Osho movement – created a community in Antelope, Oregon, who voted the city council out of office and legalized public nudity (among other things). He was deported in 1985. Witchcraft-practicing Wiccans, despite their positive exposure on popular TV shows like *Buffy the Vampire Slayer* and *Charmed*, fear persecution and continue their tradition of secrecy; in fact, revealing oneself to others is called 'coming out of the broom closet.'

POPULATION & PEOPLE

Combined, the current population of Oregon and Washington is about 10 million, which amounts to about 3.6% of the total US population. By far the greatest concentrations of people huddle in Washington's Puget Sound area and Oregon's Willamette Valley. Oregon and Washington are among the fastest-growing states in the USA.

The Canadian $20 bill features the artwork of BC native Bill Reid.

With a population of 4.3 million, BC is the fastest-growing Canadian province, due both to immigration largely from Hong Kong and to movement within Canada. The greater Vancouver area is home to about half those people.

Most US Northwesterners are white; minority groups include Latinos (9%), Asians (5%) and African Americans (3%). BC, while largely founded by British settlers, has a much more racially mixed population. Half of Vancouver's population is made up of minority groups (one-quarter with an Asian background).

The US government recognizes around three dozen Pacific Northwestern Native American tribes, for whom reservations or trust lands have been set aside. A number of other Native American groups in the region have no federally recognized status (without which they are ineligible for government assistance to support tribal schools and cultural centers) nor any guaranteed land base. Moreover, without legal recognition, it is difficult for tribes to maintain cultural identity. The total Native American population of Oregon and Washington is around 140,000 (or 1.4% of the population).

In Canada, tribal bands control small tracts of land called reserves, the parameters of which were determined through treaties with Great Britain prior to independence (though only about a quarter of the country's native people actually inhabit these lands). Less than 1% of BC's total area is under the control of the province's 197 tribal bands, who continue to press for a more equitable distribution of territory in negotiations overseen by the British Columbia Treaty Commission. First Nations inhabitants of BC number roughly 175,000 (4.5% of BC's population).

ARTS

Music

ROCK & ALTERNATIVE

You can see the handwritten lyrics of Nirvana singer/songwriter Kurt Cobain (born in Aberdeen, Washington) at the Experience Music Project in the Seattle Center p88).

Jimi Hendrix, Anthony Ray (Sir Mix-a-Lot) and the Wilson sisters (of Heart) all grew up in the Seattle area. Bryan Adams and Sarah McLachlan have BC associations. Courtney Love was a teenage rockster in Portland. But when most people think of contemporary Pacific Northwest music, the word that immediately comes to mind is grunge – that angst-driven, heavily riffed and distorted sound born in late 1980s out of Seattle's garages. With inspiration from hardcore punk, indie rock and heavy metal, bands like Green River, Pearl Jam, Soundgarden, Alice in Chains and, of course, Nirvana helped define the genre. The record label Sub Pop tapped up most grunge bands, and helped put out Nirvana's *Nevermind* in 1991, which skyrocketed this 'Seattle Sound' into mainstream music. Grunge's general popularity lasted until 1994, when Kurt Cobain found peace with a shotgun.

Olympia, Washington is a hotbed of indie rock and riot grrls, and birthplace of the now-defunct group Sleater-Kinney. Portland is also indie band heaven, and has been inspiration to such diverse groups as folktronic hip-hop band Talkdemonic, alt-band The Decemberists and multi-genre Pink Martini. BC, meanwhile, has popular indie bands like The New Pornographers, Black Mountain and Hot Hot Heat.

ALBUMS TO CHECK OUT

Black Mountain (Vancouver, BC) *Black Mountain* (2005)
The Dandy Warhols (Portland, OR) *Thirteen Tales From Urban Bohemia* (2000)
Death Cab for Cutie (Bellingham, WA) *Plans* (2005)
The Decemberists (Portland, OR) *The Crane Wife* (2006)
Foo Fighters (Seattle, WA) *One By One* (2002)
Hot Hot Heat (Victoria, BC) *Make Up The Breakdown* (2004)
Modest Mouse (Issaquah, WA) *Lonesome Crowded West* (1997)
The New Pornographers (Vancouver, BC) *Mass Romantic* (2000)
Pearl Jam (Seattle, WA) *Ten* (1991)
Pink Martini (Portland, OR) *Sympathique* (1997)
The Postal Service (Seattle, WA) *Give Up* (2003)
The Shins (Portland, OR) *Chutes Too Narrow* (2003)
Skinny Puppy (Vancouver, BC) *Last Rights* (1992)
Sleater-Kinney (Olympia, WA) *Call The Doctor* (1996)
Talkdemonic (Portland, OR) *Beat Romantic* (2006)

CLASSICAL & JAZZ

Seattle, Portland and Vancouver have all nurtured a full array of classical-music venues, including professional symphony and opera companies. The Seattle Symphony and Seattle Opera are equally distinguished, while the Northwest Chamber Orchestra is the Northwest's only orchestra that focuses on period chamber music. The Oregon Symphony and the Portland Opera are both vibrant stars of Oregon's culture, as is BC's Vancouver Symphony Orchestra and Vancouver Opera. Smaller cities all over the Northwest, such as Spokane, Victoria and Eugene, have their own musical groups as well.

Jazz is alive and seriously kicking in the Pacific Northwest, with the major cities all boasting thriving scenes originally established by the region's early African American inhabitants. Seattle jazz was raging back in the 1930s and '40s, but even today has great music (and avante-garde musicians like Bill Frisell and Wayne Horvitz), often showcased in their Earshot Jazz Festival. Portland also has a rich jazz history and contemporary scene; check out Portland's jazz festival in February. Vancouver also has a sophisticated jazz scene, with the Vancouver International Jazz Festival drawing close to half a million people each year. Nanaimo's Diana Krall is the local celebrity here.

Vancouver is home to the Vancouver Folk Music Festival, one of the largest folk festivals in North America. The city's large Chinese population has also generated some famous canto-pop (Cantonese pop music) singers.

Literature

The Pacific Northwest is a book-lover's dream. While Seattle claims to have the most bookstores per capita in the nation (and has been declared America's most literate city), Portland boasts Powell's Books, the largest independent bookstore in the world. Vancouver's no slouch either, with many literary cafés and bookstores dotting the streets of residential neighborhoods. Maybe it's the gloomy rain-soaked winter months that keeps folks indoors and looking for something to do, but whatever the reason, Northwesterners love to snuggle up with a paperback.

Powell's Books has been a part of the Portland book culture since the early 1970s. After outgrowing the original store, the operation moved to a former car dealership, and one of Portland's seven metro stores still operates on that site.

The region also nurtures many small publishing houses, while special-interest newspapers, tabloids and zines serve just about every interest. For short stories about the region, read *Edge Walking on the Western Rim*, edited by Mayumi Tsutakawa; it's an anthology of modern Northwest writers.

Washington has produced a decent share of literary greats. The late Raymond Carver, known for his grim vision of working-class angst, most recently resided on the Olympic Peninsula with Tess Gallagher, an important figure in the poetry world. Carver's best stories are collected in the volume *Where I'm Calling From* (1988). Novelist Mary McCarthy (1912–89) inspired the play *Imaginary Friends* by Nora Ephron and was known for her satirical, semi-autobiographical prose. David Guterson is famous for his award-winning *Snow Falling on Cedars* (1994), a vivid tale of prejudice in a San Juan Island fishing community. Popular author Tom Robbins, a La Conner resident, has won numerous devotees for his wacky, countercultural novels, including *Even Cowgirls Get the Blues* (1976).

Well-known writers who call the Seattle area home include Jon Krakauer, the award-winning author of *Into Thin Air* (1997) and *Under the Banner of Heaven* (2003). Sherman Alexie is a Native American author who adapted his short story *This is What It Means to Say Phoenix, Arizona* into the excellent movie *Smoke Signals* (1998). A prolific writer of the American West is Ivan Doig. His first book, *This House of Sky* (1979), was a National Book Award nominee; he most recently finished *The Whistling Season* (2006). Jonathan Raban's *Waxwings* (2003) is a fictionalized account of two Seattle immigrant families.

Oregon's biggest literary name is the late Ken Kesey, whose *One Flew Over the Cuckoo's Nest* (1962) became a textbook of 1960s nonconformity and inspired a movie that won five Oscars; Kesey also penned the brilliant *Sometimes a Great Notion* (1971). David James Duncan wrote the best-sellers *The River Why* (1983) and *The Brothers K* (1992), while Tom Spanbauer told the tale of a Native American bisexual male prostitute in *The Man Who Fell in Love with the Moon* (1992).

Resident Oregonian Barry Lopez, often compared to Henry David Thoreau and considered one of America's premier nature writers, explores the relationship between humans and their environment in short stories (such as *Desert Notes,* 1976) and nonfiction works (such as *Arctic Dreams,* 1986). Novelist Chuck Palahniuk, best known for *Fight Club* (1996), has lived in the Portland area and written about it in *Fugitives and Refugees: A Walk in Portland, Oregon* (2003).

Portland also boasts two women novelists with a bent towards science fiction and fantasy. The prolific and multi-award-winning Ursula LeGuin is responsible for *The Left Hand of Darkness* (Hugo and Nebula Awards, 1969) and *The Farthest Shore* (National Book Award, 1972), among many other things. Jean Auel is best known for her widely read *Clan of the Cave Bear* series, a set of prehistorical fiction books that speculate on the first meetings between Neanderthals and Cro-Magnons.

The lead role for the film adaptation of Ken Kesey's *One Flew Over the Cuckoo's Nest* was originally offered to James Caan. It ended up going to Jack Nicholson, who fought with director Milos Foreman over plot and character details.

BC's ever-active literary scene has cultivated a wide range of talent. The English novelist and poet Malcolm Lowry, who's best known for his semi-autobiographical *Under the Volcano* (1947), lived in BC for many years before his death in Sussex. BC resident WP Kinsella's award-winning novel *Shoeless Joe* (1982) was adapted for the film *Field of Dreams* (1989). Douglas Coupland (*Generation X,* 1991) makes his home in Vancouver, as does science-fiction guru William Gibson, who coined the term 'cyberspace' in his 1984 novel *Neuromancer*. English author and illustrator Nick Bantock, now based in Vancouver, drew acclaim in the early 1990s with his *Griffin & Sabine* trilogy.

Seattle has become a recognized center for graphic novelists and is the home of Fantagraphics, a major publisher and distributor of independent comics. Meanwhile, Dark Horse Comics (based in Milwaukie, Oregon – a Portland suburb) is one of America's largest independent comic book publishers, and whose comics have been adapted into screenplays like *Sin City, The Mask* and *Hellboy*. And in Vancouver, Budget Monk Productions produced the popular online graphic novel *Broken Saints* (2001), which won the Audience Award for Online Animation at the Sundance Film Festival in 2003.

Cinema & Television

The Pacific Northwest keeps attracting the film and TV industries with low production costs, artistic talent and a range of gorgeous backdrops. However, many films produced in the region are set somewhere else: Oregon's Cascades doubled as the Colorado Rockies in *The Shining;* Roslyn, Washington stood in as Alaska in the TV series *Northern Exposure;* and the Vancouver area has represented everything from Tibet in Martin Scorsese's *Kundun* to New York City in Jackie Chan's *Rumble in the Bronx*.

But the Northwest often appears as itself in motion pictures, too. The skyline of Seattle and its quirky lifestyles are recognizable internationally, thanks to such productions as *Sleepless in Seattle* (1993) and the TV hit show *Frasier* (1993–2004). Some of the many other movies filmed in Washington include *An Officer and a Gentleman* (1982), *The Hunt for Red October* (1990), *My Own Private Idaho* (1991) and *The Ring* (2002).

Seattle hosts a lively community of independent filmmakers, whose works are screened during spring's Seattle International Film Festival (p102). Well-known area directors include the maverick Alan Rudolph, a Bainbridge Island resident and the creator of *Choose Me* (1994), *Mortal Thoughts* (1991) and *The Secret Lives of Dentists* (2003), among other movies. Sherman Alexie, a Native American originally from the Spokane area and now living in Seattle, is an author, comedian and filmmaker who wrote the award-winning *Smoke Signals* (1998, filmed in Idaho and Washington).

Oregon has an equally lively résumé, with a wide range of diverse movies making the scene, such as *Five Easy Pieces* (1970), *One Flew Over the Cuckoo's Nest* (1975), *Animal House* (1978), *Stand by Me* (1986), *Point Break* (1991) and *What the Bleep Do We Know?* (2004). The Portland International Film Festival (p232), which takes place each February, screens shorts and feature films from all over the world (and always includes a few local creations). Even more local is the Northwest Film and Video Festival (p232), highlighting the independent work of Northwest artists.

The TV series *Twin Peaks* was shot in Snoqualmie and North Bend, both in Washington. Chris Carter's *The X-Files,* which had a similar visual style, was shot in Vancouver, BC (later moving to California), as was Carter's follow-up series, *Millennium*.

TUNING INTO THE PACIFIC NORTHWEST

Looking for good radio? Here's where to find it:

Vancouver, BC– CKNW (AM 980) is the city's leading news, traffic, talk and weather station, with call-in shows and mostly locally based hosts.

Vancouver and Victoria, BC – Canada's National Public Radio and commercial-free CBC Radio One is available at AM 690 (Vancouver) and FM 90.5 (Victoria).

Seattle, WA – Legendary KEXP (FM 90.3) is the city's independent indie and alternative rock music station, offering influential exposure to underground bands.

Seattle, WA – National Public Radio is broadcast at KUOW (FM 94.9).

Olympia, WA – Community station KAOS (FM 89.3) supports underrepresented and minority voices, and broadcasts independent music. Inspires future on-air talent.

Portland, OR – Non-profit KBOO (FM 90.7) is a mostly volunteer-run, progressive station offering unconventional, alternative and controversial news and views.

Portland, OR – National Public Radio is broadcast at KOPB (FM 91.5).

Warm Springs, OR – Native American station KWSO (FM 91.9) heightens awareness by discussing issues affecting local Native American communities and their members.

Mt Hood's Timberline Lodge (p273) had a cameo in *The Shining* as the front exterior of the Overlook Hotel. Stanley Kubrick changed room 217 in the original script to 237 because the Timberline Lodge owners requested a nonexistent room number.

Portland often serves as a menacing backdrop for the brooding films of resident author, photographer and filmmaker Gus Van Sant. His résumé includes *Drugstore Cowboy* (1989), *My Own Private Idaho* (1991), *Even Cowgirls Get the Blues* (1993) and *Elephant* (2003), all filmed in the Pacific Northwest. He also directed *Good Will Hunting* (1997, filmed in Boston). Portland-born Matt Groening created the hit cartoon show *The Simpsons*, which has many references to Portland's streets.

BC is one of the centers of film in Canada, and Vancouver is a hot spot (production costs are lower than the US). Past movies and TV series shot in BC include *The X-Files* (1993–2002), *Roxanne* (1987), *The Butterfly Effect* (2004) and *An Unfinished Life* (2005). Noted Armenian-Canadian director Atom Egoyan, raised in BC, first drew wide notice with highly lauded *The Sweet Hereafter* (1997). One of Vancouver's new talents is Trent Carlson, who directed *The Delicate Art of Parking* (2003). The **Vancouver International Film Festival** (www.viff.org) is held yearly in September.

Painting & Sculpture

Coastal Native Americans, the original artists drawn to the Northwest's beauty, painted distinctive wood and bone carvings on masks, totem poles and canoes, depicting stylized motifs of sacred animals and geometric shapes. Good places to view such artifacts are the Seattle Art Museum (p85), the University of Washington's Burke Museum (p89), the UBC Museum of Anthropology (p364) and the University of Oregon Museum of Natural History (p251).

Bill Reid (1920–88), a contemporary Native American in BC, was an outstanding Haida artist who acquired his skills from Mungo Martin, a Kwakiutl master carver of totem poles. Yet another BC resident is Susan Point, who has combined personal style with traditional Salish art elements. BC's most famous painter, Emily Carr (1871–1945), was influenced by local Native American cultures, but her art was unappreciated until she met some influential painters called the Group of Seven.

Learn about artist Emily Carr at the Carr House in Victoria, on Vancouver Island (p384) or at the Vancouver Art Gallery (p359).

Seattle's most cutting-edge art venues are the Seattle Art Museum (p85), the Roq la Rue gallery (p88) and the Center on Contemporary Art (p91). Public art and sculpture abounds in the city, thanks to its '1% for Art' program, which earmarks capital-improvement funds for public artwork. The city's Fremont neighborhood boasts some quirky sculpture (see p90), while Olympic Sculpture Park (see p88) on Elliott Bay offers impressive outdoor works against the stunning backdrop of Puget Sound.

Just south of Seattle in Tacoma is the Museum of Glass (p106), with an amazing kiln workshop. Dale Chihuly (see opposite) is the most famous of Puget Sound's glass artists and founded the Pilchuk School; see his work at the Tacoma Art Museum (p106).

Oregon has its own impressive share of Northwestern art. The Portland Art Museum (p223) is the oldest art museum in the Pacific Northwest and an impressive venue with popular exhibitions, including a sculpture garden. The city's downtown Pearl District (p228) has become a magnet for the region's finest galleries and art schools, while Alberta Street in the Northeast (p228) attracts the city's younger and less conventional artistic talents. Outside the capital, Mt Hood's Timberline Lodge (p273) showcases the handiwork of Works Progress Administration (WPA) artists of that era, while Ashland's Schneider Museum of Art (p318) is worth a visit if you're in the area.

There are plenty of artsy pockets away from the big city lights. The San Juan Islands (and nearby Port Townsend), the Oregon coast (think Astoria) and BC's jewel-like Victoria (a work of art itself) all contain secluded enclaves of artists.

GLASSMASTER DALE CHIHULY

Dale Chihuly was born in Tacoma in 1941. After an education in design and fine arts, he studied at Murano, the renowned glassmaking center near Venice. When Chihuly returned to the Seattle area in 1971, he helped found the Pilchuck Glass School, credited with transforming glass – previously used mostly for utilitarian or decorative purposes – into a medium of transcendent artistic expression. Chihuly's blown-glass sculptures are infused with lush color, sensual textures and a physicality that is both massive and delicate.

The Seattle area boasts a number of Chihuly installations, and many local art galleries display his works. Tacoma has some huge pieces in the entrance of its Federal Courthouse (p106), and the best feature at the nearby Museum of Glass (p106) is an outdoor pedestrian bridge with glass ceiling. For smaller scale work, don't miss Chihuly's permanent collection at the Tacoma Art Museum (p106).

Today, Chihuly lives at his 25,000-sq-ft studio on Lake Union. A car accident left him blind in one eye (he wears a trademark patch); ever since, he has lacked the necessary depth perception to continue solo glassblowing. He now oversees a team of glassblowers who perform the principal construction of his works.

Architecture

Forget A-frames and yurts – the Pacific Northwest has sophisticated cities with cutting-edge high-rises, beautiful arts-and-crafts neighborhoods, preserved historic buildings and eco-green constructions that'll make your head spin. And they're not only in the big cities, so expect to run across some architectural gems in the course of your rural Northwest travels.

The Great Fire of 1889 ravaged Seattle's old wooden storefronts, but they were replaced by the brick-and-stone buildings around the city's old center. Over the years the city expanded outward, flattening hills and creating a diverse mix of styles and buildings that include downtown's uber-modern Public Library, Pioneer Square's historic buildings, the waterfront's warren-like Pike Place Market, Queen Anne Hill's gorgeous Queen Annes (makes sense), Lake Union's quaint houseboats and Wallingford's industrial Gas Works Park. And let's not forget the unmistakable Space Needle and modern, controversial Experience Music Project, both neighbors in Seattle Center (p88). The city is also very open to green building options; eco-roofs (roofs covered in living, organic material) top Seattle's City Hall and Justice Center, along with Olympia's Evergreen State College.

Portland has 10 bridges that span the Willamette River, including the world's oldest lift bridge (Hawthorne), the world's only telescoping double-deck vertical lift bridge (Steel) and the USA's longest tied-arch bridge (Fremont).

Portland's center is smaller and less diverse than Seattle's but is still dotted with notable buildings that range from the 15-story, glazed terra-cotta Meier & Frank Building (1909; soon to host Macy's and a 330-room luxury hotel) to the controversial Portland Public Service Building (designed by Michael Graves in 1982 as the first major post-modern building in the country) to the twin-spire, glass-covered Oregon Convention Center (the eastside's most prominent feature). But today, most architectural projects in Portland are relatively small due to strict height requirements, which protect some (rich) residents' views of Mt Hood.

Portland is a serious leader in sustainable building practices, thoughtful urban planning, good public transport and general livability. Tasteful, high-population-density condominiums are sprouting up all over the eastside, often near bus lines, restaurants and shops, while eco-roofs, swales and cobb structures are becoming more commonplace.

Vancouver's most interesting buildings include the Roman Colosseum–like Vancouver Public Library, the ship-shaped Canada Place and the glassy Law Courts in Robson Square. The city's skyline is changing as taller buildings are being constructed, but it still retains plenty of charm in buildings such as the 1906 Vancouver Art Gallery (p359) and neighborhoods like Gastown (with its Victorian buildings and cobbled streets).

Not so far away, pretty Victoria is full of historic streets and 19th-century buildings (don't miss the Parliament buildings and Bastion Sq, p385), many dating back to when the city was a trading post for the Hudson's Bay Company.

Theater & Dance

Seattle, Portland and Vancouver are the Pacific Northwest's most dynamic hot spots for both traditional and innovative theater and dance (with a notable highlight being Ashland, in southern Oregon, which is famous for its Shakespeare Festival (p319).

Per capita, Seattle is second only to New York City in annual live performances, hosting around 30 theater companies and a wide array of special-interest troupes; Vancouver has an equally wide range of talent, and produces fun events like Bard on the Beach (p366). Portland, meanwhile, boasts highly creative groups like **BodyVox** (www.bodyvox.com) and **Do Jump!** (www.dojump.org).

Seattle's Pacific Northwest Ballet (p103) attracts one of the nation's highest per capita dance attendances, while the Oregon Ballet Theatre, performing at the Keller Auditorium (p239), is Oregon's premier ballet company. **Ballet British Columbia** (www.balletbc.com) is BC's skirt-twirler.

SPORTS

The Pacific Northwest's only National Football League (NFL) franchise is the Seattle Seahawks. Founded in 1976, they've only made it to the Super Bowl once – in 2006, against the Pittsburg Steelers (they lost, 21-10). Owned by Microsoft cofounder Paul Allen, the Seahawks play at Seattle's Qwest Field. The American football regular season runs from September to December or early January.

Get into the lifestyle – play Ultimate Frisbee. Check out http://portlandultimate.org.

Generating at least as much enthusiasm are contests between university teams, most notably the University of Washington Huskies, the Washington State University Cougars, the University of Oregon Ducks and the Oregon State University Beavers. The season runs from September to the end of January.

Vancouver is home to the Canadian Football League's (CFL) BC Lions, who won the 2006 Grey Cup against the Montreal Alouettes (who probably deserve to lose based on their name alone). Lui Passaglia is the team's most famous name, a 25-year veteran kicker who retired from the field in 2000 (but still works backstage). The Lions play at BC Place Stadium in Vancouver; their season runs from July to early November.

The Seattle Mariners, the region's only professional baseball team, have gained fans in recent years with a few great seasons – along with star recruit Ichiro Suzuki. They play at Safeco Field, which boasts a retractable 'umbrella' roof and microbrew beers on tap. The baseball season starts the first week of April and ends in October with the World Series. Outside of Seattle, fans can enjoy minor league baseball played by teams such as the Vancouver Canadians, Spokane Indians, Yakima Bears, Eugene Emeralds and Portland Beavers.

Vancouver actually won a Stanley Cup in pre-NHL hockey, when the Vancouver Millionaires defeated the Ottawa Senators. It was 1915.

Basketball season lasts from late October until mid-June. The National Basketball Association's (NBA) Seattle SuperSonics won their first and only NBA title in 1979; they play at Key Arena in Seattle Center, though at the time of writing there was controversy surrounding a possible move to Oklahoma after 2010. Portland's Trail Blazers are Oregon's only major league franchise, and used to be called the 'Jail Blazers' for their off-court antics. They're owned by Paul Allen (who also owns the Seattle Seahawks) and play at the Rose Garden Arena.

Visiting Vancouver during the October to April hockey season? Catch Canada's favorite sport, pastime and religion. The National Hockey League's (NHL) Vancouver Canucks have never won the Stanley Cup, but they did come close in 1994 – and their loss to the New York Rangers sparked a riot in downtown Vancouver. They whack the puck at GM Place. Seattle's Thunderbirds and Portland's Winter Hawks are a couple of the region's other ice-hockey teams.

Soccer isn't a major spectator sport in the US, but the United Soccer League's (USL) First Division does have its fervent fans. The Seattle Sounders, the Portland Timbers and the Vancouver Whitecaps are the Pacific Northwest's teams, kicking it from May to mid-September.

Last but not least is the newly born Portland LumberJax, an expansion team of the National Lacrosse League (NLL). They took their first baby steps in 2006, at the Rose Garden Arena. The team is owned by Angela Batinovich, who was 24 when she acquired the LumberJax – and is the youngest owner of any professional sports franchise.

Food & Drink

Lucy Burningham

Try to think of a food that isn't grown, raised or harvested in the Pacific Northwest, and you'll realize why in-the-know foodies have been putting down roots in the region for decades. Outsiders, who have been slower to discover the abundance, now flock here for the food, seeking a taste of Northwest cuisine prepared by talented chefs who cook local, seasonal foods with an alluring simplicity.

The diverse geography and climate – a mild, damp coastal region with sunny summers and arid farmland in the east – foster all types of farm-grown produce, wild mushrooms and berries, and all types of seafood (especially the famed salmon). The bounty has spawned a food-obsessed culture that congregates at farmers markets and specialty shops, especially in the cities. Many of those same food fanatics prefer organic, sustainably produced edibles, and farmers and vintners are working to meet the demand.

Here, beverages hold just as much clout as any solid food, in particular coffee and microbrewed beer. And increasingly, many Pacific Northwest red and white wines rival their European counterparts for complexity and quality.

Early American explorers Lewis and Clark recorded enjoying one of the region's specialties: 'About Noon Sergt. Ordway Frazier and Wizer returned with 17 salmon…these fish were as fat as any I ever saw; sufficiently so to cook themselves without the addition of grease or butter; those which were sound were extremely delicious; their flesh is of a fine rose colour with a small admixture of yellow.' – Meriwether Lewis, June 2, 1806.

STAPLES & SPECIALTIES

Judging from top crops in the Northwest, the region deserves a sweet reputation. Farmers grow an impressive amount of fruit, from melons, grapes and apples to every kind of berry. (Look for wild blackberries along roadsides everywhere during summer.) But savory produce thrives, too: potatoes, lentils, corn, asparagus and Walla Walla sweet onions, all of which feed local populations and some overseas. Oregon also produces 99.9% of the hazelnuts (otherwise known as filbert nuts) in the US, and the entire region grows many herbs for harvest, including lavender and spearmint.

Finding local products has become a popular pursuit for an increasingly food-aware, eco-friendly population (most of whom believe that shipping food long distances wastes precious resources). In addition to farmers markets, many small grocery and health food stores prominently label that foods are local.

Tillamook Cheese, in the coastal town of Tillamook, Oregon, makes popular cheeses and ice creams using milk from local dairies, while a cadre of artisan cheese makers around the region crafts smaller-scale products from all kinds of milk.

With miles of coastline and an impressive system of rivers, folk from the Northwest eat plenty of seafood. Depending on the season, specialties include clams, mussels, prawns, Dungeness crab and sturgeon, but salmon remains one of the region's most recognized foods, whether it's smoked, grilled and in salads, quiches and sushi. On the coast you can always find good clam chowder, but of course, the closer you go to the source, the better quality the seafood, so don't expect small, inland towns to have the same selection.

Culinate (www.culinate.com) promotes food awareness through essays, articles and book reviews.

In fact, the further you head inland, the more the cuisine changes, especially in rural areas. Expect more 'traditional' meat and potato dishes, pizzas and burgers, and less ethnic restaurants, with the exception of Mexican food. Thanks to a large immigrant population, you can find many excellent, authentic Mexican restaurants in unexpected places, like the Yakima Valley. Rivaling California as the most vegetarian- and vegan-friendly part of the country, the Pacific Northwest caters to those with an animal product-free

TOP 10 STRAIGHT FROM THE SOURCE

Here are some of the best places to find fresh Pacific Northwest foods:

- Freshly caught fish – **Pike Place Market** (www.pikeplacemarket.org; Pike St, Seattle, WA) Expert fish-handlers throw their slippery, fresh catches in the heart of Seattle.
- Berries – **Emma Lea Farms** (☎ 604 946-8216; www.emmaleafarms.com; 2727 Westham Island Rd, Delta, BC) For strawberries, raspberries, blueberries, tayberries, loganberries, boysenberries, blackberries and black currants.
- Truffles – **ShireWood Farm** (☎ 541-953-8506; www.shirewoodfarm.com; Cottage Grove, Oregon) Private truffle hunting expeditions for individuals and groups ($200 per person) or tours of the truffle farm ($25 per person).
- Mushrooms – **Puget Sound Mycological Society** (☎ 206-527-2996; www.psms.org/field_trips) Go on a spring or fall field-trip and a 'master identifier' will verify that what you find is edible.
- Hazelnuts – **Jossy Farms** (☎ 503-647-5234; www.jossyfarms.com; Hillsboro, Oregon) Buy fresh hazelnuts in November but tour this fruit-and-nut farm any time of year.
- Organic produce – **Bellingham Farmers Market** (☎ 306-647-2060; www.bellinghamfarmers.org; 1200 Railroad Ave, Bellingham, WA) Sample Washington's leafy greens and juicy fruits at their best.
- Cherries – **Fruit Loop** (www.hoodriverfruitloop.com; Hood River, Oregon) Celebrate the 4000-ton cherry harvest by cruising this 35-mile route and getting your own taste of the 12 varieties in June and July.
- Live salmon – **The Olympic Peninsula** (☎ 360-374-6300; www.fishingnorthwest.com) Catch coho, sockeye and king salmon in coastal rivers or on the open sea.
- Pumpkins – **Sauvie Island** (p229) Cut your own pumpkin from the vine, and find fresh flowers and vegetables in the fall or berries in the summer.
- Cheese – **Salt Spring Island Cheese Co** (☎ 250-653-2300; www.saltspringmarket.com) See farm-fresh sheep and goat cheese being made or visit Les Amis du Fromage (Vancouver) for the best selection of cheeses in the region.

In some cases, chefs at high-end restaurants will cook special ingredients you bring to the restaurant. Call ahead of time to confirm their openness to the idea and ask if preparation will cost extra.

diet, although rural regions offer fewer choices, and in some cases, overwhelmingly meat-heavy menus. But you can always count on college and resort towns for more worldly cuisine.

In the cities, you'll discover impressively diverse ethnic cuisine, from Ethiopian to Ecuadorian, especially in Vancouver. And many restaurants and cafés boast Northwest cuisine, a nebulous, all-encompassing term. Just try asking a local, 'What exactly *is* Northwest cuisine?' and you might experience an uncomfortable pause followed by, 'local, seasonal and fresh,' or 'organic and sustainable.' While those words don't create an image of a specific dish or spice rack, they hint at what truly defines the fare – simplicity.

The late James Beard, a famous American chef, food writer and Oregon native, believed in preparing foods simply to allow their natural flavors to shine. Beard is considered one of the greatest influences on Northwest cuisine. In many of his writings, he describes the region's wild mushrooms, herbs, truffles, berries and seafood, which obviously shaped his culinary career; he believed such quality ingredients should take center stage.

Pacific Northwesterners don't like to think of their food as trendy, but at the same time, they love to be considered innovative, especially when it comes to 'green' eating. Don't be surprised when, sharing a meal with locals,

Cookbooks by popular local chefs include *Wildwood: Cooking from the Source in the Pacific Northwest* by Cory Schreiber, *Tom Douglas's Seattle Cooking* and *A Cook's Book of Mushrooms* by Jack Czarnecki.

the conversation turns to discussing not only how the food was prepared, but also where it was grown, harvested, slaughtered or caught.

DRINKS

Pacific Northwesterners like to say that surviving the long, gray, rainy winters hinges on two things: beer and coffee.

Beer

When Prohibition in the 1920s shut down small breweries, American beer drinkers experienced a serious drought. While large-scale commercial brewers such as Budweiser flourished, small-batch, top-quality beers only came from Europe. By the 1980s, a handful of winemakers and homebrewers in Washington, Oregon and Northern California decided to revive a lost art and began brewing beer for the public in small batches using premium ingredients. Their beer became known as microbrews and the places they served them as brewpubs.

Affectionately known as 'Beervana,' Portland boasts more breweries than any other metropolitan area in the US with a total of 28.

Today, the Northwest is still the heart of beer innovation, as a new batch of brewers quenches a thirst for hop-heavy, unfiltered beers, while some of the early pioneers, including BridgePort, Red Hook and Widmer Brothers, continue to create the beer that started a revolution. Beer aficionados (otherwise known as beer geeks) sip and savor beer as they would wine, and some restaurants even have beer 'programmes' and 'sommeliers.'

Pub culture pervades the region. Find impressive small-batch beers in unexpected places, like the Twisp River Pub (p175) in Twisp, Washington, population 920, or more predictable locales, like one of the 24 McMenamins breweries (www.mcmenamins.com) scattered around Oregon and Washington (the locally owned chain also serves its beers at its nearly 50 historic hotels, restaurants and movie theaters). See also the Microbreweries tour in the Itineraries chapter, p32.

Coffee

Locals take coffee as seriously as their beer and for the most part, prefer dark roasts, and you can't escape coffee shacks and cafés even in rural areas. In fact, much of the country's current coffee culture comes from Seattle, where the first Starbucks opened across from Pike Place Market in 1971.

The Starbucks coffee chain now operates 13,000 stores in 40 countries.

These days, the best coffee comes from small-batch roasters, who carefully roast blends and single-origin coffees to perfection. To experience the high-level cult of the coffee, attend a 'cupping' at Stumptown Coffee Roasters Annex in Portland and sample unparalleled coffees from around the world.

Wine

During the past 40 years, the Pacific Northwest has become a premier wine-growing region. With such diverse geography, the area boasts 20 wine-growing regions. In Washington, which shares the same latitude as the French Burgundy and Bordeaux regions and has two hours more sunlight than California, the Columbia Valley (east of the Cascades) produces 99% of the state's wine. A small part of that area, the Walla Walla region (p213) has become the state's 'Napa Valley' with plenty of tasting rooms, wine shops and B&Bs.

Visit Wines Northwest Wines (www.winesnw.com) for wine country itineraries, maps, lodging info, events and tasting notes.

Because of a cooler climate, Oregon produces more pinot noir and pinot gris than any other variety. For the highest concentration of vineyards and tasting rooms, visit the northern part of the 100-mile-long Willamette Valley (p241), closest to Portland. BC, which has wineries on both sides of the Cascades, produces crisp, fruity white and dessert wines, but reds are just starting to catch up in number. For more information on wine regions see p34.

After California, Washington produces the highest amount of wine in the US, with over 500 registered wineries in eight American Viticulture Areas. Reds prevail, making up 80% of all Washington bottles.

Liquors

Ever pioneering when it comes to imbibing, many inventive small-batch distilleries are popping up in Oregon. Look for bottles of delicious, unique specialty liquors, such as Eau de Vie of Douglas Fir and lava-filtered vodka, from Clear Creek Distillery, Brandy Peak, Bendistillery and House Spirits Distillery in high-end liquor stores or head straight to the source; for example, Rogue Ales Public House (p300) in Newport, Oregon, serves hazelnut spiced rum and wasabi vodka.

WHERE TO EAT & DRINK

Of course the Pacific Northwest has all the steakhouses, diners, seafood shacks and Italian joints you'd expect anywhere, but extraordinary food comes from locally owned restaurants, particularly the ones where the owner is also the chef. As a general rule, avoid chains, with the exception of Burgerville, a Washington-and-Oregon-only fast-food chain that uses fresh, seasonal, local ingredients such as sweet potatoes for fries and berries for shakes.

'I don't like gourmet cooking or 'this' cooking or 'that' cooking. I like good cooking.' James Beard, American chef, food writer and native Oregonian (1903–85).

But if you're looking for a memorable dining experience, opt for places like Paley's Place (p235) in Portland, Oregon, where chef and owner Vitaly Paley prepares only the best local produce and meats or Tilth (p100) in Seattle. But not all memorable meals must be formal dining experiences. Find an unforgettable croissant at the Pacific Way Cafe (p293) in the coastal

CULINARY CALENDAR & FOOD FESTIVALS

- **Oregon Truffle Festival** (☎ 503-296-5929; www.oregontrufflefestival.com) Workshops, cooking demos, a marketplace and a five-course dinner featuring Oregon's own white and black truffles. Held in Eugene in January.
- **Vancouver Playhouse International Wine Festival** (☎ 604-873-3311; www.playhousewinefest.com) Vancouver's biggest wine festival with thousands of bottles in the tasting tent. Held in February or March.
- **Seattle Cheese Festival** (☎ 206-622-0141; www.seattlecheesefestival.com) Tasting area features 200 artisan cheeses, wine pairings and more. Held at Pike's Place in May.
- **Portland Indie Wine Festival** (☎ 503-595-0891; www.indiewinefestival.com) Features wines from small, unknown Oregon wineries. Held in May.
- **Comox Valley Shellfish Festival** (☎ 250-897-2599; www.comoxvalleyshellfishfestival.com) Seafood tastings, dinners, tours and a market. Held in June in BC.
- **Lebanon Strawberry Festival** (www.lebanonstrawberryfestival.com) World's largest strawberry shortcake, plus a parade and outdoor fair. Held in June Oregon's Lebanon (not the other one).
- **Washington Brewers Festival** (☎ 206-447-5649; www.washingtonbeer.com) More than 150 craft beers by Washington breweries. Held in Kenmore, just outside of Seattle, in June.
- **Oregon Brewers Fest** (☎ 503-778-5917; www.oregonbrewfest.com) One of the country's most established beer festivals features about 70 Oregon craft beers. Held in Portland in July, see p232.
- **International Pinot Noir Celebration** (☎ 800-775-4762; www.ipnc.org) Sip, learn and eat at tastings, dinners and more. Held in McMinnville, Oregon, in July, see p245 for further information.
- **Wild Mushroom Celebration** (www.funbeach.com/mushroom) Workshops, forays and dinners. Runs for two weeks in October along Washington's Long Beach Peninsula.

FUNGI FANATICS

Living in the Pacific Northwest means finding mushrooms growing in unexpected places, like car trunks and manicured lawns. But it also means eating an amazing array of wild mushrooms, including the yellow-fluted chanterelle, bolete (otherwise known as porcini), morel and matsutake fresh from the forest.

While it's easy to walk into most woods and find mushrooms ripe for the picking, don't plan to eat just anything you find. Always show an experienced mushroom picker the fruits of your foray – many toxic mushrooms look identical to edible ones. Mycological societies have sprouted up around the region and welcome visitors to meetings and 'field trips.'

There you may encounter a burgeoning group of truffle enthusiasts. While Europeans have been sniffing out the expensive underground fungi with pigs and dogs for hundreds of years, Americans are newer to the hunt – three new varieties of truffles were discovered in Oregon just 30 years ago. To go on a bona fide truffle hunt or learn more about the mysterious edibles, contact the Oregon-based **North American Truffling Society** (www.natruffling.org).

town of Gearhart, Oregon, or visit John's Place (p389) in Victoria, BC, for a fantastic weekend breakfast.

Visit Food Trekker (www.foodtrekker.com) to find blogs about local restaurants and other culinary travel suggestions.

And you're likely to find better beer, coffee and wine from smaller purveyors – brewpubs where you can see the brewing vats, coffee shops with roasting machines in back, and tasting rooms that serve wines made from the vines right outside the door.

VEGETARIANS & VEGANS

More than any other part of the country, vegetarians and vegans will discover plenty of food made just for them. Café Flora (p99) and the Globe Cafe (p99) in Seattle serve strictly vegetarian and vegan foods, as does Blossoming Lotus (p234) in Portland and Naam (p371) in Vancouver, BC. So many people have animal-free diets that even small, urban cafés carry assortments of vegan pastries.

Veg-Feasting in the Pacific Northwest: Vegetarian Dining, Shopping & Living by Vegetarians of Washington features listings of restaurants, natural food stores, farmers markets and recipes from local chefs.

Even if you're not dining at a strictly vegetarian restaurant, you'll discover vegetarian-friendly menus at most eateries in the metropolitan areas. Ethnic cuisine, such as Thai and Indian, usually includes many vegetarian items, and there's no shortage of delicious main-dish salads in cafés and restaurants.

Outside of the cities, vegetarians have fewer choices and vegans, even fewer still. Avoid Mexican restaurants, which usually cook seemingly-meat-free dishes in lard, and opt for pasta and pizza joints, although restaurants of every kind usually have at least one vegetarian main meal. Don't be surprised if small towns in the eastern parts of Washington and Oregon (prime cattle country) don't have veggie burgers on the menu.

EATING WITH KIDS

In general, restaurants in the Pacific Northwest welcome children of all ages and are prepared with highchairs and booster seats. Most restaurants have special children's menus (with smaller portions and kid-friendly food like mac and cheese and chicken fingers); don't hesitate to ask for one when being seated.

Portland is considered particularly kid-friendly, with places like Peanut Butter and Ellie's (p231), an entire restaurant designed for children first (think sandwiches in silly shapes and menu items like 'squishy carrots') and adults second (they have their own, healthy menu). Most smoke-free brewpubs expect children, such as the Laurelwood Public House (p231) in Portland, and many have playrooms with toys and coloring kits. While most restaurants in Seattle qualify as kid-friendly, some excel at welcoming little ones, including Ivar's Acres of Clams (p98) and the Sky City at the top of the Space Needle (p99).

But, if you're planning a special, high-end meal, especially one that requires reservations, call the restaurant ahead of time and ask if children are welcome. Most will happily receive older children who are accustomed to fine-dining protocol.

Biodynamics, a new buzzword in the wine world adopted by some vineyards in the Northwest, focuses on the health of the soil by using organic and sustainable practices – for example, farmers deter pests with flowers or bark rather than pesticides and use farm animal manure as compost.

HABITS & ETIQUETTE

Eating patterns in the Pacific Northwest mirror those in the rest of the country – dinner serves as the primary meal of the day. Generally, breakfasts are heartier than the Euro-style pastry-and-coffee meal.

Pacific Northwesterners like eating outdoors when possible, at sidewalk tables, on patios and inside next to rolled-up garage-style doors. Even during the rainy season, you'll find diners wearing sweaters and jackets enjoying leisurely meals under covered patios peppered with heaters.

Unlike other parts of the country, most Pacific Northwesterners wear casual clothing when going out to eat, even at high-end restaurants. But dressing down isn't de rigueur. Don't be surprised to see evening gowns and jeans in the same dining room or wine bar.

COOKING COURSES

Washington

Culinary Communion (☎ 206.284.8687; www.culinarycommunion.com; 2524 Beacon Ave S, Seattle; $59-119) Seattle chefs teach night and daytime classes based on seasonal ingredients that include wine.

Farm Kitchen (☎ 360-297-6615; www.farmkitchen.com; 24309 Port Gamble Rd NE, Poulsbo; $50-60) Day and nighttime courses taught on an 18-acre organic farm with guesthouse.

Gretchen's Cooking School (☎ 360-336-8747; www.gretchenskitchen.com; 509 S 1st St, Mt Vernon; $30-50) Evening classes teach cooking techniques for global and regional cuisine.

Created by amateur foodies, food blogs hold sway over restaurant chefs, menus and patrons. To see the phenomenon in action, visit An Exploration of Portland Food & Drink (www.portlandfoodanddrink.com) or the Chowhound board for the Pacific Northwest (www.chowhound.com/boards/4).

Oregon

Caprial's Bistro (☎ 503-239-8771; www.caprialandjohnskitchen.com; 7015 SE Milwaukie Ave, Portland; $35-70) Married couple and PBS TV cooking-show stars John and Caprial teach daytime and evening classes.

In Good Taste (☎ 505-248-2015; www.ingoodtastestore.com; 231 NW 11th Ave, Portland; $95-135) Visiting chefs and writers teach dinnertime courses with wine pairings.

Pacific Coast Center for Culinary Arts (☎ 541-996-1274; www.oregoncoast.org/culinary; 801 SW Hwy 101, Suite 1, Lincoln City; $30-50) Variety of daylong classes focus on regional, coastal cuisine.

British Columbia

Edible British Columbia (☎ 888-812-9660; www.edible-britishcolumbia.com; 1689 Johnston Street, Unit 565, Vancouver; $60-90) Bi-monthly evening classes includes cooking demos and wine tasting.

Wine and Thyme Cooking School (☎ 250-768-7708; www.wineandthyme.com; 1589 Gregory Rd, Westbank; $75-100) Evening, afternoon and full-day courses taught at a vineyard overlooking Lake Okanagan.

Environment David Lukas

The Pacific Northwest is home to one of the most diverse and visually stunning landscapes in North America. From a central location like Seattle or Portland it takes mere hours to reach places as varied as dramatic coastal headlands, snowcapped mountains or vast deserts. Along the way visitors may discover majestic waterfalls, towering ancient trees and lava fields so fresh it looks as if they just erupted. This is a magical place to explore and the natural world is never far away.

Want the most entertaining guide to Pacific Northwest plants and animals? Consult *Cascade-Olympic Natural History* by Daniel Matthews for information on everything from *Giardia lamblia* to the patron saint of Northwest backpackers.

THE LAND

The easiest way to visualize the Pacific Northwest is to think of the long spine of the Cascade Range as neatly dividing the region: everything west of the Cascades is drenched in rain and wrapped in forests and vegetation so green it hurts the eyes; and everything east of the Cascades is desertlike or given over to dryland farming and ranching. In some areas west of the Cascades rainfall reaches an astonishing 100in to 195in a year and fills countless rivers and lakes, while the mighty Snake and Columbia Rivers surge out of the arid eastern hinterlands and cut through the Cascade Range along the Oregon–Washington border.

Because the North American continent is creeping inexorably westward at a rate of around 1in to 2in a year, the Pacific coastline is a 'leading-edge coast' with sheer cliffs, narrow beaches and small bays. Compared with a flat 'trailing-edge coast' like the Atlantic Coast, a leading-edge coast is rugged and dynamic because the immense forces created by the edge of the drifting continent crumple the earth's crust into a band of coastal mountain ranges.

Behind the coastal ranges the earth dips to form broad fertile valleys that are collectively called the Willamette Valley in Oregon and the Puget Sound Trough in Washington. East of the valleys are the soaring heights of the Cascade Range, a long series of rolling hills punctuated by massive snowcapped volcanoes that range from Mt Baker (10,781ft) and Mt Rainier (14,411ft) in Washington to Mt Hood (11,240ft) in Oregon. The rolling hills are the eroded remnants of an ancient Cascade chain that formed 40 million years ago, while the volcanoes signify a new period of mountain-building activity that started 12 million years ago and continues to this day.

Landscapes east of the Cascades are dominated by the Columbia Plateau, the largest lava field on the earth's surface, which formed when molten lava smothered a region crossing present-day eastern Oregon and Washington around 17 million years ago. The higher peaks of much older mountain ranges like the Blue and Wallowa Mountains in Oregon, or the Selkirk

TOP FIVE GEOGRAPHIC WONDERS

- **Crater Lake** (p285) Deepest lake in North America, 1942ft deep
- **Mt Rainier** (p179) Highest peak in the Cascade Range, 14,411ft high
- **Hells Canyon** (p342) Deepest gorge in North America, 8005ft from bottom to highest peak
- **Columbia River** (p258) Fourth-largest river in North America, 1270 miles long
- **Della Falls** (p402) Highest straight-drop waterfall (1444ft) in Canada

Mountains in Washington, punctuate this otherwise monotonous yet hauntingly beautiful terrain.

Geologic Overview

Little of today's Pacific Northwest existed more than 200 million years ago. Back then, the area was a warm, shallow ocean along the west coast of an ancient, unrecognizable continent. This all changed when North America broke off from Europe and Africa and began drifting towards the west. This westward drift had major consequences. One was that the leading edge of the continent plowed up seafloor sediments and compressed them into coastal mountain ranges. Fragments of these ancient coastal ranges are still visible today in the Blue, Wallowa and Klamath Mountains of Oregon. Another consequence was that North America began colliding with large islands that added their bulk to the growing western margin of the continent.

One hundred million years ago, North America collided with the Okanogan subcontinent, an island the size of California that now underlies much of north-central Washington and southern British Columbia (BC). Then, 50 million years ago, North America collided with the North Cascades subcontinent, a body of hard metamorphic rock seen today in the uniquely jagged peaks characteristic of the Cascade Range from Snoqualmie Pass, Washington, to northern BC. Many smaller ocean islands were also added – these created mountain ranges such as the Blue and Wallowa Mountains of Oregon.

Over millions of years the Pacific Northwest arose from this combination of seafloor sediments and islands added to the old continental coastline. Although various volcanic centers contributed lava and ash, it wasn't until 40 million years ago that a line of concentrated volcanic activity formed along the Cascades axis. This ancient Cascades chain rose high enough to block storm systems and turn eastern Oregon and Washington into an arid landscape for the first time, but once the volcanic activity abated about 25 million years ago these mountains began to erode into the Cascades landscape we see today.

From 16 to 13 million years ago, eastern Oregon and Washington witnessed one of the premier episodes of volcanic activity recorded in Earth's history. Due to shifting stresses in the earth's crust, much of interior western North America began cracking along thousands of lines and releasing enormous amounts of lava that flooded over the landscape. On multiple occasions, so much lava was produced that it filled the Columbia River channel and reached the Oregon coast, forming prominent headlands like Cape Lookout. Today, the hardened lava flows of eastern Oregon and Washington are easily seen in spectacular rimrock cliffs and flat-top mesas.

The ancient ash flows in the John Day Fossil Beds National Monument of eastern Oregon preserve one of the most complete fossil records in the world.

During the ice ages of the past two million years, the southern region of BC and the northern third of Washington were completely covered in a massive ice field, while virtually every mountain range in the rest of the region was blanketed by smaller glaciers. Even more dramatically, tongues of ice extending southward out of Canada were preventing the 3000-sq-mile glacial Lake Missoula in present-day Montana from being able to drain. Consequently, on about 40 separate occasions, these massive ice dams burst, releasing more water than all the world's rivers combined and flooding much of eastern Washington up to 1000ft deep. These floods scoured over the landscape with tremendous power, digging out paths and cutting cliffs across a region now known as the Channeled Scablands. Grand Coulee and Dry Falls of northeastern Washington are remnants of these spectacular floods, as are the crowd-pleasing waterfalls of the Columbia River Gorge that plummet over cliffs carved by the floods.

WILDLIFE

Animals

Although a wild and remarkably undeveloped landscape, the Pacific Northwest does not readily reveal its wildlife. The mix of ocean, forests and untamed mountains creates a great diversity of habitats, but visitors may overlook animals hidden in the dense vegetation and rugged terrain. However, concentrations of abundant wildlife can be found with a little searching, especially in some of the national wildlife refuges and parks.

The *Seasonal Guide to the Natural Year: A Month By Month Guide to Natural Events. Oregon, Washington and British Columbia* by James L Davis presents a seasonal breakdown and reveals the premier places to view wildlife.

LAND MAMMALS

Among the Pacific Northwest's signature animals is the elk, whose eerie bugling courtship calls can be heard each September and October in forested areas throughout the region. Full-grown males may reach 1100lb and carry 5ft racks of antlers, so it's a memorable experience to run into one of these creatures. During winter, large groups gather in lowland valleys and can be observed at a number of well-known sites such as Jewell Meadows Wildlife Area west of Portland or along the Spirit Lake Highway in Mt St Helens National Volcanic Monument.

The open plains of eastern Oregon and Washington are home to pronghorn antelope, fleet-footed mammals with two single black horns instead of antlers. Pronghorns are placed in their own family and are only found in the American west, but they are more famous for being able to run up to 60mph for long stretches. Possessing keen eyesight and acute sense of smell, pronghorns keep their distance from humans, though they are sometimes spotted along highways, for example in the Hart Mountain National Antelope Refuge (p352) in southeast Oregon.

Visitors to eastern Oregon and Washington are likely to see mule deer and coyotes, not because these animals are more common but because the openness of the terrain makes them easier to see. Deer verge on abundant in agricultural or well-watered areas, while it is not uncommon to see coyotes trotting across quiet back roads.

One of the most highly sought after animals at Mt Rainier and other parks is the ghostly white mountain goat that inhabits high peaks and grassy meadows. So superbly adapted to their environment that their kids begin instinctively climbing just hours after birth, these goats specialize in scrambling up rock faces on barely perceptible ledges that no predators can follow.

The marmot, a big rodent that looks more like a fuzz ball, is often seen around mountain parking lots and campgrounds, especially in popular places such as Olympic National Park or Manning Provincial Park, begging from unwary hikers or making itself unwelcome by burrowing into unattended bags in search of food scraps. No matter how much a marmot gazes lovingly into your eyes, you should resist the temptation to feed it and turn it into a problem for future visitors.

MARINE MAMMALS & FISH

The rich ocean environment of the Pacific Northwest creates ideal conditions for a tremendous variety of fish and for the marine mammals that feed on them. Further testament to this incredibly productive marine environment are the many harbors and small fishing towns lining the coast.

Although salmon could be considered the very lifeblood of the Pacific Northwest, even locals can be forgiven for having a hard time keeping the names of different species straight. Not only do scientists argue over how to name and separate the seven species of salmon that are currently recognized, but these important fish have been given dozens of confusing common names such as dog, chum, coho, sockeye, chinook and pink, to name but a few.

Salmon have a unique lifestyle of migrating out to sea as juveniles, then returning to the stream of their birth to breed and die as adults. The annual run of returning salmon used to be one of the greatest wildlife spectacles on the planet, with 11 to 16 million salmon in the Columbia River alone. Dams, habitat destruction, overfishing and hatcheries have reduced these majestic runs to mere shadows of their former selves, but it is still possible to view spawning salmon in sizable numbers each October.

You may also glimpse the odd-looking white sturgeon at one of the hatcheries or salmon viewing sites along the Columbia River, such as the Bonneville Fish Hatchery (see p259). This monster fish can weigh up to 1800lb and is a living fossil from the time of the dinosaurs. Found only in the Columbia River system, it has been overfished for its delicious flesh and adversely impacted by the river's many dams.

Salmon conservation includes protecting populations around the entire Pacific Rim from the Russian Far East to northern California. Learn more at www.wildsalmoncenter.org.

Anywhere on the Pacific Coast it is hard to miss seals and sea lions. Most numerous are small, leopard-spotted harbor seals that drape themselves awkwardly over rocky headlands. You might see harbor seals poking their round faces out of the surf and staring at you with their big dark eyes. From April to July the pups may be found resting on beaches while their mothers are hunting at sea. Well-intentioned people often take these pups to animal shelters without realizing that their mothers are nearby: you should leave 'abandoned' pups alone or call an animal shelter and let them decide which course of action to take.

The much larger and darker sea lions, with external ears and the ability to 'walk' on land by shuffling on their flippers, are renowned for the thick manes and roaring cries that give them their name. Sea lions easily adapt to human presence and can be common around docks and jetties, where they are sometimes blamed for stealing fish from fishermen.

The aptly named 'killer whale' or orca is one of the few predators capable of attacking adult seals. This fierce predator is the largest dolphin in the world, weighing up to 24,250lb, and is the undisputed spirit animal of Pacific Northwest waters. Living up to 100 years and spending their entire lives in groups led by dominant females, orcas have complex societies and large brains that rival those of humans. Several resident groups (or pods) live around the San Juan Islands and prey on fish, while transient pods migrate along the outer coast and hunt seals and sea lions.

Other famous marine mammals of the outer coast include gray whales that make the longest and most predictable migrations of any mammal in the world each November to December and April to June. Once hunted to near extinction, these majestic 90,390lb creatures have returned to their historic population levels and are a major reason for visiting the coast.

THAT FROG HAS A TAIL!

Not many people know that one of the Pacific Northwest's most unusual creatures is a frog with a tail. Actually it's not a tail but something even more unusual – it's a copulatory organ that engorges with blood and points forward during mating, an energetic affair that lasts 24 to 30 hours! You might think that this protopenis is a highly evolved feature, but in fact tailed frogs are considered the most primitive of all frogs and their only close relatives are found in New Zealand. No other frog in the world performs true copulation. These 2in-long olive brown frogs live along cold, fast streams in the Northwest but apparently disappear when an area is logged, making their future of some concern. Because they can't sing over the roaring water, adults are voiceless and lack eardrums, while tadpoles are unique in having a suckerlike disc on their mouths that allows them to cling to rocks in the raging torrents. The tadpoles may attach to your foot if you're wading in a creek, but don't worry because they nibble on algae, not toes.

Bird-watchers in the Pacific Northwest have a unique online resource at http://thebirdguide.com.

BIRDS

Out of the countless birds seen along the coast, none have such a prominent place as the eight types of gulls that frequent the region's beaches, rocks and parking lots. Gulls are particularly numerous during winter, but they retreat to offshore rocks to breed in April or May. Because gulls eat almost anything they can swallow, they gather wherever humans congregate in hope of getting handouts.

A similar strategy is employed by the region's two prominent jay species. The dark blue, black-crested Steller's jay occupies conifer forests throughout the Pacific Northwest and is notable for its loud screeching calls as it swoops down on picnickers and eagerly peers about for food scraps.

Hikers and skiers in the high mountains may encounter the gray jay with its soft cooing whistles and gentle demeanor. Long known by the nickname 'camp robber,' these inquisitive jays are fearless in picking food from people's hands, and may even land on your shoulders to snatch some from your lips.

The Pacific Northwest is a stronghold for bald eagles to feast on the annual salmon runs and nest in old growth forests. With a 7.5ft wingspan, these impressive birds are gather by the hundreds at places like BC's Squamish River or Oregon's Lower Klamath National Wildlife Refuge.

Plants

WEST OF THE CASCADES

The division of the Pacific Northwest by the Cascade Range has such a profound effect on the vegetation that the wet western side and the dry eastern side are two utterly different regions. An abundance of rainfall on the west side supports the most impressive gathering of conifer trees anywhere in the world, with individual trees from six of the 30 or so species exceeding 500 years in age and reaching heights of over 195ft and diameters around of 6ft to 10ft. This lofty and grand forest is not only home to many creatures but also the foundation for a vast logging economy that props up countless small rural towns throughout the region.

The most ecologically and economically significant conifers are the Douglas fir, western hemlock and western red cedar, with Sitka spruce being dominant in the coastal fog zone. Taken together, these four trees account for the majority of the forested landscapes from ocean edge to high Cascades peak.

AN OLD GROWTH PRIMER

'Old growth' is a term much bandied about in the Pacific Northwest. Referring to stands of ancient trees, it is cursed by those who make their living cutting forests, shouted as a rallying cry by environmentalists and mentioned by just about everyone who sees it written in the newspapers on an almost daily basis. At the same time, very few people understand that 'old growth' means more than a bunch of big old trees.

Because of its great age, an old growth forest has tremendous structural complexity resulting from trees of many different sizes growing together, along with a high density of dead standing trees (snags) and dead fallen trees (logs). Decaying snags provide cavities for woodpeckers, owls and small mammals, while logs hold nutrients and provide pathways for small forest creatures. You may notice that conifer seedlings grow prolifically on old 'nurse' logs rather than on the forest floor, where it is too mossy or covered in needles for seeds to germinate.

Compared with a newly logged site, where trees grow back in depressing uniformity, an old growth forest creates homes for hundreds of species and the intricate webs of life that take centuries to become established. In fact, as the few remaining pockets of old growth continue to be logged it is worth considering that we will not see these unique ecosystems return in our lifetimes.

On the west side of the Olympic Peninsula and in other coastal areas where rainfall may surpass 195in per year, these same trees reach incredible sizes and become engulfed in thick carpets of bright-green moss. These are the world-famous temperate rain forests of the Pacific Northwest.

Anyone hiking in these forests will soon come to recognize a common group of plants that form the typical understory. Included in this group are densely clumped sword ferns that cover entire hillsides, as well as taller thickets of small-leaved huckleberries bearing heavy loads of delicious fruits. The state flower of Washington, the pink-flowered rhododendron, and the state flower of Oregon, the holly-leaved Oregon grape, are abundant in these areas and add much color when in bloom.

The Great Bear Rain Forest of coastal BC is the largest intact temperate rain forest in the world and many environmental groups are working to keep it that way. See www.savethegreatbear.org.

EAST OF THE CASCADES

For an entirely different experience, journey over the Cascades to a landscape many people think of as desert. Technically, the parched regions of eastern Oregon and Washington are semiarid grassland or sagebrush steppe, but, terminology aside, they are still dry places. Forest cloaks some of the higher slopes and mountains, but the most common plant at lower elevations is the pungent sagebrush, the ubiquitous plant of the arid American west. Native grasses, cleared for crops or grazed out by cattle, are being replaced by an aggressive alien species called cheatgrass that leaves spiky seeds in your socks.

Common trees east of the Cascades include the stately ponderosa pine with its orange bark and sweet vanilla smell. A grove of ancient unlogged ponderosa pines is one of the most beautiful habitats in the Pacific Northwest. Unfortunately, most of these trees have been logged. In drier areas pines are replaced by densely foliaged western junipers, whose scaly needles look like miniature lizard tails. Junipers produce crops of attractive blue-gray berries, which provide the major food for half a dozen types of birds.

A surprising sight east of the Cascades is the fall color displayed by cottonwoods. These trees require a lot of water to survive, so look for patches of golden yellow and orange along rivers and streams.

NATIONAL & PROVINCIAL PARKS

The Pacific Northwest offers an extraordinary range of parks, monuments, forests, and wildlife refuges encompassing everything from alpine peak to rugged coast, from dinosaur fossil beds to native cultural areas. Mild coastal climates mean that if some parks are buried in snow there are always alternate destinations worth visiting.

ENVIRONMENTAL ISSUES

Just as lots of people come to the Pacific Northwest for its natural splendor, so do others to profit from its natural resources, and the conflict simmering between the two camps sometimes erupts into angry confrontation. In fact, there is little room for compromise when there is value both in leaving resources intact and removing them.

Unfortunately, efforts to regulate these problems have stalled. For example, Oregon's landmark 1973 decision to dampen urban sprawl by creating a Land Conservation and Development Commission has done little to stem burgeoning urban populations or the heedless development of Oregon's precious coastline. Though Oregon is touted as having one of the most forward-thinking urban planning processes in the nation, you would hardly know it when you drive through its more populated parts.

The same could be said for the Pacific Northwest's most contentious issue, the logging of its sprawling coniferous forests. Through the 1970s and '80s, logging was proceeding at such a breathtaking pace that it exploded into a

THE BEST NATIONAL & PROVINCIAL PARKS OF THE PACIFIC NORTHWEST

Park	Location	Features	Activities	Best time to visit	Page
Crater Lake	Oregon	ancient volcano, deepest lake in North America	sightseeing, cross-country skiing	Jul-Oct	p285
John Day Fossil Beds	Oregon	technicolor landscape of prehistoric ash flows, one of the world's foremost fossil sites	sightseeing	year-round	p346
Mt Rainier	Washington	alpine peaks, wildflowers; black bear, mountain goat, elk	hiking, climbing	Jul-Sep	p179
Mt St Helens	Washington	spectacular volcano; elk, black bear, deer	hiking, sightseeing	Jun-Oct	p186
North Cascades	Washington	alpine peaks, remote wilderness; mountain goat, grizzly bear, wolf	backpacking, climbing, fishing	Jul-Sep	p168
Olympic	Washington	alpine peaks, lush rain forests, wild coasts; black bear, elk, spotted owl	backpacking, climbing, fishing	year-round	p137
Oregon Dunes	Oregon	vast dune field, remote coastlines; bald eagle, osprey	off-road vehicles, hiking, horseback riding, canoeing, swimming	year-round	p305
Pacific Rim	British Columbia	wild coast, giant rain forest trees, world-famous Coast Trail; bald eagles, black bear, cougar	hiking, kayaking	Jun-Sep	p397
Strathcona	British Columbia	remote wilderness, solitude, highest Canadian waterfall; wolf, black-tailed deer, elk	backcountry hiking and adventure	Jul-Sep	p402

national issue. In 1993 President Clinton spearheaded the passage of what came to be known as the Northwest Forest Plan as a compromise solution to allow some logging while setting aside 80% of the remaining old growth forest. By the time President Bush started reversing the plan during his first term in office, it had already been bogged down in lawsuits and both sides in the argument felt extreme frustration.

A visitor flying over the Northwest can't help but see the stunning patchwork of clear-cuts that blanket the region. Rather than resembling the vast primeval landscapes described by early explorers, the Northwest's forests have been largely converted into rigorously managed crops of trees dissected by a spaghetti-like maze of roads. As a result, hillsides have begun to erode, streams are warming up and filling with silt, invasive weeds are spreading like wildfire and a number of species are becoming endangered.

Another one of the Pacific Northwest's most important resources suffers when stream health degrades in logged areas. Salmon depend on cold, clear waters during the early stages of their development and their eggs can't tolerate warm, silted waters. Unfortunately, declining salmon populations are further impacted when dams are constructed on the rivers they breed in.

The Columbia River system has more than 400 dams – more than any other river system in the world.

The Columbia River system, once home to some of the greatest salmon runs in the world, is now the most hydroelectrically developed river basin in the world. As a consequence, salmon runs that once numbered in the millions have been reduced to ghosts of their former selves and there are no easy solutions in sight unless people agree to take down their dams. Since that is not likely to happen anytime soon, salmon populations are in grave danger.

Pacific Northwest Outdoors

Ellee Thalheimer

Armed with kayaks and full racks of climbing gear, people migrate to the Pacific Northwest to join the fleece-wearing, peak-bagging ranks. Outdoor enthusiasts come with mountain bikes and fly rods, with crampons and parachutes, to explore the immense diversity of landscape. Within a day, one can get to rivers, coasts, mountains, high-desert canyons, alpine lakes, lava fields, rain forests and wetlands. From niche activities to major outdoor sports, you'll find it here. You can carve fresh tracks in the champagne powder of world-class ski resorts, or you can cling to your kiteboard as you hurl across the water at ferocious speeds. If it's solitude you crave, set off with a backpack into the heart of your choice of breathtaking wilderness. See 360 degrees from Mt Rainier's summit or bike over the Cascades. Folks, the Pacific Northwest is a mecca for those who answer the call of that fair muse Mother Nature. So if you're a visiting outdoor junkie, and you have a to-do-before-I-die list, let the Pacific Northwest unroll her dirt-crusted carpets of snow and wildflowers and ask, 'Where shall we start?'

Orient yourself in BC by visiting www.bcadventure.com.

HIKING

This region is lavished with some of the most sublime landscapes and terrain imaginable. You can spend a couple of hours to a couple of weeks exploring the backcountry. In the summertime, popular places can be crowded, the bugs can bug, and bears may want your food, so take the necessary precautions. Winter weather can be abominable and summer weather is usually lovely yet volatile, so be prepared for anything. Ranger stations and visitor centers are excellent resources for the low-down on permits, fees, safety and trail conditions.

See www.cooltrails.com for details about hiking trails in the Northwest.

Washington

You'll see no foofy umbrella drinks on Olympic Coast beaches. Bring your fleece and weigh your options between strenuous backpacking trips through craggy rain forest terrain and mellow kid-friendly beach hikes. In the nearby Olympic Mountains, you can hike deep canyons and alpine meadows. The glacier-carved valleys and towering ridges of Washington's North Cascade Mountain Range create a dramatic landscape, and the Rainy Pass to Maple Pass Loop won't disappoint. In the Southern Cascades, you can explore the foothills of Mt Adams and smoldering Mt St Helens. To leave the crowds behind, try Glacier Peak which offers all the sparkly lake, alpine goodness to satiate your inner-hiker. The Wonderland Trail circumnavigates the snow-capped behemoth Mt Rainier.

Oregon

The Oregon coast's wind-swept beaches and rocky bluffs create a rugged and grandiose beauty. Cape Lookout is a magnificent year-round coastal hike. For a challenge, you can hike up Saddle Mountain for an unbeatable view of the coastal range. Just east of Portland, you can hike in the Columbia River Gorge among lush fir forests and dramatic waterfalls. Multnomah Falls is the hallmark, but there are other knock-out hikes nearby, such as at Wahkeena Falls. South of the gorge, the popular 40-mile Timberline Trail Loop circumnavigates Mt Hood through alpine forests and reveals spectacular views.

Though flooded with advertisements, www.gorp.com can be a good info source for many Pacific Northwest outdoor activities.

In the Cascades, wilderness areas like Waldo Lake and Three Sisters make loggers salivate and hikers bliss out. For views of Crater Lake – that freaky turquoise phenomenon – hike up Mt Scott. In remote Northeast Oregon, the Wallowa Mountains – boasting 20 alpine peaks over 8000ft – and Hells Canyon are definitely worth exploring if you can get yourself out there.

For an overview hiking guide of the region check out *Foghorn Outdoors Pacific Northwest Hiking: The Complete Guide to More Than 1,000 of the Hikes in Washington and Oregon* by Ron Judd and Dan Nelson.

British Columbia

Nothing short of a hiker's paradise, British Columbia (BC) has hundreds of out-of-this-world parks and innumerable trails. On Vancouver Island, trails like the 47-mile West Coast Trail in Pacific Rim National Park winds through ancient rain forests and gorgeous shorelines. Or take Whistler's gondola and enjoy wandering along on high alpine trails without making the high alpine climb. For a stellar coastal hike, you can do an extensive trip or a day hike on the Juan de Fuca Marine Trail.

CYCLING & MOUNTAIN BIKING

A cyclist could hardly ask for more than the Pacific Northwest offers. Both major and minor cities have high concentrations of cyclists. They are blessed with great urban riding, bike culture and access to the most diverse and spectacular environments: shoreline, high desert, alpine mountains and lush rain forests. The touring possibilities are limitless. Though the hardcores cycle year-round, summer is when it goes off. Logging trucks and RVs can be annoying/scary in certain places, so look for back roads. Local shops are great resources for route suggestions. The premier shop in Portland is **River City Bicycles** (www.rivercitybicycles.com), where the owner sells his homemade wooden fenders. In Seattle, **Gregg's Cycles** (www.greggscycles.com) is a fabulous store with locations all over the city.

There's plenty of online trail info for mountain bikers:
www.singletracks.com
www.mbronline.com
www.dirtworld.com

Fans of the knobby tire point their wheels towards the Pacific Northwest where the sheer diversity of terrain and abundance of public lands have cultivated an ever-growing mountain-biking community in the region. Be sure to share the trails and give hikers the right of way.

Washington

You can have an unparalleled multiday cycling experience in the San Juan Islands that incorporates kayaking and hiking, or you can just cycle for the day. Lopez Island is known for its beauty and bike-friendliness. In the Yakima Valley, wind your way through picturesque wine country. If you're cycling with kids, head to Bainbridge Island. For a challenge, cycle the scenic loop around Mt Rainier. In eastern Washington, go to Moses Lake for the loop around Potholes Reservoir.

The Seattle to Portland Bicycle Classic, is the largest multiday bicycle event in the Northwest, with up to 9000 participants riding from Seattle to Portland (200 miles) in one or two days. Join early because it sells out!

Near Mt St Helens, the Plains of Abraham/Ape Canyon Trail and the Lewis River Trail provide top-notch mountain biking in staggering Cascade scenery. The Wenatchee Lake and Leavenworth areas also deeply satisfy riders. Here you'll find Devil's Gulch, which claims the smoothest, fastest singletrack in the state.

Oregon

The Historic Columbia River Hwy and the mellow Sauvie Island loop are two classic rides near Portland. Around the Cascade Range there are magnificent rides. The Cascade Lakes Hwy (Hwy 46) will drop your jaw, as will the Diamond Lake to Crater Lake challenge, though it's crowded in the summertime. On the coast, Three Capes Scenic Hwy outside of Tillamook has brilliant scenery and burly climbs. In the remote northeast, Hells Canyon Scenic Byway weaves for hundreds of miles through dramatic landscape. You can take side trips along the Snake River.

BACKCOUNTRY ETHICS & GUIDELINES: BASED ON LEAVE NO TRACE PHILOSOPHY

Plan Ahead & Prepare

To ensure a safe backcountry trip that respects the natural resources you love, check in with the station ranger or park service about regulations on group size, environmental hazards, terrain, weather and permits. Beware of car break-ins at trail heads.

Travel & Camp on Durable Surfaces

While hiking, avoid trampling vegetation by staying on trails and in designated areas. Off-trail travel can cause unnecessary impact and soil erosion. When you leave a campsite, especially in remote locations, make sure you leave it better than you found it.

Dispose of Waste Properly

Pack it in, pack it out. It's not just a gum wrapper. Make a resealable double-bagged trash sack accessible, and respect the place you're visiting by taking all your scraps out with you. Pack out all meal leftovers – none of this slinging what you couldn't eat in the woods. Don't wash your unrinsed spaghetti pot in the creek either. When you rinse out your dishes, do it 100ft from water, pour the dirty water through a filter, screen or bandana, and pack out the chunks. Sand, dirt and snow work great to wash dishes, but if you must use soap, make sure it's biodegradable. Same goes with washing your body, except for the dirt part. Before you leave a lunch spot or campsite, inspect for trash or spilled food.

Going in the woods can be fun. Great views. However, there are important standards to follow. Take a trowel and dig a 6in hole at least 200 adult paces away from water, trails and campsites. Don't wait until the last minute and only manage to dig a 1in hole. Pack out all toilet paper, or use natural materials (not poison oak) and bury them too. Cover and disguise your hole. Hand sanitizer is the cherry on top. Use restroom facilities when available. Even if they're gross.

Leave What You Find

Leave only with memories. Seriously, put it down.

Minimize Campfire Impact

Ask a ranger about protocols and fire danger levels. Camp stoves are a great alternative. If you do have a fire, keep it small and use only downed wood. Use pre-existing fire rings. Disperse your ashes, but make sure they are cool to touch before you do.

Respect Wildlife

Avoid stressing out animals with ruckus. You are the visitor. Don't mess with, feed or disturb animals in anyway. Check with a ranger about bear protocol.

Be Considerate of Others

If you're in the vicinity of others, respect their right to listen to the birds and to pretend you aren't there. Contact **Leave No Trace** (☎ 800-322-4100; www.lnt.org) to find out more.

Oakridge, east of Eugene, has premier mountain biking. **Mountain Bike Oregon** (www.mtbikeoregon.com), a well-known three-day mountain-biking festival, is held here twice a summer. In central Oregon, the Mackenzie River Trail is touted by some as 'the best trail in Oregon.' It takes you past lakes, streams, waterfalls and lava fields. Bend is the unofficial mountain-bike capital of Oregon. You can catch a trail right out of town or choose one of many constellation rides that will bring you through alpine forests, old-growth and high desert canyons. Many people also head to Mt Hood to ride. The Surveyor's Ridge Trail has tremendous scenery and makes you work for it.

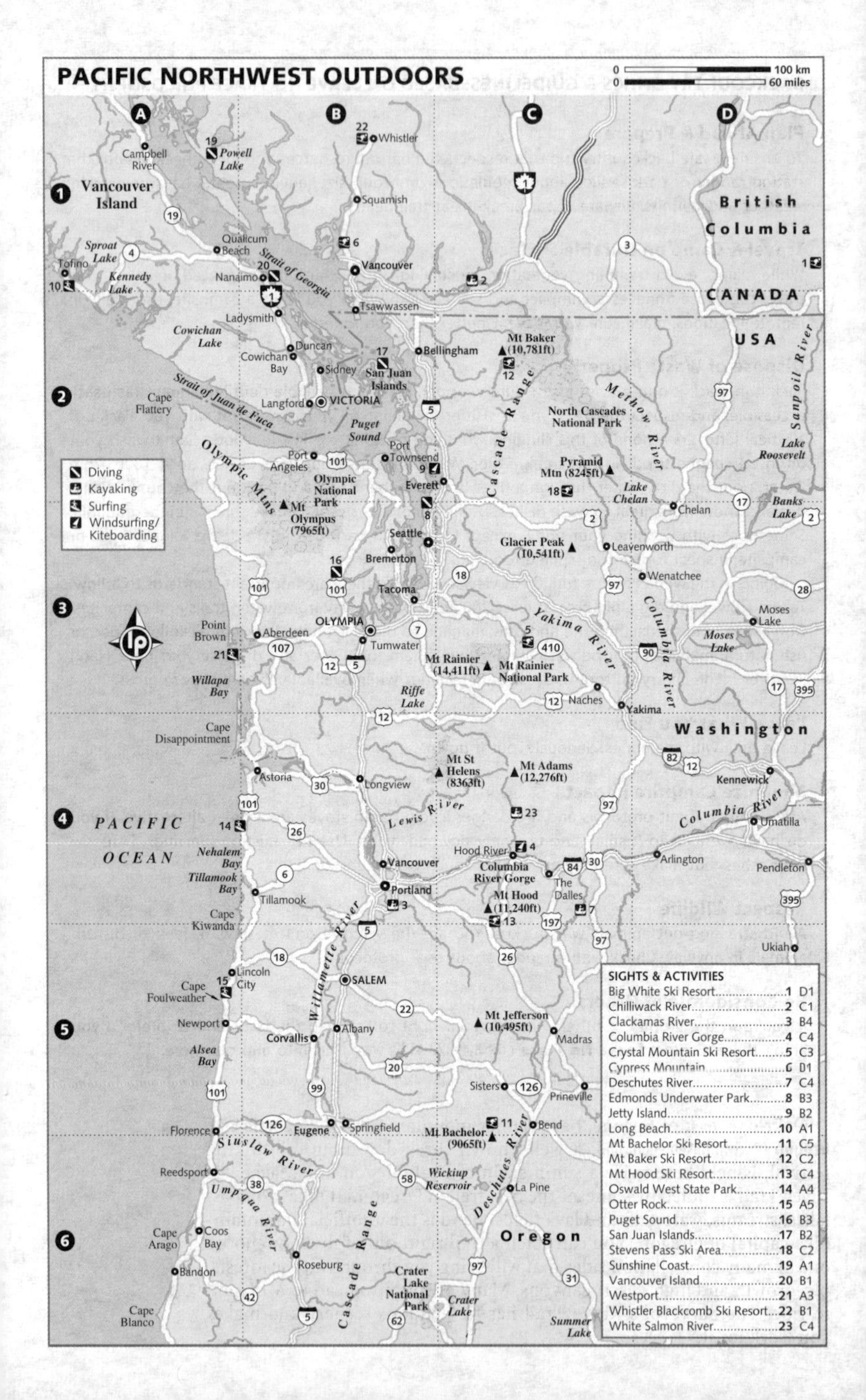
PACIFIC NORTHWEST OUTDOORS
0 100 km
0 60 miles
A
B
C
D
1
2
3
4
5
6
Vancouver Island
British Columbia
CANADA
USA
Washington
Oregon
PACIFIC OCEAN
Diving
Kayaking
Surfing
Windsurfing/ Kiteboarding
Campbell River
Powell Lake
Whistler
Squamish
Qualicum Beach
Sproat Lake
Tofino
Kennedy Lake
Nanaimo
Strait of Georgia
Vancouver
Tsawwassen
Ladysmith
Cowichan Lake
Duncan
Cowichan Bay
Sidney
San Juan Islands
Bellingham
Mt Baker (10,781ft)
Cape Flattery
Strait of Juan de Fuca
Langford
VICTORIA
Puget Sound
Port Townsend
Port Angeles
Olympic Mtns
Olympic National Park
Mt Olympus (7965ft)
Everett
Seattle
Bremerton
Tacoma
OLYMPIA
Tumwater
Point Brown
Aberdeen
Willapa Bay
Cape Disappointment
Cascade Range
North Cascades National Park
Methow River
Pyramid Mtn (8245ft)
Lake Chelan
Chelan
Sanpoil River
Lake Roosevelt
Banks Lake
Glacier Peak (10,541ft)
Leavenworth
Wenatchee
Moses Lake
Yakima River
Columbia River
Mt Rainier (14,411ft)
Mt Rainier National Park
Riffe Lake
Naches
Yakima
Mt St Helens (8363ft)
Mt Adams (12,276ft)
Kennewick
Astoria
Longview
Lewis River
Umatilla
Nehalem Bay
Tillamook Bay
Tillamook
Vancouver
Portland
Hood River
Columbia River Gorge
The Dalles
Arlington
Pendleton
Mt Hood (11,240ft)
Cape Kiwanda
Ukiah
Lincoln City
Cape Foulweather
SALEM
Willamette River
Newport
Corvallis
Albany
Mt Jefferson (10,495ft)
Madras
Alsea Bay
Sisters
Prineville
Florence
Eugene
Springfield
Mt Bachelor (9065ft)
Bend
Siuslaw River
Reedsport
Umpqua River
Wickiup Reservoir
Deschutes River
La Pine
Cape Arago
Coos Bay
Bandon
Roseburg
Cascade Range
Crater Lake National Park
Crater Lake
Cape Blanco
Summer Lake
SIGHTS & ACTIVITIES
Big White Ski Resort 1 D1
Chilliwack River 2 C1
Clackamas River 3 B4
Columbia River Gorge 4 C4
Crystal Mountain Ski Resort 5 C3
Cypress Mountain 6 D1
Deschutes River 7 C4
Edmonds Underwater Park 8 B3
Jetty Island 9 B2
Long Beach 10 A1
Mt Bachelor Ski Resort 11 C5
Mt Baker Ski Resort 12 C2
Mt Hood Ski Resort 13 C4
Oswald West State Park 14 A4
Otter Rock 15 A5
Puget Sound 16 B3
San Juan Islands 17 B2
Stevens Pass Ski Area 18 C2
Sunshine Coast 19 A1
Vancouver Island 20 B1
Westport 21 A3
Whistler Blackcomb Ski Resort 22 B1
White Salmon River 23 C4

DO IT BY BIKE

There are few places better to tour by pedal than the spectacular, bike-loving Pacific Northwest. Better yet, you can decide your vacation objectives and build a bike tour around them. Go kayaking in the San Juans and have high tea in Victoria, but arrive by bicycle. Visit the Rose Garden in Portland then windsurf in the Columbia River Gorge, but transport yourself by cycling the gorgeous landscape in between. The advantages are many: intimate experiences with the environment, staying in shape, rubbing elbows with the locals and traveling in an eco-friendly way. Maybe it seems intimidating, but once you get the hang of it, it's surprisingly pleasant and usually addictive. You can go fully-loaded with camping equipment on the cheap or travel lighter from hostel to hotel. The website www.bicycletouring101.com is a good starting point. Give bus schedules and rental car agencies the old heave ho and try it by bike.

Don't want to deal with the logistics? Try a tour company:

Adventure Cycling Association (www.adventurecycling.org) Supported and self-contained tours in Washington and Oregon. They also sell awesome cyclist-specific maps for extensive touring.

Bicycle Adventures (www.bicycleadventures.com) Runs tours in Oregon, Washington and BC.

Cascade Huts (www.cascadehuts.com) Offers hut hopping, self-guided, multi-day trips in the Mt Hood National Forest.

Randonee (www.randonneetours.com) Self-guided Gulf Islands cycling & multi-sport adventures.

Smith & Miller Productions (www.rollingpubcrawl.com) Tours Oregon by day and microbreweries by night.

Womantours (www.womantours.com) All-women company featuring a Northwest route.

For more extensive listings and information go to www.bikingbis.com.

British Columbia

This whole region is chock-full of roads begging to be cycled. Vancouver Island's Saanich Peninsula is definitely a highlight. Another destination on Vancouver Island is the rolling hills and pastoral scenery of the Cowichan Valley wine country. For short island rides with picturesque seascapes, take a couple of days hopping the Gulf Islands. Right in Vancouver, both tourists and local cyclists frequent the beautiful 1000-acre Stanley Park. Bike rentals are readily available near the park at **Bayshore Bicycle and Rollerblade** (www.bayshorebikerentals.ca).

Check out www.bikeportland.org for details on the creative, racing, funky, activist, costume-wearing mountain-bike community in Portland, OR.

Mountain biking is everywhere in BC, both free riding and cross-country. They're crazed with it. Rossland has some of the best technical rides in the region. Whistler is also famous for its diverse, world-class mountain biking. Then there is Nelson, Kamloops, Squamish, Sunshine Coast, Sun Peaks, Fernie and North Vancouver, all of which have extensive trail systems that make riders drool.

CLIMBING

Climbers love the Pacific Northwest, and it's a prime place for beginners to check out the sport. Summer is the best season to hit the rock. If you don't have your own gear, you can snag a guide service for $100 to $250 per day.

Washington

Desert crags, solitude, expansive alpine views, towering columns, old-growth forests, sandstone pinnacles, domes and slabs galore are what a climber in Washington can expect. The state has incredibly varied climbing opportunities. One of Washington's most diverse and concentrated climbing meccas is Leavenworth, which refers both to the Bavarian-themed tourist town and the surrounding climbing area. **Anew Outdoors** (www.anewoutdoors.com) is a good guide service and if you want to read about climbing then check out *Weekend Rock: Washington* by David Whilelow.

Got to www.thecrag.com for climbing route information and recommendations for the entire region.

Oregon

Don't worry when people say that Oregon has sweet cracks – it's a reference to the stellar climbing opportunities the state offers; some of the best, in fact, in the lower 48 states. Smith Rock State Park is known worldwide as a climber's haven and the birthplace of sport climbing as we know it. It's unbelievable to catch a glimpse of pros spidering up the super-advanced climbs. Yet there is a wide variety of sport and traditional routes, as well as bouldering options, that cater to all levels. Summer and shoulder seasons are crowded, especially on weekends. Shadowed by Smith's popularity are hundreds of accessible untapped climbing areas set in exquisite wilderness areas throughout the state. For specifics, look to *Rock Climbing Oregon* by Adam R Bolf and Benjamin P Ruef. A recommended guide service is **Chockstone Climbing Guides LLC** (www.chockstoneclimbing.com).

British Columbia

BC spoils its healthy climbing community with places like Squamish, home to the Stawamus Chief, a world-class granite monolith adorned with around 200 climbing routes. Flemming Beach in Victoria boasts limestone goodness that climbers love. For a guide service try **Solstice Rock Guides** (www.solsticerock.com).

SKIING & SNOWBOARDING

On Mother's Day, 300 to 400 people climb Mt St Helens in dresses then ski or snowboard down.

The powder can be prime. The slopes are killer. No wonder so many world-class snowboarders and skiers shred these slopes. The vibe can be down-to-earth and family-oriented, though many still find themselves riding the 'Ganjala' up the mountain. Locals are a significant portion of the clientele because lots of resorts don't have accommodations right on the mountain, as the government prohibits commercial development on Forest Service land. In many resorts, you'll be more likely to see a skier donning a bib from the 1970s than a fancy coat with fluffy collar.

The peak season runs from about December to March, but certain mountains, like Mt Hood, keep some slopes open year-round, primarily for kids' snowboard and ski camps. Whistler has camps as well as public summer skiing. Weekends are crazy. To avoid the chaos, go mid-week. Lift tickets run from $32 to $65 for a full day. It's more expensive during high-traffic times, but look out for deals. For instance, Ski Bowl's night skiing at Mt Hood has Ladies Night where gals pay $12.

Hells Canyon in Oregon whoops the Grand Canyon as the deepest gorge in North America.

Backcountry skiing is hugely popular in the Pacific Northwest. Ask the local mountain shops for recommendations based on the latest conditions. If you do choose the trail less traveled, know avalanche conditions and watch out for tree wells. A couple of books that have great information are *Backcountry Ski! Oregon: Classic Descents for Skiers and Snowboarders Including Southwest Washington* by Christopher Van Tilburg and *Backcountry Ski! Washington: The Best Trails and Descents for Freeheelers and Snowboarders* by Seabury Blair Jr. If you're willing to take the financial plunge, there's also heli-skiing/boarding. North Cascade Heli-Skiing is the place in Washington. In BC there's a wide variety. Check out www.heliskiguide.com.

MOUNTAINEERING

Mountaineers are a high-endurance strain of euphoria-seeking experts in the art of delayed satisfaction. To them, the taxing uphill torment followed by 15 minutes of heart-breaking 360 degree views is as addictive as crack cocaine. For some mountaineers in the Pacific Northwest, bagging peaks is a lifelong obsession. To others, a one-time summit represents a rite of passage. Whatever the reason, it's an exhilarating way to experience the brilliant mountainscape of the region. The Cascade volcanoes and jutting spires in Oregon, Washington,

TOP SKI RESORTS

Washington

Crystal Mountain (☎ 360-663-2265; www.skicrystal.com) On-hill lodging and beautiful views of Rainier plus lift-accessible backcountry.
Mt Baker (☎ 360-734-6771; www.mtbaker.us) A deep powder, 'dig the lifts out' kind of mountain with fabulous backcountry. No on-hill lodging.
Stevens Pass (☎ 206-812-4510; www.stevenspass.com) Lift-accessible backcountry and a huge variety of terrain for all skill levels. The resort is notably more eco-friendly than most. No on-hill lodging.

Oregon

Mt Bachelor (☎ 800-829-2442; www.mtbachelor.com) Very boarder friendly, with colder, drier snow. No on-hill lodging.
Mt Hood (☎ 503-337-2222; www.skihood.com) Consists of three main resort areas: Meadows, the biggest and most renowned; Timberline the only with a lodge nearby; and Skibowl, which has bargains.
Snow Cat Skiing Mt Baily (☎ 800-733-7593, ext 754; www.catskimtbailey.com) Acclaimed for its powder. Snow Cats will haul you up the mountain all day to sweet, unsullied backcountry for a base cost of $250 plus a gas fee. Very unpretentious accommodations at Diamond Lake Resort.

British Columbia

Big White Ski Resort (☎ 250-765-3101; www.bigwhite.com) Deep, dry powder combined with terrain that pleases both skier and snowboarder. There's lots of backcountry options and ski-in lodging.
Cypress Mountain (☎ 604-419-7669; www.cypressmountain.com) Home to the free-style snowboard park of the 2010 Winter Olympics, with great night skiing. Accommodations are close in Vancouver.
Whistler-Blackcomb (☎ 866-218-9690; www.whistlerblacomb.com) Gigantic, powder-laden dual-peak cohost of the 2010 Winter Olympics. The crowds are more akin to Aspen-goers than anywhere else in the Pacific Northwest. Ski village at base.

and BC present both the ascension addict and the dabbling newbie with an unprecedented number of choices, from easier day-long up-and-backs to multiday technical challenges. Just don't be classified as an unguided, inexperienced 'tourist' climber – mainly because a minute fraction of people in this category don't come back. Know your stuff or hire a guide.

In Washington, 14,411ft Mt Rainier is not only the imperial landmark of the region, it is the highest mountain in the contiguous US. Guide services, like **Rainier Mountaineering** (www.rmiguides.com), assist hardy neophytes to the top. Pouting smokily with her cap blown off, Washington's Mt St Helens is noted for being one of the more geologically interesting climbs. Mt Adams and Mt Baker are also popular. In Oregon, a layperson can summit Mt Hood, a quintessential mountain of the Northwest. Broken Top, the South Sister and Three-Fingered Jack are other favored peaks in the state. For quality Oregon mountaineering guide services, contact **Timberline Mountain Guides** (www.timberlinemtguides.com). BC's **Mountain School** (www.themountainschool.com) will take you up the towering Mt Garibaldi, as well as other challenging peaks.

CROSS-COUNTRY SKIING & SNOWSHOEING

It's said that if you can walk then you can snowshoe, yet the mobs of summer hiking enthusiasts dwindle in the snowy season leaving exquisite, white-green wilderness areas ripe for snowshoers and cross-country skiers. In the Pacific Northwest, precipitous winters make a diversity of wonderlands to explore. You can linger for a couple of hours tooling around groomed trails or commit to multiday backcountry adventures. In general, if you seek out the appropriate trail, wear the right cold-weather gear and take proper

Snowshoe Routes Washington by Dan A Nelson and *Snowshoe Routes Oregon* by Shea Andersen will lead you to pristine wintertime adventure.

precautions, snowshoeing and cross-country skiing can be accessible and appealing to anyone. Talk to local mountain-sport shops and ranger stations for specific information. Renting equipment (around $15 per day) is much cheaper than anything downhill.

Washington

Break trail through alpine meadows and evergreens in Olympic National Park. The Mt Baker area offers many spectacular jaunts. The Wenatchee National Forest also holds some prime trails with mountains vistas, ice caves, ancient forests and solitude.

Oregon

The Mt Hood area has fantastic spots like Tom, Dick and Harry Mountain. The Mt Bachelor and Three Sisters area near Bend has copious backcountry options, plus Mt Bachelor has a world-class Nordic center with extensive groomed trails. Farther south, you can check out Crater Lake National Park, without the crowds.

British Columbia

Snow by the ton doesn't keep Canadians inside one bit. Cross-country skiing and snowshoeing are hugely popular. There are endless possibilities all over the region. Ski resorts like Big White and Whistler have tremendous trail systems.

Sea Kayak guide services:

Sea Otter Kayaking (www.seaotterkayaking.com) runs trips in the Gulf Islands.

Island Outfitters (www.seakayakshop.com) out of Anacortes, WA, does San Juan tours.

Kayak Tillamook County, LCC (www.kayaktillamook.com) tours capes, bays and lakes.

WHITE-WATER KAYAKING & RAFTING

Water rampages down from ice-capped volcanoes and spires in the Pacific Northwest, creating a playland for white-water enthusiasts. The sheer number of world-class rivers titillates the rapids fiend. Plus, they have their choice of dramatic natural setting – high desert, mountains or old-growth forest. White-water crazies run rivers year-round, but most people come out from May until September. Whether you spend half a day playing on a stream or embark deep into wilderness on multiday trips, there are plenty of rivers for beginners to get their feet wet as well as enough class Vs to last a lifetime. Quality outfitters abound, and some do rentals. A full-day trip will cost around $70 to $150, but some companies offer cheaper half-day trips.

Washington

Washington's rivers are choice. Near Stevenson, the Klickitat flows through open desert valleys and, come September, the Tieton boasts the state's fastest white water. The White Salmon River is known for its smorgasbord of rapids and for hosting competitions for the extreme white-water elite. **Wet Planet Whitewater** (www.wetplanetwhitewater.com) runs these and more. Let's not forget the Wenatchee, close to Leavenworth, and the Skykomish, outside of Everett, both roaring, popular rivers. Talk to **Wave Trek** (www.wavetrek.com) about a trip.

Kayaking Puget Sound, the San Juans, and Gulf Islands: 50 Trips on the Northwest's Inland Waters by R Cary Gersten and Randel Washburne highlights the great range of kayaking trips in the region.

Oregon

There are magnificent rivers relatively close to Portland, like the Clackamas, Sandy and North Santiam (a locally known jewel). **River Drifters** (www.riverdrifters.net) can take you there. They also do a trip to the unparalleled Owyhee River, a remote, canyon-carving river over 400 miles southeast of Portland. If you want to learn to kayak from the best, or want to be guided on some sweet runs, go to Portland-based **eNRG Kayaking** (www.enrgkayaking.com). The Deschutes is your classic splash-and-giggle river, and can take you for days through stunning backcountry. **Sun Country Tours** (www.suncountry.com) runs trips there.

SEA KAYAKING

Much more patient than its distant white-water cousin, the sea kayak glides you through wilderness areas and inspires quiet exploration of the natural world (unless you're paddling through a storm or in a splash fight with your fellow kayaker, of course). To a sea kayaker, the Pacific Northwest is an oasis. It offers intricate and protected waterways, abundant marine life, coastal splendor, campsite access, alpine lakes, plentiful public parks and beautiful scenery. If you choose to paddle on the ocean, it can require technical knowledge and close attention to tides and currents. On a lake, you can piddle around knowing just the basic safety fundamentals. In temperate regions, sea kayaking can be a year-round activity, but summer is really when sea kayakers luxuriate in their sport. Renting a kayak is around $10 to $ 20 per hour, and a guided tour varies from $35 to $100 per day.

The world-renowned Gulf Islands in BC and the ever-popular San Juan Islands in Washington offer trademark Pacific Northwest sea kayaking, although the kayaking around Vancouver Island contends strongly. Excellent kayaking can also be found in Washington's Puget Sound and Olympic Peninsula, as well as Oregon's coastal bays and central lakes. A variety of extensive marine trails, like the Cascadia Marine Trail stretching from Puget Sound to the BC border, are maintained in the region. Go to www.ta.org for more information. If you're doing the big city thing in Seattle, Portland or Vancouver, BC, local outfitters can help you spruce up your urban experience with a kayak trip on waterways within the city limits. In Seattle, try **Agua Verde Paddle Club** (www.aguaverde.com). In Portland check out **Portland Kayak Company** (www.portlandrivercompany.com). In Vancouver, BC, go to **Ecomarine Ocean Kayak Centre** (www.ecomarine.com).

British Columbia

You can live it up rafting the tumbling white water of Campbell River on Vancouver Island. **Destiny River Adventures** (www.destinyriver.com) is an outfitter who will show you the way. Travel an hour and a bit outside of Vancouver, and you can be in the Cascade foothills rafting the Chilliwack River with **Hyak River Rafing** (www.hyak.com). If your visit is during May, check out Vancouver Island's **Paddlefest** (www.paddlefest.bc.ca), a major kayaking event held each year at Ladysmith.

Soggy Sneakers: A Paddler's Guide to Oregon Rivers by Pete Giordano and the Willamette Kayak and Canoe Club is a classic.

SURFING

Surfing Pacific Northwest waters is not about bikinis and picnic lunches. With the cold water, inclement weather and sometimes fickle breaks, it's about getting your surf on for the love of the swell and tube time. So head out with your wetsuit and soak up the dramatic beauty of the coast. Bro.

Washington

Stretches of Washington beaches are private land with restricted access. Even so, you still have options like Westport, the most popular spot known for consistent breaks. Westhaven State Park (aka 'the Jetty') is the most popular break there, and Half Moon Bay is a spot for the more advanced. **Steepwater Surf Shop** (www.steepwatersurfshop.com) in Westport gives lessons as well as pointers on how to meld with the local surf community. Long Beach also has decent breaks and is less crowded than Westport, but go in the morning because the break is exposed.

For the surfing skinny go to www.surfline.com. Make sure to click on the 'travel info' link for the best details.

Oregon

Oregon has sweet places to surf like Short Sands near Cannon Beach in Oswald West State Park, Otter Rock near Depot Bay, and Battle Rock near Port Orford. Prime places always have good surf shops that offer lessons, like **Otter Rock Surf Shop** (www.otterrocksurf.com) in Depoe Bay, **Cleanline Surf Shop** (www.cleanlinesurf.com) in Cannon Beach and Seaside, and the **Surf Shack** (☎ 541-332-0450)

TERRITORIALISM IN SURFING

Though rugged and hardcore in their own right, Pacific Northwest surfers living in coastal towns can be princesses. They feel entitled to the good waves first and can feel imposed upon when a non-local shares the water. After all, the surf spots are like their backyard. Visitors should be respectful. Therefore, it's best to go to local surf shops to figure out the protocol on how to not offend. Plenty of locals don't sport the attitude, so just make sure to sniff it out before playing in the waves.

in Port Orford. Take note that the surfing community can be a tight-lipped, territorial bunch (see above). Best to respect their boundaries and stay away from the renowned break near Seaside.

British Columbia

On Vancouver Island's west coast, the Tofino area is reputed as having killer waves. Go to Long Beach, between Tofino and Ucluelet, to find your spot. **Pacific Surf School** (pacificsurfschool.com) in Tofino gives lessons. For an all-female option, check out **Surf Sister** (www.surfsister.com). They have bonus mother/daughter camps and yoga/surf camps.

WINDSURFING & KITEBOARDING

The Columbia River Gorge is the gusty superstar of wind sports in the Pacific Northwest. Unlike any other river in the US, a sailor can surf with the eastbound winds and float back on the westbound current. People pilgrimage nationally and internationally to take a ride on the gorge's famously consistent and strong winds. The **2nd Wind Sports** (www.2ndwind-sports.com) in downtown Hood River is owned by a couple who have been in the area for decades and can point to a cream-of-the-crop windsurfing school. For kiteboarding, **Kite the Gorge** (www.kitethegorge.com) is a well-established school.

Beyond the gorge, other first-class wind sport sites thrive in the region. In Oregon, there are tons of great spots up and down the coast, like South Jetty in Fort Stevens State Park. Sauvie Island, near Portland, is a great place to learn. **Gorge Performance** (www.gorgeperformance.com) runs lessons and is the best shop in Portland. Locals go to Flores Lake outside of Port Orford because it's superb and less crowded than the gorge.

In Washington, Jetty Island in the Seattle area has world-class kiteboarding and is one of the top places to learn. **US Jetty Island Kite & Skim** (www.gokiting.com) is a well-reputed school. To learn to windsurf, go to Washington Lake. **Mt Baker Rowing & Sailing Center** (www.seattle.gov/parks/boats/mtbaker.htm) offers lessons for reasonable prices. Other outstanding places in Washington are Lake Wenatchee and Bellingham Bay.

The Washington shoreline has the longest stretch of roadless beach in the contiguous United States.

Stanley Park in Vancouver, BC, has loads of quality places to catch wind. **AirTime Board Sports** (www.airtimeboardsports.com) can answer questions about lessons or prime spots in the region. If you aren't the froufrou shower-needing type, Nitinat Lake, on the west side of Vancouver Island, is a spectacular place to board and surf. It's in the boon docks, but many think it's worth the journey.

PARAGLIDING & HANG GLIDING

Excellent flying sites are plentiful in the Pacific Northwest, and there are some quality schools that will help you soar over spectacular coastal terrain or verdant mountain country. Paragliding is much easier to learn and less daunting than hang gliding, so you may want to start out with that. Many places do introductory tandem lessons, or if you want to learn solo, you'll be paragliding by the end of the day. These are year-round sports, but May to September is the main season. If you're a pilot, check with locals about protocols before catching a thermal.

There are gorgeous and less-trod mountains that you can find in guide books like *Climbing the Cascade Volcanoes* by Jeff Smoot and *Classic Climbs of the Northwest* by Alan Kearny.

Washington

The **Chelan Flyers** (www.chelanflyers.com) are a group of local enthusiasts. Their website includes great info about quality schools around Washington. The organization is named for the famous Chelan Butte flying site. Other exceptional sites are Blanchard Hill, in the Bellingham area, and the Cascades Rampart Ridge near Snoqualmie. A paragliding-specific sweet spot is Twin Bowls out of Toutle.

Oregon

The folks at **Discover Paragliding** (www.discoverparagliding.com), based on the coast south of Astoria, can guide you safely on your first experience and take you to some choice places. For well-reputed hang gliding instruction, check out **Oregon Hanggliding** (www.oregonhanggliding.com) based in Corvallis. Oregon has some world-class sites, including the Tillamook Valley area, Woodrat Mountain outside of Medford, and Pine Mountain near Bend. Lakeview, a town famous for outstanding flying sites, hosts the **Umpteenth Annual Festival of Free Flight** (www.lakecountychamber.org/hang/) during Fourth of July week.

British Columbia

Go to www.bchpa.org for indepth information about the best flying sites, such as the famous Bridal Falls south of Hope and Mt Seven near Golden. There are tons of schools in BC – **Deimos Paragliding** (www.deimospg.com) in Surrey goes to highly acclaimed sites. You can get tandem flights near Vancouver at Grouse Mountain. For hang gliding, check out the **Air Dance Hang Gliding School** (www.airdancehanggliding.com) in Kamloops.

FISHING

If you're an angler visiting the Pacific Northwest, you might not leave. The region abounds with innumerable alpine lakes, rivers and bays, resplendent and worth a visit even if the fish aren't biting. On top of that, there are species galore: trout varieties, crappie, sturgeon, lingcod, rockfish and halibut. The salmon and steelhead are world famous and an inextricable part of the Pacific Northwest fabric. At any point in the year, a species is in season (salmon's peak season is in the fall). Guided trips run from $150 to $250 per day (all inclusive), or you can rent gear. Check with local shops about fee and license regulations before casting.

Originally completed in 1922, the Historic Columbia River Hwy was a marvel of road engineering and was referred to as a 'poem in stone.'

Washington

The rivers of the Olympic Peninsula, such as the Hoh, Queets and Elwha, are regarded as some of the best salmon rivers in the world. Salt-water fishing in Puget Sound is revered by anglers. North of Seattle, the Sauk and Skagit Rivers are famous for winter steelhead. For steelhead fishing contact **Dickson Flyfishing** (www.flyfishsteelhead.com).

Oregon

The Deschutes River near Bend is famous for its trout and steelhead. Close to Roseburg, the North Umpqua, with 33 miles of river set aside for fishing, is touted for steelhead. On the coast, Tillamook Bay is a primo spot for salmon in the fall because four large salmon runs converge here. In the Deschutes National Forest, there's a lake constellation (including Crane Prairie Reservoir and East Lake) which is as beautiful as it is bountiful. Both **Countrysports** (www.csport.com) out of Portland and **Scarlet Ibis Flyfishing Tours** (www.gormanflyfishing.com) out of Corvallis go to many rivers.

Great Bike Rides in Eastern Washington & Oregon by Sally O'Neal Coates is a top resource.

British Columbia

The Thompson and Skeena Rivers have made names for themselves with their plentiful salmon and steelhead. Near to Vancouver, the Pitt River is known for its trout varieties. Over on the Sunshine Coast, the fruitful lakes and inlets are the destination of many anglers. A good guide service is **West Coast Fishing Adventures** (www.westcoastfishing.ca).

DIVING

Divers of the Pacific Northwest are a distinguishably passionate, robust bunch. You need some grit to dive these cold waters. It's worth it, though, for the wrecks, cool rock formations and gargantuan marine life (like giant Pacific octopi, lingcods, wolf eel and seals). The peak season is in the winter to avoid the clouding algae bloom and plankton. The cost is usually $70 to $80 for a two-tank dive or, if you're a beginner, there are plenty of places where you can get certified.

Puget Sound and the San Juan Islands have Washington's most renowned dive spots. North of Seattle, Edmonds Underwater Park is a huge man-made underwater playground that is great for entry-level divers. The 'reefs' could be an old pickup truck with a cash register in the bed, a huge underwater bridge or a sunken vessel. In BC, Vancouver Island and the Sunshine Coast have world-class diving.

There's also diving on the Oregon coast, but riptides can be a major concern. Outside of Salem, Clear Lake is a popular lake dive, whereas diving Crater Lake is said to be more of a novelty than a good dive.

Go to local shops to get the skinny on specific dives. A good shop in Portland is **Aquatic Sports** (www.aquaticsports.com). In Seattle, **Bubbles Below** (www.bubblesbelow.com) is recommended, and **Hoodsport 'N Dive** (www.hoodsportndive.com) is one of the best shops in the Puget Sound area. On Vancouver Island, check out **Ocean Explorers Diving** (www.oceanexplorersdiving.com) in the Nanaimo area.

WHALE-WATCHING

Thousands of people flock to the coasts of the Pacific Northwest to watch these fantastically gigantic sea mammals dip and soar through the ocean.

Breitenbush Hot Springs (www.breitenbush.com) is an amazing wilderness retreat that prioritizes wellbeing and has reasonable price options. You can hike, do yoga, get a massage, soak in hot springs or go to a sweat lodge.

Washington

The San Juan Islands are far and away the premier place for watching whales. San Juan Island even has the **Whale Museum** (www.whale-museum.org) for aficionados. The most popular time is April to September, and numerous charter companies run cruises from the San Juans, Puget Sound and Seattle. On San Juan's Orcas Island, **Deer Harbor Charters** (☎ 800-544-5758) run eco-friendly, biodiesel-fueled tours and **Island Adventures** (www.island-adventures.com) out of Anacortes has whale-watching tours by boat and sea kayak.

Oregon

Gray whale migrations are in late December and late March. An organization called 'Whale Watching Spoken Here' – yes, that's its name – rallies 200 trained volunteers to assist visitors in spotting whales. Their website, www.whalespoken.org, has details about great observation points on the coast. To get a closer look, you can go on a chartered boat tour. Try **Marine Discovery Tours** (www.marinediscovery.com) in Newport, the official tour company of the Oregon Coast Aquarium.

British Columbia

Every March and April, the Pacific Rim National Park and surrounding communities celebrate the return of the gray whale during its spring migration. From May to October, killer whales roam coastal waters. There are tons of whale-watching tour companies out of Vancouver and Vancouver Island. For a listing of tours go to www.britishcolumbia.com/whalewatch.

HORSEBACK RIDING

The microbrewing, fleece-wearing lefty is a Pacific Northwest stereotype. However, a huge part of the region wears cowboy hats and plows the good earth. To get a taste of country culture and experience spectacular wilderness areas sans backpack, a horseback-riding adventure could be the answer.

Inside Out British Columbia: A Best Places Guide to the Outdoors by Jack Christie gives you possibilities for BC adventures.

Summer is the time to saddle up, and the best riding is near the Cascades where mountains, lava flows, crystal-clear lakes and sumptuous forests can be explored. In the Oregon Cascades, the **Hollow Ranch** (www.lhranch.com) out of Sisters is a well-reputed venue. In Washington's Cascades, reasonably priced day rides are available at **Happy Trails Horse Adventures** (www.happytrailsateastonwa.com) out of Easton, or, for a ranch experience, swagger over to the **Stehekin Valley Ranch** (www.courtneycountry.com) near Lake Chelan.

Though something of a cliché, coastal riding is a blast. In Oregon, **C & M Stables** (www.oregonhorsebackriding.com) has rides out of Florence. In Long Beach, WA, **Backcountry Wilderness Outfitters** (www.backcountryoutfit.com) guide day-long and more extensive pack trips. **Woodgate Stables** (www.woodgatestables.com) near Victoria will trot you to panoramic island scenery.

BC is littered with dude ranches and you can take your pick from the down-home to the hoity toity. For an extensive list of BC ranches go to www.bcadventure.com and follow the links.

Seattle & Around

The largest city in the Pacific Northwest also happens to be a perfect distillation of all the great things the region has going for it. Known as the Emerald City, it's home to about 3.3 million people (580,000 in the city proper). It's a lively, progressive urban center, lush with parks and surrounded by natural beauty. People here are fond of getting out into nature and they're serious about protecting the environment. Seattleites also love good beer, and the city has long been a cornerstone of the microbrew revolution. And on the flip side, it does coffee well enough to have launched an espresso empire.

It's a bookish, erudite place, but also a dynamic and inventive urban center – most of the city's recent economic growth has been fueled by technology, both the high-tech and the old-school, engine-parts variety. And it seems to be working: a London-based market-research company (TNS Global) recently reported that King County has 68,000 millionaires. No longer do locals shlump around in flannel shirts – the city has outgrown that stereotype. Once a slacker haven where half-employed artists moped in cafés all day and basements rented for 80 bucks a month, the city has since turned giddy on the scent of success. People here have it good, and they know it. Seattle is a dynamic place on the cusp of maturity and an exciting entry point to any exploration of the Pacific Northwest.

HIGHLIGHTS

- Soaking up culture at the newly expanded **Seattle Art Museum** (p85)
- Getting an earful of music history at the **Crocodile Cafe** (p102)
- Sampling a shot of what makes Seattle buzz at a local **coffee shop** (p102)
- Exploring the industrial-chic dive bars of **Georgetown** (p101)
- Watching Lake Union's houseboat neighborhoods from **Gas Works Park** (p91)
- Sampling local wines and brews in **Woodinville** (p102)
- Foraging for snacks in the labyrinthine **Pike Place Market** (p87)

Woodinville
Seattle
Georgetown

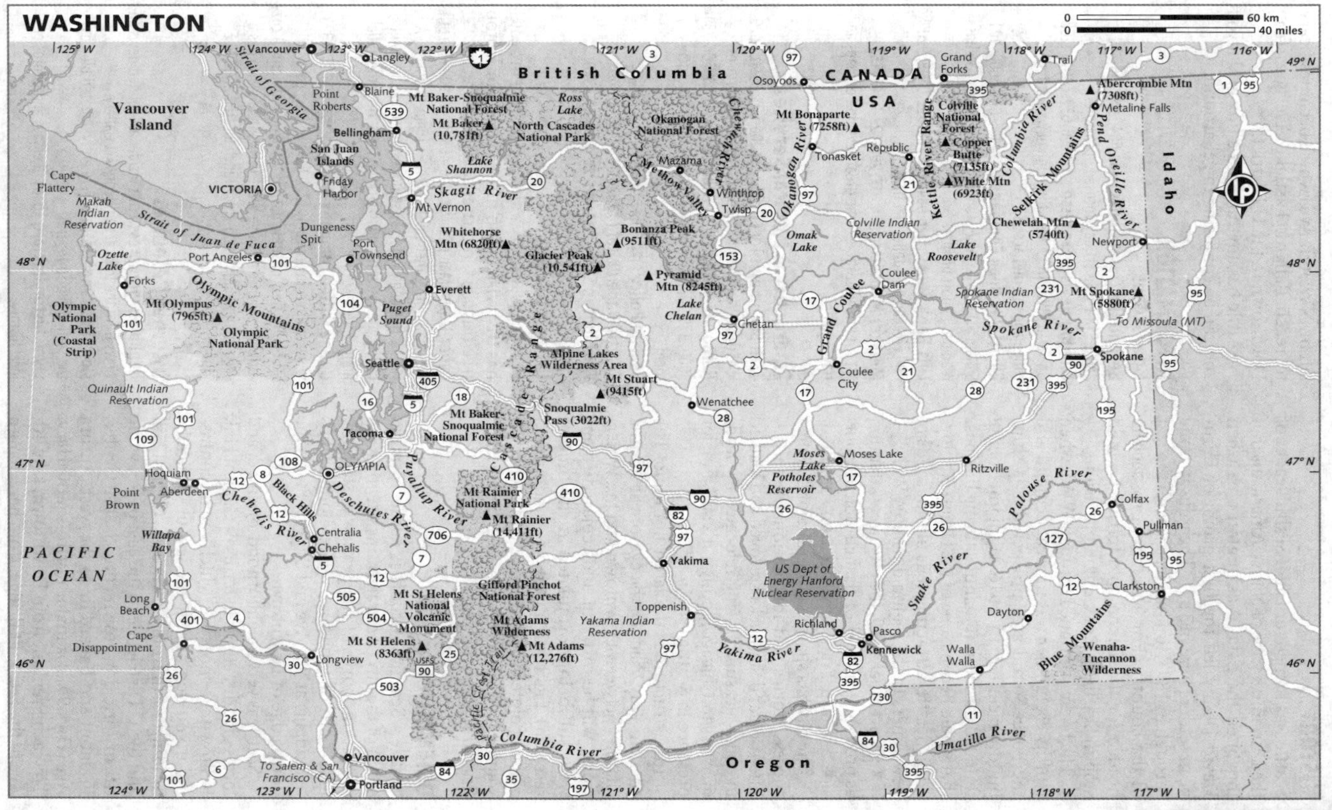
WASHINGTON
0 60 km
0 40 miles
British Columbia
CANADA
USA
Idaho
Oregon
PACIFIC OCEAN
Vancouver Island
VICTORIA
Vancouver
Langley
Point Roberts
Blaine
Bellingham
San Juan Islands
Friday Harbor
Strait of Georgia
Strait of Juan de Fuca
Cape Flattery
Makah Indian Reservation
Ozette Lake
Forks
Port Angeles
Dungeness Spit
Port Townsend
Olympic Mountains
Mt Olympus (7965ft)
Olympic National Park
Olympic National Park (Coastal Strip)
Quinault Indian Reservation
Hoquiam
Aberdeen
Point Brown
Willapa Bay
Long Beach
Cape Disappointment
Black Hills
Chehalis River
Centralia
Chehalis
OLYMPIA
Deschutes River
Tacoma
Seattle
Puget Sound
Everett
Mt Vernon
Skagit River
Lake Shannon
Mt Baker-Snoqualmie National Forest
Mt Baker (10,781ft)
North Cascades National Park
Ross Lake
Whitehorse Mtn (6820ft)
Glacier Peak (10,541ft)
Bonanza Peak (9511ft)
Pyramid Mtn (8245ft)
Alpine Lakes Wilderness Area
Cascade Range
Mt Stuart (9415ft)
Snoqualmie Pass (3022ft)
Mt Baker-Snoqualmie National Forest
Mt Rainier National Park
Mt Rainier (14,411ft)
Puyallup River
Gifford Pinchot National Forest
Mt Adams Wilderness
Mt Adams (12,276ft)
Mt St Helens National Volcanic Monument
Mt St Helens (8363ft)
Pacific Crest Trail
Longview
Vancouver
Portland
To Salem & San Francisco (CA)
Columbia River
Yakama Indian Reservation
Toppenish
Yakima
Yakima River
Wenatchee
Lake Chelan
Chelan
Okanogan National Forest
Mazama
Methow Valley
Winthrop
Twisp
Chewuch River
Osoyoos
Okanogan River
Omak Lake
Mt Bonaparte (7258ft)
Tonasket
Republic
Grand Forks
Colville National Forest
Copper Butte (7135ft)
White Mtn (6923ft)
Kettle River Range
Colville Indian Reservation
Lake Roosevelt
Coulee Dam
Grand Coulee
Coulee City
Moses Lake
Potholes Reservoir
US Dept of Energy Hanford Nuclear Reservation
Richland
Pasco
Kennewick
Walla Walla
Umatilla River
Snake River
Ritzville
Dayton
Blue Mountains
Wenaha-Tucannon Wilderness
Clarkston
Pullman
Colfax
Palouse River
Spokane
Spokane River
Spokane Indian Reservation
Mt Spokane (5880ft)
To Missoula (MT)
Chewelah Mtn (5740ft)
Selkirk Mountains
Columbia River
Trail
Newport
Pend Oreille River
Metaline Falls
Abercrombie Mtn (7308ft)
125° W
124° W
123° W
122° W
121° W
120° W
119° W
118° W
117° W
116° W
49° N
48° N
47° N
46° N

HISTORY

Seattle was named for Chief Sealth, leader of the Duwamish tribe of Native Americans that inhabited the Lake Washington area when David Denny led the first group of European settlers here in 1851. The railway came through in 1893, linking Seattle with the rest of the country. For a decade, prospectors headed for the Yukon gold territory would stop in Seattle to stock up on provisions.

The boom continued through WWI, when Northwest lumber was in great demand and the Puget Sound area prospered as a shipbuilding center. In 1916 William Boeing founded the aircraft manufacturing business that would become one of the largest employers in Seattle, attracting tens of thousands of newcomers to the region during WWII.

In November 1999, the city drew attention as protesters and police clashed violently outside a World Trade Organization summit.

The city has spawned some major business success stories and international brands – Microsoft and Starbucks are loved and loathed in equal measure. Boeing relocated its headquarters to Chicago, though it's still a major presence in Seattle.

Infrastructure is the latest hot topic. The Alaskan Way Viaduct, the eyesore of a traffic channel between Downtown and the Waterfront, will be torn out and replaced (plans were still being formulated at the time of research). Light-rail transit is expanding, and a hub of biotech companies and residences in south Lake Union will be served by the city's first streetcar in 65 years.

ORIENTATION

Seattle's Sea-Tac Airport is some 13 miles south of the city. Amtrak trains use the King St Station, north of the Seahawks stadium, just south of Pioneer Sq. Greyhound's bus terminal is at 8th Ave and Stewart St, on the north edge of Downtown.

Seattle is very neighborhood-oriented, and locals give directions in terms of Capitol Hill, Belltown, Fremont etc, which can be confusing if you don't know the layout. Basically, heading north from Downtown, Capitol Hill and the U District lie to the east of I-5, while the historic downtown core, Seattle Center, Fremont and Ballard lie to the west. Aurora Ave (Hwy 99) is a major north–south artery. To reach Fremont from Downtown, take 4th Ave to the Fremont Bridge; from here, hang a left on NW 36th Ave (which becomes Leary) to reach Ballard. Eastlake Ave goes from Downtown to the U District.

Seattle has anything but a tidy grid layout and can be confusing to get around.

INFORMATION

Bookstores

Beyond the Closet Books (Map p84; ☎ 206-322-4609; 518 E Pike St) Gay-focused bookstore.

Bulldog News & Espresso (☎ 206-632-6397; 4208 University Way NE) A very thorough newsstand, plus coffee and internet access.

Elliott Bay Book Company (☎ 206-624-6600; 101 S Main St) Labyrinthine store in historic Pioneer Sq has readings almost nightly.

Left Bank Books (Map p84; ☎ 206-622-0195; 92 Pike Pl) Left-leaning intellectual heaven.

Metsker Maps (Map p84; ☎ 206-623-8747; 1511 1st Ave) New location, same great selection of maps and travel guides.

Emergency & Medical Services

45th St Community Clinic (☎ 206-633-3350; 1629 N 45th St, Wallingford) Medical and dental services.

Harborview Medical Center (Map p84; ☎ 206-731-3000; 325 9th Ave) Full medical care, with emergency room.

Seattle Police (☎ 206-625-5011)

Seattle Rape Relief (☎ 206-632-7273)

Washington State Patrol (☎ 425-649-4370)

Internet Access

Practically every bar and coffee shop in Seattle has free wi-fi, as do most hotels. For laptop-free travelers, internet cafés include:

Cyber-Dogs (Map p84; ☎ 206-405-3647; 909 Pike St; first 20min free, then per hr $6; 🕑 10am-midnight) A veggie hot-dog ($2 to $5) stand, espresso bar, internet café & youngster hangout/pick-up joint. Note the initial limited free access.

Online Coffee Company (Map p84; ☎ 206-328-3731; www.onlinecoffeeco.com; 1720 E Olive Way; per min $0.14, 1hr free for students; 🕑 7:30am-midnight) A cozy former residence on Olive Way. The company also has a second, more utilitarian-chic branch located at 1404 E Pine St.

Internet Resources

hankblog.wordpress.com Insider art-related news and views from the folks at the Henry Art Gallery.

slog.thestranger.com A frequently updated blog by the staff of the *Stranger*.

www.historylink.org Loads of essays and photos on local history.

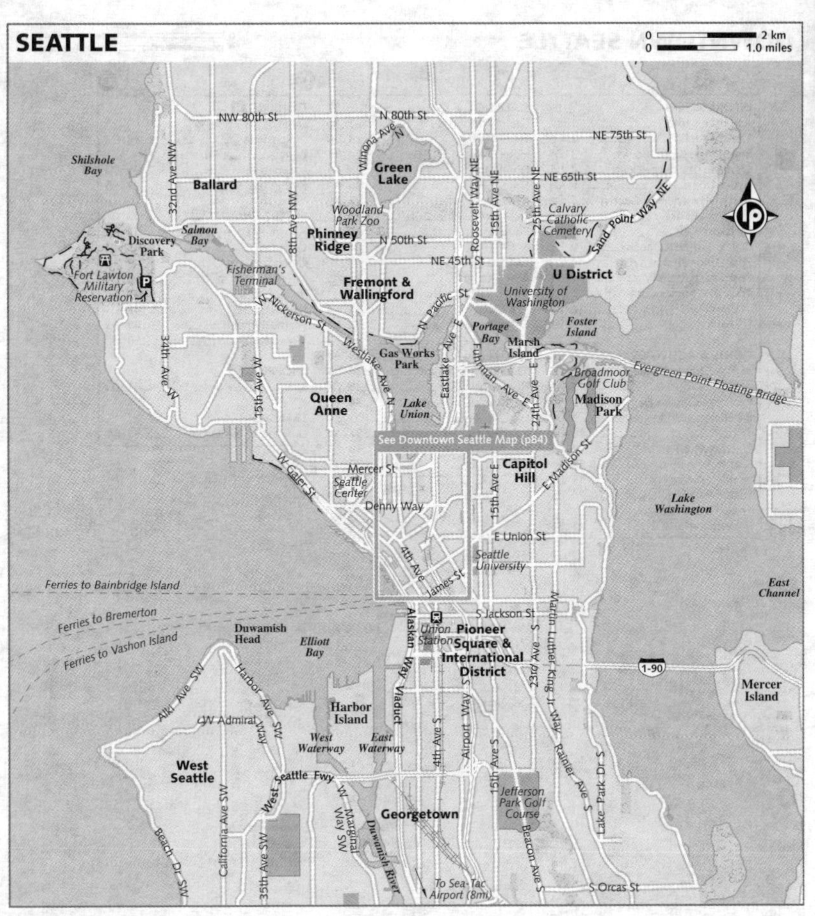

www.seattlediy.com Information on underground events and house shows.
www.seattlest.com A blog about various goings-on in and around Seattle.
www.visitseattle.org Seattle's Convention and Visitors Bureau site.

Media

KEXP 90.3 FM Legendary independent-music and community station.
KUOW 94.9 FM NPR news.
Seattle Gay News Weekly.
Seattle Post-Intelligencer (www.seattlepi.com) Daily.
Seattle Times (www.seattletimes.com) The state's largest daily paper.
Seattle Weekly (www.seattleweekly.com) Free weekly with news and entertainment listings.
The Stranger (www.thestranger.com) Irreverent weekly edited by Dan Savage of 'Savage Love' fame.

Money

American Express (Map p84; ☎ 206-441-8622; 600 Stewart St; 🕑 8:30am-5:30pm Mon-Fri)
Travelex-Thomas Cook Currency Services Airport (☎ 206-248-6960; 🕑 6am-8pm) Westlake Center (Map p84; ☎ 206-682-4525; Level 3, 400 Pine St; 🕑 9:30am-6pm Mon-Sat, 11am-5pm Sun) The booth at the main airport terminal is behind the Delta Airlines counter.

Post

Post office Main branch (Map p84; ☎ 206-748-5417; 301 Union St); Broadway Station (Map p84; ☎ 206-324-5474; 101 Broadway E); University Station (☎ 206-675-8114; 4244 NE University Way, U District)

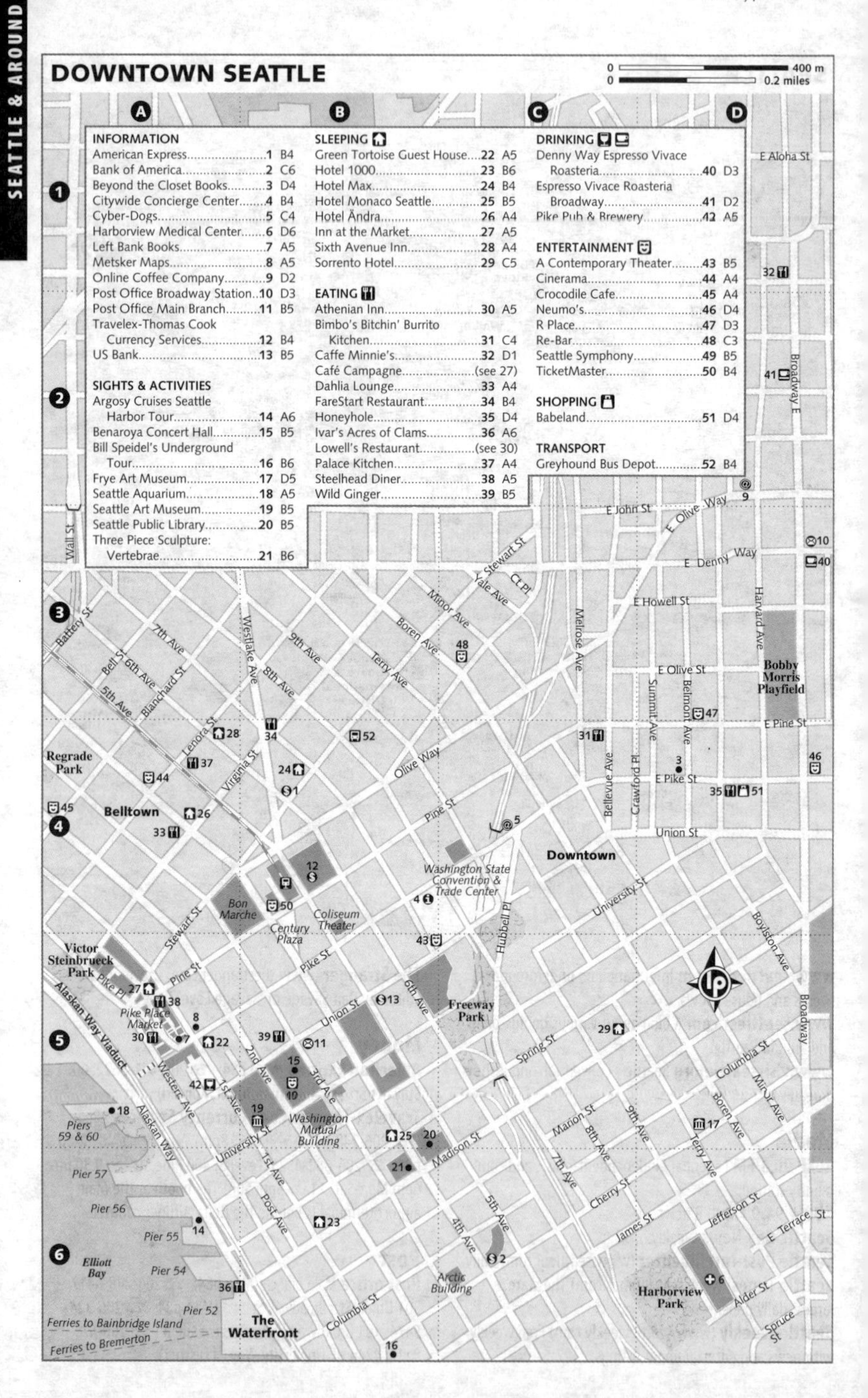
DOWNTOWN SEATTLE
0 400 m
0 0.2 miles
A
B
C
D
1
2
3
4
5
6
INFORMATION
American Express....1 B4
Bank of America....2 C6
Beyond the Closet Books....3 D4
Citywide Concierge Center....4 B4
Cyber-Dogs....5 C4
Harborview Medical Center....6 D6
Left Bank Books....7 A5
Metsker Maps....8 A5
Online Coffee Company....9 D2
Post Office Broadway Station....10 D3
Post Office Main Branch....11 B5
Travelex-Thomas Cook Currency Services....12 B4
US Bank....13 B5
SIGHTS & ACTIVITIES
Argosy Cruises Seattle Harbor Tour....14 A6
Benaroya Concert Hall....15 B5
Bill Speidel's Underground Tour....16 B6
Frye Art Museum....17 D5
Seattle Aquarium....18 A5
Seattle Art Museum....19 B5
Seattle Public Library....20 B5
Three Piece Sculpture: Vertebrae....21 B6
SLEEPING
Green Tortoise Guest House....22 A5
Hotel 1000....23 B6
Hotel Max....24 B4
Hotel Monaco Seattle....25 B5
Hotel Ändra....26 A4
Inn at the Market....27 A5
Sixth Avenue Inn....28 A4
Sorrento Hotel....29 C5
EATING
Athenian Inn....30 A5
Bimbo's Bitchin' Burrito Kitchen....31 C4
Caffe Minnie's....32 D1
Café Campagne....(see 27)
Dahlia Lounge....33 A4
FareStart Restaurant....34 B4
Honeyhole....35 D4
Ivar's Acres of Clams....36 A6
Lowell's Restaurant....(see 30)
Palace Kitchen....37 A4
Steelhead Diner....38 A5
Wild Ginger....39 B5
DRINKING
Denny Way Espresso Vivace Roasteria....40 D3
Espresso Vivace Roasteria Broadway....41 D2
Pike Pub & Brewery....42 A5
ENTERTAINMENT
A Contemporary Theater....43 B5
Cinerama....44 A4
Crocodile Cafe....45 A4
Neumo's....46 D4
R Place....47 D3
Re-Bar....48 C3
Seattle Symphony....49 B5
TicketMaster....50 B4
SHOPPING
Babeland....51 D4
TRANSPORT
Greyhound Bus Depot....52 B4
E Aloha St
Broadway E
E John St
E Olive Way
E Denny Way
E Howell St
Harvard Ave
Bobby Morris Playfield
E Olive St
Summit Ave
Belmont Ave
E Pine St
E Pike St
Bellevue Ave
Crawford Pl
Union St
Melrose Ave
Stewart St
Yale Ave
Ct Pl
Minor Ave
Boren Ave
Terry Ave
9th Ave
8th Ave
Westlake Ave
7th Ave
6th Ave
Blanchard St
Bell St
5th Ave
Battery St
Lenora St
Virginia St
Wall St
Olive Way
Pine St
Regrade Park
Belltown
Downtown
Washington State Convention & Trade Center
Bon Marche
Century Plaza
Coliseum Theater
Hubbell Pl
University St
Boylston Ave
Broadway
Victor Steinbrueck Park
Pike Pl
Pike St
Pike Place Market
Alaskan Way Viaduct
Western Ave
1st Ave
2nd Ave
3rd Ave
Freeway Park
Spring St
Columbia St
Minor Ave
Boren Ave
Marion St
8th Ave
9th Ave
Terry Ave
Washington Mutual Building
Madison St
7th Ave
Cherry St
Jefferson St
E Terrace St
James St
Piers 59 & 60
Alaskan Way
Pier 57
Pier 56
Pier 55
Pier 54
Pier 52
Elliott Bay
Post Ave
4th Ave
5th Ave
Arctic Building
Harborview Park
Alder St
Spruce St
The Waterfront
Ferries to Bainbridge Island
Ferries to Bremerton

Tourist Office

Citywide Concierge Center (Map p84; ☎ 206-461-5840; www.seeseattle.org; 7th Ave & Pike St; 🕑 9am-5pm) Inside the Washington State Convention and Trade Center, this is a visitor center with useful concierge services.

SIGHTS

Most of Seattle's sights are concentrated in a fairly compact central area. The historic downtown, Pioneer Sq, includes the area between Cherry and S King Sts, along 1st to 3rd Ave. The big-name shopping area is along 4th and 5th Aves from Olive Way down to University St. Just north of Downtown is Seattle Center, with many of the city's cultural and sporting facilities, as well as the Space Needle and EMP. Across busy Alaskan Way from the Pike Place Market is the Waterfront, Seattle's tourist mecca. And as long as you account for the somewhat hilly terrain, it's easy enough to walk back and forth among all of these areas. Public transport serves the outlying neighborhoods; see Getting Around (p104) for details.

Downtown & First Hill

Downtown is home to many of the city's more important buildings, and also to a gradually escalating series of architectural statements like 'tallest building in town/in the West/made of concrete/if you count the number of floors.' Be warned that parking around here is pure hell – instead of driving take one of a dozen or more buses that serve Downtown, stopping at 3rd Ave and Union St and several other stops. Any bus that says 'Downtown' on the front will get you here.

SEATTLE ART MUSEUM

Newly renovated and expanded, the **Seattle Art Museum** (Map p84; ☎ 206-654-3100; 1300 1st Ave; adult/child/student/senior $13/free/7/10, admission free 1st Thu of month; 🕑 10am-5pm Tue-Sun, 10am-9pm Thu & Fri) now has 118,000 extra sq feet. Some have criticized the new section for having a clinical feel, but it's difficult not to be struck by a sense of excitement upon entering. Above the ticket counter hangs Cai Guo-Qiang's *Inopportune: Stage One*, a series of white cars exploding with neon. Between the two museum entrances (one in the old building and one in the new) is the 'art ladder,' a free space with installations cascading down a wide stepped hallway. And the galleries themselves are much improved. The museum's John H Hauberg Collection is an excellent display of masks, canoes, totems and other pieces from Northwest coastal Native American peoples.

BENAROYA CONCERT HALL

With a hefty bill of almost $120 million in construction costs, it's no wonder the **Benaroya Concert Hall** (Map p84; ☎ 206-215-9494; 200 University St), Seattle Symphony's primary venue, oozes luxury. From the minute you step into the glass-enclosed lobby of the performance hall you're overwhelmed with views of Elliott Bay – on sunny days you might be lucky enough to see the snowy peaks of the Olympic Range far in the distance. Even if you're not attending the symphony, you can walk through the foyer and marvel at the 20ft-long chandeliers, specially created by Tacoma glassmaker Dale Chihuly (see boxed text, p51).

FRYE ART MUSEUM

This small **museum** (Map p84; ☎ 206-622-9250; 704 Terry Ave; admission free; 🕑 10am-5pm Tue-Sat, noon-5pm Sun, 10am-8pm Thu) on First Hill preserves the collection of Charles and Emma Frye. The Fryes collected more than 1000 paintings, mostly 19th- and early 20th-century European and American pieces, and a few Alaskan and Russian artworks. If this inspires a stifled yawn, think again. Since its 1997 expansion, the Frye has gained a hipness that it once lacked; fresh ways of presenting its artwork, music performances, poetry readings and interesting rotating exhibits, from traveling painters to local printmakers, make the museum a worthwhile stop. To get there take buses 64, 303, 941 and 942 among others.

SEATTLE PUBLIC LIBRARY

As much as architecture types have carped about the new Seattle Art Museum building (see left), they've universally raved about the new **Seattle Public Library** (Map p84; ☎ 206-386-4636; 1000 4th Ave; 🕑 10am-8pm Mon-Wed, 10am-6pm Thu-Sat, 1-5pm Sun). Designed by Rem Koolhaas and LMN Architects, the $165.5 million building of glass and steel was designed to suit the functions it would need to serve: a community gathering space, a tech center, a reading room and, of course, a whole bunch of book storage. The entry-level floor is a 'living room,' with a teen center, shop and coffee stand. There's an underground level for parking ($10.50 for two hours). And near the top is the Seattle Room, a 12,000-sq-ft reading room with 40ft glass ceilings. It has amazing light, nice views of Downtown and seating for 400 people.

Pioneer Square

This enclave of red-brick buildings, the oldest part of Seattle, languished for years and was almost razed to build parking lots, until a wave of public support led to Historic Register status followed by an influx of art galleries, antique shops and cafés. It can be seedy at night, but trendy nightclubs perpetrate more crimes than individuals do.

Yesler Way was the original 'skid road' – in Seattle's early days, loggers in a camp above town would send logs skidding down the road to Henry Yesler's pier-side mill. With the slump in the timber industry and resulting decline of the area, the street became a haven for the homeless. The nickname Skid Road (or 'Skid Row') eventually came to mean the opposite of 'Easy Street' in cities across the US.

PIONEER SQUARE PARK

At Cherry St and 1st Ave, the original Pioneer Sq is a triangular cobblestone plaza where Henry Yesler's sawmill cut the giant trees that marked Seattle's first industry. Known officially as Pioneer Square Park, the plaza features a bust of Chief Sealth (Seattle), an ornate pergola and a totem pole. Some wayward early Seattleites, so the story goes, stole the totem from the Tlingit natives in southeastern Alaska in 1890. An arsonist lit the pole aflame in 1938, burning it to the ground. When asked if they could carve a replacement pole, the Tlingit took the money offered, thanking the city for payment of the first totem, and said it would cost $5000 to carve another one. The city coughed up the money and the Tlingit obliged with the pole you see today.

The decorative pergola was built in the early 1900s to serve as an entryway to an underground lavatory and to shelter those waiting for the cable car that went up and down Yesler Way. The reportedly elaborate restroom eventually closed due to serious plumbing problems at high tide. In January 2001, the pergola was leveled by a wayward truck. It has been restored and was put back where it belongs the following year, looking good as new.

OCCIDENTAL PARK

Notable in this cobblestone plaza are the totem poles carved by Duane Pasco, a nationally respected Chinookan carver and artist from Poulsbo on the Kitsap Peninsula. The totems depict the welcoming spirit of Kwakiutl, a totem bear, the tall Sun and Raven, and a man riding on the tail of a whale. Between S Main and Jackson Sts, the park turns into a tree-lined pedestrian mall bordered by galleries, sculptures and coffee shops.

KLONDIKE GOLD RUSH NATIONAL HISTORIC PARK

One of the few *indoor* national parks in the country, the **Klondike** (☎ 206-553-7220; Jackson St & 2nd Ave S; admission free; 🕑 9am-5pm) has exhibits, photos and news clippings describing what kind of provisions you would've needed were you to stake a claim in the Yukon Territory. In an early example of Seattle civic boosters clamoring to put the city 'on the map,' the *Seattle Post-Intelligencer* trumpeted the news that a ship full of gold had arrived in town on July 17, 1897. Masses of gold-fevered unfortunates swarmed the city on their way to the Klondike River area in the Yukon Territory, and local merchants made a killing. Seattle's seminal position as the outfitting and transportation hub for the Alaskan and Yukon Gold Rush is recognized at Klondike Gold Rush National Park. It's easy to miss, but worth seeking out. Park rangers demonstrate gold panning, and you can sit down and view a slide presentation about the gold rush.

SMITH TOWER

You can't miss **Smith Tower** (☎ 206-622-4004; 506 2nd Ave S at Yesler Way; observation deck adult/child/senior & student $7.50/5/6; 🕑 10am-sunset Apr-Oct, 10am-3:30pm Sat & Sun Nov-Mar), Seattle's first skyscraper. For half a century after its construction in 1914, the 42-story Smith Tower was well known as the tallest building west of Chicago. The distinctive tower was erected by LC Smith, a man who built his fortune on typewriters (Smith-Corona) and guns (Smith & Wesson). Smith died during the building's construction, so he never got to see the beauty that still bears his name. Walk into the onyx- and marble-paneled lobby, step aboard one of the brass-and-copper manually operated elevators and let it whisk you up to the 35th-floor observation deck for a great view of Seattle's Waterfront. The ride up is as exciting as the view.

International District

A lively neighborhood that's home to various Asian cultures, 'the ID' has all of the trappings of a multiethnic neighborhood, from bustling markets to fun import shops to amazing places to eat.

WING LUKE ASIAN MUSEUM

The **Wing Luke Asian Museum** (☎ 206-623-5124; 407 7th Ave S; adult/child/student $4/2/3; 🕒 11am-4:30pm Tue-Fri, noon-4pm Sat & Sun) is a cornerstone of the neighborhood. It documents the city's wealth of Asian cultures and their often fraught meeting with the West through artwork, special exhibits, historical photographs, a replica of a WWII Japanese-American internment camp and recorded interviews with people who were forced into the camps.

JACKSON STREET

The district's Jackson Street was once home to a thriving jazz scene. As teens in the late 1940s and early '50s, Quincy Jones and Ray Charles used to hustle their way into jazz clubs here and play into the wee hours of the morning.

Pike Place Market & Waterfront

The first stop for many visitors to Seattle, this area of town rewards early birds. It's particularly important to get to the market early if you want to avoid that cattle-truck feeling. Weekdays and before 10am on weekends are best. The Waterfront is more weather-dependent – it will be swarming with people on a sunny weekend afternoon, while on a misty weekday morning you'll have the place pretty much to yourself.

At the time of research, the historic Waterfront Streetcar line was closed due to various construction projects along the Waterfront, and its future was uncertain as plans for solving the problem of the decrepit Alaskan Way Viaduct were being discussed.

PIKE PLACE MARKET

The heart of Downtown Seattle is Pike Place Market (Map p84), on Pike St between Western and 1st Aves. The buzzing warren of fruit stands, cafés and little shops is excellent street theater, although it gets claustrophobically crowded on weekends. Go early on a weekday morning to avoid the crush. The Main and North Arcades are the most popular areas, with bellowing fishmongers, arts and crafts, and precarious stacks of fruits and vegetables. Don't miss the oddball shops on the lower levels.

SEATTLE AQUARIUM

Probably the most interesting sight in the Waterfront area, this well-designed **aquarium** (Map p84; ☎ 206-386-4300; 1483 Alaskan Way at Pier 59; adult/child $15/10; 🕒 9:30am-5pm) offers a great view into the underwater world of Puget Sound and the Pacific Northwest coast. In 2007 the pilings that supported the building were found to be rotten so they were replaced, and in the process the aquarium added a café, gift shop and two new exhibits. 'Window on Washington Waters' is a look at the sea floor of the Neah Bay area, where rockfish, salmon, sea anemones and more than 100 other fish and invertebrate species live. 'Crashing Waves' uses a wave tank to show how marine plants and animals cope with the forceful tides near shore.

ODYSSEY MARITIME DISCOVERY CENTER

This unique **museum** (☎ 206-374-4000; www.ody.org; 2205 Alaskan Way at Pier 66; adult/child/senior $7/2/5; 🕒 10am-3pm Tue-Thu, 10am-4pm Fri, 11am-5pm Sat & Sun) in Waterfront Park is part of the Bell Street Pier, a huge complex that also houses convention space, restaurants and a marina. A haven for boat enthusiasts, the Discovery Center is also a wonderful place for families. The four galleries and more than 40 hands-on exhibits include a simulated kayak trip around Puget Sound, a chance to navigate a virtual ship through Elliott Bay and a visual re-creation of the cruise up the Inside Passage to southeast Alaska. You can find out about boat construction and high-tech contributions to boating, learn about oceanography and environmental issues, and hear audio simulations of ocean animals. One section of the museum is devoted to fishing and another to ocean trade.

Belltown

North of Pike Place Market is Belltown, famous as the birthplace of grunge music. A few of the original clubs are still here, but the area has gone seriously upscale, with fancy restaurants and designer boutiques in converted lofts. Still, it remains one of the best parts of town for nightlife, and the new Olympic Sculpture Park provides an anchor for daytime visits.

OLYMPIC SCULPTURE PARK

Alexander Calder's 39ft red-steel *Eagle* from 1971 is the crowning jewel of the Seattle Art Museum's new **Olympic Sculpture Park** (☎ 206-654-3100; 2901 Western Ave; admission free; 6am-9pm May-Sep, 7am-6pm Oct-Apr). Hovering over the train tracks in an unlikely oasis between the water and busy Elliott Ave, the new 8.5-acre $85 million Olympic Sculpture Park is an excellent lesson in making the most of limited urban space. Worth a visit just for its views of the Olympic Mountains across Elliott Bay, the park is still in that awkward youthful phase – much of the planned vegetation has yet to fill in – but it has a lot of potential. Its Z shape slinks back and forth between Belltown and the edge of the bay, rescuing unused parcels of land and filling them with art and plant life.

ROQ LA RUE

This Belltown **gallery** (☎ 206-374-8977; 2312 2nd Ave; 1-6pm Wed, Thu & Sat, 1-7pm Fri) has secured its reputation by taking risks – the work on view here skates along the edge of urban pop culture. Since opening in 1998, the gallery, owned and curated by Kirsten Anderson, has been a significant force in the pop surrealism field, frequently featured in *Juxtapoz* magazine.

Seattle Center

In 1962 Seattle hosted a summer-longWorld's Fair, an exhibition that enticed nearly 10 million visitors to view the future, Seattle style. The vestiges, which 45 years later look simultaneously futuristic and retro, are on view at the **Seattle Center** (☎ 206-684-8582; www.seattlecenter.com; 400 Broad St).

SPACE NEEDLE

Sticking out of the skyline, impossible to ignore, the emblematic **Space Needle** (☎ 206-905-2100; adult/child/senior $16/8/14; 9am-midnight) is a 605ft-high observation station with a revolving restaurant on top (see p99).

EXPERIENCE MUSIC PROJECT

Microsoft cofounder Paul Allen's **Experience Music Project** (☎ 206-367-5483; www.emplive.com; 325 5th Ave N; adult/child/student & senior $19.95/14.95/15.95; 9am-6pm Sun-Thu, 9am-9pm Fri & Sat summer; 10am-5pm Sun-Thu, 10am-9pm Fri & Sat winter) is worth a look for the architecture alone. Whether it's worth the admission price depends on how old and music-obsessed you are. (Ideal customers are 13 to 15 and totally into guitar.) The Frank Gehry building houses 80,000 music artifacts, including handwritten lyrics by Nirvana's Kurt Cobain and a Fender Stratocaster demolished by Jimi Hendrix.

SCIENCE FICTION MUSEUM

Attached to the Experience Music Project is this nerd's paradise, the **Science Fiction Museum** (☎ 206-724-3428; www.sfhomeworld.org; 325 5th Ave N; adult/child $15/12; 10am-8pm summer, 10am-5pm Wed-Mon winter, free 1st Thu each month 5-8pm), filled with costumes, props and models from sci-fi movies and TV shows. Highlights include the actual alien queen from the movie *Aliens* (1986) – never fear, she's behind plexiglass in the cargo bay – and the only 3D model of the Death Star made for *Star Wars: Episode 4*. Lowlights include a bedraggled Twiki costume from the *Buck Rogers* TV series. Rare books and manuscripts – including Neal Stephenson's handwritten *Baroque Cycle*, stacked as tall as the ET figure next to it – lend credibility to the collection. But mostly it just makes you want to go and rent *Blade Runner* again.

CHILDREN'S MUSEUM

In the basement of Center House near the Monorail stop, the **Children's Museum** (☎ 206-441-1768; www.thechildrensmuseum.org; 305 Harrison St; adult & child/grandparent $7.50/6.50; 10am-5pm Mon-Fri, 10am-6pm Sat & Sun) is a learning center that offers a number of imaginative activities and displays, many focusing on cross-cultural awareness and hands-on art sessions. The play area includes a child-size neighborhood and an area dedicated to blowing soap bubbles.

PACIFIC SCIENCE CENTER

The interactive **Pacific Science Center** (☎ 206-443-2001; www.pacsci.org; 200 2nd Ave N; adult/3-5yr/6-12yr $11/6/8, IMAX Theater & Laserium with general admission $3 extra, without general admission $8/6/7; 10am-6pm), a museum of science and industry, once housed the science pavilion of the World's Fair. Today, the center features laser shows, virtual-reality exhibits, a tropical butterfly house, holograms and other wonders of science, many with hands-on demonstrations.

MONORAIL

A 1.5-mile experiment in mass transit, the **Monorail** (☎ 206-905-2600; www.seattlemonorail.com; adult/child/senior $4/1.50/2; 9am-11pm) runs every 10 minutes daily from Downtown's Westlake Center right through a crumple in the smashed-guitar hull of the Experience Music Project.

Capitol Hill

This stylish, irreverent part of town displays all the panache and vitality you'd expect from Seattle's primary gay-and-lesbian neighborhood. The junction of Broadway and E John St is the core of activity, with restaurants, bars, shops and plenty of interesting characters to watch.

Capitol Hill is about 1.5 miles northeast of Downtown. Take bus 7 or 10 and get off at Broadway. If you're driving, there is also a pay parking lot on Harvard Ave E, behind the Broadway Market. Continue north to stately **Volunteer Park**, on E Prospect St, which was originally Seattle's cemetery.

SEATTLE ASIAN ART MUSEUM

This **museum** (☎ 206-654-3100; 1400 E Prospect St, Volunteer Park; adult/child/student & senior $5/free/3; ⏰ 10am-5pm Tue-Sun, 10am-9pm Thu; P) houses the extensive art collection of Dr Richard Fuller, who donated this severe art moderne–style gallery to the city in 1932. Admission is free on the first Thursday and first Saturday of each month. Also in Volunteer Park is the glass-sided Victorian **conservatory** (admission free), filled with palms, cacti and tropical plants.

JIMI HENDRIX STATUE

Jimi Hendrix, guitar genius of the last century and Seattle's favorite son, rocks out eternally in this bronze **sculpture** (1600 Broadway) by local artist Daryl Smith, made in 1997. Hendrix fans have been known to leave flowers, candles and notes at the base of the kneeling statue.

RICHARD HUGO HOUSE

Established in honor of the famed Northwest poet, the 1902 Victorian **Richard Hugo House** (☎ 206-322-7030; 1634 11th Ave), a former mortuary, is now the center of an active segment of the city's literary life. The house contains a library, conference room, theater and café with a small stage. It hosts readings and performances, writer-in-residence programs, reading groups and writing classes.

U District

The University of Washington's 700-acre campus sits at the edge of Lake Union in a commercial area about 3 miles northeast of Downtown. The main streets are University Way, known as the '**Ave**,' and NE 45th St, both lined with coffee shops, restaurants, bars, cinemas and bookstores. The core of campus is **Central Plaza**, known as Red Square because of its brick base. Get information and a campus map at the **visitor center** (☎ 206-543-9198; 4014 University Way; ⏰ 8am-5pm Mon-Fri).

BURKE MUSEUM

Near the junction of NE 45th St and 16th Ave is the **Burke Museum** (☎ 206-543-5590; adult/student/senior $8/5/6.50, free first Thu each month; ⏰ 10am-5pm, 1st Thu of month 10am-8pm), with an excellent collection of Northwest coast Native American artifacts.

HENRY ART GALLERY

At the corner of NE 41st St and 15th Ave is the **Henry Art Gallery** (☎ 206-543-2280; adult/student/senior $10/free/6, free Thu; ⏰ 11am-5pm Tue-Sun, 11am-8pm Thu), a sophisticated space centered on a remarkable permanent exhibit by the light-manipulating sculptor James Turrell, as well as various temporary and touring collections.

UW SUZZALLO LIBRARY

Those architecturally minded will be interested in the University of Washington's UW Suzzallo Library. Designed by Carl Gould around 1926, this bibliophile's dream was inspired by Henry Suzzallo, UW's president at the time. Suzzallo wanted it to look like a cathedral, because 'the library is the soul of the university.' Unfortunately for him, his bosses disagreed – on reviewing the building, they deemed it too expensive and fired Suzzallo for his extravagance. Gould was the founder of the university's architecture program, and he created the plans for 18 campus buildings.

Fremont, Wallingford & Green Lake

These three residential neighborhoods are all fun to explore for a sense of everyday life in Seattle. Green Lake is centered on a lake-filled park circumnavigated daily by hundreds of walkers, bladers, cyclists and strollers. Wallingford is a quiet little neighborhood that branches out from NE 45th St. And Fremont, about 2 miles north of Seattle Center, is known for its lefty vibe, farmers market and wacky public sculpture, including a rocket sticking out of a building and a statue of Lenin shipped over from Slovakia. People come from all over town for the **Fremont Sunday Market** (☎ 206-781-6776; www.fremontmarket.com/fremont; Stone Way & N 34th St;

STAYING IN SEATTLE: DAREK MAZZONE

Darek was born in Poland, where he lived until age nine, but has lived in Seattle since 1992 when his and a friend's van broke down after a long road trip. 'The funny thing is I was listening to KEXP when it happened,' he says. He's now a KEXP world-music presenter and an advertising consultant.

How has the local music scene changed over the years?
Well, it's always got an eyeball on it, internationally. I do a lot of travel, and anytime I say I'm from Seattle – it depends on the person I'm talking to, how old they are – sometimes they'll go 'Jimi Hendrix,' others they'll go 'grunge.' There's always something new that's bubbling up in Seattle. Right now it's Modest Mouse and Death Cab for Cutie. But it's interesting to see it from a perspective of being *in* the city, because right now the most interesting thing that's bumping in Seattle is hip-hop. There are some phenomenal bands like Blue Scholars. They're conscious, they sing about the war and about what's really going on. They do a lot of really good work. But there's other stuff too. We've got a great jazz scene, we've got a really funky reggae scene, and one of the best Balkan groups in the world, Kultur Shock. There's always something interesting going on. It's a good town for collaboration.

What neighborhood do you live in?
Capitol Hill. This place has gone nuts. How many cranes did you see? But change is good. I rent; I'd love to buy here but there's no way I could afford it. It's a great part of town.

Favorite thing about Capitol Hill?
I love being in the center of everything. I love walking. I'm desperate for the light-rail, which is going to transform the city dramatically. This is my favorite city in the world.

Where do you take visitors?
If it's family? Space Needle, Pike Place Market. If they're hip, I take them to Georgetown, which I love. Nine Pound Hammer. I take friends to places that I know there's no way they would experience otherwise. I take them to farmers markets. This is a foodie kind of town. Seattle's the West Coast, so there's a few subcultures here. There's a pretty significant Burning Man community, there's a great heritage in amazing jazz, we've got Garfield High School, which has some of the greatest jazz players in the world coming out of it. Music plays an integral part in this town.

Any only-in-Seattle moments?
There are a lot of only-in-Capitol Hill moments. This is where the freaks live. This is where you're gonna see a 60-year-old fetish couple walking down the street with leashes. You're going to see a wide range of really interesting fashion choices. I know millionaires, billionaires who live here, so, you know, you're at the espresso stand, and there's the billionaire, there's the rock star, there's the crusty, and there's the tourist. And there really isn't the separation that you'd find in other cities, because nobody gives a fuck. That really is the definitive Seattle moment.

🕑 10am-5pm Sun in summer, 10am-4pm Sun winter), which features fresh fruits and vegetables, arts and crafts and all kinds of people getting rid of variable-quality junk.

WAITING FOR THE INTERURBAN

A much-discussed piece of public art, *Waiting for the Interurban* (N 34th St at Fremont) is a cast-aluminum statue of people awaiting a train that never comes: the Interurban linking Seattle and Everett stopped running in the 1930s (it started up again in 2001 but the line no longer passes this way). Check out the human face on the dog – it's Armen Stepanian, once Fremont's honorary mayor, who made the mistake of objecting to the sculpture.

FREMONT TROLL

Beware the scary-eyed *Fremont Troll,* a mammoth cement figure devouring a Volkswagen Beetle beneath the Aurora Bridge at 36th St. The troll's creators – artists Steve Badanes, Will Martin, Donna Walter and Ross Whitehead – won a competition sponsored by the Fremont Arts Council in 1990. The 18ft figure is now a favorite place for late-night beer drinking.

THEO CHOCOLATE FACTORY

What, perhaps you wondered, could possibly take the place of the free beer that came at the end of a Redhood Brewery tour? How about free chocolate? That's right – the old Redhood Brewery, empty for years since the company moved operations to Woodinville, has been reopened as the **Theo Chocolate Factory** (☎ 206-632-5100; www.theochocolate.com; 3400 Phinney Ave N; 11am-5pm, tours 1 & 3pm daily plus 11am Sat; $5), and it does tours. Enough said.

GAS WORKS PARK

Urban reclamation has no greater monument in Seattle than **Gas Works Park** (Meridian Ave at N Northlake Way). The former power station here produced gas for heating and lighting from 1906 to 1956. The gas works was thereafter understandably considered an eyesore and an environmental menace. But the beautiful location of the park – with stellar views of Downtown over Lake Union, sailboats and yachts sliding to and from the shipping canal – induced the city government to convert the former industrial site into a public park in 1975. Rather than tear down the factory, landscape architects preserved much of the old plant. Painted black and now highlighted with rather joyful graffiti, it looks like some odd remnant from a former civilization. It also makes a great location for shooting rock album covers and music videos. Be sure to climb the small hill in order to see the sundial at the top.

WOODLAND PARK ZOO

In Woodland Park, up the hill from Green Lake Park, the **Woodland Park Zoo** (☎ 206-684-4800; 5500 Phinney Ave N; adult/child $10.50/7.50 Oct-Apr, $15/10 May-Sep; 9:30am-4pm Oct-Apr, 9:30am-6pm May-Sep; P) is one of Seattle's greatest tourist attractions, consistently rated as one of the top 10 zoos in the country. It was one of the first in the nation to free animals from their restrictive cages in favor of ecosystem enclosures, where animals from similar environments share large spaces designed to replicate their natural surroundings. Feature exhibits include a tropical rain forest, two gorilla exhibits, an African savanna and an Asian elephant forest. Parking costs $4.

Ballard & Discovery Park

Ballard, despite its recent veneer of hipness, still has the feel of an old Scandinavian fishing village – especially around the locks, the marina and the Nordic Heritage Museum. The old town has become a nightlife hot spot, but even in the daytime its historic buildings and cobblestone streets make it a pleasure to wander through.

HIRAM M CHITTENDEN LOCKS

Northwest of Seattle, the waters of Lake Washington and Lake Union flow through the 8-mile Lake Washington Ship Canal and into Puget Sound. Construction of the canal began in 1911; today 100,000 boats a year pass through the **Hiram M Chittenden Locks** (☎ 206-783-7059; 3015 NW 54th St; 24hr), about a 0.5-mile west of Ballard off NW Market St. On the southern side of the locks, you can watch from underwater glass tanks or from above as salmon navigate a fish ladder on their way to spawning grounds in the Cascade headwaters of the Sammamish River, which feeds Lake Washington. To get here, take bus 17 from Downtown at 4th Ave and Union St.

NORDIC HERITAGE MUSEUM

This **museum** (☎ 206-789-5707; 3014 NW 67th St; adult/child under 5/child/senior $6/free/4/5; 10am-4pm Tue-Sat, noon-4pm Sun) preserves the history of the northern Europeans who settled in Ballard and the Pacific Northwest, as well as bringing in special exhibits of new work by contemporary Scandinavian artists. It's the only museum in the USA that commemorates the history of settlers from all five Scandinavian countries. A permanent exhibit, features costumes, photographs and maritime equipment, while a second gallery is devoted to changing exhibitions. The museum also offers Scandinavian language instruction, lectures and films.

To get here, take bus 17 from Downtown at 4th Ave and Union St, get off at 32nd Ave NW and walk one block east on NW 67th St.

CENTER ON CONTEMPORARY ART

This **gallery space** (☎ 206-728-1980; www.cocaseattle.org; 6413 Seaview Ave NW) has been a strong force in Seattle's contemporary art scene for two decades. After floundering for a few years and moving around a lot, it has recently opened a new branch in Belltown (at 2721 1st Ave) as well as this primary space in the Shilshole Bay Beach Club. Call for opening hours.

DAYBREAK STAR INDIAN CULTURAL CENTER

In 1977, Native American groups laid claim to the land in this area, now Discovery Park, and 17 acres of parkland were decreed native land on which now stands the Daybreak Star Indian Cultural Center, a community center for Seattle-area Native Americans. Discovery Park has over 7 miles of hiking trails, several of

SEATTLE'S BEST

- Best brewpub: **Pike Pub & Brewery** (p102)
- Best view: **Gas Works Park** (p91)
- Best feel-good meal: **FareStart Restaurant** (p96)
- Best walk/cycle route: **Burke-Gilman Trail** (below)
- Best oddity: **Fremont Troll** (p90)

which lead to the Daybreak Star Center. Except for a small art gallery, there are few facilities for outside visitors. The vista point in front of the center affords beautiful views of the Sound, and several steep trails lead down through the forest to narrow, sandy beaches.

ACTIVITIES

Seattle's location lends itself to hiking, cycling and all kinds of water sports.

Hiking

There are great hiking trails through old-growth forest at Seward Park, which dominates the Bailey Peninsula that juts into Lake Washington, and longer (but flatter) hikes in 534-acre Discovery Park northwest of Seattle. The **Sierra Club** (☎ 206-523-2019) leads day-hiking and car-camping trips on weekends; most day trips are free.

Cycling

A cycling favorite, the 16.5-mile **Burke-Gilman Trail** winds from Ballard to Log Boom Park in Kenmore on Seattle's Eastside. There, it connects with the 11-mile **Sammamish River Trail**, which winds past the Chateau Ste Michelle winery in Woodinville before terminating at Redmond's Marymoor Park.

More cyclists pedal the oft-congested loop around **Green Lake**. Closer in, the 2.5-mile **Elliott Bay Trail** runs along the waterfront.

Get a copy of the *Seattle Bicycling Guide Map*, published by the City of Seattle's **Transportation Bicycle & Pedestrian Program** (☎ 206-684-7583; www.cityofseattle.net/transportation/bikemaps.htm), online or at bike shops.

The following are recommended for bicycle rentals and repairs:

Gregg's Cycles (☎ 206-523-1822; 7007 Woodlawn Ave NE) Here since 1932, Gregg's is a higher-end shop with two new storefronts in Bellevue and Lynwood; rentals are still out of the Green Lake shop. Fancy road bikes rent for $30 to $56 per hour, or you can get a more standard model for $18/135 per hour/week.

Bicycle Center (☎ 206-523-8300; 4529 Sand Point Way; rentals $3/15 per hr/24hr) This is another longstanding bike shop that does rentals and repairs; it's right off the Burke-Gilman Trail.

Recycled Cycles (☎ 206-547-4491; 1007 NE Boat St; bike rental 6/24hr $20/40) In the U District, toward the water at the lower end of the 'Ave.'

Water Sports

On Lake Union, **Northwest Outdoor Center Inc** (☎ 206-281-9694, 800-683-0637; www.nwoc.com; 2100 Westlake Ave N; kayaks $10-15 per hr) rents kayaks and offers tours and instruction in sea and white-water kayaking.

The **UW Waterfront Activities Center** (☎ 206-543-9433; canoe & rowboat per hr $7.50; 🕑 approx 10am-7pm, closed Nov-Jan), at the southeast corner of the Husky Stadium parking lot off Montlake Blvd NE, rents canoes and rowboats. Bring ID or a passport.

The **Agua Verde Paddle Club** (☎ 206-545-8570; 1303 NE Boat St; single kayak per 1/2hr $15/25, double kayak $18/30; 🕑 10am-dusk & 10am-6pm Sun Mar-Oct), near the university on Portage Bay, provides rental kayaks.

COURSES

Seattle is home to several institutions of higher education, but those looking for fun or casual classes while visiting are also in luck. Look under 'Classes' on seattle.craigslist.org for a plethora of options, or try the following:

PCC Cooks (www.pccnaturalmarkets.com/pcccooks) offers a number of cooking classes in various Seattle neighborhoods, including the free Walk, Talk & Taste classes.

Try your hand at glassblowing with a course at the **Seattle Glassblowing Studio** (☎ 206-448-2181; www.seattleglassblowing.com; 2227 5th Ave). Classes are small and intensive, but the studio is always open to the public if you just want to check it out.

SEATTLE FOR KIDS

The whole of Seattle Center will fascinate youngsters, but they'll get the most out of the **Pacific Science Center** (see p88), which entertains and educates with virtual-reality exhibits, laser shows, holograms, an IMAX theater and a planetarium, and the **Children's Museum** (p88).

Downtown on Pier 59, the newly renovated **Seattle Aquarium** (p87) is another fun way to learn about the natural world of the Pacific Northwest.

Seattle's numerous parks are all good places to let the tykes run free, and **Gas Works Park** (p91) is particularly good for flying kites.

Most of Seattle's restaurants are fine places to take the little ones along to, but **Ivar's Acres of Clams** (p98), **Sky City** (p99) at the top of the Space Needle, **Caffe Minnie's** (p98) and the **5 Spot** (p99) are all particularly kid-friendly eateries.

OFFBEAT SEATTLE

Most of Seattle is a little left of the mainstream, and that's even more true at a place like **Left Bank Books** (p82), a corner shop near **Pike Place Market** (p87) where you'll find 'how-to's on everything from vegan cupcakes to anarchist network-building. There's also plenty of excellent poetry and fiction for armchair activists.

A similarly freethinking vibe powers the Belltown gallery **Roq La Rue** (p88), which has a reputation for provocative exhibits of artwork from pop culture's underbelly.

And speaking of the undersides of things, the first thing you'll be told to go see in Seattle is the **Fremont Troll** (p90) beneath the Aurora Bridge at 36th, everyone's favorite 'wacky' piece of public art. Not recommended for Volkswagon fans.

TOURS

Argosy Cruises Seattle Harbor Tour (Map p84; ☎ 206-623-1445, 800-642-7816; www.argosycruises.com; adult/child $18.61/7.81; departs from Pier 55) Argosy's popular Seattle Harbor Tour is a one-hour narrated tour of Elliott Bay, the Waterfront and the Port of Seattle.

Bill Speidel's Underground Tour (☎ 206-682-4646; 608 1st Ave; adult/child/senior $14/7/12; 11am-5pm, schedule varies) This famous 'underground' tour, though corny at times, delivers the goods on historic Seattle as a rough-and-rowdy industrial town.

See Seattle Walking Tours (☎ 425-226-7641; www.see-seattle.com; per person $20; 10am Mon-Sat) See Seattle runs a variety of theme tours, from public-art walks to scavenger hunts.

FESTIVALS & EVENTS

Northwest Folklife Festival (☎ 206-684-7300; www.nwfolklife.org) Memorial Day weekend in May. International music, dance, crafts, food and family activities at Seattle Center.

Seafair (☎ 206-728-0123; www.seafair.com) Late July and August. Huge crowds attend this festival on the water, with hydroplane races, a torchlight parade, an air show, music and a carnival.

Bumbershoot (☎ 206-281-8111; www.bumbershoot.com) Labor Day weekend in September. A major arts-and-cultural event at Seattle Center, with live music, author readings and lots of unclassifiable fun.

SLEEPING

From mid-November through March 31, most Downtown hotels offer Seattle Super Saver Packages – generally 50% off rack rates, with a coupon book for savings on dining, shopping and attractions. Call the **Seattle Hotel Hotline** (☎ 800-535-7071; www.seattlesupersaver.com) or you can make reservations any time of year on its website.

Downtown & First Hill

Green Tortoise Hostel (Map p84; ☎ 206-340-1222; www.greentortoise.net; 105 Pike St; dm $24-29, r $77-80;) Newly situated around the corner from its old home, this hostel is one of the few budget options in the city and has an unbeatable location right across the street from Pike Place Market. Once pretty crusty, the place has moved to the Elliot Hotel Building and now offers 30 bunk rooms and 16 European-style rooms (shared bath and shower). The free breakfast includes waffles and eggs. Three nights a week the hostel offers a free dinner, and there are weekly events such as open-mic nights.

Sixth Avenue Inn (Map p84; ☎ 206-441-8300, 800-627-8290; www.sixthavenueinn.com; 2000 6th Ave; s/d from $119/129; P wi-fi) This motor inn, just five minutes north of the Downtown shopping frenzy, has an old-fashioned glamour, thanks mostly to its clubby, low-lit bar and lounge area, full of big comfy chairs and a fireplace. Spacious rooms feature vehemently 1980s-style brass beds and square lamps – if unironic retro is your thing, you're in luck. There's room service, a fitness room, and free wi-fi in the lobby and lounge. Parking costs $10.

Hotel Max (Map p84; ☎ 206-441-4200, 800-426-0670; www.hotelmaxseattle.com; 620 Stewart St; s/d from $179/199; P) There's something mildly obnoxious about a place (or a person) that describes itself as hip and artistic, but in the case of Hotel Max, the description fits. Original artworks by local and national artists hang in the (small but cool) guest rooms and public areas of the hotel, and it's tough to get any hipper than the supersaturated color scheme – not to mention unique package deals like the Grunge Special and the Gaycation. Rooms include not only a pillow menu, but also one for spirituality. Best of all: for $50,000 or so, you can buy your entire hotel room and have it delivered to your home. Parking costs $15.

Hotel 1000 (Map p84; ☎ 206-957-1000; www.hotel1000seattle.com; 1000 1st Ave; r/ste from $225/325; P ⊠ 💻) If you love the clean lines and simple elegance of IKEA but have just won the lottery, you might design a hotel like this. Leather-clad egg chairs cuddle around a fireplace made of concrete and steel tube in the lounge; rooms have round-square bedside tables made of chrome and wood; bathrooms have granite counters and freestanding tubs that fill from the ceiling; beds are curtained off in luxurious earth-tone textiles. Each room has individually adjustable art and a 40-inch high-definiton TV with surround sound. Some have a private bar, and some are pet friendly. There is also virtual golf.

Hotel Monaco Seattle (Map p84; ☎ 206-621-1770, 800-945-2240; www.monaco-seattle.com; 1101 4th Ave; r from $325; P ⊠ 💻) The hip Hotel Monaco is housed in the old Seattle Phone Building, which sat vacant before the Kimpton group from San Francisco converted it. The suite-style rooms have stripy wallpaper and heavy curtains, and leopard-print bathrobes are part of the deal. If you're lonely for your pet, you can borrow a goldfish for the length of your stay. The hotel's restaurant, Sazerac, is a popular New Orleans–style joint with a following of its own. Parking costs $26 to $36.

our pick **Sorrento Hotel** (Map p84; ☎ 206-622-6400, 800-426-1265; www.hotelsorrento.com; 900 Madison St; r from $339; P ⊠ 💻) William Howard Taft, 27th US president, was the first registered guest at the Sorrento, an imposing Italian-style hotel known since its birth in 1909 as the jewel of Seattle. The combination of luxurious appointments, over-the-top services and a pervasive sense of class add up to a perfect blend of decadence and restraint. The hotel's award-winning restaurant, the Hunt Club, is worth a stop whether you're staying here or not. Parking costs $19.

Pioneer Square

Best Western Pioneer Square Hotel (☎ 206-340-1234, 800-800-5514; 77 Yesler Way; r $179-259; P ⊠ 💻) Rooms and common areas at this historic hotel feature period decor and a comfortable atmosphere. The only hotel in the historic heart of Seattle, it can't be beaten for location – as long as you don't mind some of the saltier characters who populate the square in the off-hours. Nightlife, restaurants and shopping are just steps from the door. Parking costs $15.

Pike Place Market & Waterfront

Pensione Nichols (☎ 206-441-7125; www.pensionenichols.com; 1923 1st Ave; s/d $98/125, ste $230; P 💻) In a town with few cheap hotels and hardly any B&Bs in Downtown, Pensione Nichols is a treat. In the urban thick of things between Pike Place Market and Belltown, this charmingly remodeled European-style pensione has 10 rooms that share four retro-cool bathrooms, two large suites and a spacious common area that overlooks the market. Rooms come with a complete and tasty breakfast. Parking is in a nearby garage and costs $12.

Inn at the Market (Map p84; ☎ 206-443-3600, 800-446-4484; www.innatthemarket.com; 86 Pine St; r $175-300, water views $230-400; P) Right in the thick of things, the Inn at the Market is an elegant and architecturally interesting hotel and the only lodging in the venerable Pike Place Market. This 70-room boutique hotel has large rooms, many of which enjoy grand views onto market activity and Puget Sound. Its two restaurants, Campagne and Cafe Campagne, are renowned for their excellent French cuisine. Parking costs $20.

Hotel Edgewater (☎ 206-728-7000, 800-624-0670; www.edgewaterhotel.com; 2411 Alaskan Way, Pier 67; city/water views from $299/439; P) Perched over the water right in Elliott Bay, the Edgewater is one of the few places that lives up to its storied past. The timber-lodge theme, with its rock fireplaces and rough-hewn pine furniture, is pure Pacific Northwest, but a seriously classed-up version thereof. Half of the 223 rooms have bay views and the rest overlook the Seattle skyline; many contain gas fireplaces. OK, so you can't fish out the windows anymore, but that's probably just about the only wish this place won't fulfill. Valet parking is $26.

Belltown

Moore Hotel (☎ 206-448-4851, 800-421-5508; 1926 2nd Ave; s/d $52/64, with private bathroom $67/79, ste $104-156; ⊠ 💻) The once-grand Moore Hotel offers 135 bedrooms, small and not fancy but refurbished with an understated elegance. The turn-of-the-20th-century lobby, with its molded ceiling and marble accoutrements, speaks of the building's long history, which is echoed in the better rooms (ask for one with a view of the Sound). Don't miss the great little lounge next door, the Nitelite, whose clientele is a mix of young hipsters and regulars at least as old as the hotel.

our pick **Ace Hotel** (☎ 206-448-4721; www.acehotel.com; 2423 1st Ave; r without/with bathroom $99/190; P) Each of the Ace's 28 hospital-tidy rooms is unique and so stylish you quickly get the feeling you're the star of an art film. Ranging from European style with shared bathrooms to deluxe versions with private bathrooms, CD players and enough mirrors to make you paranoid, the rooms are stocked with condoms and, a copy of the *Kama Sutra* sits where your average midwestern motor inn would place the Gideon Bible. Obviously this isn't the place for the uptight – it's also bad for light sleepers, as the always-hopping Cyclops bar and restaurant is just downstairs. Rock and roll types have it made. Parking costs $15.

Hotel Ändra (Map p84; ☎ 206-448-8600, 877-448-8600; www.hotelandra.com; 2000 4th Ave; r from $219, ste $249-309; P) Wild fabric patterns and vivid colors combine with sleek Scandinavian-influenced design to give this hotel (formerly the Claremont) a calming yet sharply modern feel. Its 119 rooms have a sense of luxury without being claustrophobically over-furnished with the usual trappings of decadence. The trappings here, in fact, are quite unusual: alpaca headboards, anyone? There are blue-glass wall sconces, brushed-steel fixtures, gigantic walnut work desks – even the fitness room has spartan prints and plasma TVs on the walls. Some of the suites have plasma TVs too. Bathroom toiletries come from Face Stockholm. The hotel is attached to chef Tom Douglas's Greek-via-Northwest restaurant Lola.

Seattle Center & Queen Anne

Travelodge by the Space Needle (☎ 206-441-7878, 800-578-7878; 200 6th Ave N; r from $139; P) Quieter than anything on Aurora Ave N, this hotel offers amenities including a year-round Jacuzzi, outdoor pool (open in summer), in-room coffeemakers and a free continental breakfast (though it's fairly skimpy).

Best Western Executive Inn (☎ 206-448-9444, 800-351-9444; 200 Taylor Ave N; r from $189-209; P) In the shadow of the Space Needle, the Executive Inn has an exercise spa and a complimentary shuttle to Downtown. Pillowtop beds, inroom coffee and tea, microwaves and refrigerators, room service, a fitness room and a sports lounge are also available. Parking costs $5.

MarQueen Hotel (☎ 206-282-7407, 888-445-3076; www.marqueen.com; 600 Queen Anne Ave N; r from $190; P) An old 1918 apartment building, the MarQueen Hotel has hardwood floors throughout and a variety of rooms, all with kitchenettes leftover from their days as apartments. There's a free courtesy van that takes guests to nearby sights. Parking costs $16.

Capitol Hill

Gaslight Inn (☎ 206-325-3654; www.gaslight-inn.com; 1727 15th Ave; r $88-158;) The Gaslight Inn has 15 rooms available in two neighboring homes, 12 of which have private bathrooms. In summer, it's refreshing to dive into the outdoor pool or just hang out on the sun deck. No pets – the Gaslight Inn has a cat and a dog already.

Bacon Mansion (☎ 206-329-1864, 800-240-1864; www.baconmansion.com; 959 Broadway E; r $89-209) Bacon Mansion is an imposing place at first glance, but this very welcoming 1909 house is a four-level B&B on a quiet residential street just past the Capitol Hill action. It has a grand piano in the main room that guests are invited to play. The 11 rooms come in a variety of configurations, including a carriage house that's wheelchair-accessible, and include TV and voicemail. One large suite has a view of the Space Needle, one has a fireplace and another an Italian fountain as a backdrop.

Salisbury House (☎ 206-328-8682; www.salisburyhouse.com; 750 16th Ave E; s $119-139, d $129-149, suite $179; wi-fi) Salisbury House, in a quiet, tree-lined neighborhood near Volunteer Park, is a 1904 home with four elegant corner rooms and one suite, all equipped with private bathrooms, phone with voicemail, and wireless internet access. It's comfortably modern, not the floral overload of a typical B&B. The full breakfast is vegetarian. Downstairs there's a library with a fireplace. Two cats roam the grounds, and children over 12 are welcome.

U District

our pick **College Inn** (☎ 206-633-4441; www.collegeinnseattle.com; 4000 University Way NE; s/d from $55/75;) The closest thing this district has to a hostel, the College Inn is a great budget option.

Built for the 1909 Alaska-Yukon Exposition, the building has 27 European-style guest rooms – meaning shared bathrooms down the hall. There's no TV, but there's a ton of atmosphere, and some of the rooms have a view of the Space Needle. South-facing rooms get the most light. Rates include a continental breakfast served in the communal lounge. Downstairs there's a coffee shop that serves full meals, a convenience store and a lively pub. Note that the building lacks elevators, and the 'front desk' is four flights up a narrow stairway.

Chambered Nautilus B&B (☎ 206-522-2536, 800-545-8459; 5005 22nd Ave NE; r $94-169, ste $104-199; ⊠ 💻) The 1915 Georgian-style Chambered Nautilus has six guest rooms decorated with authentic British antiques, as well as an annex with one- and two-bedroom suites. All B&B rooms come with private baths, down comforters, handmade soaps and a teddy bear. The communal living room has a welcoming fireplace, and the full gourmet breakfast is reason enough to stay here. It's a handy but quiet location, tucked into the forested hillside between the university and Ravenna Park.

University Inn (☎ 206-632-5055, 800-733-3855; www.universityinnseattle.com; 4140 Roosevelt Way NE; s $109-145, d $129-155; P ⊠ 💻 wi-fi) What pushes this spotless, modern, well-located place over the edge into greatness is, believe it or not, the waffles served at the complimentary breakfast. They're amazing. The hotel is three blocks from campus, and its 102 rooms come in three levels of plushness. All of them offer such basics as a coffee maker, hair dryer and wi-fi; some have balconies, sofas and CD players, and some are pet-friendly ($20 fee). There's a Jacuzzi, an outdoor pool, laundry facilities and a guest computer in the lobby. Attached to the hotel is the recommended Portage Bay Cafe, and there's a free shuttle to various sightseeing areas.

EATING

The most fun way to assemble a budget meal is by foraging in Pike Place Market (p87) for fresh produce, baked goods, deli items and take-out ethnic foods. But Seattle has an embarrassment of riches when it comes to restaurants – without much effort, you can find everything from an Argentinean steak to a vegan cupcake.

Downtown & First Hill

This is the place to find classic Northwest food in old-fashioned oyster bars and cavernous steakhouses, as well as a couple of celebrity chef Tom Douglas's flagship restaurants.

our pick FareStart Restaurant (Map p84; ☎ 206-443-1233; www.farestart.org; 700 Virginia St; mains $8-12; ⏲ 11am-2pm Mon-Fri, 6-8pm Thu; V) Now in an attractively designed and much larger new space, FareStart continues to serve substantial meals that benefit the community. The constantly changing lunch menu is pretty darn gourmet for the price – try the veggie reuben or a flatiron steak in blue-cheese sauce. Proceeds from lunch and the popular Thursday-night Guest Chef dinners – where FareStart students work with a famous local chef to produce fantastic meals – go to support the FareStart program, which provides intensive job training, housing assistance and job placement for disadvantaged and homeless people. Reservations are recommended for dinner.

Wild Ginger (Map p84; ☎ 206-623-4450; 1401 3rd Ave; mains $10-25; ⏲ 11am-3pm Mon-Sat, 5-11pm Mon-Thu, 5pm-midnight Fri, 4:30pm-midnight Sat, 4-11pm Sun) Seattle was more or less introduced to the satay bar by this popular Indonesian restaurant, where throngs of diners sit and sample bite-size, skewered bits of fiery grilled chicken, vegetables or scallops, luscious soups and daily specials. More substantial dishes include Burmese curry crab and cinnamon-and-anise-spiced duck. The bar is a happening place and there's a live-music venue, the Triple Door, downstairs.

Palace Kitchen (Map p84; ☎ 206-448-2001; 2030 5th Ave; mains $12-25; ⏲ 5pm-1am) This is a see-and-be-seen hot spot that really picks up for the late-night cocktail scene. Daily dinner specials present such wonders as spaetzle-stuffed pumpkin or traditional pork loin. Snack on appetizers – including a terrine of smoked salmon and blue cheese or a sampler plate of regional cheeses – or go for the whole shebang with grilled trout, leg of lamb or roasted chicken with blackberries and nectarines. After 10pm there's a 'late-night breakfast' that includes a king crab omelette ($14).

Dahlia Lounge (Map p84; ☎ 206-682-4142; 2001 4th Ave; mains $22-36; ⏲ 11:30am-2:30pm Mon-Fri, 5-10pm Mon-Thu, 5-11pm Fri & Sat, 5-9pm Sun) Owner Tom Douglas started fusing flavors at this Seatle institution in the late 1980s and single-handedly made Seattleites more sophisticated. His empire has grown a lot since then and includes Palace Kitchen (see below), but this, his flagship restaurant, remains a local favorite.

There's a bakery next door where you can pick up one of the Dahlia's fabulous desserts to go. Reservations are recommended.

Pioneer Square

The historic core of the city has a surprising number of good budget-friendly dining options scattered amid its atmospheric old saloons and steakhouses.

Elliott Bay Cafe (☎ 206-682-6664; 101 S Main St; mains $3-8; 8am-9pm Mon-Fri, 9am-9pm Sat, 10am-6pm Sun) This cozy crypt underneath Elliott Bay Book Co is a clean, well-lit place to settle in with a book and a bowl of soup or salad, or a Bukowski's Ham on Rye sandwich (named for the grisly old barfly poet), and browse the book-lined walls while you eat.

Bakeman's (☎ 206-622-3375; 122 Cherry St; mains $4-6; 10am-3pm Mon-Fri) Legendary for its theatrically surly counter service and its roasted-fresh-daily turkey-and-cranberry sandwich, this subterranean diner demands that you know what you want and aren't afraid to ask for it.

Zaina (☎ 206-624-5687; 108 Cherry St; mains $4-9; 10am-9pm Mon-Fri, 11am-9pm Sat) This friendly café, bejeweled with a mishmash of sparkly decorations and pulsing with Middle Eastern pop music, dishes out juicy falafel sandwiches stuffed to overflowing, as well as shawarma, tabbouleh, hummus, great baklava and fresh-squeezed lemonade. On weekend nights the vibe goes clubbish, with hookahs and belly dancers in the house.

Grand Central Baking Co (☎ 206-622-3644; 214 1st Ave S; mains $5-9; 7am-5pm Mon-Fri, 8am-4pm Sat) This artisan bakery in the Grand Central Arcade builds sandwiches on its own peasant-style loaves and baguettes, with soups, salads, pastries and other treats.

our pick Salumi (☎ 206-621-8772; 309 3rd Ave S; mains $7-14; 11am-4pm Tue-Fri) Sure, you'll have to wait in line. This is Mario Batali's dad's place, after all. But the line to get a Salumi sandwich is like its own little community. People chat, compare notes, talk about sandwiches they've had and loved…it's nice. When you finally get in the door of this long-skinny shopfront, you're further teased by display cases of hanging meats and cheeses. Sandwiches come with any of a dozen types of cured meat and a handful of fresh cheese on a hunk of bread – you can't go wrong. There are only a couple of seats, so be prepared to picnic. On Tuesday, Aunt Izzy makes gnocchi in the window.

International District

The International District is a great neighborhood for cheap eats, or you can go all-out on a sumptuous eight-course dinner banquet. It's also a good place to seek out decent food after the bars close. The many Vietnamese, Thai and Chinese restaurants that line Jackson St between 6th and 12th Aves give you plenty of options. East of 8th Ave S and I-5, Little Saigon takes over and the flavor becomes decidedly Vietnamese.

House of Hong (☎ 206-622-7997; 408 8th Ave S; dim sum $2-3 per item; 9am-2am Mon-Sat, 9am-midnight Sun) This giant yellow mainstay of the neighborhood now serves dim sum from 10am until 4:30pm every day – handy if you're craving a hit in the middle of the day.

Pho Bac (☎ 206-568-0882; 1240 Jackson St; mains from $5; 8am-9pm) You can get three sizes of pho at this well-established restaurant on the edge of 14th Ave and Jackson St, with its huge windows gazing onto Little Saigon. Excellent spring rolls come wrapped in fresh herbs, and there are other classic Vietnamese dishes available.

Purple Dot Cafe (☎ 206-622-0288; 515 Maynard Ave S; mains $5-12; 9am-1am Sun-Thu, 9am-3:30am Fri & Sat) The Purple Dot looks like the inside of an 1980s video game (it is actually purple) and draws a late-night disco crowd on weekends. But most of the time it's a calm, quiet place to get dim sum and Macao-style specialties (meaning you can feast on spaghetti and toast along with your Hong Kong favorites).

China Gate (☎ 206-624-1730; 516 7th Ave S; mains $6-12; 10am-2am) Like House of Hong (see above), the China Gate now has all-day dim sum. The Hong Kong–style menu offers a couple of hundred choices, and the building is interesting in its own right – it was built in 1924 as a Peking Opera house.

Pike Place Market & Waterfront

Explore the market on an empty stomach and commit to a few hours of snacking – you'll be full by the time you leave, and it doesn't have to cost much. And if you're looking for serious dining, you can find that here too – some of Seattle's favorite restaurants are tucked in mysterious corners in the market district.

Lowell's Restaurant (Map p84; ☎ 206-622-2036; 1519 Pike Pl; mains $6-12; 7am-8pm) If you want a sit-down meal but nothing fancy, head to Lowell's, well loved by shoppers, businesspeople and fellow market operators for its classic, eye-opening breakfasts and cheap-and-cheerful lunches. Order up eggs Benedict, salmon omelettes or fish and chips from the chalkboard menu, lunch counter-style, then take it over to a window seat and enjoy the view.

Athenian Inn (Map p84; ☎ 206-624-7166; 1517 Pike Place Market; mains $8-12; 6:30am-6:30pm Mon-Sat) There's nothing fancy about the Athenian, but it's a landmark and a bastion of unpretentious, frontier-era Seattle – it opened in 1909, long before the days of Starbucks and Grand Central Bakery. It's been a bakery and a lunch counter and now seems to have settled in as a diner-bar combination where, especially in the off-hours, you can snuggle into a window booth and gaze over Elliott Bay with a plate of fried fish.

Ivar's Acres of Clams (Map p84; ☎ 206-624-6852; Pier 54, 1001 Alaskan Way; mains $12-20; 11am-10pm Mon-Thu, 11am-11pm Fri & Sat, 9am-10pm Sun) Ivar Haglund was a beloved local character famous for silly promotional slogans ('Keep clam!'), but he sure knew how to fry up fish and chips. Ivar's is a Seattle institution that started in 1938. Forgo the dining room for the outdoor lunch counter – the chaotic ordering system involves a lot of yelling, but it seems to work, and then you can enjoy your clam strips and chips outdoors on the pier.

Steelhead Diner (Map p84; ☎ 206-625-0129; www.steelheaddiner.com; 95 Pine St; mains $15-33; 11am-10pm Tue-Sat, 10am-3pm Sun) 'Highbrow diner' sounds like an oxymoron, but the Steelhead does it right – hearty, homely favorites like fish 'n chips, grilled salmon or braised short ribs and grits become fine cuisine because they're made with the best of what Pike Place Market has to offer. The awesome gumbo features Uli's sausage, 'Squimbled Eggs' come poached over Dungeness crab on toast, a fried-chicken sandwich is fall-apart moist and lemony, and the crab cakes have been making local foodies swoon. The place is all windows, which is great considering it's perched right over the market and Elliott Bay, and decorations include tied flies in glass. Reservations are recommended.

Café Campagne (Map p84; ☎ 206-728-2233; 1600 Post Alley; mains $16-19; 11am-5pm Mon-Fri, 5-10pm Sun-Thu, 5:30-11pm Fri & Sat, 8am-4pm Sat & Sun) At the casual younger sibling of the upscale Campagne, inside the Inn at the Market (p94), the quality of the French-style cooking is what you'd expect from such a talented kitchen. The prices are more manageable, and you don't have to dress up for dinner.

Belltown

A hodgepodge of dining options, Belltown has everything from chic to sushi, with plenty of casual noodle houses, pizza joints and cafés thrown into the mix.

Caffe Minnie's (☎ 206-448-6263; 101 Denny Way; mains $5-11; 24hr) At the northern end of Belltown, almost in Lower Queen Anne, is this appealingly worn-in 1950s-style diner, a blessing for insomniacs, bar-crawlers, truckers, fugitives or those with the munchies after 2am. You can have breakfast all day while looking out the window at the pokey little cake shop and costume-rental store.

Black Bottle (☎ 206-441-1500; blackbottleseattle.com; 2600 1st Ave; mains $8-9; 4:30pm-1:30am) The huge crowd congregating outside the front door of this new Belltown restaurant is your first clue that something interesting is happening inside. The menu has a lot more clues: octopus carpaccio, lemon squid salad and saffron risotto cakes. It's a spartanly decorated but warm-looking space, with friendly service and a chic atmosphere. Plus, you can't beat a Belltown menu where nothing tops $9.

Belltown Pizza (☎ 206-441-2653; 2422 1st Ave; mains $11-22; 4-11pm, bar until 2am) Pizza and beer is great, but pizza and liquor works quicker. Started as a tiny bar serving New York–style pizza, Belltown Pizza has expanded a lot since then but maintains its original mission of good food and good fun at grown-up hours. A large pie is enough to feed four hungry people. You can also get salads, pasta and sandwiches.

our pick Shiro's Sushi Restaurant (☎ 206-443-9844; 2401 2nd Ave; mains $20-21; 5:30-9:45pm) Kyoto-born sushi master Shiro Kashiba spent 20 years running Seattle's first sushi restaurant, Nikko. He now spends a lot of time shopping for the freshest ingredients, hence his reputation as the go-to guy for raw fish in Seattle. He's a cheerful-looking fellow but takes his sushi very seriously – get a seat at the bar if you can, and watch him work.

Flying Fish (☎ 206-728-8595; 2234 1st Ave; mains $18-38; 5pm-1am, bar menu until 2am daily, 11:30am-2pm Mon-Fri) Still the reigning king of fish dishes in Seattle, or at least in Belltown, Flying Fish is a reliable spot for seafood. Combine several small plates, share a platter of oysters, or go with a main dish, such as yellowtail with eggplant and soy ginger sauce, or monkfish in coconut peanut sauce. The dining room is bustling and energetic, the service friendly and top-notch. The menu changes daily depending on what's fresh.

Seattle Center & Queen Anne

Queen Anne has plenty of eateries – the 5 Spot being a favorite – and it's hard not to notice Seattle Center's most prominent restaurant, from its perch atop the Space Needle.

5 Spot (☎ 206-285-7768; 1502 Queen Anne Ave N; mains $10-14; 8:30am-midnight) In Upper Queen Anne, everyone's favorite breakfast and hangover diner is the 5 Spot. Good strong coffee keeps the staff ultra-perky. Try a local legend, like the red flannel hash, or get crazy with the wild salmon cakes. On weekends, go for breakfast early to avoid the lines snaking out the door – or go for lunch or dinner; this is an excellent place for a quiet meal featuring good American cooking.

Sky City (☎ 206-905-2100; 219 4th Ave N; mains $34-54; 11am-3pm Mon-Fri, 9am-3pm Sat & Sun, 5-10pm daily) You don't really go to Sky City, the revolving restaurant atop the Space Needle, for the food, which locals deem uninspiring and overpriced. The view's the thing, and it is tremendous from 500ft up in the air. The ride up the elevator is free if you have meal reservations.

Capitol Hill

The scene on Capitol Hill is almost as much about style as food. It's no use enjoying a fabulous dinner if no one can see how chic you look while you're eating it. Then again, ambience hardly detracts from a fine dining experience, so who's complaining?

Honeyhole (Map p84; ☎ 206-709-1399; 703 E Pike St; mains $5-10; 10am-2am) Cozy by day, irresistible at night, the Honeyhole has a lot to recommend it: big stuffed sandwiches with cute names (the Luke Duke, the Texas Tease), greasy fries, a full bar, DJs and a cool cubbyhole atmosphere at night.

Bimbo's Bitchin' Burrito Kitchen (Map p84; ☎ 206-329-9978; 506 E Pine St; mains $5.50-7.50; noon-11pm Mon-Thu, noon-2am Fri & Sat, 2-10pm Sun) A godsend for anyone prowling Capitol Hill late at night, Bimbo's slings fat tacos, giant burritos and juicy quesadillas until closing time. The tiny space is crammed with kitschy knickknacks, including velvet matador portraits, oil paintings with neon elements, and a hut-style thatched awning. Have a margarita with your meal or check out the adjoining Cha-Cha Lounge.

Globe Cafe & Bakery (☎ 206-324-8815; 1531 14th Ave; mains $6-9; 9am-3pm; V) The Globe serves incredibly rich vegan food, such as tempeh-and-yam gyros dripping with onions and tahini sauce. It's an industrial gallery-type space with features including a huge comic-book panel on the ceiling, giant plexiglass bookplates hanging like curtains between low booths, funky art on the walls, and a ragtag clientele of workmen, young punks, homeless people and middle-aged intellectual poets. Hipster boys in an open kitchen churn out tofu scrambles, french toast and sandwiches to die for.

Cafe Septieme (☎ 206-860-8858; 214 Broadway E; mains $10-18; 9am-midnight) The fact that Septieme has gone from super-trendy to warmly familiar probably says as much about the changing neighborhood as the place itself. A pretty, Euro-style restaurant-bar with red walls and white-clothed tables, Septieme serves filling but sophisticated burgers, salads, pastas and fish dishes. The bacon-provolone cheeseburger is great. In nice weather, outdoor tables provide first-rate people-watching. It's equally comfortable as a morning coffee shop or a classy late-night cocktail bar.

our pick **Coastal Kitchen** (☎ 206-322-1145; 429 15th Ave E; mains $14-20; breakfast 8am-3pm, lunch & dinner until 11pm) This longtime favorite turns out some of the best food in the neighborhood – it has an eclectic mix of Cajun, Mayan and Mexican inspirations, and the Italian-language instruction tape running in the bathroom gives a clue about its influences. Menus rotate by theme – a recent at the time of writing Catalan ensemble included fish stew and pan-seared chicken in Amontillado sherry-mushroom sauce. If there is a pasta lunch special, do not hesitate: get it! There's also a great 'blunch' ($8.75) between 8:30am and 3pm on weekdays.

Cafe Flora (☎ 206-325-9100; 2901 E Madison St; mains $15-17; 11:30am-5pm Mon-Fri, 9am-2pm Sat & Sun, 5-9pm Sun-Thu, 5-10pm Fri & Sat; V) Just beyond Capitol Hill in Madison Park is this longtime favorite for vegan and vegetarian food. Flora has a gardenlike feel and a creative menu, with dinner treats like seitan spring rolls and breaded coconut tofu dipped in chili sauce, a portobello French dip, caprese pizza and black-bean burgers. Or go for the hoppin' john fritters or tomato asparagus scrambles at brunch.

U District

This is one of the best districts in Seattle for cheap and authentic ethnic food, and there are good vegan and vegetarian options. When you're browsing for lunch or dinner, don't be put off by unappetizing-looking storefronts – some of the most interesting food comes from places that have the outward appearance of rundown five-and-dime stores. The adventurous will be rewarded.

Agua Verde (☎ 206-545-8570; 1303 NE Boat St; mains $6.50; 🕑 11am-9pm Mon-Sat, takeout window 7:30am-2pm Mon-Fri) On the shores of Portage Bay at the southern base of University Ave, the Agua Verde is a little gem that overlooks the bay and serves fat tacos full of lemony cod, shellfish or portabella mushrooms, plus other Mexican favorites. There's usually a wait for a table, but you can have a drink and hang out on the deck, or order from the takeout window. You can rent kayaks in the same building, in case you want to work off your dinner.

Flowers (☎ 206-633-1903; 4247 University Way NE; mains $5-12; 🕑 11am-2am; V) One of the most stylish places in the U District, Flowers has a vegetarian buffet served until 5pm, with dinners including meat choices. The lunch menu includes 20 different sandwiches, each around $5. After hours, the place becomes an inviting place to sip a cocktail, munch on an appetizer and 'do homework' with a promising study partner.

Ruby (☎ 206-675-1770; 4241 University Way NE; mains $7-9; 🕑 11am-2am) The menu at this attractive space next to Flowers reflects the room's Casablanca feel, with fragrant jasmine rice bowls ($8 to $9), a ginger-onion-chili breakfast omelette ($6) and soups like yellow dhal with tofu, spinach, lemon, garlic and ginger or lemongrass miso with shiitake mushrooms. The joint's bar is hopping at night, and all the drinks are large and well crafted.

Cedars Restaurant (☎ 206-527-5247; 4759 Brooklyn Ave NE; mains $7-13; 🕑 11:30am-10pm Mon-Sat, 1-9pm Sun; V) This place serves enormous curries and vindaloos so smooth and creamy you want to dive into them. Eat at Cedars just once and you will dream about it later. There's also a great selection of Mediterranean specialties like shish kebabs, falafel and gyros, much of which is vegetarian. The covered wooden patio is a cool hangout when the weather's nice.

Fremont, Wallingford & Green Lake

These residential neighborhoods have a number of well-loved restaurants, old and new.

Tilth (☎ 206-633-0801; 1411 N 45th St; mains $10-29; 🕑 5:30-10pm Tue-Thu & Sun, 5:30-10:30pm Fri & Sat, 10am-2pm Sat & Sun) The only ingredients on chef Maria Hines's menu that aren't organic are those found in the wild, like mushrooms and some seafood. Everything else, from asparagus to cheese, is carefully selected to meet certified-organic standards, and prepared in a manner that preserves its essence. Try the Duck Three Ways, made with the first organically raised ducks in Washington. Staff in the small restaurant are unpretentious and friendly, and will gamely answer any questions about the food or wine. Reservations are recommended; there's also a small bar in the corner.

Bizzarro (☎ 206-545-7327; 1307 N 46th St; mains $12-18; 🕑 5-10pm) With a name like Bizzarro you'd never guess that this Wallingford hotbed is an excellent neighborhood Italian café. When you learn that it's actually someone's garage crammed with kitschy art and weird antiques, the name makes sense. Deliciously buttery pasta dishes, a good wine list and frequent live music add to the experience.

Ballard & Discovery Park

Ballard boasts an ever-changing restaurant scene, so don't hesitate to ask around and check local papers for the latest recommended places.

Hattie's Hat (☎ 206-784-0175; 5231 Ballard Ave NW; mains $6-10; 🕑 11am-2am Mon-Fri, 9am-2am Sat & Sun) This might be the best place in town to make that ever so delicate transition from weekend breakfast to dinner and drinks – you can get coffee with eggs and toast all day long, and nobody will find it odd when you switch to beer, even if it's not quite noon yet. The dinner menu is, unsurprisingly, not super ambitious, but the food is plenty filling and better than your average greasy spoon.

Old Town Ale House (☎ 206-782-8323; 5233 Ballard Ave NW; mains $8-10; 🕑 11:30am-10pm Sun & Mon, 11:30am-11pm Tue-Thu, 11:30am-midnight Fri & Sat) This cavernous, warmly lit, red-brick pub serves giant sandwich 'wedges,' stacks of delicious fries and microbrewed beer in a convivial atmosphere.

Madame K's (☎ 206-783-9710; 5327 Ballard Ave NW; mains $10-20; 🕑 5-10pm Mon-Thu, 5-11pm Fri, 4-11pm Sat, 4-9:30pm Sun) An elegant, red-and-black pizza parlor with an old bordello feel (the building was once a brothel), this small, chic place is packed at dinner. It's also popular for drinks and desserts. There's a nice patio out the back, or you can let history repeat itself in the upstairs dessert room with a decadent 'Chocolate Chip Orgasm.'

DRINKING

You'll find cocktail bars, dance clubs and live music on Capitol Hill. The main drag in Ballard has brick taverns old and new, filled with the hard-drinking older set in daylight hours and indie-rockers at night. Belltown has gone from grungy to fratty, but has the advantage of many drinking holes neatly lined up in rows. Industrial Georgetown is an up-and-coming barfly's paradise, still rough around the edges. And, this being Seattle, you can't walk two blocks without hitting a coffee shop.

BARS

our pick **Brouwer's** (☎ 206-267-2437; 400 N 35th St; 🕐 11am-2am) This dark cathedral of beer has rough-hewn rock walls and a black metal grate on the ceiling. Behind an epic bar are tantalizing glimpses into a massive beer fridge. A replica *Mannequin Pis* statue at the door and the Belgian crest everywhere clue you in to the specialty.

Shorty's (☎ 206-441-5449; 2222 2nd Ave) An unpretentious oasis in a block of *très chic* lounges, Shorty's has cheap beer and hotdogs, alcohol slushies and a back room that's pure pinball heaven.

Blue Moon (☎ 206-633-626; 712 NE 45th St) Legendary haunt of literary drunks, the Blue Moon is exactly a mile from campus, thanks to an early zoning law. Be prepared for impromptu poetry recitations, jaw-harp performances and inspired rants.

Copper Gate (☎ 206-706-3292; 6301 24th Ave NW) Formerly one of Seattle's worst dives, the Copper Gate is now an upscale bar-restaurant focused on meatballs and naked ladies. A Viking longship forms the bar, with a peep-show pastiche for a sail and a cargo of helmets and gramophones.

BREWPUBS

Jolly Roger Taproom (☎ 206-782-6181; 1514 NW Leary Way; 🕐 closed Sun) Less scurvy-barnacle than placid-yachtsman, Maritime Pacific Brewing's Jolly Roger Taproom is a tiny, pirate-themed bar with a nautical chart painted onto the floor, good seafood and about 15 taps.

Hale's Ales Brewery (☎ 206-706-1544; www.halesales.com; 4301 Leary Way NW) Hale's makes fantastic beer, notably its ambrosial Cream Ale. Its flagship brewpub feels like a business-hotel lobby,

INDUSTRIAL-STRENGTH BOOZE

The newly hip warehouse district of Georgetown is the latest off-the-beaten-path neighborhood for beerhounds to explore. If Ballard's already too 'over' for you, head out here to find the preferred drinkeries of those in the know.

Georgetown Liquor Company (☎ 206-763-6764; 5501B Airport Way S) This odd mishmash of a bar has an elegant industrial-chic design, a vegetarian menu and an astounding collection of retro video games. Plus, you know, beer and liquor.

Nine Pound Hammer (☎ 206-762-3373; 6009 Airport Way S) You can bring your dog to this darkened beer hall – the place is generous with the pours and the peanuts, and the mixed crowd of workers, hipsters, punks and bikers vacillates between energetic and rowdy.

Jules Maes Saloon (☎ 206-957-7766; 5919 Airport Way S) Built in the late 1800s, this traditional saloon now benefits from punk rock and tattoos, a regular schedule of live music, pinball and other vintage games to play, and no need to hide its booze from the authorities (the place operated as a speakeasy during Prohibition).

Smartypants (☎ 206-762-4777; 6017 Airport Way; 🕐 11am-2am Mon-Fri, 10am-2am Sat, 10am-3pm Sun) A meeting place for scooterists and sport-bike riders, this giant industrial hangout has vintage motorcycles propped up in the windows, a hearty sandwich menu (plus a weekend brunch), and an obvious fondness for two-wheeled mischief of all types. Ask owner Tim Ptak about ice racing! Wednesday is Bike Night, when fans watch the week's recorded MotoGP, SuperMoto and superbike races. The kitchen is open until midnight Monday to Saturday. There's a covered patio outdoors for smokers.

but it's worth a stop. There's a self-guided tour near the entrance.

Pike Pub & Brewery (Map p84; ☎ 206-622-6044; 1415 1st Ave) This Pike Place Market pub serves great burgers and brews in a funky neo-industrial multi-level space.

Elysian Brewing Co (☎ 206-860-1920; 1221 E Pike St) On Capitol Hill, the Elysian's huge windows are great for people-watching – or being watched, if your pool game's good enough.

COFFEEHOUSES

Seattle gave the world Starbucks, and the homegrown-turned-overgrown chain is hard to avoid. But small independent coffeehouses abound.

B&O Espresso (☎ 206-322-5028; 204 Belmont Ave E) Full of understated swank, this is the place to go for Turkish coffee – if you can get past the pastry case up front.

Café Allegro (☎ 206-633-3030; 4214 University Way NE) Supposedly the city's first espresso bar, Allegro keeps students and professors wired.

Denny Way Espresso Vivace Roasteria (Map p84; ☎ 206-860-5869; 901 E Denny Way) Asked what's the best coffee in Seattle, most people will mention Vivace. There's also a walk-up window (Espresso Vivace Roasteria Broadway) further north at 321 Broadway E (Map p84).

Panama Hotel Tea & Coffee House (☎ 206-515-4000; 607 S Main St) The Panama, a historic 1910 building that contains the only remaining Japanese bathhouse in the USA, doubles as a memorial to the neighborhood's Japanese residents forced into internment camps during WWII.

Zeitgeist (☎ 206-583-0497; 171 S Jackson St; wi-fi free) A lofty, brick-walled café, the pretty Zeitgeist has great coffee and sandwiches.

ENTERTAINMENT

Consult the *Stranger*, *Seattle Weekly* or the daily papers for event listings. Tickets for major events are available at **TicketMaster** (☎ 206-628-0888), which operates a discount **ticket booth** (Map p84; ☎ 206-233-1111) at Westlake Center.

LIVE MUSIC

our pick **Crocodile Cafe** (Map p84; ☎ 206-441-5611; 2200 2nd Ave) A beloved institution in Belltown and famous as a launching pad for the grunge scene, the Croc still hosts great local and touring bands.

Neumos (Map p84; ☎ 206-709-9467; 925 E Pike St) The 'new Moe's' fills the big shoes of its long-gone namesake in booking some of the best local and touring rock shows in town.

Chop Suey (☎ 206-324-8000; 1325 E Madison St) Chop Suey is a dark, high-ceilinged space with a ramshackle faux-Chinese motif and eclectic booking.

Tractor Tavern (☎ 206-789-3599; 5213 Ballard Ave NW) This spacious, amber-lit venue in Ballard mainly books folk and acoustic acts.

CINEMAS

The biggest event of the year for Seattle cinephiles is the **Seattle International Film Festival** (SIFF; ☎ 206-464-5830; www.seattlefilm.org; tickets $5-10, passes $300-800). The festival uses a half-dozen theaters but also has its own dedicated theater, in McCaw Hall's **Nesholm Family Lecture Hall** (321 Mercer St, Seattle Center), and is the largest film festival in the US. It typically starts in mid-May.

The **Seattle Lesbian & Gay Film Festival** (☎ 206-323-4274; admission $6-8), a popular festival in October, shows new gay-themed films from directors worldwide.

WINE DOWN IN WOODINVILLE

The suburban community of Woodinville, 14 miles north of Bellevue off I-405, is home to two popular wineries and a brewpub.

One of Washington's original wineries, **Chateau Ste Michelle** (☎ 425-415-3633; 14111 NE 145th St; 10am-5pm) pioneered efforts to cultivate vineyards in the Columbia Valley, where most Washington wine production goes on today. The historic 87-acre estate lends itself to picnics and concerts in the summer. Noted for its cabernets and merlots, **Columbia Winery** (☎ 425-482-7490; 14030 NE 145th St; 10am-6pm) offers tours on weekends.

Another beverage trailblazer of sorts, Redhook led Washington's microbrewing wave. Redhook's Woodinville facility showcases its signature ales at the **Forecasters Public House** (☎ 425-483-3232; 14300 NE 145th St). Brewery tours are offered at 1pm, 3pm and 5pm weekends, 2pm and 4pm weekdays ($1 per person).

Cool theaters include:

Cinerama (Map p84; ☎ 206-441-3653; 2100 4th Ave) One of the very few Cineramas left in the world, it has a fun, sci-fi feel.

Harvard Exit (☎ 206-781-5755; 807 E Roy at Harvard) Built in 1925, Seattle's first independent theater.

Northwest Film Forum (☎ 206-329-2629; www.wigglyworld.org; 1515 12th Ave) Impeccable programming, from restored classics to cutting-edge independent and international films.

THEATER & PERFORMING ARTS

Check local newspapers for reviews and schedules.

A Contemporary Theatre (ACT; Map p84; ☎ 206-292-7676; www.acttheatre.org; 700 Union St) One of the three big companies in the city, ACT fills its $30 million home at Kreielsheimer Place with performances by Seattle's best thespians and occasional big-name actors.

Intiman Playhouse (☎ 206-269-1900; www.intiman.org; 201 Mercer St) The Intiman Theatre Company, Seattle's oldest, takes the stage at this theater.

Pacific Northwest Ballet (☎ 206-441-9411; www.pnb.org) This is the foremost dance company in the Pacific Northwest and does more than 100 performances a season from September through June.

Seattle Opera (☎ 206-389-7676; www.seattleopera.org) The Seattle Opera features a program of four or five full-scale operas every season, including a summer Wagner's *Ring* cycle that draws sellout crowds. They perform at McCaw Hall in the Seattle Center (p88).

Seattle Symphony (Map p84; ☎ 206-215-4747; www.seattlesymphony.org; 200 University St) A major regional ensemble; plays at the Benaroya Concert Hall, Downtown at 2nd Ave and University St.

SPORTS

Seattle Mariners (☎ 206-628-3555; www.mariners.org; admission $7-60) The beloved baseball team plays in Safeco Field just south of Downtown.

Seattle Seahawks (☎ 425-827-9777; www.seahawks.com; admission $42-95) The Northwest's only National Football League (NFL) franchise plays in the 72,000-seat Seahawks Stadium.

Supersonics (☎ 206-283-3865; www.nba.com/sonics; admission $10-235) Seattle's National Basketball Association (NBA) franchise draws huge crowds at Seattle Center's Key Arena.

Huskies (☎ 206-543-2200; www.gohuskies.com; admission $6-65) The University of Washington Huskies football and basketball teams are another Seattle obsession.

GAY & LESBIAN VENUES

Re-Bar (Map p84; ☎ 206-233-9873; 1114 Howell St) This storied dance club, where many of Seattle's defining cultural events happened (Nirvana album releases etc), welcomes gay, straight, bi or undecided revelers to its dancefloor.

Neighbours (☎ 206-324-5358; 1509 Broadway Ave E) For the gay club scene and its attendant glittery straight girls, check out this always-packed dance factory.

R Place (Map p84; ☎ 206-322-8828; 619 E Pine St) Three floors of dancing to hip-hop/R&B DJs and plenty of sweaty body contact make this club a blast for pretty much everyone who isn't terribly uptight.

SHOPPING

The main big-name shopping area is Downtown from 3rd to 6th Aves and University to Stewart Sts. Pike Place Market is a maze of arts-and-crafts stalls, galleries and small shops. Pioneer Sq and Capitol Hill have locally owned gift and thrift shops.

These are some only-in-Seattle shops.

Archie McPhee (☎ 206-297-0240; www.mcphee.com; 2428 NW Market St, Ballard; 🕒 10am-7pm Mon-Sat, 11am-7pm Sun) Famous for its mail-order catalog, Archie McPhee is a browser's heaven, and you'll almost certainly wind up buying something you never realized you needed – like bacon air fresheners or a ninja lunchbox.

Babeland (Map p84; ☎ 206-328-2914; www.babeland.com; 707 E Pike St; 🕒 11am-10pm Mon-Sat, noon-7pm Sun) The answer to the question 'Where can I buy pink furry handcuffs and a glass dildo?'

Sonic Boom (☎ 206-568-2666; www.sonicboomrecords.com; 514 15th Ave E; 🕒 10am-10pm Mon-Sat, 10am-7pm Sun) A local institution, Sonic Boom record store now has several locations and frequently hosts in-store performances by bands coming through town.

Uwajimaya (☎ 206-624-6248; www.uwajimaya.com; 600 5th Ave S; 🕒 9am-10pm Mon-Sat, 9am-9pm Sun) All you need to prepare an Asian feast – fresh and frozen meat and fish, produce, canned and dried and intriguingly labeled treats of all kinds, as well as cooking tools, spices, cookbooks, toiletries and gift items.

GETTING THERE & AWAY

Air

Seattle's airport, **Seattle-Tacoma International Airport** (Sea-Tac; ☎ 206-433-5388; www.portseattle.org), 13 miles south of Seattle on I-5, has daily service to Europe, Asia, Mexico and points throughout the USA and Canada, with frequent flights to and from Portland and Vancouver, BC.

Boat

Victoria Clipper (☎ 800-888-2535, 206-443-2560; www.victoriaclipper.com; Seattle-Victoria 2 to 6 times daily, round trip adult/child from $117/58) operates several high-speed passenger ferries to Victoria, BC, and to the San Juan Islands. It also organizes package tours which can be booked through the website.

The **Washington State Ferries** (☎ in Washington 206-464-6400, 888-808-7977, for ferry traffic info 551; www.wsdot.wa.gov/ferries) website has maps, prices, schedules, trip-planners, weather updates and other news, as well as estimated waiting time for popular routes. Fares depend on the route, size of the vehicle and duration of the trip, and are collected either for round-trip or one-way travel, depending on the departure terminal.

Bus

A **biodiesel bus** (☎ 503-502-5750; www.sharedroute.org; Portland-Seattle one-way/round-trip $20/$50; once daily Fri-Sun) runs from Portland and Olympia to Seattle and back on weekends.

Greyhound (☎ 800-231-2222, in Seattle 206-628-5561, baggage 206-628-5555; www.greyhound.com; 811 Stewart St; 6am-midnight) connects Seattle with cites all over the country, including Chicago (three daily, two days, $195), Spokane (three daily, five to seven hours, $38), San Francisco (four daily, twenty hours, $95), and Vancouver, BC (six daily, three to four hours, $25).

Train

Amtrak (☎ 800-872-7245; www.amtrak.com) serves Seattle's **King Street Station** (303 S Jackson St; 6am-10:30pm, ticket counter 6:15am-8pm). Three main routes run through town: the *Cascades* (connecting with Vancouver,BC, Portland and Eugene), the *Coast Starlight* (connecting with Oakland and Los Angeles) and the *Empire Builder* (connecting with Spokane, Fargo and Chicago).

These are common one-way ticket prices.

Seattle–Chicago, daily, 46 hours, from $309
Seattle–Oakland, daily, 23 hours, $135
Seattle–Portland, five daily, three to four hours, $28-31
Seattle–Vancouver, BC, five daily, three to four hours, $28-43

GETTING AROUND

To/From the Airport

There are numerous options for making the 13-mile trek from the airport to Downtown Seattle.

Shuttle Express (☎ 800-487-7433; www.shuttleexpress.com; $26-53) has pick-up and drop-off on the third floor of the airport garage. Gray Line's **Airport Express** (☎ 206-626-6088; www.graylineseattle.com; one way adult $10-13, child $7-10) fetches passengers in the parking lot outside door 00 at the south end of the baggage-claim level.

Taxis and limousines (about $35 and $40, respectively) are available at the parking garage on the third floor. Rental car counters are located in the baggage claim area.

Catch Metro buses ($1.25 to $1.75 one-way) outside door 6 by baggage carousel 5, on the baggage claim-level. Buses 194 Express and 174 go to Downtown. From there, the free bus 99 goes to the Waterfront, Pioneer Square and the International District, or use the online **trip-planner** (☎ rider information system 206-553-3000; transit.metrokc.gov).

Car & Motorcycle

Seattle traffic has been among the worst in the country for years and isn't improving. If you do drive, take a friend: some Seattle freeways have High-Occupancy Vehicle Lanes for vehicles carrying two or more people. National rental agencies have offices at the airport and around town.

Public Transportation

Buses are operated by **Metro Transit** (☎ schedule info 206-553-3000, customer service 206-553-3060; www.transit.metrokc.gov; fares $1.25-1.75), part of the King County Department of Transportation.

Taxi

All Seattle taxi cabs operate at the same rate, set by King County; at the time of research the rate was $2.50 at meter drop, then $2 per mile.

Any of the following offer reliable taxi service:

Orange Cab Co (☎ 206-444-0409; www.orangecab.net)
Redtop Taxi (☎ 206-789-4949; www.yellowtaxi.net)
Yellow Cab (☎ 206-622-6500; www.yellowtaxi.net)

AROUND SEATTLE

Blake Island

An easy way to get from Seattle onto the Sound is with **Tillicum Village Tours** (☎ 206-933-8600, 800-426-1205; www.tillicumvillage.com; adult/child/senior $79/30/72; Mar-Dec). The four-hour trip to Blake Island, the birthplace of Seattle's namesake Chief Sealth, includes a salmon bake, a native dance and a movie at an old Duwamish Native American village. Tours depart from Pier 55

Bainbridge Island

The island is a popular destination with locals and visitors alike. It's the quickest and easiest way to get out on the water from Seattle, and the ferry ride provides stunning views of both Seattle and the Sound. Prepare to stroll around lazily, tour some waterfront cafés, taste unique wines at the **Bainbridge Island Winery** (☎ 206-842-9463; 4 miles north of Winslow on Hwy 305; ⌚ tastings 11am-5pm Fri-Sun) and maybe rent a bike and cycle around the invitingly flat countryside.

Washington State Ferries (☎ 206-464-6400, in Washington 888-808-7977, for ferry traffic info 551; www.wsdot.wa.gov/ferries; Seattle to Bainbridge, adult/child/car & driver $6.70/5.40/14.45, bicycle surcharge $1) run several times a day.

Vashon Island

More rural and countercultural than Bainbridge, Vashon Island has resisted suburbanization – a rare accomplishment in the Puget Sound area. Much of Vashon is covered with farms and gardens; the small community centers double as commercial hubs and artists' enclaves. Cascade views are great, with unencumbered vistas of Mt Rainier and north to Baker.

Vashon is a good island to explore by bicycle or car, lazily stopping to pick berries or fruit at a 'U-pick' garden or orchard. There's also the option to plan a hike in one of the county parks.

An option for budget travelers in summer is **AYH Ranch Hostel** (☎ 206-463-2592; www.vashonhostel.com; 12119 SW Cove St; dm HI member $17, non-HI members 20; ⌚ May 1-Sep 30).

From Pier 50 in Seattle, a passenger-only ferry leaves eight times each weekday for Vashon Island ($8.70, 25 minutes). However, the ferry deposits you far from the centers of Vashon commerce and culture, so you'll need to bring a bike ($1 extra charge) or have a lift arranged. From Fauntleroy in West Seattle, a car ferry leaves over 30 times daily for Vashon (passenger/car and driver $4.30/18.50, 15 minutes). For either ferry, fares are collected only on the journey to the island.

Travelers from Seattle can make a visit to Vashon into a loop trip by taking the Tahlequah ferry from the southern end of the island to Tacoma, returning via the mainland's I-5.

Bremerton

Seattle's other ferry destination is Bremerton, the largest town on the Kitsap Peninsula and Puget Sound's principal naval base. The main attractions here are the **Naval Museum** (☎ 360-479-7447; 402 Pacific Ave; ⌚ self-guided tours daily in summer, Thu-Sun in winter) and the historic destroyer **USS Turner Joy**, right next to the ferry terminal.

The car ferry to Bremerton makes frequent daily trips from the terminal at Pier 52 (passenger/car and driver $6.70/14.45, one hour). Passengers are charged only on the westbound journey; those with vehicles pay both ways.

Boeing Factory

Near the city of Everett is the facility where most of Boeing's wide-bodied jets – the 747, 767 and 777 – are produced. Tours of the **factory** (☎ 360-756-0086, 800-464-1476; adult/senior & child $15/8) are given 9am to 3pm weekdays. No photography is allowed. Reservations must be made at least 24 hours in advance; call between noon and 3pm to get on the list.

To reach the Boeing factory, follow I-5 north to exit 189; turn west and drive 3 miles on Hwy 526.

Museum of Flight

Aviation buffs wholeheartedly enjoy the **Museum of Flight** (☎ 206-764-5720; 9494 E Marginal Way S, Boeing Field; adult/child/youth/senior $14/free/7.50/13, 5-9pm 1st Thu each month free; ⌚ 10am-5pm Fri-Wed, 10am-9pm Thu), while others traipse through suppressing yawns, so be choosy who you come with. The museum presents the entire history of flight, from Da Vinci to the Wright Brothers to the NASA space program. More than 50 historic aircraft are displayed, including a recently acquired British Airways Concorde. The restored 1909 Red Barn, where Boeing had its beginnings, contains exhibits and displays. The six-story glass Great Gallery has 20 airplanes suspended from its ceiling. Vintage fliers reside on the grounds outside the buildings. There's also a hands-on area where visitors get to work the controls and sit in the driver's seat. Films about flight and aircraft history are shown in the small theater, and there's a gift shop and café.

About ten miles south from Downtown, to get here by car, take I-5 south to exit 158, turn west and follow East Marginal Way north. Or take bus 174 from Downtown.

Eastside

Almost universally scorned by Seattleites, but growing at an alarming rate, **Bellevue**, on the eastern shores of Lake Washington, is an upscale burg with high-income housing, attractive parks and some interesting shops and boutiques. Civic and social life centers on Bellevue Sq, at Bellevue Way NE and NE 8th St, the shopping mall that sets the tone for the downtown and the surrounding communities. Across from the mall is the **Bellevue Art Museum** (☎ 425-519-0770; 510 Bellevue Way NE; adult/student & senior $7/5; 🕑 10am-5:30pm Tue-Thu & Sat, 10am-9pm Fri, 11am-5:30pm Sun), featuring changing exhibits of contemporary Northwest art. To reach Bellevue from Downtown Seattle, take I-90 east and exit onto I-405 northbound. By bus, take 550 from Convention Place or any of the 3rd Ave tunnel stations (regular/peak $1.25/1.75).

North of Bellevue on I-405 is **Kirkland**, known for its lakefront business district, marinas and antique shopping malls. Some of the best public access to Lake Washington is along Lake Ave W. Lots of waterfront restaurants are found here, some with docks for their boat-transported customers. East of Kirkland is **Redmond**, a sprawling suburb and the center of Seattle's high-tech industry. Computer giant Microsoft dominates life here. To reach Kirkland and Redmond from central Seattle, take Hwy 520 over the Evergreen Point Bridge or catch bus 251 along 4th Ave.

Tacoma

Tacoma gets a bad rap as a beleaguered mill town known mostly for its distinctive 'Tacom-aroma,' a product of the nearby paper mills. Its nickname, 'City of Destiny,' because it was the Puget Sound's railroad terminus, once seemed like a grim joke. But destiny has started to come through for Tacoma. A renewed investment in the arts and significant downtown revitalization make it a worthy stop on the Portland–Seattle route.

Find information at the **visitor center** (☎ 253-305-1000, 800-272-2662; www.traveltacoma.com; 1001 Pacific Ave; 🕑 8:30am-5pm Mon-Fri).

Tacoma's tribute to native son Dale Chihuly, the **Museum of Glass** (☎ 253-396-1768; 1801 E Dock St; adult/child $10/4; 🕑 10am-5pm Mon-Sat, noon-5pm Sun, 10am-8pm Thu in summer), with its slanted tower called the Hot Shop Amphitheater, has art exhibits and glassblowing demonstrations. Chihuly's characteristically elaborate and colorful **Bridge of Glass** walkway connects the museum with the enormous copper-domed neobaroque 1911 **Union Station**. Some huge pieces by Chihuly greet visitors to the city's **Federal Courthouse** (1717 Pacific Ave). For smaller-scale work, don't miss Chihuly's permanent collection at the **Tacoma Art Museum** (☎ 253-272-4258; 1701 Pacific Ave; adult/student $7.50/6.50; 🕑 10am-5pm Mon-Sat, noon-5pm Sun).

Take Ruston Way out to **Point Defiance** (☎ 253-591-5337; zoo admission adult/child $10/8; 🕑 9:30am-5pm), a 700-acre park complex with free-roaming bison and mountain goats, a logging museum, zoo, aquarium and miles of trails.

The **Antique Sandwich Company** (☎ 253-752-4069; 5102 N Pearl St; mains $5-8) is a funky luncheonette and coffee shop near Point Defiance.

For B&Bs, call the **Greater Tacoma B&B Reservation Service** (☎ 253-759-4088, 800-406-4088). Moderately priced hotels are scattered south of the center between I-5 exits 128 and 129.

Sound Transit bus routes 590 and 594 use the station behind the **Tacoma Dome** (510 Puyallup Ave; Seattle $3). The free Downtown Connector service makes a loop between the station and Seattle city center every 15 minutes. **Amtrak** (☎ 253-627-8141; 1001 Puyallup Ave) links Tacoma to Seattle and Portland.

Northwestern Washington & the San Juan Islands

Washington's northwestern corner is its coastal Shangri-la, a colorful mosaic of fir-covered islands, sparkling ocean, undulating mountain foothills and flat, fertile river valleys.

Towering over the engaging regional hub of Bellingham lies the omnipresent hulk of Mt Baker, the area's snowcapped backdrop, while nestled on the flat Skagit River delta nearby, historic La Conner comes alive in the spring with a rich patchwork of colorful tulip, daffodil and iris fields.

Though the busy I-5 corridor has its fair share of crawling traffic and ugly sprawl, northwestern Washington has so far resisted the urban inquietude of Seattle. Flush up against the southern Canadian border, towns such as Mt Vernon and Anacortes are slow-paced and low-key places with nary a skyscraper to break the natural vista.

But with a written history not much older than most folk's great-grandparents, the region's enduring lure is the great outdoors. Lying in the rain shadow of the Olympic Mountains, the sheltered waters of Upper Puget Sound and the Georgia Strait are ideal for kayaking, boating, scuba diving and whale-watching. Sprinkled along the tree-punctuated coastline, meticulously preserved lumber towns and barnacled old boat wharfs provide visitors with poignant reminders of early American pioneering life.

No excursion here is complete without a side-trip to the incomparable San Juan archipelago, a jewel-like collection of small, rural islands, replete with sheep-filled pastures and homey B&Bs, that could compete for a top 10 listing in any reputable 'Best of' USA guide.

HIGHLIGHTS

- Scanning the Haro Strait for whales from rocky coast at **Lime Kiln Point State Park** (p123)
- Standing atop of **Mt Constitution** (p126) on Orcas Island soaking up one of the Pacific Northwest's most awe-inspiring views
- Cycling around the back roads of laid-back **Lopez Island** (p129) exchanging salutations with the congenial locals
- Meandering between oyster bars on **Chuckanut Drive** (p113)
- Searching for photo ops in **La Conner's** (p115) springtime tulip fields
- Staying in a quaint and quirky B&B on **Whidbey Island** (p116)

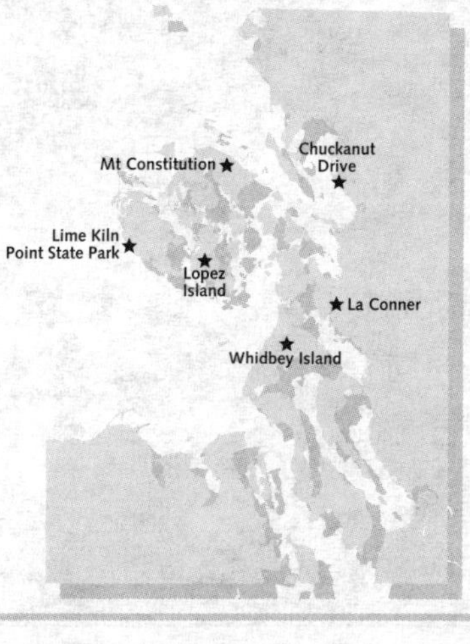

NORTHWESTERN WASHINGTON

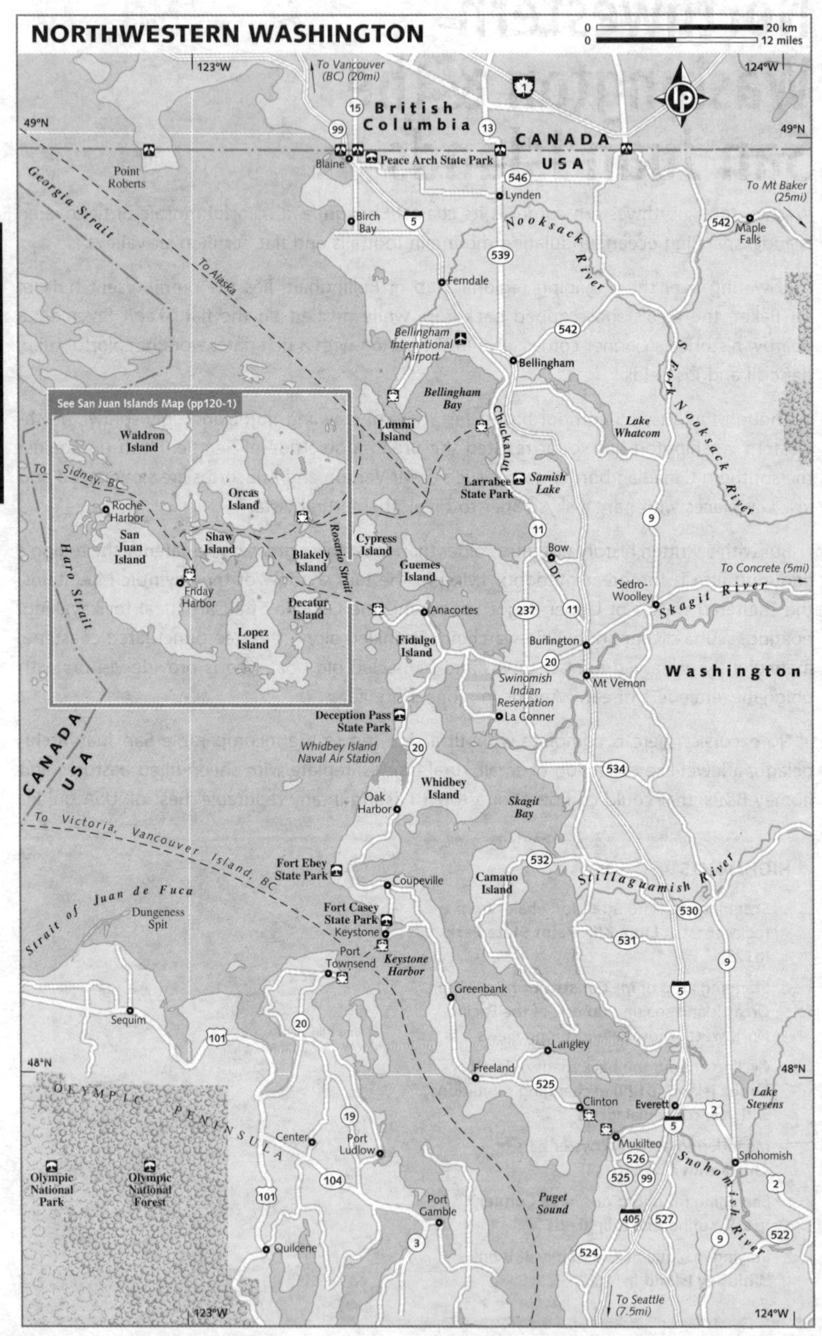

Geography & Climate

Northwestern Washington's climate is mild and wet, although notably less rain falls here than in the Olympic Peninsula, or on Mt Rainier. In Bellingham the average yearly high and low temperatures are 59°F (15°C)and 44°F (7°C) respectively and the annual rainfall tops 35in. Caught between escarpment and sea, the terrain between the Canadian border and Seattle is infringed by the foothills of the Cascade Mountains and intersected by numerous river valleys – most notably the fertile Skagit River Valley with its large tracts of reclaimed land. Relief on the San Juan Islands varies from precipitous Orcas to pancake flat Lopez.

Getting There & Away

Bellingham airport is the area's main air nexus offering daily flights to Seattle, Salt Lake City and Canada. The city is also the Washington terminal for year-round ferries to Alaska, as well as a May to October service to Victoria, Canada (p112). Further south, Anacortes offers another seasonal ferry option to Sidney, British Columbia (BC), that runs from April to December.

By road, northwestern Washington is well served by **Greyhound** (www.greyhound.com) buses with the Seattle–Vancouver, BC, service running four times a day along I-5 in both directions, stopping at Bellingham and Mt Vernon. If you're arriving by car via the northern route there are four US–Canada border crossings at Peace Arch (I-5), Pacific Highway/Truck Crossing (I-5), Lynden-Langley (SR539) and Sumas (SR9).

The scenic Amtrak Cascades (www.amtrakcascades.com) train line runs from Seattle to Vancouver, BC, five times a day with one daily stop at Bellingham and Mt Vernon.

Getting Around

Northwestern Washington is surprisingly well-served by public transport. **Whatcom Transportation Authority** (☎ 360-676-7433) serves the Bellingham area as far north as the Canadian border and as far east as Kendall on the Mt Baker highway. Further south, **Skagit Transit** (☎ 360-757-4433) runs buses from Mt Vernon out to Anacortes, La Conner and Concrete, while on Whidbey Island, **Island Transit** (☎ 800-240-8747) links the major centers fare free!

If you arrive without a car you can pick up a rental at Bellingham airport starting at around $25 a day.

BELLINGHAM

pop 67,171

Mild-mannered Bellingham – or the 'City of Subdued Excitement' as it sometimes (humorously) known – is Washington's 10th largest population center and a settlement widely lauded by real estate agents as being one of the Pacific Northwest's most livable communities. Embellishing the sidewalks of the revitalized city center you'll find secondhand bookstores, cozy coffee bars, myriad ethnic restaurants, and a bustling and vibrant farmers market that sells everything from Bavarian pretzels to organic furniture. 'Green' in both its surroundings and politics, Bellingham's allegiances have always swung inexorably leftwards, boasting such prophetic environmental innovations as bike lanes, recycling bins, slow food movements and a growing trickle of hybrid cars spruced up with the odd 'Impeach Bush!' bumper sticker.

Bellingham's love affair with the great outdoors began in 1911 with the inaugural Mt Baker marathon – one of the world's first ultra-marathon races – a multifaceted

LUMMI ISLAND

The most easily accessible and least-visited of the populated Bellingham Bay islands, Lummi Island – a six-minute ferry ride (round-trip $9, hourly) from Gooseberry Point near Bellingham – is a dreamy bucolic idyll, that mixes unhurried rural friendliness with the kind of sparkling ocean vistas that will revive even the dampest of West Coast spirits. Leave your 'to do' list at home, bring a bike or kayak, and enjoy nature at its exquisite best on this 8.2-sq-mile slither of land that is home to artists, eagles and the world's only reef net salmon fishery.

Devoid of any RV parks or campsites, accommodation options on Lummi are limited to the gorgeously located **Willows Inn** (☎ 360-758-2620; www.willows-inn.com; 2579 West Shore Dr; r low season $125, high season $145; ⊠ ⁙) that sits perched above a pristine beach on the island's western shore. Aside from a hot tub, pleasant rooms and a lively café, the Willows also boasts a top-notch restaurant where you can enjoy fresh local fish and organic vegetables over a to-die-for view.

118-mile pain-fest that involved a mad scramble from the town center up to the summit of Mt Baker and back. The tradition lives on today in the equally masochistic Ski to Sea Race, an annual seven-leg team relay that incorporates skiing, running, cycling, canoeing, mountain biking and kayaking, from the frigid heights of Baker ski resort down to the choppy waters of Bellingham Bay.

A one-time blue-collar town whose early fortunes were tied to lumber, Bellingham has diversified in recent decades to incorporate artists, professionals, realtors and the enlightened students of Western Washington University, now one of the city's main employers. With excellent transport links to Vancouver and Seattle, as well as its close proximity to Mt Baker and the San Juan Islands, tourism is another crucial draw card and a number of important bodies, including the American Alpine Institute, have chosen Bellingham as their base.

A couple of miles south of downtown lies historic Fairhaven, once a separate city that grew up in the 1880s around speculation that it would be selected as the Great Northern Railroad's Pacific Coast port city. When the Great Northern chose Seattle as its main terminus, Fairhaven – rather like Port Townsend across the water – fell into a long decline, though recent renovation has turned the handsome old buildings and warehouses into an intriguing collection of shops and restaurants. In 1904 Fairhaven joined with the two other local settlements of Whatcom and Sehome to form a single civic entity named after the bay.

Orientation & Information

Bellingham is 18 miles south of the Canadian border crossing at Blaine and 89 miles north of Seattle on I-5. The current city center is west of I-5; exit 253 leads to Holly St, a major downtown artery and one of the few streets to cut through the area without getting caught up in conflicting street grids.

The best downtown tourist information can be procured at the **Visitor Info Station** (☎ 360-527-8710; www.downtownbellingham.com; 1304 Cornwall St; 🕑 9am-6pm).

BOOKSTORES

Bellingham is a genuine readers' haven, with a number of great bookstores; it's also a major center for book collectors. Music fans will be equally enamored by Bellingham's clutch of offbeat record stores, many of which stock old vinyl.

Henderson Books (☎ 360-734-6855; 116 Grand Ave) A veritable warehouse, this place stocks an estimated quarter million titles, both new and used. You could spend the better part of a day browsing the well-organized shelves.

Michael's Books (☎ 360-733-6272; www.michaelsbooks.com; 109 Grand Ave) Across the street, Michael's carries a formidable selection of rare and out-of-print books.

Village Books (☎ 360-671-2626; 1210 11th St) This is a real community resource in Fairhaven, with lots of literary activities, to say nothing of being the home of the popular Colophon Cafe (p112).

Sights

The **Whatcom Museum of History & Art** (☎ 360-676-6981; 121 Prospect St; admission by donation; 🕑 noon-5pm Tue-Sun) is housed in the imposing and fanciful 1892 Whatcom City Hall, Bellingham's most eye-catching building. It features Native American basket weaving, some photos from the 1950s and a large selection of 19th-century household and farming implements. There's also a small shop.

The Whatcom Museum has formulated an **Old Town Bellingham Walking Tour** that starts close to the museum and incorporates 20 sites in and around West Holly St. Pick up a map and leaflet when you visit the museum.

There are two other museums situated close by. The **Children's Museum** (☎ 360-733-8769; 227 Prospect St; admission $2.50; 🕑 noon-5pm Sun, Tue & Wed, 10am-5pm Thu-Sat) has a puppet theater, art and crafts, and educational materials for kids aged from one to eight. The **American Museum of Radio and Electricity** (☎ 360-738-3886; 1312 Bay St; adult/child $5/2; 🕑 11am-4pm Wed-Sat) showcases over 2000 exhibits relating to the early days of electricity and the golden age of radio. It houses the largest collection of its kind in the US.

Also worth a quick visit is **Western Washington University** founded in 1893 as a teacher training institute and redesignated as a university in 1977. Environmental Studies is a popular specialty here. The **WWU Visitors Information Center** (☎ 360-650-3424; 🕑 7am-5pm Mon-Fri) at the end of South College Dr, can provide details of a self-guided tour of the campus' two dozen outdoor sculptures and you can also pop into the **Western Gallery** (☎ 360-650-3963; 🕑 10am-4pm Mon-Fri, noon-4pm Sat) to view the art exhibits.

Activities

Wedged precariously between mountains and sea, Bellingham offers outdoor activities by the truckload. Lakes Whatcom, Samish and Padden, all within a few minutes of town, make for great picnicking and boating, while walkers and hikers can trace the well-paved trail through Fairhaven to Larrabee Park.

Acting as a mini Kathmandu for the ever-active Northwest climbing community, the city is home of the highly regarded **American Alpine Institute** (☎ 360-671-1505; 1515 12th St, Fairhaven; 9am-5:30pm Mon-Fri) who organize everything from Everest ascents to guided trips up Mts Baker and Rainier.

Bellingham also offers a number of scenic and wildlife cruises; pick up brochures at the visitors center or the Bellingham Cruise Terminal and shop the options. **Victoria/San Juan Cruises** (☎ 360-738-8099; 355 Harris Ave) offers narrated day trips around Bellingham Bay (from $14) or further afield to the San Juan Islands (from $49) and Victoria, BC (from $79), stopping for some whale-watching along the way.

If you're interested in renting kayaks, try **Moondance Sea Kayak Adventures** (☎ 360-738-7664; www.moondancekayak.com; Apr-Sep) who runs a full-day trip in Chuckanut Bay, launching from Larrabee Park, for $85. **Fairhaven Boatworks** (☎ 360-714-8891; 501 Harris Ave) rents kayaks/sailboats/rowboats from $30/40/40 per day.

Fairhaven Bike & Mountain Sports (☎ 360-733-4433; 1103 11th St), rent bikes from $20 a day and has all the info (and maps) on local routes. It also rents out cross-country skis and snowshoes ($22/14 per day).

Sleeping

Larrabee State Park (☎ 360-676-2093; Chuckanut Dr; tents/hookups $17/24) Seven miles south of Bellingham, along scenic Chuckanut Dr, these campsites sit among Douglas firs and cedars with access to Chuckanut Bay and 12 miles of hiking and biking trails.

Birch Bay Hostel (☎ 360-371-2180; 7467 Gemini St off Alderson Rd; dm/d $17/45; May-Sep) If you're on your way to or from Canada, you can stay at this HI hostel at Bay Horizon County Park in Blaine, just south of the border. Clean dormitory beds and private rooms for up to four are housed in old military barracks, with a cozy social space. At breakfast, eat your fill of pancakes for $1. Nearby are the beach and waterfront restaurants.

Val-U Inn (☎ 360-671-9600; 805 Lakeway Dr; s/d $79/89; wi-fi) This clean, well-managed motel just off I-5 is an easy walk from downtown Bellingham, and makes up for its rather insipid, just-off-the-highway setting by its proximity to all of the major transport arteries. Even better the Vancouver–Seattle Airporter Shuttle (p113) stops here making it an ideal base for overnight travelers who want to explore the Bellingham area.

Hotel Bellwether (☎ 360-392-3100; 1 Bellwether Way; r $129-229, lighthouse $399; wi-fi) Bellingham's finest and most charismatic hotel is positioned on the waterfront with views over the harbor toward the whale-like hump of Lummi Island. Billing itself as a European hotel on the basis of its Italian furniture and Hungarian duvets, the Bellwether advertises 66 luxury rooms none of which are exactly the same. Its crowning glory is the celebrated lighthouse condominium, an old converted three-story lighthouse that offers substantially more comfortable amenities today than in the seafaring days of yore.

Fairhaven Village Inn (☎ 360-733-1311; 1200 10th St; r with bay view/park view $169/189; wi-fi) Downtown Bellingham lacks a decent number of well-appointed independent hotels, but one good alternative option is this prime place in gentile Fairhaven. Well in keeping with the vintage tone of the historic district, the Village Inn is a class above the standard motel fare with prices to match. In this instance, they're probably justified.

Eating

Mallards (☎ 360-734-3884; 1323 Railroad Av) An institution for a whole generation of Bellingham residents who made their first date or stole their first kiss on the bright red art-deco style seats here, Mallards is an ice-cream parlor extraordinaire with a whole range of strange and scrumptious flavors. Come here before or after a show and sample the vanilla-and-pepper or green-tea varieties – all organic, of course!

Old Town Cafe (☎ 360-671-4431; 316 W Holly St; mains $5-7; till 3pm) This is a classic bohemian breakfast haunt where you can get to know the locals over fresh pastries, espresso and a garden tofu scramble. Wandering musicians sometimes drop by to enhance the happy-go-lucky atmosphere.

Swan Café (☎ 360-734-0542; 1220 N Forest St; sandwiches $5-7; V) The Swan Café is pure

Bellingham: a Community Food Co-op with an onsite café/deli that sells fresh, organic, fair-trade, and guilt-free food. It's also a vegetarian and vegan's heaven offering such items as vegan muffins, organic beer and a delicious daily selection of fresh, interesting salads. Take-out or eat on-site in a bright and airy seating area that offers plenty of decent snacks.

our pick **Colophon Cafe** (☎ 360-647-0092; 1208 11th St, Fairhaven; mains $7-10) Linked with Fairhaven's famous literary haven, Village Books (see p110), the Colophon is a multiethnic eatery for people who like to mix their paninis with Proust. Renowned for its African peanut soup and chocolate brandy creams pies, the café has indoor seating along with an outside wine garden and is ever popular with the local literati.

Boundary Bay Brewery & Bistro (☎ 360-647-5593; 1107 Railroad Ave; mains $7-11) Perennially popular Boundary Bay crafts its own soulful ales and serves hearty Northwest-influenced fare for lunch and dinner, including pastas, pizzas and salads. The smoked salmon chowder hits the spot on a rainy night.

House of Orient (☎ 360-738-4009; 115 E Holly St; mains $8-11) Despite the delicious complexities of Thai cooking, one of the best ways to judge if a Thai restaurant has got 'what it takes' is to sample its standard no-frills Pad Thai noodles. Using this theory as a yardstick, the House of Orient firmly comes up trumps. It adds to the kudos with great green curry, economical prices and a pleasantly refurbished decor.

Pepper Sisters (☎ 360-671-3414; 1055 N State St; mains $9-13; 🕑 from 5pm Tue-Sun, closed Mon) People travel from far and wide to visit this colorful restaurant that serves what it bills as American southwestern cuisine with a Northwestern twist: if the definition sounds confusing, pull up a pew and taste the cilantro-and-pesto quesadillas, blue corn rellenos and potato-garlic burritos. You won't be disappointed.

Dirty Dan Harris (☎ 360-676-1011; 1211 11th St, Fairhaven; mains $16-20) Named after Fairhaven's notoriously unhygienic founder, Dirty Dan's has been knocking out excellent steaks, ribs and seafood from this historic Victorian tenement for over 30 years.

Entertainment

Wild Buffalo (☎ 360-752-0848; 208 W Holly St) Bellingham's 'house of music' is hidden in this inviting century-old building and bereft of the traditional pub foibles of cigarette smoke, games machines and unsubtly positioned TV sets. Come here to enjoy local and national acts play jazz, blues, funk, salsa, rock and roll, and much more. Microbrew ales are served and dancing is de rigueur.

Pickford Cinema (☎ 360-738-0735; 1416 Cornwall Ave) If you can't face getting in the car to catch the latest blockbuster at a satellite mall, check out the latest art movie at the 88-seat Pickford, run by the Whatcom Film Association. Plans are currently afoot to move the venue to a refurbished historic downtown theater.

Mt Baker Theatre (☎ 360-734-6080; 106 N Commercial St) With its minaret-like tower and elaborately designed interior, this grand old historic theater, built in 1925, has become one of Bellingham's signature buildings. Showcasing everything from live music to dance to plays, the theater regularly draws in top name acts.

WWU Performing Arts Center (☎ 360-650-6146; www.pacseries.wwu.edu) WWU's Performing Arts Center usually features an intriguing lineup of international music and dance figures. See the website for the current program.

Getting There & Away

Bellingham International Airport is northwest of town off I-5 exit 258 and is served by **Horizon Air** (☎ 800-547-9308; www.horizonair.com) with daily flights to Seattle. **San Juan Airlines** (☎ 800-874-4434; www.sanjuanairlines.com) flies daily from Bellingham to the San Juan Islands and BC.

Bellingham is the terminal for the **Alaska Marine Hwy Ferries** (☎ 360-676-8445), which travel once a week up the Inside Passage to Juneau, Skagway and other southeast Alaskan ports. Passenger fares to Skagway start at $363; add a small car (up to 15ft), and the fare jumps to $1183. Cabins for the three-day trip cost an additional amount and can be hard to come by, so reserve well in advance.

The **San Juan Islands Shuttle Express** (☎ 888-373-8522; www.orcawhales.com) travels daily (March to October only) from the Fairhaven ferry terminal to San Juan and Orcas Islands ($20/33 one way/round-trip). Bicycles are welcome on board with a $3/5 surcharge.

Ferries run by **Victoria San Juan Cruises** (☎ 360-738-8099; Bellingham Cruise Terminal, 355 Harris Av, Ste 104) run between Bellingham's Alaska Ferry Terminal and Victoria's Inner Harbor daily between May and September at 9am (from $49.50 one way, three hours).

DETOUR: CHUCKANUT DRIVE

Motor speedily along I-5 and you could be forgiven for thinking that northwestern Washington is an ugly hotchpotch of sprawling suburbs and uninspiring big box superstores. But veer a couple of miles to the west into the surrounding countryside and a whole new world unfolds before your eyes.

Chuckanut Dr, or state route 11, is one of the West Coast's most spectacular and understated coastal back roads, a thin ribbon of winding asphalt that provides a refreshing alternative to the car chaos of the traffic-choked interstate. Running 21 miles from Burlington in Skagit County to Old Fairhaven in Bellingham, the route traverses pastoral farmland, craggy coastline, hidden beaches and a 2500-acre state park, offering such myriad diversions as hiking, cycling, beach-combing and fine dining along the way.

Defying steep oceanside terrain, the 'drive' was first laid out in 1896 to link Whatcom County with Mt Vernon and Seattle to the south. In 1912 a railcar was added on the northern part of the route and in 1915 local entrepreneur Charles Larrabee donated 20 acres of Chuckanut Mountain to make Washington's first state park. But in the 1920s, as traffic demands between Seattle and Vancouver exploded, Hwy 99 (now I-5) was constructed further east to ply an easier route through the coastal lowlands, leaving Chuckanut as something of a rural road relic.

Scenery rather than speed has always been Chuckanut's raison d'être and these days the drive is a haven for walkers, cyclists (who ply the 6-mile Inter-urban trail from Fairhaven to Larrabee), oyster lovers (the drive boasts a trio of excellent oyster restaurants) and people showing off their fancy soft-top sports cars. If you're ambling by in the early afternoon be sure to pull over at the quirky Northwest meets ethnic **Rhododendron Café** (☎ 360-766-6667; 5521 Chuckanut Dr; 🕒 11am-9pm Wed-Sun) or the spectacularly located **Oyster Bar** (☎ 360-766-6185; 2578 Chuckanut Dr; 🕒 11.30am-10pm) for a laid-back lunch.

Greyhound buses serve Bellingham on the Seattle–Vancouver run, with four heading north to Vancouver ($16.50, two hours) and another four going south to Seattle ($17, 2½ hours). The **depot** (☎ 360-733-5251) is in the same building as the Amtrak station in Fairhaven.

The **Airporter Shuttle** (☎ 800-235-5247; www.airporter.com) runs around the clock to Sea-Tac airport ($34/60 one way/round-trip) and stops at the Val-U Inn Motel, just off I-5 exit 253; and at Bellingham airport. **Quick Shuttle** (☎ 800-665-2122; www.quickcoach.com) runs between downtown Vancouver and Bellingham airport five times a day ($22/40 one way/round-trip).

Daily Amtrak trains from Vancouver, BC (from $13, one hour 50 minutes), and Seattle (from $20, two hours 25 minutes) stop at the **train depot** (☎ 360-734-8851) at the end of Harris Ave, near the ferry terminal.

Getting Around

The city has a fairly extensive local bus system run by **Whatcom Transportation Authority** (☎ 360-676-7433). Bus 15 connects downtown Bellingham with the Bellis Fair shopping mall, buses 105 and 401 run to Fairhaven and the Alaska ferry terminal, and bus 50 runs out to Gooseberry Point and the ferry embarkation for Lummi Island. Fares start at 75¢ for local trips.

ANACORTES

pop 14,370

As the primary embarkation point for the San Juan Islands, Anacortes is often looked upon as being a 'mainland' settlement, though in reality this venerable port town is on an island itself (Fidalgo Island) – albeit one that is attached to the rest of the US by a bridge.

Most travelers view Anacortes from the ugly urban thoroughfare of Commercial Ave (SR 20), with its humdrum motels and insipid fast-food franchises, on their way through to the ferry terminal. But downtown Anacortes – if you make it that far – is a fetching mix of appetite-quenching restaurants and stately old buildings embellished by life-sized cutouts of past city residents that have been tacked onto almost every available wall. If your ferry doesn't show up, there are far worse places to pass an evening.

Orientation & Information

Anacortes is on Fidalgo Island, separated from the mainland by a narrow channel, 17 miles west of I-5 on Hwy 20. The downtown harbor skirts the edge of the business district, giving the town a detectable maritime air. If you're planning on a stopover, drop by the **Visitor Information Center** (☎ 360-293-3832; www.anacortes-chamber.com; 819 Commercial Ave; 9am-5pm Mon-Fri, 10am-3pm Sat & Sun).

Sights & Activities

The **Anacortes History Museum** (☎ 360-293-1915; 8th St & M Ave; 11am-5pm daily Jun-Aug, weekends only Apr, May, Sep & Oct) has photo exhibitions showcasing the area's maritime history. Nearby the **Snagboat Heritage Center** (713 R Ave; admission $2) contains the restored hulk of the *W.T. Preston* Snagboat that operated on Puget Sound between 1929 and 1981 removing navigational hazards from the waterways.

For prime picnic spots and attractive oceanside hiking and biking trails make your way over to **Washington Park** just west of the ferry terminal.

Sleeping & Eating

Islands Inn (☎ 360-293-4644; 3401 Commercial Ave; r from $64;) The coziest of the cluster of motels on Commercial Ave, this well-equipped inn is run by a Dutch couple from Amsterdam and offers a wide variety of spacious rooms, some with whirlpool tubs. Le Petite Restaurant is also onsite.

Majestic Inn & Spa (☎ 360-299-1400; www.majesticinnandspa.com; 419 Commercial Ave; r queen/king bed $129/159; wi-fi) Housed in Anacortes' most eye-catching construction, the Majestic Inn & Spa offers the best of both worlds, with plush modern amenities adding value to a building of longstanding historical significance. Expect bathrobes in your closet and whirlpool tubs in your bathroom. If you're fresh from a muscle-wrenching outdoor adventure in the San Juan Islands, the in-house spa could be an appropriate tonic.

La Vie en Rose (☎ 360-299-9546; 418 Commercial Ave; 8am-5:30pm Mon-Sat) The French name lures you into this local bakery in historic downtown and, while it's unlikely that you'll encounter Johnny Hallyday escaping through the door with a baguette under his arm, you *will* find delicate pastries, artisan breads and delicious desserts, all made from scratch onsite. Start loading up for the ferry.

Rockfish Grill/Anacortes Brewery (☎ 360-588-1720; 320 Commercial Ave; fish and chips $7) If you're in the area, this place is worth a visit in its own right on two counts: firstly, the local brew beer and secondly, the hearty pub grub. Try the halibut and chips washed down with a pilsner, or plump for the Aviator Doppelbock in which case you'll probably want to skip lunch.

Getting There & Away

The **Airporter Shuttle** (☎ 800-423-4219; www.airporter.com) offers eight runs a day from Mt Vernon to Anacortes and the San Juan ferries (one way/round-trip $6/10). The shuttle picks up passengers from the Ferry Terminal and the Texaco station on 14th St and Commercial Ave (no reservations required). Connections can be made in Mt Vernon to Bellingham and Sea-Tac airport.

Skagit Transit (☎ 360-757-4433; www.skat.org) bus 410 travels hourly between Anacortes (10th St and Commercial Ave) and the San Juan ferry terminal. Bus 513 connects Anacortes with Mt Vernon's Skagit Station four times a day.

LOWER SKAGIT RIVER VALLEY

The Lower Skagit River Valley is prime farming country with a climate and terrain not dissimilar to that of Holland. As a result many of the region's early settlers (some of whom were Dutch) reclaimed land and built dikes across this rich river delta in an attempt to replicate the fertile fields of northern Europe. Not by coincidence, tulips, daffodils and irises are cultivated here during the spring months when the fields become a colorful patchwork of blooming flowers grown primarily for their bulbs and seeds. The best time to visit is during the annual tulip festival that runs from late March to early May.

Mt Vernon

pop 22,059

The rather unlikely winner of the 1998 'Best Small City in America' prize, Mt Vernon is a place that most people only see the back end of as they race through on their way to Seattle or Vancouver on I-5. And, despite its prominence as a local farming center and headquarters for Skagit County's annual tulip festival, they're not missing much. Aside from a summer farmers market and a rather quaint theater (the Lincoln), Mt Vernon is a bit of a damp squib. Far more alluring are La Conner to the west or Mt Baker to the east.

For a cheap stopover try the **West Winds Motel** (☎ 360-424-4224; 2020 Riverside Dr; r from $47;) just off I-5, a 40-room motel that was renovated a couple of years ago. For a tasty tipple check out the **Skagit River Brewing Company** (☎ 360-336-2884; 404 S 3rd St) an atmospheric pub that sells its own home-brew beers including English-style bitter, IPAs and the famous Trumpeter stout. You can also load up on savories here, including fine pizza.

La Conner

pop 760

Undisturbed by modern development and unblemished by the passage of time, La Conner, established in 1867, is one of the Lower Skagit River Valley's oldest trading posts and still retains much of its 19th-century charm. Characterized by a vintage row of classic wooden house-fronts set on the narrow Swinomish Channel, this small, unpretentious rural settlement has changed little since the 1890s when its position as northwestern Washington's transport nexus was stolen by nearby Mt Vernon.

La Conner is geographically compact consisting of a small grid of architecturally appealing houses and shops that fan out along with the commercial hubs of Morris and First Sts. But what the town lacks in size it makes up for in its imperceptible atmosphere, an aura that has lured in such prestigious writers as Tom Robbins to set up homes and search for artistic inspiration among the blooming tulips.

In what passes for downtown La Conner, specialist shops flaunt olive oil, cafés sell traditional tea and scones, and wild turkeys roam the streets as if Christmas has never happened. Across the Swinomish Channel on Fidalgo Island the river's eponymous Native American reservation provides plenty of extra local color.

SIGHTS & ACTIVITIES

La Conner's three small, yet interesting, museums are highly informative and well-maintained. The **Museum of Northwest Art** (☎ 360-466-4446; www.museumofnwart.org; 121 S 1st St; admission $5; 10am-5pm Tue-Sun) endeavors to portray the 'special Northwest vision' through the works of representative artists. The ground floor is dedicated to changing shows by regional artists, and the upstairs space houses pieces from the permanent collection.

Perched atop a hill that affords impressive views of Skagit Bay and the surrounding farmlands, the **Skagit County Historical Museum** (☎ 360-466-3365; 501 S 4th St; adult/6-12yr & senior $4/3; 11am-5pm Tue-Sun) presents indigenous crafts, dolls, vintage kitchen implements and other paraphernalia utilized by the region's early inhabitants.

Of more specialized interest is the **La Conner Quilt Museum** (☎ 360-466-4288; 703 S 2nd St; admission $4; 10am-4pm Wed-Sat, noon-4pm Sun), displaying quilt art of several generations. The museum is housed in the old Gaches mansion, which has stood here since 1891.

La Conner really comes alive in spring when the annual **Skagit County Tulip Festival** (☎ 360-428-5959; www.tulipfestival.org) lights up the surrounding countryside with all shades of red, purple, yellow and orange. Events include wine tasting, bike tours and bird's-eye helicopter rides over the expansive fields.

You can pick up helpful maps to orientate yourself at the **La Conner Chamber of Commerce** (☎ 360-666-4778; Morris St). A good place to kick off is at the renowned **Roosengaarde Display Garden** (☎ 360-424-8531; 15867 Beaver Marsh Rd, Mt Vernon; admission $5; 9am-6pm Mon-Sat, 11am-4pm Sun) half-way between La Conner and Mt Vernon. The 3-acre garden plants 250,000 tulip bulbs annually and, with Mt Baker and a Dutch inspired windmill glimmering in the background, photo opportunities abound. Bring a camera!

SLEEPING

Hotel Planter (☎ 360-466-4710, 800-488-5409; fax 360-466-1320; 715 S 1st St; d $75-129; ⊠) This refurbished hotel offers a decent blend of c 1907 charm and modern amenities, including a covered hot tub in the courtyard. Children are allowed on weekdays only.

our pick **The Queen in the Valley Inn** (☎ 360-466-4578; www.queenofthevalleyinn.com; 12757 Chilberg Rd; r $109-149) Half a mile out of town, this super-friendly B&B is well worth the hike. Beautifully furnished with a designer's attention to detail, four rooms and a suite are geographically themed as Africa, West Indies, India and Hong Kong, and boast some fascinating round-the-world memorabilia. Bonuses include old-fashioned bathtubs, an extensive book-and-magazine collection (including old *Life* magazines), homemade cake and a scrumptious breakfast served in a glassed-in wraparound porch. Memorable.

La Conner Channel Lodge (☎ 360-466-1500; 205 N 1st St; r $149-289;) Though of recent vintage, this handsome luxury lodge does its best to look in keeping with the rest of old La Conner. Large and airy rooms have fireplaces and decks facing the channel and a polished grand piano adorns the lounge.

A few hundred yards away, the **La Conner Country Inn** (☎ 360-466-3101; 107 S 2nd St) offers similar facilities and prices.

EATING

Calico Cupboard (☎ 360-466-4451; 720 S 1st St; mains $7-12; 🕑 7:30am-4pm, until 5pm weekends) A busy local bakery-café that has now expanded its operations to two further outlets in Anacortes and Mt Vernon, the Calico is good for take-out and sit-down. Among the many specialties are bread pudding, fresh pastries, omelettes and light lunches. The atmosphere is congenial and inviting.

La Conner Brewing Co (☎ 360-466-1415; 117 S 1st St; pizzas $8-9, sandwiches $7-8; 🕑 11:30am-10pm, till 11pm Fri & Sat) A polished-pine eating and drinking joint that manages to combine the relaxed atmosphere of a café with the quality beers (including IPA and stout) of an English pub. Bonuses include wood-fired pizzas, fresh salads and eight home brews on tap.

Kerstin's (☎ 360-466-9111; 505 S 1st St; lunch $11-19, dinner $18-25; 🕑 noon-9pm Wed-Mon) This is La Conner's most sophisticated dining experience where gourmet food and a romantic candlelit interior have sent many a culinary reviewer home happy. The ever-changing menu features whatever's in season, from oysters to king salmon to fresh summer veggies – most of which is grown locally. Market fresh fish is an in-house staple.

WHIDBEY ISLAND

Measuring 41 miles north to south, Whidbey Island is one of the largest contiguous islands in the US. It is also quite possibly one of the greenest. Endowed with six state parks, a unique National Historical Reserve, a budding artist and writer's community, plus a free – yes free – island-wide public bus service, there's more to this little emerald oasis than meets the eye. For those in doubt check out tiny Coupeville, Washington's third established settlement, or jaw-dropping Deception Pass with its hostile gushing rapids, or one of approximately 140 meticulously restored B&Bs that vie for top 10 ranking among thousands of refugee Seattleites who head here every summer.

Whidbey's independent spirit comes largely from its insularity coupled with the fact that – along with nearby Camano Island – it comprises a separate county (Island County). However, despite successive inroads of major mainland influences – in particular the air naval base at Oak Harbor – the Whidbey Islanders have carefully managed to retain vestiges of their 19th-century pioneer history; first and foremost through the establishment of Ebey's Landing National Heritage Reserve (p118), the first venture of its kind in the US. Comparisons between Whidbey and the San Juans are common, though not entirely fair. With its handy bridge link to nearby Fidalgo Island and closer proximity to Lower Puget Sound, Whidbey Island is inevitably more hectic than the likes of Orcas and Lopez (Deception Pass State Park is actually Washington's busiest state park). But stick around here after the crowds have gone home and you'll gradually note a distinctive 'Whidbey-ness' amid the surrounding greenery.

Orientation & Information

Elongated and narrow, Whidbey Island is bisected north to south by Hwy 525, which links the island by ferry to the mainland suburb of Mukilteo; and by Hwy 20, the main northern artery, which crosses dramatic Deception Pass via two narrow bridges on its way to Anacortes and the San Juan Island ferries. The two highways join near the center of the island, at the intersection of the Keystone–Port Townsend ferry spur.

Deception Pass State Park

Captain George Vancouver originally supposed Whidbey Island to be a peninsula. Eventually Joseph Whidbey – who set off in a small boat to explore and map Puget Sound – found this narrow cliff-lined crevasse churned by rushing water, that Whidbey's insularity was confirmed. Deceived no more, the spectacular narrow passage got a name – though even today it remains a challenge to navigate a motorized boat through it.

Emerging from the flat pastures of Fidalgo Island, Deception Pass leaps out like a mini Grand Canyon, its precipitous cliffs overlooked by a famous bridge made all the more dramatic by the sight of the churning, angry water below. The bridge consists of two steel arches that span Canoe Pass and Deception Pass, with a central support on Pass Island between the two. Visitors to the 5.5-sq-mile

park (☎ 360-675-2417; 41229 N State Hwy 20) usually introduce themselves to the spectacular land and seascape by parking at the shoulders on either end and walking across the bridge. Built during the 1930s by the Civilian Conservation Corps (CCC), the bridge was considered an engineering feat in its day. The park also spans the channel, with facilities – including campgrounds – on both the north and south flanks of the passage.

More than 3.5 million visitors per year visit Deception Pass, which makes it Washington's most popular state park. Besides the dramatic bridge overviews, the park's attractions include over 15 miles of saltwater shoreline, seven nearby islands, three freshwater lakes, boat docks, hundreds of picnic sites and 27 miles of forest trails. Scuba divers and sea kayakers explore the area's reefs and cliff-edge shores. Organized kayak tours (from $30 per person) depart from Bowman Bay; contact the **Deception Pass Adventure Center** (☎ 360-293-3330) to reserve.

The park sports three **campsites** (☎ 888-226-7688; standard $17, full utility $24) with over 300 spaces nestled in the forests located beside a lake and a saltwater bay. Facilities include running water, flush toilets, hot showers and snack concessions. Reserve well ahead for summer weekends, as competition can be fierce.

Oak Harbor

pop 19,795

There are two main distinctions between the San Juan Islands and Whidbey Island. Firstly, Whidbey has a mainland bridge connection (via Deception Pass) and secondly it has Oak Harbor, a modern mishmash of box-like chain stores and uninspiring urban development that looks rather like a Seattle suburb, relocated and shunted 70 miles to the north. Dominated by Naval Air Station Whidbey Island, completed in 1942, Oak Harbor is a military town with a distinguished Irish and Dutch heritage dating back to the late 19th century. Today it accommodates the island's largest marina, a notable playhouse and – surprise, surprise – plenty of indigenous Garry oak trees.

Ever keen to shake off its lackluster image, Oak Harbor has embarked upon a major charm offensive in recent years with a redevelopment plan emphasizing its nautical heritage and waterfront amenities. The helpful **Oak Harbor Visitor Center** (☎ 360-675-3755; 32630 State Rte 20; 10am-5pm Mon-Fri), situated on the main drag through town, should be able to put you straight on the town's not-always-so-obvious attractions.

Oak Harbor's most striking and culturally distinctive lodging has to be the **Auld Holland Inn** (☎ 360-675-2288; 33575 State Rte 20; r $49-149;), an admirable nod at the town's Dutch heritage that dominates SR-20 with its long timber-beamed frontage and towering old-fashioned windmill. Run by a family from Holland, the rooms and service here live up to their European promise, and extra bonuses include an outdoor swimming pool, a gym, a children's playground and a gift shop that sells authentic clogs. The hotel also has an excellent onsite restaurant.

Coupeville

pop 1723

The third oldest town in Washington, Coupeville is the county seat of Island County and an integral part of Ebey's Landing National Historical Reserve. As attractive as nearby Oak Harbor is ugly, the town's tiny village-sized seafront is filled with arty craft shops, antique stores and old inns facing Penn Cove, a small bay that is noted for its oyster and mussel production. Named after Nova Scotia sea captain, Thomas Coupe – who made the first land claim here in 1852 – Coupeville's vintage main street and charmingly barnacled wharf (the oldest in Puget Sound) doesn't look like it's changed much since the lumber shipping days of the 1890s, bar the odd iPod-wielding Seattleite or two.

Coupeville's **Visitor Information Center** (☎ 360-678-5434; www.centralwhidbeychamber.com; 107 S Main St; 10am-5pm) is just south of Hwy 20.

SIGHTS & ACTIVITIES

The island's most comprehensive museum, the **Island County Historical Society Museum** (☎ 360-678-3310; 908 NW Alexander St; admission $3; 10am-5pm May-Sep, 10am-4pm Fri-Mon Oct-Apr) has plenty of local historical testimonies showcased in meticulous and well-presented display cases. Also on offer are self-guided walking tour maps of Coupeville's vintage homes. The helpful staff can also enlighten you on the highlights of Ebey's Landing National Historical Reserve (p118).

Ten miles south of Coupeville lies **Whidbey's Greenbank Berry Farm** (☎ 360-678-7700; www.greenbankfarm.com; Hwy 525 off Wonn Rd; 10am-5pm) the world's largest producer of loganberries, a sweet, blackish berry rather like a black raspberry. The winery-style farm is open daily for touring, tasting and picnicking.

SLEEPING & EATING

Captain Whidbey Inn (☎ 360-678-4097; 2072 W Captain Whidbey Inn Rd; s/d $85/95, cabins $175, cottages $275, all incl breakfast) They don't come any more outlandish than this. The Captain Whidbey is a 1907 inn built entirely out of rust-colored madrone wood. The result is a construction that is as captivating as it is surreal. Indeed, with its low ceilings, creaky floors and cozy lounge strewn with faded copies of *National Geographic*, the inn feels more like something out of a medieval forest than a 21st-century tourist island. Lodging is in 12 wonderfully quaint guest rooms in the main lodge (with a bathroom down the hall), as well as wood-heated cottages and a more modern building with verandahs facing a lagoon.

Anchorage Inn (☎ 360-678-5581; www.anchorage-inn.com; 807 N Main St; r $89-149) Continuing the Northwestern penchant for Victorian-style B&Bs, this place comes up trumps with plenty of lace curtains, patterned wallpaper and old-fashioned upright chairs. Seven rooms with private bathrooms are encased in a turreted house overlooking Penn Cove and the owners even run a course on inn-keeping. As is often the case in houses replete with antiques and china, children under 14 aren't permitted.

Coupeville Inn (☎ 360-678-6668; www.coupevilleinn.com; 200 Coveland St; d $90-120;) It bills itself as a motel, but with its French architecture, oak furniture and rather plush interior this is far from your standard highway sleepover. Situated close to Coupeville's tiny town center, this plush place is a bargain given the fancy furnishings and complimentary continental breakfast.

Knead & Feed (☎ 360-678-5431; 4 Front St; sandwiches & salads $6-8; 10am-3pm Mon-Fri, 9am-4pm Sat & Sun) Perched on the waterfront with great views over mollusk strewn Penn Cove, this charming waterfront eatery serves fresh bread and pastries, as well as deli-style salads and soups.

Toby's Tavern (☎ 360-678-4222; 8 Front St; mains $7-13) A quintessential Coupeville pub housed in a vintage mercantile building dating from the 1890s, Toby's historic setting is personified by its polished back bar that was originally shipped here around Cape Horn in the year 1900. These days the attention to detail is no less fastidious, with home-produced microbrews and a menu spearheaded by such local classics as beer butter onion rings, clam strips, and halibut and chips.

Ebey's Landing National Historical Reserve

This unique National Historical Reserve was the first of its kind in the nation and was created in 1978 in order to preserve Whidbey Island's historical heritage from the encroaching urbanization that had already partly engulfed Oak Harbor. Ninety percent privately owned, **Ebey's Landing** (☎ 360-678-3310; admission free; 8am-5pm Oct 16-Mar 31, 6:30am-10pm Apr 1-Oct 15) comprises 17,400 acres encompassing working farms, sheltered beaches, two state parks and the town of Coupeville itself. A series of interpretive boards shows visitors how the patterns of croplands, woods (or the lack of them) and even roads reflect the activities of those who have peopled this scenic landscape, from its earliest indigenous inhabitants to 19th-century settlers.

For information on Ebey's Landing, contact the Island County Historical Museum in Coupeville (p117), which distributes a brochure on suggested driving and cycling tours through the reserve.

At the reserve's south end is **Fort Casey State Park** (☎ 360-678-4519), with facilities for camping and picnicking. Fort Casey was part of the early 1900s military defense system that once guarded the entrance to Puget Sound. Visitors can investigate the old cement batteries and underground tunnels that line the coast. Other recreational activities here include scuba diving, boating and bird-watching – best along Keystone Spit on the southwest tip of Crockett Lake. **Admiralty Head Lighthouse**, built in 1861, houses the park's interpretive center. From here, it's a 4-mile walk north along the beach to **Fort Ebey State Park** (☎ 360-678-4636), a wonderfully secluded spot with eroded cliffs and old WWII-era coast defenses, where further trails meander off into the surrounding woodland.

Fort Casey State Park offers 38 campsites overlooking Keystone Harbor, and Fort Ebey has 53 sites ($17) plus four with RV hookups ($24). Facilities include flush toilets and running water.

A unique lodging option is **Fort Casey Inn** (☎ 360-678-8792; www.fortcaseyinn.com; 1124 S Engle Rd; r $125). The inn consists of a series of five c 1909 houses that served as WWI officers' quarters and are now rented as overnight accommodations (the rooms sleep up to four guests). Perched on a bluff overlooking the lighthouse at Fort Casey, the houses have restful porches with oak armchairs.

Langley

pop 959

Langley, like Coupeville, is a tiny seafront community that is little changed since the late 19th century. Encased in an attractive historical center lie small cafés, antique furniture shops, funky clothes boutiques and a couple of decent B&Bs. While there's little to do here activity-wise, Langley provides a perfect antidote to the hustle and bustle of nearby Seattle and is a great place to relax and unwind, after numerous hours packed bumper to bumper on I-5.

Langley is 8 miles north of Clinton and the ferry service from Mukilteo, making this the closest of the Whidbey Island communities to the urban areas of northern Seattle.

SLEEPING & EATING

Eagles Nest Inn (☎ 360-221-5331; www.eaglesnestinn.com; 4680 E Saratoga Rd; r $125-175) A unique octagonal house located on a forested hill, the Eagle's Nest is a veritable B&B gem even by Whidbey Island's high standards. Four lovingly furnished rooms blend perfectly with their natural surroundings, while luxurious extras such as locally roasted coffee, aromatherapy shampoos, private lounge (with piano) and well-stocked cookie jar add a memorable touch. The property is adjoined by 400 acres of public trails.

The Inn at Langley (☎ 360-221-3033; www.innatlangley.com; 400 1st St; r incl breakfast $189-325; wi-fi) This contemporary, condo-esque inn is the trendsetter in style and expense. The 26 beautifully furnished waterfront rooms have large windows, whirlpool tubs and fireplaces. A full-service spa provides Swedish massage and seaweed body masks. There's just the small matter of the cost.

Cafe Langley (☎ 360-221-3090; 113 1st St; lunch under $10, dinner $11-17) Ah, at last: some choice Mediterranean cuisine; with a few deft Northwest seafood infusions (eg mussels) thrown in for good measure. There are some amazing lamb options here (at least five), an Andalusian steak, Italian pasta, Greek moussaka and a memorable sweet, sticky baklava for dessert. Delicioso!

Getting There & Around

The **Airporter Shuttle** (☎ 800-235-5247; www.airporter.com) offers frequent bus service to Oak Harbor from Sea-Tac ($34/60 one way/round-trip) or from Bellingham ($12/22); transfer at Mt Vernon for the Whidbey-bound connection. Prepaid reservations are required to ensure a seat.

Services from Washington State Ferries run between Clinton and Mukilteo (car and driver/passenger $8.60/$3.95. 20 minutes) and between Keystone and Port Townsend ($11.15/$2.60, 30 minutes).

Island Transit buses run the length of Whidbey daily except Sunday, from the Clinton ferry dock to Greenbank, Coupeville, Oak Harbor and Deception Pass. Other routes reach the Keystone ferry dock and Langley on weekdays. Service is hourly and free. For more information, call ☎ 360-678-7771 or check out the website www.islandtransit.org.

SAN JUAN ISLANDS

Sailing to the San Juan archipelago is like entering another world; a greener, cleaner America where bark-stripped madrone trees outnumber buildings, and cars play second fiddle to bicycles. There's no big city hustle here, and the small cluster of populated islands are bereft of the tainting influences of street crime, big box supermarkets or anything resembling a coffee franchise. Instead the San Juan Islands float like tree-carpeted time capsules at the nautical nexus of the Georgia Strait, Puget Sound and the Strait of Juan de Fuca just as they have done for centuries; a small slice of Old World Americana cut out and preserved for posterity.

There are 450 landfalls in this expansive archipelago if you count every rock, sandbar, islet and eagle's perch between Anacortes and the Canadian border, though only about 200 of these islands are named, and of these, only a handful are inhabited. Washington State Ferries service the four largest – San Juan, Orcas, Shaw and Lopez Islands – while others are only accessible to the select few, lucky enough to brandish a private boat or sea plane.

Inhabited for centuries by native peoples, the Spanish were the first Europeans to chart this region and they were closely followed by the British under Captain George Vancouver in 1792. The domain of lime merchants

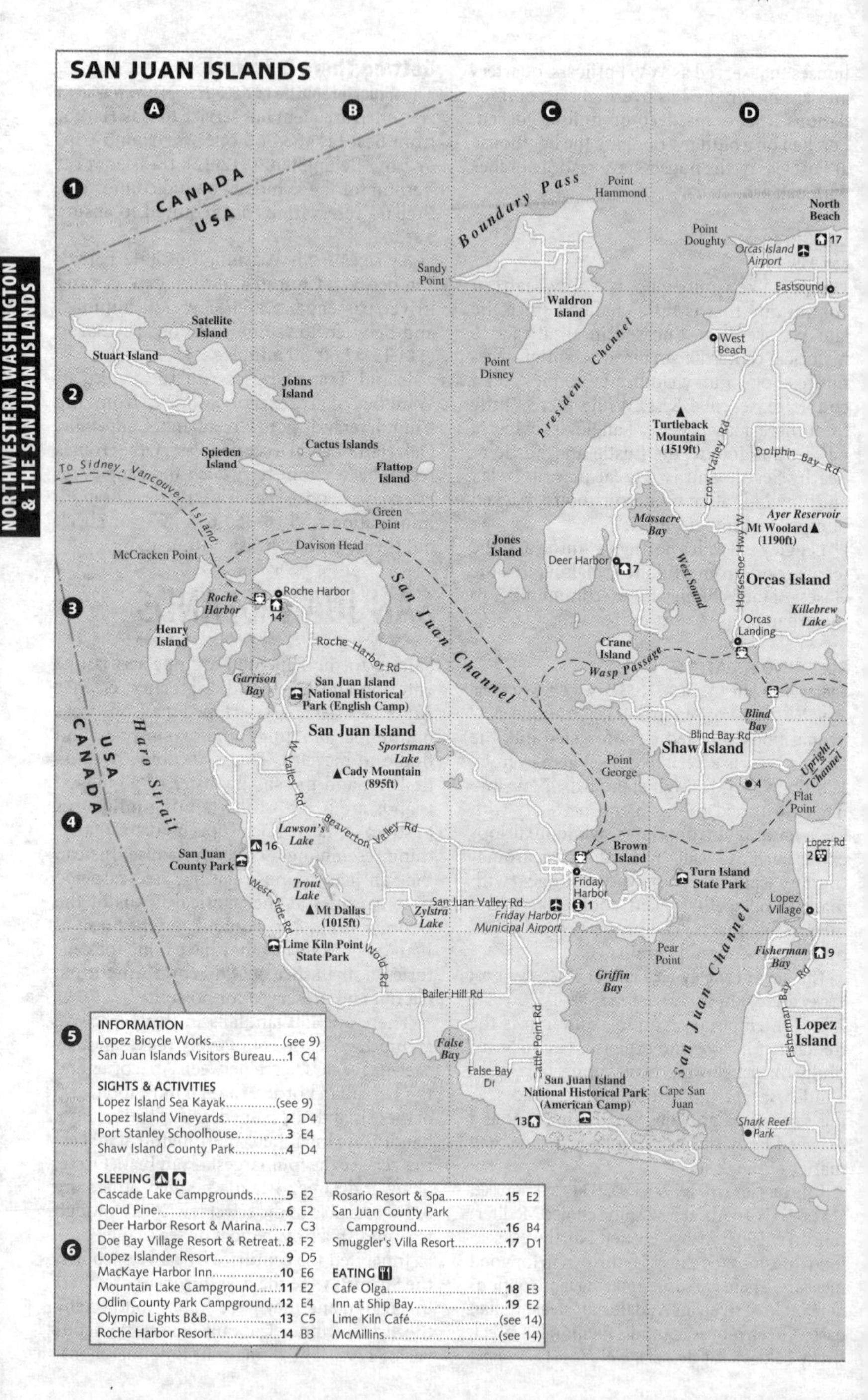
SAN JUAN ISLANDS
A
B
C
D
1
2
3
4
5
6
CANADA
USA
Boundary Pass
Point Hammond
North Beach
Point Doughty
Orcas Island Airport
17
Eastsound
Sandy Point
Waldron Island
Satellite Island
Stuart Island
West Beach
Johns Island
Point Disney
President Channel
Turtleback Mountain (1519ft)
Crow Valley Rd
Dolphin Bay Rd
Spieden Island
Cactus Islands
Flattop Island
To Sidney, Vancouver Island
Green Point
Massacre Bay
Ayer Reservoir
Mt Woolard (1190ft)
Horseshoe Hwy W
Davison Head
Jones Island
Deer Harbor
7
West Sound
Orcas Island
McCracken Point
Roche Harbor
14
Killebrew Lake
Henry Island
Orcas Landing
Crane Island
Roche Harbor Rd
San Juan Channel
Wasp Passage
Garrison Bay
San Juan Island National Historical Park (English Camp)
Blind Bay
San Juan Island
Blind Bay Rd
Shaw Island
USA
CANADA
Haro Strait
Sportsmans Lake
Cady Mountain (895ft)
W Valley Rd
Point George
4
Upright Channel
Flat Point
Lawson's Lake
Beaverton Valley Rd
16
San Juan County Park
Brown Island
Lopez Rd
2
Friday Harbor
Turn Island State Park
West Side Rd
Trout Lake
Mt Dallas (1015ft)
San Juan Valley Rd
Zylstra Lake
Friday Harbor Municipal Airport
1
Lopez Village
Lime Kiln Point State Park
Wold Rd
Pear Point
Fisherman Bay
9
Griffin Bay
Bailer Hill Rd
Fisherman Bay Rd
False Bay
Cattle Point Rd
Lopez Island
False Bay Dr
San Juan Island National Historical Park (American Camp)
Cape San Juan
13
Shark Reef Park
INFORMATION
Lopez Bicycle Works....................(see 9)
San Juan Islands Visitors Bureau.....1 C4
SIGHTS & ACTIVITIES
Lopez Island Sea Kayak..............(see 9)
Lopez Island Vineyards.................2 D4
Port Stanley Schoolhouse.............3 E4
Shaw Island County Park...............4 D4
SLEEPING
Cascade Lake Campgrounds.........5 E2
Cloud Pine.....................................6 E2
Deer Harbor Resort & Marina.......7 C3
Doe Bay Village Resort & Retreat..8 F2
Lopez Islander Resort....................9 D5
MacKaye Harbor Inn....................10 E6
Mountain Lake Campground.......11 E2
Odlin County Park Campground..12 E4
Olympic Lights B&B....................13 C5
Roche Harbor Resort...................14 B3
Rosario Resort & Spa..................15 E2
San Juan County Park Campground...........................16 B4
Smuggler's Villa Resort...............17 D1
EATING
Cafe Olga....................................18 E3
Inn at Ship Bay...........................19 E2
Lime Kiln Café.........................(see 14)
McMillins.................................(see 14)

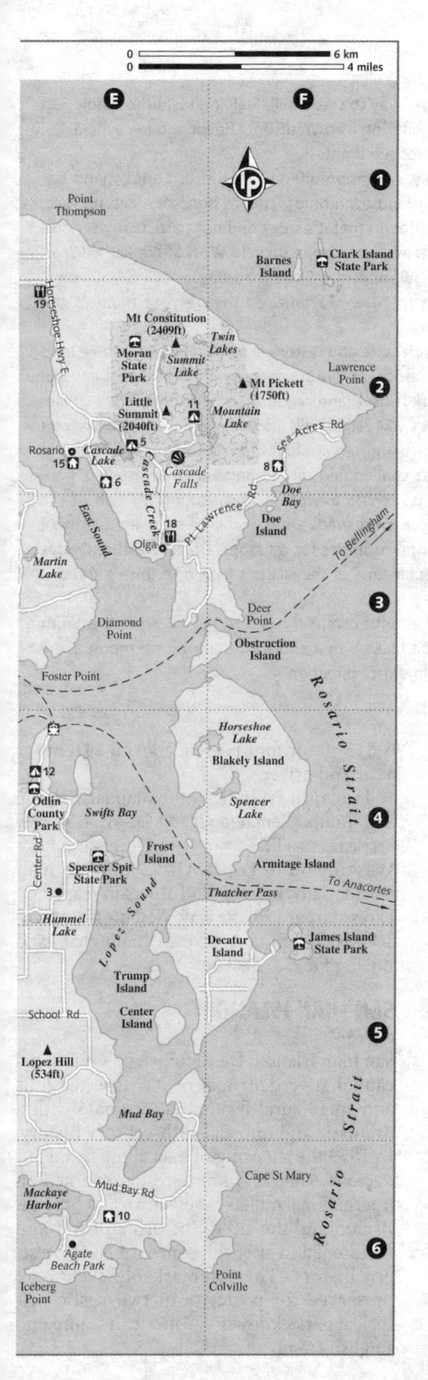

and small-scale farmers for much of the 20th century, tourism first arrived on the islands rather controversially during the 1980s and '90s, when vacationing Puget Sounders discovered the San Juan's quiet, rural ambience and slower, laid-back style of living to be the perfect antidote to the stresses of modern urban living.

Information

For general information about the San Juans, contact the **San Juan Islands Visitors Bureau** (☎ 360-468-3663, 888-468-3701; www.guidetosanjuans.com; The Technology Center, 640 Mullis St, Bldg A, Ste 210/215, San Juan Island; 10am-2pm Mon-Fri). Its website provides links to numerous San Juan businesses and organizations. In addition, the chambers of commerce of San Juan, Orcas and Lopez Islands maintain their own visitor walk-in information centers – see those sections for details.

Getting There & Away

The majority of people who visit the San Juans arrive on **Washington State Ferries** (WSF; ☎ in Washington 800-843-3779, elsewhere 206-464-6400; www.wsdot.wa.gov/ferries) who run a fleet of comfortable and efficient car ferries. The principal port on the mainland is Anacortes, and ferries for the four principal islands of Lopez, Shaw, Orcas and San Juan depart from here. From April to December, one Washington State Ferry a day continues on to Sidney, near Victoria, on Vancouver Island before returning in the opposite direction. There is no US–Canada service from January to March.

You can pick up an easy-to-decipher WSF timetable at any ferry outlet or access it on the website. The timetable varies depending on the season, but follows a standard route of Anacortes–Lopez–Shaw–Orcas–Friday Harbor–Sidney. Four or five ferries a day are inter-island in that they don't call at either Sidney or Anacortes.

You can only reserve tickets for the Sidney sailing. All other ferries operate on a first-come, first-served basis. In winter, drivers are advised to arrive 45 minutes before sailing; in summer, two hours.

Travel time from Anacortes to the closest island, Lopez, is roughly 45 minutes; to the most distant island port, Friday Harbor on San Juan, it's 1¼ hours; and to Sidney, it's three hours.

CYCLING THE SAN JUANS

The best – some would go so far to say the *only* – way to see, smell, feel and taste the scenic San Juan Islands is on two wheels. With each island offering its own distinct flavor and idiosyncrasies, the possibilities for memorable biking adventures are limitless.

With its exceptionally flat terrain and friendly, salutation-offering motorists, Lopez Island has long been a traffic weary cyclist's heaven. The island even holds its own bona fide cycling race, the annual Tour de Lopez – a typical Lopezian affair in that it's short and not particularly serious. You can rent bikes on Lopez from May to September at **Lopez Bicycle Works** (☎ 360-468-2847; 2847 Fisherman Bay Rd; mountain bikes per hr/day $7/30), opposite Fisherman Bay or bring your own. Either way, don't forget to adjust your watch to '*Slow-pez* time' and wave your hand at the trickle of passing motorists.

San Juan Island is undulating and studded with state and historical parks. The classic bike loop starts in Friday Harbor, spins north to Roche Harbor, before tracking south along the beautiful West Coast in time for a sparkling Lime Kiln Park sunset (and possibly some spontaneous whale-watching). Bikes can be hired at **Island Bicycles** (☎ 360-378-4941; 380 Argyle Ave; mountain bikes per hr/day $7/35) handily located in Friday Harbor, two-and-a-half blocks from the ferry terminal.

Hilly Orcas Island offers the San Juan's most challenging terrain and Lance Armstrong wannabes shouldn't miss the tough 5-mile climb up to the top of Mt Constitution for one of the West Coast's most awe-inspiring views. Elsewhere most roads are paved, and there are plenty of well-placed cafés and juice bars offering ideal opportunities for pit-stops. Orcas' **Wildlife Cycles** (☎ 360-376-4708; 350 North Beach Rd, Eastsound) details nine of the island's best bike routes and can deliver hire bikes to the ferry landing.

While secluded Shaw Island has only one overnight campsite, its forested 7.5-sq-mile interior is a cyclist's dream and the island can easily be tackled in a short morning or afternoon. Ferry shuttles from the other islands pass regularly in either direction.

There are three additional privately owned passenger-only ferries (no cars) that travel to the San Juans. **Victoria San Juan Cruises** (☎ 360-738-8099; www.whales.com; 355 Harris Ave, Suite 104, Bellingham) operates between Bellingham, San Juan Island, Orcas and Victoria from May to September; the **Puget Sound Express** (☎ 360-385-5288; www.pugetsoundexpress.com) runs from Port Townsend to Friday Harbor from March to September; and the **Victoria Clipper** (☎ Seattle & Victoria 206-448-5000, elsewhere 800-888-2535; www.victoriaclipper.com) is a Seattle/Friday Harbor link, with service on to Victoria, BC. It only runs from late June to late September.

On Washington State Ferries to the San Juans, fares are collected on westbound journeys only. High-season fares for a car and driver from Anacortes start at $23.35 to Lopez Island, $27.95 to Shaw and Orcas Islands and $33.25 to San Juan Island, plus a surcharge for each additional passenger. Foot passengers pay $9.60 and cyclists pay a surcharge of $2 for bikes. Foot passengers and cyclists can ride inter-island ferries free in either direction.

The peak season one-way fare for the international ferry between Anacortes and Sidney is $15.60 for foot passengers and $41.90 for a car and driver.

Two airlines fly from the mainland to the San Juans. **Kenmore Air** (☎ 866-435-9524; www.kenmoreair.com) flies from Lake Union and Lake Washington to Lopez, Orcas and San Juan Islands daily on three- to 10-person seaplanes. Fares start at $75 one way. **West Isle Air** (☎ 800-874-4434) flies from Anacortes, Bellingham and Boeing Field in Seattle.

SAN JUAN ISLAND

pop 6894

San Juan Island is the archipelago's unofficial capital, a verdant mix of low forested hills and small rural farms that resonate with a dramatic and unusual 19th-century history. In 1859 the shooting of a local pig by an audacious American homesteader sparked an international military showdown that brought Britain and the US to the brink of war and threatened to alter the course of Northwestern history. These remarkable events are preserved for posterity in two rustic historical parks known as American Camp and English Camp.

Splaying out from the commercial hub of Friday Harbor (the archipelago's only incorporated town) San Juan's undulating terrain is more varied than Lopez but less precipitous than Orcas. The west coast is the island's scenic highlight, a picturesquely wooded shoreline studded with rust-colored madrone trees and craning firs where the rocky foothills of Mt Dallas (1036ft) plunge dramatically into the deep Haro Strait, creating a form of oceanic upwelling that provides an ideal feeding ground for marine mammals such as Orcas, porpoise and seals.

Orientation & Information

The ferry terminal is at Friday Harbor, on the eastern side of the island. The main route south from here is Cattle Point Rd, while Beaverton Valley Rd heads to the west coast. To get to Roche Harbor, take 2nd St to Guard St, then turn right on Tucker Ave; from there it's a 10-mile drive to the resort.

San Juan Island's **chamber of commerce** (☎ 360-378-5240; Spring St) is inside a small arcade and is a good place to pick up free maps and other information.

Sights & Activities

SAN JUAN ISLAND NATIONAL HISTORICAL PARK

More coveted for their scenery than their history, the San Juans nonetheless hide one of the 19th-century's oddest political confrontations, the so-called Pig War between the USA and Britain. This curious 19th-century 'cold war' is showcased in two separate historical parks on either end of the island that once housed opposing American and English military encampments.

On the southern flank of the island, the **American Camp** hosts a small **visitors center** (☎ 360-378-2902; ⌚ 8:30am-4:30pm Thu-Sun, daily Jun-Sep) and is a good place to start your historical excursion. Among the remnants of an old fort are the officers' quarters and a laundress' house, while a series of interpretive trails lead to earthwork fortifications, a British farm from the dispute era and desolate South Beach. The 1.8-mile hike along the ridge of Mt Finlayson makes for a pleasant hike with splendid views and unlimited bird-watching potential.

At the opposite end of the island **English Camp**, 9 miles northwest of Friday Harbor, contains the remains of the British military facilities dating from the 1860s. A path from the parking area leads down to a handful of restored buildings that lie in an attractive setting overlooking Garrison Bay. Hikes from here lead to an old British cemetery and the top of 650ft Young Hill.

LIME KILN POINT STATE PARK

Clinging to the island's rocky west coast, this beautiful park overlooks the deep Haro Strait and is, reputedly, one of the best places in the world to view whales from the shoreline. There is a small **interpretive center** (☎ 360-378-2044) in the park open from Memorial Day (last Monday in May) to Labor Day (first Monday in September) along with trails, a restored lime kiln and the landmark Lime Kiln lighthouse built in 1919. Orca and minke whale sightings are more common in summer after the June salmon run. Offering exceptional views of Vancouver Island and the Olympic Mountains, the park is best enjoyed at sunset.

FRIDAY HARBOR

With a population of approximately 2000 people, Friday Harbor is the San Juan's only real town, with restaurants, shops and a couple of interesting museums providing enough diversions to fill a good morning's exploration. In recent years a growing contingent of realty offices has added to the disquiet. But realtors aside, Friday Harbor is still a low key, pedestrian-friendly kind of place where the worst kind of hassle you're likely to face is an uneven paving stone.

If you've only got time for one sight, be sure to pop into the **Whale Museum** (☎ 360-378-4710; 62 1st St; adult/5-18yr $6/3; ⌚ 10am-5pm), a small but cleverly arranged display space dedicated to the life of the orca (killer whale), which has become something of a San Juan Island mascot. Among whale skeletons and life-size models of orcas, there are eloquent DVD presentations, interactive maps and details of local research projects, all of which will teach you everything you need to know about these magnificent but cruelly misunderstood sea mammals.

In an 1890s farmhouse on the outskirts of town, the **San Juan Historical Museum** (☎ 360-378-3949; 405 Price St; adult/6-18yr $2/1; ⌚ 10am-4pm Thu-Sat, 1-4pm Sun May-Sep, 1-4pm Sat Mar-Apr & Oct) commemorates early pioneer life on San Juan Island. While the building itself is interesting for its vernacular architecture, the displays of kitchen and parlor furnishings – like the pump organ and massive wood range – are also worth checking out.

SEA KAYAKING & BOATING

Fishing trips for black bass and tiger rockfish can be arranged through **Trophy Charters** (☎ 360-378-2110; www.fishthesanjuans.com) who do half-day fishing tours aboard a 29ft sport fisher from $95 per person. Bareboat charters are available from **Charters Northwest** (☎ 360-378-7196; www.chartersnw.com; 2 Spring St) at $1250 a week for a 30ft vessel.

WHALE-WATCHING

Western Prince Cruises (☎ 800-757-6722; www.orcawhalewatch.com) is the San Juan Island's oldest whale-watching tour company and its year-round eco-friendly excursions keep an eye out for eagles, seals and porpoises as well as the formidable orcas. Tours on the Western Prince, which accommodates up to 30 people, depart daily from June to August (adult/child under 13 years $65/45), less often and less expensively in spring and fall. You can make reservations via its website or visit the office right next to the ferry dock in Friday Harbor.

SCUBA DIVING

Friday Harbor is the home of **Island Dive & Water Sports** (☎ 360-378-2772; www.divesanjuan.com; 2A Spring St Landing), the San Juan Island's only fully fledged dive operator. Chartered half-day expeditions cost $79/94 for two/three tanks and you can arrange a NAUI open water certification for $325, plus $50 for equipment hire.

Sleeping

San Juan County Park Campground (☎ 360-378-1842; 380 West Side Rd; hiker/biker sites per person $5, sites $20) San Juan's best campsite is beautifully located in a county park on the scenic western shoreline. The site includes a beach and boat launch, along with 20 pitches, flush toilets and picnic tables. At night the lights of Victoria, BC, flicker theatrically from across the Haro Strait. Reservations are mandatory during peak season.

Wayfarer's Rest (☎ 360-378-6428; 35 Malcolm St; dm $30, r $60) At last, a San Juan backpacker's hostel nestled amid all the $100 plus hotels and inns. Even better, the Wayfarer's is only a short hike from the Friday Harbor ferry terminal. Budget travelers will love this breezy place with its comfortable dorms and cheap private rooms. Linen, blankets, tea, coffee and fresh eggs are all part of the package, as is use of a fully equipped kitchen and cozy living space, but beware – this place gets busy.

Orca Inn (☎ 877-541-6722; 770 Mullis St; r low season from $49, high season $59; ❄) Seven blocks from Friday Harbor ferry terminal, the budget Orca is more motel than inn, with the barracks-like atmosphere not exactly in keeping with the rather luscious surroundings. But if price is your main parameter, the Orca's small, simple rooms with air-con and private bathrooms are an acceptable option.

Roche Harbor Resort (☎ 800-451-8910; www.rocheharbor.com; Roche Harbor; r $79-99, condo $143-205, 2-bedroom townhouse $375-425; ❄) Located on the site of a former lime kiln and country estate, this seaside 'village' is a great getaway for all budgets. More than 100 years after its initiation as the company hotel of limestone king John McMillin, the place is still taking guests, who enjoy its slightly faded gentility. The centerpiece of the resort is the old world Hotel de Haro whose pokey rooms and shared bathrooms are enlivened by the fact that John Wayne once walked the corridors and Teddy Roosevelt is known to have brushed his teeth in the sink. Brand new townhouses are stacked up behind the harbor, and modern condominiums are discreetly tucked behind a stand of trees. Waterfront restaurants, a 377-berth marina with boat rentals and an old dockside general store make the place pretty self-contained.

Olympic Lights B&B (☎ 360-378-3186; www.olympiclightsbnb.com; 146 Starlight Way; r $99-150; ⊠) Once the centerpiece of a 320-acre estate, this splendidly restored 1895 farmhouse now hosts an equally formidable B&B that stands on an open bluff facing the snow-coated Olympic Mountains. The four rooms are imaginatively named Garden, Ra, Heart and Olympic; sunflowers adorn the garden and the hearty breakfasts include homemade buttermilk biscuits. The wintertime room rates are a relative bargain at $99.

Friday Harbor House (☎ 360-378-8455; www.fridayharborhouse.com; 130 West St; r low season $150, high season $250; ❄) The town's most exclusive lodging is a modern boutique hotel with great views over the harbor. All 20 rooms have a fireplace, open-plan bathroom/Jacuzzi tub and other upscale niceties, and the whole place exudes a surgical level of cleanliness.

Eating

Doctor's Office (☎ 360-378-8865; 85 Front St; ⏰ 5am-9pm) A venerable coffee/sandwich joint conveniently situated next to the ferry line up which is locally famous for its home-made ice-cream. On a hot summer's day it's worth arriving 15 minutes early for the creamy luxury.

our pick **Lime Kiln Cafe** (☎ 800-386-3590; Roche Harbor; mains $5-9; ⏰ 8am-2pm) Perched on the end of the Roche Harbor marina wharf, this simple but pleasurable establishment serves up mouth-watering American breakfasts that feature organic eggs in an enticing San Juan scramble with avocado and sour cream. The lunch menu offers deli sandwiches. Even better, fresh home-cooked doughnuts are served all day.

Rocky Bay Cafe (☎ 360-378-5051; 229 Spring St; brunch $5-9; ⏰ 6:30am-3pm) Hit this cheerful establishment for a classic all-day breakfast or brunch. Highlights include eggs benedict, huge buttermilk pancakes and a hearty serving of oatmeal with cranberries, walnuts and brown sugar. Service is down-to-earth and friendly, and you'll likely find the whole family – including baby – in the kitchen.

Hungry Clam (☎ 360-378-3474; 130 1st St; seafood baskets $6-9; ⏰ 11am-7pm) A good option if you've got a long wait for your ferry ride but, while the fish and chips here aren't bad, they're not really worthy of their 'world famous' label.

Friday's Crabhouse (☎ 360-378-8801; Front St; seafood platters $10; ⏰ seasonally) It's on the harbor and sells fish al fresco – what more could you want? This place serves big platters of oysters, calamari or scallops on three open-air decks. Dungeness crab is the house specialty.

Front Street Ale House & San Juan Brewing Company (☎ 360-378-2337; 1 Front St; supper $10-17; ⏰ 11am-11pm Mon-Thu, 11am-midnight Fri & Sat) The island's only brewery serves up British-style beers, including Royal Marine IPA, in a real spit-and-sawdust style pub. Traditional pub grub features shepherd's pie and bangers-and-mash, and it ain't 'arf bad (as they say in London).

McMillin's (☎ 360-378-5757; Roche Harbor; mains $17-25; ⏰ 5-10pm) Set in the former house of lime and cement entrepreneur John S McMillin, this intimate dining room offers the best of Pacific Rim cooking. Favorites include hazelnut crusted halibut, and local spot prawn and Dungeness crab ravioli.

Getting Around

From May to October, **San Juan Transit** (☎ 360-378-8887) shuttles visitors from the ferry landing to Roche Harbor, plus points along the west coast, including Lime Kiln Point State Park and the English Camp. Buses run hourly between 9am and 6pm (round-trip $8, day pass $15). Otherwise, call **San Juan Taxi** (☎ 360-378-3550).

Susie's Mopeds (☎ 360-378-5244; 125 Nichols St), just up from the ferry dock, rents mopeds at $25 an hour, $62.50 a day; or Geo Tracker jeeps from $96 a day.

ORCAS ISLAND

pop 4593

Precipitous, unspoiled and ruggedly beautiful, Orcas Island is the San Juan's emerald jewel: a steeply wooded and lightly populated rural outpost that is home to wealthy retirees, traditional farmers, eccentrics, innkeepers, back-to-the-landers, second homers and plenty of other assorted drop-outs from the big city rat race.

Lapped by the ebbing waters of Upper Puget Sound and nestling in the dry rain shadow of the storm-lashed Olympic Mountains, the island was once an important trading post for the North Straits Salish Native Americans who maintained a permanent settlement in present day West Sound. The first European homesteaders arrived in the 1860s and within a couple of years they had set about clearing the old growth rain forest for crops and fruit orchards. Another early industrial project was lime production and by the early 20th century 35 lime kilns dotted the island, burning huge amounts of local wood.

The growth of tourism is a distinctly modern development and an inevitable consequence of Orcas' enviable natural beauty and refreshing get-away-from-it-all location. Former Seattle mayor, Robert Moran, opened the doors to the deluge in the early 1900s when he constructed a Xanadu-like mansion, the Rosario (now a hotel; see p127), overlooking the shimmering waters of East Sound and donated large tracts of his private land to create Moran State Park.

These days, of all the San Juan Islands, Orcas is perhaps the most diverse, offering the best mix of isolation and integration. You can eat well here or stay in a luxury cliff-top cottage, but the island's forte is still its good old-fashioned friendliness and refreshing closeness to nature.

Orientation & Information

Orcas Island is shaped like a saddlebag, with two distinct lobes very nearly cleaved by East Sound. The ferry terminal is at the tiny community of Orcas Landing, on the western half of the island. Roads lead north and then west to the village of Deer Harbor and, on the other side of Turtleback Mountain, to West Beach. The island's main population center is Eastsound, at the northern extreme of the eponymous fjord, where the two halves of the island meet. Most tourist and commercial facilities are available here, including a post office, laundry, bank, grocery store and gas station. The eastern half of the island is essentially comprised of Moran State Park and of resorts scattered along the coastline, most notably Rosario Resort, whose centerpiece is a mansion and spa built in 1910 by a former mayor of Seattle.

For more information, contact the **Orcas Island Chamber of Commerce** (☎ 360-376-2273; www.orcasisland.org; North Beach Rd, Eastsound; 🕑 8am-5:30pm Mon-Fri, 10am-3pm Sat).

Sights & Activities

Housed in a series of six original homesteader cabins dating from the 1880s, the **Orcas Island Historical Museum** (☎ 360-376-4849; www.oracsmuseum.org; 181 North Beach Rd, Eastsound; admission $2; 🕑 10am-3pm Tue-Sun, to 6pm Fri, late May-late Sep) relates the pioneer and local history of Orcas and the San Juan Islands. Besides the usual collection of household goods, tools, weapons and photographs, there's a history of the lime kiln industry and a focus on Orcas' first residents, the North Straits Salish.

The fourth-largest state park in Washington, 7-sq-mile **Moran State Park** (☎ 360- 376-2326; 🕑 6:30am-dusk Apr-Sep, 8am-dusk Oct-Mar) on the island's eastern saddlebag has enough attractions to consume the best part of a day. The park is dominated by 2409ft **Mt Constitution**, the archipelago's highest point and a mountain with the grandeur of a peak twice its size. To say that the view from the summit is jaw-dropping would be an understatement. On a clear day you can see Mt Rainier, Mt Baker, Vancouver's north shore and a patchwork of tree-carpeted islands floating like emerald jewels on a blue crystalline ocean. To see above the lofty firs a 53ft **observation tower** was erected in 1936 by the Civilian Conservation Corp.

For drivers, the mountain has a paved road to the summit, though the view is infinitely better if you earn it via a 4.3-mile hike up from Cascade Lake's North End Campground or a 5-mile cycle that begins just past Cascade Lake. Beginners beware; the grade is a persistent 7% (7ft vertical rise for every horizontal 100ft) with frequent hairpin turns.

The park's two major bodies of water, **Cascade Lake** and **Mountain Lake**, offer campgrounds, good trout fishing, rentable paddle boats and rowboats, picnic areas, and swimming beaches. The lakes are also ringed by hiking trails and linked via a pleasant wooded ramble that passes the spectacular 100ft-high **Cascade Falls**.

Of the more than 30 miles of trails in Moran State Park, about half are open seasonally for mountain biking. Get a trail map from the park headquarters at the south end of Cascade Lake.

BOATING & WHALE-WATCHING

Deer Harbor Charters (☎ 800-544-5758; Deer Harbor Resort) offers year-round whale-watching trips departing from either Deer Harbor or the Rosario resort. The boats run on biodiesel and sightings of orca and minke whales are common. Prices are $49/59 low/high season, for a half-day cruise.

Orcas Boat Rentals (☎ 360-376-7616; www.orcasboats.com) at Deer Harbor Marina, has powerboats and sailboats from $175 per half-day.

Sleeping

Moran State Park (☎ 360-376-2326; hiker/biker sites $6, standard sites $13) The largest camping area in the San Juans has more than 150 campsites (no hookups) at four lakeside locations: one at Mountain Lake and three at Cascade Lake. Reservations are a must in summer.

Doe Bay Village Resort & Retreat (☎ 360-376-2291; www.doebay.com; hostel dm $16, tree house/yurt from $49, cabin d $67-89, additional person $14) There are resorts, and then there's Doe Bay, 18 miles east of Eastsound on the island's easternmost shore – as lovely a spot as any on Orcas. By far the least expensive resort in the San Juans, Doe Bay has the atmosphere of an artists' commune, cum hippie retreat cum New Age center. Accommodations include campsites, a small hostel with dormitory and private rooms, and various cabins and yurts, most with views of the water. There's a natural-foods store and a café where healthy meals

ROBERT MORAN

The story of Robert Moran is a classic rags-to-riches tale with a rather inauspicious ending. A native of New York City, Moran first arrived in the frontier town of Seattle in 1875, aged 18, with only 10¢ in his pocket. Settling down to run a ship repair business with his brother he worked hard, profiting well out of the Klondike Gold Rush in 1897–98 when Moran Bros built 12 paddle steamers to run prospectors along the Yukon River. In 1888 at the age of just 31, Moran was elected Seattle's first mayor and he presided heroically over the city during the great fire of 1889 when 30 blocks of the central business district were reduced to piles of smoldering rubble. Post 1890, Moran sunk his efforts back into shipbuilding with ever larger contracts culminating in the construction of the destroyer USS *Nebraska* in 1904.

It was in the same year that, after a routine visit to his doctor, the 47-year-old Moran was told that, due to an escalating heart condition brought on by stress, he only had a year to live. Concluding that his days were numbered, he retired to the island of Orcas where he bought a 7800-tract of land upon which he constructed his dream retirement home – the exquisite Rosario estate (see below).

Not surprisingly, the rarified atmosphere of Orcas worked wonders for Moran's health and within a year or two he was back to his salutary best. But rather than return to his shipbuilding business (which he sold in 1906), the maverick former entrepreneur became something of a local environmentalist donating over 2000 acres of his own private estate to form the Moran State Park in 1921.

Falling on hard times during the Great Depression Moran was forced to sell his estate to a Californian industrialist for only $50,000 in 1938. It was a sad, if respectful, farewell. Seeing out the last five years of his life in a small house on Orcas, he died at the advanced age of 86 in 1943, a lasting testament to the convalescing powers of the salubrious San Juan Islands.

are served up family-style. The sauna and clothing-optional hot tub are set apart on one side of a creek.

Outlook Inn (☎ 360-376-2200, 888-688-5665; www.outlook-inn.com; Main St, Eastsound; r with shared bathroom $84, motel r $140, ste $245) Eastsound's oldest and most eye-catching building, the Outlook Inn (1888) is an island institution that has kept up with the times by expanding into a small bayside complex. The cheapest rooms have shared bathrooms, while rooms in the motel-style east building have private bathrooms. The positively luxurious bay view suites boast Jacuzzi tubs. Also onsite is the rather fancy New Leaf Cafe (p129).

Orcas Hotel (☎ 360-376-4300; www.orcashotel.com; Orcas Landing; r $89-208; ☒) This quintessential Orcas hotel was built in 1904 and is one of the island's oldest and most attractive buildings. Refurbished in the 1990s the place still retains a quaint 'English' feel, with narrow corridors, patterned wallpaper and a carefully manicured garden. Perched on a bluff above the ferry terminal there are a dozen individually crafted rooms here, along with a restaurant and a small coffee/sandwich bar. While not in the luxury bracket it oozes plenty of old world charm.

Cloud Pine (☎ 360-376-41100; cottage from $125) An astounding location plus a whole host of fantastic extras make this hidden treasure one of the San Juan's best rural retreats. Cloud Pine is a delightfully furnished cottage – big enough to accommodate at least four people – perched scenically on a cliff overlooking Eastsound amid rustling Douglas firs and craning madrone trees. Cocooned in a wonderfully private setting, the accommodation consists of a kitchen, sitting room, bedroom, bathroom and outdoor hot tub, while the congenial owner welcomes guests with a cupboard full of basic groceries, plus a complimentary bottle of wine. Unforgettable.

Smuggler's Villa Resort (☎ 360-376-2297; www.smuggler.com; N Beach Rd; r low season $129-225, high season $259/325;) A little windswept on the north shore, this small complex comprises 20 reasonably sized holiday houses with fireplaces, right on the beach. Facilities include a marina, an outdoor pool and a tennis court, and it's packed with families in summer.

our pick Rosario Resort & Spa (☎ 360-376-2222; www.rosario-resort.com; Rosario Way; r $188-400; wi-fi) This magnificent seafront mansion built by former shipbuilding magnate Robert Moran (above) in 1904 is now an upscale resort,

SHAW ISLAND

The quietest and, in many ways, the quirkiest of the four main San Juan Islands, tranquil Shaw is famous for its restrictive property laws and handsome Benedictine monastery. Here enveloped in a pristine, tree-carpeted time warp, Catholic nuns tend to llamas, wild deer forage on deserted roadways and idyllic sandy beaches are sprinkled with a plethora of rather foreboding 'no trespassing' signs.

Aware of the rising property prices and burgeoning resort development of their larger and swankier neighbors, Shaw islanders have steadfastly resisted the lure of the tourist dollar and chosen to remain private. That's not to say that travelers aren't welcome. Plenty of ferries arrive daily on Shaw but with only one campsite offering just 12 overnight berths, opportunities to linger are limited.

For purists that is what the island is all about. Shaw is fondly redolent of Orcas 30 years ago (and the rest of America 60 years ago), a close-knit rural community where neighbor still helps out neighbor and kids play happily in the countryside free from the constrictions of modern living. Until recently, the ferry wharf and the island's only store were managed by three Franciscan nuns who collected tickets and directed traffic in bright yellow safety vests worn over their dark brown habits. But in 2004 the Franciscans moved on and today only the Benedictine and the Sisters of Mercy orders remain.

For curious travelers, Shaw is well worth a spin on a mountain bike or an afternoon of quiet contemplation. History buffs should make a beeline for the **Shaw Island Historical Museum** (☎ 360-468-4068; Blind Bay Rd) while perennial peace-seekers can find lazy serendipity on luscious South Beach in **Shaw Island County Park** (☎ 360-378-1842; Squaw Bay Rd).

though the setting has lost none of its F Scott Fitzgerald–style romance. While the old mansion remains the resort's centerpiece, the 180 modern rooms sprawled across the surrounding grounds retain deft design touches and the complex includes tennis courts, a swimming pool, a marina and elaborately tiled spa facilities.

Deer Harbor Resort & Marina (☎ 888-376-4480; www.deerharbor.com; cottage $189-259, ste $209-399) Nearly every building in this little hamlet, set alongside one of the island's loveliest harbors, is for rent, ranging from motel-style bungalows to quaint old-fashioned cottages, all featuring deck-top hot tubs. Boat and bike rentals, tennis courts, and a small restaurant and market are all on the premises.

Eating

Homegrown Market (☎ 360-376-2009; North Beach Rd, Eastsound; 9am-8pm; V) In keeping with Orcas Island's granola-eating, New Age image, this well-stocked natural-foods store offers the best in muesli, tofu and meat-free garden burgers; it's a great place to put together an organic, spray-free, fair-trade picnic lunch.

Enzo's Italian Caffé (☎ 360-376-8057; Orcas Landing; sandwiches $6-8) The island's newest food haven has filled a gap in the ice-cream market with first-class gelati greeting passengers fresh off the ferry. If you're traveling in the opposite direction, you can also preempt your return to 'civilization' with a tasty panini or an eye-opening Italian-style coffee.

Cafe Olga (☎ 360-376-5098; Olga Rd; mains $9-11; Mar-Dec) The definitive Orcas hangout is a quiet and relatively isolated café/art gallery in the tiny settlement of Olga on the island's secluded eastern saddlebag. Living up to the hype, the scones, cinnamon buns and pies here are stupendous and if you've just burnt 2000 calories cycling up and down Mt Constitution this place is a guaranteed lifesaver.

our pick **Bilbo's Festivo** (☎ 360-376-4728; 310 A St, Eastsound; mains from $14; 4-9pm) Even if Mexican isn't your *fuerte,* it's difficult to go wrong in this funky restaurant slap bang in the middle of Eastsound with its rustic Mexican furnishings and decorative restroom hand basins. Try the generous 'Fiesta platter' with refried beans, homemade guacamole, warm tortillas and some of the best enchiladas you'll taste this side of Tijuana. There's also a wide selection of margaritas.

Inn at Ship Bay (☎ 360-376-5886; 326 Olga Rd, Eastsound; mains $17-22; 5:30-11pm Tue-Sat) It ain't cheap but the locals swear by this upmarket place that quite possibly offers some of the best fare on the island. Seafood is the specialty and it's served in an attractive 1860s orchard house a couple of miles south of Eastsound. There's also an 11-room hotel here (doubles $175 to $195).

New Leaf Cafe (☎ 360-376-2200; Main St, Eastsound; mains $17-25; 5:30-11pm Thu-Mon) A great bayside setting within the historic Outlook Inn, the great crab cakes, delicious fondue and a formidable lamb shank make this place a winner, even if the price is a little tough on the wallet.

Getting Around

If you're not biking, the **Orcas Island Shuttle** (☎ 360-376-7433; www.orcasislandshuttle.com) can meet most of your transport needs, arranging car rental (from $59.95), 24-hour taxis ($1.50 per mile plus $5 per passenger) and a May to September public bus ($5 one way).

LOPEZ ISLAND

pop 2590

Lopez – or *Slow-pez* as locals prefer to call it – is the archetypal friendly isle, a bucolic blend of pastoral farmland and forested state parks where motorists wave congenial greetings and the pace of life hasn't changed much since Captain George Vancouver first sauntered by in 1792. The closest of the larger San Juans to the Anacortes ferry terminal, Lopez's 29.5 sq miles of largely flat terrain are a well-known haven for cyclists, while its sheltered bays and picturesque shoreline are a favorite destination for boaters and sea kayakers.

Though less well set up for tourism than its two more populous neighbors, Lopez's tight-knit community and well-organized infrastructure offer a surprisingly varied selection of campgrounds and B&Bs. Lopez village is the island's centerpiece, a tiny low-rise settlement that holds a weekly summer farmers market and boasts a couple of enterprising restaurants, while a couple of miles to the north, Lopez Island Vineyards showcase the island's local wine production. Every April Lopez stages the colorful Tour de Lopez, a laid-back noncompetitive cycle race where winning is incidental. The balloons are out again on July 4, when the island temporarily breaks out of its sleepy stupor to host one of the state's most electrifying firework displays.

Orientation & Information

The ferry terminal is at the extreme north end of the island and consists of little more than a ticket office and a drinks machine. To reach civilization you have to travel 3 miles to the south to Lopez village, the island's main settlement which consists of a small collection of shops and restaurants, along with a bank (with ATM), post office and tiny historical museum. Just to the south of Lopez Village lies Fisherman Bay, home to a resort hotel and marina complex.

For information about businesses and recreation on Lopez Island, contact the **Lopez Island Chamber of Commerce** (☎ 360-468-3663; www.lopezisland.com). For a taxi, call **Angie's Cab** (☎ 360-468-2227).

Sights

The diminutive **Lopez Island Historical Museum** (☎ 360-468-2049; noon-4pm May-Sep) exhibits antiquated farm machinery, early pioneer photos and various rotating exhibitions. What it lacks in scale it makes up for in charm. The restored 1917 **Port Stanley Schoolhouse** in the settlement of the same name is run by the local historical society and offers a good photo op.

Lopez Island Vineyards (☎ 360-468-3644; 724 Fisherman Bay Rd; noon-5pm Fri & Sat May-Sep) has been making wines from grapes grown organically on the island since 1987. Drop by to sample its Madeleine Angevine and Siegerrebe varieties.

Activities

Skippered day and overnight fishing trips are available from **Harmony Charters** (☎ 360-468-3310; countess@interisland.net; 973 Shark Reef Rd) and **Kismet Sailing Charters** (☎ 360-468-2435), both of which operate out of Fisherman Bay. Visitors select from a number of organized packages, or they can schedule individualized tours or cruises. A lunch cruise on Harmony Charters' 63ft yacht costs $60 per person, while an overnight cruise with meals is $200 per person.

Sleeping

Odlin County Park (☎ 360-378-1842; 148 Odlin Rd; hiker/biker sites $10, standard sites $15) Handily situated a mile south of the ferry landing and 3 miles north of Lopez village, this pleasant waterfront campground features a picnic area, vault toilets and mooring buoys. There is an adjacent sandy beach, and hiking trails disappear off into the surrounding woods.

Lopez Islander Resort (☎ 800-736-3434; www.lopezislander.com; Fisherman Bay Rd; s/d/ste $90/129/249;) Equipped with a full-service restaurant,

KAYAKING THE SAN JUANS

With a large clutch of closely packed islands interspersed with calm, azure sea channels, exploring the San Juan archipelago by sea kayak is an increasingly popular activity. From a unique watery vantage point you'll spot whales, eagles, porpoises and harbor seals, and quickly begin to see these pristine emerald islands from an exciting new perspective. Kayak rentals and expeditions can be organized on San Juan Island with **San Juan Kayak Expeditions** (☎ 360-378-4436; www.sanjuankayak.com; Friday Harbor), a small owner-operated company with over 25 years local experience. Personally-guided kayak trips incorporating camping, whale-watching, birding and hiking run from June to September for $420/520 for three/four days. Alternatively you can rent an individual kayak for $70 a day.

On Orcas Island, **Shearwater Adventures** (☎ 360-376-4699; www.shearwaterkayaks.com) is a well-set up kayaking establishment based in Eastsound village. Aside from a fully equipped shop that sells new and used kayaks, the company offers everything from small guided half-day trips ($55) to custom tours.

Lopez Island Sea Kayak (☎ 360-468-2847; Fisherman Bay) offers similar facilities from May to September.

Kayaks can be transported on Washington State Ferries, both by vehicles and by accompanying pedestrians.

swimming pool and Jacuzzi, this bona fide 'resort' sits alongside a 64-slip marina in Fisherman Bay, where sea planes soar and eagles hover. Rooms run the gamut of singles, views, deluxe, suites and bungalows. What it lacks in intimacy, it makes up for in amiability and good service.

MacKaye Harbor Inn (☎ 360-468-2253; www.mackayeharborinn.com; 949 MacKaye Harbor Rd; r $99-159; ☒) Relatively isolated on Lopez's southern reaches, this 1927 farmhouse contains four bedrooms and one harbor-view suite and regularly gets good press. The cheap kayak rental and complimentary mountain bikes make it one of the best deals on the island.

Edenwild Inn (☎ 360-468-3238; www.edenwildinn.com; Lopez Rd, Lopez Village; r $165-185) Eden is the word at this Victorian-style mansion in Lopez village with its lovely formal gardens, wide porch and meticulous attention to detail. Encased in what must be the island's most sumptuous setting, are eight individually-crafted rooms all with private bathrooms. All of the island's low-key facilities are within shouting distance.

Eating

In keeping with their salutary 'waves' Lopezians are congenial and hospitable people who are always happy to engage visitors in casual chit-chat. Hang around in one of the village's small cafés long enough and you'll be sure to strike up a conversation with somebody.

Holly B's Bakery (☎ 360-468-2133; Lopez Rd; ⏲ Apr-Nov) With a welcome dearth of Northwest coffee chains, Holly's heads the early-morning latte and pastry rush. Follow the smell of freshly baked bread.

Isabel's Espresso (☎ 360-468-4114; Lopez Rd) A funky wood-paneled coffee bar that offers a fine selection of java coffee, herbal teas and fruit shakes, and features colorful furnishings and a small book collection.

Cafe La Boheme (☎ 360-468-2294; Lopez Rd; ⏲ 7am-4pm) Puffed cushions and Middle Eastern–style sofas lure you into this tiny local caffeine station where you can listen to a cacophony of local opinions – everything from George 'Dubya' to the merits of biodiesel versus gas – over coffee and cookies.

Vortex Juice Bar (☎ 360-468-4740; Lopez Rd S; lunch $4-6) Fresh juices are Vortex's forte, made with whatever fruits and vegetables are on hand. Hearty salads and wraps are among its other healthful offerings.

The Bay Cafe (☎ 360-468-3700; 9 Old Post Rd; mains $17-23) Lopez's plushest restaurant offers sunset dining right on the water with classic fish dishes, including Dungeness crab and seafood tapas.

Olympic Peninsula & Washington Coast

Hidden away in the nation's extreme northwest, Washington's spectacular coastline and heavily forested interior showcases over 350 miles of wild, storm-lashed beaches along with some of the country's most untainted and pristine rural ecosystems.

The jewel in the crown is the unique Olympic Peninsula and its eponymous national park, a remote and rugged amalgamation of glacier-coated mountains, misty cliffs and lush, temperate rain forest that encases a vast primeval wilderness where human habitation has been kept to a minimum. Untouched in over a millennium lie placid, sapphire lakes, ancient cedar and spruce forests, and steep, craggy mountain slopes that govern one of the wettest microclimates in the US – a weather system that dumps up to 200in of rain and snow annually on the Olympic's western mountains. Isolated from the rest of the state, the biodiversity astounds with a rich variety of plants offering a thousand different shades of green.

While the population centers in this region can't compete in size with the likes of Seattle and Spokane, cities such as Olympia, Port Townsend and Vancouver are colorful and distinct, encompassing everything from alternative music and Victorian architecture to the pioneering history of the British Hudson Bay Company.

East of this verdant Eden, the region is bordered by the craning Cascade Mountains and the arterial I-5 while, to the south, expansive beaches and small-scale resorts pepper Washington's premier coastal playground.

HIGHLIGHTS

- Discovering a precocious new band on a nighttime romp around Olympia's innovative **music scene** (p135)
- Watching inclement weather roll in over stormy **Hurricane Ridge** (p139)
- Seeking solitude on mist-enshrouded **Rialto Beach** (p153)
- Relaxing after a bracing hike in front of a fireplace at the **Lake Quinault Lodge** (p143)
- Remembering a bygone age at Port Townsend's nostalgic **Victorian Days festival** (p147)
- Flying a kite on expansive **Long Beach** (p158)

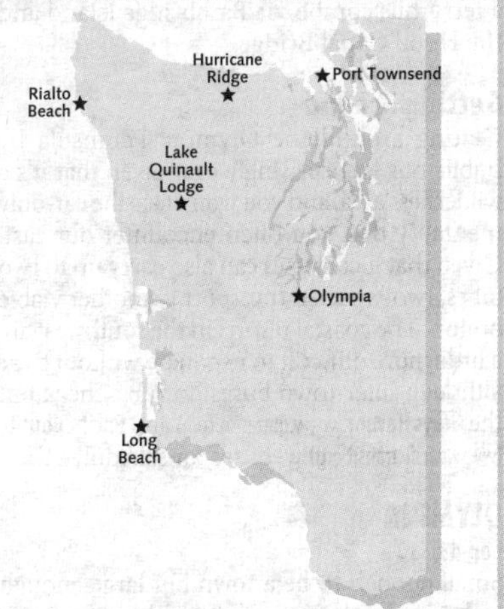

Geography & Climate

Rain, rain and yet more rain! It will come as no surprise to regular visitors that parts of the precipitous Olympic National Park are among the wettest places on earth. If you thought Seattle's 37 annual inches was hard to bear, try snapping open your umbrella in the Hoh Rain Forest where 200in of rain/snow is the norm. There are a few bright spots, however, most notably Sequim in the Northeast of the Olympic Peninsula where a marked rain shadow effect has resulted in the growth of a popular retirement community.

National Parks

The Olympic National Park is headquartered in Port Angeles and protects 922,561 acres of mountains, forest and coast. Earmarked as a national monument by President T Roosevelt in 1909, the area officially took on national park status in 1938 under President FD Roosevelt. It became an International Biosphere Reserve in 1976 and in 1981 was designated as a UNESCO World Heritage Site. Seven years later its protection was further assured by the formation of the Olympic Wilderness area.

Getting There & Away

Greyhound buses ply I-5 daily, stopping in Vancouver, Kelso, Centralia, Olympia, Tacoma and Seattle. Amtrak trains follow approximately the same route. Daily ferries from Victoria, Canada, serve Port Angeles in the north while the quickest access from Seattle and Sea-Tac International Airport is a ferry-bus combo via Bainbridge Island and the Hood Canal Bridge.

Getting Around

Getting around the Olympic Peninsula by public bus is surprisingly easy given that it's a wilderness area, and you won't face the car-only mentality that you often encounter out east. Given that local buses can also carry up to two bikes, two-wheeled transport is another viable option. The coastal resorts in the southwest are a little more difficult to negotiate without a car although inter-town buses do run. Check out the **Grays Harbor** (www.ghtransit.com) and **Pacific County** (www.pacifictransit.org) websites for schedules.

OLYMPIA

pop 43,330

Small enough to be a town but large enough to boast the dynamic cultural life of a more populous city, Washington's engaging state capital is full of unexpected surprises. Aside from being home to the magnificent State Capitol, Olympia sports other eye-catching architecture, a formidable oyster restaurant, an enlightened student population, a cluster of excellent brew pubs, numerous independent coffeehouses and a music scene that has helped define everything from grunge rock to riot grrrl feminism.

Characterized by its cool urban energy and revered for its close proximity to the scenic wonders of Mt Rainier and the Olympic National Park, Olympia has been attracting both indoor artists and outdoor adventurers for decades. Grunge pioneers Nirvana played some of their earliest gigs in the bars and pubs of downtown; Matt Groening, creator of *The Simpsons*, once edited the campus newspaper at progressive Evergreen College; and pioneering brewer, Leopold Schmidt chose the artesian water of nearby Tumwater to craft his smooth and flavorful Olympia beer. Under the circumstances, Olympians could be forgiven for being a little smug about their culture-defining city heritage. From its neo-Romanesque Old State Capitol Building in placid Sylvester Park to its exciting clutch of DIY musicians who enliven the nightspots of 4th Street, Washington's charismatic capital is a city that fully lives up to its grand, classical-sounding name.

Orientation & Information

Olympia is at the southern end of Puget Sound (an arm of the Pacific Ocean). I-5 passes through the town, running north to Seattle (60 miles) and south to Portland (114 miles).

Olympia is dominated by the Washington State Capitol campus, which rises on a bluff above Capitol Lake (formed by damming the Deschutes River). The fingerlike intrusion of Budd Inlet is Olympia's outlet to the sea and a docking area for boats and pleasure craft.

The **State Capitol Visitor Center** (☎ 360-586-3460; cnr 14th Ave & Capitol Way) offers information on the capitol campus, the Olympia area and Washington state. Backcountry permits for wilderness camping in Olympic National Park can be obtained from the **USFS office** (☎ 360-956-2300; 1835 Black Lake Blvd), west of town.

Sights & Activities

Looking like a huge Grecian temple, the **Washington State Capitol** complex dominates the town. Its beautiful setting, in a 30-acre park overlooking Capitol Lake with the Olympic Mountains glistening in the background, is a visitor favorite. The campus' crowning glory is the magnificent **Legislative Building** (admission free; 8am-4:30pm). Completed in 1927, it's a dazzling display of craning columns and polished marble, topped by a 287ft dome that is only slightly smaller than its namesake in Washington, DC.

As well as the Legislative Building, visitors are welcome to peek inside both the supreme court or **Temple of Justice** (admission free; 8am-5pm Mon-Fri) flanked by sandstone colonnades and lined in the interior by yet more marble, and the **Capitol Conservatory** (admission free; 8am-4pm Mon-Fri), which hosts a large collection of tropical and subtropical plants.

The oldest building on the campus is the **Governor's Mansion** (360-902-8880), (built in 1908. The home of the governor is open for tours only on Wednesdays; call to reserve a space. Outdoor attractions include the Vietnam War Memorial, a sunken rose garden, a replica of the Roman-style fountain found in Tivoli Park, Copenhagen, plus a Story Pole carved by Chief William Shelton of the local Snohomish tribe in 1938. The manicured grounds are an attraction in themselves and a well-marked path zig-zags down to Capitol Lake where it connects with more trails.

The **State Capital Museum** (360-753-2580; 211 W 21st Ave; adult/student/senior $2/1/1.75; 10am-4pm Tue-Fri, noon-4pm Sat & Sun) is housed in the 1920s Lord Mansion, a few blocks south of the campus, and preserves the general history of Washington state from the Nisqually tribe to the present day.

On the northeast corner of the State Capitol campus is the fun-filled **Hands On Children's Museum** (360-956-0818; 106 11th Ave; adult/child $7/4.50; 10am-5pm Tue-Sat, noon-5pm Sun) where creative exhibits on human anatomy and nature include a simulated X-ray machine and a TV studio where children can create their own weather reports.

The **Old State Capitol** (360-753-6725; 600 S Washington St; admission free; 8am-noon, 1-5pm Mon-Fri), in Sylvester Park was constructed in 1892 in an unusual Romanesque-revival style and now acts as an office for the State Superintendent of Public Instruction. Its nine-story central tower was badly burned in 1928, and the building's 11 turrets fell off during a 1949 earthquake. Nonetheless, the old capitol, with its castle-like facade and fairytale flourishes, is still a head-turner. Pick up a brochure for a self-guided tour at the 2nd-floor reception area.

When Olympia was founded, its narrow harbor was a mudflat during low tides, but after years of dredging, a decent harbor was established. **Percival Landing Park** is essentially a boardwalk along the harbor that overlooks the assembled pleasure craft and provides informative display boards that tell of Olympia's past as a shipbuilding port and a center of the lumber and cannery trades.

In the same vicinity is the **Olympia Farmers Market** (360-352-9096; 700 Capitol Way N; 10am-3pm Thu-Sun Apr-Oct, Sat & Sun Nov-Dec), the state's second-biggest farmers market after Seattle's Pike Place, and a great place to shop for organic herbs, vegetables, flowers, baked goods and the famous specialty oysters. Close by, the **Bartorf and Bronson Tasting Room** (360-753-4057; 200 Market St NE; 9am-4pm Wed-Sun), located in the company's coffee-roasting house, allows caffeine junkies to sample choice brands from Africa, Indonesia and Latin America. Knowledgeable staff provide the background facts.

The small **Yashiro Japanese Garden** (360-753-8380; 900 Plum St; admission free; 10am-10pm) adjacent to the city hall marks a collaboration between Olympia and its Japanese sister city, Yashiro. Highlights include a bamboo grove, pagoda and a pond and waterfall; stone lanterns and other gifts from Yashiro adorn the grounds.

Sleeping

Olympia Inn (360-352-8533; 909 Capitol Way S; s/d $50/57;) This unpretentious downtown motel is the city's cheapest and most central accommodation option. No-frills rooms are clean and kitted out with the usual fridge/microwave/cable TV triumvirate. Plus, rather than being stuck out in the suburbs, you're situated just blocks from both the State Capitol complex and the downtown coffee bars.

Phoenix Inn Suites (360-570-0555; www.phoenixinn.com; 415 Capitol Way N; s/d $99/109; wi-fi) The modern Phoenix is good value and dazzles guests with its sparkling modern interior and indoor pool and hot tub. What this small chain hotel lacks in character and charm, it makes up for in cleanliness, service and all-round comfort. The location, adjacent to Percival Landing, also puts you within baseball-pitching distance of one of Olympia's best oyster restaurants.

Swantown Inn (☎ 360-753-9123; www.swantowninn.com; 1431 11th Ave; r $99-179; wi-fi) In the true tradition of Washington state B&Bs, the Swantown Inn features great personal service and meticulous attention to detail in a 1887 Queen Anne–style mansion that is listed on the state historical register. Within sight of the imposing capitol dome, there are four elegantly furnished rooms, plus wi-fi internet access and a formidable breakfast that features the local specialty, ginger pancakes.

Governor Hotel (☎ 360-352-7700; www.olywagov.com; 621 Capitol Way S; d $160; wi-fi) The Governor seems to have suffered a little since its Ramada Inn days with the question 'refurbishment?' hot on the lips of many recent guests. But with its downtown location overlooking serene Sylvester Park plus its outdoor pool, fitness center, restaurant and convention facilities, it's still Olympia's largest and most obvious central accommodation choice.

Eating

Spar Cafe Bar (☎ 360-357-6444; 114 4th Ave E; breakfast $4-5, lunch $5-8; 7am-9pm) A legendary local café and eating joint where the coffee is strong and the banana caramel pancakes are something to write home about. But the ultimate draw card is its bustling, wood panel interior, complete with cigar displays and coffee pot–wielding waitresses, that hasn't changed much since the 1930s.

Urban Onion (☎ 360-943-9242; 116 Legion Way E; lunch $7; V) This low-key vegetarian place (with meat options) is accessed through a small shopping mall that once served as the old Hotel Olympian. It caters for tofu-lovers, vegans, plus anyone who just can't go much more than 24 hours without resorting to some variation of chicken. Highlights include the ravioli with mushrooms and a hearty lentil soup.

Mekong Restaurant (☎ 360-352-9620; 125 N Columbia St; entrees $7-9; V) Olympia is renowned for its ethnic eateries, but if you only have time for one, try the unfussy Mekong, a basic Thai place where the service is quick and the Pad Thai noodles are pan-fried to perfection. In typical Olympian fashion, the restaurant also has a wide selection of vegetarian and vegan options.

Trinacria (☎ 360-352-8892; 113 Capitol Way N; mains $10-12; V) A local legend for almost two decades, this hole-in-the-wall Sicilian-run restaurant evokes memories of *The Godfather* with its intimate interior and loud Italian music emanating from the kitchen. The delicious menu is heavy on garlic, homemade pasta and vegetarianism, and the place offers only one regular meat dish, the exquisite spaghetti ragu.

Oyster House (☎ 360-753-7000; 320 W 4th Ave; seafood dinners $15-20; 11am-11pm, till midnight Fri & Sat) Olympia's most celebrated restaurant also specializes in it's most celebrated cuisine, the delicate Olympia oyster, best served pan-fried and topped with a little cheese and spinach. Try them with the delicious potato skins in a booth overlooking the placid harbor and watch the boats come in.

Drinking

Batdorf & Bronson (☎ 360-786-6717; 513 Capitol Way S; 6am-7pm Mon-Fri, 7am-6pm Sat & Sun) Olympia's most famous coffee outlet is a reason in itself to visit this dynamic caffeine-fuelled city. If you like your morning brew fair trade, shade-grown and certified organic, this is the place to come. For travelers with an insatiable caffeine addiction, mosey on down to the company's new roasting house (p133) for some delicious coffee-tasting opportunities.

Fishbowl BrewPub (☎ 360-943-3650; 515 Jefferson St) Threatened with bankruptcy less than a decade ago, the Fishbowl has returned to brew with a vengeance, its classic selection of organic beers and India Pale Ales making it Washington's second-largest microbrewery. The company's cozy pub just across the road from its famous brewery is a must for all visiting beer aficionados and serves great oyster burgers.

Entertainment

Washington Center for the Performing Arts (☎ 360-753-8586; 512 Washington St) Comedy, art, ballet and plays – this is Olympia's primary venue for national touring shows and other cultural activities, and brings the city to center stage in Washington's surprisingly varied cultural life.

State Theater (☎ 360-786-0151; 202 4th Ave E) Harlequin Productions stages an eclectic lineup of contemporary plays and classics in this recently restored theater. Expect everything from Shakespeare to little-known musicals.

Capitol Theatre (☎ 360-754-6670; 206 E 5th Ave) Of 1924 vintage, the Beaux Arts–inspired Capitol Theater is the headquarters of the Olympia film society and shows art house

OLYMPIA'S MUSIC SCENE

With a small population and a workforce more attuned to drafting legislation than turning up guitar amps, Olympia is certainly one of America's most unlikely musical breeding grounds. But, thanks to a combination of lousy weather, a progressive state college (Evergreen) and the presence of plenty of forward-thinking local innovators such as Calvin Johnson (former member of the band Beat Happening and founder of K Records), the city has spawned a music culture that has reached far beyond the confines of Puget Sound. While the local scene may have quieted down somewhat since the distorted days of grunge and riot grrrl in the early 1990s, innovative local artists are still very much alive in many of Olympia's bars, brewhouses and theaters, and seeking them out is a proverbial rite of passage. Dip into *Volcano*, the weekly South Puget Sound music paper, or start your search at one of the following places:

4th Ave Tavern (☎ 360-786-1444; 210 4th Ave E) This retrofitted bar, with pool tables, pinball machines and an excellent selection of microbrews, is one of the best places to catch local bands on Friday and Saturday nights.

Le Voyeur (☎ 360-943-5710; 404 4th Ave E) Monday is movie night, Wednesday is trivia night and the rest of the week is reserved for showcasing the latest names on the ever-innovative Olympia music scene.

Manium (421 4th Av) Home of Olympia's underground punk, metal and indie scenes, Manium bills itself as a 'collectively organized music and performance venue.' Shows here just sort of 'happen,' so be sure to keep your eye on the local posters and music press.

Brotherhood Lounge (☎ 360-352-4153; 119 Capitol Way N; 🕑 4pm-2am) Strange art, precariously hung Bollywood film banners and big, polite tattooed dudes working the bar await at this favored meeting place for Olympia's hip and arty crowd which hosts regular music concerts with everything from punk to Black Sabbath impersonators, plus a Sunday night DJ.

movies and foreign films, along with regular releases. There is a film festival held every November and the occasional rock or rap concert.

Getting There & Away

Five Greyhound buses a day link Olympia to Seattle ($11.50, 1½ hours) and other I-5-corridor cities from its **station** (☎ 360-357-5541; 107 7th Ave E). **Grays Harbor Transportation Authority** (☎ 360-532-2770; www.ghtransit.com) offers a bus service to Aberdeen on the Pacific Coast ($2, 1½ hours).

Amtrak (☎ 360-923-4602) stops at its station in Lacey at 6600 Yelm Hwy; three trains a day link Olympia with Seattle ($14) and two with Portland ($20). Bus 64 goes between the station and downtown hourly 6:30am to 7:30pm.

Getting Around

The **Capital Aeroporter** (☎ 360-754-7113) has frequent service to Sea-Tac, leaving from Phoenix Inn Suites, 415 Capitol Way N ($24, two hours). Reservations are suggested.

Olympia's free public bus system is **Intercity Transit** (☎ 360-786-1881; www.intercitytransit.com). The downtown transit center is at State Ave and Washington St.

OLYMPIC PENINSULA

Cut off by water on three sides from the rest of the state, the remote Olympic Peninsula exhibits all the insular characteristics of a separate island. Dominated by the Olympic National Park, the region's main population centers are located in the northeast and include Port Angeles, Port Townsend and the drier, balmier settlement of Sequim, now a budding retirement community. Protected climatically by the Olympic Mountains, outdoor activities abound here.

Exempt from strict wilderness regulations, the area outside of the Olympic National Park is largely given over to the lumber industry. Further west, clinging to the wild Pacific Coast, you'll find a couple of large Native American reservations.

History

Some of the peninsula's Native American history is well-documented in the Ozette excavations that unearthed a 500-year-old Makah village in 1970. Other native groups included the Quileute and the Quinault.

European sailors were exploring the Northwest coast as early as 1592 but contact

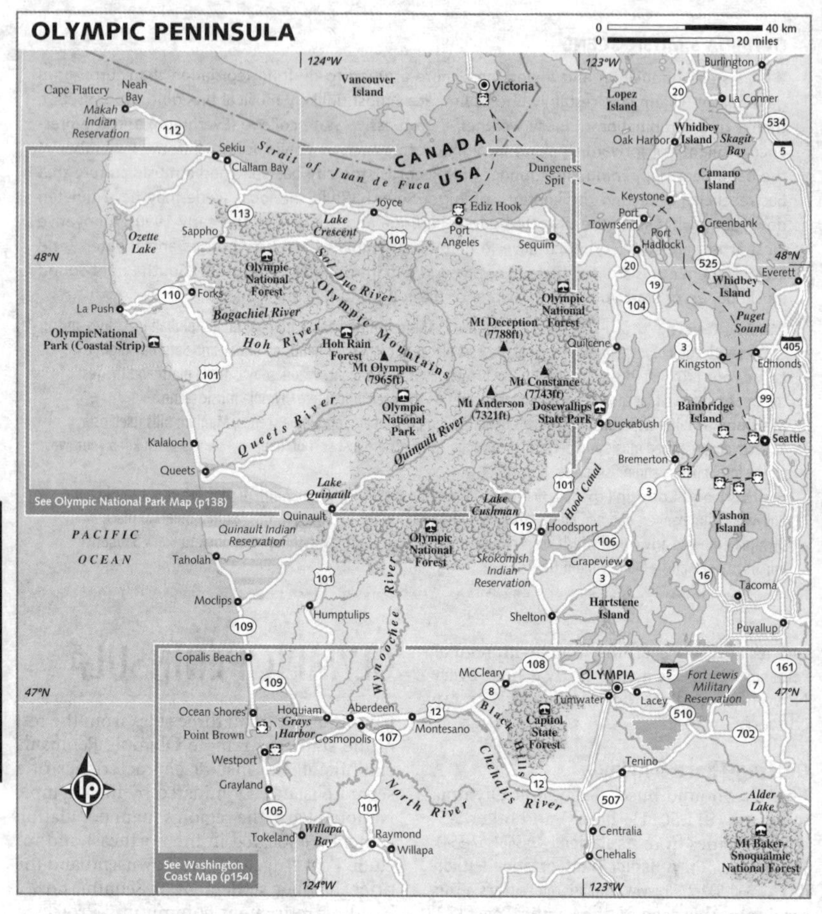

with the local people didn't occur until some two centuries later, when the land was claimed by the Spanish, who subsequently planted a colony at Neah Bay.

Port Townsend was established as the peninsula's premier settlement in 1851 and the first expanses of virgin forest began to fall to the lumberer's saws in the 1880s when the mill towns of Aberdeen and Hoquiam sprang up in the south.

Early attempts to explore the interior were limited until the 1930s, when US 101 pushed through the deep forests, linking longtime coastal communities by road for the first time. Finally, in 1938, following a 40-year struggle among conservationists, industrialists and logging companies, the Olympic National Park was established in the heart of the peninsula.

Orientation

US 101, which rings basically the whole Olympic Peninsula, is the main road in these parts. Various minor roads penetrate deeper into the Olympic National Park's interior. The fastest access from the population centers of Puget Sound is via either the Seattle–Bainbridge Island ferry or the Edmonds–Kingston ferry. You can also take the Whidbey Island ferry from Keystone to Port Townsend on the peninsula's northeast corner. Passenger and car ferry service is available from Port Angeles to Victoria, British Columbia (BC) year-round.

OLYMPIC NATIONAL PARK

Declared a national monument in 1909 and a national park in 1938, the 1406-sq-mile Olympic National Park shelters a unique rain forest, copious glaciated mountain peaks and a 57-mile strip of Pacific coastal wilderness that was added in 1953. One of North America's last great wilderness areas, most of the park remains relatively untouched by human habitation, with 1000-year-old cedar trees juxtaposed with pristine alpine meadows, clear glacial lakes and a largely roadless interior.

Opportunities for independent exploration in this huge backcountry region abound, with visitors enjoying such diverse activities as hiking, fishing, kayaking and skiing. The park's distinct and highly bio-diverse ecosystem is rich in plant and animal life, much of it – such as the majestic Roosevelt elk – indigenous to the region. Boasting 17 large, car-accessible campgrounds and 95 backcountry campgrounds, overnight excursions in the park are both easy and rewarding.

Information

About a mile south of Port Angeles is the **Olympic National Park Visitor Center** (☎ 360-565-3130; www.nps.gov/olym; 3002 Mt Angeles Rd; 9am-4pm), the park's most comprehensive information center. Aside from giving out excellent free maps and leaflets, the center offers children's exhibits plus a bookstore, replica of a prehistoric Makah seal-hunting canoe and a 25-minute film entitled *Mosaic of Diversity* shown in a small auditorium. A decent map is essential to see the various walking trails in the park.

For information on the Olympic National Forest, a 630,000-acre area that borders much of the park's perimeter, contact the **USFS headquarters** (☎ 360-956-2400; www.fs.fed.us/r6/olympic; 1835 Black Lake Blvd SW; 8am-4:30pm Mon-Fri) outside Olympia. Or you can try the field offices in Hoodsport, Quilcene, Quinault and Forks. These offices distribute free backcountry permits for wilderness camping in the park as well as Northwest Forest Passes ($5), required for parking at trailheads in the forest.

Park admission fees are $15 per vehicle and $5 per pedestrian/cyclist, and are valid for seven days for park entry and re-entry. An annual 'passport' for one year's unlimited entry costs $30. Fees are collected year-round at the Hoh and Heart o' the Hills entry points, and from May to October at Elwha, Sol Duc and Staircase entrances. (Payment is not mandatory where there is no entrance station or when an entrance station isn't open.)

Backpackers must register for overnight stays in backcountry areas. There's a $5 permit fee for groups of up to 12, valid for two weeks from purchase, plus a $2-per-person nightly fee for anyone over 16 years old. You can get permits from the **Wilderness Information Center** (☎ 360-565-3100; http://www.nps.gov/olym/planyourvisit/wic.htm; 600 E Park Ave, Port Angeles; 8am-4:30pm Apr-Sep), behind the visitor center. You can also get them from the Hoh visitor center (p142) or from ranger stations throughout the park.

Eastern Entrances

The eastern entrances to Olympic National Park are less developed than the north and west, but are handy for visitors traveling over the Hood Canal from Seattle and the 'mainland.'

DOSEWALLIPS RIVER VALLEY

This narrow valley (*doe*-sey-*wal*-ups) is surrounded by some of the highest mountains in the Olympics, including Mt Anderson and Mt Deception. The gravel Dosewallips River Rd terminates at the ranger station 15 miles from US 101, where hiking trails begin.

The northbound **Dosewallips Trail** climbs up to beautiful Dose Meadows (10 miles from Dose Forks) before crossing Hayden Pass and dropping into the Elwha Valley and the Elwha Trail. The southerly **West Fork Dosewallips Trail** leads to Honeymoon Meadows (9 miles from Dose Forks), a spring-filled basin beneath the glaciers of precipitous 7321ft Mt Anderson. The trail continues up to Anderson Pass and into the East Fork Quinault River trail system.

STAIRCASE

Staircase is another favorite entrance for hikers, and is popular with families, anglers and boaters bound for nearby Lake Cushman State Park. The **Staircase Ranger Station** (☎ 360-877-5569) is just inside the park boundary, 16 miles from US 101 and the small town of Hoodsport.

The trail system here follows the drainage of the North Fork Skokomish River, which is flanked by some of the most rugged peaks in the Olympics. The principal long-distance trail is the **North Fork Skokomish Trail**, which leads up this heavily forested valley, eventually

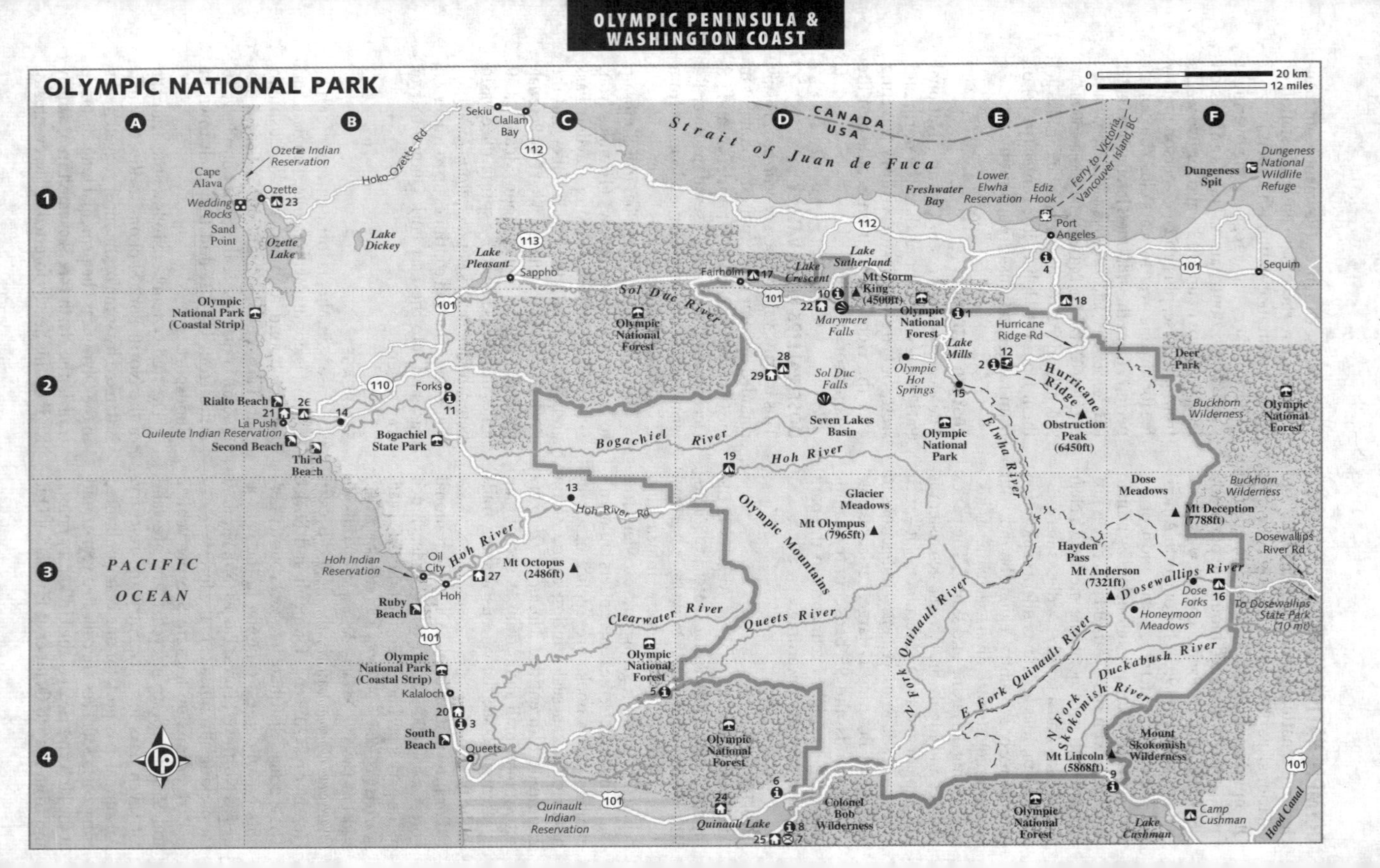
OLYMPIC NATIONAL PARK
0 20 km
0 12 miles
Strait of Juan de Fuca
CANADA
USA
Ferry to Victoria, Vancouver Island, BC
Dungeness National Wildlife Refuge
Dungeness Spit
Sequim
Port Angeles
Ediz Hook
Lower Elwha Reservation
Freshwater Bay
Lake Sutherland
Lake Crescent
Fairholm
Mt Storm King (4500ft)
Marymere Falls
Sol Duc Falls
Sol Duc River
Seven Lakes Basin
Olympic Hot Springs
Lake Mills
Hurricane Ridge Rd
Hurricane Ridge
Obstruction Peak (6450ft)
Deer Park
Buckhorn Wilderness
Mt Deception (7788ft)
Dosewallips River Rd
To Dosewallips State Park (10 mi)
Dose Meadows
Dosewallips River
Dose Forks
Honeymoon Meadows
Hayden Pass
Mt Anderson (7321ft)
Duckabush River
N Fork Skokomish River
Mount Skokomish Wilderness
Mt Lincoln (5868ft)
Camp Cushman
Lake Cushman
Hood Canal
Elwha River
Olympic National Park
Olympic National Forest
Glacier Meadows
Mt Olympus (7965ft)
Olympic Mountains
Hoh River
Hoh River Rd
Bogachiel River
Queets River
Clearwater River
N Fork Quinault River
E Fork Quinault River
Colonel Bob Wilderness
Quinault Lake
Quinault Indian Reservation
Mt Octopus (2486ft)
Sekiu
Clallam Bay
Sappho
Lake Pleasant
Hoko-Ozette Rd
Lake Dickey
Ozette Indian Reservation
Ozette
Ozette Lake
Cape Alava
Wedding Rocks
Sand Point
Olympic National Park (Coastal Strip)
Forks
Bogachiel State Park
Rialto Beach
La Push
Quileute Indian Reservation
Second Beach
Third Beach
Hoh Indian Reservation
Oil City
Hoh
Ruby Beach
Kalaloch
South Beach
Queets
PACIFIC OCEAN
101
110
112
113

crossing into the Duckabush River valley to intercept other trans-park trail systems. Ambitious day-hikers might consider following this trail 3.7 miles to the **Flapjack Lakes Trail**, an easy 4-mile climb up to several small lakes that shimmer beneath the crags of the Sawtooth peaks.

A popular short hike follows the south bank of the North Fork Skokomish River through lush old-growth forest along the **Staircase Rapids Loop Trail**. Continue up the trail a short distance to the Rapids Bridge, which crosses over to the North Fork Skokomish Trail and makes for a nice 2-mile loop.

SLEEPING

Dosewallips State Park (☎ 888-226-7688; tent sites/hookups $17/24) Near Brinnon along US 101 is this 425-acre, year-round campground situated in an expanse of meadow, close to the mouth of the Dosewallips River and facing Hood Canal. There are 100 tent spaces, 40 utility spaces, a dump space and two showers.

Camp Cushman (☎ 360-877-6770; 7211 N Lake Cushman Rd; tent sites/hookups $20/26) Eight miles northwest of Hoodsport, this campground is centered on a large reservoir on the Skokomish River, popular with anglers, water-skiers and campers. There are 82 campsites open from early April to late October.

Northern Entrances

The most popular access to Olympic National Park is from the north. Port Angeles is the park's urban hub, and other good access points are Hurricane Ridge, the Elwha Valley and Lake Crescent, the park's largest lake.

HURRICANE RIDGE

South of Port Angeles the Olympic Mountains rise up to Hurricane Ridge, one of the park's most accessible viewing points and an active ski station in the winter. Starting in Race St, the 18-mile Hurricane Ridge Rd climbs up 5300ft toward extensive wildflower meadows and expansive mountain vistas often visible above the clouds.

The **Hurricane Ridge Visitor Center** (9:30am-5pm daily when road is open, Fri-Sun & Mon holidays in midwinter) has a snack bar, gift shop, toilets and ski and snowshoe rentals, but no overnight accommodation or camping. The weather here can be fickle. Call ☎ 360-565-3131 or tune in to 530AM in Port Angeles for the latest conditions.

Hurricane Ridge is a good base for many activities including cross-country and downhill skiing, and snowboarding from mid-December to March, weekends only. The area has two rope tows and a lift, and is one of only two national park ski areas in the US.

Hurricane Ridge is also the takeoff point for a number of short **hikes** leading through meadows to vista points. **Hurricane Hill Trail**, which begins at the end of the road leading up, and the **Meadow Loop Trails** network, starting at the visitor center, are popular, moderately easy hikes. The first half-mile of these trails is wheelchair accessible.

From Hurricane Ridge, you can drive a rough, white-knuckle 8-mile road to **Obstruction Peak**, laid out by the Civilian Conservation Corps (CCC) in the 1930s. Here, hikers looking for long-distance treks can pick up either the **Grand Ridge Trail**, which leads 7.5 miles to Deer Park, much of the way above the timberline, or the **Wolf Creek Trail**, an 8-mile downhill jaunt to Whiskey Bend, where it picks up the Elwha Trail.

ELWHA RIVER VALLEY

The Elwha, the largest river on the Olympic Peninsula, and Lake Mills (actually a reservoir) are popular **trout fishing** havens. Elwha River Rd turns south from US 101 about 8 miles west of Port Angeles. Follow it for 10

INFORMATION
Elwha Ranger Station....1 E2
Hoh Rain Forest Visitor Center....(see 19)
Hurricane Ridge Visitor Center....2 E2
Kalaloch Ranger Station....3 C4
Lake Ozette Ranger Station....(see 23)
Olympic National Park Visitor Center....4 E1
Queets Ranger Station....5 C4
Quinalt Ranger Station....6 D4
Quinault Post Office....7 D4
Quinault USFS Office....8 D4
Staircase Ranger Station....9 F4
Storm King Information Station....10 D2
USFS/NPS Information Station....11 B2
Wilderness Information Center....(see 4)

SIGHTS & ACTIVITIES
Hurricane Ridge Ski Area....12 E2
Rain Forest Paddlers....13 C3
Three Rivers Resort....14 B2
Whiskey Bend....15 E2

SLEEPING
Dosewallips State Park....16 F3
Fairholm Campground....17 D1
Heart o' the Hills Campground....18 E2
Hoh Campground....19 D2
Kalaloch Lodge....20 B4
La Push Ocean Park Resort....21 B2
Lake Crescent Lodge....22 D2
Lake Ozette Campground....23 B1
Lake Quinault Inn....24 D4
Lake Quinault Lodge....25 D4
Mora Campground....26 B2
Queets Campground....(see 5)
Rain Forest Hostel....27 C3
Sol Duc Campground....28 D2
Sol Duc Hot Springs Resort....29 D2

OUTDOOR ACTIVITIES IN THE OLYMPICS

Hiking

With over 600 miles of trail, the Olympic National Park is a mecca for hikers of all abilities. For beginners there are a plethora of easy but scenic day hikes that will put you in close touch with this unique wilderness (p142). Beachcombers will love the rugged but rewarding coastal hikes (p144), while those up for a bit of backcountry bushwhacking can tackle one of a handful of challenging trans-park trails (p150).

Rafting, Kayaking & Fishing

A number of outfitters run white-water rafting trips on the park's rivers, including the Hoh, Elwha and Sol Duc. Start your search at **Rain Forest Paddlers** (☎ 1-866-457-8398; 4883 Upper Hoh Rd) who offer half-/full-day guided trips for $44/79. Rivers and lakes in the park are noted for their trout and salmon fishing. No license is needed, although those fishing for trout or steelhead are required to fill out a Washington state catch record card, and all wild fish must be released. Canoe and kayak rentals are available at many of the larger lakes.

Skiing

In winter, the area around Hurricane Ridge has over 20 miles of trails for cross-country skiing, snowboarding and snowshoeing. Downhill skiers will find a 665ft vertical drop and a couple of rope tow lifts. For more information contact the **Hurricane Ridge Winter Sports Club** (☎ 360-417-1542; www.hurricaneridge.net) in Port Angeles

Climbing

Rugged Mt Olympus (7965ft) is the park's highest and most commonly climbed peak, though, thanks to extensive glaciers and fickle weather, ascents are taxing and should not be undertaken lightly. Access is via the Hoh Trail, which ends at Glacier Meadows, 17 miles from the Hoh visitor center, and the campground here is frequently used as a base camp for ascents of the mountain. Much of the remaining climb is on glaciers and along craggy escarpments. Most people make the ascent between June and early September, although adventurous souls begin to climb as early as April. Each year Mt Olympus causes injuries and claims several lives, usually from falls into glacial crevasses or exposure during storms. Guided climbs are available through various agencies. Try **Mountain Madness** (☎ 206-937-8389; www.mouintainmadness.com) who are based out of Seattle and offer guided five-day summit attempts starting from $875.

miles to the **Elwha Ranger Station** (☎ 360-452-9191; 480 Upper Elwha Rd). The road immediately forks. Turn west to reach the Olympic Hot Springs trailhead, or turn east toward Whiskey Bend to reach the Elwha River and other trailheads.

Commercially developed as a resort in the 1930s, the **Olympic Hot Springs** once featured cabins that have long since disappeared. In 1983, park supervisors closed the road out, and the area has largely returned to nature. The 2.2-mile **hike** along the old roadbed is well worth it – what's left of the old pools steam alongside the rushing Boulder Creek, all in a verdant deep-forest grove.

From Whiskey Bend, the **Elwha Trail** leads up the main branch of the Elwha River and is one of the primary cross-park long-distance hikes (see p150). Day-hikers may elect to follow the trail for 2 miles to Humes Ranch, the remains of a homestead-era ranch.

LAKE CRESCENT

If you're heading anticlockwise on the Olympic loop from Port Angeles toward Forks, one of the first scenic surprises to leap out at you will be luminous Lake Crescent, a popular boating and fishing area and a departure point for a number of short national park hikes. The area also boasts the Lake Crescent Lodge (opposite), one of the park's most celebrated accommodation options. The best stop-off point is in a parking lot to the right of SR 101 near the **Storm King Information Station** (☎ 360-928-3380) only open in the summer. A number of short hikes leave from here including the **Marymere Falls trail**, a 2-mile round-trip to a 90ft cascade that drops down over a basalt cliff. For a more energetic hike, climb up the side of **Mt Storm King**, the peak that rises to the east of Lake Crescent. The steep, 1.7-mile ascent splits off the Barnes Creek Trail.

Trout fishing is good here – the lake is deep with steep shorelines – though only artificial lures are allowed. Rowboat rentals ($9/25 per hour/half day) are available at Lake Crescent Lodge (see right) in the summer months.

SOL DUC RIVER VALLEY

The 14-mile interior road that leads off US 101 into the heart of the national park along the headwaters of the Sol Duc River is worth a turn for some great day hikes, a dip in a natural spa and a vivid glimpse of the amazing Olympic rain forest. Note how the trees along the roadside become taller and more majestic almost immediately.

As Native American legend tells it, the geological phenomenon at Sol Duc is the legacy of a battle between two lightning fish. When neither fish won the contest, each crawled beneath the earth and shed bitter tears, forming the heated mineral springs here. These springs have been diverted into three large tiled pools for health and recreation at Sol Duc Hot Springs Resort (see right). Entry costs $10/3/6.75/7.50 for an adult/baby/child/senior. There's also a standard swimming pool to cool off in, as well as a restaurant, snack bar, gift shop and overnight accommodations.

The road ends 1.5 miles past the resort, and this is where most of the trails start. The most popular hike is the 0.75-mile **Sol Duc Falls Trail**, where the river plummets 40ft into a narrow gorge. Other more strenuous hikes cross the bridge at the falls and climb the **Deer Lake Trail** along Canyon Creek. This sometimes-steep, 8-mile round-trip trail reaches the tree-rimmed lake then joins the **High Divide Trail** before tracking back via the Seven Lakes Basin, a popular overnight destination. Another good leg-stretcher is the 2.5-mile **Mink Lake Trail**, departing from the resort. The marshy lake is noted for its bird- and wildlife-viewing.

SLEEPING

Fairholm Campground (☎ 360-928-3380; sites $10; year-round) The only national park campground on Lake Crescent features 88 sites, a general store and boat rentals. It's on the lake's west end.

Heart o' the Hills Campground (☎ 360-452-2713; 876 Hurricane Ridge Rd; sites $10) Five miles south of Port Angeles, this is the closest campground to Hurricane Ridge, with 105 sites.

Sol Duc Campground (☎ 360-327-3534; sites $12) This 82-site facility is immediately upstream from the Sol Duc Hot Springs Resort and, with its tall fir and cedar trees and mossy undergrowth, offers a quintessential Olympic rain forest experience. It's also handy for both the local trails and the spa.

Sol Duc Hot Springs Resort (☎ 360-327-3583; RV sites $23, r $115-169; late Mar-Oct;) While Sol Duc lacks the classic touches of the more luxurious Lake Quinault and Kalaloch lodges, this well-known spa retreat packs a punch with its therapeutic spring waters and easy access to surrounding forest. Furthermore, while there are enough facilities onsite – mineral pools, small store and restaurant – to make the place feel self-contained, you still get the tangible sense of being in a remote wilderness area. Thirty-two modern but basic cabins offer private baths and, in some cases, a kitchenette. Aside from the steaming waters there is also a massage service available. Day-hikers and visitors can use the Spring Restaurant or poolside deli. There are 17 RV sites for hire, but no tent sites.

Lake Crescent Lodge (☎ 360-928-3211; 416 Lake Crescent Rd; lodge r with shared bath $68-85, cottages $132-211; May-Oct; wi-fi) Built in 1915 as a fishing resort, this venerable shake-sided building is the oldest of the Olympic National Park lodges and, along with the Lake Quinault Lodge (p143), leads the way in style and coziness. To add star appeal, President FD Roosevelt stayed here in 1937 – the lodge's fanciest rooms are still known as the 'Roosevelt cottages.' Located lakeside and endowed with a impressive restaurant that serves up grilled duck breast and elk rib rack, the lodge is reasonably priced, fantastically placed and well-known for its environmentally sustainable practices. Make reservations in advance, as it is only open May to October.

Western Entrances

The Pacific side of the Olympics is the most remote part of the park and home to the unique, temperate rain forests. It is also the wettest area, receiving 12ft of rain annually, and you can expect a soaking at any time.

US 101 is the only road that accesses this vast, heavily wooded area. Paved roads

'TOUCH THE WILDERNESS' HIKES

If the thought of squat toilets and camping out in bear country makes you quiver in your hiking boots, don't worry. Help is at hand. Thanks to a dozen or so easily accessible 'touch the wilderness' hikes, there's no reason why you can't take in the awesome natural beauty of the Olympic National Park and still make it back to your hotel in time for a relaxing hot tub.

Situated at various points on and around the Olympic perimeter road (US 101), these interactive and well-marked walking trails are split into four different categories: temperate rain forest, mountains, lowland forests and coast. They're ideal for day-hikers who want to get a brief yet close-up look at the park's 1000-year-old cedar trees and storm-lashed sea stacks. Most hikes are between 0.5 and 3 miles long, and a number are wheelchair accessible and suitable for families with young kids.

For an excellent introduction to the Olympics try the **Hall of Mosses Trail** (0.8 miles) in the Hoh Rain Forest, the **Maple Glade Trail** (0.5 miles) in Quinault, **Marymere Falls** (1.8 miles) at Lake Crescent or the **Klahhane Ridge** (2.8 miles) at Hurricane Ridge, all of which provide maximum wilderness exposure with minimal effort. For more trails and information, pick up a generic leaflet at the Olympic National Park Visitor's Center (p137).

penetrate the interior at the Hoh Rain Forest and Lake Quinault, but are sometimes washed out.

HOH RAIN FOREST

The most famous section of the Olympic rain forest, the Hoh River area offers a variety of hikes and an interpretive center. If you have room for only one stop on the western side, this should be it. The paved Upper Hoh Rd winds 19 miles from US 101 to the visitor center passing a **giant Sitka spruce tree** along the way. This lord of the forest is 270ft high and over 500 years old.

At the end of Hoh River Rd, the **Hoh Rain Forest Visitor Center** (☎ 360-374-6925; ⏰ 9am-4:30pm Sep-Jun, 9am-6pm Jul & Aug) offers displays on the ecology of the rain forest and the plants and animals that inhabit it, as well as a bookstore. Rangers lead free guided walks twice a day during summer.

Leading out from the visitor center are several excellent **day hikes** into virgin rain forest. The most popular is the **Hall of Moss Trail**, an easy 0.75-mile loop through the kind of weird, ethereal scenery that even Tolkien couldn't have invented. Epiphytic club moss, ferns and lichens completely overwhelm the massive trunks of maples and Sitka spruces in this misty forest. The 1.25-mile **Spruce Nature Trail** is another short interpretive loop leading out from the visitor center. There is also a short wheelchair-accessible nature trail through a rain forest marsh.

The **Hoh River Trail** is the major entry trail into the wide, glacier-carved Hoh River Valley. It is also the principal access route to Mt Olympus (p140). The trail follows an easy grade for 12 miles, and day-hikers can use it as a pleasant out-and-back excursion.

QUEETS RIVER VALLEY

The Queets Corridor was added to the park in 1953 in an attempt to preserve one of the peninsula's river valleys all the way from its glacial beginnings to the coast. It is one of the park's least accessible areas.

The unpaved Queets River Rd leaves US 101 and almost immediately drops into the national park. The road then follows the river for 13 miles before ending at **Queets Ranger Station** (☎ 360-962-2283). From here, there is one popular day hike – the gentle 3-mile **Queets Campground Loop Trail**.

Experienced or adventurous hikers can elect to ford the Queets River in late summer or fall and explore the **Queets Trail**, which leads up the river for 15 miles before petering out in heavy old-growth rain forest.

LAKE QUINAULT

Situated in the extreme southwest of the Olympic Peninsula, the enchanting Quinault River Valley is one of the park's least crowded corners. Clustered around the deep-blue glacial waters of Lake Quinault lie forested peaks, a historic lodge and some of the oldest (and tallest) Sitka spruce, Douglas fir and western red cedar trees in the world.

The lake itself offers plenty of activities such as fishing, boating and swimming, while upstream both the north and south branches of the Quinault River harbor a couple of important trans-park trails.

The lake may be accessed from both the north and the south. The south shore hosts the tiny village of Quinault, complete with the luscious Lake Quinault Lodge, a **USFS office** (☎ 360-288-2525; 353 S Shore Rd), restaurant, couple of stores, **post office** (S Shore Rd) and gas station. The North Shore Rd passes the **Quinault Ranger Station** (☎ 360-288-2444) before climbing up to the North Fork Quinault trailhead.

Lake Quinault is part of the Quinault Indian Reservation, and fishing is regulated by the tribe; check locally for tribal licenses and regulations. Boat rentals are available from Lake Quinault Lodge (right).

A number of short **hiking trails** begin just below Lake Quinault Lodge; pick up a free map from the USFS office. The shortest of these is the **Quinault Rain Forest Nature Trail**, a half-mile walk through 500-year-old Douglas firs. This short trail adjoins the 3-mile **Quinault Loop Trail**, which meanders through the rain forests before circling back to the lake. The Quinault region is also renowned for its huge trees. Close to the village is a 191ft Sitka spruce tree, and nearby are the world's largest red cedar, Douglas fir and mountain hemlock trees.

Beyond the lake, both the north and south shore roads continue up the Quinault River Valley before merging at a bridge just past Bunch Falls. From here, more adventurous hikers can sally forth into backcountry. The area's sparkling highlight is the photogenic **Enchanted Valley Trail** which climbs up to a large meadow (a former glacial lake bed) traversed by streams and springs, and resplendent with wildflowers and thickets of alders. To the north rise sheer cliff faces and peaks craning 2000ft from the valley floor; during spring snowmelt, the 3-mile precipice is drizzled by thousands of small waterfalls.

The **Enchanted Valley hike** starts out from the Graves Creek Ranger Station at the end of the S Shore Rd, and is a 26-mile trip there and back. Long-distance hikers can continue up to Anderson Pass (19 miles from Graves Creek) and link up with the **West Fork Dosewallips Trail** to complete a popular trans-park trek.

The classic Seattle Press Expedition hike (p150) passes through the North Fork Quinault River valley to join the lengthy Elwha River trail system further north.

SLEEPING

Rain Forest Hostel (☎ 360-374-2270; 169312 US Hwy 101, Forks; dm/ r $8.50/18; 💻) Eight miles south of the Hoh Rain Forest road turnoff on US 101, this isolated independent hostel is 35 minutes on the Jefferson Transit bus from Forks. Facilities include a full kitchen, common room, fireplace and internet access. In the grand old tradition of youth hostels, guests are expected to do a housekeeping chore before they leave.

Queets Campground (☎ 360-962-2283; sites $10) Located at the end of Queets River Rd (not recommended for RVs), this small campground with 20 primitive sites is tucked amid temperate rain forest.

Hoh Campground (☎ 360-374-6925; sites $12) Adjacent to the Hoh Rain Forest Visitor Center (opposite), the campground features 88 sites, most alongside the Hoh River.

Lake Quinault Inn (☎ 360-288-2714; Amanda Park; s/d $60/65; ❄) Quinault's only motel is handily positioned on US 101 and ticks the usual boxes of clean bathrooms, decent-sized beds and copious TV channels. That said, the establishment's positioning just off the park's main ring road a good mile away from the lake doesn't really make the best of the area's serene enivronment. If it's wonderful vistas you're after, pay a few dollars more and head closer to the lake.

our pick **Lake Quinault Lodge** (☎ 360-288-2900, www.visitlakequinault.com; 345 S Shore Rd; cabin $125-243, lodge $134-167; ❄ 🏊) Everything you could want in a historic national park lodge and more, the 'Quinault' boasts a huge, roaring fireplace, peek-a-boo lake views, a manicured cricket-pitch-quality lawn, huge comfy leather sofas, a regal reception area and – arguably – the finest eating experience on the whole peninsula. The latter is thanks to the rather scrumptious sweet potato pancakes with hazelnut butter that are served up in the beautiful lakeside restaurant for breakfast (and are worth trying even if you're not staying here). Built in 1926, the Quinault's warmth and character are no secret and advance reservations are recommended. Trails into primeval forest leave from just outside the door.

OLYMPIC COASTAL STRIP

Crashing surf, untamed beaches, ghostly mists and 57 miles of isolated Washington coastline are just four of the reasons why you should include the Olympic coastal

PACIFIC COASTAL HIKES

There are two main long-distance beach hikes along the isolated Washington coast. The easiest and most popular route is the 20-mile stretch between Ozette and Rialto Beach in the north which commonly makes up a moderate four-day/three-night trek. While there are few awkward headlands or difficult streams to cross along this part of the coast, hikers should be aware of the large sections of slippery rock and the presence of numerous meddlesome raccoons who'll steal your food at a moment's notice (hang all food in hard-sided containers while camping).

The second, more arduous hike is another three-nighter that reaches from Third Beach (near La Push) to Oil City at the mouth of the Hoh River. This 17-mile trek is tougher, muddier and presents more tide problems than the northern route, though it is noticeably less crowded.

Long-distance hiking along the Pacific Ocean should not be entered into lightly. If you are contemplating a trek along the coast, request information from the **National Park Service** (www.nps.gov/olym), buy good maps and learn how to read tide tables. In all but the height of summer, hikers should be prepared for bad weather.

strip on any national park itinerary. Here, in America's extreme northwest corner, sea stacks brave pounding Pacific waves, thick forests meld imperceptibly into rocky bays, and marine mammals such as gray whales, sea otters and harbor seals claim rich pickings, undisturbed by the clawing tentacles of human development.

In true wilderness fashion, the coastline is only accessible by road at a few small nooks, and human settlement in the area is almost nonexistent. Consequently, to gain the best views of this glorious and refreshingly underdeveloped area you'll need, at some point, to switch to a boat or a good pair of legs.

Ozette

Former home of the Makah tribe, whose ancient cliff-side village was destroyed in a mudslide in the early 18th century before being unearthed in the 1970s, Ozette is more than just a well-excavated archaeological pit. It is also one of the most accessible slices of isolated beach on the Olympic coastal strip.

The Hoko-Ozette Rd leaves Hwy 112 about 3 miles west of Sekiu and proceeds 21 miles to **Lake Ozette Ranger Station** (☎ 360-963-2725; 🕑 8am-4:30pm), on Ozette Lake. There is no village here but, from the ranger station, two boardwalk trails lead out to one of two beaches at Cape Alava and Sand Point. The 3.3-mile **Cape Alava Trail** leads north to the westernmost point of land in the continental US and is the site of the ancient Makah village, where archaeologists unearthed 55,000 artifacts, many of which are on display at the Makah Museum (p151) in Neah Bay. The southern **Sand Point Trail** from Lake Ozette Ranger Station leads 3 miles to beaches below a low bluff; whale-watchers often come here in the migration season.

The two Ozette trails can easily be linked as a long day-hike by walking the 3 miles between Cape Alava and Sand Point along the beach (beware of the tides) or overland (although the trail is brushy and primitive).

The high point of this hike is the **Wedding Rocks**, the most significant group of petroglyphs on the Olympic Peninsula. Approximately a mile south of Cape Alava, the small outcropping contains carvings of whales, a European square-rigger and fertility figures. The site was traditionally used for Makah weddings and is still considered sacred.

Ruby Beach to South Beach

This southernmost portion of the Olympic coastal strip, located between the Hoh and Quinault Indian Reservations, is abutted by US 101, making it more accessible – if a little less dramatic – than the beaches further north. Your first stop here should be **Ruby Beach**, where a short 0.2-mile path leads down to a large expanse of windswept beach embellished by polished black stones and wantonly strewn tree trunks. Heading south toward Kalaloch (*klay*-lock), other accessible beachfronts are unimaginatively named Beach One through to Beach Six, all of which are popular with beachcombers. At low tide, rangers give talks on tidal-pool life at Beach Four and on the ecosystems of the Olympic coastal strip. For information about this area, contact the **Kalaloch Ranger Station** (☎ 360-962-2283; 🕑 9am-5pm May-Oct).

Sleeping

Between May and September, advance reservations are required to stay at the designated campsites along the beach at Cape Alava and Sand Point. To make a reservation contact the Wilderness Information Center (p137) or reserve online. In addition, campers must obtain a wilderness permit.

Lake Ozette Campground (☎ 360-963-2725; sites $12) The 15 sites fill every day before noon at this small camp on Lake Ozette, a popular playground for boats and kayaks.

Mora Campground (☎ 360-374-5460; sites $12) Along the Quillayute River, 2 miles east of Rialto Beach, Mora offers 95 regular sites. Guided nature walks take off from here in the summer.

Kalaloch Lodge (☎ 360-962-2271; www.visitkalaloch.com; 157151 US 101; lodge $134-285, cabins $143-289;) Up with Lake Quinault and Lake Crescent lodges in terms of quality, the Kalaloch (built in 1953) is perched overlooking the Pacific and is quite possibly the most evocative retreat on the Washington coast. In addition to rooms in the old lodge, there are log cabins and motel-style units, and a family-friendly restaurant and store that offers incomparable ocean views. Various trails lead down to the nearby beaches.

NORTHEASTERN OLYMPIC PENINSULA

Hugging the protected coast of the Strait of Juan de Fuca, the northeast corner of the Olympic Peninsula is the region's most populated enclave and provides a popular gateway to the national park. Famous for its dry climate (courtesy of the Olympic rain shadow), outdoor activities such as sea kayaking and whale-watching abound, while a rare historical treat awaits travelers in time-warped Port Townsend. Thanks to numerous ferry connections (Port Angeles to Victoria/Canada, Port Townsend to Whidbey Island and Seattle to Bainbridge Island), the area is easily accessible from the population centers of Puget Sound.

Port Townsend

pop 8344

Port Townsend is one of the architectural showpieces of the Pacific Northwest and a sight for sore eyes after the urban sprawl of Puget Sound. It is also a North American rarity in that it has successfully managed to evade the onslaught of modern commercialization and survive into the 21st century with its historical legacy firmly intact. Caught in a late-19th-century time warp, the port perches at the nautical entrance to busy Puget Sound and first prospered in the 1890s when speculators streamed in from the south and east, hailing it as the 'New York of the West' (p148). The boom that followed went bust in 1893 and the bottom rapidly fell out of Port Townsend's economy. Time effectively stood still until the 1970s, when the much vaunted 'City of Dreams' rediscovered its soul and began to transform into the artsy community that it is today.

ORIENTATION & INFORMATION

Generally speaking, there are two vintage districts in Port Townsend, both filled with Victorian-era structures. Downtown is the main commercial hub, which stretches down Water St along the waterfront. Uptown is atop the bluff, with the main business activity at Lawrence and Tyler Sts.

Pick up a useful walking-tour map and guide to the downtown historic district at the **Port Townsend Visitor Center** (☎ 360-385-2272, 888-365-6978; www.ptchamber.org; 2437 E Sims Way; 9am-5pm Mon-Fri, 10am-4pm Sat, 11am-4pm Sun).

SIGHTS

Port Townsend is a sight in itself and just exploring the Victorian shop fronts of Water St can make for a pleasant morning or afternoon stroll. Art galleries are the town's forte and you can pick up a map of 15 of the best, all clustered within four blocks of the ferry dock, at the visitor center. Higher up on the bluff, be sure to stop and admire the 100ft clock tower of the **Jefferson County Courthouse** (1892) and also **Manresa Castle** (now a hotel – see p147), and **Rothschild House** (☎ 360-379-8076; cnr Jefferson & Taylor Sts; admission $4; 11am-5pm May-Oct), a historic home now open to the public and run by the local historical society. The society also runs the **Jefferson County Historical Society Museum** (☎ 360-385-1003; 210 Madison St; adult/12yr & under $4/1; 11am-4pm Mon-Sat, 1-4pm Sun, Mar-Dec), a well-maintained exhibition area that includes mock-ups of an old courtroom and jail cell, along with the full lowdown on the rise, fall and second coming of this captivating port town.

Also located within Port Townsend's city limits is the attractive **Fort Worden State Park** (☎ 360-344-4400; www.parks.wa.gov/fortworden;

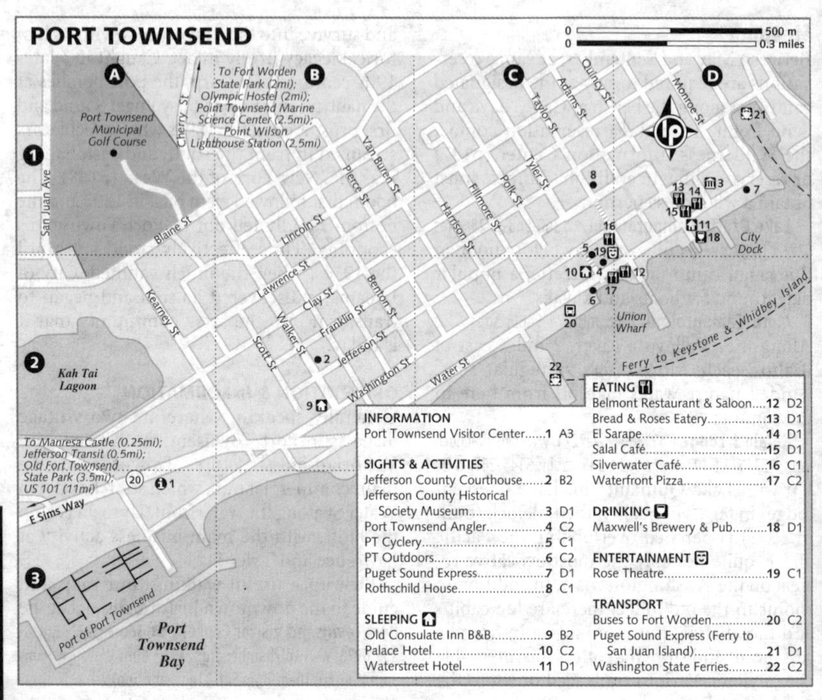

200 Battery Way; 6:30am-dusk Apr-Oct, 8am-dusk Nov-Mar), the remains of a large fortification system constructed in the 1890s to protect the strategically important Puget Sound area from outside attack. The extensive grounds and array of historic buildings have been refurbished in recent years into a lodging, nature and historical park, and sharp-eyed film buffs will recognize the setting as the backdrop for the movie *An Officer and a Gentleman*. The **Commanding Officer's Quarters** (admission $1; 10am-5pm Jun-Aug, 1-4pm Sat & Sun Mar-May & Sep-Oct), a 12-bedroom mansion, is open for tours, and part of one of the barracks is now the **Puget Sound Coast Artillery Museum** (admission $2; 11am-4pm Tue-Sun), which tells the story of early Pacific coastal fortifications.

Fort Worden offers a number of camping and lodging possibilities (opposite). Hikes lead along the headland to **Point Wilson Lighthouse Station** and some wonderful windswept beaches. On the park's fishing pier is the **Port Townsend Marine Science Center** (☎ 360-385-5582; 532 Battery Way; adult/17yr & under $5/3; noon-6pm Tue-Sun Jun 15-Labor Day, noon-4pm Sat & Sun Apr 1-Jun 14 & Labor Day-Oct 31), featuring four touch tanks and daily interpretive programs.

ACTIVITIES

It's not all history. Port Townsend is the center for sea kayaking on Puget Sound and Fort Worden is a stop on the Cascadia Marine Trail. **PT Outdoors** (☎ 360-379-3608; 1017B Water St) rents single kayaks from $25 an hour or offers guided tours from $55 for two to three hours. **Puget Sound Express** (☎ 360-385-5288; www.pugetsoundexpress.com; 431 Water St) offers four-hour whale-watching tours from May to October for $70/55 per adult/child. **Port Townsend Angler** (☎ 360-379-3763; www.ptangler.com; 940 Water St) specializes in catch-and-release tours for fly fishers.

PT Cyclery (☎ 360-385-6470; 252 Tyler St; rentals per hr/day $7/25), on a back lot on Tyler St, has mountain bikes and tandems for rent. They also provide local trail maps.

FESTIVALS & EVENTS

Port Townsend's plethora of annual events are led by **Centrum** (☎ 360-385-3102; www.centrum.org), a nonprofit arts foundation based at Fort Worden State Park, which sponsors an endless stream of arts and music festivals and seminars, many held at the fort. Among the most popular are the Festival of American Fiddle Tunes and Jazz Port Townsend, both in July. Contact Centrum for a schedule.

For those who want to learn more about the port's early life, **Victorian Days** (☎ 360-379-0668; www.victorianfestival.org) in late March offers an array of exhibits, walking tours and crafts workshops. Horses and carriages are dusted off, refined manners are polished and half the town dons asphyxiating corsets or austere waistcoats to relive the days when lamb-chop whiskers and handlebar mustaches were the height of fashion.

SLEEPING

Olympic Hostel (☎ 360-385-0655; 272 Battery Way; dm member/nonmember adult $17/20, child $7/10) A hostel with a bit of a difference, this 30-bed HI-affiliate is situated in the historic barracks at Fort Worden with great views over the bay toward Mt Rainier. Private rooms are available (add $8 to per-person rate), along with shared showers, a kitchen, common room and an all-you-can-eat pancake breakfast.

Fort Worden State Park (☎ 360-344-4400; www.parks.wa.gov/fortworden; 200 Battery Way; sites $30 plus $7 reservation fee) Of a total 80 RV hookup sites at this popular destination, 50 are between the beachfront and a wooded hillside, and 30 are on a field beside the old officers' quarters. Five more hiker/biker sites ($14) are also on this field. Amenities include kitchen shelters, flush toilets and hot showers. Campers can email reservations up to five months in advance.

Waterstreet Hotel (☎ 360-385-5467; 635 Water St; r $45-120; wi-fi) Of Port Townsend's old dockside hotels, the easy-on-the-wallet Waterstreet has to be the best bargain in town. There is a price for the giveaway room fees, however. The hotel is above a pub, hence late-night noise – though generally good-natured and exuberant – can infringe annoyingly on your pre-hiking beauty sleep. If it's peace and tranquility you're after, hit the uptown B&Bs. If Victorian furnishings, easy pub access and plenty of old-world charm are more your line, this could be the place for you.

our pick **Palace Hotel** (☎ 360-385-0773; 1004 Water St; r $59-109;) Built in 1889, this beautiful Victorian building is a former brothel that was once run by the locally notorious Madame Marie, who did her dodgy business out of the 2nd-floor corner suite. Each of the 15 rooms is named after the girl who used to occupy it. Reincarnated as an attractive period hotel with antique furnishings and old-fashioned claw-foot baths, the Palace's former seediness is now a thing of the past, as a quick glance inside the exquisite lobby will testify.

Old Consulate Inn B&B (☎ 360-385-6753; www.oldconsulateinn.com; 313 Walker St; r $99-189) Another Queen Anne masterpiece, this former residence of the German consul is a splendid eight-room B&B adorned with the kind of authentic 19th-century decor that will leave you thinking you've wandered into the pages of a Henry James novel. The only trouble is, you'll want to linger here all day, sampling the scrumptious breakfast, shooting balls in the pool room or relaxing in a hot tub set rather romantically in an outdoor gazebo.

Manresa Castle (☎ 360-385-5750; www.manresacastle.com; cnr 7th & Sheridan Sts; r $99-199) One of Port Townsend's signature buildings has been turned into a historic hotel/restaurant that's light on fancy gimmicks but heavy on period authenticity. This 40-room mansion/castle, built by the town's first mayor, sits high on a bluff above the port and is one of the first buildings to catch your eye as you arrive by ferry. The vintage rooms may be a little Spartan for some visitors, but in a setting this grandiose it's the all-pervading sense of history that counts. The most expensive room is in a turret.

Also try the Belmont (p148).

EATING

Silverwater Café (☎ 360-385-6448; 237 Taylor St; lunch $6-10, dinner $10-17; 11:30am-10pm, till 11pm Sat & Sun) The Silverwater provides a romantic atmosphere in the not-too-fancy setting of a classic Port Townsend Victorian-era building. Renowned for its creatively prepared local dishes such as ahi tuna and artichoke parmesan pâte, the restaurant also rustles up more homely desserts such as the not-to-be-missed blackberry pie.

El Sarape (☎ 360-379-9343; 628 Water St; mains $6-13; V) Decked out in traditional red, white and green, El Sarape is proudly Mexican, with plenty of seafood and vegetarian options for those who just can't face another chicken burrito. The interior is funky and inviting.

Salal Café (☎ 360-385-6532; 634 Water St; breakfast $7-8, lunch $8-9; 7am-2pm) Often considered Port Townsend's best restaurant and the winner of numerous culinary awards, the Salal specializes in eggs. Scrambled, poached, frittatas, stuffed into a burrito or served up as an omelette, you

THE 'NEW YORK OF THE WEST' THAT NEVER WAS

Located at the strategic nexus of Puget Sound, the Strait of Georgia and the Strait of Juan de Fuca, Port Townsend's position as the Pacific Northwest's most geographically viable coastal port looked unassailable in the late 19th century. Earmarked as the western terminus of the expanding Union-Pacific railroad and touted as a burgeoning New York in the making, this one-time sleepy fishing village was quickly transformed into a much-vaunted 'City of Dreams' where the Yankee dollar ruled and fast fortunes were there for the taking.

Seduced by a mixture of hype, hope and over-speculation, businessmen and prospectors started descending on Port Townsend in their droves and, by 1890, the settlement had become a bustling and bawdy boomtown. On the docks, housed in a tight cluster of sturdy Victorian buildings were six banks, two electric street railways and a $100,000 hotel, while up on a bluff in an opulent grid of genteel mansions, rich merchants' wives sipped wine and tried to avoid the raucous revelers who plied the waterfront bars below.

But after four years of whirlwind expansion, a nationwide depression took the wind out of Port Townsend's entrepreneurial sails rather dramatically in 1893. With the abrupt economic downturn, the railroad went into receivership before it ever reached the town, and as trade and commerce prospered in eastern Puget Sound, steamships began to bypass Port Townsend in favor of the growing urban hub of Seattle.

So acute was the town's slump that local authorities couldn't even find the money to demolish Port Townsend's once stately downtown buildings. For years they became squatter havens and pigeon coops until, in the early 1970s, new urban dwellers, recognizing their historical value, began to turn them into B&Bs, craft shops and wonderfully restored hotels and restaurants.

Today Port Townsend is one of only three Victorian seaports on the US' National List of Historic Places and a mecca for artists, tourists and architectural buffs who travel the breadth of the country to unlock the historical secrets of the 'New York of the West' that never was.

can ponder all varieties here during a laid-back breakfast or a zippy lunch.

our pick **Bread & Roses Eatery** (☎ 360-379-3355; 230 Quincy St; lunch $7-10; ⏰ 7am-7pm Wed-Mon, till 9pm Fri & Sat; V) Quite possibly the Olympic Peninsula's best sandwich bar–style eatery, this commodious place takes the notion of the lunchtime 'snack' to a whole new dimension, with deli salads, homemade cakes and cookies, eye-poppingly good organic coffee and – the pièce de résistance – a delicious rosemary roast lamb sandwich on fig bread. The indoor/outdoor café also features live music and art exhibitions.

Belmont Restaurant & Saloon (☎ 360-385-3007; 925 Water St; mains $7-12) Dine in a private lace-shaded booth or on a dais overlooking the water in the lovely dining room of the Belmont Hotel, a one-time dockside saloon constructed in 1885 that once heaved with crowds of brokers, hustlers and merchant seamen. Local seafood and produce highlight the wide-ranging international menu and there are a number of well-presented hotel rooms upstairs ($69 to $109).

Waterfront Pizza (☎ 360-385-6629; 951 Water St; large pizzas $11-19) Quite simply the best pizza in the state, this buy-by-the-slice outlet inspires huge local loyalty and will satisfy even the most querulous of Chicago-honed palates. Don't leave town without trying it.

DRINKING & ENTERTAINMENT

Rose Theatre (☎ 360-385-1089; 235 Taylor St) A Northwest diamond and an architectural emblem for the city, this gorgeously renovated movie theater lay woefully abandoned for 37 years before being brought back to life in the 1990s as an art cinema, replete with bohemian café and buttered popcorn. If only there were more like it.

Maxwell's Brewery & Pub (☎ 360-379-6438; 126 Quincy St) Shoot pool, play darts, eat seafood, swig beer, chat up the locals, swig more beer… Maxwell's is not Port Townsend's only spit-and-sawdust brew pub, but it's arguably the best.

GETTING THERE & AROUND

Washington State Ferries (☎ 206-464-6400) operates 15 trips every day to Keystone on Whidbey Island from the terminal in downtown (car and driver/passenger $11.15/2.60, 30 minutes).

Puget Sound Express (☎ 360-385-5288; 431 Water St) boats depart to San Juan Island at 9am between March and October (one-way/round-trip adult $52/72, child $42/49, bicycles and kayaks $13 round-trip, 2½ hours). Whale-watching tours are also available (p146).

Jefferson Transit (☎ 360-385-4777; www.jeffersontransit.com; 1615 W Sims Way) serves Port Townsend and outlying areas in Jefferson County. Buses travel as far west as Sequim, where connections can be made to Port Angeles and points west on Clallam County's intercity transit system. To the south you can connect with Mason County transit in Brinnon. The basic fare is $1.25.

To reach Port Townsend from Seattle on weekdays, take the ferry from downtown Seattle to Bainbridge Island (35 minutes). At the ferry dock catch Kitsap Transit bus 90 to Poulsbo (20 minutes), and transfer to the Jefferson Transit bus 7 to Port Townsend (one hour).

For a more direct journey, **Olympic Bus Lines** (☎ 360-417-0700; www.olympicbuslines.com) offers connections to and from its Port Angeles–Seattle run, by reservation (see p151). Shuttles arrive and depart from the Haines Place Park and Ride on E Sims Way. Fares are in the $30 bracket to downtown Seattle.

Port Angeles

pop 18,397

Larger, yet less historically interesting, than venerable Port Townsend, Port Angeles is a solid fishing and lumber town which, by right of geography, acts as the main headquarters for the nearby Olympic National Park. Backed by the steep-sided Olympic Mountains that rise like sugar-coated sentinels out of the Strait of Juan de Fuca, the town's impressive natural setting is complemented by numerous inexpensive motels and a clutch of surprisingly good restaurants, making it a good base for exploring the peninsula.

Named Puerto de Nuestra Señora de los Angeles by Spanish explorer Francisco Eliza in 1791 (the name was later anglicized), Port Angeles entered history in 1862 when President Abraham Lincoln created a navy and military reserve around the natural harbor and made it only the second planned city in the US (after Washington, DC). While the fishing industry has declined in recent years with the fall in Pacific salmon stocks, Port Angeles still maintains a couple of pulp mills (that churn out paper for telephone directories) and has added dynamism to its cultural life with a fine arts center and numerous public sculptures. A direct ferry service to Victoria, Canada, and good links with Puget Sound ensure a regular stream of tourists.

INFORMATION

Adjacent to the ferry terminal you'll find the **Port Angeles Visitor Center** (☎ 360-452-2363, 877-456-8372; www.portangeles.org; 121 E Railroad Ave; 🕑 8am-8pm May 15-Oct 15, 10am-4pm rest of yr). Olympic National Park's visitor center (p137) is 1 mile south of town, off Race St.

SIGHTS & ACTIVITIES

For a pre-Olympic limber-up hike, walk along the **Waterfront Trail**, stretching more than 6 miles along the Port Angeles waterfront through downtown and out to the end of **Ediz Hook**, the sand spit that loops around the bay. You can pick up the trail at the base of the City Pier, site of the **Feiro Marine Life Center** (☎ 360-417-6254; adult/5-12yr & senior $2.50/1; 🕑 10am-6pm Tue-Sun Jun-Sep, noon-4pm Sat & Sun Oct-May) where hands-on touch tanks are inhabited by the aquatic denizens of the strait.

The **Clallam County Museum** (☎ 360-452-2662; cnr 1st & Oak Sts; admission free; 🕑 8:30am-4pm Mon-Fri, closed holidays), housed in the 1927 Federal Building, retells the story of the community's growth. The **Port Angeles Fine Arts Center** (☎ 360-457-3532; 1203 E Lauridsen St; admission free; 🕑 11am-5pm Tue-Sun) exhibits the work of many of the professional artists who live on the peninsula. The gallery is high above the city amid a 5-acre sculpture garden with views over the strait.

If you'd like to see the area by bicycle, visit **Sound Bikes & Kayaks** (☎ 360-457-1240; 120 Front St; bike rental per hr/day $9/30).

SLEEPING

Thor Town (☎ 360-452-0931; www.thortown.com; 316 N Race St; per person $14; 💻) The Olympic Peninsula's gateway hostel is a neat, relaxed place in a handsome Dutch colonial home near the Waterfront Trail. Dormitories and two private rooms accommodate 18 people. The congenial hosts offer a full kitchen, internet ($1 per hour), bike rental at a very reasonable $8 per day and useful information on how to get around the peninsula without a car.

Downtown Hotel (☎ 360-565-1125; 101 E Front St; d/ste $65/85; ⊠ ❄) Rather scruffy on the outside but surprisingly elegant within, this family-run place down by the ferry launch is Port Angeles' secret bargain. Bright rooms are decked out in wicker and wood, and showers and communal hallways are kept surgically clean. The Corner House diner downstairs (below) is an ideal place for breakfast.

Port Angeles Inn (☎ 360-452-9285; www.portangelesinn.com; 111 E 2nd St; r $80-125; wi-fi) A better-than-average family-run motel perched on the bluff above downtown, with views over the harbor, this inn offers a complimentary breakfast and inroom wi-fi access.

Tudor Inn (☎ 360-452-3138; www.tudorinn.com; 1108 S Oak St; r $125-160;) With its black-and-white wood beam exterior, this inn manages to look authentically Tudor, although it was built a good 400 years after Henry VIII chopped off Ann Boleyn's head. Constructed by – guess what? – an Englishman in 1910, this refurbished home juxtaposes modern bathroom amenities with fine antiques and an alluring library. Five guestrooms retain their own individual quirks and surprises, and a full English breakfast fortifies hikers striking out for the Olympics.

EATING

Corner House (☎ 360-452-9692; 101 E Front St; entrees $6-8) Head to this quaint diner tucked beneath Downtown Hotel for hot sandwiches and burger-and-fries inspired comfort food with no frills attached. With a 6am opening it's a good place to catch an early breakfast before the morning ferry sailing to Victoria.

Thai Peppers (☎ 360-452-4995; 222 N Lincoln St; mains $8-10) There aren't many ethnic eateries in this neck of the woods, so stock up on your green curry and Pad Thai noodles at this friendly establishment where the congenial waitresses will offer you spicy sauces, sharp service and plenty of tasty food.

Bella Italia (☎ 360-457-5442; 118 E 1st St; mains $11-19; from 4pm) Well-known for its comprehensive wine list (with an astounding 500 selections) and some rather tempting seafood suggestions, Bella Italia is a Port Angeles icon that is often used as a last splurge for hikers facing up to a week or more of camping rations. The restaurant's large glass windows, along with the amiable buzz of the appreciative clientele within, lure hungry travelers inside to sample the Mediterranean/West Coast delights of clam linguine, chicken marsala and smoked duck breast.

Crab House (☎ 360-457-0424; 221 N Lincoln St; mains $15-30; 5:30-11pm) Dungeness crabs are the featured item on the menu at the Crab House and in the light of your location – a few miles from the region's eponymous spit – they don't come much fresher than this. The restaurant is situated in the waterfront Red Lion Hotel and has striking views across the water. Halibut, salmon and an array of steaks are also served here.

THE SEATTLE PRESS EXPEDITION HIKE

In the fall of 1889, the *Seattle Press* newspaper proposed a plan to open up the Washington wilderness to the general public by calling upon hardy amateur adventurers to 'acquire fame by unveiling the mystery which wraps the land encircled by the snow-capped Olympic range.' First to answer the call was a former arctic explorer named James H Christie, who proceeded to lead a party of five men into the uncharted mountains in December 1889, heading south along the Elwha River Valley. After six months of thrashing their way through an unexplored and inhospitable wilderness, the party emerged from the Quinault River Valley on the Pacific Coast in May 1890 half-starved and dressed in rags. It had been an arduous and taxing undertaking, but Christie and his men had successfully mapped the area, reported on its unique flora and fauna, and given names to over 50 peaks, lakes and other landmarks.

Today one of the most popular cross-park treks roughly follows the pioneering route taken by Christie's group and is often referred to as the Seattle Press Expedition hike. Starting at the Whiskey Bend trailhead on the Elwha River, the modern journey to Lake Quinault is 44 miles long, moderately strenuous and commonly takes walkers five days to complete. To tackle it, potential hikers should first take stock of local weather conditions (June to September are the recommended walking months), wise up on wilderness rules and regulations, and pack all of the relevant camping equipment and supplies. Hikers will also need to acquire a backcountry pass from the Wilderness Information Center (p137) in Port Angeles before commencing. For more information on this and other backcountry hikes check out the national park website at www.nps.gov/olym.

THE OLYMPICS BY PUBLIC BUS

Negotiating a remote wilderness area by public transportation might seem like a slightly strange proposition – especially in the car-crazy US – but with some simple planning and less than $5 – yes, five dollars! – in spare change you can circumnavigate the whole Olympic Peninsula by local bus.

To complete the full national park loop you'll need to decipher the timetables of four different transportation authorities and change buses at various transit points, but with comprehensive bus schedules and plenty of handy pit stops en route, the journey is far from onerous.

Port Townsend or Olympia (or even Seattle) are good starting points for the journey. Overnight stops can be arranged in the convenient transit hubs of Port Angeles, Forks, Lake Quinault and Aberdeen. Many day hikes start from the main Olympic ring road (US 101) and, with a quick word to the driver, you can disembark at trailheads in Lake Crescent, Ruby Beach or Kalaloch Lodge to stretch your legs, have a picnic and wait for the next bus to come along.

For Forks to Lake Quinault, or Brinnon to Sequim via Port Townsend, use **Jefferson Transit** (☎ 360-385-4777; www.jeffersontransit.com); from Sequim to Forks use **Clallam Transit** (☎ 360-452-1315; www.clallamtransit.com); from Lake Quinault to Olympia and on to Shelton try **Grays Harbor Transit** (☎ 360-532-2770; www.ghtransit.com); and from Shelton to Brinnon check out **Mason Transit** (☎ 360-426-9434; www.masontransit.org). All public buses have space to carry two bicycles.

GETTING THERE & AROUND

Horizon Air (☎ 360-547-9308, 800-547-9308; www.horizonair.com) has six direct flights daily from Seattle to Fairchild International Airport, just west of Port Angeles. There are other Horizon flights that link Port Angeles to interstate Portland.

Black Ball Transport's **MV Coho ferry** (☎ 360-457-4491; www.cohoferry.com) provides passenger and automobile service to Victoria (adult/child/car and driver $11.50/5.75/44 one-way, 1½ hours), with three crossings a day from May to September. There are two crossings a day the rest of the year, although service is briefly halted during January for maintenance. The passenger-only **Victoria Express** (☎ 360-452-8088) runs three or four times a day from late May through September (adult/child $12.50/7, one hour); there's a $2 fee to transport a bicycle.

Olympic Bus Lines (☎ 360-417-0700; www.olympicbuslines.com) runs two buses a day to/from Sequim (adult/child under 12 $8/4, 30 minutes), the Seattle Greyhound terminal (adult/child under 12 years $39/20, 2½ hours) and Sea-Tac Airport (adult/child $32/16, 3½ hours). Buses arrive and depart from the transit terminal at Front and Oak Sts.

Clallam County's **The Bus** (☎ 360-452-4511; www.clallamtransit.com) travels as far west as Neah Bay and La Push and as far east as Diamond Point. In Port Angeles, the main transfer center is at Oak and Front Sts, conveniently near the ferry dock and visitor center.

NORTHWESTERN OLYMPIC PENINSULA

Despite not falling within the boundaries of the Olympic National Park, the northwest section of the Olympic Peninsula remains sparsely populated and refreshingly remote. Logging is a primary industry here and, in the cultural sphere, four different Native American reservations offer plenty of local legends and history.

Forks is the area's only major settlement, though the fishing town of Neah Bay is reachable by public bus and boasts one of the finest museums of Native American history in the US. The beautiful coastline around La Push in the west provides another worthwhile diversion.

Neah Bay

pop 794

Isolated Neah Bay is a rather lackluster settlement that sits amid breathtaking coastal scenery at the end of Hwy 112 in North America's extreme northwestern corner. Hit hard by the decline in the salmon fishing industry, this small fishing town, characterized by its weather-beaten boats and craning totem poles, is home of the Makah Indian Reservation. The reservation hosts the **Makah Museum** (☎ 360-645-2711; 1880 Bayview Av; admission $5; 10am-5pm daily, closed Mon-Tue Sep-May), which displays artifacts from one of North America's most significant archaeological finds and is reason enough to visit the town. Exposed by tidal erosion in 1970, the 500-year-old Makah village of Ozette proved to be a treasure trove of native history, containing a huge range of materials including whaling weapons, canoes, spears and combs. The museum's centerpiece is a mock-up of an old Ozette longhouse.

The end of the road (in the literal sense) is at a parking lot at the end of a 4-mile gravel track west of the Makah Tribal Center. From here a 0.75-mile boardwalk leads out to a dramatic promontory known as **Cape Flattery**, the most northwesterly point in the lower 48 states. From the four observation decks atop this wild, wind-buffeted point, cliffs fall 60ft to the raging Pacific. Just offshore is Tatoosh Island, with a lighthouse and Coast Guard station. The Cape is frequented by 250 species of bird and is a good place to watch for whales during migration season.

Users of the trail are required to purchase a permit ($10) issued by the Makah Cultural Center (inside the Makah Museum) or at the marina.

SLEEPING & EATING

Cape Motel (☎ 360-645-2250; Neah Bay; r $45-75;) Like most accommodations in Neah Bay, this place doesn't aspire to much beyond the regular fishing crowd, but having reached the end of the road in mainland America, what more could you want than four walls, a roof and a small kitchenette? There's also an RV park and tent spaces available.

Makah Maiden Café (☎ 360-645-2924; 1471 Bayview Av; mains $5-17; 4am-11pm) A great waterfront vista, cozy booths and a pre-dawn opening time make this a favorite hangout for local fishers. But, as well as providing your essential early morning caffeine jolt, the 'Maiden' is also a good bet for seafood, and is renowned for its summer salmon bakes on the beach. Don't miss 'em!

Forks

Forks is a one-horse lumber town on US 101 that boasts the rare distinction of possessing the first and last set of traffic lights for 160 miles. The biggest settlement of note west of Port Angeles and north of Aberdeen, it is often used as a launching pad for sorties into the Hoh Rain Forest, Neah Bay and the Olympic coastline. Forks is not as pretty as the landscapes that surround it, but is friendly and low-key, with enough lodges and eating joints to persuade you to make an overnight stop.

Get orientated at the **Forks Chamber of Commerce** (☎ 360-374-253; www.forkswa.com; 1411 S Forks Ave). Olympic National Park and the USFS share a **Recreation Information Station** (Map p138; ☎ 360-374-7566; 551 S Forks Ave) along the southern approach to Forks. Staffed by knowledgeable rangers, this is the place to get backcountry permits, maps, tide charts and animal-resistant containers for coastal camping.

Next door, the **Timber Museum** (☎ 360-374-9663; admission by donation; 10am-4pm mid-Apr–Oct) commemorates the early settlers and loggers of the region. Included in the museum's collection is a steam donkey (used to transport logs), pioneer farming implements and a fire lookout tower.

You can organize **fishing trips** for steelhead and coho salmon from $250/320 for one/two people per day on the local rivers at the **Three Rivers Resort** (☎ 360-374-5300; 7764 La Push Rd), 8 miles west of Forks on Hwy 110. The lodge also rents surf and boogie boards for Pacific Coast adventurers.

SLEEPING & EATING

Bogachiel State Park (☎ 360-374-6356; Hwy 101; tents/hookups $17/24) The most convenient campground is 6 miles south of Forks, right on the Bogachiel River, with 37 sites, piped water and flush toilets.

Forks Motel (☎ 360-374-6243; 432 S Forks Ave; s/d $65/70; wi-fi) Forks' archetypal motel is glued to the side of US 101, tempting tired drivers to call it a day and put their feet up. Above-average in the standard motel stakes, this place has 73 straightforward units including two kitchen suites and a Jacuzzi suite. There's a laundry, plenty of local fishing information and – better than most – a swimming pool.

The In Place (☎ 360-372-6258; 320 S Forks Ave; sandwiches $4-7, mains $9-17) A quaint little diner that draws in a steady stream of visitors and locals to taste some *real* home cooking. Take a burger, salad or soup in one of the well-worn booths and polish it off with a slice of bumbleberry pie – a luscious blend of blackberries, blueberries, rhubarb and apple. Situated on US 101, this place can get busy in the summer, so be prepared for a wait.

La Push

La Push, 12 miles west of Forks on Hwy 110, is a small fishing village at the mouth of the Quillayute River and home of the Quiluete

Indian tribe, some of the peninsula's oldest inhabitants.

Known for its raw, untamed beaches, La Push is popular with surfers and sea kayakers who love to ride the dramatic Pacific waves, especially in January. Outside of this, the settlement is revered primarily for its remoteness and isolation. Tracking north along the Mora road will bring you to **Rialto Beach** and the start of a 24-mile coastal hike north to Cape Alava (p144). Just outside of La Push are the trailheads to rugged Third and Second Beaches (1.4 miles and 0.8 miles respectively). Third Beach is the starting point for a popular three-day beach hike (p144) to Oil City, 17 miles south, at the edge of the Hoh Indian Reservation.

Sitting above one of Washington's most beautiful beaches, the tribe-owned-and-operated **La Push Ocean Park Resort** (☎ 360-374-5267; tent/RV sites $15/25, motel r $55-78, cabins $80-160, townhouse $120-160) has accommodations ranging from basic A-frame cabins with sleeping-bag loft and toilet (no shower) to deluxe ocean-front cottages with stone fireplaces and whirlpool tubs. Somewhere in the middle are standard motel rooms in two buildings with balconies. No reservations are accepted for camping or RVs.

La Push's only restaurant, **River's Edge Restaurant** (☎ 360-374-5777; 41 Main St; mains $8-25), is one of the best on this stretch of coast with three or four freshly caught seafood options on the menu daily; look out for outdoor barbecues in the summer when salmon is deliciously baked in the Quileute tradition. Located in an old boathouse, the restaurant is famous for its free ornithological shows courtesy of the resident eagles and pelicans.

WASHINGTON COAST

The stretch of Washington coast from Ocean Shores down to Cape Disappointment at the mouth of the Columbia River, with its expansive beaches and locally run oyster farms, is the state's maritime playground. Free of the wild coves and stormy sea stacks more common further north, this is where the whole of Washington (and beyond) comes to sail, fish, fly kites and hang out.

None of the various resorts that scatter the coast in this region are particularly large – or legendary. But, though pockets of modern commercialism may have diluted the quaintness of places such as Long Beach and Ocean Shores, there are still enough state parks, wildlife refuges and lonesome stretches of sand to hide an abundance of unheralded local secrets.

Anchored between Seattle and Portland in the I-5 Corridor, Centralia is a small town with an interesting history and a formidable pub/club/hotel combo. Further south, the US incarnation of Vancouver splays along the northern shores of the Columbia River and provides occasional confusion for misguided travelers who think they've already arrived in Canada (the other Vancouver is 300 miles further north!).

GRAYS HARBOR AREA

Once home to the Chehalis tribe, Grays Harbor was first charted by non-native explorers in 1792, when American Robert Gray arrived in the bay, which acts as an estuary for the Chehalis River. Farming, fishing and fur trading were the staple of the settlers in the 1840s and '50s, though this was quickly replaced by lumber in the 1880s. With most of the mills now closed, Grays Harbor has become a sleepy backwater, although the area is doing its best to lure in tourism with a variety of charter fishing and beachcombing activities.

Ocean Shores

Washington state's most popular coastal resort is a manufactured beach haven known as Ocean Shores that was constructed in the 1960s on a scenic stretch of shoreline some distance south of the Quinault Indian Reservation. While the settlement boasts its fair share of clichéd resort activities including golf, dune buggy–riding and gambling at the Quinault Beach Resort and Casino, the area is far from spoiled with kite-flying, canoeing (there are over 20 miles of interconnecting canals) and razor clamming (digging in the sand for razor clams) also enduringly popular.

You can rent boats to ply the region's ubiquitous canals at **Runabout Cart & Pedal Boat Rental** (☎ 360-289-5001; 598 Point Brown Av SE). Beach horseback riding can be arranged through **Nan-Sea Stables** (☎ 360-289-0194; 255 State Route 115). If the weather turns ugly (and it often does), check out the local history, wildlife and geology at **Ocean Shores Interpretive Center** (☎ 360-289-4617; 1013 Catala Av SE; admission free; 🕑 10am-4pm Apr-Sep).

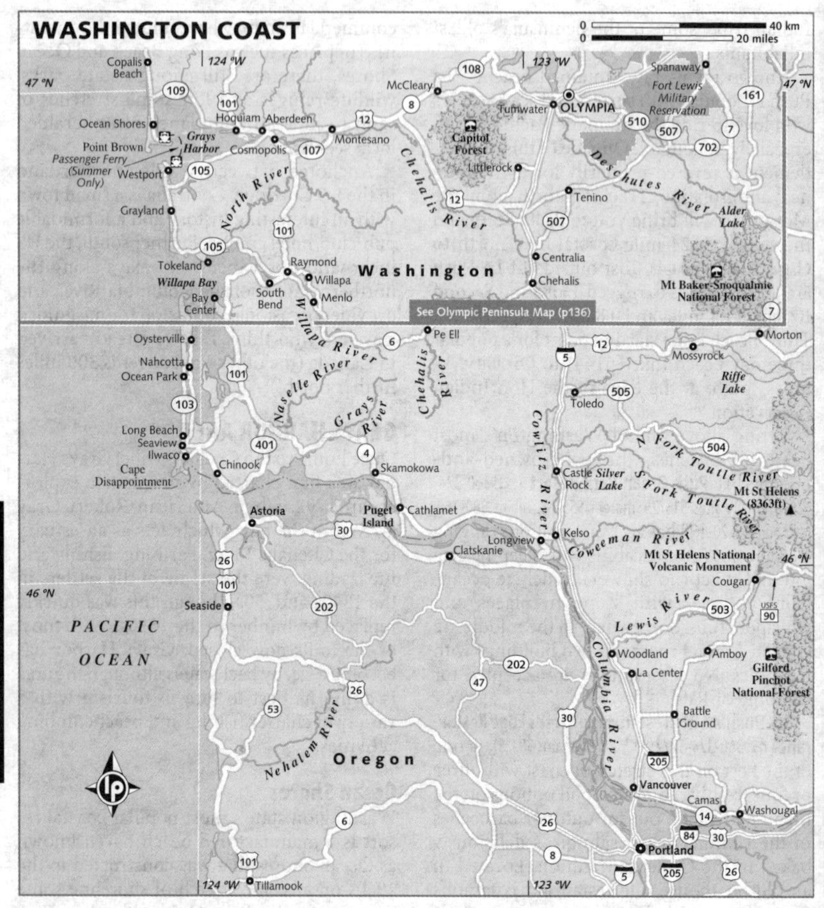

For further information, you can contact **Ocean Shores Chamber of Commerce** (☎ 360-289-2451; www.oceanshores.org; Catala Mall, 899 Point Brown Ave).

Just south of Moclips, the **Ocean Crest Resort** (☎ 360-276-4465; Hwy 109, Sunset Beach; studio $52-159, ste $112-177;) is a stellar self-contained resort and hotel overlooking the Pacific with a good selection of room prices and a decent, if exceedingly expensive, restaurant. Bonuses include a heated indoor pool, sauna and upstairs lounge where you can snuggle down and keep your eye out for passing whales. Private beach access is down a winding, wooded path.

The **Galway Bay Irish Pub** (☎ 360-289-2300; 880 Point Brown Ave) is a long way from the Emerald Isle and the food is way too good to be authentically Irish, but if you're missing your Guinness, Harps or Paddy Burke's white Irish stew, pack your fiddle and roll up here for fine music, loquacious locals and plenty of humorous hospitality.

Aberdeen & Hoquiam

Although they may not make up the prettiest conurbation in Washington state, the twin mill towns of Hoquiam and Aberdeen, referred to alternatively as the 'Birthplace of Grunge Music' and 'the Gateway to the Olympics', have produced enough national celebrities to initiate their very own Hall of Fame: Nirvana cohorts Kurt Cobain and Krist Novoselic were born and raised in Aberdeen; Denver Broncos footballer John Elway spent most of his youth in Hoquiam; aviation pioneer William Boeing made his first inroad into big business by buying up extensive tracts of timberlands around Grays Harbor.

Despite the big names, the twin towns' history has been anything but easy. Aberdeen developed around a salmon-packing plant in the 1870s and Hoquiam's first lumber mill opened in 1882. By 1910 there were over 30 lumber mills ringing the harbor and the burgeoning twin towns had earned a reputation as the roughest places in the nation, replete with whorehouses, gambling dens and a sky-high murder rate. Following the Great Depression, when the lumber mills were reduced to less than a dozen in number, Grays Harbor hit a long decline exacerbated by an equally catastrophic fall in Pacific salmon stocks. When a planned nuclear facility went bust in 1982 the unemployment rate doubled and the city's gritty rough-around-the-edges feel can still be felt today.

In response to the area's ongoing hardships, Aberdeen and Hoquiam have cultivated a thick skin over the years, with a boisterous local spirit fuelling plenty of artistic creativity. The twin towns' **Grays Harbor Chamber of Commerce** (☎ 360-532-1924, www.graysharbor.org; 506 Duffy St) affords visitors a warm welcome. Pop by for free maps and plenty of informative leaflets.

SIGHTS & ACTIVITIES

There's more to Aberdeen and Hoquiam than meets the eye. For history, check out the full-scale replica of the **Lady Washington** in Aberdeen, one of the ships piloted by Captain Robert Gray when he first sailed into Grays Harbor. The ship is open for tours when moored at **Grays Harbor Historical Seaport** (☎ 360-532-8611; www.ladywashington.org; 813 E Heron St; adult/12yr & under/student & senior $3/1/2; 🕑 10am-5pm). It's still used as a working boat.

Other aspects of the harbor's past are found in Hoquiam at the **Arnold Polson Museum** (☎ 360-533-5862; 1611 Riverside Ave; adult/child $2/0.50; 🕑 11am-4pm Wed-Sun Jun 1-Labor Day weekend, noon-4pm Sat & Sun rest of yr). Built in 1924 by one of the timber barons of Hoquiam, the 26-room edifice is filled with period furniture, clothing, a doll collection and logging implements. The nearby **Aberdeen Museum of History** (☎ 360-533-1976; 111 E Third St; admission by donation; 🕑 10am-5pm Tue-Sun) plots the history of this tough mill town from its earliest days, with a strong focus on the lumber industry. You can also ask here about the self-guided **Kurt Cobain Tour** around some of the former houses and hangouts of the late Nirvana star. Cobain and other local luminaries are honored in a Hollywood-style **Walk of Fame** that exhibits star-shaped plaques to former famous residents (and there are many) along Heron St.

SLEEPING & EATING

Westwood Inn (☎ 360-532-8161; 910 Simpson Ave, Hoquiam; s/d $55/69;) You can't miss this sprawling complex just off Hwy 101 near the center of Hoquiam. It's clean, friendly and good value for money, and makes a good sleepover if you can't afford the grandiosity of Hoquiam Castle.

Hoquiam's Castle (☎ 360-533-2005; 515 Chenault Ave, Hoquiam; r $145-195; wi-fi) Part museum (adult/child $4/1), part B&B, part local landmark, this ornate Victorian mansion was built in 1897 on a hill above Hoquiam by Robert Lytle, a wealthy lumber tycoon. The lavish furnishings and meticulous period details are some of the most authentic you'll see in the state and include lots of dark wood, delicate antiques and even a fully working Victorian bathroom. The four rooms are labeled king's, queen's, princess' and knight's, and there's an opulent lobby where traditional afternoon tea can be taken. Nonguests are welcome to view the house most afternoons.

Billy's Bar & Grill (☎ 360-533-7144; 322 E Heron St, Aberdeen; mains $10) If you're passing through on your way to the national park, this place makes a worthwhile pit stop. In the rootin' tootin' days of yore, the bars in Aberdeen were haunted by Billy Gohl (better known as Billy Ghoul), a murderous fellow who robbed and killed drunken sailors and loggers. Billy and the era are both commemorated at this handsome old bar and restaurant with good sandwiches, full dinners and regional microbrews. The place has a split entry, meaning children and non-drinkers can use the dining area.

GETTING THERE & AWAY

Grays Harbor Transit (☎ 360-532-2770, 800-562-9730; www.ghtransit.com) offers daily service between Aberdeen and Westport (bus 55, 40 minutes), Ocean Shores (bus 51, 50 minutes) and Lake Quinault in Olympic National Park (bus 60, 1½ hours), with ongoing connections to North Olympic Peninsula points by Jefferson Transit. Fares start at $0.50. On weekdays, bus 40 makes six trips to/from the Olympia

Greyhound station ($2, 1½ hours); on weekends, it makes three. Buses stop in Aberdeen at Wishkah and G Sts, in Hoquiam at 7th and J Sts.

Westport

Guarding the entrance to Gray's Harbor, storm-lashed Westport is famous for its deep-sea fishing, rugged surfing and isolated beachcombing possibilities. Once the largest whaling port on the West Coast and the largest charter fishing center in the Northwest, the town has suffered since restrictions were placed on salmon fishing in the last couple of decades. In a bid to reinvent itself as Washington's most happening coastal destination, Westport has invested heavily in a chain of restaurants, condos and golf courses. Still on offer are the ever-popular chartered fishing trips and whale-watching expeditions, though the backbone of the fishing industry disappeared years ago.

For more information, contact the **Westport-Grayland Chamber of Commerce & Visitors Center** (☎ 360-268-9422; www.westportcam.com; 2985 S Montesano St; 9am-5pm Mon-Fri, 10am-3pm Sat & Sun), located at the turnoff from Hwy 105.

SIGHTS & ACTIVITIES

A former Coast Guard station, **Westport Maritime Museum** (☎ 360-268-0078; 2201 Westhaven Dr; adult/child $3/1; 10am-4pm Memorial Day-Labor Day, noon-4pm Thu-Mon Sep-May) was built in 1939 and boasts some great period photos and artifacts of seafaring days gone by. A separate building houses the six ton, 18ft-high **Fresnel lens**, manufactured in France in 1888, that beamed for over 70 years from the lighthouse of Destruction Island, 50 miles north of Westport.

Westport's own beacon, the **Grays Harbor Lighthouse** (☎ 360-268-6214; 1020 West Ocean Av; admission $3; 10am-4pm May-Sep, noon-3pm Oct-Apr), also used a Fresnel lens until recently, when it was replaced by a simpler electronic device. To reach the lighthouse – the tallest in the state at 107ft – return to uptown Westport and head west on Ocean Ave. You can also bike or hike there along the **Westport Maritime History Trail**, a 6.5-mile pedestrian pathway that passes the marina and treks along a dune trail into Westhaven State Park. Tours of the lighthouse are available through the maritime museum. Just beyond the lighthouse, **Westport Light State Park** has wind-screened picnic sites and access to a stretch of beach that's closed to motor vehicles in summer.

Charter Fishing & Whale Watching

Charter fishing is still a hot draw card in Westport. The best fishing season runs from April through October (depending on the fish). Regular trips target black rockfish, Ling cod, salmon, halibut and tuna, using live bait and conforming to set fishing limits. One-day licenses can be purchased with the excursion. Deckhands can filet your fish for an extra fee and even arrange to have it vacuum-packed, smoked or stored. Prices tend to start at

DETOUR: CENTRALIA

From its historic founding by an African American slave in 1852 to the violence of the 1919 Centralia Massacre when laborers from the Industrial Workers of the World labor union (the 'Wobblies') opened fire on members of the American Legion, Centralia has provoked its fair share of historical notoriety.

But the overriding reason to make this small, yet engaging, mining and lumber town a pit stop on the long drive north or south along I-5 is to taste the atmosphere at one of Washington's funkiest and most innovative gathering spots, the legendary **Olympic Club Hotel** (☎ 360-736-5164; 112 N Tower Ave; bunk/queen/king $40/60/70). A boisterous bar, restaurant, billiard hall, movie theater and hotel, the Olympic dates from 1908, when it was billed as a 'gentlemen's resort' designed to satisfy the various drinking, gambling and sexual vices of local miners and loggers. In 1996 this perfectly preserved turn-of-the-century building was taken over by McMenamins brewers from Portland, who redecorated the hotel interior in period style with creaking floorboards, Tiffany lamps and art-deco murals. Downstairs you'll still find a bar, billiard hall, restaurant and small movie theater where friendly waitresses will bring in your food orders as the opening credits roll while, upstairs, quaint hotel rooms sport arty graffiti chronicling the misdemeanors of past guests. Stop by for a value-for-money sandwich washed down with one of half a dozen handcrafted ales.

around $90 per person per day for salmon fishing and up to about $165 for halibut, but shop around.

Most of these charter companies also run whale-watching excursions in the spring. Stroll along the marina and check the offerings. An hour-long excursion will generally cost around $30/20 per adult/child.

For more about charter fishing contact **Coho Charters** (☎ 360-268-0111; www.westportwa.com/coho; 2501 N Nyhus, Westport) or **Deep Sea Charters** (☎ 360-268-9300, 800-562-0151; www.deepseacharters.biz; 2319 Westhaven Dr, Westport), or procure a full list at the Visitors Center (opposite).

SLEEPING & EATING

Glenacres Inn B&B (☎ 360-268-0958; 222 N Montesano St, Westport; d $90-125) Westport's contribution to the vintage B&B scene is a good midrange option if you don't mind lace curtains, grandma's rocking chair and an old sewing machine located at the end of your bed. Built in 1898, this recently renovated 19th-century beauty boasts eight rooms and a charming gazebo gracing its tranquil wooded grounds.

Anthony's Restaurant (☎ 360-268-9166; 421 Neddie Rose Dr; mains $20-30) The toast of Westport, this swish new place situated in the port's all-purpose vacation complex serves up classic Dungeness crab cakes for appetizers, followed by such scrumptious delights as pesto salmon (what else?) and an 8oz filet mignon wrapped in bacon. The setting is intimate and the delicious food easily worth the hefty prices.

GETTING THERE & AWAY

Grays Harbor Transit (☎ 360-532-2770; www.ghtransit.com) bus 55 offers service to/from Aberdeen ($0.50, 40 minutes), with connections for Olympia and the Long Beach Peninsula. Buses stop at the bottom end of Montesano St, near Twin Harbor State Park, and at the dock area.

A passenger ferry crosses from Westport to Ocean Shores six times daily mid-June to Labor Day, and on weekends only May to mid-June and September ($6/10 one-way/round-trip). Purchase tickets at Float 10. Call **Westport/Ocean Shores Ferry** (☎ 360-268-0047) for information.

LONG BEACH PENINSULA

Long Beach Peninsula, the narrow sand spit north of the Columbia River, claims to have the world's longest beach. And with 28 unbroken miles of it, the boast has to be taken seriously. However, the adjoining 28 miles of rather lackluster development are a disappointment, and the beach itself is overrun with pickup trucks (as Washington state beaches are considered highways). Purists might prefer the Willapa Bay side of the peninsula, with its old towns, oyster beds and wildlife viewing.

Oysterville & Nahcotta

The charm of these old communities – the only ones on the bay side of the Long Beach Peninsula – derives not just from their history but also from the absence of the beachfront towns' carnival atmosphere. Here, wildlife viewing, oyster harvesting and gracious dining occupy residents and visitors alike. Oysterville stands largely unchanged since its heyday in the 1870s, when the oyster boom was at its peak.

SIGHTS & ACTIVITIES

Oysterville is filled with well-preserved Victorian homes including the 1863 **Red Cottage** (Territory Rd) near Clay St, which served as the first Pacific County courthouse, and the **Big Red House** (cnr Division St & Territory Rd), the original home of Oysterville cofounder RH Espy, built in 1871. Other historic buildings include a one-room schoolhouse and the 1892 **Oysterville Church** (cnr Clay St and Territory Rd); pick up a walking-tour brochure here.

The 807-acre **Leadbetter Point State Park Natural Area** (☎ 360-642-3078; Stackpole Rd), 3 miles north of Oysterville, is a kind of buffer between the straggling developments of Long Beach Peninsula and a section of the Willapa National Wildlife Refuge, a narrowing band of dunes increasingly breached by Pacific waves. Though most people just meander down to the reedy shores of Willapa Bay, two hiking trails lead through forest and marshes to reach these lowering dunes, as good a place as any in the Northwest to watch for shorebirds.

SLEEPING & EATING

Moby Dick Hotel & Oyster Farm (☎ 360-665-4543; www.nwplace.com/mobydick.html; 25814 Sandridge Rd, Nahcotta; d incl breakfast $90-140) You can take yoga classes in a yurt or get intimate with the whale vertebrae that furnishes the patio in this 1929 structure which once served as a Coast Guard barracks. Other features include a sauna, three communal lounge rooms and a celebrated restaurant that serves up delicious oysters picked from its very own oyster beds. Bold colors and eclectic themes characterize the 10 well-appointed rooms (two of which have a private bath) and a scrumptious three-course breakfast should keep you going all day.

Ark (☎ 360-665-4133; www.arkrestaurant.com; 3310 273rd St, Nahcotta; mains $18-25; ⏰ evenings Tue-Sat Aug & Sep, Wed or Thu-Sat Mar-Jul, Oct, Fri-Sun Dec-Mar) Giving away little from the outside, this unassuming red wooden building is a long-standing West Coast phenomenon that was championing the advantages of fresh, local ingredients, recycling and grow-your-own herbs when Al Gore was still in dungarees. The specialties are whatever grows or lives nearby, including fried oysters, Dungeness crabs, cranberries and wild mushrooms. At least 50% of what's on the menu is organic. To work up an appetite you can enjoy a pre-meal stroll through the restaurant's herb and flower gardens overlooking Willapa Bay.

Long Beach & Seaview

Long Beach and Seaview comprise the major population center on the peninsula. Both towns began as beach resorts in the late 1880s. A few old inns from this era have been beautifully restored, but most visitors will probably find that much of the area's local charm has been overrun by aggressive commercialization. Hwy 103, the main drag, is lined with T-shirt shops, middlebrow boutiques, fast-food mills and bumper-car arenas, though the beach – if often crowded – is undeniably appealing.

ORIENTATION & INFORMATION

Hwy 103 (also known as 'Pacific Hwy') runs along the west side of the peninsula from Seaview to Leadbetter Point State Park. On the east (bay) side, Sandridge Rd extends from just east of Seaview to Oysterville. Local access roads cross the peninsula at various points, linking these parallel routes.

The **Long Beach Peninsula Visitors Bureau** (☎ 360-642-2400; www.funbeach.com; cnr Hwy 101 & Pacific Hwy, Seaview; ⏰ 9am-5pm Mon-Sat, 10am-4pm Sun) can help you get reservations for the area's motels and lodgings.

SIGHTS & ACTIVITIES

Primary **beach access** points in Long Beach are off 10th St SW and Bolstad Ave; a 0.25-mile boardwalk links the two entryways. In Seaview, take 38th Place, just south of Hwy 101. Cars and trucks aren't allowed on these busy beaches in summer, but the beach north of Bolstad Ave to Ocean Park is open to vehicles year-round.

Note that surf swimming here is dangerous due to strong waves and quickly changing tides. Instead of plunging into the water, you might hit the saddle and ride on horseback along the endless dunes. Several Long Beach outfitters offer horseback-riding tours (solo riding is discouraged); try **Skippers Equestrian Center** (☎ 360-642-3676; cnr S 10th St & Ocean Beach Blvd). Biking along the boardwalk is another fun activity. **OWW** (☎ 360-642-4260; cnr 10th St & Ocean Beach Blvd) rents out bicycles ($5 per hour) and mopeds ($18).

Thousands of people descend on Long Beach during the third week of August for the **Washington State International Kite Festival**, billed as the largest such event in the western hemisphere. Festival-goers seek to gain new world records: the greatest number of kites in flight at one time, the largest kite flown, the longest time aloft and so on.

With some 150,000 people attending the festival annually, it was just a matter of time before someone opened the **World Kite Museum & Hall of Fame** (☎ 360-642-4020; 303 Sid Snyder Dr; adult/child $5/3; ⏰ 11am-5pm daily Jun-Aug, Fri-Mon Sep-May). If you think a museum devoted to the history and artistry of kites might be a bore, think again. Kites have been used for scientific research, aerial photography, mail delivery and reconnaissance – as well as for amusement – for centuries. The whole story's here, along with the largest, smallest and wackiest kites.

SLEEPING & EATING

Historic Sou'wester Lodge (☎ 360-642-2542; 38th Place, Seaview; tent/RV sites $18/20, trailers $39-104, lodge r $59-69, lodge ste $71-109, cabins $81) Built in 1892 by an Oregon senator, this three-story lodge – now owned by a well-traveled couple from South Africa who arrived here via Israel – has a self-amused air of funkiness, eclecticism and nonchalance. It's heavy on irreverence: the proprietors insist that the establishment is a B&(MYOD)B, or 'bed and make your own damn breakfast.' In the original lodge, there are both simple bedroom units that share a kitchen, bathroom and living area, and also apartment-style suites. Worth investigating (even if you're not staying here) are the 'TCH! TCH!' units, or Trailer Classics Hodgepodge –

a collection of 1950s Spartan house trailers, each one renovated and individually decorated à la Sou'wester. There are also sites for tents and RVs with hot showers and laundry.

Shoalwater Restaurant (☎ 360-642-4142; 4415 Pacific Way; mains from $20; ⏲ from 5:30pm) Many consider the restaurant at the Shelburne Country Inn one of the showplaces of Northwest cuisine. The dining room, dominated by arched stained-glass windows salvaged from an English church, is certainly one of the most charming you'll find. Local seafood, fish, poultry and lamb are served with a consistently inventive flair. The inn itself is a Washington classic with 17 elegant guestrooms starting at $145 per night.

GETTING THERE & AROUND

Pacific Transit System (☎ 360-642-9418) runs buses throughout Pacific County, from Aberdeen to towns along the Long Beach Peninsula via South Bend and Raymond, and as far south as Astoria, Oregon. Bus 20 runs approximately once an hour between Ilwaco and Oysterville from around 6am to 7pm weekdays ($0.50, 40 minutes), less often on Saturday and not at all on Sunday.

Ilwaco

pop 950

The major fishing port on Washington's southern coast, Ilwaco still bustles with charter and commercial craft. The early growth of the salmon-canning industry here was aided by the development of salmon traps, a method of catching the fish that was made illegal in the 1930s.

Unlike the rest of the Long Beach Peninsula, Ilwaco is hemmed in by rocky hills. West of town, on a rugged promontory above the mouth of the Columbia River in Cape Disappointment State Park, are the remains of Fort Canby, a Civil War–era bulwark designed to protect river shipping from Confederate interference.

SIGHTS

The **Ilwaco Heritage Museum** (☎ 360-642-3446; 115 SE Lake St; adult/6-11yr/12-17yr/senior $3/1/2/2.50; ⏲ 10am-4pm Mon-Sat, noon-4pm Sun) investigates ancient Chinook culture, along with the exploration and trade of successive Spanish, Russian, British and American explorers. There's also a restored narrow gauge passenger train known as the *Nahcotta*.

Although little remains of the original Fort Canby that once stood in what is now **Cape Disappointment State Park** (☎ 360-642-3078; Hwy 100; ⏲ dawn-dusk), 2 miles southwest of Ilwaco, the location is of considerable interest because of its interpretive center, wild beach area and hiking trails to the dramatic lighthouse.

Established in 1852, Fort Canby was heavily armed during the Civil War to prevent Confederate gunboats from entering the Columbia River. Upgraded dramatically during WWII, the fort stood as the principal defender of the river. Although no shots were fired from Fort Canby, a Japanese submarine did manage to penetrate close enough to the Oregon side to fire on Fort Stephens in 1942.

Lewis and Clark camped near here in 1805 and climbed up onto the bluff for their first real glimpse of the Pacific Ocean. Their journey is faithfully recounted at the **Lewis & Clark Interpretive Center** (☎ 360-642-3029; Hwy 100; adult/youth $5/2.50; ⏲ 10am-5pm), located inside the state park.

From the interpretive center, a hiking trail leads half a mile to **Cape Disappointment Lighthouse**. Built in 1856, it's the oldest such structure still in use on the West Coast. Nearby, the **North Head Lighthouse**, built in 1896, offers tours from $2.50. Call the park for more details.

ACTIVITIES

Unsurprisingly, Ilwaco has plenty of charter fishing options, with expeditions sallying forth in search of salmon, sturgeon, tuna or bottom fish, depending on the season. Charters start at $85 per person and set sail at the crack of dawn. Try **Pacific Salmon Charters** (☎ 360-642-3466; 191 Howerton Ave) for some of the best organized trips.

SLEEPING & EATING

Cape Disappointment State Park Campground (☎ 360-642-3078; Hwy 100; tent/RV sites $17/24, yurts & cabins $35) There are nearly 250 sites in two zones: by the beach and around a lake near the park entrance. Coin-operated hot showers and flush toilets are within easy reach. Yurts, cabins and three former lightkeeper's residences provide further unique accommodation options.

Inn at Harbor Village (☎ 360-642-0087; www.innatharborvillage.com; 120 Williams Ave NE; r $115-185; ⊠ wi-fi) One of Washington's most improbable and creative accommodations is this recently refurbished 1928 Presbyterian church, with its sloped ceilings and nine exquisite guestrooms. The parlor has an old grandfather clock, plus you can enjoy the delights of a complimentary breakfast and wine. The inn is set in woodland, an easy walk from Ilwaco port.

Don's Portside Café/Pizzeria (☎ 360-642-3477; 303 Main St; breakfast from $4, lunch $7-9) The oldest of Ilwaco's old staples, Don's is located at the same address as the Ilwaco fruit packing company, meaning its pies are exemplary even if its coffee is not quite up to Seattle standards.

VANCOUVER

pop 143,560

Fast-growing Vancouver, Washington, suffers from the same affliction as London, Ontario, or Paris, Texas: it shares its name with a far more illustrious and populous counterpart. To add to the ignominy, the city also lives in the shadow of fashionable Portland just across the Columbia River and is often overlooked by transient travelers as being little more than a glorified suburb.

The generalizations are only partly true. While Vancouver can't compete in cultural terms with the metro giants of Seattle or Portland, the city does boast a refurbished central park, a thriving farmers market, and some of the state's earliest and most important pioneering history. Fort Vancouver is one of the oldest military installations in the Pacific Northwest and a key piece of Washington's historical jigsaw. Elsewhere the city offers a county museum, a handful of ethnic restaurants and plenty of interesting Lewis and Clark memorabilia. But with a dearth of decent downtown hotels and little to do after dark, few travelers linger here for long.

Orientation & Information

Vancouver sits on the northern bank of the Columbia River, 164 miles from Seattle and only 8 miles from downtown Portland across the I-5 Bridge. Hwy 14 follows the north bank of the river, joining I-5 and continuing east to the Columbia River Gorge. Downtown Vancouver is directly west of I-5. Main St and Broadway, the principal streets, parallel the freeway.

For information about the Vancouver area, contact the **Southwest Washington Visitors & Convention Bureau** (☎ 360-750-1553; 101 E 8th St, Ste 240).

Sights & Activities

The **Vancouver National Historic Reserve** (☎ 360-992-1800; www.vnhrt.org), situated within easy walking distance of the city center, is Vancouver's – and one of Washington's – most important historical monuments. Comprising an archaeological site, the region's first military post, a waterfront trail and one of the nation's oldest operating airfields, the complex's highlight is the reconstructed **Fort Vancouver Historic Site** (☎ 360-696-7655; adult/family $3/5; 🕑 9am-5pm Mar-Oct, 9am-4pm Nov-Feb). Here resident rangers and actors in period costume skillfully summon up the era from 1825 to 1845, when the fort was under the sole administration of the British Hudson Bay Company (the so-called Oregon Country was run jointly by the British and the Americans until 1846). Within the stockaded grounds, you can learn how the fort was once a center for the burgeoning Northwest fur trade and a bulwark in a shaky 40-year alliance between the Americans and the British. As historical presentations go, it's one of the most entertaining and educational walkabouts in the state. Tours generally leave on the hour.

Travelers should also pop into the **Visitor's Center** (☎ 360-816-6230; 612 E Reserve St; admission free; 🕑 9am-5pm Mar-Oct, 9am-4pm Nov-Feb), which boasts a small museum and a fascinating video on the Lewis and Clark expedition which wound up near here in November 1805.

Along the north side of E Evergreen Blvd are the historic homes of **Officers Row**. Built between 1850 and 1906 for US Army officers and their families, they are currently rented out as offices and apartments. Three of the homes are open for self-guided tours. **Grant House** (☎ 360-693-3103; 1101 Officers Row; admission free; 🕑 11am-9pm), built in 1850 from logs and later covered with clapboard, now houses a restaurant (opposite). **Marshall House** (🕑 9am-5pm), home to General George Marshall in the 1930s, is a grand Queen Anne–style mansion. The **OO Howard House** (☎ 360-992-1800) built in 1879 was a non-commissioned officer's club during WWII and was restored to its former elegance in 1998. It now houses a small gift shop. Ask at the visitor's center about guided walks. Elsewhere, the lovely open spaces of the Historic Reserve are a great place to enjoy a picnic, fly a kite or take a stroll. At the time of writing, a land bridge was being built to connect the reserve with the Columbia River waterfront.

Just east of Fort Vancouver is the new **Pearson Air Museum** (☎ 360-694-7026; 1115 E 5th St; adult/6-12yr/13-18yr/senior $5/2/3/4; 🕑 10am-5pm Tue-Sun), devoted to the colorful history of Northwest aviation. A number of historic planes are on display in the main hangar, surrounded by exhibits on the golden age of flight.

Sleeping & Eating

Briar Rose Inn (☎ 360-694-5710; www.briarroseinn.com; 310 W 11th St; r with shared bath from $75; wi-fi) A 1908 Craftsman-style home turned B&B with antique-laden rooms, the Briar Rose is one of the few accommodations in the vicinity of downtown Vancouver. Venture further out and you're in big chain hotel/motel land and a substantial hike from the downtown core.

Farmers Market (W 8th St, cnr Columbia St; 🕑 10am-6pm) One of the best and cheapest places to eat in Vancouver is at this daily indoor/outdoor farmers market in Esther Short Park. Inside you'll find German deli sandwiches, tasty pastries and excellent Pad Thai noodles for as little as $5. Outside, in the summer, look out for the huge paellas that are concocted out on the street accompanied by an ebullient cooking commentary.

Grant House Restaurant (☎ 360-696-1727; 1101 Officers Row; mains from $15; 🕑 lunch Mon-Fri, dinner Tue-Sat, brunch Sun) A more refined experience can be found at the Vancouver National Historic Reserve in this original restaurant.

Getting There & Away

Three Greyhound buses a day stop in Vancouver on their way between Portland and Seattle. Amtrak trains run a coastal service to Seattle in the north and Portland in the south. The Empire Builder stops in Vancouver before heading west to Pasco, Spokane and, ultimately, Chicago. **Tri-Met Transit** (☎ 503-238-7433) offers frequent service between downtown Portland and Vancouver's 7th Street transit center.

Washington Cascades

The magical Cascade Mountains run from southern British Columbia (BC) all the way down to Northern California and dominate the history, geography and climate of the land west of the Rockies. Part of the Pacific Ring of Fire, a ribbon of active volcanoes that encircles the Pacific Ocean, Washington's part of the range contains some of America's tallest peaks and five picturesque but potentially lethal volcanoes: Mt Baker, Glacier Peak, Mt Rainier, Mt Adams and Mt St Helens. St Helens erupted with devastating consequences in May 1980.

Close to the Pacific Ocean, the Cascades' steep ridges and lava-sculpted summits cause a substantial amount of precipitation to fall on their exposed western flanks (Mt Baker broke the world record for snowfall in a single season in 1999). Dense forests filled with western hemlock, Douglas fir and red cedar have traditionally flourished in these well-watered zones while, on the mountain's dryer eastern slopes, ponderosa pine and western larch predominate.

Renowned for their harsh, impregnable terrain and copious crevasse-covered glaciers, the highest Cascade peaks are vast stand-alone mountains that dominate their surroundings for miles around. Standing high above the nearby crest-lines, snowcapped giants such as Rainier and Baker rise like powerful natural monuments over the bustling population centers of Upper and Lower Puget Sound and are imbued with local legends.

Protected by a string of overlapping wilderness areas, national forests and national parks, the Cascades offer some of the best backcountry adventures in the USA, if you don't mind braving the elements and getting to grips with tent camping and freeze-dried food. For the less outdoor-minded, tantalizing snapshots of the region's rarified beauty can be glimpsed traveling through by car, bus or train.

HIGHLIGHTS

- Standing on the **Diablo Dam Overlook** (p170) and gazing out over the inhospitable, yet awe-inspiring, North Cascades wilderness
- Hiking up to **Cascade Pass** (p170) to the sound of crashing glaciers
- Enjoying scrumptious food and fork-dropping views in the **Sun Mountain Lodge's** (p173) celebrated restaurant
- Cross-country skiing on a sunny winter's day in the **Methow Valley** (p185)
- Catching your first glimpse of **Mt Rainier** (p179) as it breaks through the hazy morning mist
- Watching new life re-emerge on **Mt St Helens** (p186)

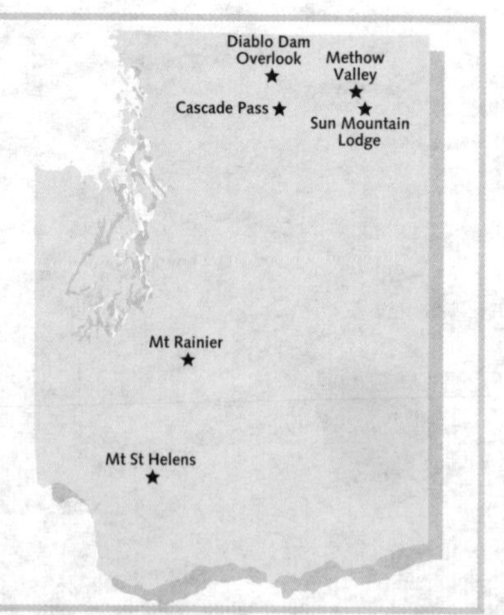

WASHINGTON CASCADES

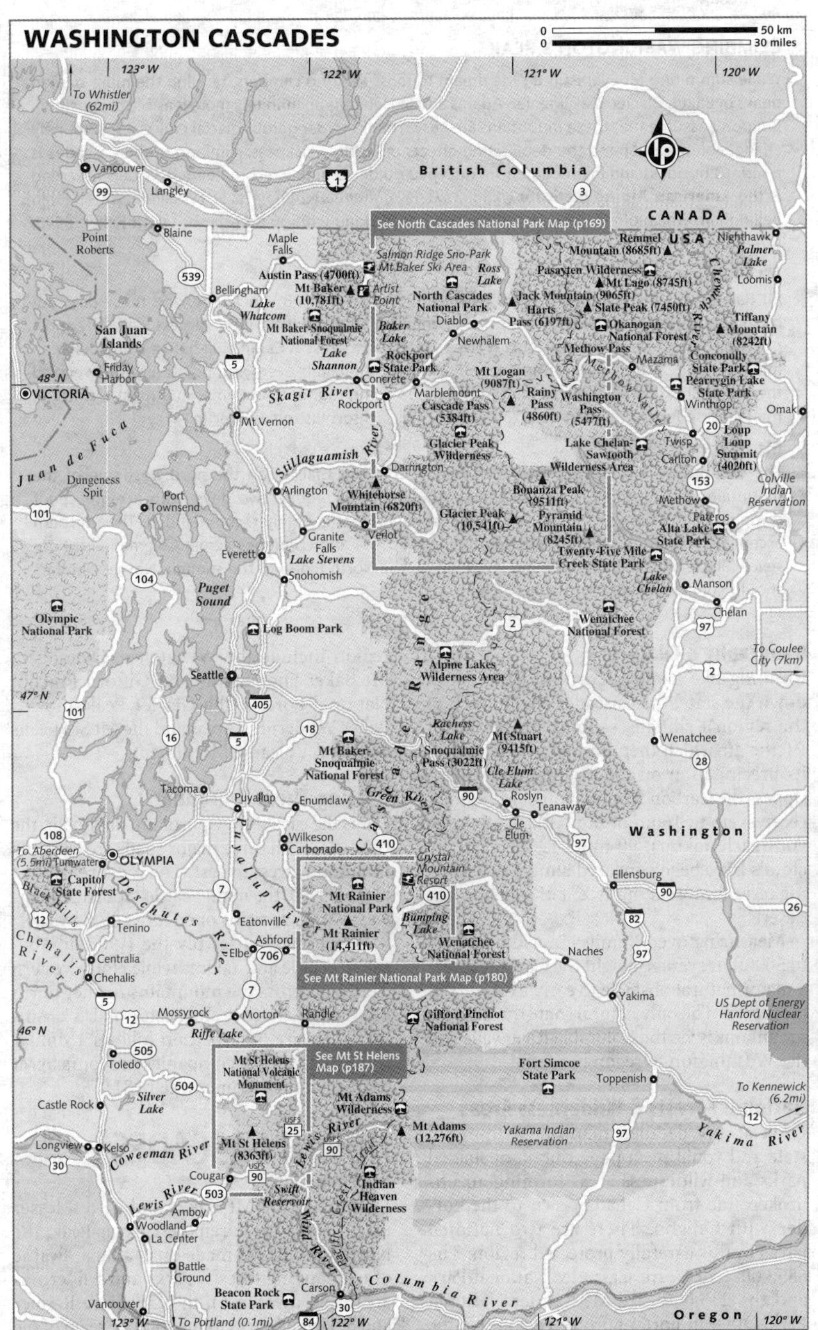

CLIMBING WASHINGTON'S PEAKS

While summiting Mt Everest is a pipe dream to most aspiring climbers, tackling the more benign peaks of Baker, Glacier Peak, Rainier, Adams and St Helens is an infinitely more feasible proposition. But don't assume that these mountains are easy. Thanks to dangerous glacial crevasses, extremely changeable weather and the debilitating effects of altitude sickness, climbing in the Cascades is a serious business and instruction from qualified guides is highly recommended. Widely regarded is the **American Alpine Institute** (☎ 360-671-1505; www.aai.cc; 1515 12th St, Bellingham, WA 98225) in Bellingham which offers general training programs, along with guided climbs up Mt Baker ($570, three days) and Mt Rainier ($1540, five days).

Mt Rainier

Mt Rainier was first climbed in 1870 by Hazard Stevens and PB Van Trump, and these days approximately 10,000 climbers attempt the summit annually with a 60% success rate. The most popular route starts at Paradise and involves a brief night's rest at Camp Muir before rising between midnight and 2am to don crampons and ropes for the climb over Disappointment Cleaver and the Ingraham Glacier to the summit. All climbers going higher than Camp Muir must register at the Paradise Ranger Station next to the Henry M Jackson Visitors Center (p181).

Mt Baker

The two principal routes up Mt Baker ascend Coleman Glacier, on the northwest side of the mountain, and Easton Glacier, on the south side. Both require two days, with a night spent camping at the base of the glacier. Technical equipment is highly recommended. The northern ascent begins at the Heliotrope Ridge trailhead (p166) and continues across Coleman and Roosevelt Glaciers for a final steep and icy climb up the North Ridge to the summit. Novice climbers should consider classes and guided climbs.

Geography & Climate

Running like a spinal cord north to south down the state, the Cascades affect much of the region's climate, sapping up the moist Pacific air which then dumps a large part of its precipitation on the mountain's western slopes (the Carbon River region of Mt Rainier receives up to 160in of rainfall). By the time you reach Yakima, 90 miles to the east, the clouds have been squeezed almost dry, leaving terrain more reminiscent of a steppe-like desert.

Measuring over 80 miles in width and up to 5000ft in average height the Cascades were a major natural obstacle to early explorers in the region. The only natural route through the mountains is via the Columbia River valley on the Washington–Oregon border.

National Forests & Wilderness Areas

Look at any detailed map of Washington state and you'll see a huge ribbon of shaded parks and wilderness areas forming an unbroken line from Canada down to the border with Oregon. There are two national parks in this carefully protected region: The 685,000-acre North Cascades National Park and the 235,000-acre Mt Rainier National Park. Other important protected zones in the region include the Wenatchee, Okanogan, Mt Baker-Snoqualmie and Gifford Pinchot National Forests, the Glacier Peak and Mt Baker Wilderness Areas and the Mt St Helens National Volcanic Monument.

Getting There & Around

Car is the easiest transportation method in the Cascades with three major roads crossing the mountains west to east. The most reliable of these is I-90, the main Seattle–Spokane highway, which remains open most of the year.

Greyhound buses ply the I-90 daily between Seattle and Yakima while Northwestern Trailways cross the mountains further north between Wenatchee and Seattle on US 2. Amtrak's *Empire Builder* train follows a similar route. Various bus companies run tours to Mt Rainier in the summer (see p181).

NORTH CASCADES

Dominated by Mt Baker and – to a lesser extent – the more remote Glacier Peak, the North Cascades is made up of a huge swathe of overlapping forests, parks and wilderness areas that dwarf even the expansive Rainier and St Helens parks to the south. Cream of the

Mt Adams

Mt Adams is one of the easiest Cascade peaks to climb, and is often used as a trial peak for beginners. While most climbs are non-technical slogs up a glacier, even these require basic climbing gear. The easiest approach (grade II) is from the south, via Cold Springs Campground, and up the South Spur to the summit. The climb is best between May and August. Climbers should sign in and out at the USFS ranger station at either Trout Lake or Randle.

Mt St Helens

Due to Mt St Helens delicate volcanic state, climbers must obtain a permit to ascend the peak from the **Mt St Helens Institute** (☎ 360-449-7887; www.mshinstitute.org). Permits should be purchased online and cost $22. Although no technical climbing abilities are needed, the hike is no walk in the park and many summit-seekers camp by the trailhead at Climber's Bivouac the night before climbing, 14 miles northeast of Cougar at the end of USFS Rd 830 (a narrow gravel road that spurs off USFS Rd 83 at Cougar Sno-Park). From here, the Monitor Ridge Trail (No 216A) ascends 1100ft in 2.3 miles to reach the timberline from where you must scramble 5 miles over lava chunks and loose pumice fields to reach the summit cliffs. Allow at least eight hours to make the round-trip.

Glacier Peak

This wilderness volcano is usually tackled from the White Chuck River Trail which begins at a trailhead off the Mountain Loop Hwy. Joining briefly with the Pacific Crest Trail 1.5 miles past Kennedy Hot Springs you then turn north and hike about a half-mile to the Glacier Trail and Sitkum Ridge and the timberline base camp. The push to the summit takes you across the Sitkum Glacier, a relatively non-technical but steep route to the 10,541ft summit. Due to a storm in 2003 much of this route is still damaged. Check ahead.

crop is the North Cascades National Park, one of the country's most remote and least-visited national parks but – as a result – also one of its most attractive.

Geologically different to the South Cascades, the northern mountains are peppered with sharp, jagged peaks, copious glaciers and a preponderance of complex metamorphic rock. This gives them their distinctive alpine feel and has helped create the kind of irregular, glacier-sculpted characteristics that have more in common with the mountains of Alaska than the less crenellated ranges further south. Thanks to their virtual impregnability, the North Cascades were a virtual mystery to humans until relatively recently. The first road was built across the region in 1972 and, even today, it remains one of the Northwest's most isolated outposts.

Orientation

You can pick up Hwy 20, the only road across the North Cascades, in the west at Burlington at exit 230 on I-5 from where it tracks east up the Skagit River Valley. From the east, Hwy 20 can be picked up at Omak, Okanogan or Twisp. Due to heavy winter snowfalls, the section of this road between Marblemount and Mazama is generally closed between late November and early April. Call ☎ 888-766-4636 for road conditions.

MT BAKER AREA

Rising like a snowy sentinel above the sparkling waters of upper Puget Sound, Mt Baker's luminous ethereal beauty has been mesmerizing visitors to the Northwest for centuries.

The Native Americans admired the mountain they called Koma Kulshan for its glowering craggy mystique, and Captain George Vancouver named its 10,781ft summit after his third lieutenant, Joseph Baker who was the first European to sight it in 1792. These days snowboarders venerate the peak's steep slopes and rollercoaster downhill runs for their record-breaking winter snowfalls and annual 'Legendary Baker Banked Slalom' race.

Formed approximately 30,000 years ago, during a series of explosive volcanic eruptions, Baker's distinctive conical summit sits atop a much older volcanic cone known to geologists as the Black Buttes. Modern-day summit cinder cones suggest that Baker may have experienced further significant eruptions less than 1000 years ago, while major ash showers were recorded as recently as the 1850s.

Despite its relatively modest height compared to the taller mountains further south, Mt Baker retains a number of interesting idiosyncrasies. The most northerly of the American Cascades, Baker is also the range's second-most heavily glaciated mountain (after Mt Rainier) and – thanks to an extraordinary seasonal snowfall in 1999 of 95ft – it can also claim to be one of the snowiest places on earth. Mt Baker is the second most active volcano in the region and increased fumarolic activity during the mid-1970s led some experts to bet on it blowing its top before Mt St Helens. Fortunately for aspiring snowboarders and peace-loving Bellingham residents, the predictions proved wrong and Baker has retained its icy majesty to seduce another generation of proud Washingtonians.

Orientation

Well-paved Hwy 542 – known as the Mt Baker Scenic Byway – climbs 5100ft to the aptly named Artist Point, 56 miles from Bellingham and is generally open year-round. The last gas station is in Maple Falls (25 miles from Bellingham) and the last motels and restaurants are in Glacier (33 miles).

Information

Jointly run by the national forest and park services, **Glacier Public Service Center** (☎ 360-599-2714; 1094 Mt Baker Hwy; 🕓 8:30am-4:30pm Memorial Day-Oct) is just east of Glacier. At this handsome stone lodge built by the Civilian Conservation Corps is a small bookstore, interpretive displays on the park and a ranger to answer questions. In summer, there's also a staffed visitors center at **Heather Meadows** (MP 56 Mt Baker Hwy; 🕓 8am-4:30pm May-Sep).

For more information about the wilderness area, contact the folk at **Mt Baker Ranger Station** (☎ 360-856-5700; ☎ year-round), located at the junction of Hwy 9 and Hwy 20 in Sedro-Woolley.

Mt Baker Scenic Byway

The 56-mile drive east along Hwy 542 from metropolitan Bellingham to the other-worldly **Artist Point** through moss-draped forests and past gushing creeks is one of the Northwest's most rewarding drives. Glacier, 33 miles in, is the last main settlement on the route. Seven miles further on turn right on Wells Creek Rd and after half a mile you'll encounter **Nooksack Falls**, which drop 175ft into a deep gorge. This was the site of one of America's oldest hydropower facilities built in 1906 and abandoned in 1997. Back on Hwy 542 the road begins to climb in earnest until you reach **Heather Meadows** at mile post 56. The Mt Baker Ski Area is here, and just up the road is **Austin Pass**, a picnic area and the starting point of several hiking trails.

Activities

HIKING

While Mt Baker offers plenty of advanced hikes for experienced walkers, there's also a handful of easier options that leave from the Artist Point parking lot and are manageable for families. The interpretive **Artist Ridge Trail** is an easy 1-mile loop through heather and berry fields with the craggy peaks of Mts Baker and Shuksan scowling in the background. Another option is the 0.5-mile **Fire and Ice Trail** adjacent to the Heather Meadows Visitors Center which explores a valley punctuated by undersized mountain hemlock. Or the 7.5-mile **Chain Lakes Loop** that starts at the Artist Point parking lot before dropping down to pass a half-dozen icy lakes surrounded by huckleberry meadows.

Many of Mt Baker's best trails start lower down on Hwy 542 from a series of unpaved forest roads. The **Heliotrope Ridge Trail** begins 8 miles down unpaved USFS Rd 39, 1 mile east of Glacier and within 2 miles takes hikers from thick old-growth forest to flower-filled meadows replete with huckleberries. At the 2-mile point a left fork takes (experienced) summit-seekers up the popular Coleman Glacier climbing route (p164) while the right fork follows a 0.5-mile trail to the breathtaking Coleman Glacier overlook.

The 7-mile out-and-back **Skyline Divide Trail** is another spellbinding stroll through forests and meadows on the edge of the Mt Baker Wilderness with eye-to-eye views of the main mountain and countless other more distant peaks. Access is via USFS Rd 37 which branches off USFS 39 soon after Hwy 542 and runs for 12 miles to the 4400ft trailhead.

SKIING

Baker is a well-known skiing mecca and, while luxury facilities might be a little thin on the ground, the fast, adrenaline-fueled terrain has many dedicated admirers. It was also one of the first North American ski locations to accommodate and encourage snowboarders.

Situated at the end of Hwy 542, the Mt Baker ski area receives heavy annual snowfall and, as a result, enjoys one of the longest seasons in the US. For more info on access and facilities see p185.

WHITE-WATER RAFTING

Rafters can put in just above the Douglas Fir Campground and ride down the North Fork Nooksack, a class-III river, to Maple Falls, a total of 10 miles. For a guided raft trip, contact **River Riders** (☎ 800-448-7238; www.riverrider.com).

Sleeping & Eating

Glacier Creek Lodge (☎ 360-599-2991; 10036 Mt Baker Hwy; r $60, 4-person cabin $135;) This lodge is pretty much your last port of call before heading east up the Scenic Byway. In true Baker-esque style, it is rustic but friendly, with a choice between 12 cozy cabins or 10 tiny motel rooms. There's a complimentary serve-yourself breakfast in the reception area, and plenty of books, maps and videos to keep you entertained if the weather closes in.

The Inn at Mt Baker (☎ 360-599-1359; www.theinnatmtbaker.com; 8174 Mt Baker Hwy; r $140) When Mt Baker breaks through the clouds, the views from this attractive, well-run B&B are unsurpassable. Situated 7 miles east of Maple Falls, uncluttered rooms and ample skylights give this place a light, airy feel. Scrumptious breakfasts are taken on a spectacular deck – weather permitting in the summer. When the weather gets rough you can enjoy heated floors, comfortable rocking chairs and a cozy communal reading room.

Milano's Restaurant & Deli (☎ 360-599-2863; 9990 Mt Baker Hwy; dinner $10-14) In common with much of the Mt Baker area, Milano's doesn't win any 'wows' for its fancy interior decor. But when the pasta's al dente, the bread's oven-fresh and you've got an appetite that's been turned ravenous by successive bouts of white-knuckle snowboarding, who's complaining? This is one of two eating choices in the small settlement of Glacier and your last potential chow before you hit the mountain proper. Not surprisingly, it's a local legend.

Douglas Fir Campground and **Silver Fir Campground** (☎ 360-599-2714; Mt Baker Hwy; campsites $16) are two attractive USFS campgrounds positioned along Hwy 542 and the North Fork Nooksack River, which are 3 and 13 miles east of Glacier, respectively. Both have drinking water and pit toilets.

Getting There & Away

Mt Baker is accessed by Hwy 542 (Mt Baker Scenic Byway), from Bellingham via Kendall or the Baker Lake Rd, off Hwy 20 west of Concrete which dead-ends at the northern end of Baker Lake.

Public transportation is scant and many boarders hitchhike (though there are always risks). From Christmas to February, the **Bellair Baker Shuttle** (☎ 360-380-8800) carries skiers from Sunset Square, Bellingham up to Heather Meadows (round-trip $16, two hours).

UPPER SKAGIT RIVER VALLEY

Tracking up through the foothills of the North Cascades the youthful Skagit River becomes increasingly narrow and fast-flowing. Settlement here is spread out and thin on the ground. Blink and you'll miss the small roadside towns of Concrete (population 790) and Rockport (population 102) and, aside from a sprinkling of campgrounds and a couple of scruffy motels, your next decent accommodation will be in Mazama on the other side of the mountains. Due to snow blocks the stretch of Hwy 20 between Marblemount and Mazama is usually closed to traffic between mid-November and early April.

Baker Lake & Lake Shannon

Just north of Concrete are these two reservoirs, which were formed by a pair of dams on Baker River. Washington's largest colony of nesting osprey is found at Lake Shannon. Baker Lake is a popular place to launch a boat and go **fishing** for kokanee salmon or rainbow trout. There are also several hiking trails.

Baker Lake Rd runs along the west side of the lake, passing several campgrounds and the **Shadow of the Sentinels**, a wheelchair-accessible trail through old-growth Douglas firs. Beyond the end of the road, the relatively flat **Baker River Trail** makes a good family hike, running 3 miles up the jade river past huge old cedars and beaver ponds.

To reach the lakes, turn north off Hwy 20 onto Baker Lake Rd, which is 6 miles west of Concrete.

Upper Skagit Bald Eagle Area

The Bald Eagle area is essentially the 10-mile stretch of the Skagit River between Rockport and Marblemount. After salmon spawn, their spent carcasses become meals for the more than 600 eagles who winter here. January is the best time to view the eagles, which are present from November through early March.

Those who want to learn more about these illustrious raptors should visit the **Bald Eagle Interpretive Center** (☎ 360-853-7626; www.skagiteagle.org; Alfred St, Rockport; 🕒 10am-4pm Sat, Sun & holidays late Dec–mid-Feb). Guided walks of the eagle sanctuary leave from here, one block south of Hwy 20, at 1:30pm weekends and holidays.

Sleeping

Baker Lake Resort (☎ 360-757-2262; Baker Lake Rd; campsites $15-20, cabins $45-75; 🕒 year-round) All of the cabins here, 24 miles north of Hwy 20, include kitchenettes, and the pricier ones have bathrooms. Guests must bring their own linen and towels. Rod-and-reelers will find boat rentals and a small store.

Rockport State Park (☎ 360-853-8461; Hwy 20, campsites/RV sites $17/24; 🕒 Apr-Oct) Set in a lush old-growth forest at the base of 5400ft Sauk Mountain, this popular park, a mile west of Hwy 530, has good facilities, including showers and flush toilets. Backpackers and cyclists will find a few secluded walk-in sites.

Cascade Mountain Lodge (☎ 360-853-8870; 44618 Hwy 20; r from $75) If you need an early pit stop on the Cascade Loop, you can always bed down in this recently refurbished place right on Hwy 20 with its polished antiques and extensive collection of old wheels! The deluxe king suites come with flat-screen TVs and plush feather pillows. The restaurant next door serves burgers, sandwiches and southern fried catfish.

Eating

Cascadian Farms (☎ 360-853-8173; Hwy 20 milepost 100; milkshakes $5; 🕒 May-Oct) The first of half a dozen or so similarly orientated snack huts on the Cascades Loop (a map outside will tell you where the rest are), this choice place, 3 miles east of Rockport, stands beside the free-flowing Skagit River and sells local jams, coffee and delicious organic blueberry fruit shakes. Housed in an Indonesian-style Batak hut you can relax at an outdoor picnic table or take a self-guided tour around the adjacent organic farm.

Buffalo Run Restaurant (☎ 360-873-2461; 60084 Hwy 20, Marblemount; lunch $7-9, mains $15-20; V) The first and last decent restaurant for miles is (fortuitously) friendly and tasty as long as you don't mind being greeted by the sight of several decoratively draped buffalo skins and a huge animal head mounted on the wall. It is perhaps surprising then that among the buffalo stroganoff and buffalo burgers there are also quite a few palatable vegetarian options.

NORTH CASCADES NATIONAL PARK

With no settlements, no overnight accommodations and only one unpaved road, the North Cascades National Park is off the radar as far as standard tourist facilities are concerned. But for the backcountry hiker and adventurer, therein lies the beauty.

In reality, few places in America can match the crystal-clear air and sweeping pristine landscapes of this dramatic yet largely uncharted region. For outsiders, the park's spine-chilling names are scary enough in themselves. Desolation Peak, Jagged Ridge, Mt Terror and Mt Despair; the titles dot the map like epitaphs in a graveyard and say much about the Cascades' stark barrenness and foreboding impregnability.

Indeed, so impenetrable were these lofty mountains to early pioneers, with their formidable combination of precipitous peaks and fickle weather, that the region didn't even acquire a road until 1972 – and even today the arterial US 20 is only operational from April through October.

Packed with over 300 glaciers – almost half the total number in the lower 48 states and more than Glacier National Park in Montana – the North Cascades' wild, alpine-like terrain supports small populations of gray wolves, grizzly bears, mountain lions and sleepy marmots.

For administrative reasons, the park is split into two sections – north and south – separated in the middle by the Ross Lake National Recreation Area which encases a spectacular 20-mile section of the North Cascades Highway (US 20). Bordering the park's southern border around Stehekin lays a third region, the Lake Chelan National Recreation Area, a 62,000-acre protected park that surrounds the fjord-like Lake Chelan. To avoid confusion, these three complementary zones are managed as one contiguous area and overlaid by the Stephen Mather Wilderness, created in 1988.

While it is possible to get a basic overview of this vast alpine wilderness by motoring through in a car on US 20 making use of the numerous pullouts and short interpretive hikes that litter the route, to taste the

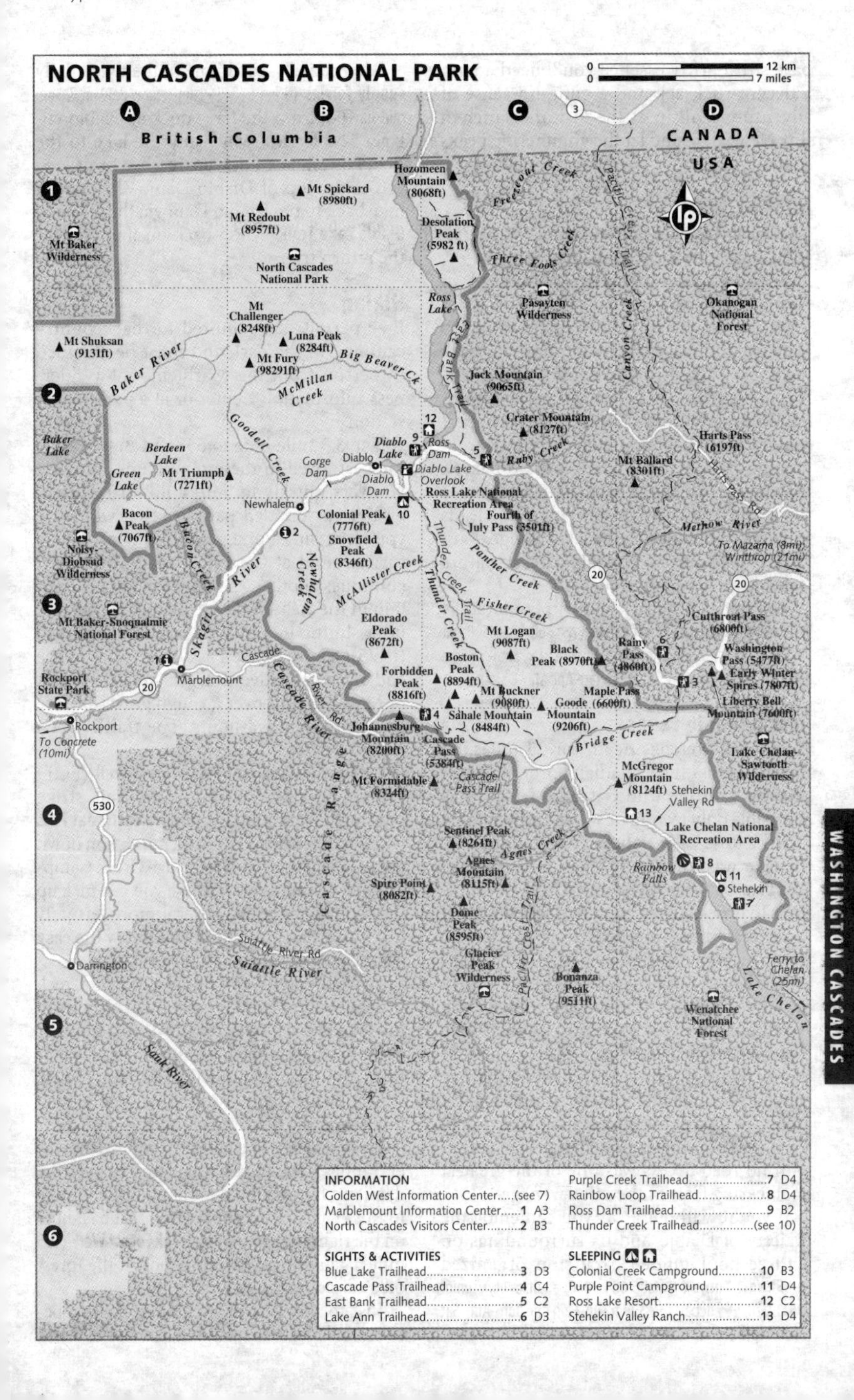
NORTH CASCADES NATIONAL PARK
0 12 km
0 7 miles
British Columbia
CANADA
USA
Mt Baker Wilderness
Mt Spickard (8980ft)
Mt Redoubt (8957ft)
Hozomeen Mountain (8068ft)
Desolation Peak (5982 ft)
North Cascades National Park
Freezeout Creek
Three Fools Creek
Pacific Crest Trail
Ross Lake
Pasayten Wilderness
Canyon Creek
Okanogan National Forest
Mt Challenger (8248ft)
Luna Peak (8284ft)
Mt Fury (98291ft)
Mt Shuksan (9131ft)
Baker River
Big Beaver Ck
McMillan Creek
East Bank Trail
Jack Mountain (9065ft)
Crater Mountain (8127ft)
Baker Lake
Goodell Creek
Berdeen Lake
Green Lake
Mt Triumph (7271ft)
Gorge Dam
Diablo
Diablo Lake
Ross Dam
Diablo Lake Overlook
Diablo Dam
Raby Creek
Harts Pass (6197ft)
Mt Ballard (8301ft)
Harts Pass Rd
Ross Lake National Recreation Area
Newhalem
Colonial Peak (7776ft)
Fourth of July Pass (3501ft)
Bacon Peak (7067ft)
Bacon Creek
Methow River
To Mazama (8mi); Winthrop (21mi)
Noisy-Diobsud Wilderness
Snowfield Peak (8346ft)
Newhalem Creek
Panther Creek
Skagit River
McAllister Creek
Thunder Creek Trail
Thunder Creek
Fisher Creek
Mt Baker-Snoqualmie National Forest
Eldorado Peak (8672ft)
Mt Logan (9087ft)
Cutthroat Pass (6800ft)
Black Peak (8970ft)
Rainy Pass (4860ft)
Washington Pass (5477ft)
Early Winter Spires (7807ft)
Marblemount
Cascade
Forbidden Peak (8816ft)
Boston Peak (8894ft)
Mt Buckner (9080ft)
Rockport State Park
Cascade River
Cascade River Rd
Sahale Mountain (8484ft)
Goode Mountain (9206ft)
Maple Pass (6600ft)
Liberty Bell Mountain (7600ft)
Rockport
To Concrete (10mi)
Johannesburg Mountain (8200ft)
Cascade Pass (5384ft)
Bridge Creek
Lake Chelan-Sawtooth Wilderness
Cascade Range
Mt Formidable (8324ft)
Cascade Pass Trail
McGregor Mountain (8124ft)
Stehekin Valley Rd
Lake Chelan National Recreation Area
Sentinel Peak (8261ft)
Agnes Creek
Agnes Mountain (8115ft)
Rainbow Falls
Stehekin
Spire Point (8082ft)
Dome Peak (8595ft)
Suiattle River Rd
Suiattle River
Darrington
Glacier Peak Wilderness
Bonanza Peak (9511ft)
Ferry to Chelan (25mi)
Lake Chelan
Wenatchee National Forest
Sauk River
INFORMATION
Golden West Information Center.....(see 7)
Marblemount Information Center......1 A3
North Cascades Visitors Center..........2 B3
SIGHTS & ACTIVITIES
Blue Lake Trailhead.............................3 D3
Cascade Pass Trailhead........................4 C4
East Bank Trailhead.............................5 C2
Lake Ann Trailhead..............................6 D3
Purple Creek Trailhead.........................7 D4
Rainbow Loop Trailhead.......................8 D4
Ross Dam Trailhead.............................9 B2
Thunder Creek Trailhead..............(see 10)
SLEEPING
Colonial Creek Campground..............10 B3
Purple Point Campground.................11 D4
Ross Lake Resort.................................12 C2
Stehekin Valley Ranch.......................13 D4

park's real gritty essence you'll need a tent, a decent rucksack and a gung-ho sense of adventure. Call in at the visitors center in tiny Newhalem and let the glimmering peaks seduce you.

Information

The **North Cascades Visitors Center** (☎ 206-386-4495; 502 Newhalem St; 🕑 9am-4:30pm daily mid-Apr–Oct, Sat & Sun Nov-Mar, extended hr mid-Jun–Labor Day), in Newhalem, is an essential orientation point for visitors, even for those just sticking to Hwy 20 and not strictly entering the park itself. A walk-through exhibit mixes informative placards about the park's different ecosystems with nature videos. Expert rangers will enlighten you on everything from melting glaciers to the chances of Mt Baker's blowing its top. In the back of the building, a short, wheelchair-accessible boardwalk leads to views of the glaciated Picket Range. Park rangers give interpretive talks or lead nature walks from here in the summer.

You can pick up backcountry permits at the **Wilderness Information Center** (☎ 360-873-4500, ext 39; 7280 Ranger Station Rd, Marblemount; 🕑 8am-4:30pm daily Memorial Day-Sep, Sat & Sun late Apr-May & Oct).

Ross & Diablo Lakes

Ross Lake stretches north for 23 miles, all the way across the Canadian border but – in keeping with the wild Cascades terrain – is accessible only by trail or water. Incorporated into the Ross Lake National Recreation Area, the lake was formed by the building of the **Ross Dam** between 1937 and 1949, an ambitious hydroelectric project that was designed to generate much-needed electricity for the fast-growing Seattle area.

Just below Ross Lake, Diablo Lake is held back by the similarly huge 389ft **Diablo Dam**. A pullout off Hwy 20 known as the **Diablo Dam Overlook** provides spellbinding views of the turquoise-green lake framed by glacier-capped peaks. Diablo was the world's highest arch-type dam at the time of its completion in 1930, and building it in such a hostile region with no road access was one of the greatest engineering feats of the inter-war age.

If you're without a car you can enjoy the majesty of Diablo and its surroundings on a three-hour guided excursion organized by **Skagit Tours** (☎ 206-684-3030; adult/6-11yr/senior $25/12/20; 🕑 departs 12:30pm Thu-Mon mid-Jun–Aug, Sat & Sun Sep). Reservations are required.

Alternatively, catch one of the twice-daily **supply ferries** (ticket $10; 🕑 departures 8:30am & 3pm mid-Jun–Oct) from the ferry dock at Diablo village. The ferries, which ply the lake to the Ross Powerhouse dock, are reached by driving across the top of Diablo Dam. Visitors can hike back to the Diablo Dam via the 4.5-mile **Diablo Lake Trail** or hop back on the ferry for the return trip.

Hiking

Free permits are required for backcountry camping in the park and must be obtained in person from the Marblemount Wilderness Information Center or at a park ranger station.

The 3.5-mile hike to 5384ft **Cascade Pass** is the best loved in these mountains, and gets you very quickly up into a flower-carpeted, glacier-surrounded paradise that will leave you struggling for superlatives. Most hikers turn around at Cascade Pass, but the trail continues another 7.5 miles to Glory Mountain in the **Stehekin Valley** where you can pick up a shuttle bus to take you into Stehekin (p175). The Cascade Pass trailhead is at the end of Cascade River Rd, a 23-mile drive east of Marblemount over a rough gravel surface that's prone to washouts. The trail is open July to October.

At Rainy Pass, the **Pacific Crest Trail** (PCT) crosses Hwy 20. To sample the trail, strike out north from here for 6800ft **Cutthroat Pass** (4 miles). Heading in the other direction down the PCT will bring you to Bridge Creek Campground, 12 miles away, where you can pick up the road to Stehekin. Several more leisurely hikes also start from Rainy Pass. Try the easy 2-mile walk to cirque-cradled **Lake Ann**.

From the south end of the Colonial Creek Campground (4 miles east of Diablo Dam), the long **Thunder Creek Trail** leads to a number of interesting sights. It's only a 1.3-mile jaunt from the campground to Thunder Creek, where a surprising number of wildflowers flourish in the dank, creek-bottom forest.

From its Hwy 20 trailhead, the **Ross Dam Trail** (1.5 miles) descends 1 mile, crosses over the dam and follows the west bank of Ross Lake to Ross Lake Resort (opposite). Just past here on the right the easy **Happy Creek Forest Walk** (0.5 miles) gets you an up-close look at the forest on a raised boardwalk.

Just to the west of Washington Pass, between mileposts 161 and 162, the **Blue Lake Trail**

JACK KEROUAC IN THE CASCADES

In the summer of 1956, American beatnik novelist Jack Kerouac spent 63 days as a fire lookout atop Desolation Peak in the remote North Cascade Mountains. Passing countless solitary hours in a small hut with panoramic views of the surrounding wilderness, Kerouac had plenty of time to contemplate life, the universe and his ever-evolving Buddhist philosophy, as he gazed out wistfully over Ross Lake and the twin-peaked majesty of looming Hozomeen (8066ft), a mountain he referred to rather chillingly as 'the Void.'

It is undocumented how many fire alarms Kerouac raised during his time in the Cascades, though he did famously use the setting in two of his subsequent novels *Dharma Bums* and *Desolation Angels*. In the latter book, published in 1965, Kerouac is said to have transcribed his Cascades journal almost word for word, providing a fascinating insight into both the mountain scenery and the writer's ongoing battle with his inner demons.

It is still possible to hike the trail up to Desolation Peak (6102ft) and ponder the fire lookout – built in 1933 – where Kerouac once sat. The hike is 6.8 miles one way and pretty strenuous although you'll be richly rewarded with the same stunning vistas that inspired Kerouac. The trailhead, on the shores of Ross Lake, is best accessed via water taxi from the Ross Lake Resort (below).

is an ambling 2-mile climb through sub-alpine meadows to Blue Lake, at 6250ft.

Rafting

Although it doesn't offer the heart-in-the-mouth white-water runs of less tamed waterways, the dam-controlled Upper Skagit makes for a good class-II or -III family trip through old-growth forest offering plenty of opportunities for wildlife-watching. A number of companies offer excursions here including **Alpine Adventures** (☎ 800-926-7238; www.alpineadventures.com). Prices start at $79/63 per adult/child.

Sleeping & Eating

Colonial Creek Campground (☎ 206-386-4495; Hwy 20 milepost 130; campsites $15; ⌚ year-round) These 167 campsites skirt the Thunder Arm of Diablo Lake on either side of the highway. On the south side, several walk-in campsites among dense woods offer a chance to get away from the cars; the lakeside spots are the most coveted and the most crowded. In summer, naturalist programs are given nightly in the amphitheater.

Ross Lake Resort (☎ 206-386-4437; www.rosslakeresort.com; Rockport, WA 98285; d cabin $112-136, q cabin $239; ⌚ mid-Jun–Oct) The floating cabins at this secluded resort, on the lake's west side just north of Ross Dam, were built in the 1930s for loggers working in the valley soon to be flooded by Ross Dam. There's no road in – guests can either hike the 2-mile trail from Hwy 20 or take the resort's tugboat-taxi-and-truck shuttle from the parking area near Diablo Dam. Cabins vary in size and facilities, but all feature electricity, plumbing and kitchenettes. Bunkhouse cabins accommodate 10 people ($130 for up to six, plus $8 per each additional person). Bedding and kitchen supplies are provided, but guests should bring food. The resort rents canoes ($22 per day), kayaks ($30) and motorboats ($67), and operates a water-taxi service for hikers destined for trailheads around the lake (see Hiking, opposite).

If you need to pick up some food, stop by the Skagit General Store in Newhalem, which has sandwiches, fudge and hot coffee.

METHOW VALLEY

Named after the Methow Native American tribe (now part of the Colville Indian Reservation), the Methow (*met*-how) River valley arises in the Pasayten Wilderness Area near the Canadian border and flows south towards its confluence with the Columbia. Along the way it is substantially engorged by both the Chewuch and Twisp Rivers.

British-Canadian David Thompson, a trader for the North West Company, was the first European geographer to explore these parts in 1811 where he encountered the Salish-speaking Methows who survived primarily by fishing for salmon at the river's mouth.

Gold was the original lure in this green yet surprisingly sunny valley though this was gradually replaced by agriculture as the prime economic activity by the late 19th century. With the opening of Hwy 20 in 1972, the Methow's combination of powdery winter snow and abundant summer sunshine transformed the valley into one of Washington's primary recreation areas with unlimited opportunities to bike, hike, fish and cross-country ski.

Orientation & Information

The upper Methow River Valley begins to widen around Mazama and becomes fairly open by the time it hits Winthrop and Twisp. It joins the Columbia at Pateros, 40 miles southeast of Winthrop.

The US Forest Service maintains the **Methow Valley Visitors Center** (☎ 509-996-4000; 24 West Chewuch Rd; 🕑 8am-5pm May-Oct) on Hwy 20 at the western end of Winthrop.

Harts Pass

If you prefer white-knuckle car rides to white-water rafting trips, consider taking the single lane gravel track up to Hart's Pass (6197ft), Washington's highest drivable road, and also its most terrifying. If the narrow, winding route and scary unguarded drop-offs don't take your breath away, the panoramic views certainly will. To get to Harts Pass head northwest on Lost River Rd (also known as Mazama Rd) past the Mazama Country Inn to USFS Rd 5400. The road is paved for the first 12 miles and the last dozen are gravel. At Harts Pass, there's still more of a climb for the intrepid driver; head another 3 miles up to **Slate Peak** (7450ft), where – after a short hike from the road's end – the view from an abandoned fire lookout is breathtaking. Slate Peak is also the site of the northernmost road access to the Pacific Crest Trail in the USA.

Activities

Good, dry snow and plenty of trails make Methow Valley famous for its cross-country skiing (p185). In summer, some of the same trails become routes for hikers, mountain bikers and horseback riders. Bikes can be rented at the Freestone Inn (right) for $35 a day. For horseback riding, cattle drives, and fishing and hunting trips contact **Early Winters Outfitting** (☎ 509-996-2659; www.earlywintersoutfitting.com; HCR 74 Box B6, Mazama, WA 98833) in Mazama.

Most of the best trails start on Harts Pass Rd (USFS Rd 5400).

Mountain Transporter (☎ 509-996-8294) is a local shuttle service offering trailhead drop-offs and pick-ups for mountain bikers, skiers and hikers ($5).

Sleeping & Eating

Mazama Country Inn (☎ 509-996-2681; www.mazamacountryinn.com; 42 Lost River Rd, Mazama; lodge r $80-125, cabin $150-300; wi-fi) The word 'inn' doesn't really do justice to this comprehensive place, a self-contained rustic oasis situated on the edge of the Pasayten Wilderness close to the tiny settlement of Mazama. Aside from 18 simple but comfortable rooms, the inn lies at the nexus of countless outdoor activities in the area with numerous ski and bike trails radiating out from its cozy interior (rentals are available). Other facilities include a pool, gym, squash and tennis courts, sauna and the best restaurant for miles. The inn also rents a number of self-contained cabins around Mazama.

Freestone Inn (☎ 509-996-3906; www.freestoneinn.com; 17798 Hwy 20; r/ste from $185/235, cabin from $235; ☒) Freestone Inn is a more luxurious version of the Mazama Inn with similar facilities encased in a more expensive wrapping. The on-site Jack's Hut adventure center can put you in touch with at least a dozen outdoor adventures, everything from snow-mobiles to balloon tours. The Kids Venture program is great for children.

WINTHROP & AROUND

Winthrop (population 349) is – along with Leavenworth – one of two themed towns on the popular Cascade Loop. This once-struggling mining community has been made over to resemble an old town from the American West (think *High Noon*).

The area was first settled by Europeans in 1891 by Harvard-educated Guy Waring, who built a trading post at the confluence of the Chewuch (*chee*-wok) and Methow Rivers. When the mining business dried up after 1915, Winthrop teetered catastrophically on the brink of extinction, until an enterprising local couple drafted in Robert Jorgenson, the architect who had redesigned Leavenworth, to rebuild the town with false-fronted shops and assorted cowboy memorabilia in the hope of attracting tourists.

The idea quickly caught on and Winthrop's renaissance was bolstered further in 1972 when the opening of the North Cascades Hwy brought in a new flood of visitors.

Orientation & Information

Winthrop is 13 miles southeast of Mazama on Hwy 20. After crossing the Methow, the highway makes a 90-degree turn as it comes into town and becomes the main drag, sometimes referred to as Riverside Ave. Twisp is 8 miles further southwest, and it's 38 miles to Omak.

The **Winthrop Chamber of Commerce** (☎ 509-996-2125, 888-463-8469; www.winthropwashington.com; 202 Riverside Ave) is at the corner where Hwy 20 enters downtown.

Sights & Activities

It's hard to differentiate the reconstructed buildings in the **Shafer Museum** (☎ 509-996-2712; 285 Castle Ave; admission by donation; 10am-5pm Memorial Day-Labor Day) from the present day structures in Winthrop itself, such is the town's eerie authenticity. However, the museum does retain one original construction – a log cabin known as 'the Castle' built by Winthrop founder Guy Waring in 1896 as a present to his wife.

Back in town, Winthrop's photogenic core is compact and cheery with plenty of gift shops, coffee bars and a decent bookstore.

Few Washington outsiders will know the first thing about smoke-jumping – a method of fire-fighting that involves parachuting out of a plane into a rural area to tackle a forest fire before it gets out of control. Few people anywhere can avoid feeling humbled by the heroic exploits of the people who have been trained to do it. The Methow Valley is often seen as the birthplace of modern smoke-jumping (which was first pioneered in the 1930s) and you can learn all about it by visiting the **North Cascade Smokejumper Base** (☎ 509-997-2031; 23 Intercity Airport Rd; admission free; 8am-5pm Jun-Oct) halfway between Winthrop and Twisp.

The Winthrop area is famous for its cross-country ski trails (p185) with the best network of trails congregated around Sun Mountain Lodge (right) 10 miles to the west. During the summer months the trails are given over to hiking, mountain biking and horseback riding. Trails range from the 2.5-mile **Sunnyside Loop**, with jaw-dropping vistas of the North Cascades, to the more adventurous **Pete's Dragon** with its white-knuckle twists and turns. Horseback riding around Beaver Pond and Patterson Lake is another popular summertime option. You can rent bikes from Sun Mountain Lodge for $35/8/24 per day/hour/four hours (helmet included). Guided horseback treks go for $32/27 per adult/child for 1½ hours, or $85/65 per adult/child for a half-day.

Fishing for steelhead trout and chinook salmon is popular in the Methow River, but anglers are required to use catch-and-release techniques for these endangered species. **Moccasin Lake**, a mile-long hike from Patterson Lake Rd, has very good fly-fishing, with rainbow trout averaging 3lb to 5lb.

Sleeping

Duck Brand Hotel (☎ 509-996-2192; www.methownet.com/duck; 248 Riverside Ave; s/d $69/79;) Stuffed with curiosities and oozing character, the handsome 'Duck' bills itself as an alternative to the ordinary – which it surely is. Perched above the popular cantina slap bang in the middle of the town are six small but cozy rooms that should leave you with enough change to hit the Winthropian gift shops. All rooms have private baths with tubs and air-con.

Chewuch Inn (☎ 509-996-3107; www.chewuchinn.com; 223 White Ave; r $75-95, cabins $100-125;) One of Winthrop's more economical options, the attractive Chewuch is situated off Twin Lakes Rd, a short stroll from the main action. Rooms and cabins are handpainted and decorated with outdoorsy objects like snowshoes, and balconies look out over the meadows and mountains. There's a games room, outdoor spa and breakfast, including homemade scones.

Hotel Rio Vista (☎ 509-996-3535; www.methow.com/~riovista; 285 Riverside Ave; d $110-145; wi-fi) A splendid Wild West–themed central option, the Rio Vista lives up to its Spanish name with glorious views over the fast-flowing Methow River that flows directly outside the rear deck. Fall asleep to the lulling sound of the water after enjoying a riverside Jacuzzi or a lazy evening on your private balcony admiring a magnificent Methow sunset.

our pick **Sun Mountain Lodge** (☎ 509-996-2211; www.sunmountainlodge.com; Box 1000, Winthrop, WA 98862; lodge r $160-346, cabin $160-620; wi-fi) Without a doubt one of the best places to stay in Washington, the Sun Mountain Lodge benefits from its incomparable natural setting perched like an eagle's nest high above the Methow Valley. The 360-degree views from its highly lauded restaurant are awe-inspiring and people travel from miles around just to enjoy breakfast here. Inside, the lodge and its assorted cabins manage to provide luxury without pretension, while the outdoor attractions that are based around its

LLAMA TREKKING

With their sharp, crenellated ridges and brooding, snowcapped volcanoes, the North Cascades share much in common with the Andes in South America. And now, thanks to the foresight and creativity of one Washington company, the mountains even have their own llamas.

Deli Llama Adventures (☎ 360-757-4212; 17045 Llama Lame, Bow) is a small, well-established local outfit that offers llama trekking and hiking excursions in both the North Cascades and the adjoining Pasayten Wilderness Area for groups of up to 10 people from May through September. Prices start at $140 per person per day (depending on group size) and include tents, cooking gear, all meals and – of course – the llamas themselves who, with their sure-footed dignity and instinctive climbing skills, can penetrate the rugged backcountry like a fleet of environmentally friendly SUVs.

extensive network of lakes and trails could keep a hyperactive hiker occupied for weeks. Not surprisingly, the Sun Mountain is pricey, but if you have just one splurge in Washington wilderness east of Seattle, this should be the place.

Eating

Sheri's (☎ 509-996-3834; 201 Riverside Av) This delightful outdoor coffee bar and ice-cream parlor adjacent to Sheri's Sweet Shoppe is the best place to snatch an espresso and hot sticky cinnamon bun (the buns are placed tantalizing on a counter on the sidewalk as soon as they leave the oven). In keeping with the surroundings, the bar stools are made out of horse saddles and behind the coffee cabin you can enjoy a quick round of crazy golf while they blast steam into your grande cappuccino.

Winthrop Brewing Company (☎ 509-996-3183; 155 Riverside Ave; mains $7-13) An unusual pub – even by Winthrop standards – that occupies a little red schoolhouse on the main street and knocks out an impressive range of handcrafted ales. Opt for the light bodied Black Canyon Porter or the heavier, darker Grampa Clem's Brown Ale. Classic pub grub highlights fish and chips (with a Japanese twist) and the Outlaw Chili. There's live music and an open mic on Friday.

Duck Brand Cantina (☎ 509-996-2192; 248 Riverside Ave; mains $7-15) Although the 'Duck' is no standard Mexican restaurant, the quesadillas, enchiladas and tacos served up here could roast the socks off any authentic Monterey diner. To add variety to the mix, the cantina – which from the outside resembles a movie prop from *The Good, the Bad and the Ugly* – also sports a bakery and, legend has it, churns out a mean breakfast.

Arrowleaf Bistro (☎ 509-996-3920; 253 Riverside Ave; mains $15-27) Winthrop's newest restaurant, with its starched white tablecloths and polished wine glasses, is a notable departure from the saloon-bar staples of yore. But the Arrowleaf works hard to justify its price tag with knowledgeable waiting staff, an excellent riverside setting and a menu that contains such mouthwatering treats as pistachio-crusted halibut and maple brined pork chops.

TWISP

pop 938

Twisp, founded in 1897, is a diminutive one-horse lumber town situated at the confluence of the Twisp and Methow Rivers. While at first glance, it might appear that there is little to do here apart from fill up on gas and shoot a few games of pool in the local bar, Twisp is actually the crucible of a small local arts scene and boasts outdoor activities aplenty. If you found Winthrop too faux and Lake Chelan too crowded, this could make a good Methow Valley base.

Orientation & Information

South of Twisp, Hwy 153 splits off Hwy 20 and follows the Methow River south, joining US 97 and the Columbia River at Pateros. Hwy 20 continues east through the Okanogan and Loup Loup forests for 29 miles to the Okanogan Valley.

The **Twisp Visitor Information Center** (☎ 509-997-2926; www.twispinfo.com; 201 S Methow Way) operates out of the Methow Valley Community Center. **Twisp Ranger Station** (☎ 509-997-2131; 502 Glover St; 🕑 7:45am-4:30pm Mon-Fri), on Twisp's main street, has information on trails and campgrounds in the Okanogan National Forest.

Sights & Activities

Diminutive Twisp boasts a small art gallery in the shape of the **Confluence Gallery & Art Center** (☎ 509-997-2787; 104 Glover St; admission free; ⏲ 10am-3pm Mon-Sat) but, outside of this, the main attractions are outdoors related. Hikes in the area are popular with a number of them fanning off the Twisp River Rd that proceeds west of town along the banks of the Twisp River. Try the 7-mile **Eagle Creek Trail** that starts from the trailhead on W Buttermilk Creek Rd (11 miles west of Twisp) or strike out further into the **Lake Chelan-Sawtooth Wilderness Area.**

If you don't mind a few snowmobiles, **cross-country skiing** is easy along the flat Twisp River Rd. Nearer to downtown, trails start at the Idle-a-While Motel (below) and meander around Twisp and along the Methow River.

Sleeping & Eating

Idle-a-While Motel (☎ 509-997-3222; 505 N Hwy 20; r $64-79, cottage $74-94; ☒) You could quite easily idle here for a night or two, as you sally forth in a clockwise direction on the Cascade Loop. Situated on Hwy 20 with basic but perfectly comfortable rooms, it might not be the Sun Mountain Lodge, though it does have a number of winter skiing trails starting directly outside its door.

Twisp River Pub (☎ 509-997-6822; 201 Hwy 20; ⏲ 11:30am-11pm Wed-Sun) Twisp might look like the back of beyond, but inside the walls of this feisty establishment there's enough food, music and beer variations to keep the most fidgety of travelers happy. Encircling the culinary world from Africa to Asia, the menu includes bratwurst, Thai peanut stir-fry, Greek salad and the good old steak sandwich. Made-from-scratch beers are brewed on the premises and music rocks the rafters at least twice a week.

STEHEKIN

After Bavarian Leavenworth and Wild West Winthrop comes wondrous Stehekin (steh-*hee*-kin), a refreshingly unique Cascade settlement renowned, not for its lederhosen-wearing waiters or its lasso-wielding cowboys, but rather for its splendid isolation. The secret lies in the location. Nestled in the craggy Cascade Mountains at the north end of Lake Chelan, Stehekin is completely cut off from the state road network and can only be reached by sea plane, boat or an arduous 11-mile hike over lofty Cascade Pass. Such purposeful inaccessibility has worked wonders for the settlement's beauty and charm. Untouched by the foibles of 21st-century consumerism, Stehekin (population 76) has become a byword for solitude, and a mecca for backcountry adventure enthusiasts keen to escape the pleasure cruisers and waterskiers who ply Lake Chelan further south.

Contrary to what you many believe, Stehekin *does* have roads and cars (all of which have been ferried here from Chelan or elsewhere) and in March 2007 it finally elected to join the Washington telephone grid – much to the chagrin of many of the solitude-seeking locals. The vast majority of visitors arrive in the settlement as part of a 90-minute stopover on a day trip from Chelan on one of two different passenger boats (p176). Those who stay longer rarely regret it.

Orientation & Information

Stehekin is 55 miles north of Chelan, at the tip of Lake Chelan. Stehekin Valley Rd (the town's only road) is referred to most often as just 'the road.' From the boat landing, it continues to the northwest for 23 miles, only 4 miles of which are paved. East of Stehekin, the road dead-ends after 4 miles.

The **Golden West Information Center** (☎ 360-854-7365; PO Box 7, Stehekin, WA 98852; ⏲ 8:30am-5pm mid-May–Sep, 10am-2pm mid-Mar–mid-May & early Oct) is a short walk up the hill from the boat landing. Here you'll find rangers, summer naturalist programs, a 10-minute video on the surrounding area and the Golden West Art Gallery.

Activities

HIKING

Backpackers planning an overnight stay will need a backcountry camping permit, which can be obtained at Golden West or from the Chelan Ranger Station.

If you're not staying overnight, it's hard to get very far on a hike with only a few hours. **Buckner Orchard**, near Rainbow Falls, is one of the Stehekin area's oldest settlements and makes for a refreshing walk. Once there, you'll find a homestead cabin built in 1889, plenty of old farm equipment and trees that keep on bearing apples. Head 3.4 miles up Stehekin Valley Rd, turn left at the far end of the Rainbow Creek bridge and look for a sign about 20 yards off the road, marking the Buckner Orchard Walk, an easy 1-mile round-trip to the apple orchards. From just past the bridge, there's also a short path leading to the 312ft **Rainbow Falls**.

The easy **Lakeshore Trail** starts at the Golden West Visitors Center and heads south near Lake Chelan's shore. It's 6 miles to views of the lake and valley at Hunts Bluff. It's also possible to make this into a backpacking trip; Moore Point is 7 miles from the trailhead, while Prince Creek, the trail's endpoint, is 17 miles. Watch out for rattlesnakes along the way.

Other treks include the 5-mile **Rainbow Loop Trail** with great lake and valley views and the **Purple Creek Trail** toward 688ft Purple Pass, 7.5 miles away.

OTHER ACTIVITIES

The **Courtney Log Office** (☎ 509-682-4677; www.courtneycountry.com) should be your first stop for other activities. You can rent bikes from **Discovery Bikes** (☎ 509-682-4677; per hr/day $3.50/20) at the office. Discovery Bikes can also shuttle cyclists and their bikes up the road to the Stehekin Valley Ranch, which is just far enough to bike back down the valley in time to catch the 2pm boat back to Chelan.

The lower Stehekin River is open for seasonal catch-and-release fishing with both cutthroat and rainbow trout living in the upper river. Stop by **McGregor Mountain Outdoor Supply** (mcgregormountain@starband.net; PO Box 68, Stehekin, WA 98852) at the landing for fishing advice.

The **Stehekin Adventure Company** (day trips adult/child $50/40) offers raft trips on the Stehekin River in the spring and summer. Stehekin Valley Ranch's **Cascade Corrals** leads three-hour horseback rides to Coon Lake ($45 per person), as well as guided hikes into the mountains with gear carried on horseback. Make bookings for all these activities at the Courtney Log Office.

Sleeping

Golden West Information Center (☎ 360-856-5700, ext 340, then ext 14) Provides information and backcountry camping permits for the 11 NPS-maintained primitive campsites along the road up the valley. All camps have pit toilets, but only the Purple Point Campground provides potable water.

Stehekin Valley Ranch (☎ 509-682-4677; www.courtneycountry.com; r shared/private bathroom $85/95) All number of activities go on at this well-organized place 9 miles upriver from the boat landing, including cycling, horseback riding, kayaking and hiking. Even better, the price for lodging in the ranch's rustic cabins includes all meals at one of Stehekin's few proper dining establishments, along with a bus to get there. Most of the cabins are simple, canvas-topped affairs, with screened windows and showers in a nearby building, but a few have their own bathrooms.

Stehekin Landing Resort (☎ 509-682-4494; www.stehekin.com; PO Box 457, Chelan, WA 98816; r $119-159, kitchenette units $159-179; ⊠) Under new management since January 2007, this resort was in the throes of a renovation while this book was being updated. Aside from spiffing up the rooms, the project promised an upgraded restaurant, new Jacuzzi and small recreation center. The lodge currently has 28 rooms of varying sizes and styles.

Eating

Stehekin Pastry Company (☎ 800-536-0745; Stehekin Valley Rd; pastries $2-6) In a large city this delectable coffee/pastry shop would do a roaring trade. Out in the middle of a wilderness area it's a godsend, guaranteed to give fresh ardor to even the most challenging of hikes. Two miles up the valley from the boat landing, this is where to come for espresso, cinnamon buns, pies and baked-from-scratch pastries. You can take the 'bakery special' shuttle service to get there.

Stehekin Valley Ranch (☎ 509-682-4677; breakfast & lunch $5-8, dinner $13-18; 🕒 breakfast 7am-9am, lunch noon-1pm, dinner 5:30-7pm; V) Reservations are required here for the daily set-dinner menu (there's a $3 shuttle service from the dock to the lodge at 5:30pm). Grill items, like burgers (beef and veggie) and fish, are also available.

Getting There & Away

Chelan Airways (☎ 509-682-5555; www.chelanairways.com; 1328 W Woodin Av, Chelan) provides seaplane service between Stehekin and Chelan for $94/159 one way/round-trip.

The **Lake Chelan Boat Company** (☎ 509-682-4584; www.ladyofthelake.com; PO Box 186, Chelan, WA 98816) operates the 285 passenger *Lady of the Lake II* ferry (no cars) leaving from Chelan boat dock daily at 8:30am and arriving at Stehekin at 12:30pm. It makes a 90-minute stopover before returning at 2pm (arriving back in Chelan at 6pm). The round-trip cost is $39. Alternatively, you can travel on the faster *Lady Express*, which cuts the four-hour boat trip in half (leave Chelan 8:30am, arrive Stehekin 10:45am). The *Lady Express* lays over in Stehekin for one hour before heading back at 11:45am (arriving back in Chelan at 2:20pm). The round trip cost is $59. Both boats stop on the way at Lucerne.

The most popular **hike** into Stehekin is via the 11-mile Cascade Pass Trail that is accessed from a trailhead on the Cascade River Rd, 23 miles east of Marblemount and US 20. The trail will bring you out at Glory Mountain where – road conditions permitting (from June to September) – you can catch a shuttle bus (below) down into Stehekin.

Getting Around

Although there are roads and cars *in* Stehekin, there are no roads *to* Stehekin. Courtesy transportation to and from the boat landing is included in most lodging prices.

Bicycles are the easiest way to get around. See opposite for rental options. If you'd prefer to bring your own, the Lake Chelan Boat Company charges $15 round-trip for bike transportation.

From late May to early October, the NPS runs the **Stehekin Shuttle Bus** (☎ 360-856-5700) up and down Stehekin Valley Rd four times a day, the 11 miles from the boat landing to High Bridge costs $5/2.50/3 per adult/child/bike. To travel the further 9 miles to Glory Mountain you'll need to double the fare.

CHELAN & AROUND

pop 3522

A natural lake as opposed to man-made reservoir, Lake Chelan lies in a deep, glacier-gouged valley that was once a prime fishing ground for Native Americans. Situated in the dry side of the Cascade Mountains and surrounded by scree-scattered hills and distant snowy peaks, the lake is 55 miles long and 1500ft deep, making it the third deepest lake in the USA and the ninth deepest in the world.

Clustered around the lake's southern shore, the small town of Chelan is a summer vacation destination and a popular center for all kinds of water recreation.

Orientation & Information

Chelan is 37 miles northeast of Wenatchee and 54 miles southwest of Omak. Woodin Ave (US 97) is the main drag into and out of town. S Lakeshore Rd, as US 971 is named, follows Lake Chelan's western shore up as far as Twenty-Five Mile Creek State Park; on the opposite side of the lake, Hwy 150 stops at Greens Landing, a few miles past Manson.

If it's tourist information you seek, don't miss the **Lake Chelan Visitors Center** (☎ 509-682-3503; www.lakechelan.com; 102 E Johnson Ave).

Therer is a wealth of information on Wenatchee National Forest, and other protected areas available from **Chelan USFS/NPS Ranger Station** (☎ 509-682-2576; 428 W Woodin Ave; 🕑 7:30am-4:30pm Mon-Fri).

Sights & Activities

WATER RECREATION

Lake Chelan shelters some of the nation's cleanest water and has consequently become one of Washington's premier water recreation areas. Not surprisingly, the place is packed in summer, with all number of speedboats, jet-skis and power-craft battling it out for their own private slice of water space. To avoid any high-speed collisions, try renting a kayak from **Clear Water Kayaking** (☎ 509-630-7615; PO Box 688, Manson; single/double per day $60/80) and paddling up the lake to see some undiluted Cascadian nature at first hand.

There are public beaches at **Lakeside Park**, near the west side of town, and at **Lake Chelan State Park**, 9 miles west on S Lakeshore Rd. Continuing west till the end of the road, you'll find boat launches at **Twenty-Five Mile Creek State Park**.

On the north shore, **Don Morse Memorial Park** is an in-town water funland, with a beach, boat launch, bumper boats and go-carts.

The swimming area at **Manson Bay Park** (☎ 509-687-9635) features several floating docks, and there's a four-lane boat launch at **Old Mill Bay Park** (☎ 509-687-9635), 2 miles east of Manson.

If you have kids, don't even think they'll let you sneak past **Slidewaters Water Park** (☎ 509-682-5751; 102 Waterslide Dr; day pass adult/child $16/13; 🕑 10am-6pm May-Sep) off W Woodin Ave. It's on a hill above the *Lady of the Lake* boat dock.

Fishing is popular in Lake Chelan with lake trout, kokanee salmon, ling cod and small-mouth bass relatively abundant. For guided fishing excursions, try **Darrell & Dad's Family Guide Service** (☎ 509-687-0709; 231 Division, Manson, WA 98831; per person half/full day $125/175).

OTHER ACTIVITIES

Mountain bikers should stop by the ranger station and pick up a map of USFS roads open to **cycling**. One popular trail follows the north fork of Twenty-Five Mile Creek, climbing steeply for 3 miles before leveling out through pine forest and eventually meeting the **Devil's Backbone** trailhead. At Echo Ridge near Manson, cross-country ski trails are taken over by mountain bikes in summer.

There are plenty of good places to go **cross-country skiing** around Chelan during the short Christmas-to-February season. Over 20 miles of trails are run by the **Chelan Nordic Club** (☎ 800-424-3526; Cooper Gulch Rd). For **downhill skiing** and **snowmobiling**, check out the **Echo Valley Ski Area** (☎ 509-682-4002, 509-687-3167; Cooper Mountain Rd; Sat & Sun), featuring three tow-ropes and one Poma lift. **Uncle Tim's Toys** (☎ 509-687-8467; Lakeshore Marina & Park) rents out bikes and ski equipment.

Sleeping

Lake Chelan State Park (☎ 509-687-3710; S Lakeshore Rd; campsites/RV sites $17/24) A guarded swimming beach, picnic areas and a boat launch make this a busy summertime destination. Of the nearly 150 sites, there are some nice lakeside spots and 35 RV hookups. Reservations are necessary in summer.

Midtowner Motel (☎ 509-682-4051, 800-572-0943; www.midtowner.com; 721 E Woodin Ave; s/tw $75/85;) This bargain is a healthy five blocks from the town center and lake, a small price to pay considering the reasonable fee and the above-average motel facilities. These include free internet in the reception, coffee on tap, a Jacuzzi and an indoor/outdoor swimming pool. Rooms have the cleanliness of one would expect in a five-star hotel.

Campbell's Resort (☎ 509-682-2561; www.campbellsresort.com; 104 W Woodin Ave; r $148-188, ste $198-308;) The plushiest place in town, Campbell's hogs the waterfront along Manson Hwy with its 170 guest rooms, marina, two swimming pools, restaurant, pub and 1200ft stretch of sandy beach. Modern rooms are spotless and have balconies, but the privilege of staying here doesn't come cheap – especially in the summer when rates triple.

Best Western Lakeside Lodge (☎ 509-682-4396; www.lakesidelodge.net; 2312 W Woodin Ave; d $199-259;) This trusty chain has nabbed the best location in town aside grassy Lakeside Park which boasts Chelan's most idyllic municipal setting along with the town's best stretch of sand-and-shingle beach. There's a lovely pool, complimentary breakfast, top lake views, and suitably well-furnished rooms, though you may spend a lot of time dodging the plethora of passing convention delegates.

TWIN PEAKS TERRITORY

You don't have to be a trivia-obsessed TV geek to appreciate the twin western Washington towns of Snoqualmie and North Bend, but it certainly helps. In the early 1990s, iconic US film director, David Lynch, set his cult TV classic *Twin Peaks* in these two atmospheric Cascade settlements. *Twin Peaks* was a surrealistic serial-drama about murder and intrigue in the seedy underbelly of small town America that spawned a host of imitations.

But there's far more to this region than decade-old TV nostalgia. The larger of the two towns, Snoqualmie, boasts one of the most stunning waterfalls in the state, a 268ft cascade of spray and foam that quickly became an international icon when it starred in the opening title sequence of Lynch's much-vaunted TV show. Perched at the top of the falls, the **Salish Lodge & Spa** (☎ 425-888-2556; 6501 Railroad Ave) is equally spectacular. It's a historic retreat that is justly famous for its sumptuous spa, gourmet restaurant and bit-part in *Twin Peaks* as the fictional Great Northern Hotel.

If you're in town, be sure not to miss the **Northwest Railway Museum** (☎ 425-888-3030; 38625 SE King St; admission free; 10am-5pm), a unique interpretive museum that runs 75-minute train trips up the Snoqualmie Valley in antique railway carriages (adult/child $9/6). Visitors pay for their tickets in the original Snoqualmie Depot which dates from 1890 and now serves as the museum's main exhibition hall.

Three miles to the east of Snoqualmie, the town of North Bend is dominated by Mt Si, the famous 'twin peaks' in the TV show. As a mountain, it's often touted as the most-climbed summit in USA, tackled via a short-but-bracing 4-mile trail to Haystack Basin near the top. The trailhead is in the Mt Si Natural Resources Conservation Area parking lot.

Eating

BC MacDonald's (☎ 509-682-1334; 104 E Woodin Ave; mains $8-16; until 2am) Don't be fooled by the name – you won't find any Big Macs or Chicken McNuggets at this kid-friendly pub-restaurant which possesses what must be one of the longest bars in the Pacific Northwest. The burgers are good, the calamari makes a stalwart appetizer and the beer is possibly the best in town. It ain't fancy, but it works. And no clowns.

Campbell House Restaurant & Second Floor Pub (☎ 509-682-4250; 104 W Woodin Ave; mains $14-20; V) Chelan's fanciest dining spot, Campbell House rises above the burger banality with the dizzying delights of scallop vol-au-vent, Northwest mixed grill (duck, salmon and beef), stuffed Portobello and coconut prawns. A decent batch of non-meat alternatives (including eggplant parmesan) should surprise the salad-weary vegetarians. The upstairs pub serves pricey snacks and fancy vodka cocktails.

Vogue (☎ 509-888-5282; 117 E Woodin Ave; wi-fi) On the surface, Vogue seems like a fresh, new Seattle-style coffee bar. but there's a lot more to this place than meets the eye. Putting aside the ubiquitous chai lattes and blueberry muffins, this venerable and popular 'café' showcases everything from live music (at weekends) and local art to a selection of its own jams and vinaigrettes. It also acts as a popular tasting room for aspiring wine connoisseurs. There's alfresco seating out front and wi-fi access inside to boot.

Getting There & Around

Chelan Airways operates a daily seaplane service to Stehekin from the airfield, 1 mile west of town on Alt US 97 (see Stehekin, p176, for details).

The *Lady of the Lake II* and the *Lady Express* board at least one boat daily for trips across Lake Chelan to Lucerne and Stehekin. The **dock** (☎ 509-682-4584, schedule info 509-682-2224; www.ladyofthelake.com) is located on the south shore, just a mile west of downtown on Alt US 97.

The Wenatchee-based **Link** (☎ 509-662-2183) provides bus services between Manson and Wenatchee (1½ hours) via Chelan (15 minutes) on route 21. For those traveling to or from Chelan, buses stop on the south side of Johnson Ave, right next to the local visitors center.

SOUTH CASCADES

Splitting the state climatically in two, the South Cascades extend from Snoqualmie Pass on the arterial I-90 down to the Columbia River and the border with Oregon. Here you'll find Washington's highest and most explosive peaks including lofty Mt Rainier, understated Mt Adams and infamous Mt St Helens, the peak that blew its top in May 1980, knocking 1300ft off its summit in the process.

Most of the South Cascades are protected by an interconnecting patchwork of national parks, forests and wilderness areas. The largest and most emblematic of these is Mt Rainier National Park inaugurated in 1899, while the most unusual is the Mt St Helens National Volcano Monument formed two years after the mountain's eruption in 1982.

While development inside the parks is refreshingly light, keen downhill skiers can find solace at Crystal Mountain just outside the limits of Mt Rainier National Park which – while no Whistler – is the largest ski resort in Washington State.

Elsewhere the protected forests, lush river valleys and sub-alpine flower meadows are the domain of hikers and backcountry campers during a short but intense summer season that runs from late May to early September.

MT RAINIER NATIONAL PARK AREA

Majestic Rainier is the nation's fifth highest peak (outside Alaska), and is also one of its most beguiling. Rising commandingly over the bustling population centers of Puget Sound, one brief glimpse of this indomitable and often cloud-enshrouded mountain – with its 26 glaciers and notoriously fickle weather – is enough to inspire a sharp gasp in most visitors. At 14,411ft, Rainier is the Cascades' highest peak and a longstanding Northwestern icon. Encased in a 368-sq-mile national park (the world's fifth national park when it was inaugurated in 1899), the mountain's snow-capped summit and forest-covered foothills harbor numerous hiking trails, huge swathes of flower-carpeted meadows and an alluring conical peak that presents a formidable challenge for aspiring climbers.

But beneath Rainier's placid exterior, much darker forces fester. As an active stratovolcano that recorded its last eruptive activity as recently as 1854, Rainier harnesses untold

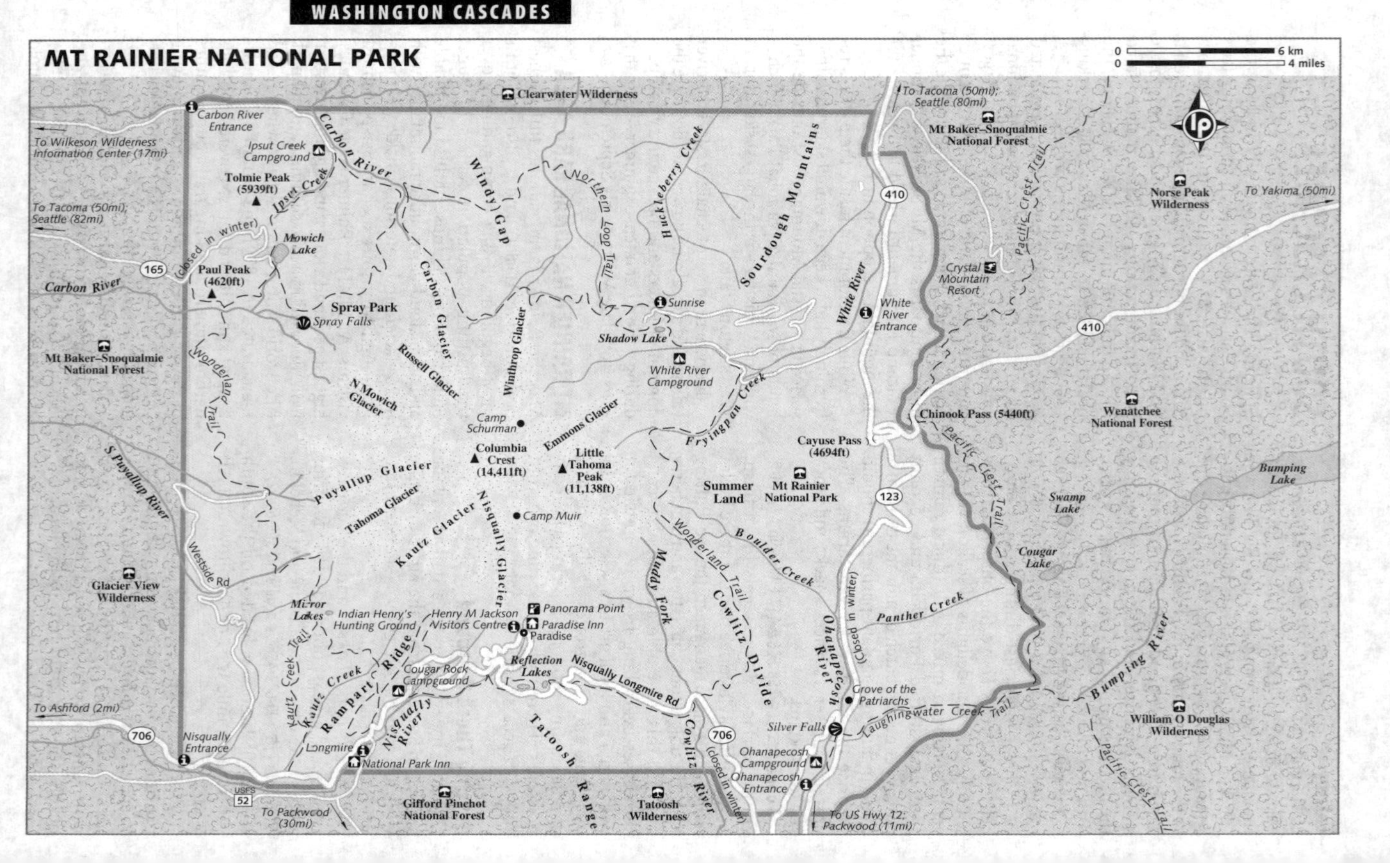
MT RAINIER NATIONAL PARK
0 6 km
0 4 miles
Clearwater Wilderness
Carbon River Entrance
To Wilkeson Wilderness Information Center (17mi)
Ipsut Creek Campground
Carbon River
Tolmie Peak (5939ft)
Ipsut Creek
To Tacoma (50mi); Seattle (82mi)
(closed in winter)
Mowich Lake
165
Paul Peak (4620ft)
Carbon River
Spray Park
Spray Falls
Windy Gap
Carbon Glacier
Northern Loop Trail
Huckleberry Creek
Sourdough Mountains
Sunrise
Shadow Lake
White River Campground
White River
White River Entrance
Winthrop Glacier
Russell Glacier
N Mowich Glacier
Mt Baker–Snoqualmie National Forest
Wonderland Trail
Camp Schurman
Columbia Crest (14,411ft)
Emmons Glacier
Little Tahoma Peak (11,138ft)
Fryingpan Creek
Cayuse Pass (4694ft)
Chinook Pass (5440ft)
S Puyallup River
Puyallup Glacier
Tahoma Glacier
Kautz Glacier
Nisqually Glacier
Camp Muir
Summer Land
Mt Rainier National Park
123
Westside Rd
Glacier View Wilderness
Mirror Lakes
Indian Henry's Hunting Ground
Henry M Jackson Visitors Centre
Panorama Point
Paradise Inn
Paradise
Reflection Lakes
Nisqually Longmire Rd
Muddy Fork
Wonderland Trail
Boulder Creek
Cowlitz Divide
Ohanapecosh River
(Closed in winter)
Panther Creek
Kautz Creek Trail
Kautz Creek
Rampart Ridge
Cougar Rock Campground
Nisqually River
Tatoosh Range
Grove of the Patriarchs
Silver Falls
Laughingwater Creek Trail
To Ashford (2mi)
706
Nisqually Entrance
Longmire
National Park Inn
706
(closed in winter)
Cowlitz River
Ohanapecosh Campground
Ohanapecosh Entrance
USFS 52
To Packwood (30mi)
Gifford Pinchot National Forest
Tatoosh Wilderness
To US Hwy 12; Packwood (11mi)
To Tacoma (50mi); Seattle (80mi)
Mt Baker–Snoqualmie National Forest
Norse Peak Wilderness
To Yakima (50mi)
410
Pacific Crest Trail
Crystal Mountain Resort
410
Wenatchee National Forest
Pacific Crest Trail
Bumping Lake
Swamp Lake
Cougar Lake
Bumping River
William O Douglas Wilderness
Pacific Crest Trail

destructive powers that, if provoked, could threaten downtown Seattle with mudslides and cause tsunamis in Puget Sound. Not surprisingly, the mountain has long been imbued with myth. The Native Americans called it Tahoma or Tacoma, meaning the 'mother of waters,' George Vancouver named it Rainier in honor of his colleague and friend Rear Admiral Peter Rainier, while most Seattleites refer to it reverently as 'the Mountain' and judge the weather by its visibility.

In truth Rainier creates its own weather – a climate that dumps some of the world's heaviest snowfalls on its higher slopes and has given rise to one of the planet's few inland temperate rain forests in the vicinity of the remote Carbon River region. But take the rain out of Rainier and you'll encounter a far friendlier natural giant. When the clouds finally lift during one of those long, clear days in August, the mountain becomes one of Washington's most paradisiacal playgrounds, loaded with leisure possibilities and awash with a dazzling array of wild flowers.

Orientation & Information

Situated 95 miles southeast of Seattle as the eagle flies, the Mt Rainier National Park is accessible by four separate entrances. By far the most popular (and the only year-round option) is the Nisqually entrance on Hwy 706, about an hour and a half southeast of Seattle, traffic permitting. Seven miles east of here lays Longmire with its store, lodge and trailheads, and 12 miles further on is Paradise at 5400ft.

In the summer you can follow Hwy 706 beyond Paradise to hook up with the southeastern Ohanapecosh and the eastern White River entrances with access to lofty Sunrise (6400ft).

Carbon River in the northwest is the most remote entrance despite its geographic proximity to Seattle. Facilities here are scant and the road is closed for most of the winter.

For information on the park check out the National Park Service website at www.nps.gov/mora which includes downloadable maps and descriptions of 50 park trails.

Park entrance fees are $15 per car and $5 for pedestrians and cyclists (those under 17 admitted free), and are valid for seven days from purchase. A $30 annual pass admits the pass-holder and accompanying passengers for 12 months from date of purchase.

Getting There & Around

Between May and October, **Rainier Shuttle** (☎ 360-569-2331) runs scheduled service between Sea-Tac Airport and the park. Three shuttles travel daily to and from Ashford ($42 one way), and one continues on to Paradise ($51). From Ashford to Paradise the fare is $12. Fares are reduced by $5 if reserved more than two days in advance. **Ashford Mountain Center** (☎ 360-569-2604) offers van service to and from the airport, as well as trailhead drop-off and pick-up throughout the park.

Gray Line of Seattle (☎ 206-626-5208; www.graylineofseattle.com) runs bus tours of the park mid-June–late September. The 10-hour tour leaves from the Seattle Sheraton Hotel at 8am daily (adult/child $59/29.50).

Nisqually Entrance

This southwestern corner of Mt Rainier National Park is its most developed (and hence most visited) corner. Here you'll find the park's only lodging, the only year-round road and the strung-out gateway settlement of Ashford that offers plenty of useful park-related facilities.

Hwy 706 enters the park about an hour and a half's drive southeast of Seattle just past Ashford and adjacent to the Nisqually River. After the entry toll booth, a well-paved road continues east offering the first good views of Mt Rainier – weather permitting – a few miles further on at Kautz Creek.

At the 7-mile mark you'll pass Longmire, the park's main nexus point replete with lodging, food and hiking trailheads. From here the road climbs steeply for 12 miles, passing numerous hairpin turns and viewpoints until it emerges at the elevated alpine meadows of Paradise.

INFORMATION

The best source of information outside the park is at the **Ashford Visitors Center** (☎ 360-569-2142; 30027 SR 706; 9am-5pm daily, until 8pm May-Oct), 6 miles before the Nisqually entrance, which has a shop, maps, leaflets and helpful staff. In Longmire, the museum (p182) can field basic questions. Otherwise head east to the flying saucer–shaped **Henry M Jackson Visitors Center** (☎ 360-569-2211, ext 2328; 9am-7pm daily May-Sep, 10am-5pm Sat & Sun Oct & Apr) at Paradise, where expert park rangers can answer questions on anything and everything. In the same building you'll find some stuffed-animal displays, an excellent expose of Rainier geology and history, a 360-degree viewing gallery, a shop and a basic cafeteria.

Park naturalists lead free interpretive hikes from the Jackson Visitors Center daily in summer, and snowshoe walks on winter weekends.

LONGMIRE

Worth a stop to stretch your legs or gain an early glimpse of Rainier's awesome old-growth forest, Longmire was the brainchild of a certain James Longmire who first came here in 1883 during a climbing trip when he noticed the hot mineral springs that bubbled up in a lovely meadow opposite the present-day National Park Inn (right). He and his family returned the following year and established Longmire's Medical Springs, and in 1890 he built the Longmire Springs Hotel. Since 1917 the National Park Inn has stood on this site – built in classic 'parkitecture' style – and is complemented by a small store, some park offices, the tiny **Longmire Museum** (☎ 360-569-2211, ext 3314; admission free; 🕑 9am-6pm Jun-Sep, 9am-5pm Oct-May) and a number of important trailheads. Long-distance walkers can pick up the famous **Wonderland Trail** (opposite) here, or test their mettle on the precipitous **Eagle Peak Trail**, a steep 7.2-mile out-and-back hike. For a more laid-back look at some old-growth forest and pastoral meadows try the sign-posted **Trail of the Shadows** loop, a 0.8-mile trail that begins across the road from the museum and is wheelchair accessible for the first 0.4 miles.

PARADISE

Paradise, situated at 5400ft, has a much shorter hiking season than Longmire (snow can persist into late June), but its dazzling wildflowers, which include avalanche lilies, western anemones, lupine, mountain bog gentian and paintbrush, make the experience spectacular.

Paradise is crisscrossed with trails, of all types and standards, some good for a short stroll (with the kids) others the realm of more serious hikers. To get a closeup of the Nisqually Glacier follow the 1.2-mile **Nisqually Vista Trail**. For something more substantial hike the 5-mile **Skyline Trail**, starting behind the Paradise Inn and climbing approximately 1600ft to **Panorama Point**, with good views of Mt Rainier and the neighboring Tatoosh Range.

Intrepid day-hikers can continue up the mountain from Panorama Point via the **Pebble Creek Trail** to the permanent snowfield track that leads to **Camp Muir**, the main overnight bivouac spot for climbing parties. At 10,000ft, this hike is not to be taken lightly. Take sufficient clothing and load up with a good supply of food and water.

During the winter the road is generally plowed as far as Paradise, and people take to the trails on cross-country skis and snowshoes. The **Longmire Ski Touring Center** (☎ 360-569-2411; 🕑 8am-6pm Sat & Sun Thanksgiving-Apr), in the Longmire General Store, has trail information, lessons and cross-country ski and snowshoe rentals.

SLEEPING

Cougar Rock Campground (☎ 360-569-2211; campsites late June-Labor Day $15, rest of season $12. 🕑 late May–mid-Oct) Cougar Rock, 2.3 miles north of Longmire on the way to Paradise, has 173 individual campsites and flush toilets. Rangers lead campfire talks on summer evenings.

Whittaker's Bunkhouse (☎ 360-569-2439; 30205 SR 706 E; dm $30, s & d $85) Another Rainier gem, Whittaker's is the home base of legendary Northwestern climber Lou Whittaker who first summited Mt Rainier at the age of 19 and has guided countless adventurers to the top in the years since. Down-to-earth and comfortable, this place has a good old-fashioned youth-hostel feel to it and the inviting onsite espresso bar is a great place to hunker down for breakfast – none of those serum-wrapped day-old muffins here.

Nisqually Lodge (☎ 360-569-8804; 31609 SR 706 E; r $85;) With an expansive lobby complete with crackling fireplace and huge well-stocked rooms, this lodge is far plusher than an average motel. The outdoor Jacuzzi, simple help-yourself breakfast and easy access to the park, seal the deal in this price bracket.

Paradise Inn (☎ 360-569-2413; http://rainier.guestservices.com; 🕑 mid-May–Sep) Rainier's classic national park inns was closed as of 2006 for a $30 million earthquake-withstanding revamp. At the time of writing it was due to reopen for the 2008 summer season.

our pick **National Park Inn** (☎ 360-569-2411; www.guestservices.com/rainier; r with shared/private bathroom $104/139, 2-room unit $191; 🕑 year-round;) The only in-park accommodation at the time of writing, the National Park Inn goes out of its way to be rustic with no TVs or telephones

THE WONDERLAND TRAIL

Sweet-scented alpine air, narrow bridges across yawning canyons and a smorgasbord of spectacular Cascade scenery – the Wonderland Trail is a hike that well and truly lives up to its name. Laid out in 1915, the trail initially served as a patrol beat for park rangers and, in the 1930s, briefly faced closure when it was earmarked as a paved ring road for four-wheeled traffic. Fortunately the plan never came to fruition, and today the original 93-mile route that completely circumnavigates Mt Rainier via a well-maintained unbroken path remains one of the most challenging and rewarding hikes in the Pacific Northwest.

Wonderland is a tough backcountry hike with a cumulative elevation gain of 20,100ft, making good physical fitness and planning prerequisites. The most common starting point is at Longmire near the Nisqually entrance and the majority of hikers tackle the route over 10 to 12 days progressing in a clockwise direction around the mountain west to east. Along the way there are 18 trailside campgrounds spaced approximately three to 7 miles apart, each equipped with two to eight cleared campsites, toilet pits and a nearby water source (which you'll need to treat, filter or boil). The best – and hence the most popular – hiking window is in July and August when rain is less common, but when mosquitoes descend in their droves. Bring repellent! Before embarking you'll need to organize a free backcountry permit from the **Wilderness Information Center** (www.nps.gov/mora; 55210 238th Av E, Ashford). Forms are available online. Camping reservations ($20) are recommended in peak season.

in the rooms and small yet cozy facilities. But with fine service, fantastic surroundings and delectable complimentary afternoon tea and scones served in the comfortable dining room who needs HBO and Discovery Channel? Book ahead in the summer.

EATING

The **cafeteria** (daily May-Sep, Sat & Sun Oct-Apr) in the Jackson Visitors Center (p181) is the only food fare at Paradise at present. If you're fresh from a meadow hike or wintertime snowshoeing expedition plump for the revitalizing chili served in cheery plastic dishes.

our pick **Copper Creek Inn** (360-569-2326; 35707 SR 706 E; breakfast $5-8, sandwiches & burgers $5.50-8; 7am-9pm) This is one of the state's greatest rural restaurants, and breakfast here is an absolute must if you're heading off for a lengthy hike inside the park itself. Situated just outside the Nisqually entrance, the Copper Creek has been knocking out pancakes, wild blackberry pie and their own home-roasted coffee successfully for over 50 years. Stop by to taste the food and soak up the ambience and you'll soon understand why.

National Park Inn (360-569-2411; lunch $6-9, dinner mains $15-18; year-round) Hearty hiking fare is served at this homely inn-restaurant and – in the absence of any real competition – it's surprisingly good. Try the pot roast or the chicken with honey glaze, and make sure not to miss the huge blackberry cobbler with ice cream that will require a good 2-mile hike along the Wonderland Trail (which starts just outside the door) to work off.

Ohanapecosh Entrance

Ohanapecosh (o-*ha*-nuh-peh-*kosh*) in the park's southeastern corner is accessed by the small settlement of Packwood, 12 miles to the southwest on US 12 which harbors a small number of eating and sleeping options. Shoehorned between Mt Rainier and it two southern neighbors, Mt St Helens and Mt Adams, this is a good base for travelers wanting to visit two or more of the mountains. Linked to Paradise by Hwy 706, Ohanapecosh's roads are generally closed in the winter months due to adverse weather conditions, making it less accessible than Nisqually.

INFORMATION

The **Ohanapecosh Visitors Center** (360-494-2229; 9am-5pm May–mid-Oct) is at the park's southeastern corner on Hwy 123. The displays here focus on tree identification and the local old-growth forest. Rangers also offer information on hiking trails.

The **Packwood Information Center** (360-494-0600; 13068 US Hwy 12; 8am-4:30pm Mon-Fri year-round, Mon-Sat Jun-Sep), near the north end of town, is a good source of information on the Goat Rocks Wilderness Area.

HIKING

Starting just north of the Ohanapecosh Visitors Center, the 1.5-mile **Grove of the Patriarchs Trail** is one of the park's most popular short hikes and explores a small island in the Ohanapecosh River replete with craning Douglas fir, cedar and hemlock trees, some of which are over 1000 years old.

SLEEPING & EATING

Ohanapecosh Campground (☎ 360-494-2229; Hwy 123; campsites $12 May-Jun, Sep-Oct, late Jun-Labor Day $15) Near the visitors center, this NPS facility has 188 campsites and flush toilets. Rangers lead campfire talks on summer evenings.

Hotel Packwood (☎ 360-494-5431; 104 Main St; tw/d $29/39, d with bathroom $49; ⊠) A frontier-style hotel with a wraparound verandah, the Packwood wouldn't win any design show awards, but at this price, who's arguing. There are nine varied rooms at this renovated 1912 establishment, two of which can accommodate four people.

Cowlitz River Lodge (☎ 360-494-4444; Hwy 12 at Skate Creek Rd; s/d incl breakfast $70-85; ⊠) Probably the most convenient accommodation for both Mts Rainier and St Helens, the Cowlitz is the sister lodge to Ashford's Nisqually Lodge and offers 32 above-average motel rooms along with the obligatory outdoor Jacuzzi.

Peters Inn (☎ 360-494-4000; Hwy 12 near Skate Creek Rd; lunch specials $8, mains $11-15) This local steak house features a lunch counter and a cozy dining area, but is best for its breakfasts which include endless coffee refills, pancakes, eggs and homemade country fries on the side.

White River Entrance

Rainier's main eastern entrance is the gateway to Sunrise, which at 6400ft marks the park's highest road. Thanks to the superior elevation here, the summer season is particularly short and snow can linger well into July. It is also noticeably drier than Paradise resulting in an interesting variety of sub-alpine vegetation, including masses of wildflowers.

The views from Sunrise are famously spectacular and – aside from stunning close-ups of Mt Rainier itself – you can also, quite literally, watch the weather roll in over the distant peaks of Mts Baker and Adams. Similarly impressive is the glistening Emmons Glacier which, at 4 sq miles in size, is the largest glacier in the contiguous USA.

ORIENTATION & INFORMATION

The White River entrance road is accessed from Hwy 410 via Seattle to the north and Yakima to the east. From the turning the entrance is approximately 1 mile to the west. The road comes to an end at Sunrise, another 15 miles further on (and also 2400ft higher up).

The **Wilderness Information Center** (☎ 360-663-2273; 🕒 8am-5pm daily late May-Sep, extended hr Thu-Sat Jul-Labor Day) at the White River entrance dispenses backcountry permits and hiking information. You can also get information at the **Sunrise Visitors Center** (☎ 360-569-2425; 🕒 9am-6pm late Jun–mid-Sep).

HIKING

Day hikes from Sunrise offer dramatic scenery and rewarding mountain vistas, and while the crowds here can be thick in the summer, the lack of tour buses makes it substantially quieter than Paradise.

A trailhead directly across the parking lot from the Sunrise Lodge Cafeteria provides access to the **Emmons Vista**, with good views of Mt Rainier, Little Tahoma and the Emmons Glacier, the largest glacier in the lower 48 states. Nearby, the 1-mile **Sourdough Ridge Trail** takes you out into pristine sub-alpine meadows for stunning views over the Washington giants of Mt Rainier, Mt Baker, Glacier Peak and Mt Adams.

To get to **Emmons Glacier**, you'll need to set off from the White River Campground (see below), 13 miles by road from Sunrise. Look out for both mountain goats and mountain climbers ascending the Inter Glacier as you track west along the **Glacier Basin Trail.** The official overlook is about 1 mile from the campground along a spur path to the left.

SLEEPING & EATING

White River Campground (☎ 360 663-2273; campsites $12; 🕒 late Jun-Sep) This 112-site campground is 10 road miles or 3.5 steep trail miles downhill from Sunrise. Facilities include flush toilets, drinking water and crowded, though not unpleasant, camping spaces.

Sunrise Lodge Cafeteria (☎ 360-569-2425; snacks $5-7; 🕒 10am-7pm daily Jun 30-Sep 16) As the only eating joint in a 30-mile radius, Sunrise's post-hike chili can look deceptively appetizing. There's not a lot else here apart from the ubiquitous hot dogs and hamburgers, and there is no overnight accomodation here.

SKIING IN THE CASCADES

While they can't compete with Whistler or Aspen for fancy après-ski facilities, the Washington Cascades *do* offer snow adventurers some of the wildest and most rugged terrain in North America. Mt Baker is a shrine for aspiring snowboarders, Crystal Mountain offers family-friendly facilities within easy driving distance of Seattle, while the Methow Valley is a cross-country skiing center almost without equal.

Mt Baker

Boasting the greatest annual snowfall of any ski area in North America, Mt Baker is a skier's paradise lauded by purists for its quality powder and fine mountain scenery. It's also the site of the world's premier snowboarding event, the Legendary Baker Banked Slalom, held every January on a narrow, winding creekbed buried under 20ft of snow.

Situated on the dry, eastern side of the mountain, the **Mt Baker Ski Area** (☎ 360-734-6771; www.mtbakerskiarea.com) has 38 runs, eight lifts and a vertical rise of 1500ft. Due to its rustic facilities, ungroomed terrain and limited après-ski options, the resort has gained something of a cult status among skiers and boarders who revere its difficult steeps, chutes and woods.

Mt Rainier

Washington's largest and most popular ski area is situated just outside the northeast entrance of Mt Rainier National Park at the **Crystal Mountain Resort** (☎ 360-663-2265; www.skicrystal.com; 33914 Crystal Mountain Blvd). More commercialized than Mt Baker, downhill skiers nonetheless give Crystal Mountain high marks for its steep chutes and remote, unpatrolled backcountry trails. Its summit (Silver King) tops out at 7012ft and the vertical drop is 3120ft. Crystal has 50 named runs, more than 50% of which are rated intermediate and is served by 10 lifts, including four high-speed chairs. There's night skiing Friday through Sunday till 8pm and lodgings in the area are plentiful, if a little pricy (p186).

Methow Valley

When it comes to cross-country skiing, the sun-splashed Methow Valley northeast of Winthrop is difficult to match. The more than 125 miles of groomed trails maintained here comprise the second largest cross-country skiing area in the USA. Managed by the **Methow Valley Sports Trails Association** (MVSTA; ☎ 509-996-3287; www.mvsta.com) the area has three main hubs at Mazama, Rendezvous and Sun Mountain (near Winthrop) with interconnecting trails progressing from easy to difficult and enabling hut-to-hut and lodge-to-lodge skiing. One- and three-day trail passes cost $18 and $42.

Passes, maps and ski rentals are available from **Jack's Hut** (☎ 509-996-2752; 17798 Hwy 20), at the Freestone Inn (p172), or from the Sun Mountain Ski Shop at the Sun Mountain Lodge (p173).

Carbon River Entrance

The park's northwest entrance is its most isolated and undeveloped corner with two unpaved (and unconnected) roads and little in the way of facilities, save a lone ranger station and the very basic Ipsut Creek Campground. But while the tourist traffic might be thin on the ground, the landscape lacks nothing in magnificence or serendipity.

Named for its coal deposits, Carbon River is the park's wettest region and protects one of the few remaining examples of inland temperate rain forest in the contiguous USA. Dense, green and cloaked in moss, this verdant wilderness can be penetrated by a handful of interpretive trails that fan off the Carbon River Rd.

For closeup mountain views head for Mowich Lake on a separate road which branches off a few miles outside the park entrance. This is Rainier's largest and deepest lake and a starting point for various wilderness hikes including the marathon Wonderland Trail (p183). In close proximity to Mowich is the Carbon Glacier, the nation's lowest glacier whose snout touches an elevation of 3520ft.

You can pick up permits for backcountry camping and for northside climbs at the **Wilkeson Wilderness Information Center** (☎ 360-829-5127; 8:30am-4pm May-Nov, 7:30am-7:30pm Jun-Aug), located 21 miles from the Carbon River entrance.

HIKES

To experience the rare thrill of walking inside a thick canopied temperate rain forest venture out on the 0.3-mile **Rainforest Trail**, just inside the park entrance, that loops via a raised boardwalk past huge-leafed ferns and giant dripping trees.

The 3520ft snout of the **Carbon Glacier** can be accessed via a trail from the Ipsut Creek Campground (see below), which proceeds southeast for 3.5 miles to a constructed overlook. Hikers are warned not to approach the glacier, as rockfall from its surface is unpredictable and dangerous. This hike is technically part of the longer Wonderland Trail (p183).

From Mowich Lake, one extremely popular trail heads south and passes **Spray Falls** on its way to **Spray Park**, flush with wildflowers late in the summer. It's just under 3 miles to Spray Park, but with numerous steep switchbacks above the falls the trail is far from easy.

SLEEPING

Ipsut Creek Campground (☎ 360-829-5127; campsites $8 late May-Labor Day, no fee rest of year; year-round, weather permitting) The campground, at the end of the Carbon River Rd, has 31 campsites but no drinking water. The road up is not recommended for trailers.

Crystal Mountain Resort

Just outside the northeast corner of the national park lies Rainier's popular ski area, 39 miles east of Enumclaw off Hwy 410. On weekends and holidays from December to March luxury buses transport skiers from Seattle and Tacoma for $70/30 adult/child including lift ticket. Call ☎ 800-665-2122 for schedules and points of departure.

SLEEPING & EATING

Alpine Inn (☎ 360-663-2262; r $75-90) Tun by Crystal Mountain Hotels, this Bavarian-style inn looks as if it's been dragged across from kitschy Leavenworth on the other side of the Wenatchee National Forest. Cozy, comfortable and playing deftly on its European image, the inn boasts a restaurant, rathskeller, deli and ski/snowboard shop. Watch out for the Wiener schnitzel in the restaurant.

Alta Crystal Resort (☎ 360-663-2500; www.altacrystalresort.com; 2-6 person ste $129-239;) The Alta Crystal Resort is popular year-round thanks to its proximity to the Crystal Mountain ski resort (winter) and the Sunrise Lodge Cafeteria and trailheads (summer). It's one of the area's plushest accommodations (though it's technically outside the park). Encased in 22 wooded acres and bisected by bubbling Deep Creek, the resort consists of 24 suites housed in three chalets surrounding a pool and Jacuzzi. One-bedroom suites sleep up to four and loft suites accommodate up to six. All have kitchenettes and wood stoves or fireplaces.

MT ST HELENS

Thanks to a 1980 eruption that set off an explosion bigger than the combined power of 21,000 atomic bombs, Washington's 87th tallest mountain needs little introduction. What it lacks in height Mt St Helens makes up for in fiery infamy; 57 people perished on the mountain on that fateful day in May 1980 when an earthquake of 5.1 on the Richter scale sparked the biggest landslide in recorded history and buried 230 sq miles of forest under millions of tonnes of volcanic rock and ash.

When the smoke finally lifted, Mt St Helens sported a new mile-wide crater on its north side and had lost 1300ft in height. Resolving to leave nature to its own devices, the Reagan Administration created the 172-sq-mile **Mt St Helens National Volcanic Monument** in 1982. A visit here today will demonstrate how, nearly three decades on, nature has restored much life to the mountain, although the devastation wreaked by the explosion is still hauntingly evident.

Orientation & Information

There are two principal entry routes to Mt St Helens. The most popular is the one-hour drive east on Hwy 504 from Castle Rock off I-5, one hour north of Portland. The route here is sprinkled with five different visitors centers, most notably the ones at Coldwater Ridge and Johnston Ridge. A second entry point is available at Windy Ridge, accessible via US 12 which connects with both I-5 and the Nisqually and Ohanapecosh Mt Rainier entrances, or Hwy 503 in the south.

The **Mt St Helens Visitors Center** (☎ 360-274-2100; 3029 Spirit Lake Hwy; admission $3; 9am-5pm) is situated 5 miles east of Castle Rock on Hwy 504 and, with its films, exhibits and free information on the mountain, serves as an excellent introduction to the monument. Twenty-two miles further on you'll come to the **Hoffstadt Bluffs Visitors Center** (☎ 360-274-7750; 15000 Spirit Lake Hwy; adult/child $3/1; 9am-6pm daily May-Sep, 10am-4pm

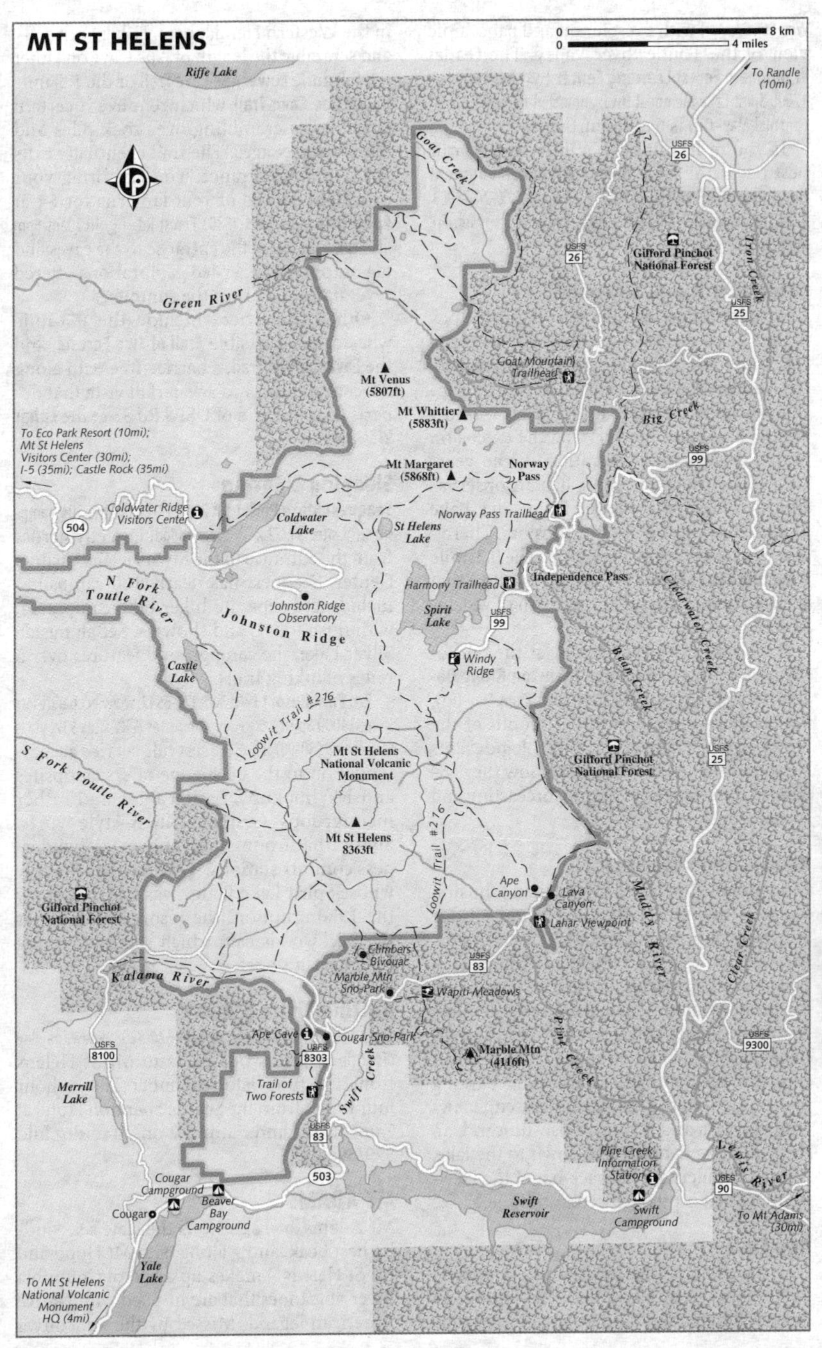
MT ST HELENS
0 8 km
0 4 miles
Riffe Lake
To Randle (10mi)
Goat Creek
Green River
Gifford Pinchot National Forest
Iron Creek
Mt Venus (5807ft)
Mt Whittier (5883ft)
Goat Mountain Trailhead
Big Creek
To Eco Park Resort (10mi); Mt St Helens Visitors Center (30mi); I-5 (35mi); Castle Rock (35mi)
Mt Margaret (5868ft)
Norway Pass
Coldwater Ridge Visitors Center
Coldwater Lake
St Helens Lake
Norway Pass Trailhead
Independence Pass
N Fork Toutle River
Harmony Trailhead
Johnston Ridge Observatory
Johnston Ridge
Spirit Lake
Clearwater Creek
Windy Ridge
Bean Creek
Castle Lake
Loowit Trail #216
S Fork Toutle River
Mt St Helens National Volcanic Monument
Mt St Helens 8363ft
Gifford Pinchot National Forest
Ape Canyon
Lava Canyon
Lahar Viewpoint
Muddy River
Gifford Pinchot National Forest
Climbers Bivouac
Marble Mtn Sno-Park
Wapiti Meadows
Kalama River
Clear Creek
Ape Cave
Cougar Sno-Park
Marble Mtn (4116ft)
Pine Creek
Swift Creek
Merrill Lake
Trail of Two Forests
Lewis River
Pine Creek Information Station
Cougar Campground
Beaver Bay Campground
Cougar
Swift Reservoir
Swift Campground
To Mt Adams (30mi)
Yale Lake
To Mt St Helens National Volcanic Monument HQ (4mi)
USFS 26
USFS 25
USFS 99
USFS 83
USFS 8100
USFS 8303
USFS 9300
USFS 90
504
503
WASHINGTON CASCADES

Wed-Sun Oct-Apr) with a restaurant and panoramic view of the Toutle River Valley. The **Charles W Bingham Forest Learning Center** (☎ 360-414-3439; 17000 Spirit Lake Memorial Hwy; admission free; 🕑 10am-6pm mid-May–Oct) is 6 miles further up.

If you're heading to Windy Ridge your best bet is the **Mt St Helens Volcanic Monument Headquarters** (☎ 360-247-3900, 24-hr info 360-247-3903; 42218 NE Yale Bridge Rd, Amboy, WA; 🕑 8am-5pm Mon-Fri, Mon-Sat Jun-Sep).

Coldwater Ridge & Around

Coldwater Ridge, 43 miles east of Castle Rock is the site of the **Coldwater Ridge Visitors Center** (☎ 360-274-2131; 🕑 10am-6pm May-Oct, 9am-5pm Nov-Apr) with views over toward Mt St Helens' gaping northern crater. Exhibits focus on how animal and plant life survived the explosion and tracks their regeneration in the years since. The modern center has an observation deck with views over Coldwater Lake created during the 1980 explosion. There's also a bookstore and a cafeteria. The 0.3-mile **Winds of Change Trail** is an interpretive hike that seeks to demonstrate the regrowth of vegetation in the area.

A few miles further along, at the end of Hwy 504, you'll find the **Johnston Ridge Observatory** (☎ 360-274-2140; 🕑 10am-6pm May-Oct), which looks directly into the mouth of the crater. Exhibits here depict the geologic events surrounding the 1980 blast and how they advanced the science of volcano forecasting and monitoring.

Windy Ridge Viewpoint

More remote but less crowded than Johnston Ridge is the harder-to-reach Windy Ridge viewpoint on the mountain's eastern side, accessed via USFS Rd 99. Here visitors get a palpable, if eerie, sense of the destruction that the blast wrought with felled forests, desolate mountain slopes and the rather surreal sight of lifeless Spirit Lake, once one of the premier resorts in the South Cascades. At the parking lot, steps climb the hillside for closeup views of the crater and you can also descend on the mile-long **Harmony Trail** down to the lake. There are toilets and a snack bar at the viewpoint, which is often closed until June.

Ape Cave

Ape Cave is a 2-mile-long lava tube formed 2000 years ago by a lava flow that followed a deep watercourse. It's the longest lava tube in the Western Hemisphere. Hikers can walk and scramble the length of Ape Cave on either the 0.8-mile **Lower Ape Cave Trail** or the 1.5-mile **Upper Ape Cave Trail** which requires a certain amount of scrambling over rock piles and narrower passages. The trail eventually exits at the upper entrance. You can bring your own light source or rent lanterns for $4 at **Apes' Headquarters** (8303 Forest Rd; 🕑 10:30am-5pm Jun-Sep), located at the entrance to the caves and tag onto free ranger-led explorations offered several times daily in the summer.

Other trails here include the 0.3-mile wheelchair-accessible **Trail of Two Forests**, and the **Lava Canyon Trail**, a barrier-free path along a recent mudflow to a waterfall vista that departs from the end of USFS Rd 83 at the **Lahar Viewpoint**.

Sleeping & Eating

Seaquest State Park (☎ 206-274-8633; Hwy 504; campsites/RV sites $17/24; 🕑 year-round) Directly across from the entrance to the Mt St Helens Visitors Center, Seaquest has nearly 100 campsites, including a separate hiker/bike camp area, with flush toilets and showers. Set alongside Silver Lake, the campground features over 5 miles of hiking trails.

Eco Park Resort (☎ 360-274-6542; www.ecoparkresort.com; 14000 Spirit Lake Hwy; campsites & RV sites $17, yurts $60, cabins $80-90) The closest full-service accommodation to the blast zone offers campsites and RV hookups, basic cabins and rather incongruous Genghis Khan–style yurts. Shared bathrooms are known as 'wilderness comfort stations.' Owned by the family whose Spirit Lake Lodge was swept away by the 1980 eruption, the resort also features the Backwoods café which serves anything as long as it's beef.

Getting There & Away

Gray Line of Seattle (☎ 206-626 5208, www.graylineofseattle.com) runs bus tours to Mt St Helens from mid-June–late September. The 11-hour tour leaves from the Seattle Sheraton Hotel at 7am Friday and Saturday only (adult/child $79/39.50).

MT ADAMS

Mt Adams, at 12,276ft, is the state's second-highest peak, and – along with Mt Hood and Mt St Helens – makes up a trio of Columbia River volcanoes that are imbued with Native American legend. Missed by the Vancouver expedition in 1792, the mountain was first logged by Lewis and Clarke in 1805 and remained nameless until 1832 when, in a mix up with nearby Mt Hood, it was named for second US president, John Adams. The oversights have continued to the present day. Further from Seattle than Mts Rainier and St Helens, and covered on its eastern flanks by the Yakima Indian Reservation, Mt Adams receives nowhere near as many visitors as its more famous neighbors. Not that this detracts from its enchanting beauty. Protected in the 66-sq-mile Mt Adams Wilderness, Adams sports plenty of picturesque hikes including the much-loved **Bird Creek Meadow Trail**, a 3-mile loop that showcases the best of the mountain's meadows, wildflowers and waterfalls.

Another unique activity in the area is blue- and huckleberry picking in the high meadows around the Indian Heaven Wilderness. For huckleberry permits and information on hiking and climbing, consult the **Mt Adams Ranger District USFS Office** (☎ 509-395-3400; 2455 Hwy 141; 🕑 8am-4:30pm Mon-Sat, daily Jun-Sep) in Trout Lake.

The easiest access to Mt Adams is from the Columbia River Gorge near Hood River (Oregon). From here Hwy 141 proceeds north for 25 miles to the tiny community of Trout Lake. Access from north is from Randle on US 12 and is only passable in the summer.

Sleeping

Takhlakh Lake Campground (☎ 509-395-3400; campsites $11) Sixty-two campsites with running water and pit toilets are situated here 25 miles north of Trout Lake on USFS Rd 23.

Serenity's (☎ 509-395-2500; www.serenitys.com; 2291 Hwy 141; cabin $99-129; wi-fi) A mile south of Trout Lake on Hwy 141, Serenity's offers four beautifully presented cabins in the woods in the shadow of snow-sprinkled Mt Adams. Wonderfully landscaped and amply equipped with kitchens, bathrooms, wood stoves, Jacuzzis, welcome cookies (homemade) and a bottle of wine, this is true luxury in the wilderness.

Central & Eastern Washington

Nestled in the rain shadow of the Cascade Mountains and cut off from the coast by the crenellated crags of Mts Baker, Rainier, Adams and St Helen's, central and eastern Washington is a different world to the rain embattled urban centers further west. Here, amid the sun-baked hills and big blue skies of Yakima, Richland, Okanogan and Walla Walla you'll find privately run wineries, abundant apple orchards, colorful Native American Reservations and a strong and vibrant Hispanic community.

If western Washington is dominated by its smoldering volcanoes and vast evergreen forests, the east's geographic identity is intrinsically linked to its rivers. The state's longest waterway, the mighty Columbia River, has transformed both the landscape and the economy in this once-parched rural region with a series of gargantuan dams and ambitious irrigation projects that have converted barren valleys and scrubby steppe into a veritable Garden of Eden. As a result, eastern Washington now churns out over half of the country's apple crop and produces some of the nation's youngest, fruitiest and most promising new wines.

Despite scant transportation links, a less-developed tourist infrastructure and a reputation for being something of a bucolic backwater, the east offers a refreshing antidote to travelers who've had their fill of West Coast adrenaline adventures or grown tired of the urban cool of Seattle. Understated Spokane boasts a rich and eclectic architectural heritage, diminutive Ellensburg holds a nationally renowned Labor Day rodeo, while up-and-coming Walla Walla is a new and emerging wine destination where subtle syrahs and fruity cabernet sauvignons vie with California's well-established Napa Valley for international recognition.

HIGHLIGHTS

- Washing down Bratwurst with German beer in Bavarian **Leavenworth** (opposite)
- Stealing a serendipitous moment in the **Alpine Lakes Wilderness** (p196)
- Catching cowboy fever at the **Ellensburg Rodeo** (p200)
- Pulling on your sports shoes for a companionable **Bloomsday run** (p207) in Spokane
- Admiring the after-dark laser show at the **Grand Coulee Dam** (p209)
- Supping a syrah in a **Walla Walla** (p214) tasting room

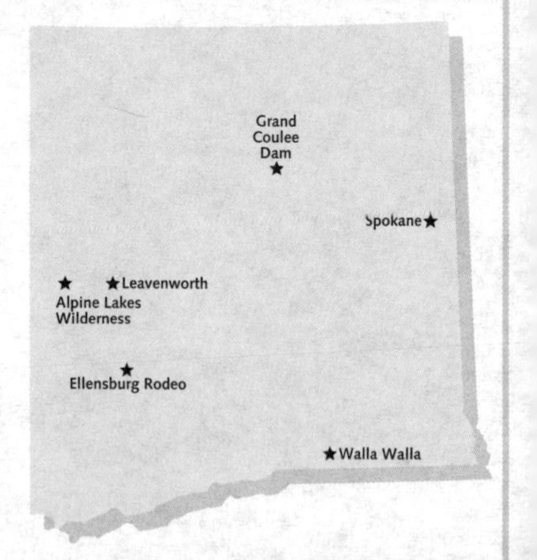

Geography & Climate

Cocooned between the Cascades and the Rockies, central and eastern Washington lies on top of the vast Columbia River plateau created millions of years ago when one of the largest flood ballasts in recorded history covered much of the Pacific Northwest. Caught in the rain shadow of the Cascade Mountains, the land is notably drier here, with the boreal forests of the Okanogan National Forest folding gradually into the dry, barren steppe more common in the Tri-Cities region. While eastern winters can be frigid, the summers in the Columbia and Yakima River valleys are notably hotter than Olympia or Seattle, with temperatures in excess of 100°F not uncommon.

Getting There & Away

Spokane is the east's biggest transportation hub with regular air links to Seattle, Portland, Denver and Salt Lake City. The daily *Empire Builder* train connects the city to Chicago in the east and Seattle and Portland in the west. There's a thrice-daily Greyhound bus service to Seattle and a daily connection to Boise in Idaho.

Getting Around

Getting around central and eastern Washington presents one of the state's biggest transportation challenges – unless, of course, you have a car. Despite having slashed a number of its routes in recent years (including the link to Walla Walla), Greyhound buses still run a service between Pasco and Spokane, and Pasco and Seattle via Yakima. There's also a daily service between Seattle and Wenatchee.

CENTRAL WASHINGTON

Caught in the foothills of the grandiose Cascade Mountains, central Washington is a geographic crossroads where dramatic alpine peaks fold imperceptibly into a barren steppe-like desert broken only by the Nile-like presence of the Columbia River and its irrigating manmade dams.

Wenatchee and Leavenworth are the most interesting urban centers here and both are popular stopping off points on the scenic Cascade Loop. They also make good bases for a plethora of exciting outdoor adventures nearby.

Leavenworth

pop 2074

Dust off your lederhosen, brush up on your German drinking songs, and get ready to swap your burgers for bratwurst and your T-bone steak for Weiner schnitzel. Welcome to Leavenworth, Washington's very own themed Bavarian 'village,' a former lumber town that went Teutonic back in the 1960s in order to stop an economic rot of catastrophic proportions from putting it permanently out of business. Rather amazingly, the ploy worked. Leavenworth's reincarnation as a quintessential *Romantische Strasse* village has transformed a once dull Cascadian pit stop into a thriving and surprisingly authentic tourist haven. The settlement's picturesque alpine setting on the eastern edge of the craggy North Cascade Mountains certainly helps; as does the fact that well over a quarter of the current population is effectively German. But, surreal as the concept may sound, Leavenworth is no Disneyland theme park. Nor is it by any means a Bavarian monopoly. If the beer and sausages get too much, simply lace up your hiking boots, fill your rucksack with a day or two of supplies and head off into an untamed and adventure-filled wilderness.

ORIENTATION & INFORMATION

Front St, Leavenworth's main drag, runs parallel to US 2, one block south. Icicle Rd, on the west side of town, traces Icicle Creek south to an assortment of recreational possibilities bordering the Alpine Lakes Wilderness.

If you're not immediately sold on the town's rather unusual German makeover, head to the **Leavenworth Chamber of Commerce & Visitor Center** (☎ 509-548-5807; www.leavenworth.org; 940 US 2; 🕑 8am-5pm Mon-Thu, 8am-6pm Fri & Sat, 10am-4pm Sun), where they'll soon convince you otherwise. The **Leavenworth Ranger Station** (☎ 509-548-6977; 600 Sherbourne; 🕑 7:30am-4:30pm daily Jun 15-October 15, 7:45am-4:30pm Mon-Fri rest of year) is off US 2 at the east end of town, and provides information on recreational opportunities and issues various types of permits.

SIGHTS

Leavenworth's small Bavarian hub is centered on Front St where gabled alpine houses nestle cozily in the shadow of the craggy Tyrolean peaks of the North Cascade Mountains. A leisurely stroll through this diminutive, if

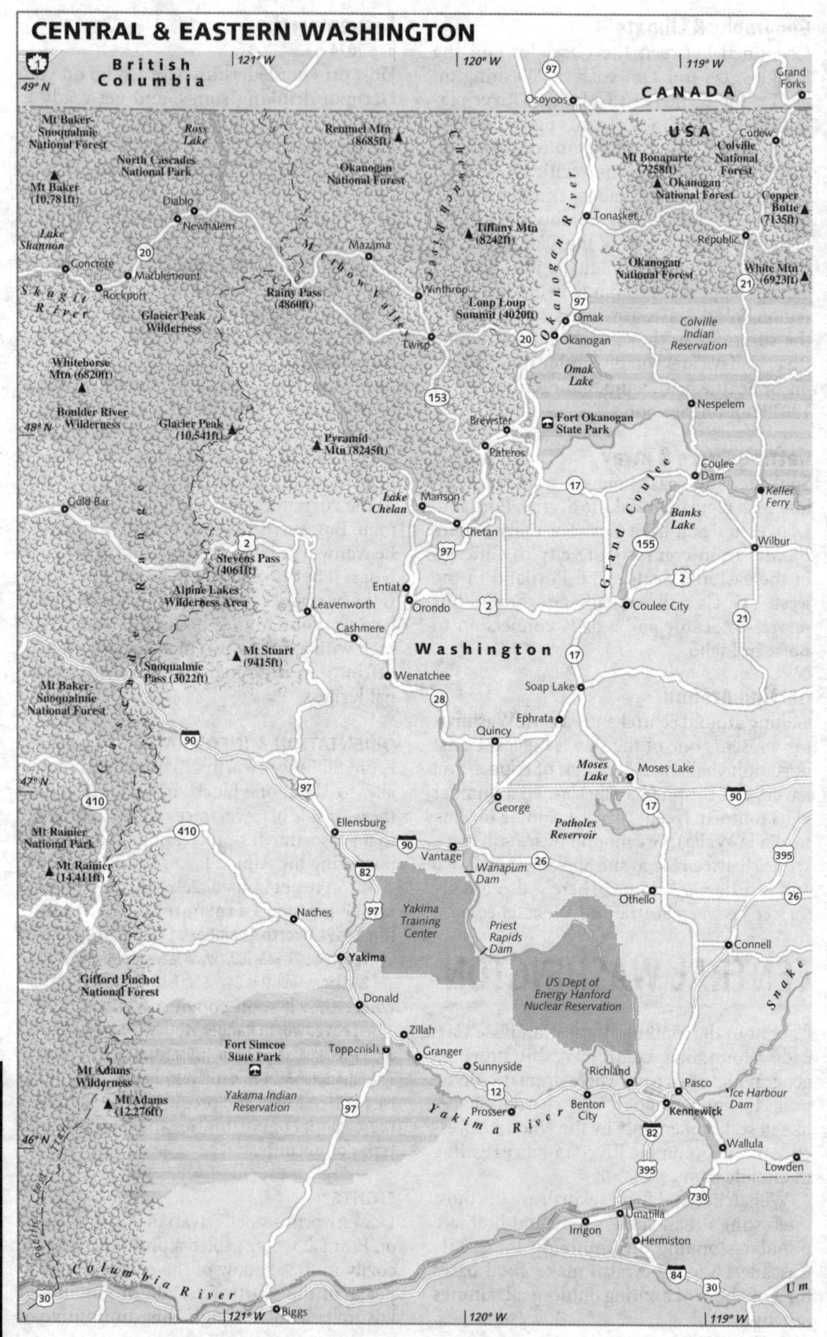
CENTRAL & EASTERN WASHINGTON
British Columbia
CANADA
USA
121° W
120° W
119° W
49° N
48° N
47° N
46° N
Mt Baker-Snoqualmie National Forest
Ross Lake
North Cascades National Park
Mt Baker (10,781ft)
Diablo
Newhalem
Lake Shannon
Concrete
Marblemount
Rockport
Skagit River
Glacier Peak Wilderness
Whitehorse Mtn (6820ft)
Boulder River Wilderness
Glacier Peak (10,541ft)
Remmel Mtn (8685ft)
Okanogan National Forest
Chewuch River
Methow Valley
Mazama
Rainy Pass (4860ft)
Winthrop
Twisp
Tiffany Mtn (8242ft)
Loup Loup Summit (4020ft)
Osoyoos
Okanogan River
Omak
Okanogan
Omak Lake
Tonasket
Mt Bonaparte (7258ft)
Okanogan National Forest
Curlew
Colville National Forest
Grand Forks
Copper Butte (7135ft)
Republic
White Mtn (6923ft)
Colville Indian Reservation
Nespelem
Brewster
Pateros
Fort Okanogan State Park
Pyramid Mtn (8245ft)
Lake Chelan
Manson
Chelan
Coulee Dam
Keller Ferry
Grand Coulee
Banks Lake
Wilbur
Gold Bar
Stevens Pass (4061ft)
Alpine Lakes Wilderness Area
Cascade Range
Entiat
Orondo
Leavenworth
Cashmere
Coulee City
Washington
Mt Stuart (9415ft)
Snoqualmie Pass (3022ft)
Wenatchee
Soap Lake
Ephrata
Quincy
Mt Baker-Snoqualmie National Forest
Moses Lake
George
Potholes Reservoir
Ellensburg
Vantage
Wanapum Dam
Mt Rainier National Park
Mt Rainier (14,411ft)
Othello
Naches
Yakima Training Center
Priest Rapids Dam
Yakima
Connell
US Dept of Energy Hanford Nuclear Reservation
Gifford Pinchot National Forest
Donald
Zillah
Toppenish
Granger
Sunnyside
Fort Simcoe State Park
Mt Adams Wilderness
Mt Adams (12,276ft)
Yakama Indian Reservation
Richland
Pasco
Prosser
Benton City
Kennewick
Ice Harbour Dam
Snake
Yakima River
Wallula
Lowden
Pacific Crest Trail
Umatilla
Irrigon
Hermiston
Columbia River
Biggs
Um
1
20
97
153
17
155
2
21
28
90
410
26
395
82
12
730
84
30

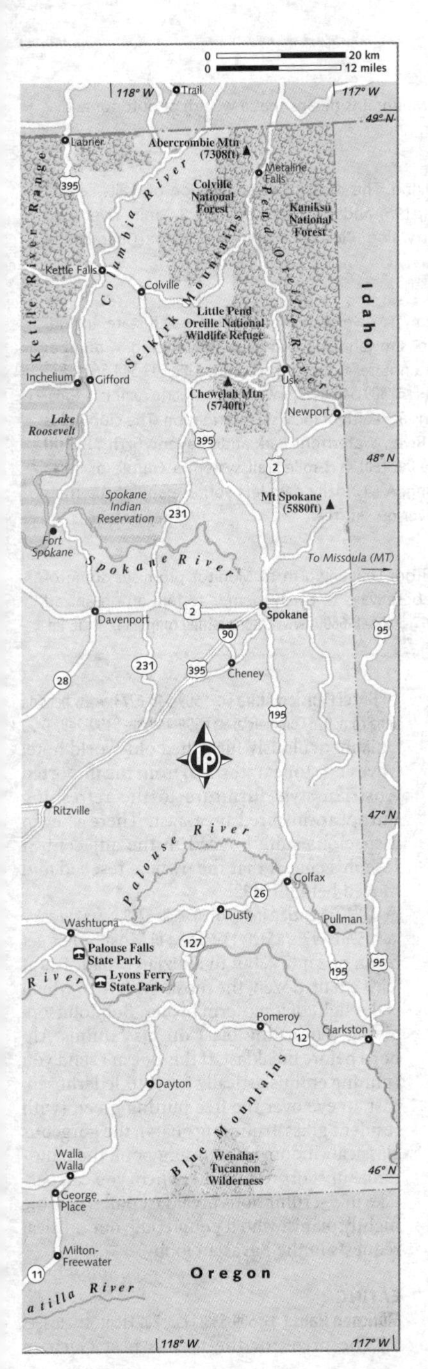

distinctly surreal, alpine community with its European cheese mongers, dirndl-wearing waitresses, wandering accordionists and neatly stacked log piles, is one of Washington state's oddest, but at the same time, most endearing experiences.

If you have a penchant for obscure, highly specialized museums, stop by the **Nutcracker Museum** (☎ 509-548-4573; 735 Front St; admission $2.50; 2-5pm) in Leavenworth's main drag which specializes in nutcracker dolls. Ebony, metal, boxwood, ivory and porcelain, there are numerous varieties here; 5000 of them in fact, along with a shop downstairs where you buy your very own nut-cracking souvenirs.

Tucked out of view but surprisingly close is **Waterfront Park**, which provides Leavenworth with access to the Wenatchee River. Wander down 9th St and follow the leafy domain over a footbridge and onto Blackbird Island where you can catch a glimpse of Sleeping Lady Mountain ringed by a border of green foliage. Interpretive signs furnish the route and help explain the local plant and animal life.

Of three thriving fish hatcheries on the Columbia River, the **Leavenworth National Fish Hatchery** (☎ 509-548-7641; 12790 Fish Hatchery Rd; admission by donation; self-guided tours 8am-4pm) is the largest and, quite possibly, the most interesting. Created to provide a spawning ground for salmon that had been blocked from migrating upriver by the construction of the Grand Coulee Dam in the 1930s, this on-going fish-rearing project produces some 1.6 million Chinook salmon a year. The young smolt are released into Icicle Creek each spring from where they migrate to the Pacific.

From the hatchery, you can hike the mile-long **Icicle Creek Interpretive Trail** and learn about the local ecology and history.

SLEEPING

Eightmile Campground (☎ 800-274-6104; 4905 Icicle Rd; $8-10) Of the half-dozen or more campgrounds situated along Icicle Rd on the way to the Alpine Lakes Wilderness this is the closest to Leavenworth with 45 campsites and access to the Enchantment Lakes area. Should it be full, keep driving and you should get lucky further on.

Mrs Anderson's Lodging House (☎ 509-548-6173; www.quiltersheaven.com; 917 Commercial St; r with shared bath $58-82, r with private bath 58-146; ☒) A block from the main action, Mrs. Anderson's B&B has 10 functional but reasonably priced

LEAVENWORTH OUTDOOR ADVENTURES

Leavenworth's proximity to the North Cascade Mountains means that a wealth of outdoor activities lie less than an hour from the town center.

Hiking

Leavenworth offers ample opportunities for hiking. The most diverse selection of trails can be found in the nearby Alpine Lakes Wilderness (p196) and vary from an easy 3.5-mile river loop to a challenging two- to three-day backcountry slog. Pick up a trail map at the Chamber of Commerce (p191).

Skiing

The area around Leavenworth has some of the most diverse skiing facilities in the state, including downhill skiing, cross-country skiing, tubing, snowshoeing and even ski jumping. A number of hotels rent skis and equipment, or you can enquire at **Der Sportsman** (☎ 509-548-5623; 837 Front St). The **Leavenworth Winter Sports Club** (☎ 509-548-5477; www.skileavenworth.com) is a local umbrella organization, and their website contains a wealth of local ski information. The club helps maintain 5 miles of mostly level trails at Icicle River, Waterfront Park and **Leavenworth Ski Hill** (☎ 509-548-6975; lift tickets $9; Wed, Fri-Sun late Dec-Feb), a 3-mile trail system a couple of miles to the north of town that is good for night skiing. A $12 daily pass lets you use any of the trails in the system; children under 13 and seniors over 69 ski free.

Rafting

The 18.5-mile stretch of the Wenatchee River from Leavenworth to Monitor promises some of the biggest rapids in the state and one of the best ways to catch them is to join an organized rafting trip. Locally run **Osprey Rafting Co** (☎ 509-548-6800; www.ospreyrafting.com; 4342 Icicle Rd,

rooms, two of which have shared baths. Options range from the one-bed Flying Geese room to the five-bed Trees in the Park room. This place is above a quilt shop and offers a simple buffet breakfast of fruit, oatmeal, bread and coffee.

Bavarian Ritz (☎ 509-548-5455; 633 Front St; d $89-139, ste $249-269; wi-fi) Wedged into Bavarian-style Front St, the Ritz is a vintage 1903 inn that was reincarnated in Leavenworth's 1960s German makeover. Promoting a wide selection of room types and a couple of decent downstairs restaurants, the facilities fall short of full-blown luxury status, though the vista-studded sundeck and the extravagant four-poster beds in the Royal King suites should keep visiting Europhiles happy.

Bavarian Lodge (☎ 509-548-7878; 810 Hwy 2; r $99-119, ste $145-189; wi-fi) Leavenworth's newest hotel addition takes the Bavarian theme to luxury levels in this plush, clutter-free establishment with modern – but definably German – rooms complete with gas fires, king beds, funky furnishings and a serve-yourself buffet breakfast. Outside there's a heated pool and hot tub, while the suite rooms upstairs have huge Jacuzzi baths wedged into a cozy Bavarian turret.

Hotel Pension Anna (☎ 509-548-6273; www.pensionanna.com; 926 Commercial St; r $99-149, ste $199-249;) This meticulously furnished old-world hotel leaves no stone unturned, from the imported Austrian-style furniture to the refreshing European-inspired breakfast. There is even a spacious suite housed in the adjacent St Joseph's chapel that the owners rescued and moved here in 1992.

our pick **Enzian Inn** (☎ 509-548-5269; www.enzianinn.com; 590 Hwy 2; s/d $120/135; wi-fi) Most hotels get by on one quirk, but the Enzian broadcasts at least a half-dozen, the most obscure of which is the sight of long-term owner, Bob Johnson, giving a morning blast on his famous Alp horn before breakfast. If this doesn't send you running enthusiastically for your lederhosen, cast an eye over the free putting green (with resident grass-trimming goats), the gorgeous classical (indoor) swimming pool, the panoramic upstairs restaurant (where you can partake in a scrumptious breakfast buffet), or the nightly pianist who'll pound out your musical requests in the Bavarian lobby.

EATING

München Haus (☎ 509-548-1158; 709 Front St; sausages $5) The prize for the town's best German

Leavenworth) offer everything from high-adventure white-knuckle rides on class-III and -IV rapids ($90, 4.5 hours) to contemplative downstream floats on rented inner tubes ($15, all day). The May and June snowmelt season sees the river at its wildest.

Climbing

A well-known nexus point for Washington's ever-evolving climbing community, Leavenworth's classic climb is situated at **Castle Rock** in Tumwater Canyon about 3 miles northwest of town off US 2. A newer focal point for climbers is the Icicle Creek Canyon in the Alpine Lakes Wilderness, where challenging rock climbing requires a USFS permit (for details, see the Alpine Lakes Wilderness section, p196). **Snow Creek Wall** is an old stalwart in this area, but there are several hundred other climbs here, most of which have been developed in the last 15 years. **Leavenworth Mountain Sports** (☎ 509-548-7864; 220 US 2; 🕑 10am-6pm Mon-Fri, 9am-6pm Sat & Sun) rents rock shoes, harnesses and other climbing gear.

Cycling

The Devil's Gulch (25 miles, four to six hours) and Mission Ridge (26 miles, four to seven hours) trails are two of the most popular off-road bike trails in the state. Freund Canyon is an intermediate 8.3-mile loop and is classed as the best single-track bike trail in the Leavenworth area. It is also home of the annual Bavarian Bike and Brews Race. Der Sportsman (see opposite) rents bikes from $25 a day.

Horseback & Sleigh Riding

For the archetypal Leavenworth wintertime experience, contact the **Eagle Creek Ranch** (☎ 509-548-7798; www.eaglecreek.ws; 7951 Eagle Creek Rd) which offers *Jingle Bells*-evoking sleigh rides from $15 per person. When the snow clears you can try your hand at **horseback riding** on four- to six-hour trail rides ($28 to $40).

sausage has to go to München Haus in lively Front St, which backs up its formidable bratwurst with fresh-from-the-oven pretzels, ice-cold German beer and lashings of ciderkraut relish.

Gingerbread Factory (☎ 509-548-6592; 828 Commercial St; 🕑 8am-5pm, closed Wed) No Bavarian village is complete without its apple strudel and you'll find plenty of it here, along with gingerbread biscuits, gingerbread houses and a decent cup of coffee. The 'factory' actually ships its gingerbread products all over the country and there's a gift shop inside full of enticing gingerbread memorabilia.

Gustav's Onion Dome (☎ 509-548-4509; 617 US 2; sausages & sandwiches $5-6) It's hard to miss this church-like building on Hwy 2, but, out of keeping with its ecclesiastical appearance, Gustav's boasts a rooftop beer garden and lots of Northwest brews on tap (including their own Icicle Ale) to complement the sausages and deli sandwiches.

Renaissance Café (☎ 509-548-6725; 217 8th St; breakfast/lunch $5-7, dinner $12-14) You can get all kinds of food specialties at this fine restaurant, including the ubiquitous German sausage platter. Hearty breakfasts include a design-it-yourself omelette with a choice of 21 ingredients intended to satisfy hungry hikers; or you can carbo-load on granola, pancakes, oatmeal or – if you're in need of a really quick sugar rush – pastries. The Renaissance also packages 'lunch to go' for hikers, kayakers, skiers or horseback riders.

our pick **Café Christa** (☎ 509-548-5074; upstairs 801 Front St; lunch $7-9, dinner $14-18) If you came to Leavenworth to sample authentic German cooking, you won't be disappointed by what's on offer here. Christa's features quaint European decor, discreet yet polite service and a menu that rustles up a plethora of old-world classics such as Bratwurst, Wiener schnitzel and Jäger schnitzel served with sauce, red cabbage and spätzle. Even better, you can wash it all down with an accompanying stein of Hofbräuhaus Munich lager.

Andreas Keller (☎ 509-548-6000; 829 Front St; sausages $10, mains $15) The definitive Leavenworth experience can be found in this cavernous basement or *rathskeller*. It conjures up a genuine Oktoberfest atmosphere, with lederhosen-clad accordionists and rousing medlies of drinking songs. To add to the authenticity, the head chef is German and prepares wonderful Wiener schnitzels, potato salad, sauerkraut, red cabbage and rye bread.

ENTERTAINMENT

Leavenworth Summer Theater (☎ box office 509-548-2000; Hwy 2 & Icicle Rd; tickets $12-20; ⌚ shows Jul-Aug) Leavenworth's flirtation with kitsch doesn't just end in the Bavarian village. If the thought of a Julie Andrews sound-alike singing *Do-Re-Mi* doesn't send you rushing back to Seattle for a distorted grunge fix, proceed to the Ski Hill Amphitheater during the summer months for a full-length production of Roger's and Hammerstein's *The Sound of Music*, performed against an authentic alpine backdrop.

GETTING THERE & AROUND

Northwestern Trailways (☎ 509-662-2183) buses stop in Leavenworth twice daily on their way between Seattle ($28, three hours) and Wenatchee ($8, 40 minutes). The bus stop is on Hwy 2 by the post office. Call ☎ 800-366-3830 (in Washington) for schedules.

Link Transit (☎ 509-662-1155; www.linktransit.com) bus 22 passes up US 2 between Leavenworth and Wenatchee ($1, 50 minutes), via Peshastin and Cashmere, 20 times daily Monday to Friday (no weekend service).

Around Leavenworth

ALPINE LAKES WILDERNESS

The Alpine Lakes Wilderness is a 614-sq-mile protected area of rough crenellated mountains, glacier-gouged valleys, and – as the name implies – gorgeous sapphire lakes (over 700 of them, in fact). Crisscrossed by trails and popularly accessed from the Icicle Canyon Rd west of Leavenworth, the wilderness offers a handful of easy day hikes along with plenty more substantial backcountry jaunts that require good fitness, shrewd forward planning and a decent pair of walking boots.

The area's close proximity to Seattle make this former logging-and-mining region popular with hikers, and the Enchantment Lakes area requires a $3 permit in the summer (enquire at Leavenworth Ranger Station, p191). Good entry points are from the Icicle Rd (USFS Rd 7600) off Hwy 2 and on a dirt road just north of Tumwater campground on US 2.

The **Icicle Gorge Trail** is the most accessible hike here, an easy 3.6-mile river loop that gives you an enticing taste of what this pristine wilderness is all about. Other trailheads dot the Icicle Rd and lead off into a patchwork of popular trails. Pick up a leaflet at the Chamber of Commerce (p191).

LAKE WENATCHEE

Swimming, boating and fishing entertain summertime visitors to Lake Wenatchee, 23 miles north of the city of Wenatchee (and actually much closer to Leavenworth). You can hike the 4.5-mile trail up Dirtyface Peak, cycle around the lake, or sign on with one of the rafting companies on Hwy 207 for a float trip.

Once there's snow on the ground, Lake Wenatchee becomes a great cross-country ski area, with 20 miles of marked and groomed trails, though skiers may have to dodge weekend snowmobilers. More trails crisscross the Lower Chiwawa River area off the Chumstick Hwy, including a five-mile scenic loop trail (closed to snowmobiles) that follows the Wenatchee River. Alternatively you can head further west into the Henry M Jackson Wilderness on USFS Rd 6500 (off Hwy 207) at Little Wenatchee Ford campground where a number of trails hook up with the Pacific Crest Trail.

To reach the lake, head north on Chumstick Hwy, or take US 2 west of town, then turn north onto Hwy 207. Link Transit (left) runs a bus up here six times daily (35 minutes). For further area details contact the **Lake Wenatchee Ranger Station** (☎ 509-763-3103; 22976 Hwy 207; ⌚ 8am-4:30pm Mon-Fri, also Sat Mar-Sep).

Wenatchee

pop 27,856

Apples are to Wenatchee what dates are to Morocco or olives are to southern Spain. The scenic run into town along the placid Columbia River will quickly drive the point home. Orchards are everywhere in this dry, yet perfectly irrigated rural oasis, their carefully tended branches and symmetrically planted trunks providing a perfect contrast to the lifeless desert that encroaches elsewhere. After such an idyllic introduction to this rural central Washington region, Wenatchee itself is a bit of an anticlimax. Infested with boring strip malls and robbed of any real urban character by the ugly tentacles of modern development there's not much to do here apart from loll lazily on the banks of the Columbia River and chomp on some of the crispest and juiciest Golden Delicious apples you're ever likely to taste.

ORIENTATION & INFORMATION

Wenatchee is situated at the confluence of the Columbia and Wenatchee Rivers. Hwy 97 and US 2 follow the Wenatchee River from Leavenworth, 22 miles to the west, bypassing the city to the north and continuing up the east side of the Columbia to Chelan, 38 miles north.

Stop by the **Wenatchee Valley Convention & Visitors Bureau** (☎ 800-572-7753; www.wenatcheevalley.org; Ste C111, 25 N Wenatchee Ave) for information and walking tour maps. **Wenatchee National Forest Headquarters** (☎ 509-664-9200; 215 Melody Lane) is north of town at the junction of Hwy 285 and US 2.

SIGHTS & ACTIVITIES

The **Wenatchee Valley Museum & Cultural Center** (☎ 509-664-3340; 127 S Mission St; adult/child $3/1; 10am-4pm Tue-Sat, closed major holidays) places its main focus on – surprise, surprise – apples. Exhibits include a re-creation of a 1920s apple packing shed and a farm shop from the 1890s.

Washington's, America's and – quite possibly – the world's self-styled apple capital is also home to the **Washington Apple Commission Visitors Center** (☎ 509-662-3090; 2900 Euclid Ave; admission free; 8am-5pm Mon-Fri, 9am-5pm Sat, 10am-4pm Sun May-Dec), a little-visited yet surprisingly interesting expose on Gala, Fuji, Golden Delicious et al. Find out how apples are grown, harvested, transported and sold in a number of interpretive displays and an enlightening 20-minute video.

To sample some of the crispest and juiciest apples this side of paradise, head for the refrigerated sales room at **Stemilt Retail Store** (☎ 509-888-0823; 524 S Columbia St; 8:30am-5:30pm Mon-Fri, 9am-4:30pm Sat).

Three miles north of town on Alt US 97, **Ohme Gardens** (☎ 509-662-5785; www.ohmegardens.com; 3327 Ohme Rd; adult/child $7/3.50; 9am-6pm mid-Apr–mid-Oct, 9am-7pm late May-early Sep) showcase the mighty Columbia River at its best with 9 acres of terraced alpine gardens emerging like an oasis from the barren rock.

Wenatchee's inter-urban trail can be found in Riverfront Park, a 10-mile walk- and cycleway that stretches along both sides of the Columbia River adjacent to downtown. Locals and visitors alike come here to stroll, cycle or rollerblade along this rather industrial stretch of the river. Access to the park can be gained at the end of 5th St or by crossing a railway footbridge at the end of 1st St. Once on the trail, head north to Wenatchee Confluence State Park, or south to reach a footbridge across to East Wenatchee, where the trail continues along the Columbia's somewhat more pastoral east bank. You can rent bikes or in-line skates at **Arlberg Sports** (☎ 509-663-7401; 25 N Wenatchee Ave), next to the Convention Center.

If you feel like **ice skating**, go to the **Riverfront Park Ice Arena** (☎ 509-664-3396; 2 5th St; $4; daily Oct-Mar).

Downhill skiers covet the dry powder covering the slopes of **Mission Ridge** (☎ 509-663-6543; www.missionridge.com; full-day lift tickets adult/student & senior $46/28; 9am-4pm Wed-Sun Dec-early Apr) located 12 miles southwest of Wenatchee. The resort features a vertical drop of 2200ft and 35 runs with four lifts and two rope-tows.

SLEEPING

Wenatchee Confluence State Park (☎ 509-664-6373; 333 Olds Station Rd; tent/RV sites $17/24) The park is divided in two by the Wenatchee River where it flows into the Columbia. The campground, with 51 hookups and eight tent spaces, is on the north bank. It's an ideal spot for active travelers: besides the swimming beach, there are athletic fields, tennis and basketball courts and 4.5 miles of trails.

WestCoast Wenatchee Center Hotel (☎ 509-662-1234; 201 N Wenatchee Ave; r $79-114; wi-fi) If you don't go in for chain hotels, it will be a struggle to find an independent lodging in franchise-filled Wenatchee, where the arterial N Wenatchee Ave is studded with all number of Travelodges, Super 8s and Econo Lodges. Best of a boring bunch is this large central franchise that is handily connected to the Convention Center by a sky-bridge and draws a regular business crowd. Rooms are well furnished, if a little characterless, and there's an above-average rooftop restaurant (the Wenatchee Roaster and Ale House) and a fitness center.

Warm Springs Inn (☎ 509-662-8365; 1611 Love Lane; r $95-130; wi-fi) Situated on 10 acres by the Wenatchee River, this 1917 mansion turned B&B has won awards and a glance inside its lovingly furnished interior and you'll soon understand why. As well as six individually crafted rooms, there's a living room with fireplace, a 'Great Room' with gorgeous river views, and a perfectly manicured English garden with a (very) private hot tub hidden away behind the trees.

EATING

Owl Soda Fountain (☎ 509-664-7221; 25 N Wenatchee Ave; ⏲ until 5pm) A classic old-fashioned soda fountain of 1950s vintage, with lurid color schemes, peanut-butter-and-jelly sandwiches, and humongous milkshakes plunked down on the bar in front of you. All that's missing is an Elvis impersonator with stick-on sideburns.

Cuc Tran Café (☎ 509-663-6281; 7 N Wenatchee Ave; mains $5.50-7; ⏲ closed Sun) A quirky, inconspicuous little place tucked away in the bowels of another building, the Cuc Tran offers cheap authentic Vietnamese food in narrow, train seat–sized booths. The rice, noodles and soup make a welcome change from the usual burger and pizza combos.

Inna's (☎ 509-888-4662; 26 N Wenatchee Ave; mains $8-13; ⏲ closed Sun) Central and eastern Washington is not renowned for its ethnic eateries (Leavenworth aside) but if you were craving borscht, piroshki or good old-fashioned Ukrainian dumplings, the search ends here. Run by a Ukrainian couple from Odessa Inna's has added an Eastern European flavor to Wenatchee's clutch of above-average eateries. The menu even dares to venture a few time-zones to the West with a Paris salad, Greek gyros and Italian meatballs.

The Windmill (☎ 509-665-9529; 1501 N Wenatchee Ave; mains $23; ⏲ 5-9pm Mon-Sat) Sitting pretty amid North Wenatchee's ugly mall-and-motel strip is this eye-catching Dutch-style windmill, in business since 1931 and still knocking out a fine selection of steaks, scintillating seafood and homemade desserts. If in doubt, try the New York whiskey pepper steak with a baked potato. Not surprisingly, the Windmill's reputation precedes it and you may have to arrive early in order to reserve some elbow room ahead of the adoring locals.

GETTING THERE & AROUND

Horizon Air services the **Pangborn Memorial Airport** (☎ 509-884-2494; www.pangbornairport.com) in East Wenatchee, with four or five flights daily to/from Seattle (from $125 one way).

All bus and rail transit services are centralized at **Columbia Station** (300 S Columbia Ave), at the foot of Kittitas St. **Northwestern Trailways** (☎ 509-662-2183) runs daily buses to Seattle direct, Spokane via Moses Lake, and Pasco via Yakima.

You can get to the nearby towns of Leavenworth via Cashmere (bus 22, $1, 50 minutes) and Chelan via Entiat (bus 21, $1, one hour) on frequent **Link Transit buses** (☎ 509-662-1155; www.linktransit.com). Buses run until 5pm or 6pm Monday to Friday and are equipped with bike racks.

Amtrak's *Empire Builder* train stops daily in Wenatchee on its way between Seattle and Chicago, westbound at 5:38am, and eastbound at 8:42pm.

YAKIMA VALLEY

With its scorched hills interspersed with geometrically laid-out vine plantations and apple orchards, the Yakima River Valley glimmers like a verdant oasis in an otherwise dry and barren desert. Arising from the snowy slopes of Snoqualmie Pass and flowing deceptively southeast (and away from the Pacific) until it joins courses with the mighty Columbia, the fast-flowing Yakima River supports a lucrative agricultural industry that churns out copious amounts of cherries, hops, vegetables

BUYING LOCAL PRODUCE

Forget imported apples or grapes flown in from Chile. When it comes to growing fruit and vegetables, Washington state is a veritable Garden of Eden and you can buy almost all the produce you need from local sources. Wenatchee is nationally famous for its apples, Walla Walla nurtures excellent asparagus, while in the verdant Skagit River Valley they sow everything from pumpkins to potatoes.

One of the surest ways to load up on the freshest local ingredients is to visit one of the colorful farmers markets that lie scattered throughout the state. Outside of Seattle, the largest of these markets is in Olympia, an all-weather indoor affair that runs from April to December and specializes in fresh Olympia oysters. Other significant markets can be found in Ellensburg, Bellingham, Vancouver and Wenatchee, while some of the smallest but quirkiest options kick off during the summer months on the San Juan Islands. Aside from fruit and vegetables, farmers markets also sell such varied items as fresh bread, homemade cakes, fair trade coffee, local crafts and often host live music.

and peaches, along with the world's largest yield of apples.

Markedly drier and hotter than Washington's wet west coast, much of the valley survives on as little as 8in of rain a year (Seattle gets 37in) and temperatures can rise to over 100°F in the summer.

A huge demand for agricultural labor to work in the fields and orchards during the fruit-picking season has brought a large Mexican population to the valley and, with 40% of Yakima county's population now registered as Hispanic, you'll hear as much 'buenos dias' as 'good morning.' The vast Yakama Native American Reservation to the southwest adds a strong Native American element to the population mix.

Ellensburg

pop 15,414

Juxtaposing the state's largest rodeo with the laidback coffee-bar sophistication of a thriving university town, Ellensburg presents one of central Washington's most interesting dichotomies. While the rowdy cow-pokers may rule the roost for a few days every September, during the rest of the year this proud, yet unpretentious, agricultural settlement, is given over to artists, wine aficionados, antique sellers and the cerebral students of central Washington University, one of the state's most prestigious academic institutions.

Once touted as the 'Pittsburg of the West' for its plentiful coal and iron-ore deposits, Ellensburg suffered the fate of many western towns in 1889 when a fire tore the heart out of nine blocks of its central business district. The present-day historical core, though small in size, is the result of an industrious post-fire rebuilding process. Thanks to meticulous restoration efforts, Ellensburg – along with New Orleans and West Hollywood – recently made the top 12 in a nationwide poll of 'distinctive US destinations.' Organizers hailed the town as representing a 'microcosm of the frontier experience in Washington.'

Nestled in the fertile Yakima River Valley and within binocular-viewing distance of the snowcapped Cascade Mountains, Ellensburg is a good base for wine-touring excursions or activity-based sorties into the surrounding countryside. With a vibrant student population, a couple of classy restaurants and – allegedly – more coffee bars per head than anywhere else in the world, the town remains an ideal escape for rain-embattled Seattleites, outdoor-adventure enthusiasts and anyone who harbors a serious addiction to caffeine.

ORIENTATION & INFORMATION

Bypassed by both the Seattle–Spokane I-90 and the Ellensburg–Yakima I-82, Ellensburg lies a couple of miles east of exit 106 and a mile or so north of exit 109. The Yakima River also misses the diminutive downtown grid which is centered on Main St and bisected by numbered avenues running west to east. Take 8th Ave east off Main to reach the university.

For maps and information, drop by the helpful **Ellensburg Chamber of Commerce** (☎ 509-925-2002; www.ellensburg-chamber.com; 609 N Main St; 🕓 8am-5pm Mon-Fri, 10am-2pm Sat). The building is shared by the US Forest Service and Ellensburg Rodeo offices.

SIGHTS & ACTIVITIES

Beautified by a compact yet charismatic grid of Victorian buildings, central Ellensburg deserves an unhurried morning or afternoon's exploration. Kick off at the friendly chamber of commerce where you can procure clear, informative maps of the downtown **historic district**, roughly contained between Main St, 6th and 3rd Avs. Sprinkled with engaging antique shops, galleries and cafés, the quarter is dominated by the **Davidson Building**, Ellensburg's signature postcard sight built in 1889 by local attorney, John B Davidson. Also worth checking out is the **Kittitas County Museum** (☎ 509-925-3778; 114 E 3rd Ave; donations accepted; 🕓 10am-4pm Mon-Sat Jun-Sep, noon-4pm Tue-Sat Oct-May), housed in the 1889 Cadwell Building, known mostly for its petrified-wood and gemstone collections, but also boasting a cleverly laid out history section documenting the backgrounds of Croatian, Arabic and Welsh immigrants. Equally intriguing are the paintings of native son John Clymer at the **Clymer Museum** (☎ 509-962-6416; 416 N Pearl St; admission free; 🕓 10am-5pm Mon-Thu & Sat, 10am-8pm Fri, noon-5pm Sun), whose all-American subjects graced *Saturday Evening Post* covers during the 1950s and '60s.

For kids try the **Children's Activity Museum** (☎ 509-925-6789; 400 N Main St; admission $3.50; 🕓 10am-3pm Wed-Fri, 6:30-8:30pm Fri, 1-4pm Sun, 10am-4pm Sat) which has a miniature cowboy ranch, science lab and other engaging hands-on exhibits.

Outside of town the historical theme continues at the **Olmstead Place State Park Heritage**

Area (☎ 509-925-1943; 921 N Ferguson Rd; admission free; 8am-5pm), 4.5 miles southeast of Ellensburg off the I-90 where log cabins, pioneer barns and other farm buildings dating from 1875 to 1890 depict early homestead life in the Kittitas Valley. Another view of frontier agriculture is on display at the **Thorp Grist Mill** (☎ 509-964-9640; admission free; 1-4pm Wed-Sun Jun-Sep), once a de facto meeting place for local farmers and now a rural museum.

As well as boasting a rather picturesque campus, Central Washington University has gained some renown for its studies of communication between humans and chumpanzees. Four of its chimps – Washoe, Loulis, Dar and Tatu – have learned to communicate using American Sign Language. On weekends the **Chimpanzee & Human Communication Institute** (☎ 509-963-2244; www.cwu.edu/~cwuchci; cnr Nicholson Blvd & D St; adult/student $10/7.50; 9:15am & 10.45am Sat, 12:30pm & 2pm Sun) presents an informative, hour-long 'Chimposium' workshop that includes an audience with the chimps. The discussions on linguistics and primate behavior are interesting, and reservations are recommended.

South of Ellensburg, Hwy 821 through the Yakima Canyon offers a scenic alternative to the busy I-82. Rafting on the Yakima River is a popular activity here with **Rill Adventures** (☎ 509-964-2520; www.rillsonline.com) offering raft and kayak hire. Catch-and-release fishing is another draw card. In Ellensburg, **Coopers Fly Shop** (☎ 509-962-5259; 413 N Main St) has tackle and gear, and can arrange guide services.

FESTIVALS & EVENTS

Ellensburg's ultimate festival, the **Ellensburg Rodeo** (☎ 509-962-7831, 800-637-2444; www.ellensburgrodeo.com) takes place on Labor Day weekend in tandem with the Kittitas County Fair. It's ranked among the top 10 rodeos in the nation and is one of central Washington's biggest events. Come prepared to see some hard riding and roping – participants take this rodeo very seriously, as there is big money at stake.

SLEEPING

Nites Inn (☎ 509-962-9600; 1200 S Ruby St; s & d $57;) This is one of a plethora of motels at the southern freeway exit (109), but a park out the back and super friendly staff put it a cut above the usual motel monotony. Standard-issue rooms come with fridge and microwave, and there are BBQ grills and picnic tables to enjoy on the landscaped grounds.

Inn at Goose Creek (☎ 509-962-8030; 1720 Canyon Rd; r from $99; wi-fi) Surely one of the most imaginative B&Bs around, this establishment off the I-90 is not your standard fancily restored period piece – at least, not from the outside. Inside is a different story, however, and the Victorian Honeymoon Suite is just one of 10 eclectic room choices, a list that also includes the Ellensburg Rodeo Room (complete with cowboy memorabilia) and the I Love Christmas Room (with its red-and-green Santa carpet).

Guesthouse Ellensburg (☎ 509-962-3706; 606 Main St; r $135) This unique guesthouse, handily located opposite the chamber of commerce on Main St, doubles as a wine shop and tasting room and the proprietors certainly know their enology. Two restored Victorian rooms are furnished with English antiques, four-poster beds and flat-screen TVs, while downstairs in the tasting room you can discuss viticulture until the grapes ripen with free tasting sessions and generous discounts for guests.

EATING

D&M Coffee (☎ 509-925-5313; 301 N Pine St; coffee $2-3) With allegedly more coffee bars per head than anywhere else in the world, you're certainly spoiled for choice when it comes to satisfying your morning caffeine habit in Ellensburg. D&M is the local roasting company and the best of its quintet of local outlets is situated opposite the Kittitas County Museum. Funky stools and an academic atmosphere make it an ideal place to linger.

Dakota Café (☎ 509-925-4783; 417 N Pearl St; 7am-9pm) The Dakota is a hybrid café and restaurant that offers casual lunch options along with more formal evening fare. Formidable sandwiches on focaccia bread will satisfy the most insatiable of rodeo appetites, while the quiches and soups offer lighter choices.

Valley Café (☎ 509-925-3050; 105 W 3rd Ave; lunch $7.50, dinner mains $8.50-25) This diminutive art-deco construction boasts a restaurant and café, along with an excellent selection of Washington wines, nicely paired with the accompanying food. Check out the cioppino for $10, the rack of lamb or the ahi tuna. The interior is furnished with unpretentious booths.

our pick **Yellow Church Café** (☎ 509-933-2233; 111 S Pearl St; breakfast $8-10, dinner $13-22) Top in the Ellensburg 'quirky' stakes is this former church built by the German Lutherans in 1923 and now converted into a homey restaurant that serves spiritually enlightening food. The breakfast – including the aptly named St Benedict's eggs – has won widespread recommendations, while the elegant dinner options have been well matched with local wines from the expert owners who also run the nearby Wineworks store.

GETTING THERE & AROUND

Although Ellensburg is a busy crossroads for regional buses, there's no real bus station. Greyhound buses stop at the Pilot gas station at I-90 exit 106, 2 two miles from the town center. The **ticket window** (☎ 509-925-1177) is in the Subway sandwich shop. Buses here leave for Seattle ($22.50, two hours, five daily), Spokane via Moses Lake ($32, four hours, three daily) and Yakima ($11, 45 minutes, three daily). Some Yakima buses continue on to the Tri-Cities and beyond.

From the bus station, **Rodeo Town Taxi** (☎ 509-929-4222) can get you downtown for $5.

Yakima

pop 71,845

Central Washington's largest city is also the center of one of its most productive wine-growing regions. But unlike Walla Walla – which is currently reaping the rewards of the burgeoning wine-tourist industry – Yakima's rather lackluster city center coupled with its dearth of any notable hotels and restaurants leaves it trailing well behind other more attractive stopovers. As if to prove the point, years three downtown department stores, an entire shopping mall and the Northwest's oldest microbrewery have folded over the last five, leaving the city that once dubbed itself the 'Palm Springs of Washington' facing increasing problems with unemployment and recession.

Nestled among the dry foothills of the Eastern Cascades and characterized by a vibrant Hispanic population, Yakima's sprawling and rather modern downtown is punctuated by a handful of interesting structures. Art-deco aficionados will appreciate the craning Larson building on East Yakima Ave with its ornate – some would say, ostentatious – lobby, while culture vultures will find solace in the grand Italianate Capitol Theater that hosts everything from live music concerts to public speaking events. The city's rather compact 'historic' district consists of one square block downtown – half of which is given over to a parking lot – and is noteworthy for its old station depot and the bizarre Track 29, a collection of antique railcars now converted into a row of eye-catching knick-knack shops.

Founded on its present site in 1884, Yakima takes its name from the Yakama Native American people who inhabited this valley for centuries before an 1855 treaty created the Yakama Native American Reservation.

ORIENTATION & INFORMATION

Yakima lies 145 miles east of Seattle, and 76 miles west of Richland. I-82 runs along the Yakima River, east of Yakima's main downtown area; exit 33 leads to East Yakima Ave, the quickest route to downtown. The main north–south strip running through town is 1st St, which can be accessed from exit 31. Yakima Ave and Front St (essentially the train tracks) divide the city into directional quadrants.

The best source of local information is the **Yakima Valley Visitors & Convention Bureau** (☎ 509-575-3010; www.visityakima.com; 10 N 8th St).

SIGHTS

The **Yakima Greenway** is a pleasant oasis in an otherwise unremarkable city. Best accessed via Sarg Hubbard Park at I-82 exit 33, it's a 10-mile path for walkers and cyclists that tracks the fast-flowing Yakima River through a string of parks and recreation areas. One potential stopping-off point is the **Yakima Area Arboretum** just east of exit 34, where a collection of over 2000 species of trees and shrubs spreads out over 46 acres of landscaped gardens. Stop at the **Jewett Interpretive Center** (☎ 509-248-7337; 1401 Arboretum Dr; admission free; 🕑 9am-4pm Tue-Sat) for a walking-tour brochure.

One of the city's proverbial highlights is the educational **Yakima Valley Museum** (☎ 509-248-0747; 2105 Tieton Dr; adult/senior $5/3; 🕑 10am-5pm Mon-Fri, noon-5pm Sat & Sun) which tells the story of the region from a geographic and historical viewpoint with a strong emphasis on agriculture and the Yakama Native American heritage. Prize exhibits include a number of horse-drawn conveyances and some early motor vehicles, plus a full working mockup of a 1930s Depression-era Soda Fountain. In yet another section, the **Children's Underground** (🕑 1-5pm Wed-Sun) does a good job of incorporating Yakima's human and natural history into a number of hands-on exhibits for kids.

Adjacent to the museum is **Franklin Park**, a broad lawn planted with evergreens that features a playground, picnic tables, and – an important feature in sunbaked Yakima – a swimming pool.

SLEEPING

Cedars Inn & Suites (☎ 509-452-8101; 1010 East A St; s/d $56/66;) A motel with a few extra trimmings justify the 'suites' title at this affordable place on the busy accommodations strip on the town's eastern edge. Aside from the usual fridge-microwave provision they lay out milk and cookies in the evening, and can rustle up quite a tasty breakfast.

Hilton Garden Inn (☎ 509-454-1111; 607 E Yakima Ave; r $109-159; wi-fi) This brand new city-center facility still looks (and smells) unused and adds a touch of elegance to the usual downtown business-style stopover. Aside from spotlessly presented rooms, the hotel offers a decent-sized gym, an indoor pool, a lounge and an American grill, along with highly professional service.

Birchfield Manor (☎ 509-452-1960; www.birchfieldmanor.com; 2018 Birchfield Rd; manor r $119-159, cottage r $139-219; wi-fi) Renowned for its flavorful food and well-stocked Washington wine cellar, the Birchfield offers unusual antique-filled rooms in a pleasant park-like setting 2 miles east of Yakima off Hwy 24. Five manor rooms are complemented by six guest cottages, some with double Jacuzzi. The manor, which makes a great alternative to the standard Yakima hotel chains, also serves as a first-class restaurant that is revered by locals.

EATING

Tequila's Family Mexican Restaurant (☎ 509-457-3296; 1 W Yakima Ave; lunch $6, dinner $9) With a vibrant Hispanic population, Yakima is the crucible of Washington-Mexican food, and a good place to sample the stuff is at this off-beat place that occupies three vintage railcars at the rear end of the Track 29 shopping mall. Emphasizing seafood, the atmosphere attempts to replicate the Jalisco coast with Corona umbrellas shading the boardwalk deck. A *torta* (overstuffed sandwich with refried bean spread) makes a hearty lunch.

Yakima Sports Center Restaurant (☎ 509-453-4647; 214 E Yakima Ave; mains $10-18) There are no pretensions at this young happening place bang in the city center which presents live bands every Friday and Saturday. Dive into the mix and sample from an extremely varied menu with such luscious treats as fish and chips, gnocchi, and blue cheese crusted tenderloin. The beer menu is equally voluminous.

Santiago's Gourmet Mexican (☎ 509-453-1644; 111 E Yakima Ave; mains $15-17) Discover gourmet Mexican cuisine among Yakima's thriving Latino community at this venerable establishment that arose from the ashes of a previous restaurant burnt down in a 1985 fire. Old favorites such as burritos and tacos are presented with extra attention to detail using real homemade ingredients, and winning numerous awards in the process – most notably for the celebrated *chili con queso*.

The Greystone (☎ 509-248-9801; 5 N Front St; 3-course dinner around $25; from 6pm Mon-Sat) A long-time Yakima staple housed in one of the city's original saloons at the base of the century-old Lund Building, the Greystone is widely considered to be the city's premier venue for fine Northwest cuisine. The excellent rack of lamb goes for $32.

SHOPPING

Known as **Track 29** (1 W Yakima Ave), the old train platform has been given over to a string of false-fronted eateries and quirky boutiques, some housed in old railroad cars, that makes for a pleasant boardwalk stroll. You'll find a smattering of antiques and collectibles, gemstones, essential oils and herbs. In summer, a Saturday market is held on the boardwalk with local produce and crafts vendors.

GETTING THERE & AROUND

The **Greyhound bus station** (☎ 509-457-5131; 602 E Yakima Ave) is located at the corner of 6th St. There are three departures daily to and from Seattle via Ellensburg ($27.50, three hours) and four to Spokane via Ellensburg or Pasco ($32, four hours plus). Other buses continue on to Portland, the Tri-Cities and beyond.

Yakima Transit (☎ 509-575-6175) runs a local service Monday to Saturday, from 6:30am until around 6:30pm. The transit center is on the corner of S 4th St and E Chestnut Ave. Adult fare is $0.50.

Yakima Valley Wine Country

The Yakima Valley is sprinkled with over 50 wineries, most of them small family-run affairs. While it's not quite the Napa Valley in terms of tourist facilities and dining potential, a drive or cycle through these dry yet deceptively fertile fields breezing past vineyards, orchards, hop pastures and roadside vegetable stalls is a great way to get acquainted with the local wine culture.

Decent stopovers between Yakima and the Tri-Cities include the communities of Zillah, Sunnyside and Prosser, while the Yakima Valley Hwy (old US 12), or 'Wine Country Rd,' which parallels the busy I-82, makes for a pleasant pastoral alternative drive.

There are literally dozens of wineries that offer tasting and scenic picnic opportunities in this area. Start your search at **Sagelands Vineyard** (☎ 509-877-2112; 71 Gangl Rd, Wapato; ⏰ tastings 10am-5pm) which has a tasting room that showcases excellent merlots and cabernet sauvignons with stunning views of Mt Adams. **Chinook Wines** (☎ 509-786-2725; Wine Country Rd, Prosser; ⏰ tastings noon-5pm Sat-Sun May-Dec) is another gem known for its classy whites, particularly its chardonnay and sauvignon blanc.

An excellent source of information for the entire valley can be found online at www.yakimavalleywine.com.

TOPPENISH

pop 8946

If you make one stop in the Yakima Valley you would do well to check out off-the-wall Toppenish, a living art festival that has become locally famous for its 60 or more historic **murals** adorning most of the downtown buildings. Chronicling the events from Yakama and Northwest history, the first mural was painted back in 1989. Later additions include an evocative tableau of the valley's more recent Mexican immigrants employed in the agricultural sector.

Further information and mural guides can be procured from the **Toppenish Mural Society** (☎ 509-865-6516; 5A S Toppenish Ave; ⏰ 10am-4pm Mon-Sat).

Another rather unique Toppenish institution is the **American Hop Museum** (☎ 509-865-4677; 22 S B St; admission by donation; ⏰ 11am-4pm May-Sep), a must for all beer-lovers, that chronicles the history of the American hop-growing industry from its humble beginnings in New England in the early 1600s.

The history of the Yakama Native Americans is well documented at the **Yakama Indian Nation Cultural Center** (☎ 509-865-2800; 280 Buster Rd; adult/senior/child $4/2/1; ⏰ 8am-5pm) which exhibits costumes, baskets, beads and audio-visual displays, and includes a gift shop, library, restaurant and heritage theater (with occasional tribal dances).

An interesting historical curiosity is contained in an old fort complex preserved in the 200-acre **Fort Simcoe State Park** (☎ 509-874-2372; 5150 Fort Simcoe Rd; ⏰ interpretive center 9am-4:30pm Wed-Sun Apr-Oct, Sat & Sun Nov-Mar), an oasis of green in the midst of scorched desert hills that was built in 1855, but served as a fort for only three years until the creation of the Yakama Reservation in 1859. Listed on the National Register of Historical Places, the park now acts as an interpretive center with a handful of original buildings still intact.

NORTHEASTERN WASHINGTON

Bordered by Canada to the north and Idaho to the east, northeastern Washington is dominated by the understated yet populous city of Spokane and is internationally famous for producing one of the 20th century's greatest engineering marvels, the gargantuan Grand Coulee Dam. However the region is little visited and only a few small towns scatter the protected hills and boreal pine forests of the Okanogan and Colville National Forests. Climatically, the northeast is a transition zone with a dry belt running immediately east of the Cascade Mountains, while wetter, more humid air seeps into the verdant Kettle River and Selkirk Mountain ranges closer to Idaho. This precipitous region marks Washington's only real incursion into the Rocky Mountains.

SPOKANE

pop 195,629

In the cultural wilderness of central and eastern Washington, Spokane is a hidden gem. Here, on the muddy banks of the Spokane River, with its gushing waterfalls and expansive municipal parks, lies a city of understated elegance. The secret, for in-the-know locals, lies in the details. Nestled among the modern skywalks and kitschy relics of the much lauded 1974 World's Fair you'll find lovingly restored steam mills, classic art-deco skyscrapers and one of Washington's – and America's – most intricately decorated hotels. And that's just for starters. Though it may lack the urban

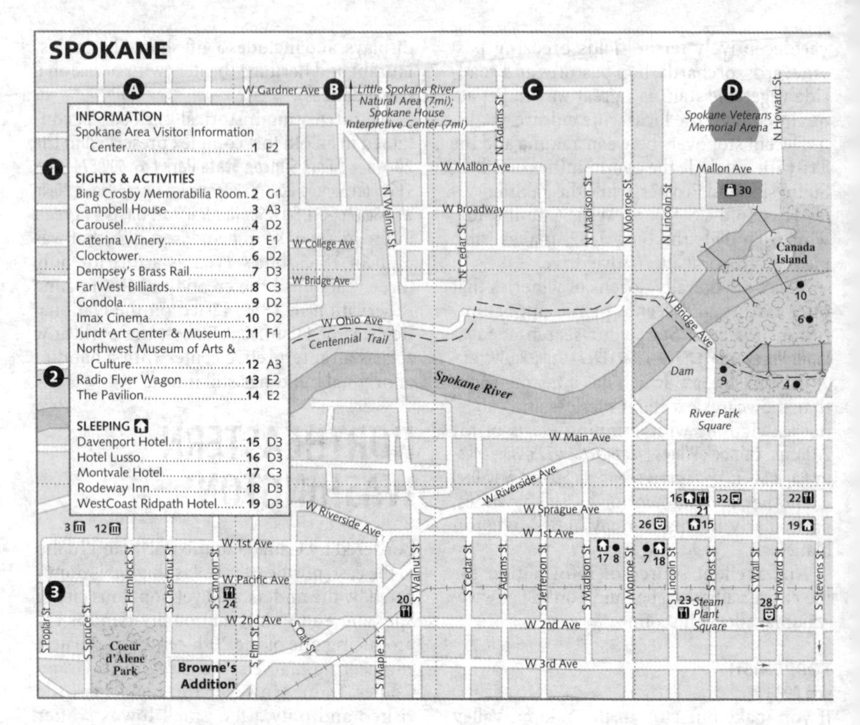

swagger of Seattle or the coffee bar sophistication of Olympia, Spokane does modesty to a tee. This, after all, is the adopted home town of Bing Crosby (the planet's most successful ever recording artist), the crucible of one of the nation's top college basketball teams and the venue for the annual 'Bloomsday,' the world's largest organized running race.

Established as Washington's first trading post in 1810 by the English-Canadian explorer David Thompson, Spokane was promptly superseded in importance by Fort Colville, 70 miles to the north. Reincarnated in the wake of the Idaho gold rush in the 1880s, the city developed as a major terminus for the new transcontinental Great Northern Railway, a move which quickly opened it up to thousands of new immigrants eager for fresh opportunities in trade and manufacturing. After the burgeoning business district was destroyed by a fire in 1889, the downtown area was rebuilt, and the city began to develop into highly distinctive neighborhoods, spearheaded by the prestigious Browne's Addition. Many of the revivalist architectural creations built during this era by local architect Kirtland Cutter still survive, including the magnificent Davenport Hotel (p207), refurbished and reopened in 2002.

Orientation & Information

Spokane is just 18 miles from the Idaho border and is 110 miles south of Canada. The I-90 is the main east–west route through town. The main downtown area, including the skywalk, is between I-90 and Riverfront Park.

Stop by the **Spokane Area Visitor Information Center** (☎ 509-747-3230; www.visitspokane.com; 201 W Main Ave at Browne St) for a raft of information.

Sights

The former site of Spokane's 1974 World's Fair and Exposition, the **Riverfront Park** (☎ 509-456-4386; www.spokaneriverfrontpark.com) provides a welcome slice of urban greenery in the middle of downtown. It has been redeveloped in recent years with a 17 point **sculpture walk**, along with plenty of bridges and trails to satisfy the city's plethora of amateur runners.

The park's centerpiece is **Spokane Falls** a gushing combination of scenic waterfalls and foaming rapids that can get pretty tempestuous

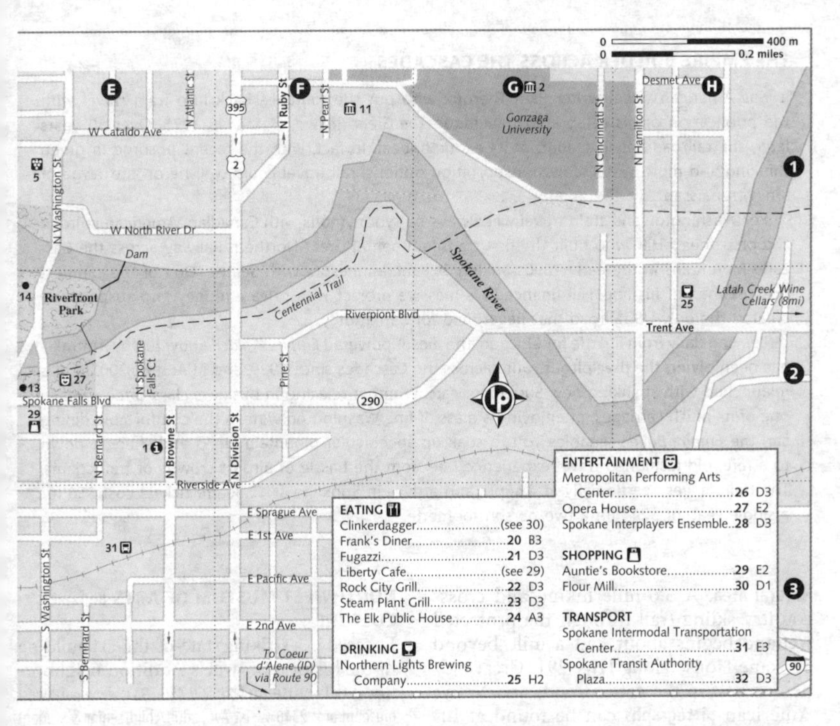

after heavy rain. There are various viewing points over the river, including a short **gondola ride** (admission $7; 11am-6pm Sun-Thu, till 10pm Fri & Sat Apr-Sep) which takes you directly above the falls, or the cheaper and equally spectacular **Monroe St Bridge**, built in 1911 and still the largest concrete arch in the USA.

In the center of the park the 151ft **clocktower** has become the city's signature sight and was originally part of a railway depot built in 1902. The kitschy **Pavilion**, is a small amusement park in the summer and an **ice rink** (noon-8pm Mon-Thu, noon-5pm & 7-10pm Fri & Sat, noon-5pm Sun Nov-Mar) in the winter. The adjacent **IMAX Theater** (509-625-6686; adult/child/senior $8/6/7; noon-7pm daily Mar-Oct, Fri-Sun & holidays Oct-Mar) seats 385 people and boasts a 53ft-high screen. Films screen hourly.

Like some relic from an old-fashioned fairground, the 1909 handcarved **carousel** (noon-5pm weekends & holidays) is a kid's classic and, along with the larger-than-life **Radio Flyer Wagon** sculpture, should keep families occupied for a couple of hours. A miniature tour train ($4.75) can cart you from A to B in the park, or you can join the walkers and joggers on the **Spokane River Centennial Trail** (509-624-7188), which extends for 37 miles to the Idaho border and beyond.

Track the trail three miles to the west and you'll end up in **Riverside State Park** (509-456-3964; www.riversidestatepark.org), 10,000 acres of protected forest and trails where you run, walk or cycle till your heart's content. Among the park's natural highlights is the **Bowl & Pitcher**, a deep gorge with huge boulders at a bend in the river 2 miles north of the southern entrance. A swinging suspension bridge, built in the 1930s by the Civilian Conservation Corps, crosses the river here.

History also has its place here. Fur trader David Thompson of the North West Company built a trading post in 1810 just north of Nine Mile Falls, beyond the Centennial Trail's northern endpoint. The site is commemorated by the **Spokane House Interpretive Center** (admission free; 10am-6pm Thu-Mon Jun-Aug), where several modest exhibits tell the story with photos and dioramas.

Nearby, you can explore one of Thompson's trapping routes, much as it may have looked in his time, at the **Little Spokane River**

THE EMPIRE BUILDER ACROSS THE CASCADES

It was American travel writer Paul Theroux who put the romance back into train travel with the publication of his celebrated travelogue *The Great Railway Bazaar* in 1975. Over 30 years later, the railroad has lost none of its exotic appeal. In fact, with the recent upsurge in green thinking and more sustainable transportation options, rail travel could well be on the verge of a new renaissance.

For Washingtonians, train travel will always be synonymous with Canadian-American railroad tycoon James J Hill, who built the first transcontinental Great Northern Railway across the Cascade Mountains in the early 1890s linking St Paul, Minnesota with Seattle. One of the canniest businessmen of his age, Hill financed his massive project with private money and auspiciously created the only US railroad that never filed for bankruptcy.

Leaving daily from Seattle for Chicago, the diesel-powered *Empire Builder* – now run by Amtrak – has been plying the precipitous route across the Cascades since 1929, and in August 2005 it was relaunched with spanking new Superliner cars. Whether relaxing in business class–sized seats in one of its plush carriages, or enjoying a glass of fine Washington wine in the comfortable dining car, the *Empire Builder* enables you to soak up spectacular mountain views and snuggle down to a rare, old-fashioned travel experience free from the hassle of airport crowds or traffic jams. The train leaves Seattle daily at 4.45pm and arrives in Spokane at 12.30am. Tickets cost $56 for a single seat, or $244 for a two-person roomette.

Natural Area. A 3.6-mile hiking and cross-country skiing trail through the protected wetland begins about half a mile beyond Spokane House along Hwy 291. Great blue herons nest in the cottonwoods and Native American **pictographs** can be found at Indian Painted Rocks. The area is perhaps best appreciated in a kayak.

GONZAGA UNIVERSITY

Founded in 1887 by the Jesuit Order, **Gonzaga University** (☎ 509-323-6398) is famous for its college basketball team, and one particularly celebrated former student, the incomparable Harry Lillis 'Bing' Crosby who came here to study in 1920. The immortal Bing donated a comprehensive collection of his recordings and paraphernalia to the college in later life, and these are displayed in the **Bing Crosby Memorabilia Room** (☎ 509-328-4220, ext 4097; 502 E Boone Ave; 🕑 8am-midnight daily during school year; hrs vary Jun-Sep), at the Crosby Student Center. A bronze statue of the crooner – who moved to Spokane at the age of three in 1906 – stands out front, with his prized golf clubs in tow.

In the university art center at the end of Pearl St is the **Jundt Art Museum** (☎ 509-323-6611; 202 E Cataldo Ave; 🕑 10am-4pm Mon-Thu, 10am-9pm Fri, noon-4pm Sat, hrs vary Jun-Sep) housing a good collection of classical sculpture and painting, as well as an 18ft chandelier by glass artist Dale Chihuly.

NORTHWEST MUSEUM OF ARTS & CULTURE

Encased in a striking state-of-the-art building in the historic Browne's Addition neighborhood this **museum** (☎ 509-456-3931; www.northwestmuseum.org; 2316 W 1st Ave; adult/child/senior & student $7/free/5; 🕑 11am-5pm Tue-Sun, till 8pm Wed & Fri) has – arguably – one of the finest collections of indigenous artifacts in the Northwest. Leading off a plush glass foyer overlooking the Spokane River are four galleries showcasing Spokane's history, as well as a number of roving exhibitions that change every three to four months. Your ticket also earns you the right to visit the adjacent English Tudor revival **Campbell House**.

WINERIES

While Walla Walla and the Yakima Valley are the most obvious stops on the Washington wine-tasting circuit, Spokane has also developed a decent clutch of wineries and tasting rooms with knowledgeable staff on hand to help decipher the flavors. For wholesome reds, including some widely lauded cabernet sauvignons, try the kid-friendly **Caterina Winery** (☎ 509-328-5069; 905 N Washington; 🕑 tastings noon-5pm) on the northern outskirts of Riverfront Park. If white's more your tipple try the riesling and chardonnays at the **Latah Creek Wine Cellars** (☎ 509-926-0164; 13030 E Indiana Ave; 🕑 9am-5pm), east of the city off I-90 exit 289.

Activities

Running aside, Spokane's outdoor activities center around golf and skiing. The refreshingly unhyped ski resort can be found at the **Mount Spokane Ski & Snowboard Park** (☎ 509-238-2220, daily snow report 509-238-4025; www.mtspokane.com), located 31 miles northeast of Spokane at the end of Hwy 206. It features a 2100ft vertical drop, and there are several trails for cross-country in, and just past, nearby Mt Spokane State Park.

Festivals & Events

With as many runners pounding the streets as New York's Central Park, it's not surprising that Spokane is the proud host of the pioneering **Bloomsday Run**, the world's biggest timed road race that attracts up to 60,000 runners, walkers and wheelchair racers on the first Sunday in May. The 7.2-mile (12km) course bisects downtown and garners plenty of local enthusiasm.

Hoopfest (☎ 509-624-2414; www.spokanehoopfest.net) is an enormous outdoor basketball tournament held at Riverfront Park and in the downtown streets in late June.

Sleeping

Rodeway Inn (☎ 509-747-1041; 901 W 1st Ave; s/d $43/45;) OK, it's a chain (of sorts), but it's family run, and its location right opposite the exquisite Davenport in the middle of downtown is a bargain at this price. Standard motel features are complemented by a tiny gym and steam room, plus Belgian waffles for breakfast. Service is fast and cheerful(ish).

WestCoast Ridpath Hotel (☎ 509-838-2711; 515 W Sprague Ave; r $99; wi-fi) While it's not in the same league as the Davenport or the Lusso, this huge old downtown hotel has an outdoor pool (open year-round) and a penthouse lounge. A skywalk connects the newer wing with the remodeled former Spokane Hotel.

Montvale Hotel (☎ 509-747-1919; 1005 W 1st Ave; r queen/king $139/179; wi-fi) One of a trio of independent downtown hotels, the Montvale is situated in a former brothel and dazzles after a recent renovation. Don't be fooled by the small, rather plain lobby. Upstairs has an inner courtyard to rival anything in Madrid or Paris. Rooms continue the European theme and mix plush old-world furnishings with plenty of up-to-date technological gadgets. Down in the basement you'll find Catacombs, a medieval-themed restaurant.

Hotel Lusso (☎ 509-747-9750; www.hotellusso.com; N One Post St; r $155-295; wi-fi) A classy accommodation option worth of any city, the Lusso is forced to play second fiddle to the delectable Davenport in the hotel heaven of Spokane. Offering gorgeously plush rooms that are on a par with its illustrious neighbor, the Lusso's luxurious lobby boasts Italian-style fountains and the exquisite Cavallino lounge, while upstairs the European theme continues with glittering marble bathrooms and solid wooden furnishings. The service is equally spiffy.

our pick **Davenport Hotel** (☎ 509-455-8888; 10 S Post St; r standard/deluxe $219/239; wi-fi) Big, historic and loaded with charm, the Davenport is quite simply, one of the most memorable hotels in the US. The winner of numerous awards – including a 2007 Expedia poll that listed it as one of America's top 10 hotels – this AAA four diamond beauty was constructed in 1914 on the designs of talented local architect Kirtland Cutter. The ostentatious lobby extracts a sharp intake of breath from most visitors, with everything from the huge fireside vases to the garbage buckets in the restrooms exhibiting an incredible attention to detail. Even if you're not staying here, be sure to check out the ornate Marie Antoinette Ballroom, the truly lavish guest rooms with their beautifully handcarved and locally crafted beds. The new Davenport Tower wing that showcases an improbable safari theme (think stuffed animals and zebra-striped chairs) and still somehow manages to look sophisticated.

Eating

Frank's Diner (☎ 509-747-8798; 1516 W 2nd Ave; breakfast $5-8) A little west of downtown, but worth the walk is this enchantingly restored vintage railway car, that knocks out a classic breakfast including extraordinarily good eggs and scrumptious biscuits and gravy. Frank's operated as a Seattle diner from 1931 until it was moved to Spokane in 1991. Arrive early to beat the queues.

Rock City Grill (☎ 509-455-4400; 505 W Riverside Ave; lunch $6-10, dinner $12-19) New-wave American-Italian *cocina* glows translucent blue in this atmospherically-lit shopping-mall favorite. The menu offers foods to go, an expansive wine list and items such as one-person artichoke hearts and Dungeness crab pizza for as little as $13.

Elk Public House (☎ 509-363-1973; 1931 W Pacific Ave; lunch $7-9) Situated on a leafy street corner in the salubrious Browne's Addition, the Elk is a favorite neighborhood pub that turns out a kicking soup and sandwich lunch menu best enjoyed alfresco on the street. Also featured is a rotating menu of Northwest beers plus live music at weekends.

Steam Plant Grill (☎ 509-777-3900; 159 S Lincoln; wraps & sandwiches $7-9, mains $15-23) It's amazing how attractive a rusty old coal elevator and a hulk of obsolete steam and electrical equipment can be made to look. Set in the neo-industrial confines of Kirtland Cutter's once-legendary old Steam Plant, this unfussy and eye-catching restaurant serves everything from a Thai chicken wrap to a plate of New Zealand lamb chops, followed up with a Kahlúa mousse–filled pastry.

Fugazzi (☎ 509-624-1133; 1 N Post St; lunch $7-9, dinner $15-27; ⏲ from 6am) A trendy lunch and dinner venue (tortilla-crusted halibut, tofu stir-fry with shiitake mushrooms), Fugazzi is one of Spokane's most stylish restaurants, affiliated with the luscious Hotel Lusso.

Clinkerdagger (☎ 509-328-5965; 621 W Mallon Ave; mains $20) If you want good food and a classic Spokane Falls view, this is the place. Wedged into the old-fashioned Flour Mill, the Clinkerdagger has wraparound windows and a dining deck jutting out over the river. The food is as elegant as the setting and includes grilled king salmon and rock-salt roasted prime ribs.

Entertainment

From opera to billiards, Spokane has the best nighttime entertainment scene east of the Cascades.

PERFORMING ARTS

Opera House (☎ 509-353-6500; www.spokanecenter.com; 334 W Spokane Falls Blvd) Part of the Spokane Convention Center at Riverfront Park the Opera House hosts touring companies and the Spokane Symphony (☎ 509-624-1200).

Metropolitan Performing Arts Center (☎ 509-455-6500; www.metmtg.com/themet; 901 W Sprague Ave) The Met presents concerts, plays, film festivals and the Spokane Opera (☎ 509-533-1150) in a fairly intimate setting.

Spokane Interplayers Ensemble (☎ 509-455-7529; www.interplayers.com; 174 S Howard St) Spokane's local theater offers Broadway-style entertainment from September to June.

Spokane Veterans Memorial Arena (☎ 509-324-7000; 720 W Mallon Ave) Catch major touring acts at this 12,500-seat hall opposite the Flour Mill.

LIVE MUSIC & CLUBS

Northern Lights Brewing Company (☎ 509-242-2739; 1003 E Trent Ave) A student hangout situated near the Gonzaga University, Spokane's best microbrewery serves all kinds of weird and wonderful flavors including an enticing blueberry crème ale and an eye-watering chocolate dunkel, all of which are brewed right on the premises. Foodwise, check out the cod and chips cooked in batter made with the brewery's own pale ale.

Far West Billiards (☎ 509-455-3429; 1001 W 1st Ave) An un-intimidating pool hall and gallery space next to the Montvale Hotel that serves about two dozen beers to accompany your game. If you need a snack, they've got falafel and fajitas.

Dempsey's Brass Rail (☎ 509-747-5362; 909 W 1st) Dempsey's offers alternative entertainment with drag cabaret shows and a dancefloor, all against a crimson background. It's definitely gay-friendly, but fun-loving straights venture in as well.

Shopping

The signature twin smokestacks visible all over Spokane comprise the **Steam Plant Square** (☎ 509-777-3900; 159 S Lincoln St), an upgrade of a 1915 power facility where shops, cafés and restaurants now mingle with the factory's former boilers and pipes. Another historic building-cum-mall is the **Flour Mill** (621 W Mallon Ave), built in 1890 as the region's major wheat-grinding facility. Remodeled for the 1974 Expo, the mill now houses restaurants, pricey boutiques and galleries.

Auntie's Bookstore (☎ 509-838-0206; 402 W Main Ave) is a fantastic bookshop with an excellent travel section, plenty of erudite book readings and the fine onsite Liberty Café with salads, sandwiches and coffee.

Getting There & Away

From **Spokane International Airport** (☎ 509-455-6455), 8 miles southwest of downtown off US 2, Alaska, Horizon, Southwest and United airlines all offer daily services to/from Seattle and Portland.

All buses arrive at and depart from the **Spokane Intermodal Transportation Center** (221 W 1st Ave), a combination bus-and-train station

DETOUR: SPOKANE TO THE IDAHO PANHANDLE

East of Spokane on the I-90 and tipping up toward Canada, the Idaho Panhandle is an alluring region, speckled with resorts, lakes and old mining haunts. **Coeur d'Alene** is the regional hub, while **Kellogg** and **Sandpoint** are prime destinations for skiers, anglers and water-sports enthusiasts, and the old silver-mining town of **Wallace** exudes preserved Western flavor. Sixty lakes lie within 60 miles of Coeur d'Alene, including Hayden, Priest and Pend Oreille, all surrounded by campgrounds. Opportunities for outdoor activities are everywhere: white-water rafting the class-III run of the St Joe National Wild and Scenic River, jet-skiing on Lake Coeur d'Alene and backpacking through the primeval forest around Priest Lake.

The **Coeur d'Alene Visitor Center** (☎ 208-665-2350; 115 Northwest Blvd; 10am-5pm Jun-Aug, 10am-3pm Tue-Sat rest of year) is a good regional information starting point.

served by the *Empire Builder* (p206) and **Greyhound** (☎ 509-624-5252; www.greyhound.com). Buses head off daily to Seattle ($34.50, six hours) and Pasco ($34, 2½ hours) the latter via Moses Lake, Wenatchee and Leavenworth.

Getting Around

Spokane Transit (☎ 509-328-7433; www.spokanetransit.com) buses depart from streets bordering the Plaza, a huge indoor transit station at Sprague Ave and Wall St. Bus fare is $0.75. Bus 64 runs hourly on weekdays between the Plaza and Spokane International Airport, from 6:20am to 5:50pm.

GRAND COULEE DAM AREA

The colossal Grand Coulee Dam is the country's largest hydroelectric project, one of the great engineering marvels of the modern world. The lynchpin of 11 Columbia River dams, Grand Coulee has a generating capacity of 6809 megawatts, about a quarter of the hydropower generated along the river. Built in the Depression era (beginning in 1933) by the US Bureau of Reclamation it is still one of the world's largest concrete structures and has transformed the once arid Columbia Basin into a fertile agricultural land.

While many people come here to marvel at the remarkable Grand Coulee itself, an equal number are drawn by the fishing, hunting and swimming opportunities that the dam has created. Indeed, the dam now sits at the center of a vast recreation area spearheaded by placid Lake Roosevelt that extends 150 miles to the east and north.

Grand Coulee Dam

The **Grand Coulee Visitor Arrival Center** (☎ 509-633-9265; 9am-5pm) details the history of the dam and surrounding area with movies, photos and interactive exhibits, while free guided **tours** of the facility run on the hour from 10am until 5pm (May to September) and involve taking a glass-walled elevator 465ft down an incline into the Third Power Plant, where you can view the tops of the generators from an observation deck.

Similarly spectacular is the nightly **laser show** (May-Sep after dark) – purportedly the world's largest – which illustrates the history of the Columbia River and its various dams against a gloriously vivid backdrop.

Accommodations in Grand Coulee itself can be found in a number of places, none better than the **Columbia River Inn** (☎ 509-633-2100; www.columbiariverinn.com; 10 Lincoln St, Coulee Dam; r $95-105;) opposite the Visitor Arrival Center, which offers a swimming pool, gym/sauna and rooms with dam-view balconies. For no nonsense café grub, try the **Melody Restaurant** (☎ 509-633-1151; 512 River Dr; mains $6-10) which has a well-placed exterior deck for laser-show viewing.

Lake Roosevelt National Recreation Area

A 150-mile-long reservoir held back by the Grand Coulee Dam, Lake Roosevelt is a major recreation area that is popular with anglers, boaters, canoeists and water-skiers.

Dry, sunny weather prevails here, drawing people to camp and play on the lake's southern white-sand beaches. As the lake inches its way north to Canada, the desert cliffs and high coulee walls give way to rolling hills and orchards, becoming dense forests of ponderosa pine around Kettle Falls.

As recreation areas go, Lake Roosevelt remains refreshingly undeveloped, and few roads penetrate its isolated shoreline. To explore the area in any great length you'll need a boat.

THE 51ST STATE?

The splitting of Washington into two separate states along a line running down the Cascade Mountains is an idea that has been floated since the 1850s when Walla Walla made a brief, but futile, attempt to break away from the newly formed Washington Territory. A decade later, in 1864, separatists in Idaho came up with a similar idea, proposing to link the Idaho Panhandle with eastern Washington in a new super-state to be known tentatively as Lincoln, after the then US President.

Though these early proposals were easily quashed, dissenters from within the 'Inland Empire' (as eastern Washington, along with parts of Idaho, Oregon and Montana, has historically been known), refused to put the idea to bed. Championing the political, economic and cultural differences of their dry and traditionally conservative agricultural heartland, successive generations of ardent easterners continued to keep the issue alive and in 1984 the Spokane *Spokesman-Review* newspaper conducted a poll that audaciously proposed a possible name for the hypothetical new entity (the winner was 'Columbia').

Undaunted by the mirth that such proposals have inspired, state legislators have been equally vociferous in their support for the idea of eastern statehood. To prove the point, a succession of (as yet, unsuccessful) bills has been presented to the Washington state senate during the last decade. The most recent of these – officially endorsed by 11 state senators – was rejected in February 2005.

The lake offers a plethora of boat launches, with fees starting at $6 for seven days and $40 for a year. One of the best places to organize other water-based activities – such as fishing, canoeing and water skiing – is at the **Keller Ferry Campground** (☎ 509-633-9188; campsites $10 May-Sep, $5 Oct-Apr), located 14 miles north of the town of Wilbur. The **Keller Ferry** crosses Lake Roosevelt (free; 6am to 11pm) near the campground, linking Hwy 21 and providing access to the Sanpoil River and the town of Republic to the north.

To uncover the history of the area visit **Fort Spokane Visitor Center** (☎ 509-725-2715; admission free; 10am-5pm May 26-Oct 10) off Hwy 25, 23 miles north of Davenport, where original fort buildings from 1880 tell the story of how white settlers attempted to quell the region's Native American tribes.

Your best bet for general information about the area is the **Lake Roosevelt National Recreation Area Headquarters** (☎ 509-633-9441; www.nps.gov/laro; 1008 Crest Dr; 8am-fpm), in Coulee Dam. Park admission is free.

OKANOGAN RIVER VALLEY

The lightly settled and relatively remote Okanogan River Valley is an extension of the popular Okanagan (note: different spelling) region in Canada. Dominated by the boreal forests and grassy steppe of the Okanogan National Forest, the area makes up Washington's largest county (Okanogan County). The area is marked by the historic Fort Okanogan, founded by the Pacific Fur Company in 1811 at the confluence of the Okanogan and Columbia Rivers and generally recognized as being the first permanent *American* settlement in present-day Washington State. Rather ironically, the fort was sold back to the British-administered Hudson Bay Company in 1821.

To get acquainted with the local history call in at the interpretive center at **Fort Okanogan State Park** (☎ 509-923-2473; junction of US 97 & Hwy 17; admission free; 10am-5pm Wed-Sun Jun-Aug), 4 miles northeast of the town of Brewster, which tells the story of the valley's original Native American inhabitants and relates how three different fur-trading companies successively occupied the site of the old fort in the early 19th century.

Okanogan – which derives from the native Salish word for 'rendezvous' – is also the name of the diminutive county capital (population 2484) which lies 29 miles to the east of Twisp at the nexus of US 20 and US 97. In recent decades Okanogan has effectively merged with the nearby town of Omak (population 4721) and though neither settlement is a budding tourist center, travelers can make a quick but interesting pit stop at the **Okanogan County Historical Museum** (☎ 509-422-4272; 1410 N 2nd St; admission $2; 10am-4pm Memorial Day-Labor Day) to admire the pictures of frontier photographer Frank Matsura who first visited this lonely region in 1890.

Omak is famous for its annual Omak Stampede (held in August), a well-known local spectacle that includes the notorious 'Suicide Race,' a 210ft plunge down a 60-degree slope on horseback followed by the fording of the 50yd-wide Okanogan River. Not surprisingly the event has raised the ire of numerous animal rights groups.

The varied landscape around Okanogan and Omak offers plenty of outdoor possibilities including a wintertime ski center at the **Loup Loup Ski Bowl** (☎ 509-826-2720; www.skitheloup.com; Dec-Mar), just off US 20, 18 miles west of Okanogan. Hiking and biking are also popular here in the summer. Contact the **USFS headquarters** (☎ 509-826-3275; 1240 S 2nd St) in Okanogan for trail information. The **Bike Shop** (☎ 509-422-0710; www.theokbikeshop.com; 137 S 2nd Ave) in Okanogan rents bikes, skis and snowshoes from $15 a day. More regional tourist information is available from the **Omak Visitor Information Office** (☎ 509-826-1880, 800-225-6625; omakvic@northcascades.net; 401 Omak Ave) just east of downtown.

If you're staying the night try the simple but friendly **Cariboo Inn** (☎ 509-422-6109; 233 Queen St, Okanogan; r $38-50) which is more inviting than first impressions might suggest. It's next door to a no-nonsense coffee shop that offers some 'healthy' specials in among all the steaks.

COLVILLE NATIONAL FOREST

Wedged into Washington's northeast corner abutting the borders of Idaho and Canada, lies the Colville National Forest, a vast and relatively remote corner of the state that spans the Kettle River and Selkirk Mountain ranges and is bisected in the west by the Columbia River and Lake Roosevelt. Lying in the foothills of the Rocky Mountains, this wild region is home to grizzly bears, cougars and the last remaining herd of caribou in the lower 48 states. Some of the loveliest scenery can be found in the isolated Salmo-Priest Wilderness Area which is crisscrossed by hiking trails. Colville makes a good base for exploring the Selkirks and the Pend Oreille River area, while Kettle Falls, on Lake Roosevelt, is replete with Columbia River history.

Kettle Falls

pop 1527

Kettle Falls was once a favored fishing spot for Native Americans before the Hudson Bay Company arrived in 1825 to set up a fur-trading post at Fort Colville. The small settlement that subsequently grew up in the area had to be relocated in the 1930s when the area was flooded by the building of the Grand Coulee Dam. These days Kettle Falls is largely a blue-collar lumber town set in an attractive valley with some nearby water-based activities and some interesting snapshots of Columbia River history.

To get a glimpse of the town before its relocation, drop by the **Kettle Falls Interpretive Center** (☎ 509-738-6964; 11am-5pm Wed-Sat May-Sep) just north of US 395 to see a giant photo mural showing the pre-dam Columbia as it crashed through Kettle Falls.

Eleven miles west of Kettle Falls on Hwy 20 (at Canyon Creek, milepost 335) you'll find the **Log Flume Heritage Site** (☎ 509-738-6111) in the middle of a ponderosa pine forest. The site provides a snapshot of logging history and several interpretive displays along a mile-long winding, wheelchair-accessible trail.

As well as camping facilities, the **Kettle Falls Campground** (☎ 509-738-6266; Boise Rd; campsites $10 May-Sep, $5 Oct-Apr; year-round) offers biking, beaches, boating, hiking, fishing and NPS rangers who lead talks and activities during the summer months. For something a little less rustic try the **Grandview Inn Motel & RV Park** (☎ 509-738-6733; 978 US 395 N at junction with Hwy 25; s/d $46/50) which has a pleasant grassy lawn overlooking Lake Roosevelt.

Colville

pop 4988

Colville is a small town, embellished with parks and some gracious older buildings, that acts as a good base camp for exploring Lake Roosevelt and the 1.1-million-acre Colville National Forest.

For local information, contact the **Colville Chamber of Commerce** (☎ 509-684-5973; www.colville.com; 121 E Astor St) or the **Colville National Forest Ranger Station** (☎ 509-684-7000; 765 S Main St) has the lowdown on hiking and camping.

The town's most notable attraction is the **Keller Heritage Center** (☎ 509-684-5968; 700 N Wynne St; admission by donation; 1-4pm daily May, 10am-4pm Mon-Sat, 1-4pm Sun Jun-Sep). Its centerpiece is Keller House, a rather large bungalow with attractive Craftsman details, built in 1910. Dispersed around the house are reconstructed versions of a pioneer blacksmith's shop, schoolhouse, trapper's cabin, sawmill and fire lookout tower.

Bird-watchers should swing down to the **Little Pend Oreille National Wildlife Refuge**, where McDowell Lake attracts waterfowl. To reach the **refuge headquarters** (☎ 509-684-8384; 1310 Bear Creek Rd; 7:30am-4pm), take US 20 for about 8 miles east of Colville, then turn south on Narcisse Creek Rd.

Eastern Washington's downhill skiers head to **49 Degrees North** (☎ 509-935-6649, snow report 509-880-9208; www.ski49n.com; 3311 Flowery Trail Rd, Chewelah; ski area closed Wed & Thu except holidays). Located about 30 miles southeast of Colville near Chewelah, it's a small ski area with four chairlifts and an 18ft vertical drop.

Cheap accommodations around Colville is plentiful in motels and campgrounds. Try **Douglas Falls Grange Park Campground** (☎ 509-684-7474; Douglas Falls Rd; free; May-Sep) alongside Mill Creek 7 miles north of town or **Benny's Colville Inn** (☎ 509-684-2517; 915 S Main St; r from $53;) which has decent rooms, a gym, Jacuzzi and two racquetball courts, and is a steal at the price. For coffee, espresso, microbrews, paninis and other snacks head to **Café al Mundo & Espresso** (☎ 509-684-8092; 100 S Main St; mains $6-9).

SOUTHEASTERN WASHINGTON

Parched, remote, and barely served by public transportation, southeastern Washington is the state's loneliest corner and is characterized by the dry volcanic plateaus and denuded lava flows of the inhospitable 'Scablands' region exposed by the Missoula floods at the end of the last ice age. Tourism – and its attendant attractions – was on a backburner here until the early 1990s when wine growers in and around Walla Walla began to realize the town's potential as a tourist center and wine connoisseurs started flocking in from around the globe.

For many it was as if the region's fortunes had turned full circle. Established as one of Washington's first permanent settlements in 1836 when Marcus Whitman rolled off the Oregon Trail and founded a mission in the foothills of the Blue Mountains, the southeast was once a hive of commercial activity that sat on the cusp of Washington's burgeoning frontier. But as the settlers pushed west in the late 19th century, the Columbia River Basin slipped into a self-imposed coma, made all the more terminal when the US government opened up the Hanford nuclear complex near Richland in 1942. Not surprisingly, the stigma of secret bomb-making factories and contaminated waste sites has been hard to dislodge.

TRI-CITIES

Pasco, Kennewick and Richland – known communally as the Tri-Cities – are infamous for the Hanford Nuclear Reservation, built north of Richland in the 1940s as a plutonium-refining plant for the top-secret Manhattan Project. In 1945 Hanford supplied the plutonium to manufacture 'Fat Man,' the atomic bomb that the Americans dropped on Nagasaki, and after WWII the facility continued to research and develop nuclear energy. Shut down bit-by-bit between 1967 and 1987, Hanford is currently engaged in the world's largest environmental clean up, a process that will last until 2030 and is estimated to cost the US government in the vicinity of $50 billion.

Unless you have a morbid fascination for fading Cold War anachronisms, the Tri-Cities offer little in the way of traveler facilities and attractions. Of the three cities, Kennewick boasts the most greenery, while newer Richland sports one of the highest per-capita incomes in the state. Pasco is largely a Latino community, and home to most of the area's agricultural workers.

Sights & Activities

To see the Tri-Cities in their best light, stay close to the broad Columbia River which reveals its only stretch of free-flowing water at the **Hanford Reach National Monument**.

Kennewick's **Columbia Park** (☎ 509-783-3711) is a vast greenway complete with a golf course, playing fields, campground and boat moorage, while the 23-mile paved **Sacagawea Heritage Trail** acts as a connecting hiking and biking artery between the three cities using the river as its marker.

Museum-wise Richland has the comprehensive **Columbia River Exhibition of History, Science & Technology** (CREHST; ☎ 509-943-9000; 95 Lee Blvd; adult/student/senior $3.50/2.50/2.95; 10am-5pm Mon-Sat, noon-5pm Sun) which documents Columbia River history, the journey of Lewis and Clark (who passed though here in 1805) and the inevitable chronicling of the Hanford project. Meanwhile, over in Kennewick, the **East Benton County Historical Museum** (☎ 509-582-7704; 205

Keewayden Dr; admission $2; noon-4pm Tue-Sat) tracks local history and has some exhibits on 'Kennewick Man,' a 9300-year-old skeleton of a Caucasian male found on the banks of the Columbia in 1996 that blew the anthropological history of North America wide open.

Sleeping & Eating

Clover Island Inn (509-586-0541; 435 Clover Island Dr, Kennewick; r $79;) You won't have trouble finding an economical motel in the Tri-Cities but, if you want something a little plusher, hit the locally owned Clover Island Inn which is situated on its own island in the Columbia River. This unique establishment boasts 150 rooms, its own boat dock and panoramic views from the top-floor Crow's Nest Restaurant.

Atomic Ale Brewpub & Eatery (509-946-5465; 1015 Lee Blvd; pizzas $9-12, sandwiches $6; closed Sun) A perceptible 'gallows humor' pervades this cheery microbrewery and eatery, well-known for its wood-fired specialty pizzas and top-notch soups (try the red potato). But first blast off with a locally crafted Half-Life Hefeweizen, Plutonium Porter or Atomic Amber.

Getting There & Around

Greyhound (509-547-3151) and **Amtrak** (509-545-1554) share a new terminal at 535 N 1st Ave in Pasco. Greyhound buses go to Spokane ($31.50, 2½ hours), Portland ($37, four hours) and Seattle ($32, 4½ hours) via Yakima and Ellensburg. Amtrak's *Empire Builder* stops here en route to Portland at 5:35am ($35, 4½ hours); eastbound, it passes through at 8:57pm on the way to Spokane ($33, 3½ hours) and Chicago.

WALLA WALLA

pop 29,686

With a reputation that is growing stronger by the year, Walla Walla has converted itself from an obscure agricultural backwater, famous for its sweet onions and large state penitentiary, into the hottest wine-growing region outside of California's Napa Valley. Indeed, for many wine aficionados, this laid-back and historic college town – which claims, not unjustly, to be one of Washington's oldest settlements – is the *new* Napa Valley with its fruity merlots, classy cabernet sauvignons and memorable syrahs.

For the local inhabitants, the kudos is not surprising. Armed with one of the prettiest main streets in the Northwest, and beautified with a fine clutch of magnificent Queen Anne, neoclassical and Craftsman-style homes, Walla Walla has long been a sleeping giant awaiting a glitzy reincarnation. While venerable Marcus Whitman College is the town's most obvious cultural attribute, you'll also find zany coffee bars here, along with cool wine-tasting rooms, salubrious parks and one of the state's freshest and most vibrant farmers markets.

Located in a rich agricultural area, Walla Walla supplements its much-sought-after sweet onions with pea and asparagus production, vineyards and apple orchards. Equally distinctive in the undulating countryside that surrounds the town are the 454 wind turbines belonging to the massive Stateline Wind Energy Center, a groundbreaking environmental project that is a vital source of Washington's renewable energy.

Orientation & Information

Walla Walla is in a fertile basin where several smaller streams meet the Walla Walla River. Rising behind the town are the Blue Mountains; only 6 miles south is the Oregon border, with Pendleton 35 miles farther south on Hwy 11. The main road through the area is US 12, which leaves the Columbia River at Wallula, 29 miles to the west, and heads up to the Idaho border at Lewiston, 99 miles northeast.

The **Walla Walla Valley Chamber of Commerce** (509-525-0850; www.wallawalla.org; 29 E Sumach St; 8:30am-5pm Mon-Fri, 9am-3pm Sat & Sun) provides four excellent walking-tour maps of the town plus plenty of information on wine tours.

Sights & Activities

Few cities take as much pride in their historical and cultural heritage as Walla Walla, and to help bring the settlement to life for visitors, the local chamber of commerce has concocted four fascinating walking tours, each explained in a free leaflet that includes a map and numbered icons (leaflets can also be picked up from a dispenser in Heritage Park on Main St).

The 1.5-mile **Downtown Walk** starts at the 1928 Marcus Whitman Hotel and proceeds in a loop around the historic buildings of Main and Colville Sts. The 2-mile **Historic Homes Walk** begins and ends at the Mill Creek Brewpub and takes in the various Queen Anne, neoclassical and Gothic

Carpenter–style homes that dot the city's suburbs. Walk three is called the 3-mile **Up Boyer to Pioneer Park Walk** and explores the gorgeous Whitman College campus as well as the lush confines of Pioneer Park.

The final walking tour takes you inside **Fort Walla Walla Park**, and showcases the original buildings from a US army installation that existed here from its inception in 1858 until 1910. You can view everything from the officer's quarters to the quartermaster's stable on the grounds of what is now the Department of Veteran's Affairs Medical Center. Slightly west of here is the **Fort Walla Walla Museum** (☎ 509-525-7703; 755 Myra Rd; adult/child/senior & student $7/3/6; ⏰ 10am-5pm Apr-Oct) off W Poplar St, which consists of a pioneer village of 16 historic buildings, including a blacksmith shop, the 1867 schoolhouse, log cabins and a railway depot, arranged around a central meadow. On a hill above the village, the fort's old cavalry stables house the museum proper, with collections of farm implements, ranching tools, Native American artifacts and what could be the world's largest plastic replica of a mule team.

WINERIES

With its laidback, small-town feel; excellent syrahs and plethora of unpretentious local wineries, Walla Walla is the best place in the state to indulge in a bit of spontaneous wine touring in the style of the film *Sideways* (it's probably only a matter of time before they cut their own wine-inspired movie here).

The best of the local wineries are found around Lowden, roughly 12 miles west of Walla Walla on US 12. **Canoe Ridge** (☎ 509-527-0885; 1102 W Cherry St; ⏰ 11am-4pm Oct-Apr, until 5pm May-Sep) has a tasting room in an old street car engine house. Try the Merlot Reserve and the Gewürztraminer.

Woodward Canyon Winery (☎ 509-525-4129; 11920 US 12; ⏰ 10am-5pm) has one of the best chardonnays in Washington.

Back in town you can stop by at an ever-expanding number of tasting rooms. The salon of **Waterbrook Winery** (☎ 509-522-1262; 31 E Main St; ⏰ 10:30am-4:30pm) is a good starting point, a tasting room which doubles up as a gallery, enabling you to admire paintings and pottery while sipping on its signature chardonnay. **Forgeron Cellars** (☎ 509-522-9463; 33 W Birch St; ⏰ 11am-4pm) is headed up by a Parisian woman who studied viticulture at Dijon University before heading west. Check out their smooth and balanced cabernet sauvignons and full bodied syrahs.

Festivals & Events

The **Walla Walla Sweet Onion Blues Fest** (☎ 509-525-1031), held in mid-July at Fort Walla Walla, celebrates the valley's renowned crop now upstaged by the region's wine. There are food booths and recipe contests, as well as live music provided by touring blues acts.

The mid-May **Balloon Stampede** sees competitors launch dozens of hot-air-filled craft into the air at 6am.

Sleeping

City Center Motel (☎ 509-529-2660; 627 W Main St; s/d $55/60; ❄ 🚭) At last, a motel with a sense of humor: the inaptly named 'City Center' is on a peripheral road a good eight blocks from historic downtown but what the hell? This is Walla Walla where walking (without an umbrella) is a rare pleasure and distances are never far. Rooms here are small and the advertised swimming pool a bit of a joke, but it's family-run, friendly and flexible with check-out times.

Marcus Whitman Hotel & Conference Center (☎ 509-525-2200; www.marcuswhitmanhotel.com; 6 W Rose St; r/ste $139/$279; ❄ wi-fi) Walla Walla's best known landmark is also the town's only tall building, impossible to miss with its distinctive rooftop turret visible from all around. In keeping with the settlement's well-preserved image, the red-bricked 1928 beauty has been elegantly renovated in an authentic old-world style, with ample rooms kitted out in rusts and browns, and embellished with Italian-crafted furniture, huge beds and killer views over the nearby Blue Mountains. The onsite Marc restaurant is one of the town's fanciest eating joints.

Green Gables Inn (☎ 509-525-5501; www.greengablesinn.com; 922 Bonsella St; r $140-175; ❄) While it's a long way from Prince Edward Island – the setting for the novel *Anne of Green Gables* – this comfortable inn in a 1909 Craftsman-style home plays heavily on the classic book's literary themes, featuring five rooms named after instances in Lucy Maud Montgomery's famous novel. Come here to enjoy candlelit breakfasts, a wraparound porch with shade from the summer sun, and rooms that are equipped with bathrobes, fresh flowers and cable TV.

WASHINGTON WINE

A relative newcomer to the viticulture world, Washington's position as the US's second-largest wine-producing region (after California) is no longer in question. In 2006 the state opened up an average of three new wineries a week and, thanks to unrestrictive growing practices and liberal irrigation laws, even experienced French growers were heading out west to sow their vines in such unlikely places as Walla Walla and the Yakima Valley.

The secret, for aficionados, is in the soil. Enriched over 15,000 years ago when the gushing Missoula floods deposited a thick layer of muddy sediment around the rugged Columbia River gorge, the grape growing potential in this arid region is second only to France. Add in dry climate (allowing farmers to control the amount of water the grapes receive), plenty of annual sunshine, and a northerly latitude that ensures long hours of daylight during the summer, and you've got a formula favorable enough to satisfy even the fussiest wine connoisseurs.

If Washington wines have a weakness, it is in their relative youth. The most mature vines in this part of the world are barely 30 years old and, while the flavor of the wines is agreeably fruity and sufficiently full-bodied, the grapes tend to lack the darker, earthier essence of old-world European vines.

Not that this has served to slow down the unstoppable vine-planting onslaught. Never keen to rest on its laurels, the Washington wine industry now boasts over 500 private wineries in nine different AVAs (American Viticultural Areas), producing an eclectic mix of different wines – 80% of which are red – including merlot, cabernet sauvignon and the much-vaunted syrah.

Walla Walla, where the soil is particularly rich, has quickly become the Napa Valley of the state with the best hotels and restaurants to support a burgeoning wine-tourist culture. Other good bases include Yakima, Ellensburg and the large yet unpretentious city of Spokane.

Inn at Abeja (☎ 509-522-1234; 2014 Mill Creek Rd; r $210-280; wi-fi) Ever wanted to stay at a full working winery? Well, if you've got your own transportation and approximately $250 in spare change you can spend a night at this historic farmstead set in the foothills of the glowering Blue Mountains 4 miles east of Walla Walla. Luxury accommodation is provided in five self-contained converted buildings (the largest of which is over 800 sq ft). It's the perfect base for a wine tour.

Eating & Drinking

our pick **Merchants Ltd Delicatessen & French Bakery** (☎ 509-525-0900; 21 E Main St; breakfast & sandwiches $5-7; closed Sun) A one-off deli-coffeehouse-bakery-breakfast stop, Merchants is housed inside the 1885 Barrett Building and is a delightful place to soak up the small-town ambience of Walla Walla's Main St. Feast on eggs Benedict, bagels, oatmeal, pastries and cheese, and sup on locally roasted fair trade coffee in a picturesque alfresco setting.

Coffee Perk (☎ 509-526-0636; 4 1st St; sandwiches $6; wi-fi) In the same building as Starbucks but infinitely perkier, this caffeine house is popular with Whitman students who research their carefully crafted college essays using the café's free wi-fi service. An old-fashioned bookcase on the back wall contains everything from Dickens to Mark Twain's famous traveler's bible *Innocents Abroad*.

Grapefields (☎ 509-522-3993; 4 E Main St; snacks $6-9, mains $12-16) A popular Main St staple, Grapefields offers light snacks, larger meals and excellent wine-tasting possibilities without driving a huge wedge into your wallet. Housed in a small European-style bistro you can enjoy cheese, pâté and preserved meats here, or plump for something more substantial, like the stone-oven pizza.

26 Brix (☎ 509-526-4075; 207 W Main St; mains $15-27; 5-10pm Mon, Thu-Sat, 9am-2pm & 5-9pm Sun) A new fine-dining establishment that has helped elevate Walla Walla into a wine-tasting destination extraordinaire, 26 Brix was set up by a respected Seattle-area chef who has crafted an interesting cordon bleu menu around fruity Washington wines and fresh local ingredients. Getting off to a shaky start, the restaurant now seems to have found a delicate balance between the posh and the personable, and dishes such as BBQ Muscovy duck and the enticing Artisan Cheese tour are winning kudos.

Whitehouse-Crawford Restaurant (☎ 509-525-2222; 55 W Cherry St; mains from $20; from 5pm Wed-Sun) If you're feeling flush, bypass the town's ample cafés and make a beeline for this fine-dining establishment housed in an impressively renovated woodworking mill dating from 1905. Great local seafood and produce highlight the seasonally (and daily) varying menu. It's an excellent place to sample the bounty of Walla Walla's vineyards, with more than 60 local vintages in the cellars.

Mill Creek Brewpub (☎ 509-522-2440; 11 S Palouse St) Walla Walla's only brewpub is an accommodating place with outdoor seating and decent snacks such as mushroom burgers and fish and chips. Situated at the top end of Main St and close to Whitman College it welcomes minors and sells small 6oz taster glasses of the local microbrews, including the smooth Walla Walla Wheat and the ever-popular English-style IPAs.

Entertainment

Walla Walla Symphony (☎ 509-529-8020; www.wwsymphony.com) Yes, the supposed rural backwater of Walla Walla has had a symphony orchestra since 1907 and the group is currently led by musical director Yaacov Bergman. Tackling everything from Holst to Gershwin, they run an annual six-concert series in the Cordiner Hall at Whitman College.

Harper Joy Theatre (☎ 509-527-5180; N Park St & Boyer Ave; adult/senior $10/7) WallaWalla's culture vultures wander over to Whitman College's theater department for renditions of Shakespeare, Rodgers and Hammerstein, and plenty of local fare.

Getting There & Around

Now for the hard bit. Walla Walla is currently off the state bus-and-rail grid and hence notoriously difficult to get to without your own car. **Budget** (☎ 509-525-8811) can sort out rentals at the airport.

Horizon Air (www.alaskaair.com) and **Northwest Airlines** (www.nwa.com) have flights to Seattle and Portland from the Walla Walla Regional Airport, which is northeast of town off US 12.

The local bus service is operated 6:30am to 5:30pm weekdays by **Valley Transit** (☎ 509-525-9140; www.valleytransit.com).

The cheapest taxis to Walla Walla from Pasco Greyhound station are with **RAB** (☎ 509-585-2944). One-way will set you back approximately $70.

PULLMAN & THE PALOUSE REGION

Another of Washington's liberal university towns, Pullman (population 24,675) lies in midst of the golden Palouse region, a fertile pastiche of rolling hills and well-tilled agricultural fields replete with wheat, lentils, barley and peas that is excellent for cycling.

Situated 7 miles west of the Idaho state line, most of Pullman's sights are related directly to expansive **Washington State University** (WSU) which accommodates over 22,000 students and boasts one of Washington's leading agricultural schools. Worth seeking out in this small 'city within a city' is the WSU's **Museum of Art** (☎ 509-335-1910; admission free; 🕑 10am-4pm

HELLS GATE STATE PARK

Located 4 miles south of downtown Lewiston, Idaho, this 960-acre state park beside the majestic Snake River is a popular departure point for jet-boat tours of Hells Canyon (p342), 50 miles upriver on the Oregon/Idaho border. The canyon – which is part of the deepest river gorge in North America (deeper even than the Grand Canyon) – is a wild and spectacular natural region that offers wilderness adventurers everything from hiking and camping excursions to exciting white-water rafting trips.

For the full tour itineraries descend on the Hells Gate State Park marina where you can choose from a whole range of half day, full day or overnight excursions to Hells Canyon by shopping around among the various operators that line the dock. Expect to pay up to $200 for a day trip and substantially more for an overnight stop. For a full list, contact the **Clarkston Chamber of Commerce** (☎ 509-758-7712; 502 Bridge St, Clarkston), 4 miles west of Lewiston.

Hells Gate State Park is a worthwhile destination in its own right with plenty of hiking, biking, swimming and horseback-riding possibilities available along with an exciting new **Lewis and Clark Discovery Center** that includes a 2-acre riverside interpretive plaza plus a ton of additional animated and informative material. You can stay overnight in the park in cabins ($45), RV hook-ups ($20) or campsites ($12). For more details contact the **park office** (☎ 208-799-5015; 5100 Hells Gate Rd, Lewiston).

Greyhound buses run a twice daily service from Seattle to Lewiston via Yakima and Pasco.

Mon-Fri, 1-5pm Sat & Sun, Tue 10am-10pm), in the Fine Arts Center at Stadium Way and Wilson Rd, which mounts some lively, well-curated shows featuring Northwest artists.

Other WSU museums include the **Jacklin Collection** (☎ 509-335-3009; admission free; 8am-5pm Mon-Fri), in room 124 of the Webster Physical Sciences Building. It showcases more than 2000 specimens of petrified wood. The **Museum of Anthropology** (☎ 509-335-3936; 110 College Hall; admission free; 9am-4pm Mon-Fri) documents fossils relating to human evolution.

Possibly one of Pullman's most famous eateries is **Ferdinand's** (☎ 509-335-2141; 101 Food Quality Bldg at the WSU Creamery; milkshakes $3; 9:30am-4:30pm Mon-Fri) which sells the locally concocted Cougar Gold cheese (white sharp cheddar, sold by the can) along with milkshakes and a decent espresso.

If you're staying over, a spiffy hotel is the **Hawthorne Inn & Suites** (☎ 509-332-0928; 928 NW Olsen St; r $70-90;) a mile outside town with views over toward the university.

Northwestern Trailways (☎ 509-334-1412) links Pullman to other cities via Spokane ($18, 1½ hours) and Lewiston ($20, one hour) from the **bus station** (NW 1002 Nye St), behind the Dissmore supermarket.

For a full lowdown on the area and its facilities drop by or call the **Pullman Chamber of Commerce** (☎ 509-334-3565; www.pullman-wa.com; 415 N Grand Ave).

Portland & the Willamette Valley

Just south of the Washington state border and 65 miles inland from the Pacific Ocean, dynamic Portland is Oregon's superstar city. It's the state's largest metropolis and features a bustling, vibrant downtown alongside charming neighborhoods full of friendly (and often zany) people. Portland is laid-back, highly livable, proud to be ultra-green – both politically and physically – and boasts countless brewpubs, bookstores, gardens and coffeehouses. It's a highly addictive, unmissable spot to slap your backpack down while adventuring in the region.

Oregon City, within Portland's southern suburbs, is the place to go for the history of the Pacific Northwest. This was the last pit stop for settlers on the Oregon Trail, where they finally dug in their heels, parked their dusty covered wagons and set up the region's first homesteads. South of Portland is the Willamette Valley, Oregon's very own wine-lovers' paradise. Let your taste buds explore the wineries around McMinnville, sampling the region's exquisite varietals and fine cuisine. Visit humble Salem, Oregon's capital city, and its surrounding attractions (which include a waterfall-filled state park and a 2.5-lb hairball – but not in the same place!). Pause and let your hair down in dynamic and liberal Eugene, full of energetic college students, pretty riverside parks and fine restaurants.

Portland and the Willamette Valley are also supremely located: head east to the Columbia River Gorge, north to Washington and west to the coast. Everything is so close by you'll want to linger for longer than you planned, so stretch that schedule and put on your explorer's hat – you'll need it.

HIGHLIGHTS

- Tromping Silver Falls State Park's 8-mile **Trail of Ten Falls Loop** (p248)
- **Wine tasting** around areas like McMinnville or Eugene (p244)
- Joining the parades, street fairs and the fun crowds in the September **Eugene Celebration** (p251)
- Exploring the many restaurants and art galleries in Portland's chic **Pearl District** (p228)
- Sampling the wide variety of microbrews in **Portland** (p237), which boasts around 30 breweries and brewpubs
- Snatching a history lesson in Oregon City at museums like the **Museum of the Oregon Territory** (p241)

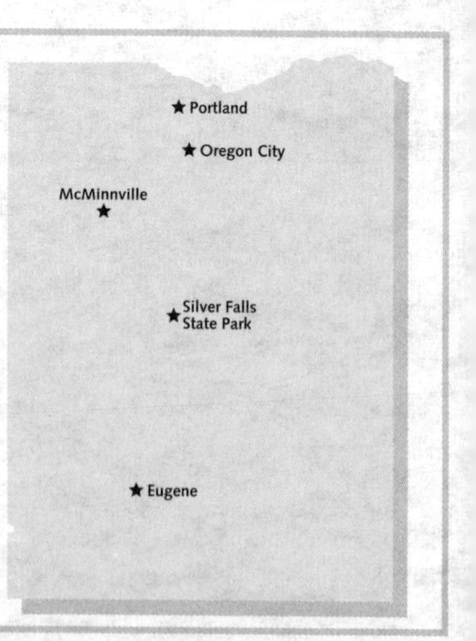

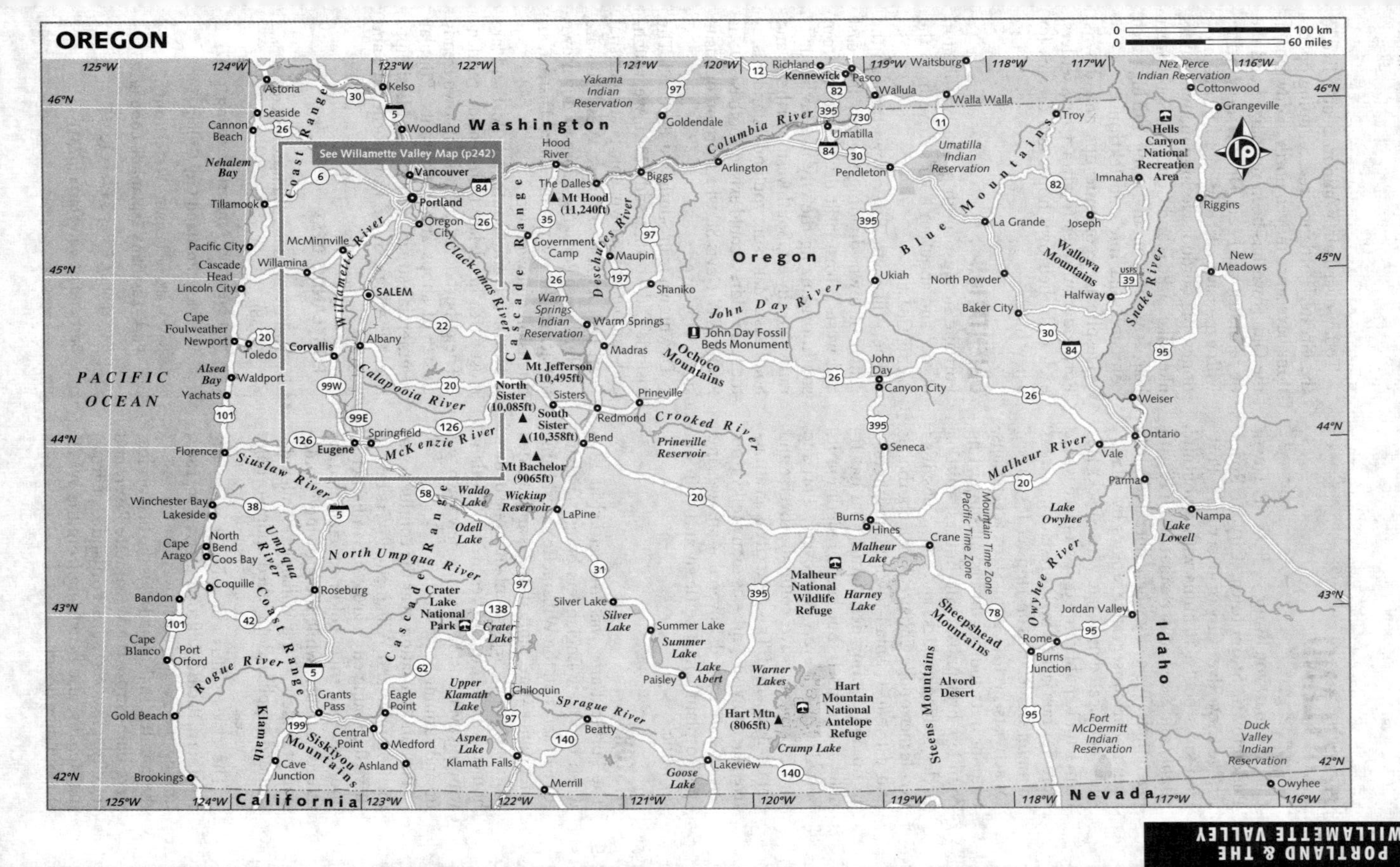
OREGON
0 100 km
0 60 miles
125°W
124°W
123°W
122°W
121°W
120°W
119°W
118°W
117°W
116°W
46°N
45°N
44°N
43°N
42°N
PACIFIC OCEAN
Washington
Oregon
Idaho
Nevada
California
See Willamette Valley Map (p242)
Astoria
Seaside
Cannon Beach
Nehalem Bay
Tillamook
Pacific City
Cascade Head
Lincoln City
Cape Foulweather
Newport
Toledo
Alsea Bay
Waldport
Yachats
Florence
Winchester Bay
Lakeside
North Bend
Coos Bay
Cape Arago
Coquille
Bandon
Cape Blanco
Port Orford
Gold Beach
Brookings
Kelso
Woodland
Vancouver
Portland
Oregon City
SALEM
McMinnville
Willamina
Corvallis
Albany
Eugene
Springfield
Roseburg
Grants Pass
Central Point
Medford
Ashland
Eagle Point
Cave Junction
Klamath
Klamath Falls
Merrill
Chiloquin
Beatty
Lakeview
Paisley
Summer Lake
Silver Lake
LaPine
Bend
Redmond
Sisters
Prineville
Madras
Warm Springs
Shaniko
Maupin
Government Camp
Hood River
The Dalles
Biggs
Goldendale
Arlington
Richland
Kennewick
Pasco
Umatilla
Wallula
Pendleton
Walla Walla
Waitsburg
Ukiah
La Grande
North Powder
Baker City
Halfway
Joseph
Imnaha
Troy
John Day
Canyon City
Seneca
Burns
Hines
Crane
Vale
Ontario
Parma
Weiser
Nampa
Riggins
New Meadows
Grangeville
Cottonwood
Jordan Valley
Rome
Burns Junction
Owyhee
Coast Range
Cascade Range
Blue Mountains
Wallowa Mountains
Ochoco Mountains
Sheepshead Mountains
Steens Mountains
Siskiyou Mountains
Alvord Desert
Mt Hood (11,240ft)
Mt Jefferson (10,495ft)
North Sister (10,085ft)
South Sister (10,358ft)
Mt Bachelor (9065ft)
Hart Mtn (8065ft)
Columbia River
Deschutes River
John Day River
Crooked River
Snake River
Malheur River
Owyhee River
Willamette River
Clackamas River
Calapooia River
McKenzie River
Siuslaw River
Umpqua River
North Umpqua River
Rogue River
Sprague River
Lake Owyhee
Lake Lowell
Malheur Lake
Harney Lake
Warner Lakes
Crump Lake
Lake Abert
Summer Lake
Silver Lake
Goose Lake
Upper Klamath Lake
Aspen Lake
Crater Lake
Odell Lake
Waldo Lake
Wickiup Reservoir
Prineville Reservoir
Crater Lake National Park
Hells Canyon National Recreation Area
John Day Fossil Beds Monument
Malheur National Wildlife Refuge
Hart Mountain National Antelope Refuge
Nez Perce Indian Reservation
Umatilla Indian Reservation
Yakama Indian Reservation
Warm Springs Indian Reservation
Fort McDermitt Indian Reservation
Duck Valley Indian Reservation
Mountain Time Zone
Pacific Time Zone
USFS 39
5
6
12
20
22
26
30
31
35
38
42
58
62
78
82
84
95
97
99E
99W
101
126
138
140
197
199
395
730

PORTLAND

Call it what you want – PDX, P-Town, Puddletown, Stumptown, City of Roses, Bridge City, River City or Beervana – Portland kicks booty. It hums with a youthful vitality and personal style that aren't easy to pigeonhole. It's a city where liberal idealists outnumber conservative stogies by a landslide, but located in a state where backroads brim with Republican red. It's a place where Gore-Tex rain jackets in fine restaurants are as common as sideburns on a hipster. It's a haven for activists, cyclists, grungsters, vegetarians, outdoor nuts and dog-lovers, all supporting countless brewpubs, coffeehouses, knitting circles, lesbian potlucks and book clubs. It's a livable metropolis with pretty neighborhoods and a friendly, small-town atmosphere – an up-and-coming destination that has finally found itself, but keeps redefining its boundaries with every controversy. Portland is racially progressive, culturally diverse and politically charged. This great city is an attractive place to visit, and – as many folks from out of state have discovered – an awesome spot to plant roots, settle in and chill out for while.

HISTORY

The Portland area was first settled in 1844 when two New Englanders bought a claim for 640 acres on the Willamette's west bank. They built a store, plotted streets and decided to name the new settlement after one of their hometowns: a coin toss resulted in Portland winning over Boston, and the new town was up and running.

Portland's location near the confluence of the Columbia and Willamette Rivers helped drive the young city's growth. San Francisco and the Californian gold rush clamored for Oregon lumber, while the growing population of settlers in the Willamette Valley demanded supplies. Both relied upon Portland for services.

The city's status got a boost when the Northern Pacific Railroad arrived in 1883, linking the Pacific Northwest to the rest of the country. In the late 1880s the first bridges were built across the Willamette River, and the city spread eastward. Portland kept growing steadily, also benefiting from the WWII shipbuilding boom.

Today over half a million people live in the Greater Portland area. Shipping operations have since moved north of downtown, the Old Town has been revitalized and the once-industrial Pearl District now brims with expensive lofts and sophisticated boutiques. Big outdoor-clothing manufacturers like Nike, Adidas and Columbia Sportswear help drive the economy, along with high-tech companies like Intel and Tektronix.

Despite its economic ups and downs, Portland continues to attract new settlers, each with their own hopes and dreams for a new life.

ORIENTATION

Portland lies just south of the Washington border and about an hour's drive from the Pacific Coast.

The Willamette River flows through the center of town, dividing the city into east and west. Burnside St divides north from south, organizing the city into four quadrants: Northwest, Southwest, Northeast and Southeast. Make sure you understand this, as the same address could exist on both NE Davis St and NW Davis St, which are on opposite sides of the river!

Downtown is in Southwest Portland. The historic Old Town, trendy 23rd Ave, rough-and-tumble Chinatown, chic post-industrial Pearl District and exclusive West Hills are in Northwest Portland. Close to downtown but across the river is the Lloyd District, an extension of downtown.

Northeast and Southeast Portland are mostly tree-lined, late 19th-century residential neighborhoods, each with its own trendy cluster of shops and restaurants. Popular commercial streets include N Mississippi Ave, NE Alberta St, SE Hawthorne Blvd and

PORTLAND'S BEST

- Best coffeehouse: **Stumptown Coffee** (p238)
- Best brewpub: **Amnesia Brewing** (p237)
- Best view: **Portland City Grill** (p234)
- Best walk/cycle route: **Waterfront Park–Eastbank Esplanade Loop** (p223)
- Best dinner: **Paley's Place** (p235)
- Best oddity: **Velveteria** (p231)

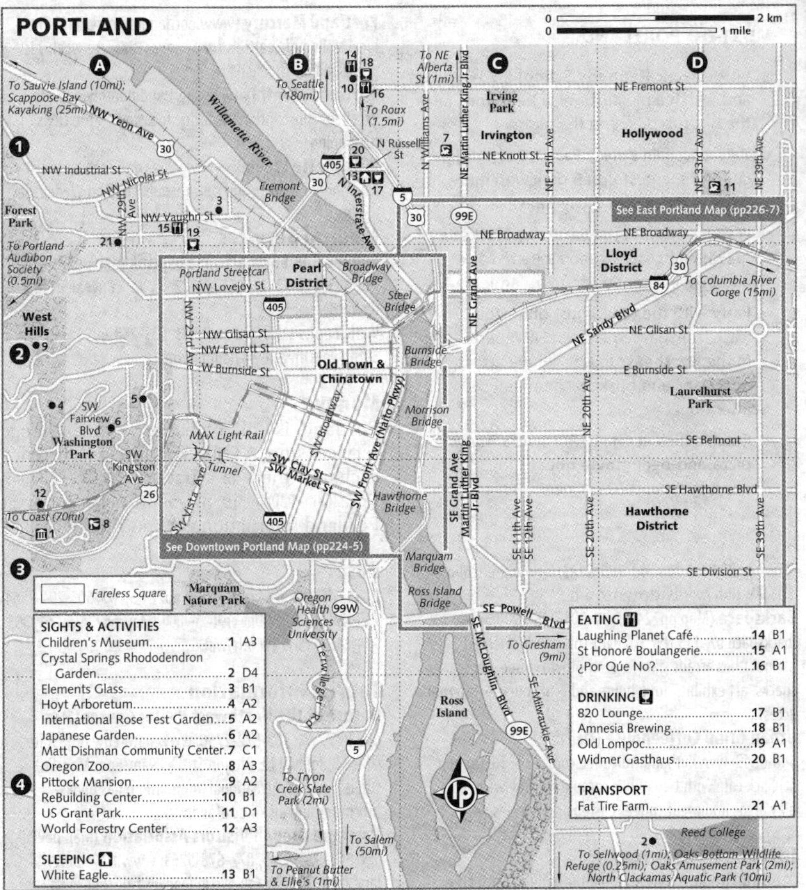

SE Division St. Sellwood is furthest south and a pretty neighborhood with antique stores and yuppies.

INFORMATION

Bookstores

Broadway Books (Map pp226-7; ☎ 503-284-1726; 1714 NE Broadway) Good general bookstore with especially strong literary fiction, biography and Judaica sections.

CounterMedia (Map pp224-5; ☎ 503-226-8141; 927 SW Oak St) Liberally minded books on fringe culture and vintage erotica.

In Other Words (off Map pp226-7; ☎ 503-232-6003; 8 NE Killingsworth St) Feminist bookstore and resource center.

Powell's City of Books (Map pp224-5; ☎ 503-228-4651; www.powells.com; 1005 W Burnside St) The USA's largest independent bookstore, with a whole city block of new and used titles. Has other branches around town, including at 3723 SE Hawthorne.

Reading Frenzy (Map pp224-5; ☎ 503-274-1449; 921 SW Oak St) Emporium of indie zines, comics and books that supports Portland writers and artists.

Emergency

The **police station** (Map pp224-5; ☎ 503-823-0000; 1111 SW 2nd Ave) is downtown. Call ☎ 911 for medical, fire or crime emergencies.

Internet Access

Practically all cafés have wi-fi. A city-wide wireless network is being finished. All Multnomah County (Portland's county) libraries have free internet access. The **Central Library**

MUST-DO PORTLAND

- Visit eclectic **Kennedy School** (p234) and watch a movie, drink a beer, soak in the hot tub or spend the night.
- Take a walk in **Forest Park** (p229), the country's largest urban park with more than 70 miles of woodsy trails.
- Wander through the **Saturday Market's** (p225) crafts stalls, grab a bite to eat and take in street performers' antics.
- Party with the hip (or just obnoxious) 'Last Thursday' crowds on NE Alberta in the **Northeast** (p228), where artists, musicians and buskers compete for attention.
- Catch a flick at one of Portland's many pizza-and-beer **movie houses** (p238), offering second-run screenings for $3.

(Map pp224-5; ☎ 503-988-5123; www.multcolib.org; 801 SW 10th Ave) is downtown.

Backspace (Map pp224-5; ☎ 503-248-2900; www.backspace.bz; 115 NW 5th Ave) This youth-oriented hangout has arcade games, Stumptown coffee, vegetarian snacks, art exhibits, long hours and – of course – internet access.

Urban Grind Coffeehouse (Map pp226-7; ☎ 503-546-0649; www.urbangrindcoffee.com; 2214 NE Oregon St) Slick café with two public computers, free wi-fi, kids' play areas and great coffee roasted on premises.

Internet Resources

Around the Sun (www.aroundthesunblog.com) Free things going on around Portland.

City of Portland (www.portlandonline.com) Stumptown's official website.

Gay Oregon (www.gaypdx.com) A resource for Portland's gay and lesbian communities.

PDX Guide (www.pdxguide.com) Fun and spot-on food and drink reviews, plus other happenings around town.

Portland Independent Media Center (www.portland.indymedia.org) Open publishing source of community news and lefty activism.

Portland Picks (www.portlandpicks.com) A gal's trendy list of restaurants, shops, services and events.

Media

Just Out (www.justout.com) Free bi-weekly serving Portland's gay community.

KBOO 90.7 FM Progressive local radio station run by volunteers; alternative news and views.

Portland Mercury (www.portlandmercury.com) The local sibling of Seattle's *The Stranger*, this free weekly is published on Thursday.

Portland Monthly (www.portlandmonthlymag.com) Excellent subscription magazine focusing on the city's happenings.

Willamette Week (www.wweek.com) Free alt-weekly covering local news and culture, published on Wednesday.

Medical Services

Legacy Good Samaritan Hospital (Map pp224-5; ☎ 503-413-7711; 1015 NW 22nd Ave) Convenient to downtown.

Walgreens (Map pp226-7; ☎ 503-238-6053; 940 SE 39th Ave) Offers a 24-hour pharmacy.

Money

Portland is full of banks with exchange services and ATMs. For foreign-currency exchange there is a **Travelex** (☎ 503-281-3045; 5:30am-4:30pm) in the main ticket lobby at Portland International Airport (p240).

Post

Post office main branch (Map pp224-5; ☎ 503-294-2564; 715 NW Hoyt St); University Station (Map pp224-5; ☎ 503-274-1362; 1505 SW 6th Ave).

Tourist Information

Nature of the Northwest Visitor Center (Map pp226-7; ☎ 503-872-2750; www.naturenw.org; State Office Bldg, 800 NE Oregon St; 9am-5pm Mon-Fri) Offers outdoor recreational information; has books, brochures and all kinds of maps.

Portland Oregon Visitors Association (Map pp224-5; ☎ 503-275-8355, 877-678-5263; www.travelportland.com; 701 SW 6th Ave in Pioneer Courthouse Sq; 8:30am-5:30pm Mon-Fri, 10am-4pm Sat, 10am-2pm Sun) A small theater shows a 12-minute film about the city. Tri-Met bus and light-rail offices are also here.

SIGHTS

Downtown

Downtown Portland is an urban success story. An activist city government began work in the 1970s to ensure that Portland's business and nightlife did not flee the city center. They were successful, and downtown Portland remains a vibrant destination both day and night.

But with success comes certain problems – like parking. You can get lucky by finding a metered street space, but for a similar price there are seven **SmartPark** parking buildings that charge $1.25 per half-hour. Check www.portlandonline/smartpark for their locations.

PIONEER COURTHOUSE SQUARE

The heart of downtown Portland, this brick **plaza** (Map pp224–5) is nicknamed 'Portland's living room' and is the most visited public space in the city. When it isn't full of hacky-sack players, sunbathers or office workers lunching, the square hosts concerts, festivals, rallies – and even summer Friday night movies (aka 'Flicks on the Bricks'; details at www.pioneercourthousesquare.org).

One of Portland's grandest Victorian hotels once stood here, but it fell into disrepair and was torn down. Later the city decided to build Pioneer Courthouse Square, and grassroots support resulted in a program that encouraged citizens to buy and personalize the bricks that eventually built the square. Names include John F Kennedy, Bruce Springsteen and Frodo Baggins.

Across 6th Ave is the **Pioneer Courthouse** (Map pp224–5). Built in 1875, this was the legal center of 19th-century Portland.

SOUTH PARK BLOCKS

Two important museums flank the South Park Blocks, the 12-block-long greenway that runs through much of the downtown. The blocks themselves are a fine leafy refuge from downtown's bustle, and host a farmers market and occasional art shows.

The **Oregon Historical Society** (Map pp224-5; ☎ 503-222-1741; www.ohs.org; 1200 SW Park Ave; adult/6-18yr/senior $10/5/8; 10am-5pm Tue-Sat, noon-5pm Sun) is the state's largest historical museum, and includes a research library. It has limited hours in winter.

Across the park, the **Portland Art Museum** (Map pp224-5; ☎ 503-226-2811; www.portlandartmuseum.org; 1219 SW Park Ave; adult/student 5-18yr/senior $10/6/9; 10am-5pm Tue, Wed & Sat, Thu & Fri till 8pm, noon-5pm Sun) has an especially good collection of Asian and Native American art. Upstairs galleries contain a small international collection, and blockbuster exhibits (extra cost) are mounted regularly.

At the southern end of the South Park Blocks is **Portland State University** (Map pp224–5), the city's largest university.

PORTLAND BUILDING & PORTLANDIA

This notoriously controversial **building** (Map pp224-5; cnr SW 5th Ave and SW Main St) was designed by Michael Graves and catapulted the postmodern architect to celebrity status. People working inside the blocky, pastel-colored edifice, however, have had to deal with tiny windows, cramped spaces and a general user-unfriendliness. The Portland Building suffered from major design flaws that later proved very costly to fix. Not a great start for what was considered to be the world's first major postmodern structure.

Towering above the main doors of the Portland Building is **Portlandia**, an immense statue of the Goddess of Commerce – Portland's supposed patroness. This crouching figure is, at 36ft, the second-largest hammered-copper statue in the world (after the Statue of Liberty).

TOM MCCALL WATERFRONT PARK

This popular riverside **park** (Map pp224–5), which lines the west bank of the Willamette River, was finished in 1978 after four years of construction. It replaced an old freeway with 2 miles of paved sidewalks and grassy spaces, attracting heaps of joggers, in-line skaters, strollers and cyclists. During the summer, the park is perfect for hosting outdoor events like the Oregon Brewers Festival. Walk over the Steel and Hawthorne bridges to the **Eastbank Esplanade** (Map pp224–5), making a 3-mile loop.

Salmon Street Springs Fountain (Map pp224–5), on Salmon St near the river, cycles through computer-generated patterns. On hot days, kids (and adults) take turns plunging through the jets. North of the Burnside Bridge is the Japanese-American Historical Plaza, a memorial to Japanese Americans who were interned by the US government during WWII. **River Place** (Map pp224–5), at the southern end of Waterfront Park, is a hotel, restaurant and apartment complex overlooking a marina.

OLD TOWN & CHINATOWN

The core of rambunctious 1890s Portland, the once-seedy Old Town used to be the lurking grounds of unsavory characters, but today disco queens outnumber drug dealers. It's one of the livelier places in town after dark, when nightclubs and bars open their doors and the hipsters start showing up.

Running beneath Old Town's streets are the **shanghai tunnels**, a series of underground corridors through which unscrupulous people would kidnap or 'shanghai' drunken men and sell them to sea captains looking for indentured workers. Call the **Cascade Geographic Society** (☎ 503-622-4798; tours by appointment; adult/12yr & under $12/7) for tours.

DOWNTOWN PORTLAND

A B C D
1 2 3 4 5 6

To Forest Park (1.75mi)
To Sauvie Island (10mi)
To Forest Park (0.75mi)
Northwest
Pearl District
Couch Park
North Park Blocks
Union Station (Amtrak)
Pioneer Courthouse Square
Downtown
Lownsdale Square
Chapman Square
South Park Blocks
Portland State University
Portland Heights
Pettygrove Park
Portland Streetcar
MAX Light Rail
NW Overton St
NW Northrup St
NW Marshall St
NW Lovejoy St
NW Kearney St
NW Johnson St
NW Irving St
NW Hoyt St
NW Glisan St
NW Flanders St
NW Everett St
NW Davis St
NW Couch St
W Burnside St
SW Ankeny St
SW Oak St
SW Stark St
SW Washington St
SW Alder St
SW Morrison St
SW Yamhill St
SW Taylor St
SW Salmon St
SW Main St
SW Madison St
SW Jefferson St
SW Columbia St
SW Clay St
SW Market St
SW Mill St
NW 23rd Ave
NW 22nd Ave
NW 21st Ave
NW 20th Pl
NW 20th Ave
NW 19th Ave
NW 18th Ave
NW 17th Ave
NW 16th Ave
NW 15th Ave
NW 14th Ave
NW 13th Ave
NW 12th Ave
NW 11th Ave
NW 10th Ave
NW 9th Ave
NW Park Ave
NW 8th Ave
NW Broadway
NW 6th Ave
SW Vista Ave
SW 14th Ave
SW 13th Ave
SW 12th Ave
SW 11th Ave
SW 10th Ave
SW 9th Ave
SW Park Ave
SW Broadway
SW 6th Ave
SW 5th Ave
SW 4th Ave
405
26

INFORMATION

Backspace.......1 E3
Central Library.......2 C4
CounterMedia.......3 D3
Legacy Good Samaritan Hospital.......4 A1
Police Station.......5 D5
Portland Oregon Visitors Association..6 D4
Post Office Main Branch.......7 D2
Post Office University Station.......8 C5
Powell's City of Books.......9 C3
Reading Frenzy.......10 D3

SIGHTS & ACTIVITIES

Chinatown Gates.......11 E3
Classical Chinese Garden.......12 E2
Jamison Square Fountain.......13 C1
Mill Ends Park.......14 E4
Museum of Contemporary Craft.......15 D2
New Market Theater.......16 E3
Oregeon Historical Society.......17 C4
Pioneer Courthouse.......18 D4
Portland Art Museum.......19 C4
Portland Building.......20 D4
Portland River Company.......21 E6
Salmon Street Springs Fountain.......22 E5
Saturday Market.......23 E3
Skidmore Fountain.......24 E3

SLEEPING

Ace Hotel.......25 D3
Benson Hotel.......26 D3
Governor Hotel.......27 C3
Heathman Hotel.......28 D4
Hotel deLuxe.......29 B3
Hotel Lucia.......30 D3
Hotel Monaco.......31 D3
Hotel Vintage Plaza.......32 D3
Inn at Northrup Station.......33 B1
Mark Spencer Hotel.......34 C3
Northwest Portland Hostel.......35 B2

EATING

Bijou Café.......36 E3
Blossoming Lotus.......37 D2
Bluehour.......38 C2
Jake's Famous Crawfish.......39 C3
Ken's Artisan Bakery.......40 A2
La Buca.......41 A1
Laurelwood Public House & Brewery.42 A1
Mother's Bistro.......43 E3
Paley's Place.......44 A1
Portland City Grill.......45 D3
Silk.......46 D2
Voodoo Donuts.......(see 54)

DRINKING

Anna Bananas.......47 A1
Brazen Bean.......48 A2
BridgePort Brewpub.......49 C1
Saucebox.......50 D3
Thirst Wine Bar.......51 E6

ENTERTAINMENT

Arlene Schnitzer Concert Hall.......52 D4
Artists Repertory Theatre.......53 B3
Berbati's Pan.......54 E3
Cinema 21.......55 A2
Crystal Ballroom.......56 C3
Dante's.......57 E3
Darcelle XV.......58 E2
Embers.......59 D3
Hobo's.......60 E2
Jimmy Mak's.......61 D2
Keller Auditorium.......62 D5
Mission Theater.......63 B2
Portland Center Stage.......64 D2

TRANSPORT

Greyhound Bus Station.......65 D2
Waterfront Bicycle Rentals.......66 E6

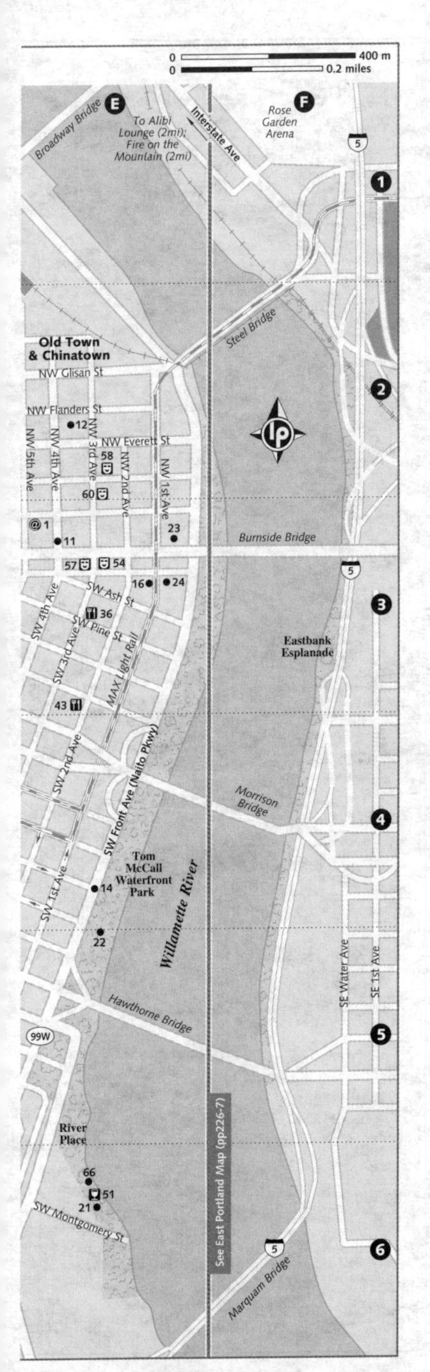

The ornate **Chinatown Gates** (Map pp224–5) define the southern edge of Portland's so-called Chinatown – you'll be lucky to find any Chinese people here at all (most are on 82nd Ave over to the east). There are a few token Chinese restaurants, but the main attraction is the **Classical Chinese Gardens** (Map pp224-5; ☎ 503-228-8131; www.portlandchinesegarden.org; NW 3rd Ave & Everett St; adult/senior $7/6; 10am-5pm). It's a one-block haven of tranquility, reflecting ponds and manicured greenery. Free tours available with admission.

SATURDAY MARKET & SKIDMORE FOUNTAIN

Victorian-era architecture and the lovely **Skidmore Fountain** (Map pp224–5) give the area beneath the Burnside Bridge some flair. Hit it on a weekend to catch the **Saturday Market** (Map pp224-5; ☎ 503-222-6072; www.portlandsaturdaymarket.com; 108 W Burnside St; 10am-5pm Sat & 11am-4:30pm Sun Mar-Dec), a fun outdoor crafts fair (also open Sunday) with street entertainers and food carts.

Beside the fountain is the **New Market Theater** (Map pp224–5), built in 1871 as Portland's first theater for stage productions. It's now home to shops and restaurants.

West Hills

This area is known for its exclusive homes, windy streets and Forest Park (see p229).

The **Portland Audubon Society** (off Map p221; ☎ 503-292-6855; www.audubonportland.org; 5151 NW Cornell Rd; 10am-6pm store, trails open dawn-dusk) is nestled in a gulch beside Forest Park. Visit the bookstore and wildlife rehabilitation center, then walk along 4 miles of forested trails in their nature sanctuary.

The grand and beautiful 1914 **Pittock Mansion** (Map p221; ☎ 503-823-3623; www.pittockmansion.com; 3229 NW Pittock Dr; adult/6-18yr/senior $7/4/6; 11am-4pm) was built by pioneer/entrepreneur Henry Pittock, who revitalized the *Oregonian* newspaper. Guided tours are available, but it's worth visiting the (free) grounds simply to have a picnic while taking in the spectacular views.

WASHINGTON PARK

This enormous park complex (Map p221), which includes the city's zoo, rose gardens and an arboretum, is perched on the slopes of the West Hills.

The **International Rose Test Gardens** (Map p221; ☎ 503-823-3636; 400 SW Kingston Ave) practically

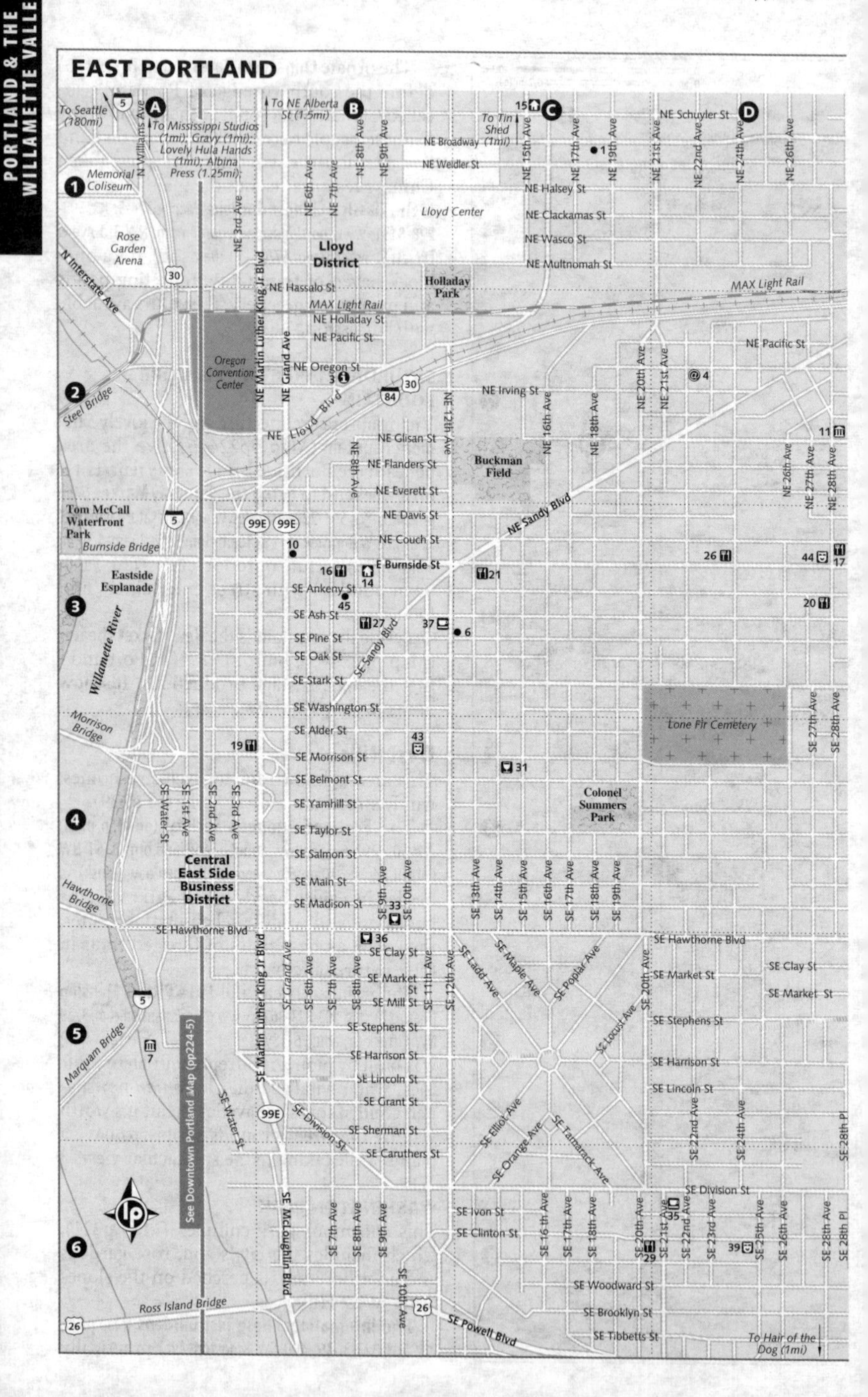
EAST PORTLAND
To Seattle (180mi)
To Mississippi Studios (1mi); Gravy (1mi); Lovely Hula Hands (1mi); Albina Press (1.25mi)
To NE Alberta St (1.5mi)
To Tin Shed (1mi)
Memorial Coliseum
Rose Garden Arena
Lloyd District
Lloyd Center
Holladay Park
Oregon Convention Center
Buckman Field
Tom McCall Waterfront Park
Eastside Esplanade
Willamette River
Lone Fir Cemetery
Colonel Summers Park
Central East Side Business District
MAX Light Rail
Steel Bridge
Burnside Bridge
Morrison Bridge
Hawthorne Bridge
Marquam Bridge
Ross Island Bridge
N Interstate Ave
NE Lloyd Blvd
NE Sandy Blvd
SE Sandy Blvd
SE Hawthorne Blvd
SE Division St
SE Powell Blvd
SE McLoughlin Blvd
NE Martin Luther King Jr Blvd
NE Grand Ave
E Burnside St
See Downtown Portland Map (pp224-5)
To Hair of the Dog (1mi)

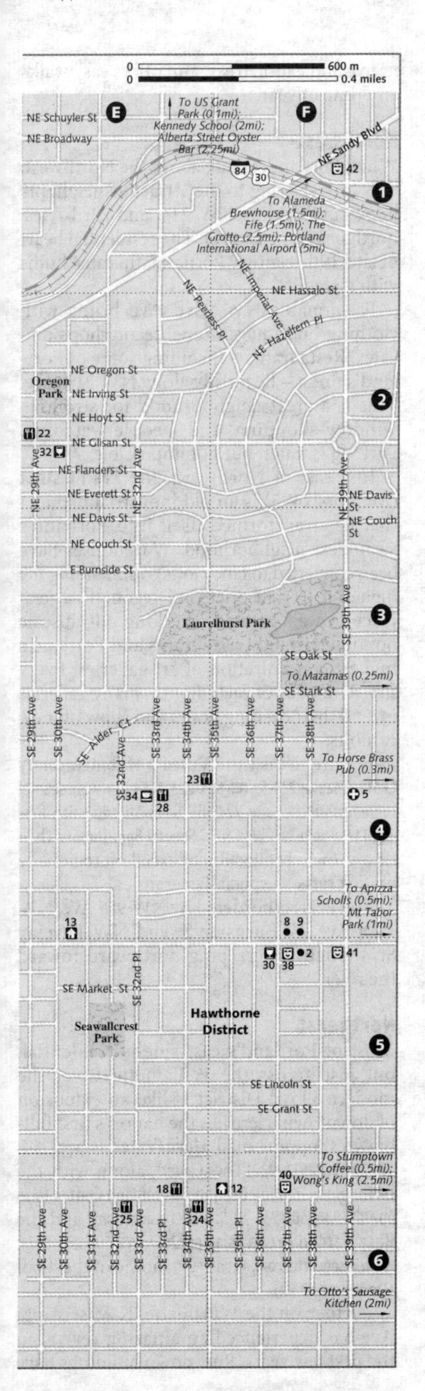

INFORMATION

Broadway Books......1 C1
In Other Words......2 F5
Nature of the Northwest Visitor Center......3 B2
Urban Grind Coffeehouse......4 D2
Walgreens......5 F4

SIGHTS & ACTIVITIES

FH Steinbart Co......6 C3
Oregon Museum of Science & Industry (OMSI)......7 A5
Powell's on Hawthorne......8 F4
Powell's Books for Cooks......9 F4
Stark's Vacuum Museum......10 B3
Velveteria......11 D2

SLEEPING

Bluebird Guesthouse......12 F6
Hawthorne Portland Hostel......13 E4
Jupiter Hotel......14 B3
Lion & the Rose......15 C1

EATING

Farm Café......16 B3
La Buca......17 D3
Lauro......18 E6
Montage......19 A4
Noble Rot......20 D3
Old Wives' Tales......21 C3
Pambiche......22 E2
Paradox Café......23 E4
Pix Patisserie......24 E6
Pok Pok......25 E6
Screen Door......26 D3
Simpatica Dining Hall......27 B3
Utopia Café......28 E4
Vindalho......29 C6

DRINKING

Back Stage Bar......(see 38)
BridgePort Ale House......30 F5
Crush......31 C4
Doug Fir......(see 14)
Laurelthirst Pub......32 E2
Lucky Labrador Brewing Company......33 B4
Pied Cow Coffeehouse......34 E4
Red & Black Café......35 D6
Roots Organic Brewing......36 B5
Three Friends Coffeehouse......37 B3

ENTERTAINMENT

Bagdad Theater......38 F5
Clinton Street Theatre......39 D6
Egyptian Room......40 F6
Hawthorne Theatre......41 F5
Hollywood Theatre......42 F1
Holocene......43 B4
Laurelhurst Theater......44 D3

TRANSPORT

City Bikes Annex......45 B3

TALK LIKE A LOCAL – A PRONUNCIATION PREMIER:

Aloha – Uh-LOW-uh (Portland suburb)
Couch – Cooch (Portland street)
Multnomah – Mult-NO-muh (Portland's county name)
Oregon – OR-uh-gun (Portland's state)
Tigard – Tie-gird (Portland suburb)
Willamette – Will-ammit (Portland's river)

gave Portland its 'Rose City' nickname. The gardens sprawl across 4.5 acres of manicured lawns, fountains and flowerbeds, and on a clear day you can catch peeks of downtown and Mt Hood. Over 400 rose varieties grow in the permanent gardens, including many old and rare varieties. From May to October, the scent and colors are intoxicating. Call ahead for tours.

Just uphill from the roses lie the tranquil, formal **Japanese Garden** (Map p221; ☎ 503-223-1321; www.japanesegarden.com; 611 SW Kingston Ave; adult/6-17yr/senior $8/5.25/6.25; 10am-7pm Tue-Sun, noon-7pm Mon). The grounds encompass 5 acres of tumbling water, koi ponds, ornamental cherry trees, a ceremonial teahouse (no drinks served!) and a sand garden. Tours are available, and hours are limited in winter.

In summer, ride the Zoo Train from the rose gardens to the excellent **Oregon Zoo** (Map p221; ☎ 503-226-1561; www.oregonzoo.org; 4001 SW Canyon Rd; adult/3-11yr/senior $9.75/6.75/8.25; 8am-6pm in summer). There's a primate house, a 'penguinarium' and exhibits on the Alaskan tundra and Amazon flooded forest. Enclosures are spacious and semi-natural, and big-name summer music concerts take place on the zoo's lawns.

Nearby is the **Children's Museum** (Map p221; ☎ 503-223-6500; www.portlandcm.org; 4015 SW Canyon Rd; admission $7; 9am-5pm Mon-Sat, 11am-5pm Sun), a great place to entertain the kids, and the **World Forestry Center** (Map p221; ☎ 503-228-1367; www.worldforestry.org; 4033 SW Canyon Rd; adult/3-18yr/senior $7/5/6; 10am-5pm), which informs the public about the importance of the world's forests.

Twelve miles of trails wind through the **Hoyt Arboretum** (Map p221; ☎ 503-865-8733; www.hoytarboretum.org; 4000 Fairview Blvd; admission free; visitor center 9am-4pm Mon-Fri, 9am-3pm Sat; park 6am-10pm), a 187-acre ridge-top garden above the zoo. It's home to over 1000 species of both native and exotic trees, and offers easy walks any time of year.

Northwest

When Portlanders talk about the Northwest, they are referring to the attractive neighborhood surrounding NW 21st and 23rd Aves, north of W Burnside St. The residential heart of late-19th-century Portland, this area hums with street life.

Fashionable NW 23rd Ave brims with clothing boutiques, home decor shops and cafés. Restaurants – including some of Portland's finest – lie mostly along NW 21st Ave. This is a great neighborhood for strolling, window-shopping and people-watching. Parking is tough but not impossible.

Just east of Northwest, the **Pearl District** (Map pp224–5) is an old industrial precinct that has transformed itself into Portland's swankiest neighborhood. Warehouses have been converted to fancy lofts commanding the highest real estate prices in Oregon. It's a great place to walk around, checking out upscale boutiques, trendy restaurants and Portland's highest concentration of art galleries. Every first Thursday of each month, many galleries extend their evening hours and show off new exhibits.

Be sure to visit the **Museum of Contemporary Craft** (Map pp224-5; ☎ 503-223-2654; www.museumofcontemporarycraft.org; 724 NW Davis St; admission free; 11am-6pm Tue, Wed & Fri-Sun, till 8pm Thu) with a fine, growing collection of excellent regionally made crafts – especially ceramics.

The Pearl is bordered by NW 9th Ave, NW 14th Ave, W Burnside St and NW Lovejoy St, though it's creeping northward toward the river.

Northeast

Most of Portland's east side is residential, but just across the Willamette River the modern Lloyd District is like an extension of downtown. Here lies the nation's first full-blown shopping mall, **Lloyd Center** (Map pp226-7; ☎ 503-2822511; 2201 Lloyd Center), along with the twin-glass-tower **Oregon Convention Center** (Map pp226-7; ☎ 503-235-7575; www.oregoncc.org) and the **Rose Garden Arena** (Map pp226-7; ☎ 503-235-8771; www.rosequarter.com; 1 Center Crt), home of the Trail Blazers (p239).

Further up the Willamette, N Mississippi Ave has experienced an amazing revival in the past few years. Run-down buildings have been transformed into trendy shops, cafés and restaurants – with the main anchor being the **ReBuilding Center** (off Map pp226-7; ☎ 503-331-1877; 3625 N Mississippi Ave; 9am-6pm Mon-Fri, 10am-5pm Sun), a cool recycling warehouse full of donated housing materials where you can find nearly anything building-related. Amnesia Brewing (see p237) is also based here.

Northeast of Mississippi, creatively spunky NE Alberta St is another success story. The stretch between NE 15th and NE 33rd Aves has revamped itself from a ribbon of vacant buildings, dubious bars and drug dealing into one of Portland's hippest streets. Despite the gentrification, it's still ethnically diverse and home to small art galleries, boutiques, studios and cafés. Don't miss the summertime street party that takes place every last Thursday of the month – it's an absolute hoot.

Southeast

The **Oregon Museum of Science & Industry** (OMSI; off Map pp224-5; ☎ 503-797-6674; www.omsi.edu; 1945 SE Water St; adult/3-13yr/senior $9/7/7; 9am-9pm) offers hands-on science exhibits for kids. There's also an Omnimax theater, planetarium shows and a submarine tour (all separate charge). The museum has limited winter hours.

Southeast is laced through with several trendy streets and good walking parks. The corner of E Burnside and 28th Ave boasts a few blocks' worth of wine bars, fine restaurants and cafés. Nearby is pretty **Laurelhurst Park** (Map pp226–7), with towering conifers, flocks of ducks and a murky lake. To the south is SE Belmont St (between 28th and 35th Sts), with its own stretch of casual eateries, bars and shops.

For a dose of hippie-hipster culture, visit the bohemian SE Hawthorne Blvd (between 30th and 45th Aves). It's a dynamic string of bookstores, cutesy shops, vintage clothing stores, brewpubs and cafés. You're almost guaranteed to be accosted by panhandlers or political activists; to escape them, head east to **Mt Tabor Park** (off Map pp226–7), home to a small extinct volcano that has great walking trails and good city views. Nearby is also Division St, another stretch of popular restaurants and shops surrounded by residential neighborhoods.

To the south is the 9.5-acre **Crystal Springs Rhododendron Garden** (Map p221; ☎ 503-771-8386; admission $3), near Reed College at SE 28th Ave and SE Woodstock St. Its large, beautiful grounds are covered with more than 2000 full-grown rhododendrons and azaleas and a large lagoon. Finally, way to the south lies Sellwood, an old working-class neighborhood known for its antique stores. **Oaks Bottom Wildlife Refuge** (off Map p221) is a large wetland with bike trails and good bird-watching, while the **Oaks Amusement Park** (off Map p221; ☎ 503-233-5777; www.oakspark.com; SE Oaks Park Way; admission free, ride bracelets $11.25-14) attracts families.

ACTIVITIES

Hiking

With over 5000 acres under its belt, **Forest Park** (Map p221) is the USA's largest park within city limits. There are more than 70 miles of trails for hikers, runners and dog-walkers,

OFF THE BEATEN PATH: SAUVIE ISLAND

About a 20-minute drive from downtown is Sauvie Island, an agricultural oasis providing an excellent break from Portland's bustle. Its flat, 12-mile country-road loop also make it a popular place for weekend cyclists.

The 12,000-acre **Sauvie Island Wildlife Area** includes a wetland sanctuary for thousands of migratory ducks, geese, tundra swans, bald eagles and Sandhill cranes. Permanent residents include peregrine falcons, great blue herons, foxes and beavers. The refuge is closed from October to mid-April and requires a $3.50 parking permit; get one from the **Fish & Wildlife Office** (18330 NW Sauvie Island Rd) or an island store.

During summer, don't miss the opportunity to pick strawberries, peaches, corn and flowers – try **Kruger's** or **Sauvie Island Farms**, both on NW Sauvie Island Rd. Plant lovers can head to the excellent, 2-acre **Cistus Nursery** (22711 NW Gillihan Rd), which specializes in Mediterranean and Southern Hemisphere plants.

Beach-heads should visit **Walton Beach**, a decent stretch of sand on the island's eastern side. Leashed dogs are allowed, but fires and camping are not. The $3.50 parking permit applies here too. Nudies can head towards **Collins Beach** at the northern end, past the pavement.

and some excellent fire roads for cyclists. The **Wildwood Trail** starts at the Hoyt Arboretum and winds through 30 miles of forest, with many spur trails allowing for loop hikes. Other trailheads into Forest Park are at the western ends of NW Thurman and NW Upshur Sts.

Out past Lewis & Clark College, in Southwest Portland, is 645-acre **Tryon Creek State Park** (off Map p221; ☎ 503-636-9886; 11321 SW Terwilliger Blvd). This verdant forest offers 8 miles of trails, including a 3-mile paved bike path, along with streamside wildlife. Late March brings wondrous displays of trillium, a wild marsh lily.

Cycling

Portland has been voted the USA's top bike-friendly city, and also boasts the highest percentage of bicycle commuters. For you, this means that great trails for both road and mountain bikes exist, including the fine **Springwater Corridor**. It heads from near the Oregon Museum of Science & Industry (p229) all the way to the suburb of Gresham – over 21 miles long, though until a connector is finished you'll have to pedal a few blocks of Sellwood's pleasant residential streets.

Mountain bikers shouldn't miss **Leif Erikson Dr**, a great old dirt logging road leading 11 miles into Forest Park (Map p229) and offering occasional peeks over the city. Avoid riding on hiking paths here, as you'd be poaching the trails.

For scenic farm country, head to **Sauvie Island** (p229), 10 miles northwest of downtown Portland. This island, the largest in the Columbia River, is prime cycling land – it's flat, has relatively little traffic and much of it is a wildlife refuge.

Cycling events worth taking part in include mid-August's **Bridge Pedal**, where thousands of Portlanders bike over bridges closed or partially closed to vehicular traffic; and mid-June's **Pedalpalooza**, a two-week celebration of the city's uniquely creative bike culture – including a naked ride.

Try to snag a free *Portland by Bicycle* or *Bike There!* map from the visitor center (p222) or a bike shop; both detail friendly bike streets and trails.

For bicycle rentals, see p240.

On the Water

Summer in Portland means finding cool things to do on hot days, and fortunately there's a few.

On hot days, visit the **Salmon Street Springs Fountain** (see p223) or the **Jamison Square Fountain** (Map pp224-5; NW Johnson & 10th), both of which attract splashing kids as the mercury rises.

Swimmers should grab their suits and beeline to the indoor pool at **Matt Dishman Community Center** (Map p221; ☎ 503-823-3673; 77 NE Knott St; admission $2-3.25).

For an outdoor experience, try the pool at **US Grant Park** (off Map pp226-7; ☎ 503-823-3674; cnr NE 33rd Ave & US Grant St; admission $2-3.25). Hours at both pools vary for different activities, so call beforehand.

About 10 miles south of downtown Portland are the water slides and indoor wave pool of **North Clackamas Aquatic Park** (off Map p221; ☎ 503-557-7873; 7300 SE Harmony Rd, Milwaukie; adult $10, child $5-7). There's also an outdoor volleyball court and deck, along with adults-only hot tub. Hours vary widely, so call ahead.

Kayakers can contact **Portland River Company** (☎ 503-229-0551; www.portlandrivercompany.com), which offers kayak tours around Ross Island in the Willamette River. To get away from the city, head to **Scappoose Bay Kayaking** (☎ 503-397-2161, 877-272-3353; www.scappoosebaykayaking.com; 57420 Old Portland Rd) in serene Scappoose Bay, 25 miles northwest of downtown Portland. Both companies also have rentals.

COURSES

If you're in the area for while and want to take a specific class, consider **Portland Community College** (www.pcc.edu), which offers courses on nearly anything you can think of. For food courses, see p59.

Glass-artist wannabes can take a beginning course at **Elements Glass** (off Map pp224-5; ☎ 503-228-0575; www.elementsglass.com; 1979 NW Vaughn St), Portland's largest glassblowing shop.

Plug into the adventure outdoor community with **Mazamas** (off Map pp226-7; ☎ 503 227-2345; www.mazamas.org; 527 SE 43rd Ave), an educational organization which gives courses on mountaineering, rock climbing and Nordic skiing, among others.

Beer-lovers can brew their own at **FH Steinbart Co** (Map pp226-7; ☎ 503-232-8793; www.fhsteinbart.com; 234 SE 12th Ave), a store which offers seasonal classes, along with a great selection of home-brewing equipment.

Learn to make avocado daiquiris with Lucy Brennan, voted one of America's top 10 bartenders by www.playboy.com. Two-hour classes cost $75 per person and take place once monthly at **820 Lounge** (off Map pp224-5; ☎ 503-284-5518; www.mintand820.com; 820 N Russell St).

PORTLAND FOR KIDS

Portland is a great place to raise a family, and sunny weekends mean the city's lush parks, shopping streets and farmers markets are filled with parents pushing baby strollers and dragging toddlers. If you're looking to entertain some kids here, there are some excellent options to consider.

The **Oregon Zoo** (p228) is a perennially popular destination; don't miss 'zoolights' during the holiday season, when the zoo becomes a winter wonderland filled with lit-up trees and animal figures. Parents also love the nearby **Children's Museum** (p228), a great place to keep the kids busy with hands-on learning activities and exhibits. Next door, **World Forestry Center** (p228) offers similar experiences but with a woodsy twist.

Another big family spot is the **Oregon Museum of Science & Industry** (p229), which combines fun with learning and has grown-up attractions as well. For outdoor laughs, head south to the riverside **Oaks Amusement Park** (p229). There are dizzying rides, go-karts and a skating rink. Hours vary widely, so call or check their website.

Hot day? Get ideas from the On the Water section on opposite.

Really great kid-friendly eateries include **Peanut Butter & Ellie's** (off Map p221; ☎ 503-282-1783; 4405 S W Vermont St), **Old Wives' Tales** (Map pp226-7; ☎ 503-238-0470; 1300 E Burnside St), **Laurelwood Public House & Brewery** (Map pp224-5; ☎ 503-228-5553; 2327 NW Kearney St) and **Urban Grind Café** (p222).

OFFBEAT PORTLAND

Portland is certainly eccentric – 'Keep Portland Weird' is the city's unofficial motto. For more oddball museums than those listed below, check www.hiddenportland.com.

Having the largest park (Forest Park) within city limits perhaps isn't an oddity in itself, but having the smallest one might be. Stop by **Mill Ends Park** (Map pp224–5) – located on the median strip at SW Naito Pkwy and Taylor St – and look for the circle of green 24in in diameter.

For strange museums, visit **Stark's Vacuum Museum** (Map pp226-7; ☎ 503-232-4101; www.starks.com; 107 NE Grand Ave; free admission; 🕒 8am-7pm Mon-Fri, 9am-5pm Sat, 11am-4pm Sun), located in a vacuum cleaner store (no surprise there). Truly unique, however, is the **Velveteria** (Map pp226-7; ☎ 503-233-5100; www.velveteria.com; 518 NE 28th Ave; admission $3; 🕒 noon-5pm Fri-Sun), a treasure-trove

PORTLAND PUB GURU: MIKE MCMENAMIN

A Portland native, Mike is one of two brothers who started the Pacific Northwest McMenamins empire that includes over 50 quirky brewpubs, hotels, restaurants, music venues and movie theaters – most located in historic buildings and decorated in highly eccentric style. They're all fun places to visit – see Kennedy School (p234), Edgefield (p259) or Bagdad Theater (p238) for exceptional examples, or visit www.mcmenamins.com.

Best things about Portland?

I think the neighborhoods here are fabulous; there are dozens of them that feel good and are not overly wrought. They have their own life and the buildings are great, beautiful. Northwest Portland has nearly every style imaginable and a lot of fun stuff. Portland is charming; rolling hills, proximity to a lot of stuff; it's a good spot, small-town feel…but it's getting faster, or I'm getting slower; that has to be it – it can't be me.

How do you find buildings to restore?

In the early days, we used to have to drive around and snoop stuff out; it was just gut feel and availability. But now we get piles and piles of suggestions, photos, brochures and calls from people that like that we preserve things and not change them dramatically. It's rewarding that they think of us like that, but it's also kind of unfortunate because we can't do everything.

How did Portland's microbrew movement get started?

There was a group of people – Portland Brewing, Widmer, us and Bridgeport – that were instrumental in getting that whole thing going. In 1985 it became law [that pubs could legally brew their own beer] and it's been a great thing. Every little pub could make their own beer, it's like making your own bread…you tend to think of a brewery as a vast thing, but it can be in the corner of the kitchen. That's what it's going back to.

full of stunning velvet paintings that will make you appreciate the art form; don't miss the Nudes Room.

There's nothing quite like **Voodoo Donuts** (Map pp224-5; ☎ 503-241-4704; www.voodoodonut.com; 22 SW 3rd Ave; 24hr) This standing-room-only, downtown hole-in-the-wall (pun intended) bakes up creative though sickly sweet treats – go for the surprisingly good bacon maple bar or 'cock & balls.' Check out their mid-week jam sessions (tiny stage above the bathroom), enter their annual cockfest (guys, stack them donuts you-know-where) and even get married for $175 (includes donuts and coffee for 10 people).

Finally, there's the **Grotto** (off Map pp226-7; ☎ 503-254-7371; www.thegrotto.org; NE 85th & Sandy Blvd; 9am-5pm), a 62-acre shrine-and-garden complex complete with *Pieta* replica in a carved out basalt cave.

TOURS

For kayak tours, see Activities section on p230.

Ecotours of Oregon (☎ 503-245-1428, 888-868-7733; www.ecotours-of-oregon.com) Naturalist tours of northwest Oregon, including the Columbia River Gorge, Mt St Helens and the wine country.

Portland Ducks (☎ 877-462-9382; www.portlandducks.com) Two-hour tours on amphibious vehicles that run on both land and water.

Portland Spirit (☎ 503-224-3900, 800-224-3901; www.portlandspirit.com) Tour Portland from the water; cruises offer sightseeing, historical narratives and/or meal combinations.

Portland Walking Tours (☎ 503-774-4522; www.portlandwalkingtours.com) Art, food, neighborhood, history, underground and even ghost-oriented tours.

FESTIVALS & EVENTS

There's some sort of festival in Portland nearly every summer weekend; even each neighborhood seems to have its own. See the visitor center for a complete list of events.

Portland International Film Festival (☎ 503-221-1156; www.nwfilm.org; mid-late Feb) Oregon's biggest film event highlights almost 100 films from over 30 countries, screened in several movie houses downtown.

Portland Rose Festival (☎ 503-227-2681; www.rosefestival.org; late May-early Jun) Rose-covered floats, dragon-boat races, a riverfront carnival, fireworks, roaming packs of sailors and the crowning of a Rose Queen all make this Portland's biggest celebration.

Queer Pride Celebration (☎ 503-295-9788; www.pridenw.org; mid-Jun) Keep Portland queer: enjoy a kick-off party, take a cruise or join the parade along with Dykes on Bikes.

Waterfront Blues Festival (☎ 503-973-3378; www.waterfrontbluesfest.com; early Jul) Enjoy top blues acts, music and partying at Waterfront Park; proceeds go to the Oregon Food Bank.

Oregon Brewers Festival (☎ 503-778-5917; www.oregonbrewfest.com; late Jul & early Dec) Quaff microbrews from near and far during the summer in Waterfront Park and during the winter at Pioneer Square. It's quintessential Portland.

Mt Hood Jazz Festival (☎ 503-661-2700; www.mthoodjazz.org; early Aug) Local and national jazz musicians whoop it up in Gresham, 12 miles east of Portland.

Northwest Film & Video Festival (☎ 503-221-1156; www.nwfilm.org/festivals/nwfvf.php; early Nov) A judged collection of the work of the Northwest's independent film and video makers.

SLEEPING

Tariffs listed are for high summer season, when reservations are a good idea. Prices at top-end hotels depend on occupancy, so are variable. Portland's 12.5% hotel tax is included below; parking costs listed are per day.

Downtown & Northwest

Northwest Portland Hostel (Map pp224-5; ☎ 503-241-2783; 425 NW 18th Ave; dm $25, d $39-79; P wi-fi) Perfectly located between the Pearl District and NW 21st and 23rd Aves, this friendly hostel takes up two buildings and features plenty of common areas (including a small deck), good rooms and bike rentals. Non HI-members pay $3 extra.

Ace Hotel (Map pp224-5; ☎ 503-228-2277; www.acehotel.com; 1022 SW Stark St; d with shared/private bathroom from $95/129; P) Currently Portland's trendiest place to sleep is this unique hotel fusing classic, industrial, minimalist and retro styles together. From the photo booth and sofa lounge in its lobby to the recycled fabrics and furniture in its rooms, the Ace makes the warehouse feel work. A Stumptown coffee shop on the premises adds even more comfort. Parking costs $20.

Mark Spencer Hotel (Map pp224-5; ☎ 503-224-3293, 800-548-3934; www.markspencer.com; 409 SW 11th Ave; d incl breakfast from $110; P -fi) A no-nonsense, downtown option is this simple yet slightly refined choice hosting spacious, unmemorable rooms, all with kitchens. There's complimentary tea with cookies in the afternoon. Don't be afraid of the alleyway-like entrance – they're friendly inside. Parking costs $16.

Benson Hotel (Map pp224-5; ☎ 503-228-2000, 800-663-1144; www.bensonhotel.com; 309 SW Broadway; d from $119; P wi-fi) The lobby is most impressive at this decadent hotel; it's lined with walnut and filled with huge chandeliers, marble floors and an elegant bar-restaurant. Some rooms can be small, but all boast Tempur-Pedic or pillowtop mattresses, and there's tea and wine service every afternoon. Parking costs $28.

Hotel Vintage Plaza (Map pp224-5; ☎ 503-228-1212, 800-243-0555; www.vintageplaza.com; 422 SW Broadway; d from $130; P wi-fi) For muted luxury there's this historic and tasteful hotel with low-key winery theme. It's a Kimpton, which means they do their part for the environment, so you can feel good while sipping pinot at their daily wine reception. Parking costs $27.

Hotel deLuxe (Map pp224-5; ☎ 503-219-2094, 866-895-2094; www.hoteldeluxeportland.com; 729 SW 15th Ave; d from $139; P wi-fi) Renovated historic hotel with old Hollywood movie theme, small but classy rooms and choose-your-own-pillow menu. Try for a corner room for the best light, and an upper floor for mountain views. Parking costs $24.

Inn at Northrup Station (Map pp224-5; ☎ 503-224-0543, 800-224-1180; www.northrupstation.com; 2025 NW Northrup St; d incl breakfast from $139; P) Almost over the top with its bright color scheme and funky decor, this super-trendy hotel boasts huge artsy suites, many with patio or balcony. There's a cool rooftop patio with plants.

Governor Hotel (Map pp224-5; ☎ 503-224-3400, 800-554-3456; www.governorhotel.com; 614 SW 11th Ave; d from $165; P wi-fi) Those not looking for frills will likely appreciate the Governor, with a grand lobby and classy executive-style rooms. For even more hedonistic comfort, go for the penthouse suites with glamorous terrace overlooking the city ($395). Parking costs $24.

Hotel Lucia (Map pp224-5; ☎ 503-225-1717, 877-225-1717; www.hotellucia.com; 400 SW Broadway; d from $175; P wi-fi) Those seeking luxurious tranquility in busy downtown Portland should head to this minimalist hotel, with limited color scheme (black and white are big here) and cutting-edge artwork in the lobby. There are iPod docking stations and flat-screen TVs, and plush robes come standard. Parking costs $26.

Hotel Monaco (Map pp224-5; ☎ 503-222-0001, 888-207-2201; www.monaco-portland.com; 506 SW Washington St; d from $179; P wi-fi) A lavishly loud lobby is decorated with Asian wallpaper, sensual furniture, patterned carpeting and brightly painted walls. Luckily the rooms are a bit quieter – though still somewhat extravagant in their decoration. Supremely pet friendly, with a lab roaming the premises and goldfish available for company. Parking costs $27.

Heathman Hotel (Map pp224-5; ☎ 503-241-4100, 800-551-0011; www.heathmanhotel.com; 1001 SW Broadway; d from $185; P wi-fi) A Portland institution, the Heathman has top-notch service and one of the best restaurants in the city. It also boasts high tea in the afternoons, jazz in the evenings and a library stocked with signed books by authors who have stayed here. Rooms are elegant, stylish and luxurious. Parking costs $30.

Northeast & Southeast

Hawthorne Portland Hostel (Map pp226-7; ☎ 503-236-3380; www.portlandhostel.org; 3031 SE Hawthorne Blvd; dm member/nonmember $22/25, d $48/54; wi-fi) With good vibes and a great Hawthorne location, this eco-friendly hostel offers artsy atmosphere, good homey rooms, a clean kitchen and fine grassy garden. Fine private rooms, co-ed dorms and open-mic night in summer; check out their planted eco-roof. Computer and bike rentals available.

White Eagle (off Map pp224-5; ☎ 503-335-8900, 866-271-3377; www.mcmenamins.com; 836 N Russell St; dm $30, d $39-59) In a small but hip industrial part of town is this old renovated hotel, another in the McMenamins empire. Nightly live rock-and-roll music creeps up from the downstairs saloon, but the 11 Spartan rooms (all with shared bathrooms) are a great deal.

Bluebird Guesthouse (Map pp226-7; ☎ 503-238-4333, 866-717-4333; www.bluebirdguesthouse.com; 3517 SE Division; d incl breakfast $54-79; wi-fi) Nicely located on a lively section of SE Division, this pleasant guesthouse is in a beautiful old arts-and-crafts house with country kitchen and small grassy backyard. There are seven tasteful rooms, two with private bathroom, and they're all different sizes. It's a good deal in an area without many accommodation options.

Jupiter Hotel (Map pp226-7; ☎ 503-230-9200; www.jupiterhotel.com; 800 E Burnside St; d $89-129 Sun-Thu, $112-155 Fri & Sat; wi-fi) The hippest hotel in town, this slick, remodeled motel is within walking distance of downtown and right next to Doug Fir (see p236), a top-notch live music venue. Standard rooms are tiny – go for the

WHERE TO GO FOR...

Bread – **Ken's Artisan Bakery** (Map pp224-5; ☎ 503-248-2202; 338 NW 21st Ave)
Dessert – **Pix Patisserie** (Map pp226-7; ☎ 503-232-4407; 3402 SE Division St)
Dim Sum – **Wong's King** (off Map pp226-7; ☎ 503-788-8883; 8733 SE Division St)
Kids meals – **Peanut Butter & Ellie's** (see p231)
Late-night snacks – **Montage** (Map pp226-7; ☎ 503-234-1324; 301 SE Morrison St)
Pizza – **Apizza Scholls** (off Map pp226-7; ☎ 503-233-1286; 4741 SE Hawthorne Blvd)
Vegan food – **Blossoming Lotus** (Map pp224-5; ☎ 503-228-0048; 925 NW Davis St; V)

Deluxe Metro instead, and ask for a pad away from the bamboo patio if you're more into sleeping than staying up all night. Check in after midnight for a discount.

Blue Plum Inn B&B (off Map pp226-7; ☎ 503-288-3848, 877-288-3844; www.bluepluminn.com; 2026 NE 15th Ave; d $95-130; wi-fi) Located at the edge of Portland's fancy Irvington neighborhood, this pretty B&B offers comfortable and unpretentious rooms. They use eco-products to clean and buy local products for the breakfast table. Close to shops, bars, cafés and Tri-Met's light-rail MAX line.

Kennedy School (off Map pp226-7; ☎ 503-249-3983, 888-249-3983; www.mcmenamins.com; 5736 NE 33rd Ave; d $99-125; wi-fi) Portland's most unusual institution, this former elementary school is now home to a hotel (sleep in old classrooms), restaurant (great garden courtyard), several bars, a microbrewery and movie theater. There's a soaking pool, and the whole school is decorated in McMenamins' funky art style – mosaics, fantasy paintings and historical photographs.

Lion & the Rose (Map pp226-7; ☎ 503-287-9245, 800-955-1647; www.lionrose.com; 1810 NE 15th Ave; d $155-189; wi-fi) Located at the edge of upscale Irvington, this turreted Queen Anne mansion is almost over the top with its fine antiques and flowery decoration. There are pastries and beverages available all day, and a lovely garden patio outside. This gay-friendly place is close to shops, bars, cafés and the MAX.

EATING

Portland holds its own when it comes to gourmet cuisine, boasting plenty of fine restaurants and seemingly a new one every week. Casual clothes are acceptable even at top-notch places, where reservations are a good idea. Fast-food lovers should consider looking up the various branches of Burgerville (local, healthier meats) and Laughing Planet (very vegetarian-friendly).

Downtown & Northwest

Office workers flock to SW 5th Ave and SW Stark St for international food carts. If it's raining and you want food that's cheap, quick and indoors, head to the basement food court of Pioneer Place shopping center.

St Honoré Boulangerie (Map p221; ☎ 503-445-4342; 2335 NW Thurman; light meals $5-7; 7am-8pm) Insanely popular for its luscious breads and pastries, this modern-rustic bakery also serves tasty panini sandwiches, vegetarian soups, seasonal salads and oven-fired pizzas. Try your luck at snagging a sidewalk table on a warm sunny day.

La Buca (Map pp224-5; ☎ 503-279-8040; 2309 NW Kearney St; mains $8-12; 11:30am-9pm Mon-Wed, till 10pm Thu & Fri, noon-10pm Sat, 5-9pm Sun; V) Some of the best value Italian food in town, as long as you like pasta, panini and salmon – that's about the extent of the menu. It's all good, however, with a contemporary and laid-back atmosphere. Also has a branch at 40 NE 28th Ave.

Silk (Map pp224-5; ☎ 503-248-2172; 1012 NW Glisan; mains $9-12; 11am-10pm Mon-Sat) Vietnamese-food lovers are in for a treat at this gorgeous Pearl District restaurant. Everything is fresh and delicious, from the banana blossom salad to claypot catfish to the beef noodle soup. Try the mango daiquiri. Also at 3404 SE Hawthorne and 1919 SE 82nd, both with the old name (Pho Van) and a slightly less fancy menu.

Jake's Famous Crawfish (Map pp224-5; ☎ 503-226-1419; 401 SW 12th Ave; mains $17-32; 11am-11pm Mon-Thu, till midnight Fri, noon-midnight Sat, 3-11pm Sun) Saunter into this classic joint, reservation in hand. You'll need it – some of Portland's best seafood can be found here within an elegant old-time atmosphere. The oysters are divine, the crab cakes a revelation and the horseradish salmon your ticket into heaven. Come at 3pm for (cheap) happy hour.

Portland City Grill (Map pp224-5; ☎ 503-450-0030; 111 SW 5th Ave; mains $18-47; 11am-midnight Mon-Thu, till 1am Fri, 4pm-1am Sat, 4-10pm Sun) Located on the 30th floor of Big Pink, Portland's tallest building, this aerie has views that are out of sight – but so are the prices. You'll have to get here early for a good table, or consider just dropping in for happy hour and some small plates. Good international menu.

Paley's Place (Map pp224-5; ☎ 503-243-2403; 1204 NW 21st; mains $20-32; ⏰ 5:30-10pm Mon-Thu, till 11pm Fri & Sat, 5-10pm Sun) Vitaly and Kimberly Paley have established one of Portland's premiere restaurants, offering a creative blend of French and Pacific Northwest cuisines. Whether it's the duck confit, Kobe burger or veal sweetbreads, you can count on fresh ingredients, excellent service and a memorable experience.

Bluehour (Map pp224-5; ☎ 503-226-3394; 250 NW 13th Ave; mains $21-29; ⏰ 11:30am-10pm Mon-Thu, till 10:30pm Fri & Sat, 10am-9pm Sun) This is one of Portland's snazziest restaurants, housed in an old warehouse converted into a hip post-industrial space with tall curtains softening the minimalist atmosphere. The food is first-rate – try the luscious wild salmon or bacon-wrapped scallops. Dessert is equally delicious, and the service is spot-on.

Northeast & Southeast

Noble Rot (Map pp226-7; ☎ 503-233-1999; 2724 SE Ankeny St; small plates $5-16; ⏰ 5pm-midnight Mon-Sat) Wine lovers should head to this upscale (but not pretentious) wine bar near the gourmet strip at 28th Ave and E Burnside St. Chef Leather Storrs whips up small creative plates that are great for sharing, while the daily wine flights (samplers) make varietal comparisons easy. Score a sidewalk table for best exposure.

Fire on the Mountain (off Map pp226-7; ☎ 503-280-9464; 4225 N Interstate Ave; mains $6-10; ⏰ 11am-10pm Sun-Thu, till 11pm Fri & Sat) The buffalo wings are pretty much the one reason to visit this BBQ joint – the buffalo wings. You have a choice in homemade sauces: try the Jamaican jerk, tequila chipotle or peanut raspberry habañero. There's even a veggie version, along with BBQ-oriented salads and sandwiches.

Pok Pok (Map pp226-7; ☎ 503-232-1387; 3226 SE Division St; mains $8-11; ⏰ 11.30am-10pm Mon-Fri, 5-10pm Sat) This popular Thai eatery gives you two seating options. Sashay up to the hole-in-the-wall counter and place your order, then have a seat outside on the patio or head down to the Whiskey Soda Lounge for much fancier inside seating. Either way it's great food and worth the inevitable wait.

Lovely Hula Hands (off Map pp226-7; ☎ 503-445-9910; 4057 N Mississippi; mains $10-21; ⏰ 5-10pm) Still testing its wings at a new location, this neighborhood favorite has that elegant yet homey feel, serving up a wide range of dishes like North African seven-vegetable stew, green garlic soufflé and rib-eye with asparagus fritto. Those in the know go for the less pricey hamburgers – some of the best in Portland. Try for a patio table in summer.

Pambiche (Map pp226-7; ☎ 503-233-0511; 2811 NE Glisan St; mains $11-17; ⏰ 11am-10pm Sun-Thu, till midnight Fri & Sat) Portland's best Cuban food, with a trendy and riotously colorful atmosphere. All your regular favorites like *ropa vieja* are available, but leave room for dessert. Lunch is a good deal, but happy hour is even better (2pm to 6pm Monday to Friday, 10pm to midnight Friday and Saturday). Be prepared to wait for dinner.

Farm Café (Map pp226-7; ☎ 503-736-3276; 10 SE 7th Ave; mains $12-20; ⏰ 5pm-11:30pm; V) From outside it's just an old white house, and you'll wonder what all the fuss is about. This is it: well-priced, very vegetarian-friendly food (plus good fish options) that's lovingly prepared and made using only local and organic ingredients. Add some good cocktails, a relaxing front deck and backyard patio, and you've got a memorable dining experience.

Vindalho (Map pp226-7; ☎ 503-467-4550; 2038 SE Clinton St; mains $14-17; ⏰ 5-10pm Tue-Sat) Modern with a traditional twist, this fancy Indian restaurant utilizes arousing Asian spices and an 800°F tandoori oven to create tasty and original dishes like lamb *boti kabob* (Oregon lamb in yogurt and mustard seed), *jhinga* prawns (in a chile and ginger sauce) and *theeyal* (Kerala-style vegetable curry with tamarind).

Lauro (Map pp226-7; ☎ 503-239-7000; 3377 SE Division St; mains $16-21; ⏰ 5-9pm Sun-Thu, till 10pm Fri & Sat) Renowned owner-chef David Machado opened his SE Division restaurant in 2003, beginning a neighborhood revitalization that continues today. Mediterranean-inspired dishes like chicken tagine and stuffed lamb shoulder grace Lauro's menu. Only the freshest, most local ingredients are used.

Alberta Street Oyster Bar (off Map pp226-7; ☎ 503-284-9600; 4926 NE Alberta St; mains $17-25; ⏰ 4:30-11pm) One of Alberta St's finer eateries, this lauded restaurant features about half a dozen of the tastiest shellfish – from Pacific oysters (Tomales Bay, California) to Kumamotos (Netarts Bay, Oregon). Appetizers and main dishes

BRUNCH ANYONE?

Here are some of Portland's favorites:

Screen Door (Map pp226-7; ☎ 503-542-0880; 2337 E Burnside St) Southern specialties and exceptional French toast.

Tin Shed (off Map pp226-7; ☎ 503-288-6966; 1438 NE Alberta) Hot NE Alberta spot with an awesome outside patio.

Mother's Bistro (Map pp224-5; ☎ 503-525-5877; 212 SW Stark St) Upscale downtown brunchery offering a guaranteed wait.

Gravy (off Map pp226-7; ☎ 503-287-8800; 3957 N Mississippi Ave) Hip N Mississippi joint serving up huge portions.

Utopia Café (Map pp226-7; ☎ 503-235-7606; 3308 SE Belmont St) Homey place with great blue corn pancakes and scrambles.

Bijou Café (Map pp224-5; ☎ 503-222-3187; 132 SW 3rd Ave) Best hashes in town, whether they be corned beef or oyster.

are a bit seafood-oriented, but the burger and cocktails are good alternatives.

Fife (off Map pp226-7; ☎ 971-222-3433; 4440 NE Fremont St; mains $18-22; 5-9pm Tue-Thu, till 10pm Fri & Sat) One of Portland's top restaurants in supporting sustainable agriculture, Fife buys almost exclusively from small organic farmers and ranchers within 100 miles. The excellent menu changes daily, but can include treats like buffalo tri-tip with cherry compote and rabbit with nettle-potato dumplings.

Simpatica Dining Hall (Map pp226-7; ☎ 503-235-1600; 838 SE Ash St; prix fixe $40-45; 7pm Fri, 7:30pm Sat, 9am-2pm Sun) Why bother, you might think. It's pricey prix fixe, dinner requires reservations and it's open weekends only at a certain time. It also tends to be heavy on the meat (vegetarians beware), some seating is at a long communal table (though can be fun) and there's always a wait for Sunday brunch. Why? Yes, there is indeed a reason…

Also recommended:

Otto's Sausage Kitchen (off Map pp226-7; ☎ 503-771-6714; 4138 SE Woodstock Blvd; sausage sandwiches $2-3; 11am-4:30pm) Awesome house Wieners, chicken sausages and pork links grilled up outside a deli in the Woodstock neighborhood. Look for the smoke.

¿Por Qúe No? (off Map 221; ☎ 503-467-4149; 3524 N Mississippi Ave; tacos $2.50) The most expensive cheap taquería in town, but the ingredients are good and so is the vibe.

Paradox Café (Map pp226-7; ☎ 503-232-7508; 3439 SE Belmont St; mains $6-9; 8am-9pm Mon-Wed, till 10pm Thu-Sat, till 3pm Sun; V) Small, funky retro café with mostly vegan and vegetarian fare; a few burgers also available.

Roux (off Map p221; ☎ 503-285-1200; 1700 N Killingsworth Ave; mains $14-22; 5-10pm Mon, Wed-Sat, 10am-2pm & 5-9pm Sun) Fine north Portland restaurant serving gourmet Creole dishes like pork ribs and roasted rabbit.

DRINKING

Check out www.barflymag.com for opinionated, spot-on reviews. At the time of writing, Oregon bars and pubs were to become non-smoking as of 2009.

Bars

Brazen Bean (Map pp224-5; ☎ 503-234-0636; 2075 NW Glisan St) Located in a sweet Victorian house, this popular bar is best known for its designer martinis – over 25 different kinds. Compete for space on the romantic veranda during happy hour (5pm to 8pm weekdays), when the prize drinks are $4 and service slows to molasses.

Saucebox (Map pp224-5; ☎ 503-241-3393; 214 SW Broadway) Metro-sleek restaurant with pretty bar staff serving upscale Asian-fusion cuisine, but also very popular for its wide selection of drinks – including creative cocktails (try the chocolate-coffee Foxy Brown). DJs fire up at 10pm, with snappy tunes and dancing potential.

Horse Brass Pub (off Map pp226-7; ☎ 503-232-2202; 4534 SE Belmont St) Portland's most authentic English pub, cherished for its dark wood atmosphere, smoke-filled air (cigars OK), excellent fish 'n chips (or try the artery-clogging scotch egg) and 50 beers on tap (that's right). Play some darts, watch soccer on TV or just take it all in.

Doug Fir (Map pp226-7; ☎ 503-231-9663; 830 East Burnside St) Paul Bunyan meets the Jetsons at this ultra-trendy venue that has transformed the

LoBu (lower Burnside) neighborhood from seedy to slick. Doug Fir books edgy, hard-to-get talent, drawing crowds from tattooed youth to suburban yuppies. Sample their restaurant (open 21 hours), then stumble next door to the rock-star quality Jupiter Hotel (p233).

Crush (Map pp226-7; ☎ 503-235-8150; 1400 SE Morrison St) Slip into this sexy lounge with all the pretty people, order one of their exotic cocktails and speak up – it gets loud, especially when the DJs get going. The menu's gourmet (try the brunch) and there's a Vice Room just for smokers. Great for a girls' night out, straight or lesbian.

Laurelthirst Pub (Map pp226-7; ☎ 503-232-1504; 2958 NE Glisan St) Great acoustic bands spill the crowds onto the sidewalk at this dark, funky and sometimes smoky neighborhood joint. The music – which plays nearly every night – is free until the evening, when you'll likely cough up just a $3 cover. Good beer and wine selection (but no liquor), along with fine breakfasts.

Also recommended:

Back Stage Bar (Map pp226-7; ☎ 503-236-9234; 3702 SE Hawthorne Blvd) Hidden gem behind the Bagdad Theater (p238) with seven-story-high space, pool tables galore and tons of personality.

Alibi Lounge (off Map p221; ☎ 503-287-5335; 4024 N Interstate) Tiki-bar heaven, with karaoke on weeknights, fun crowds and great Polynesian kitsch. Greasy-spoon grub.

Thirst Wine Bar (Map pp224-5; ☎ 503-295-2747; 315 SW Montgomery St) Best on a warm summer day, when the sidewalk tables tempt passersbys with a fine river view.

Brewpubs

It's crazy, but Portland has about 30 brewpubs within its borders – more than any other city on earth. This makes choosing difficult, so here's a starting list.

For funky atmosphere there's no beating **McMenamins** (www.mcmenamins.com). This empire includes brewpubs found all over the Pacific Northwest, each offering their own ales along with brews from other producers. Meanwhile, thirsty parents should head to family-friendly Laurelwood Public House & Brewery (p231), though many brewpubs welcome kids until 9pm or so.

Amnesia Brewing (off Map pp226-7; ☎ 503-281-7708; 832 N Beech St) This is hip Mississippi St's main brewery, with casual feel and picnic tables out front. For excellent (and despite the name, memorable) beer, try the Desolation IPA. Other good drops are Amnesia Brown or Wonka Porter. An outdoor grill offers burgers and sausages, and there's live music on weekends.

Widmer Gasthaus (off Map pp226-7; ☎ 503-281-3333; 929 N Russell St) Located in a trendy industrial area, this yuppified brewery-restaurant offers very tasty beers – some available only here. Their Hefeweizen (unfiltered wheat beer) is a good choice, and goes well with the schnitzel. Widmer Gasthaus has weekend tours, and sports on TV, and it's close to live music at the White Eagle.

Lucky Labrador Brewing Company (Map pp226-7; ☎ 503-236-3555; 915 SE Hawthorne) This is a large, no-nonsense beer hall (good for groups) with a wide selection of brews – though limited bar menu. 'Miser Mondays' means pints under $3, and their back patio is dog-friendly and shows movies in summer. Also has an outlet at 1945 NW Quimby St in the Pearl.

New Old Lompoc (off Map pp224-5; ☎ 503-225-1855; 1616 NW 23rd Ave) The main branch of this pub is housed in an old building with low-key atmosphere and creaky wood floor. Over a dozen taps offers treats like Condor Pale Ale, Sockeye Cream Stout and Bald Guy Brown. The leafy back patio is a must on warm days, and there's a decent pub menu too.

Hair of the Dog Brewing (off Map pp226-7; ☎ 503-232-6585; 4509 SE 23rd Ave) An awesome local microbrewery, Hair of the Dog doesn't have a brewpub so you'll have to check their website for outlets. It brews unusual beers, some of which are 'bottle-conditioned' – the brewing cycle is finished inside the bottle. Look for Fred, a barley wine–style ale with 10% alcohol.

Also recommended:

Alameda Brewhouse (off Map pp226-7; ☎ 503-460-9025; 4765 NE Fremont St) Creative dishes and at least a dozen beers on tap – try the Siskiyou Golden Ale.

Roots Organic Brewing (Map pp226-7; ☎ 503-235-7668; 1520 7th Ave) Relative newcomer on the scene focusing on fully organic brews.

BridgePort Brewpub (Map pp224-5; ☎ 503-241-7179; 1313 NW Marshall St) Almost too-fancy brewery with bakery, espresso bar, atrium and rooftop bar. Also at 3632 SE Hawthorne Blvd.

Coffeehouses

Portland is full of good coffee shops, and everyone has their neighborhood favorite. Here are just a few to try:

Stumptown Coffee (off Map 226-7; ☎ 503-230-7797; 4525 SE Division St) Generally considered Portland's best coffee – what else do you need? Also at 3356 SE Belmont St and downtown at 128 SW 3rd Ave.

Pied Cow Coffeehouse (Map pp226-7; ☎ 503-230-4866; 3244 SE Belmont St) Gorgeous, colorful and bohemian Victorian house with lots of atmosphere and a lovely garden patio. Hookahs available.

Albina Press (off Map pp226-7; ☎ 503-282-5214; 4637 N Albina Ave) Pure nirvana for its delicious cups of coffee, artistically constructed by award-winning baristas.

Red & Black Café (Map pp226-7; ☎ 503-231-3899; 2138 SE Division St) Worker owned-run spot with progressive ideals; enjoy live music, art exhibits and even the occasional gender-queer puppet show. At the time of writing, Red & Black was looking for a new location, so it's worth calling ahead.

Anna Bannanas (Map pp224-5; ☎ 503-274-2559; 1214 NW 21st) Funky hangout in an old renovated house with comfortable feel, gourmet food and a good crowd.

Three Friends Coffeehouse (Map pp226-7; ☎ 503-236-6411; 201 SE 12th Ave) Gay-friendly but not exclusively so, with outdoor seating, open-mic nights and live music.

ENTERTAINMENT

The best guide to local entertainment is the free *Willamette Week*, which comes out on Wednesday and contains complete listings (and cover charges) of all theater, music, clubs, cinema and events in the metro area.

Live Music

See also Doug Fir (p236) and Laurelthirst Pub (p237). For summer outdoor entertainment, check what's happening at the Oregon Zoo (p228). Yes, really.

Dante's (Map pp224-5; ☎ 503-226-6630; www.danteslive.com; 1 SW 3rd Ave) This steamy red bar books vaudeville shows along with national acts like the Dandy Warhols and Concrete Blonde. The stage is intimate and the lighting low – everybody looks good. Drop in on Monday night for the ever-popular Karaoke from Hell.

Berbati's Pan (Map pp224-5; ☎ 503-248-4579; www.berbati.com; 10 SW 3rd Ave) Big and buzzing, this established rock club nabs some of the more interesting acts in town. Expect big band, swing, acid rock and R&B music, along with a crowd of all ages. Outdoor seating and pool tables are a plus.

Crystal Ballroom (Map pp224-5; ☎ 503-225-0047; www.mcmenamins.com/crystal; 1332 W Burnside St) Major acts have played at this historic ballroom, including the Grateful Dead, James Brown and Jimi Hendrix. The 'floating' dancefloor bounces at the slightest provocation, making for some pretty wild (but fun) times while you're cutting up the rug.

Mississippi Studios (off Map pp226-7; ☎ 503-288-3895; www.mississippistudios.com; 3939 N Mississippi Ave) Very intimate venue that's perfect for checking out budding acoustic talent, along with more established musical groups. Excellent sound system – it's also a recording studio. Located right on trendy Mississippi Ave.

Jimmy Mak's (Map pp224-5; ☎ 503-295-6542; www.jimmymaks.com; 221 NW 10th Ave) Stumptown's premier jazz venue, serving excellent Mediterranean food in their fancy dining room. There's a casual smoking bar-lounge in the basement. Music starts at 8pm and reserving for dinner helps nab you a seat.

Hawthorne Theatre (Map pp226-7; ☎ 503-233-7100; www.hawthornetheatre.com; 1507 SE 39th Ave) All-ages music venue in the heart of hip Hawthorne Blvd, good for live rock, reggae, punk, pop, metal and country music. Intimate stage, high balcony and 21-and-over section for the legal boozehounds.

Cinemas

Portland has plenty of multiplex cinemas, but it's the great selection of old personality-filled theaters – often selling beer and pizza, along with $3 tickets – that makes going to the movies a joy here.

Cinema 21 (Map pp224-5; ☎ 503-223-4515; www.cinema21.com; 616 NW 21st Ave) Portland's premiere art- and foreign-film theater.

Kennedy School McMenamins' premiere Portland venue. Watch movies in the old school gym. See p234.

Bagdad Theater (Map pp226-7; ☎ 503-236-9234; www.mcmenamins.com; 3702 SE Hawthorne Blvd) Another awesome McMenamins venue with bargain flicks.

Mission Theater (Map pp224-5; ☎ 503-223-4527; www.mcmenamins.com; 1624 NW Glisan St) Come early for a front-row balcony seat at this beautiful McMenamins theater.

Laurelhurst Theater (Map pp226-7; ☎ 503-232-5511; www.laurelhursttheater.com; 2735 E Burnside St) Great pizza-and-beer theater with nearby nightlife.

Clinton Street Theater (Map pp226-7; ☎ 503-238-8899; www.clintonsttheater.com; 2522 SE Clinton St) Old neighborhood theater screening independent and revival films.

Hollywood Theatre (Map pp226-7; ☎ 503-281-4215; www.hollywoodtheatre.org; 4122 NE Sandy Blvd) Historic art-deco spot playing classic, foreign and quirky independent movies.

Theater & Performing Arts

Arlene Schnitzer Concert Hall (Map pp224-5; ☎ 503-228-1353, 800-228-7343; www.pcpa.com/events/asch.php; 1037 SW Broadway) The Oregon Symphony performs in this beautiful, if not acoustically brilliant, downtown venue.

Artists Repertory Theatre (Map pp224-5; ☎ 503-241-1278; www.artistsrep.org; 1516 SW Alder St) Some of Portland's best plays, including regional premieres, are performed in this intimate space.

Keller Auditorium (Map pp224-5; ☎ 503-248-4335; www.pcpa.com/events/keller.php; 222 SW Clay St) The Portland Opera, Oregon Ballet Theatre and Oregon Children's Theatre all stage performances here.

Portland Center Stage (Map pp224-5; ☎ 503-445-3700; www.pcs.org; 128 NW 11th Ave) The city's main theater company, now performing in the Portland Armory – a newly renovated Pearl District landmark boasting state-of-the-art features.

Gay & Lesbian Venues

For current listings see *Just Out*, Portland's free gay bi-weekly. Or grab a *Gay and Lesbian Community Yellow Pages* (www.pdxgayyellowpages.com) for other services. For an upscale, mixed-crowd bar, check out Crush (p237).

Darcelle XV (Map pp224-5; ☎ 503-222-5338; 208 NW 3rd Ave) Portland's Vegas-style cabaret show, featuring glitzy drag queens donned in big wigs, fake jewelry and over-stuffed bras. Musical performances are spiced with corny comedy while hapless audience members are picked out and teased. Male strippers perform at midnight on weekends.

Holocene (Map pp226-7; ☎ 503-239-7639; 1001 SE Morrison St) Best for lesbians on Tart Night every second Sunday of the month. Otherwise it's your typical hipster-mixed crowd dance scene in a modern industrial space, with a bleak little smoking room in the back.

Embers (Map pp224-5; ☎ 503-222-3082; 110 NW Broadway) Regulars come to meet up for the music (from '80s tunes to techno to pop), amateur drag shows, fun dancefloor and friendly camaraderie. There are different themes on different nights (Wednesday is Goth) and everyone is welcome, whether they be gay, lesbian, straight or undecided.

Egyptian Room (Map pp226-7; ☎ 503-236-8689; 3701 SE Division St) Portland's main lesbian hangout, where guys are (barely) tolerated and girls are (mostly) butch dykes. It's hardly fancy, heavy on the hip-hop and full of chain-smokers, with karaoke and pool tables to distract.

Hobo's (Map pp224-5; ☎ 503-224-3285; 120 NW 3rd Ave) Past the old historic storefront here is a classy restaurant-piano bar popular with older gay men. It's a quiet, relaxed place and good for a romantic dinner or drink; for some activity, head to the pool tables in back. Live music starts at 8pm from Wednesday to Sunday.

Spectator Sports

Portland's only major league sports team is the **Trail Blazers** (www.nba.com/blazers), who play basketball at the Rose Garden Arena (p228). The **Winter Hawks** (www.winterhawks.com), Portland's minor-league hockey team, and the **LumberJax** (www.portlandjax.com), the city's lacrosse team, both play here too.

Renovated a few years back, **PGE Park** (Map pp224-5; ☎ 503-553-400; www.pgepark.com; 1844 SW Morrison) hosts the Portland's minor-league baseball team, the **Portland Beavers** (www.portlandbeavers.com), along with the A-League soccer team the **Portland Timbers** (☎ 503-553-5555).

SHOPPING

Portland's downtown shopping district extends in a two-block radius from Pioneer Courthouse Square. Pioneer Place, an upscale mall, is between SW Morrison and SW Yamhill Sts, east of the square. The Pearl District is dotted with high-end galleries, boutiques and home-decor shops – don't miss Powell's City of Books (p221). On the first Thursday of each month galleries stay open longer and people fill some of the Pearl's streets amidst a party atmosphere. And on weekends there's the very-Portland Saturday Market (p225).

Eastside has lots of trendy shopping streets that also host a few restaurants and cafés. SE Hawthorne Blvd is the biggest of these, N Mississippi Ave is the most recent and NE Alberta is the most artsy and funky. On the last Thursday of each month, NE Alberta throws its own wild street party with budding artists, musicians and performers of all kinds.

GETTING THERE & AWAY

Air

In 2006, **Portland International Airport** (PDX; off Map pp226-7; www.flypdx.com) was voted 'best US airport' by readers of *Conde Nast Traveler* magazine. PDX provides service all over the country, as well as to seven international destinations. Amenities include restaurants, money-changers, bookstores (including three Powell's branches) and other services like free wi-fi. It's also well connected to downtown and other parts of Portland via light rail (see Getting Around, below).

Bus

Greyhound buses leave from their **depot** (Map pp224-5; ☎ 503-243-2357; www.greyhound.com; 550 NW 6th Ave) and connect Portland with cities along I-5 and I-84. Destinations include Chicago, Boise, Denver, San Francisco, Seattle and Vancouver, BC.

If you're traveling between Portland, Olympia and Seattle, consider patronizing the **Shared Route** (☎ 503-502-5750; www.sharedroute.org), which provides service three times weekly on a biodiesel bus.

Train

Amtrak (Map pp224-5; ☎ 503-241-4290; www.amtrak.com), at Union Station, NW 6th Ave at Irving St, offers services up and down the West Coast. *Empire Builder* trains travel through the Columbia River Gorge on their way to Chicago. Destinations include Chicago (via Spokane, Washington), Los Angeles and Seattle.

GETTING AROUND

To/From the Airport

PDX is about 10 miles northeast of downtown, along the Columbia River. Tri-Met's light-rail MAX line takes 45 minutes to get from downtown to the airport. If you prefer a bus, **Blue Star** (☎ 503-249-1837; www.bluestarbus.com) offers shuttle services between PDX and several downtown stops ($14, 30 minutes).

Taxis charge around $30 from the airport to downtown.

> **FARELESS SQUARE**
>
> One of downtown Portland's greatest features is Fareless Square, the area bordered by the Willamette River, NW Irving St and I-405 (and extending across the river, all the way through to the Lloyd Center District). Whether it's the MAX, streetcar or bus, all trips that start and end within these areas cost nothing; pay only if you wind up leaving this magical zone.

Bicycle

It's easy to get around Portland on a bicycle (see p230). Rent bikes from **City Bikes Annex** (Map pp226-7; ☎ 503-239-6951; www.citybikes.coop; 734 SE Ankeny St), **Fat Tire Farm** (Map p221; ☎ 503-222-3276; www.fattirefarm.com; 2714 NW Thurman St) or **Waterfront Bicycle Rentals** (Map pp224-5; ☎ 503-227-1719; www.waterfrontbikes.net; 315 SW Montgomery St).

Bus, Light Rail & Streetcar

Local buses and the MAX light-rail system are run by Tri-Met, which has an **information center** (☎ 503-238-7433; www.trimet.org; 🕑 8:30am-5:30pm Mon-Fri) at Pioneer Courthouse Square (Map pp224–5). A streetcar runs from the university through Pearl District to NW 23rd Ave. Within the downtown core, public transportation is free (see boxed text left); outside downtown, fares run $1.70 to $2.

Tickets for MAX must be bought from ticket machines at MAX stations; there is no conductor or ticket-seller on board. Bus, light-rail and streetcar tickets are completely transferable within two hours of the time of purchase. If you're a night owl, be aware that buses and light-rail both stop running at 1:30am.

Car

Most major car-rental agencies have outlets both downtown and at Portland's airport (PDX). Many of these agencies have added hybrid vehicles to their fleets; Enterprise has biodiesel options. For an interesting car-sharing option, see www.flexcar.com.

Avis (☎ 503-227-0220, 800-831-2847; PDX 503-249-4950; www.avis.com)

Budget (☎ 503-222-5421, 800-527-0700, PDX 503-249-4556; www.budget.com)

Dollar (☎ 503-228-3540, 800-800-4000, PDX 503-249-4792; www.dollar.com)

Enterprise (☎ 503-274-7313, 800-261-7331, PDX 503-254-0771; www.enterprise.com)

Hertz (☎ 503-249-5727, 800-654-3131, PDX 503-249-8216; www.hertz.com)

Pedicab

For something different, contact **PDX Pedicab** (☎ 503-839-5174; www.pdxpedicab.com), which utilizes bicycle pedicabs with 'drivers' that pedal you around downtown. Unique and eco-friendly to boot.

Taxi

Cabs are available 24 hours by phone. Downtown, you can often just flag them down.

Broadway Cab (☎ 503-227-1234)
Radio Cab (☎ 503-227-1212)

Tram

Not particularly helpful to the tourist and many locals, Portland's controversial **aerial tram** (www.portlandtram.org; round-trip fare $4) started operating in 2006 and connects the South Waterfront district to the Oregon Health & Science University hillside campus. It went over-budget by tens of millions of dollars, but at least makes an interesting conversation piece as you drive under it on I-5.

THE WILLAMETTE VALLEY

Best known as a top-notch, wine-producing region, the Willamette Valley offers fun day trips from Portland, but can also hold its own as a destination in itself. Visiting wineries (or, more importantly, their tasting rooms) is the major attraction. The surrounding B&Bs make for serene nights in the country. Salem and Eugene are the largest cities in this region and have good services, urban highlights and distinct personalities.

OREGON CITY

pop 30,000

This nondescript little Portland suburb, nestled next to the Willamette River, was the final stop on the Oregon Trail and the first US city founded west of the Rockies. Despite its historic status and good location, Oregon City is visually plagued by an expanse of ugly paper-mill buildings and electric generators corseted around the 42ft Willamette Falls. The city features a bit of historic character downtown, a variety of old homes in surrounding neighborhoods and a free municipal elevator (between Railroad and 7th Sts) that offers good views of the area.

Sights

The 1845 **McLoughlin House** (☎ 503-656-5146; 713 Center St; admission free; 🕑 10am-4pm Wed-Sat, 1-4pm Sun) was built by John McLoughlin, who was called the 'father of Oregon' for his hand in helping found Oregon City – the West's first. At the time, most settlers lived in log cabins, and this two-story clapboard home was then considered a mansion. Free tours are offered.

To visit the following three attractions, buy an Oregon City Pass for the same price as admission to any one place.

The **End of the Oregon Trail Interpretive Center** (☎ 503-657-9336; www.endoftheoregontrail.org; 1726 Washington St; adult/5-17yr/senior $9/5/7; 🕑 9:30am-5pm Mon-Sat, 10am-5pm Sun) commemorates the struggle of the Oregon pioneers on their overland journey and the challenges they faced when they arrived in Oregon. Look for the two giant covered wagon frames; hours are limited in winter. Also located here is the **visitor center** (☎ 800-424-3002; www.historicoregoncity.org; 1726 Washington St; 🕑 9:30am-5pm Mon-Sat, 10:30am-5pm Sun).

History exhibits at the engaging **Museum of the Oregon Territory** (☎ 503-655-5574; 211 Tumwater Dr; adult/5-17yr/senior $9/5/7; 🕑 11am-4pm) offer a good interpretation of the local moonshine trade and of the Willamette Meteorite, the largest meteorite found in the US. Other displays include collections of intricately etched military mess kits and Native American basketry. Head up to the 3rd floor for a good view of the dam and falls.

For a taste of the past, step into the 1907 **Stevens-Crawford House Museum** (☎ 503-655-2866; 603 6th St; 🕑 noon-4pm Wed-Sat). Owned by a pioneering family, the house still boasts most of its original furniture and hosts occasional exhibits, plant sales, tea parties and a Christmas celebration.

For a cold beer and decent pub fare, head to **McMenamins Oregon City Pub** (☎ 503-655-8032; 102 9th St; mains $7-10; 🕑 11am-midnight Mon-Thu, till 1am Fri & Sat, noon-11am Sun), a casual, family-friendly brewpub with wood booths and partial view of the river.

Getting There & Around

Tri-Met bus 35 connects downtown Portland to Oregon City (45 minutes). In town, the free summertime Oregon City Trolley stops at museums and historic homes between the Oregon Trail Interpretive Center and the Museum of the Oregon Territory.

CHAMPOEG STATE HERITAGE AREA

One of the very first settlements in Oregon, Champoeg ('shampoo-e') was located on a

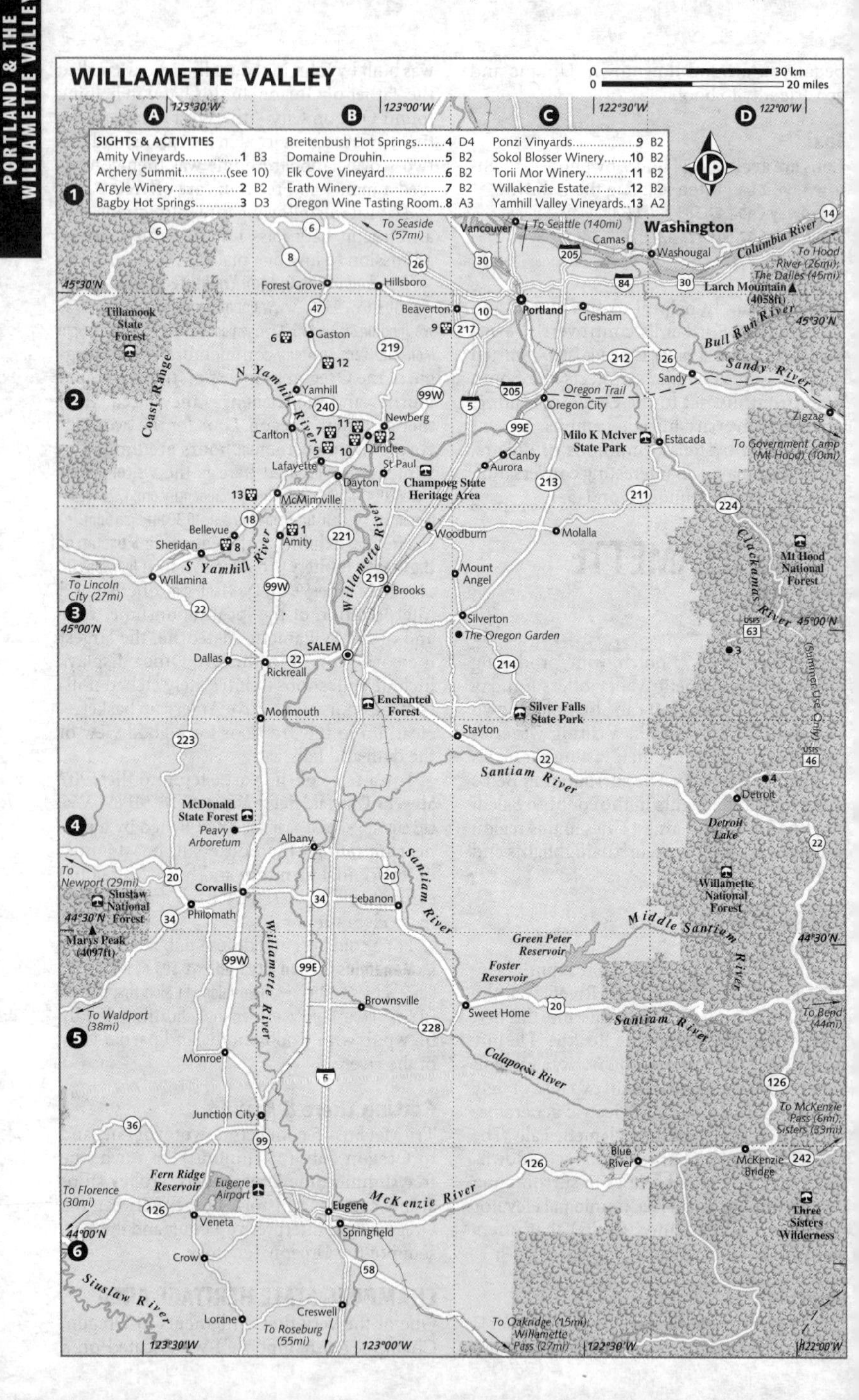
WILLAMETTE VALLEY
SIGHTS & ACTIVITIES
Amity Vineyards....1 B3
Archery Summit....(see 10)
Argyle Winery....2 B2
Bagby Hot Springs....3 D3
Breitenbush Hot Springs....4 D4
Domaine Drouhin....5 B2
Elk Cove Vineyard....6 B2
Erath Winery....7 B2
Oregon Wine Tasting Room....8 A3
Ponzi Vineyards....9 B2
Sokol Blosser Winery....10 B2
Torii Mor Winery....11 B2
Willakenzie Estate....12 B2
Yamhill Valley Vineyards....13 A2
0 30 km
0 20 miles
123°30'W
123°00'W
122°30'W
122°00'W
45°30'N
45°00'N
44°30'N
44°00'N
To Seaside (57mi)
Vancouver
To Seattle (140mi)
Washington
Camas
Washougal
Columbia River
To Hood River (26mi); The Dalles (45mi)
Larch Mountain (4058ft)
Forest Grove
Hillsboro
Beaverton
Portland
Gresham
Bull Run River
Tillamook State Forest
Gaston
Coast Range
N Yamhill River
Yamhill
Sandy River
Sandy
Oregon Trail
Oregon City
Zigzag
Newberg
Carlton
Dundee
Milo K McIver State Park
Estacada
To Government Camp (Mt Hood) (10mi)
Lafayette
St Paul
Canby
Aurora
Dayton
Champoeg State Heritage Area
McMinnville
Willamette River
Clackamas River
Bellevue
Sheridan
Amity
Woodburn
Molalla
Mt Hood National Forest
S Yamhill River
Willamina
Mount Angel
To Lincoln City (27mi)
Brooks
Silverton
The Oregon Garden
SALEM
Dallas
Rickreall
Enchanted Forest
Silver Falls State Park
(Summer Use Only)
Monmouth
Stayton
Santiam River
Detroit
Detroit Lake
McDonald State Forest
Peavy Arboretum
Albany
Santiam River
To Newport (29mi)
Corvallis
Lebanon
Willamette National Forest
Siuslaw National Forest
Philomath
Marys Peak (4097ft)
Middle Santiam River
Green Peter Reservoir
Foster Reservoir
Willamette River
Brownsville
Sweet Home
To Waldport (38mi)
To Bend (44mi)
Santiam River
Calapooia River
Monroe
To McKenzie Pass (6mi); Sisters (33mi)
Junction City
Blue River
McKenzie Bridge
Fern Ridge Reservoir
Eugene Airport
To Florence (30mi)
McKenzie River
Eugene
Three Sisters Wilderness
Veneta
Springfield
Crow
Siuslaw River
Creswell
Lorane
To Roseburg (55mi)
To Oakridge (15mi); Willamette Pass (27mi)

flood plain along a bend in the Willamette River. After the historic 1843 vote, the town continued to grow as the era of riverboat travel brought increasing trade to the Willamette Valley. However, this bounty only lasted until December 1861, when an enormous flood swept through the Willamette drainage and the settlement, destroying most of it.

Now a state heritage area and popular family destination, **Champoeg State Heritage Area** (☎ 503-678-1251; www.oregonstateparks.org; 7679 Champoeg Rd NE; day-use fee $3) is 25 miles southwest of Portland, off I-5 exit 278. There are 615 acres of old-growth woodland, grassy meadows, nature trails, historic sites and campgrounds. Films and displays at the visitors center explain the events that led up to the famous vote at Champoeg. There are also exhibits on the Calapooians and the flood patterns of the Willamette River. On summer weekends, various walks, tours and programs are offered.

The **Pioneer Mothers Memorial Cabin** (☎ 503-633-2237; adult/child/senior $4/2/3; 1-5pm Fri-Sun Mar-Oct) is a reconstructed log cabin built by the local Daughters of the American Revolution. It's filled with objects brought across the Oregon Trail and other articles of frontier life. The 1852 **Newell House** (☎ 503-678-5537; www.newellhouse.com; adult/child/senior $4/2/3; 1-5pm Fri-Sun Mar-Oct) houses Native American artifacts and inaugural gowns worn by the wives of Oregon governors.

Be sure to reserve in summer for the pleasant sites, yurts and cabins at the **Champoeg Campground** (☎ 800-452-5687; campsites/RV sites/yurts/cabins $16/20/27/35).

NEWBERG & DUNDEE

The gateways to wine country, these small cities were originally founded as Quaker settlements. Little of those original quiet ways remain however, and now strip malls and modern services are much of what you'll see. At least there's fine dining in the area, along with upscale countryside places to sleep. Dundee is 2 miles west of Newberg, on Hwy 99W.

The **Hoover-Minthorn House** (☎ 503-538-6629; 115 S River St, Newberg; adult/10yr & under/senior $3/0.50/2; 1-4pm Wed-Sun) is where Herbert Hoover (the 31st president of the USA) grew up. Built in 1881, the restored home is now a museum of period furnishings and early Oregon history. It has limited hours outside summer.

Get a bird's-eye view of the wine country from **Vista Balloon Adventures** (☎ 800-622-2309; www.vistaballoon.com), which offers summertime hot-air balloon flights with champagne breakfast. For pamphlets and information there's the **Chamber of Commerce** (☎ 503-538-2014; 415 E Sheridan St, Newberg; 9am-5pm Mon-Fri, 10am-3pm Sat & Sun).

Sleeping & Eating

The closest camping is at Champoeg State Heritage Area (p241), about 7 miles southeast of Newberg. Dundee has the area's best restaurants.

our pick **Abbey Road Farm B&B** (☎ 503-852-6278, www.abbeyroadfarm.com; 10501 NE Abbey Rd, Carlton; d $175-195) For the ultimate country experience, head 8 miles west of Newberg to this 82-acre working farm with cherry orchard, lush vegetable garden and farm animals. Your hosts John and Judy have created a serene spot with modern comforts – you'll sleep in unique silos converted into five contemporary rooms with simple luxuries like Jacuzzis and memory-foam beds. You can milk goats in the morning and sample the cheese Judy makes. A cutting-edge wine-tasting room is also in the works.

Springbrook Hazelnut Farm B&B (☎ 503-538-4606, 800-793-8528; www.nutfarm.com; 30295 N Hwy 99W, Newberg; d $225) If you've ever wanted to stay on a 70-acre hazelnut farm, here's your chance. This estate offers just two large suites, the Rose Cottage and Carriage House, both with kitchen, living room and comfortable furnishings. There's a swimming pool and tennis court, but no TV. Walk the extensive grounds, canoe in the pond and check out the barn winery – there's plenty of space to spread out.

Dundee Bistro (☎ 503-554-1650; 100 SW Seventh St, Dundee; mains $14-24; 11:30am-9pm) It's a good idea to reserve ahead at this very popular restaurant, a magnet in central Newberg. Tasty dishes like wild Chinook salmon and Muscovy duck confit grace the menu, while the gourmet pizza offers a more casual option. On warm days go for the great back patio.

Red Hills Provincial Dining (☎ 503-538-8224; 276 Hwy 99W, Dundee; mains $24-32; 5-9pm Tue-Sat, till 8pm Sun) Overlooking the highway is this unassuming, yet excellent and award-winning restaurant. It offers a changing menu which reflects the area's agricultural riches, along

OREGON'S WINE BOUNTY

Oregon's first wineries started up in the 1850s, but it took until the 1980s for savvy viticulturists to realize this region's winemaking potential. The Northern Willamette Valley's mild climate and long, relatively mild summers allow pinot gris, chardonnay and riesling grapes to flourish here – but it's the delicate and fruity pinot noirs that steal the spotlight.

Most vineyards are family-owned and -operated and welcome visitors to their tasting rooms, which range from grand edifices to homey affairs tucked into the corner of fermentation rooms. If you're short on time, visit the **Oregon Wine Tasting Room** (☎ 503-843-3787; 19690 Hwy 18; 🕒 11am-5:45pm), just a few miles southwest of McMinnville. It's a gourmet market with about 20 local wines available for tasting. Get a winery map at McMinnville's Chamber of Commerce (see opposite), or check www.willamettewines.com. Also, call or check wineries' websites for tasting-room hours and tasting fees (usually $5 to $10).

Hwy 240 leads west from Newberg to **Willakenzie Estate** (☎ 503-662-3280; www.willakenzie.com; 19143 Laughlin Rd), which is tucked in the rolling Chehalem Hills near Yamhill. Beautiful **Elk Cove Vineyards** (☎ 877-355-2683; www.elkcove.com; 27751 NW Olson Rd), off Hwy 47 near Gaston, has a nice riesling.

In the Dundee area, **Erath Winery** (☎ 800-539-9463; www.erath.com; 9409 NE Worden Hill Rd) is a topnotch winery with a good pinot noir. Nearby, **Torii Mor** (☎ 503-538-2279; www.toriimorwinery.com; 18325 NE Fairview Dr) produces small batches of quality wines, and has a pretty Japanese garden. A view of Mt Hood goes nicely with the chardonnay at **Sokol Blosser Winery** (☎ 800-582-6668; www.sokolblosser.com; 5000 Sokol Blosser Lane). **Archery Summit** (☎ 503-864-4300; www.archerysummit.com; 18599 NE Archery Summit Rd) makes some of Oregon's very best pinot noirs (aged in caves), while **Argyle Winery** (☎ 888-427-4953; www.argylewinery.com; 691 Hwy 99W) does good sparkling wines. For grand atmosphere and panoramic views, there's **Domaine Drouhin** (☎ 503-864-2700; www.domainedrouhin.com; 6750 Breymen Orchards Rd).

Try the pinot gris at **Yamhill Valley Vineyards** (☎ 800-825-4845; www.yamhill.com; 16250 NW Oldsville Rd), located west of McMinnville. Southward, near the Eola Hills area around Amity, the low-key and informal **Amity Vineyards** (☎ 888-264-8966; 18150 Amity Vineyards Rd SE) produces a variety of good wine. For something closer to Portland, head to Beaverton's **Ponzi Vineyards** (☎ 503-628-12227; www.ponziwines.com; 14665 SW Winery Lane), one of Oregon's pioneer vineyards; it also has a wine-tasting room in Dundee (100 SW 7th St).

If you'd rather just sit back, drink and be driven, wine tours are offered by **Oregon Wine Tours** (☎ 503-681-9463; www.orwinetours.com), **Grape Escape** (☎ 503-283-3380; www.grapeescapetours.com) and **Ecotours of Oregon** (☎ 503-245-1428).

with regional meats and seafood. There's a European influence in the dishes enhanced by an exceptional wine list and desserts.

Tina's (☎ 503-538-8880; 760 Hwy 99W, Dundee; mains $25-30; 🕒 11:30am-2pm, 5-9pm Tue-Fri, 5-9pm Sat-Mon) Located a block from Dundee Bistro, Tina's offers a fine French dining experience, cooking up dishes like local Oregon lamb in a port-garlic sauce and roasted duck breast with corn fritters. Mostly local organic ingredients are used. Look for the nondescript house on the main road.

our pick **Painted Lady** (☎ 503-538-3850; 201 S College St, Newberg; prix fixe from $45; 🕒 5-10pm Wed-Sun) Accomplished chefs Allen Routt and Jessica Bagley-Routt have used their wide travel and culinary experiences to open up this gourmet destination in a 1890s Victorian house. Choose from three of four courses: appetizer, seafood, main dish and dessert – it'll likely be a very tasty and memorable experience.

MCMINNVILLE

pop 30,400

At the heart of the region's wine industry lies busy and modern McMinnville, mostly charmless except for its historic, red-brick downtown district. Here you'll find older buildings, art galleries, boutiques and fine restaurants, along with a small-town feel as kids play on sidewalks and tourists stroll up and down the main artery of 3rd St. The main regional attractions are the area's fine wineries, of course.

The **Evergreen Aviation Museum** (☎ 503-434-4180; www.sprucegoose.org; 500 NE Captain Michael King

Smith Way; adult/3-17yr/senior $13/11/12; 9am-5pm), a mile east of McMinnville, showcases the Howard Hughes' *Spruce Goose*, the world's largest wood-framed airplane. In 1947, with Hughes at the wheel, the airplane flew for just under a mile (and it never took off again). The museum also has an IMAX theater with separate admission rates, along with a wine-tasting room.

Held at Linfield College in McMinnville the last weekend of July, the **International Pinot Noir Celebration** (800-775-4762; www.ipnc.org) is an important testing ground for pinot noir wines from all over the world. The three-day festival is immensely popular despite costing $795 per person (including some meals); there's a public tasting ($125) on Sunday. For a more egalitarian event, attend the **McMinnville Wine & Food Classic** (503-472-4033; www.macwfc.com); it's held at the aviation museum in March.

Pick up a pamphlet to historic downtown McMinnville at the **Chamber of Commerce** (503-472-6196; www.mcminnville.org; 417 NW Adams St; 8am-5pm Mon-Thu, 9am-5pm Fri).

Sleeping

Surrounding McMinnville are many B&Bs, with more opening all the time. The chamber of commerce can give details about more than those listed here.

Paragon Motel (503-472-9493, 800-525-5469; 2065 Hwy 99W; d incl breakfast $54-58; wi-fi) For decent cheap rooms with pillow-top mattresses, cable TV and a swimming pool, check into this motor lodge on the western edge of town. Rooms are priced slightly cheaper on weekdays.

McMenamins Hotel Oregon (503-472-8427, 888-472-8427; www.mcmenamins.com; 310 NE Evans St; d $59-109; wi-fi) For a budget stay with personality, there's this awesome downtown hotel. Expect the typical McMenamins eccentricities, like three pubs, eclectic artwork everywhere and an unbeatable rooftop restaurant. Most of the classic old rooms share bathrooms, which are kept in good order.

Steiger Haus B&B (503-472-0821; www.steigerhaus.com; 360 Wilson St; d $85-135;) This friendly, casual home offers a little paradise right in downtown McMinnville. It's on a half-acre and features a hilly, woodsy backyard. Five comfortable bedrooms are available, each with its own bathroom. A patio and deck are pluses.

Mattey House B&B (503-434-5058; www.matteyhouse.com; 10221 NE Mattey Lane; d $120-135;) Outside town, on 10 acres, is this 1892 Victorian farmhouse featuring country-style atmosphere, charming old details and four comfortable rooms with quilts and lace. There's a great wraparound porch, plus a vineyard right past the lawn.

Youngberg Hill Vineyard & Inn (888-657-8668; www.youngberghill.com; 10660 Youngberg Hill Rd; d $150-245;) There's no doubt about it – you're on this 700ft hill for the spectacular panoramic views which span four mountain ranges and three valleys. The seven suites and common areas at this large inn are luxurious, but you'll need to reserve way ahead of time – especially for summer weekends, which are popular for weddings on the premises.

Eating

There's good eating in McMinnville. For average pub fare with above-average views, head to the Hotel Oregon's restaurant (see left).

Cornerstone Coffee Roasters (503-472-6622; 216 NE 3rd St; 7am-10pm Mon-Thu & Sat, till 11pm Fri, 11am-5pm Sun) Busy, friendly coffee shop with comfy couches, airy atmosphere and a laid-back feel. There's a back patio for sunny days and live music on Friday night.

Bistro Maison (503-434-1888; 729 NE 3rd St; mains $18-25; 11:30-2pm & 6-9pm Wed-Thu, 11:30am-2pm & 5-9pm Fri, 5-9pm Sat, noon-8pm Sun) This European eatery is one of McMinnville's better restaurants, serving up all the stereotypical but tasty French treats like escargots, fondue, bouillabaisse, coq au vin and steak tartare. Grab a patio seat in summer.

La Rambla (503-435-2126; 238 NE 3rd St; mains $18-27; 11:30am-2:30pm, 5-9pm Mon-Fri, 11:30am-10pm Sat & Sun) Spanish cuisine comes to McMinnville at this beautiful, dark and atmospheric restaurant with artsy glass lights. Try as much as possible by ordering several tapas, or go for the gusto with a complex main dish. Don't miss dessert – there are churros, crema catalana and flan.

Joel Palmer House (503-864-2995; 600 Ferry St, Dayton; mains $20-37; 5-9pm Tue-Sat) Renowned especially for its dishes laced with wild mushrooms (hand-picked by the chefs – the Czarnecki family), this highly lauded restaurant is housed in an antique-filled 1857 plantation house in Dayton. It's one of Oregon's finest restaurants, turning local ingredients into unforgettable Northwest-cuisine creations.

Nick's Italian Cafe (☎ 503-434-4471; 521 NE 3rd St; prix fixe $45; ⏰ 5:30-9pm Tue-Thu, till 10pm Fri & Sat, 5-8pm Sun) Located next to the Hotel Oregon, Nick's doesn't offer slick, contemporary decor – but you're here for the five-course fixed-price dinner, which goes through antipasti, zuppa, pasta, insalata and secondi dishes. For the meek, à la carte choices are also available. Choose from over 100 local wines.

SALEM

pop 145,000

Hardly the most exciting state capital in the country, Salem is a peaceful and homely university city that exudes a slightly conservative air. It would make a good day trip from Portland as it's just an hour's drive south. Highlights include the state capitol itself and a few museums, along with a pleasant riverfront park complete with carousel. Outside the city limits are more interesting destinations like a spectacular state park, several gardens and some wineries.

Salem's biggest party of the year is the **Oregon State Fair**, held at the fairgrounds and Expo Center for the 10 days prior to Labor Day. Over 200 artists from around the country bring their work to the **Salem Art Fair & Festival**, the state's largest juried art show, held the third weekend of July at Bush Pasture Park. For more city tips, there's the **Visitors Information Center** (☎ 503-581-4325, 800-874-7012; www.travelsalem.com; 1313 Mill St SE; ⏰ 8:30-5pm Mon-Fri, 10am-5pm Sat).

If you're around on a Saturday in summer, check out the **Saturday Market** (☎ 503-585-8264; www.salemsaturdaymarket.com; cnr Marion St NE & Summer St NE), a crafts and farmers market that offers a taste of Salem's local culture.

Sights

OREGON STATE CAPITOL

The state's first capitol building burned down in 1855, and a domed neo-Greek edifice was built to replace it. Unfortunately, that building also burned down (in 1935), and the current **capitol building** (☎ 503-986-1388; www.leg.state.or.us; Court & Capitol Sts; ⏰ 7:30am-5pm Mon-Fri, 9am-4pm Sat), designed by Francis Keally, was completed in 1938. Bauhaus and art-deco influences are apparent, especially in the strident bas-relief in the front statuary and the hatbox-like cupola. The building is faced with gray Vermont marble, and the interior is lined with brown travertine from Montana. The legislative chambers are paneled with Oregon oak and walnut.

The most notable features of the capitol are four Works Progress Administration–era **murals** lining the interior of the rotunda, each depicting a turning point in Oregon history. There's also a galleria with exhibits put on by the local historical society. Surmounting the capitol building's top is the gleaming **Oregon Pioneer**, a 23ft-high gilded statue depicting a stylized, early male settler. The grounds are landscaped with native plants and trees, and home to a gaggle of squirrels.

Free tours run are offered daily from mid-March to mid-September. Call ahead to check schedules.

WILLAMETTE UNIVERSITY

Just south of the capitol, **Willamette University** (☎ 503-370-6300; www.willamette.edu; 900 State St) was the first university in the western USA and well respected for its liberal-arts undergraduate program and law school. See Salem's visitor center for a walking tour leaflet of the university.

The oldest remaining building on the campus is **Waller Hall**, built between 1864 and 1867. The **Hallie Ford Museum of Art** (☎ 503-370-6855; 700 State St; adult/senior $3/2; ⏰ 10am-5pm Tue-Sat, 1-5pm Sun) houses works from Europe and Asia, along with the Pacific Northwest.

BUSH PASTURE PARK

One of Oregon's leading citizens of the late 19th century was Asahel Bush, a newspaperman and a highly successful banker who began building his rambling Italianate mansion in 1877. Designed to be a self-sufficient farm, the estate and mansion are now preserved as Bush Pasture Park. The extensive grounds include a large rose garden, a playground, picnic areas and walking trails.

The **Bush House Museum** (☎ 503-363-4714; www.salemart.org; 600 Mission St SE; adult/child/senior & student $4/2/3; ⏰ noon-5pm Tue-Sun May-Sep, 2-5pm Oct-Apr) is open as a showplace of Victorian design. Note the marble fireplaces, 10 in all. Most of the wallpaper is from the original 1887 construction and was made in France. The house is open for guided tours only, which leave on the half-hour.

The reconstructed livery stable is the **Bush Barn Art Center** (☎ 503-581-2228; www.salemart.com; ⏰ 10am-5pm Tue-Fri, noon-5pm Sat & Sun), which features three galleries. The main floor is given over to the work of local and regional artists and craftspeople – all art is for sale.

Not too far from the Bush House is **Deepwood Estate** (☎ 503-363-1825; www.historicdeepwoodestate.org; 1116 Mission St SE; adult/6-12yr/senior & student $4/2/3; ⏲ tours noon-5pm Sun-Fri), a 1894 Queen Anne mansion topped by turrets and bejeweled with decorative moldings. Especially beautiful are the stained-glass windows. There's free access to the grounds, which contain a nature trail and a formal English tea garden. The mansion is only open for guided tours, and Saturday is reserved specifically for weddings. Hours are limited outside summer.

AC GILBERT'S DISCOVERY VILLAGE

Built to honor Salem native AC Gilbert, who invented the Erector Set, this hands-on **children's museum** (☎ 503-371-3631; www.acgilbert.org; 116 Marion St NE; admission $5.50; ⏲ 10am-5pm Mon-Sat, noon-5pm Sun) is half technology-and-science workshops and half playroom. There's a wide range of fun activities, from an all-ages bubble room to a frozen shadows room to an outdoor tower maze. Toddlers have their own section too.

MISSION MILL MUSEUM

More than a mill, this 5-acre **complex** (☎ 503-585-7012; www.missionmill.org; 1313 Mill St SE; adult/6-12yr/senior $8/4/7; ⏲ 10am-5pm) houses several gift stores, the Salem Visitors Center and a clutch of restored pioneer buildings.

The **Jason Lee House** (1841), the **John Boon House** (1847), the **Methodist Parsonage** (1841) and an **old Presbyterian church** all look pretty much as they did in the 1840s. The **Thomas Kay Woolen Mill** was built in 1889 and was powered by Mill Creek, which still runs through the grounds and still turns waterwheels in the powerhouse.

Also on the grounds is the **Marion County Historical Society Museum** (☎ 503-364-2128; www.marionhistory.org; adult/senior $4/3.50; ⏲ noon-4pm Tue-Sat), with an exhibit highlighting historic sites in the region.

ELSINORE THEATRE

This dazzling oriental-style **landmark** (☎ 503-375-3574; www.elsinoretheatre.com; 170 High St), once a silent-movie theater, is now a venue for big name performers and local talent. Silent movies are shown monthly from October to May, with live accompaniment on a 1778-pipe Wurlitzer organ – one of the finest in the country.

Sleeping & Eating

Salem Campground & RVs (☎ 503-581-6736, 800-826-9605; 3700 Hagers Grove Rd SE; campsites/RV sites $18-26) Located behind Home Depot, Salem's closest campground features 202 jam-packed campsites not far from a noisy highway. There are showers, a market and playground, but for a bit more nature head to Silver Falls State Park (p248).

City Center Motel (☎ 503-364-0121; 510 Liberty St; d $45-55; ❄) For those who don't mind slightly plain and outdated rooms, this centrally located motel is a good enough deal. Fridge and microwave are included, but smell your room before paying up.

Creekside Garden Inn (☎ 503-391-0837; www.salembandb.com; 333 Wyatt Court NE; d $75-105; ⊠ ❄ wi-fi) Five pleasant rooms (two that share an outside bath) are available at this little paradise in busy Salem. The best part is the large grassy yard, lined with flowery garden beds and located right next to a flowing creek.

Phoenix Grand Hotel (☎ 503-540-7800, 877-540-7800; 201 Liberty St; d from $150; ❄ 🏊 💻 wi-fi) Salem's best lodgings are at this downtown hotel next to the city's conference center. Even standard rooms have sitting areas, and all are stylish, modern and elegant. There's an indoor pool and spa on the 2nd floor, a breakfast buffet is included and the service is great.

Coffee House Café (☎ 503-371-6768; 135 Liberty St NE; ⏲ 6am-10pm Mon-Sat, 7am-10pm Sun) Fine hangout spot with classic touches and an open feel. The coffee is so-so, but the atmosphere is awesome and there's live music on weekends.

Wild Pear (☎ 503-378-7515; 372 State St; mains $6-9; ⏲ 10am-5pm Mon-Sat) Popular modern deli serving up tasty sandwiches, homemade soups and gourmet meals like lobster melts or salmon salads. Also makes exceptional pastries.

Bentley's (☎ 503-779-1660; 291 Liberty St; mains $10-22; ⏲ 11am-10pm Mon-Thu, till midnight Fri & Sat, 4-10pm Sun) Located at the Phoenix Grand Hotel, this upscale restaurant offers fine (but conservative) cuisine like seared halibut, artichoke ravioli, prime rib and a house burger.

Best Little Roadhouse (☎ 503-365-7225; 1145 Commercial St SE; ⏲ 11am-11pm Sun-Thu, till midnight Fri & Sat) This very family-friendly dining spot has a modern atmosphere. Surrounding the restaurant is a unique mini-golf course with waterfalls and fake-rock features. There are local microbrews on tap, and the menu is lined with your typical meat-and-salad items.

Getting There & Around

The Salem Airport is about 4 miles west of downtown; bus 21 links the two. The **Hut Airport Shuttle** (☎ 503-364-4444) provides frequent service between Salem and Portland International Airport.

For long-distance bus services there's the **Greyhound depot** (☎ 503-362-2407; 450 Church St NE). Trains stop at the **Amtrak Station** (☎ 503-371-7230; 500 13th St SE).

Cherriots (☎ 503-588-2877; www.cherriots.org) buses serve the city and are free downtown; there's no Sunday service. Get schedules and maps from the main Courthouse Square transit station, at High and Court Sts. In downtown, **Bike Peddler** (☎ 503-399-7741; 174 Commercia St NE; 9am-7pm Mon-Fri, till 5:30pm Sat, 11am-4pm Sun) offers just a couple of cruisers for rent.

AROUND SALEM

Enchanted Forest

Located 7 miles south of Salem, this children's **theme park** (☎ 503-363-3060; www.enchantedforest.com; 8462 Enchanted Way SE, Turner; adult/3-12yr/senior $9/8/8.50) is a fun fantasyland offering roller-coaster rides (extra charge), a castle, haunted house, European village and storybook themes, among other things. There are water light shows and a comedy theater in summer. Picnic grounds, gift shops and food services are also available. Opening hours vary widely so check ahead.

Wineries

One of Oregon's most-respected wine-growers is **Willamette Valley Vineyards** (☎ 800-344-9463; www.willamettevalleyvineyards.com; 8800 Enchanted Way, Turner), on an imposing hilltop south of town. **Strangeland Vineyards & Winery** (☎ 503-581-0355; www.stangelandwinery; 8500 Hopewell Rd NW), north of Salem in the Eola Hills, is a smaller winery with good pinot noir.

The Oregon Garden & The Gordon House

Garden-lovers shouldn't miss the **Oregon Garden** (☎ 877-647-2733; www.oregongarden.org; 879 W Main St; adult/students 6-17yr/senior $10/8/9; 10am-6pm), located 15 miles east of Salem outside Silverton. Over 20 specialty gardens are showcased on 80 acres, with a Northwest plant collection, children's garden and miniature conifer section. There are plans to build a large hotel resort on the premises with wedding and conference facilities, outdoor pool and spa. Opening hours and admission prices are limited outside summer.

Next to the Oregon Garden is the **Gordon House** (☎ 503-874-6066; www.thegordonhouse.org; tours $5 by reservation only) a home designed by Frank Lloyd Wright. It was built in 1964 and moved to its present location in 2002.

Mount Angel

The little town of Mount Angel, with its Bavarian-style storefronts and lovely Benedictine abbey, is like an old-world holdover in the Oregon countryside. Visit the third weekend of September, during **Oktoberfest** (☎ 503-845-9440; www.oktoberfest.org), for maximum effect. It is one of the state's largest harvest festivals, and thousands show up for brass bands, beer and dancers. Gothic-like **St Mary Catholic Church** (1910) is worth a visit for its mural-covered walls.

Open to everyone, the **Mount Angel Abbey** (☎ 503-845-3345; www.mtangel.edu; off College St) is a delightful Benedictine monastery on grassy grounds set atop a hill that overlooks town. There's a modernist library designed by Finnish architect Alvar Aalto, plus a quirky museum featuring a 2.5lb hairball and deformed calves. There's also a Russian Museum on the premises; pick up a self-guided walking-tour map at the bookshop. Lodging is available to those seeking a spiritual retreat.

Mount Angel is 18 miles northeast of Salem on Hwy 214.

Silver Falls State Park

Oregon's largest state park, **Silver Falls** (☎ 503-873-8681; day-use fee $3), 26 miles east of Salem on Hwy 214, is an easy day trip from Portland, Salem and Eugene. It offers camping, swimming, picnicking and horseback riding. Best of all are the hikes, the most famous being the **Trail of Ten Falls Loop**, a relatively easy 8-mile loop that winds up a basalt canyon through thick forests filled with ferns, moss and wildflowers. Featured on this hike are 10 waterfalls, several of which you can walk behind. A few roadside trailheads access this hike, but the most services are at the South Falls day-use area, the park's main entrance. This includes the **campground** (campsites/RV sites/cabins $16/20/35).

IN HOT WATER

A couple hours' drive east of Salem is one of Oregon's best free soaks – **Bagby Hot Springs**. You'll need to hike 1.5 miles through lush forest to reach these springs, but then you'll be rewarded with rustic private bathhouses and hollowed-log tubs. Be prepared to wait your turn on weekends. A $5 Northwest Forest Pass is required at the parking lot, where you shouldn't leave any valuables.

From Estacada, head 26 miles south on Hwy 224 (which becomes Forest Rd 46). Turn right onto Forest Rd 63 and go 3.5 miles to USFS Rd 70. Turn right and go about 6 miles to the parking area.

For a more developed soaking experience there's **Breitenbush Hot Springs** (☎ 503-854-3320; www.breitenbush.com), located east of Salem off Hwy 46, just past the town of Detroit. This peaceful, off-the-grid retreat offers beautiful hot springs, along with massages, yoga, vegetarian food and simple lodgings. Day-use fees range from $12 to $25 and require reservations. Call or check the website for directions.

CORVALLIS

pop 54,000

Proud to be home of Oregon State University (OSU), Corvallis is a bustling, youthful city at the base of the Oregon Coast Range. It lies on the edge of the Willamette River and is surrounded by miles of farms, orchards and vineyards. Downtown storefronts are filled with bakeries, bookstores and cafés, while the upscale riverfront area offers pleasant walking along with stylish restaurants and pubs. The university campus dominates just a few blocks to the west, where over half of the city's population studies or works.

Corvallis is an easy place to spend a day just hanging out in bookstores or cafés, and it's also a good base from which to explore the surrounding region. To find more information (not to mention free wi-fi access), check out the **Corvallis Convention & Visitors Bureau** (☎ 541-757-1544, 800-334-8118; www.visitcorvallis.com; 553 NW Harrison Blvd; 9am-5pm Mon-Fri). **Greyhound** (☎ 541-757-1797; www.greyhound.com; 153 NW 4th St) provides the city's long-distance bus services.

Peavy Arboretum & McDonald State Forest

Both of these areas are administered by OSU and are very popular with dog walkers. Peavy Arboretum has several interpretive trails that wind through 40 acres of forest. You can continue into McDonald State Forest, a research forest with 8 miles of hiking and mountain-bike trails. Take Hwy 99W north for 5 miles, then turn left at Arboretum Rd and go almost a mile.

Marys Peak

At 4097ft, Marys Peak, in the Siuslaw National Forest, is the highest peak in the Coast Range. A favorite with student hikers, the 4.2-mile hike to the top climbs quickly through dense hemlock before finally breaking out into a wildflower meadow. On a clear day there are views across the valley to the glacier-strewn Central Oregon Cascades.

To reach the trailhead, which is 16 miles from Corvallis, head towards Philomath on Hwy 20. Continue past the Hwy 34 junction 1.8 miles, then turn left onto Woods Creek Rd. After 7.5 miles of mostly gravel road you'll see an unmarked parking area where the trail starts. There's alternate access via Hwy 34 (8.5 miles past the Hwy 20 junction), which winds up Marys Peak Rd for 9 miles. This road is closed above milepost 5.5 from 1 December to 1 April. A $5 Northwest Forest Pass is required at either trailhead.

Festivals & Events

Kinetic sculpture and home-built electric-car races are highlights of **da Vinci Days** (www.davinci-days.org), a funky arts-and-science celebration held the third weekend in July.

Costumed players roam an Elizabethan marketplace, engaging visitors in late-16th-century small talk at the **Shrewsbury Renaissance Faire** (☎ 541-929-4897; www.shrewfaire.com), held in early to mid-September in nearby Kings Valley.

Corvallis' premier **Fall Festival** (☎ 541-752-9655; www.corvallisfallfestival.com) takes place in mid-September. Live music fills the streets and top Northwest artists showcase their work.

Sleeping & Eating

Corvallis/Albany KOA (☎ 541-967-8521, 800-562-8526; www.koa.com; 33775 Oakville Rd; campsites/RV sites/cabins $20/30/45) Pleasant RV-oriented campground with small pool, mini-golf course and playground. Located 5 miles east of Corvallis just off Hwy 34.

Super 8 Motel (☎ 541-758-8088; www.super8.com; 407 NW 2nd St; d from $56) Your basic budget motel, but with a pleasant location right next to the river and its walking trail. Expect prices to skyrocket during key football games (check ahead).

Harrison House B&B (☎ 541-752-6248, 800-233-6248; www.corvallis-lodging.com; 2310 NW Harrison Blvd; d from $80; wi-fi) Dutch colonial B&B near the campus offering four tasteful and comfortable rooms, each with private bathroom. The friendly hosts have plenty of information on the area, and there are cozy common areas in which to socialize with other guests. A cottage is also available ($150).

The Beanery (☎ 541-757-0828; 2541 NW Monroe Ave; snacks $4-6; 6am-10pm Mon-Fri, 7am-10pm Sat, 8am-10pm Sun) Popular, casual student coffee shop grinding up local beans and offering fine light snacks like sandwiches, quiches and enchiladas. Another branch downtown at 500 SW 2nd St has live music on weekends.

McMenamins (☎ 541-758-6044; 420 NW 3rd St; mains $7-10; 11am-midnight Mon, till 1am Tue-Sat, noon-midnight Sun) You can't go wrong with any McMenamins venue, where comfort foods like cheeseburgers, BLTs and Cobb salads (along with microbrews) are served up either in the stylish interior or on sidewalk tables. Another branch at 2001 NW Monroe Ave boasts an amazing copper trellis (with sinks).

Big River Restaurant (☎ 541-757-0694; 101 NW Jackson Ave; mains $15-23; 11am-2pm & 5-9:30pm Mon-Thu, till 11:30pm Fri & Sat) This is a lively bistro with excellent fare like penne with roasted red peppers, Dungeness crab gnocchi and 16oz T-bone steak. Pizza and calzones are available too, and homemade pugliese is offered as a complimentary appetizer. It's an open barn-like interior with quieter upstairs area and patio seating for sunny days.

EUGENE

pop 149,000

Full of youthful energy, liberal politics, alternative lifestylers and fun-loving atmosphere, Eugene is a vibrant stop along your I-5 travels. Also known as 'Tracktown,' the city is famous for its track-and-field champions – Nike was born here, after all. And while Eugene maintains a working-class base in timber and manufacturing, some of the state's most unconventional citizens live here as well – from ex-hippie activists to upscale entrepreneurs to high-tech heads.

Eugene offers a great art scene, exceptionally fine restaurants, boisterous festivals, miles of riverside paths and several lovely parks. Its location at the confluence of the Willamette and McKenzie rivers, just west of the Cascades, means plenty of outdoor recreation in the area – especially around the McKenzie River region (p256), Three Sisters Wilderness (p277) and Willamette Pass (p284).

Sixty miles to the west is the Oregon coast, easily accessible via pretty Hwy 126. The city is also at the south end of the Willamette Valley, which boasts several world-class wineries. Eugene is an awesome place, for both energetic visitors and those lucky enough to settle here.

Confirm all this for yourself at the **Convention & Visitors Association of Lane County** (☎ 541-484-5307; 800-547-5445; www.visitlanecounty.com; 754 Olive St; 8am-5pm Mon-Fri, 10am-4pm Sat & Sun). There is also a **post office** (520 Willamette St).

Sights

MARKETS

At E 5th Ave and Pearl St is the **5th St Public Market** (www.5stmarket.com), an old mill that now anchors several dozen restaurants, cafés and boutique stores around a pretty central courtyard. Musicians and other performers occasionally entertain here.

For great fun and a quintessential introduction to Eugene's peculiar vitality, don't miss the **Saturday Market** (☎ 541-686-8885; www.eugenesaturdaymarket.org), held each Saturday from March through November at E 8th Ave and Oak St. Between Thanksgiving and Christmas it's renamed the **Holiday Market** (www.holidaymarket.org) and moves indoors to the Lane Events Center at 13th Ave and Jefferson St.

UNIVERSITY OF OREGON

Established in 1872, the **University of Oregon** (☎ 541-346-1000; www.uoregon.edu) is the state's foremost institution of higher learning, with a focus on the arts, sciences and law. The campus is filled with historic ivy-covered buildings and includes a **Pioneer Cemetery**, with tombstones that give vivid insight into life and death in the early settlement. Campus tours are held in the summer.

Housed in a replica of a Native American longhouse, the **University of Oregon Museum of Natural History** (☎ 541-346-3024; http://natural-history.uoregon.edu; 1680 E 15th Ave; adult/3-18yr & senior $3/2; 11am-5pm Wed-Sun) contains the state's best display of fossils, Native American artifacts and geologic curiosities. On Wednesday admission is free; tours are available.

The renowned **Jordan Schnitzer Museum of Art** (☎ 541-346-3027; http://jsma.uoregon.edu; adults/seniors $5/3; 1430 Johnson Lane; 11am-8pm Wed, till 5pm Thu-Sun) offers a 12,500-piece rotating permanent collection of world-class art, from Korean scrolls to Rembrandt paintings. Free admission on the first Friday of each month. Marché restaurant has an excellent café here.

LANE COUNTY HISTORICAL MUSEUM

Old logging tools and technology are prominent among the collection of historic artifacts preserved at this local **museum** (☎ 541-682-4239; 740 W 13th Ave; adult/child/senior $2/0.75/1; 10am-4pm Tue-Sat). One exhibit details the experiences of Oregon Trail pioneers who traversed the continent to settle in Lane County.

SKINNER BUTTE

A hike up wooded Skinner Butte, directly north of downtown, provides a good orientation and a little exercise (drive up if you're feeling lazy). Eugene Skinner established the city's first business on the narrow strip of land along the Willamette River below, which is now **Skinner Butte Park**; there's a great playground for kids. And if you're a rock climber, don't miss the columnar basalt formations along the butte's lower western side (at W 1st Ave).

ALTON BAKER PARK

Heaven for cyclists and joggers is this popular riverside park, which provides access to the **Ruth Bascom Riverbank Trail System**, a 12-mile bikeway that flanks both sides of the Willamette. There's good downtown access via the DeFazio Bike Bridge.

Follow the path around the north side of Skinner Butte to the **Owens Memorial Rose Garden**, a lovely park with carefully trained climbing roses (best in June) and the country's oldest Black Tartarian cherry tree, supposedly planted in 1847.

See Paul's (p256) for bike rentals.

HENDRICKS PARK RHODODENDRON GARDEN

Thousands of varieties of rhododendron and azalea erupt into bloom here in the spring, along with dogwoods and daffodils, peaking in May. The garden is part of a larger park that features native trees and shrubs, and during the rest of the year it's a quiet, vernal retreat with lovely views worthy of a picnic. To get there head south on Agate St, turn left on 21st and left again on Fairmont, then right on Summit.

SCIENCE FACTORY

Families with young kids can visit this **children's museum** (☎ 541-682-7888; www.sciencefactory.org; 2300 Leo Harris Pkwy; adults/seniors $4/3; noon-4pm Wed-Sun). Hands-on exhibits, a kids' construction zone and a live iguana are among the highlights; weekend planetarium shows cost extra.

WINERIES

Nestled in the hills at the southern end of the Willamette Valley are some exceptional wineries. Take a picnic to lovely **Silvan Ridge** (☎ 541-345-1945; www.silvanridge.com; 27012 Briggs Hill Rd; noon-5pm), 11 miles southwest of Eugene. Nearby is **Sweet Cheeks** (☎ 541-349-9463; 27007 Briggs Hill Rd; noon-6pm), with its beautiful tasting room. **King Estate** (☎ 541-942-9874; www.kingestate.com; 80854 Territorial Rd; 11am-8pm) is a huge producer with outdoor marketplace and fine restaurant. At the other end of the spectrum is **Iris Hill** (☎ 541-345-1617; 82110 Territorial Rd; www.iris-hill.com; noon-5pm Thu-Sun), a small family-run operation.

Festivals & Events

The great composer takes center stage at the **Oregon Bach Festival** (☎ 800-457-1468; www.oregonbachfestival.com; late Jun–mid-Jul), but other classical heavyweights like Beethoven, Brahms and Dvorak get a look in as well. The **Oregon Country Fair** (☎ 541-343-4298; www.oregoncountryfair.com; mid-Jul) is a riotous celebration of Eugene's folksy, hippie past and present.

American music is celebrated at the **Oregon Festival of American Music** (OFAM; ☎ 541-434-7000; www.ofam.org/festival.aspx; early Aug), a week-long concert series of jazz and contemporary show tunes. The **Eugene Celebration** (☎ 541-681-4108; www.eugenecelebration.com; mid-Sep) takes over downtown with parades, artisans, political activists and a lively street fair.

EUGENE

INFORMATION
- Convention & Visitors Association of Lane County....1 E4
- Main Post Office....2 E3

SIGHTS & ACTIVITIES
- 5th St Public Market....3 E3
- Jordan Schnitzer Museum of Art..4 G5
- Lane County Historical Museum..5 C5
- Saturday Market....6 E4
- Science Factory....7 H3
- University of Oregon Museum of Natural History....8 H5

SLEEPING
- Campus Inn....9 F4
- C'est La Vie Inn....10 B4
- Eugene Whiteaker Hostel....11 C3
- Excelsior Inn....12 F5
- River Walk Inn....13 C1
- The Campbell House....14 E3
- The Oval Door B&B....15 D4
- The Secret Garden B&B....16 G6
- Timbers Motel....17 E4
- Valley River Inn....18 C1

EATING
- Ambrosia....19 E4
- Beppe & Gianni's Trattoria....20 H6
- Café Zenon....21 E4
- Keystone Café....22 D3
- Morning Glory Café....23 E3
- Newman's Fish & Chips....24 E5
- Oregon Electric Station....25 E3
- Papa's Soul Food Kitchen....26 C3
- Red Agave....27 E3
- Ring of Fire....28 A4
- Sweet Life Patisserie....29 C4
- The Kiva....30 E4

DRINKING
- McMenamins East 19th St Café..31 H6
- McMenamins High St Brewery & Café....32 E5
- McMenamins North Bank....33 F2
- Steelhead Brewing Co....34 E3
- The Beanery....35 D3
- Wandering Goat....36 C3

ENTERTAINMENT
- Jo Federigo's....37 E3
- Sam Bond's....38 C3

TRANSPORT
- Greyhound....39 E4
- LTD Transit Station....40 E4
- Paul's....41 E3

A B C D 1 2 3 4 5 6
Owens Memorial Rose Garden
Skinner Butte Park
Skinner Butte
1st Ave W
W 2nd Ave
W 3rd Ave
W 4th Ave
W 5th Ave
W 6th Ave
W 7th Ave
W 8th Ave
W Broadway
W 10th Ave
W 11th Ave
W 12th Ave
W 13th Ave
W 14th Ave
W 15th Ave
W 16th Ave
W 17th Ave
W 18th Ave
W 19th Ave
W 20th Ave
Blair Blvd
Van Buren St
Jackson St
Chambers St
Fillmore St
Almaden St
Taylor St
Polk St
Tyler St
Adams St
Monroe St
Madison St
Jefferson St
Washington St
Lawrence St
Lincoln St
Charnelton St
To Airport (7mi); Corvallis
To Florence (60mi); Wineries (10-15mi)
126 99 105
Lane Events Center
Amazon Creek
Westmoreland Park

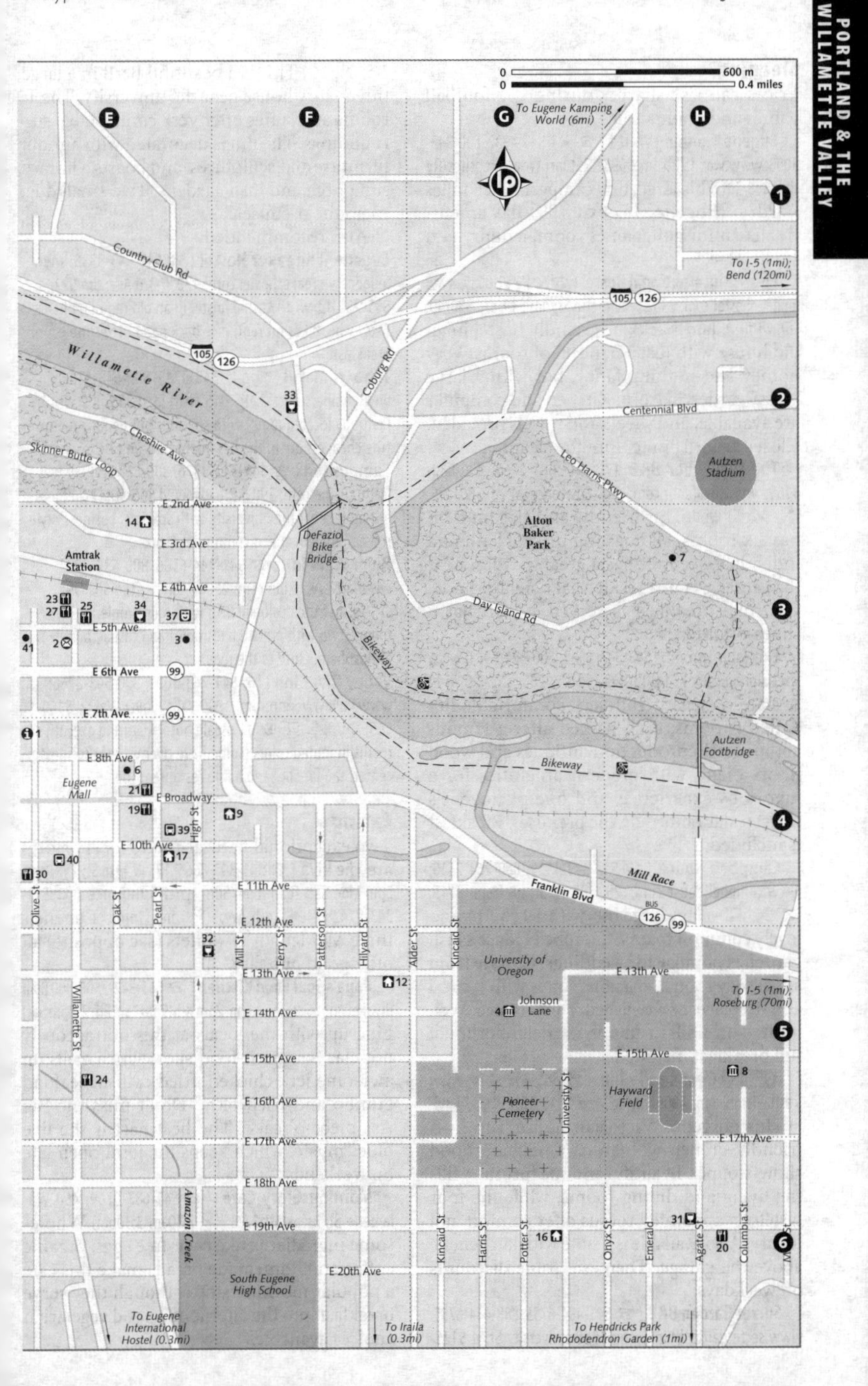

0 600 m
0 0.4 miles
E
F
G
H
To Eugene Kamping World (6mi)
To I-5 (1mi); Bend (120mi)
Country Club Rd
Willamette River
Coburg Rd
Centennial Blvd
Cheshire Ave
Skinner Butte Loop
Leo Harris Pkwy
Autzen Stadium
Alton Baker Park
E 2nd Ave
E 3rd Ave
E 4th Ave
E 5th Ave
E 6th Ave
E 7th Ave
E 8th Ave
E Broadway
E 10th Ave
E 11th Ave
E 12th Ave
E 13th Ave
E 14th Ave
E 15th Ave
E 16th Ave
E 17th Ave
E 18th Ave
E 19th Ave
E 20th Ave
DeFazio Bike Bridge
Amtrak Station
Day Island Rd
Bikeway
Autzen Footbridge
Eugene Mall
Mill Race
Franklin Blvd
High St
Olive St
Oak St
Pearl St
Mill St
Ferry St
Patterson St
Hilyard St
Alder St
Kincaid St
University of Oregon
Johnson Lane
To I-5 (1mi); Roseburg (70mi)
Willamette St
Pioneer Cemetery
University St
Hayward Field
Amazon Creek
Harris St
Potter St
Onyx St
Emerald
Agate St
Columbia St
South Eugene High School
To Eugene International Hostel (0.3mi)
To Iraila (0.3mi)
To Hendricks Park Rhododendron Garden (1mi)

Sleeping

Prices can rise sharply during key football games and graduation.

Eugene Kamping World (☎ 541-343-4832, 800-343-3008; www.woodalls.com; 90932 S Stuart Way; campsites/RV sites $18/30) This large, tidy campground 6 miles north of Eugene (I-5 exit 199) has amenities like mini-golf, games room, laundry and small store.

Eugene International Hostel (☎ 541-349-0589; www.eugenehostel.com; 2352 Willamette St; dm $19, s/d $30/40; wi-fi) A laid-back and friendly hostel in an old house with just a handful of rooms. Very homey and nothing fancy, but with a large grassy garden in front. Kitchen and computer are available, and sheets and towels provided. Closed from 1pm to 4pm for cleaning.

The Oval Door B&B (☎ 541-683-3160, 800-882-3160; www.ovaldoor.com; 988 Lawrence St; d $85-195; wi-fi) This friendly and elegant B&B has six rooms, all boasting private bath and individual decor. It has a great location near the center, yet in a residential neighborhood. Gourmet breakfast is served, and it has a shoes-off interior.

Excelsior Inn (☎ 541-342-6963, 800-321-6963; www.excelsiorinn.com; 754 E 13th Ave; d $99-265; wi-fi) A stately, elegant and very comfortable inn with 14 rooms, each named after a famous composer. Reproduction antiques and wood floors blend with modern amenities for a luxurious experience, and one of Eugene's finest restaurants is on the premises. Breakfast is included.

Campbell House (☎ 541-343-1119, 800-264-2519; www.campbellhouse.com; 252 Pearl St; d from $119; wi-fi) A large inn with 19 rooms and lovely common spaces, Campbell House's lush garden is popular for weddings. Choose from small cozy rooms, spacious suites with Jacuzzi and fireplace, or a two-bedroom cottage. Well located on a hill in an upscale neighborhood; full breakfast included.

OUR PICK **C'est La Vie Inn** (☎ 541-302-3014; www.cestlavieinn.com; 1006 Taylor St; d $119-155; wi-fi) This gorgeous Victorian house, run by a friendly French woman, is a neighborhood show-stopper. Beautiful antique furniture fills the living and dining rooms, while the four tastefully appointed rooms offer comfort and luxury. Also available is a suite with kitchenette above the garage. There are some discounts on weekdays.

Secret Garden B&B (☎ 541-484-6755, 888-484-6755; www.secretgardenbbinn.com; 1910 University St; d $125-245;) This is a beautiful B&B in a large, three-story house near the university. The 10 rooms and suites offer very comfortable surroundings. The inn is decorated with antique furniture and sculptures, and boasts a library, sun porch and lush gardens. Two small dogs roam the premises.

Also recommended:

Eugene Whiteaker Hostel (☎ 541-343-3335; www.eugenewhiteakerhostel.com; 970 W 3rd Ave; dm $22, d $35-75; wi-fi) Casual hostel in an old rambling house. Artsy vibe, bikes for rent, nice back patio, free simple breakfast.

Timbers Motel (☎ 541-343-3345, 800-643-4167; www.timbersmotel.net; 1015 Pearl St; d $55; wi-fi) Centrally located motel with spacious but generic rooms (the cheapest are in the basement but can't be reserved).

Campus Inn (☎ 541-343-3376, 800-888-6313; www.campus-inn.com; 390 E Broadway; d $65-90;) Pleasant motel near the university with spacious business-style rooms, small gym and communal Jacuzzi.

River Walk Inn (☎ 541-344-6506, 800-621-2904; www.ariverwalkinn.com; 250 N Adams St; d $69-99; wi-fi) Dutch colonial B&B with four simple, pretty rooms (two with private bathroom) and casual, homey atmosphere. Close to the river.

Valley River Inn (☎ 541-743-1000, 800-543-8266; www.valleyriverinn.com; 1000 Valley River Way; d $140-165;) Upscale hotel featuring executive rooms in muted colors (some have river views). Business center, sauna, pool and a fine restaurant too.

Eating

Two exceptional natural-food grocery stores are **The Kiva** (☎ 541-342-8666; 125 W 11th St; 9am-8pm Mon-Sat, 10am-6pm Sun) and **Sundance** (☎ 541-343-9142; 748 E 24th Ave; 7am-11pm). Eugene's three McMenamins outlets (see opposite) all offer good pub fare.

Papa's Soul Food Kitchen (☎ 541-342-7500; 400 Blair Blvd; mains $6-9; noon-2pm & 5-9pm Tue-Fri, 2-9pm Sat) Line up with the locals at this outrageously popular Southern-food spot, which grills up awesome jerk chicken, fried catfish, seafood gumbo and fried okra. Don't miss the Big Ass piece o' cake. The best part is the live blues music, which keeps the joint open late on weekends.

Morning Glory Café (☎ 541-687-0709; 450 Willamette St; breakfast $7-8; 7:30am-3:30pm) Wholesome ingredients like cage-free eggs, organic coffee and homemade breads make this café a popular morning stop – though they serve breakfast into the afternoon. Good vegetarian choices available.

Ring of Fire (☎ 541-344-6475; 1099 Chambers St; mains $12-17; 🕑 11am-10pm Mon-Thu, till 11pm Fri & Sat, noon-9:30pm Sun) Thai food dominates the menu and you get to dictate the spiciness at this restaurant. Try the calamari marinated in sake and lemongrass as an appetizer, then go for a noodle, curry or stir-fried dish. The attached Lava Lounge stays open late for hipsters sipping cocktails.

ourpick **Beppe & Gianni's Trattoria** (☎ 541-683-6661; 1646 E 19th Ave; mains $14-16; 🕑 5-9pm Sun-Thu, till 10pm Fri & Sat) One of Eugene's most beloved restaurants and certainly its favorite Italian food. Homemade pastas are the real deal here, and the desserts excellent. Reservations only for groups of eight or more; otherwise, expect a wait.

Iraila (☎ 541-684-8400; 2435 Hilyard St; mains $14-20; 🕑 5-9pm Wed-Sun; V) This small, modest eatery has made a name for itself with good Mediterranean dishes sporting a Middle Eastern twist. Main dishes are excellent, but to sample more than one thing try ordering several small plates off their tapas menu. Vegan choices available.

Café Zenon (☎ 541-343-3005; 898 Pearl St; mains $18-21; 🕑 8am-11pm Sun-Thu, till midnight Fri & Sat) Going on 25 years, this flashy restaurant cooks up French-inspired main dishes, but it's the appetizers, salads and desserts that have folks coming back for more. Noteworthy breakfasts as well.

Red Agave (☎ 541-683-2206; 454 Willamette St; mains $19-25; 🕑 5:30-9pm Mon-Thu, till 10pm Fri & Sat) Caribbean and Latin American cuisine is featured here – consider the lamb shank with chipotle and tomatillos, or the corn masa crepes. Especially popular, however, are the chicken enchiladas topped with green mole and ancho pepper sauce. And tequila? *¡Sí señor!*

Also recommended:

Sweet Life Patisserie (☎ 541-683-5676; 755 Monroe St; pastries $2.50-5; 🕑 7am-11pm Mon-Fri, 8am-11pm Sat & Sun) Eugene's best dessert shop; also serves organic coffee.

Keystone Café (☎ 541-342-2075; 395 W 5th Ave; mains $6-9; V) Organic omelettes, vegan pancakes, tofu scrambles, salmon burgers. Get the idea?

Newman's Fish 'n Chips (☎ 541-344-2371; 1545 Willamette St; mains $6-8; 🕑 11am-7pm Mon-Fri, till 6:30pm Sat) Fish market offering Eugene's best fish 'n chips. Limited counter seating.

Ambrosia (☎ 541-342-4141; 174 E Broadway; mains $14-22; 🕑 11:30am-9:30pm Mon-Thu, till 11:30pm Fri, 4:30-11pm Sat, 4:30-9pm Sun) Beautiful restaurant offering northern Italian cuisine and wood-fired pizzas.

Oregon Electric Station (☎ 541-485-4444; 27 E 5th Ave; mains $19-27; 🕑 11:30am-2:30pm, 5-10pm Mon-Fri, 4:30-10:30pm Sat, 4:30-9:30pm Sun) Fancy and attractive steakhouse located in a remodeled railroad station.

Drinking & Entertainment

The Beanery (☎ 541-342-3378; 152 W 5th Ave; 🕑 6am-11pm Mon-Sat, 7am-11pm Sun) Warm, modern loft space hosting a great organic coffeehouse. Enter through the alley in back.

Wandering Goat (☎ 541-344-5161; 268 Madison; 🕑 7am-11pm Mon-Fri, 9am-11pm Sat, 9am-9pm Sun) For the best macchiato in town, hunt out this small artsy coffee shop next to the railroad tracks. They roast their own organic beans. DJs spin on Thursday night and there's live music on weekends.

Steelhead Brewing Co (☎ 541-686-2739; 199 E 5th Ave; 🕑 11:30am-11:30pm Sun-Thu, till 1am Fri & Sat) Classic yuppie pub with all the usual suspects on the menu, plus around a dozen homemade brews from their light Hairy Weasel Hefeweizen to a hoppy Bombay Bomber IPA to a fruity chocolate-covered cherry porter. Bottoms up.

McMenamins North Bank (☎ 541-343-5622; 22 Club Rd; 🕑 11am-11pm Sun-Thu, till midnight Fri & Sat) Gloriously located on the banks of the mighty Willamette, this relatively modest (for a McMenamins) pub-restaurant boasts some of the best views in Eugene. Grab a riverside patio table on a warm, sunny day and order their Hammerhead ale – you can't get more stylin'. Their two other locations (1243 High St and 1485 East 19th St) lack water views but offer similar fare.

Sam Bond's (☎ 541-343-2635; 407 Blair Blvd) Eugene's favorite live music venue, located in an old garage. Nightly entertainment from 4pm on, with good organic pizza, happy hour pints for $2.50, free bluegrass jams on Tuesday and nice outdoor patio for those sweltering summer nights.

Jo Federigo's (☎ 541-343-8488; 259 E 5th Ave) Walk into a restaurant above and jazz venue below. Local bands play on weekdays and visiting bands jam on weekends. Shows start at 8:30pm or 9pm.

Getting There & Around

The **Eugene Airport** (☎ 541-682-5430; www.eugeneairport.com) is about 7 miles northwest of center. **Greyhound** (☎ 541-344-6265; www.greyhound.com) is at 987 Pearl St. The **Amtrak station** (☎ 541-687-1383; www.amtrak.com) is at E 4th Ave and Willamette St.

Local bus service is provided by **Lane Transit District** (LTD; ☎ 541-687-5555; www.ltd.org). To get around on your own pedal power, head to **Paul's** (☎ 541-344-4150; 152 W 5th St; 🕑 9am-7pm Mon-Fri, 10am-5pm Sat & Sun) for bike rentals.

MCKENZIE REGION

The single name 'McKenzie' identifies a beautiful and mysterious river, a mountain pass, a spectacular historic highway and one of Oregon's most extraordinary and wondrous natural areas. Premiere recreational opportunities abound, from fantastic fishing to exceptional hiking to racy rafting trips.

The little community of McKenzie Bridge, 50 miles east of Eugene on Hwy 126, offers a few cabins and a market. Four miles east from here the highway splits and continues east as Hwy 242 (the Old McKenzie Hwy) over the Cascades toward McKenzie Pass on its way to Sisters, 34 miles distant (the pass is closed November to June). Hwy 126 continues north along the McKenzie River to US 20, which crosses the Cascades at Santiam Pass (4817ft, open year-round).

The **McKenzie Ranger Station** (☎ 541-822-3381; www.fs.fed.us/r6/willamette; 57600 McKenzie Hwy; 🕑 8am-4:30pm) can help with trails and campgrounds, and sells permits. **Lane Transit District** (☎ 541-687-5555; www.ltd.org) bus 91 from Eugene provides services along Hwy 126 to the McKenzie Ranger Station.

Hiking

One of Oregon's showcase 'Wild & Scenic Rivers,' the McKenzie is graced with the 26-mile **McKenzie River National Recreation Trail**, which follows the here-again, gone-again cascading river from its inception near the town of McKenzie Bridge. There are entry trailheads at several places along Hwy 126.

A good day hike is the 5-mile **Clear Lake Loop**, accessible via either Clear Lake Resort or Coldwater Cove Campground. It circles Clear Lake while passing a large spring, several groves of old-growth forest and an extensive lava flow.

Another series of easy hikes begins at the **Sahalie Falls**, where a footbridge crosses the upper falls viewpoint to join the McKenzie River Trail for a 2-mile stroll to Carmen Reservoir past **Koosah Falls**. On the highway side of the river is the more-developed and shorter **Waterfall Trail**, which links Sahalie with Koosah Falls. Parts of this trail are wheelchair accessible.

Day hikes also reach the calm, emerald-colored **Tamolitch Pool** from the south. To reach the trailhead, turn off Hwy 126 at Trail Bridge Reservoir, following the gravel road to the right. The 2-mile trail passes through a mossy lava flow before coming upon the mighty McKenzie River surging up in a cliff-lined bowl of rock.

Fishing

The McKenzie River is one of the best fishing streams in Oregon, and the slower water and deep pools west of Blue River also offer good fishing. Check regulations with the **Fish & Wildlife office** (☎ 541-726-3515) in Springfield. For fishing trips and equipment rental contact **Jim's Oregon Whitewater** (☎ 541-822-6003; 56324 McKenzie Hwy) in McKenzie Bridge.

Rafting

White-water rafting trips are popular on the McKenzie River's class I to III rapids from April to October. **High Country Expeditions** (☎ 888-461-7238; www.hcexpeditions.com) and **Oregon Whitewater Adventures** (☎ 541-746-5422; 800-820-7238; www.oregonwhitewater.com) operate on the McKenzie.

Sleeping & Eating

There are many lovely summer campgrounds (campsites $12) in the area, which include Paradise (old-growth grove near white water), McKenzie Bridge (Douglas fir and cedar trees), Delta (scenic and enchanting) and Ice Cap Creek (cliff-top location near a reservoir and waterfalls). Limited reservations are possible (☎ 877-444-6777). Contact the Ranger Station for more information.

Reserve rooms in summer.

Belknap Hot Springs Lodge (☎ 541-822-3512; www.belknaphotsprings.com; 59296 Belknap Springs Rd; campsites/RV sites $25/30, d $75-185, cabins $85-400; P ⊠ ⊠) This large mountain resort has something for everyone – camping, RV sites, rustic cabins, modern lodge rooms and even fancy houses. The reason to visit or stay here, however, are the spring-fed pools (nonguest fee $10.50).

Clear Lake Resort (☎ 541-967-3917; www.clearlakeresort-oregon.org; Hwy 126; cabins $58-106) These rustic lakeside cabins, 4 miles south of Hwy 20, are great – except for the diesel generators. More modern cabins are available, though the older ones don't have bathrooms. Rowboat rentals, store and café are on premises. Bring bedding.

Harbick's Country Inn (☎ 541-822-3805; www.harbicks-country-inn.com; 54791 McKenzie Hwy; d $65-110; ⊠ ⁜ wi-fi) Friendly and attractive motel with both older rooms and gorgeous newly remodeled ones. Eventually all will be converted (and prices will rise), but this might take years. There's also a large apartment available ($122).

Horse Creek Lodge (☎ 541-822-3243; www.hclodge.com; 56228 Delta Dr; cabins $85-88, 4-bedroom house $340; ⊠) Three one- and two-bedroom cabins with fireplace and kitchens are available at this lovely, secluded spot with artsy feel. The Delta House is great for large groups, and it's a quarter-mile walk to the river.

Caddisfly Resort (☎ 541-822-3556; www.caddisflyresort.com; 56404 McKenzie Hwy; cabins $90; ⊠) Friendly place with just three rustic, two-bedroom 'cottages' with kitchenette, fireplace and decks near the river.

Eagle Rock Lodge (☎ 541-822-3630; www.eaglerocklodge.com; 49198 McKenzie Hwy; d $130-225; ⁜ ⊠) This gorgeous B&B has eight rooms (some with fireplace and Jacuzzi) and over 4 acres of lovely lawns and gardens. Located right next to the river, with a great deck nearby, next door is the McKenzie River Inn, another B&B.

Rustic Skillet (☎ 541-822-3400; 54771 McKenzie Hwy; mains $6-10; ⏲ 7am-9pm) Go back in time at this very casual diner, which offers up three-egg omelettes for breakfast, a variety of sandwiches and burgers for lunch and steaks for dinner. Homemade breads and pies are the highlights.

our pick **Holiday Farm Resort** (☎ 541-822-3725; 54455 McKenzie River Dr; mains $16-19; ⏲ 5-9pm) This elegant restaurant almost seems out of place in this 'rustic' region, but may be a sign of things to come. Enjoy upscale dishes like fresh trout, fettuccine alfredo, portobello mushroom ravioli and filet mignon. There's a lounge for hanging out, and they rent cottages as well.

Columbia River Gorge

Cleanly dividing Oregon and Washington is the spectacular Columbia River Gorge, which was carved some 15,000 years ago by cataclysmic glaciers and floods. Driving east on I-84 (or, more leisurely, on the scenic Historic Columbia River Hwy) has you passing high waterfalls and nearly vertical mountain walls, all while paralleling the mighty Columbia.

Hikers have plenty to keep them busy in the gorge, which features lots of steep, lovely trails that lead through canyons lined with ferns and pretty waterfalls, and across wildflower fields to grand vistas. Summer wind sports are legendary – the gorge channels westerlies inland against the current, creating world-class windsurfing and kiteboarding conditions. There are also mountain biking and rafting possibilities, especially around Hood River.

Not into strenuous activity? The gorge offers highlights such as exceptional waterfall viewing, impressive museums and pleasant hot springs. You can also sample nearby Hood River Valley's agricultural bounty in the right seasons (don't miss the cherries in July!) and go wine tasting in the area's fine vineyards. And, on a clear day, keep your eyes peeled for Mts St Helens, Adams and Rainier (all in Washington), along with Mts Hood and Jefferson (both in Oregon). As you pass through the gorge's fine scenery, these white-topped mountains will only enhance your views of this special place.

HIGHLIGHTS

- Enjoying the incredible panorama from **Vista House** (opposite)
- Counting **waterfalls** (p261) up and down the gorge
- Hiking up the **Eagle Creek Trail** (p261) to heart-skipping heights
- Soaking away your aches at **Bonneville** or **Carson Hot Springs** (p262)
- Learning to catch the wind on your kiteboard at **Hood River** (p262)
- Exploring the **Maryhill Museum of Art** (p267), on the Washington side

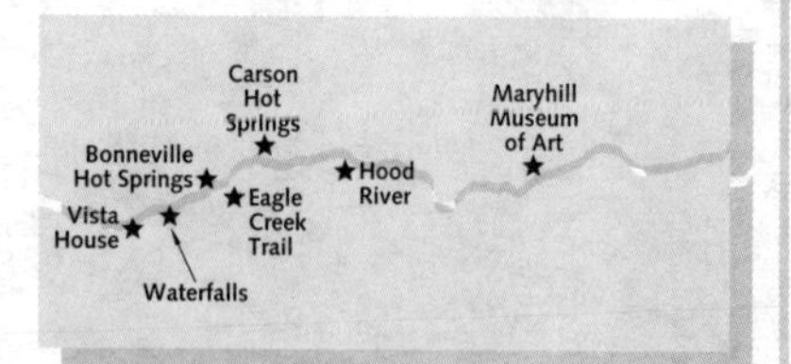

THE WESTERN GORGE & COLUMBIA RIVER HIGHWAY

Finished in 1915, the Historic Columbia River Hwy winds its scenic way between Troutdale and The Dalles. Also known as US 30, this thoroughfare was the first paved road in the Northwest and America's first scenic highway; it was also the last leg of Lewis and Clark's Corps of Discovery expedition and the hellish finale for Oregon Trail pioneers.

The Columbia River Hwy offers access to gushing waterfalls in spring, wildflower displays in summer and awe-inspiring views all year round. Hikers have plenty of trailheads to choose from, and cyclists can cruise two stretches of the old highway renovated for non-vehicle use (cars 'detour' onto I-84). It's slow going on busy weekends, however, and windy enough that trailers are not recommended.

For great views, head to **Portland Women's Forum Park** – it's just a parking lot but one of the best viewpoints into the gorge. Another great must-see panoramic spot is nearby **Crown Point**, which marks the western edge of the gorge. Here, the 1916 **Vista House**, an art nouveau-style rotunda, houses an **information center** (☎ 503-695-2230; 🕑 9am-6pm). And everyone stops at **Multnomah Falls** – Oregon's tallest waterfall at 642ft – with a one-hour hike to the top. There's a **US Forest Service visitors center** (☎ 503-695-2372; 🕑 9am-5pm) here with plenty of area information. Finally, hikers will love the very popular **Eagle Creek Trail**, the gorge's premier tromp; just be prepared for high trails with steep drop-offs.

There's camping at **Ainsworth State Park** (☎ 503-695-2301, 800-551-6949; www.oregonstateparks.org; tents/hookups $14/16) though it caters more to RVs with crowded campsites and highway noise. For unique atmosphere stay at the unforgettable **McMenamins Edgefield** (☎ 503-492-3086; www.mcmenamins.com; 2126 SW Halsey St, Troutdale; dm $35, d $58-108, d with private bathroom $120; ⊠ wi-fi), worth a visit for its bars and restaurants alone. The **Multnomah Falls Lodge** (☎ 503-695-2376; 🕑 8am-9pm) offers several dining options, from casual snacks to weekend summer BBQs to fine Northwest-style dinners.

To reach the historic highway, take exit 17 or 35 off I-84.

CASCADE LOCKS & AROUND

An early transportation center and present-day summer home to the sternwheeler *Columbia Gorge*, Cascade Locks derives its name from the navigational locks, completed in 1896, that cut through the treacherous rapids here. The town flourished throughout the 1930s, when the area was home to thousands of Bonneville Dam construction workers. Bonneville Lake (ie the backed-up dam waters) flooded the rapids in 1938 and they remain submerged.

The **Cascade Locks Historical Museum** (☎ 541-374-8535; Port Marina Park; admission free; 🕑 noon-5pm May-Sep), housed in an old lockmaster's residence, features Native American artifacts, a fish wheel and period furniture. Don't miss the basement, which is full of tools, a wooden wheelchair and a taxidermy collection including a skunk, beaver and a very surprised bobcat.

Sightsee the Columbia River aboard the **Columbia Gorge Sternwheeler** (☎ 800-643-1354; www.sternwheeler.com; adult/4-12yr $25/15). Embark from the eastern end of Marine Park, where there's a pleasant café and gift shop. There are also jet boat rides and other types of cruises.

A couple of campgrounds, a few motels and some diners offer the basics. Most travelers stay in Hood River, 14 miles to the east, or across the river at elegant Skamania Lodge (see p261).

Bonneville Dam

The **Bonneville Dam** (☎ 541-374-8820; admission free; 🕑 9am-5pm) was one of the largest Depression-era New Deal projects. Completed in 1937, it was the first major dam on the Columbia River. Dam construction brought thousands of jobs, and the cheap electricity produced by the dam promised future industrial employment. Bonneville's two hydroelectric powerhouses back up the Columbia River for 15 miles and together produce over 1 million kilowatts of power.

The visitors center has good exhibitions on the dam and local Native American culture; there are also theaters showing videos of the dam's history. Downstairs, underwater windows allow visitors to watch salmon (and lampreys!) swim by. From the roof you can clearly see the fish ladders, which allow migrating fish to negotiate around the dams.

Nearby, the **Bonneville Fish Hatchery**, located on pretty grounds, is a visitor-friendly facility. There are several ponds full of rainbow trout and massive sturgeon – including a 10-footer named Herman – along with a few educational exhibits and a gift shop.

To reach the dam and fish hatchery, take exit 40 off I-84.

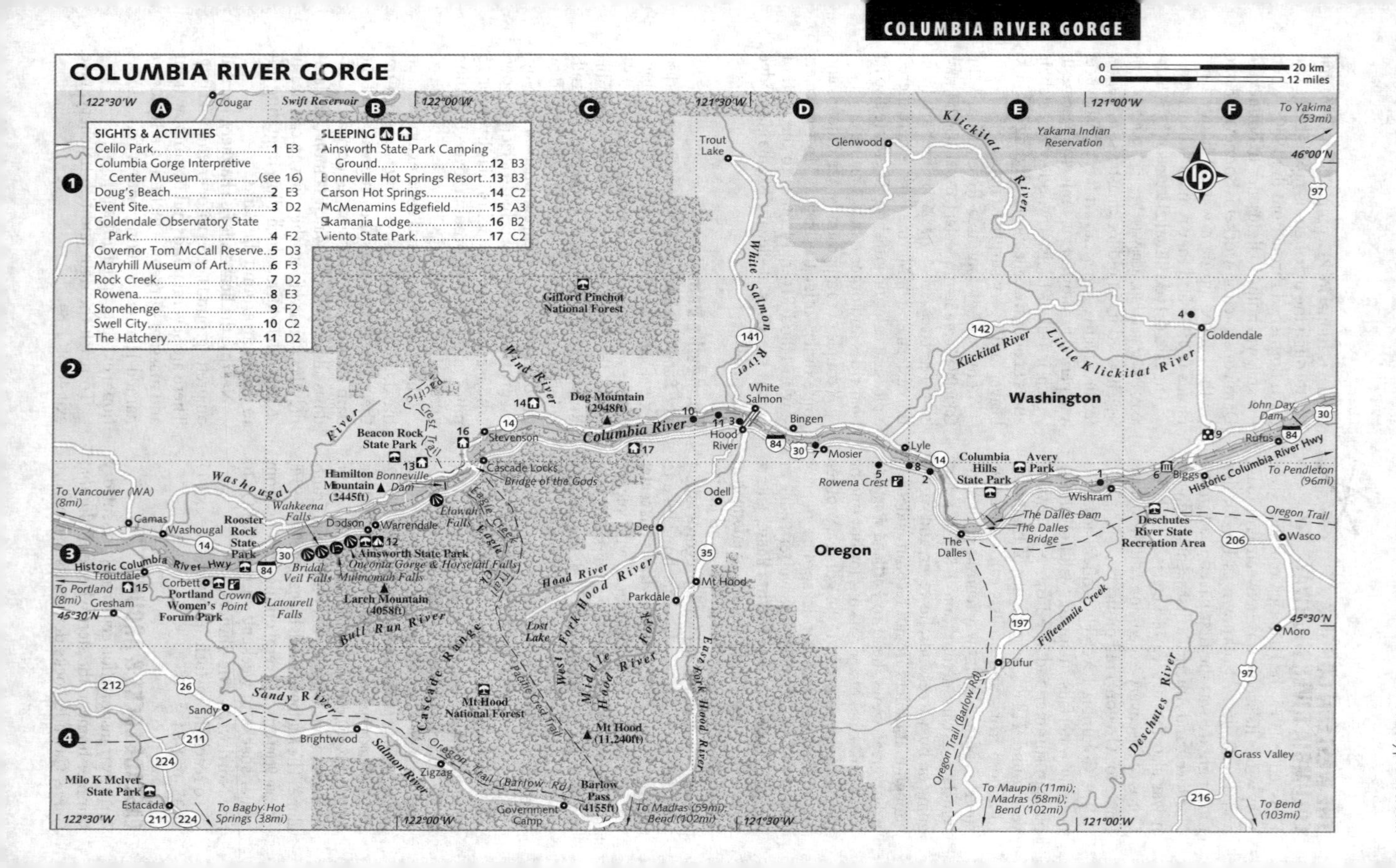
COLUMBIA RIVER GORGE
0 20 km
0 12 miles
SIGHTS & ACTIVITIES
Celilo Park....1 E3
Columbia Gorge Interpretive Center Museum....(see 16)
Doug's Beach....2 E3
Event Site....3 D2
Goldendale Observatory State Park....4 F2
Governor Tom McCall Reserve..5 D3
Maryhill Museum of Art....6 F3
Rock Creek....7 D2
Rowena....8 E3
Stonehenge....9 F2
Swell City....10 C2
The Hatchery....11 D2
SLEEPING
Ainsworth State Park Camping Ground....12 B3
Bonneville Hot Springs Resort..13 B3
Carson Hot Springs....14 C2
McMenamins Edgefield....15 A3
Skamania Lodge....16 B2
Viento State Park....17 C2
122°30'W
122°00'W
121°30'W
121°00'W
46°00'N
45°30'N
Cougar
Swift Reservoir
Trout Lake
Glenwood
Klickitat River
Yakama Indian Reservation
To Yakima (53mi)
Gifford Pinchot National Forest
White Salmon River
Goldendale
Klickitat River
Little Klickitat River
Wind River
Pacific Crest Trail
Dog Mountain (2948ft)
Washington
White Salmon
Bingen
Columbia River
Stevenson
Hood River
Mosier
Lyle
Columbia Hills State Park
Avery Park
John Day Dam
Rufus
Historic Columbia River Hwy
To Pendleton (96mi)
Biggs
Wishram
Beacon Rock State Park
Hamilton Mountain (2445ft)
Bonneville Dam
Cascade Locks
Bridge of the Gods
Rowena Crest
Washougal River
To Vancouver (WA) (8mi)
Camas
Washougal
Rooster Rock State Park
Wahkeena Falls
Dodson
Warrendale
Elowah Falls
Eagle Creek
Eagle Creek Trail
Odell
Dee
The Dalles Dam
The Dalles Bridge
The Dalles
Deschutes River State Recreation Area
Oregon Trail
Wasco
Oregon
Ainsworth State Park
Oneonta Gorge & Horsetail Falls
Multnomah Falls
Bridal Veil Falls
Historic Columbia River Hwy
Troutdale
To Portland (8mi)
Gresham
Corbett
Portland Women's Forum Park
Crown Point
Latourell Falls
Larch Mountain (4058ft)
Hood River
West Fork Hood River
Lost Lake
Mt Hood
Parkdale
Bull Run River
Cascade Range
Middle Fork Hood River
East Fork Hood River
Fifteenmile Creek
Moro
Dufur
Deschutes River
Sandy River
Sandy
Mt Hood National Forest
Pacific Crest Trail
Mt Hood (11,240ft)
Brightwood
Salmon River
Zigzag
Oregon Trail (Barlow Rd)
Barlow Pass (4155ft)
Milo K McIver State Park
Estacada
To Bagby Hot Springs (38mi)
Government Camp
To Madras (59mi); Bend (102mi)
To Maupin (11mi); Madras (58mi); Bend (102mi)
Grass Valley
To Bend (103mi)

Eagle Creek Recreation Area

The beautiful, 13.2-mile **Eagle Creek Trail** is the gorge's most popular hike; on summer weekends, get here early to snag a parking spot. Early gorge promoters engineered this historic trail in 1910 to coincide with the opening of the Columbia Gorge Hwy.

The trail passes 11 waterfalls as it meanders up wooded slopes and sheer rock walls through a narrow basalt canyon. Parts of the trail are perilously high and lack guard rails, making them dangerous for children and dogs. These sections have metal aid ropes, but even so those with vertigo issues should be extra careful.

It's 6 miles to Tunnel Falls, which passes a swimmable pool at the foot of a cliff and crosses a dizzying bridge over a 150ft chasm before reaching a tunnel carved behind a waterfall. Backpack overnight at 7.5 Mile Camp (1.5 miles past Tunnel Falls) to turn a tiring day hike into an easy two-day trip. Punchbowl Falls (4.2 miles round-trip) and High Bridge (6.5 miles round-trip) are turning points for shorter hikes.

The trail continues past Tunnel Falls for longer backcountry loops to viewpoints at Wahtum Lake and Benson Plateau, accessible via connections with the Pacific Crest Trail, Wy'East Trail No 434 and Ruckel Creek Trail No 405.

ACROSS THE BORDER

Driving the Columbia River Gorge on the Washington side has its advantages, and in some ways offers better views than the Oregon side. There are roadside recreational lakes and fewer trees to block views, plus the two-lane highway is slower and curvier than I-84. You can reach it via a few key bridges, including Cascade Lock's **Bridge of the Gods** ($1 toll), named after a mythical (and geologically possible) natural bridge over the Columbia River.

Skamania Lodge

our pick **Skamania Lodge** (☎ 509-427-7700, 800-221-7117; www.skamania.com; 1131 SW Skamania Lodge Way; d $250-392; wi-fi) Up the hill from the bridge is the gorge's biggest and cushiest resort. Facilities include hiking trails, tennis courts, a spa, an indoor swimming pool and an 18-hole golf course. There are over 250 comfortable lodge rooms and suites with either forest or river views, and the fine restaurant emphasizes local ingredients.

Columbia Gorge Interpretive Center Museum

Located below Skamania Lodge, this **museum** (☎ 800-991-2338; 900 SW Rock Creek Dr; adult/6-12yr/senior $6/4/5; 10am-5pm) attempts to weave together the many threads that form the area's history – Native Americans, early explorers, pioneer settlers, logging, fishing, shipping, power generation and recreation. However, the center also claims to have the 'world's largest rosary collection.'

Beacon Rock State Park

Washington's Beacon Rock, the core of an ancient volcano, is a pleasant **state park** (☎ 509-427-8265; Hwy 14 milepost 35) about 7 miles west

WATERFALL SPOTTING

Waterfalls are at their gushiest in spring. The following are all off US 30.

Latourell Falls (249ft) The first major waterfall as you come east on US 30. Hike 10 minutes to reach it, or go a mile to the top.

Bridal Veil Falls (160ft) Two-tiered falls reached via an easy half-mile walk. A separate wheelchair-accessible trail passes through a meadow.

Wahkeena Falls (242ft) Hike up the Wahkeena Trail, join Trail No 441 and head down to Multnomah Falls. Return via the road for the 5-mile loop.

Multnomah Falls (642ft) The gorge's top attraction. Trail No 411 leads to the top (1 mile). Continue to Multnomah Creek and the top of Larch Mountain (7 miles).

Oneonta Falls (75ft) Located within the lovely, 0.5-mile Oneonta Gorge. Carefully scamper over log jams and wade in water up to waist-high. Fun and worth it!

Horsetail Falls (176ft) Just east of Oneonta Gorge. A 3-mile loop begins here, passing through Ponytail Falls. Walk a half-mile east on US 30 to return.

Elowah Falls (289ft) More isolated but pretty falls located a mile off the highway. Hike to the top, then to McCord Creek Falls (2.5 miles round-trip).

THE FRUIT LOOP

You'll come across promotional literature and maps on the Hood River County Fruit Loop at all Columbia River Gorge information offices. Covering 35 miles along scenic fertile lands, this driving loop takes you by family fruit stands, U-pick orchards, lavender fields, alpaca farms and winery tasting rooms. There are blossoms in spring, berries in summer, and apples and pears in fall – with plenty of festivals and celebrations also throughout the seasons (except for winter). It's a good way to sample the area's agricultural bounties while appreciating the local scenery too. Jump on the agritourism wagon; for more information and a list of events, check www.hoodriverfruitloop.com.

of the Bridge of the Gods. It offers hiking, mountain-bike trails, picnicking, camping (tents/hookups $19/24) and river access.

The ascent up 848ft Beacon Rock is a 0.75-mile trail with 53 switchbacks. For a longer hike, climb 2445ft Hamilton Mountain (five hours round-trip). Going just 1 mile leads to Hardy and Rodney Falls. For something easy, try the short, easygoing hike along the park's nature trail to tiny Riddell Lake.

Beacon Rock is one of the few rock-climbing sites in the gorge. The majority of climbs are on the south face of Beacon Rock and are for experienced climbers only.

Mountain bikers and horseback riders share old logging roads to the upper reaches of Hardy Creek and the back of Hamilton Mountain. Road access begins at a locked gate about half a mile up the Group Camp road.

Carson Hot Springs Resort

Featuring a fine golf course with a clubhouse, this **spa** (☎ 509-427-8292; www.carsonhotspringsresort.com; 372 St Martin Rd; d from $80; ☒) also offers claw-foot tub soaks ($20) and wraps with massage ($60). There's a sauna, but don't expect anything too fancy. There are several kinds of rooms available, all excellent and the newest ones are even semi-luxurious.

Bonneville Hot Springs Resort

For a more luxurious experience, there's this fancy **spa** (☎ 866-459-1678; www.bonnevilleresort.com; 1252 E Cascade Dr; d from $160; ☒ ⊠). With a grand, five-star lobby and stylish rooms (some with private hot tubs), this resort offers fine dining and full spa services. There's an elegant, 25m indoor pool filled with mineral water, and indoor and outdoor Jacuzzis.

Dog Mountain

It's a steep 4 miles up the popular Dog Mountain Trail, but this is the best place in the gorge for late-spring wildflowers. Once on top the views of the Columbia River and nearby Cascade volcanoes are spectacular. Allow approximately six hours round-trip.

For other hiking and recreational information, visit the **US Forest Service visitors center** (☎ 509-427-2528; ⏲ 9am-5pm) in Skamania Lodge (p261).

HOOD RIVER

One of the best windsurfing and kiteboarding destinations in the world is the dynamic town of Hood River. Strong river currents, prevailing westerly winds and a vast body of water provide the perfect conditions for these wind sports, attracting sometimes hundreds of photogenic enthusiasts who zip back and forth across the wide Columbia River.

But Hood River offers more than awesome winds. South of town, the Hood River drains a wide fertile valley planted with orchards. During spring, the area fills with the scent and color of pink and white blossoms, and roadside fruit stands peddle apples, pears, cherries, berries and vegetables. Premiere wineries have also taken hold in the region, providing good wine-tasting opportunities. Hwy 35, which traverses the valley, continues south 40 miles to Mt Hood (p269), Oregon's best-known mountain and a mecca for more great outdoor activities.

The Hood River Valley springs to life the third weekend of April with the **Blossom Festival**. Local orchard tours are the highlight, along with food, music and crafts in town. And if you happen to be around on a Saturday, check out the **Saturday Market** at 5th and Columbia Sts for crafts, live music and a farmers market.

For details there's the **chamber of commerce** (☎ 541-386-2000, 800-366-3530; www.hoodriver.org; 405 Portway Ave; ⏲ 9am-5pm Mon-Fri, 10am-5pm Sat & Sun).

Sights & Activities

The **Hood River County Historical Museum** (☎ 541-386-6772; 300 E Port Marina Dr; admission free; ⏲ 10am-4pm Mon-Sat, noon-4pm Sun) includes Native American artifacts, pioneer quilts and early logging equipment among its displays. Open April to October only; limited hours in fall.

The **Mt Hood Railroad** (☎ 541-386-3556, 800-872-4661; www.mthoodrr.com; 110 Railroad Ave; adult/2-12yr/senior/from $25/15/23) built in 1906, once transported fruit and lumber from the upper Hood River Valley to the main railhead in Hood River. The vintage trains now transport tourists beneath Mt Hood's snowy peak and past fragrant orchards. Reserve in advance.

Lovers of the grape can visit over a dozen wineries in the region for **wine-tasting** adventures. Stop by the chamber of commerce for a 'Columbia Gorge Wine Map,' which outlines all of them; you can also check www.columbiagorgewine.com.

Take your own postcard photo of Mt Hood from **Lost Lake**, which frames the white peak rising from a deep-blue lake amid thick green forest. This inland side trip offers relief when the gorge gets too hot. To reach Lost Lake, which is 25 miles south of Hood River, take Hwy 281 from Hood River to Dee and follow the signs. Canoe rentals are available at the resort here.

Head south of town for great **mountain biking**. Most of the area's trails are off Hwy 35 and Forest Rd 44 (which branches off Hwy 35 about 20 miles south of Hood River). Good local rides include Post Canyon, Surveyor's Ridge and Nestor Peak. **Discover Bicycles** (☎ 541-386-4820; 116 Oak St; 10am-6pm Mon-Sat, till 5pm Sun) rents mountain bikes and can give advice.

For **white-water rafting**, head to the White Salmon, Hood or Klickitat Rivers. For organized trips check out **Wet Planet** (☎ 509-493-8989, 800-306-1673; www.wetplanetwhitewater.com), located nearby in White Salmon, WA. In Hood River, **Kayak Shed** (☎ 541-386-4286; 6 Oak St; 9am-5pm) rents kayaks for $40 per day.

Cyclists, walkers, runners and skaters share the pavement on the refurbished stretch of the Historic Columbia River Hwy between Hood River and Mosier. No cars are permitted on the 4.5-mile road, which passes through two old highway tunnels and is popular with families. To reach the trailhead, head east out of downtown, cross Hwy 35, and continue up the hill to the parking area ($3 parking fee).

Sleeping

Hood River is a popular place; you'll need reservations in summer. Listed here are summer weekend rates; during the off-season and on weekdays prices tend to drop.

Viento State Park (☎ 541-374-8811, www.oregonstateparks.org; exit 56 from I-84; tents/hookups $14/16) Located 8 miles west of Hood River is this campground near the highway and river; there's river access and walking trails.

Columbia River Gorge Hostel (☎ 509-493-3363; www.bingenschool.com; cnr Cedar & Humboldt Sts; dm $21, d $55) Across the Columbia River in Bingen, WA, this quirky hostel is located in an aging school two blocks up from the main highway. Lodgings are in the old basic classrooms (sometimes oddly shaped), and facilities include a kitchen and old gym with basketball court. Reception hours are limited.

Gorge View B&B (☎ 541-386-5770; 1009 Columbia St; dm $43, d $104; wi-fi) Catering to outdoor sports enthusiasts more than an exclusive clientele is this tasteful yet casual B&B. There's a four-bunk room for single travelers, along with peeks at the river views from the living room. Most rooms share a common bathroom; open May to September only.

Vagabond Lodge (☎ 541-386-2992; 4070 Westcliff Dr; d $72-115;) Some rooms at this basic motel have river views, and suites come with amenities like fireplace, kitchenette and Jacuzzi. It's next to the highway but near woodsy areas and next door to the Columbia Gorge Hotel (and its pleasant gardens).

Hood River Hotel (☎ 541-386-1900, 800-386-1859; www.hoodriverhotel.com; 102 Oak St; d $99-186; wi-fi) Located right in the heart of downtown, this fine 1913 hotel offers comfortable old-fashioned rooms with four-post or sleigh beds. The suites and riverview rooms have the best amenities and views. Kitchenettes are also available, and there's a small restaurant, sauna and Jacuzzi on the premises.

Inn at the Gorge (☎ 541-386-4429; www.innatthegorge.com; 1113 Eugene St; d $130-164; wi-fi) Surrounded by a wrap-around porch and lush grounds is this comfortable 1908 house with five rooms, three of which are two-bedroom suites with kitchenettes. The owners are friendly and have DVDs to rent, and there's a nice grassy lawn and patio in the back.

Lakecliff B&B (☎ 541-386-7000; www.lakecliffbnb.com; 3820 Westcliff Dr; d $192;) Sitting on 3.5 acres overlooking the Columbia River, this artsy and colorful B&B offers four simple but spacious rooms, most with electric fireplace and some with views. There's a grassy lawn that's popular for weddings in summer, along with a back patio with a great view. No children allowed.

SLICING UP THE COLUMBIA

On hot summer days, the inland desert climate of Eastern Oregon attracts cool air from the Pacific Coast, creating fierce winds that shoot westwards 80 miles through the narrow walls of the Columbia River Gorge. These westerlies, which directly oppose the river's flow, create some of the world's most optimal conditions for **windsurfing**, popular around Hood River since the 1980s. **Kiteboarding**, a relative newcomer on the block, offers greater speeds and more airy acrobatics. On a good day you can witness hundreds of colorful sails cutting through the water at breathtaking speeds, a daring display of athleticism and beauty.

Good put-in spots in Washington include Swell City, the Hatchery and Doug's Beach. In Oregon, Hood River's Event Site is a major put-in location; other good ones include Rock Creek and Rowena. Wind conditions change frequently, making some locations better than others on any given day; for current conditions check www.iwindsurf.com.

For beginners, taking a lesson will make a world of difference. **Big Winds** (☎ 888-509-4210; www.bigwinds.com; 207 Front St, Hood River) is the biggest operator in the area, and the only one open year-round. **Brian's Windsurfing** (☎ 541-386-1423; www.brianswindsurfing.com; 100 Marina Way, Hood River) is another good option.

Columbia Gorge Hotel (☎ 541-387-5428, 800-345-1921; www.columbiagorgehotel.com; 4000 Westcliff Dr; d $219-330; ⊠ wi-fi) Hood River's most famous stay is this historic Spanish-style hotel, though it won't be your best value. While service is good, the atmosphere classy and the grounds lovely, some rooms are smallish and 'river views' can be blocked by trees. It's the classiest place in town, however.

Eating

Sage's Cafe (☎ 541-386-9404; 202 Cascade Ave; sandwiches $4-7; 7:30am-4pm Mon-Fri, 8am-4pm Sat, 9am-4pm Sun) A good variety of breakfast dishes, along with over 25 kinds of sandwiches, are the main deal at this casual spot. Wraps, soups, salads and plenty of espresso choices round out the menu.

Full Sail Brewpub (☎ 541-386-2247; 506 Columbia St; mains $8-14; 11:30am-9:30pm Sun-Thu, till 10:30pm Fri & Sat) Hood River's main brewpub offers limited food selections – there are only a handful of appetizers, sandwiches and main dishes – but the river views are great, and there's decent beer too. An outdoor patio is a plus on sunny days, and you can also take free 20-minute tours in the afternoon.

6th Street Bistro & Loft (☎ 541-386-5737; 509 Cascade Ave; mains $13-19; 11:30am-10:30pm Sun-Thu, till 10:30pm Fri & Sat) This is a long-running bistro with good sandwiches and hamburgers for lunch, and fancier dishes like chipotle-lime glazed chicken, and morel and asparagus linguine for dinner. There are also choice microbrews and a fantastic outdoor deck and patio.

Celilo (☎ 541-386-5710; 16 Oak St; mains $15-21; 11:30am-3pm & 5-9:30pm Sun-Thu, till 10pm Fri & Sat) For upscale dining there's slick Celilo, a modern and beautiful restaurant with walls that open to the sidewalk on warm afternoons. Main dishes like the housemade tagliatelle pasta and seared Pacific halibut are made from local, organic ingredients, and other sustainable practices are also utilized.

our pick **Stonehedge Gardens & Bistro** (☎ 541-386-3940; 3405 Cascade Ave; mains $22-27; 5-9pm) Located at the end of a 0.3-mile gravel road, at the top of a hill, is this fine restaurant in a 1898 restored house. On a warm night, snag a table on the huge stone patio and order the seafood linguini, seared ahi or gorgonzola sirloin. Reserve way in advance for summer weekends.

Getting There & Around

Columbia Area Transit offers **Greyhound** buses (☎ 541-386-4202; 600 E Marina Way), Amtrak's *Empire Builder* stops at Bingen, on the Washington side of the gorge, daily along its Portland–Spokane leg.

THE DALLES & AROUND

Located about 85 miles east of Portland, The Dalles features a decidedly different climate – much drier and sunnier. Though steadfastly unglamorous and down-to-earth, the city offers good outdoor recreation; there's decent camping and hiking, and fierce winds excellent for windsurfing and kiteboarding. The region hosts several good wineries and is also the nation's largest producer of sweet cherries.

The Dalles has gone high-tech – Google has built a large server facility here to utilize the area's cheap hydroelectric power – bringing jobs, higher real estate prices and a bit of attention to this homely city.

The Dalles was likely named by French Canadian trappers after the trough-like shape of the Columbia River just upstream from town, which they may have associated with the stones used to pave gutters back home (the name is French for 'flagstones'). The region is full of basaltic formations, and south of downtown The Dalles is built on a series of steep terraces, with rocky outcroppings jutting up in the middle of streets and in people's backyards. For a good view across to Washington and some greenery, head uphill to Sorosis Park on Scenic Dr.

One of The Dalles' biggest summer events is **Fort Dalles Day**, held in July. There's music, dances, a parade and a popular rodeo. The **Chamber of Commerce** (☎ 541-296-2231, 800-255-3385; www.thedalleschamber.com; 404 W 2nd St; 8:30am-6pm Mon-Fri, 10am-4pm Sat, 11am-3pm Sun) caters to your monkey curiosity; staff can also hand you a walking tour map of the city's interesting buildings and murals.

There are bus services at **Greyhound** (☎ 541-296-2421; 201 1st St). Amtrak stops at Wishram, on the Washington side of the Columbia River.

Sights & Activities

COLUMBIA GORGE DISCOVERY CENTER

This **museum** (☎ 541-296-8600; 5000 Discovery Dr; adult/6-16yr/senior $8/4/7; 9am-5pm) Covers the history of the gorge, from its creation by cataclysmic floods to the hardships pioneers had traversing it, to early settlements and transport in the area to the construction – and consequences – of its dams. The Lewis and Clark wing has an exhibit on animals the corps had to kill (including 190 dogs and a ferret); there's also a frightfully large pewter syringe similar to the one used to give Sacagawea's ailing son an enema.

Other amenities include a large theater, plenty of video narratives and a nice café with an outside deck. The discovery center is a couple miles west of the city.

FORT DALLES MUSEUM

Located at the corner of W 15th and Garrison Sts, this **museum** (☎ 541-296-4547; 500 W 15th St; adult/7-17yr/senior $5/1/4; 10am-5pm) was once part of an 1856 fort and Oregon's oldest history museum. It's a fascinating place full of mostly donated historical items; highlights include an albatross-feather muff, human hair wreaths, a child's casket with window face hole and a bonnet worn at Ford Theatre the night Abraham Lincoln was assassinated. There are several antique cars, stagecoaches and even a horse-drawn hearse. Across the street is a rare example of the area's Swedish architecture.

THE DALLES DAM & LOCK

The Dalles Dam, built in 1957, produces enough electricity to power a city of a million inhabitants. Access to this power came at a price, however. The dam's reservoir, Lake Celilo, flooded the culturally rich area around Celilo Falls, which was for thousands of years a Native American meeting place and fishery (see boxed text, p266).

In Seufert Park, east on the frontage road from I-84 exit 87, is the **Dalles Dam Visitors Center** (☎ 541-296-9778; Clodfelter Way; 9am-5pm spring & summer only). This information center contains the usual homage to hydroelectricity, along with exhibits on local history. From here, a small train (no charge) leaves every half-hour to visit the dam.

COLUMBIA HILLS STATE PARK

Some of the most famous remaining **pictographs** (painted figures) along the Columbia River are at this Washington **state park** (☎ 509-767-1159; Hwy 14 milepost 85; Apr-Oct). The pictograph area can be visited only on a free guided tour, at 10am on Friday and Saturday; reservations are required. The park's **petroglyphs** (carved figures) can be seen any time, without a tour.

Rock climbers practice their moves on the basalt walls of **Horsethief Butte**, just east of the park entrance, and this section of the Columbia River is a good place for beginning windsurfers to catch some wind without strong river currents. The park also offers fishing and swimming in the lake, as well as camping (see p266) and hiking.

ROWENA CREST

Between Hood River and The Dalles, the heavy vegetation of the western gorge diminishes, and the basaltic architecture of the gorge appears.

On top of Rowena Crest are spectacular views and vast meadows now preserved as a wildflower sanctuary. Established by the

THE FALL OF CELILO

On March 10, 1957, the newly constructed gates of the Dalles Dam closed for the first time, nearly halting the mighty Columbia. Eight miles upstream, it took only a few hours for Celilo Falls – an important Native American fishing ground – to be forever buried under the rising floodwaters. It was the end of a Native American identity, tradition and livelihood that dated back 10,000 years.

Over millennia, thousands of native peoples from as far away as the Great Plains and Alaska would gather at Celilo Falls – also known as *Wyam* ('the echo of falling water') – to fish for salmon, trade goods and socialize. Lewis and Clark stopped by in 1805 and were amazed by the variety and numbers of people they encountered here.

Celilo Falls' tallest drop only stood at 22ft – but in volume, the falls were the sixth largest in the world. Native Americans would risk their lives on rickety wooden platforms over the rushing currents while using dip nets to catch their 60lb quarry. It was a dangerous occupation – if they fell, survival was unlikely – but a good day could yield tons of fish per day.

Native American tribes were financially compensated for submergence of the falls, but their cultural loss is priceless. Today, 50 years later, Celilo Falls is still mourned by those who remember its glory – and recall the impact the area had on their ancestors' lives.

Nature Conservancy, the **Governor Tom McCall Reserve**, on Rowena Plateau, is one of the best places to see native plants. Springtime wildflowers include balsamroot, wild parsley, penstemon and wild lilies. Watch out for poison oak.

To reach this section of the Historic Columbia River Hwy from The Dalles, follow W 6th St westward out of town until it becomes US 30. From the west, take I-84 exit 69 at Mosier, and travel east on US 30.

WINDSURFING

Hood River may be the gorge's windsurfing capital, but the wind blows hard at The Dalles too. Right in town, **Riverfront Park** (exit 85) is a good spot for beginners. **Avery Park**, 8 miles from town, offers access to the river from the Washington side. A favorite entry point, with strong west winds, is **Celilo Park**, about 10 miles east of town.

Sleeping & Eating

Columbia Hills State Park (☎ 509-767-1159; www.stateparks.com; Hwy 14 milepost 85; tents $14-19, hookups $25; Apr-Oct) This park is across the Dalles Bridge in Washington (2 miles east on Hwy 14) near the site of an old Native American village where Lewis and Clark camped. It offers two boat ramps and plenty of other activities (see p265).

Columbia Windrider Inn (☎ 541-296-2607; www.windriderinn.com; 200 W 4th St; r $49-65;) This casual guesthouse has only four simple but comfortable rooms, each with its own bathroom (though two have them down the hall). It caters mostly to longer-term tenants, but doesn't turn away brief visitors if there's room. Fun amenities include a pool table, hot tub and swimming pool. Kitchen use and continental breakfast is included.

Oregon Motor Motel (☎ 541-296-9111; 200 W 2nd St; d $60; wi-fi) The Oregon is a basic motel with nothing-special rooms, though they do come with microwave and fridge. The best thing about this place is its central location (right downtown) and the morning doughnuts. Weekday prices are $5 cheaper.

Best Western River City Inn (☎ 541-296-9107; www.bestwesternoregon.com; 112 W 2nd St; d from $69;) The Dalles nicest downtown lodging, with typical Best Western amenities like pleasant rooms, all the regular appliances and even a small outdoor pool out the front. Breakfast is included; reserve in summer.

our pick **Lyle Hotel** (☎ 509-365-5953, 800-447-6310; www.lylehotel.com; 100 7th St, Lyle, WA; d $77; wi-fi) Cross the river and head 8 miles west on Hwy 14 to tiny Lyle, where this old hotel has 10 nicely restored warm rooms. This isn't a luxurious place – shared bathrooms are down the hall and there are no TVs – but it is charming and relaxed. A continental breakfast is included, and the restaurant serves good dinners (Wednesday to Sunday) to both hotel and outside guests.

Holstein's Coffee Co (☎ 541-298-2326; 811 E 3rd St; 5am-8pm Mon-Fri, 5:30am-8pm Sat, 6am-8pm Sun) For good coffee, stop at this pleasant joint which offers a dozen kinds of fancy java drinks (think raspberry mochas), along with plenty of smoothies (peanut butter?!) and exotic 'coffee alternatives' like chai, yerba mate and Italian sodas. There are pastries and a nice deck too.

Baldwin Saloon (☎ 541-296-5666; 205 Court St; mains $9-15; 🕑 11am-10pm) It doesn't look like much from the outside, but this 1876 building holds a colorful past – it's been a bar, a brothel and a coffin storage warehouse. Today it's a casual restaurant with interesting brick interior full of large oil paintings. The menu is simple but good, with tasty natural beef burgers and exceptional desserts. There's an historic bar, plus live piano music on weekends.

Romul's (☎ 541-296-9771; 312 Court St; mains $16-20; 🕑 11am-9pm Sun-Thu, till 10pm Fri & Sat) Italian murals and faux-marble statues decorate the inside of this upscale restaurant, which serves up The Dalles' fanciest dinners. Pastas are the main show; try the penne in a light vodka cream sauce or the vermicelli with house-made meatballs.

EASTERN GORGE

Deschutes River State Recreation Area

The Deschutes River, Oregon's second largest, cuts through Central Oregon and meets the Columbia at this fine **state park** (☎ 541-739-2322, 800-452-5687; www.oregonstateparks.org; tents/hookups $8/16). Reserve sites in summer.

Rafting parties finish up here after excursions on the Deschutes, while boaters head onto the Columbia from here. This is a great place to find sage-scented warmth and sun, in spring especially, when western Oregon is wet and dank.

From the south end of the park, riverside **hiking trails** pass old homesteads, springs and groves of willow and locust trees. Keep an eye out for raptors and migrating songbirds. There is also a **mountain-biking trail** (originally a rail bed) that runs about 16 miles upriver from here.

Maryhill Museum of Art

Eccentric Sam Hill is responsible for some of the most famous building projects in the gorge, including this impressive and worthwhile **museum** (☎ 509-773-3733; www.maryhillmuseum.org; 35 Maryhill Museum Dr, WA; adult/child/senior $7/2/6; 🕑 9am-5pm Mar 15-Nov 15).

Spectacularly located on a bluff above the Columbia, this old mansion boasts an outstanding collection of Native American baskets and other artifacts, including a seal intestine parka and carved walrus tusks. Other notable exhibits include a large and amazing collection of chess sets, a variety of French fashion dolls and drawings by Auguste Rodin. Outside are garden sculptures, picnic tables with fine views and roaming peacocks. There's also a café on premises.

The museum is in Washington, just across the Columbia; cross the US 97 bridge and follow the signs.

Stonehenge

Not one for small gestures, Sam Hill built a full-scale replica of Salisbury Plain's Stonehenge on the cliffs above the Columbia River. Dedicated as a memorial to Klickitat County's soldiers killed in WWI, his Stonehenge was built of poured concrete and represents an intact site (unlike its tumbled-down English cousin).

Hill planned that his Stonehenge would line up for celestial events such as equinoxes, but many local Stonehenge scholars think the keystone is in the wrong place. At any rate, this is a popular place for odd rites and ceremonies.

To reach Sam Hill's Stonehenge from Maryhill, continue east on Hwy 14 past the US 97 junction. One mile later, follow signs to the right for Stonehenge.

Goldendale Observatory State Park

Located in Washington state, about 10 miles from the Columbia River, this **observatory** (☎ 509-773-3141; 1602 Observatory Dr; 🕑 2-5pm & 8pm-midnight Wed-Sun Apr-Sep; 2-5pm & 7pm-10pm Fri-Sun Oct-Mar) sits atop a 5-acre park. There's a 24.5in reflecting telescope inside, and free tours and evening programs are available. In the evening there's also the chance to view heavenly bodies through the telescopes. If you arrive in the daytime, however, don't despair – there are great vistas from the top, even if they're not of planets, galaxies, stars and comets.

Central Oregon & the Oregon Cascades

Love mountain tops? Well, that's what Central Oregon and its Cascades are all about. You can practically skip your way from peak to snowy peak through this whole region – from Mt Hood, to Jefferson, to Bachelor, to Three-Fingered Jack and the Sisters volcanoes, through Thielsen and finally to Crater Lake's Mt Scott. As you can imagine, there's plenty of awesome skiing and mountaineering here, along with exceptional hiking and camping. And it's not just mountain-lovers who come – there's also great biking, golfing, rafting, kayaking, fishing and rock climbing in Central Oregon. And did we mention the weather is great here too? Boasting over 300 days of sunshine a year, what more could you ask for?

How about the amazingly stunning Crater Lake, which started life as a 12,000ft puffy volcano before blowing its top and then collecting only fresh water and snow into a lake almost 200ft deep? And the Newberry National Volcanic Monument, where lava flows, lava tubes and a lava cast forest are all frozen in time? Or the gloriously cool and clear Metolius River, which flows straight out of a hillside and offers world-class trout fishing? And as much as the outdoors may beckon, when it's time for a break there's the exploding city of Bend, right smack in the middle of this region, providing the visitor with plenty of good food and accommodations (or head to nearby Sisters for a more personal atmosphere).

HIGHLIGHTS

- Taking in the surreal beauty of gorgeous **Crater Lake** (p285)
- Carving powder in winter (and summer!) above **Timberline Lodge** (p273)
- Photographing summer wildflowers in the **Three Sisters Wilderness** (p277)
- Sampling **Bend's** (p278) finest cuisine, after golfing, rafting, skiing or hiking nearby
- Setting up a multi-pitch climb at spectacular **Smith Rock** (p275)
- Peeking through a lava tube at **Newberry National Volcanic Monument** (p283)

Geography & Climate

The Cascades run the length of the state, getting higher from south to north and forming a second barrier – after the Coast Range – against the moist air that comes in from the Pacific Ocean. Their western slopes wring out much of the remaining wetness as it heads east, and this second pressing of the clouds results in precipitation totals around 50% to 75% of those on the coast (which is still an awful lot). The northern Cascades at their higher elevations get a dumping of snow that can average hundreds of inches annually. And even in the south, the highest recorded annual snowfall total for Crater Lake National Park reached almost 900in, with on-the-ground depths of more than 20ft. Though signs point toward decreasing totals and warmer winters, snow generally persists through April at 4000ft; above 7000ft it will remain year-round in the form of glaciers. Though there are enormous variations in temperature, average lows in winter in the western Cascades run in the low 20s, with summer highs in the 70s.

East of the range's summit is a different world. Most of Central Oregon lies above 2000ft in elevation, and the rain shadow cast by the Cascades makes this high desert country. Precipitation averages vary here from the low single digits to just shy of the teens, good conditions for the juniper trees and sagebrush throughout the region. Average minimum/maximum temperatures in January run in the low 20s/40s while July highs/lows are in the mid-80s/40s.

National Parks & Wilderness Areas

Crater Lake National Park, at the extreme southern end of Central Oregon, is the state's sole national park and truly a jewel in the park system's crown, holding the world's ninth deepest lake and plenty of opportunities for hiking, Nordic skiing and scoping magnificent vistas. Other outdoor joys in the region include the Three Sisters Wilderness, a mountaineers' paradise featuring scenic peaks, and the tranquil Mt Jefferson Wilderness Area, which offers exceptional camping, hiking and fishing opportunities.

Getting There & Around

The Redmond Municipal Airport, 18 miles north of Bend, is the only show of its kind around here. It sees dozens of commercial flights arrive daily from Portland, Eugene, all of Oregon's neighboring states but Idaho, and the outliers Utah and Colorado. Amtrak's *Coast Starlight* rail route, on its way between Klamath Falls and Eugene, stops at Chemult (northwest of Crater Lake National Park), with connecting buses between there and Bend. Various city and county bus systems provide service around and between several of the towns in this chapter; you may be able to cobble together an itinerary using **TripCheck** (www.tripcheck.com), a site maintained by the Oregon Department of Transportation.

MT HOOD

The state's highest peak, Mt Hood (11,240ft), pops into view over much of northern Oregon whenever there's a sunny day, exerting an almost magnetic tug on skiers, hikers and sightseers. In summer, wildflowers bloom on the mountainsides and hidden ponds shimmer in blue, making for some unforgettable hikes; in winter, downhill and cross-country skiing dominates people's minds and bodies. Timberline Lodge (p273), a handsome wood gem from the 1930s, offers glorious shelter and refreshments to both guests and non-guests all year round, and can't be missed.

Mt Hood rises above the Western Cascades, a ridge of older volcanoes stretching between Mt Rainier and Mt Shasta. These volcanoes erupted between 20 and 40 million years ago, and their peaks have long since eroded. Mt Hood began to burp toward the end of the last ice age, and geologists reckon that Mt Hood's last major eruption was about 1000 years ago.

Mt Hood is accessible year-round on US 26 from Portland (56 miles), and from Hood River (44 miles) on Hwy 35. Together with the Columbia River Hwy, these routes comprise the Mt Hood Loop, a popular scenic drive. Government Camp is at the pass over Mt Hood, and is the center of business on the mountain.

For maps, permits and information there's the **Mt Hood Information Center** (☎ 503-622-4822; www.mthood.info; 24403 E Welches Rd, Welches; 🕑 8am-5pm). Various area ranger stations provide similar services and include **Hood River** (☎ 541-352-6002; 6780 Hwy 35, Parkdale; 🕑 8am-4:30pm Mon-Sat), **ZigZag** (☎ 503-622-3191; 70220 E Hwy 26, Zigzag; 🕑 7:45am-4:30pm Mon-Sat) and **Mt Hood National Forest Headquarters** (☎ 503-668-1700; www.fs.fed.us/r6/mthood; 16400 Champion Way, Sandy; 🕑 7:30-11:30am, 12:30-4:30pm Mon-Fri).

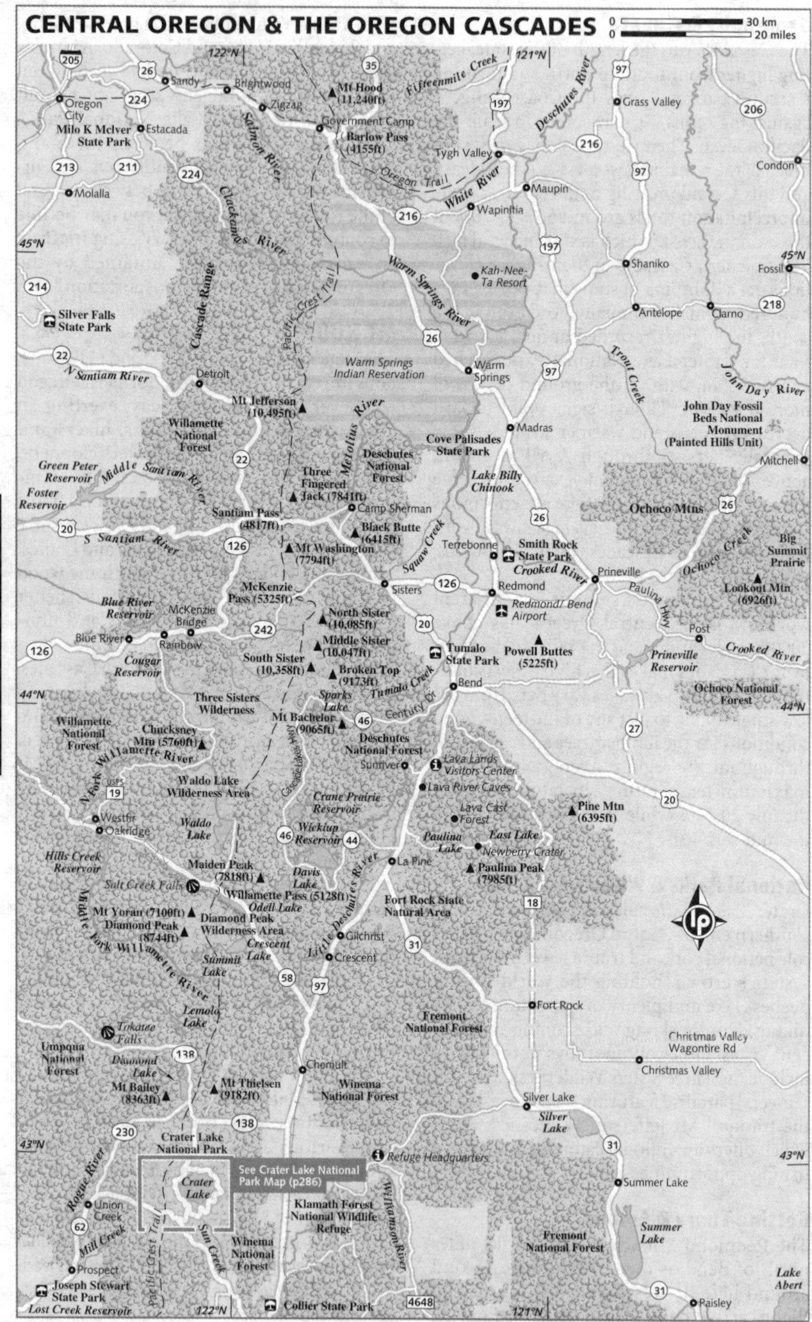

CENTRAL OREGON & THE OREGON CASCADES
30 km
20 miles
Mt Hood (11,240ft)
Sandy
Brightwood
Zigzag
Government Camp
Barlow Pass (4155ft)
Oregon City
Estacada
Milo K McIver State Park
Molalla
Grass Valley
Condon
Tygh Valley
Maupin
Wapinitia
Shaniko
Fossil
Antelope
Clarno
Kah-Nee-Ta Resort
Silver Falls State Park
Warm Springs Indian Reservation
Warm Springs
Detroit
Mt Jefferson (10,495ft)
Willamette National Forest
John Day Fossil Beds National Monument (Painted Hills Unit)
Madras
Mitchell
Cove Palisades State Park
Lake Billy Chinook
Deschutes National Forest
Three Fingered Jack (7841ft)
Camp Sherman
Santiam Pass (4817ft)
Black Butte (6415ft)
Mt Washington (7794ft)
Ochoco Mtns
Terrebonne
Smith Rock State Park
Prineville
Big Summit Prairie
Lookout Mtn (6926ft)
Sisters
Redmond
McKenzie Pass (5325ft)
Redmond/ Bend Airport
North Sister (10,085ft)
Middle Sister (10,047ft)
South Sister (10,358ft)
Broken Top (9173ft)
Blue River Reservoir
McKenzie Bridge
Blue River
Rainbow
Cougar Reservoir
Tumalo State Park
Powell Buttes (5225ft)
Post
Prineville Reservoir
Bend
Three Sisters Wilderness
Sparks Lake
Mt Bachelor (9065ft)
Ochoco National Forest
Chucksney Mtn (5760ft)
Deschutes National Forest
Sunriver
Lava Lands Visitors Center
Lava River Caves
Waldo Lake Wilderness Area
Westfir
Oakridge
Waldo Lake
Crane Prairie Reservoir
Wickiup Reservoir
Lava Cast Forest
Pine Mtn (6395ft)
Paulina Lake
East Lake
Newberry Crater
Paulina Peak (7985ft)
La Pine
Hills Creek Reservoir
Maiden Peak (7818ft)
Davis Lake
Salt Creek Falls
Willamette Pass (5128ft)
Odell Lake
Fort Rock State Natural Area
Mt Yoran (7100ft)
Diamond Peak (8744ft)
Diamond Peak Wilderness Area
Crescent Lake
Gilchrist
Crescent
Summit Lake
Fort Rock
Lemolo Lake
Fremont National Forest
Tokatee Falls
Umpqua National Forest
Diamond Lake
Mt Bailey (8363ft)
Mt Thielsen (9182ft)
Chemult
Winema National Forest
Christmas Valley Wagontire Rd
Christmas Valley
Silver Lake
Crater Lake National Park
Refuge Headquarters
See Crater Lake National Park Map (p286)
Crater Lake
Summer Lake
Union Creek
Klamath Forest National Wildlife Refuge
Fremont National Forest
Prospect
Joseph Stewart State Park
Lost Creek Reservoir
Collier State Park
Lake Abert
Paisley
Salmon River
Clackamas River
Cascade Range
Pacific Crest Trail
Oregon Trail
White River
Fifteenmile Creek
Deschutes River
Warm Springs River
Trout Creek
John Day River
N Santiam River
Metolius River
Middle Santiam River
Green Peter Reservoir
Foster Reservoir
S Santiam River
Squaw Creek
Crooked River
Ochoco Creek
Paulina Hwy
Tumalo Creek
Century Dr
Cascade Lakes Hwy
N Fork Willamette River
Little Deschutes River
Middle Fork Willamette River
Rogue River
Mill Creek
Sun Creek
Williamson River
122°N
121°N
45°N
44°N
43°N

Activities

DOWNHILL SKIING

Mt Hood Meadows (☎ 503-337-2222, snow report 503-227-7669; www.skihood.com; lift tickets adult/7-14yr & senior $52/30) is the largest ski area on Mt Hood and often has the best conditions. Facilities include two day-lodges with a dozen snack bars and restaurants.

Timberline Lodge (☎ 503-622-0717, snow report 503-222-2211; www.timberlinelodge.com; lift tickets adult/7-14yr/15-17yr $52/30/40) boasts skiing throughout summer, and its legendary lodge is a must-visit for bar drinks, fireplace sit-downs and upscale dinners.

Mt Hood Skibowl (☎ 503-272-3206; www.skibowl.com; lift tickets adult/7-12yr & senior $38/20) is the USA's largest night-ski area and is the closest skiing to Portland. It's smaller than Meadows or Timberline and popular with people who buzz out from Portland for an evening of skiing.

Cooper Spur Ski Area (☎ 503-352-7803; www.cooperspur.com/skiarea; lift tickets adult/child under 14yr & senior $20/15), on the northeast slopes of Mt Hood, caters to beginners and families with 10 runs and a tubing area. An 'all-access pass' ($30) includes equipment rentals.

CROSS-COUNTRY SKIING

Nordic Center (☎ 503-337-2222, ext 262; day pass $10) offers around 10 miles of groomed wooded trails. Several other free (ungroomed) trails start from the same parking area, including an easy mile-long trail to Sahalie Falls and a longer, more challenging one to Elk Meadows.

Teacup Lake (www.teacupnordic.org; trail fee $5) has 12 miles of groomed trails and a variety of terrain.

HIKING

An outstanding guide that includes Mt Hood hikes is William L Sullivan's *100 Hikes in Northwest Oregon*. It's also worth visiting a ranger station for maps and information on the many hikes in the area. A Northwest Forest Pass ($5) is required at most trailheads.

A popular trail loops for 7 miles via lovely **Ramona Falls**, which tumbles 120ft down a face of mossy columnar basalt. To reach the trailhead from Zigzag, turn north onto Lolo Pass Rd for 4 miles, then turn right on USFS Rd 1825 for 3 miles.

Hike 1.5 miles up from US 26 to **Mirror Lake**, which reflects Mt Hood beautifully. You can hike a half-mile around the lake, then 2 miles beyond the lake to a ridge top. The trail begins between mileposts 51 and 52 on US 26, just west of Government Camp.

Walk 2.6 miles on the mostly gentle **Old Salmon River Trail**, through riverside old-growth forests to the Salmon River Bridge. You can car-shuttle back or return the same way. To reach the trailhead, turn south from Zigzag on Salmon River Rd and drive 2.7 miles. The walk follows the road, but this doesn't detract from the hike.

The mother of all trails is the 40.7-mile **Timberline Trail**, which circumnavigates Mt Hood along a scenic wilderness of waterfalls, quiet reflecting lakes, wildflower meadows and mountain vistas. You don't have to do it all at once, however. Noteworthy portions of the trail include the hike to McNeil Point and the short climb to Bald Mountain, both offering breathtaking scenery. From Timberline Lodge, Zigzag Canyon Overlook is a 4.5-mile

CLIMBING MT HOOD

Mt Hood is the second-most-climbed peak over 10,000ft in the world, after Japan's Mt Fuji. This isn't to say Mt Hood does not require both climbing skills and stamina. Nearly every year, a few people die making the ascent. Climbing is best between May and mid-July, and a typical climb from Timberline Lodge (where registration is mandatory) on the south side takes 10 to 12 hours round-trip. Experienced climbers who wish to organize their own expedition can check www.fs.fed.us/r6/mthood/recreation/climbing for details. Otherwise, be safe and go with a guide service:

Northwest Mountain Guides (☎ 503-698-1118; www.gotrek.com)
Northwest School of Survival (☎ 503-668-8264; www.nwsos.com)
Timberline Mountain Guides (☎ 541-312-9242; www.timberlinemtguides.com)

Portland's **Mazamas** (☎ 503-227-2345; www.mazamas.org) is a mountaineering and hiking club (not a guide service) that sponsors climbs of many Northwest peaks, including Mt Hood. Membership isn't necessary, though mountaineering experience might be. And for climbing Mt Hood, experience certainly won't hurt.

round-trip through meadows of wildflowers to a canyon vista. Some trails can be snowbound until late July, so ask beforehand.

MOUNTAIN BIKING

When the snow is gone, **Mt Hood Skibowl** (see p271) is transformed into a mountain-bike downhill arena. If you're more the cross-country type, however, cross US 26 to the free Government Camp recreational trail network. The Crosstown Trail is a fairly easy 3-mile single track between Glacier View and the Summit Ski Area. More challenging trails sprout from it.

Most of the cross-country ski trails in the area are good for summertime mountain biking. Trails shoot uphill from several points around the easy Trillium Lake loop.

Sleeping

Most area campsites cost $12 to $16 and have drinking water and vault toilets. Reserve ahead on busy weekends (☎ 877-444-6777; www.reserveusa.com), though some walk-in sites are usually set aside. For more information contact the ranger stations (see p269).

Tollgate and Camp Creek Campgrounds are further down US 26 with some nice streamside sites. Still Creek Campground is near Government Camp. Large and popular Trillium Lake Campground has great views of Mt Hood. Frog Lake Campground lies on the shores of tiny Frog Lake. Off the beaten track is Cloud Cap Campground, with easy access to the Timberline Trail. Robin Hood and Sherwood Campgrounds are toward the east, on Hwy 35.

Mt Hood Village (☎ 503-622-4011, 800-255-3069; www.mthoodvillage.com; 65000 E US 26; hookups $42-49, cabins $59-200; 💻) The area's only RV hookups. Amenities include showers, indoor swimming pool, fitness center, store and a variety of sporting options.

Mazama Lodge (☎ 503-272-9214; www.mazamas.org; Westlake Rd; dm members/ nonmembers $15/20, d $45-60) Run by the mountaineering group Mazamas, this three-story lodge has dorms and three private rooms accommodating. Amenities include decks with mountain views, a great fireplace room and restaurant. Bring bedding. Open mostly on weekends in winter it's a 10-minute walk in.

Lost Lake Resort (☎ 541-386-6366; www.lostlakeresort.org; USFS Rd 1340; campsites $18, d $85-125, cabins $60-120) Six lodge rooms with kitchenettes, 127 campsites and seven very rustic cabins (bathroom outside, showers $4) are nestled here on Mt Hood's northern flank. Bring all bedding; lodge rooms are cheaper on weekdays. There's a small store and motorless boat rentals.

Cascade Ski Club Lodge (☎ 503-272-9204; www.cascadeskiclub.org; 30510 E Blossom Trail; dm members/members $12/22) This is a family-friendly and very casual lodge with 103 beds in 10 to 15-bed dorms. Bring your own bedding, pillow, towel and earplugs. Nonmembers can stay two nights maximum. Open to the public October to mid-May.

Huckleberry Inn (☎ 503-272-3325; www.huckleberry-inn.com; 88611 E Government Camp Loop; d $92-168; ⊠) Small, simple and rustic rooms are available here, though there's a 'bunk' room that sleeps up to 14. It's in a great central location in Government Camp, and there's a restaurant (come here for reception). Holiday rates go up 20%.

our pick **Timberline Lodge** (☎ 503-622-7979, 800-547-1406; www.timberlinelodge.com; d $115-270; ⊠ 💻 wi-fi) More a community treasure than a hotel, this gorgeous historic lodge offers rooms for all price ranges, from rustic bunks to luxury suites. Huge wooden beams tower over multiple fireplaces, there's a year-round heated outdoor pool, and the ski lifts are close by. Enjoy awesome views of Mt Hood, nearby hiking trails, two bars and an exceptional dining room (see the boxed text opposite).

Old Welches Inn B&B (☎ 503-622-3754; www.mthoodlodging.com; 26401 E Welches Rd; d $122-175; ⊠) Originally a hotel from 1890, this comfortable B&B offers four cozy, homey rooms (two share an outside bathroom). There's a pretty garden, and a patio overlooks the nearby Salmon River. A two-bedroom cottage is also available. Two-night minimum; reserve ahead.

Cooper Spur Mountain Resort (☎ 541-352-6692; www.cooperspur.com; 10755 Cooper Spur Rd; d $137, cabins $190-272, log house $465) This upscale resort, 2.5 miles west of Hwy 35, has six fine hotel-style rooms, two-bedroom condo/cabins and a four-bedroom, two-bathroom log house with a hot tub and boasting a Mt Hood view. Facilities include spa tubs and a fancy restaurant. Weekday rates are cheaper.

Summit Meadow Cabins (☎ 503-272-3494; www.summitmeadow.com; cabins $165-235; ⊠) These five lovely A-frame cabins, just south of Government Camp in the Trillium Lake basin, make great bases for vigorous wintertime getaways.

TIMBERLINE LODGE

The building of Timberline in 1936 and 1937 was a huge project by Oregon's Works Progress Administration (WPA), who employed up to 500 workers to hand-construct the 43,700-sq-ft log-and-stone lodge.

To emphasize the natural beauty of the area, architects quarried local stone and cut local timber, also designing the six-sided central tower to echo the faceted peak of Mt Hood. The steeply slanted wings leading away from the common rooms are meant to shed the heavy snowfalls and resemble mountain ridges.

The interior of the lodge is where the workmanship is most evident. The central fireplace rises 92ft through three floors of open lobby. All the furniture was made by hand in WPA carpentry halls, and murals and paintings of stocky, stylized workers – in the best Socialist-Realist tradition – adorn the walls.

Timberline Lodge is a hotel, ski resort and restaurant. Anyone can stop by for a refreshment and look around however – this building belongs to the wider community more than anything. And yes, some exterior shots of *The Shining* were really filmed here.

During winter, it's a 1.5 mile cross-country ski in. Trails surround the cabins. Two-night minimum; rates higher on weekends. Reservations required.

Eating

Mountain High Espresso (☎ 503-622-6334; 73265 E US 26; 6:30am-5pm Mon-Fri, till 6pm Sat & Sun) Right by Rhododendron's grocery store is this nondescript trailer serving up flavored coffees, fine teas and excellent hot chocolate. Good cookies and muffins also.

Backyard Bistro (☎ 503-622-6302; 67898 E US 26; mains $6-9; 11am-8pm Tue-Sat, 10am-4pm Sun) This tiny but elegant bistro has awesome soups, salads and sandwiches. Tasty choices include a pear salad with chicken and walnuts, and their Cuban hoagie with special sauce. The menu is livened up by specials, and there's a great patio for warm days.

Ice Axe Grill (☎ 503-272-3724; 87304 E Government Camp Loop; mains $10-15; 11:30am-10pm) Government Camp's only brewery-restaurant, the Ice Axe offers a friendly, family-style atmosphere and pub fare like good pizzas, beer-chip encrusted salmon, and gorgonzola-and-pepper bacon burgers. Veggie chili and boca burgers too.

Rendezvous Grill & Tap Room (☎ 503-622-6837; 67149 E US 26; mains $20-30; 11:30am-9pm) In a league of its own is this excellent restaurant with outstanding dishes like chargrilled porterhouse steak, Dungeness crab linguine and lamb chops with rosemary pesto. There's great desserts and an extensive wine list.

our pick **Cascade Dining Room** (☎ 503-622-0700; at Timberline Lodge; mains $24-30; 5:30-8:30pm) World-class cuisine is expertly prepared and presented at Timberline Lodge's fine restaurant. With a Northwest emphasis, chef Leif Benson uses only the freshest ingredients for his creations. The wine cellar is award-winning and the staff are knowledgeable; this is the place for that special meal with great views and atmosphere. Breakfast and lunch are available.

The Huckleberry Inn (see opposite) has a decent family diner.

Getting There & Away

BUS

On winter weekends and holidays, a **Park & Ride bus** (☎ 503-287-5438) transports skiers from three Tri-Met stops in Portland to Mt Hood Meadows. The cost is $59 for combination round-trip transportation and lift ticket. Call or check www.skihood.com for details.

Mt Hood Airporter (☎ 800-831-7433) provides winter transport from Government Camp to Timberline Lodge for $15 round-trip. It also has airport shuttles and private charter services.

CAR

For road conditions, dial the **24-hour information line** (☎ 503-588-2941, 800-977-6368). State law requires traction devices to be carried in vehicles during winter, and trailers are sometimes banned.

In winter, if you park a vehicle at most places on Mt Hood, you will need a Sno-Park permit ($5 daily, $9 for a three-day pass, $17 for a season pass). During the rest of the year, a Northwest Forest Pass ($5 daily, $30 annually) is required to park at most trailheads. Permits are available at the Mt Hood Information Center (p269), from many Government Camp businesses and at Timberline Lodge.

LOWER DESCHUTES RIVER

The Lower Deschutes River boasts some of the Northwest's most renowned **white-water rafting**, with 97 miles of mostly class III rapids flowing though stark canyon landscapes and basalt cliffs before mingling with the Columbia way to the north. Most expeditions are one-day adventures that leave from Harpham Flat, about 5 miles upstream from Maupin (the nearest town), and end about 15 miles down the river at Sandy Beach. Longer two- and three-day excursions are also available.

Maupin's outfitters include **All Star Rafting** (☎ 800-909-7238; www.asrk.com; 405 Deschutes Ave), **Deschutes River Adventures** (☎ 800-723-8464; www.800-rafting.com; 602 Deschutes Ave) and **Imperial River Company** (☎ 800-395-3903; www.deschutesriver.com; 304 Bakeoven Rd). You can also rent equipment yourself, but be sure to wear a safety vest – drownings are not uncommon.

A boater pass is required for all floaters ($2 weekdays and $8 weekends, per person, per day). It's available online at www.boaterpass.com, which also has details on this local system.

Rafting isn't the only highlight in the area. **Fly-fishing** on the Deschutes River is challenging and world renowned – the remoteness of desert canyons makes this an unforgettable experience. In May and June, the stonefly hatch drives Redside trout (and anglers) into a frenzy, while fall means steelhead trout are in the crosshairs.

The **Deschutes Canyon Fly Shop** (☎ 541-395-2565; www.flyfishingdeschutes.com; 599 S US 197) and the **Deschutes Angler** (☎ 541-395-0995; www.deschutesangler.com; 504 Deschutes Ave), both in Maupin, are great places to buy gear and get advice. Call the **Fish & Wildlife Bureau** (☎ 541-296-8026), in The Dalles, for current regulations.

For a dramatic peek at white water without getting wet, head to **Sherars Falls**, north of Maupin about 10 miles. You might see Native Americans dip-net fishing on wooden platforms right above the water (only tribal members from the Warm Springs Reservation are allowed to fish here). Maupin provides most of the area's services.

Sleeping & Eating

Near Maupin are BLM campgrounds with minimal facilities (sites $8 to $12, no reservations, bring water or a filter). Contact the **BLM Visitor Center** (☎ 541-395-2778; 10am-5pm Thu-Sun), just west of the Deschutes River Bridge, for details.

Maupin City Park (☎ 541-395-2252; 206 Bakeoven Rd; tents/hookups $16/24) Next to the Imperial River Company, this camping ground has running water, showers and RV hookups – along with a boat ramp ($3 day use).

Oasis (☎ 541-395-2611; www.deschutesriveroasis.com; 609 US 97 S; tents $15, cabins $35-75;) These 11 tiny but cute cabins are a marvel of efficient design, and while they're not luxurious they are well-equipped (most have kitchenettes). There's a small restaurant on the premises, and raft shuttle services are offered. Campsites are at a different location nearby, closer to the river.

Imperial River Company (☎ 800-395-3903; www.deschutesriver.com; 304 Bakeoven Rd; d from $75-125; wi-fi) Maupin's best stay is this modern riverside lodge, featuring a good variety of rooms that range from small and unmemorable to huge and magnificent. Only the imperial suite comes with a TV ($195). Its restaurant has an awesome patio with log furniture and river views.

Both the Oasis and the Imperial River Company have restaurants.

WARM SPRINGS INDIAN RESERVATION

Home to three groups – the native Wasco, the Tenino (from the Columbia River area) and the Northern Paiute (from Eastern Oregon) – Warm Springs stretches from the peaks of the Cascades in the west to the banks of the Deschutes River to the east. The Wasco and Tenino were confined here after a treaty with the US government in 1855; the Paiute were moved here after the Bannock Indian War of 1878.

The Pi Ume Sha Treaty Days Celebration is held on the third weekend of June at Warm Springs, with competitive dancing, horse races and a rodeo. For details contact the **Confederated Tribes of Warm Springs** (☎ 541-553-1161; www.warmsprings.com; 1233 Veterans St).

Don't miss the excellent **Warm Springs Museum** (☎ 541-553-3331; www.warmsprings.com/museum; 2189 US 26; adult/5-12yr/senior $6/3/5; 9am-5pm), a wonderful evocation of traditional Native

DETOURS: SMITH ROCK, COVE PALISADES & MILL CREEK

Best known for its glorious rock climbing, **Smith Rock State Park** (☎ 541-548-7501; www.oregonstateparks.org; day-use fee $3) boasts rust-colored 800ft cliffs that tower over the pretty Crooked River. Nonclimbers have several miles of fine hiking trails, some of which involve a little simple rock scrambling. Nearby Terrebonne has a couple of climbing outfitters that provide instruction, along with some eateries and groceries. There's **camping** (sites $4 per person) right next to the park; the nearest free campsites are at Skull Hollow (aka 'The Grasslands,' no water), 8 miles east. The nearest budget hotels are 10 miles south in Redmond: try **The Hub** (☎ 541-548-2102; 1128 NW 6th St; d $53).

Rent boats (☎ 541-546-3521) at the marina in spectacular Lake Billy Chinook, in **Cove Palisades State Park** (☎ 541-546-3412, 800-551-6949; www.oregonstateparks.org; day-use fee $3). Or hike the 7-mile **Tam-a-lau Trail** for spring wildflowers and great views. There's **camping** (sites/hookups $17/21) near the lake, or try the **Hoffy's Motel** (☎ 541-475-4633, 800-227-6865; 600 N US26; d $65;) 15 miles northeast in Madras.

The gently sloping Ochoco Mountains undulate across much of Central Oregon, offering good hikes near Prineville in the **Mill Creek Wilderness**. For a good one, follow US 26 east from town for 9 miles, and head north on USFS Rd 33 for another 9 miles to Wildcat Campground. From here a trail winds along the East Fork of Mill Creek through a lovely pine forest, eventually reaching **Twin Pillars**, a couple of spirelike volcanic crags (10 miles round-trip). The **Prineville Ranger Station** (☎ 541-416-6500; www.fs.fed.us/r6/centraloregon; 3160 NE 3rd St; 7:30am-4:30pm Mon-Fri) has a list of nearby USFS campgrounds. There are plenty of hotels in Prineville.

American life and culture, with artifacts, audiovisual presentations and re-created villages.

The tribe-owned **Kah-Nee-Ta Resort** (☎ 800-554-4786; www.kahneeta.com; teepee $72, d $146-260) is popular with families, especially sun-starved Portlanders. Facilities include a casino, golf, horseback riding, tennis, fishing and an Olympic-size spring-fed pool (nonguests $10, parking $5).

MT JEFFERSON & THE METOLIUS RIVER

The Metolius River bursts in all its glory from a ferny hillside, flowing north through a beautiful pine-filled valley as it passes beneath rugged Mt Jefferson, Oregon's second-highest peak (10,495ft). This gorgeous and peaceful region offers fine recreational opportunities that include great hiking and biking, world-class trout fishing, riverside USFS campgrounds and comfortable lodges. Summer is fabulous and popular, but consider coming in fall when the crowds disperse and temperatures remain mild. In winter there's good cross-country skiing.

To find the head of the Metolius, turn north from US 20 onto the Camp Sherman Rd (USFS Rd 14), then turn east at the 'Campgrounds' sign and continue about a mile down this road. A short path leads through a forest of ponderosa pines to remarkable **Metolius Springs**, where the river flows out of a hillside.

Hiking

Trails lead from the Metolius Valley up into the **Mt Jefferson Wilderness Area**. For a serious but fabulous day hike, head up to Canyon Creek Meadows, where summer produces a vibrant wildflower display and great views onto the rugged 7841ft **Three Fingered Jack** (4.5 miles round-trip). To reach the trailhead from Sisters, drive 13 miles northwest on US 20. Just south of Suttle Lake, turn north on the 'Jack Lake Rd,' USFS Rd 12. It's about 8 miles to the trailhead, at USFS's Jack Lake Campground.

From the same access road, there is a shorter hike that leads to three mountain lakes. One mile from the turnoff of US 20, take a west-turning fork (USFS Rd 1210) toward **Round Lake**. From here an easy 2-mile trail leads past tiny Long Lake to **Square Lake**, the highest of the trio, which is nestled in thick forest.

For less-strenuous yet still excellent walking, follow the trails on either side of the Metolius River, accessed from Camp Sherman or any campground.

Sleeping & Eating

The tiny community of Camp Sherman provides a few lodges, two restaurants, a store and not much else. For information on any of the 12 Metolius campgrounds, check with the **Sisters Ranger Station** (☎ 541-549-7700; www.fs.fed.us/r6/centraloregon; 207 N Pine St; 8am-4pm). Reserve in summer.

Metolius River Lodges (☎ 800-595-6290; www.metoliusriverlodges.com; cabins $106-205;) Just across the bridge from Metolius River Resort is this casual place with cozy, rustic and comfy cabins – both attached and stand-alone – right next to the river. Many have kitchens and fireplaces, and some boast decks over the water (the 'salmonfly' cabin is the best).

Metolius River Resort (☎ 800-818-7688; www.metoliusriverresort.com; cabins $240-255; wi-fi) More like small houses, the 11 lovely cabins at this pleasant spot all have two bedrooms and well-equipped kitchens. They sleep two to six people and are all decorated differently (as they're owned by different people). The river is nearby.

Kokanee Cafe (☎ 541-595-6420; mains $23-27; dinner May-Nov) Located at the Metolius River Resort, this log-cabin restaurant offers fine Northwest cuisine that includes the use of game, organic meats and wild fish. Reserve ahead.

Pine Rest (Forest Rd 1419; sites $14) and **Riverside** (Forest Rd 14; sites $10), north and south of Camp Sherman, respectively, are for tent campers only. Both have water and are by the river.

HOODOO MOUNTAIN RESORT

Oregon's oldest downhill **ski area** (☎ 541-822-3799; www.hoodoo.com; lift tickets adult/6-11yr & senior/youth $39/29/35) is 25 miles west of Sisters at the crest of the Cascades. Though it's small, Hoodoo has variety in its terrain, with good snow and some surprisingly challenging skiing. For conditions call ☎ 541-822-3337.

There's night skiing Friday and Saturday. Hoodoo also has groomed cross-country ski trails (Nordic pass $12) though many free, ungroomed trails start at the Sno-Parks near Santiam Pass.

SISTERS

pop 1500

Straddling the Cascades and high desert, where mountain pine forests mingle with desert sage and juniper, lies the darling town of Sisters. Once a stagecoach stop and trade town for loggers and ranchers, Sisters is today a bustling and fast-growing hot spot full of boutiques, art galleries and eateries housed in Western facade–buildings. Visitors come for the mountain scenery, spectacular hiking, fine cultural events and awesome climate – there's plenty of sun and little precipitation here. The town has also attracted a wave of migrants from nearby Bend, who've come to escape their city's own fast-growing pains. Sisters will someday outgrow its britches, but for the moment it's still beautiful and friendly – and the deer herds still happily return to nibble locals' back street gardens.

The town shows its cowboy spirit during the second weekend of June at the **Sisters Rodeo** (☎ 800-827-7522; www.sistersrodeo.com), complete with parade, toe-tappin' music and rodeo queens. A month later, in mid-July, is the wildly popular **Outdoor Quilt Show** (☎ 541-549-6061; www.sistersoutdoorquiltshow.org). Over a thousand quilts are on display throughout the packed-out town, including many hung up outside buildings.

Get the scoop at the **Chamber of Commerce** (☎ 541-549-0251; www.sisterschamber.com; 291 Main St; 9am-5pm). For camping and hiking information there's the **Sisters Ranger Station** (☎ 541-549-7700; www.fs.fed.us/r6/centraloregon; 207 N Pine St; 8am-4pm).

Porter Stage Lines connects Sisters with Eugene, stopping at the corner of Cascade and Spruce Sts. The chamber of commerce has details.

Sleeping

Unless you camp, sleeping in Sisters is expensive; head to Bend (19 miles southeast) for budget motels. Nonreservable campsites are available at the pleasant city park, at the southern end of Sisters ($10, no showers, closed in winter). Reserve accommodation in summer.

Sisters/Bend KOA (☎ 541-549-3021, 800-562-0363; 67667 US 20 W; tents/hookups/cabins from $25/25/60; Mar-Dec; wi-fi) These are comfortable sites about 3.5 miles southeast of Sisters and 15 miles northwest of Bend. Fun activities on offer include basketball, mini-golf, table-tennis, a fishing pond and a pool. There's also a store.

Sisters Inn (☎ 541-549-7829; www.sistersinnandrvpark.com; 540 US 20 W; d $87-109; wi-fi) Just outside town is this motel with great rooms and indoor pool. There's a full kitchen, library and games for everybody to use, along with a group room. RV sites available ($35 to $38).

Sisters Motor Lodge (☎ 541-549-2551; www.sistersmotorlodge.com; 511 W Cascade St; d $98-159; ☒ wi-fi) There are 11 cozy rooms at this older motel, half with kitchenettes. Expect homey decor and quilts on the beds, along with the modern comforts like DVD player. Two-bedroom suites are available.

Black Butte Ranch (☎ 800-452-7455; www.blackbutteranch.com; condos $98-265, cabins & houses $165-540; ☒ wi-fi) This is an all-encompassing mega-resort with golf, pools, horseback riding, tennis, walking trails, spa and restaurants. It's a privately-owned accommodation located 8 miles north of Sisters on US 20.

Blue Spruce B&B (☎ 541-549-9644, 888-328-9644; www.blue-spruce.biz; 444 S Spruce St; d $175; ☒ wi-fi) This is a fine B&B that's home to four spacious, themed rooms, all with fireplaces and private bathrooms (and some jetted tubs). There's a large grassy backyard and a great deck, and bicycle rental is included.

Five Pine Lodge (☎ 866-974-5900; www.fivepinelodge.com; 1021 Desperado Trail; d $219-305, cottages $260-305; ☒ wi-fi) Five Pine is a superb Craftsman-style lodge with gorgeous and luxurious rooms. Spacious townhouse rooms have two floors, fireplace, decks and bathtubs that open to the sitting area and fill from a ceiling spigot (really). Cottages are also available.

Eating

Sisters Coffee Company (☎ 541-549-0527; 273 W Hood St; 6am-6pm Mon-Sat, 7am-5pm Sun) This is a trendy coffee shop with high ceilings, wonderful rustic furniture and a bear rug. A wide variety of lattes and mochas (add extra shots and flavors) is available, as are a few snacks like pastries, oatmeal and soups.

Seasons Café & Wine Shop (☎ 541-549-8911; 411 E Hood St; sandwiches $6; 11am-3pm) Line up with the locals at this popular sandwich shop and order the turkey with cranberry sauce, pastrami with sauerkraut or roast beef with blue cheese dressing. There's also quiche and lots of wine. Lunch only.

Bronco Billy's Ranch Grill & Saloon (☎ 541-549-7427; 190 E Cascade Ave; mains $11-20; 11:30am-9pm) Right on the main drag and located in the historic Hotel Sisters is this old-time family joint. Meats highlight the menu (think steaks, ribs, hot links and hamburgers) but for less carnage there are salads, sandwiches and a vegetable sauté.

Jen's Garden (☎ 541-549-2699; 403 E Hood; mains $21-23; 5-9pm Wed-Sun) One of Sister's finer restaurants is this intimate spot cooking up gourmet dishes like grilled game hen, seafood bourride and wasabi pea–crusted salmon in plum wine broth. A prix-fixe menu is available for $49; reserve ahead.

MCKENZIE PASS AREA

From the lava fields of 5325ft McKenzie Pass you'll find stunning views of the Cascade Range and one of the youngest and largest lava flows in the continental USA. Intriguing hikes are scattered in the area.

Perched on a swell of frozen rock at McKenzie Pass, **Dee Wright Observatory** is a small fortress that was built out of lava in 1935 by the Civilian Conservation Corps. It surveys a desolate volcanic landscape, but on a clear day you can witness a dozen volcanic cones and mountain peaks from its arched windows. Nearby, a half-mile interpretive trail winds through the lava.

Two free primitive campgrounds (no water) in the area are **Scott Lake** and **Lava Camp Lake Campground**, both with lakeside campsites. The campsites can't be reserved.

A Northwest Forest Pass ($5, available at ranger stations) is required for the following activities. The **Upper & Lower Proxy Falls** tumble over glacier-carved walls to disappear into lava flows. A 1.2-mile loop trail begins directly east of milepost 64, about 12 miles east of McKenzie Bridge.

The **Pacific Crest Trail** crosses McKenzie Pass a half-mile west of the Dee Wright Observatory. It's 2.5 miles across barren lava flows to a spectacular viewpoint atop **Little Belknap Crater**. Bring water and sun protection.

The **Obsidian Trail** is a very popular access point into the Three Sisters Wilderness, but requires a free limited-entry permit (available at ranger stations). The full loop to Obsidian Cliffs and back is 13 miles, but for a shorter hike go just 2.5 forested miles to a 50ft-high lava flow with exhilarating views of the Three Sisters.

THREE SISTERS WILDERNESS

This beautiful 283,400-acre region spans the Cascade Range and is highlighted by the glaciered Three Sisters, three recent volcanic peaks each topping 10,000ft. The west slope of the wilderness is known for dense old-growth forest laced with strong rivers and streams. The glorious **Pacific Crest Trail** traverses the area, easily accessed from Hwy 242 at McKenzie Pass.

USFS Rd 19, also known as the **Aufderheide National Scenic Byway**, edges the westernmost wilderness boundary as it makes the 65-mile connection between Rainbow on Hwy 126 and Westfir (near Oakridge on Hwy 58). From **French Pete Campground**, one popular trail along this route leads up **French Pete Creek** through old-growth forest for about 3 miles.

Another good hike is to **Green Lake Basin**, on a high plateau between 9173ft Broken Top and 10,358ft South Sister. These celadon-green lakes are the centerpiece of a tremendous wildflower display in July and August, when the area throngs with crowds – especially on weekends. Park at the Green Lakes Trailhead along Hwy 46, above Sparks Lake, and hike north. The 4.4-mile trail is fairly steep but passes some great waterfalls.

Strong hikers should consider climbing South Sister. It's Oregon's third-highest peak, but during summer, the southern approach doesn't demand any technical equipment. The steep 5.6-mile trail begins near Devils Lake (just off the Cascade Lakes Hwy) and is passable only in late summer.

For more information contact the Bend–Fort Rock Ranger District (see opposite).

BEND

pop 76,000

Everyone wants to live in Bend. There aren't too many places where you can ski fine powder in the morning, paddle a kayak in the afternoon and take in a game of golf into the evening. Many more outdoor adventures abound – there's exceptional biking, hiking, mountaineering, fly-fishing and rock climbing also close by. And you'll probably be enjoying it all in great weather, as the area gets 250 days of sunshine each year. It's no wonder Bend is absolutely booming and boasts some of the country's highest-appreciating property values. This is a premiere outdoor city – just the number of shiny new SUVs tells this tale – and the secret is out.

With the lovely Deschutes River carving its way through the heart of the city, Bend offers a vibrant and attractive downtown area full of boutiques, galleries and upscale dining. Perhaps the best sign of the renewal in the city, however, is just south where the Old Mill District has been renovated into a large shopping area full of brand-name stores, fancy eateries and modern movie theaters. Anchoring the area is the old paper mill building, dominated by three landmark smokestacks and home to outdoor gear giant REI.

Not all of Bend is pretty, though – US 97 (3rd St) is a long commercial strip of cheap motels, fast-food restaurants and run-of-the-mill services. But something has to support Bend's fast-growing population, which has skyrocketed 50% in five years. Let's hope they can control future growth and sprawl while maintaining the pleasant atmosphere and lovely surroundings that brought transplants here in the first place.

There's local information at the **Visitor and Convention Bureau** (☎ 541-382-8048; www.visitbend.com; 917 NW Harriman St; 9am-5pm Mon-Fri, 10am-4pm Sat). For area camping and hiking there's the **Bend–Fort Rock Ranger District** (☎ 541-383-5300; 1230 NE 3rd St; 7:45am-4:30pm Mon-Fri). The downtown post office is at 61 NW Oregon Ave.

Sights & Activities

Drake Park, right downtown, is a good place to start exploring Bend's many miles of riverfront walking trails.

The **Deschutes Historical Center** (☎ 541-389-1813; 129 NW Idaho Ave; adult/7-12yr $5/2; 10am-4:30pm Tue-Sat) is in an old grade school and houses Native American and pioneer artifacts.

Don't miss the excellent **High Desert Museum** (☎ 541-382-4754; www.highdesertmuseum.org; 59800 S US 97; adult/5-12yr/senior $15/9/12; 9am-5pm), 6 miles south of Bend on US 97. It charts the exploration and settlement of the West, using re-enactments of a Native American camp, a hard rock mine and an old Western town. The region's natural history is also explored; kids love the live bat, snake, tortoise and trout exhibits, and watching the otters is always fun.

MOUNTAIN BIKING

Bend is laced with bike trails. The 9-mile (one way) **Deschutes River Trail** runs from Lava Island Falls, just past the Inn of the Seventh Mountain, south to Dillon Falls. It's a lovely riverside route with separate paths for bikers, hikers and horses.

There's more mountain biking up Hwy 46 at **Swampy Lakes** and **Virginia Meissner Sno-Park** areas; Nordic ski routes become bike trails in summer.

Also fun are the mountain-bike routes up Skyliner Rd. Head west out of town on Galveston Ave and 9 miles up Skyliner Rd to the Skyliner's sno-play parking lot, the start of the 4.5-mile **Tumalo Falls Trail**. Bring a lock as the last bit involves walking in; there are great views of rim rock and the 90ft-high Tumalo Falls.

Rent bikes at **Hutch's Bicycles** (☎ 541-382-9253; 725 NW Columbia St; 9am-6pm Mon-Fri, till 7pm Sat & Sun). It also offers (inexpensive) community rides and has another location at 820 NE 3rd St.

KAYAKING

Rent kayaks and canoes from **Alder Creek Kayak & Canoe** (☎ 541-317-9407; 805 Industrial Way; 9am-7pm); the company also offers paddling classes and guided trips. Raft the Deschutes (among other rivers) with **Ouzel Outfitters** (☎ 800-788-7238; www.oregonrafting.com; 63043 Sherman Rd); it also rents rafts and inflatable kayaks.

Sleeping

Tumalo State Park (☎ 541-388-6055, 800-551-6949; www.oregonstateparks.org; 64120 OB Riley Rd; tents/hookups/yurts $17/22/29) Streamside spots are best at this piney campground 5 miles northwest of Bend off US 20. Solar showers and flush toilets available.

Sonoma Lodge (☎ 541-382-4891; www.sonomalodge.com; 450 SE 3rd St; d $55;) One of Bend's cheapest accommodations, with 17 good rooms – all with microwaves and refrigerators, and some with kitchenette.

Cascade Lodge (☎ 541-382-2612, 800-852-6031; 420 E 3rd St; d $60; wi-fi) One of the better motels on this strip, with good spacious rooms set away from busy 3rd. Jacuzzi suites, kitchenettes and an outdoor pool are available.

Bend Riverside Motel (☎ 541-389-2363, 800-284-2363; www.bendriversidemotel.com; 1565 Hill St; d $70-152; wi-fi) Unmemorable rooms, but a wide range of them. Go for a river view with kitchen and fireplace for something more exciting. Indoor heated pool, sauna and Jacuzzi are pluses, as is the nearby park.

The Sather House B&B (☎ 541-388-1065, 888-388-1065; www.satherhouse.com; 7 NW Tumalo Ave; d $115-185; wi-fi) Homey antique-filled spot with rooms (each with private bathroom) decorated in country-style or flowery Victorian decor. Great location near downtown.

our pick **McMenamins Old St Francis School** (☎ 541-382-5174; www.mcmenamins.com; 700 NW Bond St; d $145-175, cottages $190-330; wi-fi) The McMenamin brothers do it again with this old schoolhouse remodeled into a classy 19-room hotel. The fabulously tiled saltwater Turkish bath is worth the stay alone, though nonguests can soak for $5. A restaurant-pub, three other bars, a movie theater and creative artwork completes the picture.

Ameritel Inn (☎ 541-617-6111, 800-600-6001; 425 SW Bluff Ave; d $155-308; wi-fi) Perched above the Old Mill District, this fancy hotel offers good views over the city, luxurious spa suites and an impressive stone-and-wood lobby with a huge fireplace. There's also an indoor pool and small workout room, plus easy access to Old Mill shops.

Pine Ridge Inn (☎ 541-389-6137, 800-600-4095; www.pineridgeinn.com; 1200 SW Century Dr; d $165-285; wi-fi) For modern luxury lodging there's this splendid place just outside the center of town. Many of the spacious suites have Jacuzzi, romantic fireplaces and views of the Deschutes River and Old Mill District. There's a morning breakfast buffet and afternoon wine reception.

Lara House B&B (☎ 541-388-4064, 800-766-4064; www.larahouse.com; 640 NW Congress Pl; d $275; wi-fi) Lara House is a supremely elegant B&B with contemporary furniture, a sun room, small back deck and six beautiful rooms with private bathrooms. It's a high class place, so behave yourself.

There's a countless supply of cheap motels and services on 3rd St (US 97).

Eating

Strictly Organic Coffee Co (☎ 541-383-1570; 6 SW Bond St; 6am-8pm Mon-Thu, till 10pm Fri & Sat, 7am-7pm Sun) Good coffee shop housed in an industrial space with outdoor front patio. The beans are roasted on the premises, and light snacks like salads, sandwiches, quiche and wraps are available.

Soba (☎ 541-318-1535; 945 NW Bond St; mains $6-7; 11am-10pm Mon-Sat) Soba is a large, airy eatery with great noodle dishes and rice bowls – the spicy shrimp soup is especially worth a shot. There's also a few appetizers and organic salads.

Victorian Café (☎ 541-382-6411; 1404 NW Galveston Ave; mains $7-12; 7am-2pm) Bend's best breakfast spot, Victorian Café is especially awesome for its eggs Benedict (nine kinds). It's also good for sandwiches, burgers and salads. Be ready to wait for a table, especially on weekends (no reservations taken).

our pick **Merenda** (☎ 541-330-2304; 900 NW Wall St; mains $15-26; 11:30am-midnight) Merenda is a wonderfully elegant, brick-walled restaurant

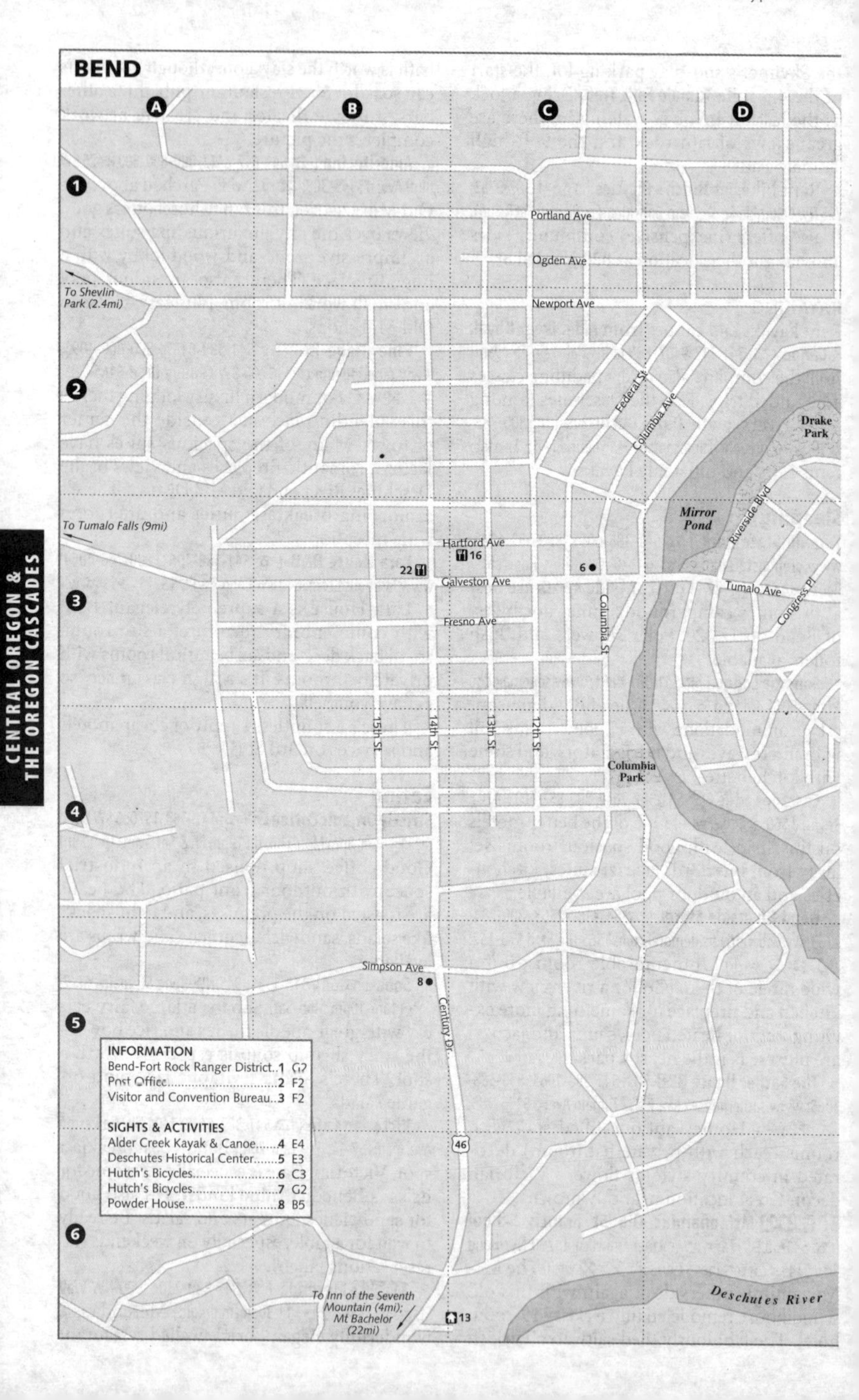
BEND
A
B
C
D
1
2
3
4
5
6
Portland Ave
Ogden Ave
Newport Ave
To Shevlin Park (2.4mi)
To Tumalo Falls (9mi)
Federal St
Columbia Ave
Drake Park
Mirror Pond
Riverside Blvd
Hartford Ave
16
22
6
Galveston Ave
Tumalo Ave
Congress Pl
Fresno Ave
Columbia St
15th St
14th St
13th St
12th St
Columbia Park
Simpson Ave
8
Century Dr
46
INFORMATION
Bend-Fort Rock Ranger District..1 G2
Post Office..............................2 F2
Visitor and Convention Bureau..3 F2
SIGHTS & ACTIVITIES
Alder Creek Kayak & Canoe......4 E4
Deschutes Historical Center.......5 E3
Hutch's Bicycles.........................6 C3
Hutch's Bicycles.........................7 G2
Powder House.............................8 B5
To Inn of the Seventh Mountain (4mi); Mt Bachelor (22mi)
13
Deschutes River

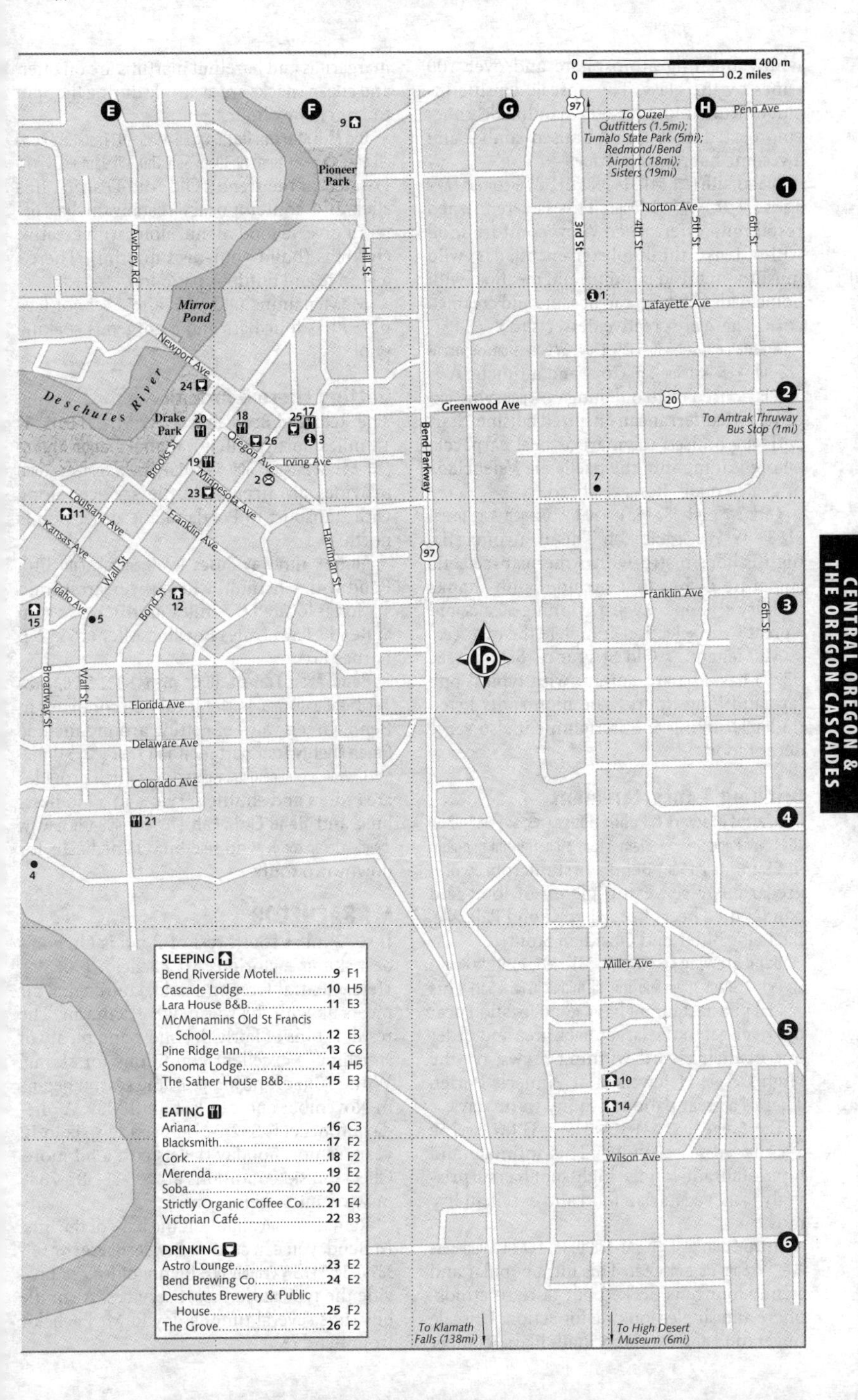

SLEEPING

Bend Riverside Motel	9	F1
Cascade Lodge	10	H5
Lara House B&B	11	E3
McMenamins Old St Francis School	12	E3
Pine Ridge Inn	13	C6
Sonoma Lodge	14	H5
The Sather House B&B	15	E3

EATING

Ariana	16	C3
Blacksmith	17	F2
Cork	18	F2
Merenda	19	E2
Soba	20	E2
Strictly Organic Coffee Co	21	E4
Victorian Café	22	B3

DRINKING

Astro Lounge	23	E2
Bend Brewing Co	24	E2
Deschutes Brewery & Public House	25	F2
The Grove	26	F2

with a bustling atmosphere and over 100 wines by the glass. The upscale cuisine includes Kumamoto oysters, handmade gnocchi, roasted halibut and braised lamb – and awesome happy hour prices.

Blacksmith (☎ 541-318-0588; 211 NW Greenwood Ave; mains $17-27; 5:30-10pm) This is a renowned restaurant offering cowboy comfort food with a twist: think lobster enchiladas, wild mushroom bread pudding and meatloaf with homemade ketchup, carrot sauté and creamed corn. There are creative desserts too.

Ariana (☎ 541-330-5539; 1304 NW Galveston Ave; mains $22-30; 5-9pm Tue-Sat) Cozy and intimate, Ariana is housed in an old bungalow, serving excellent Mediterranean-inspired cuisine. Start with the braised calamari or beef carpaccio before leading into the paella ala Valenciana or grilled quail. Reserve ahead.

Cork (☎ 541-382-6881; 150 NW Oregon Ave; mains $22-30; 5:30-9pm Tue-Sat) This is a romantic, high-caliber bistro with American-eclectic signature dishes that include lamb shanks and dry scallops. Award-winning steaks and a great wine selection complete the picture.

McMenamins Old St Francis School (see p279) has a bar-restaurant with typical pub fare and long hours. The nightspots listed under Drinking & Entertainment also serve decent food.

Drinking & Entertainment

Deschutes Brewery & Public House (☎ 541-382-9242; 1044 NW Bond St; 11am-11pm Mon-Thu, till midnight Fri & Sat, till 10pm Sun) Bend's first microbrewery, gregariously serves up plenty of food and handcrafted beers like Mirror Pond Pale Ale, Bachelor Bitter and Obsidian Stout.

Bend Brewing Co (☎ 541-383-1599; 1019 NW Brooks St; 11:30am-10pm Sun-Thu, till midnight Fri & Sat) This casual pub-restaurant has a good location near the river. Sit in the larger back area and order one of their award-winning brews; try the High Desert Hefeweizen or Pinnacle Porter. There's a great patio for sunny warm days.

The Grove (☎ 541-318-8578; 1033 NW Bond St; 5:30pm-close Tue-Sat; V) This intimate and hip restaurant-lounge nightspot has surprisingly tasty vegetarian food and excellent live music.

Astro Lounge (☎ 541-388-0116; 147 NE Minnesota Ave; 5pm-close Mon-Sat) This ultra popular and trendy lounge is decked out in retro atmosphere and singles looking for action. Upscale finger food and exotic cocktails like cucumber margaritas and hazelnut martinis are on offer, and cheap snacks are available during the 5pm to 7pm happy hour.

Old Mill Martini Bar (☎ 541-585-1011; 360 SW Powerhouse Dr; 4pm-12:30am Sun-Thu, till 2am Fri & Sat) Located in the trendy Old Mill District, this slick and contemporary restaurant-bar offers a diverse food menu, along with creative cocktails (build-your-own martini). There's a lounge and outdoor patio too.

McMenamins Old St Francis School (see p279) has four bars and a gorgeous soaking pool.

Getting There & Around

The **Redmond/Bend airport** (☎ 541-388-0019) is 18 miles north of Bend. **Central Oregon Breeze** (☎ 541-389-7469, 800-847-0157; www.cobreeze.com) provides an airport shuttle service, along with transport to Portland and other points north.

Amtrak Thruway Buses (www.amtrak.com) link Bend with Chemult, where the nearest train station is located (65 miles south). Buses stop at Bend's Lava Lanes Bowling Alley (1555 NE Forbes Rd).

Bend Area Transit (BAT; ☎ 541-322-5870; www.bendareatransit.com) is the local bus company in Bend. Green ways of getting around include **Green Energy Transportation and Tour** (☎ 541-610-6103; www.greenenergytransport.com), which provides area tours and shuttle services in a biodiesel bus; and **Bend Cycle Cab** (☎ 541-408-6363; www.bendcyclecab.com), who use bicycle pedicabs for downtown tours.

MT BACHELOR

Just 22 miles southwest of Bend is Oregon's best skiing – glorious Mt Bachelor (9065ft). Here, Central Oregon's cold, continental air meets up with the warm, wet Pacific air. The result is tons of fairly dry snow and plenty of sunshine – excellent conditions for skiing. With 370in of snow a year, the season begins in November and can last until May. A one-day lift ticket is $52/32/44 per adult/six to 12 years/senior; holiday tickets cost a bit more. Check on ski conditions at ☎ 541-382-7888 or www.mtbachelor.com.

Rentals are available at the base of the lifts. In Bend, you can stop by **Powder House** (☎ 541-389-6234; 311 SW Century Dr). Plenty of lodges provide the typical ski resort services. A shuttle bus runs several times a day to Mt Bachelor from Bend ($5).

Mt Bachelor grooms 56 miles of cross-country trails, though the $13 day pass may prompt skiers to check out the free trails at Dutchman Flat, just past the turnoff for Mt Bachelor on Hwy 46. This is as far as the snowplows maintain the highway during winter.

If there's adequate snow at lower elevations, forget Dutchman Flat and cross-country ski from the Virginia Meissner or Swampy Lakes Sno-Parks, between Bend and Mt Bachelor on Hwy 46. You'll need a Sno-Park permit, which are available from area businesses.

Sleeping

For budget sleeping there's Bend. Otherwise, the nearest rooms are at the all-encompassing resort **Inn of the Seventh Mountain** (☎ 800-452-6810; www.seventhmountain.com; 18575 SW Century Dr; d from $125; ☒ ✠ wi-fi), 14 miles from Bachelor. Expect many accommodation options, along with activities like swimming, tennis, biking, ice-skating and horseback riding.

NEWBERRY NATIONAL VOLCANIC MONUMENT

This relatively recent volcanic region (day use $5), highlighted by the Newberry Crater, showcases 500,000 years of volcanic activity. Start your visit at the **Lava Lands Visitor Center** (☎ 541-593-2421; ⏲ 9am-5pm Jul-Sep, limited hr spring/fall, closed winter), about 13 miles south of Bend. Head up the nearby road to **Lava Butte**, a perfect cone rising 500ft above the surrounding lava flows; views here are spectacular.

Four miles west of the visitors center is **Benham Falls**, a good picnic spot on the Deschutes River. About 1 mile south of the visitors center, **Lava River Cave** is the only lava tube that's developed for visitors (bring a flashlight or rent one for $3).

About 6000 years ago, a wall of molten lava 20ft deep flowed down from Newberry Crater and engulfed a forest of mature trees, resulting in the **Lava Cast Forest.** This mile-long interpretive trail is 9 miles east of US 97 on Lava Cast Forest Rd.

Newberry Crater

Newberry Crater was formed by the eruption of what was one of the largest and most active volcanoes in North America. Successive flows built a steep-sided mountain almost a mile above the surrounding plateau. As with Crater Lake, the summit of the volcano collapsed after a large eruption, creating a caldera.

Initially a single body of water, **Paulina Lake** and **East Lake** are now separated by a lava flow and a pumice cone. Due to the lakes' great depths and the constant flow of fresh mineral spring water, stocked trout thrive here. Looming above is 7985ft **Paulina Peak**.

A short trail halfway between the two lakes leads to the **Big Obsidian Flow**, an enormous deposit on the south flank of Newberry Crater. The **Newberry Crater Rim Loop Trail** encircles Paulina Lake and is a good place for hiking and mountain biking.

To get there from US 97, take Paulina East Lake Rd to Newberry Crater.

Sleeping

The 10 Newberry Crater campgrounds ($12) usually stay open from late May to October. Contact the Bend–Fort Rock Ranger District (see p278) for more information.

There are a few cheap motels and restaurants in La Pine, about 30 miles south of Bend.

La Pine State Park (☎ 541-536-2071, 800-452-5687; www.oregonstateparks.org; 15800 State Recreation Rd; hook-ups $17, cabins $38-70) Just north of La Pine on US 97, this scenic campground has sites near the Deschutes River, along with hot showers and flush toilets.

East Lake Resort (☎ 541-536-2230; www.eastlakeresort.com; 22430 E Lake Rd; d $75, cabins $110-185) This resort offers 12 rustic but comfortable cabins, most with kitchenettes and lake views. There are also four motel-type rooms with outside coin-op showers, a restaurant and boat rentals.

Paulina Lake Lodge (☎ 541-536-2240; www.paulinalakelodge.com; cabins $105-195) A good place for outdoor enthusiasts, this lodge features a handful of charming log cabins (sleeping up to 10), a restaurant, general store and boat rentals.

CASCADE LAKES

Long ago, lava from the nearby volcanoes choked this broad basin beneath the rim of the Cascade Range. Lava flows dammed streams, forming lakes. In other areas, streams flowed underground through the porous lava fields to well up as lake-sized springs. Still other lakes formed in the mouths of small, extinct craters.

Hwy 46, also called the Cascade Lakes Hwy, loops roughly 100 miles between high mountain peaks, linking together this series of lovely alpine lakes (though many of them aren't visible from the road). Cyclists pedal the road in summer, while snowmobilers take over during winter. There are several trailheads in the area. Beyond Mt Bachelor, the road is closed from November to May.

Tiny **Todd Lake** offers views of Broken Top and relative seclusion, as getting here requires a quarter-mile hike. **Sparks Lake**, in a grassy meadow popular with birds, is in the process of transforming itself into a reedy marsh. **Hosmer Lake** is stocked with catch-and-release Atlantic salmon, making it popular with anglers. It's less commercial than nearby lakes and has magnificent views of Mt Bachelor. **Little Lava Lake** is the source of the mighty Deschutes River.

The Deschutes is dammed at **Crane Prairie Reservoir**, where ospreys fish in the shallow lake water and use dead trees for nesting.

Sleeping

There are **public campgrounds** at each of the lakes along the route.

Many Cascade Lakes have cabins on their shores, ranging from rustic to upscale. Restaurants, groceries and boat rentals are usually available. These include (but are not limited to) **Cultus Lake Resort** (☎ 800-616-3230; www.cultuslakeresort.com), **Twin Lakes Resort** (☎ 541-382-6432; www.twinlakesresortoregon.com), **Elk Lake Resort** (☎ 541-480-7378; www.elklakeresort.net) and **Crane Prairie Resort** (☎ 541-383-3939; www.crane-prairie-resort-guides.com). Not all are open all year; check details ahead of time.

WILLAMETTE PASS

Southeast from Eugene, the Willamette River leaves its wide valley and is immediately impounded into reservoirs. By Oakridge, the Willamette is restored to a rushing mountain river, and Hwy 58 climbs steadily up the Cascade Range's densely forested western slope.

At the Cascade crest, near Willamette Pass, are a number of beautiful lakes and wilderness areas, as well as Oregon's second-highest waterfall, 286ft **Salt Creek Falls**. There's good hiking here, and in winter, the area is popular for downhill and cross-country skiing. Along the way, you can soak in warm waters at undeveloped **McCredie Hot Springs**; it's close to the road, popular with truckers and clothing is optional. The unpaved turnout is just past Blue Pool Campground, 45 miles east of Eugene.

The pass divides two national forests. For details on the Deschutes National Forest, contact the **Crescent Ranger District** (☎ 541-433-3200; www.fs.fed.us/r6/centraloregon; 136471 Hwy 97 North, Crescent; 7:45am-4:30pm Mon-Fri). For information on the Willamette National Forest, including Waldo Lake, contact the **Middle Fork Ranger Station** (☎ 541-782-2291; www.fs.fed.us/r6/willamette; 46375 Hwy 58, Westfir; 8am-4:30pm).

ALTITUDE SICKNESS

Be aware that the road up to Crater Lake reaches an elevation of over 7000ft, and that Cloudcap Overlook is at nearly 8000ft. Though most people are fine at this altitude, a few people can be affected by altitude sickness at these heights. If you start feeling dizzy, fatigued, sick to your stomach and/or have a headache, you may be experiencing symptoms. The best solution is to head to lower elevations immediately. Exertion can aggravate this condition. See p427 for more details.

Waldo Lake

At an elevation of 5414ft on the very crest of the Cascades, Waldo Lake has no stream inlets – the only water that enters is snowmelt and rainfall. It is one of the purest bodies of water in the world and is the source of the Willamette River. The lake is amazingly transparent – objects 100ft below the surface are visible. Not only is it Oregon's second-deepest lake (420ft), it's also the state's second-largest lake (10 sq miles). No motorized boats are allowed, but afternoon winds make the lake popular for sailing. Three lovely USFS campgrounds flank the eastern half of the lake.

The west and north sides of the lake are contained in the **Waldo Lake Wilderness Area**, a 148-sq-mile area that abuts the Three Sisters Wilderness and is filled with tiny glacial lakes, meadows and hiking trails.

Odell, Crescent & Summit Lakes

Immediately on the eastern slope of Willamette Pass is gorgeous Odell Lake, resting in a steep glacial basin. Hiking trails lead into relatively unexplored wilderness from lakeside campgrounds. In winter, the lake becomes a popular cross-country ski destination.

A rustic lodge and campgrounds ring Crescent Lake, which is popular for snowmobiling, waterskiing and swimming (in summer, that is).

USFS Rd 610 leads west from the end of the lake to reach remote Summit Lake, which is preferred by wilderness purists.

Hiking

A Northwest Forest Pass ($5) is required for all of the following hikes. Trails are snow-free from July to October.

The 20-mile **Waldo Lake Trail** encircles Waldo Lake. A less ambitious hike leads 3.4 miles from North Waldo Campground to sandy swimming beaches at the outlet of the Willamette River. Make it an 8-mile loop by returning via **Rigdon Lakes**, which lie at the base of a volcanic butte.

The Pacific Crest Trail at Willamette Pass winds through old forests to **Midnight Lake**, an easy 3.3-mile one-way hike. From nearby Trapper Creek Campground, on the west end of Odell Lake, energetic hikers should consider the 4.3-mile one-way hike to **Yoran Lake** for a great view of 8744ft Diamond Peak. A popular hike from the Odell Lake Lodge leads 3.8 miles to **Fawn Lake**, below two rugged peaks.

Skiing

The **Willamette Pass Ski Area** (☎ 541-345-7669; www.willamettepass.com; Hwy 58; lift tickets adult/6-10yr & senior $38/22), 27 miles east of Oakridge, has steep slopes, great views and night skiing. Most of the 29 runs are rated intermediate to advanced, with a vertical drop of 1563ft. Eight-person gondolas run all year for both skiers and hikers/mountain bikers. The Pacific Crest Trail is less than a mile away (no bikes).

The resort also has 12 miles of groomed cross-country ski trails. **Odell Lake** is another popular spot for cross-country skiing.

Sleeping & Eating

North Waldo Lake Campground (off USFS Rd 5897; tents $14) Campgrounds don't get much better than this lovely and rustic spot on Waldo Lake, but bring repellant. Located 11 miles off Hwy 58 at the end of USFS Rd 5898.

Odell Lake Lodge & Campground (☎ 541-433-2540, 800-434-2540; www.odelllakeresort.com; Hwy 58; sites $16, d $60-78, cabins $99-190) This casual family resort has small lodge rooms, but you'll want to hang out in the fine living room downstairs anyway. Also available are 12 cabins, each with kitchen and fireplace, that sleep up to 16. There's a restaurant onsite. Located 6 miles east of Willametter Pass, east of Odell Lake.

Westfir Lodge (☎ 541-782-3103; www.westfirlodge.com; 47365 1st St, Westfir; d $99; ⊠ ⁂) A stone's throw from Oregon's longest covered bridge is this spacious B&B with nine homey guest rooms (some with shared bathrooms) and an English-style flower garden.

Willamette Pass Inn (☎ 541-433-2211; Hwy 58; www.willamettepassinn.com; d $105-129, cabins $145; ⊠ wi-fi) This is the closest motel to the ski area, with very spacious and beautiful rooms boasting fireplaces and kitchenettes. Privately owned cabins are also available. It's seven miles east of Willamette pass.

CRATER LAKE NATIONAL PARK

The gloriously still waters of Crater Lake reflect surrounding mountain peaks like a giant dark-blue mirror, making for spectacular photographs and breathtaking panoramas. **Crater Lake** (☎ 541-594-2211; www.nps.gov/crla; admission per vehicle $10, free in winter) is Oregon's only national park and also the USA's deepest lake at 1943ft deep.

Steel Visitors Center (☎ 541-594-3100; ⌚ 9am-5pm summer, 10am-4pm winter) is 3 miles south of Rim Village (the park's center of activities) and provides good information. At Rim Village itself there's the smaller **Rim Visitors Center** (☎ 541-594-3090; ⌚ 9:30am-5:30pm summer only).

You can hike and cross-country ski in the area, but most visitors just cruise the 33-mile loop **Rim Drive**, which is open from around June to mid-October and offers over 30 viewpoints as it winds around the edge of Crater Lake. A paved side road on the east side leads to amazing views from **Cloudcap Overlook**, almost 2000ft above the lake. Another nearby side road leads 10 miles southeast to **The Pinnacles**, a valley of pumice and ash formations carved by erosion into 100ft spires called hoodoos.

The popular and steep mile-long **Cleetwood Cove Trail**, at the north end of the crater, provides the only water access at the cove. A two-hour **boat tour** (adult/3-11yr $25.50/15; ⌚ 10am-4:30pm Jul–mid-Sep) is available, some which include a brief layover at Wizard Island ($3 to $5 per person extra).

The park's popular south entrance is open year-round and provides access to Rim Village and Mazama Village, as well as the park headquarters at the Steel Visitors Center. In winter you can only go up to the lake's rim and back down the same way; no other roads are plowed. The north entrance is only open in summer.

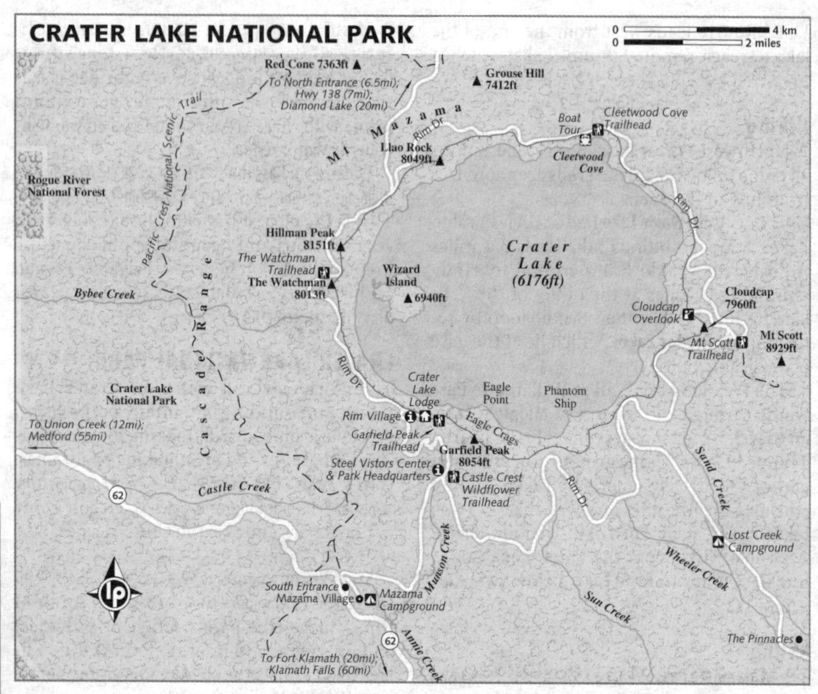

It's best to top up your gas tank before arriving at Crater Lake. There's reasonably priced gas at Mazama Village, but it can run out; the closest pumps otherwise are in Chiloquin, Prospect, Chemult and Fort Klamath.

Summer is often cold and windy, so dress warmly.

Hiking

High-elevation trails in this region generally aren't completely clear of snow until late July. From the east edge of the Rim Village parking lot, a 1.7-mile trail leads up the 8054ft **Garfield Peak** to an expansive view of the lake; in July the slopes are covered with wildflowers. A strenuous 5-mile round-trip hike takes you to an even better lake vista atop 8929ft **Mt Scott**, the highest point in the park. For a steep but shorter hike, trek up 0.7 miles to the **Watchman**, an old lookout tower on the opposite side of the lake that boasts one of the park's best views. For the enthusiasts, there is a 1-mile nature trail near the Steel Visitors Center, that winds through the **Castle Crest Wildflower Garden**.

Cross-Country Skiing

In winter, only the southern entrance road to Rim Village is kept plowed to provide access to several Nordic trails. Rentals are unavailable, so bring your own skis. Snowshoes are provided for free ranger-led **snowshoe walks**, which are held on weekends from Thanksgiving through to March. Only experienced skiers should attempt the dangerous, avalanche-prone loop around Crater Lake, which takes three days and requires a backcountry permit from park headquarters.

Sleeping & Eating

Other than Crater Lake Lodge (the only lodging at the lake itself) and Mazama Village (7 miles from the rim) – both of which are limited – the nearest accommodations are 20 to 40 miles away. Park lodging is closed from mid-October to late-May, depending on the snow pack.

Fort Klamath has several good choices (see opposite). Union Creek, Prospect (see p325) and the Diamond Lake area (see p329) all have nice, sometimes woodsy places. The drive-through towns of Chemult and Chiloquin have

MT MAZAMA

The ancient mountain whose remains now form Crater Lake was Mt Mazama, a roughly 12,000ft volcanic peak that was heavily glaciered and inactive for many thousands of years until it came back to life 7700 years ago. A catastrophic explosion scattered ash for hundreds of miles as flows of superheated pumice flowed and solidified into massive banks. These eruptions emptied the magma chambers at the heart of the volcano, and the summit cone collapsed to form the caldera.

Only snowfall and rain contribute to the lake water. This purity and the lake's great depth give it that famous blue color. Sparse forests can be seen growing in pumice and ash in the Pumice Desert, just north of Crater Lake along N Entrance Rd.

budget motels that are much less scenic. Finally, if you don't mind driving all day, there's lots of accommodations in Medford, Roseburg or Klamath Falls.

The park's eating facilities are limited as well, though you can always bring a picnic and find a fabulously scenic spot. Rim Village has a small café and there's an upscale dining room nearby at the lodge. Mazama Village has a small store and restaurant.

Lost Creek Campground (☎ 541-594-3100; tents $10) Open mid-July to mid-September, this campground is 3 miles southeast of the lake and offers just 16 tent sites. Water is available, but there are no showers. No reservations taken.

Jo's Motel (☎ 541-381-2234; www.josmotel.com; 52851 Hwy 62, Fort Klamath; tents/hookups $10/20, d $87-120; ☒ ☒) Five well-kept and wood-paneled two-room suites with kitchens are available at this friendly motel. Bigger groups can go for the stand-alone cabins with a loft that sleep six. There are sites for campers and RV fans too, along with a tiny organic grocery store.

Mazama Campground (☎ 888-774-2728; Mazama Village; tents/hookups $19/22) Open mid-June to early October, this is the park's main campground. There are around 200 wooded sites but no reservations are taken. Pay showers and a laundry are available.

Crater Lake Resort (☎ 541-381-2349; www.craterlakeresort.com; 50711 Hwy 62, Fort Klamath; d $60-97; ☒) A great deal and awesome budget spot, this friendly place is just south of Fort Klamath and boasts 10 excellent, well-maintained cabins with kitchens. There are grassy spots and a playground for the kids, a volleyball court and picnic tables.

Crater Lake B&B (☎ 866-517-9560; www.craterlakebandb.com; 52395 Weed Rd, Fort Klamath; d $90; ☒ wi-fi) With great views of the surrounding area, this friendly B&B has three simple but comfortable rooms (each with a bathroom) that might remind you of your parent's house.

Cabins at Mazama Village (☎ 541-830-8700, 888-774-2728; www.craterlakelodges.com; d $130; ☒) The cabins are open June to early October, with 40 pleasant rooms (no TV or telephones) in attractive four-plex buildings. They're 7 miles from Crater Lake, with a small grocery store and gas pump nearby.

our pick **Crater Lake Lodge** (☎ 541-594-2255, 888-774-2728; www.craterlakelodges.com; d $148-278; ☒ ☒) Open from late May to mid-October, this grand old lodge has 71 simple but comfortable rooms, but it's the common areas that are most impressive. Large stone fireplaces, rustic leather sofas and a spectacular view of Crater Lake from the outside patio make this place special. There's a fine dining room too.

Crater Lake Lodge Dining Room (☎ 541-594-1184; mains $20-28; ⏰ 7-10:30am, 11:30am-2pm, 5-9pm) Crater Lake's finest dining is at the lodge, where you can feast on Northwest cuisine like citrus-chili basted duck and artichoke chicken in gouda cream. Try for a table with a lake view. Open till 10pm in July; dinner reservations recommended.

Oregon Coast

Driving along Oregon's coast is a must-see highlight any time of year. Rocky headlands loom high above the ocean, providing astounding vistas, while craggy rocks lie scattered along the shoreline like oceanic sentinels. The Coast Range is deeply etched by great rivers and patched with forests, offering outdoor enthusiasts excellent boating, fishing and hiking opportunities. The Oregon Dunes – among the largest coastal dunes in the world – stretch for over 50 miles, and, offshore, gray whales migrate from Alaska to Mexico and back.

Thanks to a far-sighted government in the 1910s, Oregon's 362-mile Pacific Coast was set aside as public land and strung with over 70 state parks and protected areas. The northern Oregon coast has developed more quickly than the southern end, offering travelers a choice between bustling beach resorts and blissfully laid-back retreats. And everyone from campers to gourmet-lovers will find a plethora of opportunities to enjoy this exceptional region.

HIGHLIGHTS

- Nibbling fish 'n chips or crab cakes in a cheap shack or fine restaurant in towns like **Seaside** (p293)
- Spotting gray whales during their migrations up and down the coast from **Depoe Bay** (p299)
- Hiking the **Cape Falcon** and **Neahkahnie Mountain Trails** (p295) for awesome views
- Checking out the jellyfish and sea otters at Newport's **Oregon Coast Aquarium** (p299)
- Sticking to the coast when US 101 veers inland by taking the stunning **Three Capes Drive** (p296)
- Camping and hiking among the towering sand dunes of the **Oregon Dunes National Recreation Area** (p305)

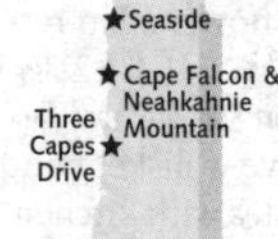

Geography & Climate

Spectacular cliffs and rocky beaches characterize much of the region (the best are in the stretches running between Yachats and Florence and between Port Orford and Brookings), and the central coast boasts some impressive sand dunes. The Pacific Ocean's moderating influence makes for mostly frost-free winters at lower elevations on the coast, with average lows in around 35°F and highs around 50°F. The barrier to the east formed by the Coast Range triggers a lot of winter precipitation, though, and annual totals reach between about 55in and 110in, depending on the area. Summers are fairly dry, with high temperatures averaging in the mid-to-upper 60s.

Getting There & Around

The entire Oregon coast – from the Washington border to the California line – is traversed by US 101. It's a mostly two-lane highway, and in summer often gets clogged with traffic. Still, considering the public transportation gaps and sometimes spotty bus schedules, your best bet for conveniently seeing the whole coast is by car.

The coast is served by a patchwork of city and county bus systems. Amtrak Thruway or Porter Stage Lines buses run between small towns along the coast to major inland cities like Portland or Eugene, providing connections to train stations. The only scheduled flights into the area are from Portland to the south coast town of North Bend (Coos Bay), on Horizon Air.

NORTHERN OREGON COAST

Oregon's northern coast stretches from the mouth of the Columbia River south to Florence. Here lie the state's biggest and most touristy beach towns – Seaside, Cannon Beach and Lincoln City – while Depoe Bay is big on whale-watching and Newport is famous for its excellent aquarium.

Because of its popularity, the northern coast tends to get clogged with weekend visitors from Portland and the Willamette Valley. Traffic can slow to 20mph in sections, since US 101 is mostly two-lane highway and there are many RVs on the windy stretches. Also, expect to join the masses during summer

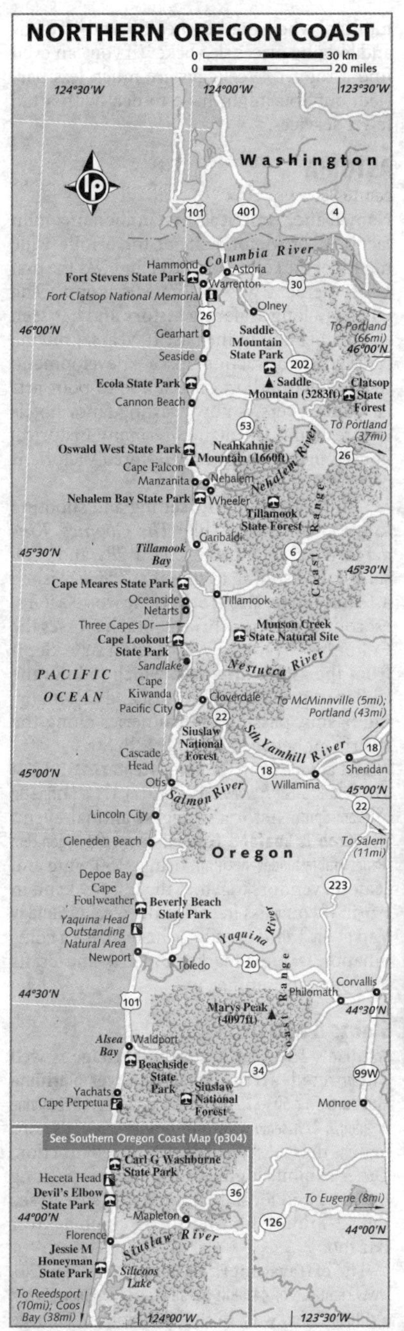

months, when the beaches fill with crowds and lodging prices skyrocket (if you can even find a room). Weekdays are much less harried, but you might have to deal with a tad fewer services.

ASTORIA

pop 10,000

Named after America's first millionaire, John Jacob Astor, Astoria sits at the 5-mile-wide mouth of the Columbia River and was the first US settlement west of the Mississippi. The city has a long seafaring history and has seen a gentrification in the past 10 years, growing rapidly and attracting upscale development; the derelict harbor, once home to poor artists and writers, is now drawing fancy hotels and restaurants. Inland are many historical houses, including lovingly restored Victorians converted into B&Bs.

Astoria has been the setting and shooting location for movies like *The Goonies, Kindergarten Cop* and the *Free Willy* and *Ring* series. And adding to the city's scenery is the 4.1-mile **Astoria-Megler Bridge**, the world's longest continuous truss bridge, which crosses the Columbia River into Washington state. See it from the **Astoria Riverwalk**, which follows the trolley route between the west and east mooring basins, passing old canneries along the riverfront between 6th and 12th Sts.

Get advice from the **visitors center** (☎ 503-325-6311, 800-875-6807; www.oldoregon.com; 111 W Marine Dr; 9am-5pm). Astoria's biggest annual event, the **Crab & Seafood Festival** (www.oldoregon.com/Pages/crabfestandevents.htm), brings 150 wine and seafood vendors together the last weekend in April. If you miss it, try for the weekly **Sunday Market** (cnr 12th & Commercial St) instead; it's a combination farmers market and arts-and-crafts fair, open in summer.

Sights & Activities

Astoria's 150-year seafaring heritage is well interpreted at the **Columbia River Maritime Museum** (☎ 503-325-2323; www.crmm.org; 1792 Marine Dr; adult/6-17yr/senior $8/4/7; 9:30am-5pm). It's hard to miss the Coast Guard boat, frozen in action. Other exhibits highlight the salmon-packing industry and local lighthouses; be sure to see the 12-minute film on the Columbia River Bar too.

The extravagant **Flavel House** (☎ 503-325-2203; www.cumtux.org; 441 8th St; adult/6-17yr/senior $5/2/4; 10am-5pm) was built by Captain George Flavel, one of Astoria's leading citizens during the 1880s. This Queen Anne has been repainted with its original colors and the grounds have been returned to Victorian-era landscaping. It has great views over the harbor.

Housed in the former city hall, the **Heritage Museum** (☎ 503-338-4849; www.cumtux.org; 1618 Exchange St; adult/6-17yr/senior $4/2/3; 10am-5pm) commemorates Astoria's various ethnic communities. Look for the Ku Klux Klan robes and the Klan letter supporting prohibition. There's also a room dedicated to the Clatsop tribe.

Rising high on Coxcomb Hill, the **Astoria Column** (built in 1926) is a 125ft tower painted with scenes from the westward sweep of US exploration and settlement. The top of the column (you'll need to go up 164 steps) offers good views over the area. The nearby 1.5-mile walking trail is another good leg-stretcher.

Five miles south of Astoria, the **Lewis and Clark National Historical Park** (☎ 503-861-2471; www.nps.gov/lewi; adult/2-15yr $5/2; 9am-6pm Jun-Aug, till 5pm rest of yr) holds a reconstructed fort similar to the one the Corps of Discovery occupied during their miserable winter of 1805–06. There's expedition history and Clatsop artifacts at the visitor center, and costumed docents demonstrate common fort pastimes such as candle-making, leather-tanning and canoe-building. In summer you can only reach the park via shuttle from a nearby parking lot.

Ten miles west of Astoria is **Fort Stevens State Park** (☎ 503-861-1671), which commemorates the historic military reservation that guarded the mouth of the Columbia River. Near the **Military Museum** (☎ 503-861-1470; www.visitftstevens.com; day-use fee $3; 10am-6pm Jun-Sep, 10am-4pm Oct-May) are grim, warren-like garrisons dug into sand dunes – interesting remnants of the fort's mostly demolished military buildings. There's plenty of beach access and camping in the park, along with 9 miles of bike trails.

Sleeping

Fort Stevens State Park (☎ 503-861-1671; off US 101; tents/hookups/yurts $18/22/30) Close to 500 sites (most for RVs) are available at this campground, one of the nation's largest, 10 miles west of Astoria. Great for families.

Hideaway Inn & Hostel (☎ 503-325-6989; www.hideawayinnandhostel.com; 443 14th St; dm $20, d $30-80; wi-fi) Well-located, this cheap option has reasonable bunks, a range of private rooms and a communal kitchen. All rooms share outside bathrooms. It's an older place but bright and tidy enough; call ahead as there's no doorbell.

Grandview B&B (☎ 800-488-3250; www.pacifier.com/~grndview; 1574 Grand Ave; d $50-132; ⊠ wi-fi) This sprawling house features nine guest rooms, each with private bath and some with great views of the city. There are old-fashioned touches but it's not a pretentious place. You won't find TVs in the rooms and there's no alcohol permitted on premises.

Crest Motel (☎ 503-325-3141, 800-421-3141; www.crestmotelastoria.com; 5366 Leif Ericson Dr; d from $60; wi-fi) Get a quieter room in the back, away from the road, at this decent motel on the eastern edge of town. View rooms are best; they overlook the Columbia and cost $87. Or save a few bucks and enjoy the view from the grassy picnic area instead.

Rose River Inn B&B (☎ 503-325-7175, 888-876-0028; www.roseriverinn.com; 1510 Franklin Ave; d $90-160; ⊠ wi-fi) This country-style B&B offers five pretty rooms, including one with a Finnish sauna and a two-bedroom suite. A Chihuahua roams the premises; kids over 12 only.

Rosebriar Inn B&B (☎ 800-487-0224; www.rosebriar.net; 636 14th St; d $90-192; ⊠ wi-fi) This large inn is beautiful and elegant, offering 12 rooms – most pretty small but perfectly comfortable. More spacious choices include a 'carriage house' that sleeps four and a 'captain's suite' with kitchenette and awesome views ($305). Kids over 12 only.

Hotel Elliott (☎ 503-325-2222, 877-378-1924; www.hotelelliott.com; 357 12th St; d from $160; ⊠ ⁂ wi-fi) Standard rooms have that charming period elegance at this historic hotel. For more space, get a suite (the presidential suite boasts six rooms, a grand piano and rooftop garden for a mere $715). There's a complimentary wine reception almost every night.

Cannery Pier Hotel (☎ 503-325-4996, 888-325-4996; www.cannerypierhotel.com; 10 Basin St; d from $170; ⊠ wi-fi) Located on a pier at the west end of town, this luxurious hotel offers fine rooms right over the water, with bridge views, contemporary furnishings and open bathtubs. Perks include a Jacuzzi, afternoon wine socials, continental breakfast and free ride in a 1939 Buick. Spa on premises.

Eating

T Paul's Urban Café (☎ 503-338-5133; 1119 Commercial St; mains $9-16; ⌚ 9am-9pm Mon-Thu, till 10pm Fri & Sat, 11am-4pm Sun) For a slick yet funky atmosphere, head to this popular café that serves up a large variety of gourmet quesadillas, sandwiches, salads and pastas. On weekends, prime rib, lamb and pork dishes are added to the menu as well.

DINING OUT WITH A VIEW

The Oregon coast boasts its share of restaurants with awesome water views – though at times, you have to hunt them out. Here are some great choices:

- Astoria's **Baked Alaska** (below)
- Lincoln City's **Bay House** (p298)
- Depoe Bay's **Tidal Raves** (p299)
- Newport's **Saffron Salmon** (p301)
- Florence's **Traveler's Cove** (p305)
- Charleston's **Portside Restaurant** (p309)
- Bandon's **Lord Bennett's** (p310)
- Gold Beach's **Riverview** (p313)

Wet Dog Cafe (☎ 503-325-6975; 144 11th St; mains $9-17; ⌚ 11am-10pm Sun-Thu, till 2am Fri & Sat) For casual dining there's no beating this large, quirky pub, which brews its own beer with names like Shark Spit IPA and Kick Ass Imperial Stout. The grub is typically pub-like, there's a good water view and you can enjoy live music on weekends.

Columbian Café (☎ 503-325-2233; 1114 Marine Dr; mains $10-19; ⌚ 8am-noon Mon-Tue, 8am-noon & 5-8pm Wed-Fri, 10am-2pm & 5-8pm Sat, 10am-2pm Sun) This old-fashioned hole-in-the-wall joint has just three booths and some counter seating, making it easy to interact with the feisty cook. There are sandwiches and omelettes earlier in the day and fresh seafood, pasta and crepes for dinner.

Baked Alaska (☎ 503-325-7414; 1 12th St; mains $18-24; ⌚ 11am-10pm) One of Astoria's better restaurants, Baked Alaska sits right atop a pier on the water. The views are pretty darn good. Lunch means 0.5lb burgers and options like blackened halibut tacos, while dinner mains range from grilled wild salmon to 10oz rib eye steak.

Silver Salmon Grille (☎ 503-338-6640; 1105 Commercial St; mains $18-33; ⌚ 11am-10pm) Right next to T Paul's is this fancy diner with booths, old-time music and an antique bar in the lounge next door. There's plenty of good seafood and steak choices, along with low-carb mains and

FUN OREGON COAST FESTIVALS

- Newport's February **Wine & Seafod Festival** (p299)
- Florence's May **Rhododendron Festival** (p304)
- Cannon Beach's June **Sandcastle Day** (opposite)
- Lincoln City's June and September **kite festivals** (p297)
- Seaside's August **Hood to Coast Relay Marathon** (below)

smaller (less expensive) portions available – a nice touch.

Getting There & Around

Amtrak Thruway buses link Portland to Astoria, stopping at the minimart next to the visitors center. Buses to Seaside and Cannon Beach leave from the **Astoria Transit Center** (☎ 800-776-6406; 900 Marine Dr). **Pacific Transit** (☎ 360-642-9418) goes over the border to Washington.

Astoria's **Riverfront Trolley** ($1) plies through the old cannery district, between the East and West Mooring Basins, daily in summer and weekends only in winter.

SEASIDE

pop 6300

Oregon's largest resort town is the brash, crowded and gaudy resort of Seaside, and its detractors would call it a tourist trap. On summer weekends and during holidays or festivals the town's central precinct – dominated by loud party hounds, video-game arcades and gift stores – is thronged with tourists. Bicycles, 'fun-cycles' and surreys have the run of Seaside's 2-mile boardwalk, called 'the Prom,' but at least the miles of sandy beach are relatively peaceful.

For more subtle attractions, inquire at the **Visitors Bureau** (☎ 503-738-3097; www.seasideor.com; 989 Broadway; 8am-5pm Mon-Sat, 11am-5pm Sun). The third weekend in August, the **Hood to Coast Relay Marathon** jams the main road between Portland and Seaside and packs out the town. The **Seaside Beach Volleyball Tourney** is held in early August.

Amtrak Thruway buses to Portland, Astoria and Cannon Beach stop daily at **Del's Service Station** (cnr N Holladay Dr & US 101).

Sights & Activities

BIKING & SURFING

Join the pedaling hordes on the promenade by renting bikes ($10 per hour) and four-wheel surreys ($15 to $36 per hour) at **Prom Bike & Hobby Shop** (☎ 503-738-8251; 622 12th Ave; 10am-5:30pm Thu-Tue). They also offer trikes, tandems, lowriders and strollers. For surfing gear and advice on where to hit the waves, there's **Cleanline Surf Company** (☎ 503-738-7888; 719 1st Ave; 9am-7pm). They rent longboards for $15 per day.

SEASIDE AQUARIUM

Families with kids might enjoy this slightly cheesy **aquarium** (☎ 503-738-6211; 200 N Promenade; adult/6-13yr/senior $7/3.50/6; 9am-7pm), which has been going since 1937 – and feels like it. Don't expect anything like Newport's cutting-edge version (p299), but rather a few fish tanks, a touch pool and a rather bleak seal tank. Limited hours outside summer.

SADDLE MOUNTAIN STATE PARK

About 13 miles east of Seaside on US 26, this **park** (☎ 503-861-1671) features a popular 2.5-mile hiking trail through alpine wildflower meadows to the top of Saddle Mountain (3283ft). Views of the Columbia River and the Pacific coastline are pretty spectacular, but the trail is steep and grueling. Storms can blow in quickly from the ocean, so be prepared for changeable weather.

Sleeping

Summer reservations are always a good idea.

Circle Creek RV Park & Campground (☎ 503-738-6070; 85658 US 101; tents/hookups $20/33; mid-Mar–late Oct) One mile south of Seaside is this fine campground with pleasant, grassy open sites and a river out back. There are laundry facilities, picnic tables and a small store.

Seaside International Hostel (☎ 503-738-7911, 888-994-0001; www.seasidehostel.net; 930 N Holladay Dr; dm/d from $21/40; wi-fi) For decent budget lodgings you can't beat this small hostel, offering good dorms in back and private rooms up front that open to the parking area. There's a kitchen and TV room, but the highlight has to be the grassy backyard overlooking a river. Non–HI members pay $3 extra per person.

Hillcrest Inn (☎ 503-738-6273, 800-270-7659; www.seasidehillcrest.com; 118 N Columbia; d $80-149; ⊠) Offering a wide variety of simple but comfortable rooms and suites is this Cape Cod–style inn. Each room has a different price, and some come with kitchenette, jetted tubs and partial ocean views (room 123 is an especially nice one). There's a nice grassy common area, and it's just a block to the beach.

Sandy Cove Inn (☎ 503-738-7473; www.sandycoveinn.com; 241 Ave U; d from $88; ⊠ wi-fi) This no-nonsense motel is away from the beach at the south end of town, but offers basic and clean rooms at a fair price. Suites and a house are available also with a two-night minimum. Prices drop 25% on weekdays.

Seaside Oceanfront Inn (☎ 503-738-6403, 800-722-7766; www.theseasideinn.com; 581 S Promenade; d $99-300; ⊠ wi-fi) The front entry is strangely unwelcoming and reception is a restaurant counter, but it's the vistas out back that really matter. All of the 15 rooms have a light theme, like 'captain's quarter' or 'the library' ('rock 'n roll' comes with a '50s Oldsmobile bed) – and many boast ocean views. A full breakfast is included.

Gilbert Inn B&B (☎ 503-738-9770, 800-410-9770; www.gilbertinn.com; 341 Beach Dr; d $119-139; ⊠ wi-fi) This 1892 Queen Anne house is located in a neighborhood of apartments, but it's just a few blocks from the beach. It has 10 guest rooms, all carpet and old-fashioned decorations like flowery bedspread and wallpaper. Breakfast is served in a glassy sunroom.

Inn of the Four Winds Motel (☎ 503-738-9524, 800-818-9524; www.innofthefourwinds.com; 820 N Promenade; d $129-235; ⊠ 💻 wi-fi) One of Seaside's better luxury values is this intimate inn with only 14 rooms. All are beautiful and come with gas fireplace and outside seating area with ocean views. Best of all, however, might be the complimentary cookies that greet you on arrival.

Eating & Drinking

Norma's (☎ 503-738-4331; 20 N Columbia; mains $14-21; 🕑 11am-10pm) Look for the lighthouse shape atop of this family-friendly restaurant, which serves up a medley of seafood dishes from halibut steaks and four kinds of fish 'n chips to Alaska king crab and Cajun scallops. Steaks, pasta and salads are available too.

Lil' Bayou (☎ 503-717-0624; 20 N Holladay Dr; mains $16-19; 🕑 5-10pm, till 11pm Sat) It's Mardi Gras every day at this colorful, Cajun-Creole restaurant, which offers some of the finest blackened catfish, seafood gumbo, crawfish pie and jambalaya this side of the Louisiana border. On Saturday nights there's also live music in its magnolia lounge.

our pick **Pacific Way Bakery & Cafe** (☎ 503-738-0245; 601 Pacific Way; mains $18-29; 🕑 11am-3:30pm & 5-9pm Thu-Mon) Located in Gearheart, about 3 miles north of Seaside, this jewel of a restaurant is well worth the trip. It serves excellent sandwiches and soup for lunch, while dinner means gourmet treats like lavender-roasted duck or prosciutto-wrapped scallops. The bakery next door (open 7am to 5pm Thursday to Monday) has folks lining up outside.

Seaside Coffee House (☎ 503-717-0111; 5 N Holladay Dr; 🕑 7am-5pm Sun-Thu, till 6pm Fri & Sat) For good coffee and an artsy atmosphere there's this comfortable café, located away from the beach madness and across from Lil' Bayou. They roast the beans themselves and also sell in bulk. Order a caramel smoothie and lose yourself in a sofa.

CANNON BEACH

pop 1730

Charming Cannon Beach is one of the most popular (and upscale) beach resorts on the Oregon coast. Several premier hotels here cater to a fancier clientele, as do the town's many boutiques and art galleries. In summer the streets are ablaze with flowers. Unlike Seaside's Coney Island–like atmosphere, Cannon Beach is toned down and much more refined. Lodging is expensive, and the streets are jammed: on a sunny Saturday, you'll spend a good chunk of time just finding a parking spot.

Just offshore is another reason for the town's popularity. The glorious Haystack Rock is an attractive magnet for beach goers, and provides great photo opportunities. Miles of sandy beaches don't hurt either. Directly behind the rock, the Coast Range rises in steep parapets.

The **chamber of commerce** (☎ 503-436-2623; www.cannonbeach.org; 207 N Spruce St; 🕑 10am-5pm Mon-Sat, 11am-4pm Sun) has local information. Cannon Beach's largest festival, **Sandcastle Day** (held in June, exact date depends on tides), has teams competing for originality and execution in sand sculpture.

Amtrak Thruway buses to Portland, Seaside and Astoria depart daily from the **Family Market** (☎ 503-436-0515; 1170 S Hemlock St). The free hourly **Cannon Beach shuttle** (☎ 800-776-6406) runs the length of Hemlock St to the end of Tolovana Beach.

Sights & Activities

BEACHES

The beaches here are some of the most beautiful in Oregon, with **Haystack Rock** and other outcroppings rising out of the surf. There's easy beach access at the end of Harrison St downtown, or at the end of Gower St, a mile south. Busy **Tolovana Beach Wayside** is at the south end of town, along Hemlock St. Other beach points are accessible at the more remote **Hug Point State Park**, 3 miles south on US 101.

If you want to check out the local surfing, visit **Cannon Beach Surf** (☎ 503-436-0475; 1088 S Hemlock St) for board rentals and lessons. Landlubbers who like to pedal can rent three-wheeled sand bicycles at **Family Fun Cycle** (☎ 503-436-2247; 1160 S Hemlock St).

ECOLA STATE PARK

Located just north of town, this **state park** (☎ 503-436-2844; day-use $3) offers seclusion and great picnicking. Short paths at Ecola Point lead over the headland to dramatic views of Cannon Beach's sandy shore, sharply punctuated by stone monoliths and all hunkered beneath the Coast Range.

Leading north from here is an 8-mile stretch of the **Oregon Coast Trail**, which follows the same route traversed by the Corps of Discovery in 1806. Highlights on this trail include a sandy cove at **Indian Beach** (popular with surfers) and **Tillamook Head** (which offers a view of an inactive lighthouse).

Sleeping

Cannon Beach is pretty exclusive; for budget choices head 9 miles north to Seaside. Reserve ahead in summer. Rates are much cheaper in the off-season. There are primitive, free, hike-in campsites at Ecola State Park.

Sea Ranch RV Park (☎ 503-436-2815; www.searanchrv.com; 415 Fir St; tents/RVs/cabins $24/27/74). Pleasant Sea Ranch, on quiet Ecola Creek, is across from the turnoff to Ecola State Park and is popular with the local feral bunny population. Horseback riding is also available.

Blue Gull Inn Motel (☎ 800-507-2714; www.haystacklodgings.com; 487 S Hemlock St; d $98-175; ☒ wi-fi) These are some of the more affordable rooms in town, with comfortable atmosphere and toned down decor, except for the colorful Mexican headboards and serapes on the beds. Kitchenettes available. Run by Haystack Lodgings, which also manages three other hotels in town and does vacation rentals.

Argonauta Inn (☎ 800-822-2468; www.thewavesmotel.com; 188 W 2nd St; d $118-415; ☒ wi-fi) This five-unit complex run by the Waves Motel features three suites, a two-bedroom townhouse and three-bedroom beach house that sleeps up to nine. All are simply decorated but casual and spacious; some have ocean views.

Waves Motel (☎ 800-822-2468; www.thewavesmotel.com; 188 W 2nd St; d $118-415; ☒ wi-fi) Disregard the word 'motel' here – this place is more like an upscale inn than a motor lodge. Furnishings are elegant and the rooms comfortable and bright, and some come with kitchens, two bedrooms and decks overlooking the beach.

Cannon Beach Hotel (☎ 503-436-1392, 800-238-4107; www.cannonbeachhotel.com; 1116 S Hemlock St; d $120-220; ☒ wi-fi) If you don't need much space, check out this classy, centrally located hotel. Standard rooms are lovely and tasteful but very small; even the suites are tight. There's a good restaurant on the premises, however.

Ocean Lodge (☎ 503-436-2241, 888-777-4047; www.theoceanlodge.com; 2864 S Pacific St; d from $250; ☒ wi-fi) Those seeking Cannon Beach's most luxurious rooms should check out this gorgeous place. Most of the contemporary, tasteful rooms come with ocean view, and all have a fireplace and kitchenette. Service is friendly but not overbearing. A complimentary continental breakfast, a 500-DVD library and pleasant sitting areas are available to guests.

Eating & Drinking

Warren House Pub (☎ 503-436-1130; 3301 S Hemlock; mains $8-17; 🕑 11:30am-1am) To get away from Cannon Beach's downtown bustle, head south to the Tolovana neighborhood and plop yourself down at this pleasant, English-style brewpub. The food is well-made, with all the usual pub fare choices available, along with some fine microbrews. It's popular with the locals and a fun place to hangout.

Lumberyard (☎ 503-436-0285; 264 3rd St; mains $9-22; 🕑 11am-10pm) This casual, family-friendly eatery has sandwiches, burgers, pizzas and steaks. There are booths for cozy dining, a front patio for warm days and a bar area for easy access to the hard stuff.

Gower St Bistro (☎ 503-436-2729; 1116 S Hemlock St; mains $10-22; 🕑 9am-3pm, 5-9pm Sun-Thu, till 10pm Fri & Sat) There are just nine inside tables at this bright and contemporary corner bistro, popular for its brunch (consider the Grand Marnier French toast), sandwiches, pasta and gourmet mains.

Newman's (☎ 503-436-1151; 988 S Hemlock St; mains $19-26; 🕑 5:30-9pm) Expect a fine dining experience at this small, quality restaurant on the main drag. Award-winning chef John Newman comes up with a fusion of French and Italian dishes like duck breast with foie gras and lobster ravioli in marsala cream sauce. Desserts are sublime.

Sleepy Monk Coffee (☎ 503-436-2796; 1235 S Hemlock St; 🕑 8am-2pm Mon, 8am-5pm Fri-Sun) For organic, certified fair trade coffee, there's this little coffee shop on the main street. Sit on an Adirondack chair on the tiny front patio and enjoy the rich brews, all roasted on the premises.

MANZANITA

pop 690

One of the more laid-back beach resorts on Oregon's coast is the hamlet of Manzanita, boasting lovely white-sand beaches and a slightly upscale clientele. It's much smaller and far less hyped than Cannon Beach, and still retains a peaceful atmosphere. You can relax at the beach, take part in a few activities and perhaps hike on nearby Neahkahnie Mountain, where high cliffs rise dramatically above the Pacific's pounding waves.

Manzanita is located near the Nehalem River, which creates a wide estuarial valley and then a bay that's protected from the ocean by a 7-mile sand spit. Just to the south and right on the river, the historic fishing villages of Nehalem and Wheeler are becoming centers for antiques and river recreation.

Tillamook County Transportation (☎ 503-815-8283) buses stop at 5th St and Laneda Ave, and connect to Tillamook, Pacific City and Portland.

Activities

Nearby **Nehalem Bay State Park** (day-use $3) has a good 2-mile walk (or sandy bike ride) on the **Spit Trail**, which finishes up at the end of a peaceful peninsula. The quiet, bird-rich waters of Nehalem Bay are good for contemplative **kayaking** and **bird watching**; there's kayak rentals at **Wheeler on the Bay Lodge & Marina** (☎ 503-368-5858, 800-469-3204; 580 Marine Dr) in Wheeler, just 5 miles south of Manzanita.

Five miles north is **Oswald West State Park** (☎ 503-368-3575), a beautiful preserve with dense coastal rain forest and two headlands. For a good hike, take the 2.4-mile trail to **Cape Falcon**, which offers expansive views and good bird-watching. For more exercise, climb 3.8 miles to the top of 1660ft **Neahkahnie Mountain**, which towers above Nehalem Bay and offers amazing views – on a clear day, you can see 50 miles out to sea.

Surfers and body boarders head a quarter-mile from the highway parking lot to **Short Sand Beach**, which offers good waves. Rent bicycles and surfboards from **Manzanita Bikes & Boards** (☎ 503-368-3337; 170 Laneda Ave).

Sleeping

Oswald West State Park (☎ 800-551-6949; tents $14) Wheelbarrows are provided for hauling gear down a short trail to 30 forested tent sites above Smuggler's Cove, 5 miles north of Nehalem Bay State Park. No reservations. Flush toilets are available.

Nehalem Bay State Park (☎ 503-368-5154, 800-452-5687; hookups/yurts $20/27) On the dunes of Nehalem Spit, 3 miles south of Manzanita off US 101, this big campground has showers, equestrian facilities and a boat ramp.

Bunk House (☎ 503-368-2865; 36315 N US 101; d $55-125; ⊠) Lying on the southern edge of town is this homely spot with seven good rooms, each differently priced (the cheapest share a bathroom). You can also opt for two small cabins with kitchens.

our pick **Old Wheeler Hotel** (☎ 503-368-6000, 877-653-4683; www.oldwheelerhotel.com; 495 Highway 101, Wheeler; d $85-99; ⊠ wi-fi) This lovely historic hotel, with views of Nehalem Bay, is located in Wheeler. The simple, old-fashioned rooms are a bit flowery but very neat and comfortable. It's a good deal, and continental breakfast is included.

Coast Cabins (☎ 503-368-7113; www.coastcabins.com; 635 Laneda Ave; d $125-275; ⊠ wi-fi) Just five luxurious cabins are available at this lovely retreat near the entrance to town. All come with contemporary furnishings and kitchenette, but three are larger, two-story affairs. The simple, lovely gardens provide plenty of privacy.

Zen Garden B&B (☎ 503-368-6697; www.neahkahnie.net/zengarden; 8910 Glenesslin Ln; d $130-175; ⊠ wi-fi) Privacy is held dear at this home, which offers just two rooms, including one with a large living space. Both have their own bathroom and separate breakfast areas, and there's a peaceful garden out back with soaking tub ($20 extra).

Inn at Manzanita (☎ 503-368-6754; www.innatmanzanita.com; 67 Laneda Ave; d $150-180; ⊠ wi-fi) This very pleasant inn is located right on the main street but within forested grounds. There are 14 cozy rooms, all with fireplace, balcony and

THREE CAPES DRIVE

Cape Meares, Cape Lookout and Cape Kiwanda are some of the coast's most stunning headlands, strung together on a slow, winding and sometimes bumpy, 30-mile alternative to US 101. Head due west on 3rd St out of Tillamook instead of continuing south on US 101.

The forested headland at **Cape Meares** offers good views from its lighthouse, which is 38ft tall (Oregon's shortest). Sea birds nest in the area, and the 'Octopus Tree' (a candelabra-shaped Sitka spruce) is also a short stroll from the parking lot.

A panoramic vista atop sheer cliffs that rise 800ft above the Pacific makes **Cape Lookout State Park** a highlight. In winter, the end of the cape, which juts out nearly a mile, is thronged with whale-watchers. There are wide sandy beaches, hiking trails and a popular campground near the water.

Finally there's **Cape Kiwanda**, a sandstone bluff that rises just north of the little town of Pacific City. You can hike up tall dunes, or drive your truck onto the beach. It's the most developed of the three, with plenty of services nearby. Watch the dory fleet launch their craft or, after a day's fishing, land as far up the beach as possible.

jetted tub. The larger suites are best for families and come with kitchenette; there's also a three-bedroom penthouse ($415).

Eating

Manzanita News & Espresso (☎ 503-368-7450; 500 Laneda Ave; 🕑 7:30am-5pm) The best thing about this friendly, cozy coffee shop is the bumper stickers they sell. Otherwise go for the drinks and pastries.

Bread and Ocean (☎ 503-368-5823; 154 Laneda Ave; mains $6-10; 🕑 7:30am-5:30pm Wed-Sat, 8am-3pm Sun) You'll have to line up and wait for good panini, pasta salads and bread at this small bakery-deli. There are a few tables inside, but the cute garden patio is the place to be.

San Dune Pub (☎ 503-368-5080; 127 Laneda Ave; mains $7-14; 🕑 4-10pm Mon, 11:30am-10pm Tue-Sat, till 9pm Sun) If you don't mind eating in a pub with sports on TV, step into this joint. Burgers dominate the menu, but they're special – try the teriyaki chicken or the blue-cheese bacon. There are also a few wraps and seafood appetizers, along with a nice back patio for sunny days.

Marzano's Pizza Pie (☎ 503-368-3663; 60 Laneda Ave; pizzas $19-27; 🕑 4.30-9pm) Thirteen kinds of top-quality pizzas are covered in choice sauces and baked on a fire-heated stone. Try the Italian sausage – it's homemade and comes with fresh mushrooms and roasted red peppers. Calzones and salads also available.

TILLAMOOK

pop 4700

Best known for its huge cheese industry, Tillamook is a nondescript town that's worth a brief stop to down some dairy. Cheese production began in Tillamook in the 1890s, when an English cheese maker brought his cheddar-making techniques to the fledgling dairies along Tillamook Bay. Thousands stop here annually to visit the famed Tillamook Cheese Visitors Center (see below), which produces over 100 million pounds of the product every year. The city's **chamber of commerce** (☎ 503-842-7525; 3705 N US 101; 🕑 9am-5pm Mon-Fri, 10am-3pm Sat) is next door.

South of Tillamook, US 101 loses the beaches and headlands and follows the Nestucca River through pastureland and logged-off mountains. The slower but prettier Three Capes Drive (above) begins in Tillamook and follows the coast.

Tillamook County Transportation (☎ 503-815-8283; www.tillamookbus.com) buses depart from 2nd and Laurel Sts to Oceanside, Netarts and Pacific City on the capes, as well as to Manzanita and Portland.

Sights & Activities

Two miles north of town is a tourist wonderland called the **Tillamook Cheese Visitors Center** (☎ 503-815-1300; www.tillamookcheese.com; 4175 N US 101; admission free; 🕑 8am-8pm). Line up for free cheese samples, lick down an ice-cream cone or peek into the factory floor assembly line. There's a bit less hype at the nearby **Blue Heron French Cheese Company** (☎ 800-275-0639; www.blueheronoregon.com; 2001 Blue Heron Dr; admission free; 🕑 8am-8pm) which also offers cheese tastings. Its farm-animal petting pen outside makes it more of a country experience.

In town, the worthwhile **Pioneer Museum** (☎ 503-842-4553; 2106 2nd St; adult/child/senior $3/0.50/2;

9am-5pm Tue-Sat, 11am-5pm Sun) has antique toys, a great taxidermy room (check out the polar bear) and a basement full of pioneer artifacts. There are also curiously carved Neahkahnie stones meant to point to a legendary buried treasure near Manzanita.

Aircraft lovers shouldn't miss the large collection of fighter planes and the 7-acre blimp hangar at the **Tillamook Naval Air Museum** (☎ 503-842-1130; www.tillamookair.com; 6030 Hangar Rd; adult/6-17yr/senior $11/6.50/10; 9am-5pm). It's located 2 miles south of town.

At Munson Creek State Natural Site, 7 miles south off US 101, an easy quarter-mile hike through old-growth spruce reaches **Munson Creek Falls**, the highest waterfall in the Coast Range at 319ft (though some figures incorrectly claim it's 266ft).

LINCOLN CITY

pop 8000

More a sprawling modern beach resort than serene seaside retreat, Lincoln City is a long series of commercial strips, motels, eateries and gift shops that front a fairly wide and lackluster stretch of sandy beach. As one local put it, 'Lincoln City is five towns brought together in 1965 by the fact they needed a sewer system.' But the resort does serve as the region's principal commercial center, while boasting the Oregon coast's most affordable beachfront accommodations. The surrounding area features some good hikes.

The self-proclaimed 'Kite Capital of the World,' Lincoln City hosts two **kite festivals** (☎ 800-452-2151), held June and September. Enormous kites – some over 100ft in length – take off to twist and dive in the ocean breezes. There's also a big sandcastle contest in August.

The **visitor center** (☎ 541-996-1274, 800-452-2151; www.oregoncoast.org; 801 SW US 101; 9am-5pm Mon-Fri, 10am-4pm Sat) sits next to the Price 'n Pride. Local **Lincoln City Transit** (☎ 541-265-4900) buses connect to Newport and Yachats. There are no long-distance bus services.

Sights

BEACHES

Lincoln City's wide sandy beaches cater to holidaymakers, especially families. Brightly colored glass floats, hand blown by local artisans, are hidden weekly along the beach for beachcombers as part of an ongoing promotion.

The main public access points are at the D River Beach State Wayside, in the center of town; at Road's End State Wayside, off Logan Rd just north of town; and south along Siletz Bay at Taft City Park.

CASCADE HEAD

Two Nature Conservancy **trails** access Cascade Head's 1200ft-high ocean vista. The first is a mile-long upper trail from USFS Rd 1861 (or Cascade Head Rd), 4 miles north of the Hwy 18 junction; the second is a 2.7-mile lower trail that scales the headland from the end of Three Rocks Rd, a mile north of town along the Salmon River. At the end of USFS Rd 1861 is the 2.6-mile trail down to **Harts Cove**, a remote meadow along a cliff-lined bay frequented by sea lions. USFS Rd 1861 and its trailheads are closed December to August in the interest of preserving rare flowers that sustain an endangered butterfly. The lower Cascade Head trail stays open year-round.

Activities

Canoeing and **kayaking** are possible on both Devil's Lake, east of town, and on Siletz Bay. **Blue Heron Landing** (☎ 541-994-4708; 4006 W Devil's Lake Rd; 9am-7:30pm) has various rentals and a bumper boat ride for the kids.

Get surfing gear and advice at **Oregon Surf Shop** (☎ 541-996-3957; www.oregonsurfshop.com; 4933 SW US 101; 10am-6pm).

Sleeping

There are endless hotels and motels lining Lincoln City's shoreline.

Devil's Lake State Park (☎ 541-994-2002, 800-452-5687; www.oregonstateparks.org; 1452 NE 6th Dr; tents/hookups/yurts $17/23/29) Located a short walk to the beach, Devil's Lake includes pluses like showers, flush toilets and fishing and boating on a freshwater lake.

Captain Cook Inn (☎ 541-994-2522, 800-808-9409; www.captaincookinn.com; 2626 NE US 101; d from $69; wi-fi) One of the area's better hotels, with 17 well-maintained, pretty rooms. The furniture is modern and there are a few flowers planted on the premises. Kitchenettes are available.

Sea Horse Oceanfront Lodgings (☎ 541-994-2101, 800-662-2101; www.seahorsemotel.com; 1301 NW 21st St; d from $89; wi-fi) Go for an oceanfront room at this fine motel with good, neat rooms. Kitchenettes, gas fireplaces and jetted tubs are available, and there's beach access and an indoor heated pool.

SO HIP IT YURTS

Many Oregon state parks – especially along the coast – have embraced the wonderful yurt: a felt-covered, lattice-framed structure used as portable homes by Central Asian nomads. Park yurts are rather permanent, however, sporting wood floors, canvas walls, windows and a skylight. They have electricity and heat, but bathrooms are outside, unless you happen upon a deluxe version, which sometimes features a kitchen, too! Furniture such as bunk beds, futon sofas and tables are included, but you need to bring all bedding and cooking equipment. Yurts are convenient, private, secure, fun and immensely popular in summer, so reserve ahead; they cost around $30 per night.

Brey House B&B (☎ 541-994-7123, 877-994-7123; www.breyhouse.com; 3725 NW Keel Ave; d $95-125; ⊠ wi-fi) For a more personal experience, stay at this Cape Cod–style B&B just a block from the beach. There are four comfortable rooms with quilts on the beds, and a suite with kitchen and fireplace is available. For the best ocean view snag the Admiral's Room on the 3rd floor.

Looking Glass Inn (☎ 541-996-3996, 800-843-4940; www.lookingglass-inn.com; 861 SW 51st; d $115-150; ⊠ 🖳) Simple but clean and comfortable rooms in various sizes are featured here; some have kitchenette, fireplace, jetted tubs and two bedrooms. There are faraway views to the beach, which is across a parking lot.

O'dysius Hotel (☎ 541-994-4121, 800-869-8069; www.odysius.com; 160 NW Inlet Court; d from $174; ⊠ wi-fi) For a classy stay near the beach there's this family-run hotel with 30 elegant rooms. The common spaces are decorated with artwork and reproduction antiques, and all rooms come with fireplace, featherbed and ocean views. There's a wine social every evening, and breakfast can be delivered to your room. Children over 12 only.

Salishan Spa & Golf Resort (☎ 541-764-2371; www.salishan.com; 7760 N US 101, Gleneden Beach; d from $180; ⊠ 🖳 🏊) This four-star luxury resort boasting a top-notch 18-hole golf course, indoor (and outdoor) tennis courts and a gorgeous spa is for those who must have the very best. Rooms are tastefully done, very spacious and sport gas fireplaces. Also onsite are fancy shops, an indoor pool and a fine dining room (right).

Eating

Sun Garden Café (☎ 541-994-2590; 1816 NE US 101; mains $5-10; 🕒 8am-8pm Mon, Wed & Thu, till 10pm Fri & Sat, 9am-3pm Sun) Breakfast is especially good at this eclectic spot on the busy highway, which plays Zen-like music to help the French toast go down easy. Indian treats like curries and *saag* (sautéed spinach) are also offered, along with chicken fried steak and Cobb salad.

McMenamins Lighthouse Pub & Brewery (☎ 541-994-7238; 4157 N US 101; mains $7-18; 🕒 11:30am-midnight Sun-Thu, till 1am Fri & Sat) Located in an ugly strip mall next to Grocery Outlet, this McMenamins chain venue features typical pub food with a seafood twist. There's plenty of sandwiches, pizza and burgers, plus house-signature microbrews and wine.

Side Door Café (☎ 541-764-3825; 6675 Gleneden Beach Loop Rd; mains $9-29; 🕒 11:30am-9pm Wed-Mon) Located 3 miles south in Gleneden Beach, this airy loft bistro exudes an upscale yet slightly funky vibe. Gourmet sandwiches, burgers and salads share the menu with mains like hazelnut encrusted pork medallions and fire-roasted rack of lamb. Worth the drive from town.

Blackfish Café (☎ 541-996-1007; 2733 NW US 101; mains $14-18; 🕒 11:30am-9pm Sun & Mon, Wed & Thu, noon-10pm Fri & Sat) One of the best restaurants on the coast, Blackfish specializes in cutting-edge cuisine highlighting fresh seafood and organic vegetables. Chef Rob Pounding is an accomplished master, creating these tasty, beautiful Northwest-inspired foods at a reasonable price.

Kyllo's Seafood Grill (☎ 541-994-3179; 1110 NW 1st Ct; mains $14-24; 🕒 11:30am-9pm Sun-Thu, till 9:30pm Fri & Sat) One of Lincoln City's few restaurants with an ocean view, Kyllo's menu offers nothing too surprising, which is just the thing for many beachgoers. There's good clam chowder, seafood, pasta and steaks, plus a small kids' menu.

Salishan Dining Room (☎ 800-452-2300; 7760 N US 101, Gleneden Beach; mains $24-37; 🕒 5-9pm) Premier Pacific Northwest cuisine is served in the Salishan's impressive, if slightly ostentatious, dining room. Chef Ken Martin whips up dishes made to perfection, and there are at least a few selections in the restaurant's legendary 10,000-bottle wine cellar. For a less stuffy atmosphere head to the casual Sun Room.

Bay House (☎ 541-996-3222; www.thebayhouse.org; 5911 SW US 101; mains $32-39; 🕒 5:30-9pm Sun-Mon, 11:30am-2pm & 5:30-9pm Tue-Sat) Chef Justin Wills presides over the kitchen at this elegant establishment, creating a fine rotating seafood and meat menu (posted daily on their website). Only the freshest top-quality ingredients are used, and the wine list is award-winning; the view should be.

DEPOE BAY

pop 1300

Located 10 miles south of Lincoln City, pleasant Depoe Bay is edged by modern timeshare condominiums but still retains some original coastal charm. It lays claim to having the 'world's smallest navigable harbor' and being the 'world's whale-watching capital' – pretty big talk for such a pint-sized town. Whale-watching and charter fishing are the main attractions in the area, though 5 miles south of town there is also Devil's Punchbowl, an impressive collapsed sea cave that churns with waves and offers good tide pools nearby.

The **visitor center** (☎ 541-765-2889; www.depoebaychamber.org; 223 SW US 101 Suite B; 🕑 11am-3pm Mon-Thu, 8:30am-4pm Fri-Sun) is next to the Mazatlan restaurant. An impressive **Whale Watching Center** (☎ 541-765-3304; 119 SW US 101; 🕑 9am-5pm) has good exhibits and provides binoculars and views out to sea.

Sleeping & Eating

Trollers Lodge (☎ 541-765-2287; www.trollerslodge.com; 355 SW US 101; d $59-90; ⊠ 💻) Anglers love this place, which offers a dozen cute rooms and two-bedroom suites (some with kitchenette), all decked out in casual country style. It's not on the water but you can hear the waves crashing.

WHALE-WATCHING

Each year, the longest migration of any mammal takes place in the Pacific Ocean, when approximately 20,000 gray whales make their annual 10,000-mile round-trip journey between the Arctic Sea and the lagoons of Baja California. The migration along the Oregon coast peaks in late December, but whales can also be spotted from March to May as they meander back north.

Viewpoints are sometimes staffed with volunteers who can help identify and interpret gray whale behavior. For a close-up view take a two-hour boat tour, which are especially accessible from Depoe Bay or Newport.

Whale Inn (☎ 541-765-2789; www.whaleinnatdepoebay.com; 416 NE US 101; d $65-119; ⊠) Just 11 cozy rooms are available at this old-fashioned homely place, each with its own personality. It's an older place with newer amenities like pillow-top beds, high-definition TVs and kitchenettes. One- and two-bedroom suites available.

Inn at Arch Rock (☎ 541-765-2560; www.innatarchrock.com; 70 NW Sunset St; d $75-185; ⊠ 💻) This friendly, upscale inn has 13 very comfortable rooms and suites, most with sea view. They range widely in size and amenities; some have fireplace, kitchenette and sitting areas. Room number 10 is a favorite.

Tidal Raves (☎ 541-765-2995; 279 US 101; mains $11-21; 🕑 11am-9pm) Both the food and the view are awesome here. Lip-smacking mains include garlic scallops, grilled wild salmon and Dungeness crab casserole. Salads are huge, and the steamed clams supremely tasty.

NEWPORT

pop 9675

Oregon's second-largest commercial port, Newport is a lively tourist city with several fine beaches and a world-class aquarium. Good restaurants – along with some tacky attractions, gift shops and barking sea lions – abound in the historic bay-front area, while bohemian Nye Beach offers art galleries and friendly village atmosphere. The area was first explored in the 1860s by fishing crews who found oyster beds at the upper end of Yaquina Bay.

One of the coast's premier events, the **Newport Wine & Seafood Festival** (www.newportchamber.org/swf/) occurs in late February. For more information there's the **Chamber of Commerce** (☎ 541-265-8801, 800-262-7844; www.newportchamber.org; 555 SW Coast Hwy; 🕑 8am-5pm Mon-Fri, 10am-3pm Sat).

Sights & Activities

OREGON COAST AQUARIUM

The region's top attraction, this **aquarium** (☎ 541-867-3474; www.aquarium.org; 2820 SE Ferry Slip Rd; adult/3-13yr/senior $13/8/11; 🕑 9am-6pm) is especially fun if you have kids along. Marine celebrities include seals, sea otters and a giant octopus, and there's an impressive deep-sea exhibit where you walk under Plexiglas tunnels and get an eyeful of sharks and rays swimming by. The jellyfish room is a surreal experience, while the touch tank appeals to everyone. Rogue Ale brewery (see right) runs the aquarium's family-friendly café.

HATFIELD MARINE SCIENCE CENTER

This excellent **science center** (☎ 541-867-0271; www.hmsc.orst.edu/visitor; 2030 S Marine Science Dr; 10am-5pm) has more modest exhibits than its flashy aquarium neighbor and provides a more educational – and less bustling – alternative. It's free, but give them a few bucks to help run programs.

YAQUINA BAY STATE PARK

Situated on a bushy bluff above the north entrance of the bay, this day-use **park** (no fee) is popular for beach access and views over Yaquina Bay. Visit the **Yaquina Bay Lighthouse** (not to be confused with the Yaquina Head Lighthouse, 3 miles north), built in 1871 but decommissioned in 1874. The living quarters are preserved as an informal **museum** (☎ 541-265-5679; admission by donation; 11am-5pm).

OREGON COAST HISTORY CENTER

This two-building **museum** (☎ 541-265-7509; www.oregoncoast.history.museum; 545 SW 9th St; admission free; 10am-5pm Tue-Sun) is located in both the 1895 Burrows House and a log cabin next door. On display are an impressive collection of Siletz artifacts, a rectangular grand piano and – most impressive of all – a large toothpick model of the Yaquina Bay Bridge. Check out the photos of wood-plank surfboards.

YAQUINA HEAD OUTSTANDING NATURAL AREA

Stretching a mile out to sea is the popular **Yaquina Head** (☎ 541-574-3100; 750 Lighthouse Dr; $5 entry; sunrise-sunset), a grassy headland just north of Newport. Short trails lead to viewing areas for shorebirds, harbor seals and whales, and the tide pools are the best-managed on the coast. Visit the excellent **interpretive center** (9am-5pm) to explore different marine environments and get a taste of the history of the coast's lighthouses. The coast's tallest, still-functioning **lighthouse** is at the tip of the headland and offers tours by docents in period costumes.

WHALE-WATCHING

Marine Discovery Tours (☎ 541-265-6200, 800-903-2628; www.marinediscovery.com; 345 SW Bay Blvd; adult/4-13yr/senior $32/16/30) sets out on two-hour cruises to stalk whales and other marine life.

Sleeping

There are plenty of economy hotels on US 101.

Beverly Beach State Park (☎ 541-265-9278, 800-452-5687; www.oregonstateparks.org; tents/hookups/yurts $17/22/29) This large campground, 7 miles north of town on US 101, has over 250 sites, 21 yurts and hookups to cable TV. Also has showers and flush toilets.

South Beach State Park (☎ 541-867-4715, 800-452-5687; www.oregonstateparks.org; tents & hookups/yurts $22/29) Two miles south on US 101, this 227-site campground is especially good for large groups, and has showers, flush toilets and 27 yurts.

Waves Newport Motel (☎ 541-265-4661, 800-282-6993; www.wavesofnewport.com; 820 NW Coast St; d $64-109;) Offers basic but good-sized motel rooms with fridge, coffeemaker and microwave. The higher floors have sea views.

Rogue Ales Public House (☎ 541-265-3188; 740 SW Bay Blvd; apt $92-130) Just three one- or two-bedroom apartments huddle above this pub-restaurant – the original Rogue Ales brewery site – all with comfortable modern furnishings (including washer/dryer) and kitchenette. Rather than breakfast, two 22oz beers come with the package, making it a true 'Bed and Beer.' Plenty of creative concoctions are supplied direct from Rogue Ale's nearby new brewery.

our pick **Sylvia Beach Hotel** (☎ 541-265-5428; www.sylviabeachhotel.com; 267 NW Cliff St; d $96-190;) This book-themed hotel offers simple and classy rooms, each named after a famous author and decorated accordingly. The best are higher up, and the 3rd-floor common room has a wonderful ocean view. Two cats roam the premises. Breakfast is included; reservations mandatory.

Grand Victorian B&B (☎ 541-265-4490, 800-784-9936; www.grandvictorianor.com; 105 NW Coast St; d $100-165,) Three rooms (two share one bathroom) are nestled in this green, three-story Victorian home. They're all beautiful and decorated with antiques; the suite is huge and awesome. A separate cottage next door, great for families, is also available ($180).

Elizabeth Street Inn (☎ 541-265-9400, 877-265-9400; www.elizabethstreetinn.com; 232 SW Elizabeth St; d $176-220;) This lovely hotel has 68 elegantly furnished rooms, all with fireplace and balcony overlooking the ocean. Continental breakfast is included, and there's a common Jacuzzi and a small fitness room.

Also recommended:

Newport City Center Motel (☎ 541-265-7381, 800-687-9099; www.newportcitycentermotel.com; 538 SW Coast Hwy; d $40-144; 💻) Cheap, but smell your room first. Apartments with kitchens available.

Tyee Lodge B&B (☎ 888-553-8933; www.tyeelodge.com; 4925 NW Woody Way; d $139-192; ⊠ 💻) Five luxury rooms with fireplace and ocean peeks. Located north of town.

Ocean House Inn B&B (☎ 866-495-3888; www.oceanhouse.com; 4920 NW Woody Way; d $199-229; ⊠ 💻) Next to Tyee Lodge; same owner and similar offerings. Cottage available ($230).

Eating

Panini Bakery (☎ 541-265-5033; 232 NW Coast St; mains $5-7; 🕒 7am-7pm) Lines form out the door at this tiny bakery-café, but gossip away the wait. The spinach focaccia is a dream and the rustic loaves get snapped up quickly. Takeout is also pizza available.

Brewer's on the Bay (☎ 541-867-3664; 2320 SW OSU Dr; mains $8-15; 🕒 11am-10pm Sun-Thu, till 11pm Fri & Sat) This casual eatery, located onsite with Rogue Ale brewery's giant tanks, serves up fare like buffalo wings, BLTs, clam chowder and Kobe burgers. The view of Yaquina Bay is a plus, and the bar's a great hangout.

Whale's Tale (☎ 541-265-8660; 452 SW Bay Blvd; mains $10-27; 🕒 9am-9pm Sun-Thu, till 10pm Fri & Sat) A local institution serving a good selection of sandwiches, soups and salads, along with fancier fare like cioppino, oysters and seafood platters. Casually eclectic and full of marine-themed knickknacks.

April's at Nye Beach (☎ 541-265-6855; 749 NW 3rd St; mains $12-20; 🕒 5-9pm Wed-Sun) This elegant, highly regarded restaurant serves excellent Mediterranean and Italian cuisine using fresh, local and sustainably harvested seafood ingredients. Try the prawn linguini, pan-seared scallops or roast duck, and top it off with a homemade dessert (prepared by their own pastry chef).

Saffron Salmon (☎ 541-265-8921; 859 SW Bay Blvd; mains $22-30; 🕒 11:30am-2:30pm & 5-8:30pm Thu-Tue) Once you get past the stellar wall-to-wall view, dig into grilled chinook salmon or herb-crusted rack of lamb. Local seafood and 'natural' beef used. Reserve for dinner.

Tables of Content in the Sylvia Beach Hotel (opposite) is open to nonguests, but reservations are necessary (prix fixe dinners $21.50). Rogue Ales Public House (opposite) serves typical pub grub (mains $8 to $15) like pizza, burgers and seafood appetizers, plus plenty of beer. Convenient for stumbling to bed if you're staying there!

Getting There & Around

Valley Retriever Buslines (☎ 541-265-2253; www.kokkola-bus.com/valleyretrieverbuslines.html; 956 SW 10th St) heads to Corvallis and other inland locations. **Lincoln County Transit** (☎ 541-265-4900; www.co.lincoln.or.us/transit) runs through Newport.

In summer there's a free daily shuttle that stops at key locations around town (runs weekends only the rest of year). For bike rentals try **Bike Newport** (☎ 541-265-9917; 152 NE 6th St; 🕒 10am-6pm Mon-Sat). At the time of writing it looked like they might move, so call beforehand.

YACHATS & AROUND

pop 635

One of the Oregon coast's best-kept secrets is the neat and friendly little town of Yachats (ya-*hots*). Lying at the base of massive Cape Perpetua, Yachats offers the memorable scenery of a rugged and windswept land. People come to small, remote inns and B&Bs just south of town to get away from the big cities, which isn't hard to do along this undeveloped coast.

Beginning at Cape Perpetua and continuing south about 20 miles is some spectacular shoreline. This entire area was once a series of volcanic intrusions which resisted the pummeling of the Pacific long enough to rise as ocean-side peaks and promontories. Acres of tide pools are home to starfish, sea anemones and sea lions. Picturesque Heceta Lighthouse rises above the surf, while tiny beaches line the cliffs. There's plenty to see in the area, especially if you're a nature fan.

For tips on area activities head to the **visitor center** (☎ 800-929-0477; www.yachats.org; US 101 & 3rd St; 🕒 10am-5pm).

Sights & Activities

BEACHES

Beaches around here are small, secluded affairs that offer tide pools and rocky promontories. Among in-town beaches at the mouth of Yachats River is **Yachats State Park**, which has a wheelchair-accessible trail along the surf.

About 4 miles south of Yachats are **Strawberry Hill Wayside** and **Neptune State Park**, which offer intertidal rocks, sandy inlets and picnic tables. Sea lions are common here.

CAPE PERPETUA

Located 3 miles south of Yachats, this volcanic remnant – one of the highest points on the Oregon coast – was sighted and named by England's Captain James Cook in 1778. Famous for its dramatic rock formations and crashing surf, the area contains numerous trails that explore ancient shell middens, tide pools and old-growth forests. Views from the cape are incredible, taking in coastal promontories from Cape Foulweather to Cape Arago. There's a day-use fee of $5.

The **visitor center** (☎ 541-547-3289; www.orcoast.com/capeperpetua; 🕑 10am-6pm Memorial Day-Labor Day, 10am-4pm Wed-Mon rest of yr) details human and natural histories, and has displays on the Alsea tribe. There are also great viewing areas to watch whales. From the visitor center turnoff, head up Overlook Rd to the Cape Perpetua Viewpoint for a spectacular ocean view.

Deep fractures in the old volcano allow waves to erode narrow channels into the headland, creating effects such as **Devil's Churn**, a mile north of the visitor center. Waves race up this chasm, shooting up the 30ft inlet to explode against the narrowing sides of the channel.

If you're looking for more than just a short stroll, start at the visitor center and climb up 1.5 miles on the **St Perpetua Trail** to a stone shelter erected by the Civilian Conservation Corps and used as a lookout for enemy vessels during WWII. The trail passes through open meadows and Sitka spruces to one of the coast's best views.

For an easier hike, the paved **Captain Cook Trail** (1.2 miles round-trip) leads down to tide pools and shell middens at Cooks Chasm, where the geyser-like spouting horn blasts water out of a sea cave.

The **Giant Spruce Trail** (2 miles round-trip) leads up Cape Creek to a 500-year-old Sitka spruce with a 10ft diameter. The **Cook's Ridge–Gwynn Creek Loop Trail** (6.5 miles round-trip) heads into deep old-growth forests along Gwynn Creek; follow the Oregon Coast Trail south and turn up the Gwynn Creek Trail, which returns via Cook's Ridge.

HECETA HEAD LIGHTHOUSE

Built in 1894 and towering precipitously above the churning ocean, this **lighthouse** (☎ 541-547-3416; day-use $3; 🕑 11am-5pm May-Sep, varies rest of yr), 13 miles south of town on US 101, is one of the most photographed lighthouses in the US. A half-mile trail winds up the bluff past the whitewashed **Heceta House**, an old lighthouse keeper's house that is now a B&B (opposite). At the end of the cape is the lighthouse, which still functions and is open for free tours.

SEA LION CAVES

Fifteen miles south of Yachats on US 101, this enormous **sea grotto** (☎ 541-547-3111; www.sealioncaves.com; adult/6-12yr/senior $9/5/8; 🕑 8am-6pm summer, limited hours rest of yr), home to hundreds of smelly, groaning sea lions, is a popular stop on the Central Oregon coast. An elevator descends 208ft to a dark interpretive area, and a nearby observation window lets you watch Steller's sea lions jockeying for the best seat on the rocks. It seems a bit overpriced for what you get, but that doesn't stop the summer crowds, who also jockey for prime (observation) positions.

Sleeping

Beachside State Park (☎ 541-563-3220, 800-452-5687; www.oregonstateparks.org; tents/hookups/yurts $17/21/29) Five miles north of town on US 101, about 80 sites and two yurts are available at this beachside campground. Showers and flush toilets available.

Carl G Washburne State Park (☎ 541-547-3416, 800-452-5687; www.oregonstateparks.org; tents/hookups/yurts $17/22/29) After traveling 12 miles south of town on US 101, hike 6 miles round-trip to Heceta Head Lighthouse (left). Over 60 woodsy sites and two yurts are available, along with showers and flush toilets.

Cape Perpetua Campground (☎ 877-444-6777; www.recreation.gov; tents $20; 🕑 May-Oct) This USFS campground, 2 miles south on US 101, has 38 beautiful sites.

Ya'Tel Motel (☎ 541-547-3225; www.yatelmotel.com; cnr US 101 & 6th St; d $59-99; ⊠) Newly remodeled by friendly proprietors, this nine-room motel has large, clean rooms; some with kitchenette. It's a good deal and includes amenities like fridges, microwave and coffeemaker; packets of hot chocolate and popcorn are thoughtful touches. Board games available.

Rock Park Cottages (☎ 541-547-3214; www.trillian.com/rockpark/rock.htm; 431 W 2nd St; d $75-85; ⊠) Five cute and comfy cottages with kitchenette are available here. Room one comes with ocean peeks. The large A-frame sleeps up to six and is great for families.

See Vue (☎ 541-547-3227, 866-547-3237; www.seevue.com; d $80-95; ⊠) This unique, lesbian-owned-and-operated motel is set high above the surf, 6 miles south of town on US 101. All 11 rooms come with a glorious ocean view, and each is decorated with its own motif. Kitchenettes and fireplaces add convenience and coziness. Two-bedroom apartment are also available.

Yachats Inn (☎ 541-547-3456, 888-270-3456; www.yachatsinn.com; 331 S US 101; d $80-135; ⊠ 💻 🏊) Simple and homely units (or more modern suites) are on tap here, some with kitchenette, fireplace and/or deck. Indoor pool and Jacuzzi available to all.

Ocean Haven (☎ 541-547-3583; www.oceanhaven.com; 94770 US 101; d $90-125; ⊠ 💻) Eight miles south of Yachats, this casual five-room inn is run by an eccentric couple who have banned Hummers from their parking lot. All rooms come with awesome ocean view, and the rustic cabin ($120) has hosted author Robert Bly. Whimsical details add personality to an already quirky place.

Oregon House (☎ 541-547-3329; www.oregonhouse.com; 94288 US 101; d $115-175; ⊠ 💻) More a retreat center than anything else, this little haven offers tranquility for spirituality-seekers or those just looking for a little peace. Eleven modern rooms and suites come with glimpses of the sea, kitchenettes, and some have fireplaces and/or Jacuzzis. Located 9 miles south of Yachats.

Shamrock Lodgettes (☎ 541-547-3312, 800-845-5028; www.shamrocklodgettes.com; 105 S US 101; d from $119, cabins from $159; ⊠ 💻) Go for a rustic log cabin here, though you won't be far from comfort – most come with fireplace, kitchenette and ocean views, and some even have jets in the tub. Simple but spacious modern rooms are also available.

our pick SeaQuest Inn B&B (☎ 541-547-3782, 800-341-4878; www.seaquestinn.com; 95354 US 101 S; d incl breakfast from $169; ⊠ 💻) This gorgeous B&B is located in a large wood-shingle, driftwood-decorated house that has stunning ocean views and down-to-earth artsy touches. Seven luxurious rooms (four with their own Jacuzzi) come with private deck and gourmet breakfast. The huge suite is heaven for romantic couples.

Overleaf Lodge (☎ 541-547-4880, 800-338-0507; www.overleaflodge.com; 280 Overleaf Lodge Lane; d $169-175; ⊠ 💻) Just north of Yachat's town center is this fancy resort-spa, the area's snazziest lodging. Luxury rooms all come with great sea views, and some also have balconies, fireplaces and Jacuzzis. It's a scenic spot with a nearby walking trail winding along the coast.

Heceta Light Lighthouse B&B (☎ 866-547-3696; www.hecetalighthouse.com; d $179-265; ⊠ 💻) This 1894 Queen Anne can't help but attract passersby. Located near the lighthouse trail (opposite), it's 13 miles south of town on US 101. Inside there are six pretty rooms, all simply furnished with period antiques, along with a classy, museum-like atmosphere. Breakfast is a gourmet sensation and reservations are definitely recommended.

Eating

Green Salmon Coffee House (☎ 541-547-3077; 220 US 101; snacks under $4; 🕑 7:30am-4pm; Ⓥ) Organic and sustainable are big words at this eclectic solar-powered café. The windows steam up early while patrons munch on tasty breakfast sandwiches (and awesome oatmeal) and sip fair-trade coffees. Homemade pastries also available.

our pick Grand Occasions Deli (☎ 541-547-4409; 84 Beach St; mains $7-12; 🕑 10am-6pm Sun-Thu, till 8pm Fri & Sat) This funky and friendly bistro offers some of the tastiest treats in town. Try the delicious Greek pita wrap or the oyster poor boy. Other offerings include a hummus plate and baked brie with tomato chutney. The pies are spectacular. There's a sea view to gaze over as you eat.

Drift Inn (☎ 541-547-4477; 124 N US 101; mains $8-19; 🕑 8am-11pm) Wood booths mean cozy dining at this casual eatery. Appetizers include nachos and pork dumplings, and main dishes run the gamut from Jamaican prawns and a Teriyaki rice bowl to crab crepes and butternut squash ravioli. For simpler fare there's also burgers and pizza.

Yachats River House (☎ 541-547-4100; 131 US 101; mains $17-29; 🕑 11:30am-2pm & 5-9pm Tue-Sun) Fine dining in Yachats is enhanced by this excellent establishment, where chef Harley Charron whips up creations like hoisin-glazed cod, roast duck with fig sauce and a comforting winter vegetable pot pie. Its sister, the nearby Wine Trader, also offers upscale cuisine and wine.

Getting There & Away

Lincoln County Transit (☎ 541-265-4900; www.co.lincoln.or.us/transit) runs through Yachats.

SOUTHERN OREGON COAST

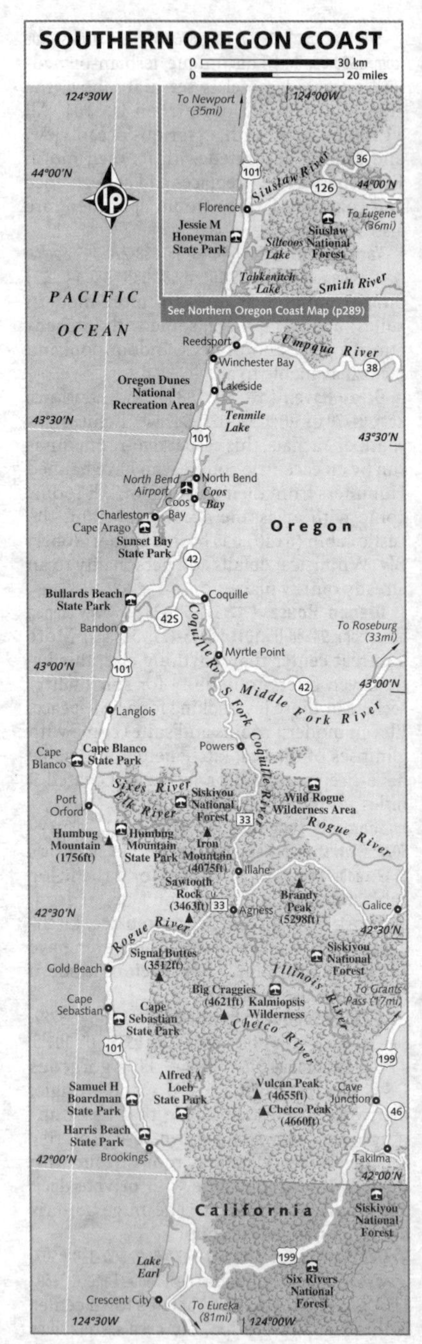

The flip side of its northern coastal counterpart, Oregon's southern coast is further from the major inland metropolises and consequently gets less attention, less traffic, less bustle and more solitude. Much of the coastline here is nearly pristine, with a more wild and dramatic feel. Beautiful clean rivers gush from inland mountainsides down to the sea, offering exceptional salmon and steelhead fishing along with boating recreation. Life is laid-back and relatively subdued; if you find a sandy beach at the end of a hiking trail, chances are you'll have it to yourself.

But despite its remoteness, the southern coast is slowly attracting development and a finer class of tourism, and you won't have a hard time finding the occasional upscale resort, world-class golf course or amazing gourmet restaurant if that's what you're looking for. Harboring a milder climate (and less precipitation) than the north has its advantages as well, and the scenic drives – especially from Port Orford to Brookings – boast some of the most memorable coastal views you'll ever set eyes on.

FLORENCE

pop 8100

Much of Florence consists of a long, mind-numbing commercial strip that in summer serves the needs of tourists and passing dune buggy enthusiasts, buzzing a path to the Oregon Dunes National Recreation Area just further south. Find your way to the Old Town area, however, and you'll see another, more charming side of the town: a quaint waterfront district nestled along the scenic Siuslaw River next to Oregon coast's prettiest harbor.

A floral parade, flower show and slug race are highlights of the **Rhododendron Festival** (☎ 541-997-3128; 🕑 3rd weekend in May), which has been celebrated for over 100 years to honor the ubiquitous shrubbery. Ask about other local events at the **visitors center** (☎ 541-997-3128; www.florencechamber.com; 290 US 101; 🕑 9am-5pm Mon-Fri, 10am-2pm Sat).

Porter Stage Lines (☎ 541-269-7183; www.kokkola-bus.com/PorterStageLines2.html) provides long-distance bus services along the coast, also connecting with Amtrak and Greyhound in Eugene.

Sights & Activities

Boardwalks, fun shops, good restaurants and great views of the Siuslaw Bridge make **Old Town** a top place to explore. The **Siuslaw Pioneer Museum** (☎ 541-997-7884; cnr Maple & 2nd Sts; admission $3; noon-4pm Tue-Sun) is located in a 1905 schoolhouse and displays exceptional farming, fishing and logging artifacts, along with typical household items from the pioneer days.

Five miles north of downtown Florence on US 101 is the **Darlingtonia Wayside**, where a short boardwalk overlooks a surreal bog of insect-eating pitcher plants (*Darlingtonia californica*, also known as cobra lilies). There's **horseback riding** on beaches and trails 8 miles north of Florence at **C&M Stables** (☎ 541-997-7540; www.oregonhorsebackriding.com; 90241 N US 101; rides per person $35-80).

Sleeping & Eating

There are good accommodation choices to the north on US 101 towards Yachats (see p302). For camping around Florence, check out the Oregon Dunes National Recreation Area (p306).

Landmark Inn (☎ 541-997-9030, 800-822-7811; www.landmarkmotel.com; 1551 4th St; d $65-100; ⊠ 💻) A fine deal, this pretty hilltop inn offers a dozen tasteful rooms and suites, some with kitchenette and one with an outdoor Jacuzzi. A great choice for families; get room number 10 for the best view.

River House Inn (☎ 541-997-3933, 877-997-3933; www.riverhouseflorence.com; 1202 Bay St; d from $100) Close to the Old Town, this remodeled motel offers a good night's sleep. Riverview rooms come with private wood balcony and are worth the extra cost; some have Jacuzzis as well.

Blue Heron Inn B&B (☎ 541-997-4091, 800-997-7780; www.blue-heroninn.com; 6563 Hwy 126; d $120-150; ⊠) Five beautiful rooms are available at this pleasant B&B. It's located 2 miles east of Florence, right on Hwy 126. Gourmet breakfasts are served, and there's a great river view from the living room.

Edwin K B&B (☎ 541-997-8360, 800-833-9465; www.edwink.com; 1155 Bay St; d $140-174; ⊠ 💻) Sitting across the street from the Siuslaw River is the flowery Edwin K, which comes with six comfortable rooms. All are spacious, and two boast romantic open bathtubs. A five-course breakfast is served on the hostess's fine china.

Traveler's Cove (☎ 541-997-6845; 1362 Bay St; mains $8-14; 9am-9pm) Good hamburgers, Caesar salads and other bistro fare is cooked up here, but you'd do well with the Mexican choices also. The wood deck out back overlooks the river and is a must on sunny days.

International C-Food Market (☎ 541-997-9646; 1498 Bay St; mains $9-21; 11am-9pm) A fabulous location right on the river makes for great views at this popular and lively eatery. Burgers, pasta, pizza and a good selection of seafood are on tap. Crab lovers should zero in on the all-you-can-eat Dungeness special ($30).

Waterfront Depot (☎ 541-902-9100; 1252 Bay St; mains $10-15; 4-9pm) This cozy, atmospheric joint is one of Florence's best restaurants. Come early to snag one of the few waterfront tables, then enjoy your Jambalaya pasta or crab-encrusted halibut. There are tapas on offer if you want to try a bit of everything. Reserve ahead.

OREGON DUNES NATIONAL RECREATION AREA

Stretching for 50 miles between Florence and Coos Bay, the Oregon Dunes form the largest expanse of oceanfront sand dunes in the USA. The dunes tower up to 500ft and undulate inland as far as 3 miles to meet coastal forests, harboring curious ecosystems that sustain an abundance of wildlife, especially birds. The area inspired Frank Herbert to pen his epic sci-fi *Dune* novels.

The lower half of the dunes is dominated by dune buggies and dirt bikes (off-highway vehicles, or OHVs); hiking is not recommended in these areas. It's possible to rent vehicles near Florence, Winchester Bay and Hauser for $30 per hour. The upper half of the dunes is closed to OHVs, and instead preserved for wildlife and less destructive human activities like hiking and canoeing.

Get informed at the Oregon Dunes National Recreation Area's **headquarters** (☎ 541-271-3495; www.fs.fed/us/r6/siuslaw; 855 Highway Ave; 8am-4:30pm Mon-Fri, till 4pm Sat & Sun May 15-Sep 15) in Reedsport (p306). Day-use fees apply at all USFS sites.

Activities

HIKING

From the **Stagecoach Trailhead** (look for 'Siltcoos Recreation Area' sign), three short trails along a river and wetlands afford good wildlife viewing. One of these, the **Waxmyrtle Trail**, winds to the beach for 1.5 miles along the Siltcoos

River, where herons, deer and waterfowl can be seen. Other trails lead to a freshwater lagoon or up to a forested vista point.

The wheelchair-accessible **Oregon Dunes Overlook** ($5), 10 miles north of Reedsport, has good viewing platforms and also serves as a trailhead for a 1-mile hike to the beach. Two miles north is **Carter Lake Campground** ($5), where the wheelchair-accessible **Taylor Dunes Trail** leads 0.5 miles to a viewing area. You can hike beyond here through dunes to meet the **Carter Dunes Trail** and head to the beach (3 miles round-trip).

A longer, 6-mile loop hike starts from Tahkenitch Campground (right), 8 miles north of Reedsport. Follow the **Tahkenitch Dunes Trail** west to reach the beach in less than 2 miles, then walk south along the beach to directional posts for the **Threemile Lake Trail**, which returns hikers to the campground via a freshwater lake and deep forests.

For some of the biggest dunes in the area, take the **Umpqua Dunes Trail** from Eel Creek Campground (right), 10 miles south of Reedsport, which leads out across a wilderness of massive sand peaks before reaching the beach. The hike there and back is 5 miles, involves some tough dune climbing and can be unpleasant in windy weather.

SWIMMING & BOATING

Jessie M Honeyman State Park (right) has two lakes. **Cleawox Lake** is the smaller of the two and especially popular for swimming. Rent canoes, kayaks and pedal boats at the park concession; kayak tours are also offered. Motor boaters prefer **Woahink Lake**.

Wildlife-viewing is good along the **Siltcoos River Canoe Trail**, which travels the Siltcoos River through forest and marsh towards the ocean. Start at Siltcoos Lake, 6 miles south of Florence.

Sleeping

The nearest hotels are at Florence (p305) and Reedsport (opposite). Campgrounds from north to south include the following:

Umpqua Lighthouse State Park (☎ 541-271-4118, 800-452-5687; www.oregonstateparks.org; tents/hookups/yurts/cabins $16/20/27/35) Pleasant, wooded campsites here are adjacent to tiny Lake Marie, which warms up nicely for summer splashing. Two deluxe yurts (with TV, kitchen and bathroom) cost $65. Situated 6 miles south of Reedsport.

William M Tugman State Park (☎ 541-759-3604, 800-452-5687; tents/yurts $16/27) Eight miles south of Reedsport on US 101, this is a large campground with grassy open areas, 16 yurts and easy access to Eel lake, popular for fishing and walking.

Carter Lake Campground (☎ 877-444-6777; tents $17) Close to US 101, 8 miles south of Florence, Carter Lake has some trails that provide easy access to dune viewpoints and further on to the beach.

Eel Creek Campground (☎ 877-444-6777; tents $17) The shrubby sites here offer refuge from OHVs and a hiking trail to the dunes. Located on US 101, 10 miles south of Reedsport.

Tahkenitch Campground (☎ 877-444-6777; tents $17) A good woodsy place to ditch those OHVs; also has trailheads. Located on US 101, 7 miles north of Reedsport.

Jessie M Honeyman State Park (☎ 541-997-3641, 800-452-5687; www.oregonstateparks.org; off US 101; tents/hookups/yurts $17/21/29) Located 3 miles south of Florence on Cleawox Lake, this campground is massively popular for its easy access to swimming and the dunes. Showers and flush toilets available; reserve in summer.

Driftwood II Campground (☎ 877-444-6777; tents $20) Set up for OHVs, Driftwood II is on Siltcoos Beach Access Rd, 7 miles south of Florence. The nearby Waxmyrtle and Lagoon Campgrounds share contact details and prices.

Horsfall Campground (☎ 877-444-6777; tents $20) On Horsfall Beach Rd, 3 miles north of North Bend, Horsfall is set up for OHVs. The Wild Mare Horse Camp, for horse riders, is nearby and has the same contact details and tent prices.

Sand camping ($10, no facilities) is allowed anywhere in the dunes, though you must register at the headquarters (p305), and you'll need an all-wheel-drive vehicle to navigate the sands.

REEDSPORT

pop 4250

Five miles from where the mighty Umpqua River joins the Pacific Ocean is Reedsport, the historic port that ushered out the immense bounty of logs cut in the wide Umpqua River drainage. Today Reedsport is a small town getting smaller, but still boasts a few area attractions. Its location in the middle of the Oregon Dunes makes it an ideal base for exploring the region.

Take the kids to **Umpqua Discovery Center** (☎ 541-271-4816; www.umpquadiscoverycenter.com; 409 Riverfront Way; adult/6-15yr/senior $8/4/7; 9am-5pm) to explore the cultural and natural history of the area through colorful murals and a few interactive displays. A free platform near the entrance offers good riverside views.

Umpqua Lighthouse State Park offers summer tours of a local 1894 **lighthouse** (☎ 541-271-4631; tours$3; 10am-4pm May 1-Oct 30). Opposite the lighthouse is a whale-watching platform, and a nearby nature trail rings freshwater Lake Marie, popular for swimming.

A herd of about 120 Roosevelt elk loiter at **Dean Creek Elk Viewing Area**, a roadside wildlife refuge 3 miles east on Hwy 38. These elk are Oregon's largest land mammal.

If you're here in mid-June, don't miss the testosterone-fueled **Chainsaw Sculpting Championships**. For more information contact the **Chamber of Commerce** (☎ 541-271-3495; 855 Highway Ave; 8am-4:30pm Mon-Fri, till 4pm Sat & Sun May 15-Sep 15).

Sleeping & Eating

For camping around Reedsport see opposite.

Salty Seagull (☎ 541-271-3729; www.saltyseagull.com; 1806 Winchester Ave; d from $60;) There's only nine units here, but they're a sweet deal (despite the hotel's name). Two- and three-bedroom apartments with full kitchen are available, along with a single regular room. Decor is a bit outdated, but there's plenty of room to stretch out in.

Don's Main Street Restaurant (☎ 541-271-2032; 2115 Winchester Ave; mains $5-10; 8am-9pm) This modern diner is a longtime favorite for families. Don's serves up a dozen kinds of cheap burgers and 20 flavors of pie, among other things. It's nothing mind-blowing, but you'll get a good look at the locals.

COOS BAY & NORTH BEND

The no-nonsense city of Coos Bay (population 16,000) and its modest neighbor North Bend (population 10,000) make up the largest urban area on the Oregon coast. Coos Bay boasts the largest natural harbor between San Francisco and Seattle, and has long been a major shipping and manufacturing center for most of Southern Oregon. It was also once the largest timber port in the world. Today the logs are gone, but the tourists have taken their place.

The **Coos Art Museum** (☎ 541-267-3901; www.coosart.org; 235 Anderson Ave; 10am-4pm Tue-Sat), in a historic art-deco building, provides a hub for the region's art culture. Rotating exhibits from the museum's permanent collection are displayed, along with occasional local artists' works. The old-style movie house **Egyptian Theatre** (☎ 541-269-8650; www.egyptian-theatre.com; 229 S Broadway; movies $4) has fun Egyptian motifs and an original Wurlitzer organ. Coos Bay's **Oregon Coast Music Festival** (☎ 541-267-0938; www.oregoncoastmusic.com) takes place over two weeks in July.

In North Bend, just south of the McCullough Bridge, the **Coos Historical and Maritime Museum** (☎ 541-756-6320; www.cooshistory.org; 1220 Sherman Ave; admission $2; 10am-4pm Tue-Sat, noon-4pm Sun) displays exhibits from Native American culture to maritime shipwrecks. Check out the fish weir lattice.

Both Coos Bay's **visitor center** (☎ 541-269-0215, 800-824-8486; www.oregonsbayareachamber.com; 50 Central Ave; 9am-5pm Mon-Wed & Fri, till 7pm Thu, noon-4pm Sat & Sun) and North Bend's **visitor center** (☎ 541-756-4613; www.northbendcity.org; 1380 Sherman Ave; 8am-5pm Mon-Fri, 10am-4pm Sat & Sun) provide good local information. Inquire at the latter about the *North Bend self-guided walking tour* pamphlet.

Sleeping

There are oceanside campgrounds to the southwest, near Charleston (p309), or north in the Oregon Dunes National Recreation Area.

Bay Bridge Motel (☎ 541-756-3151, 800-557-3156; 66304 US 101, North Bend; d from $55;) Run by the friendly 'Bay Bridge Betty,' this typical motel is located just north of the McCullough Bridge and has typical amenities, but some rooms boast very atypical (and memorable) bay views.

Old Tower House B&B (☎ 541-888-6058; www.oldtowerhouse.com; 476 Newmark Ave, Coos Bay; d $100;) This pretty Victorian B&B (1872) offers just three rooms decorated with lovely period antiques; all share two outside bathrooms. There's a great sunroom for the continental breakfast (gourmet costs $5 extra), and a cottage is available for $146.

This Olde House B&B (☎ 541-267-5224; www.bnbweb.com/thisoldehouse.html; 202 Alder Ave, Coos Bay; d $109-135;) Not every B&B can claim to have hosted Robert Plant, even if they had no idea who he was at the time. The five lovely rooms are otherwise just five lovely rooms, with the Magnolia boasting the best amenities and view. Reservations are mandatory (even if you're a rock star).

Edgewater Inn (☎ 541-267-0423, 800-233-0423; www.theedgewaterinn.com; 275 E Johnson Ave, Coos Bay; d incl breakfast $119-135;) Tucked in behind Safeway and Fred Meyer's, this pleasant motel features clean, good-sized rooms (some with kitchenette). Get an upper room for views over the river. A business center, gym and indoor pool are fun diversions.

Coos Bay Manor B&B (☎ 541-269-1224, 800-269-1224; www.coosbaymanor.com; 955 S 5th St, Coos Bay; d $139;) Nestled in this 1912 neo-colonial mansion are five gorgeous period rooms with modern amenities. It's a wonderfully interesting house, complete with 1878 piano, 2nd-floor porch and three resident pets (two cats and a dog). A large family room ($238) is also available.

Eating

Kaffe 101 (☎ 541-267-4894; 170 S Broadway, Coos Bay; snacks under $5; 6am-10pm Mon-Tue, Fri & Sat, till 5pm Wed & Thu) Settle into a sofa at this trendy modern spot, but be aware that it's a Christian establishment. (You're not required to say grace before nibbling your scone, though you will be exposed to overt friendliness.) There's also a religious bookstore here.

Café Mediterranean (☎ 541-756-2299; 1860 Union St, North Bend; mains $8-14; 11am-9pm Mon-Sat) Walk past the unspectacular facade and settle into an appetizer of baba ganoush or dolmas. Locals rave about the shish kebabs, *shawarmas* and spanakopita, but pitas, panini and hummus platters are also available. *Kali orexi!*

Blue Heron Bistro (☎ 541-267-3933; 100 W Commercial Ave, Coos Bay; mains $8-20; 11am-9pm Mon-Thu, till 10pm Fri & Sat) Seafood and bistro fare with a Euro twist are served here, from pulled pork sandwiches to Hungarian goulash to Weiner schnitzels and bratwurst. Try the 'Brussels Mussels,' oyster stew or vegetarian pizza, and wash them all down with a Spaten Oktoberfest or Belgian Chimay.

Getting There & Around

Horizon Air (☎ 541-547-9308; www.horizonair.com) serves the North Bend Airport with daily Portland connections.

Coos County Area Transit (CCAT; ☎ 541-267-7111) provides local buses. **Porter Stage Lines** (☎ 541-267-4436; www.kokkola-bus.com/PorterStageLines2.html; 275 Broadway, Coos Bay), in the old Tioga Hotel, has long-distance services.

CHARLESTON & AROUND

pop 3000

Charleston is a tiny bump of civilization on the Cape Arago Hwy, a commercial fishing port that sits just 8 miles southwest of bustling Coos Bay but feels worlds away. It makes a peaceful enough stopover and jump-off point to a trio of splendid state parks on the Cape Arago headlands. South of Charleston is Seven Devils Rd, a winding shortcut between Charleston and Bandon that accesses a number of beaches south of Cape Arago, such as Whisky Run and Agate.

The **Charleston Visitors Center** (☎ 541-888-2311; www.charlestonoregon-merchants.com; 91141 Cape Arago Hwy; ☎ 9am-5pm May-Sep) sits at the west end of the bridge.

Sights & Activities

SUNSET BAY STATE PARK

Three miles southwest of town on Cape Arago Hwy, this **state park** (☎ 541-888-4902; www.oregonstateparks.org) is nestled in a small, protected bay that once served as a safe harbor for fishing boats, and possibly pirates as well. Today it's popular with swimmers, hikers and tide pool explorers. A 4-mile, cliff-edge stretch of the **Oregon Coast Trail** continues south from here to link all three state parks. Cape Arago Lighthouse sits just offshore on a rocky crag.

SHORE ACRES STATE PARK

Beautiful rehabilitated gardens are the highlight of this unusual **state park** (☎ 541-888-2472; www.shoreacres.net; day use $3), 4 miles southwest of town on Cape Arago Hwy. Louis Simpson, an important shipping and lumber magnate, was exploring for new stands of lumber in 1905 when he discovered this wildly eroded headland. After buying up the 320 acres for $4000 he built a three-story mansion here, complete with formal gardens. It burned down in 1921. A trail leads to a glass-protected **vista point** on the cliffs where the mansion once stood, and then continues on to the beach.

CAPE ARAGO STATE PARK

A mile beyond Shore Acres is **Simpson Reef Viewpoint**, where you can spot shorebirds, migrating whales and several species of pinnipeds. Head another 0.5 miles to **Cape Arago State Park** (www.oregonstateparks.org) and the terminus of Cape Arago Hwy, where grassy picnic grounds make for great perches over a pounding sea. Trails lead down to the beach and fine tide pools, while the **Oregon Coast Trail** heads back north 4 miles to Shore Acres and Sunset Bay.

SOUTH SLOUGH NATIONAL ESTUARINE RESEARCH RESERVE

Charleston sits at the mouth of South Slough, a tidal river basin that turns into a vast, muddy estuary full of wildlife. Four miles south of Charleston on Seven Devils Rd is an excellent **interpretive center** (☎ 541-888-5558; www.southsloughestuary.org; ⌚ 10am-4:30pm Memorial Day-Labor Day, 10am-4:30pm Mon-Sat rest of yr) which has exhibits on estuarine ecology, also showcased in a 12-minute video. It runs events and programs all year long (check the website for details).

Three **walking trails** (⌚ sunrise to sunset daily), ranging from 0.25 miles to 3 miles, offer glimpses of the local ecology. Canoeing is also possible in the area, but you'll need your own canoe.

Sleeping & Eating

Sunset Bay State Park (☎ 541-888-4902, 800-452-5687; www.oregonstateparks.org; 89814 Cape Arago Hwy; tents/hookups/yurts $16/20/27) Three miles southwest of town, this is a busy, sheltered beachside campground with 130 sites, eight yurts, a playground, showers and flush toilets.

Bastendorff Beach County Park (☎ 541-888-5353, 541-396-3121, ext 354; Bastendorff Beach Rd; tents/hookups/cabins $16/20/30) Two miles southwest of town, just off Cape Arago Hwy, this park has over 90 pleasant wooded campsites in a developed campground near the beach.

Captain John's Motel (☎ 541-888-4041; www.captainjohnsmotel.com; 63360 Kingfisher Dr; d $60-70; 💻) Popular with anglers, Captain John's keeps room smells down by providing an outside crab-cooking facility for guests. It's located right near the boat docks and offers well-kept motel rooms, some with kitchenette. Flower boxes add color.

Portside Restaurant (☎ 541-888-5544; 63383 Kingfisher Dr; mains $13-25; ⌚ 11:30am-11pm) Seafood is comfort food at this excellent long-running restaurant, which offers an excellent bay view to boot. All the usual marine suspects dot the menu, along with terrestrial choices like chicken, beef and pasta. There's live music in the lounge on weekends. Reservations recommended.

BANDON

pop 2900

Optimistically touted as Bandon-by-the-Sea, this little town happily sits at the bay of the Coquille River. While Bandon as a whole may not yet be as captivating as some would like, the Old Town district has gentrified into a picturesque harborside shopping location that offers pleasant strolling and window-shopping. The city's most noteworthy industry is cranberry farming, with neighboring bogs yielding a considerable percentage of the cranberry harvest in the US.

South of town, and not obvious from the highway, are miles of sandy beaches broken by outcroppings of towering rocks – home to a large number of chattering sea birds. Ledges of stone rise out of the surf to provide shelter for seals, sea lions and myriad forms of life in tide pools.

The **Bandon Historical Society Museum** (☎ 541-347-2164; 270 Fillmore Ave; admission $2; ⌚ 10am-4pm Mon-Sat) has exhibits on the area's historical industries and the Coquille Native Americans, along with memorable photos of Bandon's two devastating fires (1914 and 1936) and various shipwrecks.

For something different, visit **Game Park Safari** (☎ 541-347-3106; www.gameparksafari.com; adult/senior $13/12, child $5.50-8.50; ⌚ 9am-7pm Mar-Nov, till 5pm rest of yr), 7 miles south on US 101, where you can meet lions and tigers and bears, among other wild (but handraised) animals. **Bandon Beach Riding Stables** (☎ 541-347-3423; 54629 Beach Loop Dr; per hr $40-50), 3 miles south of downtown, offers horseback riding.

For more information, harass the **Chamber of Commerce** (☎ 541-347-9616; www.bandon.com; cnr 2nd St & Chicago Ave; ⌚ 10am-5:30pm). The **Cranberry Festival**, Bandon's largest civic event, is held in September with a parade, craft fair and the glorious crowning of the Cranberry Queen.

Beaches

Head west to Beach Loop Dr for the best beach access points. There's good whale-watching here in the spring, and there's marine life to see all year round. At **Coquille Point**, at the end of SW 11th St, steps lead down to a beach interspersed with rocky crags and monoliths. Sea lions and shorebirds inhabit **Table Rock**, which lies just offshore and is protected as the Oregon Islands National Wildlife Refuge.

A path leads over the headland at Face Rock State Park Wayside to sandier beaches around

Face Rock, a huge monolith with a human profile. Native American legends tell of a maiden and her pet kittens turned to stone by an evil sea god; they all now rise as sea stacks. A path winds along the headland and to the beach.

West of Old Town at the end of Jetty Rd, there's beach access near the **South Jetty**, which affords views of the Coquille Lighthouse.

Two miles north of Bandon, on the north shores of the Coquille River, are the windswept sands of **Bullards Beach State Park**. Visit the **Coquille Lighthouse** (☎ 541-347-2209; 🕑 9am-4pm May-Oct, 10am-4pm Apr), out of commission since 1939 and now an historic landmark.

Sleeping

Bullards Beach State Park (☎ 541-347-2209, 800-452-5687; tents/yurts $20/27) On US 101, 2 miles north of town, there are about 185 sites available here, along with 13 yurts and easy beach access. Hot showers and flush toilets too.

Bandon Wayside Motel (☎ 541-347-3421; www.bandonwayside.com; 1175 SE 2nd St; d $65-69; 💻) Ten small, neat rooms are well cared for at this budget motor-lodge just east of town. A few RV spaces with full hookups and cable TV also available.

Sea Star Guesthouse (☎ 541-347-9632; www.seastarbandon.com; 370 1st St; d $75-109; ☒) This harborside guesthouse offers a handful of pleasant rooms, some with loft and kitchenette. If you're splashing out, go for the 'Penthouse,' which has views over the river and a back deck, and sleeps five ($160).

Table Rock Motel (☎ 541-347-2700, 800-457-9141; www.tablerockmotel.com; 840 Beach Loop Rd; d $90-129; ☒ 💻) A variety of tastefully decorated rooms are available at this fine motel, from regular rooms with pink-tile baths to multistory 'cottages' with kitchenette, covered balcony and handpainted motifs or Asian-inspired decor.

Windermere (☎ 541-347-3710; www.windermerebythesea.com; 3250 Beach Loop Rd; d $105-170; ☒ 💻) These refurbished suites at the Windermere are a decent deal for oceanfront rooms. The newest ones have kitchenette, fireplace and balcony, but all have stunning views.

Lighthouse B&B (☎ 541-347-9316; www.lighthouselodging.com; 650 SW Jetty Rd; d $140-245; ☒ 💻) With its location on the Coquille River, this five-room B&B provides some pretty impressive views. The 3rd-floor Gray Whale Room has a Jacuzzi overlooking the water. The common area is bright and pleasant enough for extended lounging sessions.

Eating

Cranberry Sweets (☎ 541-347-9475; cnr 1st St & Chicago Ave; 🕑 9am-5:30pm Mon-Sat, till 5pm Sun) Not an eatery per se, but rather an exceptional candy shop where you can fill up just on the multitude of luscious samples they always have out. Got children? Have them keep their hands in their pockets.

Bandon Coffee Café (☎ 541-347-1144; 365 2nd St; snacks under $6; 🕑 6am-6pm; 💻) This modern, casual coffee shop offers light meals such as sandwiches, burgers, pitas and bagels. The coffee is average but the atmosphere is warm. There's a computer in the back.

Lord Bennett's (☎ 541-347-3663; 1695 Beach Loop Rd; mains $16-26; 🕑 11am-2:30pm & 5-9pm Mon-Fri, 10am-2:30pm, 5-9pm Sat & Sun) A Bandon institution, this upscale restaurant has fine panoramic sea views and house specialties like wild prawns, stuffed sole, and lamb chops – all served with the appropriate sides. There's a large selection of Oregon wines by the glass, and live music fills the lounge on weekends.

Alloro Wine Bar & Restaurant (☎ 541-347-1850; 375 2nd St; mains $18-21; 🕑 3-10pm Tue-Sun) Bandon goes gourmet with this snazzy eatery, which boasts an Italian menu and wide-ranging wine list. *Primi* dishes include *Zuppa di Farro* (wild barley and pancetta soup), while *secondi* mains run from *Filetto di Maiale* (pork tenderloin) to *Ossobuco d'Agnello* (braised lamb shank).

Wild Rose Bistro (☎ 541-347-4428; 130 Chicago St; mains $18-24; 🕑 5-10pm Wed-Mon) Some of the coast's tastiest food can be found at this cozy bistro, which features a variety of dishes using the finest ingredients possible. Try seafood dishes like pan-seared scallops or the wild sturgeon with pancetta. Homemade desserts seal the deal. Reservations recommended.

PORT ORFORD

pop 1200

Perched on a grassy headland and wedged between two magnificent state parks, the small hamlet of Port Orford is one of Oregon's true natural ocean harbors (most others are situated along river mouths). The town is located in one of the most scenic stretches of coast highway and there are stellar views even from Battle Rock City Park, right in the center of town. While Port Orford is still a sleepy little place, there are signs that modern development has discovered it: an upscale retreat is nestled a half-mile from town, and, at the time of writing, a fine-art gallery was due to be

CATCHING A BREEZE

Unassuming Langlois, 14 miles south of Bandon, is the closest town to Floras Lake, a covert **windsurfing**, **kitesurfing** and **kayaking** destination. Only a thin sand spit separates this shallow spring-water lake from the ocean. Summer is the peak season, though winter storms also attract adventurers. To reach the lake, head 2 miles south of Langlois on US 101, turn west (right) onto Floras Lake Rd and follow the signs.

There are **campsites** (tent/RV $12/16) at the lake with showers available but no RV hookups. For luxury, check into the lovely four-room **Floras Lake House B&B** (☎ 541-348-2573; www.floraslake.com; 92870 Boice Cope Rd; d $160-182; ☒) nearby. There's a small market and café in Langlois, but bring groceries anyway.

Equipment rental and lessons are available at the lake from **Floras Lake Windsurfing** (☎ 541-348-9912; www.floraslake.com/flw2.html; Boice Cope Rd); take the short, unmarked path next to RV site 91, or ask at Floras Lake House for information.

opened in 2008 by renowned glass artist Chris Hawthorne, along with a fine restaurant. The town has come a long way from its fishing and logging roots, and from when it was hit by the Japanese in WWII.

A **visitor center** (☎ 541-332-8055; www.discoverportorford.com; 8am-5pm Jun-Oct, till 3pm rest of yr) is located at Battle Rock City Park.

Sights & Activities

PORT ORFORD HEADS STATE PARK

A short drive along Coast Guard Rd leads to this **state park**, which has the best location in town. A couple of 20-minute loop trails offer fine panoramic views and a closer look at coastal flora. Deer and bunnies live on the grassy picnic grounds surrounding the **Lifeboat Station Museum** (☎ 541-332-0521; 10am-3:30pm Thu-Mon Apr-Oct), which was formerly a Coast Guard station. Check out the 36ft 'unsinkable' motor lifeboat on display.

CAPE BLANCO STATE PARK

Four miles north of Port Orford, off US 101, this rugged promontory is the second-most westerly point of the continental USA and a fine **state park** (☎ 541-332-6774) with hiking trails spreading out over the headland. Sighted in 1603 by Spanish explorer Martin d'Anguilar, Cape Blanco juts far out into the Pacific, withstanding lashing winds that can pass 100mph. Visitors can tour the **Cape Blanco Lighthouse** (admission $2; 10am-3:30pm Tue-Sun Apr-Oct), built in 1870, the oldest and highest operational lighthouse in Oregon. A mile east and open the same hours is **Hughes House**, a restored Victorian home built in 1898 by Patrick Hughes, an Irish dairy rancher and gold miner.

HUMBUG MOUNTAIN STATE PARK

Six miles south of Port Orford, mountains edge down to the ocean, and heavily wooded Humbug Mountain rises 1750ft from the surf. When European settlers first came to the area in 1851, the Tututni Native Americans lived in a large village along the beach just north of here. At this **state park** (☎ 541-332-6774), a 3-mile trail leads through the coast's largest remaining groves of Port Orford cedar to the top of the mountain for dramatic views of Cape Sebastian and the Pacific Ocean.

PREHISTORIC GARDENS

Twelve miles south of Port Orford, your kids will scream at the sight of a tyrannosaurus rex in front of this **dinosaur park** (☎ 541-332-4463; 36848 US 101; adult/child $7/5; 8am-8pm, varies off-season). Replicas of extinct beasties are set in a lush rain forest. Adults might find it all a bit cheesy but the little ones will love it.

Sleeping

Humbug Mountain State Park (☎ 541-332-6774, 800-452-5687; www.oregonstateparks.org; tents/hookups $14/16) About 100 comfortable, sheltered sites with access to showers and flush toilets available at this park, 6 miles south of Port Orford on US 101.

Cape Blanco State Park (☎ 541-332-6774, 800-452-5687; www.oregonstateparks.org; tents/hookups/cabins $16/16/35) Located on US 101, 4 miles north of town on a high, rocky headland with beach access and great views of the lighthouse. Showers, flush toilets and boat ramp available.

Castaway-by-the-Sea Motel (☎ 541-332-4502; www.castawaybythesea.com; 545 W 5th St; d $85-135; ☒) Thirteen modern, pleasant and spacious ocean-view rooms are available here, some with kitchenette and fireplace. The Castaway claims to be the most westerly motel in the continental US, which might well be the case if Cape Flattery in Washington has no sea-edge motels.

Home by the Sea B&B (877-332-2855; www.homebythesea.com; 444 Jackson St; d $105-115) A true B&B, in that you can tell you're in Alan and Brenda's family house, this is a very homely place with just two bedrooms (one large and one small) and awesome views. Not fancy, but you might hear some great stories from your hosts.

Compass Rose B&B (541-322-7076; www.compassroseportorford.com; 42497 Gull Rd; d $130-140) This huge, gorgeous and newly built B&B is set on 12 acres of woodland with peeks at a nearby lake. It has four beautiful and contemporary rooms, and there are plenty of spacious common areas. You can walk to the beach from here.

Wildspring Guest Habitat (541-322-0977, 866-333-9453; www.wildspring.com; 92978 Cemetery Loop; d $225-255) Five acres of wooded serenity greet you at this quiet retreat, set in a sheltered grove a half-mile from town. A handful of luxury cabin suites, all filled with elegant furniture and modern amenities like radiant-floor heating and slate showers, make for a comfortable getaway. A spa and spectacular views from the guest hall are included, as is breakfast.

Eating

At the time of writing, a new fine cuisine restaurant called Red Fish was due to open in 2008. It might be worth a visit during your stay in the area.

Crazy Norwegian (541-322-8601; 259 6th St; mains $5-11; 11:30am-8pm) A casual family spot famous for its excellent fish 'n chips, of which it has seven kinds. Soups, salads and burger fans won't be disappointed either. There are homemade cakes and pies aplenty, plus free refills on all sodas.

Surf Shack (541-322-0450; 190 6th St; mains $6-11; 11am-8pm Tue-Sun) The Shack attracts gnarly surf dudes who order at the counter. It shows surf videos on a wall screen and looks out across US 101 to the breakers. It also serves the best food in town, including fish tacos, panini and tabbouleh salad. And there are awesome desserts, man.

Paula's Bistro (541-322-9378; 236 6th St; mains $17-25; 5-9pm Tue-Sat) Best for its traditional dishes like wild mushroom ravioli, lamb chops provencal and BBQ baby ribs; also offers great soups. Paula, the owner-chef, decorates the bistro with her own spectacular art. Live music on weekends.

GOLD BEACH

pop 1930

Situated at the mouth of the fabulous Rogue River, the ex-mining town of Gold Beach didn't amount to much until the early 20th century, when the salmon-rich waters caught the fancy of gentleman anglers such as Jack London and Zane Grey. Still a place for fishing vacations, this utilitarian town's other big attraction is jet boat excursions up the Rogue River, one of Oregon's wildest and most remote. Wildlife-viewing is good, with deer, elk, otters, beavers, eagles and osprey in the area.

The **Gold Beach Chamber of Commerce** (541-247-7526, 800-525-2334; www.goldbeachchamber.com; 29279 S Ellensburg Ave; 9:30-5:30pm Tue-Sun) shares space with the **Gold Beach Ranger Station** (541-247-3600; www.fs.fed.us/r6/siskiyou; 29279 S Ellensburg Ave), so it's easy to find local information.

The coast around Gold Beach is spectacular. Take a break at **Cape Sebastian State Park**, a rocky headland 7 miles south, for a panorama stretching from California to Cape Blanco. Flex your legs on a 1.5-mile walking trail to the cape; during migration months, keep your eyes peeled for whales.

The 40-mile **Rogue River Trail** ends (or begins) east of town at Illahe. Hike up the canyon 4.3 miles to the waterfall at Flora Dell Creek. For a shorter hike, drive 12 miles up USFS Rd 33 to the **Schrader Old Growth Trail**, which wanders for 1.5 miles through towering Douglas fir and Port Orford cedar.

The **Curry Historical Society Museum** (541-247-6113; 29410 Ellensburg Ave; noon-4pm Tue-Sat Apr-Oct, weekends only rest of yr) has displays on the beachfront gold grab in the 1850s.

Sleeping

There's more great riverside camping up USFS Rd 33.

Secret Camp RV park (541-247-2665, 888-308-8338; www.secretcamprvpark.com; 95614 Jerry's Flat Rd; tents/hookups $16/32) Three miles east of town, this nature-surrounded haven, complete with small creek, offers pretty sites for campers and full hookups for RV enthusiasts. Fire pits, horseshoes and volleyball are available.

Homemade signs attest to the manager's whimsies.

Endicott Gardens B&B (541-247-6513; www.endicottgardens.com; 95768 Jerry's Flat Rd; d $80-90; Mar-Oct;) This countryside B&B has four modern and unpretentious rooms, two with private deck. Lovely lawns and gardens grow outside, including some vegetable beds – the owner used to run a nursery. Located 3.5 miles east of town.

Azalea Lodge (541-247-6635; www.azalealodge.biz; 29481 Ellensburg Ave; d $80-92;) This is a decent hotel with small, clean, comfortable and unmemorable rooms featuring the typical amenities (fridge, microwave) in this price range. Back rooms are quieter, but some in front have peeks at the ocean across the highway.

Ireland's Rustic Lodges (541-247-7718; www.irelandsrusticlodges.com; 29346 Ellensburg Ave; d $100-160;) A wide variety of accommodation awaits you at this darling inn. There are regular suites with kitchenette, rustic one- and two-bedroom cabins, beach houses or even RV sites. A glorious garden area greets visitors in front and beach views out back. Its sister lodging next door, the Gold Beach Inn, has even more options.

Tu Tu' Tun Lodge (541-247-6664, 800-864-6357; www.tututun.com; 96550 N Bank Rogue Rd; d from $229;) One of Oregon's most exclusive hideaways is about 7 miles up the Rogue River. Sixteen luxurious rooms and suites all come with river views, while a few boast fireplaces and private outdoor Jacuzzi. It's a romantic spot with a small golf course and an excellent dining room that may be open to nonguests – call to find out.

Eating

Savory Natural Foods (541-247-0297; 29441 Ellensburg Ave; 9am-6pm Mon-Wed, till 5pm Thu & Fri; V) The best place for organic shopping, veggie sandwiches and juices.

Biscuit Coffeeshop (541-247-2495; 29707 Ellensburg Ave; snacks under $5; 7am-10pm) Nestled in an excellent Gold Beach bookshop, this cheery café has homemade pastries and espresso. It's a good way to start your day.

our pick **Patti's Rollin 'n Dough Bistro** (541-247-4438; 94257 N Bank Rogue Rd; mains $7-14; 10:30am-3pm Tue-Sat) Considered by some to be the best food in the area, this tiny bistro has a limited menu, but what's there really counts. Chef Patti Joyce has studied at the Culinary Institute of America, and it shows. Reservations recommended.

Porthole Café (541-247-7411; 29975 Harbor Way; mains $7-19; 11am-10pm) Located at the harbor, this old standby offers delicious food and river views. The menu covers a wide swathe: from Philly sandwiches and huge salads for lunch to blackened snapper and veal cutlets for dinner. Liver and onions anyone?

Spinners (541-247-5160; 29430 Ellensburg Ave; mains $9-27; 4:30-9pm) Tasty meats (whiskey strip steak, grilled duck, New Zealand lamb) and exceptional seafood (cedar-planked wild salmon, fresh Dungeness crab, sea scallops scampi) are grilled up at this great local restaurant. Black Angus and bison burgers are also available, and the sea views aren't bad, either.

Riverview (541-247-7321; 94749 Jerry's Flat Rd; mains $13-22; 4-9pm) Less than a mile east of Gold Beach, this fine waterside restaurant offers exceptional pasta, pizza and meat dishes. Views of the Rogue River add to diners' enjoyment, while the lounge offers more comfortable seating.

BROOKINGS

pop 6300

Just 6 miles from the California border, Brookings is a balmy and bustling commercial town on the bay of the Chetco River. Tourists are drawn here more for the surrounding area than anything else: there's world-class salmon and steelhead fishing upriver, and the coastline to the north is some of the most gorgeous Oregon has to offer. Winter temperatures hover around 60°F, making Brookings the state's 'banana belt' and a leader in Easter lily–bulb production. In July, fields south of town are filled with bright colors and a heavy scent.

Roads lead inland from Brookings up the Chetco River to the western edge of the Kalmiopsis Wilderness (p327). Oregon's only redwood forests are also found in this area.

The **Chamber of Commerce** (541-469-3181; www.brookingsor.com; 16330 Lower Harbor Rd; 9am-5pm Mon-Fri) is at the harbor. For regional information there's the **Brookings Welcome Center** (541-469-4117; 1650 US 101; 8am-5pm Mon-Fri, 9am-5pm Sun Apr-Oct), north of town. The **Chetco Ranger Station** (541-412-6000; www.fs.fed.us/r6/rogue-siskiyou; 539 Chetco Ave; 8:30am-12:30pm, 1:30-4:30pm Mon-Fri) is located inside a Mexican restaurant. Really.

Sights & Activities

WWII BOMB SITE

Brookings was the site of one of the two mainland air attacks the US suffered during WWII. A seaplane launched from a Japanese submarine in September 1942 succeeded in bombing Mt Emily, behind the city (there were no casualties). The main goal of the attack was to burn the forests, but they failed to ignite. The Japanese pilot of that same seaplane returned to Brookings 20 years later and presented the city with his samurai sword, which was in his plane during the bombing. The site is up S Chetco River Rd about 10 miles; the sword is in Brookings' city hall.

CHETCO VALLEY HISTORICAL SOCIETY MUSEUM

Once a stagecoach stop, the 1857 Blake House is now home to this **museum** (☎ 541-469-6651; 15461 Museum Rd; admission by donation; noon-4pm Sat & Sun). Stop in to see a quilt from 1844, an old Native American cedar canoe and an iron face cast resembling Queen Elizabeth I. Off-hours private tours are possible; call ahead.

AZALEA PARK

This is a glorious, hilly **park** (Azalea Park Rd) showcasing hundreds of azaleas, along with other pretty flora. Blooms are best in May and June. On Memorial Day weekend, the park becomes the focus of the annual **Azalea Festival**, with a floral parade and craft fair. There are Sunday concerts in summer and a holiday light show in December.

BRANDY PEAK DISTILLERY

A must for brandy lovers is this family-owned **distillery** (☎ 541-469-0194; www.brandypeak.com; 18526 Tetley Rd; 1-5pm Tue-Sat Mar-Jan, by appt rest of yr), which produces fine pear brandies, marc (young) brandies, aged grape brandies and blackberry liqueurs. Tours (which include all-important tastings) are given.

SAMUEL H BOARDMAN STATE PARK

Four miles north of Brookings, US 101 winds over 11 miles of headlands through Boardman State Park, which contains some of Oregon's most beautiful coastline. Along the highway are a number of roadside turnouts and picnic areas with short trails leading to secluded beaches and dramatic viewpoints. Marching far out to sea are tiny island chains, home to shorebirds and braying sea lions.

Secluded **Lone Ranch Beach**, the southernmost turnoff, has swimming and tide pools in a sandy cove studded with triangular sea stacks. Half a mile north is the turnoff to **Cape Ferrelo**, a popular spot for spring whale-watching. A couple of miles north is **Whalehead Beach**, with glorious views.

Just past the Thomas Creek Bridge (Oregon's highest at 345ft) is the turnoff for **Natural Bridge Viewpoint**, where you can see rock arches – the remnants of collapsed sea caves – just off the coast. At **Arch Rock Point**, 2 miles north, the volcanic headlands have been eroded to leave the arch of a lava tube. Paths down to Whiskey Creek lead to great tidal pools.

HIKING

There are short hiking trails 2 miles north of town at **Harris Beach State Park** (☎ 541-469-2021) on US 101. Enjoy views of Goat Island, Oregon's largest offshore island and a bird sanctuary, from the picnic area.

Nature trails at lush **Loeb State Park** (☎ 541-469-2021), 10 miles east of town on N Bank Chetco Rd, showcase two of Oregon's rarest and most cherished trees – redwood and myrtle. Check out the gorgeous 1.2-mile **Redwood Nature Trail** loop; the trailhead is on Chetco Rd, 0.25 miles past the park's entrance.

There's coastal access to the remote **Kalmiopsis Wilderness** (p327). For a fine 1.4-mile hike (but long drive), head 15 miles up N Bank Chetco River Rd, then right onto USFS Rd 1909 for another 15 miles to the Vulcan Lake trailhead. Get more detailed information at the Chetco ranger station (p313).

Sleeping & Eating

Alfred A Loeb State Park (☎ 541-469-2021, 800-452-5687; www.oregonstateparks.org; tents/cabins $16/35) There are almost 50 sites in a grove of myrtle trees available here, along with three riverside log cabins and showers and flush toilets. Located 10 miles east of Brookings on N Bank Chetco River Rd.

Harris Beach State Park (☎ 541-469-2021, 800-452-5687; www.oregonstateparks.org; tents/hookups/yurts $17/21/29) Two miles east of town on US 101, you can camp beachside at one of 150 sites. Six yurts, showers, flush toilets and coin laundry are among the amenities.

Westward Inn (☎ 541-469-7471; 1026 Chetco Ave; d $65;) Fine budget motel with clean, good-

OREGON COAST

sized rooms and basic amenities. One of the better cheapies on this row.

South Coast Inn B&B (☎ 541-469-5557, 800-525-9273; www.southcoastinn.com; 516 Redwood St; d $119-149; ⊠ 💻) Bernard Maybeck designed this lovely Arts and Crafts–style house in 1917, which offers four rooms (two with sea views), one cottage ($170) and an apartment ($149). It's filled with antiques, and a gorgeous stone fireplace dominates the living room.

Chetco River Inn (☎ 541-251-0087; www.chetcoriverinn.com; 21202 High Prairie Rd; d $135-150; ⊠) Seventeen miles northeast of town is this peaceful inn set on 40 acres that include vegetable and lavender gardens. Five classy rooms, decorated in a simple, casual style, offer comfort next to the Rogue's waters. A wonderful deck serves as entry and hangout spot. One cottage is available ($200); reserve ahead.

Smuggler's Cove (☎ 541-469-6006; 160011 Boat Basin Rd; mains $15-24; 🕑 7am-10pm) Right near the harbor is this modern eatery offering booths, tables and glimpses of the water. The menu is dominated by seafood, though there are decent meat, pasta and salad choices as well. Breakfast is also served.

Suzie Q's (☎ 541-412-7444; 613 Chetco Ave; mains $19-28; 🕑 7am-2pm Mon, 7am-2pm, 5-10pm Tue-Fri, 8am-2pm, 5-10pm Sat, 8am-2pm Sun) This casual yet upscale bistro serves quiche Rochelle and veggie omelettes for breakfast, tall sandwiches and killer pies for lunch, and stuffed halibut and filet mignon for dinner. Great food; reserve ahead.

Ashland & Southern Oregon

With a warm, sunny and dry climate that belongs in nearby California, Southern Oregon is the state's 'banana belt' and an exciting place to visit. Rugged and remote landscapes are entwined with a number of designated 'wild and scenic' rivers, which are famous for their challenging white-water rafting, world-class fly-fishing and excellent hiking. The marshy Klamath Basin is a supreme bird-watching sanctuary and wintering spot for hundreds of bald eagles. Toward the coast are the impressive Oregon Caves and the unique Kalmiopsis Wilderness. And the area is a great staging point for nearby Crater Lake National Park, home to the deepest lake in the country and one of its most beautiful.

A wealth of gold and timber originally brought pioneers to Southern Oregon cities, and today the migration continues with young families and California retirees coming to seek affordable housing. Ashland, Medford, Klamath Falls and Grants Pass have grown significantly in recent years, bringing new development and revitalizing downtowns. There's also plenty of culture in the area – Ashland is home to the renowned Oregon Shakespeare Festival, while nearby Jacksonville hosts the Britt Festival and its world-class music. Centrally located between Seattle and San Francisco, Southern Oregon is certainly worth more than a short gas break if you're cruising I-5.

HIGHLIGHTS

- Strutting with the Bard at Ashland's **Oregon Shakespeare Festival** (p319)
- Counting bald eagles at **Klamath Basin National Wildlife Refuges** (p332)
- Hiking up **Table Rocks** (p322), outside Medford, in flowery springtime
- Rafting down the mighty **Rogue River** (p324), Oregon's premier white water
- Spelunking the main grotto at **Oregon Caves National Monument** (p327)
- Dancing up a storm during Jacksonville's summer **Britt Festival** (p323)

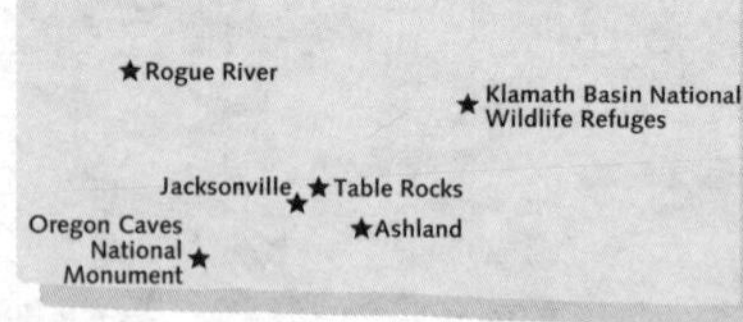

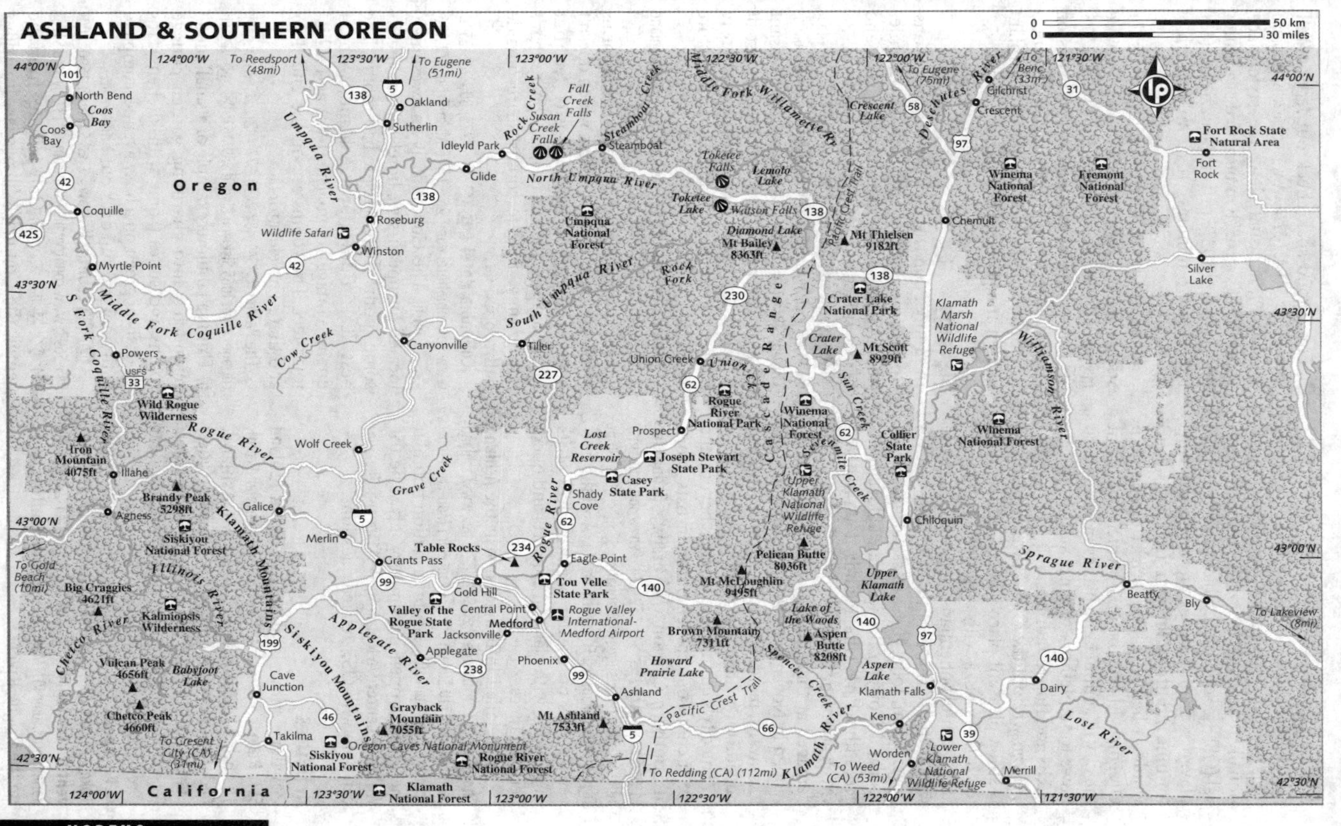
ASHLAND & SOUTHERN OREGON
0 50 km
0 30 miles
44°00'N
43°30'N
43°00'N
42°30'N
124°00'W
123°30'W
123°00'W
122°30'W
122°00'W
121°30'W
Oregon
California
To Reedsport (48mi)
To Eugene (51mi)
To Eugene (75mi)
To Benc (33mi)
To Lakeview (8mi)
To Weed (CA) (53mi)
To Redding (CA) (112mi)
To Cresent City (CA) (31mi)
To Gold Beach (10mi)
North Bend
Coos Bay
Coos Bay
Coquille
Myrtle Point
Powers
USFS 33
Illahe
Agness
Galice
Merlin
Wolf Creek
Grants Pass
Cave Junction
Takilma
Canyonville
Roseburg
Winston
Sutherlin
Oakland
Idleyld Park
Glide
Steamboat
Tiller
Union Creek
Prospect
Shady Cove
Eagle Point
Gold Hill
Central Point
Medford
Jacksonville
Applegate
Phoenix
Ashland
Keno
Klamath Falls
Worden
Merrill
Dairy
Beatty
Bly
Chiloquin
Chemult
Crescent
Gilchrist
Silver Lake
Fort Rock
Fort Rock State Natural Area
Fremont National Forest
Winema National Forest
Klamath Marsh National Wildlife Refuge
Crater Lake National Park
Crater Lake
Mt Scott 8929ft
Mt Thielsen 9182ft
Mt Bailey 8363ft
Diamond Lake
Lemolo Lake
Toketee Lake
Toketee Falls
Watson Falls
Fall Creek Falls
Susan Creek Falls
Umpqua National Forest
Rogue River National Park
Winema National Forest
Joseph Stewart State Park
Casey State Park
Lost Creek Reservoir
Collier State Park
Upper Klamath Lake
Upper Klamath National Wildlife Refuge
Pelican Butte 8036ft
Mt McLoughlin 9495ft
Brown Mountain 7311ft
Lake of the Woods
Aspen Butte 8208ft
Aspen Lake
Howard Prairie Lake
Mt Ashland 7533ft
Lower Klamath National Wildlife Refuge
Tou Velle State Park
Rogue Valley International-Medford Airport
Table Rocks
Valley of the Rogue State Park
Grayback Mountain 7055ft
Oregon Caves National Monument
Siskiyou National Forest
Klamath National Forest
Rogue River National Forest
Wildlife Safari
Wild Rogue Wilderness
Brandy Peak 5298ft
Iron Mountain 4075ft
Big Craggies 4621ft
Kalmiopsis Wilderness
Vulcan Peak 4656ft
Chetco Peak 4660ft
Babyfoot Lake
Crescent Lake
Cascade Range
Klamath Mountains
Siskiyou Mountains
Pacific Crest Trail
Umpqua River
North Umpqua River
South Umpqua River
Rock Creek
Steamboat Creek
Middle Fork Willamette Rv
Deschutes River
Williamson River
Sprague River
Lost River
Klamath River
Rogue River
Applegate River
Illinois River
Chetco River
Middle Fork Coquille River
S Fork Coquille River
Cow Creek
Grave Creek
Union Ck
Sun Creek
Sevenmile Creek
Spencer Creek
Rock Fork

ASHLAND

pop 21,000

This popular city is best known for its internationally renowned Oregon Shakespeare Festival (OSF; see opposite), which attracts 100,000 playgoers from all over the world and runs for nine months of the year. In fact, Ashland wouldn't be the cultural center of Southern Oregon without the OSF, which packs out the city in summer and brings in steady cash flows for a plethora of fancy hotels, upscale B&Bs and fine restaurants.

Even without the OSF, however, Ashland is still a pleasant place whose trendy downtown lanes buzz with well-heeled shoppers and youthful bohemians. In late fall and early winter, those few months when the festival doesn't run, folks come to ski at nearby Mt Ashland. You can also ice-skate at lovely, 93-acre Lithia Park, which winds along Ashland Creek above the center of town. (The rink was damaged at the time of writing, but due to reopen in November 2007.) In summer it offers swans, picnickers and concerts. And just outside town are a few good wineries.

The city's culture also extends beyond the OSF; check out contemporary artists' work at Southern Oregon University's **Schneider Museum of Art** (☎ 541-552-6245; www.sou.edu/sma; 1250 Siskiyou Blvd; suggested donation $3; 🕑 10am-4pm Tue-Sat, 10am-7pm first Fri of each month). And the university puts on theater performances of its own, along with classical concerts and opera performances.

For detailed information visit the **Ashland Chamber of Commerce** (☎ 541-482-3486; www.ashlandchamber.com; 110 E Main St; 🕑 9am-5pm Mon-Fri, 11am-3pm Sat, noon-3pm Sun). An information booth at the Plaza is open in summer only. The **OSF Welcome Center** (76 N Main St; 🕑 11am-6pm Tue-Sun) can help with OSF-related questions.

Activities

Powdery snow is abundant at **Mt Ashland Ski Resort** (☎ 541-482-2897; www.mtashland.com), 16 miles southwest on 7533ft Mt Ashland. Pedal-pushers can rent a bike at **Siskiyou Cyclery** (☎ 541-482-1997; 1729 Siskiyou Blvd; 🕑 10am-5:30pm Tue-Sat) and explore the countryside on Bear Creek Greenway.

Kokopelli (☎ 541-201-7694, 866-723-8874; www.kokopelliriverguides.com; 2475 Siskiyou Blvd) and **Adventure Center** (☎ 541-488-2819, 800-444-2819; www.raftingtours.com; 40 N Main St) both offer rafting trips on the Rogue River.

For a good soak check out **Jackson Wellsprings** (☎ 541-482-3776; www.jacksonwellsprings.com; 2253 Hwy 99), a casual New Age–style place, which boasts an 85°F mineral-fed swimming pool ($6) and 103°F private Jacuzzi tubs ($20 to $30 for 75 minutes). It's 2 miles north of town.

Families with children shouldn't miss the **Science Works** (☎ 541-482-6767; www.scienceworksmuseum.org; 1500 E Main St; adult/2-12yr & senior $7.50/5; 🕑 10am-4pm Wed-Sat, noon-4pm Sun). This hands-on interactive museum has plenty of fun science-oriented exhibits, along with a native plant garden and geodesic tree nursery dome.

Sleeping

In summer don't arrive without reservations. Rooms are cheaper in Medford, 12 miles north. There's also camping, RV sites and tepees at Jackson Wellsprings (see above).

Glenyan Campground (☎ 541-488-1785, 877-453-6929; www.glenyanrvpark.com; 5310 Hwy 66; tents/hookups $21/26; wi-fi) This is a shady and pleasant 12-acre campground 4 miles southeast of Ashland. Reserve a creek-side spot, as they're the best. Playground, games room and store available.

Ashland Hostel (☎ 541-482-9217; www.theashlandhostel.com; 150 N Main St; dm $23, d from $55;) There are separate men's and women's dorms at this centrally located hostel, which doesn't have your typical casual hostel feel but rather an upscale sort of atmosphere that's less grungy. Private rooms share outside bathrooms.

Columbia Hotel (☎ 541-482-3726, 800-718-2530; www.columbiahotel.com; 262-1/2 E Main St; d $72-126; wi-fi) The Columbia is an awesomely located European-style hotel – which means some rooms share outside bathrooms. The best deal in downtown Ashland, with 24 quaint vintage rooms (no TVs) and a historic feel. The rooms are on the 2nd floor and there's no elevator.

The Palm (☎ 541-482-2636, 877-482-2635; www.palmcottages.com; 1065 Siskiyou Blvd; d $89-161; wi-fi) This is a fabulous example of a small motel remodeled into charming garden cottage rooms and suites (some with kitchens). It's an oasis of green on a busy avenue, complete with pool and sun deck out back.

our pick **Country Willows** (☎ 541-488-1590, 800-945-5697; www.countrywillowsinn.com; 1313 Clay St; d $125-244; wi-fi) Only minutes from the center, the Country Willows is a luxurious

OREGON SHAKESPEARE FESTIVAL

Highly respected and wildly popular, the Oregon Sakespeare Festival (OSF) repertoire is rooted in Shakespearean and Elizabethan drama, but also features revivals and contemporary theater from around the world.

As a young town, Ashland was included in the Methodist Church's cultural education program, called the Chautauqua Series. By the 1930s, one of the venues, Chautauqua Hall, had deteriorated to a dilapidated wooden shell. Angus Bowmer, a drama professor at the local college, noted the resemblance of the roofless structure to drawings of Shakespeare's Globe Theatre. He then convinced the town to sponsor two performances of Shakespeare's plays and a boxing match (the Bard would have approved) as part of its 1935 Fourth of July celebration. The plays proved a great success, and the OSF was off and running.

Eleven productions run from February to October in three theaters near Main and Pioneer Sts: the outdoor **Elizabethan Theatre** (open June to October), the **Angus Bowmer Theatre** and the intimate **New Theatre**. There are no Monday performances.

Performances sell out quickly; obtain tickets in advance at www.osfashland.org. You can also try the **box office** (☎ 541-482-4331; 15 S Pioneer St; tickets $30-75) for unclaimed tickets. Backstage tours (adult/youth $11/8.25) also need to be booked well in advance.

Check the OSF Welcome Center (see opposite) for other events, which may include scholarly lectures, play readings, concerts and pre-show talks.

B&B in the 'countryside' (complete with a few farm animals). The nine rooms and suites sport a mix of antiques and contemporary furniture, and some suites are huge and creatively designed. A cottage is also available.

Chanticleer Inn (☎ 541-482-1919, 800-898-1950; www.ashlandbnb.com; 120 Gresham St; d $143-198; ⊠ ❄ wi-fi) This is a lovely Craftsman B&B with six elegant rooms and friendly hosts, Ellen and Howie. The common areas are comfortable, and the gardens are filled with flowers and lush plants. It's located in a residential neighborhood close to the center.

Cowslip's Belle B&B (☎ 541-488-2901, 800-888-6819; www.cowslip.com; 159 N Main St; d $157-226; ⊠ ❄ wi-fi) It's a short walk to the Plaza from this 1913 antique-filled bungalow with five good rooms and a small grassy backyard. The quietest rooms are in the back building and include a deluxe suite with a Jacuzzi and kitchen.

Ashland Springs Hotel (☎ 541-488-1700, 888-795-4545; www.ashlandspringshotel.com; 212 E Main St; d $160-249; ⊠ ❄ wi-fi) A beautiful, renovated, historic landmark hotel with modestly sized but pleasant rooms and a noteworthy restaurant. Snag a corner room for great light and views. Great downtown location.

Arden Forest Inn (☎ 541-488-1498, 800-460-3912; www.afinn.com; 261 W Hersey St; d $161-221; ⊠ ❄ 🏊 wi-fi) This is a lovely and comfortable B&B with five tastefully decorated rooms, a wonderful large garden and theater-loving hosts. It has a casual and liberal atmosphere with a kitty on the premises; supremely gay-friendly.

Ashland Creek Inn (☎ 541-482-3315; www.ashlandcreekinn.com; 70 Water St; d $212-299; ⊠ ❄ wi-fi) This gorgeous creek-side inn offers 10 impeccable and eclectic suites, each with a living area, kitchenette and private deck over the water. There's a small but pretty garden and deck areas in which to relax.

Also recommended:

Ashland Motel (☎ 541-482-2561, 800-460-8858; 1145 Siskiyou Blvd; d $55-74; ❄ 🏊 wi-fi) Cheap. Drab. Features kitchenettes and pool.

Manor Motel (☎ 541-482-2246, 866-261-9733; www.manormotel.net; 476 N Main St; d $72-94; ⊠ ❄ wi-fi) Cute motel with pleasant rooms and small garden.

Timbers Motel (☎ 541-482-4242, 866-550-4400; www.ashlandtimberslodging.com; 1450 Ashland St; d $79-115; ⊠ ❄ 🏊 wi-fi) Good comfortable motel rooms, some with kitchenette.

Cedarwood Inn (☎ 541-488-2000, 800-547-4141; www.ashlandcedarwoodinn.com; 1801 Siskiyou Blvd; d from $88; ❄ 🏊 wi-fi) Pleasant larger motel on relatively quiet avenue. Indoor and outdoor pools.

Peerless Hotel (☎ 541-488-1082, 800-460-8758; www.peerlesshotel.com; 243 4th St; d $143-198; ⊠ ❄ wi-fi) European-style boutique hotel in a historic landmark building. Fine restaurant.

Iris Inn (☎ 541-488-2286, 800-460-7650; www.irisinnbb.com; 59 Manzanita St; d $161; ⊠ ❄ wi-fi) Casual and long-running B&B with five rooms and garden deck.

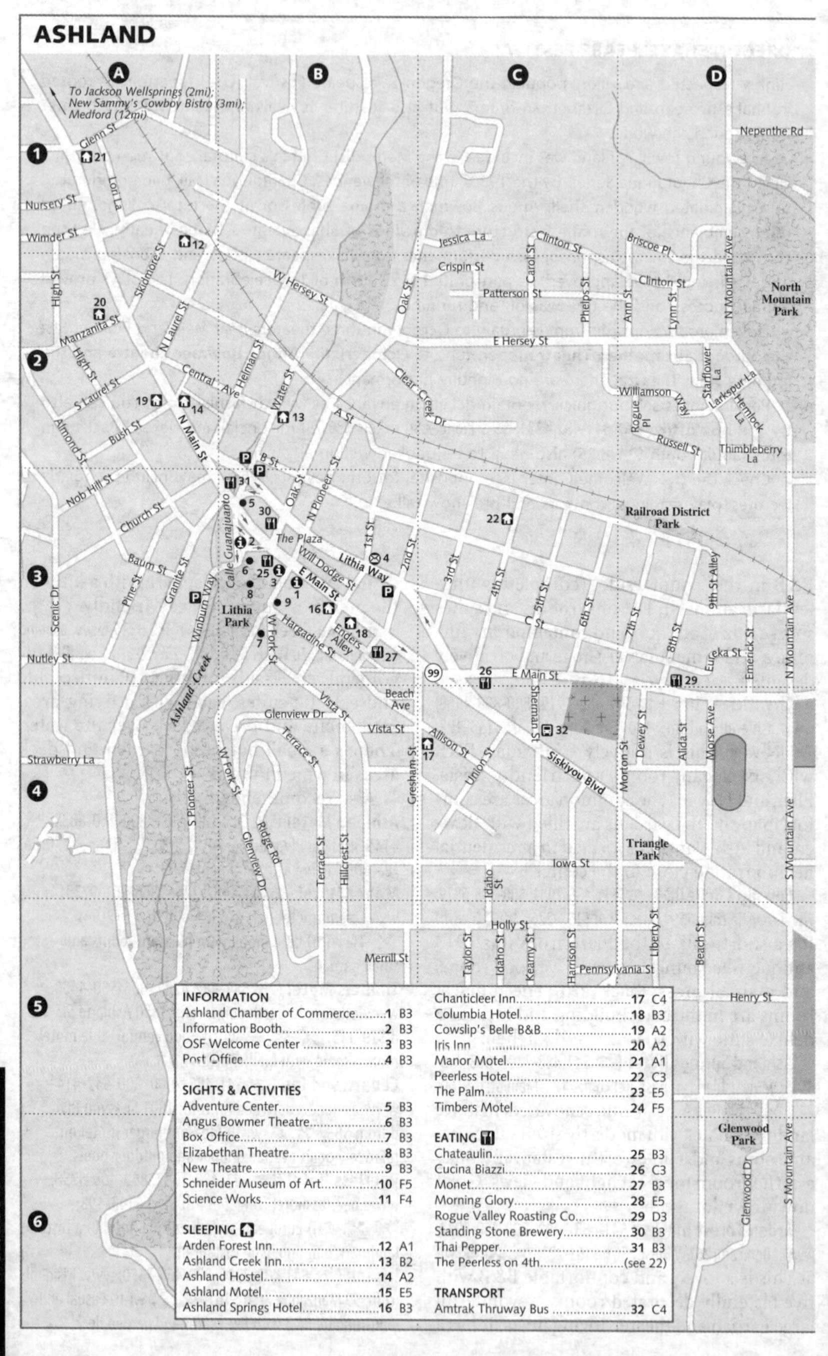
ASHLAND
A
B
C
D
1
2
3
4
5
6
To Jackson Wellsprings (2mi); New Sammy's Cowboy Bistro (3mi); Medford (12mi)
Glenn St
Lori La
Nursery St
Wimder St
Skidmore St
High St
Manzanita St
N Laurel St
S Laurel St
Central Ave
Helman St
Water St
W Hersey St
Oak St
Jessica La
Crispin St
Clinton St
Carol St
Patterson St
Phelps St
Ann St
Briscoe Pl
Lynn St
N Mountain Ave
Nepenthe Rd
North Mountain Park
E Hersey St
Clear Creek Dr
Williamson Way
Rogue Pl
Starflower La
Larkspur La
Hemlock La
Russell St
Thimbleberry La
Almond St
Bush St
N Main St
A St
B St
N Pioneer St
Nob Hill St
Church St
Calle Guanajuato
The Plaza
Lithia Way
1st St
2nd St
3rd St
4th St
5th St
6th St
7th St
8th St
9th St Alley
Railroad District Park
Baum St
Pine St
Granite St
Winburn Way
Will Dodge St
E Main St
Lithia Park
Hargadine St
W Fork St
Enders Alley
C St
Eureka St
Emerick St
Scenic Dr
Nutley St
99
E Main St
Beach Ave
Ashland Creek
Glenview Dr
Vista St
Terrace St
Allison St
Union St
Sherman St
Siskiyou Blvd
Dewey St
Morton St
Alida St
Morse Ave
Strawberry La
S Pioneer St
Ridge Rd
Gresham St
Hillcrest St
Idaho St
Iowa St
Triangle Park
S Mountain Ave
Holly St
Taylor St
Kearny St
Harrison St
Liberty St
Beach St
Merrill St
Pennsylvania St
Henry St
Glenwood Park
Glenwood Dr
INFORMATION
Ashland Chamber of Commerce 1 B3
Information Booth 2 B3
OSF Welcome Center 3 B3
Post Office 4 B3
SIGHTS & ACTIVITIES
Adventure Center 5 B3
Angus Bowmer Theatre 6 B3
Box Office 7 B3
Elizabethan Theatre 8 B3
New Theatre 9 B3
Schneider Museum of Art 10 F5
Science Works 11 F4
SLEEPING
Arden Forest Inn 12 A1
Ashland Creek Inn 13 B2
Ashland Hostel 14 A2
Ashland Motel 15 E5
Ashland Springs Hotel 16 B3
Chanticleer Inn 17 C4
Columbia Hotel 18 B3
Cowslip's Belle B&B 19 A2
Iris Inn 20 A2
Manor Motel 21 A1
Peerless Hotel 22 C3
The Palm 23 E5
Timbers Motel 24 F5
EATING
Chateaulin 25 B3
Cucina Biazzi 26 C3
Monet 27 B3
Morning Glory 28 E5
Rogue Valley Roasting Co 29 D3
Standing Stone Brewery 30 B3
Thai Pepper 31 B3
The Peerless on 4th (see 22)
TRANSPORT
Amtrak Thruway Bus 32 C4

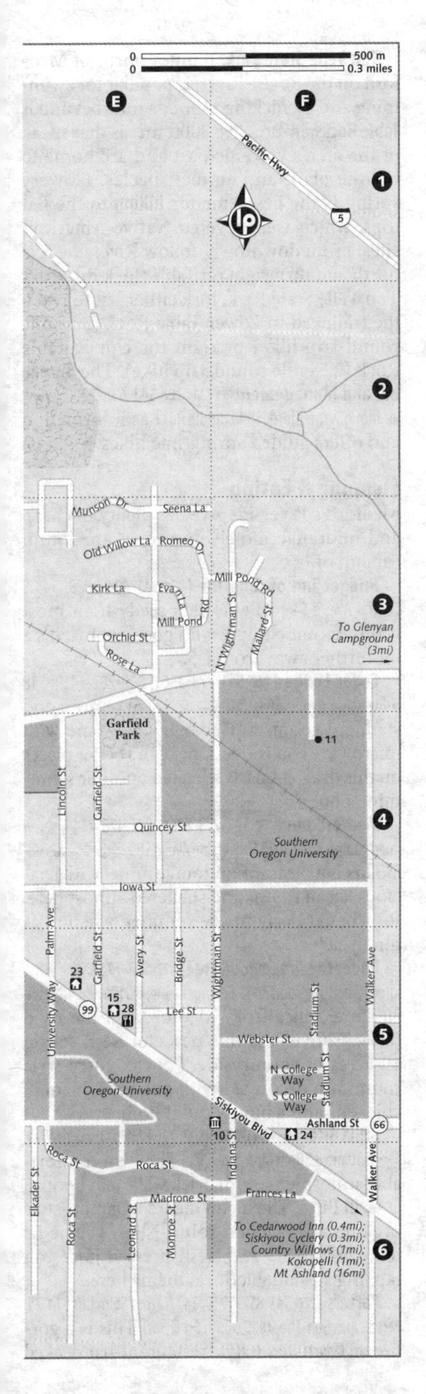

Eating & Drinking

There's plenty of great eating choices in Ashland, which levies a 5% restaurant tax. Make reservations during the Shakespeare Festival.

Rogue Valley Roasting Co (☎ 541-488-5902; 917 E Main St; ⏲ 6:45am-6pm Mon-Sat) This is a quality coffeehouse serving up typical dark roasts and organic beans, along with gourmet teas and light snacks. There's a good, modern, casual atmosphere with a touch of outdoor seating.

Morning Glory (☎ 541-488 8636; 1149 Siskiyou Blvd; breakfast $9-12; ⏲ 8am-2pm) This colorful, eclectic café is one of Ashland's best breakfast joints. Creative dishes include the Alaskan crab omelette, tandoori tofu scramble and shrimp cakes with poached eggs. For lunch there's soups, salads and sandwiches.

Standing Stone Brewery (☎ 541-482-2448; 101 Oak St; mains $9-16; ⏲ 11:30am-11pm Sun-Thu, till midnight Fri & Sat) Popular hip brewery-restaurant with burgers, salads and woodfired pizzas. Fancier dinner choices include steaks, seafood and pasta, and there's also a half-dozen microbrews. Great back patio.

Thai Pepper (☎ 541-482-8058; 84 N Main St; mains $12-16; ⏲ 5:30-9pm Mon-Sat, 5-8:30pm Sun) Small, contemporary Thai Pepper is known for its fiery Asian cooking. Choose the spicy lemongrass soup, green coconut chicken curry or sweet and soup shrimp. Creek-side tables and exotic cocktails rein in the heat.

Monet (☎ 541-482-1339; 36 S 2nd St; mains $23-29; ⏲ 5:30-8:30pm Tue-Sun) Inspired by the impressionist, this classy restaurant offers a simple menu of fine French cuisine. Chef Pierre Verger honed his cooking in the Rhone Valley and Paris, and has owned restaurants in California and New York.

our pick **New Sammy's Cowboy Bistro** (☎ 541-535-2779; 2210 S Pacific Hwy; mains $23-36; ⏲ 5-8:30pm Thu-Sun) Some consider this funky spot, run by an eclectic couple, Oregon's best restaurant. There are only six tables and the wine list is spectacular. Located in Talent, about 3 miles north of Ashland. Reserve weeks in advance; limited winter hours.

Chateaulin (☎ 541-482-2264; 50 E Main St; mains $24-36; ⏲ 5-9pm) This upscale French bistro serves a limited but fine menu. Try the herbed crepes filled with vegetables, roasted duck with mustard demi-glace or the red wine-infused rack of lamb. Prix-fixe dinners are also available ($37).

The Peerless on 4th (☎ 503-488-6067; 265 4th St; mains $24-38; 5:30-9pm) Fine Northwest cuisine is the star attraction at this upscale and contemporary restaurant. Fresh ingredients from family farms and ranches are used when possible, and the result is some of Ashland's best food. There's a patio area out front for warm nights.

Cucina Biazzi (☎ 541-488-3739; 568 E Main St; prix-fixe dinner $27-37; 5:30-8:30pm) This intimate restaurant offers four-course Italian meals that include grilled marinated vegetables (antipasto), a pasta course, a meat-based main dish and a salad to finish. The great back patio boasts a fire pit.

Getting There & Away

The nearest airport is 15 miles north in Medford (see opposite). **Cascade Airport Shuttle** (☎ 541-488-1998) provides services from the airport to Ashland for $24 (one person) or $28 (two people). Reserve ahead.

The Shuttle (☎ 541-883-2609) buses head to Medford and Klamath Falls. Local bus transportation is provided by **Rogue Valley Transportation District** (RVTD; ☎ 541-779-5821; www.rvtd.org).

MEDFORD

pop 74,000

Southern Oregon's largest metropolis, Medford is well-known for its fruit industry, especially pears and wine grapes. In the past 10 years the city has grown tremendously, drawing thousands of California retirees with its sunny warm weather. It's also well located: Ashland, Jacksonville, Crater Lake, Oregon Caves National Monument and the Rogue River valley are all a day trip away.

The **visitors center** (☎ 541-776-4021; www.visitmedford.org; 1314 Center Dr; 9am-6pm) is next to Harry and David's (see below). The **Rogue River-Siskiyou National Forest office** (☎ 541-858-2200; www.fs.fed.us/r6/rogue-siskiyou; 333 W 8th St; 8am-4:30pm Mon-Fri) is at the same address as the post office.

Sights

Medford's most famous tourist attraction is **Harry and David's Country Village** (☎ 541-776-2277; 1314 Center Dr; 9am-8pm Mon-Sat, 10am-6pm Sun), the outlet store of a giant mail-order fruit company. They offer nearby **plant tours** (☎ 877-322-8000; tours $5; Mon-Fri) with advance reservations.

Tou Velle State Park, 6 miles north of Medford on the Rogue River, is popular for swimming and picnicking. About a mile beyond is **Table Rocks**, impressive 800ft mesas that speak of the area's volcanic past and are home to unique plant and animal species. Flowery spring is the best time for **hiking** to the flat tops, which were revered Native American sites. From downtown, follow Riverside Ave north and turn right on Table Rock Rd. After Tou Velle State Park, fork either left to reach the trailhead to Lower Table Rock (3.5-mile round-trip hike) or right for Upper Table Rock (2.5-mile round-trip hike). The **Bureau of Land Management** (BLM; ☎ 541-618-2200; www.or.blm.gov/medford; 3040 Biddle Rd) has information and offers guided springtime hikes.

Sleeping & Eating

Medford's Riverside Ave has plenty of cheap and midrange motels, but most are within earshot of I-5.

Budget Inn of America (☎ 541-494-8088; 345 S Central Ave; d $46; wi-fi) Less seedy than most is this decent cheapie with good rooms; it's a bit further away from I-5.

Cedar Lodge (☎ 541-773-7361, 800-282-3419; 518 N Riverside Ave; d $63) There are good standard rooms at Cedar Lodge, some with microwave and fridge. One of the better places on this drag, it boasts a heated outdoor swimming pool.

Medford Inn (☎ 541-773-8266, 877-473-7444; www.medfordinn.com; 1015 S Riverside Ave; d $83; wi-fi) This is a pleasant midrange motel with spacious, clean rooms and sheltered atmosphere. It's a better deal outside summer, when rates dip by 30%.

Under the Greenwood Tree (☎ 541-776-0000; www.greenwoodtree.com; 3045 Bellinger Lane; d $129; wi-fi) Three miles from Medford, on the road to Jacksonville, is this peaceful B&B set on 10-acres of countryside. Four country style rooms are decorated with antiques. Llamas, chickens and a bunny call it home.

Grilla Bites (☎ 541-245-9802; 226 E Main St; mains $7-9; 7:30am-8:30pm Mon-Sat; V) There's a comfortable atmosphere, with brick walls and booths, at Grill Bites. The menu includes panino-style organic sandwiches, tofu dishes, veggie or tempeh burgers and fresh-pressed juices on tap. Big sustainable/local theme here.

Porters (☎ 541-857-1910; 147 N Front St; mains $14-25; 5-9pm Sun-Thu, till 9:30pm Fri & Sat) This is a gorgeous, Craftsman-style restaurant-bar decked out in dark-wood booths and boasting a pleasant patio next to the train tracks. Steak, seafood and pasta dishes dominate the menu.

Getting There & Around

The **Rogue Valley International-Medford Airport** (☎ 541-776-7222) is 2.5 miles north, off Biddle Rd. **Greyhound** (☎ 541-779-2103; www.greyhound.com) is at 212 Bartlett St.

Amtrak Thruway buses and the local **Rogue Valley Transit District** (RVTD; ☎ 541-779-5821; www.rvtd.org) share the transfer station at 8th and Front Sts.

JACKSONVILLE

This ex-gold-prospecting town is the oldest settlement in southern Oregon and a National Historic Landmark. Small but endearing, the town's main drag – California Street – is like step back in time, lined with well-preserved brick-and-wood buildings dating from the 1880s. Today, folks come to stroll around downtown, enjoying the old-time atmosphere while exploring the many boutiques and galleries. Although summertime is great, Jacksonville has a certain magic touch in winter, when the crowds are lighter and magical holiday celebrations take hold.

Don't miss the Britt Festival, a world-class musical experience that runs all summer long (see boxed text below). There's more information at the **Chamber of Commerce** (☎ 541-899-8118; www.jacksonvilleoregon.org; 185 N Oregon St; 10am-5pm Mon-Fri, 11am-4pm Sat & Sun). RVTD bus 30 runs from Medford.

Sights

The **Jacksonville Museum** (☎ 541-773-6536; 206 N 5th St; adult/3-12yr & senior $5/3; 1-4pm Wed-Sat) is in the former county courthouse (1883). There's a tribute to photographer Peter Britt, the first to take pictures of Crater Lake. Adjacent is a **children's museum**, in the old county jail (entry included with Jacksonville Museum admission). Peter Britt's mansion once sat in the lovely **gardens** at S 1st and W Pine Sts.

The 32-acre **Jacksonville Cemetery** is worth a wander to explore historic pioneer grave sites chronicling wars, epidemics and other untimely deaths. The chamber of commerce has helpful literature with maps.

Narrated **trolley tours** provide a good historical overview of the town and run on summer weekends.

Sleeping & Eating

Jacksonville's accommodations are mostly fancy B&Bs (reserve ahead). There's more choice and less expensive accommodations 6 miles east in Medford (see opposite).

Cantrall-Buckley Campground (☎ 541-776-7001; 10 miles west on Hwy 238; sites $10) Located in Ruch, this high and dry 30-site campground (showers available) is shaded by oak, fir and madrone trees. A pleasant river flows nearby.

Jacksonville Stage Lodge (☎ 541-899-3953, 800-253-8254; www.stagelodge.com; 830 N 5th St; d $94-104; wi-fi) This modern hotel with 27 spacious and fine contemporary rooms is outside the heart of town.

Magnolia Inn (☎ 541-899-0255, 866-899-0255; www.magnolia-inn.com; 245 N 5th St; d $137-152; wi-fi) The Magnolia is a pleasant, nine-room B&B boasting a guest kitchen with a nearby veranda. The rooms are all different and decorated with antiques, and breakfast is continental. It's across from the church.

TouVelle House (☎ 541-899-8938, 800-8466-8422; www.touvellehouse.com; 455 N Oregon St; d $148-178; wi-fi) This gorgeous Craftsman

THE BRITT FESTIVAL

In 1963, Portland conductor John Trudeau came to Jacksonville with a few friends and found themselves on the former hillside estate of Peter Britt (1819–1905), a Swiss photographer who made a name for himself after immigrating to Oregon. These musicians noticed the exceptional acoustics of the hillsides surrounding Britt's old home, and that same year built a plywood stage for a local orchestral performance. Thus was born the Pacific Northwest's first outdoor music festival.

In 1978 a pavilion was constructed and the festival continued to grow and attract top-notch artists. The nonprofit **Britt Festival** (☎ 541-773-6077; www.brittfest.org) is now a premier musical festival that also sponsors educational programs through its Britt Institute. For more information, head to the festival's website. And for more on Peter Britt and his many talents, go to www.peterbritt.org.

house offers six elegant rooms, each with feather beds, down comforters and private bathrooms. It's on spacious grounds with a pool out the back.

our pick **Jacksonville Inn** (☎ 541-899-1900, 800-321-9344; www.jacksonvilleinn.com; 175 E California St; d $152-168, cottages $263-456; wi-fi) This historic 1863 hotel is right downtown and has 12 beautiful, antique-filled rooms and cottages with flowery (but tasteful) decoration. There's an excellent upscale restaurant as well.

GoodBean Coffee (☎ 541-899-8740; 165 S Oregon St; snacks $1.50-3; 6am-7pm) This is a casual, trendy coffee shop with brick walls and sidewalk tables. Gourmet beans and bagel sandwiches are available.

Bella Union (☎ 541-899-1770; 170 W California St; mains $13-24; 11:30am-10pm) An old saloon from 1868, the Bella Union now serves up pizzas, pastas, meat dishes and sandwiches. The bar is open until much later.

THE ROGUE RIVER

The Rogue is a legendary white-water river that flows from its headwaters at Crater Lake to its terminus at Gold Beach, on the Pacific Ocean – 215 miles total. A good stretch of it has been designated 'wild and scenic' (thus protected), and celebrities such as Zane Grey and Ginger Rogers have lived along its banks. The Rogue is prized for awesome steelhead and trout fishing, along with exceptional hiking, but it's most famous for world-class rafting.

For the serious adventurer, the Rogue offers everything from pulse-thumping class-IV rapids near the **Wild Rogue Wilderness** to more gentle waters upriver. A convenient base is the busy city of Grants Pass (see p326). For those more into an afternoon float amidst natural surroundings, there's the Shady Cove area (see right).

Some of the many outfitters than run the Rogue include **High Country Expeditions** (☎ 888-461-7238; www.hcexpeditions.com), **Orange Torpedo Trips** (☎ 541-476-5061, 800-635-2925; www.orangetorpedo.com), **Rogue Wilderness, Inc** (☎ 541-479-9554; 800-336-1647; www.wildrogue.com) and **Sundance River Center** (☎ 888-777-7557; www.sundanceriver.com).

Wild Rogue Wilderness

Famous for its turbulent class-IV rapids, the Rogue River departs civilization at Grave Creek and winds for 40 untamed miles through a remote canyon preserved within rugged BLM land and the Wild Rogue Wilderness. This stretch is not for amateurs – a typical rafting trip here takes three to four days and costs upwards of $650. Hiring an outfitter is mandatory for all but the most experienced (see left).

Contact the BLM's **Smullin Visitors Center** (☎ 541-479-3735; www.blm.gov/or/resources/recreation/rogue; 14335 Galice Rd, Galice; 7am-3pm) for information. They also issue rafting permits, which are required to float the Rogue without an outfitter (for details go to www.blm.gov/or/resources/recreation/rogue/about-permits.php).

The **Rogue River Trail** is a highlight of the region, and is at the west end of the Rogue River. This 40-mile track, best hiked in spring or fall, follows the rapids from Grave Creek to Illahe. Once used to transport mail and supplies from Gold Beach, the route follows a relatively easy grade through scrub oak and laurel past historic homesteads and cabins.

The full hike takes four to five days, but rustic lodges along the way can make your itinerary flexible. These include the **Black Bar** (☎ 541-479-6507; www.blackbarlodge.net); **Marial** (☎ 541-474-2057); **Paradise** (☎ 888-667-6483; www.paradiselodge.us); **Half Moon Bar** (☎ 888-291-8268; www.halfmoonbarlodge.com); and **Clay Hill** (☎ 503-859-3772; www.clayhilllodge.com). Rates run from $102 to $130 per person and typically includes breakfast, dinner and a packed lunch; reserve ahead. Riverside camping is also a possibility; contact the **Rand Visitors Center** (☎ 541-479-3735).

A 6-mile round-trip hike to **Whiskey Creek Cabin** from Grave Creek makes a good day trip.

Shady Cove

Although the real action is far downriver, most people find more peaceful adventures in the gentle waters north of scrappy Shady Cove – which has plenty of services. For general information visit the **McGregor Park Visitors Center** (☎ 541-878-3800; 10am-5pm Fri-Sun & holidays, summer).

Raft rental options include **Raft The Rogue** (☎ 800-797-7238; www.rafttherogue.com; 21171 Hwy 62); **Raging Waters Raft Rental** (☎ 541-878-4000; www.upperrogue.org/ragingwaters; 21873 Hwy 62) and **Rogue Rafting Company** (☎ 888-236-3096; www.upperrogue.org/roguerafting; 7725 Rogue River Dr).

North of Shady Cove about 12 miles is **McGregor Park**, a popular raft put-in and picnic

BISCUIT FIRE CONTROVERSY

Named after a local creek, the 2002 lightning-started Biscuit Fire burned over 300 million acres, including most of the Kalmiopsis Wilderness. It lasted for six months, destroyed four homes and put 15,000 people on evacuation alert, but caused no human deaths. Still, it was Oregon's largest fire in history and much of the Siskiyou National Forestlands were burned. The fire also gave birth to a controversy.

In January 2006, an article written by Oregon State University (OSU) Forestry graduate student Don Donato (et al) was printed in the scientific journal *Science*. The article highlighted the effects of salvage logging on the lands burned by the Biscuit Fire, noting that the removal of dead trees hindered conifer germination rates due to possible soil disturbances and leftover logging materials.

The controversial kick is that the US Forest Service, along with a group of university professors (including six from OSU's College of Forestry), had asked *Science* to delay the publication of the article – or at least publish a side note illustrating the group's concerns (the journal refused both these requests). The Forest Service and professors' attempt to interfere with the publication of Donato's article was seen as a politically motivated attack on academic freedom; after all, the College of Forestry receives 10% of its funding from a logging tax, and some of the professors had ties to the Forest Service.

Today the Siskiyou National Forest is slowly regenerating, as forests often do after a fire – but the fight between environmentalists and logging (and possibly political) interests will go on long after any seedlings have taken hold.

spot. Up by the dam is the large **Cole M Rivers Fish Hatchery**, where you can feed the fish for $0.25.

Area campgrounds include the expansive, well-serviced **Joseph Stewart State Park** (☎ 541-560-3334, 800-452-5687; www.oregonstateparks.org; tents/hookups $13/15) and the roadside **Rogue Elk Campground** (☎ 541-776-7001; sites $17-19). For more comfort there's the outdated but decent **Royal Coachman Motel** (☎ 541-878-2481; www.royalcoachmanmotel.com; 21906 Hwy 62; d $49-68; ⊠ ⊠) and the much fancier **Edgewater Inn** (☎ 888-811-3171; www.edgewater-inns.com; 7800 Rogue River Dr; d from $102; ⊠ ⊠ wi-fi).

Prospect & Union Creek

Past Shady Cove, about 17 miles north, the valley walls close in, and the silvery river quickens and channels a gorge through thick lava flows. Dense forests robe the steep mountainsides, surrounding sparsely populated Prospect and Union Creek with uncrowded hiking trails, quiet camping and rustic lodging convenient to Crater Lake.

A mile south of Prospect on Mill Creek Dr is the 0.3-mile trail to **Mill Creek Falls** (173ft). A side shoot leads to the **Avenue of Giant Boulders**, where the Rogue River crashes through rocky boulders (scrambling required).

Upriver from Prospect, the trail through **Takelma Gorge** starts at either Woodruff Bridge picnic area (3.2 miles round-trip) or River Bridge campground (6 miles round-trip).

Trails on both sides of the river between Natural Bridge and the Rogue River Gorge form two 2.5-mile loop hikes. At **Natural Bridge**, the Rogue River borrows a lava tube and goes underground for 200ft. Upriver is the magical **Rogue River Gorge**, where a narrow, turbulent section of river cuts a sheer-walled cleft into a lava flow. Combine both sites for an 8-mile hike.

Mill Creek, **River Bridge** and **Natural Bridge** primitive campgrounds have no water (sites $6; Natural Bridge is close to a lava tube). **Union Creek** ($11) and **Farewell Bend** ($15) do have water. Make reservations at these two through www.roguerec.com.

For detailed camping and hiking information contact the **High Cascades Ranger Station** (☎ 541-560-3400; www.fs.fed.us/r6/rogue-siskiyou; 47201 Hwy 62, Prospect; 🕑 8am-4:30pm Mon-Fri).

The grand old **Prospect Hotel** (☎ 541-560-3664, 800-944-6490; www.prospecthotel.com; 391 Mill Creek Dr; d $69-97; ⊠ ⊠ wi-fi) has small, charming B&B rooms (along with modern motel rooms), a wrap-around porch and a worthy dining room (mains $19 to $24; open 5pm to 9pm summer only). The **Union Creek Resort** (☎ 541-560-3565, 866-560-3565; 56484 Hwy 62; d $49-54, cabins $74-207; ⊠) is an old 1930s lodge with nine wood-paneled rooms (shared bathrooms outside) and a couple dozen rustic cabins that sleep two to 10 people.

GRANTS PASS

pop 30,000

As a modern and not particularly scenic city Grants Pass isn't much of a destination, but its location on the banks of the Rogue River makes it a portal to adventure. White-water rafting, fine fishing and jet boat excursions are the biggest attractions, but there's also good camping and hiking in the area. If you're here on a Saturday between mid-March to Thanksgiving, be sure to check out the Outdoors Growers' Market, a farmers and craft market that draws the city together. Grants Pass is also the freeway exit for the Illinois Valley's Oregon Caves National Monument.

The **chamber of commerce** (☎ 541-476-7717, 800-547-5927; www.visitgrantspass.org; 1995 NW Vine St; 8am-5pm Mon-Fri) is right off I-5 exit 58. **Greyhound** (☎ 541-476-4513; www.greyhound.com; 460 NE Agness Ave) is off I-5 near exit 55 – about 2 miles from downtown.

Sleeping

There are plenty of economy motels lining 6th and 7th Sts.

Schroeder Park (☎ 800-452-5687; 605 Schroeder Lane; sites/hookups/yurts $14/19/27) This is a pleasant, river side campground 4 miles west of town, on the south side of the river. There are about 50 sites with showers and flush toilets, and there's a boat ramp nearby.

Valley of the Rogue State Park (☎ 541-582-1118, 800-452-5687; www.oregonstateparks.org; 3792 N River Rd; tents/hookups/yurts $15/19/25) Around 12 miles east of town, this riverside campground has 168 sites and six yurts. There are showers, flush toilets and a boat ramp.

Indian Mary Park (☎ 541-474-5285; 7100 Merlin-Galice Rd; sites/hookups $16/17) Rafters are fond of this popular 90-site, park-like campground 7 miles northwest of Grants Pass, near Galice. Amenities include a playground, boat ramp and beach.

Ivy House B&B (☎ 541-474-7363; 139 SW I St; s/d $51/60; ☒) Likely the best deal in town is this lovely Arts & Crafts B&B run by a gardening Englishwoman who uses composters and rain barrels to nourish her 100-year-old rosebushes. Five rooms decorated with antiques are available, four of which share two bathrooms.

Buona Sera Inn (☎ 541-479-4260; www.buonaserainn.com; 1001 NE 6th St; d $65-125; ☒ wi-fi) Irene and Peter have lovingly renovated this old motel into a comfortable, and even slightly luxurious, place with 14 country-style rooms. All have wood floors, quality linens and quilted bedspreads, and boast a fridge and microwave; some come with kitchenette. Breakfast is continental.

our pick **Wolf Creek Inn** (☎ 541-866-2474; www.thewolfcreekinn.com; 100 Front St; d $79-102; ☒) Located 20 miles north of Grants Pass, this historic hotel and stagecoach stop was once the lodging choice of celebrities such as Jack London, Clark Gable and Mary Pickford. There are only nine period rooms available, which include breakfast but no TV. Restaurant available.

Redwood Motel (☎ 541-476-0878, 888-535-8824; www.redwoodmotel.com; 815 NE 6th St; d incl breakfast $80-125; ☒ wi-fi) Simple, elegant and spacious rooms in muted colors the include a fridge and microwave are on offer at this central motel. Some have private Jacuzzi, but there's a communal hot tub (and pool) as well. Kitchenettes available.

Weasku Inn Resort (☎ 541-471-8000, 800-493-2758; www.weasku.com; 5560 Rogue River Hwy; d from $182, cabins from $201; ☒ wi-fi) Situated about 5 miles east of town, this grand old lodge has hosted Clark Gable. Luxuriously rustic rooms and cabins are available (get one away from the highway) and a continental breakfast, along with evening wine and cheese reception, is included.

Eating

Wild River Brewing & Pizza Co (☎ 541-471-7487; 595 NE E St; mains $7-12; 10:30am-10:30pm Sun-Thu, till 11pm Fri & Sat) This is a modern and cozy pub-restaurant serving up good burgers, salads, sandwiches, pasta and woodfired pizza, along with plenty of fresh microbrews to power it all down.

Laughing Clam (☎ 541-479-1110; 121 SW G St; mains $7-18; 11am-8pm Mon-Thu, till 10pm Fri & Sat) Exotic dishes like its cosmic Cajun catfish sandwich and magic mushroom burger are served up at this neon-lit, brick-walled eatery. More standard things like fish 'n chips, pasta and jambalaya are also available, along with a few rotating microbrews.

our pick **Summer Jo's** (☎ 541-476-6882; 2315 Upper River Loop; mains $15-24; 9:30am-2pm & 5-8:30pm Wed-Sat) An organic farm-restaurant, Summer Jo's utilizes veggies grown on the premises, along with sustainable seafood and quality meats. It offers exquisite dishes and is well worth the drive out: take G St west 1.4 miles, then turn left on Upper River Loop. A great spot for lunch – sit outside on sunny days.

OREGON CAVES NATIONAL MONUMENT

This very popular tourist destination lies 19 miles east of Cave Junction on Hwy 46. The cave (there's only one) contains about 3 miles of passages, explored via 90-minute walking tours that expose visitors to dripping chambers and 520 rocky steps. The trail – which requires ducking at times – follows an underground waterway called the River Styx.

The Oregon Caves began as seafloor limestone deposits that were eventually hoisted into the Siskiyou Mountains. Molten rock forced its way up into rock faults to form marble, and acidified groundwater seeped through cracks to carve underground channels. Surface erosion eventually created an opening for air to enter, causing water to mineralize and create myriad formations, such as cave popcorn, pearls, moonmilk, classic pipe organs, columns and stalactites.

Guided **cave tours** (☎ 541-592-2100; www.nps.gov/orca; adult/16yr & under $8.50/6; ⏰ 10am-4pm Apr-May & Oct-Nov, 9am-5pm Jun-Sep, closed Dec-Mar) run at least hourly; they run half-hourly in July and August. Dress warmly, wear good shoes and be prepared to get dripped on. Children less than 42in tall are not allowed on regular tours – they can go on special free tours when accompanied by an adult.

A handful of short nature trails surround the area, such as the three-quarter-mile **Cliff Nature Trail** (offering good views) and the 3.5-mile **Big Tree Trail** (which loops through old-growth forest to a huge Douglas fir). You can stop for snacks or a meal at the Oregon Caves Chateau, a beautiful old lodge (see p328). Also, some fine wineries are found en route to the caves.

Cave Junction, 28 miles south of Grants Pass on US 199 (Redwood Hwy), provides the region's services. The **Illinois Valley Visitor Center** (☎ 541-592-4076; 201 Caves Hwy; ⏰ 9am-5pm) has information on the area. Nearby is the **Wild Rivers Ranger District** (☎ 541-592-4000; www.fs.fed.us/r6/rogue-siskiyou; 26568 Redwood Hwy; ⏰ 8am-noon, 1-4:30pm Mon-Fri).

For something completely different, check out **Great Cats World Park** (☎ 541-592-2957; www.greatcatsworldpark.com; 27919 Redwood Hwy; adult/4-12yr/senior $12/8/10; ⏰ vary widely), a mile south of Cave Junction. This zoo/interactive big cat preserve proves cats *are* trainable – even if they're big enough to eat your head.

Sleeping & Eating

Cave Creek Campground (☎ 541-592-2166; sites $10) Fourteen miles up Hwy 46, this campground is 3.7 miles from the caves and has a trail leading there. There are vault toilets, picnic tables and drinking water; no showers or hookups.

Country Hills Resort (☎ 541-592-3406; 7901 Caves Hwy; tent sites/hookups $15/18, d $59, cabins $65-74) A friendly, rustic place, this resort has five comfortable country-style rooms and six cabins that come with kitchenettes. It also offers creek-side camping and full-hookup RV sites.

KALMIOPSIS WILDERNESS

Oregon's largest wilderness, the remote Kalmiopsis Wilderness is famous for its rare plant life and the state's oldest peaks – the Klamath Mountains. About 150 million years ago, offshore sedimentary beds buckled up into mountains separated from North America by a wide gulf. Vegetation evolved on its own, so by the time the mountains fused to the continent the plant life was very different from that of the mainland. The area also has the country's largest exposed serpentine rock formations.

Unusual and unique plant species are showcased on an easy hike to **Babyfoot Lake**. The pink-flowered Kalmiopsis leachiana and rare Port Orford cedar are found almost nowhere else on earth. Watch meadows for the carnivorous Darlingtonia (also called the pitcher plant or cobra lily) that traps insects for nourishment. To get to the trailhead, turn onto Eight Dollar Mountain Rd (USFS Rd 4201, 5 miles north of Cave Junction) and follow the signs for 18 winding miles. This road is impassable in winter.

(If you just want to see Darlingtonias without the slow, windy mountain drive, head 30 miles south on Hwy 199 from Cave Junction into California, keeping an eye peeled for the sign 'botanical trail.' A short wheelchair-accessible walk leads to a bog full of the plants.)

Another section of the Kalmiopsis is accessible from the coastal town of Brookings (see p313). For more information, enquire at the ranger stations in Cave Junction and Brookings.

It's on the way to Oregon caves; make sure you reserve in summer.

Junction Inn (☎ 541-592-3106; 406 Redwood Hwy; d from $60;) Cave Junction's largest motel, the Junction Inn has basic, no-nonsense rooms. A swimming pool cools things down in summer.

Oregon Caves Chateau (☎ 541-592-3400, 877-245-9022; www.oregoncaveschateau.com; d from $83-126; May-Oct) Situated near the cave's entrance, this impressive six-story lodge has huge windows facing the forest, 23 homely rooms and a dining room overlooking a plunging ravine. Snacks and great milkshakes are served at the old-fashioned soda fountain.

our pick **Out 'n' About Treesort** (☎ 541-592-2208; www.treehouses.com; 300 Page Creek Rd; tree houses from $106) A must for families with inquisitive kids, this rustic but fun place offers a dozen different kinds of tree houses, from small round rooms 35ft up, to more terrestrial suites with kitchens. Not all have bathrooms, and some are only for those comfortable with heights. It's in Takilma, 10 miles south of Cave Junction. Breakfast is included; reservations are crucial.

Wild River Brewing & Pizza Co (☎ 541-592-3556; 249 Redwood Hwy; pizzas $5-20; 11am-9pm Mon-Thu, till 10pm Fri & Sat, noon-9pm Sun) Another link of this small but good restaurant chain. There are large family tables inside, but if it's sunny the back deck (overlooking a small river) is the place to be. Also offers great burgers and sandwiches.

ROSEBURG

pop 21,000

Sprawling Roseburg lies in a valley near the confluence of the South and North Umpqua Rivers. The city is mostly a cheap, modern sleepover for travelers headed elsewhere, but does contain a cute historic downtown area and is surrounded by award-winning wineries. Two exceptional area sights include a regional museum and drive-through safari park.

The **Roseburg Visitors & Convention Bureau** (☎ 541-672-9731, 800-444-9584; www.visitroseburg.com; 410 SE Spruce St; 9am-5pm Mon-Fri, 10am-4pm Sat & Sun) is downtown. Want to fish the Umpqua? Contact the **Fish & Wildlife office** (☎ 541-440-3353; 4192 N Umpqua Hwy; 8am-5pm Mon-Fri).

Long-distance bus services are provided by **Greyhound** (☎ 541-673-3348; www.greyhound.com; 835 SE Stephens St).

Sights & Activities

Don't miss the excellent **Douglas County Museum** (☎ 541-957-7007; www.co.douglas.or.us/museum; I-5 exit 123; adult/child/senior $4/1/3; 9am-5pm Mon-Fri, 10am-5pm Sat, noon-5pm Sun), which displays the area's cultural and natural histories. Especially interesting are the railroad derailment photos, mammoth tusk and Victorian wreath made from human hair. Kids have an interactive area.

Ten miles southwest near Winston is the **Wildlife Safari** (☎ 541-679-6761, 800-355-4848; www.wildlifesafari.org; I-5 exit 119; adult/senior/4-12yr $14.50/11.50/12.50; 9am-6pm), where you drive your car around a 600-acre park dotted with inquisitive ostriches, camels, giraffes, lions, tigers and bears – among other exotic animals. Includes a small zoo where 'encounters' are available. Limited hours outside summer.

Sleeping & Eating

Roseburg is host to plenty of budget and midrange hotel chains, most located just off I-5 on NW Garden Valley Blvd, or on SE Stephens St.

Budget 16 Motel (☎ 541-673-5556, 800-414-1648; www.budget16.com; 1067 NE Stephens St; s/d $32/39;) One of the cheapest motels around, though you might have to deal with outdated furniture and stains on the carpet. Get a room in the back to avoid traffic noise. Kitchenettes are available.

Hokanson's Guest House (☎ 541-672-2632; www.hokansonsguesthouse.com; 848 SE Jackson St; d $88-97;) Just three charming rooms are available at this downtown B&B, each with a private bathroom. The 1882 Victorian is filled with antiques, and two cats roam the premises, along with the hosts' children.

McMenamins Roseburg Station Pub (☎ 541-672-1934; 700 SE Sheridan St; mains $7-11; 11am-11pm Mon-Thu, till midnight Fri & Sat, till 10pm Sun) This is a beautiful, cozy pub-restaurant in typical McMenamins style – old fashioned and tasteful. Burgers, sandwiches and salads dominate the menu. It's in an old train depot; sit and order a microbrew on the sunny patio in summer.

Brix (☎ 541-440-4901; 527 SE Jackson St; mains $8-10; 7am-3pm; V) A modern, hip café, Brix serves omelettes, pancakes and French toast for breakfast, and burgers, sandwiches, pastas and salads for lunch. A few veggie options are available.

NORTH UMPQUA RIVER

From Roseburg, Hwy 138 winds east toward Crater Lake along the lovely North Umpqua, a designated 'wild and scenic' river, and one of the best-loved fly-fishing streams in Oregon. Deep forests crowd the river's boulder-strewn edge while volcanic crags rise above the trees. This corridor contains one of Oregon's greatest concentrations of waterfalls, and there are short hikes to most of them.

Between Idleyld Park and Diamond Lake are dozens of mostly USFS campgrounds, many right on the river. In summer, plan on pitching a tent unless you've reserved accommodation at one of the resorts.

There's plenty of help in the area; stop by Glide's **Colliding Rivers Information Center** (☎ 541-496-0157; 18782 N Umpqua Hwy; 9am-5pm summer). Adjacent is the **North Umpqua Ranger District** (☎ 541-496-3532; 8am-4:30pm Mon-Fri). Over toward the east are the **Diamond Lake Ranger District** (☎ 541-498-2531; 8am-4:30pm Mon-Fri) and **Diamond Lake Visitors Center** (☎ 541-793-3310; 9am-5pm summer).

Steamboat & Around

Fly-fishing is heaven here, offering steelhead, cutthroat trout, and Chinook and Coho salmon. Consult Roseburg's **Fish & Wildlife Office** (☎ 541-440-3353) for limits and restrictions.

Frothy rapids above Steamboat make this part of the river good for **rafting** and **kayaking**. Contact **North Umpqua Outfitters** (☎ 888-454-9696; www.nuorafting.com) for guided raft trips.

Turn up USFS Rd 38 at Steamboat to reach **Steamboat Falls**, where sea-run salmon and steelhead struggle to the top of the fast-moving falls from May to October.

The 79-mile **North Umpqua Trail** begins near Idleyld Park and passes through Steamboat en route to the Pacific Crest Trail near Lemolo Lake. A worthwhile day hike to **Mott Bridge** travels 5.5 gentle miles upstream through old-growth forest; it starts from the Wright Creek Trailhead, a few miles west of Steamboat on USFS Rd 4711.

Another popular sideline of the North Umpqua Trail is the 0.3-mile jaunt to the sheltered, clothing-optional **Umpqua Hot Springs** (108°F), situated east of Steamboat near Toketee Lake. Follow USFS Rd 34 for 2 miles to Thorn Prairie Rd (USFS Rd 3401) and turn right to the trailhead after two more miles (Northwest Forest Pass required, or pay $5 onsite). Right off the highway at the USFS Rd 34 turnoff is the trailhead for the 0.4-mile stroll to stunning, two-tiered **Toketee Falls**, flowing over columnar basalt. Two miles past Toketee Junction on Hwy 138 is **Watson Falls**, which at 272ft is one of the highest waterfalls in Oregon. The 0.4-mile path begins at the picnic area on USFS Rd 37, but you can also see it from the parking lot.

From the Susan Creek day-use area (just west of Susan Creek campground) the 1.2-mile **Indian Mounds Trail** passes **Susan Creek Falls** before climbing up to a vision-quest site. About 4 miles east is the 1-mile hike to the double-tier **Fall Creek Falls**. Nearby, **Job's Garden Trail** is a short offshoot halfway up that leads to columnar basalt formations.

SLEEPING

Campgrounds on Hwy 38 include **Susan Creek** (sites $10), a lovely place with showers 13 miles east of Glide; **Horseshoe Bend** (sites $12), 30 miles east of Glide and popular with boats and anglers; and **Boulder Flat** (sites $8), a primitive spot with now water, 36 miles east of Glide with views of a spectacular (and phallic) lava formation down the river.

Dogwood Motel (☎ 541-496-3403; www.dogwoodmotel.com; 28866 N Umpqua Hwy; d $60-65; ☒ ❄) At the Dogwood actual log cabins house seven dark, rustic and tidy rooms, some with kitchenettes. A pretty garden in the back offers a wood gazebo and koi pond, along with a picnic area and the start of a walking trail. A house is also available for rent.

Steelhead Run B&B (☎ 541-496-0563; www.steelheadrun.com; 23049 N Umpqua Hwy; d $79-134; ☒ ❄) This country-style place has six homely rooms and suites, some with views of the river. There are pretty gardens, games to play and a swimming hole. A house is also available for rent.

our pick **Steamboat Inn** (☎ 541-496-3495; www.thesteamboatinn.com; 42705 N Umpqua Hwy; d $148-184; ☒ ❄ wi-fi) The Steamboat offers lovely wood-paneled suites and cabins next to the river, or larger modern cottages in the forest beyond. All offer comfortable amenities and some come with a fireplace, kitchenette and soaking tubs. Its renowned restaurant is open to nonguests (prix-fixe dinner $50 to $85; reserve ahead).

Diamond Lake

This beautiful, deep-blue lake attracts motorboat and RV enthusiasts in summer, with activity centered on a bustling full-service resort. There's fishing, boating, swimming possibilities, along with a 12-mile paved bike path around the lake. Winter brings cross-country skiers.

Rising to the east of Diamond Lake is pointy **Mt Thielsen**, a 9182ft basalt spire. A 5-mile trail (Northwest Forest Pass required) begins a mile north of the junction of Hwys 138 and 230 and stops 80ft short of the summit, which is attainable only with technical climbing skills.

Diamond Lake Campground (☎ 877-444-6777; USFS Rd 4795; sites $11) has 238 sites and offers plenty of camping amenities at the north end of the lake. It's such a popular place that you should reserve ahead in summer.

Diamond Lake Resort (☎ 541-793-3333, 800-733-7593; www.diamondlake.net; 350 Resort Dr; d $74-276) offers motel-type rooms, studios, Jacuzzi suites and two-bedroom cabins with kitchens. Dining options include a café, a pizzeria and a fancier dining room. Boats, canoes, kayaks, bicycles and fishing gear are available for rent.

Lemolo Lake

Ten miles north of Diamond Lake is Lemolo Lake, a much quieter, family-oriented resort with views across the reservoir to faraway Mt Thielsen.

The 1.7-mile hike to **Lemolo Falls** is worth the off-road drive. Turn off Hwy 138 onto USFS Rd 2610 (Lemolo Lake Rd) for 4.2 miles, then left onto USFS Rd 3401 (Thorn Prairie Rd) for 0.5 miles. Then turn right onto USFS Rd 800 for 1.8 miles, and another right at USFS Rd 840 for 0.3 miles.

Poole Creek Campground (☎ 877-444-6777; USFS Rd 2610; sites $9-11) is a popular USFS-maintained ground – the best sites are right near the lake. Only one group site is reservable. A boat ramp is available, but unless you're staying at the campground, you'll need a Northwest Forest Pass.

Lemolo Lake Resort (☎ 541-643-0750; www.lemololakeresort.com; 2610 Birds Point Rd; hookups $21, d $65-79, cabins $115-138) is a casual place with a nondescript RV campsite, motel-style rooms, A-frame cabins, a boat ramp, small store and a café. Boat rentals are available, but you'll have to bring your own alcohol and TV.

KLAMATH FALLS

pop 21,000

If there's a city in Oregon with up-and-coming potential, Klamath Falls is it. Sure it still suffers from unemployment problems after the decline of the timber industry, and it could certainly use an urban facelift – but K Falls has a lot going for it. Over 300 days of sunshine, affordable real estate, spectacular countryside and awesome recreational opportunities are all attracting opportunistic re-settlers, including plenty of retirees from nearby California. The economy is slowly growing with tech, medical and service industries, and the historic downtown area is gradually being spruced up.

Perhaps now is the time to see K Falls, when it's still a well-kept secret. Enjoy the city's small-town feel and friendly people. Visit the nearby Klamath Basin National Wildlife Refuge (see p332), which boasts a huge population of wintering bald eagles. Check out the surrounding high desert mountain terrain – amazing Crater Lake National Park is only 60 miles north, and there are lots of lakes and fishing streams to explore. Boat, bike and raft in summer and ski in winter. Will Klamath Falls become the next Bend? It's set on course, but only time will tell.

The **Great Basin Visitor Association** (☎ 541-882-1501; www.travelklamath.com; 205 Riverside Dr; 🕑 9am-5pm Mon-Fri, till 2pm Sat) has area information. For more on the Winema National Forest visit the **Klamath Falls Ranger District** (☎ 541-883-6714; www.fs.fed.us/r6/frewin; 2819 Dahlia St; 🕑 8am-4:30pm Mon-Fri).

Sights & Activities

Downtown has quite a few old but noteworthy buildings – take a walk and discover them (the visitors center has a pamphlet).

Learn about the area's history at the quirky **Klamath County Museum** (☎ 541-883-4208; 1451 Main St; adult/6-12yr/senior $3/1/2; 🕑 9am-5pm Tue-Sat) in the old armory. Along with natural history dioramas and fine Native American basketry, look for the pelican figurine collection. The museum also maintains historic artifacts housed in the **Baldwin Hotel** (☎ 541-883-4207; 31 Main St; adult/senior with tour $4/3; 🕑 10am-4pm Tue-Sat summer).

Native American tools, basketry and beadwork meet campy Western art at the **Favell Museum of Western Art & Indian Artifacts** (☎ 541-882-9996; www.favellmuseum.org; 125 W Main St; adult/6-16yr/senior $6/3/5; 🕑 9:30am-5:30pm Mon-Sat). Over 60,000 arrowheads are on display, including one made of opal; also check out the miniature guns.

Rent bikes at **Hutch's** (☎ 541-850-2453; 808 Klamath Ave; 9am-6pm Mon-Sat, 11am-5pm Sun). It offers free bike rides in summer, or ask about the **OC&E Woods Line State Trail**, which follows a historical rail bed for 100 miles.

Ashland-based **Adventure Center** (☎ 541-488-2819; www.raftingtours.com) offers rafting trips down the Upper Klamath River. In winter there's **cross-country skiing** west on Hwy 140 at Lake of the Woods and north at Crater Lake.

Sleeping & Eating

Rocky Point Resort (☎ 541-356-2287; www.rockypointoregon.com; 28121 Rocky Point Rd; tents/hookups $18/25, d $82, cabins $129-175) Around 24 miles northwest of town is this rustic 'resort' on the shores of Upper Klamath Lake. The RV sites, rooms and cabins are in full view of each other and not the water. Still, the country-style accommodations are popular with boaters and anglers; there's a full-service marina, tackle shop, restaurant and canoes for rent.

Klamath Falls KOA (☎ 541-884-4644, 800-562-9036; www.koa.com; 3435 Shasta Way; tents/hookups/cabins $23/32/44; wi-fi) This pleasant KOA is 3 miles southeast of the center. It has an outdoor pool and kids' playground.

Lake of the Woods Resort (☎ 541-949-8300, 866-201-4194; www.lakeofthewoodsresort.com; 950 Harriman Rte; RV sites $25-32, cabins $155-285;) Located 32 miles west of Klamath Falls is this pleasant family resort with around 30 cabins. The marina rents boats; you can also rent mountain bikes in summer and snowshoes in winter. There's a restaurant, lounge and small store on premises. Reserve ahead; it offers a discount on weekdays.

Maverick Motel (☎ 541-882-6688, 800-404-6690; www.maverickmotel.com; 1220 Main St; d $51-60; wi-fi) Your typical motel. Get a room with two beds on the 2nd floor, overlooking the back street – these are bigger, brighter and quieter than the ones in the front, and have peeks at faraway mountains for only a few bucks more. It's next door to the hip Creamery brewpub.

Quality Inn (☎ 541-882-4666; www.choicehotels.com/hotel/or413; 100 Main St; d from $89; wi-fi) There are fine, modern and spacious rooms at the Quality Inn that are a couple of steps up from basic budget motels. Amenities include a restaurant, lounge, fitness center and a heated outdoor pool. Nice and central location.

Thompson's B&B (☎ 541-882-7938; www.thompsonsbandb.com; 1420 Wild Plum Crt; d $96-106; wi-fi) Three miles west of center, in a residential neighborhood overlooking Upper Klamath Lake, is this comfortable B&B. The four rooms each have private bathrooms and two come with water views. It's like Grandma's house, run by a friendly couple.

Running Y Ranch (☎ 541-850-5500, 888-850-0275; www.runningy.com; 5115 Running Y Rd; d $186-264; wi-fi) This is only for those seeking recreational opportunities amid luxurious surroundings. The lodge is upscale western ranch style, and you can golf, play tennis, fish, swim, cycle, canoe, kayak, horseback-ride, birdwatch, ice-skate, work out and get a facial – all without leaving the premises.

Daily Bagel (☎ 541-850-0744; 636 Main St; snacks under $6; 6am-5pm Mon-Fri, 7am-4pm Sat) This is a popular café toasting up great bagel sandwiches from Nova Scotia salmon lox to corned beef and sauerkraut to pizza toppings. Soups are also available.

Antonio's (☎ 541-850-4500; 1012 Main St; mains $8-15; 11am-10pm) A pleasant, quality restaurant, Antonio's serves all the typical Italian goodies like minestrone, pasta primavera, meatball sandwiches, hand-thrown pizzas and chicken

BALD EAGLE–WATCHING

Every November, hundreds of bald eagles travel from Canada and Alaska to winter in the Klamath Basin, feeding on the area's rich waterfowl populations. December through to February are prime viewing months, when you can spot dozens of these national symbols along the Lower Klamath Refuge and Tule Lake. To catch them flying out from their night roosts at first light, head to Bear Valley Refuge, an old-growth hillside located off Hwy 97 (turn west onto the Keno-Worden road just south of Worden, and after the railroad crossing go left onto a dirt road for 0.5 miles; park on the shoulder).

In spring and summer you can also watch nesting bald eagles along the west side of Upper Klamath Lake and at Klamath Marsh National Wildlife Refuge. For more on bird life in the area, see www.klamathbirdingtrails.com; for general information on bald eagles, see www.baldeagleinfo.com.

parmesan. Leave room for the tiramisu, or spumoni ice cream.

Creamery (☎ 541-273-5222; 1320 Main St; mains $8-18; 🕐 11am-10pm Sun-Mon, till 11pm Fri & Sat) The hippest place in town, the Creamery is a large brewpub-restaurant with all the usual favorites like steaks, ribs, burgers, pastas, salads and sandwiches. Microbrews include its decent Butt Crack Brown. There's a great back deck for sunny days. Portions are huge.

There are more choices north of Klamath Falls.

Getting There & Away

The **Klamath Falls airport** (☎ 541-883-5372) is 5 miles south of town. **The Shuttle** (☎ 541-883-2609) provides regional bus services to surrounding cities. **Amtrak** (☎ 541-884-2822; www.amtrak.com) is at S Spring St and Oak Ave.

KLAMATH BASIN NATIONAL WILDLIFE REFUGES

The Klamath Basin is a broad, marshy floodplain extending from the southern base of Crater Lake into the northernmost part of California. The surrounding region offers some of the finest bird-watching in the West: six wildlife refuges, totaling more than 263 sq miles, support concentrations of up to two million birds.

In the **Upper Klamath Refuge**, tule rushes fill the northwestern shore of shallow, marshy, Upper Klamath Lake. Here there's shelter for colonies of cormorants, egrets, herons, cranes, pelicans and many varieties of ducks and geese. A 9.5-mile **canoe trail** starts at Rocky Point Resort, 24 miles northwest of Klamath Falls off Hwy 140 (canoe rentals are available; see p331).

West of Worden, down near the border, the **Bear Valley Refuge** is known mostly as a wintering area for bald eagles; 500 to 1000 gather here between December and March (see the boxed text, p331).

The 83-sq-mile **Lower Klamath Refuge** lies mostly in California. This mix of open water, shallow marsh, cropland and grassy upland offers the best year-round viewing and great access for motorists: a 10-mile **auto tour** begins off Hwy 161 (State Line Rd). Get information beforehand in Klamath Falls or at the **Refuge Headquarters** (☎ 530-667-2231; www.fws.gov/klamathbasinrefuges; 4009 Hill Rd) in Tulelake, California.

If you're in the area on President's Day weekend in mid-February, check out the four-day **Winter Wings Festival** (www.winterwingsfest.org), which draws together bird-lovers of all kinds for lectures, workshops, field trips and wildlife art at the Oregon Institute of Technology in Klamath Falls.

Eastern Oregon

Eastern Oregon will amaze you. Sure, much of it is extensive farmlands, desert plateaus and alkali lakebeds, but then there are the stunners like the Wallowa Mountains, rising up from green agricultural valleys to lofty snowy peaks. And Hells Canyon, which dips deeper than even that most-famous gorge over in Arizona. And the John Day Fossil Beds, with eerily colorful hills and brash mountain formations. Or the scenic wonders of the Steens Mountain range, with its hanging valleys and alpine meadows.

Natural beauty aside, Eastern Oregon is also the place where the settlers crossed the state, dragging themselves over hill and dale, toward the end of their arduous journey west – in certain regions you can still see where their wagon ruts carved out the Oregon Trail. Gold was discovered in the region in the 1860s, making and breaking dozens of towns and cities – ghost towns abound around Baker City, and some mines are still being worked today. Native American history is also rich, as the northeast region especially was once filled with Cayuse, Umatilla, Walla Walla and Nez Perce. Places like the Tamástslikt Cultural Institute in Pendleton, or the Four Rivers Cultural Center in Ontario are good places to catch up on Native American history.

With a rodeo in every town and the Old West still palpable in spots, Eastern Oregon is like going back in time – but forget the covered wagons and bring the digital camera.

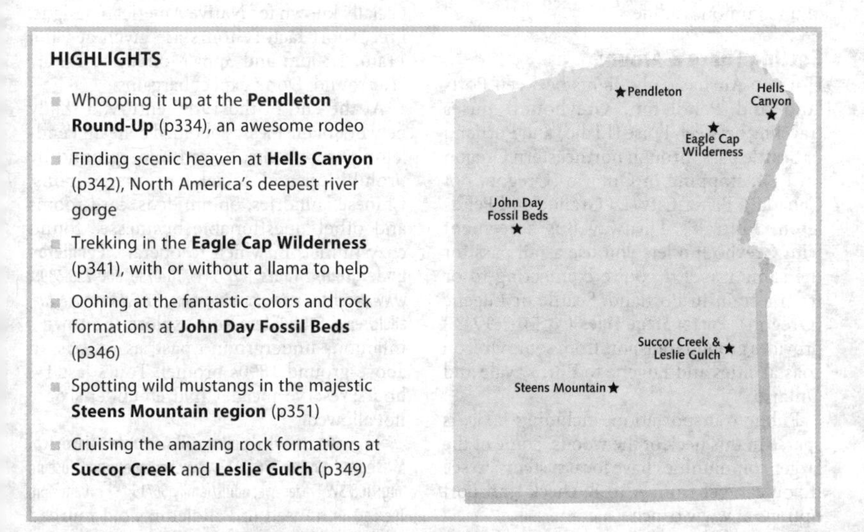

HIGHLIGHTS

- Whooping it up at the **Pendleton Round-Up** (p334), an awesome rodeo
- Finding scenic heaven at **Hells Canyon** (p342), North America's deepest river gorge
- Trekking in the **Eagle Cap Wilderness** (p341), with or without a llama to help
- Oohing at the fantastic colors and rock formations at **John Day Fossil Beds** (p346)
- Spotting wild mustangs in the majestic **Steens Mountain region** (p351)
- Cruising the amazing rock formations at **Succor Creek** and **Leslie Gulch** (p349)

Geography & Climate

Almost two thirds of Oregon's total area lies east of the Cascades. Most of it sees very little precipitation, averaging between 14in and 19in annually. The exceptions are mostly at higher elevations, some of which receive much more, often in the form of snow. In addition to its dryness, this part of the state sees the greatest thermal extremes. The records for high and low temperatures are both held by northeastern towns: 119°F (shared by Pendleton and Prineville) and –54°F (Seneca). Summer highs average in the 80s in much of the north and slightly higher in the south. Summer lows average in the 40s (north) and around 50°F to 55°F (south). Winter highs average in the 30s, with lows generally averaging in the teens.

Wilderness Areas

The magnificent alpine splendor of Eagle Cap Wilderness is a major reason to visit northeastern Oregon. The snow-topped Wallowa Mountains (several of which rise above 9000ft) provide an unforgettable backdrop for hiking, backcountry skiing and other outdoor activities in the area's 560-plus sq miles. Not far to the southwest lies the much smaller and less-visited Strawberry Mountain Wilderness. These rugged mountains, like the Wallowas, bear much evidence of their glacial past – most notably the wonderfully scenic U-valleys – and are home to a variety of uncommon wildlife.

Getting There & Around

Horizon Air has daily flights between Portland and Pendleton. Greyhound buses traveling between Boise (Idaho) and Portland or Seattle pass through northeastern Oregon on I-84, stopping in Ontario (Oregon, not Canada!), Baker City, La Grande and Pendleton. Amtrak's Thruway Bus agreement with Greyhound lets you use a rail pass for the same travel if you're connecting to or from a train in Portland, Seattle or Eugene (Oregon). **Porter Stage Lines** (☎ 541-269-7183) provides ground transport from some Oregon coastal cities and Eugene to Burns, Vale and Ontario.

Public transportation, including taxis, is sparse in this neck of the woods. Some of the larger communities have local systems; to see if you can get from A to B, check transport options at www.tripcheck.com.

PENDLETON

pop 17,300

Eastern Oregon's largest city, 'wild and woolly' Pendleton is a handsome old town famous for its wool shirts and big-name rodeo. It has managed to retain a glint of its old-time atmosphere and cow-poking past, and nestles between steep hills along the Umatilla River. All around are farms and ranchlands, though at least one small boutique winery has recently popped up as a sign of the times, along with a million-dollar steak-house complex. With its art galleries, antique shops and new businesses, Pendleton looks ready to become Eastern Oregon's trendiest destination.

Held in mid-September, the rowdy **Pendleton Round-Up** (☎ 800-457-6336; 1205 SW Court Ave), called 'the USA's best rodeo,' is an all-out Dionysian celebration featuring cowboy breakfasts, dances, bull riding and an Indian Pageant. There's also a big-name music concert. Reserve tickets and lodging way in advance.

For more information there's the **Pendleton Chamber of Commerce** (☎ 541-276-7411, 800-547-8911; www.pendletonchamber.com; 501 S Main St; 🕑 8:30am-5pm Mon-Thu, 10am-5pm Fri, 10am-4pm Sat).

Sights & Activities

World-famous **Pendleton Woolen Mills** (☎ 541-276-6911; www.pendleton-usa.com; 1307 SE Court Pl; 🕑 8am-6pm Mon-Sat, till 5pm Sun) has been weaving blankets for nearly 100 years, and is especially known for Native American designs. Free, short factory tours are given at 9am, 11am, 1:30pm and 3pm Monday to Friday year round. Don't expect bargains.

At the end of the 19th century, a shady network of businesses boomed beneath Pendleton's storefronts, driven underground by prohibition and social tensions. Saloons, Chinese laundries, opium dens, card rooms and other questionable businesses found cozy tunnels in which to operate. **Pendleton Underground Tours** (☎ 541-276-0730, 800-226-6398; www.pendletonundergroundtours.org; 37 SW Emigrant Ave; adult/senior $15/10) lets you explore the town's infamous underground past, as well as an above-ground 1890s brothel. Tours last 1½ hours; reserve ahead. Children under six are not allowed.

The worthwhile **Umatilla County Historical Museum** (☎ 541-276-0012; www.heritagestationmuseum.org; 108 SW Frazer Ave; adult/family $6/15; 🕑 10am-4pm Tue-Sat) is housed in Pendleton's old railroad

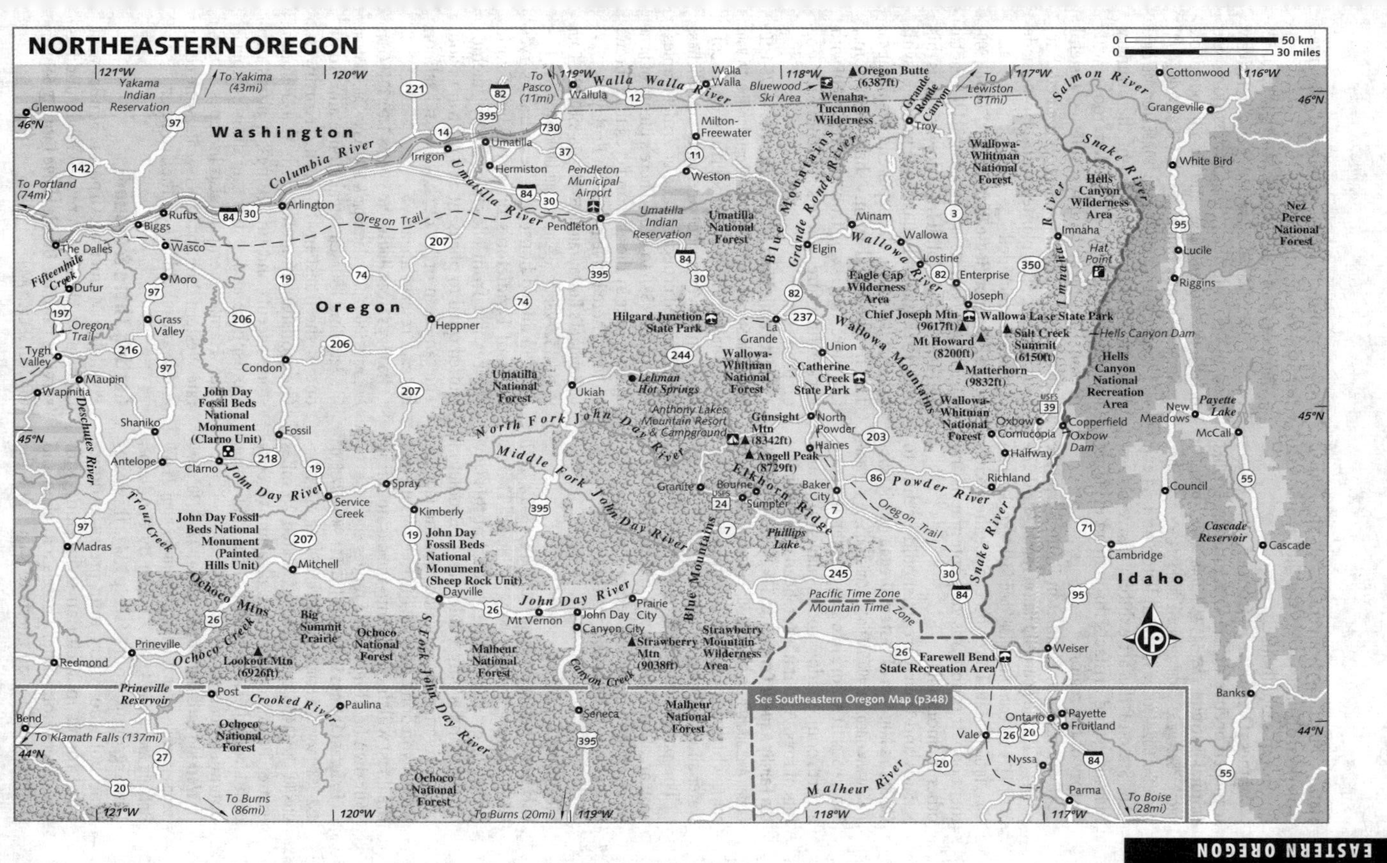
NORTHEASTERN OREGON
0 50 km
0 30 miles
Washington
Oregon
Idaho
See Southeastern Oregon Map (p348)
To Yakima (43mi)
To Portland (74mi)
To Pasco (11mi)
To Lewiston (31mi)
To Boise (28mi)
To Burns (86mi)
To Burns (20mi)
To Klamath Falls (137mi)
Yakama Indian Reservation
Umatilla Indian Reservation
Glenwood
The Dalles
Dufur
Tygh Valley
Wapinitia
Maupin
Biggs
Rufus
Wasco
Moro
Grass Valley
Shaniko
Antelope
Madras
Redmond
Bend
Prineville
Post
Paulina
Arlington
Condon
Fossil
Clarno
Mitchell
Service Creek
Spray
Kimberly
Dayville
Mt Vernon
John Day
Canyon City
Prairie City
Seneca
Heppner
Irrigon
Umatilla
Hermiston
Pendleton
Pendleton Municipal Airport
Wallula
Walla Walla
Milton-Freewater
Weston
Ukiah
La Grande
Elgin
Minam
Wallowa
Lostine
Enterprise
Joseph
Imnaha
Troy
Union
North Powder
Haines
Baker City
Sumpter
Bourne
Granite
Richland
Halfway
Cornucopia
Oxbow
Copperfield
Oxbow Dam
Weiser
Ontario
Payette
Fruitland
Nyssa
Vale
Parma
Cambridge
Council
New Meadows
McCall
Cascade
Banks
Riggins
Lucile
White Bird
Grangeville
Cottonwood
Columbia River
Deschutes River
Fifteenmile Creek
Trout Creek
John Day River
North Fork John Day River
Middle Fork John Day River
S Fork John Day River
Crooked River
Ochoco Creek
Canyon Creek
Umatilla River
Walla Walla River
Grande Ronde River
Wallowa River
Imnaha River
Snake River
Salmon River
Powder River
Malheur River
Blue Mountains
Wallowa Mountains
Elkhorn Ridge
Ochoco Mtns
Oregon Trail
Pacific Time Zone
Mountain Time Zone
Prineville Reservoir
Phillips Lake
Payette Lake
Cascade Reservoir
Hells Canyon Dam
Hells Canyon National Recreation Area
Hells Canyon Wilderness Area
Hat Point
Wallowa-Whitman National Forest
Umatilla National Forest
Malheur National Forest
Ochoco National Forest
Nez Perce National Forest
Eagle Cap Wilderness Area
Wenaha-Tucannon Wilderness
Strawberry Mountain Wilderness Area
Big Summit Prairie
Bluewood Ski Area
Oregon Butte (6387ft)
Chief Joseph Mtn (9617ft)
Mt Howard (8200ft)
Matterhorn (9832ft)
Salt Creek Summit (6150ft)
Wallowa Lake State Park
Catherine Creek State Park
Hilgard Junction State Park
Gunsight Mtn (8342ft)
Angell Peak (8729ft)
Anthony Lakes Mountain Resort & Campground
Lehman Hot Springs
Strawberry Mtn (9038ft)
Lookout Mtn (6926ft)
Farewell Bend State Recreation Area
John Day Fossil Beds National Monument (Clarno Unit)
John Day Fossil Beds National Monument (Painted Hills Unit)
John Day Fossil Beds National Monument (Sheep Rock Unit)
Grande Ronde Canyon
46°N
45°N
44°N
121°W
120°W
119°W
118°W
117°W
116°W

station. There are pioneer exhibits and Native American artifacts; check out the caboose and one-room schoolhouse.

Witness Oregon's past from a Native American perspective at the spacious **Tamástslikt Cultural Institute** (☎ 541-996-9748; www.tamastslikt.org; 72789 Hwy 331; adult/senior & child $6/4; 9am-5pm, closed Sun Nov-Mar), east of Pendleton off I-84 exit 216. State-of-the-art exhibits weave voices, memories and artifacts through an evolving history of the region.

If you miss the Pendleton Round-Up (see p334), visit the **Round-Up Hall of Fame** (☎ 541-278-0815; 1114 SW Court Ave; adult/child $3/1; 10am-5pm Mon-Fri, till 4pm Sat). Here you can see the excitement of past round-ups via photographs and other memorabilia.

Kids and their parents should beeline to **Children's Museum of Eastern Oregon** (☎ 541-276-1066; www.cmeo.org; 400 S Main St; admission $3; 10am-5pm Tue-Sun). It's more like a day center, boasting an art room, shadow room, playground and lots of toys. And if it's hot, head to the **Pendleton Family Aquatic Center** (☎ 541-276-0104; 1800 NW Carden Ave; adult/3-17yr $3.50/2.50; noon-8pm summer only), which features an Olympic-size pool, water slides and a dive tank.

The paved **Umatilla River Parkway**, located atop an old levee, follows the Umatilla for 2.5 miles and provides great recreational opportunities for residents and visitors alike.

Sleeping & Eating

Wild Horse Resort & Casino (☎ 800-654-9453; 72777 Hwy 331; campsites/tepees/RV sites $11/15/20;) There's plenty of grass and little shade, but this tidy campground is only 5 miles east of Pendleton and offers an outdoor heated pool and Jacuzzi. Even if you don't gamble, the free continental breakfast will draw you into the casino. Bring your own bedding for the tepees.

Emigrant Springs State Park (☎ 541-983-2277, 800-452-5687; www.oregonstateparks.org; I-84 exit 234; campsites/RV sites$14/16, cabins $20-35) Located 26 miles east of Pendleton, this is a pleasant woodsy campground. There's a bit of freeway noise, but quieter cabins are available.

Working Girls Old Hotel (☎ 541-276-0730; www.pendletonundergroundtours.org/main/index.htm; 21 SW Emigrant Ave; d $65-84;) Run by Pendleton Underground Tours (see p334), this one-time bordello offers four pretty antique-filled rooms in Victorian style, along with one three-room suite. There's a kitchen and dining room for all guests to share, and the downtown location is convenient. Reservations are required.

America's Best Value Inn (☎ 541-276-1400; 201 SW Court Ave; d $75; wi-fi) A good, relatively new motel with neat, clean rooms (king size beds!), decent amenities and an outdoor pool.

Rugged Country Lodge (☎ 541-966-6800, 877-778-4433; www.ruggedcountrylodge.com; 1807 SE Court Ave; d incl breakfast from $77; wi-fi) Out-of-the-ordinary motel featuring beautiful modern rooms with personal touches like down pillows, tasteful artwork and lavender sprigs on the bed. Surrounded by pretty planted strips. Homemade cookies are included.

The Pendleton House B&B (☎ 541-276-8581, 800-700-8581; www.pendletonhousebnb.com; 311 N Main St; d $109-147;) Uphill from downtown is this pink 1917 Italian Renaissance mansion with original furniture, wallpaper and even drapes. The five beautiful rooms share bathrooms, and there's a relaxing front covered patio with wicker furniture. There's a friendly pet dog on premises.

Great Pacific Wine & Coffee Co (☎ 541-276-1350; 403 S Main St; mains $5-8; 10am-8pm Mon-Thu, till 9pm Fri, 8:30am-8pm Sat) This wonderfully open coffee shop serves up hot and cold sandwiches, salads, baked croissants and gourmet Naples-style pizzas ($15 to $25). There's plenty of java choices, wine by the glass and even microbrews on tap. There is live music on Friday.

Raphael's Restaurant (☎ 541-276-8500; 233 SE 4th St; mains $20-28; 5-8pm Tue-Thu, till 9pm Fri & Sat) Located in an old house, this restaurant serves some of Pendleton's finest cuisine. Exotic choices run from elk chops and pistachio-stuffed quail to pheasant and saffron ravioli. The tame can order duck, crab and salmon instead; reserve ahead.

Hamley's Steak House (☎ 541-278-1100; 30 SE Court Ave; mains $16-28; 11am-2pm & 5-9pm Sun-Thu, till 10pm Fri & Sat) This 150-seat steak house aims to be one of the finest in the Pacific Northwest. Gorgeously remodeled with wood floors, stone accents and tin ceilings, it offers rich atmosphere and a supreme dining experience. Hamley's empire also includes a first-rate Western shop, art gallery, café, wine cellar and beautiful old bar on the 3rd floor.

Getting There & Around

Pendleton Municipal Airport is 5 miles west of town on US 30. There are Greyhound bus services from the **Double J Drive Thru** (☎ 541-966-6675; 801 SE Court Ave).

If you're driving, the Blue Mountains are notorious for severe winter weather, and Deadman Pass between Pendleton and La Grande can be especially treacherous. Call ☎ 800-977-6368 for road conditions.

LA GRANDE

pop 12,500

Early French traders, upon seeing the broad, seemingly circular valley, declared it to be La Grande Ronde, or 'the Big Circle.' Indeed, from the historical marker on US 30 above town, it does seem as if the mountain peaks form a giant ring around the valley.

The Oregon Trail crossed this valley, and the pioneers rested here in preparation of traversing the challenging Blue Mountains. Some saw the valley's agricultural potential and its pretty Grande Ronde River, and decided to settle down instead. Today La Grande is home to Eastern Oregon State College and provides services to the region; it also offers a surprising wealth of outdoor recreation, though the city itself isn't all that memorable.

Take your questions to the **Chamber of Commerce** (☎ 541-963-8588, 800-848-9969; www.visitlagrande.com; 102 Elm St; 9am-5pm Mon-Fri, till 3pm Sat).

Sights

BLUE MOUNTAIN INTERPRETIVE CENTER

Better than any other place in the Blue Mountains, this **outdoors center** (☎ 541-963-7186; I-84 exit 248; $5 Northwest Forest Pass required for parking; 8am-8pm Memorial Day-Labor Day) gives a visceral feeling of what travel was like for Oregon Trail pioneers. Paths wind through the forest to ruts left by pioneer wagons – still quite visible after 150 years. Steep grades and early snowstorms in the Blue Mountains were a huge concern to the pioneers, who usually made the crossing in early September.

The center is 13 miles west of La Grande and 3 miles on well-marked roads from the freeway exit.

GRANDE RONDE RIVER AREA

Explore the upper reaches of this scenic waterway by taking Hwy 244, 8 miles west of La Grande from I-84 exit 252.

At the site of today's **Hilgard State Park**, just off the freeway exit, Oregon Trail pioneers gathered their strength before climbing up over the Blue Mountains. Information kiosks explain how the pioneers winched their wagons down the steep slopes.

Hwy 244 follows the Grande Ronde Valley, then climbs up to a low pass. **Cross-country skiing** is popular here in winter. Stop to soak at **Lehman Hot Springs** (☎ 541-427-3015; admission $7; 10am-8pm Wed-Fri, 9am-8pm Sat & Sun), on Hwy 244, 40 miles southwest of La Grande. A huge pool has three separate areas, with water ranging from warm to sizzling hot. The pools are closed Monday and Tuesday for cleaning (except for holidays and in 'hunting season'). Camping, RV sites, rooms and cabins are available (see below under Sleeping & Eating).

Activities

There's good hiking at **Catherine Creek State Park** (☎ 800-551-6949; Hwy 203), about 26 miles southeast of La Grande. You can access the Eagle Cap Wilderness from a trail here, and there are mountain-top views from another hike nearby.

Try fishing on the Grande Ronde for rainbow trout – test your luck at Red Bridge State Park, west of La Grande on Hwy 244. Fly-fishing for steelhead is popular in winter near the little community of Troy. Contact the **Fish & Wildlife office** (☎ 541-962-8584; 3502 Hwy 30) in La Grande for current regulations and information.

Float beautiful, remote stretches of the Grande Ronde from Minam to Troy with **Wapiti River Guides** (☎ 800-488-9872; www.doryfun.com) offering multi-day float trips. Mountain biking is excellent in the area, though you'll have to bring your own bike. **Cyclesports** (541-962-7441; 1910 Island Ave) is a good resource on area trails.

Spout Springs Resort (☎ 541-566-0320; www.skispoutsprings.com; 79327 Hwy 204; lift tickets $28) is a tiny, low-key ski area. There are also 13 miles of groomed cross-country ski trails. For another nearby ski area, see Anthony Lakes (p344).

Sleeping & Eating

Keep an eye on **Hot Lake Springs** (www.hotlakesprings.com), 8 miles southeast of La Grande. It aims to become a hotel, spa and bronze foundry – among other things – in a few years' time.

Hilgard Junction State Park (☎ 800-551-6949; I-84 exit 252; campsites $8) Only 8 miles west of La Grande, this lovely (but basic) riverside park is convenient but gets highway noise. Boat launch available.

Catherine Creek State Park (☎ 800-551-6949; Hwy 203; campsites $8) Some 26 miles southeast of

La Grande, past the town of Union, this beautiful state-park campground has a clear fishing creek and trails through Ponderosa forest but few facilities.

Orchard Motel (☎ 541-963-6160; 2206 Adams Ave; d $43; wi-fi) Of the cluster of motels east of downtown, this is one of the nicer ones. Ten cozy, homey rooms come with microwave, coffeemaker and fridge. Two-bedroom units are also available.

Lehman Hot Springs (☎ 541-427-3015; www.lehmanhotsprings.com; Hwy 244, milepost 17; campsites/RV sites $12/20, cabins $75-95;) Forty miles southwest of La Grande in Ukiah, are these developed hot springs piped into swimming pools. Comfortable rooms and cabins sleep two to eight, and there's a bunkhouse that holds 48 people ($345, bring your own bedding).

Stange Manor Inn B&B (☎ 541-963-2400, 888-286-9463; www.stangemanor.com; 1612 Walnut St; d $110-133; wi-fi) La Grande's nicest accommodations are in this 1920s Georgian mansion. Four rooms (including a couple of two-bedroom suites) all have private bath and are decorated with antiques. There's a pretty sunroom with wicker furniture.

Ten Depot Street (☎ 541-963-8766; 10 Depot St; mains $12-25; 5-10pm Mon-Sat) This longtime local favorite has a pretty standard menu, but a few surprises (like emu burgers and steaks) pop out. The weeknight Blue Plate Specials are great deals, and on weekends there's live music.

Foley Station (☎ 541-963-7473; 1114 Adams Ave; mains $17-30; 10:30am-10pm Mon-Sat, 7am-10pm Sun) For breakfast there's Belgian waffles, for lunch get the halibut fish 'n chips, and for dinner go for the Jamaican jerk prawns, grilled pesto tenderloin or one of 10 kinds of steak.

Getting There & Around

Bus services run through the **Greyhound bus depot** (☎ 541-963-5165; 63276 Oregon Hwy 203), behind the Flying J truck stop. The **Wallowa Valley Shuttle** (☎ 541-398-1563) has services between Joseph, Enterprise and La Grande.

ENTERPRISE

pop 2000

Enterprise is a small, friendly place that's less expensive and pretentious than its nearby sister town of Joseph, just 6 miles away. However, it shares with Joseph an attraction for artists, as well as an exceptional location surrounded by grassy meadows, pine forests and the stunning Wallowa Mountains. Some of Enterprise's original buildings are still intact and there's a good selection of traveler's services, making it an ideal base for exploring northeastern Oregon – such as Hells Canyon (p342) and, of course, the Wallowas (p340).

In early September, Enterprise is host to **Hells Canyon Mule Days** (www.hellscanyonmuledays.com), a three-day event which features a parade, quilt show, cowboy poetry and – of course – mule and donkey races.

For information there's the **Chamber of Commerce** (☎ 541-426-4622, 800-585-4121; www.wallowacountrychamber.com; 115 Tejaka Lane; 10am-noon, 1-5pm Mon-Fri) off Hwy 82. The **Wallowa Mountains Visitor Center** (☎ 541-426-5546; www.fs.fed.us/r6/w-w; 88401 Hwy 82; 8am-6pm Mon-Sat) is an excellent information source on outdoor recreation in the area.

The **Wallowa Valley Shuttle** (☎ 541-398-1563) has bus services between Joseph, Enterprise and La Grande.

Sleeping & Eating

Note that during Chief Joseph Days (held the last weekend in July) prices tend to rise for area accommodations.

our pick **RimRock Inn** (☎ 541-828-7769; www.rimrockrestaurant.com; 83471 Lewiston Hwy; RV sites $19, tepees $36-45; May-Nov) There aren't many fine restaurants that offer RV hookups and tepee stays, but this is one of them. It's off the beaten path, 35 miles north of Enterprise in an awesome location. Book ahead, and bring bedding for the tepees (firewood provided). The restaurant (mains $10-24, open 11:30 am to 8:30pm Tuesday to Saturday) overlooks the Joseph Creek Canyon and serves fine cuisine. Order well-prepared burgers, steaks or wild salmon, along with panini sandwiches for lunch.

Mountain View Motel & RV Park (☎ 541-432-2982, 866-262-9891; www.rvmotel.com; 83450 Joseph Hwy; campsites/RV sites/r $20/24/70; wi-fi) Located 3 miles from Enterprise on the way to Joseph is this fine spot with campsites, RV hookups and small, homey rooms with kitchenettes.

Ponderosa Motel (☎ 541-426-3186; 102 E Greenwood St; d $67-74; wi-fi) Right in downtown is this well-run motel with attractive wood-and-stone facade. The excellent rooms are clean and comfortable, and each has its own fridge, microwave and coffeemaker.

Wilderness Inn (☎ 541-426-4535; 301 W North St; d $72; wi-fi) A good budget choice is this basic motel with spacious rooms and a few amenities.

ALL ABOARD!

Railroad buffs and scenery lovers shouldn't miss out on the **Eagle Cap Excursion Train** (☎ 541-963-9000; www.eaglecaptrain.com), a service that winds its way through some of northeastern Oregon's finest landscapes. Be witness to wild rivers, rugged canyons and the stunning Wallowa Mountains, among other exceptional sights. There's even a chance of seeing Rocky Mountain elk, black bears and bald eagles.

Connecting Elgin with Joseph, the Wallowa Union Railroad (aka the *Joseph Branch)* runs for 63 miles and transports freight as well as tourists. It runs mostly on Saturday from June to October, and the four- to seven-hour trips cost $65 to $85 per adult.

Rooms out the back have two beds and offer more peace as well as mountain views (from higher floors), though they'll cost a bit more.

Enterprise House B&B (☎ 541-426-4238, 888-448-8825; www.enterprisebnb.com; 508 S 1st St; d $118-180; wi-fi) Enterprise's most majestic place to stay is this 1910 colonial revival mansion with wraparound porch and fancy wine cellar. The five antique-filled rooms are all lovely, and the common places are elegant. Your hosts Jack and Judy are friendly and helpful too.

Cloud 9 Bakery & Café (☎ 541-426-3790; 105 SE 1st St; mains $5-8; 6:30am-4pm Mon-Fri) Popular for breakfast and lunch (they don't do dinner) is this downtown café serving bagels, salads, sandwiches and a few Mexican treats. They fix boxed lunches for day hikers.

Terminal Gravity Brewing (☎ 541-426-0158; 803 School St; mains $7-11; 11am-10pm Wed-Sat, 4-9pm Sun & Mon) One of Oregon's best breweries is right here in town. There's limited inside seating, but on a warm summer evening you want to be outside on the front lawn with a tasty IPA and buffalo burger anyway. Pastas, salads and sandwiches dominate the menu.

JOSEPH

pop 1200

If ever there was a trendy Eastern Oregon town, it's Joseph. You can see its wealth right on the brick sidewalks, where well-groomed planter boxes and huge bronze statues sit proudly on every downtown corner. Many of the old storefronts are now glitzy boutiques, peddling everything from nature photos to artsy screen doors to huge, expensive bronzes. There seem to be more galleries than anything else, and Valley Bronze – one of the nation's largest foundries – anchors the artistic heart of this old frontier town.

Even while Joseph feels more like Santa Fe than your typical backcountry Western town, it has just enough boots-and-jeans street life to keep it from seeming completely fake. And simply heading a few blocks out of downtown brings you back into beautiful countryside – just a mile south is Wallowa Lake, a glacial basin flanked by gorgeous towering peaks. Joseph is also a good base for exploring the region's many other recreational highlights; there's even a tiny ski resort, **Ferguson Ridge**, about 8 miles away.

Chief Joseph Days (www.chiefjosephdays.com), held the last weekend of July, features a rodeo, Native American dancing and cowboy breakfasts. And if you're here in mid-August, don't miss the **Bronze Blues & Brews Festival** (www.bronzebluesbrews.com), which sees good jazz, microbrews and bronze sculptures on display.

The **Wallowa Valley Shuttle** (☎ 541-398-1563) has a bus service between Joseph, Enterprise and La Grande.

Sights & Activities

Joseph is most noted for its cast-bronze sculpture, thanks in part to **Valley Bronze** (☎ 541-432-7551; www.valleybronze.com; 18 S Main St; 10am-5pm Mon-Sat). Foundry tours are available for $15 per person.

The **Wallowa County Museum** (☎ 541-432-6095; 110 S Main St; adult/under 12yr $2.50/free; 10am-5pm Memorial Day-late Sep), housed in an 1888 bank building, is notable for its display on Nez Perce history.

The Wallowa-Whitman National Forest and the Hells Canyon National Recreation Area are laced with **mountain biking** trails, including the pretty, 10-mile Wagon Loop Rd. When snow falls, the area is good for **cross-country skiing**.

Sleeping & Eating

Accommodations in Joseph tend to run toward B&Bs, so consider staying 6 miles north in Enterprise (opposite) for better budget choices. In either case, reserve ahead on summer weekends – especially during festivals and events.

WALLOWA MOUNTAINS VISITORS CENTER

If you plan on spending any time camping, hiking, mountain biking, skiing and otherwise recreating in the area, be sure to stop in at the Wallowa Mountains Visitor Center (p338) in Enterprise. The rangers there are a wealth of information on the Wallowa Mountains, the Eagle Cap Wilderness Area, the Hells Canyon area and the Wallowa-Whitman National Forest. They have maps and hiking-trail details, and know the area's current road conditions – especially helpful in late fall, winter and early spring, when some passes are choked with snow.

Hurricane Creek Campground (☎ 541-426-5546; Mile 7, Hurricane Creek Rd; campsites $6) In summer the real action is at Wallowa Lake, but campers seeking peace should try this primitive but beautiful campground 7 miles south of Joseph. Bring water.

Indian Lodge Motel (☎ 541-432-2651; www.indianlodgemotel.com; 201 S Main St; d $73; ⊠ wi-fi) This is Joseph's only motel, with 16 neat plain rooms and a great downtown location. Reserve well in advance.

Chandler's Inn (☎ 541-432-9765; www.josephbedandbreakfast.com; 700 S Main St; d $87-132; ⊠ wi-fi) With more of a lodge feel than B&B, this homely and casual spot offers three varied guest rooms (a couple with two bedrooms) and a country-style breakfast. It's run by an American-English couple.

Belle Pepper B&B (☎ 541-432-0490, 866-432-0490; www.belelpepperbnb.com; 101 S Mill St; d $105-154; ⊠ wi-fi) Off the main street and on an acre of grounds is this colonial-style, no-nonsense B&B that embraces green practices such as recycled building materials, composting, low-flow faucets and organic products. There are three comfy rooms and a nice garden.

our pick **Bronze Antler B&B** (☎ 541-432-0230, 866-520-9769; www.bronzeantler.com; 309 S Main St; d $132-165; ⊠ wi-fi) This lovingly restored Craftsman home offers three elegant rooms each with its own bathroom, a port or sherry refreshment in the afternoon and friendly hosts who know the area well. A cat roams the premises.

La Laguna (☎ 541-432-0380; 100 N Main St; mains $7-12; 11am-9pm) You wouldn't think to find decent Mexican food in these parts, but here it is. Everything from chorizo burritos to chicken fajitas to spinach enchiladas are available, and if you're lucky the boisterous Angelica will be here rather than at her Enterprise branch.

Caldera's (☎ 541-432-0585; 300 N Lake St; mains $8-14; 8am-9pm Thu-Mon) This small but interesting café-restaurant is gorgeously decorated in an art-nouveau style. Grilled paninis, a few salads and meat dishes line the menu, along with plenty of java drinks and some pastries. Don't miss the stunning glass-tiled bathrooms. Open late May to mid-October.

Embers Brewhouse (☎ 541-432-2739; 206 N Main St; mains $8-15; 7am-9pm Sun-Thu, till 10pm Fri & Sat) Pizza, sandwiches, salads and microbrews all go down easy in this relaxed pub. On summer evenings the place to be is on the front deck, as seating is limited inside.

WALLOWA MOUNTAINS

Rising precipitously from the flatlands in Oregon's far northeastern corner, the Wallowas have 19 peaks over 9000ft. Ice Age glaciers carved sharp crags and deep canyons into the mountains, and the moraines of one such glacier now impound Wallowa Lake. Much of the high country, including the only remaining glacier (Alpine Glacier) and Eastern Oregon's highest peak (the 9838ft Sacajawea), is part of Eagle Cap Wilderness Area, a 715-sq-mile natural area studded with alpine meadows and lakes.

Trails, campgrounds and fishing holes are popular during the high season. In particular, the lovely state park at Wallowa Lake takes on a carnival atmosphere on summer weekends. Some secondary roads over the Wallowa Mountains are closed between November and May, so check ahead.

Wallowa Lake

Wallowa Lake was formed when glaciers plowed down out of the Wallowas, pushing huge piles of displaced rock. These rock moraines eventually stopped the progress of the glacier, which melted, creating a lake basin. Today the lake is surrounded by dramatic peaks, including the 9617ft Chief Joseph Mountain. Speaking of Chief Joseph, his gravesite is located near the north shore of Wallowa Lake, just a mile south of Joseph and right on the highway.

Pretty **Wallowa Lake State Park** (☎ 541-432-4185; 72214 Marina Lane) is the center of activities at the lake's south end. A swimming beach and a boat launch bustle madly in summer, and you can rent canoes and a variety of boats here. The best **hiking** is from the end of Wallowa Lake Rd.

The **Wallowa Lake Tramway** (☎ 541-432-5331; www.wallowalaketramway.com; 59919 Wallowa Lake Hwy; adult/4-11yr/12-17yr $20/13/17; 10am-4pm late May-Sep) leaves from Wallowa Lake and climbs 3700ft to the top of 8150ft Mt Howard. The 15-minute ride is thrilling enough, but the real rewards are the easy alpine hikes around Mt Howard's summit, with views onto Hells Canyon, the Wallowas and Idaho's Seven Devils.

SLEEPING & EATING

The lake's southern shore has several popular places to stay and eat. Reservations are essential in summer.

Wallowa Lake State Park (☎ 541-432-4185, 800-452-5687; 72214 Marina Lane; campsites/RV sites/yurts/cabin $17/21/29/80) This popular lakeside state park offers over 200 campsites, along with two yurts and one cabin. Flush toilets and showers are available.

Eagle Cap Chalets (☎ 541-432-4704; www.eaglecapchalets.com; 59879 Wallowa Lake Hwy; RV sites $28, d $102-128, cabins $102-180;) Choose from simple and unpretentious motel rooms, cabins or condos. RV sites are also available. There's a mini-golf course for the kids, and indoor pool and spa for everyone.

Flying Arrow Resort (☎ 541-432-2951; www.flyingarrowresort.com; 59782 Wallowa Lake Hwy; cabins $85-212; wi-fi) This resort is awesome, boasting 28 spacious cabins of all sizes, each with its own kitchen and many with a deck overlooking the Wallowa River. One six-bedroom lodge that sleeps 14 is available ($370).

Wallowa Lake Lodge (☎ 541-432-9821; www.wallowalakelodge.com; 60060 Wallowa Lake Hwy; d $95-170, cabins $133-232;) This 1923 lodge, on the shores of the lake, has both charming lodge rooms and rustic but comfortable lakeside cabins. Two-bedroom units are available. There's a great stone fireplace in the lobby, and a restaurant on the premises (see right).

our pick **Vali's Alpine Deli & Restaurant** (☎ 541-432-5691; 59811 Wallowa Lake Hwy; mains $10-14; 7pm & 9pm seatings Wed-Sun, Memorial Day-Labor Day) Hungarian specialties like cabbage rolls, chicken paprika, beef kabobs and schnitzel are all excellent here, though dishes change daily. Credit cards are not accepted, and reservations are required.

Wallowa Lake Lodge Dining Room (☎ 541-432-9821; 60060 Wallowa Lake Hwy; mains $16-22; 8-11am, 5:30-8pm) This old-fashioned dining room serves up fancy dishes like crab-stuffed halibut, grilled chicken and Mediterranean pasta. For breakfast ($6 to $8) there are hazelnut pancakes, Belgian waffles and blintzes.

WALLOWA MOUNTAIN LOOP ROAD

From Joseph, paved USFS Rd 39 skirts the eastern Wallowas and heads south to Hwy 86, just east of Halfway. It's a scenic drive (not really a loop) that links the northern and southern halves of the Wallowas. It also provides access to **Hells Canyon Overlook**, 3 miles off USFS Rd 39 on USFS Rd 3965, the only canyon viewpoint you can drive to over a paved surface.

It's 73 miles between Joseph and Halfway along this route. USFS Rd 39 is closed in winter (though it's groomed for snowmobiles and cross-country skiing) and can stay closed into early summer. There are trailheads and campsites along the way, but no gas stations or other services.

Eagle Cap Wilderness

Glacier-ripped valleys, high mountain lakes and marble peaks are some of the rewards that long-distance hikers find on overnight treks into the beautiful Eagle Cap Wilderness, nicknamed 'America's Little Switzerland.'

A major trailhead starts at the south end of Wallowa Lake Rd. One popular trail is the six-mile one-way jaunt to **Aneroid Lake**, where the remains of a cabin settlement add to the alpine lake's mystique. A longer trek is the **West Fork Trail**, which leads though springs and lakes to the Lake Basin (9 miles one way). From the upper Lostine Valley, or from USFS Rd 39's Sheep Creek Summit, there is easier day-hike access to the Eagle Cap's high country.

For easier, organized hiking consider using horses or llamas to help out. **Eagle Cap Wilderness Pack Station** (☎ 541-432-4145, 800-681-6222; www.eaglecapwildernesspackstation.com; 59761 Wallowa Lake Hwy) offers a variety of horseback trips, from hour-long rides to extended pack tours. For llama excursions, contact **Wallowa Llamas** (☎ 541-742-2961; www.wallowallamas.com; 36678 Allstead Lane, Halfway). They run three- to seven-day trips in the region.

Go skiing in the backcountry with **Wing Ridge Ski Tours** (☎ 800-646-9050; www.wingski.com; 65113 Hurricane Creek Rd, Enterprise). Their five-day Aneroid Lake trip features stays in rustic cabins, along with days of challenging skiing (intermediate or above) in stunning country.

HELLS CANYON

Over its 13-million-year life span, the Snake River, which neatly straddles the border between Oregon and Idaho, has carved out the deepest river gorge in North America – yes, at 8000ft from highest peak to river, it's deeper even than the Grand Canyon (though not nearly as dramatic). The river originates in Yellowstone National Park and ends at the Columbia River near Pasco, Washington – running over 1000 miles in total.

The prehistoric people who dwelled along Hells Canyon left pictographs, petroglyphs and pit dwellings. The Shoshone and Nez Perce tribes battled for dominance along this stretch of the Snake, with the Nez Perce winning out.

Relics of the mining era, from the 1860s to the 1920s, are also found throughout the canyon, and tumbledown shacks remain from the unlikely settlement attempts of turn-of-the-century homesteaders.

Hat Point

High above the Snake River, the Hat Point fire lookout tower (elevation 6982ft) offers great views. On each side of the canyon, mountains soar toward 10,000ft, with the Seven Devils on the Idaho side and the towering Wallowas on the Oregon side.

From Hat Point, a hiking trail edges off the side of the canyon. It's a steep 4 miles to another vista from the top of the river cliffs, then another 4 miles down to the river itself.

To reach Hat Point from Joseph, follow Hwy 350 about 30 miles to the little community of Imnaha. From here, a gravel road (narrow at times) climbs up the Imnaha River canyon to Hat Point. Allow at least two hours each way for the 24-mile drive from Imnaha to Hat Point; you'll be stopping for photos along the way. The road is generally open from late May until October.

Imnaha River Valley

Just west of Hells Canyon, the Imnaha River digs a parallel canyon that offers pastoral scenery in addition to astounding cliff faces.

The gravel Imnaha River Rd follows this narrow valley between the hamlet of Imnaha and the junction of USFS Rd 39 for about 40 miles. The lower valley (the northern end) is very dramatic, as the river cuts more and more deeply through stair-stepped lava formations. The upper valley is bucolic, with meadows and old farmhouses flanking the river – don't be surprised to come upon a cattle drive right on the road!

North of Imnaha, a gravel road continues for 20 miles to Cow Creek Bridge, where the **Imnaha River Trail** begins (4.5 miles one way). Two miles beyond the bridge is the start of the **Nee-Me-Poo Trail** (which traces the path of Chief Joseph and the Nez Perce); it climbs 3.5 miles to a viewpoint over the Snake River. The road ends 5 miles later at Dug Bar, where the 46-mile (one way) **Snake River Trail** begins.

Hells Canyon Dam

Hells Canyon's most spectacular scenery is perhaps along the Snake River itself, following 25 miles of paved road (Idaho's Rte 454) towards Hells Canyon Dam. Here dramatic canyon walls loom almost vertically – and you're driving right next to them. The road goes up the Idaho border but is accessed via the southern end of the Wallowa Mountain Loop, near Oxbow (previously known as Copperfield, in Oregon). Just past the dam the road ends at the **Hells Canyon Visitors Center** (☎ 541-785-3395; 8am-4pm summer only) and boat launch. Miles beyond here, the Snake drops 1300ft in elevation through wild scenery and equally wild rapids, and the area can only be accessed via jet boat or raft.

There's also a gravel road that goes up the Snake River on the Oregon side, but it stops short of the dam. It accesses Bureau of Land Management (BLM) land, and some trailheads and rustic campgrounds. There's no bridge linking this gravel road to Rte 454 over the Snake.

Hells Canyon Adventures (☎ 541-785-3352, 800-422-3568; www.hellscanyonadventures.com; 4200 Hells Canyon Dam Rd, Oxbow) is the area's main tour outfitter, running a variety of raft and boat trips from May through September. Reservations are required.

There are several good hiking trails on the way to the dam; Allison Creek (on the Idaho side) and Hells Canyon (on the Oregon side) are each 2 miles one way. Longer trails are possible; check with the Hells Canyon Visitors

Center, from where there's also a mile-long hike downriver.

See the boxed text on Hells Gate State Park (p216) for tour options across the border.

Sleeping

Enterprise, Joseph and Halfway are all day trips away from Hells Canyon, but you also have closer options to the area's various access points.

There's a free primitive campsite near Hat Point. Imnaha has food and water (and some basic RV sites), but for gas you'll have to go to Joseph. Five miles north of Imnaha is the fine **Imnaha River Inn** (☎ 541-577-6002, 866-601-9214; www.imnahariverinn.com; d $128); while 3 miles south is the **River House** (☎ 541-432-4075; www.wallowa-scenic-rentals.com/riverhouse.htm; $130), a three-bedroom house that requires a three-night minimum stay and easily sleeps six people.

Two campgrounds at the southern end of the canyon, **Ollokot** (campsites $8) and **Blackhorse** (campsites $8), are right on USFS Rd 39, midway between Halfway and Joseph.

There's plenty of camping in the Hells Canyon Dam area. Opt for rustic **BLM campsites** (free) on the Oregon side of the Snake River, or head up the Idaho side to pretty **Hells Canyon Park** (☎ 800-422-3143; campsites/RV sites $10/16). At Oxbow there's the pleasant **Copperfield Park** (☎ 800-422-3143; campsites/RV sites $10/16).

There are also two B&Bs in the Oxbow area, including the great-value **Hells Canyon B&B** (☎ 541-785-3373; www.hells-canyon-bed-and-breakfast.com; d $60) and the homey and casual **Hillside B&B** (☎ 541-785-3389; d $95).

HALFWAY

pop 320

An idyllic little town, Halfway lies on the southern edge of the Wallowa Mountains and is surrounded by beautiful meadows dotted with old barns and hay fields. It's a friendly spot with just enough tourist services to make it a decent base to explore the Hells Canyon Dam area. The **Pine Ranger Station** (☎ 541-742-7511; 38470 Pine Town Lane; 7:30-11:45am, 12:30-4:30pm Mon-Thu, till 3:30pm Fri) is 1 mile south of Halfway.

The **Pine Valley Museum** (☎ 541-742-5346; admission by donation; 10am-4pm Sat & Sun summer only) is located right in the middle of the town and has a few of the region's old photos and relics. It's open on weekdays and by request for a $5 fee.

Sleeping & Eating

Halfway Motel (☎ 541-742-5722; www.halfway-motel.com; 170 S Main St; RV sites $19, d $65-70) Both old and new rooms are available at this reasonable motel. Go for the newer ones on the 2nd floor (facing the back) to enjoy peaceful meadow views – number 209 is especially large and has more amenities. Rustic older rooms are smaller and cheaper. RV hookups are available.

our pick **Pine Valley Lodge** (☎ 541-742-2027; www.pvlodge.com; 163 N Main St; d incl breakfast $87-152; wi-fi) Halfway's fanciest accommodation, with seven stylish rooms in two buildings surrounded by flowery gardens. There's a great porch with wicker rocking chairs. One cabin also available.

Inn at Clear Creek Farm (☎ 541-742-2238; www.clearcreekfarm.biz; 48212 Clear Creek Rd; d $95) This beautiful inn, 4 miles north of Halfway, is also a working cattle ranch with a small pear orchard. It offers six elegant rooms, including a suite than sleeps five ($130), and meals are extra. No shoes are allowed inside, so bring your slippers!

Mimi's Café (☎ 541-742-4646; 241 S Main St; mains $6-10; 8am-2pm Thu & Fri, 8am-1pm & 5-8pm Sat) Halfway's best eatery is this small place run by a friendly family that serves up excellent scrambles, pancakes, paninis and salmon burgers.

BAKER CITY

pop 10,000

Back in the old days, Baker City was the largest metropolis between Salt Lake City and Portland, along with being the commercial and cultural capital of Eastern Oregon. The 1860s gold rush had helped establish the town, enriching its coffers while making it party-central for the region – a heady mix of miners, cowboys, shopkeepers and loggers kept the city's many saloons, brothels and gaming halls boisterously alive.

The good old times are long gone now, but the city's wide downtown streets and historical architecture recall its rich bygone days. Today travelers come not only for a peek at the city's swaggering history, but to explore the area's outdoor attractions. There's good skiing in winter, while fishing, hiking and boating are great in summer – and the Eagle Cap Wilderness and Wallowa Mountains aren't too far away.

Area events include the **Miners Jubilee** in mid-to-late July, with art and quilt shows, and a rodeo. In June there's the **Hells Canyon Rally** (www.hellscanyonrally.com), bringing hundreds of motorcycle aficionados into town for a motorcycle show and rides into the scenic surrounding region.

The **Visitors Bureau** (☎ 541-523-3356, 800-523-1235; www.visitbaker.com; 490 Campbell St; 8am-5pm Mon-Fri, till 4pm Sat, 9am-2pm Sun) has good information. Head to the **Baker Ranger District office** (☎ 541-523-4476; 3165 10th St; 7:45am-4:30pm Mon-Fri) for details on nearby hiking trails.

Greyhound buses stop at the **Baker Truck Corral** (☎ 541-523-5011; 515 Campbell St).

Sights & Activities

The **old downtown** retains much of its late 19th-century Victorian Italianate architecture. A brochure describing a walking tour of historic buildings in the city center is available from the visitors bureau. To ogle at the 80.4oz **Armstrong Nugget**, found in the area in 1913, visit the **US Bank** (2000 Main St) during regular banking hours.

Housed in a 1921 natatorium (indoor swimming pool) is the **Oregon Trail Regional Museum** (☎ 541-523-9308; 2480 Grove St; adult/senior $5/4.50; 9am-5pm Apr-Oct). On display are machinery and antiques from Baker City's frontier days, along with plenty of semiprecious stones, fossils and petrified wood. Don't miss the fluorescent rock room and 950lb crystal.

The **Historic Alder House** (☎ 541-523-9308; 2305 Main St; admission $5; 10am-2pm Fri-Mon Apr-Oct) is great if you like old houses full of original fixtures and antiques. Planning to visit both this museum and the Oregon Trail Regional Museum? Buy an $8 ticket for both.

The excellent **National Historic Oregon Trail Interpretive Center** (☎ 541-523-1843; www.oregontrail.blm.gov; 22267 Hwy 86; adult/senior $5/3.50; 9am-6pm Apr-Oct, 9am-4pm Nov-Mar) is the nation's foremost memorial to the pioneers who crossed the West along the Oregon Trail. Lying atop a hill 7 miles east of Baker City, it contains interactive displays, artifacts and films that stress the day-to-day realities of the pioneers. Outside you can stroll along the 4-mile interpretive path system and spot the actual Oregon Trail.

Anthony Lakes, some 30 miles northwest of Baker City, offers great scenery, along with camping and fishing. Hiking trails lead to several other small lakes, including a short but steep climb up Parker Creek to Hoffer Lakes (1 mile one way). Another short hike goes from **Elkhorn Crest Trail** up to Black Lake (1 mile one way). In winter, ski-heads should beeline to nearby **Anthony Lakes Mountain Resort** (☎ 541-856-3277; www.anthonylakes.com; 47500 Anthony Lakes Hwy; 9am-4pm Thu-Sun), which offers dry, fluffy powder and the highest base elevation in Oregon (7100ft). The resort grooms nearly 20 miles of cross-country trails.

Sleeping & Eating

Union Creek Campground (☎ 541-894-2393; Hwy 7 at Phillips Reservoir; campsites $12, RV sites $18-20) Located 19 miles southwest of Baker City is this pleasant campground in a conifer forest around a reservoir popular with fishermen and boaters.

Anthony Lakes Campground (☎ 541-894-2393; 47500 Anthony Lakes Hwy; campsites $12) Though it's 35 miles from town, this rustic but splendid campground is worth the drive (bring mosquito repellent). It's high up and opens only after the snow melts, so call first.

Bridge St Inn (☎ 541-523-6571, 800-932-9220; www.bridgestreetinn.com; 134 Bridge St; d $41; wi-fi) Rooms are a bit small and their layout eccentric, but the Nitty Gritty Dirt Band once slept here and that's worth something. And part of the cast and crew of *Paint Your Wagon* also stayed here. Get a room facing the back for peace.

A Beaten Path B&B (☎ 541-523-9230; 2510 Court Ave; d $82;) Located in a residential district is this friendly and eclectic B&B in a 1888 historical home. Two casual and comfortable Victorian-style rooms are available, but only one is rented at a time since there's one bathroom (unless you're willing to share the bathroom).

our pick **Geiser Grand Hotel** (☎ 541-523-1889, 888-434-7374; www.geisergrand.com; 1996 Main St; d $105-165; wi-fi) Baker City's downtown landmark and fanciest lodging is this meticulously restored Italian Renaissance Revival building. The elegant rooms are spacious and decorated with old-style furniture, while the restaurant offers fine food and has a stunning stained-glass ceiling. There's a great old saloon, too.

Mad Matilda's Coffeehouse (☎ 541-523-4588; 1917 Main St; mains $6-8; 7am-5:30pm Mon-Thu, till 8pm Fri, 8am-2pm Sat) This colorful café comes with 15ft tin ceilings, brick walls, eclectic retro furniture and artsy decor. It's a trendy place serving breakfast wraps, sandwiches and salads, and offers live music on weekends.

THE BLUE MOUNTAINS

Rising to the west from ranchland near Baker City, the Blue Mountains were responsible for the 1860s gold strikes that established towns such as Sumpter, Granite and Baker City. Ghost-town enthusiasts will find the Blue Mountains dotted with old mining camps, but there are also high mountain lakes, river canyons and hiking trails. And if you're crazy about trains, don't miss the narrow-gauge **Sumpter Valley Railroad** (www.svry.com).

A good way to explore the Blue Mountains is via the **Elkhorn Drive Scenic Byway**, which circles Elkhorn Ridge. It takes all day to properly explore this 106-mile loop that includes Baker City, Phillips Lake, Sumpter, Granite and Haines; it also skirts the Anthony Lakes area, which offers camping, fishing and hiking. Part of the loop (between Granite and Anthony Lakes) is closed in winter, so visit the Baker Ranger District (p344) in Baker City for road conditions and a map.

Barley Brown's Brewpub (☎ 541-523-4266; 2190 Main St; mains $12-18; 4-10pm Mon-Thu, till 11pm Fri & Sat) Baker City's only microbrew pub, with comfortable atmosphere boasting tin ceilings and plenty of wooden booths. The regular pub menu features interesting items like clam linguini, teriyaki salmon and BBQ ribs – wash it all down with one of the eight brews that are on tap.

Haines Steak House (☎ 541-856-3639; 910 Front St, Haines; mains $13-22; 5-9pm Mon, Wed & Thu, till 10pm Fri, 4-10pm Sat, 1-9pm Sun) Exceptional steaks are grilled up at this Western-themed restaurant, located 10 miles north of town in Haines. Good options are the T-bone, rib-eye or top sirloin; there's also prime rib and chicken strips. Vegetarians are plumb out of luck, other than the chuck wagon salad bar and some sides.

JOHN DAY

Smack near the middle of Eastern Oregon, this unpretentious, one-stoplight town strings along a narrow passage of the John Day River Valley. It's a utilitarian but decent enough place to base yourself while exploring the scenic region, and hosts a few interesting museums as well.

Get information at the **Chamber of Commerce** (☎ 541-575-0547; www.grantcounty.cc; 301 W Main St; 8am-5pm Mon-Fri) and the **Malheur National Forest Ranger Station** (☎ 541-575-3300; www.fs.fed.us/r6/malheur; 431 Patterson Bridge Rd; 7:45am-4:30pm Mon-Fri).

Don't miss the **Kam Wah Chung State Heritage Site** (☎ 541-575-2800; 250 NW Canton St; admission free; 9am-5pm) located in a building which served primarily as an apothecary for the noted Chinese herbalist and doctor, Ing Hay. But it was also a community center, temple, general store and opium den for the Chinese population that reworked the area's mine tailings. A nearby interpretive center offers a 19-minute video.

Rodeo lovers should visit the small **Grant County Ranch & Rodeo Museum** (☎ 541-575-5545; 241 E Main St; adult/child under 13 $3/free; 10am-4pm Mon, Thu & Sat), which showcases fine saddles and lots of rodeo photos. The friendly guys there really know the local rodeo and ranch scene. Call for off-hours visits.

Two miles south of downtown John Day, in the center of tiny Canyon City, the **Grant County Historical Museum** (☎ 541-575-0362; 101 S Canyon City Blvd; adult/7-18yr/senior $4/2/3.50; 9am-4:30pm Mon-Sat May-Sep) houses gold-rush memorabilia, lots of polished agates and some stuffed two-headed calves. Outside is frontier poet Joaquin Miller's cabin.

The **People Mover bus** (☎ 541-575-2370) has services to Bend.

Sleeping & Eating

See Sleeping & Eating under John Day Fossil Beds National Monument (p347) for other accommodation in the area.

Clyde Holliday State Park (☎ 541-932-4453, 800-452-5687; www.oregonstateparks.org; Hwy 26 milepost 155, Mt Vernon; campsites/RV sites/teepees $9/17/28) Six miles west of John Day, this pleasant, shady campground lies next to the John Day River, though it's also close to the road.

Blue Mountain Lodge (☎ 541-932-4451; 150 W Main St; d $50;) Located in Mt Vernon, 8 miles west of John Day, this good motel is old fashioned but comfy and cheap.

Dreamers Lodge (☎ 541-575-0526, 800-654-2849; 144 N Canyon Blvd; d $60; wi-fi) One of John Day's better value places, this friendly motel offers good-sized rooms (the ones with two beds are huge) and it's off the main drag and more sheltered.

Sonshine B&B (☎ 541-575-1827; www.sonshinebedandbreakfast.com; 210 NW Canton St; d $75-105; wi-fi) This small, friendly B&B is located right across from the Kam Wah Chung Museum and has four homey rooms; some share a bathroom, and one comes with a kitchen.

Strawberry Mountain Inn B&B (☎ 541-820-4522; www.strawberrymountaininn.com; 710 NE Front St; d $85-120;) Located just east of Prairie City near the Strawberry Mountain Wilderness, this beautiful B&B offers five romantic rooms and great meadow views. There's also a nice grassy garden out the back. Prairie City is 13 miles east of John Day.

Snaffle Bit (☎ 541-575-2426; 830 S Canyon City Blvd; mains $8-25; 11:30am-9pm Wed-Fri, 4-9pm Sat) John Day's best hamburgers are at this no-nonsense restaurant with a nice fountain patio. Also on the menu are salads, pasta, Mexican specialties, lots of steaks and decent margaritas.

Strawberry Mountain Wilderness

Named for the wild strawberries that thrive on its mountain slopes, the Strawberry Range is covered with ponderosa and lodgepole pines growing on glacier-chiseled volcanic peaks that are 15 million years old. The Strawberry Mountains contain deceptively high country: much of the wilderness is above 6000ft, and the highest peak – Strawberry Mountain – rises to 9038ft.

A popular and rewarding 2.5-mile round-trip hike winds up a steep valley to **Strawberry Lake**. A mile past the lake is **Strawberry Falls**. To reach the trailhead, follow the signs 11 miles south from Prairie City.

Circle around to the south side of the wilderness area on Hwy 14 and paved USFS Rds 65 and 16, past old ponderosa pines and wide meadows, to find more trails. Hike into **High Lake Basin** (2.6 miles round-trip) from a trailhead high up the mountainside. From USFS Rd 16, turn on USFS Rd 1640 toward Indian Springs Campground. The trailhead is 11 miles up a steep gravel road.

There are several good campgrounds, including **Trout Farm** (☎ 541-820-3311; County Rd 62; campsites $8), a lovely stream-side spot 15 miles south of Prairie City. Water is available.

JOHN DAY FOSSIL BEDS NATIONAL MONUMENT

Within the soft rocks and crumbly soils of John Day country lies one of the world's greatest fossil collections. Discovered in the 1860s by clergyman and geologist Thomas Condon, these fossil beds were laid down between six and 50 million years ago, when this area was a coastal plain with a tropical climate. Roaming the forests at the time were saber-toothed, feline-like nimravids, bear-dogs, pint-sized horses and other early mammals.

The fossils of more than 2200 different plant and animal species have been found here. The national monument includes 22 sq miles at three different units: Sheep Rock Unit, Painted Hills Unit and Clarno Unit. Each has hiking trails and interpretive displays. To visit all of the units in one day requires quite a bit of driving, as more than 100 miles separate the fossil beds.

Visit the excellent **Thomas Condon Paleontology Center** (☎ 541-987-2333; www.nps.gov/joda; 32651 Hwy 19, Kimberly; 9am-5:30pm) 2 miles north of US 26. Displays include a three-toed horse and petrified dung beetle balls, along with many other fossils and geologic history exhibits. It offers ranger-guided trips in summer.

The nearby **Cant Ranch House** offers a peek into settlers' early lives, and has picnic grounds and a riverside trail.

Sheep Rock Unit

Featuring the most walks and hikes, this unit is also closest to the Paleontology Center. Above loom majestic, layered mountains tilted and eroding into spectacular formations that date back 28 million years ago. Fossils are continually being exposed here.

From the **Blue Basin Trailhead** there are several hikes that lead out to the fossil formations. The **Island in Time Trail** is a well-maintained, mile-long path that climbs up a narrow waterway to a badlands-basin of highly eroded, uncannily green sediments. Fossils can be seen along the trail. Several other overlook trails lead to amazing vistas of the John Day Valley.

Painted Hills Unit

Because no cap rock protects them from erosion, the Painted Hills have eroded into low-slung, colorfully banded hills that were originally formed about 30 million years ago. A series of eruptions drifted into beds hundreds of feet deep, layering the brick-red, yellow, black, beige and ochre-hued ash that you now see. It's a fabulous and uncommon sight.

RAFTING THE JOHN DAY

From Clarno Bridge (on Hwy 218) to Cottonwood Bridge (on Hwy 206), a distance of 70 miles, the John Day River cuts a deep canyon through basaltic lava flows on its way to the Columbia River. No public roads reach the canyon here; along the river are the remains of homesteads, Native American petroglyphs and pristine wildlife habitats.

Plan to float the John Day in spring or early summer, when the toughest rapids are class-III or -IV, depending on the water levels. Most trips take four days and some rafters float the John Day on their own. Shuttle service and raft rentals are available from Service Creek Stage Stop (see Service Creek Lodge, below).

Among the companies that run trips are **Oregon Whitewater Adventures** (☎ 800-820-7238; www.oregonwhitewater.com), **Ouzel Outfitters** (☎ 800-788-7238; www.oregonrafting.com) and **Oregon River Experiences** (☎ 800-827-1358; www.oregonriver.com).

For specific advice, contact the **Prineville BLM office** (☎ 541-416-6700; www.or.blm.gov/Prineville; 3050 NE 3rd St).

Interpretive walks include the easy half-mile (round-trip) **Leaf Hill Trail**, which winds over the top of a banded hill, and the 1.5-mile (round-trip) **Carroll Rim Trail**, which goes to the top of a high bluff for great views.

Clarno Unit

The oldest, most remote fossil beds in the area are at the base of the John Day River's canyon. The 40-million-year-old Clarno Unit exposes mud flows that washed over an Eocene-era forest. The Clarno Formation eroded into white cliffs topped with spires and turrets of stone. Several 0.5-mile (round-trip) interpretive trails include one that passes through boulder-sized fossils containing logs, seeds and other remains of an ancient forest, and another that leads to the base of Palisades Cliff and some petrified logs.

Sleeping & Eating

Several campgrounds provide relatively easy access to the fossil beds. **Lone Pine** (campsites $8) and **Big Bend** (campsites $8) are nice riverside places on Hwy 402, north of the Sheep Rock Unit and 2 to 3 miles east of Kimberly.

The town of John Day itself (see p345) has a few good accommodation choices.

Historic Hotel Oregon (☎ 541-462-3027; 104 E Main St, Mitchell; d $29-79; ☒) An insanely good-value place is the lovely old HIstoric Hotel. It's in the little Western town of Mitchell, about 10 miles southeast of the Painted Hills Unit. Comfortable, homey rooms are featured, most with shared bathroom; dorm bunks available for $15 each. Continental breakfast is included.

Lands Inn B&B (☎ 541-934-2333; www.landsinn.net; 45457 Dick Creek Rd; camping per person $15, cabins incl breakfast$45-95; ☎ mid-May–mid-Oct) Possibly the world's only B&B with its own airstrip, this mountain hideaway, 13 miles south of Kimberly, has several comfortable cabins (some with shared bathhouse), plus some campsites. Meals are available onsite. Reservations are required.

Fish House Inn (☎ 541-987-2124, 888-286-3478; www.fishhouseinn.com; 110 Franklin St, Dayville; RV sites $20, d $55-70; ☒ ⁙) Five nice rooms are available at this inn in Dayville, less than 10 miles east of the Sheep Rock Unit. There's also a pleasant area for RVs. Note that no breakfast is served.

Service Creek Lodge (☎ 541-468-3331; www.servicecreekstagestop.com; 38686 Hwy 19; d $75; ☒ ⁙) Twenty miles southeast of Fossil, this fine lodge has six awesome and comfortable rooms with country quilts, a restaurant and rafting services. Rates include breakfast; reception is at the restaurant.

Wilson Ranches Retreat B&B (☎ 866-763-2227; www.wilsonranchesretreat.com; 16555 Butte Creek Rd, Fossil; d $75-95; ☒ ⁙) Seven tasteful guestrooms of all sizes are available at this good B&B, which is also a working ranch. There are comfortable common spaces, and a Cowboy Breakfast is served. It's located 2 miles northwest of Fossil.

Shaniko Hotel (☎ 541-489-3441, 800-483-3441; 4th & E Sts; d $79-110; ☒ ⁙) The charming ghost town of Shaniko is home to this historic hotel, which offers good, old-fashioned rooms and a café. Strangely enough, the hotel is only open from Thursday to Monday, and reception hours are only during the day.

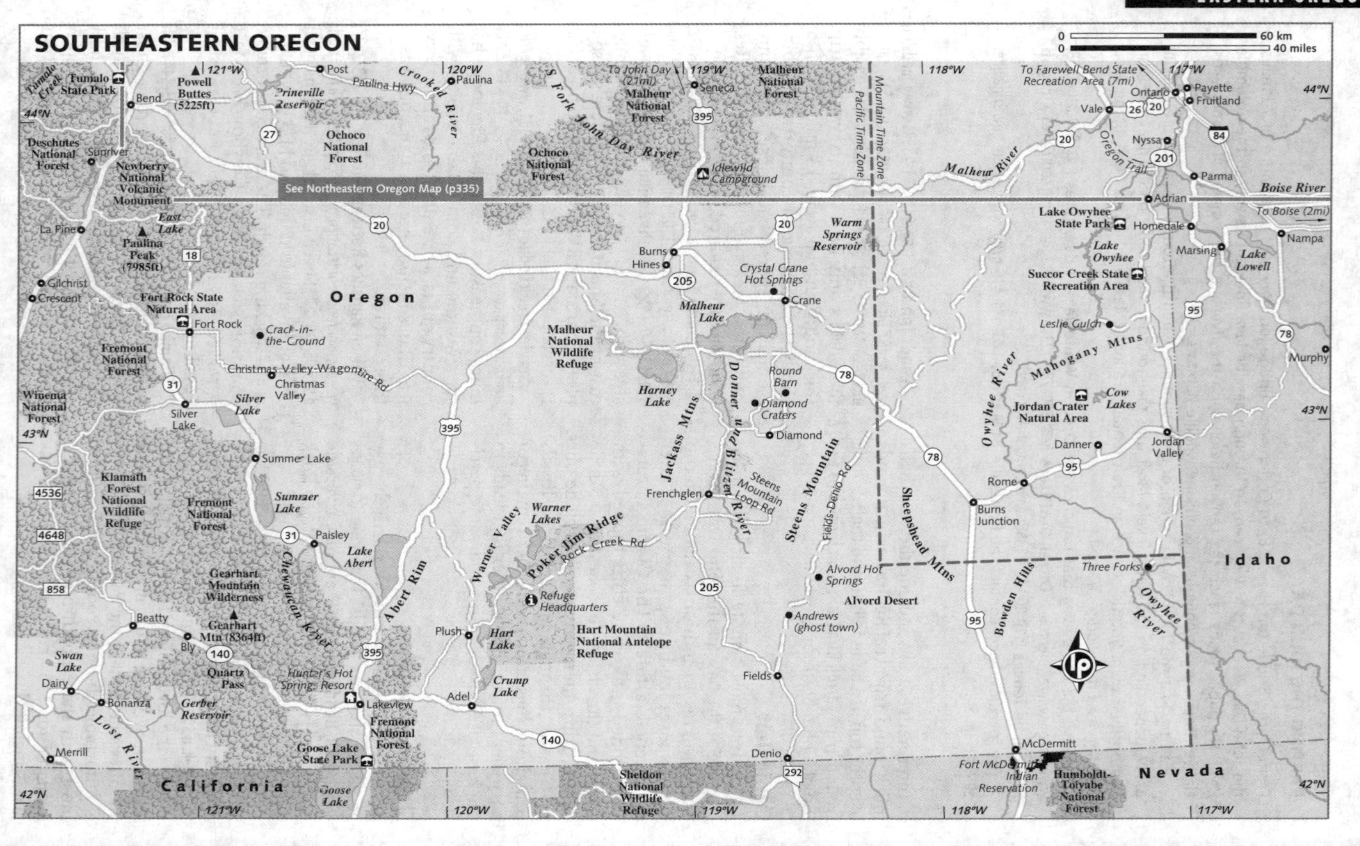
SOUTHEASTERN OREGON
0 60 km
0 40 miles
See Northeastern Oregon Map (p335)
Oregon
Idaho
Nevada
California
Mountain Time Zone
Pacific Time Zone
To Farewell Bend State Recreation Area (7mi)
To Boise (2mi)
To John Day (21mi)
Boise River
Malheur River
Owyhee River
S Fork John Day River
Crooked River
Chewaucan River
Donner und Blitzen River
Lost River
Tumalo Creek
Ontario
Payette
Fruitland
Parma
Nampa
Vale
Nyssa
Adrian
Homedale
Marsing
Lake Lowell
Murphy
Jordan Valley
Oregon Trail
Lake Owyhee State Park
Lake Owyhee
Succor Creek State Recreation Area
Leslie Gulch
Mahogany Mtns
Cow Lakes
Jordan Crater Natural Area
Danner
Rome
Burns Junction
Three Forks
Bowden Hills
McDermitt
Fort McDermitt Indian Reservation
Humboldt-Toiyabe National Forest
Sheepshead Mtns
Alvord Desert
Alvord Hot Springs
Andrews (ghost town)
Fields-Denio Rd
Steens Mountain
Steens Mountain Loop Rd
Fields
Denio
Warm Springs Reservoir
Malheur National Forest
Seneca
Idlewild Campground
Crystal Crane Hot Springs
Crane
Round Barn
Diamond Craters
Diamond
Malheur Lake
Harney Lake
Burns
Hines
Jackass Mtns
Frenchglen
Malheur National Wildlife Refuge
Ochoco National Forest
Paulina
Paulina Hwy
Post
Prineville Reservoir
Powell Buttes (5225ft)
Bend
Tumalo State Park
Deschutes National Forest
Sunriver
Newberry National Volcanic Monument
East Lake
Paulina Peak (7985ft)
La Pine
Gilchrist
Crescent
Fort Rock State Natural Area
Fort Rock
Crack-in-the-Ground
Christmas Valley
Christmas Valley-Wagontire Rd
Silver Lake
Summer Lake
Fremont National Forest
Winema National Forest
Klamath Forest National Wildlife Refuge
Sumner Lake
Paisley
Lake Abert
Abert Rim
Warner Valley
Warner Lakes
Poker Jim Ridge
Rock Creek Rd
Refuge Headquarters
Hart Mountain National Antelope Refuge
Hart Lake
Crump Lake
Plush
Adel
Sheldon National Wildlife Refuge
Lakeview
Hunter's Hot Spring Resort
Goose Lake State Park
Goose Lake
Gearhart Mountain Wilderness
Gearhart Mtn (8364ft)
Quartz Pass
Gerber Reservoir
Bly
Beatty
Bonanza
Swan Lake
Dairy
Merrill
44°N
43°N
42°N
117°W
118°W
119°W
120°W
121°W

SUCCOR CREEK & LESLIE GULCH

It takes a little doing to get to the wildly eroded Owyhee River country, but sections of this 35-mile gravel route are unforgettable. Running between Adrian and a junction with US 95, 18 miles north of Jordan Valley, it passes grand desert landscapes and bare rock peaks.

Follow the road south from near Adrian, through sagebrush and rolling hills, and after 10 miles it will start dropping onto Succor Creek. A couple of miles later you'll see vertical walls of volcanic tuff hundreds of feet high. The **Succor Creek State Recreation Area** sits at the other end of the canyon, with basic campsites (no water), informal hiking trails and stunning scenery.

The scenery is even more spectacular at **Leslie Gulch**, located further south on a 16-mile dead-end side branch off the main gravel road. A narrow creek channel goes through vividly colored volcanic rock eroded into amazing pinnacles and turreted formations, at last reaching the popular Lake Owyhee Reservoir. Rock climbing is possible, but drilling into the rock is not allowed. There's primitive camping in the area; watch for rattlesnakes.

Driving on gravel roads is slow going, so leave yourself plenty of time and take plenty of food and water.

ONTARIO

pop 11,250

Oregon's most easterly city, Ontario and its environs are often considered to be an extension of Idaho's fertile Snake River valley. The Malheur, Payette and Owyhee Rivers join the Snake's wide valley here, with irrigated farms producing a variety of crops – the region's economic backbone. The city itself is a bit homely and not worth more than a brief stop on your way somewhere more exciting.

Ontario shares the same time zone, Mountain Standard Time, with Idaho (it's one hour ahead of Pacific Standard Time). For tourist information visit the **Chamber of Commerce** (☎ 541-889-8012; www.ontariochamber.com; 676 SW 5th Ave; 8am-5pm Mon-Fri); it's located right at the Four Rivers Cultural Center.

A far cry from your typical small-town museum, the **Four Rivers Cultural Center** (☎ 541-889-8191; www.4rcc.com; 676 SW 5th Ave; adult/6-14yr & senior $4/3; 9am-5pm Mon-Sat) celebrates the region's diversity, focusing on Paiute Native Americans, Basque sheepherders, and Japanese- and Mexican-American farm workers.

Greyhound and Amtrak Thruway buses stop at the **Pilot Truck Stop** (☎ 541-889-5112; 653 East Idaho Ave).

Sleeping & Eating

Farewell Bend State Recreation Area (☎ 541-869-2365; www.oregonstateparks.org; I-84 exit 353; campsites/RV sites/cabins $15/17/38) A good camping spot relatively close to Ontario is this large oasis at the Snake River's Brownlee Reservoir, 25 miles northwest of town.

Stockmans Motel (☎ 541-889-4446; 81 SW 1st St; d $44;) It's not the best nor the worst place in town, but it's cheap and clean, with good budget rooms and convenience store nearby.

Creek House B&B (☎ 541-823-0717; www.creekshouse.com; 717 SW 2nd St; d $100-142; wi-fi) This lovingly restored, historic home offers four fine rooms, each with private bathroom. There are plenty of unique details here – check out the antique mailbox wine holder. The hosts are friendly and warm.

Brewsky's Broiler (☎ 541-889-3700; 23 SE 1st Ave; mains $7-12; 10am-midnight Mon-Sat) Experience family-friendly dining at this restaurant near the tracks. Burgers, sandwiches and Mexican specialties dominate the menu, and there's airy outside seating out front.

JORDAN VALLEY

pop 230

The closest thing to civilization in the southeastern corner of Oregon is tiny Jordan Valley. Known for its Basque heritage, this pit stop has an interesting rebuilt *frontón,* a stone ball court used for playing the traditional Basque game of *pelota.* There are a couple of motels (both with check-in at gas stations) and a surprisingly good restaurant.

Basque Station Motel (☎ 541-586-9244; 801 Main St; d $49;) is nothing fancy, with large rooms overlooking a serene meadow out the back.

Order steak, burgers and sandwiches at **Old Basque Inn** (☎ 541-586-2800; 306 Wroten St; mains $11-18; 7am-3pm, 5-9pm Mon-Fri, 5-10pm Sat, 8am-3pm Sun), an old Basque boarding house; there are a few Basque dishes as well.

RAFTING ON THE OWYHEE

The southern stretch of the Owyhee River, below Three Forks, consists of a number of class-IV rapids. Downstream from Rome the river is less turbulent, but the scenery – highly eroded desert cliffs – is top-notch. Only in spring (March through May) does the Owyhee contain enough water to be safely rafted.

Guided trips are offered by **Oregon Whitewater Adventures** (www.oregonwhitewater.com) and **Wapiti River Trips** (www.wapitiriverguides.com), among others.

BURNS

pop 2750

Named by a wistful early settler for Scottish poet Robert Burns, this isolated high desert town was established in 1883 as the watering hole and social center for incoming settlers and roving cowhands. Today, Burns has plenty of services and is a convenient jumping-off point for trips south into the Malheur National Wildlife Refuge and Steens Mountain area.

Get information at the **Chamber of Commerce** (☎ 541-573-2636; www.harneycounty.com; 76 E Washington St; 9am-noon & 1-5pm Mon-Fri), the **Bureau of Land Management office** (BLM; ☎ 541-573-4400; www.blm.gov/or/districts/burns; 28910 US 20W, Hines; 7:45am-4:30pm Mon-Fri) and the **Immigrant Creek Ranger District** (☎ 541-573-4300; 265 US 20S, Hines; 8am-4:30pm Mon-Fri).

Porter Stage Lines (☎ 541-573-5500; www.kokkola-bus.com/PorterStageLines2.html; 63 N Buena Vista Ave) runs out of Figaro's Pizza.

Lots of historical Western memorabilia are on exhibit at the **Harney County Historical Museum** (☎ 541-573-5618; www.burnsmuseum.com; 18 West D St; adult/6-12yr/senior $4/1/3; 10am-4pm Tue-Fri, 10am-2pm Sat Apr-Sep).

The rustic resort of **Crystal Crane Hot Springs** (☎ 541-493-2312; www.cranehotsprings.com; 59315 Hwy 78; 9am-9pm Mon-Sat, 2-9pm Sun), 25 miles southeast of Burns and 3 miles west of Crane, is a little oasis and worth a stop. The springs flow into a large pond ($3.50 day use) and are also piped into wooden tubs in small private bathhouses ($7.50 per person per hour).

Sleeping & Eating

Crystal Crane Hot Springs has five simple **cabins** (d $40-50), some with shared bathrooms, and a **campground** (campsites $12, RV sites $16-18).

Idlewild Campground (☎ 541-573-4300; Hwy 395; campsites $10) The closest public campground to Burns is here, 20 miles north of town on Hwy 395, in the Malheur National Forest.

Silver Spur Motel (☎ 541-573-2077; 789 N Broadway Ave; d $41; wi-fi) Your typical budget motel, with plain, small rooms and a manager with personality.

Sage Country Inn (☎ 541-573-7243; www.sagecountryinn.com; 351-1/2 W Monroe St; d $99; wi-fi) Burns' most charming lodging by far, this beautiful old house has three well-furnished rooms, each with its own bathroom. Grassy gardens surround the place, and it's located right near downtown.

Broadway Deli (☎ 541-573-7020; 530 N Broadway Ave; sandwiches $6-8; 8:30am-4pm Mon-Fri, 11:30am-3pm Sat) Good sandwiches and salads are sold at this small, simple deli. Soups, smoothies and homemade pies and cakes are also available.

MALHEUR NATIONAL WILDLIFE REFUGE

South of Burns, covering 290 sq miles of lake, wetland and prairie, is this important breeding and resting refuge for birds traveling along the Pacific Flyway. Six miles east of Hwy 205 on a side road is the **Refuge Headquarters** (☎ 541-493-2612; 8am-4pm Mon-Thu, till 3pm Fri & Sat), which has information, maps, a little museum and good bird-watching on Malheur Lake.

The refuge's two big, shallow lakes attract waterfowl, but the best place for wildlife-viewing is often south along the Donner und Blitzen River, where wide, grassy marshes and ponds shelter many animals. The gravel Central Patrol Rd runs between the refuge headquarters and Frenchglen, paralleling the river and providing 35 miles of good access into the backcountry. A few walks (most of them short) lead to ponds, a canal and reservoir; many are along the Central Patrol Rd. Snag a brochure at the refuge headquarters for details.

Waterfowl migration at Malheur peaks in March, shorebirds arrive in April, and songbirds wing-in during May. During summer, waterfowl families skim across the ponds and lakes. In fall, birds come through on their way south. Mosquitoes are around most of the time, so bring repellant.

Adjacent to the wildlife refuge, 55 miles south of Burns and east of Hwy 205, is **Diamond Craters**, a slightly underwhelming area of volcanic craters, cinder cones and other lava formations that were formed about 2500 years ago. Pick up a brochure for a self-guided tour from the BLM office in Hines to sniff out the highlights.

Northeast of the Diamond Craters area and a mile off Lava Bed Rd is Pete French's **Round Barn**, an impressive (though a bit decrepit) 100ft-wide structure used to buck out broncos in the glory days of the open range. A nearby fancy **gift shop** (☎ 888-493-2420; 🕑 9am-5pm) provides a commercial angle to this unique attraction.

Sleeping & Eating

Burns has a decent selection of budget lodging (see opposite).

Malheur Field Station (☎ 541-493-2629; www.malheurfieldstation.org; 34848 Sodhouse Lane; RV sites/dm $16/20, trailers d $60-100; ⊠) Four miles west of the refuge headquarters, this collection of rustic buildings offers RV hookups, simple dormitories, kitchenette trailers and no-nonsense meals (reserve ahead). Bring your own bedding, a towel (linen rental is $5), toiletries and flashlight – lights out at 10pm!

Hotel Diamond (☎ 541-493-1898; www.central-oregon.com/hoteldiamond; 10 Main St; d $68-90; ⊠) This small but beautiful hotel, located in the hamlet of Diamond, is decorated with antiques and offers eight lovely rooms with quilt bedspreads. Both new and older rooms are available, and some share bathrooms. Continental breakfast is included, and dinners available to guests and visitors alike (reservations required).

STEENS MOUNTAIN

The highest peak in southeastern Oregon, Steens Mountain (9773ft) is part of a massive, 30-mile-long fault-block range that was formed about 15 million years ago. On the western slope of the range, Ice Age glaciers bulldozed trenches that formed massive U-shaped gorges and hanging valleys. To the east, 'the Steens' – as the range is usually referred to – drop off to the Alvord Desert, 5000ft below.

Beginning in Frenchglen, the 66-mile **Steens Mountain Loop Rd** is Oregon's highest road and a good way to access the range's best sights, providing awesome overlooks and access to some hiking trails. You'll need a high-clearance vehicle in certain sections, however – the road gets slower and rougher the further you go in. You'll start amid sagebrush, then pass through a band of junipers into aspen forests, and finally into fragile rocky tundra.

The loop is open as weather allows, July through October – check road conditions with the Burns BLM office (see opposite). If you happen to be in the area outside these months or have a low-clearance vehicle, consider seeing the Steens via the flat eastern road through the Alvord Desert (below). Take a full gas tank and be prepared for weather changes at any time of year.

Another option is to take a guided tour, which can include lodging; **Steens Mountain Packers** (☎ 541-495-2315, 800-977-3995; www.steensmountains.com; 39269 Hwy 205, Frenchglen) offers interpretive tours of the loop road, horseback-riding trips, wild-horse viewing excursions and even cross-country skiing packages.

Sleeping & Eating

Frenchglen (population 15) has one hotel with a dining room, a campsite, a small store and not much else. There are camping options on the Steens Mountain Loop Rd, such as the BLM's pretty **Page Springs**. A couple other campgrounds, further into the loop, are accessible just in summer; only Page Springs is open year round. Water is available at all of these campgrounds (campsites $6 to $8). Free backcountry (or 'dispersed') camping is also allowed in the Steens.

Steens Mountain Resort (☎ 541-493-2415, 800-542-3765; www.steensmountainresort.com; N Steens Mountain Loop Rd; campsites/RV sites $15/25, cabins $65-160; ⊠ ⊡) Just before Page Springs, this 'resort' has nine decent single-wide trailers of various sizes spread out over a sparse hillside with low trees. Showers are available to nonguests from 9am to 5pm ($6).

Frenchglen Hotel (☎ 541-493-2825; fghotel@yahoo.com; 39184 Hwy 205, Frenchglen; d $67-100; 🕑 Mar 15-Oct 31; ⊠) This historic hotel dates from the 1910s and features eight small but cute rooms, all sharing outside bathrooms. A newer section of the hotel has five rooms, each with private bathroom. Dinners ($12, reservations required) are family style and served promptly at 6:30pm. Reserve ahead.

ALVORD DESERT

Once a large 200ft-deep lake, the stunning Alvord Basin is now a series of playas – white alkali beds that have resulted from centuries of evaporation. They alternate startlingly with irrigated alfalfa fields, sagebrush prairies and old ranches, while Steens Mountains loom dramatically above.

WILD SYMBOLS OF THE WEST

One of the highlights you might experience while exploring the Steens could be spotting a herd of wild mustangs. Descended from domesticated horses that escaped from Native Americans, early Spanish explorers and pioneers, these free-roaming herds are managed by the BLM, who cull the animals (usually for adoption) to keep them healthy, maintain desired characteristics and prevent overpopulation.

Several different herds can be seen, each with their own distinctive markings. The most famous bunch are the Kiger mustangs, who were discovered in 1977 during a round-up and are considered to have descended directly from original Spanish stock. They number less than 150 and are generally dun in color, sometimes sporting zebra-like markings on their legs and a dark dorsal stripe. Their rugged handsomeness and vitality attracted the attention of DreamWorks, whose animated 2003 film *Spirit: Stallion of the Cimarron* was based on a Kiger mustang.

Keep your eyes peeled as you explore the northern reaches of the Steens (there's a Kiger Wild Horse Viewing Area 11 miles southeast of Diamond, the nearest town). If you're lucky, you might spot some Kigers in the wild ranges of the untamed West.

The 75-mile gravel Fields–Denio Rd, between the community of Fields and Hwy 78, is well maintained and open all year. It makes a good alternative drive to the Steens Mountain Loop Rd, which is open only in summer and fall.

Directly below the summit of the Steens, a few miles north of the near-ghost town of Andrews and about a hundred yards east of the Fields–Denio Rd, is **Alvord Hot Springs** (look for the small metal shelter – it's hard to miss). As at all free, public hot springs, be respectful of other users.

For a good 3-mile **hike** up Pike Creek, look for a dirt road 1.5 miles north of Alvord Hot Springs and head west 1 mile; park at the juniper tree growing out of a boulder. There is an old cabin and an abandoned mine along this hike, which can involve two creek crossings; it ends up at a tidy campground.

There's free dispersed **camping** around the edges of the Alvord Desert and beneath the east rim of Steens Mountain. Bring food, water and sun protection. In the hamlet of **Fields**, the small store and café are a good place to stop for gas, a burger and excellent milkshakes. There's also camping and a tiny **inn** (☎ 877-225-9424; www.alvordinn.com; d $60-70).

HART MOUNTAIN NATIONAL ANTELOPE REFUGE

From the tiny town of Plush, Hart Mountain Rd crosses the Warner Lakes Basin and climbs into the spectacular, near-vertical Hart Mountain fault block (peak elevation over 8000ft). The road emerges onto the prairie-like expanses of the Hart Mountain National Antelope Refuge. Roughly 2800 pronghorn antelope are protected within the refuge's 435 sq miles – a mere shadow of the millions of pronghorns that once roamed North America – but at least their population is now steadily growing.

Pronghorns are not true antelopes, and have horns rather than antlers, shedding only the outer hairy sheath and growing a new covering each year. Pronghorns are the world's second-fastest land animal (after the cheetah), having been clocked at over 50mph.

The refuge also protects bighorn sheep, reintroduced to Hart Mountain in the 1970s and now living on the steep western side of the refuge. Cougar, bobcat, coyote, mule deer and a wide variety of birds (including sage grouse) inhabit the area, with plenty of waterfowl visiting the Warner Lakes Basin below.

Hart Mountain has an extensive network of 4WD trails and single-tracks through isolated areas, making for good hiking and mountain biking. Destinations include **Petroglyph Lake**, which is just over 2 miles from the refuge's headquarters – though you can drive to within a mile (or right up to the lake in a high-clearance vehicle). A short loop around the lake makes for great petroglyph-spotting. You can also drive south from the headquarters toward Blue Sky, park at **Lookout Point** and start on the **Skyline Trail** (open in summer), which climbs for 5 miles before hitting a ridge and great views.

The refuge's **headquarters** (☎ 541-947-2731) is often unstaffed, but you can pick up brochures at any time and utilize the area's only potable water and toilet facilities. Pitch a tent at the **Hot Springs Campground** (camping free), about 4 miles south of headquarters. There's a lovely

DETOUR: OREGON TO BOISE ALONG THE I-84

If you take I-84 southeastwards out of Oregon and into Idaho, you'll bump into the buzzing city of Boise. With an outdoors slant and hassle-free vibe, this city, where the desert meets the mountains, is more than a gateway to Idaho's wilder climes – it holds its own as a destination. Much of its late-19th-century architecture remains, cafés and restaurants stay open late, and crowds from nightspots spill onto the streets on hot summer nights. And in recent years more than a few magazines have named it as one of America's top places to live. Needless to say, it's worth the detour.

Boise has the largest population of Basque descendents outside of Europe's Basque country. Along Grove St between 6th St and Capitol Blvd, the Basque Block commemorates the early Basque pioneers. You can visit the **Basque Museum & Cultural Center** (☎ 208-343-2671; www.basquemuseum.com; 611 Grove St; admission free; 🕑 10am 4pm Tue-Fri, 11am-3pm Sat).

Built in 1905, the architecturally impressive **state capitol** (☎ 208-334-5174; 700 W Jefferson St) is the only US statehouse heated by geothermal water. Riverfront Julia Davis Park contains the **Idaho Historical Museum** (☎ 208-334-2120; 610 N Julia Davis Dr; admission $2; 🕑 9am-5pm Mon-Sat, 1-5pm Sun), which is great for a real look into the Old West and the Oregon Trail.

In the foothills above town hit the **Ridge to Rivers Trail System** (www.ridgetorivers.org), offering 75 miles of scenic to strenuous hiking and mountain-biking routes.

In summer, rent tubes or rafts at **Barber Park** (☎ 208-343-6564; Warm Spring Rd; tube rental $6) and float 5 miles down Boise River.

wooded creek plus an open-air bathhouse that traps a hot spring – just the thing you'll need after a dusty day of exploring.

If you're just passing through, allow two to three hours to travel the 75 miles between Plush and Frenchglen (about 50 miles of this is on a slow gravel surface) and make sure you have plenty of gas. Call in winter or after heavy rains to check the refuge's roads, which can be impassable at times.

LAKEVIEW

pop 2700

There's no longer any lake in view here, but at an elevation of 4800ft, Lakeview is 'the tallest town in Oregon.' It's also known as the 'hang gliding capital of the west,' with surrounding towering fault-block rims and prevailing westerly winds bringing hundreds of aficionados for summertime hang-gliding and paragliding events.

Those not interested in hovering about in the sky can visit some fun **hot springs** just outside town. There's also the **Schminck Memorial Museum** (☎ 541-947-3134; 126 South E St; 🕑 10am-4pm Tue-Sat Jun-Aug), which holds pioneer relics including pressed-glass goblets, china dolls and a few Native American artifacts. Opening days are limited outside summer.

For information see the **Chamber of Commerce** (☎ 541-947-6040; www.lakecountychamber.org; 126 North E St; 🕑 8am-5pm Mon-Fri, 9am-5pm Sat & Sun) or the **Lakeview Ranger District office** (☎ 541-947-2151; www.fs.fed.us/r6/frewin; 1301 S G St; 🕑 7:45am-4:30pm Mon-Fri). The BLM office is at the same telephone and address.

Sleeping & Eating

Goose Lake State Park (☎ 541-947-3111; www.oregonstateparks.org; US 395 at the state line; campsites & RV sites $16) This fine campground is 14 miles south of Lakeview (right on the Californian border) and offers wildlife-watching and boating opportunities.

Lakeview Lodge (☎ 541-947-2181; www.lakeviewlodgemotel.com; 301 N G St; d $62; wi-fi) Run by a British couple, this comfortable motel has good, spacious rooms; some featuring sofas. All have fridge and microwave, and there's a Jacuzzi for all guests to use.

Hunter's Hot Springs Resort (☎ 541-947-4142; www.huntersresort.com; US 395 N; d $70-90; wi-fi) This homespun resort, 1.5 miles north of town, offers a hot mineral swimming pool ($5 for nonguests) and a chance to eye the Pacific Northwest's only hot-water geyser, which erupts every minute or so (depending on the water table). Rooms are motel-like and unpretentious.

Eagle's Nest (☎ 541-947-4824; 117 N E St; mains $5-7; 🕑 11am-9pm) This old-time locals' spot is hardly fancy, serving up things like fish sticks, Jalapeño poppers, deep-fried zucchini and (interestingly enough) frogs' legs. Get similar food at the attached lounge next door, which has longer hours.

Vancouver, Whistler & Vancouver Island

From Zen-calm ferries sliding across glassy inlets between quirky island communities where fresh-caught seafood is always the main meal to a buzzing, mountain-ringed metropolis warmed by its international élan and laid-back approach to life, southern British Columbia (BC) is a smorgasbord of life-affirming experiences for most visitors.

Eminently worthy as a side-trip for those traveling up from the US or as a starting point for a cross-border Pacific Northwest odyssey, the region's highlights – Vancouver, Vancouver Island, the Sunshine Coast, Whistler and the Southern Gulf Islands – quickly explain why Canada's third-largest province is nicknamed 'Beautiful BC.'

Set your camera to 'panoramic' to shoot jaw-dropping images of snow-crowned mountains, shimmering lakes, sparkling waterfalls, breathtaking glaciers, slender fjords, lush rain forests and tree-covered islands. But it's not just about the great outdoors. Challenging BC's nature-hugging label, Vancouver is a by-word for cosmopolitanism, mixing cuisines and cultures from Asia and beyond, while vibrant smaller communities like Vancouver Island's Victoria are increasingly driven by their student populations, ensuring they don't just rely on their colonial past. Culture vultures will also enjoy dipping into the area's vibrant First Nations heritage.

With Vancouver hosting the 2010 Olympic and Paralympic Winter Games, it's worth recalling that BC has long been a hotbed of activity for those who like a little thrill-seeking in their holidays. Olympic co-host Whistler is a world-renowned ski and snowboarding resort; Vancouver Island's tempestuous west coast is a surf-dude capital; and hikers, cyclists, kayakers and campers are kept blissfully occupied on the Sunshine Coast and throughout the wider BC region.

Please note that all prices in this chapter are given in Canadian dollars unless otherwise indicated. You'll also notice that, unlike other chapters, distances here are given in metric units.

HIGHLIGHTS

- Stretching the legs with a seawall stroll around Vancouver's **Stanley Park** (p359)
- Scoffing juicy local fruit and piquant cheese at the Salt Spring Island's **Saturday Market** (p404)
- Skiing the slopes at **Whistler** (p376) and enjoying a warming après beverage while rubbing aching muscles
- Sampling some malty regional brews at a downtown Victoria **bar** (p389) or two
- Drinking in the wild, untamed beauty of **Cape Scott Provincial Park** (p403) on Vancouver Island's remote northern tip
- Exploring quirky communities by kayaking along the **Sunshine Coast** (p379)

VANCOUVER

pop 2.1 million

It's Western Canada's largest city, a magnet for 8.7 million annual visitors and host of the 2010 Olympic and Paralympic Winter Games, but Vancouver is best known around the world as a utopia of *joie de vivre* ringed by dense waterfront forest and looming snow-topped mountains.

Whether you're circumnavigating Stanley Park's sea-to-sky vistas, straining your neck as you stroll among ancient Douglas fir trees, skiing atop a mountain overlooking the downtown sprawl or kayaking along the crenulated coastline with its glimpses of mirrored tower blocks, outdoor Vancouver's appeal is undeniable. But for downtown wanderers who like dipping into heart-and-soul neighborhoods, the city turns out to be an unexpected delight for urban adventurers.

From the student-chic shopping district of South Main, the former hippy community of Kitsilano and the loft-living Yuppies of Yaletown to the bohemian coffee-suppers of Commercial Dr, the gay-friendly streets of the West End and the clamorous thoroughfares of Chinatown, the city is a smorgasbord of explorable areas, all best encountered on foot.

This diversity is Vancouver's main strength and a major reason why visitors keep coming back. If you're a first-timer, soak in the breathtaking vistas and hit the verdant forests whenever you can, but save time to join the locals and to head off the beaten path. It's in these places that you'll discover what really makes this beautiful metropolis tick.

BEST OF VANCOUVER

- Best view: Sunset at **Third Beach** (p359)
- Best walk: **Stanley Park seawall** (p359)
- Best dinner: **C Restaurant** (p369)
- Best pub: **Six Acres** (p372)
- Best oddity: The forensic coroners exhibit at the **Vancouver Police Centennial Museum** (p363)

HISTORY

Historians say First Nations people thrived in this area for as long as 16,000 years before Spanish explorers arrived in the late 1500s. When Captain George Vancouver of the British Royal Navy sailed up in 1792, he met a couple of Spanish captains who informed him of their country's long-standing claim on the region. But it was Britain's territorial demands that eventually won out, and when fur traders and gold-rush prospectors began arriving in their thousands in the 1850s, the Brits officially claimed the area as a colony.

Entrepreneur John 'Gassy Jack' Deighton seized the development initiative in 1867 by opening a bar on the forested shores of Burrard Inlet. This triggered a rash of growth nicknamed 'Gastown' that became the forerunner of modern-day Vancouver. Not every thing went to plan for the fledgling city: it was almost completely destroyed in the 1886 Great Fire. But a prompt rebuild followed and a new downtown core soon took shape.

Growing steadily throughout the 20th-century – economic setbacks like the Wall Street Crash were mitigated by increasing diversification away from resource exploitation – Vancouver added an NHL hockey team and other accoutrements of a midsized North American city. Finally reflecting on its heritage, old-school Gastown was saved by gentrification in the 1970s, becoming a popular history-flavored tourist area.

In 1986 the city hosted a successful Expo World's Fair, sparking a massive wave of new development and adding the first of the mirrored skyscrapers that now define Vancouver's downtown core. At the time of writing it's anticipated that the 2010 Olympic and Paralympic Winter Games will have a similar positive effect on the region.

ORIENTATION

Downtown Vancouver occupies a narrow peninsula bounded on three sides by Burrard Inlet, English Bay and False Creek with Stanley Park at the tip. Key downtown attractions and neighborhoods are all accessible on foot and streets are organized on an easy-to-follow grid system. Robson St and Georgia St are the main downtown east–west thoroughfares, while Granville St is the main north–south artery.

The West End, Gastown, Yaletown and Chinatown neighborhoods are all accessible from the downtown center on foot, while you'll have to travel south across False Creek to get to Granville Island, Kitsilano and the University of British Columbia.

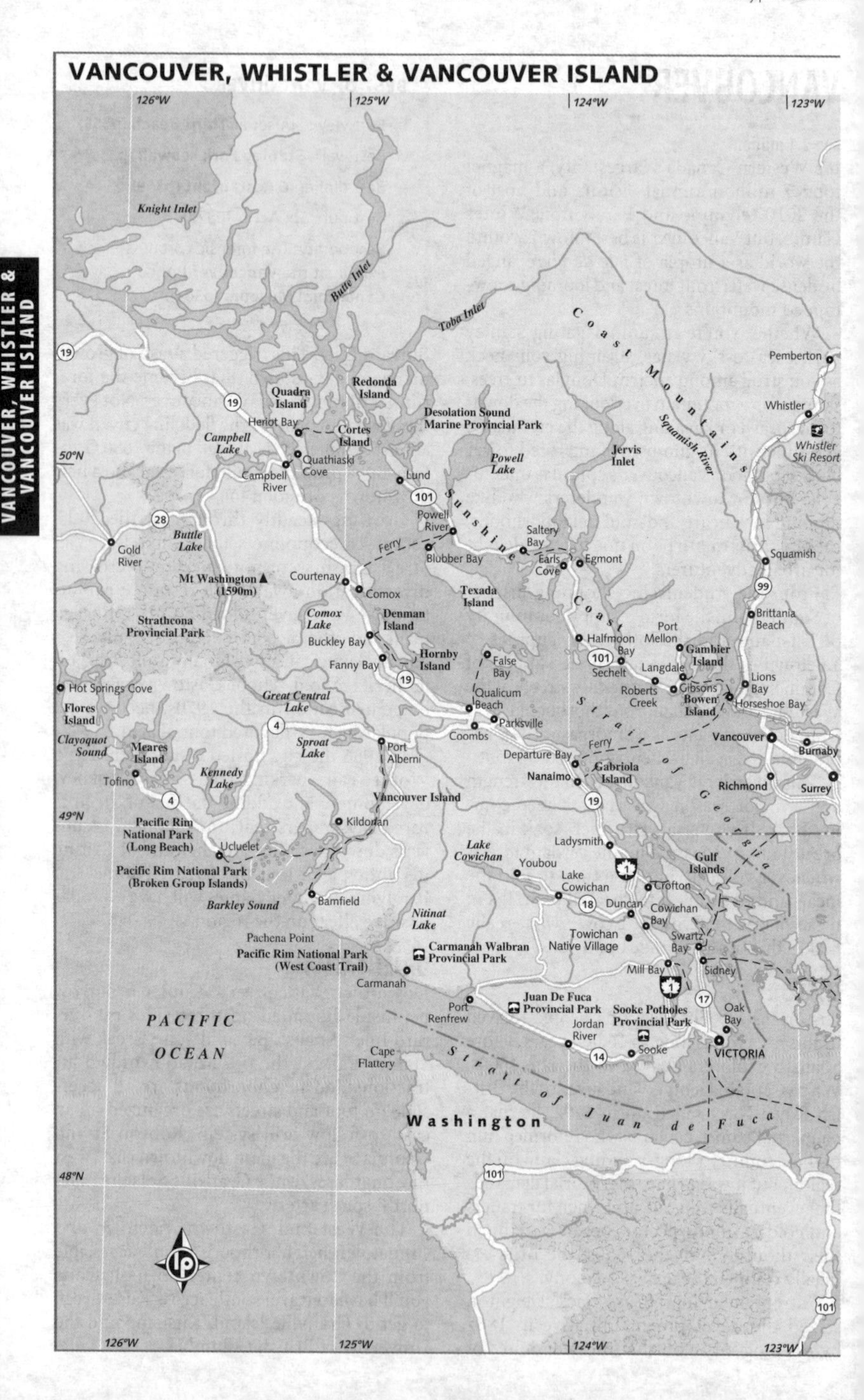
VANCOUVER, WHISTLER & VANCOUVER ISLAND
126°W
125°W
124°W
123°W
50°N
49°N
48°N
Knight Inlet
Butte Inlet
Toba Inlet
Coast Mountains
Squamish River
Pemberton
Whistler
Whistler Ski Resort
Quadra Island
Redonda Island
Desolation Sound Marine Provincial Park
Heriot Bay
Cortes Island
Campbell Lake
Quathiaski Cove
Campbell River
Powell Lake
Jervis Inlet
Lund
Sunshine Coast
Powell River
Saltery Bay
Egmont
Earls Cove
Ferry
Blubber Bay
Gold River
Buttle Lake
Mt Washington (1590m)
Courtenay
Comox
Texada Island
Squamish
Strathcona Provincial Park
Comox Lake
Denman Island
Buckley Bay
Hornby Island
Fanny Bay
False Bay
Halfmoon Bay
Port Mellon
Gambier Island
Brittania Beach
Sechelt
Langdale
Lions Bay
Gibsons
Roberts Creek
Bowen Island
Horseshoe Bay
Hot Springs Cove
Flores Island
Great Central Lake
Qualicum Beach
Parksville
Coombs
Strait of Georgia
Vancouver
Burnaby
Clayoquot Sound
Meares Island
Sproat Lake
Port Alberni
Departure Bay
Gabriola Island
Nanaimo
Richmond
Surrey
Tofino
Kennedy Lake
Vancouver Island
Pacific Rim National Park (Long Beach)
Kildonan
Ladysmith
Ucluelet
Lake Cowichan
Youbou
Gulf Islands
Pacific Rim National Park (Broken Group Islands)
Lake Cowichan
Crofton
Barkley Sound
Bamfield
Duncan
Cowichan Bay
Nitinat Lake
Towichan Native Village
Swartz Bay
Pachena Point
Carmanah Walbran Provincial Park
Pacific Rim National Park (West Coast Trail)
Mill Bay
Sidney
Carmanah
Juan De Fuca Provincial Park
Sooke Potholes Provincial Park
Oak Bay
Port Renfrew
Jordan River
PACIFIC OCEAN
Cape Flattery
Sooke
VICTORIA
Strait of Juan de Fuca
Washington
19
28
101
4
99
18
17
14
1

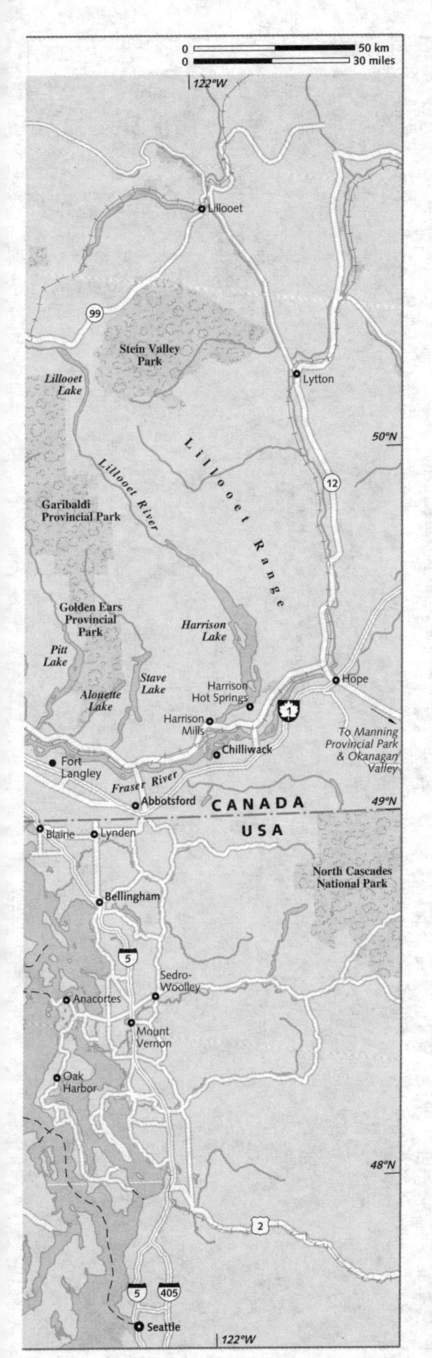

INFORMATION

Bookstores

Book Warehouse (Map pp360-1; ☎ 604-683-5711; 552 Seymour St; 🕑 10am-9pm Mon-Fri, 10am-6pm Sat & Sun) Vancouver's favorite independent bookseller.

Travel Bug (Map p358; ☎ 604-737-1122; 3065 W Broadway; 🕑 10am-6pm Mon-Wed & Sat, 10am-7:30pm Thu & Fri, noon-5pm Sun) Extensive travel guides, maps and accessories.

Internet Access

Electric Internet Café (Map pp360-1; ☎ 604-681-0667; 605 W Pender St; per 30min $1.50; 🕑 7am-3am Mon-Fri, 8am-3am Sat & Sun) Dozens of terminals plus good food specials.

Vancouver Public Library (Map pp360-1; ☎ 604-331-3600; 350 W Georgia St; 30min free; 🕑 10am-9pm Mon-Thu, 10am-6pm Fri & Sat, noon-5pm Sun) Some terminals for nonmembers.

Media & Internet Resources

CKNW 980AM (www.cknw.com) News, traffic and talk radio station.

Georgia Straight (www.straight.com) Free listings newspaper.

Tourism Vancouver (www.tourismvancouver.com) Official online visitor site with downloadable maps.

Vancouver 2010 (www.vancouver2010.com) Official online info for the 2010 Winter Olympics.

Vancouver Sun (www.vancouversun.com) The city's main daily newspaper.

Medical Services

St Paul's Hospital (Map pp360-1; ☎ 604-682-2344; 1081 Burrard St; 🕑 24hr) Downtown accident and emergency.

Ultima Medicentre Plus (Map pp360-1; ☎ 604-683-8138; Bentall Centre, 1055 Dunsmuir St; 🕑 8am-5pm Mon-Fri) A walk-in clinic where appointments are not required.

Money

American Express (Map pp360-1; ☎ 604-669-2813; 666 Burrard St; 🕑 8:30am-5:30pm Mon-Fri, 10am-4pm Sat) Full-service Amex branch.

Vancouver Bullion & Currency Exchange (Map pp360-1; ☎ 604-685-1008; 800 W Pender St; 🕑 9am-5pm Mon-Fri) Best exchange rates in town.

Post

Postal outlets are often tucked at the back of drugstores – look for the blue-and-red window signs.

Canada Post Main Outlet (Map pp360-1; ☎ 604-662-5723; 349 W Georgia St; 🕑 8am-5:30pm Mon-Fri)

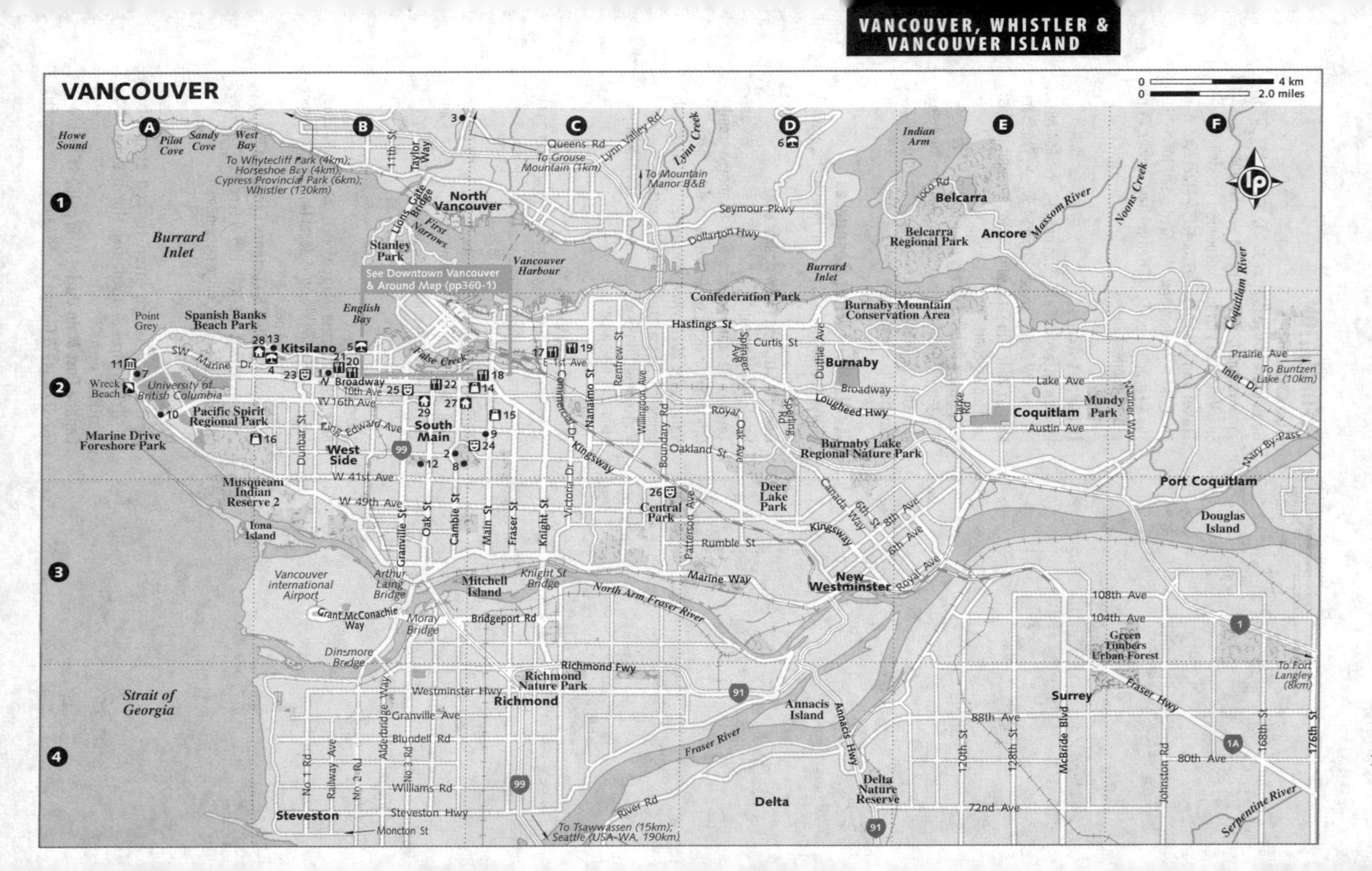
VANCOUVER
0 4 km
0 2.0 miles
Howe Sound
Burrard Inlet
Strait of Georgia
Pilot Cove
Sandy Cove
West Bay
To Whytecliff Park (4km); Horseshoe Bay (4km); Cypress Provincial Park (6km); Whistler (120km)
Point Grey
Spanish Banks Beach Park
Wreck Beach
University of British Columbia
Pacific Spirit Regional Park
Marine Drive Foreshore Park
Musqueam Indian Reserve 2
Iona Island
Kitsilano
English Bay
Stanley Park
Lions Gate Bridge
First Narrows
North Vancouver
Vancouver Harbour
See Downtown Vancouver & Around Map (pp360-1)
False Creek
South Main
West Side
To Grouse Mountain (1km)
To Mountain Manor B&B
Lynn Creek
Lynn Valley Rd
Queens Rd
Taylor Way
11th St
Dollarton Hwy
Seymour Pkwy
Burrard Inlet
Indian Arm
Belcarra
Belcarra Regional Park
Ioco Rd
Ancore
Masson River
Noons Creek
Coquitlam River
To Buntzen Lake (10km)
Prairie Ave
Inlet Dr
Mary Hill Bypass
Port Coquitlam
Douglas Island
Coquitlam
Mundy Park
Mariner Way
Lake Ave
Austin Ave
Clarke Rd
Confederation Park
Burnaby Mountain Conservation Area
Burnaby
Burnaby Lake Regional Nature Park
Hastings St
Curtis St
Duthie Ave
Broadway
Lougheed Hwy
Sperling Rd
Springer Ave
Deer Lake Park
Oak Ave
Royal Oak
Oakland St
Canada Way
6th St
8th Ave
6th Ave
Royal Ave
Kingsway
New Westminster
Central Park
Patterson Ave
Rumble St
Marine Way
Boundary Rd
Willingdon Ave
Renfrew St
Nanaimo St
E 1st Ave
Commercial Dr
Victoria Dr
Knight St
Fraser St
Main St
Cambie St
Oak St
Granville St
Dunbar St
SW Marine Dr
Broadway
10th Ave
W 16th Ave
King Edward Ave
W 41st Ave
W 49th Ave
Mitchell Island
Knight St Bridge
Arthur Laing Bridge
Moray Bridge
Grant McConachie Way
Vancouver International Airport
Dinsmore Bridge
Bridgeport Rd
Richmond
Richmond Nature Park
Richmond Fwy
North Arm Fraser River
Westminster Hwy
Granville Ave
Blundell Rd
Williams Rd
Steveston Hwy
Aldebridge Way
No 3 Rd
No 2 Rd
Railway Ave
No 1 Rd
Moncton St
Steveston
To Tsawwassen (15km); Seattle (USA-WA, 190km)
River Rd
Fraser River
Delta
Annacis Island
Annacis Hwy
Delta Nature Reserve
Surrey
Green Timbers Urban Forest
Fraser Hwy
108th Ave
104th Ave
88th Ave
80th Ave
72nd Ave
McBride Blvd
128th St
120th St
Johnston Rd
168th St
176th St
To Fort Langley (8km)
Serpentine River
A
B
C
D
E
F
1
2
3
4

INFORMATION	VanDusen Botanical Garden......12 B2	Naam......21 B2
Travel Bug......1 B2	Windsure Adventure Watersports......13 B2	Tojo's......22 B2
SIGHTS & ACTIVITIES		**ENTERTAINMENT**
Bloedel Floral Conservatory......2 B2	**SHOPPING**	Cellar Restaurant & Jazz Club....23 B2
Capilano Suspension Bridge......3 B1	Mountain Equipment Co-op.....14 C2	Nat Bailey Stadium......24 C2
Jericho Beach Park......4 B2	Smoking Lily......15 C2	Stanley Theatre......25 B2
Kitsilano Beach Park......5 B2	UBC Farm Market......16 B2	Swangard Stadium......26 C3
Mt Seymour Provincial Park......6 D1		
Nitoba Memorial Garden......7 A2	**EATING**	**SLEEPING**
Queen Elizabeth Park......8 B2	Charlatan......17 C2	Douglas Guest House......27 B2
Regional Assembly of Text......9 C2	Foundation......18 C2	HI Vancouver Jericho Beach.....28 B2
UBC Botanical Garden......10 A2	Havana......19 C2	Shaughnessy Village......29 B2
UBC Museum of Anthropology..11 A2	Lumière......20 B2	

Howe Street Postal Outlet (Map pp360-1; ☎ 604-688-2068; 732 Davie St; 7am-8pm Mon-Fri, 8am-7pm Sat)

Tourist Information

Tourism Vancouver Tourist Info Centre (Map pp360-1; ☎ 604-683-2000; www.tourismvancouver.com; 200 Burrard St; 8:30am-6pm Jun-Aug, 8:30am-5pm Mon-Sat Sep-May) Offers free maps, city guides and wider BC visitor guides, automated currency exchange and a half-price theater ticket booth. Additional airport outlet.

SIGHTS

Vancouver's most popular attractions are in several easily walkable neighborhoods, especially hot spots like Gastown, Chinatown, Stanley Park and Granville Island.

Downtown

Bordered by water to the north and south, and by Stanley Park to the west, downtown Vancouver is centered on shop-lined Robson St, the city's main promenade.

Once a regional gallery with little other than Emily Carr paintings to lure visitors, the **Vancouver Art Gallery** (Map pp360-1; ☎ 604-662-4719; www.vanartgallery.bc.ca; 750 Hornby St; adult/child/youth $19.50/6.50/14, by donation after 5pm Tue; 10am-5:30pm, to 9pm Tue & Thu) has undergone a renaissance in recent years. It now combines edgy contemporary exhibitions with blockbuster traveling shows. Consider dropping by on select Fridays for **FUSE** (admission $15), a late-night party with chin-stroking local arties.

A legacy of Expo 86, the waterfront landmark **Canada Place** (Map pp360-1; ☎ 604-775-7200; www.canadaplace.ca; 999 Canada Place Way) resembles a series of soaring white sails. Like a modern-day pier, it's worth strolling its length for some panoramic views of Stanley Park and the mountains. Inside, there's the CN IMAX Theatre (p373) and the kid-friendly **Port Authority Interpretation Centre** (Map pp360-1; ☎ 604-665-9179; admission free; 8am-5pm Mon-Fri, 10am-2pm Sat & Sun), a hands-on exploration of maritime trade.

With a recent (and long-overdue) renovation, **Vancouver Lookout** (Map pp360-1; ☎ 604-689-0421; www.vancouverlookout.com; 555 W Hastings St; adult/child/youth $13/6/9; 8:30am-10:30pm May–mid-Oct, 9am-9pm mid-Oct–Apr) is still a pricey way to get a bird's-eye view of the city and its environs. Entry includes an optional guided tour of the scenery and your ticket is valid all day so you can return for a twinkly nighttime viewing.

Home of the BC Lions (p373), Teflon-dome **BC Place Stadium** (Map pp360-1; ☎ 604-669-2300; www.bcplacestadium.com; 777 S Pacific Blvd) is also a 2010 Winter Olympics venue. Sports fans can visit the **BC Sports Hall of Fame & Museum** (Map pp360-1; ☎ 604-687-5520; www.bcsportshalloffame.com; Gate A; adult/child $10/8; 10am-5pm), complete with regional and national historic memorabilia.

Stanley Park

Vancouver's highlight is a micro-reflection of what makes BC special. Don't miss a jog, stroll or cycle around the **seawall** – still partly closed at the time of writing due to a massive storm – and consider a picnic stop at **Third Beach**, a great place to watch the sunset.

If you don't fancy walking all the way round, a free summer **shuttle bus** operates around the park. You'll likely be fighting the tour groups for photos at the eight brightly painted **totem poles** but you might also want to stop off at the nearby **artist market** (9am-dusk) for a painterly souvenir of your visit.

After you've spotted your first wild park raccoon, stop by **Lost Lagoon Nature House** (Map pp360-1; ☎ 604-257-6908; www.stanleyparkecology.ca; admission free; 10am-7pm Tue-Sun May-Sep) to learn about the region's varied ecology.

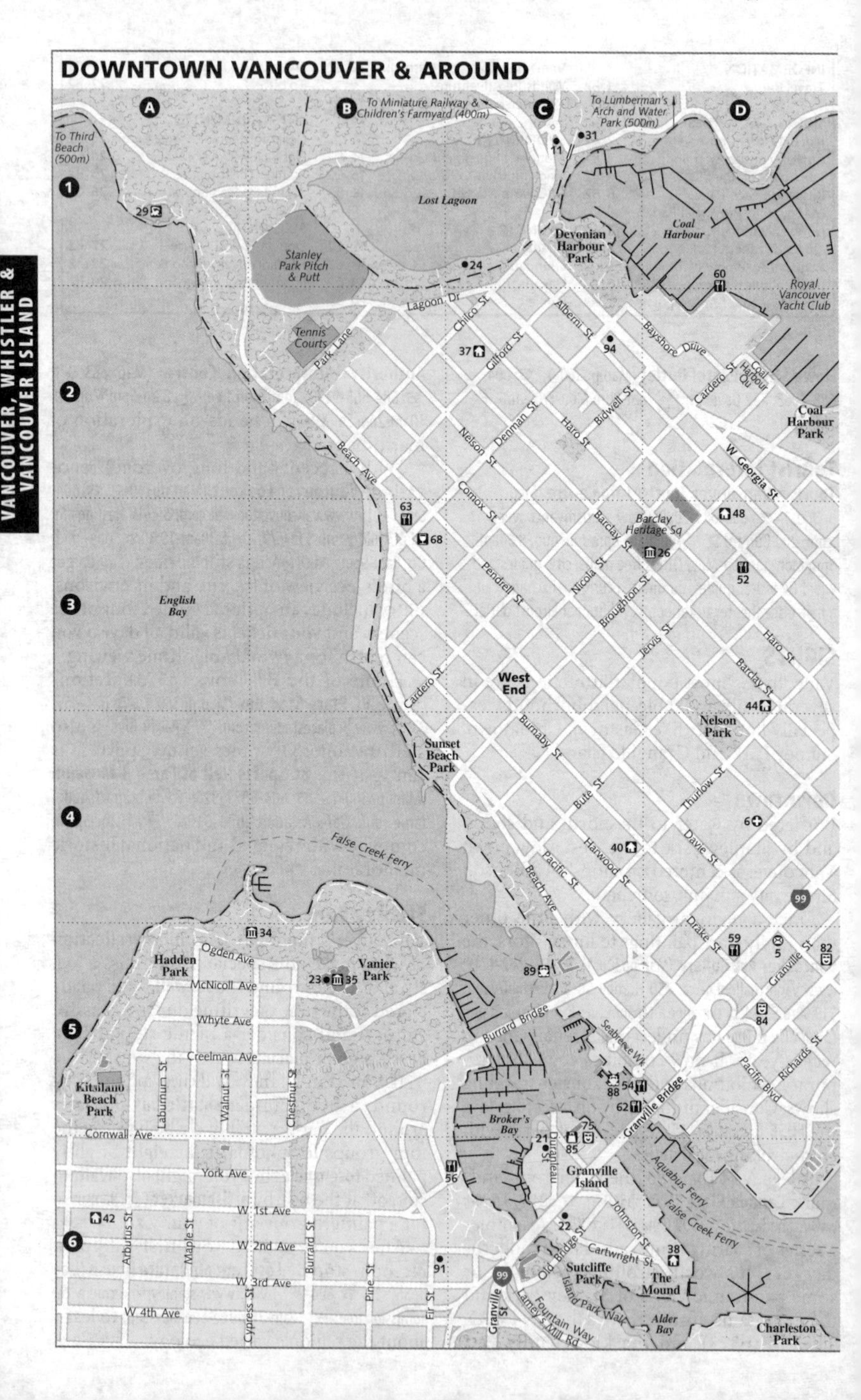
DOWNTOWN VANCOUVER & AROUND
To Third Beach (500m)
To Miniature Railway & Children's Farmyard (400m)
To Lumberman's Arch and Water Park (500m)
Lost Lagoon
Stanley Park Pitch & Putt
Tennis Courts
Devonian Harbour Park
Coal Harbour
Royal Vancouver Yacht Club
Coal Harbour Park
Lagoon Dr
Park Lane
Chilco St
Gilford St
Alberni St
Bayshore Drive
Cardero St
Bidwell St
Haro St
Denman St
Nelson St
Beach Ave
Comox St
W Georgia St
Barclay Heritage Sq
Barclay St
Nicola St
Pendrell St
Broughton St
Jervis St
English Bay
West End
Cardero St
Burnaby St
Haro St
Barclay St
Nelson Park
Sunset Beach Park
Bute St
Thurlow St
Davie St
Harwood St
Pacific St
Beach Ave
False Creek Ferry
Drake St
Granville St
Hadden Park
Ogden Ave
Vanier Park
McNicoll Ave
Whyte Ave
Creelman Ave
Burrard Bridge
Seabreeze Wk
Pacific Blvd
Richards St
Kitsilano Beach Park
Laburnum St
Walnut St
Chestnut St
Cornwall Ave
Broker's Bay
Duranleau St
Granville Bridge
Aquabus Ferry
York Ave
Granville Island
W 1st Ave
Johnston St
False Creek Ferry
W 2nd Ave
Arbutus St
Maple St
Burrard St
Cartwright St
Old Bridge St
W 3rd Ave
Pine St
Fir St
Sutcliffe Park
The Mound
Island Park Walk
W 4th Ave
Cypress St
Granville St
Fountain Way
Lamey's Mill Rd
Alder Bay
Charleston Park

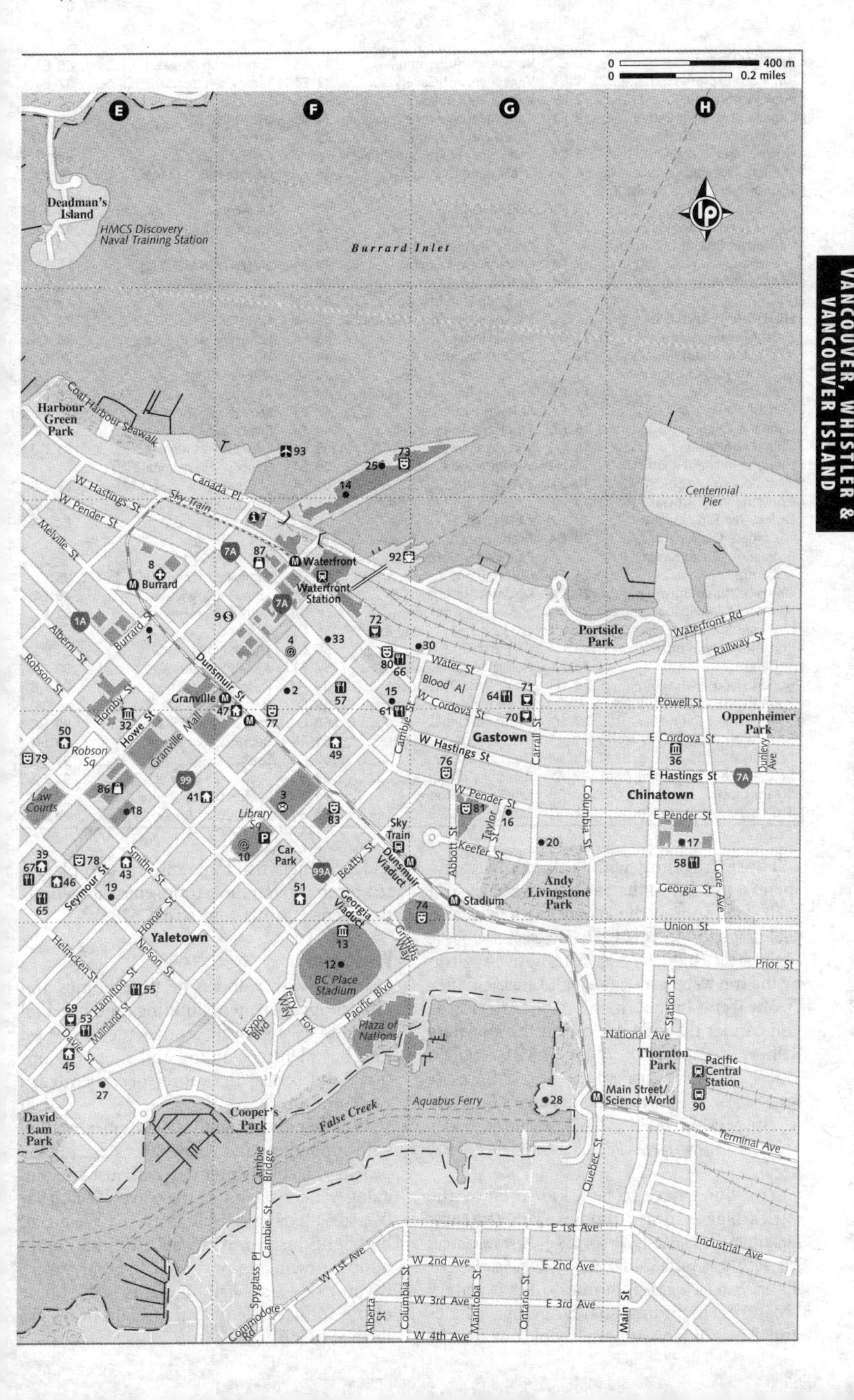

E
F
G
H
Deadman's Island
HMCS Discovery Naval Training Station
Burrard Inlet
Harbour Green Park
Coal Harbour Seawalk
Canada Pl
W Hastings St
W Pender St
Melville St
Sky Train
Waterfront
Waterfront Station
Burrard
Burrard St
Alberni St
Robson St
Hornby St
Howe St
Granville
Granville Mall
Dunsmuir St
Robson Sq
Law Courts
Library Sq
Car Park
Seymour St
Smithe St
Homer St
Nelson St
Helmcken St
Hamilton St
Mainland St
Davie St
Yaletown
Beatty St
Sky Train
Dunsmuir Viaduct
Georgia Viaduct
Griffiths Way
BC Place Stadium
Terry Fox Way
Expo Blvd
Pacific Blvd
Plaza of Nations
David Lam Park
Cooper's Park
False Creek
Aquabus Ferry
Cambie Bridge
Cambie St
Spyglass Pl
Commodore Rd
W 1st Ave
Alberta St
Columbia St
Manitoba St
Ontario St
W 2nd Ave
W 3rd Ave
W 4th Ave
Water St
Blood Al
W Cordova St
Cambie St
Gastown
W Hastings St
Carrall St
W Pender St
Abbott St
Taylor St
Keefer St
Stadium
Andy Livingstone Park
Columbia St
Portside Park
Waterfront Rd
Railway St
Centennial Pier
Powell St
Oppenheimer Park
E Cordova St
Dunlevy Ave
E Hastings St
Chinatown
E Pender St
Georgia St
Gore Ave
Union St
Prior St
Station St
National Ave
Thornton Park
Pacific Central Station
Main Street/ Science World
Terminal Ave
Quebec St
E 1st Ave
E 2nd Ave
E 3rd Ave
Main St
Industrial Ave
0 400 m
0 0.2 miles

INFORMATION
American Express....1 E3
Book Warehouse....2 F3
Canada Post Main Outlet....3 F4
Electric Internet Café....4 F3
Howe Street Postal Outlet....5 D5
St Paul's Hospital....6 D4
Tourism Vancouver Tourist Info Centre....7 F3
Ultima Medicentre Plus....8 E3
Vancouver Bullion & Currency Exchange....9 F3
Vancouver Public Library....10 F4

SIGHTS & ACTIVITIES
Artist Market....11 C1
BC Place Stadium....12 F5
BC Sports Hall of Fame & Museum....13 F5
Canada Place....14 F2
Cannabis Culture Headquarters..15 F3
Chinatown Millennium Gate....16 G4
Chinatown Night Market....17 H4
Commodore Lanes....18 E4
Contemporary Art Gallery....19 E4
Dr Sun Yat-Sen Classical Chinese Garden....20 G4
Ecomarine Ocean Kayak Centre....21 C6
Granville Island Brewing....22 C6
HR MacMillan Space Centre....23 B5
Lost Lagoon Nature House....24 C1
Port Authority Interpretation Centre....25 F2
Roedde House Museum....26 D3
Roundhouse Community Arts & Recreation Centre....27 E5
Science World at TELUS World of Science....28 G5
Second Beach Swimming Pool...29 A1
Steam Clock....30 G3
Tickets Tonight....(see 7)
Vancouver Aquarium....31 C1
Vancouver Art Gallery....32 E4
Vancouver Lookout....33 F3
Vancouver Maritime Museum...34 B5
Vancouver Museum....35 B5
Vancouver Police Centennial Museum....36 H4

SLEEPING
Buchan Hotel....37 C2
Granville Island Hotel....38 D6
HI Vancouver Central....39 E4
HI Vancouver Downtown....40 C4
Kingston Hotel....41 E4
Mickey's Kits Beach Chalet....42 A6
Moda Hotel....43 E4
O Canada House B&B....44 D3
Opus Hotel....45 E5
Samesun Backpackers Lodge....46 E4
St Regis Hotel....47 F4
Tropicana Suite Hotel....48 D3
Victorian Hotel....49 F4
Wedgewood Hotel & Spa....50 E4
YWCA Hotel....51 F4

EATING
Asahi-Ya....52 D3
Blue Water Café....53 E5
C Restaurant....54 C5
Dockside Restaurant & Brewing Company....(see 38)
Glowbal Grill & Satay Bar....55 E5
Go Fish....56 C6
Gorilla Food....57 F3
Hon's Wun-Tun House....58 H4
La Bodega....59 D5
Lift Bar & Grill....60 D1
Mouse & the Bean Café....61 F4
Nu....62 C5
Raincity Grill....63 B3
Salt Tasting Room....64 G3
Sanafir....65 E4
Social at Le Magasin....66 F3
Templeton....67 E4

DRINKING
Afterglow....(see 55)
Calling....68 B3
George Ultra Lounge....69 E5
Irish Heather....70 G4
Six Acres....71 G3
Steamworks Brewing Co....72 F3

ENTERTAINMENT
CN Imax Theatre....73 F2
Commodore....(see 18)
GM Place....74 G4
Granville Island Stage....75 C6
Honey....76 G4
Railway Club....77 F4
Republic....78 E4
Scotiabank Theatre....79 E4
Shine....80 F3
Tinseltown Cinemas....81 G4
Vancity International Film Centre....82 D5
Vancouver Playhouse....83 F4
Yale....84 D5

SHOPPING
Granville Island Public Market..85 C6
John Fluevog Shoes....86 E4
Mink Chocolates....87 F3

TRANSPORT
Aquabus Ferries....88 C5
False Creek Ferries....89 C5
Harbour Air....(see 93)
Pacific Central Station....90 H5
Reckless Bike Stores....91 B6
SeaBus....92 F3
Seaplane Terminal....93 F2
Spokes Bicycle Rental....94 C2
West Coast Air....(see 93)

Those traveling with kids could easily spend a full day in the park. Arrive early and grab your spot at the **Second Beach swimming pool** (Map pp360-1; ☎ 604-257-8370; adult/child/youth; admission $6/3/4; May-Sep). Alternatively, drop by the fun **water park** (off Map pp360-1; admission free; May-Sep) at Lumberman's Arch. Afterwards you can let the kids dry off on the **Miniature Railway** (off Map pp360-1; ☎ 604-257-8531; adult/child $5.50/4; 10:30am-5pm mid-May–Aug, Sat & Sun only Feb–mid-May & Sep) or at the **Children's Farmyard** (off Map pp360-1; ☎ 604-257-8531; adult/child $5.50/4; 11am-4pm mid-May–Aug, Sat & Sun only Feb–mid-May & Sep).

You don't have to be a kid to enjoy the park's biggest draw, though. The **Vancouver Aquarium** (Map pp360-1; ☎ 604-659-3474; www.vanaqua.org; adult/child/youth $20/12/15; 9:30am-5pm Sep-Jun, 9:30am-7pm Jul & Aug) is home to 9000 watery creatures, including sharks, beluga whales and Amazonian caimans. Look out for the iridescent jellyfish tank and the two playful sea otters. If you have time, enjoy a behind-the-scenes trainer tour (from $25).

West End

Dripping with wooden heritage homes and old-school apartment buildings and lined on one side by a seawall promenade, the West End has plenty of dining and shopping options and is also the center of Vancouver's gay community.

Whether it's a languid late-summer evening with sunbathers and volleyballers sharing the beach, or a cold winter day with just you and a dog-walker staring at the waves, **English Bay** (Map pp360-1; cnr Denman & Davie Sts) is a West End highlight. Just a 1.5km walk from the center of downtown, and next door to Stanley Park if you fancy a seawall hike, this is the home of the annual Celebration of Light fireworks festival (p366).

For a glimpse of what pioneering Vancouver looked like before the glass towers, drop by **Roedde House Museum** (Map pp360-1; ☎ 604-684-7040; www.roeddehouse.org; 1415 Barclay St; admission $5; ⏲ 10am-5pm Tue-Fri, 10am-3pm Sat, 2-4pm Sun), a handsome 1893 mansion that's one of several attractive timber-framed homes lining Barclay Heritage Sq. It's packed with period antiques and is a superb recreation of how well-heeled Vancouverites used to live. Sunday entry, which includes tea and cookies, costs $1 extra.

Yaletown

An old brick warehouse district transformed into swanky restaurants and bling-bling boutiques, pedestrian-friendly Yaletown – Vancouver's 'little Soho' – is where the city's beautiful people come to be seen, especially at night when the bars are full of designer trendies.

Roughly bordered by Nelson, Homer, Drake Sts and Pacific Blvd, the area has not completely abandoned its industrial past: old railway tracks remain embedded in the roads and the **Roundhouse Community Arts & Recreation Centre** (Map pp360-1; ☎ 604-713-1800; www.roundhouse.ca; 181 Roundhouse Mews), home of eclectic theater productions and cultural events, occupies a revamped train shed with a restored steam locomotive.

Check out the **Contemporary Art Gallery** (Map pp360-1; ☎ 604-681-2700; www.contemporaryartgallery.ca; 555 Nelson St; admission free; ⏲ noon-6pm Wed-Sun) for a glimpse of what local modern artists are up to.

Gastown & Chinatown

Vancouver's most historic district, cobbled Gastown is where the city began. A former skid row area that's slowly been restored, the heritage buildings are mostly still here but they now house souvenir shops and popular restaurants. The landmark hissing **steam clock** (Map pp360–1) – actually powered by electricity – is halfway along Water St.

The nearby Chinatown, one of North America's largest, is one of the city's most enticing areas. Check out the towering **Chinatown Millennium Gate** (Map pp360-1; cnr W Pender & Taylor Sts) and don't miss the chattery summer **Chinatown Night Market** (Map pp360-1; ☎ 604-682-8998; www.vcma.shawbiz.ca; 100-200 Keefer St; ⏲ 6:30-11pm Fri-Sun mid-May–mid-Sep).

Dr Sun Yat-Sen Classical Chinese Garden (Map pp360-1; ☎ 604-662-3207; www.vancouverchinesegarden.com; 578 Carrall St; adult/child $9/7; ⏲ 10am-6pm May–mid-Jun & Sep, 9:30am-7pm mid-Jun–Aug, 10am-4:30pm Oct-Apr) offers a tranquility break from bustling Chinatown. This intimate 'garden of ease' reveals the Taoist symbolism behind the placing of gnarled pine trees, winding covered pathways and ancient limestone formations. Entry includes a guided tour. Look out for lazy turtles bobbing in the water.

Charting the city's murky criminal past **Vancouver Police Centennial Museum** (Map pp360-1; ☎ 604-665-3346; www.vancouverpolicemuseum.ca; 240 E Cordova St; adult/child $7/5; ⏲ 9am-5pm Mon-Sat) – complete with confiscated weapons and a mortuary exhibit that's not for the faint-hearted – is an excellent little museum and one of the best historic attractions around. If you have time, its Sins of the City tour ($12) escorts visitors around the dodgy Downtown Eastside area.

A great place to bring the kids, **Science World at TELUS World of Science** (Map pp360-1; ☎ 604-443-7443; www.scienceworld.bc.ca; 1455 Quebec St; adult/youth/child $16/13/11; ⏲ 10am-6pm) occupies the mirrored geodesic 'Golf Ball' that was built for Expo '86. It's a high-tech playground of interactive exhibits and live presentations on nature, space, physics and technology. The onsite **OMNIMAX Theatre** (tickets $10), showing large-screen documentaries, is handy if you need a sit down.

South Main & Commercial Drive

Eschewing the fake tans of the Robson St shoppers, Vancouver's indie crowd has colonized an area of town that used to be a by-word for down-at-heel. Starting at the intersection of Main St and Broadway, South Main – now known as SoMa – is home to bohemian coffee bars, one-of-a-kind boutiques and bold artist-run galleries.

Jump back on bus 3 along Main St from downtown until you hit Main and 48th and you'll find yourself in the **Punjabi Market** area. Also known as 'Little India,' this little enclave of sari stores and Bangra music shops is a good spot for an all-you-can-eat curry lunch followed by a restorative walkabout.

Culinary adventurers should also consider trekking along funky **Commercial Drive**, where decades of European immigrants have created a United Nations of restaurants, coffee bars and exotic delis. The best spot in town to watch international soccer games, it's also a promenade of espresso-supping patio dwellers in summer.

Granville Island

Fanning out under the iron arches of Granville Bridge, this gentrified former industrial peninsula – it's not actually an island – is an ideal spot to spend a lazy afternoon in the city. Combining restaurants, bars, theaters and artisan businesses, it's usually crowded here on summer weekends as visitors chill out with the buskers and wrestle seagulls for their fish 'n chips.

The highlight here is the Granville Island Public Market (p373), a multi-sensory deli specializing in gourmet fish, fruit and bakery treats. It has an international food court (eat lunch early or late to avoid the rush) and a kaleidoscope of cool craft stalls.

You can take a tour at nearby **Granville Island Brewing** (Map pp360-1; ☎ 604-687-2739; www.gib.ca; 1441 Cartwright St; tours $9.75; 🕑 tours noon, 2pm & 4pm) where the guides walk you through the brewing process before depositing you in the taproom for samples like the recommended Kitsilano Maple Cream Ale.

Kitsilano

A former hippy haven where the counterculture flower children grew up to reap large mortgages, 'Kits' is a pleasant neighborhood of pricey heritage homes and highly browsable shops. Recommended for a lazy afternoon of street strolling – especially along W 4th Ave – there's also a couple of great waterfront stretches at **Jericho Beach** and **Kitsilano Beach**.

Among the cultural attractions here, Vanier Park's **Vancouver Museum** (Map pp360-1; ☎ 604-736-4431; www.vanmuseum.bc.ca; 1100 Chestnut St; adult/child $10/6.50; 🕑 10am-5pm Tue-Sun, to 9pm Thu) showcases aboriginal artifacts, although they're not as well presented as those at the Museum of Anthropology (right). Recent history is also on offer, with colorful displays covering 1950s pop culture and 1960s hippy counterculture.

The **HR MacMillan Space Centre** (Map pp360-1; ☎ 604-738-7827; www.hrmacmillanspacecentre.com; 1100 Chestnut St; adult/child $15/11; 🕑 10am-5pm Jul & Aug, Tue-Sun only Sep-Jun) is popular with kids, who hit the hands-on exhibits with maximum force.

The final member of the park's triumvirate, the **Vancouver Maritime Museum** (Map pp360-1; ☎ 604-257-8300; www.vancouvermaritimemuseum.com; 1905 Ogden Ave; adult/child $10/7.50; 🕑 10am-5pm May-Aug, 10am-5pm Tue-Sat, noon-5pm Sun Sep-Apr) combines dozens of intricate model ships with some detailed recreated boat sections and a few historic vessels.

University of British Columbia

West from Kits on a forested peninsula, the **University of British Columbia** (UBC; Map p358; ☎ 604-822-2211; www.ubc.ca) is the province's largest university. Its concrete campus is home to accessible beach and forest areas and a smattering of recommended visitor attractions.

The must-see **UBC Museum of Anthropology** (Map p358; ☎ 604-822-3825; www.moa.ubc.ca; 6393 NW Marine Dr; adult/child $9/7, by donation after 5pm Tue; 🕑 10am-5pm, until 9pm Tue mid-May–mid-Oct, 11am-5pm Wed-Sun, until 9pm Tue mid-Oct–mid-May) has Canada's best display of Northwest coast aboriginal artifacts. The totem poles alone – displayed against a wall of glass overlooking the coastline – are worth the admission. Ask about the free, twice-daily gallery tours to get the most from your visit.

Green-thumbed visitors will enjoy the 28 hectares of themed gardens at the **UBC Botanical Garden** (Map p358; ☎ 604-822-9666; www.ubcbotanicalgarden.org; 6804 SW Marine Dr; adult/child $7/free; 🕑 10am-6pm mid-Mar–mid-Oct, 10am-3pm mid-Oct–mid-Mar), including Canada's largest collection of rhododendrons and a winter garden of plants that bloom outside spring and summer. Combined entry with the nearby Nitobe Memorial Garden is $10.

Designed by top Japanese landscape architect Kannosuke Mori, **Nitobe Memorial Garden** (Map p358; ☎ 604-822-6038; www.nitobe.org; 6804 SW Marine Dr; adult/child $5/free; 🕑 10am-6pm mid-Mar–mid-Oct, 10am-2:30pm Mon-Fri mid-Oct–mid-Mar) is a perfect example of Japan's symbolic horticultural art form. Aside from traffic noise and summer bus tours, it's a tranquil retreat ideal for quiet meditation. Combined entry with the UBC Botanical Garden is $10.

West Side

With sports fields and manicured lawns, the 53-hectare **Queen Elizabeth Park** (Map p358) – located between Cambie and Ontario Sts near 33rd Ave – serves up some of Vancouver's best city views. Cresting the park's hill is the triodetic dome of the **Bloedel Floral Conservatory** (Map p358; ☎ 604-257-8584; 2099 Beach Ave; adult/child $4/2; 🕑 9am-8pm Mon-Fri, 10am-9pm Sat & Sun Apr-Sep, 10am-5pm Oct-Mar) where tropical birds and plants fill three climate-controlled environments.

Four blocks west, **VanDusen Botanical Garden** (Map p358; ☎ 604-878-9274; www.vandusengarden.org; 5251 Oak St; adult/child/youth Apr-Sep $8/4.50/6, Oct-Mar $5.70/3/4; 🕑 10am-9pm Jun-Aug, hrs vary rest of yr) offers a highly ornamental confection of sculptures, rare plants and a popular hedge maze. The gardens are a top Christmas destination, when they're covered with thousands of twinkling fairy lights.

If you fancy an enjoyable window shop stroll, **South Granville** (www.southgranville.org), an 11-block stretch of galleries, restaurants and browsable shops between 5th and 16th Aves on Granville St, is worth an afternoon of anyone's time.

North Vancouver & West Vancouver

Accessed from downtown via the Lions Gate Bridge or the SeaBus transit service, the North Shore comprises the commuter city of North Vancouver and the chichi district of 'West Van.'

The Lower Mainland's most popular attraction, **Capilano Suspension Bridge** (Map p358; ☎ 604-985-7474; www.capbridge.com; 3735 Capilano Rd, North Vancouver; adult/child/youth $27/8.30/16; 8:30am-8pm Jun & Sep, till 9pm Jul & Aug, hours vary rest of yr) is a 140m-long pedestrian walkway that sways over tree-lined Capilano Canyon, an awesome visual even for the most jaded traveler. The surrounding park houses some totem poles and a network of smaller cable bridges between the trees.

Grouse Mountain (off Map p358; ☎ 604-980-9311; www.grousemountain.com; 6400 Nancy Greene Way, North Vancouver; adult/child/youth summer $33/12/19, winter $45/20/35; 9am-10pm) offers smashing views of downtown Vancouver. In summer, gondola passengers can access restaurants, lumberjack shows, hiking trails and a grizzly bear refuge up top. In winter, Grouse becomes the locals' favorite snowy playground, with 25 ski and snowboard runs and an outdoor ice-skating rink.

Eight kilometers north of West Van via Hwy 99, **Cypress Provincial Park** (off Map p358; ☎ 604-924-2200; www.bcparks.ca; Cypress Bowl Rd, West Vancouver) offers great summertime hiking trails. In winter, the park's **Cypress Mountain** (☎ 604-926-5612; www.cypressmountain.com; adult/child/youth $47/21/40; 9am-4pm Dec, 9am-10pm Jan-Mar) attracts sporty types with its 38 ski runs and popular snowshoe trails. This is the snowboarding and freestyle skiing venue for the 2010 Winter Olympics.

ACTIVITIES

With a reputation for outdoorsy locals who like nothing better than an early morning 10km jog and a lip-smacking feast of rice cakes for breakfast, Vancouver is all about being active.

Hiking and Running

For arm-swinging strolls or heart-pounding runs, the 9km Stanley Park seawall is mostly flat – apart from a couple of uphills where you might want to hang onto a passing bike. While a devastating late-2006 storm affected many of the forested trails within the park, at the time of writing most were expected to be restored, including the popular 4km trek around Lost Lagoon. UBC (opposite) is another good running spot, with trails marked throughout the campus. Visit Grouse Mountain (left) for the Grouse Grind, an uphill slog that's a rite of passage for many locals.

Cycling

Joggers share the busy Stanley Park seawall with cyclists (and rollerbladers), necessitating a one-way traffic system that also acts to prevent bloody pile ups. The sea-to-sky vistas are breathtaking, but the exposed route can be hit with crashing waves and icy winds in winter. Slow-moving, camera-wielding tourists crowd the route during summer peaks so it's best to come early in the morning or later in the evening.

After circling the park to English Bay, bikers with energy to spare can continue along the north side of False Creek towards Science World (p363), where the route heads up the south side of False Creek towards Granville Island, Vanier Park, Kitsilano Beach and, finally, UBC. This extended route, including Stanley Park, is around 25km.

On the Water

Situated on Granville Island, the friendly folk at **Ecomarine Ocean Kayak Centre** (pp360-1; ☎ 604-689-7575, 888-425-2925; www.ecomarine.com; 1668 Duranleau St; rentals 2hr/day $34/59, tours from $54; 9am-6pm, till 9pm Fri & Sat Jun-Aug, hours vary rest of yr) offer guided tours and equipment rentals – Tuesday is two-for-one rental day.

For those who want to be at one with the sea breeze, **Windsure Adventure Waterports** (p358; ☎ 604-224-0615; www.windsure.com; Jericho Sailing Centre, 1300 Discovery St; surfboard/skimboard rentals per hr $17.50/4.50; 9am-8pm Apr-Sep) specializes in kiteboarding, windsurfing and skimboarding and offers lessons and equipment rentals from its Jericho Beach base.

VANCOUVER FOR KIDS

Stanley Park (p359) can keep most families occupied for a full day. If it's hot, make sure you hit the water park at Lumberman's Arch or consider the miniature railway and children's farmyard. The park is a great place to bring a picnic and its beaches – especially Third Beach – are highly kid-friendly. Save time for the **Vancouver Aquarium** (p362) and, if your kids have been good, consider a behind-the-scenes trainer tour.

The city's other educational family-friendly attractions include **Science World** (p363) and the **HR MacMillan Space Centre** (p364). If it's raining, you can duck inside at downtown's **Canada Place** (p359) for its hands-on Port Interpretation Centre and CN IMAX Theatre (see p373).

If you time your visit right, the city has an array of family-friendly festivals, including the **Pacific National Exhibition** (right) and the **Vancouver International Children's Festival** (right).

OFFBEAT VANCOUVER

While 'BC Bud' usually makes an appearance at most Vancouver house parties, many visitors are still mildly shocked to see hemp shops and hydroponics stores openly selling the required paraphernalia (although not the weed itself). For arguments in support of legalization, duck into the BC Marijuana Party office at **Cannabis Culture Headquarters** (Map pp360-1; ☎ 604-682-1172; www.bcmarijuanaparty.ca; 307 W Hastings St; 🕑 10am-7pm Mon-Thu, 10am-8pm Fri & Sat, noon-6pm Sun). It also houses the Vapour Lounge, where you can chill-out with like-minded buddies.

You can strike out in a more wholesome way at one of Canada's last remaining downtown bowling alleys. Hiding underneath the Granville St stores, **Commodore Lanes** (Map pp360-1; ☎ 604-681-1531; 838 Granville St; 🕑 11am-midnight Sun-Thu, 11am-1am Fri & Sat) attracts nostalgic oldsters and kitsch-loving Japanese language students pretending they're in an *Archie* comic.

For a complete change of pace, head over to the **Regional Assembly of Text** (Map p358; ☎ 604-877-2247; www.assemblyoftext.com; 3934 Main St; 🕑 11am-6pm Mon-Sat, noon-5pm Sun) shop, where you can join the hipsters for a monthly letter-writing club (7pm, first Thursday of the month), complete with stationery, tea and encouragement. This highly quirky store brims with handmade journals and lexicographical paraphernalia. Ask nicely to try out a vintage typewriter.

TOURS

Big Bus (☎ 604-299-0700, 877-299-0701; www.bigbus.ca; adult/child/youth $35/17/30) Two-day hop-on-hop-off ticket covering 20 attractions.

City By Cycle Tours (☎ 604-730-1032, 888-599-6800; www.citybycycle.com; adult/child $69/59; 🕑 tours 9am & 2pm) Offering excellent four-hour guided rides around the city's highlights, including Stanley Park, English Bay, Chinatown and Granville Island. Rates include bikes and helmets.

Edible BC (☎ 604-662-3606, 888-812-9660; www.edible-britishcolumbia.com; tours $55) Colorful three-hour foodie treks around Chinatown, Commercial Dr or Granville Island.

Gastown Historic Walking Tours (☎ 604-683-5650; www.gastown.org; departs from Gassy Jack Statue; tours free; 🕑 tours 2pm mid-Jun–Aug) A 1½-hour tour on the history and architecture of Vancouver's birthplace.

Harbour Cruises (☎ 604-688-7246, 800-663-1500; www.boatcruises.com; adult/child/youth $25/10/21; 🕑 mid-Apr–mid-Oct) View the city – and some unexpected wildlife – from the water on a 75-minute harbor tour. Departs north foot of Denman St.

FESTIVALS & EVENTS

Vancouver International Children's Festival (☎ 604-708-5655; www.childrensfestival.ca; 🕑 mid-May) Storytelling, performance and activities in the tents at Vanier Park.

Bard on the Beach (☎ 604-739-0559; www.bardonthebeach.org; 🕑 Jun-Sep) A season of four Shakespeare-related plays in the Vanier Park tents.

Vancouver International Jazz Festival (☎ 604-872-5200; www.coastaljazz.ca; 🕑 from mid-Jun) City-wide cornucopia of superstar shows and free outdoor events.

Vancouver Folk Music Festival (☎ 604-602-9798; www.thefestival.bc.ca; 🕑 mid-Jul) Folk and world music shows at Jericho Beach.

Celebration of Light (☎ 604-641-1193; www.hsbccelebrationoflight.com; 🕑 from late Jul) Free international fireworks extravaganza in English Bay.

Pride Week (☎ 604-687-0955; www.vancouverpride.ca; 🕑 from late Jul) Parties, concerts and fashion shows culminating in giant gay pride parade.

Festival Vancouver (☎ 604-688-1152; www.festivalvancouver.bc.ca; 🕑 mid-Aug) Showcases choral, opera, classical, jazz and world music performances.

Pacific National Exhibition (☎ 604-253-2311; www.pne.bc.ca; 🕑 from mid-Aug) Family-friendly shows, music concerts and a fairground midway.

Vancouver International Fringe Festival (☎ 604-257-0350; www.vancouverfringe.com; 🕑 mid-Sep) Wild and wacky theatricals at mainstream and unconventional Granville Island venues.

SHAKESPEARE AND SAND: CHRISTOPHER GAZE

Actor and artistic director of Bard on the Beach, Vancouver's waterfront Shakespeare festival.

What makes Bard on the Beach a uniquely Vancouver festival?

The exquisite beauty of the sea, the mountains and the sky becomes the backdrop of a great production of classical theater, bringing the two worlds of stage and nature together.

How do you think Shakespeare would react to seeing his plays performed in waterfront tents?

I think he would be delighted! Essentially he wrote his plays for the Globe Theatre in London, which was open above a portion of the audience. Our theater is open behind the stage, so everyone is dry.

Vancouver has a strong 'outdoorsy' reputation but how would you define the city's cultural scene?

The cultural scene in Vancouver is at an exciting precipice right now. Professional production companies are providing outstanding seasons, while emerging artists are bringing a new energy and cultural growth to the city.

Outside Bard, what other festivals do you personally enjoy visiting in the area?

Festival Vancouver, the Folk Festival and the Jazz Festival – there's a festival for everyone.

Any tips for first time visitors on how to make the most of their Bard experience?

Buy your tickets early! Once you have your tickets, plan to come down early and have a picnic in beautiful Vanier Park. Don't forget to bring something warm as it does tend to cool down once the second act gets going.

Vancouver International Film Festival (☎ 604-685-0260; www.viff.org; from late Sep) Popular two-week showcase of Canadian and international movies.

SLEEPING

While room rates peak in the summer months here, there are some great deals available in fall and early spring when the weather is almost as good. **Tourism Vancouver** (www.tourismvancouver.com) provides listings and the province's **Hello BC** (☎ 604-663-6000, 800-663-6000; www.hellobc.com) service provides further information and bookings. Be aware that many hotels charge between $10 and $15 for overnight parking.

Downtown

Samesun Backpackers Lodge (Map pp360-1; ☎ 604-682-8226, 888-203-8333; www.samesun.com; 1018 Granville St; dm/r $25/65; wi-fi) Expect a party atmosphere at this lively hostel in the heart of Granville's nightclub area – there's a hopping onsite bar if you don't quite make it out the front door. The dorms, complete with funky paintjobs, are comfortably small and there's a large kitchen plus a strong line-up of social events.

HI Vancouver Central (Map pp360-1; ☎ 604-685-5335, 888-203-8333; www.hihostels.ca/vancouvercentral; 1025 Granville St; dm/r incl breakfast $27.50/66; wi-fi) Opposite the Samesun Backpackers, this labyrinthine former hotel building has a calmer ambience, small dorms with sinks and lots of private rooms – some with en suites. If you're new to the city, ask about taking a tour with the legendary Erik, HI volunteer extraordinaire.

Kingston Hotel (Map pp360-1; ☎ 604-684-9024, 888-713-3304; www.kingstonhotelvancouver.com; 757 Richards St; s/d/tw incl breakfast $115/145/160) Many rooms at this Euro-style pension property are basic and a bit worn, except for the recommended en suite rooms, which have new furniture, flat-screen TVs and fresh floral bedspreads. There's a popular onsite patio bar and most of the city's main action is within comfortable walking distance.

Moda Hotel (Map pp360-1; ☎ 604-683-4251, 877-683-5522; www.modahotel.ca; 900 Seymour St; d from $119; wi-fi) The old, rough-and-ready Dufferin Hotel has been reinvented as a white-fronted, designer-flecked boutique property one block from the Granville St party area. The new rooms have loungey flourishes like mod furnishings and bold paintwork, and the bathrooms have been given a swanky makeover. The flat-screen TVs are a nice touch if you decide to have a night in.

Wedgewood Hotel & Spa (Map pp360-1; ☎ 604-689-7777, 800-663-0666; www.wedgewoodhotel.com; 845 Hornby St; r from $350;) The last word in boutique luxury, the elegant Wedgewood is dripping with top-hat charm. The friendly staff are second-to-none, the rooms are stuffed with reproduction antiques and the balconies enable you to smirk at the grubby plebs shuffling past below. Steam up your monocle with a trip to the spa where a shiatsu massage should work off those sore shopping muscles.

Stanley Park & West End

HI Vancouver Downtown (Map pp360-1; ☎ 604-684-4565, 888-203-4302; www.hihostels.ca/vancouverdowntown; 1114 Burnaby St; dm/r incl breakfast $28/66; 💻 wi-fi) Actually located in the West End, close to Davie St's pubs and clubs, this purpose-built hostel has a more institutional feel than its Granville St brother. It's also quieter and more popular with families. The dorms are all small and added extras range from bike rentals to internet access computers.

Buchan Hotel (Map pp360-1; ☎ 604-685-5354, 800-668-6654; www.buchanhotel.com; 1906 Haro St; r from $72) This cheerful, tidy and good-value heritage sleepover near Stanley Park combines cheaper rooms – many with shared bathrooms, dinged furnishings and older blankets – with higher-quality and pricier en suites. The smiling front-desk staff are excellent and there are storage facilities for bikes and skis.

Tropicana Suite Hotel (Map pp360-1; ☎ 604-687-6631; www.tropicanavancouver.com; 1361 Robson St; s/d $129/139; 🏊) Best of the three self-catering hotels crowding the corner of Robson and Broughton Sts, rooms at the Tropicana combine faded pink-trimmed walls and clashing green comforters. While it will never be cool, it's good value and has a great location. Most suites have full kitchens with stoves and large refrigerators, and there's a heated indoor pool and sauna.

O Canada House B&B (Map pp360-1; ☎ 604-688-0555, 877-688-1114; www.ocanadahouse.com; 1114 Barclay St; d from $210; 💻 wi-fi) The home where Canada's national anthem was penned is now an immaculate, adult-oriented B&B packed with antiques and Queen Anne flourishes. Its seven elegant rooms are a haven from the city bustle – the wraparound veranda is a popular spot to watch the world go by – and there's a guest pantry with sherry and baked goodies if you can't wait for your next meal.

Yaletown & Gastown

YWCA Hotel (Map pp360-1; ☎ 604-895-5830, 800-663-1424; www.ywcahotel.com; 733 Beatty St; s/d/tr $64/77/102; 💻) One of Canada's best Ys, this popular tower near Yaletown is a useful option for those on a budget. Accommodating singles, couples and families, it's a bustling place with a communal kitchen on every other floor and rooms ranging from compact singles to group-friendly larger quarters. All are a little institutionalized – think student study bedroom – but each has a sink and refrigerator.

Victorian Hotel (Map pp360-1; ☎ 604-681-6369, 877-681-6369; www.victorianhotel.ca; 514 Homer St; with/with out bathroom incl breakfast from $129/99; wi-fi) Housed in a couple of expertly renovated older properties, high-ceilinged rooms at the Victorian combine glossy hardwood floors, a sprinkling of antiques and bags of heritage charm. Most are en suite with summer fans, TVs and robes provided, but the best rooms are in the extension, complete with its marble-floored bathrooms.

St Regis Hotel (Map pp360-1; ☎ 604-681-1135, 800-770-7929; www.stregishotel.com; 602 Dunsmuir St; r from $149 incl breakfast; ❄ wi-fi) Upgraded in recent years, this well-located heritage hotel combines fairly pokey standard rooms with swankier quarters on its higher floors. Rates include access to a small onsite business center and entry to the gym across the street. It's a busy part of town, so ask for a back room if noise is an issue.

Opus Hotel (Map pp360-1; ☎ 604-642-6787, 866-642-6787; www.opushotel.com; 322 Davie St; d & ste from $340; ❄ 💻 wi-fi) At the time of writing, the Opus was still Vancouver's best contemporary boutique property (though things may change with the opening of the hotly anticipated Lodon Hotel). Combining designer esthetics with loungey West Coast comforts, the rooms – especially the corner suites with their feng shui bed placements – offer laid-back coziness and stylish mod furnishings.

Granville Island & Kitsilano

HI Vancouver Jericho Beach (Map p358; ☎ 604-224-3208, 888-203-4303; www.hihostels.ca; 1515 Discovery St; dm/r $27/71; 🕑 May-Sep; 💻) A waterfront retreat that's a bus ride from downtown, this giant hostel attracts beach bums and activity nuts in equal measure. The large, basic dorm rooms are fine if you like a crowd – book ahead if you want one of the private rooms. Outdoor types can rent bikes and sports equipment on-site or at the nearby beach.

Mickey's Kits Beach Chalet (Map pp360-1; ☎ 604-739-3342, 888-739-3342; www.mickeysbandb.com; 2142 W 1st Ave; d incl breakfast $120-160; wi-fi) Behind its slender, chimney-dominated exterior, the three rooms at this Whistler-style chalet –

including the gabled, top-floor York Room – are decorated in a comfortable contemporary style, although only the York Room is en suite. Family-friendly, the hosts can supply toys, cribs and even babysitters.

Granville Island Hotel (Map pp360-1; ☎ 604-683-7373, 800-663-1840; www.granvilleislandhotel.com; 1253 Johnston St; d from $215; wi-fi) Hugging the waterfront on the eastern tip of Granville Island, this laid-back hotel has a tranquil West Coast ambience. The rooms have exposed beams and earth-toned walls – the suites, with their floor-to-ceiling waterfront views, are recommended. There's also good brewpub with beers such as Johnston Pilsner and Cartwright Pale Ale.

UBC & West Side

Douglas Guest House (Map p358; ☎ 604-872-3060, 888-872-3060; www.dougwin.com; 456 W 13th Ave; r/ste from $75/145) The Douglas is a bright orange, home-style B&B in a quiet neighborhood near City Hall. The six old-school, comfortable rooms include two flowery singles with shared bathrooms, two larger doubles with en suites and two family-friendly suites. The top-floor penthouse has a nice private balcony while the downstairs Garden Suite has a kitchenette.

our pick **Shaughnessy Village** (Map p358; ☎ 604-736-5511; www.shaughnessyvillage.com; 1125 W 12th Ave; s/d $79/89;) This uniquely kitsch sleepover that feels like a 1950s Vegas hotel – think pink carpets, flowery sofas and maritime memorabilia – describes itself as a tower block 'B&B resort.' Where else can you find a petrified rock display, a gym with a bum-shaking belt machine and a tree-lined garden with crazy golf? Despite the old-school approach, the hotel is perfectly ship-shape, right down to its clean, well-maintained rooms. Like boat cabins, they're lined with wooden cupboards and have tiny en suites.

EATING

Celebrated for its international diversity, Vancouver visitors can fill up on great ethnic dishes before they even start on the region's flourishing West Coast cuisine. Whatever you choose, don't miss the seafood – it's BC's greatest culinary asset.

Downtown

Templeton (Map pp360-1; ☎ 604-685-4612; 1087 Granville St; mains $6-11; 9am-11pm, until 1am Thu-Sun; V) A funky chrome and vinyl 1950s diner with a twist, Templeton serves up organic burgers, fair-trade coffee, vegetarian sausages and perhaps the best breakfast in town (served until 3pm). Sadly, the mini jukeboxes on the tables don't work but you can console yourself with a waistline-busting chocolate ice-cream float.

Sanafir (Map pp360-1; ☎ 604-678-1049; 1026 Granville St; mains from $14; 5pm-midnight) A beacon among Granville's grubby sex shops, Sanafir is a loungey, Bedouin-themed eatery dripping with North African style. But it's not all about looks. The menu's small plates are designed for sharing and range from wine-braised short ribs to Indian-spiced scallops. Head to the decadent mezzanine level where you can lay down and eat like a king.

Nu (Map pp360-1; ☎ 604-646-4668; 1661 Granville St; mains $16-24; 11am-1am Mon-Fri, 10:30am-1am Sat, 10:30am-midnight Sun) A funky 1970s interior makes this feel like the set of an old Chinzano Bianco advert. Encouraging diners to be adventurous and share the unfamiliar French-influenced dishes with their friends, highlights here include tempura olives and duck confit with liquefied foie gras. Consider a cocktail or two, preferably on the sunset-viewing deck.

C Restaurant (Map pp360-1; ☎ 604-681-1164; 1600 Howe St; mains $18-46; 5:30-11pm) This pioneering West Coast seafood restaurant overlooking False Creek isn't cheap but its approach to fish and shellfish makes it probably the city's best. Scallops wrapped in octopus bacon and served with foie gras is a signature, while deceptively uncomplicated dishes of side-stripe prawns and Queen Charlotte scallops are highly recommended.

West End

Asahi-Ya (Map pp360-1; ☎ 604-688-8777; 1230 Robson St; mains $6-10; 11:30am-10pm) You'll be rubbing shoulders with Asian language students who know a good deal when they see one at this friendly and decidedly unpretentious Japanese diner. Good-value sushi and sashimi classics are fresh and well-presented but it's the hearty cooked combo meals – especially the sizzling chicken teriyaki – that will bring you back for more.

Lift Bar & Grill (Map pp360-1; ☎ 604-689-5438; 333 Menchions Mews; mains $17-23; 11:30am-midnight Mon-Fri, 11am-midnight Sat & Sun) Hanging over the seawall in Coal Harbour near Stanley Park, the swanky Lift provides unrivalled views of the verdant rain forest and mist-cloaked mountains from its wraparound windows and heated deck. Pull yourself away from the vistas to enjoy gourmet comfort dishes like bison strip loin and prosciutto-wrapped salmon.

Raincity Grill (Map pp360-1; ☎ 604-685-7337; 1193 Denman St; mains $20-30; 11:30am-2:30pm & 5-10pm Mon-Fri, 10:30am-2:30pm & 5-10pm Sat & Sun) This smashing English Bay restaurant was finding and serving unique BC ingredients long before the fashion for Fanny Bay oysters and Salt Spring Island lamb took hold. A great showcase for fine West Coast cuisine – the $30 three-course tasting menu served between 5pm and 6pm is recommended – you can also drop by the take-out window for gourmet $10 sandwiches.

Yaletown

Gorilla Food (Map pp360-1; ☎ 604-722-2504; 422 Richards St; mains $4-7.50; 11am-6pm Mon-Fri; V) More guerrilla than gorilla, this hole-in-the-wall take-out is a pilgrimage spot for raw-food devotees. Nothing is cooked, leading to innovative treats like lasagna with strips of zucchini substituting for pasta, and pizza made from a dehydrated seed crust and topped with tomato sauce and mashed avocado. Save room for an icy almond shake.

La Bodega (Map pp360-1; ☎ 604-684-8814; 1277 Howe St; mains $5-11; 4:30pm-midnight Mon-Fri, 5pm-midnight Sat, 5-11pm Sun) It's all about the tasting plates at this country-style Spanish tapas bar. Pull-up a chair, order a jug of sangria and decide on a few shareable treats: if you're feeling spicy, the chorizo sausage hits the spot and the Spanish meatballs are justifiably popular. There's a great atmosphere here, so don't be surprised to find yourself staying for several hours.

Glowbal Grill & Satay Bar (Map pp360-1; ☎ 604-602-0835; 1079 Mainland St; mains $14-26; 11:30am-midnight Mon-Fri, 10:30am-midnight Sat & Sun) This often clamorous restaurant has a comfortable, lounge-like feel and a menu of classy dishes fusing West Coast ingredients with Asian and Mediterranean flourishes. The grilled halibut – served with scampi butter and roasted tomato risotto – is hard to beat, but save room for some finger-licking satay sticks.

Blue Water Café (Map pp360-1; ☎ 604-688-8078; 1095 Hamilton St; mains $22-44; 5pm-midnight) Vancouver's best oyster bar also serves excellent sushi and an array of delightfully simple seafood dishes in its warm brick-and-beam dining room. If you feel like an adventure, head straight to the semicircular raw bar and watch the chef's whirling blades prepare delectable sushi and sashimi, served with the restaurant's signature soya-seaweed dipping sauce.

Gastown & Chinatown

Mouse & the Bean Café (Map pp360-1; ☎ 604-633-1781; 207 W Hastings St; mains $4-12; noon-6pm Mon-Thu, noon-8pm Fri & Sat; V) Everything – including the salsa and refried beans – is made in-house at this family-run Mexican joint. The prices are incredibly low – which may explain why the floor is still unfinished concrete – and there are many vegetarian options. Try the feast-like Plato Mixteco if you want to share.

Salt Tasting Room (Map pp360-1; ☎ 604-633-1912; Blood Alley; mains $5-15; noon-midnight) Located along a darkened nook off Carrall St, this brick-lined, dine-in charcuterie is a protein-lover's delight with a deceptively simple approach. Pull up a bar stool at the long table and choose from cured meats and local cheeses, accompanied by a glass or two of great wine. Restoring the social aspect to dining, the room is often buzzing with chat.

Hon's Wun-Tun House (Map pp360-1; ☎ 604-688-0871; 268 E Keefer St; mains $6-18; 11am-11pm Sun-Thu, 11am-midnight Sat & Sun) Vancouver's favorite Chinese restaurant mini-chain, Hon's flagship Chinatown branch is suffused with inviting cooking smells. Dishes range from satisfying dim sum to steaming wonton soup bowls, bobbing with juicy dumplings. Try the congee rice porridge, a fancy-free soul food dish that takes three hours to prepare and comes in seafood, chicken and beef varieties.

Social at Le Magasin (Map pp360-1; ☎ 604-669-4488; 332 Water St; mains $22-28; 11am-midnight Mon-Fri, 10:30am-midnight Sat, 10:30am-10pm Sun) The downstairs oyster bar will entice you through the door but the ornate tin ceiling upstairs is worth the climb. Recommended for brunch, it's also a comfortable dinner spot with West Coast specials including a mouthwatering lamb shank. The onsite deli serves great sandwiches ($4 to $9) and heaped bowls of chili ($4).

South Main & Commercial Drive

Foundation (Map p358; ☎ 604-708-0881; 2301 Main St; mains $6-12; 5pm-1am; V) SoMa's liveliest hangout, this funky vegetarian (mostly vegan) restaurant is the kind of place where artsy students and chin-stroking young intellectuals like to be seen. To fuel all that brainpower, dishes include adventurous treats like mango and coconut pasta, all served on the eatery's signature mismatched Formica tables. Beer comes from regional fave Storm Brewing.

Charlatan (Map p358; ☎ 604-253-2777; 1446 Commercial Dr; mains $6-16; 🕑 11:30am-midnight) This laid-back pub-style hangout caters to myriad tastes: sports fans can perch at the bar under the flat-screen TVs to catch a game; drinkers – the Big Rock Traditional Ale is recommended – can hit the patio to watch the buzzing streetscape; and diners can chow down upstairs on comfort food like crab cakes with avocado salsa and mussels in exotic broths.

Havana (Map p358; ☎ 604-253-9119; 1212 Commercial Dr; mains $10-20; 🕑 11am-11pm Mon-Thu, 10am-midnight Fri, 9am-midnight Sat & Sun) The granddaddy of Commercial Dr has still got it, hence its teeming summertime patio. Combining a rustic Latin American ambience with a roster of satisfying Afro-Cuban-Southern soul food dishes, highlights include a shellfish platter of clams, mussels and oysters. Arrive early for dinner or you'll be fighting the crowds.

Granville Island

our pick Go Fish (Map pp360-1; ☎ 604-730-5040; 1505 W 1st Ave; mains $8-13; 🕑 11:30am-6:30pm Wed-Fri, noon-6:30pm Sat & Sun) On the amble-friendly seawall between Granville Island and Vanier Park, this waterfront shack, favored by in-the-know locals, serves Vancouver's best fresh-caught fish 'n chips, along with excellent wild salmon tacos and scallop burgers. All dishes are made to order and include house-chopped coleslaw. There's not much seating – although it's nice to perch on a stool facing the waterfront towers of north False Creek – so take your grub to nearby Vanier Park for a sunset dine-out.

Dockside Restaurant & Brewing Company (Map pp360-1; ☎ 604-685-7070; 1253 Johnston St; mains $14-26; 🕑 7am-10pm) Wood-grilled steaks and grilled wild salmon are among the highlights in the dining room here at the Granville Island Hotel (p369), but you can also kick back and enjoy a more casual (and cheaper) meal in the adjoining microbrew lounge. Both rooms share the waterfront patio – a chatty al fresco hangout on most summer evenings.

Kitsilano & West Side

Naam (Map p358; ☎ 604-738-7151; 2724 W 4th Ave; mains $7-14; 🕑 24hr; Ⓥ) Luring city-based vegetarians for 30 years, this casual 24-hour Kits eatery still has the ambience of a cozy, old-school hippy hangout. But the menu (and weekend brunch queues) show that these guys mean business, encouraging legions of repeat diners who keep coming back for stuffed quesadillas, hearty 'Farmers Breakfasts' and sesame-fried potatoes with miso gravy. Live music is a nightly fixture and there's a convivial covered patio.

Tojo's (Map p358; ☎ 604-872-8050; 1133 W Broadway; mains $16-26; 🕑 5-10pm Mon-Sat) Hidekazu Tojo's legendary skill with the sushi knife has created one of North America's most revered sushi restaurants, but signatures here also include lightly steamed monkfish and fried red tuna wrapped with seaweed and served with plum sauce. The sushi bar seats are highly prized, so reserve as early as possible and make sure you sample a selection or two from the sake menu.

Lumière (Map p358; ☎ 604-739-8185; 2551 W Broadway; mains $18-45; 🕑 5:30-11pm Tue-Sun) A constant contender in the 'best Vancouver restaurant' stakes, this swanky eatery from Rob Feenie – the city's most famed chef – deploys deceptively unfussy preparations to create an array of French-inspired, Asian-brushed masterpieces. Choose from mouthwatering mains like sake-and-maple syrup–baked sablefish or loosen your belt and launch into one of the three multicourse tasting menus (from $110).

DRINKING

New bars and lounges are springing up in Vancouver like persistent drunks at an open bar. Wherever you end up, try some local brewers, including Nelson, Granville Island and Crannóg.

Afterglow (Map pp360-1; ☎ 604-602-0835; 1082 Hamilton St; 🕑 11:30am-midnight) Tucked at the back of Yaletown's Glowbal Bar & Grill (opposite), the city's tiniest lounge is an intimate, pink-hued room lined with naked women – at least, their silhouettes appear on the walls. Pull up a stool and experiment with cocktails like You Glow Girl and Pink Pussycat or knock yourself out with an ultra-strong Quebecois beer.

Calling (Map pp360-1; ☎ 604-801-6681; 1780 Davie St; 🕑 11am-2am Mon-Fri, 10am-2am Sat, 10am-midnight Sun) A small but swanky reinvention of the neighborhood pub – think silky hardwood floors, mod furnishings and black-clad wait staff – the main draw is the sunset-hugging patio overlooking English Bay. Gourmet pub grub like smoky bacon-and-gorgonzola burgers are served alongside exotic European brews like Belgian cherry beer.

George Ultra Lounge (Map pp360-1; ☎ 604-628-5555; 1137 Hamilton St; 4pm-2am Mon-Sat) One of hedonistic Yaletown's favorite haunts, the moodily lit George attracts the laser-whitened-teeth crowd with its giant list of high-concept cocktails. Anyone for a Sazerac, featuring bourbon in an 'absinthe-washed glass'? Work your way down the list, sink further into your comfy chair and try to figure out what the giant swirly glass thing above the bar is supposed to be.

Irish Heather (Map pp360-1; ☎ 604-688-9779; 217 Carrall St; noon-midnight) Vancouver's best traditional pub, the Heather is an unpretentious labyrinth of brick-lined rooms with a cozy rear conservatory serving properly poured Guinness and great gourmet pub grub. Warm up in winter with a restorative 'Hot Irish,' a concoction of whiskey, lemon, cloves, sugar and boiling water, or head straight for the hidden Shebeen Whiskey House out back, complete with the city's largest malt selection. Both were planning a move across the street at the time of writing.

Six Acres (Map pp360-1; ☎ 604-488-0110; 203 Carrall St; noon-midnight Tue-Thu, noon-1am Fri & Sat) A smashing, brick-lined nook capturing the spirit of what a chatty pub should feel like and fusing it with some knowing quirky flourishes like menus enclosed by used book covers and old language tapes playing in the bathrooms. There's an excellent beer selection – try the Draft Dodger from Phillips Brewing – and inspired pub grub like the Berlin, a shared plate of cheese and sausage.

Steamworks Brewing Co (Map pp360-1; ☎ 604-689-2739; 375 Water St; 11:30am-midnight Sun-Wed, 11:30am-1am Thu-Sat) A giant Gastown microbrewery in a cavernous converted brick warehouse, the signature beer here is Lions Gate Lager, a good summer tipple. A favorite place for the city's after-work crowd, the pubby downstairs can get noisy while the upstairs is all about serene views across to the North Shore.

ENTERTAINMENT

Pick up the *Georgia Straight* or West Coast Life section of the *Vancouver Sun* – both out on Thursdays – to tap into local happenings.

Live Music

Railway Club (Map pp360-1; ☎ 604-681-1625; www.therailwayclub.com; 579 Dunsmuir St; most shows $4-10) The city's most authentic live music venue, the Railway combines a grungy Brit-pub feel with an eclectic nightly roster of indie, folk, soul and everything in between.

Commodore (Map pp360-1; ☎ 604-739-4550; 868 Granville St; most shows $20-35) Vancouver's best mid-sized venue, this art-deco spot is an old but lovingly renovated upstairs ballroom. Complete with a bouncy dancefloor, it showcases great visiting bands and top local talent.

Yale (Map pp360-1; ☎ 604-681-9253; www.theyale.ca; 1300 Granville St; most shows $10-25) Blues fans should head along Granville St to this unpretentious joint with a large stage and a devoted clientele.

Cellar Restaurant & Jazz Club (Map p358; ☎ 604-738-1959; www.cellarjazz.com; 3611 W Broadway; most shows $5-15) This is the place for jazz nuts, a subterranean venue where serious tunes are reverentially performed.

Nightclubs

Honey (Map pp360-1; ☎ 604-685-777; 455 Abbott St; noon-late) A refreshing alternative to the Granville St party rabble, this restaurant-lounge transforms into a club on weekends and is especially renowned for its Friday night Mod Club, when a pretence-free crowd of young coolsters dresses up for a night of pop-soul-and-everything-else partying.

Republic (Map pp360-1; ☎ 604-669-3266; 958 Granville St; 6pm-3am Sun-Wed, 4pm-3am Thu-Sat) The city's most exciting new club combines a swanky, high-ceiling ground level with a dramatic backlit bar and a hopping upstairs dance floor dripping with grinding bodies – especially on weekends when the Granville strip turns into a carnival of all-night partiers. You can watch the anarchy unfolding outside from the glass-encased patio.

Shine (Map pp360-1; ☎ 604-408-4321; 364 Water St; 9pm-2am) With music from electro to funky house and hip-hop, Gastown's subterranean Shine attracts a younger crowd and is divided into a noisy main room and an intimate cozy cave. The club's Saturday night 'Big Sexy Funk' (hip-hop and rock) is a local legend but Thursday's 1990s retro night appeals to all those ancient 25-year-old hipsters out there.

Theater & Cinemas

Arts Club Theatre Company (☎ 604-687-1644; www.artsclub.com; tickets $30-60) Popular classics and works by contemporary Canadian playwrights are part of the mix at this company, which performs at the Granville Island Stage (Map pp360–1) and Stanley Theatre (Map pp360–1).

Vancouver Playhouse (Map pp360-1; ☎ 604-873-3311; www.vancouverplayhouse.com; cnr Hamilton & Dunsmuir Sts; tickets $40-55) Mainstream live theater in the city is staged primarily here. Presents a six-play season at its large civic venue in the Queen Elizabeth Theatre complex.

For multiplex movie fans, the **Scotiabank Theatre** (Map pp360-1; ☎ 604-630-1407; www.cineplex.com; 900 Burrard St; admission $12) is downtown's blockbuster central. Adding a few festival flicks to the mix, **Tinseltown Cinemas** (Map pp360-1; ☎ 604-806-0799; www.cinemark.com; 88 W Pender St; admission $11) is another downtown favorite. Alt-movie buffs can hit the **Vancity International Film Centre** (Map pp360-1; ☎ 604-683-3456; www.viff.org; 1181 Seymour St; admission $9.50) while Canada Place's **CN IMAX Theatre** (Map pp360-1; ☎ 604-682-4629; www.imax.com/vancouver; 201-999 Canada Place; admission $12) mainly screens large-format documentaries.

Spectator Sports

The **Vancouver Canucks** (☎ 604-899-4600; www.canucks.com; GM Place; tickets $33-$94; ⌚ Oct-Apr) National Hockey League team is the city's leading sports franchise. Book your seat at their GM Place (Map pp360–1) home way in advance – most games are sold to capacity.

Canadian Football League (CFL) side **BC Lions** (☎ 604-589-7627; www.bclions.com; BC Place Stadium; tickets $27-70; ⌚ Jun-Oct) strut their stuff at downtown's covered BC Place Stadium (Map pp360–1). Tickets are generally easy to come by, unless the Lions are closing in on the Grey Cup, last won in 2006.

For a nostalgic (and cheap) afternoon of baseball and beer (in plastic cups), it's hard to beat a **Vancouver Canadians** (☎ 604-872-5232; www.canadiansbaseball.com; Nat Bailey Stadium; tickets $8-12.50; ⌚ mid-Jun–mid-Sep) game at the recently renovated Nat Bailey Stadium (p358).

And if you want to see the **Vancouver Whitecaps** (☎ 604-669-9283; www.whitecapsfc.com; Swangard Stadium, Burnaby; tickets $16-35; ⌚ May-Sep) Western League soccer team before their proposed 2011 move to a new downtown stadium, you'll have to hit the SkyTrain to Burnaby and their old-school Swangard Stadium (p358) venue.

SHOPPING

While Robson St is fine if you're looking for chain fashion stores, it's hard to beat the edgier SoMa boutiques between 19th and 23rd Aves. For window shopping, Granville Island and Kitsilano's 4th Ave are ideal.

Granville Island Public Market (Map pp360-1; ☎ 604-666-6477; www.granvilleisland.com; Johnson St; ⌚ 9am-7pm) Towering peaks of fruit and veg dominate at the city's leading covered market, which also acts as a great spot to trawl the deli stands and tempting bakeries for picnic supplies. There's also a good food court plus many temporary stalls hawking quirky arts and crafts.

John Fluevog Shoes (Map pp360-1; ☎ 604-688-2828; 837 Granville St; ⌚ 11am-7pm Mon Wed & Sat, 11am-8pm Thu & Fri, noon-6pm Sun) While some of their footwear looks like Doc Martens on acid and others could poke your eye out from 20 paces, many of Fluevog's funky shoes also have a reduced 'green footprint.' Check out the completely biodegradable 'Earth Angels' range.

Mink Chocolates (Map pp360-1; ☎ 604-633-2451; 863 W Hastings St; ⌚ 8am-6pm Mon-Fri, 10am-6pm Sat & Sun) Avoid the usual Canuck souvenirs of maple syrup cookies and vacuum-packed salmon at this decadent designer chocolate shop in the downtown core. Trouble is, once you've selected a handful of choccy bonbons (little edible artworks embossed with prints of trees and coffee cups) you'll be lured to the drinks bar for a velvety hot chocolate. Next stop: years of addiction therapy.

Mountain Equipment Co-op (Map p358; ☎ 604-872-7858; 130 W Broadway; ⌚ 10am-7pm Mon-Wed, 10am-9pm Thu & Fri, 9am-6pm Sat, 11am-5pm Sun) Outdoorsy visitors usually gravitate towards this store stuffed with clothing, kayaks, sleeping bags, clever camping gadgets and a respectable array of regional and international travel books. You'll have to be a lifetime member to buy, but that's easy to arrange and only costs $5.

Smoking Lily (Map p358; ☎ 604-873-5459; 3634 Main St; ⌚ 11am-5:30pm Thu-Sat, noon-5pm Sun & Mon) Quirky art-student cool is the approach at this SoMa store, where skirts, belts and halter tops are whimsically accented with prints of ants, skulls or the Periodic Table, making their wearers appear interesting and complex. Men's clothing is slowly creeping into the mix, with some fish, skull and bird sketch T-shirts available.

UBC Farm Market (Map p358; ☎ 604-822-5092; 6182 South Campus Rd; ⌚ 9am-1pm Sat mid-Jun–Sep) A tasty cornucopia of regional BC farm produce hits the stalls here in summer. Highlights can include crunchy apples, lush peaches and juicy blueberries, while home-baked treats are frequent accompaniments. Additional summer market venues throughout the city include Nelson Park, Trout Lake and Nat Bailey Stadium. Check www.eatlocal.org for information.

GETTING THERE & AWAY

Air

Vancouver International Airport (Map p358; ☎ 604-207-7077; www.yvr.ca) is the main West Coast hub for airlines from Canada, the US and international locales. It's in Richmond, a 13km drive from downtown.

Intra-Canada flights arriving here include regular **Westjet** (☎ 800-538-5696; www.westjet.com) services from Calgary ($160, 1½ hours) and **Air Canada Jazz** (☎ 514-393-3333, 888-247-2262; www.aircanada.com) services from Victoria (from $91, 25 minutes).

Several handy floatplane services can also deliver you directly to the Vancouver waterfront. These include frequent **Harbour Air Seaplanes** (☎ 604-274-1277, 800-665-0212; www.harbour-air.com) services ($120, 35 minutes) and **West Coast Air** (☎ 604-606-6888, 800-347-2222; www.westcoastair.com) services ($119, 35 minutes) from Victoria's Inner Harbour.

Boat

BC Ferries (☎ 250-386-3431, 888-223-3779; www.bcferries.com) services arrive at Tsawwassen – a 35km drive south of downtown – from Vancouver Island's Swartz Bay (passenger/vehicle $10.55/35, 1½ hours) and Nanaimo's Duke Point (passenger/vehicle $10.55/35, two hours). Services also arrive here from the Southern Gulf Islands (p404).

Additional ferries arrive in West Vancouver's Horseshoe Bay – 21km northwest of downtown – from Nanaimo's Departure Bay (passenger/vehicle $10.55/35, 1½ hours). Services also arrive at Horseshow Bay from Langdale (passenger/vehicle $9.60/34, 40 minutes) on the Sunshine Coast.

Bus

Most out-of-town buses grind to a halt at Vancouver's **Pacific Central Station** (Map pp360-1; 1150 Station St).

Greyhound (☎ 800-661-8747; www.greyhound.ca) services arrive here from Whistler ($18.80, 2½ hours, eight daily), Kelowna (from $30, six hours, seven daily) and Calgary (from $70, 14 to 17 hours, six daily) among others. Traveling via the BC Ferries Swartz Bay–Tsawwassen route, frequent **Pacific Coach Lines** (☎ 250-385-4411, 800-661-1725; www.pacificcoach.com) services trundle in here from downtown Victoria ($37.50, 3½ hours).

Perimeter Tours (☎ 604-266-5386, 877-317-7788; www.perimeterbus.com) services arrive in the city from Whistler ($67, 2½ hours, seven to 11 daily).

Quick Coach Lines (☎ 604-940-4428, 800-665-2122; www.quickcoach.com) runs an express shuttle between Seattle and Vancouver, departing from downtown Seattle (US$34.20, four hours, six daily) and the city's Sea-Tac International Airport (US$46.55, 4½ hours, seven daily).

Car & Motorcycle

If you're coming from Washington State in the US, you'll be on the I-5 until you hit the border town of Blaine, then you'll be on Hwy 99 in Canada. It's about an hour's drive from here to downtown Vancouver. Hwy 99 continues through downtown, across the Lions Gate Bridge to Horseshoe Bay, Squamish and Whistler.

If you're coming from the east, you'll probably be on the Trans-Canada Hwy (Hwy 1), which snakes through the city's eastern end, eventually meeting with Hastings St. If you want to go downtown, turn left onto Hastings and follow it into the city center, or continue on along the North Shore towards Whistler.

If you're coming from Horseshoe Bay, the Trans-Canada Hwy (Hwy 1) heads through West Vancouver and North Vancouver before going over the Second Narrows Bridge into Burnaby. If you're heading downtown, leave the highway at the Taylor Way exit in West Vancouver and follow it over the Lions Gate Bridge towards the city center.

Train

Trains trundle in from across Canada and the US at **Pacific Central Station** (Map pp360-1; 1150 Station St).

Via Rail (☎ 888-842-7245; www.viarail.com) trains arrive here from Kamloops North ($115, nine hours, three weekly), Jasper ($240, 17½ hours, three weekly) and Edmonton ($325, 24 hours, three weekly), among others.

Amtrak (☎ 800-872-7245; www.amtrak.com) US services arrives from Eugene (US$56, 13½ hours, two daily), Portland (US$42, eight hours, three daily) and Seattle (from US$28, 3½ hours, five daily).

GETTING AROUND

To/From the Airport

With the new SkyTrain rapid transit airport line not expected to open until late 2009 at the time of writing, budget up to $35 for the 13km taxi ride from the airport to downtown Vancouver. Alternatively, the **Vancouver Airporter** (☎ 604-946-8866, 800-668-3141; www.yvrairporter.com; one-way/return $13.50/21; 🕑 5:30am-11:45pm) shuttle bus delivers passengers to many city center hotels.

Bicycle

With routes running across town, Vancouver is a relatively good cycling city. Pick-up a *Greater Vancouver Cycling Map & Guide* ($3.95) at convenience stores and bookshops for area information.

Bikes can be rented from the following:

Reckless Bike Stores (Map pp360-1; ☎ 604-731-2420; www.rektek.com; 1810 Fir St; half/full-day $25/32.50; 🕑 9am-7pm Mon-Sat, 10am-6pm Sun May-Aug, 10am-dusk Sep-Apr) Near the Granville Island entrance.

Spokes Bicycle Rental (Map pp360-1; ☎ 604-688-5141; www.vancouverbikerental.com; 1798 W Georgia St; adult per hr/6hr from $7/20; 🕑 9am-7pm May-Aug, 10am-dusk Sep-Apr) One block from Stanley Park's main entrance.

Boat

Running minivessels (some big enough to carry bikes) between the foot of Hornby St and Granville Island, **Aquabus Ferries** (Map pp360-1; ☎ 604-689-5858; www.theaquabus.com; adult/child from $2.50/1.25) services spots along False Creek as far as Science World.

Its cutthroat rival is **False Creek Ferries** (Map pp360-1; ☎ 604-684-7781; www.granvilleislandferries.bc.ca; adult/child from $2.50/1.25), which operates a similar Granville Island service from the Aquatic Centre, plus ports of call around False Creek.

Car & Motorcycle

The rush-hour queue to cross the Lions Gate Bridge to the North Shore frequently snakes far up Georgia St. Try the alternative Second Narrows Bridge. Other peak-time hot spots to avoid are the George Massey Tunnel and Hwy 1 to Surrey.

Parking is at a premium downtown: there are few free spots available on residential side streets, and traffic wardens are predictably predatory. Some streets have metered parking but the numerous parking lots (from $4 per hour) are a better proposition. Some early bird discounts before 9am.

Public Transportation

TransLink (☎ 604-953-3333; www.translink.bc.ca) has overseas bus, SkyTrain and SeaBus boat services. A ticket bought on any of the three services is valid for 1½ hours of travel on the entire network, depending on the zone you intend to travel in. The three zones become progressively more expensive the further you journey. One-zone tickets are $2.50, two-zone tickets are $3.75 and three-zone tickets are $5. If you're traveling after 6:30pm or on weekends or holidays, all trips are classed as one-zone fares and cost $2.50.

The bus network is extensive in the downtown area, especially along Granville St, Broadway, Hastings St, Main St and Burrard St. Many buses have bike racks and are wheelchair accessible. Exact change (or more) is required since all buses use fare machines.

At the time of writing, the SkyTrain network consisted of two routes with a third Canada Line route from downtown to the airport due to open in 2009. The 35-minute Expo Line takes passengers to and from downtown Vancouver and Surrey, via stops throughout Burnaby and New Westminster. The newer Millennium Line alights near shopping malls and suburban residential districts in Coquitlam and Burnaby.

The aquatic SeaBus shuttle operates every 15 to 30 minutes throughout the day, taking 12 minutes to cross the Burrard Inlet between Waterfront Station and Lonsdale Quay. At Lonsdale there's a bus terminal servicing routes throughout North Vancouver and West Vancouver.

WHISTLER & THE SUNSHINE COAST

One of the world's most scenic coastal mountain drives, the winding Sea to Sky Hwy delivers spectacular views of glassy Howe Sound en route to Whistler. (At the time of writing it was being upgraded as the main road artery between the two 2010 Winter Olympic sites.) The world-famous ski resort is a hive of snow-based activity in winter, when it can be just as much fun hanging around with the beautiful people in the loungey bars as actually hitting the slopes. For those who prefer toasty temperatures, the resort in summer has also become a popular hiking and biking magnet.

Travelers who like to keep their tans topped-up should also make for the Sunshine Coast, which reputedly receives more rays than Hawaii. This 139km stretch of crenulated, mostly forested waterfront northwest of Vancouver is accessible via a 40-minute ferry ride from the outskirts of the city. Many Vancouverites have little idea just how close they are to a region renowned for its diving, kayaking and quirky rival communities.

WHISTLER

Named after the furry marmots that populate the surrounding mountains and whistle like deflating balloons, this pretty alpine village is one of the world's most popular ski resorts. Sharing the 2010 Winter Olympics with Vancouver, Whistler is staging biathlon, bobsleigh, luge, alpine skiing and ski jumping events, so don't be surprised to hear construction workers hammering outside your hotel window if you're here before February 2010. But it's not all about winter activities here. The area has seen summer visitor numbers leaping in recent years, with many dropping in to try mountain biking, alpine hiking and a full roster of adventurous outdoor activities.

Orientation & Information

Approaching via Hwy 99 from the south, you'll hit Creekside, the first of Whistler's four main neighborhoods – the others are Whistler Village, Village North and Upper Village. Whistler Village is the area's commercial hub and can be a confusing maze for first-timers. Luckily, there are lots of people around to snag directions from. Pick up the *Pique* or *Whistler Question* newspapers for local insights.

Local services include the following:

Armchair Books (☎ 604-932-5557; 4205 Village Sq; 🕑 9am-9pm) Central bookstore with strong travel section

Custom House Currency Exchange (☎ 604-938-6658; 4154 Village Stroll; 🕑 9am-5pm May-Sep, 9am-6pm Oct-Apr) Handy central exchange.

Cyber Web (☎ 604-905-1280; 4340 Sundial Cres; per 10min $2.50; 🕑 9am-10:30pm May-Sep, 8am-10pm Oct-Apr) Large internet café.

Post office (☎ 604-932-5012; 106-4360 Lorimer Rd; 🕑 8am-5pm Mon-Fri, 8am-noon Sat)

Town Plaza Medical Clinic (☎ 604-905-7089; 4314 Main St; 🕑 8:30am-7:30pm Oct-Apr, 9am-5:30pm Mon-Sat, 10am-4pm Sun May-Sep) Walk-in medical center.

Whistler Activity Centre (☎ 604-938-2769, 877-991-9988; 4010 Whistler Way; 🕑 9am-5pm) Recommendations and bookings for local activities.

Whistler Visitor Centre (☎ 604-935-3357, 877-991-9988; www.tourismwhistler.com; 4230 Gateway Dr; 🕑 8am-8pm) Flyer-lined information center with friendly staff.

Activities

Once a determinedly winter-based activity capital, Whistler is also increasingly a summer destination, drawing visitors with rafting, hiking and mountain-biking opportunities. Whatever season you arrive, head to the visitor centre or activity centre (both above) for tips and recommendations.

SKIING & SNOWBOARDING

With 200 runs, Twin-mountain resort **Whistler-Blackcomb** (☎ 604-904-7060, 888-403-4727; www.whistlerblackcomb.com; 2-day lift ticket adult/child/youth $81/42/69) is one of North America's largest ski areas. Recent years have seen record snowfalls and the region generally enjoys Canada's longest resort season – November through June on Blackcomb, and November through April on Whistler. There are dozens of lifts to transport skiers and snowboarders, and a hotly anticipated 4.4km peak-to-peak gondola – linking both mountains for the first time – was due to open in 2008 at the time of writing.

Ski and board fans can beat the crowds with an early-morning **Fresh Tracks ticket** (adult/child $17/12). Book in advance at the Whistler Village Gondola and be there for a 7am start the next day. Night owls might prefer the **Night Moves** (adult/child/youth $16/11/13; 🕑 5-9pm Thu-Sat) program operated via Blackcomb's Magic Chair lift.

If you don't bring you own gear, **Mountain Adventure Centres** (☎ 604-904-7060, 888-403-4727; www.whistlerblackcomb.com/rentals; 1-day ski or snowboard rental adult/child from $38/20) runs equipment rental outlets around town.

CROSS-COUNTRY SKIING & SNOWSHOEING

A short stroll or free shuttle bus away from the village, **Lost Lake** (☎ 604-905-0071; www.crosscountryconnection.bc.ca; day pass adult/child & youth $15/7.50; 🕑 8am-9pm Nov-Mar) is the hub for 32km of wooded cross-country ski trails, suitable for novices and experts alike. Lit at night, its 'warming hut' provides rentals, lessons and

WHISTLING FOR THE OLYMPICS

While Whistler was originally developed in the 1960s with the Olympics in mind, it has taken 40 years for the five-ringed circus to finally roll into town. The region hit the international spotlight when it was selected to join Vancouver in hosting the 2010 Olympic and Paralympic Winter Games.

Visitors arriving before the Games can hit the alpine ski race runs for themselves or just drop by the **Whistler 2010 Info Centre** (☎ 877-408-2010; www.winter2010.com; 4365 Blackcomb Way; 11am-5pm) for the latest Olympic news, including plans for legacy projects due once the famous flame is extinguished.

Along with backcountry partner the Callaghan Valley, it's the scheduled home of the following events:

- Alpine skiing: Downhill, Super-G, Giant Slalom, Slalom, Combined
- Nordic: Biathlon, Cross-country Skiing, Nordic Combined, Ski Jumping
- Sliding: Luge, Skeleton, Bobsleigh
- Paralympic: Alpine Skiing, Cross-Country Skiing, Biathlon

maps. Snowshoers are also well-served here: you can stomp off on your own on marked trails or rent a guide.

Outdoor Adventures Whistler (☎ 604-932-0647; www.adventureswhistler.com; 4205 Village Sq; tours adult/child from $69/39) offers four snowshoeing tours, including a three-hour fondue excursion (adult/child $109/49). Prices include equipment rentals, and the company also offers a wide range of other tours and activities.

MOUNTAIN BIKING

Served by three lifts, **Whistler Mountain Bike Park** (☎ 604-904-8134, 866-218-9690; www.whistlerbike.com; lift access 1-day adult/child/youth $40/21/35; mid-May–mid-Oct) has 1200m of vertical drops, plus plenty of ramps, high-octane jumps and 45 forested trails (pick up a route map from the visitor centre, opposite). There are more than 100km of additional bike trails throughout the region – visit www.worca.com for more info.

HIKING

With more than 40km of alpine trails (most accessed via the Whistler Village Gondola) this region is ideal for those who like nature of the strollable variety. Favorite routes include the **High Note Trail** (8km), which traverses pristine meadows and has stunning views of Cheakumus Lake. Pick-up a general route map from the visitor center (opposite).

Whistler Alpine Guides Bureau (☎ 604-938-9242; www.whistlerguides.com; 113-4350 Lorimer Rd; guided hikes from adult/child from $89/69) organizes guided treks of the region as well as rock climbing and rap jumping activities.

RAFTING

Tumbling waterfalls and local wildlife are some of the visuals you might catch as you lurch along the Elaho or Squamish Rivers on an adrenalin-fuelled raft trip. **Whistler River Adventures** (☎ 604-932-3532, 888-932-3532; www.whistlerriver.com; Whistler Village Gondola; mid-May–Aug) offers five paddle-like-crazy excursions, including the popular Green River trip (adult/child $69/59).

Sleeping

Hotel rates can double here in winter but specials are available the rest of the year, especially in fall's shoulder season. Most hotels charge parking fees ($10 to $20 daily) and some also charge resort fees ($12 to $25 per day). The Visitor Centre (opposite) has a handy **accommodation reservation service** (☎ 604-932-0606, 800-944-7853; www.whistler.com).

HI-Whistler Hostel (☎ 604-932-5492; whistler@hihostels.ca; 5678 Alta Lake Rd; dm/r $30/68) Teetering on the edge of Alta Lake, 5km from the village, this secluded hostel is ideal for those who don't have to make it back from a wild night on the town. Dorms are predictably institutional, and there's a muscle-soothing sauna.

Riverside RV Resort & Campground (☎ 604-905-5533; www.whistlercamping.com; 8018 Mons Rd; tent/cabin $35/165) A few minutes north of town via Hwy 99 – there's a free shuttle bus in summer – this family-friendly spot is popular with campers. Aside from the tent-pitches, there's a clutch of rustic, gable-topped wooden cabins, each with porches, showers and full kitchens. The onsite restaurant serves great breakfasts (have the salmon eggs Benedict).

Alpine Lodge (☎ 604-932-5966; www.alpinelodge.com; 8135 Alpine Way; dm/r/ste $50/125/175; wi-fi) A colorful, wood-lined lodge just north of town, the centerpiece here is the cozy 'Great Room' where your free coffee-and-croissants breakfast is served. The rooms are functional rather than palatial but most have private baths and all have mountain views. There's a handy shuttle bus to and from the lifts.

Blackcomb Lodge (☎ 604-935-1177, 888-621-1117; www.blackcomblodge.com; 4220 Gateway Dr; r/ste from $109/139;) This boutique-style sleepover combines West Coast style with classy flourishes. There's plenty of rock lining the lobby but the rooms are all about deep leather sofas and black appliances. Lofts and studios come with full kitchens. Blackcomb is right in the heart of the Village Sq – you can almost shout your order to the liquor store opposite.

Crystal Lodge (☎ 604-932-2221, 800-667-3363; www.crystal-lodge.com; 4319 Main St; d/ste from $130/175;) Not all rooms are created equal at this central sleepover forged from the fusion of two quite different hotel towers. Cheaper rooms in the South Tower are standard motel-style but those in the Lodge Wing match the splendid rock-and-beam lobby, complete with small balconies. Both share excellent proximity to village restaurants and are close to the main ski lift.

Chalet Luise B&B Inn (☎ 604-932-4187, 800-665-1998; www.chaletluise.com; 7461 Ambassador Cres; r from $135) A five-minute trail walk from the village, this recently renovated Bavarian-look pension has eight bright and sunny rooms – pine furnishings and white duvets – and a flower garden that's ideal for a spot of evening wine quaffing. Or you can just hop in the hot tub and dream about the large buffet breakfast coming your way in the morning.

OUR PICK Edgewater Lodge (☎ 604-932-0688, 888-870-9065; www.edgewater-lodge.com; 8020 Alpine Way; r incl breakfast from $150; wi-fi) Three kilometers past Whistler on Hwy 99, this 12-room haven is ideal for those who like to be close to nature without sacrificing home comforts. Rooms overlook glassy Green Lake through large windows – sit in your padded alcove and watch the ospreys swooping past. Peel yourself away for breakfast in the magnificent dining room. The outdoor seating on the lake's edge is the perfect place for a dinner of juicy Queen Charlotte Islands salmon.

Adara Hotel (☎ 604-905-4665, 866-502-3272; www.adarahotel.com; 4122 Village Green; r from $160; wi-fi) Unlike all those Whistler lodges now claiming to be boutique hotels, the sophisticated Adara is the real deal, but with quirky twists like dramatic mod rooms and art-lined interiors. Fireplaces look like TVs, bathrooms are of the raindrop shower variety and faux fur throws make you feel like you're in a 1970s Christmas card. The front desk loans iPods.

Fairmont Chateau Whistler (☎ 604-938-8000, 800-441-1414; www.fairmont.com/whistler; 4599 Chateau Blvd; r from $400;) Standing sentinel near the base of Blackcomb, this castle fits its natural surroundings perfectly. The hallways, lobbies and 550 rooms are adorned in rich hues and tastefully furnished with classic West Coast elegance. Ask for a room with mountain views or spend your time at the swanky spa. Close enough to the lifts for ski-in/ski-out decadence.

Eating

Beet Root Café (☎ 604-932-1163; 129-4340 Lorimer Rd; light mains $4-8; 7:30am-6pm) The best home-style hangout in Whistler, the menu here leans towards bulging breakfast burritos and huge packed sandwiches but it's worth loitering until the baked treats are released from the oven. Buy as many cookies and muffins as you can eat: smiling and stuffing your face has never been easier.

Sachi Sushi (☎ 604-935-5649; 106-4359 Main St; mains $8-18; 11:30am-10pm Tue-Fri, 5-10pm Sat-Mon) Whistler's best sushi spot doesn't stop at mere California rolls. Serving everything from crispy popcorn shrimp to seafood salads and stomach-warming udon noodles (the tempura noodle bowl is best), this bright and breezy eatery is a relaxing hangout. Try a glass of hot sake on a cold winter day.

Citta Bistro (☎ 604-932-4177; 4217 Village Stroll; mains $8-22 10am-1am Mon-Fri, 9am-1am Sat & Sun) Pronounced 'cheeta,' this lively patio eatery on the edge of Village Sq serves up creative twists on comfort food classics – try the wild salmon club sandwich. The loungey, sometimes raucous, bar will keep you occupied past midnight when you can stagger back to wherever your hotel might be.

21 Steps Kitchen & Bar (☎ 604-966-2121; 4320 Sundial Cres; mains $14-22; 5:30pm-1am Mon-Sat, 5:30pm-midnight Sun) With small plates for nibblers, the main dishes at this cozy upstairs spot are high-end comfort food. Not a great place for vegetarians – unless you like stuffed portobello mushroom – steak, chops and seafood feature heavily. Check out the great attic bar, a local favorite.

our pick **Araxi Restaurant & Lounge** (☎ 604-932-4540; 4222 Village Sq; mains $30-45; ⏰ 5-11pm) Whistler's best splurge restaurant, exquisite Araxi combines a sophisticated menu with service that immediately puts diners at ease. The inventive main dishes are all about superb, mostly Pacific Northwest, with ingredients ranging from Queen Charlottes cod to Cowichan Valley chicken. Save room for dessert: the cheese menu is small but perfectly formed and the Okanagan apple cheesecake will have you licking the glaze off your plate.

Drinking & Entertainment

Amsterdam Café Pub (☎ 604-932-8334; Village Sq; ⏰ 11am-1am) A brick-lined party joint with a neighborhood pub vibe, this bar is in the heart of the village action and offers lots of drinks specials – the Alexander Keith's Pale Ale is recommended. You can treat your hangover to a late breakfast the next day by coming in for a good-value fry-up.

Garibaldi Lift Company (GLC; ☎ 604-905-2220; Whistler Village Gondola; ⏰ 11:30am-11pm) The closest bar to the slopes – you can watch the powder geeks on Whistler Mountain slide to a halt from the patio – the GLC is a smashing, rock-lined cave of a place defining the essence of après ski. From its wrought-iron chandeliers to its stone hearth and giant windows, you can tell anyone who will listen all about your daring escapades on the slopes. They might even believe you.

Garfinkel's (☎ 604-932-2323; 1-4308 Main St) Mixing mainstream dance grooves with Monday night live bands, Whistler's biggest club has been a regional legend for years. Thursday is the best night of the week, attracting locals with indie and funk tunes, but be prepared to line up for weekend entry when everyone within a 25km radius seems to be trying to get in.

Moe Joe's (☎ 604-935-1152; 4155 Golfer's Approach) Locals in the know will point you to this place if they want to hang out with you. More intimate than Garfinkel's, it's the best place in town if you like dancing yourself into a drooling heap. Always crowded on Friday nights (Monday's drum 'n bass night is also popular), this is where you're most likely to find the under-25 ski-bunny crowd.

Getting There & Around

While most visitors arrive by car from Vancouver via Hwy 99, you can also fly in on a **Whistler Air** (☎ 603-932-6615, 888-806-2299; www.whistlerair.ca) floatplane to Green Lake ($149, 30 minutes, two daily, May to September).

Greyhound (☎ 800-661-8747; www.greyhound.ca) bus services arrive at Creekside and Whistler Village from Vancouver ($18.80, 2½ hours, eight daily) and Squamish ($8.35, 50 minutes, nine daily).

Motor coach services from **Perimeter Tours** (☎ 604-266-5386, 877-317-7788; www.perimeterbus.com) also arrive from Vancouver ($67, 2½ hours, seven to 11 daily) and Vancouver Airport ($67, three hours, nine daily) and drop off at Whistler hotels. **Snowbus** (☎ 604-685-7669, 866-7669-287; www.snowbus.ca) operates a November to April service from Richmond ($29, three hours, two daily) and Vancouver ($21, 2½ hours, two daily).

Trainspotters can trundle into town on Rocky Mountaineer Vacations' **Whistler Mountaineer** (☎ 604-606-8460, 888-687-7245; www.whistlermountaineer.com), which winds along a picturesque coastal route from North Vancouver (from $105, three hours, daily May to mid-October).

Whistler's **WAVE** (☎ 604-932-4020; www.busonline.ca; adult/child/1-day pass $1.50/1.25/4.50) public buses are equipped with ski and bike racks. In winter, trips are free between Marketplace and the Upper Village loop and in summer there's a free service from the village to Lost Lake.

SUNSHINE COAST

Stretching from the ferry dock in Langdale to Lund, the Sunshine Coast, separated from the Lower Mainland by the Coast Mountains and the Strait of Georgia, has an independent, island-like mentality that belies the fact it's only a 40-minute ferry ride from Horseshoe Bay. With Hwy 101 linking key communities like Gibsons, Sechelt and Powell River, it's an easy and convivial region to explore, and there's plenty of local rivalry to keep things colorful. Check www.sunshinecoastcanada.com for information.

Getting There & Around

BC Ferries (☎ 250-386-3431, 888-223-3779; www.bcferries.com) services arrive at Langdale, 6km northeast of Gibsons, from West Vancouver's Horseshoe Bay (passenger/vehicle $9.60/34, 40 minutes, eight daily). The **Sunshine Coast Transit System** (☎ 604-885-6899; www.busonline.ca)

runs bus services (adult/child $2.25/1.75) from the terminal into Gibsons, Roberts Creek and Sechelt.

Buses run by **Malaspina Coach Lines** (☎ 604-886-7742, 877-227-8287; www.malaspinacoach.com) arrive twice-daily (once-daily off-season) from Vancouver, via the ferry, in Gibsons ($24, two hours), Roberts Creek ($27, 2½ hours), Sechelt ($30, three hours) and Powell River ($51, five to six hours). This service is also handy for traveling up and down the highway between the Sunshine Coast communities.

Gibsons

This gateway town's waterfront (named Gibsons Landing) is a kaleidoscope of painted buildings perched over a marina. Walk up from the waterfront and you'll hit the shops, the tiny **Visitor Info Centre** (☎ 604-886-2374, 866-222-3806; www.gibsonsbc.ca; 417 Marine Dr; 🕑 9am-5pm May-Sep, Tue-Sat Oct-Apr) and Hwy 101.

Once you've finished wandering, kayak rentals and tours are available from the friendly folk at **Sunshine Kayaking** (☎ 604-886-9760; www.sunshinekayaking.com; Molly's Lane; rentals per 4/8hr $32/45; 🕑 9am-6pm Mon-Fri, 8am-6pm Sat & Sun). Their guided sunset tour ($60) is recommended.

The best bet for a bed is just out of town at **Caprice B&B** (☎ 604-886-4270, 866-886-4270; www.capricebb.com; 1111 Gower Point Rd; d $95-125; 🏊). Nestled among the arbutus trees, it's a large waterfront home with three suites – two have handy kitchenettes. Homemade bakery treats feature on the breakfast menu and there's a small outdoor pool.

The local's favorite nosh pit, **Molly's Reach** (☎ 604-886-9710; 647 School Rd; mains $7-12; 🕑 7am-9pm) is a great spot for a heaping breakfast – try the stomach-expanding 'Constable Constable,' consisting of two eggs, two sausages, two pancakes and two slices of bacon. Aim for a window seat and you'll be overlooking the water.

Sechelt

The Sunshine Coast's second-largest town, Sechelt is a base for hiking, biking, kayaking and diving fans. It also has plenty of pit-stop amenities if you're just passing through. For info, try the **Sechelt Visitor Information Centre** (☎ 604-885-1036, 877-885-1036; 5790 Teredo St; 🕑 9am-5pm May-Aug, 10am-4pm Mon-Fri, 10am-2pm Sat Sep-Apr).

Pedals & Paddles (☎ 604-885-6440, 866-885-6440; www.pedalspaddles.com; Tillicum Bay Marina; kayak rental per 4/8hr $32/44) organizes kayak rentals and tours of the area's tranquil waters, while **On the Edge** (☎ 604-885-4888; www.ontheedgebiking.com; 5644 Cowrie St; bike rental per 4/8hr $20/34) rents bikes and also leads guided treks.

For cold-water divers and those who'd like to learn, the friendly folk at **Porpoise Bay Charters** (☎ 604-885-5950, 800-665-3483; www.porpoisebaycharters.com; 5718 Anchor Rd; dive trips from $100) offer training and trips. One of BC's best dive regions, you can check out steely eyed blue sharks and hulking shipwrecks just off the coast.

Great waterfront views are part of the attraction at **Sechelt Inlet B&B** (☎ 604-740-0776, 877-740-0776; www.secheltinletbandb.com; 5870 Skookumchuck Rd; d $109-129), which has three intimate, colorfully decorated suites. The purple-hued Maple Suite is a favorite and there's a hot tub overlooking the twinkling water.

If you feel like splurging, continue your drive along Hwy 101 past Sechelt to **Rockwater Secret Cove Resort** (☎ 604-885-7038, 877-296-4593; www.rockwatersecretcoveresort.com; 5356 Ole's Cove Rd; r/ste/cabin/tenthouse from $149/179/159/299) where the highlight accommodation is a clutch of tenthouse suites perched like nests on a steep cliff. Each luxurious canvas-walled dwelling has a heated rock floor, Jacuzzi and a private deck overlooking the bay.

The resort has a good West Coast restaurant (mains $16 to $28), but Sechelt's best eatery

SKOOKUMCHUCK NARROWS PROVINCIAL PARK

Located at the top of the lower Sunshine Coast, Egmont is home to **Skookumchuck Narrows Provincial Park** (☎ 604-885-3714; www.bcparks.ca), where a 4km hike brings you to an inlet so narrow that when the water is forced through during high tide it causes 30km/h rapids. Hop aboard a steel-hulled water taxi operated by **High Tide Tours** (☎ 604-883-9220; www.hightidetours.com; Egmont Marina; tickets $15) and take-in the roiling, unpredictable waves first-hand. The boat crisscrosses the rapids like a dive-bomber – keep a lookout for the crazy kayakers who also come here for a little white-knuckle paddling. If you're not feeling too queasy after your bouncy boat trip, the marina's laid-back **Backeddy Pub** (☎ 604-883-3614; Egmont Marina; mains $6-12) is a good spot for a bulging 'Egmont burger' and a restorative beer or two.

is the **Old Boot** (☎ 604-885-2727; 5330 Wharf St; mains $10-16; 🕑 11:30am-10pm Tue-Sun), a charming Italian nook with good pizzas and well-prepared pasta dishes. Try the prawn linguini.

Powell River

A short ferry hop along Hwy 101 brings you to this vibrant former resource town which has a strong claim to being the Sunshine Coast's heart and soul. Funkier than Sechelt and busier than Gibsons, Powell River is well worth a sleepover and is a hot spot for outdoor activities – drop by the **Powell River Visitor Centre** (☎ 604-485-4701, 877-817-8669; www.discoverpowellriver.com; 111-4871 Joyce Ave; 🕑 9am-9pm Mon-Fri, 10am-6pm Sat & Sun May-Sep, 9am-5pm Mon-Fri Oct-Apr) for information.

West of downtown, **Willingdon Beach City Park** is an ideal waterfront picnic spot. You can walk off your lunch with a guided **walking tour** (☎ 604-483-3901; tour $5; 🕑 tours 7pm Wed, 10am Sat Jul & Aug) of the town's historic quarter. Or you can hit the water with a kayak from **Powell River Sea Kayak** (☎ 604-483-2160, 866-617-4444; www.bcseakayak.com; 3hr rental $35).

For a quirky sleepover, the **Old Courthouse Inn** (☎ 604-483-4000, 877-483-4777; www.oldcourthouseinn.ca; 6243 Walnut St; s/d from $59/69) occupies the town's former court chambers and police station. In keeping with the historic theme, the rooms are nicely decorated with antique furnishings.

At the end of a long day of exploring, it's hard to beat **La Casita** (☎ 604-485-7720; 4578 Marine Ave; mains $7-14; 🕑 11:30am-10pm Mon-Sat, 5-10pm Sun; Ⓥ), an energetic Mexican eatery with lip-smacking shrimp and scallop tacos plus plenty of veggie-friendly options. If a beer and pub grub is more your style, drop by the waterfront **Shinglemill Pub & Bistro** (☎ 604-483-3545; 6233 Powell Pl; mains $8-12; 🕑 11am-10pm) instead.

VANCOUVER ISLAND

The largest populated landmass off the North American coast, Vancouver Island is 450km long and 100km wide. The island is laced with colorful, often eccentric settlements, many founded on logging or fishing and featuring the word 'Port' in their name.

Despite the general distaste among residents for the 'far too busy' mainland – a distaste that often comes from people who have never actually left the island – the locals are usually a friendly and welcoming bunch, proud of their region and its distinct differences. If you want to make a good impression, don't refer to the place as 'Victoria Island,' an oft-repeated mistake that usually provokes involuntary eye-rolls and an almost imperceptible downgrading of your welcome.

While the history-wrapped BC capital, Victoria, is stuffed with attractions and is the first port of call for many, it should never be the only place you visit here. Food and wine fans will enjoy weaving through the verdant Comox Valley farm region; outdoor activity enthusiasts shouldn't miss the surf-loving Tofino area; and those who fancy remote forested beaches far from the madding crowds should make straight for the North Island region, an undiscovered gem that's among the most rewarding wilderness areas in BC.

For an introduction to the island, contact **Tourism Vancouver Island** (☎ 250-754-3500, 888-655-3843; www.vancouverisland.travel) for listings and resources.

VICTORIA

pop 78,000

With a metro population clost to 350,000, the province's picture-postcard capital was long-touted as North America's most English city. This was a surprise to anyone who actually came from Britain, since Victoria promulgated a dreamy version of England that never really was: every garden (complete with the occasional palm tree) was immaculate; every flag pole was adorned with a Union Jack; and every afternoon was spent quaffing tea from bone china cups.

Thankfully this tired theme-park version of Ye Olde England has been gradually superseded here in recent years. Fuelled by an increasingly younger demographic, a quiet revolution has seen lame tourist pubs, eateries and stores transformed into brightly painted bohemian shops, wood-floor coffee bars and surprisingly innovative restaurants that would make any city proud. It's worth seeking out these enclaves on foot but activity fans should also hop on their bikes: Victoria has more cycle routes than any other Canadian city.

Orientation & Information

Centered on the Inner Harbour landmarks of the Parliament Buildings and the Empress Hotel, downtown Victoria is compact and

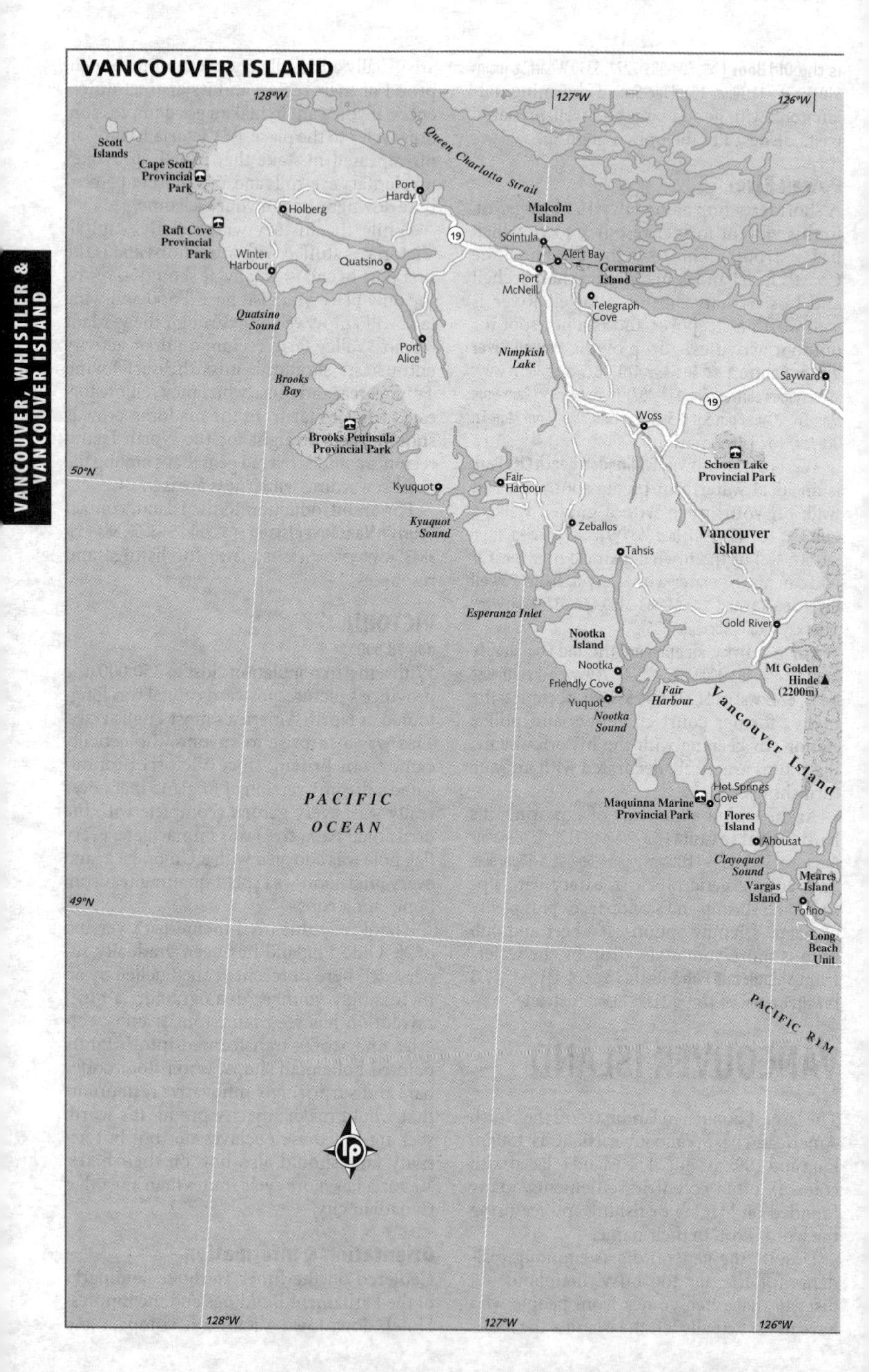
VANCOUVER ISLAND
128°W
127°W
126°W
Scott Islands
Cape Scott Provincial Park
Queen Charlotta Strait
Port Hardy
Holberg
Malcolm Island
Raft Cove Provincial Park
19
Sointula
Alert Bay
Cormorant Island
Winter Harbour
Quatsino
Port McNeill
Telegraph Cove
Quatsino Sound
Port Alice
Nimpkish Lake
Sayward
Brooks Bay
Woss
Brooks Peninsula Provincial Park
Schoen Lake Provincial Park
50°N
Kyuquot
Fair Harbour
Kyuquot Sound
Zeballos
Vancouver Island
Tahsis
Esperanza Inlet
Gold River
Nootka Island
Nootka
Mt Golden Hinde (2200m)
Friendly Cove
Yuquot
Fair Harbour
Nootka Sound
Vancouver Island
Hot Springs Cove
Maquinna Marine Provincial Park
Flores Island
PACIFIC OCEAN
Ahousat
Clayoquot Sound
Meares Island
Vargas Island
49°N
Tofino
Long Beach Unit
PACIFIC RIM

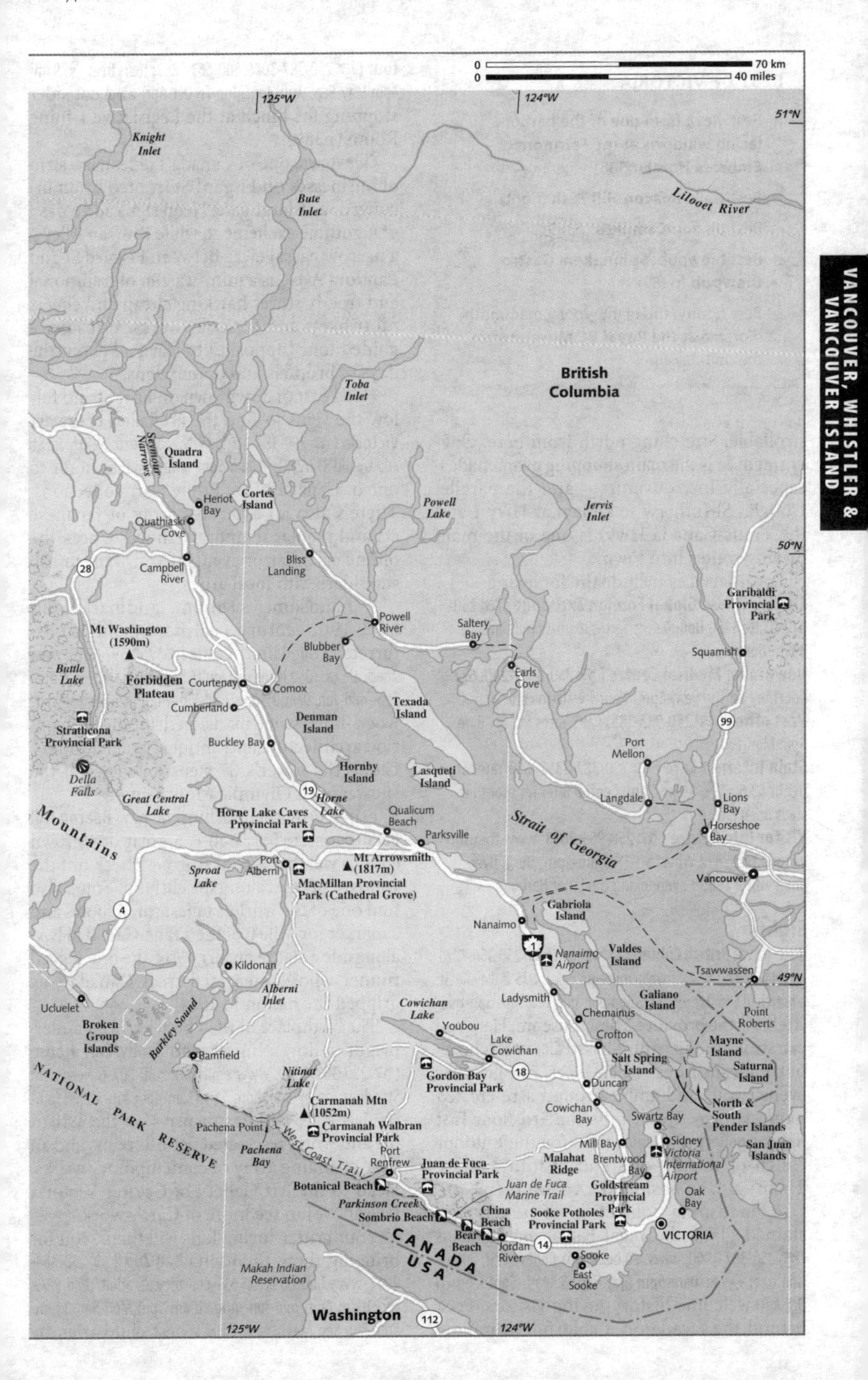

VANCOUVER, WHISTLER & VANCOUVER ISLAND

BEST OF VICTORIA

- Best view: from one of the harbor-facing windows at the **Fairmont Empress Hotel** (p388)
- Best walk: **Beacon Hill Park** (right)
- Best dinner: **Camille's** (p389)
- Best brewpub: **Spinnakers Gastro Brewpub** (p389)
- Best oddity: the giant woolly mammoth diorama at the **Royal BC Museum** (below)

strollable. Stretching north from here, Government St is the main shopping promenade – especially for souvenirs – and the parallel Douglas St (otherwise known as Hwy 1 and the Trans-Canada Hwy) is one of the main driving routes into town.

Local services include the following:

Custom House Global Foreign Exchange (☎ 250-412-0336; 1150 Douglas St; 9:30am-6pm Mon-Sat, 11am-6pm Sun)

Downtown Medical Centre (☎ 250-380-2210; 622 Courtney St; 9am-6pm) Handy walk-in clinic.

Post office (☎ 250-953-1352; 706 Yates St; 8am-5pm Mon-Fri)

Stain Internet Café (☎ 250-382-3352; 609 Yates St; per hr $3.50; 10am-2am) Central internet spot that stays open late.

Visitor Info Centre (☎ 250-953-2033; www.tourismvictoria.com; 812 Wharf St; 9am-5pm) Busy, flyer-lined visitor center overlooking the Inner Harbour.

Sights

The **Royal British Columbia Museum** (☎ 250-356-7226, 888-447-7977; www.royalbcmuseum.bc.ca; 675 Belleville St; adult/child $18/12; 9am-6pm Jul–mid-Oct, 9am-5pm mid-Oct–Jun) is the province's best museum. Here you can stroll among nature-based **dioramas** (check-out the rain forest where deer and grizzlies eyeball you) and amble around a re-created pioneer town. Don't miss the 3rd-floor **First Nations gallery** and save time for the outdoor clutch of totem poles and historic homes. There's also an onsite IMAX Theatre (p390).

A handsome confection of turrets and stained glass, the regal **Parliament Buildings** (☎ 250-387-1400; www.leg.bc.ca; 501 Belleville St; admission free; 8:30am-5pm May-Sep, 8:30am-5pm Mon-Fri Oct-Apr) welcome history-loving visitors. Peek behind the facade on a colorful 30-minute **tour** (☎ 250-387-3046, 800-663-7867; tours free; 9am-4pm May-Sep, 9am-4pm Mon-Fri Oct-Apr) and consider stopping for lunch at the Legislative Dining Room (p389).

Chinatown, one of Canada's oldest, is a strip of businesses on Fisgard St fronted by an incongruously large gate. Neon signs add a dash of nighttime excitement, while Fan Tan Alley – a narrow passageway between Fisgard St and Pandora Ave – is a mini-warren of traditional and trendy stores hawking cheap and cheerful trinkets and funky artworks. Consider a guided tour (opposite) to learn all about the days of brothels and opium dens.

Head east of downtown on Fort St and follow the signs to find the **Art Gallery of Greater Victoria** (☎ 250-384-4101; www.aggv.bc.ca; 1040 Moss St; adult/child $12/2; 10am-5pm, until 9pm Thu), home to one of Canada's best Emily Carr collections. There's also an extensive array of Japanese art and regular temporary shows. Check the online calendar of events if you want to rub shoulders with local arties.

A handsome 39-room landmark built by a 19th-century coal baron, the multi-turreted **Craigdarroch Castle** (☎ 250-592-5323; www.thecastle.ca; 1050 Joan Cres; adult/child $12/4; 10am-5pm Sep–mid-Jun, 9am-7:30pm mid-Jun–Aug) is an elegant, wood-lined stone mansion dripping with period architecture and antique-packed rooms. Climb the tower's 87 steps for views of the snowcapped Olympic Mountains.

Fringed by the crashing ocean, **Beacon Hill Park** (entrance on Douglas St) is a great downtown spot to weather a wild storm – check out the windswept trees along the cliff top. You'll also find one of the world's tallest totem poles and a marker for Mile 0 of the Trans-Canada Hwy, alongside a statue of Terry Fox, the one-legged runner whose attempted cross-Canada trek gripped the nation in 1981.

The birthplace of BC's best-known painter, bright-yellow gingerbread **Emily Carr House** (☎ 250-383-5843; www.emilycarr.com; 207 Government St; admission by donation; 11am-4pm Jun-Aug, 11am-4pm Tue-Sat Sep-May) has displays on the artist's life and work, re-created period rooms and an ever-changing array of contemporary works. Head to the Art Gallery of Greater Victoria (see above) to see more of Carr's work.

Your critter-loving kids will thank you for bringing them to **Victoria Bug Zoo** (☎ 250-384-2847; www.bugzoo.bc.ca; 631 Courtney St; adult/child $8/5; 10am-6pm mid-Jun–Aug, 10am-5pm Mon-Sat, 11am-5pm Sun Sep-May), the city's best child-friendly attraction – especially if they like ogling leaf-cutter ants and glow-in-the-dark scorpions. That doesn't mean you have to join them in the handling area, complete with a disturbingly large 400-leg millipede.

Between Government and Wharf Sts, on the site of the old Fort Victoria, **Bastion Square** is a clutch of scrubbed colonial strongholds, now home to the **Maritime Museum of British Columbia** (☎ 250-385-4222; www.mmbc.bc.ca; 28 Bastion Sq; adult/child $8/3; 🕑 9:30am-5pm mid-Jun–mid-Sep, 9:30am-4:30pm mid-Sep–mid-Jun), where 400 model ships illuminate the region's salty heritage.

Activities

WHALE-WATCHING

Raincoat-clad tourists head out by the boatload from Victoria during the May to October viewing season. The whales don't always show, so most excursions also visit the local haunts of elephant seals and sea lions.

Try the following operators:

Orca Spirit Adventures (☎ 250-383-8411, 888-672-6722; www.orcaspirit.com; 146 Kingston St; adult/child $89/59)

Prince of Whales (☎ 250-383-4884, 888-383-4884; www.princeofwhales.com; 812 Wharf St; adult/child $85/69)

KAYAKING

Paddling around the coast of Vancouver Island by kayak is the perfect way to see the region, especially if you come across a few soaring eagles, lolling seals and an occasional starfish-studded beach. You can rent equipment for your own trek or join a tour of the area's watery highlights.

Ocean River Sports (☎ 250-381-4233, 800-909-4233; www.oceanriver.com; 1824 Store St; rental per 2/24hr $25/50; 🕑 9:30am-6pm Mon-Thu & Sat, 9:30am-8pm Fri, 11am-5pm Sun) Popular 2½-hour sunset tours ($59).

Sports Rent (☎ 250-385-7368; www.sportsrentbc.com; 1950 Government St; rental 5/24hr $29/45; 🕑 9am-5:30pm Mon-Thu & Sat, 9am-6pm Fri, 10am-5pm Sun)

SCUBA DIVING

The region's dive-friendly underwater ecosystem includes popular spots like Ogden Point Breakwater, south of Beacon Hill Park, and 10 Mile Point near Cadboro Bay.

Frank Whites Dive Stores (☎ 250-385-4713; www.frankwhites.com; 1620 Blanshard St; 🕑 9am-5:30pm)

Ogden Point Dive Centre (☎ 250-380-9119, 888-701-1177; www.divevictoria.com; 199 Dallas Rd; 🕑 9am-6pm)

Tours

Architectural Institute of BC (☎ 604-683-8588, 800-667-0753; www.aibc.ca; tours depart Community Arts Council, 1001 Douglas St; tour $5; 🕑 1pm Tue-Sat Jul & Aug) Five great-value themed walking tours.

Cycle Treks (☎ 250-386-2277, 877-733-6722; www.cycletreks.com; 450 Swift St; from $50; 🕑 9:30am-6pm Mon-Sat) Three- to four-hour seafront-themed cycling tour (bikes provided). One of the best ways to encounter Victoria.

Gray Line West (☎ 250-388-6539, 800-663-8390; www.graylinewest.com; 700 Douglas St; adult/child from $20.50/10.25) Ninety-minute double-decker bus tours of the city starting from the Empress Hotel (p388).

Hidden Dragon Tours (☎ 250-920-0881, 866-920-0881; www.oldchinatown.com; 541 Fisgard St; adult/child $29/14.50) Fascinating three-hour behind-the-scenes lantern tour of old Chinatown.

Festivals & Events

Victoria Day Parade (🕑 mid-May) Street fiesta shenanigans with dancers and marching bands.

Victoria Jazzfest International (www.vicjazz.bc.ca; 🕑 late Jun) Ten days of jazz performance.

Victoria SkaFest (www.victoriaskafest.ca; 🕑 mid-Jul) Canada's largest ska music event.

Moss Street Paint-In (🕑 mid-Jul) One hundred artists demonstrate their skills at popular one-day community event.

Symphony Splash (www.symphonysplash.ca; 🕑 early Aug) Victoria Symphony Orchestra perform from an Inner Harbour barge.

Victoria Fringe Theatre Festival (www.victoriafringe.com; 🕑 late Aug) Two weeks of quirky short plays staged throughout the city.

Victoria Cycling Festival (www.victoriacyclingfestival.com; 🕑 mid-Sep) Family-friendly fiesta weekend of cycling races and bike events.

Sleeping

From heritage B&Bs to midrange motels and swanky high-end sleepovers, Victoria is stuffed with accommodation options for all budgets. Tourism Victoria's **room reservation service** (☎ 250-953-2033, 800-663-3883; www.tourismvictoria.com) can let you know what's available.

BUDGET

Ocean Island Backpackers Inn (☎ 250-385-1788, 888-888-4180; www.oceanisland.com; 791 Pandora Ave; dm/s/d from $24/39/44; 💻 wi-fi) A great place to meet fellow travelers, this funky, multicolored sleepover is a labyrinth of dorms and private rooms. There's also a communal kitchen and a licensed lounge for bands – avoid lower-floor

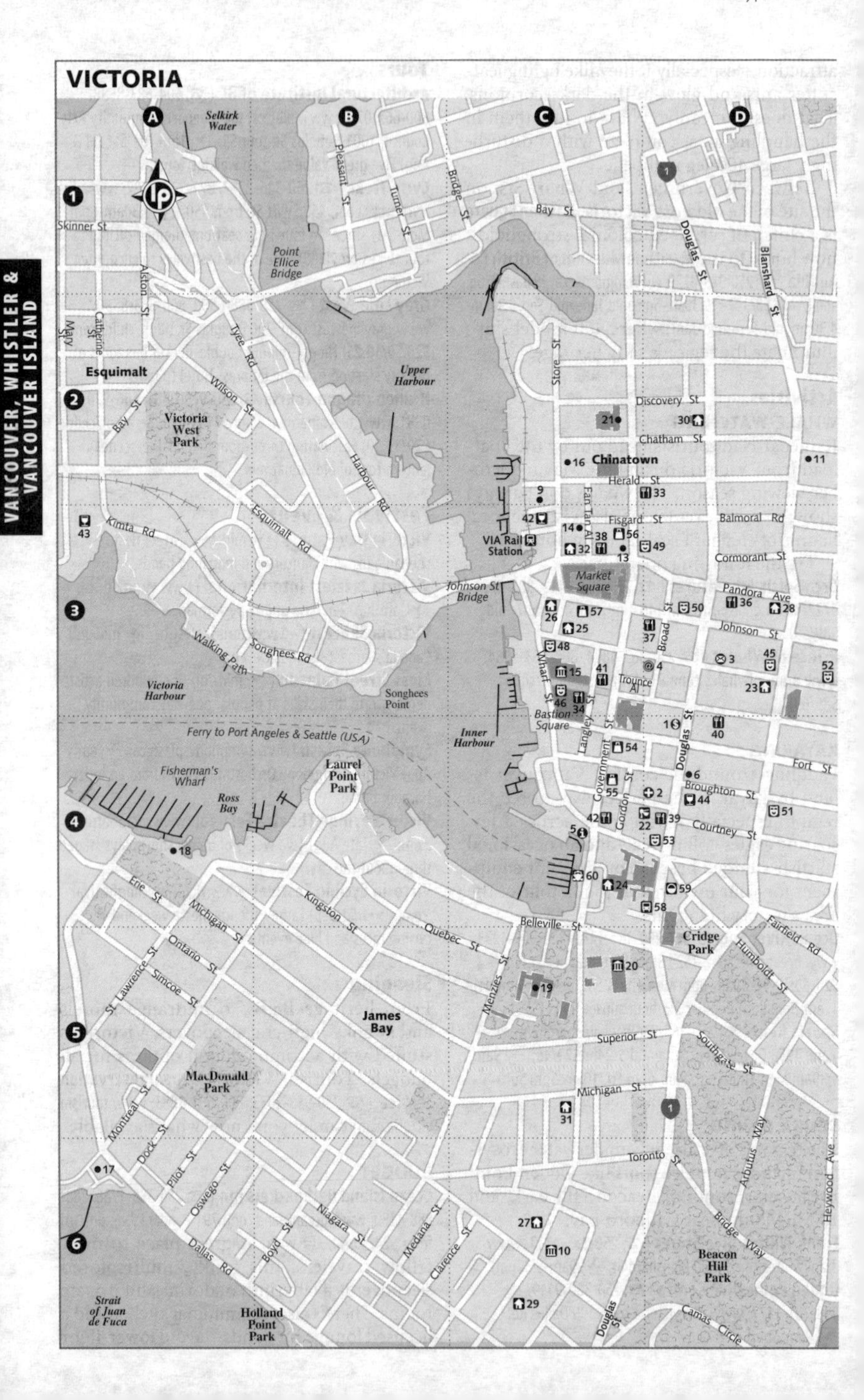

VICTORIA
Selkirk Water
Point Ellice Bridge
Upper Harbour
Esquimalt
Victoria West Park
Chinatown
VIA Rail Station
Market Square
Johnson St Bridge
Victoria Harbour
Songhees Point
Inner Harbour
Bastion Square
Ferry to Port Angeles & Seattle (USA)
Fisherman's Wharf
Ross Bay
Laurel Point Park
Cridge Park
James Bay
MacDonald Park
Beacon Hill Park
Strait of Juan de Fuca
Holland Point Park
Skinner St
Aston St
Catherine St
Mary St
Tyee Rd
Wilson St
Bay St
Pleasant St
Turner St
Bridge St
Store St
Douglas St
Blanshard St
Discovery St
Chatham St
Herald St
Fisgard St
Fan Tan Al
Balmoral Rd
Cormorant St
Pandora Ave
Johnson St
Broad St
Trounce Al
Wharf St
Langley St
Government St
Gordon St
Fort St
Broughton St
Courtney St
Harbour Rd
Esquimalt Rd
Kimta Rd
Songhees Rd
Walking Path
Belleville St
Kingston St
Quebec St
Menzies St
Erie St
Michigan St
Ontario St
Simcoe St
St Lawrence St
Superior St
Southgate St
Humboldt St
Fairfield Rd
Toronto St
Arbutus Way
Heywood Ave
Bridge Way
Camas Circle
Montreal St
Dock St
Pilot St
Oswego St
Niagara St
Boyd St
Medana St
Clarence St
Dallas Rd

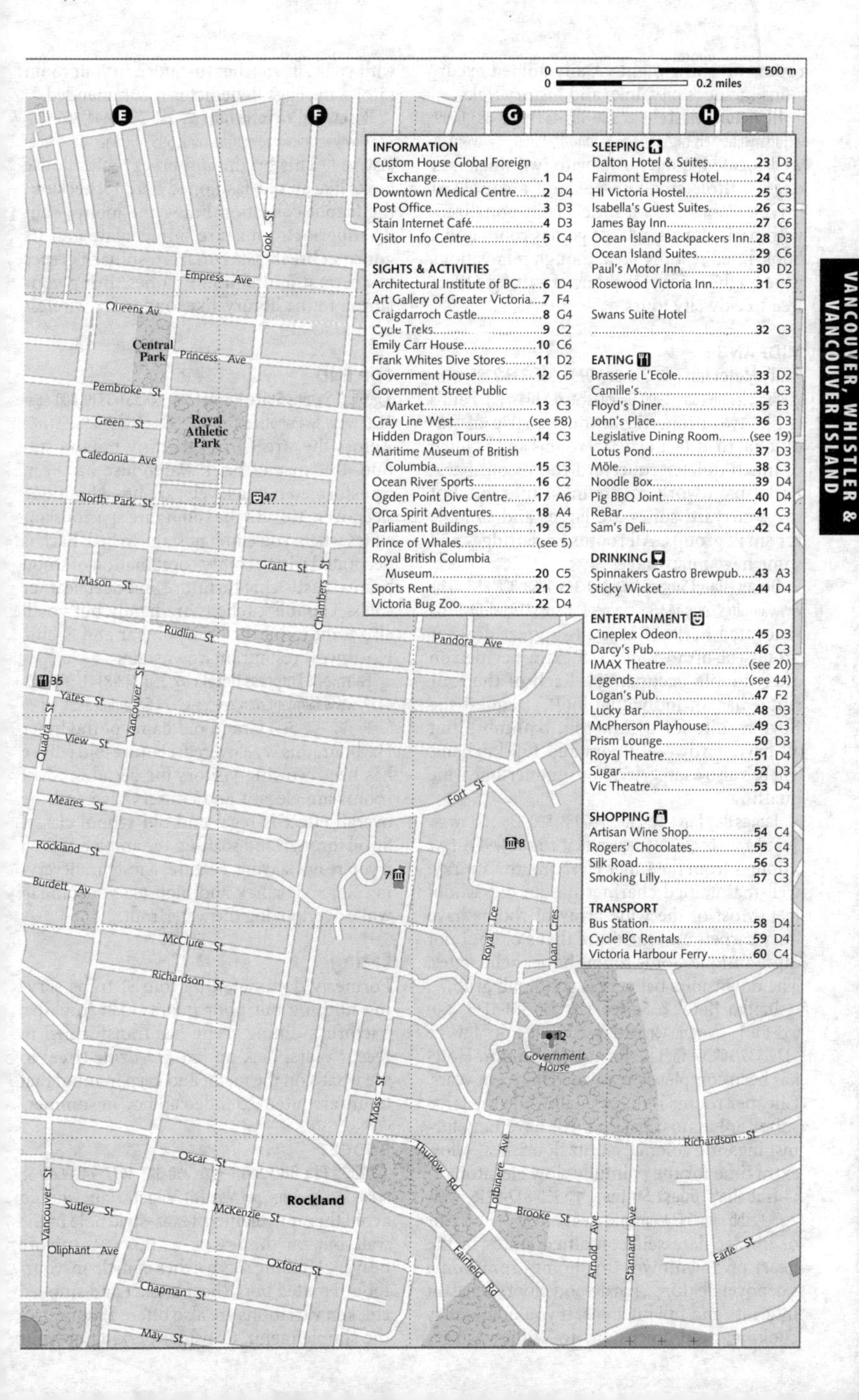
0 500 m
0 0.2 miles
E
F
G
H
INFORMATION
Custom House Global Foreign Exchange....1 D4
Downtown Medical Centre....2 D4
Post Office....3 D3
Stain Internet Café....4 D3
Visitor Info Centre....5 C4
SIGHTS & ACTIVITIES
Architectural Institute of BC....6 D4
Art Gallery of Greater Victoria....7 F4
Craigdarroch Castle....8 G4
Cycle Treks....9 C2
Emily Carr House....10 C6
Frank Whites Dive Stores....11 D2
Government House....12 G5
Government Street Public Market....13 C3
Gray Line West....(see 58)
Hidden Dragon Tours....14 C3
Maritime Museum of British Columbia....15 C3
Ocean River Sports....16 C2
Ogden Point Dive Centre....17 A6
Orca Spirit Adventures....18 A4
Parliament Buildings....19 C5
Prince of Whales....(see 5)
Royal British Columbia Museum....20 C5
Sports Rent....21 C2
Victoria Bug Zoo....22 D4
SLEEPING
Dalton Hotel & Suites....23 D3
Fairmont Empress Hotel....24 C4
HI Victoria Hostel....25 C3
Isabella's Guest Suites....26 C3
James Bay Inn....27 C6
Ocean Island Backpackers Inn....28 D3
Ocean Island Suites....29 C6
Paul's Motor Inn....30 D2
Rosewood Victoria Inn....31 C5
Swans Suite Hotel....32 C3
EATING
Brasserie L'Ecole....33 D2
Camille's....34 C3
Floyd's Diner....35 E3
John's Place....36 D3
Legislative Dining Room....(see 19)
Lotus Pond....37 D3
Möle....38 C3
Noodle Box....39 D4
Pig BBQ Joint....40 D4
ReBar....41 C3
Sam's Deli....42 C4
DRINKING
Spinnakers Gastro Brewpub....43 A3
Sticky Wicket....44 D4
ENTERTAINMENT
Cineplex Odeon....45 D3
Darcy's Pub....46 C3
IMAX Theatre....(see 20)
Legends....(see 44)
Logan's Pub....47 F2
Lucky Bar....48 D3
McPherson Playhouse....49 C3
Prism Lounge....50 D3
Royal Theatre....51 D4
Sugar....52 D3
Vic Theatre....53 D4
SHOPPING
Artisan Wine Shop....54 C4
Rogers' Chocolates....55 C4
Silk Road....56 C3
Smoking Lilly....57 C3
TRANSPORT
Bus Station....58 D4
Cycle BC Rentals....59 D4
Victoria Harbour Ferry....60 C4
Cook St
Empress Ave
Queens Av
Central Park
Princess Ave
Pembroke St
Green St
Royal Athletic Park
Caledonia Ave
North Park St
47
Grant St
Chambers St
Mason St
Rudlin St
Pandora Ave
35
Yates St
Vancouver St
Quadra St
View St
Fort St
Meares St
Rockland St
8
7
Burdett Av
McClure St
Royal Tce
Joan Cres
Richardson St
12
Government House
Moss St
Richardson St
Thurlow Rd
Lotbiniere Ave
Oscar St
Rockland
Vancouver St
Sutley St
McKenzie St
Brooke St
Arnold Ave
Stannard Ave
Earle St
Oliphant Ave
Oxford St
Fairfield Rd
Chapman St
May St
VANCOUVER, WHISTLER & VANCOUVER ISLAND

rooms on show nights. Daily guided excursions includes city, bike and history treks.

HI Victoria Hostel (☎ 250-385-4511, 888-883-0099; victoria@hihostels.ca; 516 Yates St; dm/d $25/60; 💻 wi-fi) A well-located, quiet hostel with two single-sex dorms, three small co-eds and a couple of private rooms. It's a little institutionalized, with basic dorms, a large games room and a book-lined reading area, though renovations were on the cards at the time of writing. Offers free weekly city tours.

MIDRANGE

Paul's Motor Inn (☎ 250-382-9231, 866-333-7285; www.paulsmotorinn.com; 1900 Douglas St; d $104-119) Paul's is like two properties in one: a strip of traditional road-facing motel rooms and a clutch of much quieter courtyard rooms out back. Pastel paintwork covers most interiors but the courtyard suites are larger and suitable for small groups. All rooms have fridges and some have microwaves.

Ocean Island Suites (☎ 250-385-1788, 888-888-4180; www.oisuites.com; 143 Government St; ste $120; wi-fi) This renovated heritage home is a great deal for groups of up to four ($15 extra per person after double occupancy). Each of the four suites has an individual look – request the Burma suite for a claw-foot bathtub – but all have hardwood floors and full kitchens. There's also a large deck for summertime wine quaffing.

James Bay Inn (☎ 250-384-7151, 800-836-2649; www.jamesbayinn.bc.ca; 270 Government St; r from $129) A few minutes from the Inner Harbour, this quirky, well-maintained charmer has an old-school feel. Most of the wide array of rooms have busy carpets and furniture that's old but not quite antique. Some rooms have kitchenettes. The downstairs bar serves good pub grub.

Dalton Hotel & Suites (☎ 250-384-4136, 800-663-6101; www.daltonhotel.ca; 759 Yates St; d/tw/ste $129/139/169; wi-fi) The former Dominion Hotel has been completely renovated in recent years. Cheaper rooms remain small while the large suites are almost palatial. All have new furnishings and colonial chintz flourishes. Allow extra time for the painfully slow elevator.

Isabella's Guest Suites (☎ 250-812-9216; www.isabellasbb.com; 537 Johnson St; ste from $150; wi-fi) A pair of immaculate self-contained suites in the heart of downtown, this home-from-home sleepover features hardwood floors, elegant interiors and full kitchens. If you don't fancy cooking, head downstairs to Willie's Bakery with your gift voucher (included in your room rate) – the eggs Benedict is recommended.

Rosewood Victoria Inn (☎ 250-384-6644, 866-986-2222; www.rosewoodvictoria.com; 595 Michigan St; d from $150; wi-fi) This bright and breezy guesthouse looks like an old-fashioned B&B – check out the teapot collection lining the lobby – but its superior rooms are immaculate and its gourmet breakfasts run from spinach crepes to coconut and almond scones. Bring your laptop to the library-like lounge for wireless access.

TOP END

our pick Swans Suite Hotel (☎ 250-361-3310, 800-668-7926; www.swanshotel.com; 506 Pandora Ave; d/ste $199/289) Across the street from the tiny railway station, this former brick warehouse has been transformed into a lovely, art-lined boutique sleepover. Most of the rooms are spacious loft suites where you climb upstairs to bed. Each is decorated with a comfy combination of wood beams, rustic chic furniture and deep leather sofas. The full kitchens are handy but you'll also want to hit the brewpub bar and Pacific Northwest restaurant downstairs.

Fairmont Empress Hotel (☎ 250-348-8111, 866-540-4429; www.fairmont.com/empress; 721 Government St; r from $249; ❄ 💻 ♿) Grand old dame of the Inner Harbour, this ivy-covered, century-old edifice has been wowing visitors for decades. Most rooms are elegant and conservative and the overall effect is regal and old-school classy. Stroll through and soak-up the ambience even if you're not staying. Features a restaurant serving Raj-style curry and high tea you can sip while overlooking the waterfront.

Eating

Formerly dominated by tourist traps serving nothing but poor-quality fish 'n chips, Victoria's dining scene has transformed in recent years. Pick up *Eat Magazine* (free) to see what's on the menu and keep in mind that hours are often extended ad hoc in summer.

BUDGET

our pick Pig BBQ Joint (☎ 250-381-4677; 749 View St; mains $5; 🕐 9am-7pm Mon-Fri) Vegetarians should avoid this aptly named Texas-style hole in the wall, but for the rest of us this is carnivore heaven. Hulking sandwiches of melt-in-your-mouth pulled pork (beef brisket and smoked chicken variations are also offered) dominate the simple menu. Consider perking up your order with a side of succulent cornbread, and wash it all down with homemade ice tea. Expect lunchtime queues.

Sam's Deli (☎ 250-382-8424; 805 Government St; mains $5-8; 7:30am-7pm Mon-Fri, 8am-7pm Sat, 9am-6pm Sun; V) It's not just the nearby Inner Harbour that makes this fuel-up spot permanently popular: they also make darn good sandwiches. Signature sarnies feature roast beef or pastrami but the bulging vegetarian sandwich is also recommended.

Floyd's Diner (☎ 250-381-5114; 866 Yates St; mains $6-11; 8am-5pm Mon-Fri, 9am-5pm Sat & Sun) A funky eatery with an ultra-friendly vibe, Floyd's offers a menu of serious comfort food – it's *the* spot in town to recover from a throbbing hangover. Along with the all-day breakfast menu, there are some bulging burgers and sandwiches, and a great lunch deal: a $5.50 bottomless bowl of soup.

MIDRANGE

Legislative Dining Room (☎ 250-387-3959; Rm 606 Parliament Buildings; mains $6-16 9am-3pm Mon-Thu, 9am-2pm Fri) One of Victoria's best-kept dining secrets, the Parliament Buildings has a subsidized restaurant where anyone can drop by for a silver-service menu of regional dishes, ranging from smoked tofu salads to shrimp quesadillas. It's cash-only and entry is via the security desk just inside the building's main entrance.

John's Place (☎ 250-389-0711; 723 Pandora Ave; mains $7-16; 7am-9pm Mon-Thu, 7am-10pm Fri, 8am-10pm Sat, 8am-9pm Sun) Victoria's best weekend brunch spot, this heritage room is lined with funky memorabilia and the menu is a cut above standard diner fare. Belgian waffles are served with homemade cream cheese, and those who stay for dinner can choose from a medley of international comfort foods, from calamari to pierogi dumplings.

Noodle Box (☎ 250-384-1314; 818 Douglas St; mains $8-12; 11am-9pm Mon-Thu, 11am-10pm Fri & Sat, noon-7pm Sun) Southeast Asian cuisine is the approach at this buzzing business that started out as a street vendor. A great place for take-out, it's also a chatty eat-in spot. Try the Cambodian Jungle Curry and look out for additional outlets around town.

Lotus Pond (☎ 250-380-9293; 617 Johnson St; mains $8-16; 11am-3pm & 5-9pm Tue-Sat, noon-3pm & 5-8pm Sun; V) Behind the shabby exterior of this downtown Chinese restaurant is an extensive, all-vegan menu of delights. Even meat-eaters have been known to swoon as they tuck into surprisingly tasty spring rolls, dim sum and pot sticker dumplings. Combo meals are the best option, since they offer an array of different flavors.

ReBar (☎ 250-360-2401; 50 Bastion Sq; mains $9-14; 8:30am-9pm, until 10pm Thu-Sat, until 3:30pm Sun; V) This relaxing local favorite fuses colorful interiors with a clever, mostly vegetarian menu. Hearty savory dishes like shitake-tofu pot stickers and an array of dense fruit smoothies will keep both vegetarians and omnivores happy. The weekend brunch is popular.

Möle (☎ 250-385-6653; 554 Pandora Ave; mains $10-18; 8am-3pm daily, 5:30-11pm Wed-Mon) Lined with funky local artworks, this laid-back joint is popular for breakfast (try the curry tofu scramble) but also attracts the hip crowd with its day menu featuring comfort classics and adventurous fusion dishes (think organic hamburgers and yam wraps). The beer selection includes Phillips and Lighthouse brews.

TOP END

our pick **Camille's** (☎ 250-381-3433; 45 Bastion Sq; mains $18-26; 5:30-10pm Tue-Sat) The granddaddy of Victoria's fine-dining scene, adventurous Camille's still challenges. Its charming subterranean dining room offers a lively, ever-changing menu reflecting whatever the chef can source locally: if wild strawberries are in season, they'll appear in savory dishes as well as desserts. With a great wine menu, this spot invites adventurous foodies.

Brasserie L'Ecole (☎ 250-475-6260; 1715 Government St; mains $19-28; 5:30-11pm Tue-Sun) Incongruously abutting Chinatown, this superb bistro offers country-style French cuisine in a casual atmosphere. Locally sourced produce is de rigueur, so the menu constantly changes to reflect seasonal highlights like salmonberries and heirloom tomatoes. The velvety lamb shank is recommended.

Drinking

Spinnakers Gastro Brewpub (☎ 250-386-2739; 308 Catherine St; 11am-10:30pm) A pioneering craft brewer, this local fave is a waterfront walk or taxi ride from the Inner Harbour but it's worth it for the lip-smacking beers. Summer drinkers enjoy the lighter Honey Blonde Ale, while those with darker palates should try the Nut Brown. Save room for dinner: the menu of locally sourced dishes is superior to most pubs and includes excellent seafood.

Canoe Brewpub (☎ 250-361-1940; 450 Swift St; 🕑 11:30am-midnight, until 1am Fri & Sat) The cavernous brick-lined interior here is popular on rainy days but you can also enjoy the sun on the large waterfront patio. Another good spot for food, Canoe's own-brewed beers – that's the stuff in those giant copper tanks – includes the hoppy Red Canoe Lager and the summer-friendly Siren's Song Pale Ale.

Sticky Wicket (☎ 250-383-7137; 919 Douglas St; 🕑 11am-11pm Sun-Thu, 11am-midnight Fri & Sat) The Wicket's main bar serves mainstream beers, and its menu offers heaped plates of standard pub grub. There's live sports on the TVs and a pool room upstairs if you need to exercise your cue arm. Good for a noisy night out with the locals. The highlight bar is Big Bad John's, a tiny hillbilly nook with log-lined walls and a carpet of peanut shells.

Entertainment

LIVE MUSIC

Lucky Bar (☎ 250-382-5825; www.luckybar.ca; 517 Yates St; cover free-$10) This Victoria institution offers an array of live music from ska and indie to electroclash. There are bands here at least twice a week, while the remaining evenings are occupied by club nights, including Wednesday's mod fest and Saturday's mix night.

Logan's Pub (☎ 250-360-2711; www.loganspub.com; 1821 Cook St; cover free-$15) A ten-minute walk from downtown in the Cook St Village area, this joint looks like nothing special from the outside but its roster of shows is a main fixture of the local indie scene. Fridays and Saturdays are your best bet for performances but other nights are frequently also booked – check their online calendar to see what's coming up.

Darcy's Pub (☎ 250-380-1322; www.darcyspub.ca; 1127 Wharf St) A laid-back downtown alternative, Darcy's offers free live acts every night, ranging from weekend cover bands to a Monday night open mic session. In between, it's all about singer-songwriters beloved by the local student population. It's a fun spot to hangout, with a beer menu centered on local brews from Vancouver Island Brewing.

NIGHTCLUBS

Legends (☎ 250-383-7137; www.legendsnightclub.com; 919 Douglas St; cover free-$15) Conveniently located under the Sticky Wicket pub, this is a mainstream hangout known for its Saturday Top 40, hip-hop and R&B night. Friday is also popular and there are also regular live acts.

Sugar (☎ 250-920-9950; 858 Yates St; cover free-$20; 🕑 Thu-Sat) A long-standing, popular alternative that's only open a few days a week, two-floored Sugar is another mainstreamers haunt, with Top 40 sounds (under a giant disco ball) plus live events.

Prism Lounge (☎ 250-388-0505; www.prismlounge.com; 642 Johnson St) The city's raucous gay and lesbian hangout hosts nightly events including karaoke evenings and drag fests. The Friday and Saturday night dance parties here are the main attraction.

THEATER & CINEMAS

Victoria's main stages, **McPherson Playhouse** (☎ 250-386-6121; www.rmts.bc.ca; 3 Centennial Sq) and **Royal Theatre** (☎ 250-386-6121; www.rmts.bc.ca; 805 Broughton St), both offer mainstream theater productions. The Royal Theatre is also home of the **Victoria Symphony** (☎ 250-385-6515; www.victoriasymphony.bc.ca; tickets $19-60) and **Pacific Opera Victoria** (☎ 250-382-1641; www.pov.bc.ca; tickets $25-100; 🕑 Apr-Oct).

The city's main first-run cinema is **Cineplex Odeon** (☎ 250-383-0513; 780 Yates St; tickets $8.25). Arthouse flicks hit the screen at the **Vic Theatre** (☎ 250-383-1998; 808 Douglas St; adult/child $8.50/5.50) and the Royal BC Museum's **IMAX Theatre** (☎ 250-953-4629; www.imaxvictoria.com; 675 Belleville St; adult/child $10.50/8.25) shows larger-than-life documentaries.

Shopping

Government St is a magnet for souvenir shoppers, but those looking for more worthwhile purchases should head to the Johnson St stretch between Store and Government Sts. Nicknamed 'LoJo' (Lower Johnson), this old-town area has around 40 independent stores.

Smoking Lilly (☎ 250-382-5459; 569 Johnson St; 🕑 11am-5:30pm Thu-Sat, noon-5pm Sun & Mon) LoJo's signature shop is a tiny boutique stuffed with eclectic garments and accessories that define art school chic. Tops and skirts with insect prints are hot items, but there are also lots of cute handbags, socks and brooches to temp your credit card.

Silk Road (☎ 250-704-2688; 1624 Government St; 🕑 10am-6pm Mon-Sat, 11am-5pm Sun) A pilgrimage spot for fans of regular and exotic teas, there's all manner of tea paraphernalia here. Sidle up to the tasting bar to quaff some adventurous brews. Surprisingly, there's also a small on-site spa where you can indulge in oil treatments and aromatherapy.

Artisan Wine Shop (☎ 250-384-9994; 1007 Government St; 🕑 10am-9pm) Reflecting BC's wine-producing expertise, this popular store showcases the tipples of Mission Hill, one of the Okanagan's most celebrated producers. A mini-theater walks you through the process, a tasting bar serves those who like to quaff before buying and an impressive selection of vintages is offered for sale.

Rogers' Chocolate (☎ 250-727-6851; 913 Government St; 🕑 9am-7pm, until 9pm Thu-Sat) This old-school confectionery has the best ice-cream bars in town, but repeat offenders usually spend their time guiltily hitting the variety of rich Victoria Creams, one of which is usually enough to substitute for lunch. Flavors range from peppermint to chocolate nut.

Government Street Public Market (☎ 250-598-2593; 1600 Government St; 🕑 Sun May-Sep) An eclectic mix of vendors and performers transform this stretch of Government St into a bustling pedestrian street market on summer Sundays. Expect lots of artsy trinkets and a handful of food stalls. Try to arrive early to beat the crowds.

Getting There & Away

AIR

Victoria International Airport (☎ 250-953-7500; www.victoriaairport.com) is 26km north of the city via Hwy 17. **Air Canada Jazz** (☎ 514-393-3333, 888-247-2262; www.aircanada.com) services arrive here from Vancouver (from $91, 25 minutes, up to 21 daily) while **Westjet** (☎ 800-538-5696; www.westjet.com) flights arrive from Calgary (from $180, 1½ hours, five daily). Both airlines offer connections across Canada.

Harbour Air Seaplanes (☎ 604-274-1277, 800-665-0212; www.harbour-air.com) services arrive in the Inner Harbour from downtown Vancouver ($120, 35 minutes) throughout the day. Similar **West Coast Air** (☎ 604-606-6888, 800-347-2222; www.westcoastair.com) services arrive from Vancouver ($119, 35 minutes) and from Whistler ($249, one hour).

BOAT

BC Ferries (☎ 250-386-3431, 888-223-3779; www.bcferries.com) services arrive from mainland Tsawwassen (adult/child/vehicle $10.30/5.15/34.20, 1½ hours) at Swartz Bay, 27km north of Victoria via Hwy 17. Regular services also arrive from the Southern Gulf Islands (p404).

Victoria Clipper (☎ 250-382-8100, 800-888-2535; www.clippervactions.com) services arrive in the Inner Harbour from Seattle (US$69, three hours, up to three daily). **Black Ball Transport** (☎ 250-386-2202; www.ferrytovictoria.com) boats also arrive from Port Angeles (passenger/vehicle US$11.50/44, 1½ hours, up to four daily) and **Victoria Express** (☎ 250-361-9144; www.victoriaexpress.com) services arrive from Port Angeles (US$12.50, one hour, up to four daily) and the Sun Juan Islands (US$35, three hours, daily).

BUS

Services terminating at the city's main **bus station** (700 Douglas St) include **Greyhound** (☎ 800-661-8747; www.greyhound.ca) routes from Nanaimo ($18.75, 2½ hours, six daily) and Port Alberni ($35.85, four to six hours, three daily), along with frequent **Pacific Coach Lines** (☎ 250-385-4411, 800-661-1725; www.pacificcoach.com) services from Vancouver ($37.50, 3½ hours) and Vancouver International Airport ($43, four hours).

TRAIN

The charming **Via Rail** (☎ 888-842-7245; www.viarail.com) *Malahat* service arrives in the city near the Johnson St Bridge from Courtenay ($49, 4½ hours, daily), with additional up-island stops in Nanaimo, Parksville and Chemainus, among others.

Getting Around

TO/FROM THE AIRPORT

AKAL Airporter (☎ 250-386-2525, 877-386-2525; www.victoriaairporter.com) minibuses run between the airport and area hotels ($15, 30 minutes). In contrast, a taxi to downtown costs around $45, while transit bus 70 (35 minutes, three to five daily) costs $3.

BICYCLE

Victoria is a great cycling capital with plenty of routes crisscrossing the city and beyond. Rentals are available from **Cycle BC Rentals** (☎ 250-380-2453, 866-380-2453; www.cyclebc.ca; 747 Douglas St; hr/day $7/24; 🕑 9am-5pm Nov-Feb, 9am-7pm Mar-Oct) and Sports Rent (p385).

BOAT

Victoria Harbour Ferry (☎ 250-708-0201; www.victoriaharbourferry.com; tickets from $4) covers the Inner Harbour, Songhees Park (for Spinnakers Brewpub, p389), Reeson's Landing (for the LoJo shopping area, opposite) and other stops along the Gorge Waterway with its colorful armada of bath-sized little boats.

PUBLIC TRANSPORTATION

Victoria Regional Transit (☎ 250-382-6161; www.busonline.ca) buses – including some double-deckers – cover a wide area in and around the city. All routes require a one- or two-zone ticket ($2.25/3.00) and tickets are valid for up to one hours of transfer travel. Day passes ($7) are also available from convenience and grocery stores.

SOUTHERN VANCOUVER ISLAND

Outside Victoria's madding crowds, the wider Southern Vancouver Island region is a laid-back region of quirky towns, tree-lined cycling routes and rocky outcrops bristling with gnarly Garry oaks. The wildlife here is abundant and impressive; you'll likely spot bald eagles swooping overhead and sea otters cavorting on the beaches.

Saanich Peninsula & Around

Home of Vancouver Island's main airport and ferry terminal, this peninsula north of Victoria has more to offer than transportation options. Drop by the **Saanich Peninsula Visitor Info Centre** (☎ 250-656-0525; 10382 Patricia Bay Hwy; 8:30am-5:30pm Jun-Sep) near Sidney for tips and insights on the area.

SIDNEY

A relaxing excursion from Victoria, seafront Sidney is a self-proclaimed 'booktown' (see www.sidneybooktown.ca) with an inordinate number of bookshops, including **Tanner's** (☎ 250-656-2345; 2436 Beacon Ave; 8am-10pm), with its extensive travel section, and **Beacon Books** (☎ 250-655-5283; 2372 Beacon Ave; 10am-5:30pm Mon-Sat, noon-4pm Sun), with its vast array of used tomes guarded by a portly cat.

Dominating the waterfront, the new **Sidney Pier Hotel and Spa** (☎ 250-655-9445, 866-659-9445; www.sidneypier.com; 9805 Seaport Pl; d/ste $159/299) fuses West Coast lounge cool with beach pastel colors. Many rooms have waterfront views (some side-on) and each has local artworks lining the walls. There's an excellent restaurant down below and an unmissable artifact in the lobby: a large chunk of the *Sea Shepard* Greenpeace vessel.

If you can't wait for your fish 'n chips fix, head to the nearby **Pier Bistro Restaurant** (☎ 250-655-4995; 2550 Beacon Ave; mains $9-12; 8:30am-8:30pm, until 5pm Mon), which serves stunning waterfront views and a seafood-dominated menu. The oyster burger is recommended.

Victoria Regional Transit bus 70 trundles into Sidney from Victoria ($3, one hour) throughout the day.

BUTCHART GARDENS

Industrialist Robert Butchart spotted limestone deposits here and chose this site in 1904 for his cement factory, while his more aesthetically minded wife, Jennie, planted sweet peas and a single rose bush, despite knowing little about gardening. More than a century later, the cement operation is dust but the huge, elaborately manicured **Butchart Gardens** (☎ 250-652-5256, 866-652-4422; www.butchartgardens.com; 800 Benvenuto Ave; adult/child/youth $25/3/12.50; 9am-10:30pm mid-Jun–Aug, earlier in other months) has become one of BC's leading visitor destinations.

With its year-round kaleidoscope of colors and textures, the immaculate grounds here are divided into separate garden areas. The tranquil Japanese Garden is our favorite. Summer is crowded with the usual tour bus hordes but daily afternoon and evening music performances and Saturday night fireworks (July and August) make it all worthwhile. Yuletide-loving December visitors are treated to thousands of fairy lights draped among the wintering plants.

Victoria Regional Transit bus 75 arrives from Victoria at Butchart Gardens ($3, 50 minutes) and at points around the area.

CENTRE OF THE UNIVERSE

Since 'National Research Council of Canada Herzberg Institute of Astrophysics' doesn't exactly trip off the tongue, the public part of the institute goes by the name **Centre of the Universe** (☎ 250-363-8262; 5071 W Saanich Rd; adult/child before 7pm $9/5, after 7pm $12/7; 3-11pm Tue-Sat Mar-Oct, 3-11pm Sat Nov-Feb). Perched atop Observatory Hill, this government facility houses the **Plaskett Telescope** (in use since 1918) along with several hands-on exhibits and a mini-planetarium for the astronomically inclined. Starry-eyed visitors can crash the Star Party on Friday or Saturday evenings (May to October), when the astronomers chill out, show off their equipment and tackle thorny themes from asteroids to zero gravity.

GOLDSTREAM PROVINCIAL PARK

About 16km from Victoria on the Island Hwy, this scenic **park** (☎ 259-474-1336; www.bcparks.ca) at the base of Malahat Mountain makes for a restorative nature-themed day out from the city. Dripping with ancient, moss-covered cedar trees and a moist carpet of plant life, it's known for its chum salmon spawning season (late October to December). Hungry bald eagles are attracted to the fish and bird-watchers come ready with their cameras. You'll also find good fishing and hiking here, along with natural history exhibits at the **Goldstream Nature House** (☎ 250-478-9414; ⏰ 9am-4:30pm). There's also a roster of occasional lectures on the region's human history and ecological heritage.

Highway 14

Rounding the island's southwestern tip along Hwy 14 will thread you through this progressively rugged region of forested coastline, prompting local tourism chiefs to deploy the slogan 'Where the rain forest meets the sea.' At least it's descriptive: lined with tangled trees and craggy waterfronts, the road here is like a verdant nature-themed safari park.

SOOKE & AROUND

Heading west around the end of Vancouver Island, the roads are soon flanked by towering trees and overgrown hedgerows. The houses – many of them artisan workshops – seem to skulk in the shadows of the forest. Despite the spooky feel, the area has plenty of hidden charms. Drop by the **Sooke Region Visitor Centre** (☎ 250-642-6351, 866-888-4748; www.sooketourism.bc.ca; 2070 Philips Rd; ⏰ 9am-5pm) for information.

If you can't wait to get outdoors, head to **Sooke Potholes Provincial Park** (www.bcparks.ca), a 5km drive from Hwy 14 (the turn-off is east of Sooke). With rock pools and potholes carved into the river base during the last ice age, it's a popular spot for swimming and tube floating, and is ideal for a summer picnic.

Sooke is also the end of the line for the popular Galloping Goose cycling trail (p394). Rent a bike from **Sooke Cycle** (☎ 250-642-3123; www.sookebikes.com; 6707 West Coast Rd; per hr/day from $5/20; ⏰ 9am-6pm Mon-Fri, 9am-5pm Sat & Sun) and hit the trail peddling.

You'll find B&Bs dotted along the route here but for one of the province's most delightful and splurge-worthy sleepovers, head to Whiffen Spit's **Sooke Harbour House** (☎ 250-642-3421, 800-889-9688; www.sookeharbourhouse.com; 1528 Whiffen Spit Rd; ste $399-479). With paintings, sculptures and carved wood lining its interiors, some of the house's 28 rooms have fireplaces and steam showers, and all have views across the wildlife-strewn waterfront – look for gamboling sea otters and swooping cranes.

You can eat in the hotel's excellent, regionally biased restaurant or come back down to earth at the seasonal **Smokin' Tuna Café** (☎ 250-642-3816; 241 Beecher Bay Rd; mains $8-16; ⏰ 11am-6pm Mon-Wed, 11am-8pm Thu-Sun May-Oct) which serves up delectable fresh-caught treats along with smashing seafront views from its sunny patio.

JUAN DE FUCA PROVINCIAL PARK

The highlight of this **park** (☎ 250-474-1336; www.bcparks.ca) is the 47km **Juan de Fuca Marine Trail** (www.juandefucamarinetrail.com), which joins the popular West Coast Trail (p398) as a must-do trek for Vancouver Island's outdoorsy visitors. From east to west, its trailhead access points are China Beach, Sombrio Beach, Parkinson Creek and Botanical Beach.

It takes around four days to complete the full route – the most difficult stretch is between Bear Beach and China Beach – but you don't have to go the whole hog if you want to take things a little easier. Be aware that some sections are often muddy and difficult to hike, and bear sightings are not uncommon.

The route has several backcountry campsites and you can pay your camping fee ($5) at any of the trailheads. The most popular is the family-friendly **China Beach Campground** (☎ 604-689-9025, 800-689-9025; www.discovercamping.ca; tent sites $14) which has pit toilets and cold-water taps but no showers. There's a waterfall at the western end of the beach. Booking ahead is recommended.

Booking is also required on the **West Coast Trail Express** (☎ 250-477-8700, 888-999-2288; www.trailbus.com) minibus that runs between Victoria, the trailheads and Port Renfrew (from $30, daily in each direction).

PORT RENFREW

Handily nestled between the Juan de Fuca and West Coast trails, Port Renfrew is a great access point for either route. Quiet and often stormy during the off-season, it's usually full of preparing or recuperating hikers in summer. With several spots to stock-up on supplies or just fraternize with other trekkers, it's worth dropping by the **Visitor Information Centre** (www.portrenfrew.com; ⏰ 10am-6pm May-Sep) on your left as you enter town.

If you've had enough of your sleeping bag, try Renfrew's **Trailhead Resort** (☎ 250-647-5468; www.trailhead-resort.com; 17268 Parkinson Rd; ste/cabins

$110/225), complete with motel-style lodge rooms and some two-bedroom cabins. It's an ideal place to wind down after a hike, and its facilities include barbecues and hot tubs (often welcome after a long trek).

And for a break from campground mystery meat pasta, the nearby **Coastal Kitchen Cafe** (☎ 250-647-5545; 17245 Parkinson Rd; mains $8-14; 🕑 5am-8pm) serves fresh salads and sandwiches, plus burgers and pizzas. The seafood is the star attraction, especially the Dungeness crab and chips. Hikers are often found lolling around outside on the picnic tables here.

COWICHAN VALLEY

A swift 50km drive northwest of Victoria on Hwy 1, the verdant Cowichan Valley region is ripe for discovery, especially if you're a traveling foodie who likes visiting friendly farms and boutique wineries. Contact **Tourism Cowichan** (☎ 250-746-1099, 888-303-3337; www.visit.cowichan.net) for maps and information on the area's food, wine and biking trails.

Duncan

An old logging industry outpost, latter-day Duncan has revitalized itself as a key regional hub. For visitors, it's a place to stock up on supplies, grab a coffee with the locals or check out the 50 totem poles colorfully dotted around town. Try the **Visitor Information Centre** (☎ 250-746-4636, 888-303-3337; www.duncancc.bc.ca; 381 Hwy 1; 🕑 9am-5pm mid-Apr–mid-Oct) for info on its free summertime guided pole walks.

For those interested in First Nations, go to the **Quw'utsun' Cultural & Conference Centre** (☎ 250-746-8119, 877-746-8119; www.quwutsun.ca; 200 Cowichan Way; adult/child/youth $13/2/11; 🕑 10am-5pm Mon-Fri, 10am-4pm Sat & Sun mid-Apr–Sep) to learn about carving, beading and traditional salmon runs.

Alternatively, drive 3km north to the **BC Forest Discovery Centre** (☎ 250-715-1113, 866-715-1113; www.discoveryforest.com; 2892 Drinkwater Rd; adult/child $11/6; 🕑 10am-5pm Jun-Aug, 10am-4:30pm Thu-Mon Apr, May & Sep), complete with its pioneer-era buildings, logging machinery and a working steam train.

Lake Cowichan & Around

West of Duncan on Hwy 18, this waterfront town is a good base for exploring the region. Drop by the **Visitor Information Centre** (☎ 250-749-3244; www.lakecowichan.ca; 125-C South Shore Rd; 🕑 9am-5pm Tue-Sat, 10am-2pm Sun & Mon) for tips on the area.

> **GALLOPING GOOSE**
>
> Starting north of Sooke, the **Galloping Goose Trail** – named for a noisy 1920s gas railcar that ran between here and Victoria – is a 55km bike and walking path on abandoned railway beds. If you're not wiped out by the end of your ride from Victoria, you can cycle another 29km up the Saanich Peninsula to Sidney on the **Lochside Regional Trail**. This route gets cyclists off the highways and into some usually unseen backcountry. Getting on and off the trails is easy since bus lines along both routes are bike-rack equipped. You can download free maps and guides for both these routes from the **Capital Regional District** (☎ 250-478-3344; www.crd.bc.ca/parks).

The nearby **South Shore Motel** (☎ 250-749-6482, 888-749-6482; www.cowichanlakemotel.com; 266 South Shore Rd; s/d $50/65) offers standard but comfortable rooms (some with kitchenettes), and you can indulge in some hearty sustenance at the **Shaker Mill** (☎ 250-749-6350; 72 Cowichan Lake Rd; mains $8-11; 🕑 8am-8pm), which serves home-style specials and has a couple of patios where you can watch over the town.

Chemainus

After the last sawmill shut down in 1983, tiny Chemainus became the model for BC communities dealing with declining resource jobs. Instead of submitting to a slow death, town officials commissioned a giant wall mural depicting local history. People took notice, and 34 more murals and 13 sculptures were ordered. A new tourism industry was born. Check the **chamber of commerce** (☎ 250-246-3944; www.chemainus.bc.ca; 9796 Willow St; 🕑 9am-5:30pm daily May-Oct, 9am-5pm Mon-Fri, 10am-4pm Sat Nov-Apr) for mural maps and information.

Stroll the streets on a mural hunt and you'll pass artsy boutiques and tempting ice-cream shops. In the evening, the surprisingly large **Chemainus Theatre** (☎ 250-246-9800, 800-565-7738; www.chemainustheatrefestival.ca; 9737 Chemainus Rd; tickets $29-36) stages professional productions, mostly popular plays and musicals.

Developed in partnership with the theater – ask about show packages – the **Chemainus Festival Inn** (☎ 250-246-4181, 877-246-4181; www.festivalinn.ca; 9573 Chemainus Rd; r $139-219; 🖳) is like a midrange business hotel from a much larger town.

WHAT THE..?

Make your way to Duncan's **Cowichan Community Centre** (☎ 250-748-7529; 2687 James St) and you'll come across the somewhat forlorn **World's Largest Hockey Stick**, clinging improbably to its exterior like it might fall off and clunk you on the head at any moment. The 62m, 28,000kg stick, complete with its own monster puck, was commissioned for Vancouver's Expo 86.

Rooms are slick and comfortable and many include kitchens.

You can rub shoulders with the locals at the nearby **Twisted Sisters Tea Room** (☎ 250-246-1541; 9885 Maple St; mains $5-12; 11am-11pm;), a smashing hangout with light meals, vegetarian options, a smorgasbord of tea varieties and weekend music and movie nights.

NANAIMO

pop 79,000

Nanaimo will never have the allure of tourist-friendly Victoria, but the 'Harbour City' has undergone its own quiet renaissance since the 1990s, with the downtown emergence of some good coffee shops, worthwhile indie stores and a smattering of great restaurants. With its own mainland ferry service, the city is a handy hub for exploring up-island. Drop by the **Downtown Information Centre** (☎ 250-754-8141; www.nanaimodowntown.com; 150 Commercial St; 8:30am-4:30pm Mon-Fri, 11am-3pm Sat) for local insights.

Sights & Activities

The windswept **Piper's Lagoon Park** (3600 Place Rd) is one of Nanaimo's undoubted outdoor highlights. Bring a picnic and check out the birds hanging around the lagoon, take a short hike through the gnarly Garry oak forest or give the climbing wall your best shot. Then head over to **Shack Island**, which houses a straggle of old fishermen's sheds kept as unserviced cottages for those lugging their own sleeping bags.

With picnicking, cycling, hiking and beaches, the rustic **Newcastle Island Marine Provincial Park** (☎ 250-754-7893; www.bcparks.ca) is well worth an afternoon visit. Walks or hikes range from 1km strolls to a 7.5km perimeter trek. Access is via a 10-minute trip by **ferry** (250-708-0201, 877-297-8526; www.nanaimoharbourferry.com; adult/child $8/4; Apr–mid-Oct) from the Inner Harbour.

Overlooking downtown, the colorful **Nanaimo District Museum** (☎ 250-753-1821; www.nanaimomuseum.ca; 100 Cameron Rd; adult/child/youth $2/1/2; 10am-5pm daily mid-May–Aug, 10am-5pm Tue-Sat Sep–mid-May) explores the growth of the city, from its First Nations heritage to its Hudson's Bay Company days. It's not far from the **Bastion** (☎ 250-753-1821; cnr Front & Bastion Sts; adult/child $1/free; 10am-4pm Jun-Aug), a landmark fortified tower built by the Hudson's Bay Company in 1853.

Wild Play Element Parks (☎ 250-716-7874, 888-668-7874; www.wildplayparks.com; 35 Nanaimo River Rd; adult/child/youth $39/19/29; 10am-6pm daily mid-Jun–Aug, 10am-6pm Fri-Mon Mar–mid-Jun, Sep & Oct), a former bungee jumping site, has reinvented itself with five obstacle courses strung between the trees. Once you're harnessed, you can hit ziplines, rope bridges, tunnels and Tarzan swings, each aimed at different ability levels.

Sleeping & Eating

Painted Turtle Guesthouse (☎ 250-753-4432, 866-309-4432; www.paintedturtle.ca; 121 Bastion St; dm $24, r $45-70; wi-fi) This exemplary budget property in the heart of downtown combines four-bed dorms with family and private rooms. Hardwood floors and IKEA-esque furnishings abound, and facilities range from a large and welcoming kitchen to a laundry room and en suite showers. You can book a variety of local activities through the front desk.

Buccaneer Inn (☎ 250-753-1246, 877-282-6337; www.buccaneerinn.com; 1577 Stewart Ave; s/d/ste $70/90/160; wi-fi) Handy for the Departure Bay ferry terminal, this family-run motel has an immaculate white paint job. The neat and tidy approach is carried over into the maritime-themed rooms, many with kitchenettes. Splurge on a spacious suite and you'll have a fireplace, full kitchen and flat-screen TV.

Dorchester Hotel (☎ 250-754-6835, 800-661-2449; www.dorchesternanaimo.com; 70 Church St; r $109-160; wi-fi) Downtown's signature hotel has an unbeatable location overlooking the harbor. It's been refurbished in recent years – hence the loungey look to the old rooms – but the hallways running at odd angles couldn't be changed, nor could its historic character: it's still got its Victorian moldings and sitting rooms on the southwest corners of each floor.

Inn on Long Lake (☎ 250-758-1144, 800-565-1144; www.innonlonglake.com; 4700 N Island Hwy; r/ste $159/219; wi-fi) A 2km drive north of the Departure Bay ferry terminal, this lakeside retreat offers a swanky change of pace for travelers who've been roughing it around the island. The large rooms, each with a balcony, have plenty of amenities and some have kitchenettes. There's a sauna, fitness center and lake-bound canoes to keep you occupied, along with a free continental breakfast.

Pirate Chips (☎ 250-753-2447; 1 Commercial St; mains $4-7.50; ⏰ 11:30am-10pm Mon-Wed, until midnight Thu, until 3am Fri & Sat, noon-9pm Sun) Locals started coming here for the best fries in town (the curry topping is recommended) but they keep coming back for the funky ambience and quirky pirate-themed decor. An excellent late-night hangout, you can even indulge in poutine (fries with cheese curds and gravy) and deep-fried chocolate bars here (although preferably not together).

Penny's Palapa (☎ 250-753-2150; 10 Wharf St H Dock; mains $8-14; ⏰ 11am-9pm mid-Apr–Oct; V) A floating, flower-decked hut and patio bobbing among the boats in the harbor, this seasonal gem is well worth a look. Its inventive, well-priced menu of Mexican delights includes seafood specials – the signature halibut tacos are recommended – and some spicy vegetarian options.

Wesley Street Restaurant (☎ 250-753-6057; 321 Wesley St; mains $15-29; ⏰ 11:30am-2:30pm & 5:30-10pm Tue-Sat) Like a transplant from Victoria, this long-overdue West Coast specialty restaurant combines a bright, art-lined dining room with the kind of delectable menu sophisticated Nanaimoites have been craving for years. The locally sourced ingredients mean ever-changing specials but the favorite on our visit was Pacific halibut with Dungeness crab potato salad.

Drinking & Entertainment

Nanaimo's **Old City Station Pub** (☎ 250-716-0030; 150 Skinner St) is a convivial and well-located spot for a beer or three. The impressive roster here focuses on a significant proportion of Canadian tipples, including brews from Alexander Keith's and Granville Island Brewing. The food menu is also recommended and is a cut above standard pub grub.

If you're more inclined to test your sea legs, catch the **ferry** (☎ 250-753-8244; round-trip $4; ⏰ 11am-midnight mid-May–Sep, 11am-11pm Oct–mid-May) from the harbor to the aptly named **Dinghy Dock Floating Pub** (☎ 250-753-2373; 8 Pirates Lane), which bobs offshore near Protection Island.

The city's best live music and dance spot, the **Queen's Hotel** (☎ 250-754-6751; www.thequeens.ca; 34 Victoria Cres) hosts an eclectic roster of live performances and club nights, ranging from indie to jazz and country. In contrast, the **Port Theatre** (☎ 250-754-8550; www.porttheatre.nisa.com; 125 Front St) presents local and touring live theater shows.

Getting There & Away

AIR

Nanaimo Airport (☎ 250-245-2147; www.nanaimoairport.com) is 18km south of town via Hwy 1. **Air Canada Jazz** (☎ 514-393-3333, 888-247-2262; www.aircanada.com) flights arrive here from Vancouver (from $91, 25 minutes, up to seven daily).

Frequent **West Coast Air** (☎ 604-606-6888, 800-347-2222; www.westcoastair.com) floatplane services arrive in the harbor from downtown Vancouver ($67.50, 25 minutes) and Vancouver International Airport ($55, 20 minutes), while similar services (at almost identical prices) are provided by **Harbour Air Seaplanes** (☎ 604-274-1277, 800-665-0212; www.harbour-air.com).

BOAT

BC Ferries (☎ 250-386-3431, 888-223-3779; www.bcferries.com) from Tsawwassen (passenger/vehicle $10.55/$35, two hours) arrive at Duke Point, 14km south of Nanaimo. Services from Horseshoe Bay in West Vancouver (passenger/vehicle $10.55/$35, 95 minutes) arrive at Departure Bay, 3km north of the city via Hwy 1.

BUS

Greyhound (☎ 800-661-8747; www.greyhound.ca) buses arrive from Victoria ($18.75, 2½ hours, six daily), Campbell River ($24.95, three hours, three daily), Port Alberni ($16.65, 1½ hours, three daily) and Tofino ($35.85, 3½ hours, two daily).

TRAIN

The daily **Via Rail** (☎ 888-842-7245; www.viarail.com) *Malahat* service arrives from Victoria ($26.50, 2½ hours), Parksville ($16, 35 minutes) and Courtenay ($26.50, two hours), among others.

Getting Around

Nanaimo Regional Transit (☎ 250-390-4531; www.rdn.bc.ca; single/daypass $2.25/5.75) buses stop along Gordon St, west of Harbour Park Mall. Bus 2 goes to the Departure Bay ferry terminal. No city buses run to Duke Point. **Nanaimo Seaporter** (☎ 250-753-2118) provides door-to-door service to downtown from Departure Bay ($8) and Duke Point ($16) ferry terminals.

PORT ALBERNI

pop 18,700

Although its key fishing and forestry sectors have been declining for decades, waterfront Alberni was initially slow to develop itself as a tourist destination. But the double whammy of First Nations and pioneer heritage, plus easy access to some truly outstanding natural wilderness, makes this an ideal spot for off-the-beaten-path adventuring. Drop by the **Alberni Valley Visitor Info Centre** (☎ 250-724-6535; www.avcoc.com; 2533 Redford St; 8am-6pm daily mid-May–Aug, 9am-5pm Mon-Fri, 10am-2pm Sat & Sun Sep–mid-May).

Sights & Activities

The mystical highlight of MacMillan Provincial Park, between Parksville and Port Alberni, **Cathedral Grove** (☎ 250-248-9460) is the spiritual home of tree huggers. Often overrun with summer visitors – try not to knock them down as they scamper across the highway in front of you – its accessible forest trails wind through a dense canopy of vegetation, offering glimpses of some of BC's oldest trees, including centuries-old Douglas firs more than 3m in diameter. Try hugging that.

The best way to encounter the waters of Barkley Sound is via one of the traditional packet boats – the *MV Lady Rose* or *MV Frances Barkley* – offered by **Lady Rose Marine Services** (☎ 250-723-8313, 800-663-7192; www.ladyrosemarine.com; 5425 Argyle St; return tours $40-64; departs 8am Tue, Thu & Sat) from Alberni's Argyle Pier. The vessels stop en route to deliver mail and supplies and the trip is an enjoyably scenic day excursion, plus a practical means of returning from the West Coast Trail's north end at Bamfield.

A one-stop shop for active-types, **Batstar Adventure Tours** (☎ 250-724-2050, 877-449-1230; www.batstar.com; 4785 Beaver Creek Rd) arranges everything from guided bike trips into the wilderness to multiday kayak odysseys around the Broken Group Islands. If time is an issue, take their half-day kayak harbor tour ($59) or 20km streams-and-forest bike ride along a disused railway line ($79).

Sleeping & Eating

Fat Salmon Backpackers (☎ 250-723-6924; www.fatsalmonbackpackers.com; 3250 Third Ave; dm $21-25; Apr-Sep; wi-fi) Driven by its energetic, ultra-welcoming owners, this funky and eclectic backpacker joint offers four- to eight-bed dorms, each with names like 'Knickerbocker' and 'Mullet Room.' There are lots of books to read, free hot drinks and a kitchen bristling with utensils. Make sure you say 'hi' to Lily, the friendly house dog.

Hummingbird Guesthouse (☎ 250-720-2111, 888-720-2114; www.hummingbirdguesthouse.com; 5769 River Rd; ste $125-160; wi-fi) With four large suites and a giant deck (complete with hot tub), this modern B&B has a home-away-from-home feel. There's a shared kitchen on each of the two floors but the substantial cooked breakfast should keep you full for hours. Each suite has satellite TV, one has its own sauna and there's a teen-friendly games room out back.

Clam Bucket (☎ 250-723-1315; 4479 Victoria Quay; mains $7-12; 11am-9pm Mon-Thu, 11am-10pm Fri & Sat, 11am-8pm Sun) Renowned for its fresh-catch seafood – try the Cajun-style blackened oysters – the Clam Bucket also serves unlikely treats like Japanese wings and heaping gourmet burgers. Its funky orange-and-blue interior provides a casual atmosphere indoors, or you can head to the patio for panoramic inlet views.

Getting There & Away

Greyhound (☎ 800-661-8747; www.greyhound.ca) buses arrive here from Victoria ($36, 4½ hours, three daily), Nanaimo ($16.65, ½ hours, three daily), Tofino ($21.70, two hours, two daily) and Parksville ($8.95, 50 minutes, three daily).

PACIFIC RIM NATIONAL PARK RESERVE

A wave-crashing waterfront and brooding, mist-covered trees ensure that the **Pacific Rim National Park Reserve** (☎ 250-726-7721; www.pc.gc.ca/pacificrim; adult/child $7/4) is among BC's most popular outdoor attractions. The 50,000-hectare park comprises the northern Long Beach Unit, between Tofino and Ucluelet, the Broken Group Islands in Barkley Sound, and, to the south, the ever-popular West Coast Trail.

Drop by the **Pacific Rim Visitor Centre** (☎ 250-726-4600; www.pacificrimvisitor.ca; 2791 Pacific Rim Hwy; 9am-5pm mid-Mar–Jun & Sep, till 7pm Jul & Aug, 10am-4pm Thu-Sun Oct–mid-Mar) for regional information.

Long Beach Unit

Attracting the lion's share of visitors, Long Beach Unit is easily accessible by car along the Pacific Rim Hwy. Wide sandy beaches, untamed surf, lots of beachcombing nooks and a living museum of old-growth rain forest are the main reasons for the summer tourist clamor.

Drop by the **Wickaninnish Interpretive Centre** (Wick Rd; 9am-6pm mid-Mar–mid-Oct), named after a chief of the local Nuu-chah-nulth tribe, for intriguing exhibits on regional natural history and First Nations culture.

If you're inspired to take a stroll, try one of the following trails, keeping your eyes peeled for swooping bald eagles and shockingly large banana slugs. Safety precautions apply on all trails here: never turn your back on the mischievous surf.

Long Beach (easy) Great scenery along the sandy shore.
Rainforest Trail (1km; moderate) Two interpretive loops through old-growth forest.
Shorepine Bog (800m; easy, wheelchair accessible) Loops around a moss-layered bog.

SLEEPING & EATING

Green Point Campground (☎ 250-689-9025, 877-737-3783; www.pccamping.ca; campsites $20.80; mid-Mar–mid-Oct) Between Ucluelet and Tofino on the Pacific Rim Hwy, Green Point encourages lots of novice campers to try their first night under the stars. Extremely popular in summer – book ahead – its 105 tent sites are located on a forested terrace, with trail access to the beach. Expect fairly basic facilities: the faucets are cold but the toilets are flush.

Wickaninnish Restaurant (☎ 250-726-7706; Wick Rd; mains $10-22; 11:30am-10pm) Make up for roughing it with a rewarding meal in the interpretive centre, where the crashing surf views are served with fresh-caught seafood.

GETTING THERE & AROUND

The **Tofino Bus** (☎ 250-725-2871, 866-986-3466; www.tofinobus.com) 'Beach Bus' service runs between Tofino's visitor center (opposite) and Ucluelet lighthouse up to four times daily (one-way adult/child $10/5), with stops at Long Beach, Green Point Campground and the Wickaninnish Centre.

Broken Group Islands Unit

Comprising some 300 islands and rocks scattered across 80 sq km around the entrance to Barkley Sound, the Broken Group is a serene natural wilderness beloved by visiting kayakers, especially those who enjoy close-up views of gray whales, harbor porpoises and various birdlife. Compasses are required for navigating here, unless you fancy paddling to Hawaii.

If you're up for a trek, **Lady Rose Marine Services** (☎ 250-723-8313, 800-663-7192; www.ladyrosemarine.com) can ship you and your kayak to their Sechart Whaling Station Lodge in Barkley Sound. From there, popular paddle-to points include the recommended Gibraltar Island, a one-hour kayak away. It has a sheltered campground and many explorable beaches. Willis Island (1½ hours from Sechart) is also popular. It has a campground and, at low tide, you can stroll to some of the nearby islands.

If your own kayak didn't fit in your backpack, you can rent at Sechart Whaling Station Lodge ($35 to $50 per day). Alternatively, **Broken Island Adventures** (☎ 250-728-3500, 888-728-6200; www.brokenislandadventures.com) rents kayaks and also runs popular three-hour powerboat tours (adult/child $72/26) around the region.

West Coast Trail Unit

Slowly recovering from a devastating late-2006 storm – repeat hikers will notice the missing trees from large sections – the legendary 75km West Coast Trail is one of Canada's best-known and toughest hiking routes. There are two things you need to know before tackling this rite of passage: it will hurt and you'll want to do it again.

Winding between the **West Coast Trail Pachena Bay Information Centre** (☎ 250-728-3234; 9am-5pm May-Sep), near Bamfield on the north end, and the **West Coast Trail Gordon River Information Centre** (☎ 250-647-5434; 9am-5pm May-Sep), near Port Renfrew to the south, most trekkers take between six and eight days to complete the full route.

Accessible from May to September, there is a limit of 26 overnight backpackers starting from each end each day. All overnighters must pay a trail user fee ($130) and a fee ($30) to cover the two ferry crossings you'll encounter en route. Call ☎ 250-387-1642 or ☎ 800-663-6000 for reservations ($25) from March 1 each year.

You must be able to handle rough terrain, rock-face ladders, stream crossings and adverse weather to tackle this trail. Hikers can camp at any of the designated sites along the route, most of which have solar-composting outhouses.

GETTING THERE & AWAY

West Coast Trail Express (☎ 250-477-8700, 888-999-2288; www.trailbus.com; May-Sep) runs a daily shuttle to Panchena Bay from Victoria ($65, six hours), Nanaimo ($65, four hours) and Port Alberni ($45, 2½ hours). It also runs a service to Gordon River from Victoria ($45,

2½ hours), Bamfield ($60, 3½ hours) and Panchena Bay ($60, three hours).

TOFINO & AROUND

Having rapidly transformed in recent years from a sleepy hippy hangout into a popular eco destination with high-end resorts, Tofino is like the Whistler of Vancouver Island – it's the region's most popular outdoor destination. A short drive south of town, the **Tofino Visitor Centre** (☎ 250-725-3414; www.tourismtofino.com; 1426 Pacific Rim Hwy; ⏰ 10am-6pm May-Sep) has detailed information on the area.

Sights

Check out what coastal temperate rain forests are all about by exploring the flora and fauna at the **Tofino Botanical Gardens** (☎ 250-725-1220; www.tbgf.org; 1084 Pacific Rim Hwy; 3-day admission adult/child/youth $10/free/6; ⏰ 9am-dusk), complete with a frog pond, forest boardwalk, native plants and an ongoing program of workshops and field trips. There's a $1 discount for car-free arrivals.

Hot Springs Cove is the highlight of **Maquinna Marine Provincial Park** (☎ 250-474-1336; www.bcparks.ca), one of the most popular day trips from Tofino. Tranquility-minded trekkers travel here by Zodiac boat or seaplane, watching for whales and other sea critters en route. From the boat landing, 2km of boardwalks lead to a series of natural hot pools.

Visible through the mist from the Tofino waterfront, **Meares Island** is home to the **Big Tree Trail**, a 400m boardwalk through old-growth forest that includes a stunning 1500-year-old red cedar. The island was the site of the key 1984 Clayoquot Sound anti-logging protest that kicked off the region's latter-day environmental movement.

Activities

SURFING

Live to Surf (☎ 250-725-4464; www.livetosurf.com; 1180 Pacific Rim Hwy; board rental 24hr $25) Tofino's original surf shop also supplies skates and skimboards.

Surf Sister (☎ 250-725-4456, 877-724-7873; www.surfsister.com; 625 Campbell St) Surf school offering introductory lessons (from $65) plus women-only multiday courses (from $175).

KAYAKING

Rainforest Kayak Adventures (☎ 250-725-3117, 877-422-9453; www.rainforestkayak.com; 316 Main St; multiday courses & tours from $699) Specializing in four- to six-day guided tours and courses.

Tofino Sea Kayaking (☎ 250-725-4222, 800-863-4664; www.tofino-kayaking.com; 320 Main St; tours 2/4/6hr $54/68/90) Short guided paddles, including a popular four-hour Meares Island trip.

TOURS

Clayoquot Connections (☎ 250-726-8789; tours from $25) Good-value tours on an old open-deck lifeboat, including sunset, fishing and Meares Island trips.

Tla-ook Cultural Adventures (☎ 250-725-2656, 877-942-2663; www.tlaook.com; tours 2/4/6hr $44/64/140) Learn about First Nations culture by paddling an authentic dugout canoe.

WHALE-WATCHING

Jamie's Whaling Station (☎ 250-725-3919, 800-667-9913; www.jamies.com; 606 Campbell St; adult/child $79/50) Whale, bear and sea lion spotting tours.

Ocean Outfitters (☎ 250-725-2866, 877-906-2326; www.oceanoutfitters.bc.ca; 421 Main St; adult/child $79/65) Popular whale-watching tours, with bear and hot-spring trips also offered.

Sleeping & Eating

Clayoquot Field Station (☎ 250-725-1220; www.tbgf.org/cfs; 1084 Pacific Rim Hwy; dm/d $32/120; 💻 wi-fi) In the grounds of the Botanical Gardens, this immaculate education center has a selection of four-bed dorm rooms, a large kitchen and an onsite laundry. There's also a tranquil en suite private room where the surrounding forest brushes the window. A great sleepover for nature-lovers, there's a natural history library and regular speakers and events.

Tofino Inlet Cottages (☎ 250-725-3441, 866-725-3411; www.tofinoinletcottages.com; 350 Olsen Rd; d $100-175) A five-unit clutch of old A-frame buildings on a quiet stretch of waterfront overlooking Meares Island, these vacation cottages are like sleeping in a wood-lined boat cabin. The interiors are a little faded but all is neat and well-maintained – plus your deck is an ideal spot for some beer-fueled sunset watching.

Gull Cottage (☎ 250-725-3177; www.gullcottagetofino.com; 1254 Lynn Rd; d $135-165) A short trail walk from Chesterman Beach, this fusion West Coast–and Victorian-style B&B is a cozy haven for storm-watchers and a well-located base for summer explorers. It has three immaculate rooms, each with a light, pinewood esthetic. We like the rain forest room with it's large soaker tub. There's also a book-lined TV room and a great outdoor hot tub among the trees.

Wickaninnish Inn (☎ 250-725-3100, 800-333-4604; www.wickinn.com; Chesterman Beach; r from $460) 'The

Wick,' which has the market in luxury winter storm-watching packages cornered, is a local landmark that's worth a stay any time of year. Embodying nature with recycled old-growth furniture, natural stone tiles and the atmosphere of a place grown rather than constructed, the sumptuous guestrooms have gas fireplaces, two-person hot tubs and private balconies. Pampering has rarely felt better.

Sobo (☎ 250-725-2341; 1084 Pacific Rim Hwy; mains $6-10; ⌚ 11am-9pm) This legendary purple dining truck at the entrance of the Botanical Gardens serves gourmet salads, hearty soups and polenta fries. But it's the fish treats that draw the locals: the sizzling shrimp cakes are mouth-watering and the fish tacos are a staple of every diet within a 5km radius.

Shelter (☎ 250-725-3353; 601 Campbell St; mains $27-39; ⌚ 5-10pm) An exquisite West Coast eatery with international accents, our menu favorite here is the shrimp and crab dumplings. There's a strong commitment to local, sustainable ingredients – the salmon is wild and the sablefish is trap-caught – and there are plenty of non-fishy options for traveling carnivores, including a delectable char-grilled pork chop dish.

Getting There & Around

Orca Airways (☎ 604-270-6722, 888-359-6722; www.flyorcaair.com) flights arrive at **Tofino Airport** (☎ 250-725-2006) from Vancouver International Airport's South Terminal ($159, 55 minutes, one to three daily).

Affiliated with Greyhound (you can book via www.greyhound.ca), **Tofino Bus** (☎ 250-725-2871, 866-986-3466; www.tofinobus.com) runs an express service from Vancouver ($61 plus ferry, seven hours), Victoria ($65, 5½ hours), Nanaimo ($38, four hours) and Port Alberni ($23, 2½ hours). The route runs twice daily from mid-March to mid-November and daily for the rest of the year.

The company also operates a localized 'Tofino Transit' service around the region ($2), plus a 'Beach Bus' running between Tofino and Ucluelet (one-way adult/child $10/5).

UCLUELET

Long-regarded as Tofino's ugly sister, Ucluelet (yew-klew-let) nevertheless shares the same scenery and the same activities, and is generally cheaper and more accessible. For more information, drop by the **Chamber of Commerce** (☎ 250-726-4641; www.uclueletinfo.com; 100 Main St; ⌚ 9am-5pm May-Sep).

Sights & Activities

The smashing 8.5km **Wild Pacific Trail** (www.wildpacifictrail.com) runs via untamed rain forest and coastline, with bonus views of the Broken Group Islands and Barkley Sound. Seabirds and whales are abundant here and it's also a good area for storm-watching – don't get too close to the surf when it's really crashing. In contrast, the tide pools and kelp beds at **Big Beach** make it a great kid-friendly spot.

If you want to stretch your sea legs, **Subtidal Adventures** (☎ 250-726-7336, 877-444-1134; www.subtidaladventures.com; 1950 Peninsula Rd; adult/child from $49/39) has boat tours covering whales, sunsets and bears. Alternatively, you can rent some wheels from **Ukee Bikes** (☎ 250-726-2453; 1599 Imperial Lane; 1/24hr $5/25).

Sleeping & Eating

C&N Backpackers (☎ 250-726-7416, 888-434-6060; www.cnnbackpackers.com; 2081 Peninsula Rd; dm/r $25/65) They're very protective of their hardwood floors here, so take your shoes off to enter this calm and well-maintained hostel. The dorms are mostly small and basic, but private rooms are also available and there's a spacious kitchen. The highlight is the landscaped garden overlooking the inlet, complete with hammocks and a rope swing.

Canadian Princess Resort (☎ 250-598-3366, 800-663-7090; www.canadianprincess.com; 1943 Peninsula Rd; r $89-285; ⌚ Apr-Sep) You can choose from some tiny but cool staterooms on an old steam ship moored in Ucluelet Harbour, or some much larger and more traditional hotel rooms in the lodge. Don your eye-patch and stay on the boat, which handily houses the resort's bar and restaurant.

Ukee Dogs (☎ 250-726-2103; 1576 Imperial Lane; mains $4-6; ⌚ 9am-5pm Mon-Sat) Focusing on homebaked treats and comfort foods, this bright and breezy good-value eatery offers gourmet hotdogs, made-from-scratch soups and topping-packed pizzas (the smoked garlic sausage is great, unless you're planning to kiss anyone). Drop by in the afternoon for coffee and sprinkle-topped cakes.

Getting There & Around

Tofino Bus (☎ 250-725-2871, 866-986-3466; www.tofinobus.com) runs an express service from Vancouver ($53 plus ferry, 6½ hours), Victoria ($58, five hours), Nanaimo ($34, 3½ hours) and Port Alberni ($19, two hours). The route runs daily year-round and twice daily from mid-March to mid-November. They're now affiliated with Greyhound, so you can book at www.greyhound.ca.

The company also operates a localized 'Tofino Transit' service around the region ($2), as well as a 'Beach Bus' between Ucluelet and Tofino (one-way adult/child $10/5).

COMOX VALLEY

Comprising the main towns of Comox, Courtenay and Cumberland, this is a temperate region of rolling mountains, alpine meadows and eccentric communities. A good base for outdoor adventures, its highlight is the Mt Washington resort. Drop by the area's main **Visitor Information Centre** (☎ 250-334-3234, 888-357-4471; www.discovercomoxvalley.com; 2040 Cliffe Ave, Comox; 9am-5pm mid-May–Aug, closed Sun Sep–mid-May) for information.

Vancouver Island's skiing mecca, **Mt Washington Alpine Resort** (☎ 250-338-1386, 888-231-1499; www.mountwashington.ca; lift ticket adult/child Dec-Mar $46/25, May-Sep $28/18) has 50 runs, a snowshoeing park (adult/child $16/11) and cross-country ski trails (adult/child $19/10). There are also some great summer activities here, including horseback riding, alpine hiking and mountain biking.

For watery exertions in the region, contact **Pacific Pro Dive & Surf** (☎ 250-338-6829, 877-800-3483; www.scubashark.com; 2270 Cliffe Ave, Courtenay). They offer tours and rentals to traveling surf, scuba and kiteboarding fans.

There are plenty of B&Bs around the valley, as well as one of Vancouver Island's best backpacker joints. **Riding Fool Hostel** (☎ 250-336-8250, 888-313-3665; www.ridingfool.com; 2705 Dunsmuir St, Cumberland; dm/r $22/50; wi-fi) is a restored heritage building with immaculate wooden interiors, a large kitchen and lounge area, and the kind of neat and tidy private rooms often found in hotels.

For a cozy, home-style stay, the nearby **Cumberland Gardens B&B** (☎ 250-336-2867; www.cumberland-gardens.ca; 3303 First St, Cumberland; s/d $50/75) is also worth a look. There are two basement suites each with their own entrance. The chatty host will regale you with some colorful local stories.

When it's time to eat, head to **Atlas Café** (☎ 250-338-9838; 250 Sixth St, Courtenay; mains $12-18; 8:30am-10pm Tue-Sat, until 9pm Sun, until 3pm Mon), a popular restaurant that fuses Asian, Mexican and Mediterranean approaches. The fish tacos are ace and the locals often keep this place packed at meal times.

CAMPBELL RIVER

pop 30,800

Southerners will tell you this marks the end of civilization on Vancouver Island, but Campbell River is a former resource town that's reinvented itself as a drop-off point for wilderness tourism. The **Information Centre** (☎ 250-287-4636, 866-830-1113; www.campbellriver.travel; 1235 Shoppers Row; 9am-7pm) will fill you in on local attractions and happenings.

Sights & Activities

The recommended **Museum at Campbell River** (☎ 250-287-3103; www.crmuseum.ca; 470 Island Hwy; adult/child $6/4; 10am-5pm Mon-Sat, noon-5pm Sun mid-May–Sep, noon-5pm Tue-Sun Oct–mid-May) showcases First Nations masks, an 1890s pioneer cabin and video footage of the world's largest artificial, non-nuclear blast: an underwater mountain in Seymour Narrows that caused dozens of shipwrecks before it was blown apart in 1958.

Since locals claim the town as the 'Salmon Capital of the World,' you should wet your line off the downtown **Discovery Pier** (rod rentals $6 per day) or just stroll along with the crowds and see what everyone else has caught. Much easier than catching your own lunch, you can also buy fish 'n chips here. Work off the beer batter with a **scuba dive** around the sunken *HMCS Columbia*. Contact **Beaver Aquatics Limited** (☎ 250-287-7652; 760 Island Hwy; 1-day full equipment rental $50, intensive courses from $150; 9:30am-5pm Mon-Fri, 10am-5pm Sat) for gear and lessons.

Sleeping & Eating

Heron's Landing (☎ 250-923-2848, 888-923-2849; www.heronslandinghotel.com; 492 S Island Hwy; r from $145; wi-fi) A former Bavarian-style pension with a gingerbread-house look, the new owners have done a good job of sprucing up this property. Rooms have been fitted with fresh furnishings, appliances and bathrooms, while new extras include free wi-fi and laundry facilities ($1). The loft rooms are massive and comfortably sleep up to four.

Dolphins Resort (☎ 250-287-3066, 800-891-0287; www.dolphinsresort.com; 4125 Discovery Dr; cabins from $200) A beautifully maintained nest of cedar cabins spilling down to the water's edge, this lovely mini-resort is dripping with charm. The cabins have a cozy, rustic feel and each has a full kitchen with porch (barbecue rentals available). Most also have outdoor hot tubs. There's a secluded private beach area with its own fire pit for those essential evening hangouts.

Lookout Seafood Bar & Grill (☎ 250-286-6812; 921 Island Hwy; mains $7-12; ⏰ 8:30am-10pm) This old-school diner-style eatery has a slightly more cosmopolitan menu than you might expect, considering that it's been here since 1929. Oysters, halibut burgers and fish 'n chips dot the menu, while intriguing historic photos of Campbell River dot the walls.

Getting There & Around

Greyhound (☎ 800-661-8747; www.greyhound.ca) services arrive here from Port Hardy, ($38.70, 3½ hours, daily), Nanaimo ($25, three hours, three daily) and Victoria ($46.50, five to six hours, three daily). **Campbell River Transit** (☎ 250-287-7433; www.bctransit.com) operates local buses throughout the area (adult/child $1.75/1.50).

STRATHCONA PROVINCIAL PARK

Campbell River is the main access point for Vancouver Island's largest **park** (☎ 250-337-2400; www.bcparks.ca). Its 250,000 hectares are centered on Mt Golden Hinde, the island's highest point at 2200m.

A hiker's paradise, the park's notable trails include the **Paradise Meadows Loop** (2.2km), an easy amble among wildflower meadows, and **Mt Becher** (5km), with its great views over the Comox Valley. The 9km **Comox Glacier Trail** is quite an adventure but is only recommended for advanced hikers. Those who approach from the south across the Great Central Lake can follow the 16km trail (an intermediate hike) to **Della Falls**, a spectacular waterfall.

You can get close to nature by pitching your tent at **Buttle Lake Campground** (☎ 604-689-9025, 800-689-9025; www.discovercamping.ca; tent sites $14). The swimming area and playground here make this a good choice for families.

Alternatively, the 50-year-old **Strathcona Park Lodge** (☎ 250-286-3122; www.strathcona.bc.ca; r/cabins from $50/169) on Hwy 28 still makes environmental enlightenment its main mission. In keeping with its low-impact proximity to nature, there are no telephones or TVs in the rooms, which range from college-style bedrooms to secluded timber-frame cottages.

A one-stop shop for activities including kayaking, yoga and rock climbing, the lodge's laid-back Whale Room and Canoe Club Café eateries serve wholesome buffet meals (breakfast and lunch $11, dinner $21), while the Hi-Bracer Lounge & Bar is where to head for a restorative end-of-day beer.

NORTH VANCOUVER ISLAND

South-islanders will chuckle and say, 'There's nothing up there worth seeing,' while locals here will respond, 'They would say that, wouldn't they.' Parochial rivalries aside, what this giant region (which covers nearly half the island) lacks in towns, infrastructure and population, it more than makes up for in rugged natural beauty. If your trip to BC is all about encountering the untamed wilderness, this is the place for you. Despite the remoteness, some areas are remarkably accessible to hardy hikers, especially with the long-awaited arrival of the North Coast Trail. For regional information, contact **Tourism North Vancouver Island** (☎ 250-949-9094, 800-903-6660; www.vinva.bc.ca).

Telegraph Cove

Once nothing more than a remote outpost, Telegraph Cove has reinvented itself in recent decades as a charming visitor destination. Its pioneer feel is enhanced by the dozens of wooden buildings standing around the marina on stilts, but the place can get surprisingly crowded in summer.

Head along the boardwalk to the smashing **Whale Interpretive Centre** (☎ 250-928-3129, 250-928-3117; www.killerwhalecentre.org; suggested donation $2; ⏰ Jun-Sep), stuffed with hands-on artifacts and artfully displayed skeletons of cougars, sea otters and a giant fin whale.

You can also see whales of the live variety just offshore; Telegraph Cove is one of the island's best viewing spots. **Stubbs Island Whale-watching** (☎ 250-928-3185, 800-665-3066; www.stubbs-island.com; tours $74-84; ⏰ May-Sep) will get you up close with the orcas on a boat trek and you might also see humpbacks, dolphins and sea lions. Its sunset cruise is highly recommended.

While the established **Telegraph Cove Resorts** (☎ 250-928-3131, 800-200-4665; www.telegraphcoveresort.com; tent sites/cabins from $21/99) provides tent spaces and a string of charming cabins overlooking the marina, the nearby new **Dockside 29** (☎ 250-928-3163, 877-835-2683; www.telegraphcove.ca; r $115-155; wi-fi) is a good, motel-style alternative.

The **Killer Whale Café** (☎ 250-928-3155; mains $14-18; ⏰ 10am-9pm May-Sep) is the cove's best eatery. We recommend the salmon, mussel and prawn linguini.

Port Hardy

Settled by Europeans in the early 1800s, this small north island town is best known as the arrival/departure point for BC Ferries Inside Passage trips. It's also a handy gearing-up point for treks to remote Cape Scott.

Head to the **Chamber of Commerce** (☎ 250-949-7622; www.ph-chamber.bc.ca; 7250 Market St; 🕑 8:30am-6pm Mon-Fri, 9am-5pm Sat & Sun mid-May–Sep, 9am-5pm Mon-Fri Oct–mid-May) for local information, then drop by its adjoining **museum** (☎ 250-949-8143; 7110 Market St; 🕑 10am-3:30pm Tue-Sat May-Oct) covering the area's First Nations heritage.

SIGHTS & ACTIVITIES

Hikers can book a customized guided tour into the wilderness with the friendly folk at **North Island Daytrippers** (☎ 250-956-2411, 800-956-2411; www.islanddaytrippers.com). A one-stop shop for outdoorsy types, **Sea Legend** (☎ 250-949-6541, 800-246-0093; www.sealegend.com) also offers hiking, diving and whale-watching adventures.

It's hard to beat an overnight stay with **Great Bear Nature Tours** (☎ 250-949-9496, 888-221-8212; www.greatbeartours.com; tours from $700; 🕑 mid-May–mid-Oct), who boat visitors to their floating lodge for an educational up-close encounter with the region's grizzly occupants. Take their night-viewing option and you'll be watching the nocturnal shenanigans of wolves and cougars as well.

SLEEPING & EATING

Glen Lyon Inn & Suites (☎ 250-949-7115, 877-949-7115; www.glenlyoninn.com; 6435 Hardy Bay Rd; s/d/ste from $90/95/125; 💻) This recently renovated hotel has large rooms with balconies and a decidedly aqua color scheme. Most rooms have fridges and microwaves, and some have kitchenettes and heart-shaped Jacuzzi baths – ideal if you're a visiting 1970s movie star. There's an exercise room and laundry facilities and, for ferry catchers, it's not far from the terminal.

Quarterdeck Inn & Marina Resort (☎ 250-902-0455, 877-902-0459; www.quarterdeckresort.net; 6555 Hardy Bay Rd; s/d $125/145) A suite gives you a lot more room (plus a fireplace and Jacuzzi) and is worth the extra dollars if you've been roughing it at bare-basics campsites for a few days. The upper floor waterfront rooms have excellent views. The onsite IV's Quarterdeck Pub & Dining Room (☎ 250-949-6922; mains $8 to $14) serves bar grub and comfort food including a halibut burger that's hard to beat.

GETTING THERE & AROUND

Pacific Coastal Airlines (☎ 604-273-8666, 800-663-2872; www.pacific-coastal.com) services arrive from Vancouver ($201, 75 minutes, up to six daily).

Greyhound (☎ 800-661-8747; www.greyhound.ca) buses roll in from Port McNeil, ($5.80, 45 minutes, daily), Campbell River ($38.70, 3½ hours, daily) and Nanaimo ($61.50, seven hours, daily).

BC Ferries (☎ 250-386-3431, 888-223-3779; www.bcferries.com) services arrive from Prince Rupert (passenger/vehicle $116/275, 15 hours, schedules vary) via the spectacular Inside Passage route. The company also operates a summer-only Discovery Coast Passage route (passenger/vehicle from $120/241) that departs and arrives to/from McLoughlin Bay, Shearwater, Klemtu, Ocean Falls and Bella Coola. Reservations are required.

North Island Transportation (☎ 250-949-6300; nit@island.net) operates a handy shuttle to/from the ferry terminal via area hotels ($8).

Cape Scott Provincial Park

It's 568km from Victoria to the end of the logging road at the trailhead of this remote **park** (www.bcparks.ca) on Vancouver Island's northern tip. But if you really want to experience the raw beauty of BC – wild coastlines, mossy rain forests and stunning sandy bays alive with rolling waves and beady-eyed seabirds – this should be your number one destination.

From the parking area, take the relatively easy 2.5km trail to **San Josef Bay** and you'll stroll from the shady trees right onto one of the province's best white-sand beaches, a breathtaking expanse of lapping ocean, tree-lined crags and the kind of caves that might harbor ancient smugglers. If it's not too windy – this place takes the full force of the North Pacific in its stride – consider camping ($5) right here on the beach.

If you're just here for the day, there are several tempting wood trails, most aimed at well-prepared hikers with plenty of gumption, passing between moss-covered yew trees, old-growth cedars that are centuries-old and a soft carpet of sun-dappled ferns.

One of the area's shortest trails (2km) in the adjoining **Raft Cove Provincial Park** (www.bcparks.ca) brings you to the crescent-shaped beach and beautiful lagoons of Raft Cove. You'll likely have the entire 1.3km beach to yourself, although north-islanders also like to access it for surfing.

Hiking further in the region, where you're fairly likely to come across black bears, is not for the uninitiated or unprepared. For information on the area's routes – and progress reports on the development of the **North Island Trail** that was due to open soon after the time of writing – check www.northcoasttrail.com.

SOUTHERN GULF ISLANDS

Stressed-out Vancouverites tired of languishing on their favorite Stanley Park beach often seek solace in the restorative arms of the rustic Southern Gulf Islands, handily strung like a necklace of enticing pearls between the mainland and Vancouver Island. Once colonized by hippy-dippy Canadian dropouts and fugitive US draft dodgers, Salt Spring, Galiano, Mayne, Saturna and the North and South Penders are the natural retreat of choice for many in the region. Whichever island you choose, the soothing relaxation begins once you step on the ferry to get here: time suddenly slows, your heart rate drops to hibernation level and the forested isles and glassy waters slide by like a slow-motion nature documentary.

Getting There & Around

Serving the main Southern Gulf Islands, **BC Ferries** (☎ 250-386-3431, 888-223-3779; www.bcferries.com) operates direct routes from Vancouver Island's Swartz Bay terminal to Salt Spring and North Pender. From North Pender, you can connect to Mayne, Galiano or Salt Spring. From Mayne, you can connect to Saturna.

From the mainland, there is a direct service from Tsawwassen to Galiano, which then connects to North Pender. There are also direct weekend services from Tsawwassen to both Mayne (Sunday only) and Salt Spring (Friday to Sunday). For more frequent services to these and the other islands, you will need to travel from Tsawwassen to Swartz Bay, then board a connecting ferry. For island hopping, consider a handy **SailPass** (4/7 days $169/199) which covers ferry travel around the region on 20 different routes.

Gulf Islands Water Taxi (☎ 250-537-2510; www.saltspring.com/watertaxi) runs walk-on ferries between Salt Spring, North Pender and Saturna (one-way/return $15/25) and between Salt Spring, Galiano and Mayne (one-way/return $15/25), both twice-daily September to June and once-daily July and August.

Seair Seaplanes (☎ 604-273-8900, 800-447-3247; www.seairseaplanes.com) services run from Vancouver International Airport's South Terminal to Salt Spring ($77, 20 minutes, three daily), North Pender ($82, 20 minutes, three daily), Saturna ($82, 20 minutes, three daily), Mayne ($82, 20 minutes, two daily) and Galiano (adult $82, 20 minutes, two daily).

SALT SPRING ISLAND

pop 10,500

Dominating the island chain, pretty Salt Spring receives the most visitors and has the largest population. A former hippy enclave that's now the site of many rich vacation homes, it's well worth a visit if you're looking for a picturesque escape from the city without sacrificing on amenities. Drop by the **Chamber of Commerce** (☎ 250-537-5252, 866-216-2936; www.saltspringtoday.com; 121 Lower Ganges Rd; 🕑 11am-3pm) in Ganges, Salt Spring's main community.

Sights & Activities

Check out Ganges' thriving **Saturday Market** (☎ 250-537-4448; www.saltspringmarket.com; Centennial Park; 🕑 8:30am-3:30pm Sat Apr-Oct) for luscious island-grown fruit, piquant cheeses and tons of arts and crafts.

You can also visit local artisans with a downloadable self-guided studio map from **Salt Spring Island Studio Tour** (☎ 250-537-9476; www.saltspringstudiotour.com). Among the best stops is the rustic **Blue Horse Folk Art Gallery** (☎ 250-537-0754, www.bluehorse.ca; 175 North View Dr; 🕑 10am-5pm Sun-Fri Apr-Oct) where lovely angular vases jostle for space with those leaping wooden hare carvings you've always craved.

Gather some picnic fixings then add to your feast with a bottle from **Salt Spring Vineyards** (☎ 250-653-9463; www.saltspringvineyards.com; 151 Lee Rd; 🕑 11am-5pm mid-Jun–Aug, hours vary rest of yr), where you can sample a few tipples to find the one you like best (we favor the rich blackberry port).

Consider taking your picnic to **Ruckle Provincial Park** (☎ 250-539-2115; www.bcparks.ca), a southeast gem with ragged seashores, arbutus forests and sun-kissed farmlands.

Sleeping & Eating

Lakeside Gardens (☎ 250-537-5773; www.lakesidegardensresort.com; 1450 North End Rd; cabanas/cottages $75/135;

Apr-Oct) A rustic retreat where nature is the main attraction, this tranquil, family-friendly clutch of cottages and cabanas is ideal for low-key fishing, swimming and boating. The cabanas are basic – like camping in a cabin – while the larger cottages have TVs, en suites and full kitchens.

Love Shack (250-653-0007, 866-341-0007; www.oceansidecottages.com/love.htm; 521 Isabella Rd; cabins $135) If Austin Powers comes to Salt Spring, this is where he'll stay. Love Shack is a groovy waterfront nook complete with a lava lamp, collection of vintage cameras and a record player plus albums (Abba to Stan Getz). The kitchen is stocked with organic coffee and the private deck is ideal for watching the sunset in your velour jumpsuit.

Barb's Buns (250-537-4491; 121 McPhillips Ave; mains $6-9; 7am-5pm Mon, 7am-10pm Tue-Sat, 10am-2pm Sun; V) Good wholesome treats are the menu mainstays here, with heaped pizza slices, hearty soups and bulging sandwiches drawing the lunch crowd, many of whom are grateful vegetarians. Others repeatedly fail to resist the mid-afternoon lure of organic coffee, cookies, cakes and, of course, Barb's lovely buns.

Tree House Café (250-537-5379; 106 Purvis Lane; mains $8-14; 8am-9pm Mon-Fri, 9am-9pm Sat & Sun May-Sep, 8am-3pm Oct-Apr) A magical outdoor café in the heart of Ganges, you'll be sitting in the shade of a large plum tree here as you choose from a menu of comfort pastas, Mexican specialties and gourmet burgers – the Teriyaki salmon burger is recommended, washed down with a hoppy bottle of Salt Spring Pale Ale. Live music is held here every night in summer.

Getting There & Around

BC Ferries, Gulf Island Water Taxis and Seair Seaplanes operate services to Salt Spring (opposite). If you don't have a car, the **Ganges Faerie** (250-537-6758; www.gangesfaerie.com; tickets $8-14) shuttles between the island's three ferry terminals and the Ganges, Ruckle Park and Fernwood areas.

NORTH & SOUTH PENDER ISLANDS

pop 2200

Once joined by a sandy isthmus (and still referred to in the singular) the North and South Penders are far quieter than Salt Spring. With pioneer farms, old-time orchards and almost 40 coves and beaches, the Penders – now linked by a single-lane bridge – are ideal for bikers and hikers. Drop by the **Chamber of Commerce** (250-629-6541, 866-468-7924; www.penderislandchamber.com; 2332 Otter Bay Rd, N Pender; 9am-5pm daily Jul & Aug, 9am-5pm Thu-Sun May & Jun) for information.

Sights & Activities

Enjoy the sand at **Medicine Beach** and **Clam Bay** on North Pender, as well as **Gowlland Point** on the east coast of South Pender. Just over the bridge to South Pender is **Mt Norman Regional Park**, complete with a couple of hikes that promise grand views of the surrounding islands. There's a regular Saturday **Farmers Market** (250-629-3669; 4418 Bedwell Harbour Rd) in the community hall and a smaller one at the Driftwood Centre, the region's small commercial hub.

You can paddle around with **Kayak Pender Island** (250-629-6939, 877-683-1746; www.kayakpenderisland.com; tours from $45), while **Sound Passage Adventures** (250-629-3920, 877-629-3930; www.soundpassageadventures.com) offers tempting eco-tours and scuba-diving excursions.

Sleeping & Eating

Arcadia-by-the-Sea (250-629-3221, 877-470-8439; www.arcadiabythesea.com; 1329 MacKinnon Rd, N Pender; d $105-186; May-Sep;) A 1km hop from the ferry, this tranquil, adults-only stop-off has three homely cottages (each with kitchen and deck) decorated in pastel shades and flowery bedspreads. There's also a surprisingly large outdoor pool and a tennis court, both overlooking the sea, along with a boardwalk and deck that takes you right to the waterfront.

Poet's Cove Resort & Spa (250-629-2100, 888-512-7638; www.poetscove.com; 9801 Spalding Rd, Bedwell Harbour, S Pender; r from $289;) A luxurious harborfront lodge with arts-and-crafts-accented rooms, most with great views across the glassy water. Chichi extras include a full-service spa and an activity center that books eco tours and fishing excursions around the area. There's also an elegant West Coast restaurant where you can dine in style.

Pender Island Bakery Café (250-629-6453; Driftwood Centre, 1105 Stanley Point Dr, N Pender; mains $4-9; 8am-5pm Mon-Sat, 9am-5pm Sun) The locals' fave coffee spot, this chatty nook takes an organic approach to its java as well as many of its bakery treats and light meals. Gourmet pizzas are the highlight – try the Gulf Islander (smoked oysters, anchovies, spinach and three cheeses) if you're a connoisseur.

Getting There & Around

BC Ferries, Gulf Island Water Taxis and Seair Seaplanes operate services to Pender (p404). If you don't have a car, and your accommodation can't pick you up, catch a **Pender Island Taxi** (☎ 250-629-3555).

SATURNA ISLAND

pop 325

The closest Gulf Island to the US – cell phones often welcome you to the States when you arrive here – small and tranquil Saturna is also remote enough to discourage most casual visitors. It's a stunning nature-locked retreat that represents a real escape from the hurly-burly of mainland life. Download a map and handy listings from www.saturnatourism.com. Bring cash to the island – there are no ATMs.

Sights & Activities

On the north side of the island, **Winter Cove Park** has a white-sand beach that's popular for swimming, boating and fishing. If you're here for Canada Day (July 1), you should also partake in the island's main annual event in the adjoining Hunter Field. This communal **Lamb Barbeque** (☎ 250-539-2452; www.saturnalambbarbeque.com; adult/child $18.50/10), complete with live music, sack races, beer garden and a smashing meat-lovers' feast, is centered around a pagan fire pit surrounded by dozens of staked-out, slow-roasting sheep.

Walk off your meat belly the next day with a hike up **Mt Warburton Pike** (497m) where you'll spot wild goats, soaring eagles and inspiring panoramic views of the surrounding islands. Focus your binoculars and you might catch a whale or two sliding quietly along the coast.

Sleeping & Eating

Breezy Bay B&B (☎ 250-539-5957; www.saturnacan.net/breezy; 131 Payne Rd; d $75) A 100-year-old farmhouse property with its own private beach, this cheerfully rustic sleepover is still a working farm. The main house has wood floors, stone fireplaces and even an old library, while your room – with shared bathroom – will be fairly basic, but clean and comfortable. Breakfast is in a window-lined room overlooking a garden.

Saturna Lodge (☎ 250-539-2254, 888-539-8800; www.saturna.ca; 130 Payne Rd; s/d $130/195; wi-fi) Country-style charm is the theme at this unpretentious seven-room sleepover. Rates include breakfast, but nonguests can also stop by for dinner in the restaurant (mains $24), where regional delicacies like Queen Charlotte Islands halibut (highly recommended) are offered.

Groceries and picnic fixings are available at the **General Store** (☎ 250-539-2936; 101 Narvaez Bay Rd; 🕑 9am-6pm Mon-Sat, 9:30am-5pm Sun), which also has its one excellent café (mains $8 to $16). The **Lighthouse Pub** (☎ 250-539-5725; 102 East Point Rd; mains $8-12; 🕑 11am-11pm Mon-Thu, 11am-midnight Fri & Sat) is a chatty spot for a beer, bar grub and great views along Plumper Sound.

Getting There & Around

BC Ferries, Gulf Island Water Taxis and Seair Seaplanes operate services to Saturna (p404). A car is not essential here since some lodgings are near the ferry terminal, but there are no taxis or shuttle services to get you around.

MAYNE ISLAND

pop 900

Once a stopover for gold-rush miners on their way to the mainland – they nicknamed it 'Little Hell' – Mayne is the region's most historic island. Visit www.mayneislandchamber.ca for local listings and a downloadable map of island artisans.

Sights & Activities

The heritage agricultural hall in Miners Bay hosts the lively **Farmers Market** (🕑 Sat Jul-Sep) of local crafts and produce, while the nearby **Plumper Pass Lock-up** (☎ 250-539-5286; 🕑 11am-3pm Fri-Mon late Jun-early Sep) is a tiny museum that originally served as a jailhouse.

The south shore's **Dinner Bay Park** has a top beach, and the island's north end is home to **Georgina Point Heritage Park**. The old lighthouse and keeper's cottage are still there, and it's an invigorating place to be when the waves come pounding onto the shore. The park is also home to a small beach with lots of explorable tidal pools.

For paddlers and peddlers, **Mayne Island Kayaking** (☎ 250-539-2463, 877-535-2424; www.kayakmayneisland.com; 563 Arbutus Dr; kayak rentals 2/8hr from $28/48, bike rentals 4/8hr $18/25) offers kayaks and bikes – ideal for launching yourself on a picnic trek around the island.

Sleeping & Eating

Tinkerers' B&B (☎ 250-539-2280; www.bbcanada.com/133.html; 417 Sunset Pl, Miners Bay; d $110-130; 🕑 mid-Apr–mid-Oct) This charming wood-frame house overlooking Active Pass has rooms of various configurations within a calming organic garden setting. If you fancy learning a new skill while on vacation, there are language and knife-sharpening tutorials on offer. Upstairs rooms share a shower but they have the best views.

Oceanwood Country Inn (☎ 250-539-5074; www.oceanwood.com; 630 Dinner Bay Rd; d $179-349) Nestled on the rocky, tree-lined coast, this pioneer-style inn features stylish, chintzy rooms and incredible views over Navy Channel's glassy waters. Rates include breakfast and afternoon tea in the downstairs restaurant, which is also open to non-guests for sumptuous dinners (four-course set menu $55).

Wild Fennel Restaurant (☎ 250-539-5987; 574 Fernhill Rd; mains $16-20; 🕑 6-10pm Mon-Sat) A warm, cozy dining room specializing in seasonal fresh ingredients (the menu changes every week), Wild Fennel is mostly about sampling simply prepared but exquisite local seafood. If it's available, try the Crab Three Ways – crab served in salad, bisque and lollipop form.

Getting There & Around

BC Ferries, Gulf Island Water Taxis and Seair Seaplanes operate services to Mayne (p404). For transport around the island, call **MIDAS Taxi** (☎ 250-539-3132).

GALIANO ISLAND

pop 1100

Named after a Spanish explorer who visited in the 1790s, the bustling ferry end of Galiano is markedly different to the rest of the island, which becomes increasingly forested and tranquil as you continue your drive from the dock. The Galiano Chamber of Commerce operates a **Visitor Info Booth** (☎ 250-539-2507; www.galianoisland.com; 2590 Sturdies Rd; 🕑 Jul & Aug) on your right-hand side as you leave the ferry. Check the website for maps and listings.

Sights & Activities

Visit the island's **Montague Harbour Marine Provincial Park** (☎ 250-539-2115; www.bcparks.ca) for trails to beaches, meadows and a cliff carved by glaciers. Renowned for its eagle, loon and cormorant birdlife, **Bodega Ridge Provincial Park** (☎ 250-539-2115; www.bcparks.ca) contains some spectacular drop-off viewpoints.

The protected waters of Trincomali Channel and the chaotic waters of Active Pass satisfy paddlers of all skill levels. **Gulf Island Kayaking** (☎ 250-539-2442; www.seakayak.ca; Montague Marina; 3hr/day rental from $28/50, tours from $40) can help with rentals and guided tours.

You can also explore the islands with a bike from **Galiano Bicycle** (☎ 250-539-9906; 36 Burrill Rd; 4hr/day $23/28), or if you want company consider one of the customized guided tours organized by Bodega Ridge (below).

Sleeping & Eating

Bodega Ridge Lodge & Cabins (☎ 250-539-2677; www.bodegaridge.com; 120 Manastee Rd; cabins $125-150; 💻 wi-fi) It's hard to imagine a more peaceful retreat than this north-island nest of cabins among the arbutus trees and rolling hills. The seven two-story log homes (each with three bedrooms) are furnished in rustic country fashion. Guided bike treks (per hour $20) are offered for the activity-inclined.

Galiano Inn (☎ 250-539-3388, 877-530-3939; www.galianoinn.com; 134 Madrona Dr; r $249-299; wi-fi) Close to the ferry dock, this immaculate villa has 10 elegant rooms, each with a fireplace and oceanfront terrace. The ambience is adult, sophisticated and soothing, and the amenities include a spa where you can choose outdoor flower treatments. The fine-dining restaurant (mains $18 to $29) has some inspiring regional wines.

Daystar Market Café (☎ 250-539-2505; 96 Georgeson Bay Rd; mains $4-8; 🕑 10am-5pm Mon-Wed, 9am-6pm Fri, 10am-6pm Sat, 9:30am-5pm Sun) This funky little local hangout is an ideal mid-morning pit stop (gotta love those chunky cranberry muffins). The hearty salads and thick sandwiches might entice you back for lunch and the organic juices and fruit smoothies will bring you back the next day.

Hummingbird Pub (☎ 250-539-5472; 47 Sturdies Bay Rd; mains $8-12; 🕑 11am-midnight Sun-Thu, till 1am Fri & Sat) The Hummingbird's massive log columns and chatty outdoor deck lend this pub a comfortable, down-to-earth feel. The menu is full of the usual bar grub suspects and the pub runs a seasonal shuttle to Montague Harbour, so you can feel free to drink as much as you like.

Getting There & Around

BC Ferries, Gulf Island Water Taxis and Seair Seaplanes operate services to Galiano (p404). **Fly'n Riun's Taxi Galiano** (☎ 250-539-0202; www.taxigaliano.com) provides a shuttle bus and cab service around the island.

Directory

CONTENTS

ACCOMMODATIONS

Accommodations in this book fall into one of three categories: budget (less than $75); midrange ($75 to $150); and top end (more than $150). We have marked exceptional picks within the lists, but each property we recommend meets a certain baseline standard for quality within its class.

Room prices listed in this guidebook are high-season rates. They do not include local taxes. Prices vary widely depending on the season, festivals and holidays, whether it's a weekend and sometimes even vacancy rates. Prices are generally highest in summer, and some places have two- or three-night minimum stays. Always ask about discounts, packages and promotional rates. Some places give better rates if you book online.

It's always a good idea to see a room before paying for it. Rooms can vary widely within an establishment – some are bigger and brighter and might not cost much more. Reserve ahead during festivals and holidays, or in the summer (especially on the coast). If you plan on arriving late, let your hotel know or they might give away your room.

Many lodgings have only nonsmoking rooms, but you can usually smoke outdoors. Air-conditioning (marked with our icon) is common in inland places – where it gets really hot – but nearly nonexistent along the coast, which is much cooler. Some hotels take pets, but ask beforehand. Internet computers (marked with our icon) or wi-fi access are commonplace except in backcountry towns. Children are often allowed to stay free with their parents, but the age marking the end of childhood can vary from six to 18. In this guidebook we've used the parking icon only in big cities, where parking is at a premium.

PRACTICALITIES

- Most of the Pacific Northwest lies within the Pacific Standard Time zone – GMT -0800. A tiny sliver along the Oregon–Idaho border lies in the Mountain Standard Time zone – GMT -0700.
- Voltage is 110/120V, 60 cycles.
- Distances (in the US) are measured in feet, yards and miles; weights are tallied in ounces, pounds and tons.
- National Public Radio (NPR) features a progressive yet impartial approach to news and talk radio. See p49 for other interesting radio stations in the Pacific Northwest.
- In general, the US Postal Service provides a dependable and timely service for the price. Any packages 16oz or heavier can't be placed in mailboxes and must be taken to a post office for mailing.
- Self-service, coin-operated laundries are available in nearly all towns and cities, and at many campgrounds and motels.

BOOK ACCOMMODATIONS ONLINE

For more accommodations reviews and recommendations by Lonely Planet authors, check out the online booking service at www.lonelyplanet.com. You'll find the true, insider lowdown on the best places to stay. Reviews are thorough and independent. Best of all, you can book online.

B&Bs

If you want an intimate alternative to impersonal hotel rooms, stay at a Bed and Breakfast. They're typically in large historical or country homes with charming furnishings and just a few rooms – usually with private bathrooms. The owners tend to be friendly, and are happy to offer advice on the area. Most B&Bs have limited rooms and appreciate advance reservations, though some will take the occasional drop-in. Nearly all prohibit smoking and many don't allow children. Substantial breakfasts are included in the price, which is usually between $80 and $200.

B&Bs abound throughout Oregon and Washington, but are particularly concentrated on the islands of Puget Sound and along the Oregon coast. Countless B&B websites compile lists and photos; these include the **Washington Bed & Breakfast Guild** (www.wbbg.com), the **Oregon B&B Guild** (www.obbg.org) and **Bed & Breakfast Explorer** (www.bbexplorer.com). For BC, check www.wcbbia.com.

Camping & Recreational Vehicles (RVs)

Camping is a cheap and wonderful way to appreciate the outdoors, especially in summer. The Pacific Northwest is strewn with campgrounds, both public and private, and setting up a tent usually costs $15 to $20. RV site costs depend on hookups, but generally run from $20 to $30.

Campground facilities vary widely. Basic or primitive campgrounds usually have vault toilets, fire pits and (sometimes) drinking water, and are most common in national forests and on Bureau of Land Management (BLM) land. The state- and national-park campgrounds tend to be the best equipped, featuring picnic benches, flush toilets, hot showers and RV hookups. Private campgrounds are usually close to town and tend to cater to RVers, with good services and facilities like full hookups, showers, coin laundry, swimming pools, play areas and even small convenience stores.

Most campgrounds along the coast are open all year round, but inland where it snows they close in winter. Dispersed (or backcountry) camping is only permitted in national parks with the proper permit.

Yurts, found mostly at state parks, are Mongolian-style round houses with a canvas shell; see p298 for details. It's a good idea to reserve campsites and yurts in summer, when campgrounds fill up quickly.

Hostels

Hostels are an excellent budget option; what they lack in amenities and privacy they make up for in a ready-made travelers' community. Most have cooking facilities, common lounges, information boards, tour services and computer access. Dormitory beds (sometimes segregated by sex) tend to run from $22 to $25, with private rooms priced similarly to a budget hotel. Some hostels have a small charge for sheet and towel rental.

Hostelling International (HI; in US www.hiusa.org, in Canada www.hihostels.ca) lists member hostels. Independent hostels have comparable rates and conditions to HI/AYH hostels. During high seasons, reserve ahead.

Lodges

The word 'lodge' is used with great latitude in the Northwest. Places like Timberline Lodge on Mt Hood and Paradise Lodge on Mt Rainier are magnificent old log structures with dozens of rooms infused with a sense of the woods and handcrafted venerability. Most other lodges are more modest. Those on the lakes of the Cascades have cabin accommodations, campsites, boat rentals and at least a small store if not a café. Some of these lodges are just fine; others are quite funky and unspectacular. If your standards are exacting, make careful inquiries before heading up long mountain roads to marginal accommodations best suited to hardened anglers.

Motels & Hotels

Motels are cheaper than hotels, with rooms that open to the outside and often surround a parking lot. Hotels have inside hallways, nicer lobbies and provide extra services.

As a rule, motels offer the best lodging value for the money. Rooms are unmemorable but usually comfortably furnished and clean. Amenities vary, but expect a private bathroom, cable TV, telephone with free local calls, heating and air-conditioning. Many have small refrigerator, coffeemaker and microwave. Some have kitchenette, coin laundry and swimming pools.

Rental Accommodations

In many coastal areas and in Central Oregon and Washington, owners of weekend or vacation homes depend on occasional rentals to help pay the mortgage. Most of these well-maintained, furnished homes have at least three bedrooms. For a family, or for a group of friends, these homes may represent one of the best-value lodgings in the area.

Descriptions of rental properties can usually be found on the internet. Local visitors centers should also be able to supply information. Some restrictions apply: houses are often occupied by the owners on major holiday and summer weekends, there's usually a minimum stay of two nights and there may be a housekeeping fee.

Resorts

Certain parts of Oregon and Washington are home to huge resort communities offering diverse rental options like condominiums, apartments, lodge rooms, cottages and houses. These are usually privately-owned by people who rent out their places for supplemental income. More upscale versions, such as Rosario Resort on Orcas Island (see p127) or the Running Y Ranch outside Klamath Falls (see p332) boast amenities like golf courses, tennis courts, swimming pools and guided outdoor activities.

ACTIVITIES

The Pacific Northwest offers more activities than you can shake a hockey stick at; you can go hiking, biking, skiing, kayaking, kiteboarding, windsurfing and whale-watching. See the Outdoors chapter (p67) for ideas and inspiration; for specific outfitters, check within the destination chapters.

BUSINESS HOURS

Most businesses stay open from 9am to 5pm, but there are certainly no hard and fast rules. In any large city, a few supermarkets and restaurants are open 24 hours. Shops are usually open from either 9am or 10am to 5pm or 6pm (often until 9pm in shopping malls), except Sunday, when hours are usually noon to 5pm.

Post offices and banks are usually open 8am or 9am to 5pm weekdays, and some are open until 2pm on Saturday.

CHILDREN

Successful travel with young children requires planning and effort. Don't overbook your day, as cramming too many activities often causes grumpiness on everyone's part.

Ensure that the activities you choose include something for the kids as well – balance that morning at the art museum with a visit to the zoo or the beach. Include the kids in the trip planning; if they've helped figure out where you are going, they'll be much more interested when they get there.

Kids often get discounts on such things as motel stays, museum admissions and restaurant meals; however, the definition of 'child' can vary from age zero to 18-years old. Some B&Bs don't take children under a certain age (ask ahead). Larger hotels sometimes offer a babysitting service.

The choice of baby food, infant formulas, soy and cow's milk, disposable diapers (nappies) and other necessities is great in supermarkets throughout the Pacific Northwest. Diaper-changing stations can be found in many public toilets.

For specific kid-friendly travel destinations, see p33. For more information, advice and anecdotes, read Lonely Planet's *Travel with Children,* by Cathy Lanigan.

CLIMATE CHARTS

The Pacific Northwest has a wide variety of climates, from a temperate coast to cool mountains to hot inland deserts. Rain (and, in places, snow) is abundant in winter and early spring, while Indian summers can extend into October.

DANGERS & ANNOYANCES

The Pacific Northwest is not an overly dangerous place. General travel savvy will keep you safe in most circumstances. See the Health chapter (p425) for advice on heat and cold exposure, altitude sickness and animal bites.

Crime

Crime does exist, mostly in bigger cities, but generally in neighborhoods tourists don't go.

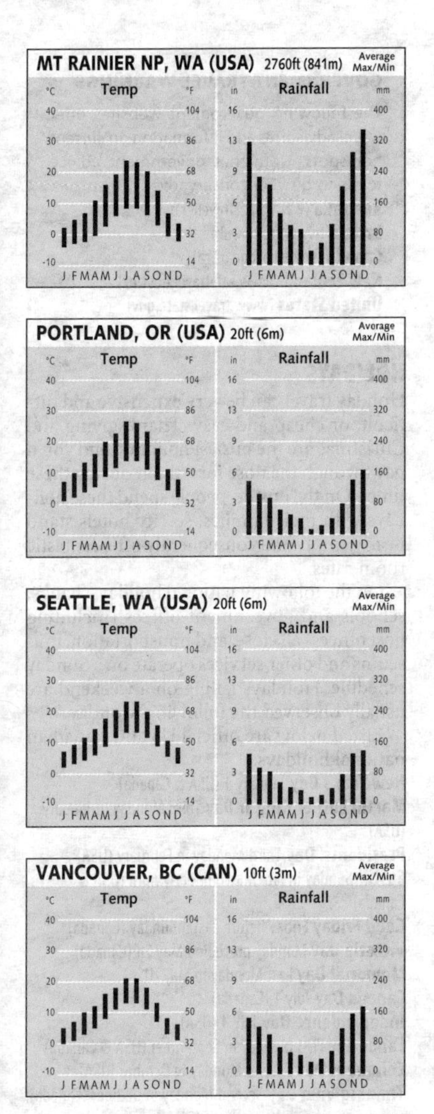

Locking cars and putting valuables out of sight (whether you are in a busy downtown street or at a remote hiking trailhead) is always a good idea. Aim to use ATMs in well-trafficked areas. In hotels, don't leave valuables lying around your room; use safety-deposit boxes, or place things in a locked bag.

If you find yourself in a questionable neighborhood, don't look at your map every few minutes – act like you know where you're going, even if you don't. If you're accosted by a mugger, always hand over the goods fast – nothing is worth getting attacked for. Some people keep two stashes of cash on themselves, one with enough money to placate a possible mugger – and the other with 'valuables' like credit cards and other cash.

Panhandlers or beggars are a problem in any city. Many suffer from psychiatric problems and drug abuse, but most are harmless. It's an individual judgment call whether to offer them anything – you might just offer food if you have it. If you want to contribute toward a long-term solution, consider donating to a reputable charity that cares for the homeless.

Ocean Hazards

Never turn your back on the ocean when beachcombing in or near the water. Large 'sneaker waves' often catch the unwary. If you're swimming and get caught in a riptide, which pulls you away from shore, don't fight it or you'll get exhausted and drown. Instead, swim parallel to the shoreline, and once the current stops pulling you out, swim back to shore.

Wildlife

In country areas you might encounter cattle on back roads, so just slow down and enjoy their company.

It's unlikely that you'll run into a bear or mountain lion while hiking or camping. Talking or making noise (to avoid surprising them) usually scares them off. Bears are attracted to campgrounds, where they may find accessible food in bags, tents, cars or picnic baskets. Get advice from the local ranger station or follow posted instructions; never feed bears or other wildlife!

You'd be very lucky to even glimpse a mountain lion (also called a cougar or puma). Adult travelers aren't much at risk of an attack, but unattended children and pets can be. Loud noises and making yourself appear bigger (hold open your jacket) will usually scare them off.

Rattlesnakes live in dry desert country and hikers can encounter them basking on trails. Give them a wide berth and they'll leave you alone. Wearing thick hiking boots offers some protection, as does staying out of thick underbrush. Bites are rare; see p427 for what to do if bitten.

DISCOUNT CARDS

Many hostels in the Pacific Northwest are members of **HI-USA** (www.hiusa.org), which is affiliated with the **Hostelling International** (www.hihostels.com). You don't need an HI-USA card in order to stay at these hostels, but having one saves you $3 a night. You can also buy one at the hostel when checking in. If you're a student bring along your student ID, which can get you discounts on transportation and admission to sights and attractions.

People over the age of 65 (or sometimes younger) often qualify for the same discounts as students; any identification showing your date of birth should suffice as proof of age. Contact the **American Association of Retired Persons** (AARP; ☎ 888-687-2277; www.aarp.org), an advocacy group for Americans 50 years and older and a good resource for travel discounts.

GAY & LESBIAN TRAVELERS

As elsewhere in North America, gay life in the Pacific Northwest is most tolerated in urban centers, while attitudes tend to be far less accepting in the hinterlands. In the major cities of Seattle, Vancouver and Portland, and even some smaller towns, such as Eugene and Victoria, travelers will find everything from gay religious congregations to gay hiking clubs, while in the rural areas, they may want to keep their orientation to themselves.

The Capitol Hill neighborhood is the center of gay life in Seattle. For information, there's the **Lesbian Resource Center** (www.lrc.net) and the **Beyond the Closet bookstore** (☎ 206-322-4609; 518 E Pike St). To get a listing of gay-friendly businesses, contact the **Gay/Lesbian Business Association** (www.thegsba.org); for news, pick up the **Seattle Gay News** (www.sgn.org). The city's **Pride Parade** (www.seattlepride.org) happens in late June.

In Oregon, a valuable source of information is Portland's gay bi-weekly newspaper **Just Out** (www.justout.com); you can also skim through www.gayoregon.com for local news. The Portland Area Business Association publishes the **Gay & Lesbian Community Yellow Pages** (www.pdxgayyellowpages.com), which lists gay-oriented businesses. Portland puts on its **Pride Festival** (www.pridenw.org) in mid-June.

On Vancouver Island look for copies of the **Pink Pages** (www.gayvictoria.ca/pinkpages) with links to local gay and lesbian resources. **Vancouver Pride Week** (www.vancouverpride.ca) takes place in late July/early August.

GOVERNMENT TRAVEL WARNINGS

The following government websites offer travel advisories and information on current hot spots. Note that government advice tends to be very conservative.

Australia (www.smartraveller.gov.au)
Britain (www.fco.gov.uk)
Canada (www.voyage.gc.ca)
New Zealand (www.safetravel.govt.nz)
United States (www.travel.state.gov)

HOLIDAYS

Holiday travel can be very expensive and difficult, or cheap and easy. Thanksgiving and Christmas are the busiest holidays, and you'll pay through the nose for a flight during these times. On the upside, people spend these holidays with their families, so city hotels stand nearly empty and consequently offer fantastic room rates.

On the following national holidays, banks, schools and government offices (including post offices) all close, and transportation, museums and other services operate on a Sunday schedule. Holidays falling on a weekend are usually observed the following Monday.

Listed below are official US and Canadian national holidays:

New Year's Day January 1 (USA & Canada)
Martin Luther King Jr Day Third Monday in January (USA)
Presidents' Day Third Monday in February (USA)
Easter Sunday in late March or early April (USA & Canada)
Good Friday Friday before Easter Sunday (Canada)
Victoria Day Monday preceding May 24 (Canada)
Memorial Day Last Monday in May (USA)
Canada Day July 1 (Canada)
Independence Day July 4 (USA)
Labor Day First Monday in September (USA & Canada)
Columbus Day Second Monday in October (USA)
Thanksgiving Day Second Monday in October (Canada); fourth Thursday in November (USA)
Veterans' Day November 11 (USA)
Remembrance Day November 11 (Canada)
Christmas Day December 25 (USA & Canada)
Boxing Day December 26 (Canada)

INSURANCE

It makes good sense to obtain a policy covering travel theft, loss, medical problems and trip cancellation or delays. Policies come in all shapes and sizes, so read the small print.

In the USA, with its exorbitant health-care costs, it's best to spring for a higher medical-expense option. Check that the policy you're considering covers ambulances or an emergency flight home.

Ask both your insurer and your ticket-issuing agency to explain the finer points, especially what supporting documentation you need to file a claim. Buy travel insurance early to cover possible delays to your flight caused by strikes or circumstances. Some policies specifically exclude 'dangerous activities' such as scuba diving, motorcycling and even trekking. If these activities are on your itinerary, search for policies that include them.

Some policies pay doctors or hospitals directly, but be aware that many health-care professionals still demand payment at the time of service. Except in emergencies, call around for a doctor willing to accept your insurance. Be sure to keep all receipts and documentation. Some policies ask you to call a center in your home country for an immediate assessment of your problem.

INTERNATIONAL VISITORS

The USA

Getting into the United States can be a bureaucratic nightmare, depending on your country of origin, as the rules keep changing. For up-to-date information about visas and immigration, check the website of the **US Department of State** (www.unitedstatesvisas.gov) and the travel section of the **US Customs & Border Protection** (www.cbp.gov).

In 2004 the US Department of Homeland Security introduced a new set of security measures called US-VISIT. Upon arrival in the US, all visitors are photographed and have their index fingers scanned. Eventually, this biometric data will be matched when you leave the US. For full details about US-VISIT, check with a US consulate or online at www.dhs.gov/us-visit.

Canada

Visitors to Canada from major Western countries need no visa, but citizens of more than 150 nations do. Visa requirements change frequently, so check before you leave. The most current information can be found at the website of **Citizenship & Immigration Canada** (www.cic.gc.ca).

Officially, US citizens don't need a passport or visa to enter Canada, and some proof of citizenship, such as a birth certificate along with state-issued photo identification, will ordinarily suffice. However, since the introduction of tighter border security in the wake of the terrorist attacks of September 2001, border officials recommend that US citizens carry a passport to facilitate entry.

Customs

US customs allows each person over the age of 21 to bring 1L of liquor, 100 cigars and 200 cigarettes duty free into the country. US citizens and permanent residents are allowed to import, duty free, $400 worth of gifts from abroad, while non-US citizens are allowed to bring in $100 worth. US law permits you to bring in, or take out, up to $10,000 (cash, traveler's checks, etc); greater amounts must be declared to customs.

Canadian Customs allows visitors 19 years and older to bring in 1.1L (40ozs) of liquor or a case of beer (24 beers), as well as 200 cigarettes. You can bring in gifts up to C$60 in value.

US & Canadian Embassies Abroad

Australia US Embassy (☎ 02-6214-5600; 21 Moonah Place, Yarralumla ACT 2600); Canadian High Commission (☎ 02-6270-4000; Commonwealth Ave, Canberra ACT 2600)
France US Embassy (☎ 01-43-12-22-22; 2 Ave Gabriel, 75008 Paris); Canadian Embassy (☎ 01 44 43 29 00; 35 Ave Montaigne, 75008 Paris)
Germany US Embassy (☎ 030-830-50; Neustädtische Kirchstr 4-5, 10117 Berlin); Canadian Embassy (☎ 030-203-120; 12th fl, Friedrichstrasse 95, 10117 Berlin)
Ireland US Embassy (☎ 01-668-8777; 42 Elgin Rd, Dublin 4); Canadian Embassy (☎ 01-417-4100; Canada House, 65 St Stephen's Green, Dublin 2)
Italy US Embassy (☎ 06-46-741; Via Veneto 119/A, 00187 Rome); Canadian Embassy (☎ 06-445-981; Via GB de Rossi 27, 00161 Rome)
Japan US Embassy (☎ 03-3224-5000; 1-10-5 Akasaka, Minato-ku, Tokyo); Canadian Embassy (☎ 03-5412-6200; 7-3-38 Akasaka 7-chome, Minato-ku, Tokyo 107-5803)
Netherlands US Embassy (☎ 070-310-9209; Lange Voorhout 102, 2514 EJ, The Hague); Canadian Embassy (☎ 070-311-1600; Sophialaan 7, 2514 JP, The Hague)
New Zealand US Embassy (☎ 04-462-6000; 29 Fitzherbert Tce, Thorndon, Wellington); Canadian High Commission (☎ 04-473-9577; 61 Molesworth St, 3rd fl, Thorndon, Wellington)
UK US Embassy (☎ 020-7499-9000; 24 Grosvenor Sq, London W1A 1AE); Canadian High Commission (☎ 020-258-6600; Canada House, Consular Services, Trafalgar Sq, London SW1Y 5BJ)

Consulates in the Pacific Northwest

Australia Washington (☎ 206-575-7446; 401 Andover Park E, Seattle); British Columbia (☎ 604-684-1177; 1225-888 Dunsmuir St, Vancouver)
Canada Oregon (☎ 503-417-2166; 805 SW Broadway Suite 1900, Portland); Washington (☎ 206-443-1777; 1501 4th Ave, Seattle)
France Oregon (☎ 503-725-5298; 393 Neuberger Hall, Portland State University, Portland); Washington (☎ 206-256-6184; 2200 Alaskan Way Suite 490, Seattle); British Columbia (☎ 604-681-4345; 1130 Pender St, Vancouver)
Germany Oregon (☎ 503-222-0490; 200 SW Market St, Suite 1695, Portland); British Columbia (☎ 604-684-8377; 999 Canada Pl, Vancouver)
Ireland British Columbia (☎ 604-683-9233; 1385 8th Ave W, Vancouver)
Japan Oregon (☎ 503-221-1811; 1300 SW 5th Ave, Suite 2700, Portland); Washington (☎ 206-682-9107; 601 Union St, Seattle); British Columbia (☎ 604-684-5868; West 1177 Hastings St, Vancouver)
Netherlands Oregon (☎ 503-222-7957; 520 SW Yamhill St Suite 600, Portland); British Columbia (☎ 604-684-6448; 475 Howe St, Vancouver)
New Zealand British Columbia (☎ 604-684-7388; 888 Dunsmuir St, Vancouver)
UK Oregon (☎ 503-227-5669; calls only); Washington (☎ 206-622-9255; 900 4th Ave, Seattle); British Columbia (☎ 604-683-4421; 1111 Melville St, Vancouver)
USA British Columbia (☎ 604-685-4311; 1095 W Pender St, Vancouver)

INTERNET ACCESS

The Pacific Northwest is also known as the 'Silicon Forest' for its computer industries; accessing the internet won't be a problem. There are a few internet cafés in cities large and small, and many hotels, coffee shops and libraries provide guests computers or wi-fi.

LEGAL MATTERS

If you are stopped by the police for any reason in the USA, there is no system of paying fines on the spot. Attempting to pay the fine to the officer may lead to a charge of attempted bribery. For traffic offenses, the police officer will explain the options to you. Most matters can be handled by mail.

If you are arrested for more serious offenses, you have the right to remain silent and are presumed innocent until proven guilty. There is no legal reason to speak to a police officer if you don't wish. All persons who are arrested are legally allowed the right to make one phone call. If you don't have a lawyer, friend or family member to help you, call your embassy. The police will give you the number upon request. If you don't have a lawyer, one will be appointed to you free of charge.

You must be at least 16 years old to drive in Oregon, Washington or British Columbia. The drinking age is 21 in Washington and Oregon, and 19 in BC, and you need photo identification that proves your age. Stiff fines, jail time and other penalties can be incurred for driving under the influence (DUI) of alcohol or drugs. It is also illegal to carry open containers of alcohol inside a vehicle. Containers that are full and sealed may be carried, but if they have been opened or are empty put them in the trunk.

Possessing illegal drugs is always a bad idea, and if you're caught expect fines, lengthy jail sentences and/or deportation (if you're a foreigner).

MAPS

Visitors centers and chambers of commerce often have good local maps, free or at low cost. The American Automobile Association (AAA) issues the most comprehensive and dependable highway maps, which are free with membership. AAA has reciprocal agreements with 65 foreign countries, including Canada's CAA.

For detailed state- and national-park trail and topographical maps, stop by park visitors centers or the forest ranger's station. The best are those published by the US Geological Survey (USGS), usually available at outdoor stores and travel bookshops. Many convenience stores and most gas stations sell detailed folding maps of local areas that include a street-name index.

MEDICAL SERVICES

See the Health chapter (p425) for details.

TIPPING

Tipping for certain services is the norm in the US and Canada. If service is truly appalling, however, don't tip. Here are customary tipping amounts:

Bartenders – 15% of the bill.
Bellhops, skycaps in airports – $1 to $2 per bag.
Housekeeping staff – $2 daily, left on the pillow each day.
Parking valets – $1 to $2.
Restaurant servers – 15% to 20% of the pretax bill (no tax in Oregon).
Taxi drivers – 10% to 15% of metered fare.

TOURIST INFORMATION

Oregon, Washington and British Columbia (BC) have state and provincial tourist bureaus that offer glossy guides, maps and plenty of other pertinent travel information. Individual cities and regions also maintain visitor centers, which are often run by the local chamber of commerce; addresses and phone numbers for these are in the regional chapters.

Oregon Tourism Commission (☎ 800-547-7842; www.traveloregon.com)
Tourism British Columbia (☎ 800-435-5622; www.hellobc.com)
Washington State Tourism (☎ 800-544-1800; www.experiencewa.com)

TRAVELERS WITH DISABILITIES

If you have a physical disability, travel within the Pacific Northwest won't be too difficult. The Americans with Disabilities Act (ADA) requires all public buildings – including most hotels, restaurants, theaters and museums – to be wheelchair accessible. Sidewalks are wide and smooth and most intersections have curb cuts and sometimes audible crossing signals.

Lift-equipped buses are the norm in Washington, Oregon and BC, and many taxi companies have wheelchair-accessible cabs. Some municipal bus networks provide door-to-door service for people with disabilities. Disabled travelers using Washington State Ferries can phone ☎ 206-515-3460 for a copy of *The Accessible Ferry, a Guide for Disabled Passengers*. Most car-rental franchises are able to provide hand-controlled models at no extra charge (but reserve well ahead). All major airlines, Greyhound buses and Amtrak trains allow service animals to accompany passengers. Airlines will also provide assistance for connecting, boarding and disembarking if requested with your reservation.

Many state and national parks in the Northwest maintain a nature trail or two for use by wheelchair-using travelers. For a list of accessible trails in Washington State, see www.parks.wa.gov/ada-rec; another useful site is www.accessibletrails.com. For a good book, check *Easy Access to National Parks,* by Wendy Roth and Michael Tompane. The Golden Access Passport, available free to blind or permanently disabled US travelers with documentation, gives free lifetime access to US national parks and wildlife refuges and 50% off campground use.

Organizations & Resources

A number of organizations and tour providers specialize in serving disabled travelers:

Access-Able Travel Source (www.access-able.com) Excellent website with good links.
Emerging Horizons (www.emerginghorizons.com) The website of a magazine about accessible travel.
Mobility International USA (www.miusa.org) Advises travelers with disabilities on mobility issues; runs educational exchange programs.
MossRehab ResourceNet (www.mossresourcenet.org) Lists extensive web contacts.
New Directions (www.newdirectionstravel.com) Specializes in developmentally challenged travelers.
Society for Accessible Travel & Hospitality (www.sath.org) Useful links and information specifically about travel.

WOMEN TRAVELERS

The Pacific Northwest is a progressive region and relatively safe place for women travelers. Use your common sense and you should be fine.

If despite your precautions you are assaulted, call the **police** (☎ 911). In some rural areas where 911 is not active, just dial 0 for the operator. Larger towns usually have rape crisis centers and women's shelters that provide help and support; check the telephone directory for listings or ask the police for referrals.

Journeywoman (www.journeywoman.com) facilitates women exchanging travel tips and includes links to other sites. Another good source is *Her Own Way,* an online booklet available on the Canadian **Consular Affairs** (www.voyage.gc.ca) website that is filled with good general travel advice for women.

Transportation

CONTENTS

GETTING THERE & AWAY

AIR

Domestic airfares fluctuate significantly depending on the season, day of the week, length of stay and flexibility of the ticket for changes and refunds. Still, nothing determines fares more than demand, and when business is slow, airlines lower fares to fill seats. Airlines are competitive and at any given time any one of them could have the cheapest fare. Expect less fluctuation with international fares.

Airports & Airlines

Most air travelers to the Pacific Northwest will arrive at one of the three main airports in the region: **Vancouver International Airport** (YVR; www.yvr.ca), **Portland International Airport** (PDX; www.flypdx.com) or **Seattle Tacoma International** (SEA; www.portseattle.org), which is known locally as 'Sea-Tac'. All offer a good selection of regularly scheduled flights to both domestic and international destinations.

AIRLINES FLYING TO & FROM THE PACIFIC NORTHWEST

International airlines include the following:

Air Canada/Air BC (☎ 888-247-2262; www.aircanada.ca)
Air New Zealand (☎ 800-262-1234; www.airnz.com)
American Airlines (☎ 800-433-7300; www.aa.com)
British Airways (☎ 800-247-9297; www.britishairways.com)
Cathay Pacific Airways (☎ 800-233-2742; www.cathaypacific.com)
China Airlines (☎ 800-227-5118; www.china-airlines.com)
Continental Airlines (☎ 800-525-0280; www.continental.com)
Delta Air Lines (☎ 800-221-1212; www.delta.com)
Japan Airlines (☎ 800-525-3663; www.japanair.com)
Lufthansa Airlines (☎ 800-645-3880; www.lufthansa.com)
Northwest Airlines/KLM (☎ 800-225-2525; www.nwa.com)
Qantas (☎ 800-227-4500; www.qantas.com.au)
Scandinavian Airlines (SAS; ☎ 800-221-2350; www.flysas.com)
Singapore Airlines (☎ 800-742-3333; www.singaporeair.com)
United Airlines (☎ 800-241-6522; www.united.com)

Domestic airlines include the following:

Alaska Airlines (☎ 800-252-7522; www.alaskaair.com)
Frontier Airlines (☎ 800-432-1359; www.frontierairlines.com)
Hawaiian Airlines (☎ 800-367-5320; www.hawaiianair.com)
Horizon Air (☎ 800-547-9308; www.horizonair.com)
Jet Blue Airways (☎ 800-538-2583; www.jetblue.com)
Southwest Airlines (☎ 800-435-9792; www.southwest.com)
United Express (☎ 800-241-6522; www.united.com)
US Airways (☎ 800-428-4322; www.usairways.com)
WestJet (☎ 800-538-5696; www.westjet.ca)

THINGS CHANGE...

The information in this chapter is particularly vulnerable to change. Check directly with the airline or a travel agent to make sure you understand how a fare (and ticket you may buy) works and be aware of the security requirements for international travel. Shop carefully. The details given in this chapter should be regarded as pointers and are not a substitute for your own careful, up-to-date research.

LAND

Border Crossings

The main overland point of entry from Washington to Vancouver, BC, is at Blaine/Douglas, on the northern end of I-5, which continues as Hwy 99 on the Canadian side. This crossing has the longest lines.

Slightly less busy on weekdays is the Pacific crossing, 3 miles (5km) east of Blaine; from I-5, take exit 275 (the one before Blaine). Northbound travelers purchasing duty-free items must use this crossing, which is busy (northbound) on weekends. A good choice during busy holidays is the little-known Lynden/Aldergrove crossing (Hwy 539 from Bellingham), about 30 miles (50km) east of Blaine. Lastly there's Sumas/Huntingdon, 62 miles (100km) east of Blaine. The latter is best for heading into BC's interior. All crossings are open 24 hours except Lynden, which is open 8am to midnight. During the week, expect to wait five to 30 minutes; on weekends, as long as an hour; and on holiday weekends, longer. For details check www.vancouver.hm/border.html.

Many travelers also cross the border by ferry, principally on journeys from Anacortes to Sidney, BC (near Victoria) and from Port Angeles to Victoria. See the Boat section under Getting Around (p420) for details. Foreigners should also check the International Visitors section of the Directory, p413.

Bus

In car-oriented societies like the USA and Canada, bus travel takes second place. Service is infrequent or inconvenient, networks are sparse and fares can be relatively high. Air travel is often cheaper on long-distance routes, and it can even be cheaper to rent a car – especially for shorter routes. However, very long-distance bus trips can be available at decent prices if you purchase or reserve tickets in advance.

The only nationwide bus company in the USA and Canada, **Greyhound** (☎ 800-231-2222; www.greyhound.com) operates to major and minor cities throughout the Pacific Northwest; check its website for destinations and schedules. Tickets can be purchased by phone or online with a major credit card and mailed to you if purchased 10 days in advance, or picked up at the terminal with proper identification. Buying tickets in advance will save you money, as will traveling during weekdays and non-holiday times. Children, students, veterans and seniors are eligible for discounts as well; check the website for specifics.

CLIMATE CHANGE & TRAVEL

Climate change is a serious threat to the ecosystems that humans rely upon, and air travel is the fastest-growing contributor to the problem. Lonely Planet regards travel, overall, as a global benefit, but believes we all have a responsibility to limit our personal impact on global warming.

Flying & climate change

Pretty much every form of motorized travel generates CO_2 (the main cause of human-induced climate change) but planes are far and away the worst offenders, not just because of the sheer distances they allow us to travel, but because they release greenhouse gases high into the atmosphere. The statistics are frightening: two people taking a return flight between Europe and the US will contribute as much to climate change as an average household's gas and electricity consumption over a whole year.

Carbon offset schemes

Climatecare.org and other websites use 'carbon calculators' that allow travelers to offset the level of greenhouse gases they are responsible for with financial contributions to sustainable travel schemes that reduce global warming – including projects in India, Honduras, Kazakhstan and Uganda.

Lonely Planet, together with Rough Guides and other concerned partners in the travel industry, support the carbon offset scheme run by climatecare.org. Lonely Planet offsets all of its staff and author travel.

For more information check out our website: lonelyplanet.com.

NORTH TO ALASKA

Waaay at the northwest tip of North America lies the country's 49th state, Alaska. It's the biggest US state by far, and home to stupendous mountains, massive glaciers and amazing wildlife. Mt McKinley lives here (the continent's highest peak), as do huge numbers of humpback whales and bald eagles. Not many folks regret having visited the unforgettable grandeur of Alaska.

You have a few choices getting to this remote place. Sure, there are daily flights from Seattle to Juneau, and you could always drive (and drive and drive); but the best way to reach Alaska is probably by ferry. Think of it as a cruise through the inside passage – but cheaper and more interesting. Bellingham, Washington (1½ hours north of Seattle) is the southern terminus of the Alaska Marine Highway System, which provides ferry transport to many destinations in coastal Alaska. Trips can take a few hours or a few days, depending on where you're going; in high season, the trip from Bellingham to Juneau costs $326 and takes nearly three days (cabins are $352 extra and small cars $739 extra). You can also make stops along the way. For more information check www.dot.state.ak.us/amhs. And enjoy the scenery!

Greyhound's fare specials include their Companion Fare, where you can buy a second ticket for 50% off, if you do it at least three days in advance. Go Anywhere fares offer good discounts if you book seven or 14 days in advance. Greyhound's **Discovery Pass** (www.discoverypass.com) allows unlimited travel and stopovers within particular regions of the USA and Canada over a certain period; it must be bought 14 to 21 days in advance. All Greyhound buses are nonsmoking.

Car & Motorcycle

Although the quickest way to get to the Pacific Northwest is usually by plane, the best way to get around is by car. (For information on buying or renting a car, see the Getting Around section, p422.) If you have time, it can be less expensive to drive to the Pacific Northwest than to fly and rent a car. And the region is blessed with many scenic highways that make driving long distances a feasible alternative.

Note that driving regulations, such as speed limits and the permissibility of right turns on red lights or making U-turns, can vary somewhat from state to state. Also, Oregon law prohibits you from pumping your own gasoline – all stations there are full service.

Train

The Pacific Northwest is well served by **Amtrak** (☎ 800-872-7245; www.amtrak.com) in the USA and **VIA Rail** (☎ 888-842-7245; www.viarail.com) in Canada. Trains are comfortable, if slow, and equipped with dining and lounge cars on long-distance routes.

Amtrak's *Coast Starlight* links Los Angeles to Portland and Seattle via Oakland and other West Coast cities. The *Empire Builder* runs from Chicago to the Pacific Northwest via Minneapolis and Spokane, where it separates to reach Portland and Seattle. VIA Rail's *Canadian* runs between Vancouver and Toronto. Note that schedules can be very fluid: Arrival and departure times become less reliable the farther you are from the starting point.

Fares on Amtrak vary greatly, depending on the season and what promotions are going. You can beat the rather stiff full-price fares by purchasing in advance – the sooner made, the better the fare. Round-trips are the best bargain, but even these can be more expensive than airfares. Children, students, veterans, military personnel, seniors and even AAA members are eligible for discounts; check the Amtrak website for details.

RAIL PASSES

The best value overall is Amtrak and VIA Rail's North America Rail Pass, which allows 30 days of unlimited travel in the USA and Canada. The peak-season fare (May 25 to October 15) is $999; off season, it's $709. Seniors, students and children receive a 10% discount. Reservations for the pass can be made by phone, and tickets can be picked up at staffed stations, or you can purchase the pass online. This pass is available to US and Canadian residents, as well as foreigners.

For non-US or Canadian citizens, Amtrak offers a USA Rail Pass, which offers 15 or 30 days of unlimited travel. Passes are available for either three separate regions or the entire USA, and can be purchased online, via travel agents outside North America or by Amtrak offices in the US (show your passport). Prices vary from $299 to $599, depending on peak periods and regions. Advanced booking is highly recommended.

SEA

Opportunities to arrive by boat in the Pacific Northwest are slim. Cities in the Puget Sound and Georgia Strait region of the Pacific Northwest are linked by ferry, and while strictly speaking they're international journeys, they are best thought of as commuter ferry routes. Probably the granddaddy of all Northwest ferry rides is the Inside Passage trip, which travels between Bellingham, Washington and destinations in Alaska. See Bellingham's Getting There & Away section (p112) for more information.

GETTING AROUND

Don't automatically assume that, once arriving in the Northwest, ground travel is going to be the cheapest method of transportation. The west coasts of the USA and Canada are home to a number of inexpensive, no-frills airlines, whose rates rival bus and train fares. Check discount airlines, or have a look at the website www.gonorthwest.com, with links to many regional carriers.

AIR

Seattle, Portland and Vancouver are the principal hubs for flights to outlying Pacific Northwest cities, which include (but are not limited to) Klamath Falls, Eugene, Medford, Salem, Yakima, Walla Walla, Spokane, Bellingham and Wenatchee. Seattle also has air destinations in the San Juan Islands and Victoria.

Regional flights are usually moderately priced if bought seven or 14 days in advance; within a week of departure you'll pay full price. Generally, fares can drop substantially if you fly very early in the morning or on specific less-used flights. Ask airlines and travel agents about special-fare flights.

Popular airlines that serve the Pacific Northwest include Air Canada, Alaska, Horizon, Southwest and United Express.

BICYCLE

Cycling is a very popular recreational activity in the Pacific Northwest, and an interesting, inexpensive and environmentally friendly way to travel. Roads are good, shoulders are usually wide, and there are many decent routes for bikes. Summer is best; during other seasons, changeable weather can be a drawback, especially at high altitudes where thunderstorms are frequent. In some areas, the wind can slow your progress to a crawl (traveling west to east and north to south is generally easier than the opposite), and water sources can be far apart. Spare parts are widely available, and repair shops are numerous, but it's still important to be able to do basic mechanical work, such as fixing a flat tire, yourself.

Seattle, Portland and Vancouver all have great bike paths and key street bike lanes. Some local buses in these cities provide bike racks, and you can also take your bikes on light-rail systems, trains and ferries. On the road, cyclists are generally treated courteously by motorists. Bicycles are prohibited on interstate highways if there is a frontage road;

BIKE RENTALS & CO-OPS IN THE BIG CITIES

If you are thinking of buying a bicycle, consider patronizing bike cooperatives (co-ops) – worker-owned, nonprofit organizations that repair bikes and/or take in donated bikes and refurbish them for sale. They often encourage cycling by renting bikes, supporting community biking events and organizing work-for-trade programs.

Vancouver's **Bike Kitchen** (☎ 604-827-7333; www.thebikekitchen.com; 6138 Student Union Blvd) is a student-run, full-service co-op that sells and rents refurbished bikes.

In Seattle, **BikeWorks** (☎ 206-725-9408; www.bikeworks.org; 3709 S Ferdinand St) is not really a co-op but a nonprofit organization with an 'earn-a-bike' youth program and offers maintenance classes and donates bikes to needy communities.

Portland has a couple of interesting groups. **City Bikes** (☎ 503-239-0553; www.citybikes.coop; 1914 SE Ankeny) is a worker-run co-op that fixes bikes, and sells and rents them from its annex on 734 SE Ankeny. The **Community Cycling Center** (☎ 503-288-8864; www.communitycyclingcenter.org; 1700 NE Alberta St) helps youths through educational bike programs and services.

TRANSPORTATION

however, where a suitable frontage road or other alternative is lacking, cyclists are permitted on some interstates.

Bicycles can be transported by air, usually in a bike bag or box, although airlines often charge an additional fee. Check this with the airline in advance, preferably before you pay for your ticket. You can rent bikes in most cities for around $20 per day; you'll find places that rent them throughout this guide. Buying a bicycle is another option, and the Pacific Northwest has lots of bike shops with a wide range of choices. For used bikes a good place to check is www.craigslist.com, but beware stolen of bikes.

In most states helmets are required by law (all under-18s must wear them) – in any case, they should be worn to reduce the risk of head injury. Wearing highly reflective clothing makes you more visible to cars, as do night-lights, which are required by law throughout most of the Pacific Northwest. Also, using the best lock you can get is a must, as bike theft is fairly common; consider using two kinds of locks at the same time. Adding ugly stickers and painting over expensive brand names to make your bike less desirable is another smart option.

A good source of information is **Adventure Cycling Association** (www.adv-cycling.org), which has suggested bike routes for all over the country, and also sells maps. For more details on cycling, see the biking section in the Outdoors chapter, p68.

BOAT

Washington and British Columbia (BC) have two of the largest state-owned ferry systems in the world, and these ferries access some of the most rewarding destinations in the Pacific Northwest. Some boats are passenger-only, while others take both vehicles and passengers. Be aware that some summertime ferry routes can have long waits if you're in a car, and bring snacks as ferry offerings are limited and expensive. For a good general information on the area's schedules and routes, check www.youra.com/ferry.

Washington State Ferries (WSF; ☎ 206-464-6400, in Washington 800-843-3779; www.wsdot.wa.gov/ferries) operates most of the ferries that run in the Puget Sound area. Popular routes go to Bremerton and to Bainbridge and Vashon Islands from Seattle. WSF also operates the ferry system through the San Juan Islands and on to Sidney (near Victoria, on Vancouver Island) from Anacortes. Check its website for fares, schedules, route maps and tourist information, plus links to other ferry services.

BC Ferries (☎ 888-223-3779; www.bcferries.com) operates most of the ferries in that BC. Primary links are between Tsawwassen (south of Vancouver) and Swartz Bay (on Vancouver Island), and to Nanaimo from Tsawwassen and Horseshoe Bay. BC Ferries services also link Gulf Islands to Tsawwassen.

Privately operated ferries are also important transportation links in this area. **Black Ball's Coho ferry** (☎ 360-457-4491 in Washington, 250-386-2202 in BC; www.cohoferry.com) connects Victoria with Washington's Olympic Peninsula via Port Angeles year round.

Clipper Navigation (☎ 206-448-5000, 800-888-2535) operates the *Victoria Clipper*, a year-round passenger ferry that connects Seattle with Victoria (on Vancouver Island). It stops at San Juan Islands during the summer.

BUS

Greyhound (☎ 800-231-2222; www.greyhound.com) generally serves the less-affluent strata of American society – those without private vehicles. Service is relatively good but infrequent, especially in more remote areas. Greyhound largely sticks to the interstate freeway system, while regional carriers provide service to outlying areas. In almost all cases, these smaller bus lines share depots and information services with Greyhound.

Generally, buses are clean, comfortable and reliable. Amenities include onboard lavatories, air-conditioning and slightly reclining seats. Smoking is not permitted. Buses break for meals every three to four hours, usually at fast-food restaurants or cafeteria-style truck stops. When you buy tickets a week in advance, discounts apply.

Bus stations are often dreary places. In small towns, where there is no station, buses stop in front of a specific business; in these cases, be prepared to pay the driver with exact change.

CAR & MOTORCYCLE

When you're traveling around the most car-oriented societies on the planet, auto transportation is well worth considering, if only to delve into the national mindset. A car is much more flexible than public transportation, and in a region where gas is still a

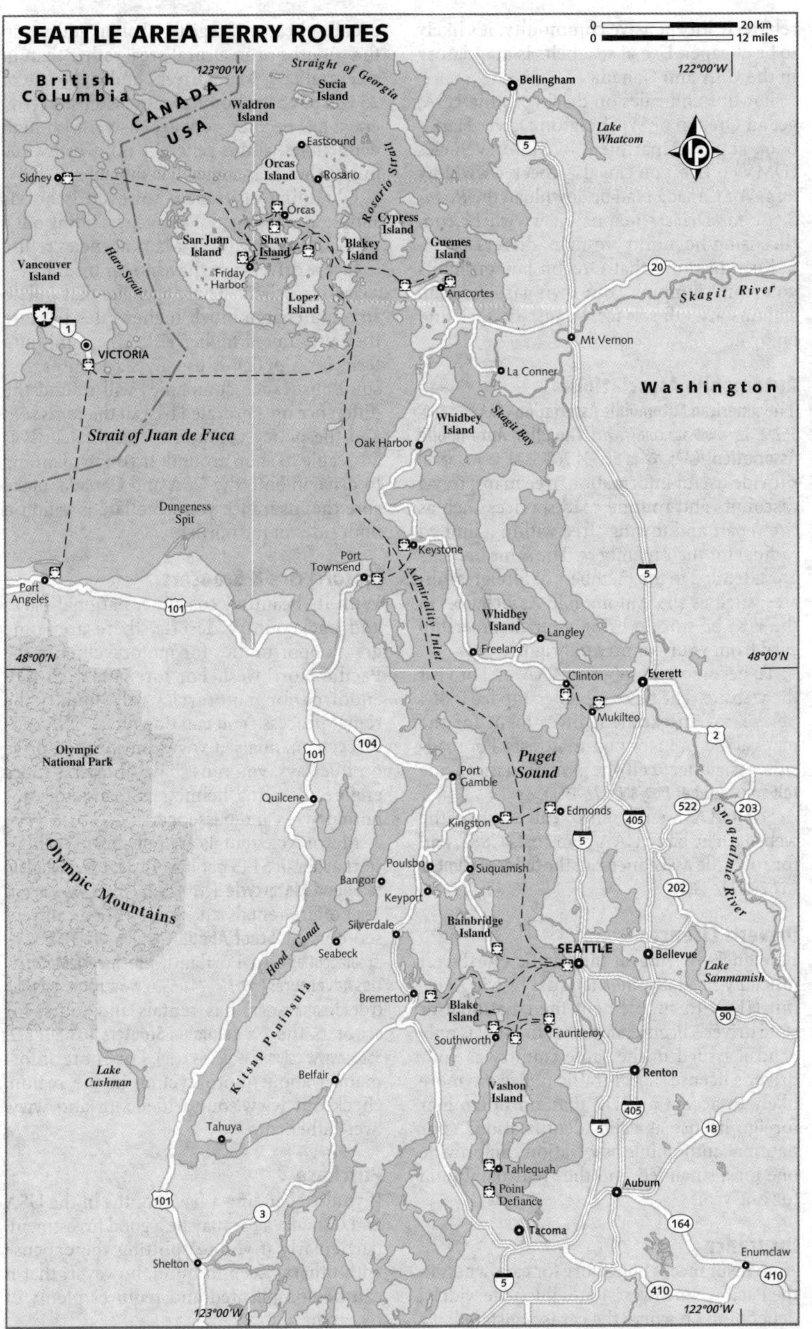
SEATTLE AREA FERRY ROUTES
0 20 km
0 12 miles
123°00'W
122°00'W
British Columbia
CANADA
USA
Straight of Georgia
Sucia Island
Waldron Island
Bellingham
Lake Whatcom
Eastsound
Orcas Island
Rosario
Rosario Strait
Sidney
Orcas
Cypress Island
San Juan Island
Shaw Island
Blakey Island
Guemes Island
Haro Strait
Friday Harbor
Vancouver Island
Lopez Island
Anacortes
Skagit River
VICTORIA
Mt Vernon
La Conner
Washington
Whidbey Island
Skagit Bay
Strait of Juan de Fuca
Oak Harbor
Dungeness Spit
Keystone
Port Townsend
Port Angeles
Admiralty Inlet
Whidbey Island
Langley
Freeland
48°00'N
Clinton
Everett
Mukilteo
Olympic National Park
Puget Sound
Port Gamble
Quilcene
Edmonds
Kingston
Snoqualmie River
Olympic Mountains
Poulsbo
Suquamish
Bangor
Keyport
Silverdale
Bainbridge Island
Hood Canal
Seabeck
SEATTLE
Bellevue
Lake Sammamish
Bremerton
Blake Island
Southworth
Fauntleroy
Kitsap Peninsula
Lake Cushman
Belfair
Renton
Vashon Island
Tahuya
Tahlequah
Point Defiance
Auburn
Tacoma
Shelton
Enumclaw
TRANSPORTATION

relatively inexpensive commodity, it's likely to be cheaper. Use of seat belts is mandatory in the USA and Canada.

For tips and rules on driving in the USA, get an Oregon or Washington Driver Handbook at any Department of Motor Vehicles (DMV) office; you can also check www.dmv.org. For Canada read or download the *Road-Sense for Drivers* manual at www.icbc.com/licensing/lic_utility_resman_drivers.asp.

Keep in mind that Oregon law prohibits you from pumping your own gasoline – all stations are full service, so just sit back and enjoy it.

Automobile Associations

The **American Automobile Association** (AAA; ☎ 800-562-2582; www.aaa.com) and **Canadian Automobile Association** (CAA; ☎ in BC 604-268-5500; www.caa.ca) provide useful information, free maps, travel discounts and routine road services such as tire repair and towing (free within a limited radius) for their members. The same benefits are extended to the members of foreign affiliates, such as the Automobile Association in the UK; be sure to bring your membership card from your country of origin.

To become a member of AAA, call or visit the website. The basic membership fee is $64 per year – an excellent investment for the maps alone, even for non-motorists. For roadside assistance, call the AAA's nationwide **toll-free number** (☎ 800-222-4357).

For CAA membership, call or visit the website. The basic CAA plan costs C$81, and for roadside assistance call the **toll-free number** (☎ 800-222-4357).

Driver's Licenses

Foreigners driving in the Pacific Northwest officially need an International Driving Permit (IDP) to supplement their national or state driver's license; note that the IDP is only valid if issued in the same country as your driver's license. Local traffic police are more likely to accept an IDP than an unfamiliar foreign license as valid identification. Your national automobile association can provide one for a small fee, and they're usually valid for one year.

Insurance

Auto insurance is obligatory for car owners in the Pacific Northwest. Rates fluctuate widely, depending on where the car is registered; it's usually cheaper if registered at an address in the suburbs or in a rural area, rather than in a central city. Male drivers under the age of 25 will pay astronomical rates. Collision coverage has become very expensive, with high deductibles, and is generally not worthwhile unless the car is somewhat valuable.

Obtaining insurance, however, is not as simple as walking into an agency, filling out a form and paying for it. Many agencies refuse to insure drivers who have no car insurance – a classic catch-22. Those agencies that will do so often charge much higher rates because they presume a higher risk. The minimum term for a policy is usually six months, but some insurance companies will refund the difference on a prorated basis if the car is sold and the policy voluntarily terminated. It is advisable to shop around. If you're planning to drive in both the USA and Canada, make sure the insurance you negotiate is valid on both sides of the border.

Motorcycles & Scooters

With its beautiful coastline, national parks and backcountry deserts, there are some great opportunities for motorcycling in the Pacific Northwest. For foreigners, an IDP endorsed for motorcycles will simplify the rental process. You can download USA motorcycle manuals at www.dmv.org. To drive on freeways, you must have at least a 150cc engine. Wearing helmets is mandatory for both drivers and passengers.

Motorcycle rentals are not cheap – rentals start at about $145 per day. In Seattle, **Mountain to Sound Motorcycle** (☎ 425-222-5598; www.mtsma.com) offers rentals and tours. Your can rent scooters at **Scoot About** (☎ 206-407-3362; www.scootabout.biz). In Portland, **Northwest Motorcycles Adventures** (☎ 360-241-6500; www.northwestmotorcycleadventures.com) has rentals and tours; for scooters there's **Columbia Scooters** (☎ 503-872-8565; www.columbiascooters.com). For more information about motorcycling in the region, check out www.soundrider.com and www.wetleather.com.

Purchase

If you're spending a few months in the USA and Canada, a car may be a good investment, particularly if you're splitting the expense with others. Keep in mind, however, that it can be complicated and requires plenty of research.

It is possible to purchase a viable used car for less than $2000, but it might eventually need repair work that could cost several hundred dollars or more. It doesn't hurt to spend more to get a quality vehicle – you can sometimes sell it for close to what you paid. It's also worth having a mechanic check over the vehicle for problems; AAA has diagnostic centers that can do this for members.

Check the official value of a used car by looking it up in the **Kelley Blue Book** (www.kbb.com), which is a listing of cars by make, model and year that gives the average resale price. Local public libraries have copies of the *Blue Book*, as well as back issues of *Consumer Reports*, an unbiased magazine that annually tallies the repair records of common makes of cars.

Recreational Vehicles (RV)

You can drive, eat and sleep in a recreational vehicle (RV). It's easy to find campgrounds with hookups for electricity and water, but in big cities RVs are a nuisance, since there are few places to park or plug it in. They're cumbersome to navigate and they burn fuel at an alarming rate, but they solve transportation, accommodations and cooking needs in one fell swoop.

Many companies rent RVs. For a state-by-state list of dealers, rentals and repairs check www.koa.com/rvfinder, which also lists its excellent campgrounds. Another good camp ground list is at www.woodalls.com; while a great source for general RV-travel tips is www.rvtravel.com.

Rental

Major international rental agencies (see right) have offices throughout the Pacific Northwest. To rent a car, you must have a valid driver's license, be at least 21 years of age and present a major credit card or a large cash deposit. Drivers under 25 must pay a surcharge over the regular rental.

Agencies often have bargain rates for weekend or week-long rentals, especially outside the peak seasons or in conjunction with airline tickets. Prices vary greatly depending on type or size of car, rental location, drop-off location, number of drivers, etc. In general, expect to pay from $30 to $50 per day and $150 to $250 per week for a midsize car, more in peak seasons. Rates usually include unlimited mileage, but not taxes or insurance.

You may be able to get better rates by pre-booking from your home country. If you get a fly-drive package, local taxes may be an extra charge when you collect the car. Several online travel reservation networks have up-to-the-minute information on car-rental rates at all the main airports. Compare their rates with any fly-drive package you're considering.

Basic liability insurance covers damage you may cause to another vehicle. Rental companies are required by law to provide the minimum level set by each state, but it usually isn't enough in case of a serious accident. Many Americans already have enough insurance coverage under their personal car-insurance policies; check your own policy carefully. Foreign visitors should check their travel-insurance policies to see if they cover foreign rental cars. Rental companies charge about $15 per day for this extra coverage.

Insurance against damage or loss to the car itself, called Collision Damage Waiver (CDW) or Loss Damage Waiver (LDW), costs about $15 per day (and may have a deductible). The CDW may be voided if you cause an accident while breaking the law, however. Again, check your own coverage to see if you have comprehensive and collision insurance.

Some credit cards cover CDW for rentals up to 15 days, provided you charge the entire cost of the rental to the card. Check with your credit-card company to determine the extent of coverage.

Most of the big international rental companies have desks at airports, in all major cities and some smaller towns. For rates and reservations, check the internet or call toll-free:

Alamo (☎ 800-327-9633; www.alamo.com)
Avis (☎ 800-831-2847; www.avis.com)
Budget (☎ 800-527-0700; www.budget.com)
Dollar (☎ 800-800-4000; www.dollar.com)
Enterprise (☎ 800-325-8007; www.enterprise.com)
Hertz (☎ 800-654-3131; www.hertz.com)
National (☎ 800-227-7368; www.nationalcar.com)
Rent-A-Wreck (☎ 800-944-7501; www.rent-a-wreck.com)
Thrifty (☎ 800-847-4389; www.thrifty.com)

Road Hazards

Seat belts are obligatory for the driver and all passengers. Oregon, Washington and BC all require that anyone (including passengers) riding a motorcycle wear a helmet.

Some backcountry roads of the Pacific Northwest region are in open-range country where cattle forage along the highway. Pay attention to the roadside, especially at night.

During winter months – especially at the higher elevations – there will be times when tire chains are required on snowy or icy roads. Sometimes such roads will be closed to cars without chains or 4WD, so it's a good idea to keep a set of chains in the trunk. Make sure they fit your tires, and practice putting them on *before* you're out there next to the highway in the cold and dirty snow. Also note that many car-rental companies specifically prohibit the use of chains on their vehicles. Roadside services might be available to attach chains to your tires for a fee.

LOCAL SERVICES

Though local bus networks are minimally developed in the hinterlands, the bigger cities have extensive services – with some planning, you can usually get wherever you want by bus. Because these systems are aimed at the commuting workforce rather than tourists, outside of peak commuting hours service may be sparse, and even unavailable on weekends.

Portland boasts one of the country's best public-transportation systems, with an efficient light-rail system, extensive bus service and downtown streetcars. Within the city center, these services are free all day! Seattle has a decent system that's getting better, with underground bus tunnels, train services, a monorail and ferries. A trolley system has been sidelined, but a light-rail project is in the works.

TRAIN

Amtrak (USA) and VIA Rail (Canada) trains provide an attractive, if costly, alternative to buses for travel between major points. Amtrak's *Cascades* train links Vancouver, BC, to Eugene, Oregon – via Seattle, Portland and Salem. This connects with Amtrak Thruway buses (actually a regional bus line under contract with Amtrak) to reach other destinations like the Oregon coast.

A branch of Amtrak's daily *Empire Builder* leaves Portland and crosses to Vancouver (in Washington, not BC) before making its scenic run up the north side of the Columbia Gorge to meet the other eastbound half of the train in Spokane. The Seattle branch of the *Empire Builder* heads north to Everett before winding east to Spokane. Note that the westbound *Empire Builder* divides in Spokane for Portland and Seattle: Make sure you're sitting in the correct portion of the train!

One thing to know about these trains – delays can be very frequent, so don't plan on getting anywhere exactly on time.

Health

Dr David Goldberg

CONTENTS

The North American continent encompasses an extraordinary range of climates and terrains, from the freezing heights of the Canadian Rockies to tropical areas in southern Florida. Because of the high level of hygiene here, infectious diseases will not be a significant concern for most travelers, who will probably experience nothing worse than a little diarrhea or a mild respiratory infection.

BEFORE YOU GO

INSURANCE

Both the United States and Canada offer some of the finest health care in the world. The problem is that unless you have either citizenship or good insurance, it can be prohibitively expensive. If your regular policy doesn't cover you when you're abroad, it is essential that you purchase travel health insurance if you want to avoid very high medical fees.

Bring any medications you may need clearly labeled in their original containers. A signed, dated letter from your physician that describes all your medical conditions and medications, including generic names, is also a good idea.

Along with purchasing some supplemental insurance if your current insurance doesn't cover you when you're traveling overseas, it's also worth finding out in advance whether your insurance provider will make payments directly to health-care providers or reimburse you later for overseas health expenditures.

MEDICAL CHECKLIST

- acetaminophen (Tylenol) or aspirin
- anti-inflammatory drugs (eg ibuprofen)
- antihistamines (for hay fever and allergic reactions)
- antibacterial ointment (eg Bactroban) for cuts and abrasions
- steroid cream or cortisone (for poison ivy and other allergic rashes)
- bandages, gauze rolls
- adhesive or paper tape
- scissors, safety pins, tweezers
- thermometer
- pocket knife
- DEET-containing insect repellent for the skin
- permethrin-containing insect spray for clothing, tents and bed nets
- sun block

RECOMMENDED VACCINATIONS

No special vaccines are required or recommended for travel to North America. All travelers should be up-to-date on routine immunizations: tetanus-diphtheria, measles, chicken pox and influenza.

INTERNET RESOURCES

There is a wealth of travel health advice on the internet. The World Health Organization publishes a superb book, *International Travel and Health*, which is revised annually and is available free online at www.who.int/ith/. Another website of general interest is **MD Travel Health** (www.mdtravelhealth.com), which provides complete travel health recommendations for every country, updated daily, also at no cost.

It's usually a good idea to consult your government's travel health website before departure, if one is available:

Australia (www.smarttraveller.gov.au)
Canada (www.hc-sc.gc.ca)
United Kingdom (www.doh.gov.uk/traveladvice)
United States (www.cdc.gov/travel/)

IN THE USA & CANADA

AVAILABILITY & COST OF HEALTH CARE

In general, if you have a medical emergency, the best bet is to find the nearest hospital and go to its emergency room. If the problem isn't urgent, you can call a nearby hospital and ask for a referral to a local physician, which is usually cheaper than a trip to the emergency room.

Pharmacies are abundantly supplied, but you may find that some medications that are available over the counter in your home country require a prescription in the US or Canada and, as always, if you don't have insurance to cover the cost of prescriptions, they can be shockingly expensive.

INFECTIOUS DISEASES

In addition to more common ailments, there are several infectious diseases that are unknown or uncommon outside North America. Most are acquired by mosquito or tick bites.

Giardiasis

This parasitic infection of the small intestine occurs throughout North America and the world. Symptoms may include nausea, bloating, cramps and diarrhea, and may last for weeks. Avoid drinking directly from lakes, ponds, streams and rivers, which may be contaminated by animal or human feces. The infection can also be transmitted from person to person if proper hand washing is not performed. Giardiasis is easily diagnosed by a stool test and then readily treated with antibiotics.

HIV/AIDS

As with most parts of the world, HIV infection occurs throughout the US and Canada. You should never assume, on the basis of someone's background or appearance, that they're free of this or any other sexually transmitted disease. Be sure to use a condom for all sexual encounters.

Lyme Disease

Most documented cases occur in the northeastern part of the US and southern Canada. Lyme disease is transmitted by tiny deer ticks. Most cases occur in the late spring and summer. The US-based Centers for Disease Control and Prevention (CDC) has an informative, if slightly scary, **Lyme disease website** (www.cdc.gov/ncidod/dvbid/lyme/).

The first symptom is usually an expanding red rash that is often pale in the center, known as a bull's eye rash. However, in many cases, no rash is observed. Flu-like symptoms are common, including fever, headache, joint pain, body aches and malaise. When the infection is treated promptly with an appropriate antibiotic, usually doxycycline or amoxicillin, the cure rate is high. Luckily, since the tick must be attached for 36 hours or more to transmit Lyme disease, most cases can be prevented by performing a thorough tick check after you've been outdoors.

Rabies

Rabies is a viral infection of the brain and spinal cord that is almost always fatal. The rabies virus is carried in the saliva of infected animals and is typically transmitted through an animal bite, though contamination of any break in the skin with infected saliva may result in rabies. In the US and Canada, most cases of human rabies are related to exposure to bats. Rabies may also be contracted from raccoons, skunks, foxes and unvaccinated cats and dogs.

If there is any possibility that you have been exposed to rabies, you should seek preventative treatment, which consists of rabies immune globulin and rabies vaccine and is quite safe. In particular, any contact with a bat should be discussed with health authorities, because bats have small teeth and may not leave obvious bite marks.

West Nile Virus

Cases of West Nile virus were unknown in North America until a few years ago, but have now been reported in most of the continent. The virus is transmitted by culex mosquitoes, which are active in late summer and early fall and generally bite after dusk. Most infections are mild or asymptomatic, but the virus may infect the central nervous system, leading to fever, headache, confusion, lethargy, coma and sometimes death. There is no treatment for West Nile virus. For the latest update on the areas affected by West Nile, go to the **US Geological Survey website** (http://westnilemaps.usgs.gov/) or the **Health Canada website** (www.hc-sc.gc.ca/english/westnile).

ENVIRONMENTAL HAZARDS

Altitude Sickness

Acute Mountain Sickness (AMS), aka 'Altitude Sickness,' may develop in those who ascend rapidly to altitudes greater than 8200ft. Being physically fit offers no protection. Those who have experienced AMS in the past are prone to future episodes. The risk increases with faster ascents, higher altitudes and greater exertion. Symptoms may include headaches, nausea, vomiting, dizziness, malaise, insomnia and loss of appetite. Severe cases may be complicated by fluid in the lungs (high-altitude pulmonary edema) or swelling of the brain (high-altitude cerebral edema).

The best treatment for AMS is descent. If you are exhibiting symptoms, do not ascend. If symptoms are severe or persistent, descend immediately. When traveling to high altitudes, avoid overexertion, eat light meals and abstain from alcohol. If your symptoms are more than mild or don't resolve promptly, see a doctor. Altitude sickness should be taken seriously; it can be life-threatening when severe.

Bites & Stings

Commonsense approaches to these concerns are the most effective: wear boots when hiking to protect from snakes; wear long sleeves and pants to protect from ticks and mosquitoes. If you're bitten, don't overreact. Stay calm and follow the recommended treatment.

MOSQUITO BITES

When traveling in areas where West Nile virus or other mosquito-borne illnesses have been reported, keep yourself covered (wear long sleeves, long pants, hats, and shoes rather than sandals) and apply a good insect repellent, preferably one containing DEET, to exposed skin and clothing. In general, adults and children over 12 should use preparations containing 25% to 35% DEET, which usually lasts about six hours. Children between two and 12 years of age should use preparations containing no more than 10% DEET, applied sparingly, which will usually last about three hours. Neurologic toxicity has been reported from DEET, especially in children, but appears to be extremely uncommon and generally related to overuse. DEET-containing compounds should not be used on children under age two.

Insect repellents containing certain botanical products, including oil of eucalyptus and soybean oil, are effective but last only 1½ to two hours. Products based on citronella are not effective.

TICK BITES

Ticks are parasitic arachnids that may be present in brush, forest and grasslands, where hikers often get them on their legs or in their boots. Adult ticks suck blood from hosts by burrowing into the skin and can carry infections such as Lyme disease.

Always check your body for ticks after walking through high grass or thickly forested area. If ticks are found unattached, they can simply be brushed off. If a tick is found attached, press down around the tick's head with tweezers, grab the head and gently pull upwards – do not twist it. (If no tweezers are available, use your fingers, but protect them from contamination with a piece of tissue or paper.) Do not rub oil, alcohol or petroleum jelly on it. If you get sick in the following couple of weeks, consult a doctor.

MAMMAL BITES

Do not attempt to pet, handle or feed any animal, with the exception of domestic animals known to be free of any infectious disease. Most animal injuries are directly related to a person's attempt to touch or feed the animal.

Any bite or scratch by a mammal, including bats, should be promptly and thoroughly cleansed with large amounts of soap and water, followed by the application of an antiseptic such as iodine or alcohol. The local health authorities should be contacted immediately for possible post-exposure rabies treatment, whether or not you've been immunized against rabies. It may also be advisable to start a course of antibiotics, since wounds caused by animal bites and scratches frequently become infected.

SNAKE BITES

There are several varieties of venomous snakes in North America, but unlike those in other countries they do not cause instantaneous death, and antivenins are available. First aid is to place a light constricting bandage over the bite, keep the wounded part below the level of the heart and move it as little as possible. Stay calm and get to a medical facility as soon as possible. Bring the dead snake for identification if you can, but don't risk being bitten again. Do not use the mythic 'cut an X and suck out the venom' trick; this causes more damage to snakebite victims than the bites themselves.

SPIDER BITES

Although there are many species of spiders in the USA and Canada, the only ones that cause significant human illness are the black widow, brown recluse and hobo spiders. The black widow is black or brown in color, measuring about half an inch in body length, with a shiny top, fat body, and distinctive red or orange hourglass figure on its underside. It's found throughout North America, usually in barns, woodpiles, sheds, harvested crops and bowls of outdoor toilets. The slightly smaller brown recluse spider is brown in color (unsurprisingly), with a dark, violin-shaped mark on the top of the upper section of the body. It's usually found in the South and southern Midwest, but has spread to other parts of the USA in recent years. The brown recluse is active mostly at night, lives in dark sheltered areas such as under porches and in woodpiles, and typically bites when trapped. Hobo spiders are found chiefly in the northwestern US and western Canada.

If bitten by a black widow, apply ice or cold packs and go immediately to the nearest emergency room. Complications of a black widow bite may include muscle spasms, breathing difficulties and high blood pressure. The bite of a brown recluse or hobo spider typically causes a large, inflamed wound, sometimes associated with fever and chills. If bitten, apply ice and see a physician. The symptoms of a hobo spider bite are similar to those of a brown recluse, but milder.

Cold

Cold exposure may be a significant problem, especially in the northern regions of the countries. To prevent hypothermia, keep all body surfaces covered, including the head and neck. Synthetic materials such as Gore-Tex and Thinsulate provide excellent insulation. Because the body loses heat faster when it is wet, stay dry at all times. Change inner garments promptly when they become moist. Keep active, but get enough rest. Consume plenty of food and water. Be especially sure not to have any alcohol. Caffeine and tobacco should also be avoided.

Watch out for the 'umbles' – stumbles, mumbles, fumbles and grumbles – which are important signs of impending hypothermia. If someone appears to be developing hypothermia, you should insulate them from the ground, protect them from the wind, remove wet clothing or cover them with a vapor barrier such as a plastic bag, and transport them immediately to a warm environment and a medical facility. Warm fluids (but not coffee or tea – noncaffeinated herbal teas are OK) may be given if the person is alert enough to swallow.

Heat

Dehydration is the main contributor to heat exhaustion. Symptoms include weakness, headache, irritability, nausea or vomiting, sweaty skin, a fast but weak pulse and a normal or slightly elevated body temperature. Treatment involves getting out of the heat, fanning the victim and applying cool wet cloths to the skin, laying the victim flat with their legs raised and rehydrating with water containing a quarter of a teaspoon of salt per liter. Recovery is usually rapid and it is common to feel weak for some days afterwards.

Heatstroke is a serious medical emergency. Symptoms come on suddenly and include weakness, nausea, a hot, dry body with a body temperature of over 106°F, dizziness, confusion, loss of coordination, fits and eventually collapse and loss of consciousness. Seek medical help and commence cooling by getting the person out of the heat, removing their clothes, fanning them and applying cool, wet cloths or ice to their body, especially to the groin and armpits.

The Authors

SANDRA BAO

Coordinating Author, Destination, Getting Started, Itineraries, History, The Culture, Portland & the Willamette Valley, Columbia River Gorge, Central Oregon & the Oregon Cascades, Oregon Coast, Ashland & Southern Oregon, Eastern Oregon

After years of traveling, Sandra finally got tired of not having a vegetable garden and settled down in Portland, Oregon. She finally has her heirloom tomatoes, but their health is constantly compromised by her continued trips. Researching Oregon has been a highlight of Sandra's Lonely Planet career, which has spanned six years and as many countries. She's come to realize of how beautiful her home state is, how much it has to offer and how friendly people are in those tiny countryside towns in the middle of nowhere.

JOHN LEE

Vancouver, Whistler & Vancouver Island

Born in the UK, John first moved to British Columbia to attend the University of Victoria where he studied utopianism in the Department of Political Science. Shocked at the paucity of jobs in the utopian field, he transformed his student visa into permanent citizenship and waded into a full-time travel-writing career. John has been a Vancouver-based journalist since 1999, and his work has appeared in 120 publications around the world, including the *Guardian, Los Angeles Times, Chicago Tribune* and *National Geographic Traveler.* Specializing in Canadian and UK destinations, his favorite BC trek was the wintertime, way-up-north Skeena railroad.

BECKY OHLSEN

Seattle & Around

Originally drawn to the Pacific Northwest 12 years ago by a hopeless crush on Mudhoney singer Mark Arm, Becky didn't even make it all the way up to Seattle on her first try. Instead she settled in Portland, Oregon, biding her time, until one day the promise of unlimited pinball games and high-altitude trespassing drew her to the Emerald City to work on the previous edition of this book. Since then she's spent enough time mooching around the city to have seen it from the water, the gutter and the tops of numerous buildings, with wildly varying degrees of clarity. She has yet to leave any impression whatsoever on Mark Arm.

LONELY PLANET AUTHORS

Why is our travel information the best in the world? It's simple: our authors are independent, dedicated travelers. They don't research using just the internet or phone, and they don't take freebies in exchange for positive coverage. They travel widely, to all the popular spots and off the beaten track. They personally visit thousands of hotels, restaurants, cafés, bars, galleries, palaces, museums and more – and they take pride in getting all the details right, and telling it how it is. Think you can do it? Find out how at lonelyplanet.com.

BRENDAN SAINSBURY
Northwestern Washington & the San Juan Islands, Olympic Peninsula & the Washington Coast, Washington Cascades, Central & Eastern Washington

An expat Brit, Brendan's first exposure to Pacific Northwest culture came via a well-used copy of *Nevermind* by Washington grunge merchants Nirvana purchased in London's Oxford St in 1992. Moving to British Columbia in 2004, he made his first sorties across the US–Canadian border to the evergreen state in search of snowcapped volcanoes, enlightening music and a half-decent cup of coffee. Somewhere between Mt Baker and downtown Seattle he found all three.

CONTRIBUTING AUTHORS

Lucy Burningham wrote the Food & Drink chapter. Lucy is a fulltime freelance writer living in Portland, Oregon. She covers travel, food and drink, and the outdoors for a variety of publications, and has traveled in the Americas and Europe.

David Goldberg, MD wrote the Health chapter. David completed his training in internal medicine and infectious diseases at Columbia-Presbyterian Medical Center in New York City, where he has also served as voluntary faculty. At present, he is an infectious diseases specialist in Scarsdale, New York, and the editor-in-chief of the website MDTravelHealth.com.

David Lukas wrote the Environment chapter. Born and raised in the Pacific Northwest, David is an avid student of natural history who has traveled widely on biological research projects, including all US states west of the Rocky Mountains. David now works as a professional naturalist and writer, published in many national magazines.

Ellee Thalheimer wrote the Pacific Northwest Outdoors chapter. As freelance writer based in Portland, Oregon. She has explored the area as a professional wilderness guide, bike tour leader and recreationist. Ellee's favorite way to travel is touring by bike, which she has done extensively in the US and Latin America.

Behind the Scenes

This 4th edition of *Washington, Oregon & the Pacific Northwest* was written by a team of authors led by Sandra Bao. The team consisted of Brendan Sainsbury, Becky Ohlsen, John Lee, David Lukas, Lucy Burningham and Ellee Thalheimer. Dr David Goldberg wrote the Health chapter. The 3rd edition was written by Daniel C Schechter, Jennifer Snarski, Debra Miller and Judy Jewell. This guidebook was commissioned in Lonely Planet's Oakland office, and produced by the following:

Commissioning Editor Heather Dickson
Coordinating Editor Daniel Corbett
Coordinating Cartographer Erin McManus
Coordinating Layout Designer Clara Monitto
Managing Editor Bruce Evans
Managing Cartographer Alison Lyall
Managing Layout Designer Adam McCrow
Assisting Editors Carolyn Bain, Trent Holden, Rowan McKinnon, Branislava Vladisavljevic, Helen Yeates
Assisting Cartographers Ross Butler, Owen Eszeki, Karen Grant, Sophie Reed
Cover Designer Pepi Bluck
Project Manager Eoin Dunlevy

Thanks to Sean Egusa and Michelle Godfrey at Travel Oregon, Carrie Wilkinson at Washington State Tourism, Heather Bryant at Seattle's Convention and Visitors Bureau, Jay Cooke, Andrea Dobbin, Jennifer Garrett, James Hardy, Geoff Howard, Lisa Knights, Naomi Parker, Laura Jane, Amanda Sierp, Celia Wood

THANKS

SANDRA BAO

My husband, Ben Greensfelder, deserves top honors for conceding to drive me everywhere around Oregon – though he really enjoyed the trips as well. My co-authors Becky, Brendan and John – along with expert authors Elle, Lucy and David – all helped me in some way or another, and I truly appreciate it. My commissioning editor, Heather Dickson, was ace as well. Neighbors and friends (especially Stacey Henke and Todd Guren) showered me with tips and opinions. Thanks to you all, and to the many Oregonians who also helped me find my way.

JOHN LEE

Thanks to Lana at Tourism Vancouver Island for her help on this and other projects, as well as the host of area tourism staff and generous locals who chatted to me along the way – it's amazing how well a free beer can loosen the tongue on regional rivalries and spill the beans on in-the-know tips. Thanks also to my friends and family for their support and for forcing me to take occasional but very necessary breaks during my bleary-eyed, hibernation-style

THE LONELY PLANET STORY

Fresh from an epic journey across Europe, Asia and Australia in 1972, Tony and Maureen Wheeler sat at their kitchen table stapling together notes. The first Lonely Planet guidebook, *Across Asia on the Cheap*, was born.

Travellers snapped up the guides. Inspired by their success, the Wheelers began publishing books to Southeast Asia, India and beyond. Demand was prodigious, and the Wheelers expanded the business rapidly to keep up. Over the years, Lonely Planet extended its coverage to every country and into the virtual world via lonelyplanet.com and the Thorn Tree message board.

As Lonely Planet became a globally loved brand, Tony and Maureen received several offers for the company. But it wasn't until 2007 that they found a partner whom they trusted to remain true to the company's principles of travelling widely, treading lightly and giving sustainably. In October of that year, BBC Worldwide acquired a 75% share in the company, pledging to uphold Lonely Planet's commitment to independent travel, trustworthy advice and editorial independence.

Today, Lonely Planet has offices in Melbourne, London and Oakland, with over 500 staff members and 300 authors. Tony and Maureen are still actively involved with Lonely Planet. They're travelling more often than ever, and they're devoting their spare time to charitable projects. And the company is still driven by the philosophy of Across Asia on the Cheap: 'All you've got to do is decide to go and the hardest part is over. So go!'

write-up period. Finally, thanks to my favorite English soccer team, Queen's Park Rangers, for being a constant source of amusement.

BECKY OHLSEN

Becky Ohlsen thanks Maureen O'Hagan and Bob Young, Margo Debeir, Darek Mazzone, Tom Douglas, Sarah Novotny, Cathy McCown, Dawn Mucha, Danella Anderson, Thomas Kohnstamm and Heather Dickson for all their help in putting together the guide, and the Sang-Froid Riding Club, Janice Logan, Peter Kahn, Scott Elder, Bradford Duval, Paul Gaudio and all the CB160 folks for providing the best possible means of escaping the office during write-up.

BRENDAN SAINSBURY

A hearty thanks to all the untold park rangers, taxi drivers, tourist info reps, ski bums and innocent bystanders who helped me during my research, particularly to Heather Dickson, my commissioning editor, and coordinating author, Sandra Bao. Special thanks also to Connie Ruffo for her invaluable tips on northwest Washington and to my wife and son for accompanying me for most of the research.

OUR READERS

Many thanks to the US: travelers who used the last edition and wrote to us with helpful hints, useful advice and interesting anecdotes:

Shona Addison, Larry Andrews, Mark Bartlett, Harbinder Basan, Joshua Bash, Roger Bennett, Ewa Blachno-Held, Malynda Boyle, Diane Bright, Alex Buchanan, Jessica Byers, Steven Chmielnicki, Karen Clark, Gee Gee Clemency, Mandy Comish, Creighton Connolly, Nancy Corrie, Arthur Corte, Ben Davenport, Charlotte Dinolt, Chris Dipalma, Christopher Edwards, Tom Elvin, Andy Foltz, Jim Gibson, Dayna Gorman, Mathieu Gosselin, Eleanor Grant, Deborah Gravrock, Andrea Gray, Katherine Grubstein, Janine Harris, Jan Harvey-Smith, Katja Hefter, M Hempton, Karen Hensley, Alain Hottat, Jeff Howlett, Elizabeth Hutchison, Vikramjit Kanwar, Yu Fay Khan, Arvid E Koetitz, Fil Lewitt, Kathryn Mcfarlane, Miki & Julie Mcgehee, Sonia Mcleskey, Don Mcmanman, Jason & Katie Mead, Marc Mentzer, Heinz Mostosi, Laura Napier, Suparto Bambang Oetomo, Chad Perry, Dorothy Roberts, Frank Rohl, Markus Rudolph, Susan Scott, David Simmonds, Dawn Stover, Qadri Syed, Lee & Beverley Treanor, Jessica Troy, Andrea Ursillo, Darian Weir, JJ Wentworth, Jerry White, Ben Wimmer, Skip Winitsky

ACKNOWLEDGMENTS

Many thanks to the following for the use of their content:

Globe on title page ©Mountain High Maps 1993 Digital Wisdom, Inc.

SEND US YOUR FEEDBACK

We love to hear from travelers – your comments keep us on our toes and help make our books better. Our well traveled team reads every word on what you loved or loathed about this book. Although we cannot reply individually to postal submissions, we always guarantee that your feedback goes straight to the appropriate authors, in time for the next edition. Each person who sends us information is thanked in the next edition – and the most useful submissions are rewarded with a free book.

To send us your updates – and find out about Lonely Planet events, newsletters and travel news – visit our award-winning website: **www.lonelyplanet.com/contact**.

Note: we may edit, reproduce and incorporate your comments in Lonely Planet products such as guidebooks, websites and digital products, so let us know if you don't want your comments reproduced or your name acknowledged. For a copy of our privacy policy, go to www.lonelyplanet.com/privacy.

Index

INDEX

000 Map pages
000 Photograph pages

000 Map pages
000 Photograph pages

N

O

000 Map pages
000 Photograph pages

000 Map pages
000 Photograph pages

Y

Z

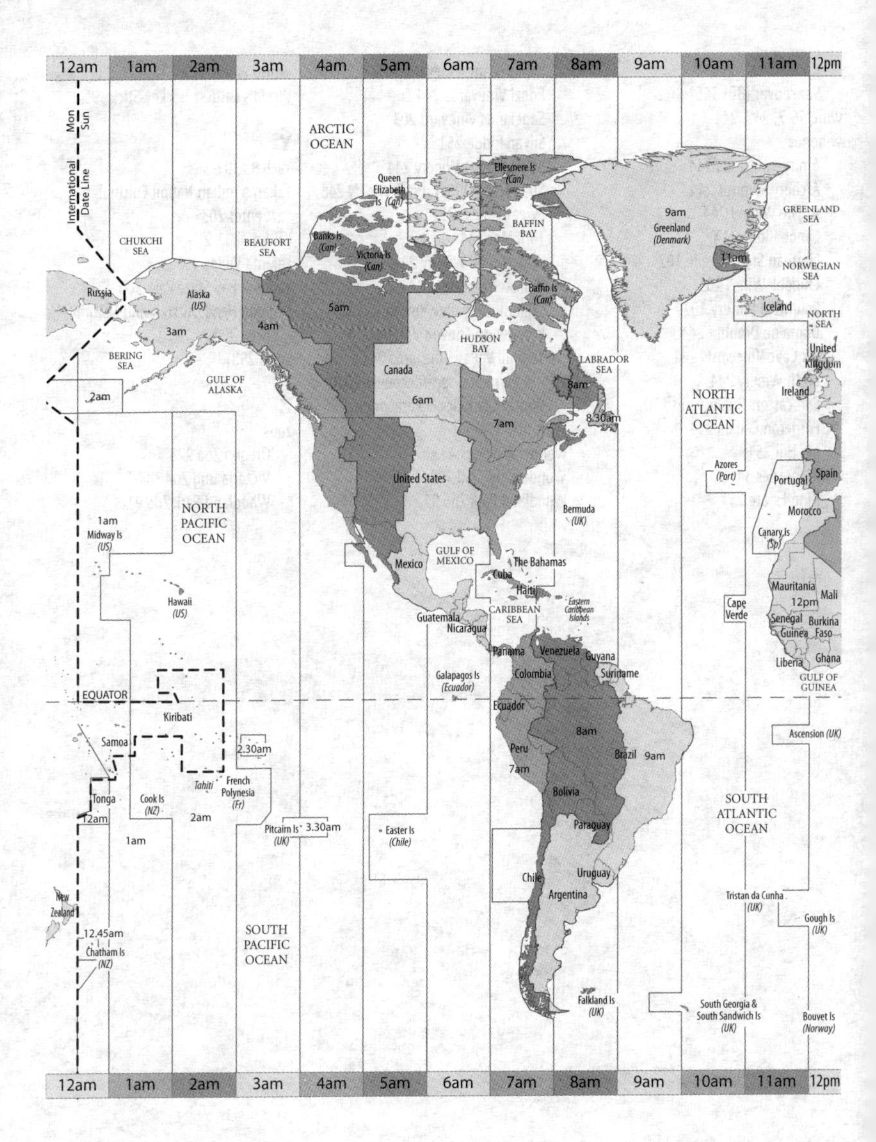
12am
1am
2am
3am
4am
5am
6am
7am
8am
9am
10am
11am
12pm
Mon
Sun
International Date Line
ARCTIC OCEAN
Queen Elizabeth Is (Can)
Ellesmere Is (Can)
Greenland (Denmark)
GREENLAND SEA
NORWEGIAN SEA
BAFFIN BAY
CHUKCHI SEA
BEAUFORT SEA
Banks Is (Can)
Victoria Is (Can)
Baffin Is (Can)
Russia
Alaska (US)
Iceland
NORTH SEA
HUDSON BAY
United Kingdom
BERING SEA
GULF OF ALASKA
LABRADOR SEA
Canada
Ireland
NORTH ATLANTIC OCEAN
8.30am
United States
Azores (Port)
Portugal
Spain
Morocco
NORTH PACIFIC OCEAN
Bermuda (UK)
Midway Is (US)
Canary Is (Sp)
GULF OF MEXICO
Mexico
The Bahamas
Cuba
Haiti
Hawaii (US)
Eastern Caribbean Islands
Mauritania
Mali
Cape Verde
Guatemala
CARIBBEAN SEA
Nicaragua
Senegal
Burkina Faso
Guinea
Panama
Venezuela
Guyana
Liberia
Ghana
Colombia
Suriname
Galapagos Is (Ecuador)
GULF OF GUINEA
EQUATOR
Ecuador
Kiribati
Ascension (UK)
Samoa
2.30am
Peru
Brazil
Tahiti
French Polynesia (Fr)
Bolivia
Tonga
Cook Is (NZ)
SOUTH ATLANTIC OCEAN
Paraguay
Pitcairn Is (UK)
3.30am
Easter Is (Chile)
Uruguay
Chile
Argentina
Tristan da Cunha (UK)
New Zealand
Gough Is (UK)
12.45am
Chatham Is (NZ)
SOUTH PACIFIC OCEAN
Falkland Is (UK)
South Georgia & South Sandwich Is (UK)
Bouvet Is (Norway)

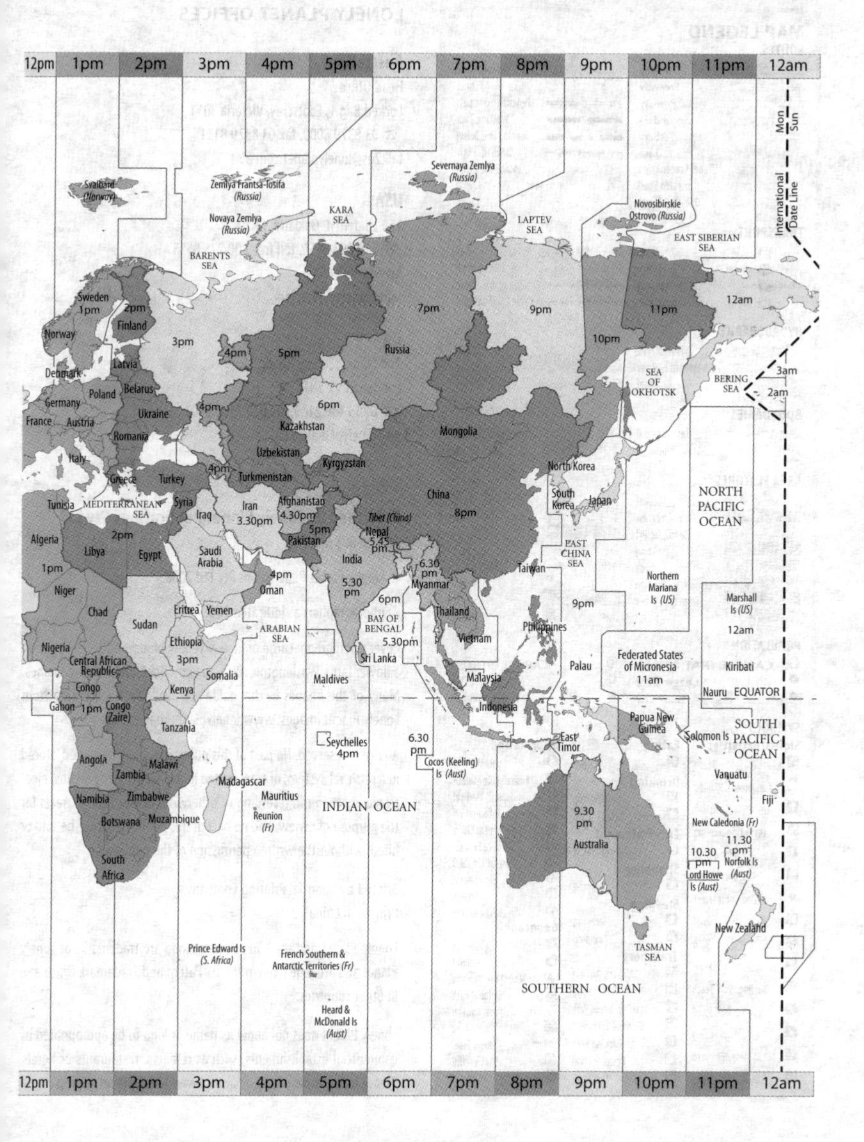
12pm
1pm
2pm
3pm
4pm
5pm
6pm
7pm
8pm
9pm
10pm
11pm
12am
Mon
Sun
International Date Line
Svalbard (Norway)
Zemlya Frantsa-Iosifa (Russia)
Severnaya Zemlya (Russia)
Novaya Zemlya (Russia)
KARA SEA
LAPTEV SEA
Novosibirskie Ostrovo (Russia)
EAST SIBERIAN SEA
BARENTS SEA
Sweden 1pm
2pm
Finland
Norway
3pm
4pm
5pm
7pm
9pm
11pm
12am
10pm
Russia
Denmark
Latvia
Belarus
Poland
Germany
France
Austria
Ukraine
Romania
Italy
Greece
Turkey
4pm
6pm
Kazakhstan
Uzbekistan
Turkmenistan
Kyrgyzstan
Mongolia
SEA OF OKHOTSK
BERING SEA
3am
2am
North Korea
South Korea
Japan
China
8pm
Tunisia
MEDITERRANEAN SEA
Syria
Iraq
Iran 3.30pm
Afghanistan 4.30pm
Tibet (China)
Nepal 5.45 pm
5pm
Pakistan
Algeria
2pm
Libya
Egypt
Saudi Arabia
India
5.30 pm
NORTH PACIFIC OCEAN
EAST CHINA SEA
Taiwan
6.30 pm
Myanmar
1pm
4pm
Oman
Niger
Chad
Eritrea
Yemen
Sudan
ARABIAN SEA
BAY OF BENGAL
6pm
Thailand
Vietnam
Philippines
9pm
Northern Mariana Is (US)
Marshall Is (US)
12am
Nigeria
Ethiopia
3pm
5.30pm
Sri Lanka
Central African Republic
Somalia
Maldives
Malaysia
Palau
Federated States of Micronesia
11am
Kiribati
Congo
Kenya
Nauru
EQUATOR
Gabon
1pm
Congo (Zaire)
Indonesia
Papua New Guinea
Tanzania
Seychelles 4pm
6.30 pm
East Timor
Solomon Is
SOUTH PACIFIC OCEAN
Angola
Malawi
Zambia
Cocos (Keeling) Is (Aust)
Madagascar
Vanuatu
Namibia
Zimbabwe
Mauritius
Fiji
INDIAN OCEAN
Botswana
Mozambique
Reunion (Fr)
9.30 pm
New Caledonia (Fr)
Australia
11.30 pm
10.30 pm
Norfolk Is (Aust)
Lord Howe Is (Aust)
South Africa
New Zealand
Prince Edward Is (S. Africa)
French Southern & Antarctic Territories (Fr)
TASMAN SEA
SOUTHERN OCEAN
Heard & McDonald Is (Aust)

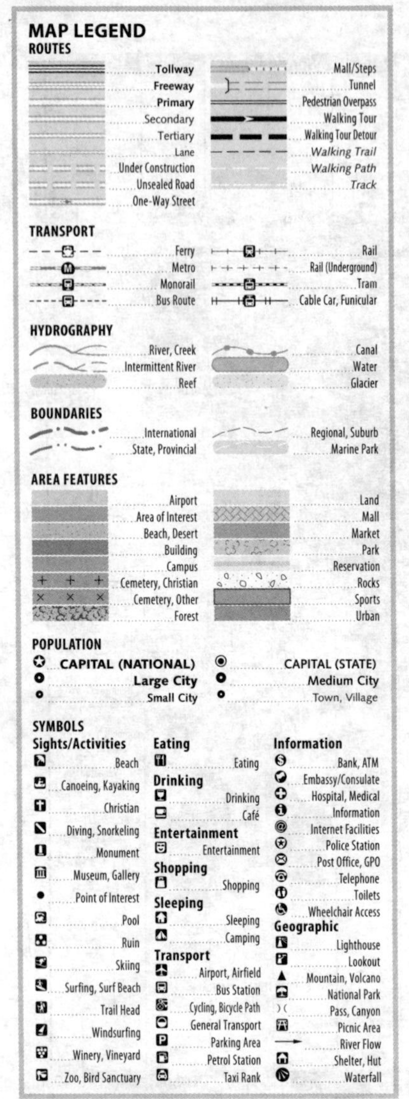

LONELY PLANET OFFICES

Australia
Head Office
Locked Bag 1, Footscray, Victoria 3011
☎ 03 8379 8000, fax 03 8379 8111
talk2us@lonelyplanet.com.au

USA
150 Linden St, Oakland, CA 94607
☎ 510 893 8555, toll free 800 275 8555
fax 510 893 8572
info@lonelyplanet.com

UK
2nd Floor, 186 City Road,
London ECV1 2NT
☎ 020 7106 2100, fax 020 7106 2101
go@lonelyplanet.co.uk

Published by Lonely Planet Publications Pty Ltd
ABN 36 005 607 983

Cover photograph: Large orange & yellow blooms and a red barn on a flower farm, Washington, Richard Cummins/Lonely Planet Images. Many of the images in this guide are available for licensing from Lonely Planet Images: www.lonelyplanetimages.com.

Printed by Hang Tai Printing Company.
Printed in China.